Ole Miss A&M football game, Starkville, Thanksgiving 1930

Ballgame at Morton's Stadium, Booneville, 1931

Ballgame at Morton's Stadium, Booneville, 1931

Rosewood Park

Detroit during National American Legion Convention, September 1931

Snow covered Booneville in 1929

Picking up hose after Price Jeweler fire, 1931

Mauvalene Pugitt

Archie Gurratt's Gulf Station

Picking up hose after Price Jeweler fire, 1931

Claude Branson's Home, Memphis

George Roberts

Sutherland Building

Prentiss County, Mississippi

History and Families

TURNER PUBLISHING COMPANY

Turner Publishing Company
412 Broadway • P.O. Box 3101

Copyright © 2002 Prentiss County Genealogical and Historical Society.
Publishing Rights: Turner Publishing Company.
This book or any part thereof may not be reproduced with the written consent of
the Prentiss County Genealogical and Historical Society
and Turner Publishing Company.

ISBN: 978-1-68162-444-0
Library of Congress Control Number: 2002100537
Project Coordinator: Herbert C. Banks II.
Designer: Peter A. Zuniga

Limited Edition.

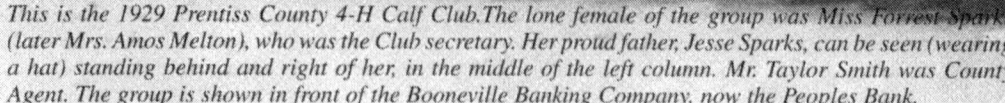

This is the 1929 Prentiss County 4-H Calf Club. The lone female of the group was Miss Forrest Sparks (later Mrs. Amos Melton), who was the Club secretary. Her proud father, Jesse Sparks, can be seen (wearing a hat) standing behind and right of her, in the middle of the left column. Mr. Taylor Smith was County Agent. The group is shown in front of the Booneville Banking Company, now the Peoples Bank.

Contents

Dedication 4
Foreword 5
History of Prentiss County, MS 6
Schools 22
Sports 25
Churches 27
Timeline 46
Special Pages 85
Biographies 89
Index 220

DEDICATION

DEDICATED TO

MRS. MAUREEN HOLLEY CROWE

AND

MRS. MARY FLOYD SUMNERS RICKARD

In appreciation of

years of genealogical research done

on Prentiss County families

by these two ladies.

Mrs. Crowe's papers were left by her estate to the George E. Allen Library.

Mrs. Rickard's papers were given by her estate to the Prentiss County Genealogical and Historical Society.

FOREWORD

In March 1983, the Prentiss County Historical Association was formed in order to record the history of our county. In 1984, PRENTISS COUNTY HISTORY was published by the Prentiss County Historical Association and Curtis Media Corporation. This fine volume, the product of many months of dedicated work on the part of Association members H. H. Daws, Marie Gullett, Kathryn Houston, Eudora Kemp, Louise Peeler, Thomas Wallis, and Martha and Bill White, has become an heirloom in the homes of many Prentiss Countians near and far. Many who missed out on that volume have searched in vain for an available copy, but that book is out of print. Fortunately there are copies in all the Prentiss County Libraries and indeed in many libraries all over the country.

Ann Sparks, first President of the Prentiss County Genealogical & Historical Society, working at the George E. Allen Library in 1998, was at the right place at the right time to be aware of the many requests for the History Book, and initiated the forming of the Society with the goal of a companion volume to the PRENTISS COUNTY HISTORY.

Prentiss County Genealogical and Historical Society charter members are Ann Sparks, President; Brenda Scott, Vice President; Laura Hall, Secretary-

Reporter, and Ann Sparks, Acting Treasurer; (Mitch Burchell was the first elected treasurer but resigned due to health reasons) Catherine Ashcraft, Jo Carolyn Beebe, Peggy Chase, Travis Childers, Betty Browning Ford, Billy Glover, Sandra Gray, Bettie Parker Gustafson, Debbie Joy Hamby Hampton, Wayne A. Holley, Belinda & Nelwyn Houston, Kathryn Houston, Webber & Melba Isbell, Bernice Janeway, ZuAnn King, Carolyn Lambert, Melvin V. Lambert, Cindi Lovell, Edward McCoy, JoAnn Massey, Deborah Moseley, Karen Newcomb, O'Neil Parker, Nancy M. Perez, Sara Pounds, Waylon Provins, Charles H. Rhoads, Jim M. Robertson, Ruby Rorie, Pete Scott, Crandall Storey, Margaret Vanstory, Carole Eastridge Waters, Marjorie Waters, and Margaret Barnes Woods. Recently joined members are Howard Q. Allen, Bonnie Lee Coatney, Pamela Cay Crabb Devin, Joseph and Bettye Earnest, Jimmy G. Lawrence, Doris A. Weatherbee Oakes, Christine Pike, Wm. D. Scroggin, Eric & John Sparks, Gloria Smith, and Jeanne Spain.

Book committee members (for this volume) were Ann Sparks- Chairman, Catherine Ashcraft, Belinda Houston, ZuAnn King, Deborah Moseley, Sara Pounds, and Ruby Rorie. Also, contributing invaluable help were Laura Hall, Sandra Gray and Marjorie Waters.

We sincerely thank Mr. Dave Turner and Mr. Herbert C. Banks II of Turner Publishing Company of Paducah, Kentucky for making this volume possible. We never dreamed the realization of our primary goal would come so soon after our society's founding.

We appreciate all who have contributed family and community histories and photos.

PRENTISS COUNTY, MS HISTORY

PRE-HISTORY

Scientists tell us that our planet Earth is very ancient. Thus so, is the area now known far and wide as Prentiss County, Mississippi, U.S.

Ages ago the North American continent was much smaller and the oceans much larger.

Judging by fossils found in this area, the earliest inhabitants of what is now known as Prentiss County were sea creatures. Browning Cretaceous Fossil Park near Frankstown in Prentiss County is the site of excavation and studies by paleontologists because of the many sharks teeth and fossils found there. There have been no major dinosaur finds in this area, but dinosaur teeth have been found.

Ages passed and the waters slowly receded and abundant wildlife and man appeared. The earliest human inhabitants of our area were aboriginals of the Mississippian culture, the so called native Americans. They lived in this area from about 700 to 1200 AD and some of their mounds still remain. One may view some of these mounds on the nearby Natchez Trace Parkway.

HISTORY

About 1541, Hernando de Soto explored the present day Prentiss County area and was hindered by attacks from Chickasaw Indians, descendants of the Mississippians, who then occupied the land. These southeastern Indians lived by farming, hunting and fishing. The Chickasaws successfully resisted being overun by both the French and the Spanish and never lived under the flags of those nations. The most prominent of the Chickasaw chiefs was Tishomingo.

Tishomingo was a warrior of great distinction. It is known that he was one of the chiefs who served with a company of Chickasaws under General Anthony Wayne in his expedition against hostile tribes in the northwest. He was present at the Battle of Fallen Timbers where General "Mad" Anthony Wayne defeated Little Turtle and crushed the hostile tribes.

For these services Tishomingo received a great silver medallion from George Washington. Two other medals went to Chief Piomingo and Chief William Colbert.

An old Tupelo newspaper story tells of Chief Tishomingo losing his medal and it's being returned to him by a resident of Baldwyn, Mississippi some years before the great chief migrated to the Indian Territory.

An Arkansas newspaper reported the medal was in the chief's possession when he died about 1838.

The Colbert chiefs were half-breed Indians who were diplomats and had the best interest of the Chickasaw Indians at heart.

Pictured with the W.M. Browning Cretaceous Fossil Park are W.M. Browning's children and their spouses. From left to right: Emmy and William Browning and Anne (Browning) and Lamar Walker.

Eric and John Sparks of Louisville, KY, with Prentiss County roots, exploring the Browning Cretaceous Fossil Park.

George Colbert, born in Muscle Shoals, Alabama, was one of the sons of James Logan Colbert, a Scotsman who is thought to have come over on *The Prince of Wales* in January 1736 and who landed at Savannah, Georgia.

George Colbert had an Indian mother and acquired the Indian name, Tootemastubbe. He became a colonel in the U.S. Army and had two ferrys on the Tennessee River. He had large farms, one of which was about four miles south of Booneville, Mississippi on Wolf Creek. He exerted considerable influence over the Chickasaws and the settlers in this area.

Brown's Creek in eastern Prentiss County was most likely named for Jim Brown, a noted individual of half Indian descent.

Confederates goin' to meet the enemy

He was the husband of Jincy Brown who also has a creek named for her. Jim and Jincy Brown lived about where Little Brown Church now stands near the New Site, Mississippi Post Office. Jim Brown was a commanding officer of a company or battalion under General Andrew Jackson in the Creek Indian War.

In 1729 warfare broke out between the Natchez Indians, allied with the Chickasaws, and the French over land ownership. The Natchez were slaughtered and dispersed.

In 1763 the Treaty of Paris ended the French and Indian War and France ceded to to England all claims to what is now Alabama.

Reverend Joseph Bullen was likely the first minister to preach a sermon to the Chickasaws. He came to the Chickasaw village of Long Town, located northwest of the present day city of Tupelo on May 20, 1799. In his diary he described the town as having 200 houses made of poles 3 to 5 inches thick and and plastered with mortar and 16 by 22 feet on the ground floored with earth and covered with capboards.

Reverend Charles Riddle was a Primitive Baptist preacher who was born in or around Chatham County, North Carolina July 10, 1782. He preached in Hardin County, Tennessee and often came to Burton Community in Prentiss County to deer hunt. He traveled over the same trail each time and it became known as the Riddle Wind Trail. He moved his family over this same trail to the Burton area and settled on Riddle's Creek. He and his wife and another family member are buried in Mackey's Creek Cemetery. It is interesting to note that the Riddle name is still common in Prentiss County.

In 1800 this area was part of Georgia and was sold to land speculators. The "Yazoo Land Fraud", as it was known, was rescinded and in 1802 Georgia ceded the territory to the United States government and in 1804 it became part of the Mississippi Territory.

During the War of 1812, General Andrew Jackson broke the power of the Creek Indians in the Mississippi Territory and Georgia, assisted by the ancestors of many present day Prentiss Countians, who came with Jackson from South Carolina to Tennessee and Mississippi Territory, and later migrated from Alabama to old Tishomingo and Prentiss County.

In 1817 the western half of the Mississippi Territory became the state of Mississippi, and the eastern half became the Alabama Territory. In 1832 a land office was set up in Pontotoc, Mississippi and between 1832 and 1834 the Chickasaws, one of the Five Civilized Tribes, were removed to Oklahoma, and an excellent class of white settlers, mostly farmers, started pouring into northeast Mississippi from Alabama, Georgia, the Carolinas and Virginia.

OLD TISHOMINGO COUNTY

The part of the Chickasaw nation lying in Mississippi was divided into ten counties in 1836, the largest of those counties being Tishomingo,

Often called the Free State of Tishomingo, or Old State of Tishomingo. This old Tishomingo County included all of present Alcorn, Prentiss and Tishomingo Counties. Commissioners appointed to organize the county were Peter G. Rives, James Davis, James McMathews and A. M. Cowan, who called for an election May 6 & 7, 1836. At the June session the county was divided into five districts with each district electing two Justices of the Peace and one Constable for each police district. The act of creating the county provided that the county seat be no more than five miles from the geographical center of the county. The board was then offered 60 acres of land by Armstead Barton. The new town and county seat was first named Cincinnati. Citizens objected to the northern name and it was soon changed to Jacinto. From the time of the county's formation until 1860, it had become one of the wealthiest counties in the South. The pioneers that had pushed their way across the southern boundary of Tennessee and the western counties of Alabama had made Tishomingo County a place of importance. Today the descendants of these hardy settlers are to be found in every part of the world and many remain right here on the land their pioneer families settled.

Long before the first shots of the Civil War were fired at Fort Sumter, the seeds of sectional dissension were sown because of economic and political rivalry and the argument over States Rights and the right of a state to secede.

In 1859, the state legislature passed a resolution to the effect that Mississippi would secede if a Republican were elected to the Presidency. When Abraham Lincoln was elected President a convention was summoned at Jackson. Delegates elected from

Tishomingo County were A. E. Reynolds, W. W. Bonds, T. P. Young and J. A. Blair.

Mississippi was the second of the southern states to secede and that terrrible war, called by some simply The Civil War, by some the War Between the States, and by others The War of Northern Agression, began in 1861.

Although no major battles were fought in present day Prentiss County, important battles took place in old Tishomingo County: the Battle of Corinth and the Battle of Iuka. There were other area battles, the Battle of Shiloh and the Battle of Brice's Crossroads. Booneville and the surrounding communities were subjected to Union occupation, skirmishes and much hardship and deprivation. Ancestors of many Prentiss Countians volunteered at Jacinto and fought and died on distant battlefield.

Confederate units from old Tishomingo County area were the Anna Perry Guards, Co. F, 26th Reg. Inf.; the Beauregard Rifles, Co. H, 32nd Reg. Inf.; the Blackland Gideonites, Co. F, 23rd Reg. Inf; the Blount Guards, Co. A, 23rd Reg. Inf.; the Bob Davenport Grays, Co. C, 26th Reg. Inf.; the Boone Avengers, Co. B, 26th Reg. Inf.; the Buckner Boys, Co. K, 32nd Reg. Inf.; the Burnsville Blues, Co. E, 17th Reg. Inf.; Capt. Burton's Co., Co. I, 26th Reg. Inf.; Capt. Duncan's Co. (aka Inge's Co. and Tishomingo Rangers), independent cavalry; the Cape Horn Rifles, Co H, 26th Reg. Inf.; Capt. Belsher's Co., Co. D, 26th Reg. Inf.; Capt. Kizer's Co., Co K, 26th Reg. Inf.; Capt. Polk's Co., 1st Battalion Inf.; Capt. Reid's Co., Co A, 26th Reg. Inf.; Carter's Co., Co. C, Davenport's Battalion State Cavalry; Corinth Minute Men, Co. B, 2nd Reg. Inf.; Corinth Rifles, Co. A/C, 9th Reg. Inf.; Corona Guards, Co. D, 2nd Reg. Inf.; Davenport Rifles, Co. E, 42nd Reg. Inf.; Dixie Boys,Co. A, 2nd Reg. Inf. (Davidson's, Army of 10,000); Dixie Guards, Co. D, 1st Battalion Inf. (Beckett's, Army of 10,000); Forrest's Cavalry (aka Ford's Co.), Co. A 1st Reg. Partisan Rangers (Falkner's) (Also Co. A, 7th Reg. Cav.); Gates' Co, Co. C, Ham's Reg. Cav.; Ham's Co., Co. B, Ham's 1st Battalion State Cav. (aka 16th Battalion State Cav); Hatchie Tigers, Co. E, 32nd Reg. Inf.; Iuka Rifles, Co. K, 2nd Reg. Inf.; Jake Thompson Guards, Co. K, 19th Reg. Inf.; James Creek Volunteers, Co. H, 1st Reg. Inf.; Johnston Avengers, Co. I, 32nd Reg. Inf.; Johnston Guards, 1st Battalion Inf. (Beckett's, Army of 10,000); Jones' Company, Co. B, 3rd Reg. Cav. Reserves; Kossuth Volunteers, Co. D, 23rd Reg. Inf.; Lowrey Guards (aka Lowrey Rebels), Co. D, 32nd Reg. Inf.; Lowrey Guards, Co. G, 2nd Reg. Inf. (Davidson's, Army of 10,000)' Lowrey Invinicibles, Co. G, 32nd Reg. Inf.; Lowrey's Company, Co. L, 2nd Reg. State Cav.; Marietta Rifles, Co. G, 26th Reg. Inf.; Mary Davis Guards, Co. E, 2nd Reg. Inf. (Davidson's, Army of 10,000); Mayes' Company, Co. G, Ham's 1st Battalion State Cav.; Melson's Company, Co. E, 2nd Reg. Cav. Reserves; Moore's Company, Co. F, 12th Reg. Cav. (aka 16th Reg. Confederate Cav.); Outlaw Guards, Co. C, 1st Battalion Inf. (Beckett's, Army of 10,000); Reason's Company, Co. F, 2nd Reg. Partisan Rangers (Ballentine's); Tishomingo Avengers (aka Tishomingo Rifles), Co. A, 32nd Reg. Inf.; Tishomingo Rangers (aka Roddey's Company), 4th Battalion Cav. (aka 2nd Battalion Cav. and Pope Walker Battalion) (Baskerville's); Tishomingo Rangers, Co. A, Ham's 1st Battalion State Cav.; Tishomingo Reapers, Co. K, 2nd Reg. Inf. (Davidson's, Army of 10,000); Tishomingo Rebels, Co. C, 32nd Reg. Inf.; Tishomingo Riflemen, Co. A, 2nd Reg. Inf.; Volunteer Cavalry of Tishomingo County, Co. A, Ashcraft's Reg. Cav. (aka 11th Reg. Cav.); W. R. Nelson Guards, Co. B, 32nd Reg. Inf.; Wallis' Company, Co. C, Ashcraft's Reg. Cav. Consol.;White's Company, Co. D, Ham's 1st Battalion State Cav.; Wince Price Guards, Co. E, 26th Reg. Inf.; and Yates' Company, Co. C, Ham's 1st Battalion State Cav.

Davis' Brigade of the Army of Northern Virginia included the 1st Confederate Battalion, the 2nd Mississippi Infantry, the 11th Mississippi Infantry, the 26th Mississippi Infantry, and the 42nd Mississippi Infantry.

There was an engagement on the Blackland Road at Booneville, Mississippi, July 1, 1862, between Confederates under General James R. Chalmers and a Union force under Colonel Phil Sheridan. As a result of this action, Phil Sheridan was promoted to Brigadier-General. However there is much controversy as to whether it was merely a skirmish or a minor battle.

Virgil Robinson, a Booneville historian, did much research on the subject and found that Major William B. Hankee, United States Air Force, Retired, a Research Analyst with the U. S. Army Combat Developments Command Strategic Studies Institute, did a paper entitled "Fire and Maneuver at the Battle of Booneville."

Excerpt from the Banner Independent, Booneville, Mississippi, Centennial Edition, quoting General Chalmers:

"...I do remember that I was greatly amused at the accounts given of it then and since. The facts are these: General Withers was ordered to move with his division of infantry from Tupelo to Ripley, Mississippi, and I was ordered to move with the cavalry to protect his right flank from attack by the enemy, who then held the Mobile and Ohio railroad from Booneville up to Corinth. A short time before this, Col. Sheridan had made a bold dash into the Confederate camp at Blackland, where Col. W. C. Richards, of Columbus, Mississippi, was seriously wounded and escaped with very small loss. In passing Booneville I determined to return his visit and did so. In making the attack at Booneville, I used but three regiments, Wirt Adams' Mississippi regiment, Clanton's 1st Alabama, and the 1st Confederate under Col. Wm. Wade. Col. Sheridan made a gallant resistance, but fell back before us, as our command was largely superior to his in number. When beaten in front, Col. Sheridan made a spirited attack from our rear, which was repulsed by a squadron of Wirt Adams' regiment under Capt. Isaac Harrison of Louisiana... Having accomplished my object here, I moved on to Ripley, in obedience to my instructions, covering the flank of Gen. Withers, with my command in perfect order and without any molestation from Col. Sheridan or anyone else, either going to or returning from Ripley. Col. Sheridan captured some of my wounded, who were left at a farmhouse, and this perhaps gave rise to the idea that I had been routed. This report made Phil Sheridan a brigadier general and gave him an opportunity to show to the world that he was a great soldier. His attack at Blackland, and his resistance against superior numbers at Booneville, showed the courage and genius of a true soldier. But to say that he with 728 men routed 4,000 Confederate cavalry is simply ridiculous.

James R. Chalmers, Memphis, Tennessee, Aug. 22, 1888"

Another excerpt from the Booneville Banner, Booneville, Mississippi, July 11, 1912, concerning a casualty of the Battle of Corinth:

"We found a dead Confederate soldier lying on his back, his outstretched fingers stretched across the stock of the rifle lying by his side. He was one of the Rogers' Texans. Fifty seven of them we had found lying in the ditch of Fort Robinette. I covered his face with a slouch hat and took off the haversack slung to his neck, that it might not swing as we carried him to his sleeping chamber, so cool and quiet and dark, after the savage tumult and dust and smoke after that day of horror. 'Empty, isn't it?' asked the soldier working with me. I put my hand in it and drew forth a handful of roasted acorns; I showed them to my comrade. 'That's all,' I said. 'And he has been fighting like a tiger for two days on that forage,' he commented. We gazed at the face of the dead soldier with new feelings. By and by he said, 'I hate this war and the things that caused it. I was taught to hate slavery before I was taught to hate sin. I love the Union as I love my mother-better. I think that this is the wickedest war that was ever waged in modern times. But this,' and he took some of the acorns from my hand, 'this is what I call patriotism.' 'Comrade,' I said, 'I am going to send these home to the Peoria Transcript. I want them to tell the editor this war won't be ended until there is a total failure of the acorn crop. I want the folks at home to know what manner of men they and we are fighting.'…I was more and more devoted to the Union as the war went on. But I never questioned the sincerity of the men in the Confederacy again. I realized how dearly a man must love his own section who would fight for it on parched acorns… I understood him, I hated his attitude toward the Union as much as ever but I admired the man and after Corinth I never could get a prisoner half way to the rear and have anything left in my haversack. Oh, I too have suffered the pangs of hunger for my dear country, as all soldiers have done, now and then. But not as that Confederate soldier did. We went hungry at times when rain and mud or the interference of the enemy detained the supply train. But that man half starved. That's different. Other haversacks we found that night on Corinth field with a slight ration in them. Sometimes it was a chunk of corn pone… so the southern people loved the states for which they suffered.

Rev. Robert J. Burdette" (a gallant Union soldier)

JAMES WRIGHT BONDS

On July 1, 1997, the 134th anniversary of the Battle of Gettysburg, the bones of a Civil War soldier were reburied in a solemn ceremony after being washed up by rains in the railroad cut where the 2nd Mississippi was entrenched on the first day of the battle, July 1863.

Private James Wright Bonds, Co. A, 2nd Mississippi Infantry, from Jacinto, Mississippi, was killed at Gettysburg on July 1 1863 and his body was never recovered.

The program from the 1997 ceremony states:

"Today we offer a final resting place, with full military honors, for a soldier who perished during the Battle of Gettysburg. We may never know his identity, or even which side he fought for, but it is fitting that we honor him today and that he rest here at the Gettysburg National Cemetery, where Lincoln gave his immortal address.

In March 1996, a park visitor accidentally found eroded skeletal remains along a railroad embankment, on the first day battlefield, northwest of town. A National Park Service archeological investigation determined that the discovery was a Civil War battlefield burial, probably a battle participant, slain near the Railroad Cut where intense fighting took place on July 1, 1.863. There was no conclusive evidence regarding the soldier's identity."

No conclusive evidence? Perhaps. But there is much circumstantial evidence that the bones were those of James Wright Bonds. Records show that James Bonds was with the 2nd Mississippi and that he was killed on that day in that place and an archive record shows that he was 5'9" as was the skeleton.

Articles in various newspapers mentioned Jim Bonds from Jacinto, Mississippi as fitting the profile arrived at by Smithsonian scientists who did tests on the bone samples.

Bernice Bonds Janeway and Sara Bonds Pounds, great granddaughters, and Ann Sparks, great great granddaughter of James Wright Bonds, made the long drive from Booneville, Mississippi to Gettysburg, Pennsylvania, to attend the 1997 ceremony. They are convinced they attended the funeral of their ancestor.

The ceremony was a big draw for the anniversary. And if the powers that be had admitted that the soldier was a Rebel, he would not have been reburied at Gettysburg. He would have been reburied at Richmond, Virginia. And if they had gone so far as to admit it was or probably was Jim Bonds from Jacinto, Mississippi, the bones should and could have been returned to his home state. This writer believes it's the same old story, the powers that be in the North giving short shrift to us Southerners!

Descendants attend reburial at Gettysburg. From left: Sara Bonds Pounds, Ann Sparks, Bernice Bonds Janeway Behind: Curt Johnson, the visitor from Oregon who discovered the bones.

Ann, Bernice, and Sara were impressed with the respect, solemnity and grandness of the ceremony. But Ann still feels unsettled at the thought that this young soldier, her ancestor, died so far from home and was given a second chance so to speak, and unfortunately is still buried so far from home and the state for which he fought and died.

James Wright Bonds was the son of Wright Walker Bonds 11 and Sarah Nicholson. His grandparents were Wright Walker Bonds and Priscilla Eley. Wright Walker Bonds and Priscilla Eley have many, many descendents in Prentiss, Tishomingo, and Alcorn Counties and indeed all over the country. Priscilla Eley was descended from Robert Eley. One of Robert Eley's descendants, who became President of the United States, was Lyndon Baines Johnson!

James Wright Bonds left a widow, Mary A. Ledbetter Bonds, and two small sons, Wright Walker III and James Andrew, who became the first mayor of Mantachie, Mississippi. Andrew's home in Mantachie, the Bonds House, is now a museum.

In the interest of history and science, some believe DNA should have been done on the bones, at the expense of the government, of course. Lord knows, they spend money on some really stupid studies, such as the sex life of gnats

All that aside, in June 2000 his great great granddaughter had a memorial Confederate marker for James Wright Bonds placed beside the grave of his son, Wright Walker Bonds, at Holley Cemetery, east of Booneville, in Prentiss County, Mississippi.

JAMES MATLOCK KITCHENS

"The State of Ala. February 15' 1863 Very dear children I avail my-self of this favorable opportunity of riting you a few lines to let you know that we are well in common health and the connection with the one exception of Zack Dutton. I understand he is sick though I don't know what his complaint is. Your aunt Susan Hamilton is dead she died sometime last spring. Hear son James and one of the girls is living with John Hamilton in Walker's. Some of the children is living with John Long. I would inform you that George Dutton was captured in the Fort Donelson fight. George is dead. Sarah is married to Christopher Witt and Frances

Brick building that replaced frame building in 1920's - corner 3rd St. and Thomas St. Baldwyn First Christian Church

Street scene in Baldwyn looking west on Main Street between Front Street and 2nd Street

Baldwyn N. 2nd Street in early 1940's. Prather Auto Co. in lower left corner.

Original First Christian Church Baldwyn, corner of 3rd St. and Thomas Street.

to Stephen Dutton. Frances has a son and Sarah a daughter. I received a letter from Matlock Kitchens (the writer's son) dated 13 January. He was in Rome,, Georgia wounded in the right foot at the Murfersborough fight. I have nothing of interest to rite to you. Times are very distressing with us particular with (?) Salt has been selling at 60 to 65 per pound, pork at 12 1/2 to 15 here and at Tuscaloosa from 20 to 25 per hundred. Your cousin L. W. Baker is dead he died at Chattanooga Tennessee. 4 of Harvey H. Hamilton's sons is in the army (?). Your uncle Jesse Kitchens was captured in Kentucky and paroled. He is now gone back to the army. I heard from him a few days past. He was well. He belongs to the 28 Alabama Reg't and Matlock to the 22. 1 will close my letter for the present hoping these few lines may reach and find you all in good health and doing (?) well is the wish of yours T. (?)

Farewell

James M. Kitchens"

(From a clipping of a letter which appeared in the Dallas Semi-Weekly Farm News perhaps around 1916-date unknown)

My great-grandfather Price was born in Ireland; came to the United States when a single young man and was a soldier in the Revolutionary War. My father, David S. Price, was born in East Tennessee; came to Coffeeville, Yalobusha County, Mississippi, when a young man. He was there married to Miss Agatha Collicoatte on February 26, 1835. There were five children, three boys and two girls born to them in Coffeeville. About the year 1845, my father moved over near Aberdeen, Mississippi, where my dear mother died, June 26, 1847, leaving an infant babe. My father was again married to Mrs. Salenah Vandiver (nee Hughes). We lived in several counties in North Mississippi, and were living in Corinth, Miss., when my father died of pneumonia, November 7, 1856.

When the War Between the States opened I was living with Ben Boydston, five miles east from Water Valley, Mississippi. I enlisted in a company made up by Captain Aldridge in and around Coffeeville, Mississippi, the old town in which I was born, April 20, 1843. After several weeks' training, we went to Corinth; were then thrown into the Fifteenth Mississippi Infantry Regiment. From there we went to Union City, Tennessee, and thence to Knoxville. By this time I had completely lost my health. Was discharged a short time before the command was ordered into Kentucky. I returned to near Baldwyn, Miss. In the fall of 1862 1 had partially regained my health, when General Cabell returned to Baldwyn from the Iuka battle. There I re-enlisted in Captain S.E. Nobles' company, Third Texas Dismounted Cavalry. After a few days' rest we marched from Baldwyn to Corinth. On the third and fourth days of October, 1862, we made a desperate effort to retake the town. There the Federals made it dear for us, as they had the advantage of the ditches and the fort around the town. There could not have been anything harder than this battle. In our last charge on the fort, which was a life and death struggle, while capping my gun, a grape or cannister shot struck my left arm at the wrist and left my arm nothing more than a pulp up to my elbow. It was amputated that night. The wounded went into the hands of the Federals as our leader found we were overpowered by about six men to one. In eight or ten days after the battle all the wounded that there was any hope for were moved to Iuka, Miss.

A few things took place at this time I can never forget. First, there was a captain who was mortally wounded. A Federal chaplain wanted to help the poor captain to make ready for a hasty death, but the poor dying captain's blood was at boiling heat. His answer was he knew he was bound to die, but he expected to die and go to hell cursing Yankees. The preacher saw he was only adding fuel to fire and gave the poor captain up. A few days after

Burton School, 1923

the battle my clothing was taken off to have the blood washed out. I suppose had they ever been washed I would have gotten them by this time. I was sent to Iuka just as I came into this world, but thanks to the Lord for the good and kindhearted women around Iuka and of Northwest Alabama who flocked in to our rescue with clothing, which I was ready for; also great boxes of provisions and the best of all is yet to come. They stayed there and administered to our wants; saw to it that we were not neglected. May the Lord bless such women. I think at least half our wounded died there of blood poison. Had all of us Confederates gone after the Federals like the two I read about who ran a little squad through two or three picket lines into their ditches, went in on them, brought them out by the hair of the head, I don't think we would have had four long years of war. But I suppose they were just buttermilk cavalry and had no guns.

The Corinth battle wound up my fighting, as the Federals had my home country in their possession. Soon after this battle I went back to my command on Big Black and around Oakland, Miss. The last year of the war I was buying and shipping corn from the prairies of Mississippi into Tishomingo County. The Federal Government was good enough to allow a train to run for the express purpose of furnishing bread for the old people and children. When the war was over we had a country in ruin, "neither law nor gospel".

On Dec 29, 1867, I was married to Miss Mary E. Jowell, near Guntown. I soon took the Texas fever, left from near Geeville in an ox wagon, March 25, 1869, landed near Lexington, Burleson County, Texas. Lived on G. W. Cook's place three years. I left there in the fall of 1872; stopped four miles west of Ennis, Ellis County. I came very near dying there with pneumonia. Moved to Coryell County, near where I now live, in the fall of 1874. Lost my wife, June 19, 1875. Was left with three helpless children.

I was again married in Ellis County to Mrs. Sarah Heard (nee Garner), Sept. 17, 1876. I then moved to Palo Pinto County, then back to Coryell in 1885. Have made no move since then. I hope, through this sketch of my life,, I may find some lost relatives and old friends.

Thomas B. Price, Bee House., Coryell Co., Texas

Thomas Benton Price was born in Yalobusha County, Mississippi on April 20, 1843 and died in Bee House, Texas on January 28, 1924. He was the brother of Martha Price Brinkley, grandmother of Kathryn R. Houston of Booneville (see Prentiss County History Vol. I).

Submitted by Kathryn Houston, great niece of Thomas Benton Price

PRENTISS COUNTY

In 1870, Prentiss County was formed from part of old Tishomingo County. The new county was named for Sargent Smith Prentiss, a gifted statesman, jurist and orator.

BALDWYN

The town of Baldwyn received its name from a Mr. Baldwyn who was one of the principal projectors of the Mobile and Ohio Railroad. In November of 1860 the first train came to Baldwyn and they turned the locomotive on a turntable that was located back behind where the old Oil Mill and the Outlaw-Lewellen Cotton Gin building was located.

The first store building was built by a man named Andy Mannin. He cleared away a small space on a wooded hill and built at a location that would have been about directly behind where the Kirk Hardware and the Lu-Ru Flower Shop stands today (in 1984). The timber that was used for erecting the building was cut from the part of the hill that the town now stands on. The logs were so huge that it only took six to eight of these timbers split to form one wall of the store building. The second building was a log blacksmith shop put up and built by Isom Wallis approximately where the Houston Drug Store now stands.

In the beginning the store buildings were built pretty well overlooking the depot which was the center of attraction back in those days. The old Home Hotel was built right there by the railroad and depot and was originally built facing east on the railroad. It was remodeled in 1920 and the front put on the north side. The post office and barber shop was built on up the hill there on front street overlooking the railroad and depot. Col. Robert Lowery and Zebedee Williams also built store buildings there before the Civil War. The population in 1890 was 500.

For the most part, most of the main store buildings were bricked by World War I. It might be interesting to note that as far back as the 1830s, 20 Mile Creek or bottom as well as Okeelala were called by those names in that day. It is also interesting to note the way they referred to how thick and dense the undergrowth were and how thick the woods were in those bottoms and how abundant they were with wildlife. It might also be interesting to know that when they were originally dredged out the 20 Mile Creek specs for the canal or creek were 20 feet wide and 20 feet deep. I have heard of two or three ideas of how 20 Mile Creek got its name but for right now, I think it came from this: They used to say years ago that it was 20 miles from where it originates back up in the hills to where it empties into the Tombigbee.

Baldwyn is located on the southern boundary line of Prentiss County and partly in Lee County. The town is surrounded by very fertile lands and is one of the best cotton markets in North Mississippi, size considered. Many thousand bales are handled annually and the highest market price is always paid.

Baldwyn has two banks, progressive business houses in every line, cotton oil mill, large timber interests, and a municipally owned waterworks. Much street improvement work has been done, and the beautiful location on the crest of a bluff, with natural drainage in every direction, makes Baldwyn both attractive and healthful.

Hundreds of golden opportunities are lying in wait for the thrifty man's grasp, and the co-operative and hospitable welcome of Baldwyn's entire population is ever in evidence.

Baldwyn's people believe in Baldwyn, and this one thing is the great factor in her material growth and development.

Homeseekers will do well to include Baldwyn in their itinerary.

History portion by Simon (Buddy) Spight

BURTON

Burton is a small, close knit community of about 300 people. It's situated on either side of highway 30 fifteen miles east of Booneville, Mississippi. In the backyard of Burton is the Tenn Tom Waterway and recreation area. Space is more than adequate for picnicking, swimming, camping, hiking, biking., etc. The avid fisherman can fish for bass, crappie or catfish and have the time of his life. There"s plenty of water for boating and skiing should one prefer that sport. Indians were the earliest known settlers of this region. The most obvious sign that Indians have occupied this land is arrowheads and shale. Shale is the residue that was chipped from rock to form arrowheads. After a rain on freshly plowed dirt, arrowheads can still be found. Before the day of cars and rocket engines this community was blessed with an abundance of doctors. Early records show that Dr. Robert G. Smith was born in 1851. He married Amanda S. Smith and began to practice medicine in the Burton area. He is the grandfather of Robert G. Smith, Myra Smith Holley, and Mildred Smith. After Dr. Smith died in 1887 at the age of thirty-six, the family convinced his brother Dr. Bolivar R. Smith (1853-1930) to move his medical practice to Burton. In 1887 Dr. Bolivar Smith and his faithful horse (Dolly) relocated to Burton where he practiced un-

Girls in front of Burton School. Hester Rushing, Venus Lester, Hazel (Woodruff) Browning, Thena Owens, Mabel Smith, Grace Brown, Ena (Pace) Akers.

Marshall Woodruff's Store, Burton Community, the post office was in this store from 1841 to 1906.

til 1928. If you were born in or around Burton from 1887 to 1928 the stork didn't deliver you, Dr. Smith did. This doctor loved to fox hunt and would go every time he had an opportunity.

Another doctor from Burton,, Dr. L. L. McDougal, took training under Dr. Bolivar Smith and practiced in the vicinity. During those years Myers McDougal was born. The story is told that Dr. McDougal wanted the baby to be just like Dr. Smith. So he was brought to the home of Dr. Smith when only a few days old to get acquainted with the good doctor. As it turned out Myers did not even remotely resemble Dr. Smith. His interest was not in medicine. After completing his early education in the Prentiss County Schools he enrolled at Ole Miss where he received three degrees before attending Oxford University as a Rhodes Scholar. He became a professor of Law at Yale Law School. Shortly before his death he was presented the Lifetime Achievement Award by the Old Miss Alumni Chapter.

Ernest Brown, another Burton scholar who furthered his education in law, became a judge. He is retired, living in Brooksville, Mississippi.

Over the years a large number of young people became teachers, others became carpenters, brick layers, farmers, saw millers, molasses makers, seamstresses,, small business owners') beauticians,, etc.

During the early years Mr. Burton operated the post office which was in Mr. Marshall Woodruff's country store. There was a well in front of the store with two watering troughs positioned nearby for watering their horses. Mail was delivered to the larger towns (Booneville and Paden) by train where it was picked up by a local mail carrier who delivered by horseback from Paden one day and from Booneville the next day. Burton was named after Mr. Burton who operated the post office.

Mr. Thomas Lacey had a store that was near the Burton school in the 1930's and early 1940's. He may have been responsible for Charles McCoy becoming an avid fisherman as Mr. Lacey often gave him fishhooks. He must have been a kind and caring person.

From the center of Burton one will need travel only a short distance to find the church of his choice. Forked Oak Missionary Baptist church is believed to date back to the 1800's. Dates on tombstones are evidence that Forked Oak cemetery existed in 1804. Most of the dates are illegible in the oldest section of the cemetery; however, those that are readable lend credence to the belief that Forked Oak church was in existence in the very early 1800's.

According to records, Mackey's Creek Primitive Baptist church was organized in 1845. New Burton was organized in the 1960's as Southern Baptist. Just outside Burton's borders are the following churches: Shady Grove (Missionary Baptist), New Hope (Primitive Baptist), Fairview (Church of God), Mt. Nebo (Methodist) which had land donated by an Indian in 1835 to build the church on.

Schools tend to draw people together. Although the Burton schoolhouse, constructed in 1922-1923 no longer functions as a school it is significant in the history of education in rural Prentiss County for being one of the earliest consolidated schools and for being one of the first brick schools in the county. This building served as an educational facility for thirty-five years.

On August 25, 1995, the property was designated a Mississippi Landmark by the Department of Archives and History. Much has already been done toward renovation and preservation of this landmark. When restored, the building will continue to be significant in the community as it will house an educational museum, have an area for public presentations, provide space that may be rented for private/public functions, etc. This ongoing project will serve as a memorial to all who sacrificially gave of themselves while erecting Burton school.

Today if you were to tour Burton, as you enter from the west on highway 30, your first stop will be Claude Wilemon's quilt museum. If you have an appreciation for beautiful and unique quilts as I do you will browse for quite a spell.

Continuing on highway 30 about one quarter of a mile is Lee's One Stop. Most anything can be purchased there from headache powder to fishing supplies, sandwiches, etc.

Evelyn's Beauty Shop is also on highway 30 about a quarter of a mile

from Lee's One Stop. It's best to make an appointment before you go for a hair style; however, drop ins are welcome. An hour spent in her shop can boost morale and send you on your way with confidence.

Continue on another quarter of a mile. On the left there is a video house owned by the Slacks. They always have the latest videos along with the oldies.

In the same building is Burton's Kountry Kitchen. Their food is delicious and is served by the friendliest waitresses you could ever hope to meet.

Directly across the highway from the cafe' is the Burton schoolhouse, sometimes called the place of memories. Since August 1995, we refer to it as a Mississippi Landmark.

Still on highway 30 the last stop is a discount store operated by Stephen Carter on Fridays and Saturdays. He has a variety of items to select from.

To conclude the "History of Burton" a few people were interviewed and asked the question: "What is your most vivid memory of Burton?'"

My most vivid memory of Burton is picking cotton. It was a " really fun thing" to do because Grandmother always prepared a picnic lunch which was spread on the tailgate of a pickup truck at noon on a tablecloth. In our family everyone worked. Daddy believed it was good therapy. Submitted by Judy McCoy Griffin who grew up in Burton and now lives in Ripley, Ms.

"Living on a farm in Burton is just a dream." Christy Tennison Ryan made this statement when she was in the first grade at Hills Chapel. She is 27 years old and still lives in Burton.

"The ball games we had on the dirt court at Burton school stands out in my memory. Mr. Elmore Owens would bring bags of parched peanuts and sell them for five cents." Said Vivian Hodges Tennison who has lived in Burton all her life.

"I started to school at Burton in 1923 when I was in first grade and finished high school there, then came back as a teacher. The years at Burton school were extraordinary for me." said Majorie Tennison Harper who lives in Burton.

When Mr. Prentiss Crabb was principal of Burton school and Bernard Burks was assistant principal, Mr. Crabb got the mumps, which allowed Mr. Burks to be in charge of running the school. He sent two tenth-grade girls to his house (which was across the road) to baby sit while his wife coached a play. When Mrs. Burks returned, the sitters were free to leave. A group of students came by going to Burton Lake so these girls made a quick decision to go along. The students still remember sixty five years later the severe punishment they received for a few minutes of fun. Mr. Crabb came back to the school with mumps holding his coat over his mouth and nose. For some reason Mr. Burks had not whipped Coleman Wilemon so Coleman took the switch, handed it to Mr. Crabb and said, "You whip me." He gave him three light licks on the pant leg. Mildred Smith likes to add, "The only reason I wasn't with them ... I'd gone shopping with my aunt! Submitted by Mauvelene Smith Wilemon.

Burton Community RC DC hosted a musical program with the Slim Rhodes Band performing. I remember Speck Rhodes in his black and white plaid suit, and snaggled tooth grin blowing his nose on the stage curtains during the performance. Submitted by Vaughanda McCoy Hall who attended Burton 1956-57 and 1957-58.

Submitted by Ruth McCoy

CARROLVILLE

Today all that is left of the glory of the past is the boyhood home of Private John Allen, the Anne Spencer Cox home, known in later years as the "Allen Homestead". It was built in 1842 and was added to in later years and restored by Joe Horace Bishop, a showplace to remind people of what existed long ago at Carrollville, two miles northwest of downtown Baldwyn. It is believed to be the only remaining structure of what was once Carrollville.

Pontotoc was the capital of the Chickasaw nation. The road from Pontotoc to Carrollville was known as the Wire Road due to the fact that a telegraph line ran along it. Carrollville grew into a sizable settlement, due mainly to it's location on the Pontotoc-Eastport route to the Tennessee River, some 60 miles to the northeast. Eastport on the Tennessee River was the shipping center for river traffic, merchandise, and farm produce for the northeast area of Mississippi, northwest Alabama and southwest Tennessee.

In 1840 David Allen and his wife Sally Spencer Allen left their home in Henry County, Virginia, and headed southwest with their household effects, livestock, and a few farm implements. They settled in the almost-wilderness around Carrollville.

In the 1840s Carrollville was a flourishing settlement, a crossroads. The Tuscumbia to Pontotoc road and the Jacinto to Pontotoc road crossed through Carrollville. There was a road leading from Carrollville to Fulton and the Carrollville to Pontotoc road passed through Brice's Crossroads, the scene in later years of the Battle of Brice's Crossroads which was an overwhelming victory for the south under the command of General Nathan Bedford Forrest.

The Civil War started in 1861. The Allens had six sons to serve in the Confederate Army. One was killed, and five were wounded. John M. Allen, later known as Private John Allen, went into national prominence by serving 16 years in the United States Congress from the first congressional district of Mississippi.

The little town of Carrollville grew in size and influence. There were from two to five doctors, an inn run by Wiley Belcher, two or three saloons, two blacksmiths, a tannery, five dry goods stores, three saddle shops, two shoe shops, two tailoring shops, a mill and a gin, a post office, a jail and a church used for all denominations, a school and a masonic hall. But the thriving little settlement was doomed to die in the not too distant future.

It was only natural that the town should move to the railroad. As far back as 1854 they were working on the right-of-way for the Gulf-Mobile and Ohio Railroad to the east of Carrollville. The railroad bypassed Carrollville and merchants from Carrollville started building at the new location as early as 1858 and in the summer of 1860 all that was left of the old settlement of Carrollville was one store and the post office.

*Compiled with information from Mr. Claude Gentry
And Mr. Simon (Buddy) Spight*

GEEVILLE

The Geeville Community, located approximately four miles west of Frankstown on Mississippi Highway 30, was settled about 1850. The majority of the settlers came from Anderson County, South Carolina and settled there because "the ground was higher and looked to be more healthful than the land they had left". The community, then located in Tishomingo County, was named for the McGee family who was among the pioneer settlers.

Surnames of early settlers included the following: McGee, Nelson, McElroy, Garrison, Franks, Gamer, Gardner, Wallis, Randolph, Lominick, Jones, Ashley, Brock, Davis, Roberts, Burress, Morris, Murdock and others.

The majority of these early settlers fanned for a living. Some acquired large tracts of fine farm and timber land. Some of the farm labor was done by slaves. After a few years a number of two-story white houses dotted the landscape.

Geeville had a post office, two general stores and a school. In June 1851, Mt. Olive Baptist Church was organized and from that time to the present it has been the focal point of the community (see the history of Mt. Olive Baptist Church, this edition).

At least three medical doctors, Drs. J. C. McGee, F. E. Lewellen and Tom Randolph, practiced in Geeville. They also practiced dentistry. Dr. McGee's office was located in his store while the other two doctors practiced in their homes and traveled throughout the community.

The school operated as an elementary school, grades 1-8, for many years. In the 1930s the ninth and tenth grades were added to the curriculum for a few years, then it reverted back to an elementary school. In the 1950s the school closed during Mississippi's Rural School Consolidation program. Students then attended either Baldwyn or Wheeler schools.

The stores located in the community supplied residents with most of their needs for home and farm. Sometime around 1900, McElroy's store opened and carried a larger line of merchandise. W. E. McElroy and Dalton Lominick were the owners. This store burned in 1916. The Geeville Mercantile was then built and was operated by the Lominick family for a number of years. The last store to operate in Geeville was a small structure operated by May Lominick Prather until her death in 1972. This building is still used as the polling place for the Geeville precinct.

For many years people came in great numbers to the Geeville hills to harvest chestnuts which grew there in great abundance. Of course this tradition ended with the demise of the chestnut trees.

Although Geeville no longer has stores or other institutions (except Mt. Olive Baptist Church), it is an active community. Many newcomers have built homes and the number of residents has 'increased during the last several years.
Submitted by Thomas Wallis.

Home of Private John Allen, relative of George E. Allen, at Carrollville, the earliest community in Pentiss County.

Old Geeville Store, currently in use only as voting precinct, built circa 1916.

Hobo Station Grocery

HOBO STATION

About ten miles east of Booneville at the fork of Highways 4 and 371 is the community of Hobo Station. Now there is only signs and a convenience store with an auto service department to mark what once was a bustling community.

This community began many years ago at a fork in the road. At a time when few people owned cars, one could walk to this fork in the road and catch a ride to Booneville, Tupelo, or Belmont with a passerby who happened to be going that way. Eventually someone constructed a shack or small building to be used for protection against the weather and the area came to be known as Hobo Station.

Walter Odom was the first person to establish a grocery store at this location. His store was across the road from the present day store. Walter's brother Bob owned and operated a grist mill only a few hundred yards down the road. The grist mill was operated by a kerosene engine and Bob would often take his pay for grinding the corn by filling a small box with a portion of the corn.

In the late 1930's Fester Horn, Jesse Horn, Will Caver, Marvin Breedlove, and Lonie Breedlove decided to set up a cotton gin at Hobo Station. The Breedloves and the Horns already owned an interest in the Marietta and Hills Chapel gins and felt that establishing one between those two locations would benefit the community. This gin was operated by a diesel engine that powered a generator for electric lights. Lester and Maureen Crowe were the last owners of the gin. It operated until the late 1970's.

In a small building near the store Vick Champion and Hershel Spencer built large hog vats used for killing and dressing hogs that were brought in. The store carried the spices and necessary ingredients for preparing the meat for storage as sausage and ham, etc. This small building is still on the grounds of the present day store, but it is no longer used.

The present owners of the Hobo Station Grocery purchased the store in 1956 from H.L. Caldwell. The building they purchased was a small one room plank building with a small side room. They remodeled the store into the present day building.

Information supplied by Reba and Cayce DePoyster, Ralph Caver, and W.V. Horn

JACINTO

Although, Jacinto is now in Alcorn County, it is just over the line from Prentiss and is so much a part of the history of our county, which was prior to 1870 a part of Tishomingo County, of which Jacinto was the county seat.

Jacinto., first named Cincinnati, was later named Jacinto after people objected to a northern name their growing town. It was named after the Battle of San Jacinto. This territory was alloted to the Chickasaw Indians in the Hopewell Treaty of 1786. The Chickasaws relinquished their claim. A land office was set up at Pontotoc. Old State of Tishomingo, embracing present Tishomingo, Prentiss and Alcorn, was the largest county in the state with 923,040 acres. Persons were appointed to organize the county, officers were elected, and fifty-three lots were sold for a total of $10,000. A courthouse of crude logs was built for $199.00. Taverns came in 1836. By 1838, hundreds moved to Jacinto, a number of acres were cleared and planted. Businesses, dwelling houses and roads were built. A county jail was built for $3,957. A sawmill, gristmill and a male academy were established. There was a mail service, three days each way. Chisley Key was Jacinto Postmaster. In 1845 a Baptist Church was erected at the crossing of Eastport and Fulton Roads. Ministers were granted the authority to perform the rites of matrimony. A telegraph line was built along the stage road, but a drought came in 1850 and people thought the telegraph line was the cause of the drought and that it was the work of the devil, so they tore the line from its posts.

A poor house was built for $50.00. The surplus produce shipped from Eastport was bringing in thousands of dollars annually.

The need for a new courthouse arose, and plans to build a wood building were changed to a two story brick, with an octagon shaped belfry, for the sum of $6.798. Plans for the courthouse were commissioned in 1852 and it was completed in 1854, and is an impressive example of federal style architecture.

The toll road between Rienzi and Jacinto was the best paying institution in the county with 5,457 people crossing in 1857. Residents of Jacinto included a professor, a medical doctor, and a dentist. There was the Jacinto Hotel.

It is told that when old Tishomingo County was divided in 1870, people thought that the coming railroad was a thing of the devil and voted that it should not come to Jacinto. Thus,, the town declined.

The courthouse was later, at different times, used as a school and as the jail. Mrs. Zelma Brimingham's father, C. P. Rinehart, was one of the students taught there by Mrs. Opal Rutledge. A school, A Line, was later built south of the courthouse, where students from Prentiss and Alcorn Counties attended. It had at different times, four or five teachers. It still stands and was used for many years by the Jacinto A.C.D.C.

A community club set out pine seedlings, had auction sales and paid $300.00 to Alcorn County. The Jacinto Senior Citizens met five days a week. C. P. Rinehart was the first Site Manager, followed by Willard Newborn and Dewey Bain. Randall Eldridge is the current Site Manager. They quilt, play checkers, pitch dollars, and have good gospel singing each Wednesday, led by R. C. "Jack' Woodruff, with Nita Dees playing piano.

The Jacinto Courthouse and Park is open May through September except on Mondays, and open on holidays. Hours are 1-5 Sunday through Friday and 10-5 on Saturday. Loren Chase oversees the courthouse and park. The Country Store, across from the courthouse, owned by the Jacinto Foundation, has the same hours as the courthouse. Zelma Brimingham and Avis Crum operate the store, with extra help on the 4th of July, when there is a celebration on Saturday of the holiday weekend. Quilting is done there. Bonnets and aprons, etc. are made and sold. Courthouse souvenirs and hand dipped ice cream are available.

There are five churches and one grocery store in Jacinto. There was once several grocery stores, a grist null, blacksmith shop and a school and library.

Submitted by Zelma Bimingha

JUMPERTOWN

A brief history beginning with the birth of James Alvin (Jimmy) Jumper in November, 1822, through the present date, May, 2000.

The Jumpertown community has not always been as it is known today. The original community is about three miles south of Jumpertown High School. It consisted of many hardy families. There were Greens, Eatons, Englishes, Yates, Windhams, and Jumpers, just to mention a few. It will not be too misleading to call these families pioneers and settlers. They were farmers and had to clear the land before crops could be planted.

As stated earlier, there were many families living in this sprawling, unnamed community. One of the largest and best known was the family of Jimmy Jumper. He was the son of immigrants from Europe. Jimmy married Eliza James, who was a relative of the notorious James brothers.

To Jimmy and Eliza were born nine children, five boys and four girls. With so many offspring marrying into other families, the community was quickly populated with Jumpers, and the name of the community was established, Jumpertown.

Front row L to R- Jane Gilley Davidson, Barbara Huddleston Beard, Leaverne Bumpers Henderson, Mary Faye Lauderdale Spencer. Back row L to R- L.L Bethay, Bobby Jean, Henderson Holloway, Venus Stevens Johnson, Janie Carpenter Ellis, Elizabeth Pike Mathis, Peggy Allen Bates, Tolbert Brown.

L to R- (seated) Noonan Hopkins, L.Q. Mathis, Dewey Burcham, Ophelia Waddle (standing) L to R- Stanley Eldridge, Herman Saylors, Marvin Christian, Guy Woods.

No community is complete without a church. Therefore, a church building was erected in the vicinity of the Bud and Paulette Sims home. After the Civil War, several of the freed slaves settled in the area of the church. The slaves had taken the name of their owners, some of whom took the Jumper name. The church was used by Methodists, Baptists and the Negro community. When most of the white families moved out of the area, the church became known as the Negro Jumpertown Church.

The Methodists bought or were given land where the home of the late Leroy Brumley now stands. A wood building was erected there and served as both church and school for the growing community. This building was used until another one was erected where the present Jumpertown Methodist Church now stands. The dates of erection and use of the different buildings can be found in "The History of Jumpertown Methodist Church".

Until the early 1870's, there was no single burying place for the community. In that year, a family from Tippah County by the name of Yates bought land on the east side of Dry Creek canal and started building a house where the home of the late Sam and Ada English now stands. The infant son of the Yates family, John William Yates, died on August 14, 1872, and he was buried on. the land the Yates had bought. His body was the first one buried in what came to be known as the Jumpertown Cemetery. A small piece of the original gravestone still marks the grave in the center of the cemetery. Also in the center of the cemetery is a large area with no grave markers, and when attempts were made to dig graves in this area, other graves were found. It is told as fact that freed slaves of the Jumpers and others are occupants of those unmarked graves.

As the community grew in area and populace, so did the need for grocery stores and other businesses. Tom English, who was a son-in-law of Jimmy Jumper, and his son, Sam, opened a grocery store in the yard of Sam and Ada English. Since this was a farming community, it was only natural for a blacksmith to set up shop. The clearing of the land brought about the need of a sawmill. The cotton had to be processed, and so a cotton gin was installed. The corn had to be ground into meal, thus a grist mill was built. As the community increased, so did the services.

As mentioned earlier, the Methodist Church was used as the school in the beginning. Later, a separate building was erected for the school, and a new church was built across the road where the present Jumpertown Methodist Church now stands. This new school building was used until land was donated for another, larger school. The donated land was in a very distinct, separate community by the name of Cross Roads. This building burned in the late 1920's, and the first building of the present Jumpertown High School was built. This brick structure with a dome roof is still in use today.

The first expansion of the Jumpertown community came about when the school was moved into the Cross Roads community. Today, most people think Cross Roads is only the little Methodist Church. Does anyone wonder or even care enough to ask why the voting precinct is called Cross Roads precinct?

Through the years, other communities have been included in the general geographics of Jumpertown. Some of these communities are Pisgah, Hatchie, Carolina, parts of Blackland and Dry Creek. Most of these inclusions came about due to consolidation and changing school boundary lines.

With these area expansions came more churches into Jumpertown. Some of these are Jumpertown, Cross Roads, Pisgah, and Carolina United Methodist Churches, Lambs Chapel Ind. Methodist, Jumpertown First Baptist, Antioch Baptist, and Oak Hill Missionary Baptist. All of these churches are well grounded in Christian theology and serve the community well.

More businesses were established as the community grew. Some of the grocery store owners in the old community were Tom and Sam English, Will English, Olis English, Rich Hill, and Willie Keenum. In the bigger community: Padgetts, Colsons, Morris, Green, Knight, Geno, Windham, Mauneys, Jumpers, Prentiss, and Hallmark.

With the growth of the community continuing, it became apparent that there was a need for a governing body, other than the County government. The direction seemed to be toward incorporation. In the latter part of 1974, a group of civic-minded citizens met and with an attorney giving advice, the legal process of incorporation was started with the State of Mississippi for Jumpertown to be incorporated into a township. In 1975, incorporation was granted and later in the same year, the first election was held. A mayor and a five-member Board of Aldermen was elected. The secretary's minutes of meetings were lost in a fire prior to the hiring of the present secretary, therefore, the records of the early years of the township are left to the memory of those who were there. It is a fact that a great-grandson of the founding father, Jimmy Jumper, was the first mayor elected to serve with a board of aldermen. Ruey Eaton was this mayor.

Today, Jumpertown is a thriving town and community with several businesses including two grocery stores, a feed and fertilizer store, a cafe, a furniture manufacturing company, a trucking company, a public park, and other private enterprises. The incorporated town is 2 miles east to west and 3 miles north to south. The 1990 Census shows the population to be 437 good souls. Jumpertown is approximately seven miles from down town Booneville on State Highway No. 4. It is ironic that Jumpertown city limits do not include the old, original Jumpertown community. The greater community is served by the Jumpertown water system and volunteer fire department.

The history of Jumpertown would not be complete without the names of the children of James Alvin and Eliza James Jumper. Being unsure of order of birth, they will just be listed with their spouses:
1) William A. (Uncle Bill) and Sarah Crowell Jumper
2) Sarah Elizabeth Jumper and Thomas Jefferson Engli sh
3) Samuel P. and Virginia Hunt Jumper
4) Phillip (Tip) and Margaret Yates Jumper
5) David and Julia Hasting Jumper
6) Mary Jumper and Hardin Yates
7) George and Mollie Quinn Jumper
8) Nancy Ann (Nan) Jumper and Frank Yokum
9) Jane Jumper and Sam Yokum

The lists of families, churches, and businesses are not complete dates and locations are approximates. If anyone has information that should be added or if you think some information is incorrect, just be patient. Maybe you will get your chance next time. This is not intended to be a genealogical family tree, just a brief history.

In closing, it should be said, "Strangers and newcomers, you are very welcome, but don't make derogatory remarks about any of us because we are all kinfolks either by blood or by marriage."

LEBANON

Lebanon Community is located approximately seven miles west of Frankstown along Mississippi Hwy 30 in both Prentiss and Union Counties.

The area was located in Tippah County until Prentiss and Union Counties were organized in 1870. The community was named for Lebanon Mountain, the second highest point in the state, located within the community. The view from the summit of this mountain is spectacular.

The community was settled in much the same manner as other communities 'in the area. Beginning about 1845, pioneer settlers began coming to the area from the Carolinas, Georgia, Alabama and Tennessee.

Surnames of early settlers included the following: Arnold, Davis, Pruitt, Pannell, Palmer, McGill, Wallis, Owen,, Steele, Fowler, Graham, Hickey, Little, McCary, Gullett and others.

Sometime prior to the Civil War (exact date unknown) Lebanon United Methodist Church was organized. A large cemetery, which has served as the burial ground for the Geeville-Lebanon area since the communities were settled, is located across the road from the church. The cemetery contains several hundred graves. A few Confederate veterans are interred there.

Lebanon had a school for a number of years. It was located in at least two different places near the church and finally on Highway 30 at the present site of Mrs. Leonard Brown's home. In the 1930s the school was consolidated with Geeville School.

In the early days of the community, a tannery was operated by Jack Davis. Later two grist mills were operated, one by Jeff Davis and the other by George Palmer. Mr. Palmer also operated a steam-powered cotton gin.

Will McElroy operated a grocery store for a number of years. Later the community had two small stores. One store was operated by Monroe Pannell and the other by Ferd Fowler. Other businesses included a barber shop and a feed crusher.
Submitted by Thomas Wallis

TUSCUMBIA

The Tuscumbia community accquired it's name from the local Chickasaw indian chief, Tuscumbia. The tribal burial site still sits on a hill known as the old indian mound just west of brush creek. In the late 1700s and the early 1800s Tuscumbia was a very wooded area. Wild hogs,, deer, wolves,, bears, panthers and turkeys roamed the woods and meadows... Beautiful clear streams meandered through the hills and valleys, providing fresh water to drink, as well as fish and game to eat. Some of Tuscumbia's earliest white settlers prior to the Civil War were the Thomas Smith family. My grandfather Noonon Hopkins once related the following story,, "During the Civil War, Thomas Smith took several wagons full of cotton to the old indian mound, to hide from the Yankee soldiers prowling the area. In July 1862, during the civil war,, some records state that as many as 15 to 20 thousand federal troops were encamped in the Tuscumbia bottom.

According to writings by Mr. Walter Nunley. Good roads played a big part in the development of this community. Prior to the formation of Prentiss County in 1870, Jacinto was the county seat. Travelers would camp overnight at a spring East of the Tuscumbia canal where the upper and lower Jacinto roads came together. These roads were under the supervision of Mr. Walker smith,, who also owned the land and with the help of his road gang built a camp site at this location. They split rails and built corrals that could be divided into four parts. Troughs were also built for feeding the horses. They made seats of split logs, with legs made from pegs driven into the bored holes on the rounded side of the log. The tops were hewn then hand planed until very smooth. A place to cook was also constructed near this site. An old horse cotton gin was located nearby. The low land roads became very difficult if not impossible to travel by foot or horse when the rains and ice came. At this time the road was crosslayed with logs5 a practice called causeway. The old causeway road was accidentally found in the late 1950s by clyde hopkins while plowing with his new tractor on the james lewis farm. The reason it hadn't been discovered before was the soil wasn't tilled as deep with mules as with tractor plowing.

Two schools served the community, the old providence

Tuscumbia School 1945

school sat in back of where the roy gray home sits today and the old stringfellow school was to the south west of the community. These two schools were combined when Mr. John Ashcraft gave four acres of land for the building of the Tuscumbia school in 1925. The Tuscumbia school closed its door in 1957 and area students were then consolidated into the thrasher school district.

The 1900s brought new families to our community. The Lauderdale,, Ashcraft, Lovell, Jones, Allen, Mize, Dodds, Fraiser, Curtiss, Stokes, Deaton, Goodwin, Nunley, Thompson, Saylors, Gray, Henderson, Stevens, Johnson, Tittle, Lambert, King, Morton, Cunningham, McCoy, Timbes, Church, Huddleston, Bolt, Swinney and Winfield.

We had two stores in the 1920s. Uncle Bud and Aunt Ella stokes had a store where the challis barron home now sits. Mr. John ashcraft's store was where the Jewel Ashcraft white house sits across from the Tuscumbia community center.

Our community grew with the famlies of Henson, Stanley, Hopkins, Barker, Sheffield, Waddle, Cole, Barron, White, Mathis, Mooney and Kelton.

Our dead were usually buried at the local Smith cemetery, dating back to the 1850s and started by the Thomas Smith family.

Mr. Carey Pike later bought this land and saw the need for a church. He told his neighbor, Mr J.C. Henderson, the community needed a church, also a place for funerals and for getting out of the weather while digging the graves. (Mrs. Elizabeth Pike Mathis said she remembered that most of the graves were dug at night if during farming season. "I would hold the lantern while the men dug the grave.")

Mr. Carey Pike said he would deed the cemetery and extra land for a church if he could get enough petitions to build it. Mr. Henderson then contacted Mr. Noonon Hopkins, Mr. Herman Saylors, and Mr. Tim Huddleston. They got enough money to buy the materials and with the help of good neighbors built the church and deeded it to Mr. J.C. Henderson. The church started to deteriorate over time and Mr. Henderson deeded it to the Freewill Baptist. Later Mr. Carey Pike donated more land to the cemetery for a much needed expansion.

In the late 1940s the community decided it needed another church and met in the old Tuscumbia school building until Mr. Oscar L. Waddle donated the land and the Tuscumbia Southern Baptist Church was built at its present location.

Our community had three stores in the late Mr. W.E. (Bill) Barker's store was located across the road from the James Lewis home. Mr. Junior Stevens' store was to the north across the road from the Smith Chapel Church and Mr. Carley Timbes' store was to the southwest.

Beginning in the 1940s and continuing through the early 1970s came the nightmare of war. Here is a partial listing of our brave men who served: Horace Allen,, James Hardin Lewis,, John Edward Timbes, Prentiss Ray Waddle, Hollis Waddle, J.C. Hopkins, Noonon Clyde Hopkins, Bobby Thompson, Leslie Thompson, Lester Thompson, Floyd Dodds, Gerald Dodds, J.R. Tittle, Cloys Stevens, Cleovis Stevens, John Watson Lambert, O.D. Stites, David Richard Stites, J.W. Church, James Stanley Southern, Arthur Southern, Raymond Gray, Claude Gray, Tommy Gray, Troy Henderson, Paul Ray Henderson, Jerry Pike, Terry Hester, Caroll Rampley, Oscar Stevens, Cleo Bumpers, Edward Smith, Cullen Swinney, Jimmy Shook, Smith Burcham, Benny Burcham,, James Burcham, Clifton Mize, Freemon Stokes . Travis Stokes, Warren Mathis, L.Q. Mathis. Selby McCoy, Clettis Floyd, Jimmy Floyd, David Church, Michael Joseph Smith, Gary Breedlove, Randall Breedlove, Horace H. Huddleston, David Earl Jones, Ovie J. Henderson, John Tittle, David Tittle, Richard Tittle, Bobby Lambert, Hershel Lambert, and Charlie Gene Lambert.

A partial listing of those who gave the ultimate sacrifice for their country are as follows: William Homer Saylors, Hubert Thompson, Melvin Grady Mathis, Larry F. Dodds, and James Ralph Stevens.

The mid 1960s brought great change,, we got our own voting precinct and in 1967 we receivd a paved road.

In the 1970s we got our own water system. In the 1980s we got a fire department and a community center, in the late 1980s we got the Tuscumbia watershed.

Caterpillar Inc. located in our community in the late 1990s.

Although in recent years a part of our community has been incorporated into the city, many descendants of our charter families still dwell in this lovely community.

Submitted by: Sandra Lewis Gray

WHEELER

Wheeler is located in a wide valley between the long, sloping hills leading to Hodges Chapel and the steep rounded hills of Frankstown. The western side of the valley is the "bottom" where Wolfe Creek, Little Twenty-Mile, and Osborne Creek merge to form Twenty-Mile on its way to the Tombigbee.

Wheeler was not so named in the first years of its existence. Before the Civil War, a few farmers lived on the hills both east and west of the valley but the bottom itself was covered with trees and vegetation and often flooded.

The Carrollville-Jacinto Road crossed Twenty-Mile somewhere near the present Ritchie farm. The road then turned north until it reached the present location of Wheeler where it made another turn toward the east and then northeast. When the railroad was built a numbered station was designated at the place where the Carrollville Road crossed the railroad. This station immediately became known as the Five-Mile Crossing. The opening of a depot at the Five-Mile Crossing with trains stopping to load and unload freight and take on passengers brought a new way of life to the people. Some of them built business houses near the station, erected homes, conducted religious services, and organized a school.

Originally written by Martha Ruth Martin Much of the land in the new-born community was poorly drained. Mr. George Aiken whose family came to the Crossing soon after the railroad was built could remember that his favorite fishing place was a big shallow lake covering what is now the location of Wheeler High School and the grove of trees near the gym. He also remembered that the railroad was built on an embankment so high that as a boy when he rode by the side of the levee he could barely see across. (Mr. Aiken related his memories of Five-Mile Crossing to MS. Martha Ruth Martin a few years before he died.) Two vivid memories of his childhood at the Crossing remained very strong as long as Mr. Aiken lived. One was of the day when a messenger rushed through the village warning that the Yankees were marching down the railroad from Corinth and that General Forrest was moving from the west to meet them. If true, they would clash somewhere near Five-Mile Crossing. The majority of the village men were away in the army, but he remembered that his mother and other women took the children and fled into the hills east of the Crossing. One night they spent in a field near Meadow Creek. His other memory, he said, was probably just a tale without "even the smack of truth" in it; but every child in the community knew the story of the man who was hanged from a walnut tree whose branches extended over the Carrollville Road. Henceforth the place was supposed to be haunted, and the bad part about that was that the tree stood directly in front of the one-room school. (Mr. and Mrs. E. C. Floyd live in a house on the site of this first school.)

All of the people of Five-Mile Crossing were directly or indirectly dependent on farming, and they hoped to see the day when the rich bottom lands would be drained and prices of farm produce would rise. But on the heels of the confusion caused by the reconstruction came even ftirther declines. About this time early settlers became aware of the Farmers' Movement in America carried on by such organizations as the Grange. By 1880 the Grange was exerting influence on politics and splinter organizations were fielding candidates for president. One such party was the Wheeler's, whose strong agrarian platform appealed to a group of farmers and business men of the Crossing. More in derision than anything else, their friends began to refer to them as the Wheeler's. Very soon the name began to be used in referring to anyone from Five-Mile Crossing. Although the little national party never got off the ground, the people of Five-Mile Crossing liked the name and adopted it, always with the apostrophe s. The railroad retained that spelling, but the post office dropped it in favor of Wheeler.

Around the turn of the century, Wheeler began to grow and in the first decades of the new century it reached its peak. During this time the dredging of a canal through the bottom drained the rich fanning lands of the community. Mr. Tom Gordon had bought from the Shinnaults all of the land between what is now Frankstown and Wheeler except that part inherited by Mrs. Crawford. After the death of Mr. Gordon, the land was divided into farms now owned by Vance and Joe Wayne Garner, Wilmer Keeton, T. V. Strange, Sale Martin, and Sam Ritchie. In the early part of the century the bottom land south of the Gordon land was owned by George Grisham, David Pritchard, Kirk Glover, and the Gooch family.

As their businesses prospered around the turn of the century the residents of Wheeler began to build better homes for themselves. Many of the houses were large, some with two stories and all but a few painted white. When electricity became available, these homes were wired to take care of lights only; and as more electrical appliances were added, the inadequate wiring caused the houses to bum. No more than a dozen remained. Many of these survivors are the smaller houses. Among those who built homes in Wheeler in the boom days were J. H. Wallace, Aaron Ricks, R.E.L. Sutherland, Tandy Caver (the Callie Bruce house), Jim Hardin Grisham (the Larkin Lokey house, 1906), Dr. W. W. Sutherland, (the Milton home), Dr. W. H. Sutherland, Frank Elder, Sam Ritchie, George Maness, E. T. Keeton, Bud Chisholm, Doc Hill, Van Grisham, Will Grisham, Mrs. Nelson, John Miller., Otho Miller,, Clay Michael, John Gardner, Bob Gooch, Jim Olive, and Martin Franks.

On the hills to the east, the Ritchie home and the Pryor Gardner home were already aging gracefully. The Gardner house still stands as one of the oldest landmarks of the community.

Early in its development, Wheeler became a cotton buying center. Van Grisham became known over a wide area as an expert cotton grader and in addition to operating a mercantile business did a big business buying and selling cotton. His brother Jim Hardin Grisham also was engaged in the mercantile business. When a bank opened in Wheeler, Van Grisham and H. P. Elder were selected to operate it. The new brick building on the east side of the railroad, in addition to housing the bank, had room for a general store owned and operated by Sam Ritchie, grandfather of the present boys basketball coach of Wheeler High School.

When George Maness moved to Wheeler in 1905 he built a big white store just east of the railroad. The front of the store was high off the ground and steps led up to a small porch. An ell was added to the building which was located where Wheeler Cash Grocery now stands. Mr. Maness kept groceries and notions in his store. Next door in the ell, Alee Prather Tinkle had a millinery store which drew customers from a wide area. No one could trim a leghom hat with ribbons and flowers in such a charming way as could Miss Allee. Her creations with their bows and streamers were unforgettable.

From time to time other businesses operated in parts of the Maness building.

Between the Maness building and the railroad was a small building that housed the post office until 1906. In 1920 when R. S. Oakley moved from Gloster to Wheeler, he bought the Maness building and stocked it as a general mercantile store. Later he moved into the brick building still known as the bank building and remained in business there until his death. After Mr. Oakley's death, his son George carried on the business until he retired.

The town pump and watering trough were located just west of the bank building and long after the horse and buggy days were gone it remained as a gathering place for the exchange of news or gossip of the day. On the south side of the road and facing north were the John Miller store and Lokey's blacksmith shop. When Miss Agnes Harrison was appointed postmistress in 1906, Martin Franks built a small building between the blacksmith shop and the railroad for a post office. Mrs. Eva Lou Keeton, who succeeded Miss Agnes bought the building and remodeled it. Later when Arvil Smith was postmaster he added more space to the building. Sometime later H. P. Elder built a store and filling station east of the Miller building.

The Masonic Building built in the heyday of Wheeler was a big square building that opened onto the sidewalk on the comer just across from the present home of James Moore. The upstairs part was the meetmig place of the masons. The downstairs housed the office of the town doctor. Both Dr. W. W. Sutherland (known as old Dr. Sutherland) and Dr. Wade Sutherland, (known as young Dr. Sutherland) practiced 'in Wheeler. In 1915 the younger Dr. Sutherland moved to Booneville to become head of the new hospital there. Dr. J. C. Vandiver came to Wheeler at that time and practiced here for a number of years before moving to Baldwyn. No other doctor located in Wheeler.

In the first quarter of the new century, Mr. Shelt Rutherford built a very large store facing the railroad on the west side. (This store was about where Joe Wayne Garner's tool house is now.) A road in front of his store leading to the depot ran parallel to the railroad. At one time Mr. Rutherford set up a drug store in the back of the building. Several old-timers remember a startling event that took place one summer afternoon. Business in Rutherford's store was slow that afternoon, and the clerks and loafers alike were almost asleep when one of the young gallants of the town rode his horse into the store and down the aisle to the back where he pulled his steed to a halt and demanded that the store keeper serve the horse a cold drink.

The stunned store keeper brought the bottle and tipped it up to the horse's mouth. The horse drank with gusto. With an exaggerated bow and an elaborate "thank you", the dashing young horseman turned his mount and galloped out.

Between Rutherford's store and the old gin owned by Bud Chisholm were the livery stable, blacksmith shop, and grist mill owned and operated by E.T. Keeton, with the help of his sons, Lindsey, Ed, Varner, and Wilmer. The sons could spin many a tale about the traveling men who rented rigs and hired the Keeton boys to drive them to country stores in the area. Wilmer Keeton remembered firing the grist mill boiler with wood and working far into the night to fmish grinding the turns of meal for the people of the community.

Across from Rutherford's store on the north side of the road Martin Franks built and operated a store until he moved into the brick building built by Bud Chisholm. Somewhat back from the road up the slope from the brick store was a sawmill owned and operated by Charles Nagel.

About the turn of the century and all through the heyday of Wheeler, one of the most familiar sights around the community was Mr. George Aikens with his dray wagon pulled by Red, a horse so well trained he could skillfully back the wagon to the exact place for loading or unloading without any help from his master. When the homemakers of Wheeler bought ice boxes, Mr. Aikens; and Red made routine trips to the ice plant in Booneville and delivered ice to the customers in Wheeler.

Wheeler never had a caf6 as such, but from time to time someone would open a place that served hamburgers. Lonnie Blankfield was perhaps the most successful vendor, but the most famous of the hamburger joints was the *Dead Rat* operated by Walter Martin and Cotton (Clarence) Anderson while they were in high school.

At the peak of its growth, Wheeler became an incorporated town, replete with mayor, marshall, and board of aldermen. More for a symbol of determent than as a place of punishment, a jail was designed and built by the town fathers. Knowing the ingenuity of its bright young men, the authorities were aware that no ordinary fragile building would suffice. Consequently, they constructed the small edifice of two-by-fours laid flat on top of each other and so securely nailed together that nothing short of a tornado could destroy the building. Located near the railroad track in the "cut" below the Maness home, the jail was sufficiently isolated. Nobody knew for sure who was responsible, but under cover of darkness a cable was wrapped securely around the little building and fastened to the caboose of a freight train. As the train left the water tank and picked up speed, the little jail left its mooring and banged against the cross ties until finally like the onehoss Shay it fell completely apart and its pieces were scattered like matchsticks for a considerable distance down the railroad track. The jail may not have gone out in a burst of glory, but no one can say that it did not end with a decided burst of some kind.

Until its waning days, Wheeler always had a barber shop. Among the barbers were Clyde Rogers, Will Hicks, and R.B. Loveless.

The first telephone exchange was installed by Mr. George Owens in his home near the school. His sons Van, Jack, and Boyd helped Mr. Owens install telephones and maintain the lines. Oliver Wilson bought the exchange and house and he and his family ran the exchange. After the death of MrNilson, Ralph and Verdie Mae Labbeare operated the telephone service. During the depression, the exchange went out of business.

The town depot was the general gathering place for the young men of the village. On cold nights they built roaring fires in the stove and sat around until very late. Those who had dates bade the young ladies an early goodnight so they could join their friends around the stove. In the daytime the chief social event for both old and young was meeting the passenger trains. Conductors often teased passengers bound for Wheeler that the engineer might not be able to see so tiny a speck as Wheeler and consequently might go rushing through. But they never did.

The first post office in Wheeler opened in February 1888 with George A. Prichard as postmaster. From that time until 1906, several people served short terms as postmaster: George N. Williams, 1888-1890; Henry D. Caver, 1890-1891; William B. Wileman, 1891-1892; George H. Williams, 1892-1897; James C. Glover, 1897-1900; John Seay, 1900-1902; Thomas Hale, 1902-1906. Since 1906 only four people have served: Miss Agnes Harrison, 1906-1942; Eva Lou Keeton Nabors, 1942-1960; William A. Smith, 1960-1980; and Elizabeth Gardner Glover, 1980 until the present. One rural mail delivery route went out from Wheeler, and for many years Mr. Doc Hill was the caiTier. This route was discontinued and the territory added to the Booneville delivery.

The old plank sidewalks of early days were replaced by concrete walks under a ATA grant during the depression. During the depression, in order to save taxes the people decided to dissolve the incorporation and no longer fimction as a town. The last mayor was Donald Franks under whose administration the streets were made wider.

Although Wheeler has four churches, it has never had a burial ground.

The second decade of the new century ushered in the age of the automobile and trucks. Wheeler had been created by the railroad, and as the railroad began to lose business to the trucking industry, business in Wheeler declined. A new highway which shortened the distance from Baldwyn to Booneville brought disaster to Wheeler. The new road missed Wheeler by more than a mile and that along with the depression of the thirties caused businesses in Wheeler to close or move elsewhere. Only two stores remained: Franks' and Oakley's. After the depression, Luke Crawford and Wilson Williams operated a thriving grocery store, followed by Gardner and Sappington. At the present only one store remains. It is owned and operated by Willie Moore.

Although the business section of Wheeler decreased, the community itself continued to grow. In 1993 the fire department built a new building and purchased a new fire truck, making it one of the most well-equipped volunteer fire departments in the state. Randy Moore is the fire chief. Sherry Pannell Prather has a beauty shop in the old post office building and a new post office was built just south of the Baptist Church. The school has added a new larger elementary building, renovated the lunch room, built a new gymnasium, and added a Tech-Prep building. A new Head Start building was built in 1999 on the road leading to Meadow Creek.

A Civitan Club was organized in 1994, with Ted Hill President, and built a walking track next to the old gym location.

Submitted by Sharon Hill as originally written by Martha Ruth Martin

THE OLDEST HOUSE IN WHEELER

This house was built by Robert Beall Gardner and wife, Mary Maria Eugenia (Hightower) Gardner, probably before the Civil War. The original structure has five bedrooms, front and back porch and a breezeway that leads to the kitchen and dining area. It has a stairway that leads to a full attic with beams put together with wooden pegs instead of nails. They had a slave who lived as a family member and shared the Gardner name. Robert and Mary are buried in the Hodges Chapel Cemetery near Wheeler, Mississippi.

The Gardners had nine children: John Hightower, Obadiah Benjamin, James Wood (died in childhood), Judge Brantley, Charlotte Emily, Robert Beall, Mary Lou, Sterling Pryor, and William Flournoy.

At the death of Robert and Mary, the house was inherited by Pryor Gardner and at his death the house was inherited by a daughter, Eva Lou (Gardner) Keeton Nabors. The house is presently owned by McEllis Nabors, a stepson of Eva Lou Nabors. The cedar trees in front are probably 100 years old or more. Photo caption: Robert Beall Gardner house, the oldest in Wheeler.
Submitted by Max E. Wilson

Robert Beall Gardner house. Oldest house in Wheeler, MS.

SCHOOLS

BOONEVILLE SCHOOL DISTRICT

Before the Civil War, the first school was established in Booneville as a two-room frame house across from the courthouse by a Presbyterian minister Reverend O.F. Rogers. In 1872 the Methodist Episcapal Church bought ten acres of land and built an all-male high school known as Paine High School. The six room brick building opened in 1874 with Professor C.M. Verdell as principal and was under the oversight of the Methodist Conference. In 1876 The town of Booneville purchased the property but retained the name. In 1887 J.C. Benedict became principal and changed the name to Booneville Normal School with five departments including the primary, preparatory, teachers, scienctific, and classic.

By 1900 the old school building was torn down. A new ten room building was opened in 1902 named Booneville High School with D.A. Hill serving as surperintendent. He served for nineteen years. Because the enrollment was growing so rapidly, another school was built in 1916 and named the D.A. Hill School in honor of the superintendent. This school was located on the cast side of town near some of the oldest homes. A new structure was erected in 1948 and the name was changed to Booneville Grammar School.

A tornado in 1936 damaged the high school so severely that it had to be torn down. A school building and gymnasium was begun but destroyed by fire in 1937. The new school and gym were completed in 1940 with seventeen classrooms and an auditorium. Labor and material were furnished under the WPA Works Progress Administration program, a Rooseveltian emergency measure. Materials amounted to 80% and labor 20% of the total cost and a replica of the school was exhibited at the Worlds Fair in New York in 1940 demonstrating the WPA worksmanship. In 1950 eight classrooms were added to the south end of the existing building.

Located in the center of the colored district, a colored school was built in 1921. In 1960 a new school replaced it and dedicated to Dr. W.H. Anderson for the work he had done. Mr. James Triplett was principal. The Wick Anderson High School became Anderson Junior High with integration.

Because of the proximity to the college, land was bought near the college property for additional buildings for the school district. The land was purchased in 1959 and by 1961 Booneville Junior High School was completed to accomodate fifth, sixth, seventh, and eighth grades. It included a cafeteria, eighteen classrooms, a gym, conference room, and clinic. The name was changed to Booneville Middle School and in 1994 renamed R.L. Long Booneville Middle School in honor of Howard Long, the retiring principal.

In 1980 the Booneville City Schools were separated from the county system and became the Booneville Seperate School District. Mr. Troy Henderson was superintendent for one year and in 1981 Robert Griffin became superintendent. At this time there were four schools in the district: Booneville Elementary School (grades 1-3, Booneville Middle School (grades 4-6), Anderson Junior High (grades 7-8), and Booneville High School grades 9-12).

After a separation in the wall, the auditorium was condemed and the school began plans for a new high school. Two bond issues failed to pass in 1982 and 1983. After the failure of the 1983 bond issue, the old elementary building was closed and classes were consolidated into the remaining buildings. In 1986 the laws changed allowing school bonds to be issued and a new building to be completed in 1988. The new building was located on the property occupied by the Middle School and connected to it.

Made possible through a cooperative effort of the State of Mississippi Department of Education, contributing partners, and the community, the Booneville Environmental Education Center was opened in 1998. Located adjoining the Middle School, it contains the latest technology both in the classrooms and an auditorium.

Three separate additions were made to Anderson Elementary School in the fall of 1988, 1994, and 1998. In 1997 the Booneville School District received a level 5 rating from the Mississippi Department of Education recognizing excellence in education and meeting all academic and performance standards. This is the highest rating that can be attained.
Submitted by Brenda Pike Scott.

BURTON SCHOOL

Burton, MS is home of the Old Burton Schoolhouse, located on Hwy 30, 12 miles east of Booneville. This property became a Mississippi Landmark in July 1995.

The school is significant in the history of education in Prentiss County not only for being one of the earliest consolidated schools, but also for being one of the earliest brick school buildings in rural Prentiss County - possibly the only one with solid brick walls (13" thick).

The Burton schoolhouse, constructed in 1922-1923, is a red brick, one story, hipped roof structure, whose doors and windows have a double brick segmented arch. Exterior walls have a triple layer of bricks. Interior brick walls have a plaster finish. All other walls, ceilings, and floors are finished with tongue and groove lumber.

Dr. Bolivar Smith, whose medical office was in Burton, served as a general practitioner for more than 40 years. Recognizing the need for better school facilities, he donated 7 acres of land (the deed now calls for 5 1/3 acres) on which to build the school.

Reputable people who lend historical significance to the school and have made meaningful contributions to Prentiss County - and to the state of Mississippi - are former teachers: Mr. Raymond T. Jarvis (a judge), Ms Rebecca Thompson (wife of Representative Jamie Whitten), and Mr. Elmer McCoy (a state Representative who served four terms).

Mr. Lieuallen Riddle, a landholder and sawmiller, provided the first school transportation (covered wagon pulled by mules).

After the school closed in 1958, it was not used at all for eight years. Then, it was leased to a church as a place to worship from 1966-1982. In 1983 it was leased to five men from Burton to be used as a Community Center. When the five year lease expired in 1988, it was not renewed.

SINGING SCHOOL AT BURCHAM SCHOOL

Singing School at Burcham School, previous page. Picture from about 1914 First at left end is John Lovel, teacher in dark suit 1st top row: Elton Gray, Anna Liza Smith, Gale Garrett, Ida Lovel, Louis, Woodruff, Eliza Schoggins, Henry Smith, Maggie Pollard, Lena, Hare, John Pollard, Angie. Rogers, Maggie Borden, Elzie Brimingham, Jessie D. Jones, Mark Lambert, Joe Clark, Luther Borden k 2nd row: Lee Garrett, Rozie Smith, Maggie Thompson, Mable Carpenter, Mattie Lou Rogers, Mabelle Brimingham, Will Hutchins, Alma Gray, Ola Butler, Mary Lizzie Brimingham, Elmanzie Rogers, Mary Lou Woodruff, Lillie Flanagan, Sherman Jones, Chalmus Laster, John William Carpenter, Robert Burcham 3rd row: John Garrett, Vada Carpenter, Edna Lovel, Essie Lovel, Contenea Lee, Lucy McAnally, Bettie Lee, Autie Beard, Ottie Massey, Willie Beard, Essie Massey, Nettie Borden, Lena Caddle, Hattie Parson, Coleman Rogers, Ada Tidwell, Wyatt Jones, Andrew Burcham 4th row: Sam Caddle, Lonnie Tidwell, Verna Brimingham, Letha Carpenter, Velma Caddle, Alma Carpenter, Lois Brimingham, Oscar Lambert or Ernest Massey ? not sure, Claude Lambert ? not sure, Guy Beard, Leonard Massey, and Guy Scoggins. Submitted by Charles Smith.

Burton School

At this time Ernestine Cunningham and the Burton Hunting Club led the way in trying to keep the schoolhouse repaired and usable; however, with limited funds and lack of interest, it soon became too much of a burden for a few people to deal with. Being without a caretaker put the schoolhouse in serious jeopardy.

Planning for restoration of the Burton schoolhouse began in mid-December 1994 when Maxine and Ruth McCoy, looking for a suitable place to have their family Christmas dinner, found the schoolhouse in need of much repair. The roof, ceilings, and floors were heavily damaged but repairable. io

Money was needed fast r stabilizing the building. Estimated cost to restore was $500,000. We were not deterred. A community meeting was held on January 23, 1995, committees were appointed. The next meeting would be on February 13, 1995 when every committee was expected to give a report. Every committee did a great job.

At this meeting the Burton Community Historical Society was formed and officers were elected. A motion was made to apply for listing as a Mississippi Landmark, in hopes of receiving federal funds - none were received. But, in August of 1996 confirmation was received signifying that Burton School had been declared a Mississippi Landmark. This recognition has brought prestige and rejuvenation to the Burton community.

Every able-bodied person in Burton has assisted in the work. Early in the spring of 1995 we started a massive cleanup inside and out of the old schoolhouse and were amazed at it's beauty.

A welcome sign was hung inviting everyone to our first event on the first Saturday in May, 1995. Thus began "fund raising" which continued twice monthly until September, 1996 when work actually began on the roof.

By this time, in excess of $30,000 ($3,325 were donations) had been raised. Hardly a drop in the bucket of what was needed, but a great start.

In 1995 the legislature appropriated a grant of $250,000 for restoring old schoolhouses. Our need was great so we applied for $250,000 and received $110,000 in the fall of 1996. Much has been done and much remains to be done.
Submitted by Ruth McCoy.

MOSE THOMAS HILL

Mose T. Hill is the man for whom Hills Chapel School, in Prentiss County, Mississippi, was named. Moses T. Hill was born in Wayne County, Tenneseee on August 7, 1864 to T. M. Hill and Malinda K. Taylor. On July 10, 1887 he married Miss Dora Alice Newborn, born on November 22, 1870, the daughter of James Haswell Newborn and Nancy Elizabeth Davis. To this union eight children were born, one of whom died in infancy. Their children were Ada (June 16, 1889-1964) who married Harve T. Free, Walter L. (Sep 3, 1891-May 2, 1962) who married first Delma Cooper and second Emily Lowenstein, Daisy Ester (Jan 19, 1894-Nov 6, 1919) who married Beryl McClain, Betre Ethel (Feb 4, 1897-Jan 23, 1964) who married first John Cooper and second Woodward Brazil (these children were born in Clifton, Tennessee), Sydney Clyde (Jan 21, 1902-Mar 23, 1991) who married Hazel Louise Holder, Earl (Aug 15, 1906) who married Mable Smith, and Queenie Jewel (Apr 2, 1909-Nov 1930) who married a Radcliff (these last three children were born in Booneville, Mississippi).

Mose T. Hill moved from Tennessee to Mississippi in 1897 and from there to New Mexico in 19 10, settling on a homestead some miles east of Kenna. Then in 1918 he, with his family, moved to Portales, New Mexico.

He bought the Boucheru Wagon Yard in 1919 and operated it for a while. When the new high school was built in 1922, he was

caretaker for it for 13 years. Mose T. Hill died on October 6, 1938 in Portales, New Mexico and his wife, Dora Alice, died on May 18, 1940 in Portales.
Submitted by Jennifer Dill Source: Earl Hill, Hogales, Az

ROARING HOLLOW

Roaring Hollow was a school, a frame building with seats hewed out of logs. It stood on the south side of county road 4140 until it was destroyed by a storm in about 1913. The rebuilding, from what I can find out, was a community effort. Men of the area who donated time and materials to rebuild on the north side of the road were Jim Pounds, who donated lumber; Oscar Sanders, who drug up the seals for the building; George Brumbley and his boys; Elis Sanders and many others that I can't name who donated their time to building the building that is there now.

After the building was completed they held school in it for a while as well as church services. Roaring Hollow used to be a place known far and wide for its gospel meetings, singings and dinners on the ground. Many preachers held gospel meetings at Roaring Hollow. Even I can remember meetings with Brother J.A. Thornton, Brother Calvin Barber, Brother Charles Leonard, Brother J.T. Smith, Brother Haskel Sparks, and Brother L.D. Willis just to mention a few.

People from miles away came to Roaring Hollow; the building would be packed, not even standing room was available. I've been told that at times there would be people standing outside with the windows raised to hear the gospel. Those must be wonderful memories of friendships of days past.

I guess the memories became final in about 1994 when the men decided, with only about eight members and four of them in regular attendance, to discontinue services at Roaring Hollow Church of Christ.

Through the years Roaring Hollow endured the 20th century and the memories that people have win last on into the 21st century.
Submitted by Marie Hester Thom.

7 of Moses children are in this picture

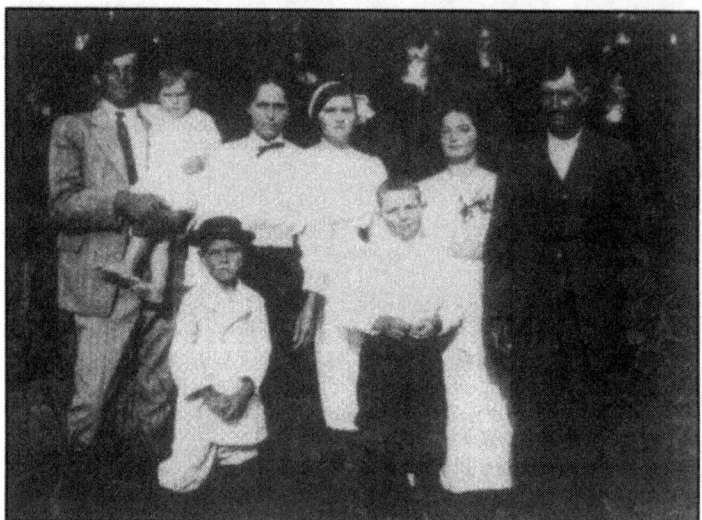
The M.T. Hill Family. Front row - Left Earl, Clyde, Back row - Left Walter, Jewel, Alice Betre, Ester, Rose Hill. THis picture was made about 1912 in New Mexico. The Hill Family attended school at Hills Chapel in 1907. Mose Hill helped build the school and the school is named after him.

Row 1 - Sandra Senter, Randall Breedlove, Billy Frost, Bobby Marshall, Joe Guy Kelio, Lloyd Stacy, and Hoyle Lambert. Row 2. Barbara Searcy, Peggy Pippin, Kathlene Kendrick, Billy Frost, Arion Mason and Clifton Bullard. Row 3 - Jeweldeen Jones, Lavern Trimbel, Sue Lovell, Sandra Lewis, Kenneth Harris, Doyle Lambert, Larry Hutchens and Mr. Ted Ledbetter. ow 4 - Carolyn Shackelford, Regetta Smith, Ann Taylor, Louise Cole, Billy Holland, Bobby Cole and Horace Huddleston. Row 5 - Ann Palmer, Evelyn Lindley, Linda King, Eugene Michels, Gene Burress and Charlie Gene Lambert.

SPORTS

ARNOLD, HARRISON AND BONNER

Harrison Arnold and his younger brother, Bonner, were each called "Mister Basketball" by some.

The big brother of the pair, Harrison, is looked upon as the dean of high school coaches in Mississippi. His record of 44 years in the classroom and 37 on the basketball court at Wheeler and at other places like Jumpertown, Baldwyn and Booneville speaks for itself. During his coaching career he coached his own brother, his two sons, Coach Jimmy Arnold and Coach Richard Arnold, and his daughter who was a star for her dad's Baldwyn High School team. Besides his son, his daughter and his kid brother, Harrison Arnold developed such great stars as DeVoy and Cecil Graham, Googe Prather of University of Alabama fame, John Ray Ricks and his brother Arlis Ricks of Delta State, Milton Steele of Mississippi State and Milton's brother, Fats Steele, Jerry Keeton of Mississippi State, the Saylors boys of Wheeler High School, and more too numerous to name. His teams appeared in 16 state tournaments; his 1929 team at Wheeler won the state championship and placed high in the National High School Tournament in Chicago, and his 1955 Wheeler High Boys won the state B-BB championship and went all the way to cop the Overall Tournament of Champions in Jackson. In 1973 he was named to the Mississippi Association of Coaches first Hall of Fame.

Bonner Arnold played on three state championship teams at Wheeler High, in 1925, 1926, and 1929. As a member of the 1929 team, coached by big brother Harrison, Bonner made the all-state team, the all-Tri-State team, and the all-National team. After his own school days were over, he coached for several years at Belmont High and Northeast Mississippi Junior College. At Belmont, his teams won two state titles. His Belmont boys won the championship in 1943 and his Belmont girls won two years later. In 1943, his team opposed brother Harrison's Jumpertown team, when he outdid big brother. When Bonner's Belmont boys beat Harrison's Jumpertown boys in the final game of the state meet, it was the first time in the history of Mississippi tournament play that two brothers opposed each other for the state championship as rival coaches.

Bonner's junior college teams won seven state junior college titles and twice his team was No. 2 in the National Junior College Tournament.

Hills Chapel Ball Team

Thrasher High School 1939 Basketball Team. Seated Inez Henson, Moeise Hopkins, Maxine Olive, Charlene Davis, Marie Hopkins. Standing - Helen Hester Williams, Marie Brown, Imojene Daniels, Zee Hopkins, Willie Hopkins.

Sam's sixth State Championship as Wheeler State Champions March 1992. Pictured are: Kate Richey, Sam Richey, Gabriel Richey, Clark holding Gabe, and Gardner Richey.

SAM RICHEY

Coach Sam Richey has coached varsity high school boys' basketball for thirty-three years in Prentiss County at Jumpertown, Wheeler, and Baldwyn. He holds several state records and is listed in the National High School Sports Record Book. as one of the top twenty coaches for wins in boys' basketball in the United States.

Coach Richey's state accomplishments include 17 state tournament boys' teams including 6 state championships, 4 state runners-up, and 7 state semi-finals. He has 23 North Half teams and 17 District/Division championships. His won/loss record at the end of the 1999-2000 season was 840/345 that is third in all-time Mississippi Boys' Basketball.

Coach Richey is the son of the late Robert Richey and Katherine Richey both of Prentiss County. He is married to Dale Gardner Richey. They have two sons - Clark Richey and his wife Rothann McGee Richey, and Clay Richey and his wife Lorie Bishop Richey. Kate, Gardner, Gabe, Reggie, and Rob Richey are their five grandchildren.

CHURCHES

BOONEVILLE CHURCH OF CHRIST

The Booneville Church of Christ began in 1903 when three Christian ladies, Clarissa and Fannie Wright, and Jessica Bums began meeting in their homes. In 1906 J.E. Wright moved his family to Booneville from Marietta and readily opened his home to the church as a meeting place. Following his death, the church began meeting in a rented building on Church Street in downtown Booneville.

In 1919 the church bought property on Main Street and built a frame building in 1920 which was used until 1950. In 1950 the frame building was torn down and a new brick building was built. The church quickly outgrew the building on Main Street and in 1960 a choice five-acre plot was purchased on Highway 45 and *in 1961 the congregation moved into its present facilities.

Doug Greenway has been the pulpit minister for the Booneville church of Christ since April, 1982. The immediate predecessor of Greenway was Bill Huggins, who served from 1970-1982. His predecessor was J.A. Thornton, who served from 1956-1970. Brother Thornton returned to work with the Booneville church in July, 1986 as associate minister. Larry Morgan has served as education director and youth worker since 1976 and Tommy Baragona, began working as the involvement and youth minister in April, 1999. Other ministers who have served full-time with the Booneville church of Christ are: W.A. Black, V.P. Black, Athelson Crowson, JW. Evans, W.R. Ward, Joe K. Alley, and Jimmy Powell. Jim Archer served as associate minister for many years.

Presently the Booneville Church of Christ is overseen by five elders, Jack Arnold, Billy Deaton, James Googe, Donnie Sweeney and Jim Wilson, and is served by eighteen deacons, Eddie Allen, Tommy Baragona, J.T. Beard, Adrian Edge, Milton Floyd, Buster Green, Roger Griffin, Joel Johnson, Jr., Ronny L. Johnson, Dale Kendrick, Bobby Maddox, Billy Martin, Eddie Mauney, Larry Morgan, Tommy Palmer, Stan Pounds, Doyle Trolliger, and Gordon Tyra. The membership is made up of 315 families and 530 members and continues to grow.

Some of the numerous ministries, programs and areas of service that the Booneville church of Christ offers are: an extensive education program offering Bible classes to all ages including home Bible studies and Bible correspondence courses, community benevolence program, two yearly blood drives, food ministry, transportation to all services, Vacation Bible School, visitation program, helping hands program, tape ministry (all sermons are recorded and mailed upon request, presently 130 families locally, throughout the country and overseas receive the tapes), daily radio program, two weekly tv programs, and regular activities for youth, college age, and semior citizens. Our ladies host the annual North Mississippi Ladies Retreat each year at Tishomingo State Park and the church conducts its own summer Bible Camp.

Booneville First United Methodist Church

The Booneville Church of Christ is dedicated to the restoration of New Testament Christianity, respecting both the authority and the silence of the scriptures. It is our sincere desire to worship the Lord to the best of our ability, using only the New Testament as our pattern.

The Booneville Church of Christ extends a cordial invitation to everyone to visit our services, and sincerely hopes that we can be of assistance to all as we strive to spread the Gospel in our community and in all the world.

BOONEVILLE FIRST UNITED METHODIST CHURCH

The church was organized in 1867 by a small band of Christians who met in a frame building, used for a schoolhouse, and organized the first Methodist Church in Booneville. That first building was located on Fourth Street, and it was a part of the Rienzi Circuit, where J. W. Honnoll was the pastor.

In 1875, after the church-school property was sold, the M & O Rail Road Company gave the church a corner lot near the old railroad station. Efforts began in 1895 to build a new brick church, and the building was completed in 1897. That structure was at the corner of Main and East Church Street, where the Prentiss County Chancery Court building is presently located. The 1897 church was destroyed by fire, but was rebuilt.

In 1928, the present building was completed (400 West Church Street). The Deed to the lot where the present church is located is in the Prentiss county Chancery's Clerk's Office in the Town of Booneville, in Book No. 39, Page 147, dated November 10., 1927.~ Special Ceremonies took place in 1941 when the note was burne8 wh:~n the final debt was paid off.

The Education Building was erected in 1963. The Church Bell had been purchased in 1904; however, the Bell Tower was not constructed until 1970. The Waters Patio was dedicated in 1971.

The Woman's Missionary Society (The Home Missionary Society and the Foreign Missionary Society) began in the 18901 s. They were combined in 1910. In 1921, the Wesleyan Service Guild was organized, and in 1940, it became a part of the Women's Society of Christian Service. Then in 1972, they became known as United Methodist Women.

Sue Robinson, daughter of one of the ministers, W. L. Robinson, has been a missionary in Africa and has worked with the United Methodist General Board of Global Ministries.

The church at 400 West Church Street in Booneville is the Booneville First United Methodist Church. However, it has been known as the Methodist Episcopal Church, Methodist Episcopal Church South, The Methodist Church before becoming a United Methodist Church. There are approximately 500 members.

The following is a corrected list of pastors/ministers of the First United Methodist Church since its beginning in 1867:

1868-69	J. W. Honnoll
1870-71	John Barcroft
1872	J. W. Honnoll (Returned)
1873-1875	Thomas Cameron
1876	J. A. Babb (One Year)
1877-78	John Parcroft (Returned)
1879	Eugene Johnson (Served One Year)
1880	J. T. Harris (Served One Year)
1881	John H. Mitchell
1882	Jimmie B. Johnson
1883	J. W. Anderson (Served Part of Year)
1883	P. R. Hoyle (Filled Out This Year)
1884	E. L. Spraggins
1885-86	D. W. Babb
1887	George S. Inge
1888-91	K. M. Harrison
1892-93	B. F. Phillips
1894	H. R. Tucker
1895	John C. Park
1896	A. P. Sage
1897	George H. Lipscomb
1898	Thomas B. Clifford
1899-1901	J. M. Bradley
1902-1903	B. P. Jaco
1904-1905	T. C. Weir
1906-1907	W. G. Harbin
1908-1910	J. H. Holder (He also served part of 1907)
1911-1914	S. A. Brown
1915	Lee M. Lipscomb
1916-17	J. M. Wyatt
1918-1921	J. W. Ward
1922	H. P. Lewis
1923-24	E. G. Mohler
1925-26	E. E. McKeithen (The Centenary Pledge Paid in Full.)
1927-1929	W. H. Mounger
1930-1934	J. V. Bennett
1935-1937	P. F. Luter
1937-1941	W. L. Robinson
1941-1944	Thad H. Ferrell
1944-47	J. J. Baird
1947-1952	W. M. Jones
1952-54	J. A. George
1954-58	J. C. Christian
1958-61	W. V. Stokes
1961-65	W. L. Wallace, Jr.
1965-68	W. R. Richerson
1968-73	E. S. Furr
1973-78	Shelby Hathorn
1978-85	Charles L. Potts
1985-1989	William V. (Bill) Kemp
1989-2000	Bobby W. Hankins

Additional and more detailed information can be found in the first edition of the History of Prentiss County, Mississippi 1984. This is merely a condensed version of our history that was published in that first edition. Because of errors in the first edition, a complete listing of the pastors/ministers is given.

Prepared by Laura Windham Cartwright Historian, Booneville First United Methodist Church

BOONEVILLE PRESBYTERIAN CHURCH

The Booneville Presbyterian Church was organized March 3, 1871, with nineteen members transferred from Ebenezer Church which was located where Gaston Baptist Church is now. The church has been at the present location, 801 W. George E. Allen Drive, since early 1973. The service of dedication was held on Sunday, May 27, 1973. The former location was on Bridge Street, present site of the Bridge Apartments.

Booneville Presbyterian Church is a member of the Presbytery of St. Andrew, Synod of Living Waters, Presbyterian Church, USA. As a connectional church, the mission, programs of service, and giving follow guidelines set forth by the General Assembly, Presbyterian Church, USA. The overall program of Presbyterian Women is part of a similar pattern. However, the church and the

Booneville Presbyterian Church 801 W George and Allen Drive

Chandler's Chapel Baptist Church, 1999

Christ United Methodist Church of Booneville

PW organization also take an active part in local missions and community activities.

Dr. Eldridge E. Fleming of Tupelo has served as pastor since May 1994. Worship service is at 9:00 a.m. each Sunday, followed by Sunday School at 10:30 a.m.

A fuller history of this church and histories of earlier different branches of Presbyterian Churches in the county appear in the first edition of the Prentiss County History.

CANDLER'S CHAPEL BAPTIST CHURCH

On September 29, 1895, after preaching by Bro. J.S. Berry in Blythe's Chapel, the brethren met for the purpose of organizing a Baptist Church. Rev. E.S. Candler, Jr. acted as clerk pro. tem. Candler's Chapel Baptist Church was organized with 31 charter members.

A building committee was appointed in October 1895. The R.C. Anderson Estate deeded one acre and F.M. Whitlow deeded one acre for a church building. It is not known when the first building was completed.

The following was taken from the minutes of the church. "Bro. C.S. Wales held a meeting in August 1924. At that time the church was almost dead. Bro. Wales and others worked hard to restore the church. There were 28 additions during this meeting." The old church was reborn! It is said that this meeting was held in a brush arbor. A new building was built during the summer of 1924.

According to Ida Lee (Sparks) McCutchens, a few efforts were made in the early years to organize a Sunday School but it did not last. Then in 1936, she and her first husband, Ernest Houch, moved into the community. The pastor, Bro. Joe Crawford, asked Ernest to organize a Sunday School. She bought cheap material and curtained off the corners of the church for classrooms. Charley Holley taught the adults, Ernest the teenagers, she took the middle age group but does not remember who taught the little children. This was the beginning of a continuous Sunday School at Candler's Chapel.

The church moved into the present building in 1957. In 1966 land was purchased from Mr. and Mrs. Clyde Shook and a pastor's home was built. In 1991 a new Family Life Center was built and the sanctuary of the church was completely redecorated.

On October 29, 1995, Candler's Chapel celebrated 100 years of service to the Lord. The day began with Sunday School at 10:00 a.m. followed by a note burning and worship service at 11:00 a.m. A wonderful meal and fellowship followed in the Family Life Center. Approximately 125 members, former members and friends helped celebrate this joyous occasion.

Pastors to serve at Candler's Chapel are as follows: Perry Duncan 1895-1896, C.S. Wales 1903-1911, L.O. Roberts 1911-1916, Joe Crawford 1925-1936, J.O. Gunthrop 1936-1937, Joe Crawford 1938-1948, Malcolm Jones 1949-1950, Bro. Butler 1950-1953, James Smith 1954-1956, Charles Smith 1956-1959, Dewey Wallis 1960-1964, Eugene Tennison 1964-1964, Lon Brown 1965, Herman Dykes 1965-1966, Alton Byrd 1966-1970, Dale Prince 1971, Mike Tyson 1972-1973, Steve Hardwick 1973-1976, F.A. Collins 1976-1985, Tommy Wilder 1985-1987, Jay Houston 1988-1989, Roger Kennedy 1990-1992, Ed Lowrey 1992-present.

Submitted by Mrs. Winna Cunningham

CHRIST UNITED METHODIST CHURCH

Christ United Methodist Church, located just west of Booneville on the Booneville Blackland Road was born of a dream of the Rev. Huey Wood, former Prentiss County preacher, in 1966.

As pastor of the West Prentiss Parish, which at that time consisted of the Blackland, Carolina, Crossroads, Jumpertown, and Oak Grove churches, he saw that the Blackland and Oak Grove churches, which were only 3 miles apart, could be merged to form one larger, more effective church. This was the dream. In 1966 he shared this with the church members from both churches, and the dream became a vision.

Although he was the moving force behind the vision, Rev. Wood was denied the opportunity to organize the new church as he was moved in June of 1967, and a new pastor was appointed. Thus it was that in July of 1967, Rev. Henry Wimberly organized the Christ United Methodist Church.

The history of the new church did not begin in 1967 when it was organized; neither did it begin in 1966 with a dream. The history of the church could be traced back to John Wesley and the first Methodists and even back to the apostolic church if we wanted to go that far.

But it is sufficient for our purpose to trace this history back to the middle of the 1800's and the beginning of the Blackland Methodist Episcopal Church-South.

While it is difficult to determine the exact date from official records, it seems clear from available sources that Rev. J. M. Wells organized a Methodist Episcopal Church-South sometime in the late 1850's or early 1860's. Of the original church, located on what is now the Archie Saylor's farm, about 1 mile north of the present church location, all that is left are the remains of a brick chimney and a cemetery. This cemetery is known as the Mitchell Cemetery and was named after the early settlers on whose farm it was located.

In 1871 two acres of land on which the present building is located were deeded to the Methodist Episcopal Church-South by Solomon Dalton and L. W. Redus. This land was to be used for a church and cemetery. The first trustees of this property were L. W. Redus, Mrs. E. J. Redus, Kader Miller, H. B. Barber and Pat Perkins.

The Blackland Methodist Church, located as it was, next to the Blackland School (now the Blackland Community Center) served as one of the centers of the community.

This church stood for many years. A new building was erected in 1933 and still stands today. It was sold after the Christ United Methodist Church was built and is presently serving as the house of worship for the Church of the Lord Jesus Christ.

The beginning of the Oak Grove United Methodist Church is well documented. In 1903 members of the Booneville Methodist Church living in the Osborne Creek Community wanted to build their own church, mainly because bad winter weather made travel to town impractical.

On July 25, 1903, a building committee consisting of Aaron Spain, James Taylor, Robert B. Smith, and J. P. Tays met at the parsonage in Booneville to discuss building a church in the Osborne Creek Community. It was decided to construct a 30 x 50 feet, 14 feet high frame building. The plans and specifications were to be prepared by Rev. B. P. Jaco, Presiding Elder, Aaron Spain, and Robert B. Smith.

The first services were held on November 25, 1903, with 18 male and 26 female members. In 1912 the membership was 51. At the time of merger in 1968, Oak Grove had 63 members.

The Oak Grove church and property were sold to help building the new church. The building is now occupied by an independent congregation.

Christ United Methodist Church, located on the Blackland Road, half way between the former Blackland and Oak Grove United Methodist Churches, on land given by Mr. and Mrs. Millard Lothenore, has seen many changes since its beginning. The average attendance has grown from 58 in 1968 to its present 93. The membership *now* stands at 145. It began life as part of the 5 point West Prentiss Parish, but in 1970 was placed with Wheeler to form a 2 point charge. In 1980, the church was named "Church of the Year" for the New Albany District of the United Methodist Church.

The Planning Committee met on June 29, 1977, to plan for the Fellowship Hall. Plans were drawn up for a 40 x 50 addition and $15,000 was borrowed for the construct-Ion. The Fellowship Hall was paid for within the next three years.

In the Spring of 1982, lightning struck the church and caused extensive damage. It was also in 1982 that the church separated from Wheeler and joined with the Lebanon United Methodist Church to form the Christ-Lebanon Charge. And, having bought a parsonage, began a new era with its first resident pastor.

In 1985 a new altar rail was built in the church and the parsonage was improved with new carpet, new shingles and an additional carport. Also new church hymnals were purchased.

In September, 1989, the church had a 50-Year Celebration for any church member who has been a Christian for 50 years or longer. These Christians were honored with a dinner and singing and a plaque with their names engraved thereon was erected in the Fellowship Hall as a memorial.

A new Family Life Center was built in August, 1989, at a contract cost of $36,368.00. With a $3500 grant from the conference and with tithes and offerings from the local church the indebtedness on the Family Life Center was paid in full within three years.

In 1990 the parsonage was redecorated. The extra carport was made into a laundry room with additional closet space and new landscaping around the parsonage.

Also in 1990, a new sound system was installed in the church sanctuary, new stained glass windows were added along with new vinyl siding and gutters, new landscaping around the church, redecoration of the Library and bathrooms.

In 1992 additional acreage was bought around the parsonage and in 1993 the MS Conference made The Wesley Foundation at Northeast MS Community College a permanent part of Christ United Methodist Church with the pastor of Christ Church being the Director.

In June, 1994, Christ United Methodist Church again received the "Small Membership Church of the Year" for the New Albany District. Also in 1994, the Sunday School rooms were renovated and new carpet was installed in the northex, hallway, and Sunday School rooms.

In June, 1997, the new stained glass window was installed behind the pulpit. Also new carpet was installed in the Fellowship Hall and new folding cushioned chairs were purchased for the Fellowship Hall and the Prayer Room.

With the Lord's blessings and the dedication, hopes and prayers of each church member, this dream that became a vision and now a reality, is that Christ United Methodist Church will be a light to guide the way to bigger and better rewards in the years to come.

Pastors of Christ United Methodist Church:
1967-1968	Rev. Henry L. Wimberly
1968-1973	Rev. Faban Clark
1973-1977	Rev. Jimmy Grisham
1977-1980	Rev. W. G. (Bill) Garrison
1980-1982	Rev. Gerald Chaffim
1982-1985	Rev. Paul Daniel
1985-1986	Rev. Leslie Mills
1986-1990	Rev. Doug Pepper
1990-1993	Rev. Bill Beavers
1993-1997	Rev. Jim Genesse
1997-2000	Rev. Randy Owen

THE CHURCH OF JESUS CHRIST OF LATTER DAY SAINTS

The Church of Jesus Christ of Latter-day Saints in Booneville is located at 204 George E. Allen Drive, one block west of the Booneville High School. Prior to 1968, members of the congre-

The Church of Jesus Christ of Latter Day Saints, in Booneville, was built in 1968.

Concord Baptist Church

gation met in a wooden frame chapel in the Tuscumbia area, built on land donated by R.C. Fugitt. Today, that oriqinal location is the site of the "Old Mormon" Cemetery.

A complete history of the Prentiss County LDS Church may be found in the Prentiss County History, published in 1984. The following information refers only to events that have occurred since then.

Bishops of the Ward have been: Bobby Smith, Arthur Byrd, Jimmy Burcham and, currently, John T. Larsen. In 1991, the Tupelo, MS Stake was formed and Booneville Ward became a part of that stake.

Missionary work is an important part of the LDS church. Those who have served missions include: Andy Pollard, Stephen Christian, Bob Floyd, Steve Collins, Jason McCreary, Johnny Murphy, Steven Ericksen, Jana Murphy, Evan Brown, Benjamin Murphy, and Wesley Hayes. Latter-day Saints are Christians who accept Jesus Christ as their Savior and Redeemer, followinq His teachinqs and commandments.

Scoutinq is a vital part of the church's youth program, and a number of LDS youth have become Eagle Scouts.

The church is known for its beautiful temples, where sacred ordinances are performed. Booneville Ward members attend the temple in Memphis, dedicated on April 23, 2000. This temple, so near, is the answer to many prayers and much faithfulness.

The public is always welcome at church activities.
Submitted by Deborah Moseley

CLAUSEL HILL INDEPENDENT METHODIST CHURCH

From reading the church record of Clausel Hill Church, believe the church was built in the year of 1894. The land was donated by Bro. Jonathan White, a Methodist preacher.

The charter members were Charley White, Virginia White. James W. White, Henrietta White, William T. White, John A. Davis, L. Ellen Davis, Benjamin F. Robinson, Lafayette Coker, Nora Coker, George W. Moses and Thomas Nixon.

Bro. Charley White had a sawmill. The men went to work cutting logs and hauled to the mill where they were cut into lumber.

The church they built was a little wood frame building where they could worship together, hear the Gospel preached and lost souls would be saved. Since there was a cemetery near the church house named Clausel Hill Cemetery, the church was named Clausel Hill. In it's day there were several pastors. The pastors were sent by the Methodist Conference. Conference assessed how much money the church had to pay. Some of the money was spent for things this church did not approve of. For this reason and because they wanted to pick their pastors, the church withdrew from the Methodist Conference in 1950 and became Independent. Bro. W. E. Sharp was the first pastor selected in the year 1950.

As time went by the little church began to decay. The members decided it was time to build another building. In 1952 a new block church was started a few feet west of the old one. The blocks were hauled from Alabama by Brothers Harold and Lowell Sims. Bro Olen White gave logs for most of the lumber that was needed. Bro. Lamar Umfress hauled the logs to Bro. Clint Trimble's sawmill where they sawed the logs into lumber. Bro. Lowell Sims and Bro. Wallace South hauled the lumber to the planer and back to the church site.

The blocks were laid. Some of the best lumber in the old church was used in the new one. The men of the church worked together and on April 25, 1954-services were held in the new building. The church was used without a floor until January 1956.

In 1968 Clausel Hill became a member of (AIM) Association of Independent Methodist.

In 1973 Brothers Earl Lentz, Lamar Umfress, Kenneth Sims, Marshal Trimble and Lowell Sims would meet at night and work on the church, partitioning off Sunday School class rooms and a rest room, and putting up paneling.

Bro. W. E. Sharp served this church for thirty three years. Many souls were saved by his ministry. There has been several pastors since Bro. Sharp. Bro. Gary Redd is the pastor now.

A new sanctuary is in the process of being built. The old one will be used for extra Sunday School class rooms, nursery and fellowship hall.

I grew up in this church. It has been a very important part of my life.

It's a nice church and has a warm welcome spirit. We welcome you to come worship with us.
Submitted by Pauline L. Henry

CONCORD BAPTIST CHURCH

Concord Baptist Church is located in the Dry Creek Community on the Prentiss-Tippah County line. Membership consists of individuals living in both counties. The church was organized prior to 1848 by settlers from North Carolina and named for their former church in Bostic, North Carolina. Some early settlers were families with names like Green, Ledbetter, Kurkendall, Michaels, Bridges, Geno, Carpenter, Rinehart, Morgan, Tollison, Murley, Harden, Dees, Jumper, Bartlett,Cox, Ivey, Smart, Blassingame and others. Many of these family names are to be found in the Bostic, North Carolina Concord Baptist Church cemetery as well.

Pastors who have served the church are: Edmund B. Reynolds (1848); Prier Scally (Most of the years -1848-1870); Drewery D. Roach, 1858; John Howard Byrd, 1867,1874; Elder S. D. Chapman 1887-1889; J. M. McElroy, 1890; William David Lancaster, 1892-1894; J. L. Morris, 1895; L R. Randolph, 1896; 1. P. Randolph, 1897; Lafayette F. Carmichael, 1898; A. C. Vandiver, 1903; Marion Francis Hill, 1906,1909,1915; John Allen (Reece) Gullett, 1907,1916; G. T. Kilpatrick, 1910-1911; C. C. Clark, 1913; Bascrum Luther Crawford, 1918-1920; Joseph H. Crawford, 1922-1934 and 1945-1957; Dewey Wallis, 1935; Loyd Ellis Horton, 1936-1944; Willie Booth Colter, 1958-1964; Rev. Luther Edd McCafferty, 1966; Robert Eugene Walker, 1967-1978 and 1993 to the present; William Gullick, 1979-1980; Excail Burleson, 1980-1985; William Gray Dowdy, 1986-1992. As noted above Robert Eugene Walker is presently serving his second tenure as pastor. Some of these pastors were distinguished in other ways beside the

Crossroads United Methodist Church

ministry. Pastor Scally was a wealthy landowner (1,400 acres) and operated a grist mill, cotton gin and lumber mill. Pastor John H. Byrd was father of 18 children. Lafayette Carmichael was a successful merchant in the Mitchell community. Pastor A. C. Vandiver lost an arm on the battlefield as a confederate soldier. Bascrum Crawford represented Prentiss, Tippah and Union Counties in the State legislature two different times. Pastor Loyd Ellis Horton served as Superintendent of Education for Tippah County. Robert E. Walker, present pastor, has been a public and private school teacher, worked as surveyor and enviromentalist for the Mississippi Highway Department and is a published author and genealogist. Every pastor has distinguished himself in particular and unique ways.

Concord has been a member of three associations: Chickasaw 1848-1860; Tishomingo 1860-1921; Tippah 1922-Present. Presently, Concord has over 275 members. It has six paid staff members including a Minister of Music and Youth, Mr. Gary Kennedy, graduate of Blue Mountain College.

The church was originally located about 2 miles north of its present site and operated a church school until 1923. Concord moved to its present site in 1914 on land donated by Blake and Polly Rinehart. The new sanctuary was built with donated lumber and manpower for the cost of $1,000. A cemetery was added to the property in 1925. Many improvements have been made through the years to the church facilities. A new pastorium and educational annex were added during the first pastorate of Robert E. Walker. Later a fellowship hall was added during the pastorate of Excail Burleson. Additional land surrounding the church sanctuary was recently purchased bringing the value of church property to almost $350,000.

Many descendants of the original settlers from North Carolina are stiff faithfully attending and supporting the church today. Deacons in the church today are James D. Crawford, T. C. Mauney, Gaston Ford, Freddie Corbin, Billy Tigrett, Luke Ledbetter, Bobby Smart, Enoch Stacy, Ivan Blassingame and Stephen Walker. Some of these are presently either retired or inactive.

Through the Gerald C. Mauney Scholarship fund Concord annual presents one or two scholarships to deserving mission or ministerial students. Most, though not all, of these scholarships have gone to Blue Mountain College students. A large part of the church's annual budget is directed to missions. Several thousand dollars in its benevolent fund is used annually to minister to the needs of needy families in the community and church. Additionally, the church gives to mission endeavors throughout the world through the Cooperative Program, State, American and International missions.

Concord has been associated with the Southern Baptist Convention for most of it's 150 year history and believes the future holds great promise for future growth and progress in preaching the gospel and reaching the unsaved.
Submitted by Robert E. Walker

CROSSROADS UNITED METHODIST CHURCH

On the first Sunday in May each year, there is a large crowd at the Crossroads United Methodist Church. It's homecoming time for this country church located seven miles west of Booneville at Jumpertown.

On that day the building is filled to capacity – every seat taken. There are Methodists to be sure. But there are also Baptists Presbyterians, and a number of other denominations.

The rest of the year, the building is not quite so filled. According to the pastor, W.C. Alexander, there are about 40 on roll; however, there are only about 20 active members. The church is located in the middle of Jumpertown, across the street from Jumpertown School. Older residents remember leaving school and going "across the road" to the daytime services at revival time.

The church had its beginning in the 1840's – beginning with a white plank building built sometime during that time.

Some of the older residents have believed that it had its beginning as a Presbyterian Church that was located across the street from the present building.

Windhams were a big part of the church, and in 1897, Simeon Windham was the pastor. Under "Bro. Sim's" leadership, patriotic Fourth of July celebrations were held for many years. After Bro. Sims retirement, the pastorship was handed down to his son Willam Wesley Windham. In the 1920's, Laura Windham, Bro. Sims wife, was one of the oldest members in the church.

In 1904, Crossroads and Jumpertown were organized as a charge to share preachers. Some of these ministers include Jess Sharp, Cleve Ivy, Leonard Jumper, Bro. Roberts, B.G Whitehurst, Carl and Alson Wasson, Bill White, Garland Knott, Bro. Hamilton, Huey Wood, Fabian Clark, Henry Wimberly, Jake Barnes, Maston Prewitt, Ronald Winzell, James P. Perry, Robert McCoy, Charles McGill, Dr. Ray Clarke and W.C. Alexander.

The present brick building was constructed in 1968 and was paid for and dedicated in 1976. The fellowship hall was built in 1982. The beautiful stained glass windows were donated by Ruby and Murray Davis, long-time members of the church.

According to minutes taken at a church meeting in 1926 — and kept by Doris Geno (a member since 1931), the church was called a Methodist Protestant Church, later it would be The Methodist Church, and eventually the Crossroads United Methodist Church. Mrs. Geno is the wife of Charlie Geno, a grandson of Simeon and Laura Windham, and is today one of the oldest members.

The first Sunday in May – usually referred to by members and relatives as "First Sunday" – is the church's annual Homecoming Day. This day was a celebration of Laura Windham's birthday at her home. Before she died, she requested that her family members move the celebration to the church, and it was called the Windham Reunion. Years later, this reunion was changed to Homecoming Day for everyone to remember their loved ones who were buried in the church cemetery.
Submitted by Darlene Hurt.

EAST BOONEVILLE BAPTIST CHURCH

East Booneville Baptist Church, currently located at 602 East Church Street, was organized June 18, 1948 with thirteen members. Worship services began on the third Sunday in September. The first church building was located on a one acre tract of land

East Booneville Baptist Church

East Pleasant Ridge Baptist Church

on Hatchie Street across from the old Sale Barn. The church was originally organized as a Missionary Baptist Church. Members of the church requested admittance into the Prentiss Baptist Association October 15, 1948. The Association approved admittance and welcomed East Booneville into Southern Baptist fellowship. The church building was moved to its current location in May, 1954. Through the years the church has purchased adjoining properties to provide room for growth.

The vision for growth was never restricted to its own location. During the years 1966-1968, the members of East Booneville saw the need for a church in the Burton community and sponsored a mission church. Due to the efforts of the church, as well as the people at the mission point, the mission was established as the Burton Baptist Church in June, 1968.

Love for the Lord, love for every member, and love to the community has continued through the years. Today East Booneville Baptist Church is a committed community of believers with ongoing ministries for all ages. Construction began in 2000 for a new sanctuary, choir suite, and additional education class rooms.

EAST BOONEVILLE PENTECOSTAL CHURCH

The East Booneville (Independent) Pentecostal Church, 1400 East Church St, began as the Home Missionary Band. On December 1st, 1954 a business meeting was held in the home of J. C. Cain. At this meeting the name was changed to its present name The East Booneville (Independent) Pentecostal Church. Constitution and By-Laws were approved and a statement of faith was established. January 18th, 1955 the Reverend V.A. Smith of Selmer TN. was elected as the first Pastor. The present property was purchased from the Assembly of God organization 'in 1955. At that time, the budding was only the basement of the current church. The floor was not concrete, but sawdust covered the dirt floor. Folding chairs were borrowed from the Amen-can Legion for the first services. In 1961 the upper floor was started. Members picked cotton and had bake sales to pay for the new budding. Most of the labor was donated by members of the church. By 1964 the present building was finished and completely paid for. Over the years many improvements have been made. Many pastors have come and gone, but the same good work, that was started back in 1954, still goes on today. The East Booneville (Independent) Pentecostal Church still remains strong in the Lord and the power of His insight. Our present Pastor is the Reverend Jeff Jones. Assistant Pastor is the Reverend Kenneth Edge.
Submitted by Jeff Jones.

EAST PLEASANT RIDGE BAPTIST CHURCH

East Pleasant Ridge Baptist Church is located about 4 miles northeast of f5aldwyn on CR 5011.

In 1945 the Lord began to implant in the hearts of the people of the community the need for a church. Under the direction of Bro. John B. Laney, then the Prentiss County Missionary, the church was finally organized in 1947 with 16 charter members. Land was donated by Jim Watson and Lihue Reid. The building was completed in 1949 with the men of the community doing most of the work. After several renovation projects, this building is presently our fellowship hall and educational space. The present sanctuary was built in 1975 and has undergone several renovations. Currently a Family Life Center is in progress.

In the summer of 1949, Bro. Martin Gilbert led a revival and 51 members were added to the church. Shortly thereafter, Bro. Malcolm Jones was called as the first pastor. Other pastors that have served the church down through the years are: Bro. Charles Skutt. Bro. Ivan Lowery, Bro. B.A. Wilson, Bro. Wallace Pannell, Bro. Morris Stevens, Bro. L.S. Hearn, Bro. D.S. Tidwell, Bro. Kenneth Bishop, Bro. Gary Gardner, Bro. Ray Bennett, Bro. Jimmy Wallis, Bro. Neil Davis, Bro. Rick Parks, Bro. Adron Horne as interim pastor until our present pastor, Bro. Greg Smart came in 1995.

Music Ministers have been: Ron Boone, Fred Shearon, Gerald Thompson, Tim Ledbetter and presently, Donnie Wallis.

Deacons: W.D. Pruitt, Lee Swinney, Billy Gray, Howard Holmes, Glen Skelton, Mike McBrayer, Mark Cagle and Marty Roberts.

We have 194 members.

Through the years and changes at East Pleasant Ridge, our goal remains the same, to win the world to Jesus Christ. Our greatest challenge is to work together more faithfully at the task that is before us, to proclaim through word and deed the "Good News" of God's love.

FIRST APOSTOLIC CHURCH OF JUMPERTOWN

When Bro. and Sis. A.L. "Buddy" Marshall moved to Northeast Mississippi in 1980, it was their dream to establish an Apostolic church in an area in which there was no Apostolic church. Upon looking toward Jumpertown, they found that there was no established Apostolic church in that community. So with faith in God and a desire to establish a church, they set out to make their dream a reality.

The church was established on May 13, 1984. The very first service was held under a tent in the yard of Mrs. Bernice Michaels. God began to bless and two weeks later land was purchased where the church now stands. Services were held under the tent for approximately 4 months. As God continued to bless, a double-wide trailer was purchased and completely remodeled. The first service was held on September 23, 1984. Today, this facility houses part of out Sunday School Department as well as Fellowship Hall.

God continued to bless, and the church grew under the leadership of Bro. and Sis. **Marshall.** Soon, the need arose to build a larger facility. Once the new facility was finished, the first service was held on July 24, 1986. Within a short period of around 9 years, the church membership grew and soon the need arose again for larger facilities. A new sanctuary which seats 400 - 500 people was built, and the former church was converted to more Sunday School rooms. The first service was held in the new sanctuary on March 9, 1995.

Bro. and Sis. Marshall have been with the church since establishment. Today, the church has evangelistic quarters across the street. God has steadily blessed since day 1, and under the leadership of our pastor the church continues to grow. As of this printing, we nave in attendance around 150 people. Our church is considered one of the most beautiful churches inside and out in this area. Because of the leadership and outreach of our church, Bro. and Sis. Marshall have had the privilege of traveling to foreign countries such as the former Soviet Union. There they have established smaller branches of the First Apostolic Church of Jumpertown.

Ephesians 2:20 "And are built upon the foundation of the apostles and prophets, Jesus Christ himself being the chief corner stone."

Submitted by Larry Jackson

FIRST UNITED PENTECOSTAL CHURCH

In 1935, on East Church Street, from a large gospel tent, the late Reverend A. D. Gurley, who was a church pastor and official at Pentecostal Church, Inc. from Corinth, Mississippi, conducted a revival meeting that marked the beginning of First Pentecostal Church of Booneville. Prior to 1935, groups of Pentecostal believers had worshiped together in revivals and meetings throughout the area including "Happy Holler" and "Friendship Church" in Lake City, with several different preachers, including Reverend Jim Jones, leading the services.

Following the tent revival in 1935, the Booneville Pentecostal Church was organized and the infant church with 26 charter members purchased the old "Friendship Church" property in the Lake City Community where the Fairview Baptist Church is now located. 'Mere the young church worshiped until 1940.

The growing little church realized the need for larger facilities, and purchased three acres on North Lake Street where the present church buildings now stand. In 1942, after months of laboring together for the glory of God, a new House of Worship was set upon that hill to become a light to the City of Booneville.

There were 26 charter members of the Church. These include: Vera Lee Kennedy, Mollie Ricketts, Ollie Maddox, Mary Lee Spencer, Antlean Nicholson Jones, J. W. England, Clemmie Nicholson Kennedy, Mamie Nichols, R. C. Nichols, Lum Gentry, Cora Gentry, James Gentry, Dalton Ricketts, Vermer England, W. T. (Tuggle) Jones, Pearl Nicholson Bristow, Sarah Allen, Annie Duke, Devel Reece, Juanita Gentry, R. R(Brown) Kennedy, Parker Nichols, Thomas Allen, Cecil Gahagan, Rheba Duke and Bro. Jessie Smith.

These ministers have served this local congregation as pastor: the Reverends RH. Kemp, H. B. Lee, R. B. Boyd, Samuel Scott, Floyd H. Coleman, James A. Boutwell, Lloyd W. Shaw, M. D. Padfield, C. Holiday Charles Comb, Robert Forbush, Hulon Sanford, Danny Odle, Bobby Upchurch, Larry E. Hill, and since 1996, Jimmy C. Hicks.

The Original Board of Trustees were: Dalton Ricketts, W. T. Jones, and R. k Kennedy. Vera Lee Nicholson Kennedy served as the first secretary treasurer of the church.

The present trustees are: Kim Billingsley, Chesterjackson, Hoyle Lambert, Gary Smith and James Young.

The Present Church Board of Deacons is Marty Barnes, Clyde Hicks, James Southern and Jerry Wallace.

During the administration of the first full time pastor, the Reverend R. B. Boyd, 1946-1952, the congregation constructed a six room frame parsonage on the church property which provided a home for the pastors' family until 1976 when a spacious, brick pastors' home was built near the church.

The small frame Church building originally constructed in 1942, with the addition of a Sunday School wing added during Reverend James Boutwell's pastorate, served the needs of a growing congregation until 1963 when a large, modern, brick sanctuary was dedicated to the service of the Lord by the congregation.

With the Church experiencing tremendous growth, in 1979, Pastor Larry E. Hill and the Church family realized the need for additional space to accommodate the needs of the church. A Family Life Center, which contained classrooms, a kitchen, and a gym, was constructed to help meet the needs of the growing church.

In 1995, a major renovation to the Church facilities was completed. The sanctuary was enlarged, a foyer and classrooms added; the Family Life Center expanded; and the parking facilities were enlarged and re-paved.

Under the leadership of Pastor Jimmy C. Hicks, the Church continues to grow. With an expanding vision to reach this area with the gospel of Jesus Christ, new souls are being added regularly to God's Church. First Pentecostal Church is a revival church, which reaches into the community to help to provide for the needs of the people.

The credit for the continued growth of the Church goes first to God, whose blessings to us can not be measured, and to a group of dedicated believers who love God with all their hearts; who worship God in the "old fashioned" way; and, who, under the leadership of our Pastor, are anxious to work for the building of the Kingdom of God.

Whether it was gathering rocks and clearing the hillside to build that original frame structure, selling donuts the ladies made in the Donut House in Lake City to help meet the needs of additional space for the congregation, or spending Sunday afternoon down in the woods at the young people's prayer meeting; we have a great tradition left to us by those who have paved the way for us.

Many hours of prayer are encircling the throne room which was sent up by the Ladies from their Tuesday morning cottage prayer meetings; hours of chain prayers have strengthened the spiritual growth of this Church; and hundreds of hard earned dollars have gone to spread the gospel to out area and to the many missionary families the congregation supports through the United Pentecostal Church International.

For the past 65 years, the people who have made up the First Pentecostal Church of Booneville have established a legacy for those who now are left to carry the banner of the Church and to be the light which has been set upon that hill on North Lake Street which cannot be hidden. It is the challenge of the church family to continue into this new millennium with a renewed dedication to see that the church presents the whole gospel" to each person with whom the members come in contact and to be certain that, aware of the great heritage, the congregation prepares for the future, by living so that others might see Jesus through each person in his present day life.

First Pentecostal Church of Booneville is a Bible believing, family centered, group of followers of Jesus Christ who want to fulfil the great commission of reaching the World with Bible salvation.

FORKED OAK BAPTIST CHURCH

Forked Oak Baptist Church is an old landmark located on old highway 30 about a mile north of Burton, just east of highway 365 near the Tishomingo County line. It is perhaps one of the oldest churches in Prentiss County. It is said that Forked Oak got its name from some forked oak trees near where the church now stands.

At one time there was a school and a Masonic Lodge. The building was two stories. The lodge moved to Paden in the 1920's and the top story was removed.

The first records of the church burned, thus we do not know exactly when the church was organized. However, records in the Prentiss County Courthouse describe a two acre tract of land, deeded to the church by W. M. Gibson on July 24, 1874, recorded on page 379 Deed Book 8. According to that deed, the meeting-house was on the land at that time. The description of the land deeded was "commencing at a stake three rods due east of the center of the meeting house now on the land." The description continues laying out a tract of land around the meeting-house. We have every reason to believe the church is over 125 years old. It is possible that when it was organized it was located in Old Tishomingo County, as Prentiss County did not come into existence until 1870.

Our records begin with August 6, 1904. The church was called Mt Providence Baptist Church in 1874 on the deed. In 1920 the name changed to Forked Oak Baptist Church. The records between January 31, 1920 and September 4, 1920 are missing, so we do not know the exact date they voted to change the name. The new name is used in the October 2, 1920 minutes.

Mrs. Flora Pinson on December 26, 1931, page 144-145 of Deed Book 83, also deeded Two acres of land to the deacons of Forked Oak Missionary Baptist Church. Later A. C. Roberts deeded additional land for the cemetery.

There is a large cemetery, in four sections; with the earliest date legible on the tombstones is 1879. Some of the stones are so old the date cannot be seen. Because of the difficulty in maintaining the cemetery, a Foundation Fund was set up and free will offerings were asked ror. People responded liberally. Holly Patterson, one of the committee members was very instrumental in this. He was also the flrst donor contributing one thousand dollars. A caretaker was employed and today the cemetery is neatly kept.

On the fifth Sunday in August 1930 revival services began with Brother C. C. Kerr as the evangelist. Brother W. G. Gray was the Pastor at that time. Eight additions were added to the church by experience and baptism. The church decided to hold another revival meeting beginning on the third Sunday in September - three (3) weeks later. Brother G. S. Rayburn was the evangelist. In the words of the church clerk Brother M. T. Searcy, taken from the minutes: "The results of this meeting was a great revival, the likes which has never been seen at this church, with twenty (20) additions to the church, three (3) by letter and seventeen (17) by experience and baptism."

In 1959 a parsonage was built under the pastoral leadership of Brother Alan Powers. It was a modest three-bedroom frame house. Brother Vester Tennison gave the land for the building site, about six tenths of an acre.

In 1989, Mrs. Belva Sparks, who was 95 years old and the oldest living member of the church, said: "I started coming to church at the age of 8 and was baptized at the age of 16". Services were held once a month on Saturday evening and Sunday Morning. Not many came on Saturday evening, but a lot of people came on Sunday. She said: "At the services, the women sat on the left and the men sat on the right side. The men carried on the business. The first time I ever heard a woman pray in church was Mrs. Artie Rushing, wife of the Rev. Elton Rushing. There were eight of us when I was baptized, in, four sets of sisters, my sister Lora and me, Bessie and Blanche Rushing, Elma and Ruth Woodruff, and Ora and Clemmie Timbes. Brother Wells from Arkansas baptized us."

Mrs. Sparks was the daughter of Willie Sanders and Margaret Tennison Sanders. She said: "My daddy was a Mason and my mother was a member of the Eastern Star. My grandfather, Hiram Tennison, was a deacon at Forked Oak Baptist Church. Lora and I loved to go to church. Decoration Day was an annual day for cleaning the cemetery. It was always on Friday. We'd have a lemonade stand and a good meal. The men worked until every grave was clean." Decoration Day was changed to Sunday by the vote of the church in 1965.

Mrs. Sarah McCoy was another of our longtime members in 1989. She was the daughter of J. W. Phifer and Mary Elizabeth Johnson Phifer. She remembered, as a child, sleeping on a pallet during church services. Hqr husband, 0. C. McCoy, was a deacon and chairman of the building committee in 1965 when, under the leadership of Rev. Milton Wright, the present sanctuary was built.

The church had a note burning ceremony April 11, 1971. Pastor Horace McCombs read Psalms 45. Brethren Otis McCoy and A. C. Roberts burned the note.

In 1973 the church built a fellowship building. The dedication service was the first Sunday of December 1973.

Forked Oak Baptist Church (before 1965)

Forked Oak Baptist Church

Gaston Baptist Church

The current pastor, Rev. Ricky Johnson, has served since 1991. Some of the former pastors of Forked Oak Missionary Baptist Church were: J. E. Glenn, D.R. Raper, W. P. Elledge, S. Barber, D. R. Robison, Oneal Estes, B. Taylor, Buford Harper, T. Whitaker, Harold Cosby, W.T. Grigory, Bill Tutor, W H Hamilton, L G Hankins, W N Tindley, Milton Wright, G.S. Rayburn, Alan Powers, W.G. Gray, B A Nolan, J. M. Young, Harold Holifield, W Carroll Patterson, Horace McCombs

The following ministers surrendered to preach and were ordained at Forked Oak: Elton Rushing, Buford Harper, W Carroll Patterson, W.C. Patterson Jr., Horace McCombs

The current Deacons are: Aaron Bullard, A. C. Roberts, Leness Woodruff, Ronnie McCombs, Vick Johnson

Some of the former Deacons were: Hiram Tennison, Curtis Holley, Johnny Tennison, Lester Tennison, O.C. McCoy, W. Carroll Patterson, Vester Tennison, Robert G. Smith, Luther Sanders, Horace McCombs, R.G. McCutchens., Geraldine Houston Roberts has been Church Clerk since 1961.

Forked Oak Baptist Church has 98 members.
Submitted by Belinda Houston

GASTON BAPTIST CHURCH

Gaston Baptist Church was organized on August 18,1883 under the leadership of ministers W.L.Skinner and W.G.Thompson with about thirty members.

On February 21,1903 the congregation bought the Ebenezer Presbyterian church building and in 1904 a new one room building was built.

Gaston became a full time church in July 1953. The Pastorium was built and work done on cemetery.

The present sanctuary was completed and dedicated in 1962.

In 1976 the church bought 4.8 acres of land remodeled and additions made to Pastorium. A member gave the church Choir robes. Parking lot paved, and in 1977 the Gaston Gospel (Monthly Mailout) was begun. The Tennis Courts completed and Family Life Center begun.

The church adopted it's first constitution and by-laws on February 25, 1979.

In 1980 Gaston started a mission at Jumpertown, now a full time church. The Gaston deacons increased from six to nine and then to twelve.

The Sanctuary was remodeled, balcony completed, new choir robes purchased, and a new Organ in 1982. In 1983 the note on Family Life Center burned. The Church celebrated its 100th Anniversary. New by-laws were drawn up to include the rotation of deacons.

In the years 1986-90 a new Piano and new Van purchased. Note on Sanctuary was paid and burned, 11. 5 acres of land purchased. The WMU completed the Centennial quilt and presented it to the church. Larry Garner, Mike Hatfield, Billy Staggs, and Terry Hurt surrendered and ordained to full Gospel Ministry. Brenda Williams to full time Youth Ministry.

Another van purchased in 1996. In 1997 the sanctuary and education space was renovated with new paint, wall paper, and carpet. The Family Life Center was renovated with new paint, drop ceiling, central air and heat, with a large puff door at center court Total cost approximately $96,000. Now paid and note burned.

In 1998-99 the western parking lot enlarged and resurfaced. Gaston initiated a new outreach ministry called GROW or "God Rewards Our Worw'. The outreach involves contacting community members, visitors, and prospects through letters, phone calls, and personal contacts.

Gaston has continued to be blessed by the Lord with resources to be utilized for outreach, people with a desire to work and to give, and a desire to provide spiritual growth opportunities for members as well as the community. Gaston is moving and there is a lot of promise for the future with so many young families. Our gratitude goes to God fbr His care and leadership. May the church activities be surrounded by His Grace, May Love abound at Gaston.
Submitted By Avanelle Worley

GRACE UNITED METHODIST CHURCH

Grace United Methodist Church was organized on January 18, 1953, as East Booneville Methodist Church. The congregation purchased the old Miller Lumber Company building, known as the Corinth Planing Mill. It was located on Hwy 30 E at Miller Crest Subdivision. In March of 1954 the building program began and was completed in 1955 and the Church name changed to Grace. On March 8, 1959 the Church building was dedicated and at that time there were 92 members.

The roots of Grace Church are entwined in the progress of Booneville and the surrounding area. The current membership stands at 250. Many converts throughout the year serve as a solid foundation as Grace continues to grow and serve. With a modem parsonage next door and a spacious Family Center adjoining the Sanctuary, Grace is dedicated to reaching its area for Jesus Christ, through Bible preaching and a strong music ministry. With a sincere love and concern for this community, Grace lives up to its motto, "Small enough to care, large enough to share".
Submitted by C.D. Edge

HILL'S CHAPEL BAPTIST CHURCH

Hills Chapel Baptist Church is a vision that became a reality on March 10, 1990, when the official ground breaking occurred. The church is centrally located in the Hills Chapel community;

Grace United Methodist Church, Jan. 1999

Hill's Chapel Baptist Church building in 1999

HILL'S CHAPEL CHURCH OF CHRIST

This is the old Hill's Chapel School building where the Hill's Chapel Church of Christ met until the 1940's.

The first frame building was built in the 40's. This building was used until 1968.

This modern brick building was built in 1968. Then an addition was built in 1990.

off Hwy 30 east and just north of the Hills Chapel School. The Hills Chapel Baptist Church is situated on the original 5 acre plot that was donated by Mr. Bill Smith.

The church was sponsored as a mission of Southern Baptist Ministries through the First Baptist Church of Booneville and their pastor Bro. Bill Duncan. Bro. Jerry Mitchell held the first worship service at the church on Easter Sunday, April 15, 1990. The vision at Hill's Chapel Baptist continues to grow under the dedicated leadership of Bro. Jerry Mitchell. Additional property has been purchased for the future use of a cemetery and renovation is currently under way for a temporary fellowship hall. Phase two of construction is soon to begin and will accommodate us with a new sanctuary.

The family of Hill's Chapel Baptist gives God the glory for allowing us to have this facility and it is our prayer that God will richly bless the individuals and families who were initially involved in the organization and construction of the I-Ell's Chapel Baptist Church.
Submitted by Wanda Harris

JUMPERTOWN UNITED METHODIST CHURCH

Jumpertown United Methodist Church as we know it today wasn't always so, neither in size nor location. Its three buildings and parsonage are approximately ten miles from Booneville on Highway 4 West and one and one-half miles from the Tippah County line. In fact, the first organized church, 1840, was about three miles south of the present location and was named Liberty Methodist Protestant Church. It was a crude log building. Split logs with no backs nor foot rests were the "pews."

The building was used by both Methodists and Baptists. Whites and blacks used this building for about 27 years. White members moved out of this church and erected another log building in 1867 near the present site. As the community surrounding the original building was mostly composed of Negroes, that church was known locally as "Negro Jumpertown Church". Negroes in this community had taken the surname of their former owners, Jumper, thus the name just mentioned.

The building erected in 1867 was still Liberty Methodist Protestant Church and was served by Pastors S. W. Mask, Z. D. Tatum, H. Freeman and Larkin Cathie. Liberty Church was re-named Jumpertown Mission in 1878. Rev. S. M. Windham was named pastor of Jumpertown Mission.

In 1880, a third building was built across the road from the present site on the property now owned by Leroy Brumley. Rev. John Stone was the pastor. This building was also used as a school and was later torn down to erect a school building.

In 1883, another frame building was erected on the site of the present church. This building was used for seventy plus years. It had been renovated, updated and added on to in order to serve a fast-growing congregation.

In 1962, at approximately $17,000.00 and donated labor and furnishings, the present sanctuary was built. The Milton English Fellowship Hall and the Newell Brown Family Life Center were built in recent years as the needs arose and at this writing, November, 1999, another need has arisen. We have outgrown our church and plans are now under way for a larger sanctuary.

Jumpertown Methodist Church has always been the center of our community and continues to offer spiritual guidance to everyone in the community at large.

Jumpertown Methodist Church, Jumpertown School and the community were named for the founding family of Jumpers. This created a very unique situation in that almost everyone in this community and the Methodist Church are related. This heritage is one that everyone is proud to boast of!

Submitted by Ruth English Grisham

LAMB'S CHAPEL INDEPENDENT METHODIST CHURCH

In 1952, in order to end a controversy of long standing among the members of Cross Roads Methodist Church, certain members decided to leave. These people, with minister L. J. Ivey as their leader, formed Lambs Chapel Church. In 1953 a block building, which housed a General Store, was purchased. Church services were held in this building for several years. The church was formed as non-denominational. The first Board of Trustees included Pete Corbin, Cliff Bridges, Henry Smart and Frank Jumper. J. S. Windham was the first Sunday School Superintendent.

In 1964 a more suitable building was built. In 1967 Lambs Chapel joined the Association of Independent Methodist. In 1983 the membership agreed that a new church was needed. The old plank church was sold and moved and the money was borrowed and, through faith in God, the present brick church was built. Trustees at this time were C. D. Windham, Kirby Windham, Tommy Prentiss and James E. Windham.

In 1996 a beautiful brick fellowship hall was built behind the church. Construction on the fellowship hall was headed by Archie Smith, Marlin Cartwright, Jerry Thrasher, Clayton Pace and Bob Michael.

Pastors have included Bro. L. J. Ivey followed by Bro. W. E. Sharp until his health failed in 1987. At this time Bro. Gene Coltharp was chosen as pastor and remains to this time. Bro. Teddy Cornelius serves as assistant pastor. The present Board of Trustees include Archie Smith, Jerry Thrasher, Bobby Gene Michael and Clayton Pace.

The first Sunday in April has been set aside as Homecoming Day at the church.

Lambs Chapel has two singing groups, The Prayer Warriors and The Lyfe Tyme Believers.

Mrs. Carolyn Smith has been pianist for over forty years. Her daughter Danita Cartwright, who plays the keyboard, has joined her. Reba Bums plays the bass guitar and Charlie Smith plays the rhythm guitar. Other guitarists are Archie Smith and Matthew Windham.

Mrs. C.D. (Jack) Windham has served as song leader for over forty years and has now been joined by Ruth Moore, Becky McDowell, Reba Bums and Glenda Thrasher.

Teachers include: Jerry Thrasher, Randy Estes, Alex Bums, Scott Bane, Marlin Cartwright, Clayton Pace, Charlie Smith, Glenda Thrasher, Rhonda Pace, Susan Bane, Christi Smith and Danita Cartwright.

Lamb's Chapel Independent Methodist Church

Liberty United Methodist Church

The church is serviced by two vans, with Marlin Cartwright and Clayton Pace serving as bus drivers.

Bro. Teddy Cornelius preaches on fourth Sundays and Bro. Jesse Sharp preached on fifth Sunday for many years.

The church also holds three revivals and a Vacation Bible School each year, gospel singing on fifth Sunday nights and a nursing home ministry twice monthly.
Submitted by Carolyn Smith.

LIBERTY UNITED METHODIST CHURCH

The Liberty United Methodist Church as been a part of its community for over a hundred years. It is located just a short distance east of Booneville. Liberty United Methodist Church is on the left side of the road and the cemetery is on the right side of Highway 30 East.

According to sources when the history was written in the First Edition of the Prentiss County History written in 1984, one of the earliest persons associated with the Liberty Methodist Church was Arch Street, a Confederate soldier, who recruited soldiers at that location.

After the war, a few Methodists in the community saw the need for a church nearby, and the first building was built. There is no confirmation of the exact date of the first church, but there is a deed (dated 1859) to some land that described the same spot where the church is now located; however, it was called Old Friendship.

It is not known whether there was a building known as Liberty Church; however, there is a deed (dated 1874), that read in part "from the Northwest corner of the Methodist Church building located on said land and known as Liberty Church."

The church was used by several denominations – Free Will Baptists, Holiness, as well as the Methodist. The completed church was indeed the center of activity in the community, and was at one time used as a schoolhouse.

In 1946, the cemetery purchased more land for further burial use. New Sunday School rooms were to be built in 1947, but in making plans, it was decided to not only build Sunday School rooms, but a new church as well. It was erected around the old building.

Over the years, Sunday school rooms have been added as well as a kitchen, Fellowship Hall, and rest rooms. New pews have also been installed.

Additional and more detailed information can be found in the 1984 Prentiss County History, written by Mrs. Orien C. Hare.

In 1999, the pastor is Bro. Jack Williams, who is officially retired. He retired as a United Methodist Minister — serving all over North Mississippi with forty-one years of experience. In 1993, he and his wife Vetrice came to Liberty, and they have been there since that time — with Vetrice a very vital part of his ministry.

Liberty United Methodist Church is a small country church. The congregation may be small with just about 75 members. There are usually 55 to 60 of those members present at the Sunday morning service.

These folks, along with Bro. Jack and Vetrice, may be small in number, but they are large in friendliness and love and companionship for each other — and to all those who come through the church's doors.

The following is a list of the ministers over the years at the Liberty Methodist/United Methodist Church:

1933-36	W. J. Wood
1936-39	R. W. Threet
1939-40	R. W. Ledbetter
1940-42	J. E. Roberts
1942-48	L. K. Alexander
1948-50	R. A. Thornton, Jr.
1950-51	T. W. Rankin, A. R. Beasley
1951-56	L.A. Wasson, R. A. Thornton, Jr., W. M. Hester
1957-59	Garland Knott
1959-60	Huey Wood, Minister, and Ruth Wood, Associate Minister (Without Pay)
1960-67	Ruth Wood
1967-70	H. D. Robinson, Don Bishop, Henry C. Moorehead
1970-73	Betty Marie Grisham
1973-75	H. G. Storey
1975-77	W. E. Ludlam
1977-80	Don Sparks
1980-83	C. D. Edge
1983-84	John Savoy
1984-86	Gerald Carpenter, J. R. Grisham, Smith Whiteside
1986-87	Kenneth Duke
1987-93	Donnie Riley
1993-2000	Jack Williams

Submitted by: Laura W. Cartwright.

LITTLE BROWN MISSIONARY BAPTIST CHURCH

The exact date of the beginning of Little Brown Missionary Baptist Church is not known but it goes back a good many years. The original location of the Church was near Little Brown Creek which was named for a Chickasaw Indian.

In 1953, the Church voted to tear down its building and join with the Freewill Baptist in building a new Church building across the road. The site of the Missionary Baptist Church building would be added to the existing cemetery. Each Church would have charge of the services twice a month. The Missionary Baptist would have services the second and fourth Sundays with Decoration Day the second Sunday in May. The Freewill Baptist would have services the first and third Sundays with Decoration Day the third Sunday in October.

In 1976 the two churches separated with the Freewills remaining in the existing building. The Missionary Baptist chose a site by Highway 4 near the Hobo Station to build their new building. Dedication services for the new building were held October 2, 1977.

The Little Brown Missionary Baptist Church now has Homecoming Services on the first Sunday in October. At present the Church does not have a cemetery but the members have been trying to obtain land for one.

The Church has been a member of two Associations, the Judson and the Big Bear Creek.

Marietta Church of Christ

The present pastor is Bro. B. P. Thornton, a World War II veteran who celebrated his 80th birthday December, 1999.

MARIETTA CHURCH OF CHRIST

According to a survey of the churches of Christ in Mississippi by Bro. Joe K. Alley in 1953-1954, the Marietta Church of Christ is the oldest in Prentiss County. It was established in 1879 when Bro. Sewell preached in the community. A meeting house was built in 1880.

Some of the early preachers of this congregation were: G. W. Archer, W. A. Simmons, N. B. Patten, G. A. Dunn, Sr., J. E. Dunn, P. G. Wright, W. R. Wilcut, W. W. Heflin, Sr., J. W. Howell, John T. Underwood and Hal P. McDonald.

In meetings held by different preachers such as Bro. W. H. Owens, Bro. J. W. Brent, Bro. A. G. Freed, Bro. W. T. Lemmons, Bro. W. W. Heflin, Bro. Nichols, Bro. Tim Walker, Bro. W. R. Wilcut, Bro. J. W. Howell, Bro. V. H. Bradley, Bro. W. A. Black, Bro. Everet Day, Bro. Athelson Crowson, Bro. J. G. Pounds, Bro. Joe K. Alley and others; many people were converted. A large number of those have died, and some have moved to other places.

The attendance has varied down through the years, the assembly runs around 70 to 100 at the present time.

The oldest man in this congregation, Bro. James G. (Grafton) Burns, served as an elder for 33 years. When all the other elders died he resigned. Since then the men of the church have met regularly and attended to the business matters. The church meets once a month for a fellowship meal and also meets once a month for practice singing. The members are very close to one another in Christian love. The youth are doing a great work participating in Bible Trivia over the county and also in a larger one in Cookeville, TN. The young men from age six through teens have charge of services one time in each month, and they do a really good job. Some of the members are aged. There are a few ladies that have been members of this congregation for 70 years.

Some of the regular preachers for this congregation in late years have been: Bro. Frank Newcomb, Bro. E. W. Wade, Bro. Calvin Barber, Bro. Richard Gooch, Bro. Hershel Orick and Bro. Ronnie Livingston who has been with the church for 5 years or around 1994 when he began.

MT. OLIVE BAPTIST CHURCH

The first page of the church minute book states that on June 28, 1851, seventeen people having a common faith assembled themselves for the purpose of constituting a Baptist Church. These people were recent settlers of the Geeville community of present-day Prentiss County. The name "Mt. Olive" was chosen, no doubt, because of the hilly terrain somewhat like that of the Mount of Olives mentioned in the New Testament.

The presbytery was composed of elders Martin Ball and Lewis Ball. The charter members were W.A. Davis, Thomas Burress, James R. Brock, J. B. Jones., Joseph Ashley, J.O. Nelson,-J.C. McGee, and A.W. Brock; the women were E. Saylors, M. Davis, S. R. Davis, N. E. Davis, Sarah A. Burress, H. E. Jones, Lettie Ashley, S. M. McGee and S. A. Brock. Rules of Decorum were set up immediately. Elder Martin Ball was called as the first pastor and served until November 1852.

On September 27, 1851, plans were made for a church house to be built of "hewed logs covered with thirty inch board and that the building committee determine the height of the house and all the particulars relating to the building".

In July 1852 the first colored members, Culle and Gracie, the property of Thomas Burress, joined the church.

In January 1861 A. H. Booth was called to the pastorate, but after a few months he was called into the chaplaincy of the Confederacy. A full year elapsed before another pastor was called. H. S. Archer served for a few months,, but in May 1862, A. H. Booth returned as pastor. In October 1863 H. G. Savage became pastor and served until 1867. Other references to the Civil War include the receipt of a certificate from Bro. M. P. Lowry, Brigdr. Gen., Army of Tenn., certifying that he had baptized Josiah Wallis, Co. B. 32'd Regt, Miss Vol on the first day of May 1864 on profession of faith in Christ. Bro. Wallis by his request was received into full fellowship of the church. An entry for March 1865 states that R. R. Brock was killed by soldiers.

In August 1867 a proposal was made to the colored members of the church that they transact their own business, have their own days of meeting, call their own preacher, but still be under the supervision of the white church. The proposal was accepted and Bro. Henderson Young (colored) was called to be the first pastor.

Luther R. Burress was ordained into the full work of the ministry by the church in October 1867. In November of that same year he was called to be the pastor. Bro. Burress served until 1905 except for a year in 1876-1877 while he served as Centennial agent. J. S. Berry served in Bro. Burress's absence.

Elaborate tributes of respect were written into the minutes for deceased members during the early years. Instances of church discipline can also be found several different times.

Through the years Mt. Olive has consistently entertained the association meetings and held homecomings. In September 1897 the association meeting had to be postponed because of Yellow Fever. The first homecoming was held in 1892 on the 41't anniversary of the church. A centennial celebration was held on July 1, 1951.

In October 1907, a building committee was appointed to draw up plans for a new church. The members were J. H. McGee, J. F. Morris, H. Youngblood, W. E. McElroy, R. A. Morris, J. A. Jones and J C. Milton. The church burned in November 1921. A structure similar in size and appearance was built during the summer of 1922. Also in 1922, Arthur Flake . noted Southern Baptist leader, who was a member of Mt. Olive at one time, organized a B.Y.P.U. which was one of the first in the state of Mississippi.

Pastors who have served since 1905 include L. P. Randolph, 190519151) 1926-1936, F. C. Flowers 1916-1917, J. J. Cloar 1918-1919, Mark Harris 1919-1922, C. C. Weaver 1922, T. T. Harris 1922-1926, B. G. Basden June-Oct 1937 and Feb-Sept 1945, C. E. Patch 1937-1944, N. D. Story 1946-1949, Charles Gentry 1950-1953, James Moore 1953-54, Hugh Conwill 1954-1960, Stanley Bryan 1960-1962, H. T. Curbow 1963-1967, J. C. McIntire 1967-199 1, Chuck Baggett 1991-1992, Chester W. Harrison Apr 1993-June 1998, Rayborn Richardson Sept 1999-.

Beginning in 1965 Mt. Olive has undertaken several building programs . First, a three bedroom pastorium was built on the church grounds. In December 1969 a new sanctuary was dedicated. In 1975 an Educational Building was annexed to the sanctuary. This building accomodates four of the five divisions of the Sunday School. During the summer of 1990 a Family Life Center measuring 150 x 60 feet was built behind the Educational Building. This structure includes a spacious kitchen/fellowship area, a full gymnasium and bathrooms on the first floor. Addditional recreational space and a bedroom are included in the upper level.

Mt. Olive has a membership of approximately 350. A full program of activities is offered to its members and all who will come worship and fellowship. It reaches out to the world through its generous giving to local, state, and foreign missions. The church has a long and interesting history and in 2000 it looks to the future with the motto of the great English missionary, William Carey, "Expect great things from God; attempt great things for God."
Submitted by Thomas Wallis, Church Historian

NEW SITE BAPTIST CHURCH

The New Site Baptist Church was organized in 1937. The land was donated by Mr and Mrs Jack Green. The church was built by the members and the community.

There were nine charter members: Mr and Mrs Jack Green, Mr and Mrs Dalton Green, Mr and Mrs J. E. Lindley, Travis and Faye Lindley, and Evelyn Sparks.

The oldest living member of the church is Grace Moore age 95.

The present pastor of the church is Bro. Richard Denson. The Sunday School Superintendent and adult teacher is Holley Sparks. The Music Director is Walter Rorie. The Church Clerk is Sarah Stephens who is the grandaughter of Travis and Faye Lindley and Great-grandaughter of Mr and Mrs J.E. Lindley. The present deacons are Holley Sparks, Chairman, Walter Rorie and Rodney Beasley.

The Church has Decoration on the first Sunday in June.

OAK GROVE UNITED METHODIST CHURCH

A church burning in the Osborne Creek Community brought back lots of memories to many in the community — but especially former members like Merril Cartwright, Marjorie Waters, and Virginia Smitherman.

A local Apostolic church burned down on a Sunday night in early 1999. It was an Independent Pentecostal church at the time of its demise. Its official name was Jesus Name House of Prayer Apostolic Church. However, for its first years — better than fifty years, it was the Oak Grove Methodist Church.

It was in that church that Merril Cartwright went to church all his growing up years. He joined the church at the alter of that church.

He had such wonderful teachers like Marjorie Waters and Virginia Smitherman. However, they were Marjorie Oakley and

Oak Grove Methodist Church

Virginia Smith during those years. This was home for both "girls" at that time.

He learned to sing good old songs like "Jesus Loves Me", "In the Sweet By and By, 11 and "I Love to Tell the Story" there.

"Cousin" Mary Oakley (as he called her) played the piano. And he thinks that her daughter Marjorie led the singing. However, according to Marjorie, Lena Parker was the song leader also. Mrs. Mary Oakley not only played the piano, but she was Sunday School Superintendent for 35 years.

He was in the MYF (Methodist Youth Fellowship) there, and became the district president of the group. The church meant so much to him — as it did to Virginia and Marjorie. He had ministers that he knew and loved — B. G. Whitehurst, Bob Thornton, and Thomas Rankin.

Sunday School classes were held in various places within the church. Some of the classes were taught in the teachers' cars.

It was so much a part of Merril's life that when he got married, that is where it had to be. Life for him and his bride therefore started at the Oak Grove Methodist Church.

It is located on the Osborne Creek Road near the Osborne Creek Baptist Church, and what was at one time the Osborne School.

It was particularly sad for people like these three — Merril, Marjorie, and Virginia. It was a part of the life they had known when they were young. And it brought back memories of the people who had been a part of it then.

Marjorie could remember names of so many people who had been a part of the church in the thirties and forties. Folks like Sidney Spain, Eugenia and Gordon Smith, Reuben and Louella Smith, "Uncle" Bobby Smith and his family, the Mary Oakley Family, the Dee Jackson Family, and the Charley Parker Family.

Marjorie Oakley Waters said, "My Aunt was married — not inside - - but just outside the Oak Grove Methodist Church." Flemma Dupree Carpenter and Albert Jackson Tucker became man and wife on the grounds of Oak Grove Methodist Church on November 24, 1904.

O'Neil Parker, a former Booneville resident who now lives in Memphis, remembered, "The Charlie Parkers (O'Neil's grandparents) moved to the Gardner farm near the church in 1904, and were members of the church until their death. Charlie's funeral was there in 1962 and his wife, Lula, in 1960.

And Virginia Smitherman remembered, "My parents met at that church — Mary Virginia Sanford and Walter Smith. She came to play the piano and my grandfather and his family had lived in the community. The young couple were married about a year later."

Marie Robertson Spain, who lives in the Osborne Creek Community, said, "My grandmother, Fannie Tays (Mrs. A. A.) gave the church its name."

According to documents from the Christ United Methodist Church (the union of the Oak Grove and Blackland Methodist Churches), the beginning of the Oak Grove United Methodist Church was well documented.

In 1903, members of the Booneville Methodist Church living in the Osborne Creek Community, wanted to build their own church -mainly because bad winter weather made travel to town impractical.

On July 25, 1903, a building committee consisting of Aaron Smith, James Taylor, Robert B. Smith, and J. P. Tays met at the parsonage in Booneville to discuss building a church in the Osborne Creek Community. It was decided to construct a 30 by 50 feet, 14 feet high frame building. The plans and specifications were to be prepared by Rev. B. P. Jaco, Presiding Elder, Aaron Spain, and Robert B. Smith.

The first services were held on November 25, 1903, with 18 male and 26 female members. In 1912, the membership was 51. At the time of the merger in 1968, Oak Grove had 63 members.

Virginia also remembered, "The great time we had at the ,dinners on the ground'. A particular memory that we have was of the huge amounts of food on the long table, and the time my Mother was passing around both angel food and devil's food cakes, and passing them to the preacher, who said, 'Perhaps I'd better take the angel cake'."

The Oak Grove church and property were sold to help build the new church. The building was then occupied by an independent congregation.

Today — 1999, the old Oak Grove Methodist Church just lives in the memories of the families who were a part of it. And the independent church that continued in the white plank building can only be seen in their memories too.

However, today a new building is going up. I t may have changed its name -and possibly its people — but a church will remain in the community. Within the area there IS a place of worship.
Submitted by:Laura W. Cartwright.

OAK HILL BAPTIST CHURCH

Oak Hill Baptist Church had its beginning August 27 J. B. Roberts was the first pastor, he was pastor for eight years, resigned and was pastor again in 1899. J. S. Browny, J. P. Randolf and L. R. Brosness were pastors before the turn of the century. Beginning in 1877 preaching services were scheduled once a month "Saturday before the fourth Lord's day." The church also had its conference or business meeting on the same day following preaching. Preaching would continue for one time per month until the 1960's when services were held twice a month and the 1970's when they were full-time.

The name, Oak Hill Baptist Church is used today although it was changed several times. In 1889 the church was renamed, The Baptist Church of Christ, in 1897-it. was designated as Oak Hill Baptist Church of Christ. In 1901 the phrase, "Church of Christ", was dropped and the name remains Oak Hill Baptist Church.

J. R. Russell, J. A.. Landers, and Dan Waters served as pastors in the early 1900's. In 1925 the community of Oak Hill contained a store and gin. During the twenties the pastors were E. S. Summers, Clarence Palmer, D. H. Waters and Joe Crawford, During the 1930's Joe Crawford, S. V. Gullett, Lloyd Horton and Bynum Basden were pastors. In 1948 Spurgeon Mullikin was the pastor. W. B. Coulter and Vaster Carter were pastors in the 1950's. During the.1960's Hulon Chaney,W. D. Ross, D. S. Tidwell and John Dugard were pastors. Edward Lowery began his pastorate in the fall of. 1970. Lowery accepted the church full-time.

Joe McIntire accepted the pastorate after Lowery resigned a W-A i. in 1973. During this time we built a new auditorium and Sunday School space, with a pastor's study and a baptistry. Chuck Hampton accepted the pastorate in the fall of 1976. We constructed sidewalks, new kitchen facilities, road signs and a yard sign while he was pastor.

Eugene Tennison was pastor from June, 1979 until December 1981. Marion Payne served from December, 1981, until April, 19,84. We built a pastors home in 1984; Dwight Massengill was first pastor to live there. Charles Farmer, came in October, 1985. We built a Fellowship Building in 1988. Ray Burks, served from December, 1989, until June, 1991. Dan Mobley, came October, 1991; he retired

August, 1999 after eight years. During this time we paved the Church parking lot. We Incorporated the church, November, 1996, remodeled the church, choir loft and put Stain Glass Windows in.1998.

We called Mark Cagle, November 7, 1999.
Submitted by Ann Floyd.

OAKLEIGH CHURCH OF CHRIST

The meeting house of Oakleigh church of Christ is located at 101 Oakleigh Drive, just off Hwy.4/30 between Hwy. 145 and Hwy. 45. This congregation had its beginning in April, 1994. For a time the church met in temporary quarters until the present building was completed in February, 1995. Initially, there were approximately 15 members. By September, 1999, Oakleigh had grown to 41 members. During the first five years of existence–except for a period of approximately 18 months in which David Dodd worked as full-time evangelist–preaching was carried on by the men of the congregation with the assistance of evangelists from Tupelo and Corinth. In May of 1999, Jim Allen came to work as a full-time evangelist, joined in July, 1999 by Elmo Wilson as the second full-time evangelist. On August 29, 1999 Jim Allen and Elmo Wilson were appointed as elders of Oakleigh church of Christ.

The first Sunday of July, 1999, Oakleigh church began a weekly TV program on local station 53 airing from 9:30 to 10:00 A.M. on Sunday. The program is titled "Let the Bible Speak." Regular weekly services are at 9:45 and 10:30 on Sunday morning, 4:00 Sunday afternoon and 7:00 on Wednesday evenings.

This congregation of God's people have as their plea a return to the old paths, calling Bible things by Bible names; doing Bible things in Bible ways; speaking where the Bible speahs and being silent where it is silent.
Submitted by Diane Wilson

OSBORNE CREEK BAPTIST CHURCH

On Saturday, May 29,1850 Osborne Creek Church was organized with twelve charter members of the Baptist faith and Rev. P.H. Roberts as pastor. The twelve charter members are unknown but earlier writings state that the church's first worship structure was a bush arbor. A log building was built next and used until a frame building was constructed in 1854 at a cost of $98.50.

Regular services were held by the congregation on through the Civil War except for about two years. Records show that before the War Between the States, colored members were counted. This suggests members with slaves wanted them to be churched in moral values.

In 1866 the records show that the church membership was 115 of which 2S were colored. In the following year there were no colored members listed since they have become separate organizations.

The brick church where the congregation now worships was built in 1925/1926 and the church note was burned in a special service May, 1929. The church has not been in debt since this date.

Osborne Creek Baptist Church

Paul's Chapel Methodist Church

The church parsonage was built in 1956 and in the 1980's the fellowship hall next to the church was added. Many other improvements have been made in recent years.

Records indicate that the Osborne Creek Church has always taken a leading part in denominational activities. It was first a member of the old Chickasaw Association. Later it. became a member of the Tishomingo Association. The church has been a member of the newly formed Prentiss Baptist Association since its conception on Oct., 20 1920.

At present, the Pastor is Rev. Clyde L. Patton; Deacons, John Morrow, James Davis, John Gambill, and Guy Spain Chairman. Dorothy Gambill - Music Director, Martha Parker - Children and Youth Director. Guy Spain - Treasurer, Kathy Brinkley - Sec.

Osborne Creek Baptist Church will celebrate its sesquicentennial in the summer of 2000.

The church is known for its friendlyness, warmth, and love for their fellow man. It's goal for the future is to grow in Christ, spread the Gospel, provide spritual need for the community and surrounding areas.

Our prayer is to joyfully carry on with the work of all the God fearing Saints that preceded our generation.

May we all give Glory to God and His Son, Jesus Christ.
Submitted by Guy Spain

PAUL'S CHAPEL METHODIST CHURCH

Paul's Chapel Church is a small country church in the Dry Creek Community on Tippah County Road 600 — near the Prentiss/Tippah County Line.

No one knows the exact organizational date of Paul's Chapel Church, but it is believed to be sometime prior to 1848. Mrs. Ira Parks said that her parents, Colonel and Lottie Jumper, were two of the first members.

The land for the church was donated by the grandfather of Mrs. Parks; Mrs. Parks attends the church regularly. Besides the Jumper family, the families of Ernest Green, Marvin Yates and Ruby Bartlett have made the church their home. The great grandchildren of Mr. Yates and Mr. Bartlett are now attending this church.

Until 1971, Paul's Chapel Methodist Church was a part of the North Mississippi Conference of the United Methodist Church.

However, in 1971, the church petitioned the North Mississippi Annual Conference to withdraw, forming and operating an independent Methodist Church.

The church in its earlier days was a white plank building. Today, it is a small brick building with a fellowship hall adjacent to the sanctuary. There is a cemetery about a mile from the church, but there is a new cemetery behind the church buildings.

Some of the ministers over the years have been Bro. W. B. Ward, Bro. Mask, Bro. Obie Richardson, Bro. W. R. Timmons, Bro. Mincey, Bro. W. E. Sharp, Bro. Irvin Dees, Bro. Fabian Clark, and Bro. T. L. Parker.

Bro. W. E. Sharp served the church for 15 years until he became ill. At that time, some 13 years ago, Bro. Excail Burleson became the pastor.

Older members remember overflowing crowds with folks standing the windows outside to listen, and big revivals under a brush arbor. However, today the congregation numbers between 22-25 average attendance.

Laura W. Cartwright (Information obtained from Bess Jumper Parks, Catherine Jumper Yates, Dean Michael Tollison, Ragan Sharp Davis, and gleaned from The Mississippi Ozarks by Rev. Robert E. Walker.

PLEASANT GROVE BAPTIST CHURCH

The church was constituted in 1917, and the old Hester School House was used as a meeting place for church. The land had be donated by Mr and Mrs. Hugh Counce, to be used for a school. The deed was changed in 1918, to be deeded to the church. The Pastor may have been Squire Shook. In 1938, a new church building was built and the church was named Pleasant Grove Baptist. Brother Lewsford was the Pastor at that time and several years afterwards. In 1962 a new brick building was built. In 1970, a new addition was built for a fellowship hall, kitchen and three rooms to be used as two Sunday school rooms, nursery and two new bathrooms. Brother Doyle was the Pastor at that time. Brother Kennth White is the Pastor at this time.

"The first beginning of a church."

The first beginning of any kind of meeting at Hester Church was when Miss Betty Fughum (who never married) rode in a buggy that her father had bought for her. On Sunday afternoons in Hester Community she notice all the children along the road playing. She stoped her horse and buggy in the shade and gathered the children and taught them about Jesus. The men in the community got together and built a little brush arbor to meet under. This is what later became Hester Church and later Pleasant Grove Baptist Church. This is the story Miss Betty Fulghum told me a few years before she died.
Submitted by Pauline Counce and Linda Burns

SNOWDOWN CHURCH OF CHRIST

In 1912, the Church of Christ was established about two miles north of the present location. The church got its name when they finished the building. It began to snow, and someone asked

"What will we call it?" Someone answered, "Snowdown," and the name stuck.

Joseph Hightower Woodruff preached the first sermon in the building. He wanted to be the very first buried in the new church, cemetery

P.J. Stanley, W.V. Woodruff, Alonzo Wren, and S.T. Clark donated land at the present location where another building was built, in 1916. The building served as a church and a school.

Around 1940 yet another building was erected, and a young man by the name of Flavel Nichols held a revival He was a very zealous minister. Mr. Nichols led singing and preached the sermons. and several people were baptized. After the revival, interest grew and more people came to worship.

Once again another building was built. Twenty-five to thirty people were in attendance, and worship was only held on the second and fourth Sundays. By this time A.L. Armstrong (Archie) had begun to attend. Mr. Armstrong only had one hand. He would hold a song book with his good hand and lead with the arm with no hand. Archie Armstrong and his wife Jessie were a big asset to the church

Down through the years Snowdown Church of Christ had a number of preachers. They included: J.H. Woodruff, Ab Woodruff, Ed Taylor, Frank Cole, Frank Newcomb, Jasper Rogers and a few more.

The first elders of the Church were elected around 1963. They were Blunt Woodruff, Carl Green, Glen Armstrong, and William Floyd.

The present building was constructed in 1971. The congregation began to grow, and the attendance grew to about 150.

Bro. W. Archer started preaching for Snowdown Church of Christ in 1956. At first, he onlv came two times a month and for Bible Study on Friday nights which was later moved to Wednesday.

Bro. Archer has been of great value to the church in the 43 years he has served there. His name is synonymous with Snowdown Church of Christ.

ST. FRANCIS OF ASSISI

In the fall of 1961, Father Charles Reiner, O.S.B. visited Booneville in hopes of locating Catholic families. At that time he was the Benedictine Priest at St. James Catholic Church in Corinth and St. Thomas Catholic Church in Saltillo. Father Reiner located six families.

At that time, all six families were going to Mass either in Corinth or Saltillo. However, occasionally Mass was held in the home of Mr. & Mrs. Barney Shiplett of Booneville. Confessions were held in the home of Gladys and John Kellam.

Father Reiner and John and Gladys Kellam went all over Booneville and out in the country looking for property. Six acres of soybean land, four miles south of Booneville, was purchased from Mr. Wade Trantham. The Infant Jesus of Prague Church was erected with the financial support of the Extension Society.

Dedication services were held on Sunday, April 29, 1962, at 4:00 p.m. Following the services, a dinner was held in the dining room of the Town Motel that is now the Regency Inn.

The Church began to grow as more families moved to the Booneville area. The Fulper family started a Dairy Farm. The Buchberger family established Marathon Cheese. The Lawyer family came here with American Seating, which later became Schweiger's furniture.

While Father Reiner was here Benedictine Sisters came during the summers from Cullman, Alabama to hold Vacation Bible School. While here they would stay at the homes of the parishioners, mainly the Buchberger family. Meals were taken with different families within the parish.

In 1967, Sacred Heart Southern Missions, took on the responsibility of the nine counties in Northeast Mississippi. Prentiss County has been served spiritually and financially since that time by Sacred Heart Southern Missions.

Father Patrick Tierney, S.C.J. was the first priest from Sacred Heart Southern Missions, succeeding Father Reiner, O.S.B., in 1967. While serving in Booneville, Father Tierney resided in Corinth.

In 1969, Father Kenneth Stoll, S.C.J., came to Booneville. While here, he was assisted by Brother David Caranfor, S.C.J., who worked with the young people for approximately one year. The also resided in Corinth.

Father George Pinger, S.C.J., became the first full-time Priest in' 1977. Father Pinger made his home in the back of the Church.

When Father Pinger retired due to poor health in 1981, Father Charles Flood, S.C.J., then served as Priest. While here, he lived in a rented house at 101 Evergreen in Booneville. During his period of service, however, a house was purchased at 200 Washington. This now serves as our Parish House.

Father Richard Zelones, S.C.J., succeeded Father Flood in 1982. He was in Booneville until August 25, 1986.

Father Leonard, S.C.J., arrived on August 29, 1986. He was in Booneville for the 25th anniversary of the church. Mass was held in the Church followed by a dinner at Northeast Mississippi Junior College.

Father Steve Weise, S.C.J., held a meeting on August 18, 1987. At that time Father Weise informed the parish that due to the shortage of priests, Booneville would no longer have a resident priest. A sister would be hired to be a Resident Pastoral Minister. She would be the pastor with a priest coming for the Sacraments. If we could not accept a Sister, the doors would be closed.

Having agreed to accept a. Sister, the parish welcomed Sister Jane Eschweiler, S.D.S., on September 3, 1987. Sister Angelo Segoria, S.D.S, was here for a short time. She left Booneville on July 3, 1988. Sister Lorene Schuster, S.N.J.M. came in 1988 as an Associate Minister.

During this time Father John Young, S.C.J, came every other Sunday for Mass. A communion and word service was held on Sundays when there was not a Mass. Sister Jane left on June 30, 1990. Sister Lorene left in July 1990.

Daughters of Charity sisters from Holly Springs came on alternate Sundays during the summer of 1990. Father John presided at Mass the other Sundays.

Sister Kathleen Dede, S.P. moved to Booneville on August 30, 1990. After her arrival, a hall was rented at 203 West Market. Classrooms and an office were built in it. We were also able to

St. Francis of Assisi Catholic Church

have a place for social gatherings. Sister Kathleen and Father John alternated Sunday Service until Sister was able to get a priest for each weekend.

Father Tom Lind, S.C.J. came to Booneville from Holly Springs on September 1, 1991. At that time he began to preside at Mass every Saturday evening or Sunday morning. Father Lind left on June 20, 1992 and Father John Young, S.C.J. returned on July 1, 1992.

In the fall of 1992, plans were made for a new Church. Land was purchased on College Avenue across from Northeast Community College. At the direction of Bishop Houck, this was to be the location of the Catholic Church and Catholic Student Center.

On March 28,1993, groundbreaking took place for a new Church and hall. The Extension Society and a very small number of families made the first Church possible. The second Church was made possible by the Sacred Heart Southern Missions, a grant from Marathon Cheese in Wisconsin, and contributions both financially and through service, by parishioners.

On June 1, 1993, the Infant Jesus of Prague Church was sold. During the interim, services were held at the rented hall facilities on Market Street.

Father Tom Burns arrived as Sacramental Minister in July of 1993 and continues to hold this position to this day.

The Congregation moved to the new church facility in December 1993, and a beautiful dedication ceremony took place on April 10, 1994.

The new church was named St. Francis of Assisi Catholic Church. Sister Kathleen left in December 1994 and Sister Marian Jochum, OS.F., served from 1994 - 1996. Sister Dorothy Pashuta, C.S.J., from the Congregation of the Sisters of St. Joseph arrived August 25, 1997 and continues to serve as the Resident Pastoral Minister and resides at the Parish House at 200 Washington Street.

Church membership continues to steadily grow and members of the Congregation are proud of caring for the present Church, Social ' Hall and grounds. We have been richly blessed and ask you to join us in thanking God for graces received through all these years. Anyone is welcome to stop by to see our facilities or join us for services on Sundays at 11:15 a.m.

Wheeler United Methodist Church

In 1961 Brother Grady Gunthorpe became the first full time pastor. Later that same year a new auditorium and more Sunday school rooms were added, a steeple was constructed and the entire church building was bricked. New pews and a pulpit were also purchased.

In the spring of 1979, the church members voted to remodel and add on to the church building. This project resulted in new Sunday school rooms, new restroom facilities, a nursery, and a fellowship hall. This construction was dedicated to the service of the Lord on November 25, 1979 and the note was paid in full by 1983.

In 1984, Tuscumbia purchased twenty acres of land surrounding the church and a house, located on this land, to be used for a parsonage. Approximately two acres were set aside for a cemetery. The church was again debt free in 1990.

In July 1993, the members of Tuscumbia voted to build a new sanctuary and do some reconstruction to the existing building. This new church building was dedicated to the Lord on June 26, 1994.

Pastors according to church records: Grady Gunthorpe, Billy Hester, Dewey Wallis, Jim Wooten, Jimmy Wallis, Ed Lowery, Billy Dowdy, Ben Griffin, Roger Kennedy, Dwayne Kelly, and Jason Pilcher.
Submitted by Cindy Deaton.

TUSCUMBIA BAPTIST CHURCH

Tuscumbia Baptist Church was founded in 1948. The members met in the Tuscumbia School from 1947 until the fall of 1948. At this time Mr. Oscar Waddle donated land for a church building. When the building was constructed, it consisted of only an auditorium and a few Sunday school rooms. Baptism was held in nearby ponds. The pews were hand-made by church members. Members of the community donated a table, piano, and church sign.

Tuscumbia shared a preacher with Gaston and Thrasher Baptist Churches for several years. Therefore, preaching services were held only twice a month. Sunday school, training union and prayer meeting were held every week.

In January of 1952, Tuscumbia ordained its first deacons. Sunday school officers and teachers were also elected for the first time and a budget was submitted.

WHEELER UNITED METHODIST CHURCH

The church was erected in 1927 under the leadership of Rev. W.C. McCay. There was already a Methodist Church in Wheeler, located in the same spot, which was organized in 1898.

Many improvements have been made to this church since it was built. A fellowship hall, kitchen and bathroom were added. After that, more room was needed and the fellowship hall and kitchen were made larger. Two Sunday school rooms were added. Concrete was poured for a tennis court which later has been used as a basketball court.

In 1989 the front porch was enclosed for a vestibule in memory of Estelle (Gooch) Gardner and also a bathroom was added. The last project in 1999 was the paving of our parking lot. We members are proud of Wheeler United Methodist Church.
Submitted by Mrs. Gene Sappington

TIMELINE

Since 2000 marked the beginning of a millennium, it seems appropriate to give highlights of the last millennium in our history. And since this past millennium saw the colonization of our country and many of our ancestors were among those colonists, it is doubly appropriate. Therefore, following (with credit to Prentiss County History, World Almanac, Millennium Year by Year, and the Banner Independent) is

A Millennium Timeline of World Events, County Happenings and "Banner" News Items:

c1000   Vikings discover another new land, "Thule" (possibly Iceland).
Polynesians arrive in New Zealand.
With the 1000th anniversary of the birth of Christ, many feared 'end of world'.

1009   In Jerusalem, Caliph al-Hakim destroys the church of the Holy Sepulchre, apparently in a fit of madness, prompting calls for a Christian crusade to recover the Holy Land.

1013   Danes invade England.

1014   In Ireland, the Vikings are defeated at the battle of Clontarf by the Irish army of King Brian Boru, who is killed in the battle.

1019   King Canute unites England and Denmark.

1033   Famine causes fresh panic for "end of world".

1066   William of Normandy conquers English at Hastings.

c1085   Thule Eskimo culture spreads across North American Arctic area as far as Greenland and Siberia; they used large canoes and dog sleds to traverse the continent, hunting whales.

1086   Domesday Book gives William a record of conquered England.

1096   The world's first university founded at Salerno, Italy.

1099   The Crusaders take Jerusalem.

1149   A university is founded at Oxford, England.

1170   Archbishop Thomas Becket murdered at Canterbury.

1175   Famine, fire, anarchy and revolution destroy the Toltec empire in Central America.

1179   Maya city of Chichen Itza in Central America sacked, burned and abandoned.

1189   Troops assembled in France for Third Crusade. Richard Lionheart crowned King of England.

1190   Anti-semitic riots spread in England; 500 Jews died at York, England.

1192   Crusade ends in failure for Richard.

1199   Richard Lionheart dies.

1210   Moslems crushed in Spanish crusade.

1215   English King John seals Magna Carta.

1227   In China Ghengis Khan dies.

1244   Moslems regain Holy Land.

1255   In Rome, the Church approves use of torture in hunt for heretics.

1260   Kublai Khan heads the Mongol empire in China.

1290   England to expel affluent Jews.

c1300   In London gunpowder being manufactured; changing warfare.

1347   Mystery plague heads west after hitting Russian cities.

1348   Black Death claims third of European populatin.

1391   Private armies of mercenaries roam and plunder Europe.

1429   In France, Joan of Arc defeats English at Orleans.

1431   Joan is burnt at stake.

1434   Portuguese find new way to the east.

1440   In Mexico Montezuma becomes leader of the Aztecs.

1455   German Gutenberg prints Bible.

1470	Incas extend power over South America.
1477	Music, maps and posters roll off the new Gutenberg printing presses.
1484	Portuguese calculate latitude by the sun.
1492	All Jews are ordered out of Spain. Christopher Columbus lands on an island he calls San Salvador (in the Bahamas); arrives in Cuba believing it to be Japan.
1493	Columbus leaves Cadiz, Spain on a second voyage of exploration.
1494	Columbus lands on an island, which he names Santa Gloria (Jamaica). Spain and Portugal divide up the world.
1496	Columbus introduces pipe smoking of tobacco from America to the Europeans.
1497	The Italian navigator John Cabot reaches North America and starts to explore the coastline. Columbus imposes a system of forced labor on the Indians in Hispaniola (Santo Domingo).
1498	Toothbrush invented in China. Columbus leaves on his third voyage. All Jews are expelled from Portugal.
1499	The Italian navigator Amerigo Vespucci explores the northeast coastline of South America.
1502	Columbus begins his fourth voyage. Peter Henlein, a German locksmith, invents a portable timepiece.
1503	The Saragossa Instruction sets out a series of measures intended to encourage the Indians in the New World to adopt a settled way of life and to spread the gospel among them.
1507	German map calls new world "America" after Amerigo Vespucci who claims to have discovered the mainland in 1497-a year before Columbus arrived, when in fact all indications are that Vespucci's expedition took place two years later.
1508	In search of a north-west passage, Sebastian Cabot reaches Hudson Bay. Spanish settlers make slaves of Indians.
1511	First African slaves arrive in the Americas.
1513	Ponce de Leon claims Florida for Spain.
1514	Spain orders New World natives to convert to Christianity under threat enslavement or death.
1522	Martin Luther translates Bible into German for common people.
1524	The Portuguese Diogo Gomes, in the service of Spain, explores the whole American coastline from Nova Scotia to Florida. Italian explorer, Giovanni da Verazanno, under the French flag, explores coast of North America.
1526	First bibles appear in English language.
1527	Spain sends five ships and 600 men to explore and settle the lands between Florida and Mexico.
1528	Panfilo de Narvaez lands at Tampa bay with 400 colonists, most of whom died of hunger and thirst; Narvaez was lost at sea.
1536	In London King Henry VIII beheads his second wife, Anne Boleyn.
1540	Hernando de Soto encounters Temple Mound Indian culture at Coosa (Alabama). Priests accompanying de Soto conduct the first recorded baptism in the New World, that of an Indian guide.
1541	De Soto reaches a large river which he names Rio de Espiritu Santo (the Mississippi).
1542	Henry VIII's fifth wife, Catherine Howard, is beheaded for sins she committed before she married the king.
1550	The Spanish bring the first beef cattle to Florida and North America.
1554	Mary Tudor, daughter of Henry VIII, beheads Lady Jane Grey.
1556	Mary Tudor burns Thomas Cranmer, archbishop of Canterbury, at the stake.
1565	San Agostin (St. Augustine) settlement founded in Florida by Spanish; they introduce the game of billiards into America.
1568	A French force slaughters hundreds of Spanish at San Mateo fort near San Agostin.
1569	Jesuits work among the Indians, hoping to establish permanent missions (in present day Florida, Georgia and South Carolina).
1579	Aboard his ship, *The Golden Hind,* docked in San Francisco Bay, Sir Francis Drake conducts the first Protestant service in the New World.
1581	The first English attempt at establishing a colony, at Roanoke (Virginia).
1585	A group of 108 English colonists arrive at Roanoke. A Flemish mathematician invents the decimal system.
1586	Sir Francis Drake burns the Spanish settlement at San Agostin. Sir Richard Grenville leaves Roanoke leaving 20 settlers behind.
1587	Queen Elizabeth beheads Mary, queen of Scots. First English child, Virginia Dare, born in New World.

John White leaves 177 colonists at Roanoke, having found no trace of the colonists left by Richard Grenville.

1587 Christians ordered out of Japan.

1588 The Spanish Armada defeated by the English.
Phillip II authorizes half-castes in America to become priests provided that they are legitimate, which is rarely the case.

1590 The colonists of Roanoke (about 100, including Virginia Dare) are found to be completely vanished when governor (and grandfather of Virginia Dare) John White returned with two ships and supplies.

1595 Having decided that conversion of Indians is preferable to conquest, Spain divides southeastern North America into mission provinces.
Hundreds burned in German witch hunts.

c1596 The first wheeled vehicles, wagons similar to German farm carts, appear in the New World. They are used to haul supplies as the Spanish continue to explore and settle the southwest.

1597 Simon Ferdinano, a Portuguese navigator working for the English crown, lands on the coast of Maine looking for treasure.
The marquis of la Roche, elected lieutenant general of Canada, founds a colony on Sable Island.
In England the first crop of domestically grown tomatoes is produced and eaten.
Catholics crucified on hill in Nagasaki on orders of Japanese warlord.

1598 The marquis le la Roche leaves France with 40 convicts to colonize Sable Island, off Nova Scotia.

1600 The French found a fur trading post at Tadoussac, on the St. Lawrence River.
Two products discovered in the New World, tobacco and potato tubers, becoming popular in Europe.
In the North American plains, Spanish horses fall into Apache hands.

1601 Germany and France agree to co-operate in the establishment of a new postal service.

1602 Sir Walter Raleigh sends a final party in search of the Roanoke settlers in Virginia. It is feared the 225 colonists have died at the hands of Indians or Spaniards.
The English Captain Bartholomew Gosnold, having given up his Colonisation efforts in the northeast, has left Falmouth and has discovered and named Cape Cod after the fish he found there, and Martha's Vineyard in honor of his daughter, and is now returning to England.

1603 Colonisation of Sable Island, where 50 petty criminals and their guards were left in 1597, has been abandoned. They were sending sealskins and oil back to France, but last year nothing was heard from them and envoys sent to the colony found the guards had been killed and the prisoners had turned on each other with only 11 surviving.
Bartholomew Gilbert is killed by Indians during a search for the Roanoke colonists who were last seen in 1587.

Elizabeth the Great dies and English and Scottish thrones are united under the Scottish King James VI.

1604 French explorer Pierre du Guast, the sieur du Monts, founds the first French colony in the northeast region, on the St. Croix River.
In London King James describes the habit of tobacco smoking as "vile and stinking" and "dangerous".
In New Spain the term "Mexican" appears in print for the first time in *La Gazetta Mexicana,* published by the creole Balbuena.

1605 Port Royal is established in Acadia (Nova Scotia).
George Weymouth returns to England from the northeastern coast of America (Maine) with glowing reports of agricultural development, notably barley and pea cultivation.
European diseases, smallpox, measles, dysentery, typhoid and tuberculosis, are decimating the American Indians. Alcohol is also reported to be having a disastrous effect on Indian communities.

1606 A French performance of *La Theatre de Neptune en la Louvelle France* in Port Royal is one of the first plays staged in the New World.
The London Company dispatches the ships *Sarah Constant, Discovery* and *Goodspeed*, led by Captain Christopher Newport, to Virginia.
The Virginia Company is given the task of colonising the area around Florida and Delaware, while the Plymouth Company is to colonise territory inland from Cape Cod Bay.
Breakaway sect calling themselves Baptists plan to leave England for Amsterdam. Having rejected the Church of England and unable to accept orthodox Calvinism, they are led by a former Gainsborough preacher, John Smith, who in turn has broken away from the dissenting Separatists. They face continuous persecution in England whereas in Amsterdam, tolerance is the norm.

1607 Captain Christopher Newport and 105 followers have founded the colony of Jamestown at the mouth of the James River on the coast of Virginia. By June they build James Fort to defend themselves against attacks by the Spanish and Indians.
Newly arrived Jamestown colonists have lived on sturgeon and sea Crab all summer, and have buried at least 50 people in the last four Months, lost to disease and starvation.
In December John Smith heads up Chickahominy River in search of food. Indian Chief Powhatan spares Smith's life after the pleas of his daughter Pocahontas.

1608 A Spanish royal decree legalizes the slavery of Chilean Indians.

1609 In London, the American province of Virginia is granted a new charter, extending its territory "from sea to sea".
In his second attempt to locate a passage to China, the English navigator Henry Hudson sails his ship, the *HalfMoon*, up the river near Manhattan island (the Hudson) far enough to determine that it does not lead to the Orient, a great disappointment to Hudson.

1610 Sir Thomas Gates institutes "Laws Divine Morall and Martial", a harsh civil code, for Jamestown.
During a winter of appalling hardship in Jamestown, a man is put to death for eating his wife's body.
Colonists in Jamestown play bowls. This is the first game that settlers in the English colonies have found time for.

1611 The "Dale Code" codifies two years of harsh laws passed by Dale and others in Virginia.
King James Version of Bible appears.

1612 The Dutch send the ships *Tiger* and *Fortune* to trade with Indians on Hudson's river and build huts and establish a settlement. Settlers begin to cultivate tobacco plants.

1613 In France workers in a sandpit in the Dauphine discover the skeleton of what is alleged to be a 30-foot tall man, the remains, it is thought, of the giant Theotobocus, a legendary Gallic king who fought the Romans.
The governor of Virginia rents three acres of land to each colonist, abandoning unsuccessful collectivism.
In Canada, Champlain, the French governor, explores lakes Huron and Erie
In France the publication of the *Voyages du Sieur Champlain, Saintongeois,* a "faithful Journal of the Observations and Discoveries of New France whilst seeking a northern route to China".
In Mexico government troops attempt unsuccessfully to storm a settlement of runaway slaves in the mountains.

1616 The population of the colony of Virginia is 351 including 205 officials and workers on company land, 81 tenants and 65 women and children.

1617 Captain John Rolfe returns to Virginia to find that settlers have nearly deserted Jamestown to grow tobacco in the hinterlands.
The British set up a penal colony in Virginia.
Dutch traders abandon the Fort Nassau settlement set up in 1614 on Hudson's River.

1618 The governor of Virginia decrees that those who miss church will be jailed "lying neck and heels in the Corps of Gard the night following and be a slave the week following."
Headright laws offer 50 acres per colonist to each investor who pays the cost of the trans-Atlantic passage.
Colonists begin to cultivate wheat.

1619 The first general assembly in the provincial capital, Jamestown, has passed a series of stern laws against drinking, gambling, immorality, idleness and "excess in apparell". Setters have been prohibited from planting Mulberrry trees, grapes and hemp, all of which could be used to produce intoxicants. Each city, borough or plantation is also required to educate the Indian children.
A Dutch frigate lands 20 Africans, who are to be indentured servants in the port of Jamestown, the first cargo of its kind to arrive in a British North American colony. In a separate transaction, 90 "willing maidens" were sold at the cost of their passage to become brides of settlers.
Some 1200 new settlers this year bring the population in Virginia to over 3,000. The newcomers are "choice men, born and bred up to labor and industry", plus 90 women and 100 London slum children.

1620 Leaders of the colony write to the Virginia Company asking for more orphaned apprentices for employment.
The crown bans tobacco growing in England, giving the Virginia Company a monopoly in exchange for a tax of one shilling per pound.
The *Mayflower* brought 120 anti-Catholic Puritans to the shores of what they call "New England" and the harbor "New Plymouth".
Leaders of the *Mayflower* expedition gathered in the ship's main cabin today, 21 November 1620, to prepare a social contract designed to bolster unity. The document is meant to placate settlers angered by their arrival on land which has not been granted to them by charter.
The "Mayflower Compact" establishes a civil body politic that will set up "just and equal laws" based on church covenants.
The first public library in Virginia is founded at the site of a proposed college in Henrico. Landowners donate the books for the library.

1621 England gets its world news on paper, the king having licensed certain members of the Stationers' Company to issue pamphlets on a regular basis.
The Privy Council orders all exports from colonies to have customs paid in England.
The governor of New Plymouth prevents newcomers from playing cards.
The first ironworks in the colonies are constructed at Falling Creek.
The first Jewish colonial settler, Elias Legardo, settles in Virginia.
At Thanksgiving a year after landing, the New Plymouth settlement is at peace with the Indians thanks to Squanto, an English-speaking member of the Wampanoag tribe.

1622 Indian attack in Virginia leaves 350 colonists dead in their fields and homes. Jamestown inhabitants are saved by a warning from Chanco, an Indian who had converted to Christianity.

1623 Colonists at New Plymouth established the system of trial by 12-man jury in the American colonies, originally instituted in the 1100s by King Henry II.
Captain John Mason of Hampshire has established the territory of New Hampshire from land granted to him by King James.

1624 After years of unprofitable operation, Virginia's charter is revoked and it becomes a royal colony.

1626 Salem is founded as the capital of Massachusetts.
Following negotiations, a Dutch group led by Peter Minuit agrees to pay the Canarsee Indians the value of 60 guilders, or $24, in beads and trinkets, for the 22-square-mile island of Manhattan at the mouth of the river explored by Henry Hudson.

1627 George Calvert arrives in Newfoundland to develop his 1622 land grant.

More than 1,500 children who were kidnapped from the streets of London arrived in Virginia.
Despite opposition from the pope and King James, tobacco exports total 500,000 pounds, up from 18,000 in 1617.

1628 Lord Baltimore arrives in Virginia to form a colony.
The New England Company is established, an English joint-stock venture to promote trade and colonization in North America, and given a patent to land along the coast between the Merrimack and Charles rivers.
Self-appointed Governor John Winthrop of Massachusetts and his assistants passed resolutions declaring that Trimontaine, on the Shawmut peninsula, "shall be called Boston" and will replace Salem as the colony's capital.
The first ferry route in the colonies opens, from Boston to Charlestown on the Charles River.

1631 The first American-built ship, the 30-ton sloop *Blessing of the Bay* is launched in Boston harbor.

1634 The French explorer Jean Nicolet crosses a great lake (Lake Michigan) wearing a Chinese robe, and enters what he thinks is the Orient. Instead, he finds himself in the wilds of the American continent, Probably the first white man to set foot in the area.
Maryland is founded by Lord Baltimore.

1635 The Charter of the Council for New England, founded in 1620, is returned to the English crown after repeated defiance of its authority by the New England settlers.

1636 The Puritan John Harvard founds the first American University, at Cambridge, Massachusetts.
The Dutch are granted the first patents on Long Island. English Puritan Roger Williams leads colonists to settle Rhode Island. A Puritan force from the Connecticut River area, supported by Indian allies, attacks a Pequot village and slaughters 500 Indian men, women and children. The battle brings to an end several years of war between the settlers and the Pequot.

1637 The English offer a reward for every Indian killed—on production of the victim's scalp.

1638 Disillusioned by the autocratic rule of their leaders in Boston, a group of 100 Puritans, led by Thomas Hooker, a Congregationalist minister, establish a anew settlement at Hartford, Connecticut.
The Swedes and the Finns land in the Delaware estuary and lay the foundations of a colony (New Sweden), with a capital at Christiania.

1639 The first printing press in America, at Cambridge, Massachusetts, issues its first volume, *Oath of a Free Man*, a broadside lambasting the vow of allegiance that colonists must swear to the English crown.
Representatives from three Connecticut towns band together to write the Fundamental Orders, the first constitution in the New World. It establishes a general assembly, the office of governor and the right to tax. It guarantees the political rights of free men, but makes no mention of allegiance to the English crown.

1641 The general court of the Massachusetts Bay Colony establishes the *Body of Liberties*, a code of 100 laws.

1642 Dutch settlers slaughter lower Hudson Valley Indians, who are seeking refuge from Mohawk attacks.

1643 Religious leader Anne Hutchinson, expelled with her husband from the Massachusetts Bay Colony by Governor John Winthrop because of their religious beliefs, is killed with her family in an Indian attack.
The Puritan colonies of Plymouth, Massachusetts, Connecticut and New Haven unite to form the dominion of New England.
The Dutch, on the orders of General Kieft, massacre the Algonquin Indians.

1646 The Virginia colony's first law for the education of the poor is passed, providing for the apprenticeship of poor children.

1648 The first woman lawyer in the colonies, Margaret Brent, has been denied a vote in the Maryland Assembly. She has protested that proceedings were unlawfully conducted without her, since all landowners should be represented.
Margaret Jones of Plymouth found guilty of witchcraft and sentenced to be hanged by the neck. Trade with the Canaries, Madeira and Spain begins to help the Massachusetts colony out of an economic depression.

1649 The Maryland Assembly passes an act permitting any form of Christian worship in the colony. This religious toleration and the fine position of the colony at the head of Chesapeake Bay attract numerous settlers.

1650 French Jesuits abandon the last of the Huron missions (Michigan) following the destruction of the Huron population by the Iroquois.

1651 Two leading Baptists are arrested in Boston for holding an unauthorized religious meeting. One of them is whipped in the streets as a deterrent.
Laws are passed in Massachusetts forbidding the poor to adopt excessive styles of dress.
Anthony Johnson, a free Negro, imports five servants and forms a Negro community on the Pungoteague river.

1652 The royalist governor of the Virginia colony, Sir William Berkeley, submits to warships sent by the English parliament.
A law is passed in Rhode Island banning slavery in the colonies, but it Causes little stir and seems unlikely to be enforced.
Under Puritan leadership the colony of Massachusetts defies Parliament and declares itself to be an independent commonwealth.

1653 In New France (Canada), the Iroquois League has signed a peace treaty with the French.

1655 Women's illiteracy rate in Massachusetts is put at 50 per cent.
In New Netherland (New York), 60 per cent and in Virginia, 75 per cent.

1656 In Virginia, suffrage is extended to all free men, regardless of their religion.
The first Quakers to enter the Boston colony, Mary

Fisher and Ann Austin, are met with strip searches, jail and banishment.

1657 Rhode Island becomes the third colony to defy the British ban on trade with the Dutch.

1658 The Governor of New Amsterdam, Peter Stuyvesant, has prohibited tennis-playing while religious services are being held. The neighboring colony of Massachusetts has gone even furthur: during 1655 and 1656 colonists were punished for eavesdropping, scolding, meddling, naughty speeches, profane dancing, making love without the consent of the congregation, playing cards, pulling hair and pushing their wives.

1659 Two Quakers, Will Robinson and Marmaduke Stevenson, were hanged on Boston common for preaching their non-violent doctrine in defiance of the Puritan government. A third, Mary Dyer, was reprieved at the last moment in response to her son's pleas.

1660 The Quaker Mary Dyer is hanged in Boston for continuing to spread the doctrines of Quakerism.
The crown strengthens the Navigation Act, requiring that certain colonial goods are to be shipped only to Britain.

1663 Parliament passes a second Navigation Act, requiring all good for the colonies to travel in British ships from British ports.

1664 The Dongan treaty makes the Iroquois subjects of the English king.
Horse racing becomes the first organized sport in North America, as Governor Nicolls establishes the Newmarket course at Hempstead Plains, Long Island. The Dutch settlement of New Amsterdam has surrendered without firing a shot to British forces under King Charles II. Britain now controls ports from Virginia to Massachusetts and will be better able to enforce the Navigation Act.
In Carolina the proprietors split the northern part of the colony into The counties of Albemarle and Clarendon.

1665 There are about 75,000 English colonists in the New World, compared with 7,500 French settlers.
Londoners flee from the city in panic as plague kills 100,000.

1666 Fire devastates London; finally halted by the Duke of York who brings in naval gunpowder teams to blow up buildings in the path of the flames.

1668 In New England Governor Edmund Andros takes personal control of colonial militias to quiet unrest.

1669 Father Jacques Marquette establishes the first colony in the northern plains; in Virginia, a German, Johann Lederer, has been granted a permit to explore westwards, (into the Blue Ridge Mountains and Kentucky); Robert Cavalier explores the mid-west.

1670 In Virginia a law is passed ruling that Negroes who arrive in the colonies as Christians cannot be used as slaves; Sir William Berkeley estimates that there are 2,000 slaves and 6,000 white servants in an overall population of 40,000.

1672 The Dutch regain control of New York from the English.
Colonists in Elizabeth Port, New Jersey opposed to the payment of the land taxes known as quitrents form an assembly.

1673 A regular mounted mail service begins between New York and Boston delivered by a "post road" along which men and horses are posted at intervals.

1674 John Winslow is elected governor of Plymouth, becoming the first native-born colonial governor.
Philip Carteret, governor of New Jersey, launches a campaign to enforce the payment of quitrents, which have sparked a rebellion in the colony.

1676 Nathaniel Bacon, leader of an armed rebellion in the colony of Yorktown, which was sparked by governor's refusal to support Bacon's raids on Indians, dies.

1677 Colonel Jeffreys succeeds William Berkeley as governor and halts execution of followers of the rebel leader Nathaniel Bacon.

1678 The French explorer Robert Cavalier and his chaplain are the first Europeans to see the Niagara Falls.

1679 Robert Cavalier de la Salle explores an uncharted region in the north central part of the continent (Indiana). The French sell slaves in the West Indies.

1680 The expulsion of the Spanish from Santa Fe by Indians sets off a war.

1682 Robert Cavalier, sieur de la Salle, claims possession of the entire Mississippi valley for France naming the region Louisiana in honor of his king, Louis XIV.
Spaniards fleeing the New Mexican Pueblo revolt found the first Settlement in Texas.
The English Quaker William Penn founds Philadelphia and the colony of Pennsylvania.

1683 In New York a Charter of Liberties is enacted banning taxation without consent.

1685 The renunciation of the Edict of Nantes spurs the migration of French Huguenots to South Carolina.

1687 La Salle is murdered by his own men while searching for the mouth of the Mississippi River along the Gulf of Mexico coast.

1688 In Pennsylvania the radical Protestant sect known as Mennonites, which evolved out of the Anabaptist movement, is the first religious group in the colonies to condemn slavery.
The English exile their Catholic monarch, James II; William of Orange rides into London in a "bloodless revolution".

1689 Emboldened by the victory of William and Mary in England, the residents of Boston oust Governor Andros and break up the Dominion of New England

In New York a German born militia captain leads a rebellion of supporters of William and Mary against a pro-Jacobite faction and sets up a provisional government.

The war of the Grand Alliance spreads to North America, where it is known as King William's war.

1690 In the first major engagement of King William's war, British troops from Massachusetts seize Port Royal in Acadia (Nova Scotia and New Brunswick) from the French.

1691 Maine and Plymouth are incorporated within Massachusetts.

1692 Twenty people are executed in Salem, Massachusetts for witchcraft.

1693 Governor Ponce de Leon completes the reconquest of New Mexico for Spain.

1700 Judge Samuel Sewall writes *The Selling of Joseph*, the first outright appeal for the abolition of slavery to appear in America.

The port of Boston has become the most important colonial center of the slave trade.

1701 Antoine de La Mothe Cadillac establishes a French fort at Detroit.

1702 A British raid on the Spanish town of St. Augustine extends the European war of the Spanish succession.

1704 A French massacre of the Puritan colony at Deerfield, Massachusetts intensifies the war in which the French and their Indian allies have been attacking English settlements throughout New England.

1706 Juan de Uribarri claims a vast area in western North America (Colorado) for Spain.

1711 With the arrival of 64 British ships in Boston, carrying 5,000 troops and 6,000 seamen, preparations begin for an advance on Canada against the French.

Upset by a new wave of settlements, Indians attack colonists on the Roanoke and Chowan rivers, launching the Tuscarora war.

1712 In New York after one of the first slave uprisings in North America, 12 slaves are executed and six commit suicide before they can be hanged. Before the militia arrived to arrest them, the slaves killed nine whites.

1713 Troops from North and South Carolina capture Fort Nohucke, a Tuscarora base, and force the Indians to negotiate.

1715 In South Carolina Yamassee Indians, goaded by Spanish agitation, kill hundreds of English settlers.

In Massachusetts, with six 30-ton whaling sloops, the whale-oil industry is booming in Nantucket.

1717 Colonial ships, now allowed to trade in the West Indies, begin bringing back French molasses which they use to distill cheap rum in New England.

1718 The infamous pirate Edward Teach, known as Blackbeard, is killed by an English naval officer. A reward of 100 pounds was offered by the government of Virginia for his capture.

Governor Bienville founds a new city at the mouth of the Mississippi River, calling it New Orleans in honor of the French regent, the duke of Orleans.

1719 In South Carolina the colonists overthrow British proprietors.

1720 Two years of hostilities between French and Spanish troops in Florida and Texas, caused by the war of the Quadruple Alliance in Europe, are over. Spanish possession of Texas has been confirmed.

Population of the British colonies now stands at 474.000. Boston is the largest city at 12,000; Philadelphia has an estimated 10,000 and New York some 7,000 inhabitants.

1721 A group of women taken from a house of correction in France arrives in New Orleans to relieve the shortage of females in the colony; many are married almost immediately and the rest parcelled out to various French settlements to appease the lonely bachelors.

During an outbreak of smallpox, Dr. Zabdiel Boylston of Boston experiments with inoculation at the prompting of Cotton Mather who heard of the technique from his African slave Onesimus. All but six of the 240 Boylston inoculated have survived.

1723 Benjamin Franklin, 17-year-old publisher of an irreverent weekly, the *New England Courant*, leaves Boston for Philadelphia after a fight with his brother, writing under the pseudonym Silence Dogood.

1729 Natchez Indians massacre most of the 300 French soldiers and settlers in Fort Rosalie, in the most vicious attack yet in the Louisiana colony, triggered by the demand that the Natchez give up their sacred burial ground and temple.

1730 In retribution for last year's attack, French soldiers take prisoner the chief of the Natchez Indians, Sun.

In Philadelphia Benjamin Franklin publishes *A Witch Trial at Mount Holly,* satirizing superstition of witchcraft.

1732 The *Philadelphia Zeitung*, is the first foreign language newspaper in the British colonies, is published by Benjamin Franklin.

A law is passed in London prohibiting the export of American hats to England, another example of the so-called mercantile system which seems to benefit the mother country only.

1739 England goes to war with Spain over borderlines in Florida.

1740 Some 50 slaves are hanged in Massachusetts after the exposure of alleged plans for an insurrection.

The South Carolina assembly makes it illegal to teach Negroes to Write or to hire them as scribes.

1741 Following a series of arson attacks in New York City,

29 slaves are executed—11 are burned at the stake and 18 are hanged.

Scots-Irish Presbyterian immigrants are arriving in the colonies in droves, driven out of the Irish province of Ulster by renewed religious persecution.

1743 The printing magnate Benjamin Franklin sells his businesses to his partner, intending to devote his life to science, in particular the study of electricity.

John Woolman, an itinerant Quaker clergyman, begins preaching about the evils of slavery.

1745 The French fort of Louisbourg on Cape Breton Island falls to British colonial forces from New England, intensifying hostilities in what is known as King George's war.

The French and their Indian allies carry out a series of raids on English settlements.

1746 Princeton University is founded in New Jersey.

1749 The University of Pennsylvania is founded in Philadelphia.

Some 2,500 settlers sent by Lord Halifax to consolidate the British, hold on Nova Scotia found the town of Halifax.

1750 The population of the colonies passes the one-millionth mark.

1752 The French overrun the English trading post of Pickawillany in an effort to re-establish control over the Ohio River Valley region.

1753 George Washington, adjutant of Virginia, delivers an ultimatum to the French forces at Fort Le Boeuf, south of Lake Erie, reiterating Britain's claim to the entire Ohio River Valley.

1754 The site of a British fort at the fork of the Allegheny and Monongahela Rivers in the Ohio River Valley is captured by the French.

At the Albany Congress, which brings together delegates from the 13 British colonies, Benjamin Franklin calls for the establishment of a Common council of defense to fight the French and the Indians.

British forces under George Washington are defeated by the French Near Fort Necessity in the Ohio River Valley.

1755 George Washington takes command of the British forces after their defeat by the French at the Battle of the Wilderness, near Fort Duquesne (Pittsburgh).

British forces under William Johnson defeat the French and the Indians at the Battle of Lake George.

British expedition against the French at Fort Niagara ends in failure.

The British admiral Edward Hawk takes possession of 300 French merchant ships.

The British expel about 7,000 Acadians for refusing to take an oath of loyalty to Britain.

The first regular passenger ship service begins between Britain and the colonies.

1756 A stagecoach line opens between Philadelphia and New York. By travelling at 18 hours a day, the distance can be covered in three days.

Louis Montcalm de St Veran takes Fort Oswego from the British; the British surrender Fort William Henry to Louis Montcalm.

1758 British attack on Fort Carillon at Ticonderoga (in New York state) is foiled by the French;

British forces under James Wolfe capture Fort Louisbourg on Cape Breton Island; after losing Louisbourg and Fort Frontenac to the British, the French are forced to evacuate Fort Duquesne, which the British rename Fort Pitt.

1759 British forces defeat the French at Fort Niagara.

The French blow up Forts Carillon and Fort St Frederic and flee from The British.

1760 Major Robert Rogers takes possession of Detroit on behalf of Britain.

People of African descent are said to constitute 30 per cent of the population of the 13 British colonies.

1762 France cedes to Spain all lands west of the Mississippi, the territory known as Louisiana.

1763 Pontiac, the chief of the Ottawa Indians, begins an all-out war on British garrisons in the region west of Niagara, which fails after he is unable to gain French support.

A large area on the Canadian border, which is claimed by both New Hampshire and New York, is given the name Verd-mont, meaning green mountain.

Two English surveyors, Charles Mason and Jeremiah Dixon, begin surveying a boundary line between the colonies of Pennsylvania and Maryland.

The British prohibit settlement in the entire region west of the Appalachian Mountains.

The Touro synagogue, the first major center of Jewish culture in America, opens at Newport, Rhode Island.

1764 A French trading post is established at St. Louis on the west bank of the Mississippi river, not far below the mouth of the Missouri.

British parliament passes a Sugar Act, its first law specifically aimed at raising revenue from the colonies.

Parliament passes a Currency Act banning the colonies from printing paper money.

The lawyer James Otis denounces "taxation without representation" and calls for the colonies to unite in demonstrating their opposition to Britain's new tax measures.

Boston city merchants organize a boycott of luxury goods from Britain, inaugurating a policy of non-importation.

The British farmer John Bartram discovers vast groves of wild oranges in Florida.

1765 Parliament passes the Stamp Act, taxing stamps affixed to certain printed matter, in order to raise money in the colonies to support British troops stationed there.

Parliament passes the Quartering Act, requiring the colonies to Provide shelter and food for British soldiers and their horses.

The passage of the Stamp Act provokes widespread protests and riots In British colonies.

1766	Parliament repeals the Stamp Act, the cause of bitter and violent opposition in the colonies. Thomas Gage, the commander of the British forces, closes the New York Assembly, which has resolutely refused to comply with the Controversial Quartering Act. Benjamin Franklin invents bifocal spectacles. Southwark theatre in Philadelphia, the first building in the colonies Designed expressly for the staging of drama, opens.
1767	Parliament passes the Townshend Acts, spearheaded by Charles Townshend, the chancellor of the exchequer, imposing new taxes on the colonies and suspending the New York Assembly until it complies with the Quartering Act. Boston leads a revival of the boycott of British goods.
1768	Samuel Adams, the first American leader to deny the authority of the British Parliament over the colonies, calls for united action to oppose the Townshend Acts. Lord Hillsborough, British secretary of state for the colonies, sends two regiments to Boston to quell unrest provoked by the Townshend Acts. In Louisisana Germans and Acadians join French Creoles in an armed Revolt against the Spanish governor, Antonio de Ulloa. Wesley Chapel, the first Methodist church in the colonies, is dedicated in New York City. William Johnson, the northern Indian commissioner, signs a treaty with the Iroquois Indians to acquire much of the land between the Tennessee and Ohio Rivers for future settlement.
1769	The Spanish begin to settle in California, establishing a mission at San Diego. The Virginia House of Burgesses condemns the policies of London. Dissolved by the governor of Virginia, the House decides to boycott British merchandise. North Carolina joins South Carolina in adopting the Virginia Association's ban on trade with Britain pending the repeal of the Townshend Acts. The explorer Daniel Boone penetrates the fabled territory west of the Blue Mountains, which the Iroquois Indians call Kentake. Thomas Jefferson, the scientiest and free thinker who was recently elected to the House of Burgesses, calls for the emancipation of slaves. Virginia's boycott of British goods is joined by Maryland, South Carolina, North Carolina, Delaware and Connecticut.
1770	A group of New Yorkers called the Sons of Liberty engage British troops in a pitched battle in New York City over British demands for compliance with the Quartering Act. In what immediately becomes known as the Boston Massacre, British Soldiers open fire on demonstrators, killing five. Parliament repeals all the duties on the colonies imposed by Charles Townshend except the tea tax. The British soldiers responsible for the massacre in March are acquitted on murder charges.
1771	William Tryon, governor of North Carolina, puts down a group called the Regulators, who have been in rebellion against the Eastern elite in the colony since 1764.
1772	Patriots led by Abraham Whipple seize and destroy the British customs boat *Gaspee* after it runs aground near Providence, Rhode Island. During the case of James Somesett, a black slave who had escaped from his master, the lord chief justice Lord Mansfield declares that slavery is illegal on English soil. In the face of a growing number of clashes between the English authorities and the settlers over the imposition of customs measures, radical Americans set up Committees of Correspondence.
1773	To keep the troubled East India Company afloat, Parliament passes the Tea Act which allows the company to export tea directly to the colonies and keeps the Townshend duty of three pence a pound on tea. Patriots board three British tea ships moored in Boston harbor, open all the tea chests and dump their contents into the harbor.
1774	Parliament passes the Coercive Acts to punish the American colonists for their anti-British actions. The Acts close the port of Boston and reduce the power of the Massachusetts legislature. Parliament reactivates the Quartering Act. Continental congress in Philadelphia criticizes British interference in the colonies and affirms the right to "life, liberty and property". George Washington signs the Fairfax Resolves which bar the further Importation of slaves and threaten to stop all colonial exports to Britain. Fort William and Mary captured by a group of militia led by lawyer John Sullivan in the first military action against the British "Redcoats" by colonial "Minutemen".
1775	British parliament declares Massachusetts to be in a state of rebellion. Thousand British soldiers killed in battle of Bunker Hill at Charlestown.
1776	American Independence is declared and the United States is born. Britain's Cornwallis forces Washington to retreat across Delaware River. Washington retaliates in a surprise attack, killing 100 Hessian mercenaries and taking 900 prisoner.
1777	Washington defeats the British at Princeton. Fort Ticonderoga in New York lost to British. British capture Philadelphia. British defeated at Saratoga.
1778	British defeated at Monmouth. The British capture Savannah, Georgia.
1779	American privateers capture British warship off coast of England.
1780	Russian czarina Catherine II protests Britain's indiscriminate attacks on ships at sea whether or not they are involved in American Revolution. American general Benedict Arnold turns traitor.

Britain declares war on Holland who had been supplying French and Spanish arms to the rebels.
Gen. Washington orders offensive against Iroquois Indians in Mohawk River region in New York.

1781 French and American allies defeat the British at Yorktown and Cornwallis surrenders.

1782 Parliament votes to abandon further prosecution of the American war.
In his *Notes onVirginia* Thomas Jefferson says of the British Empire, "The sun of her glory is fast descending the horizon".
Virginia passes legislation making it legal for any man to free his slaves.

1783 Some 100,000 loyalists leave the United States with a majority failing to return to England by taking advantage of land grants in Canada and Nova Scotia.
Slave trade is banned in northern states.
United States of America (which includes the 13 colonies and the Northwest Territory) is recognized.

1784 First Russian colony in North America is founded on Kodiak Island in the Gulf of Alaska.

1785 New York makes slavery illegal.

1786 In Massachusetts 1200 farmers stage an armed protest against seizures of farms, livestock and household goods for non-payment of debts.

1787 Congress adopts the Northwest Treaty providing for the incorporation of new states into the union.
United States Constitution is approved.

1788 Almost all of New Orleans is destroyed by fire.
Congress declares New York as the federal capital.

1789 The first congress meets in New York.
In April, George Washington is inaugurated as the first U.S. President.
The Department of Foreign Affairs, headed by Thomas Jefferson, is established.
The War Department is created with Henry Knox as head.
The Treasury Department with Alexander Hamilton as head, is created.
Congress creates circuit and district courts and Supreme Court with the Federal Judiciary Act.
Congress proposes 12 amendments to the constitution known as the Bill of Rights.
Congress votes to create a U.S. Army.
Social revolution in France with storming of Bastille by mob of angry citizens and workers.

1790 Twenty thousand attend the funeral of Benjamin Franklin in Philadelphia.
The first census taken in the U.S. shows a population of almost four million.
In Rhode Island, Samuel Slater opens the first cotton mill in the U.S.

1791 Vermont becomes the 14th state.
Anti-slavery bill vetoed in London's House of Commons.
U.S. troops suffer humiliating defeat in a battle with Ohio Indians under Chief Little Turtle.

1792 First silver dollar minted in the U.S. bears the head of an eagle.
President Washington declares American neutrality in the war in Europe.
New York Stock Exchange is created on Wall Street.
In Paris, the first execution is carried out by guillotine, which is thought to be a more humane manner of execution.
Thomas Paine arrived in Paris fleeing charges of treason in England for his views as expressed in his *Rights of Man*.
George Washington is re-elected as President of the U.S.
Monarchy abolished in France and republic declared.

1793 In Paris, Louis XVI is guillotined.
Britain, Austria, Prussia, Spain, the Netherlands, Sardinia, Tuscany, and Naples form a coalition against France; the U.S. officially proclaims its neutrality.
In Philadelphia over 4,000 die in epidemic of yellow fever.
In Washington, DC President Washington lays the foundation stone of the Capitol, the intended seat of U.S. government.
In December, Thomas Jefferson resigns as Secretary of State.

1794 General "Mad Anthony" Wayne defeats the Ohio Indians at Fallen Timbers in the Northwest Territory.

1796 Napoleon Bonaparte wins a brilliant victory against the Austrians at Lodi Bridge in Italy.
The Southwest Territory becomes the 16th state of Tennessee.
President Washington makes his farewell address after 20 years as President.
In Russia, Czarina Catherine II (the Great) dies.

1797 Vice-President John Adams is sworn in as President of the U.S.
The U.S. agrees to pay tributes to Algiers, Tunis and Tripoli in an effort to halt piracy against American ships.

1798 Congress passes the Sedition Act.
Threat of war with France grows.

1799 In Philadelphia, the first organized labor action in the U.S.
The Federal Society of Cordwainers (shoemakers) wins a nine-day strike.
A U.S. Navy frigate, the *Constellation*, wins a significant duel with the French *Insurgente*.
Retired President George Washington dies.
In Paris, Napoleon Bonaparte sets himself up as first consul.

1801 The House of Representatives chooses Thomas Jefferson as the new president and Aaron Burr as Vice President after the two men tie in the electoral college.
Pasha Yusuf Karamanli of Tripoli declares war on the United States when the latter refuses to pay more tribute; U.S. fleet blockades Tripoli; the U.S. schoo-

ner *Enterprise* captures the barbary corsair *Tripoli*, heaves its 14 guns into the sea and chops off its mast.

1803 United States negotiates the Louisiana Purchase from France.
Captain Meriwether Lewis leaves Pittsburgh on the first government-sponsored exploration of the far west.

1804 Lewis is joined by William Clark on a journey to reach Pacific.
U.S. Lieutenant Stephen Decatur launches night attack on Tripoli.

1805 Lewis and Clark reach the Pacific coastline.

1808 United States Congress bars importation of slaves.

1812 War with Britain declared over freedom of the seas for U.S. vessels. USS *Constitution* sinks British frigate.

1814 British capture and burn Washington but fail to take Fort McHenry at Baltimore. Andrew Jackson repulses assault on New Orleans after Treaty of Ghent ends war. War settles little but strengthens U. S. as independent nation. George Stephenson builds first practical steam locomotive.

1820 Missouri Compromise—Missouri admitted as slave state but slavery barred in rest of Louisiana Purchase north of 30 30' N.

1823 United States Monroe Doctrine warns European nations not to interfere in the Western Hemisphere.

1830 Morman Church formed in the U.S. by Joseph Smith.

1833 Slavery is abolished in the British Empire.

1834 McCormick patents the reaper.

1836 Mexicans besiege Texans at Alamo. Texans gain independence from Mexico after winning the Battle of San Jacinto.

1837 Victoria becomes Queen of Great Britain.
A mob kills Elijah P. Lovejoy, an Illinois abolitionist publisher.

1841 U.S. President Harrison dies one month after inauguration. Tyler becomes first Vice President to succeed the presidency.

1844 Samuel F. B. Morse patents the telegraph.

1846 W. T. Morton uses ether as anesthetic.
Elias Howe patents the sewing machine.

1848 The U.S.-Mexican War ends.

1849 The California Gold Rush begins.

1850 Henry Clay opens the great debate on slavery and heeds the South against secession.

1854 The Kansas-Nebraska Act allows local option on slavery; rioting and bloodshed.

"Cunningham House" in Booneville where Gen. Nathan Bedford Forrest is reputed to have spent the night prior to the Battle of Brice's Crossroads.

Antislavery men in Michigan form Republican Party.

1855 Armed clashes in Kansas between pro- and anti-slavery forces.

1857 Supreme Court in Dred Scott decision rules that a slave is not a citizen.

1858 Pro-slavery constitution rejected in Kansas.
Abraham Lincoln makes strong antislavery speech in Springfield, Illinois: "…this government cannot endure half slave and half free."

1859 John Brown raids Harpers Ferry; is captured and hanged. Work begins on Suez Canal.

1861 U.S. Civil War begins as attempts at compromise fail.
Mobile and Ohio Railroad completed and joined twenty miles to the north at Cross City (Corinth), with the Memphis and Charleston Railroad.
Old Tishomingo County mustered out 2,000 troops after state voted to secede and join the Confederate States of America. The first army sent to join the Confederate troops in Virginia. The second army was sent to Tennessee.

1862 Third and last Army is organized.
Battle of Shiloh. Corinth evacuates after the Battle of Corinth.
Battle of Booneville, May 30, actually might be regarded as a skirmish. Two or three other Yankee visits.

1863 Booneville is visited by Yankees on April 2, May 22, damage was slight.
2nd Mississippi from Jacinto, suffers intense fire on first day of Battle of Gettysburg.

1864 General Nathan Bedford Forrest moves toward Rienzi. June 10, Battle of Brice's Crossroads. (General Forrest spent the night in Booneville, allegedly in what is known as the Cunningham house, where he planned the Battle of Brice's Crossroads.)

1865 Lee surrenders to Grant at Appomattox and the War Between the States ends.
Lincoln is shot at Ford's Theatre by John Wilkes Boothe.

Vice President Johnson is sworn in as successor.

1867 First Methodist Church is organized, with Rev. J. W. Honnell as the first pastor.
U.S. President, Andrew Johnson, just escapes impeachment.
Teenage emperor's coup in Japan.
Britain dithers over self-rule for blacks in Africa.
Irish bombs rock England.

1868 Booneville's first industry is started, a brick manufacturing plant, owned and operated by Rufus Peyton Walthall.
Spain's rebel generals oust Queen Isabella.
The 14th Amendment to the Constitution gives full U.S. citizenship to African Americans.
General Ulysses S. Grant, a Republican who was in ultimate command of all union armies during the Civil War, is elected President.
The Oglala Sioux Indians led by chief Red Cloud sign a peace treaty with General William Sherman of the U.S. government at Fort Laramie, Wyoming. The pact ends two years of fighting between gold miners and the Sioux.
The U.S. Seventh Cavalry under George A. Custer defeats a combined force of Arapaho and Cheyenne Indians led by Chief Black Kettle on the Washita River, east of the Texas Panhandle.
The 15th Amendment, requires all Southern states to allow Negroes to vote, is passed.
In Germany, Wilhelm Liebknecht founds the Social Democratic Workers' Party.

1869 First Baptist Church is organized on January 20, with Rev. H. S. Archer as the first pastor.
U.S. joined east to west with the completion of the world's longest railroad track, joining the Union and Central Pacific lines at Promontory, Utah.
Women in the territory of Wyoming are given the right to vote.
The press agencies of Havas, Reuter and Wolff sign an agreement between them whereby, they can cover the whole world.

1870 The first newspaper, *Prentiss Recorder,* is established by J.M. Norment. (Followed later in their turns by *The Pleader, Prentiss Plaindealer, Prentiss County Advocate,* and the *Prentiss County News.*)
Mississippi Legislature approves division of Tishomingo County into Prentiss, Alcorn, and Tishomingo, on April 15.
Booneville becomes county seat of Prentiss County with a county population of 9,348.
Joseph H. Rainey becomes the first Negro member of the U.S. House of Representatives.
The Rev. Hiram R. Revels becomes the first Negro member of the Senate.
In Central Africa, Swahili slave trader, Tippu Tib, sets himself up as ruler west of Lake Tanganyika.
France declares war on Prusssia.
Novelist Charles Dickens' death is hastened by overwork.

1871 Booneville Presbyterian Church organized under the direction of Rev. O.F. Rogers, a school teacher.
Britain's most famous explorer, David Livingstone, found alive in Central Africa by *New York Herald* journalist, Henry Morton Stanley.
Indian Appropriations Bill makes Indian land prey to railroads. U.S. Democratic party boss, William "Boss" Tweed, faces huge fraud charge.
Maritime world baffled by finding of *Marie Celeste,* abandoned in the Atlantic ocean with the saloon laid for tea, with no sign of crew nor captain and no sign of struggle.
In Chicago, a great fire kills 300 people, making 90,000 homeless.
In Los Angeles, 19 Chinese are killed in anti-Chinese riots.
The National Association of Professional Baseball Players is founded.
Charles Darwin publishes *The Descent of Man* which expounds his theory of natural selection.
In West Africa, the British take over the Dutch forts in Gold Coast (Ghana).

1872 Congress gives amnesty to most Confederates.
The first Prentiss County courthouse is built.
Ulysses S. Grant elected for a second term as president of U.S.

1873 Bank failures and bad harvests hit U.S.

1874 In Vietnam, France signs a treaty with the emperor Tu Duc which acknowledges a French protectorate over Cochin China.
In Hawaii rioting breaks out among islanders who support the claim to the throne of Queen Emma, the widow of King Kamehameha IV.
In the U.S., the National Women's Christian Temperance Union is founded.
In the Sudan, Zubair Pasha, a former slave-trader, conquers Darfur on behalf of the Turkish viceroy of Egypt.
The U.S. Congress passes the Civil Rights Act, guaranteeing equal rights in transport, theatres and inns and on juries.
Hawaii signs a treaty giving exclusive trading rights with the islands to the U.S.
Thomas Adams of Brooklyn, New York manufactures the first chewing gum.

1876 Sioux kill General George Armstrong Custer and 264 troopers at Little Big Horn River.
Alexander Graham Bell patents the telephone.

1877 Electoral Commission gives votes to Rutherford B. Hayes as U.S. President despite Tilden's popular majority.
Reconstruction ends in the South.
Thomas Edison patents the phonograph.

1880 Claude Price, son of Mr. Dan T. Price, first Boonevillian to receive appointment to Annapolis.

1881 President Garfield is fatally shot by an assassin.
Vice President Chester A. Arthur succeeds.

1885 *The Prentiss Plain Dealer* started publication.

1886 Statue of Liberty is dedicated.
Geronimo, an Apache Indian chief, surrenders.

Booneville Hardware, the town's oldest business and a downtown landmark.

1888 Booneville Hardware is founded.
George Eastman introduces his box camera, the Kodak.
Jack the Ripper murders in London.

1889 Indian Territory in Oklahoma opened to settlers.

1890 Booneville Fish Lake is developed by a company formed by many of the citizens of the town.
Sitting Bull is killed in a Sioux uprising.

1894 The first elected Mayor and Board of Aldermen (From 1870 to 1894 Booneville and Prentiss County had a cooperative plan of government); were elected: G.B. Kimbell, Mayor; Aldermen L.K. Peeler, P.H. Perkins, L.L. Brown, W.H. Collins and A.G. Smith, who was also secretary for the board.

1895 X-rays are discovered by German physicist, Wilhelm Roentgen.

1896 City officials elected: G.B. Kimbell, Mayor; Aldermen J.C. Stanley, L.K. Peeler, J.T. Price, P.H. Perkins, and S.M. Barnett; John W. True, Marshall. This group was re-elected consecutively and served until 1915.
Supreme Court's *Plessy v. Ferguson* decision—"separate but equal" doctrine.

1897 McMillan Funeral Home in Booneville is founded.

1898 *The Booneville Banner* is established by Thomas L. Bettersworth.
Spanish-American War.

1900 Prentiss County population grows to 15,788.
Martin Hill School is built.
Daltonville Post Office opens.

1901 Livingstone Hotel and *Booneville Banner* building are destroyed by fire.
President McKinley begins his second term and is assassinated. Theodore Roosevelt is sworn in as successor.

1902 The first store opened at Thrasher, owned by Clarence Rugg.

1903 Booneville Church of Christ is founded.
Wright brothers fly the first powered, controlled, heavier-than-air plane at Kitty Hawk, North Carolina.
Henry Ford organizes Ford Motor Company.

1905 Approximate date of the first electric lights in Booneville.
The first County Courthouse burns.

1906 Eastern Star, Prentiss County Chapter, No. 12, receives its charter.
T. G. Rees opens a generating plant in Prentiss County.

1907 Financial panic in U.S.
The town of Marietta, Mississippi is incorporated.
Marion Pruitt Nagles opens a sawmill in the Cairo community.

1908 Oak Ridge Church of Christ in Blackland is founded.

1909 United Daughters of the Confederacy organized in January, as D. T. Beall Chapter, No. 1185.
The town of Wheeler was incorporated.

1910 One of the earliest automobiles is brought to the city by the Rineharts.

1911 Ferris wheel falls during a July carnival, killing two and injuring others.
Football comes to Booneville in form of "Pigskin Pounders".

1912 Balkan Wars.
Titanic sinks on maiden voyage drowning 1,500.
The first picture show in Booneville is opened by Mr. Mortimer.
Old Snowdown School is destroyed by fire.
First Baptist Church in Booneville is also destroyed by fire.

Booneville Depot, built in 1913, now houses the Chamber of Commerce.

1913 Suffragettes demonstrates in London.
Garment workers strike in New York and Boston.
Sixteenth Amendment (income tax) adopted.
Ninety percent of the town of Marietta is destroyed by "the great tornado".
A new depot is built in Booneville.
Town of Rienzi is ravaged by storm.

1914 World War I begins.
The Panama Canal officially opens.
U.S. Marines occupy Vera Cruz, Mexico to protect American interests.
Hill Chapel Church is established.

1915 Booneville elections: T.P. McCullar, Mayor; L.O. Rinehart, clerk.
U.S. protest German submarine actions and British blockade Germany.
U.S. banks lend $500 million to France and Britain.

1916 Many good citizens lose lives from seige of influenza throughout the county.
City elections: T.P. McCullar, Mayor; L.O. Rinehart, clerk; Aldermen Jule Smith, Thomas A. Cook, Guy Young, and S.E. Hodges; and J.H. Huffman, marshal.
President Wilson is re-elected with "he kept us out of war" slogan.
Easter Rebellion in Ireland is put down by British troops.

1917 Twelve-bed hospital opens by Dr. W.H. Sutherland, which included a training school for nurses; Miss Ozella Thomas is the first trained nurse.
Smallpox epidemic hits town.
Many sons leave to serve country in WW I.
Gray's Department Store is founded.
First U. S. combat troops in France as U.S. declares war on April 6.
Russian Czar Nicholas and his family are executed by revolutionaries.

1918 Dr. W.H. Anderson brings the first closed car to Prentiss County.
In the U.S. alone, 500,000 perish from worldwide influenza epidemic.

1919 Hospital sold to the town of Booneville and the name changed to Northeast Mississippi Hospital.
Paris Peace Conference.
Versailles Treaty.
President Wilson's Covenant of League of Nations signed by Allies and Germany.

1920 American Legion and Boy Scout Troops are organized.
Booneville establishes the first high school for blacks.
Women's Suffrage (19th) Amendment is ratified.
In Germany, the National Socialist Workers' Party, led by Adolph Hitler, publishes a program for a third *reich*.
America spurns the League of Nations.

1921 City elections: J.E. Cunningham, Mayor; W.H. Huffman, clerk; Aldermen W.L. Newhouse, Jule Smith, Jim Moore and F.W. Duckworth; and W.C. Weems, marshal.

McMillan Funeral Home in 2000, one of the oldest "institutions" in Booneville and Prentiss County.

Princess Theatre in Booneville opens.
President Harding signs a peace decree, formally ending the war with Germany and Austria.
The first Congress of the Chinese Communist Party is held in Shanghai.

1922 Booneville Street lights are first turned on.
Booneville Woman's Club is organized.
Mussolini marches into power in Italy.
In Munich, Germany, the National Socialist (Nazi) Party holds its first rally.

1923 *The Booneville Independent* is founded by Sam W. Tapscott.
President Calvin Coolidge succeeds to the presidency following the sudden death of Warren Harding.
In Mexico, Pancho Villa, the revolutionary turned rancher, is shot dead by gunmen.

1924 Booneville Water Company changes ownership.
The old dome-topped courthouse burns and is rebuilt without a bond issue.
In Germany, Adolph Hitler is jailed for five years for his abortive beer-hall attempt to overthrow the government.

1925 The water tank is erected.
Home Telephone System is converted to common battery and is moved to a permanent office.
City elections: J.E. Friday, Mayor; W.L. Newhouse, clerk; Aldermen J.M. Moore, W.R. Fulghum, E.P. Brown and A.L. Bryant; and T.J. Pike, marshal.
Wheeler won its first basketball championship.
In the Dayton, Tennessee "Monkey Trial", John Scopes was found guilty of teaching evolution and fined $100.
Hitler tells his tale in *"Mein Kampf (My Struggle)"*.

1926 The Natchez Trace Chapter of Daughters of the American Revolution is organized by Mrs. W.L. Newhouse.
In London, John Logie Baird, a Scottish engineer, invents a process he calls "television".

1927 City elections: J.E. Cunningham, Mayor; Aldermen A.L. Bryant, W.R. Fulghum, L.L. McDougal, H.L. Walden and J.M. Moore; H.R. Spight, clerk; and V.O. Fugitt, marshal.
In New York, Al Jolson in "The Jazz Singer" enthrals cinema audience with the first spoken voice in a feature film.
A soundtrack is added to Booneville's picture show by M. W. McCuiston.

1928 Dr. W.H. Anderson purchases the *Booneville Mississippi Independent,* and forms Booneville Printing Company to publish newspaper and the *Doctor,* monthly medical journal, both of which he edited.
In Britain, the *Oxford English Dictionary* is completed after 70 years work.
Republican Herbert C. Hoover is elected president of the U.S.
In New York, a mouse called Mickey steams into action.
In Chicago, seven members of "Bugsy" Morans gang are machine- gunned to death in the St. Valentine's Day Massacre.

Gray's Department Store, founded in 1917, one of the oldest businesses in downtown Booneville.

1929 Joseph W. Sanders scatters circulars from his airplane, campaigning for J.E. Friday as chancellor.
City elections: J.B. Alexander, Mayor; Aldermen J.M. Moore, F.W. Duckworth, Jule Smith, W.K. McMillan, and S.M. Hamm; H.R. Spight, clerk.
Sewerage is installed in the Booneville business district.
President Hoover sends warplanes to the Arizona-Mexico border after the deaths of American troops in a crossfire between Mexican rebels.
Financial panic hits as Wall Street dives.

1930 Hitler is runner-up in German elections.
In the U.S, a new planet discovered beyond Neptune by astronomer Clyde Tombaugh and it is named Pluto.

1931 City elections: J.B. Alexander, Mayor; Aldermen J.M. Moore, F.W. Duckworth, H.L. Walden, W.K. McMillan, and Jule Smith; H.R. Spight, clerk; and W.F. Fulghum, marshal.
The Burton basketball team won the state championship.
Killing of United States Deputy Marshal, for which Ruey Eaton is convicted.
Death in New Jersey of Thomas Alva Edison, inventor of the electric light bulb, the phonograph, the ticker tape machine, and much of the technology of moving pictures.
Denmark, Norway, Sweden and Egypt abandon the gold standard.
The "Star Spangled Banner" becomes the U.S. national anthem.

1932 Franklin D. Roosevelt wins the Democratic nomination for president.
In Switzerland, the allies vote to ease Germany's economic crisis by suspending the repayments of war debts.
Also in Switzerland, the World Bank calls for a return to the gold standard.
Worldwide unemployment and hunger are in the dark days of a depression.

1933 City elections: Marion W. Smith, Mayor; Aldermen L.A. Wright, J.M. Moore, W.K. McMillan, H.L. Walden, and Murray T. Spain; H.R. Spight, clerk.
President Franklin Roosevelt passes through Booneville, enroute to Tupelo.
President FDR declares war on depression and repeals prohibition, telling Congress, "I think this would be a good time for a beer."
Adolph Hitler, a rabble-rousing demagogue who never before held office, became Chancellor of Germany.
Official confirmation that the Nazis are sending Jews to concentration camps.

1934 In Louisiana, the famous outlaws, Bonnie and Clyde, are killed in a police ambush.
In Germany, in the "Night of the Long Knives" Hitler purges the Fascist Party, crushing the Brownshirts and establishing the supremacy of the Blackshirts, or SS.

1935 Prentiss County Electric Power Association is formed.
New Scout Hut is dedicated.
Miss Rachel Smith is selected as first "Miss Mississippi".
First Pentecostal Church is founded in Booneville.
President Roosevelt signs the Social Security Bill, introducing welfare for the old, sick and unemployed.
In the USSR, Nikita Krushchev is elected as Chief of the Communist Party.
France, Britain and Italy agree to form a united front against German rearmament.

1936 A disastrous tornado hits the northeast Mississippi area. Four people killed and many others injured in Booneville.
Kraft Cheese plant opens.
Black American athletic star, Jesse Owens, upstages Nazis at Berlin Olympic Games winning four gold medals. Nazi leader Adolph Hitler who had intended to greet winners, stormed out of the stadium after Owens' second win.
Civil War erupts in Spain.
In Britain, Edward VIII makes his abdication speech and Prince Albert is proclaimed King as George VI.

1937 The Rotary Club is organized with Seth Pounds as first President.
City elections: Marion W. Smith, Mayor; Aldermen F.W. Duckworth, W.K. McMillan, J.M. Moore, J.E. Price and L.A. Wright who was also chosen as clerk; and Clyde Carter, marshal.
Italy joins the anti-communist pact between Germany and Japan.
Sigmund Freud arrives in London, fleeing Nazi persecution.
In London, Anthony Eden resigns as Foreign Secretary in protest against Chamberlain's appeasement.
"Nylon" and "Polaroid" camera invented.

1938 The Lions Club is organized with Donald Franks as first President.
Tuscumbia School burns.
British Prime Minister Neville Chamberlain announces that Britain will fight for France and Belgium.
Britain and the U.S. abandon the London Naval Treaty to allow for the building of battleships.

World War II U.S. Navy supply ship based in Philippine Islands.

1939 City elections: Marion W. Smith, Mayor; Aldermen J.M. Moore, L.A. Wright, F.W. Duckworth, W.K. McMillan and H.R. Spight; and Clyde Carter, marshal.
Lions Club is founded with Donald Franks as President.
Allies, Britain and France, declare war on Germany; President Roosevelt announces U. S. neutrality; Hitler orders U-boats to hit neutral ships.

1940 Fairview Baptist Church is founded on September 20, with Milton Stone first pastor.
Harold Prichard elected state president of the Future Farmers of America.
Official re-opening of the Booneville Library, December 21.
First run of "The Rebel", GM & O streamliner, through Booneville.
Sewerage is extended to residences in Booneville.
In London, Winston Churchill becomes Prime Minister.
Italy declares war on Britain and France; the *Luftwaffe* carries out its first bombing raid on London; British planes bomb Berlin; the Japanese join the Nazi-Fascist axis.

1941 Northeast Mississippi Junior College is created, but no funds are made available until 1946.
City elections: Marion W. Smith, Mayor; Aldermen E.D. Floyd, J.E. Price, Kyle Lindsey, Les McCullar and Phil Mitchell; Les McCullar, clerk.
Japanese launch surprise attack on U. S. base at Pearl Harbor. 'IT'S WAR!'; U.S. joins the Allies; U.S. takes Iceland; Allies Iran; *Bismarck*, pride of German fleet, is sunk!

1942 Mayor Marion Smith, youngest Mayor in the state at time of his first election, resigns to enter service. (He was re-elected upon his return.)
J.S. Finch became Mayor.
Seth Pounds is appointed chairman of the Prentiss County War Bond Drive, also chairman of the Rationing Board.
Chinese peasants beat Japanese veterans; U.S. Navy trounces Japanese at Midway; British put Japanese to flight in Burma; British Commander Montgomery "Monty" hits the Germans in Egypt.

1943 During WW II, Dr. David L. Hill participated and worked in initial research on the atomic bomb. He directed the first chain reaction experiments on Stag Field.
Arrival of American troops clinches victory for allies in North Africa; the RAF and U.S. bomb pulverise Hamburg, Germany; German U-boats on the run; Italy is out of the war; Russians win Stalingrad.
General Dwight D. Eisenhower to be Supreme Commander of Allied invasion of western Europe.

1944 J.E. Cunningham is elected as Mayor.
Arlin Rushing opens large store in Cairo.
East Pleasant Ridge Baptist Church is organized.
New Site wins the state basketball championship.
Allies liberate Rome; allied forces take Normandy beaches; the Russian Red Army sweeps the Germans out of the Crimea.
The "Desert Fox", Erwin Rommel, takes poison rather than being executed for conspiracy against Hitler's life; German flying bombs devastate London; American warships land in Phillipines; Paris falls to the Allies; Allied air raids reduce Dresden, Germany to rubble.
President Franklin Delano Roosevelt wins unprecedented fourth term.

1945 Partisans kill Mussolini and his mistress; Allies march into Berlin; Adolf Hitler commits suicide; Allied soldiers enter concentration camps where millions of Jews, Poles, gypsies, homosexuals, communists and others have been systematically put to death.
The U.S. Navy sinks Japan's biggest battleship, the *Yamamoto*.
American President and Statesman, Franklin D. Roosevelt, dies and Harry S. Truman is sworn in as President.
In Berlin, Field-Marshal Keitel signs Germany's final act of surrender.
Himmler kills himself while in British custody; Allied Supreme Commanders sign a pact for the occupation of Germany; The first atomic bomb tests take place in the New Mexico Desert; Nazi murderers are put on trial by victors at Nuremberg; The atom bomb wipes out Hiroshima.

1946 City elections: John Lee Richie, Mayor; Aldermen E.D. Floyd, Phil Mitchell, Cullen Morton, J.E. Price and Marion W. Smith; Les McCullar, clerk.
World food shortage as result of the war.
U.S. scientist claims smoking could be cause of lung cancer.
President Truman formally ends World War II.
Nazi war criminals are hanged in Nuremberg.
Goering kills himself.
The United Nations is formed to insure world peace and has first session.
Vietnam sparks war with French.

1947 National Guard Unit Company B organized under the command of Capt. Maurice I. Hill.
Mid South Manufacturing Co. Plant is purchased by Blue Bell, Inc.
President Truman tells Congress U.S. must abandon traditional isolationism to combat Communism.

1948 Prentiss Manufacturing Company begins operations on January 2.
Caver Milling begins its operations.
An ordinance passed to put up parking meters on the streets of the town.
One hundred mercury-vapor lamps are installed along the streets of the city.
East Booneville Baptist Church is established with

Prentiss Countian John Sparks (on left in front), who "re-upped" for second hitch after war, and crew aboard USS YW-123 stationed in Philippines, Subic Bay.

Smith Windham as first Pastor.

Northeast Mississippi Agricultural High School – Junior College opens its doors on September 3.

Dr. W.H. Anderson is appointed to the Mississippi Commission on Hospital Care.

In one of the major upsets in political history, President Harry Truman has won a full term in the White House, confounding the prophets.

1949 Northeast Mississippi Hospital formally opens on December 14.

Northeast Mississippi Junior College wins Mississippi Valley Basketball Championship

Booneville High School wins Mississippi State Basketball Championship.

The U.S., Canada, Britain, France and the Benelux nations write and sign the North Atlantic Treaty Organization (NATO).

1950 National Guard Armory explosion; seven men killed; called the first domestic casualty of the Korean War.

Miss Gwen Michael wins the first "Miss Hospitality".

WBIP radio station opens.

U. S. Government Housing Authority begins work on housing projects known as College View Apartments and Sunflower Apartments.

Booneville Library moves to the north section of American Legion Building.

Kiwanis Club is organized with Thomas Comer as first President.

City elections: Marion W. Smith, Mayor; Aldermen A.C. Wheeler, Phil Mitchell, V.E. Crawford, Kyle Lindsey and Bennie Yaeger.

Two Vietnams vie for recognition; Communists and West fight in Korea; McCarthy launches U.S. anti-Red crusade.

Figures show average U.S. income is $1,436.

In West Germany, Deutsche Grammophon launches the first 33 RPM 'long playing' record.

1951 Grace Methodist Church, formerly known as the East Booneville Methodist Church is organized on January 18 with Harold C. Vaughn as the first full time pastor.

City Park property is purchased from Mrs. Lucille Smith.

Shannon Manufacturing Company moved to Booneville.

John Mahaffy is elected to vacancy on Board of Aldermen when Bennie Yaeger moved from Booneville.

The Business and Professional Women's Club is organized with Miss Mabel Cunningham as the first president.

Booneville wins first place in the State Hospitality contest in its first Year of competition.

The largest crowd ever attends the 46th annual Prentiss County Singing Convention.

Rube's Variety Store opens in the Schultz building.

Ben Franklin 5 & 10 is remodeled.

U.S. detonates the H-bomb and the French break Viet Minh attack on Hanoi.

1952 James Godwin opens a law office in the Duckworth Building.

Drive-in theatre opens north of Booneville on Highway 45.

Business and Professional Women's Club chartered, with Mabel Cunningham as president.

Booneville's first Christmas parade is held.

General Dwight D. Eisenhower is elected as 34th President in a Republican landslide.

1953 Booneville wins first place in Hospitality Contest.

Mayor and Board of Aldermen are elected for the first four year term: Marion W. Smith, Mayor; Aldermen Wayne Hunter, A.C. Wheeler, V.E. Crawford, Kyle Lindsey and John Mahaffy; Miss Sude Walker, Deputy Clerk (for 20 years); Ovid Robertson, tax collector; N.E. Chaffin Police chief; and James A. Cunningham, Jr., attorney.

Elizabeth II is crowned in spectacular London ceremony.

DNA is shown as a double not alpha helix.

Dr. Salk's polio vaccine is used successfully.

1954 East Booneville Pentecostal Church organized in December with U. A. Smith as first pastor.

Honorable mention in Hospitality competition.

Booneville's Carolyn Cunningham wins first alternate in Miss Mississippi pageant.

Gentle Hosiery Mill begins operation.

Town Motel opens.

Senate condemns Joseph R. McCarthy.

1955 Junior Chamber of Commerce is organized with Billy Cook as first president.

Brown Shoe Company opens on April 6 with R.E. Jessup as first Superintendent.

Booneville wins first place in State Hospitality Contest.

Dr. W.H. Anderson is elected District Governor of Rotary International for the year of the Golden Jubilee.

Elvis Presley, originally from Tupelo and now living in Memphis, appears in Booneville in a show sponsored by the Kiwanis at Northeast Junior College Auditorium.

Lamar Ratliff sets a new world's record for corn growing, with 304.38 bushels per acre.

In Alabamas Mrs. Rosa Parks refuses to take back seat on bus.

James Dean is killed in a car crash.

Dr. Albert Einstein dies.

Disneyland opens in Anaheim, California.

1956 Booneville Nursing Home is established in November by Mr. and Mrs. Leland Mullinix.

Thomas Comer is elected Lieutenant Governor of the Kiwanis.

Elvis Presley appears at the Von Theatre in Booneville along with Johnny Cash and the Tennessee Two.

The new East Booneville Baptist Church is dedicated.

Record viewers watch Elvis "The Pelvis" on Ed Sullivan's *Toast of the Town* show.

President Eisenhower is re-elected with a bigger majority than in 1952.

1957 Booneville wins first place for the third time in the Hospitality Contest.

Mrs. Josephine Holliday is elected District Governor of Pilot Club.

A $50,000 swimming pool is added to the City Park.

Downtown seen from Booneville landmark "overhead bridge", most prominent buildings, the four sotry Dickerson's Furniture and Prentiss County Courthouse.

City elections: Marion W. Smith, Mayor; Aldermen Leland George, Kyle Lindsey, J.W. Mahaffy, W.K. Wallace, and A.C. Wheeler; Floyd W. Cunningham, attorney; O.J. Robertson, clerk; and N.E. Chaffin, police chief.
Troops are sent to Little Rock, Arkansas schools.
Sputnik, the first man-made satellite to be launched into orbit, is sent into orbit by USSR

1958 Brown Shoe Company begins making high-heel Smartaire shoes.
School of Nursing is added to NEMJC.
Fred's Dollar Store opens.
Mid-South Quality Egg Company starts operations.
Teenage fans distraught over the drafting of Elvis into the Army.
Krushchev replaces Bulganin as leader of the Soviet Union.

1959 Premier showing of "It Happened in Booneville", the story of Northeast Mississippi Hospital.
New overhead bridge is erected and dedicated.
First fishing rodeo is held in Booneville on Kemp's Lake.
Charles Vail serves as page in Congress.
Booneville's first Music Festival Year.
Civitan Club is organized with Carmon Lovell as the first president.
Unions voted down in the city election.
Two monkeys come back alive after being shot into space by U.S.
Hawaii is proclaimed as the 50th state.
Fidel Castro's soldiers conquer Cuba.
Soviet premier Nikita Krushchev ends a 12-day tour of the U.S, after signing accords with President Eisenhower.

1960 Unions are again voted down.
Prentiss County Home Bank is reorganized.
Marion Smith elected to high Shrine post, Oriental Guide of the Hamasa Temple.
American Seating Company announces plans to locate a church furniture factory in Booneville.
Wick Anderson High School is dedicatedon July 10.
Booneville City Planning Commission is organized.
Walden-Rowland Big Star holds its grand opening.
U-2 spy plane destroys Big 4 summit.
Israelis bring SS head Eichmann to trial.
JFK wins presidency by a close shave.

1961 Lancer Industries begins its operations.
Booneville celebrates its Centennial Year.
New Junior High School building opens for the fall season.
New $200,000 Church of Christ is completed on Highway 45 location.
City elections: Marion W. Smith, Mayor; Aldermen: Charles Crabb, Charles Steen, John Mahaffy, Leland George and E.T. Sartin; Floyd W. Cunningham, attorney; O.J. Robertson, city clerk; and W.W. Stacy, police chief.
Russia wins space race, the first to put a man in space.
The disaster of U.S. Bay of Pigs invasion; U.S. helps Vietnam stop infiltration.

1962 Catholic Church is founded south of Booneville.
Kraft Foods opens in Booneville.
Eula Dees Library at Northeast Junior College is built.
Teenager machine-gunned by East Berlin police as he was trying to get over Berlin Wall to West Berlin and freedom.
John Glenn is the first American astronaut to orbit earth; The telstar communications satellite is put into orbit.

1963 Aletha Lodge (Longwood Manor) opens.
Marietta Manufacturing opens.
Paul B. Johnson is elected as Governor of Mississippi in a record turnout.
President Kennedy is slain by an assassin in Dallas,

Eula Dees Memorial Library, NE Mississippi Community College, Librarian Carol Killough

Bonneville-Baldwyn airport.

Texas; Vice President Lyndon Johnson is sworn in as President; Alleged assassin Lee Harvey Oswald is shot as television cameras roll.

1964 Jimmy R. Isbell, from Marietta, is killed in Vietnam, he was the first Prentiss Countian to die in that conflict.
Beatles frenzy takes over in America.
Cassius Clay (later known as Muhammed Ali) TKOs Sonny Liston for world title.
Dr. Martin Luther King collects the Nobel Peace Prize.
Brezhnev replaces deposed Krushchev.

1965 City elections: Marion W. Smith, Mayor; Aldermen Charles Crabb, Charles Steen, John Mahaffy, George Bullard, and Leland George; Floyd W. Cunningham, attorney; O.J. Robertson, city clerk; and W.W. Stacy, police chief.
Harold T. White is named President of Northeast Junior College.
Heavy damage by a tornado in Wheeler and Frankstown area.
Sunflower Grocery holds its grand opening.
Bonds are sold for construction of the Booneville-Baldwyn Airport.
U.S. goes on an offensive in Vietnam.
Johnson is elected to full term as President.
Americans protest against the Vietnam War.

1966 Twelve railroad cars of the GM&O Railroad derailed north of Booneville on Christmas Eve.
A construction worker was killed in a fall while painting the Jumpertown Water Tower.
Miniskirt craze: "men can't believe their eyes".
Opposition to the Vietnam War grows.
Ronald Reagan is elected Governor of California.

1967 A tornado kills one person in Pisgah community.
Westside Community Center is completed.
Prentiss County Rescue Squad is organized.
Thrasher and Hills Chapel has tornado damage.
Nelwyn Murphy becomes the first female Superintendent of Education.
Israel smashes Arabs in Six Day War.
Ali won't serve and loses his boxing title.
Astronauts Gus Grissom, Edward White, and Roger Chaffee are killed in flash fire in Apollo I spacecraft during a simulation launch.

1968 Prentiss County integration plan gets underway.
The Jeran Theatre burns.
Jacinto Courthouse, built in 1854, opens as a tourist site.
Mrs. Orien Hare becomes the first woman summoned for jury duty in Prentiss County.
The Bank of Mississippi holds its grand opening.
Dr. Martin Luther King is killed in Memphis.
Bobby Kennedy is also killed in Los Angeles.
Richard Nixon wins the presidency in one of closest races in history.

1969 City elections: Marion W. Smith, Mayor; Aldermen Charles Crabb, Charles Steen, W. S. (Bill) Chittom, Robert Floyd, and Norman Young; Floyd W. Cunningham, attorney; and W.W. Stacy, police Chief.
The Church of Jesus Christ of Latter Day Saints opens.
Commentator Paul Harvey visits Booneville.
Neil Armstrong, first man to walk on moon, is followed by "Buzz" Aldrin.
Manson "family" slays actress and seven others.
Thousands of people flock to Woodstock festival.
Massive anti-war rallies across the U.S.

1970 Construction begins on a county vo-tech school.
The movie 'Tomorrow', starring Robert Duval, is filmed in the area.
Kent State shootings shock the nation.
10,000 women march for equal rights.
Paul McCartney splits, breaking up the Beatles.

1971 The Marietta School burns.
The new Booneville City Hall opens.
U.S. astronauts David Scott and James Irwin take a "four-wheeler" ride on the moon.
Frazier outpoints Ali to hold on to the heavy-weight boxing title.
China joins the UN; Britain joins the Common Market.

1972 Nixon wins his second term by a landslide; Nixon visits China; seven indicted in the Watergate break-in.
Arabs massacre 11 Israeli Olympians in Munich.
Astronauts John Young and Charles Duke, Jr. spend a record 71 hours on the moon and bring back sample moon rocks.
Americans bomb Hanoi and Haiphong.

1973 Booneville Mayor Marion Smith steps down after 13 terms in office.
City election: Charles Steen, Mayor; Aldermen Wade Lambert, Charles Crabb, Leland Barnett, J.W. Timbes, and Jack Arnold; Eugene B. Gifford, attorney; O.J. Robertson, city clerk; and W.W. Stacy, police Chief. (June Hutcheson took over as city clerk in 1975.)
George E. Allen, a Booneville native and adviser to three U. S. Presidents, dies and is buried in the Booneville Cemetery.
The Watergate hearings begin.
The U.S. role in Vietnam comes to an end.
Vice President Spiro T. Agnew resigns.
Gerald Ford, house minority leader, is sworn in.

1974 ETV Channel 12 is dedicated and a county wide ambulance service is begun.
Heiress Patricia Hearst is kidnapped from her apartment in San Francisco by "Symbionese Liberation Army"; Hearst caught on film assisting her SLA captors in bank robbery.
President Richard Nixon, faced with impeachment, resigns from office of President in aftermath of the Watergate scandal; Vice President Ford is sworn in as President; Ford pardons Nixon;
Scientists warn that aerosol gases threaten the ozone layer.
Ali KOs Foreman and regains his title.

1975 Wal-Mart comes to Booneville.
Ground-breaking ceremonies for the George E. Allen Library in Booneville are held.
Ten Illinois Central Gulf cars derail in Booneville.
Saigon surrenders to Communists; Communists capture Cambodia.
Britain's Conservative Party elects its first woman leader, Margaret Thatcher.
CIA plots the deaths of foreign leaders.

George E. Allen library in Booneville, funded and named for Mr. Allen, friend of the Presidents.

Anne Spencer Cox library in Baldwyn.

1976 Jumpertown is incorporated.
Northeast Mississippi Junior College changes its name to Northeast Mississippi Community College.
Democrat Jimmy Carter is elected as President defeating President Ford.
Patty Hearst is found guilty of an armed robbery.
The U.S. celebrates its 200th birthday.

1977 City elections: Charles Crabb, Mayor; Aldermen Charles Steen, Wade Lambert, J.W. Timbes, Jack Arnold and Norman Young; Eugene B. Gifford, attorney; June Hutcheson, city clerk; and W.W. Stacy, police Chief. (J.W. Timbes died in 1980 and Bluford Allen was elected, beginning Jan 1, 1981.)
Native Mississippian, Elvis Presley, dies at age of 42.

1978 The official groundbreaking of Baldwyn's library takes place Tuesday, July 11, 1978 to commemorate the beginning of the construction. Those taking part in the ceremony were Alderman Wayne Griffin, 1st District Supervisor Jessie Burcham, Library Committee Members: Mrs. Betty Jo Dobbs, Julia McElroy, Jim Cunningham, and Dr. Lee Roberts, 3rd District Supervisor J.P. Davis, Chairwoman of Library Committee Mrs. Loreda Windham, and City Attorney Paul Haynes, Jr. Others attending were Jackie Cole, Harold Dobbs, and Dr. John White, Alderman, 2nd District Supervisor Jimmy Moore, 5th District Supervisor V.W. Horn, and 4th District Supervisor Ross Pharr, and Mayor Merle Rowan. Booneville mayoral office becomes full time position; Indian skeletons dating from about A.D. 1000 are found at a construction site on the Natchez Trace Parkway.

1979 Board of Supervisors votes to consolidate the county schools.
Iran welcomes the fanatic Ayatollah Khomeini back after 15 years in exile, forcing the Shah of Iran to leave the country; Iranian militants seize the U.S. embassy in Tehran;
Mother Teresa is given Nobel Peace Prize.
Egypt and Israel sign a peace treaty.
A U.S. nuclear accident at Three Mile Island in Pennsylvania scare nation.

1980 Dr. Cliff Cartwright, a Booneville native, returns to set up a practice of family medicine.
Ruey Eaton, Jumpertown's first Mayor and author of the book *"In Prison and Out"*, dies.
Marion Smith, longtime Booneville Mayor and banker, dies.
A U.S. mission to rescue Iran hostages fails.
The British storm Iran's embassy, freeing 19.
Mt. St. Helens, a volcano in Washington State, dormant since 1857, erupts.
Former actor and California Governor, Ronald Reagan, is elected 40th President of the United States.
Former Beatle, John Lennon, is shot and killed outside his home in New York City by David Chapman.

1981 City elections: Charles Crabb, Mayor; Aldermen Charles Steen, Wade Lambert, Norman Young, R.G. Houston and Bluford Allen; Eugene B. Gifford, attorney; June Hutcheson, city clerk; and John O. Lambert, police chief.
Pope John Paul II is shot in Rome.
AIDS is identified for the first time.
Iran releases 52 hostages.
President Reagan is shot and gravely wounded by John W. Hinckley, Jr.; also wounded are Reagan's press secretary, James Brady and two security officers.
In London, Prince Charles and Lady Diana Spencer marry in splendor.

1982 Prentiss County becomes the 14th community in the state to successfully complete the requirements of the "Key Community" program.
The stadium at Northeast, formerly known as Tiger Stadium, is renamed for Thomas D. Keenum of Booneville.
In Australia, a mother who claims a dingo killed her baby, went on trial for murder.
Princess Grace of Monaco is killed in a car crash on a mountain road.

1983 After almost two years of delays, due to federal budget

Keenum Stadium, home of the Northeast Tigers of Northeast Mississippi Community College.

cuts, the go ahead was given for construction of a new post office in Booneville.
Booneville Elementary classes are shifted from the old school on Bryant Street to the middle school and Anderson.
Booneville Head Start starts meetings in the building on Bryant Street.
In Beirut, 216 U. S. Marines die in a terrorist bombing.
The space shuttle Challenger is launched on a six day mission that made Sally K. Ride, 32, the first United States woman in space.
The Soviets down a Korean jetliner, killing 269.
U.S. Marines take Grenada amidst protest.

1984 Illinois Central & Gulf Railroad announces it will sell a section of its line that parallels the Tenn-Tom Waterway in northeast Mississipppi, Corinth to Prichard, Alabama line.
Prentiss County's only remaining indoor theatre, The Princess, is destroyed by fire.
The city contracts with a private garbage collection service, Refuse Systems of Corinth.
Brown Shoe Company closes its Booneville plant after almost 30 years of continuous operation, laying off about 425.
Phase one of a multi-million-dollar expansion and renovation project is completed at Baptist Memorial Hospital in Booneville.
The State Education Finance Committee recommends that the Booneville, Baldwyn and Prentiss County School Districts to be combined.
New sheriff, W.V. Horn, and new county superintendent of education, J.W. Green are elected.
Site of new post office is announced
In February, Margaret Rinehart Floyd is named Booneville's Out-Standing Citizen at Jr. Auxiliary VIP dinner.
In March, Dr. David Greenhaw, formerly of Wheeler, opens an office for the practice of Internal Medicine
Court date is set for 16th Section lawsuit – which con-

The new Booneville Post Office.

tested the inequities between the Chickasaw Cession counties in north Mississippi.
In May, an estimated 10,000 people attend the dedication service for Bay Springs Lock and Dam.
In June, a new industry, Parker-Hannifin, opens, employing some 200 people.
In August, Julian Graddick announces Booneville will go on the air with a low power TV station, TV-53.
The Baldwyn Implement Company, a John Deere farm equipment Dealer in Prentiss County for 45 years, closes due to the "present agricultural economy".
In September, Dr. Joe Putnam, formerly of Jackson, opens an office in Booneville for the practice of Internal Medicine, sharing offices with Dr. David Greenhaw.
In October, it was announced that Blue Bell would have a "temporary layoff" affecting 223 employees.
In November, following a national trend, Prentiss Countians give Republican President Ronald Reagan and Vice President George Bush, the majority of votes in the general election, with a 50 % turnout in Prentiss County.
In December, James Franks' museum and sorghum mill is sold to the City of Huntsville, Alabama.
In California, a gunman runs amok in a McDonald's and kills 20.

Baptist Memorial Hospital in Booneville.

In Beirut, a suicide bomber blows up 40 people at the U.S. embassy.

1985 In February, Charles Walden is named Outstanding Citizen at the Jr. Auxiliary third annual Charity Dinner.
In March, Baldwyn teachers picket in Prentiss County's first teacher's strike for higher pay.
In April, a severe afternoon thunderstorm and possible funnel cloud causes $500,000 damage to Booneville homes and businesses and Northeast Mississippi Junior College.
In May, the city of Booneville elects its first woman Mayor, Nelwyn Murphy, and elects it's first black Alderman, Robert Swinney.
In June, the 50th anniversary of Prentiss County Electric Power Association and the rural electrification program is celebrated.
On June 22, 1935, Prentiss County citizens form the PCEPA
In July, TV-53 (W53AF) begins broadcasting.
Ex-police chief W. W. Stacy, who served for 20 years, dies of a heart attack
On October 8, Stacie Dianne Pannell, a Northeast Mississippi Junior College freshman, is found apparently murdered in her dorm room.
An Air India jet plunges into the sea off the Irish Coast killing all 325 on board; a terrorist bomb suspected.
In Japan, a JAL plane crashes killing 517 people, making 1985 the worst year ever for air disasters.
Wheel-chair bound American, Leon Klinghoffer, is killed by Arab hijackers of an Italian cruise ship, the *Achille Lauro.*

1986 The Challenger space shuttle explodes as a horrified nation watches.
The new post office opens in June
Veterans Day unveiling of Prentiss County War Memorial and the lighting of an eternal flame at the Prentiss County Courthouse.
Marietta gets a new water system and expansion of Marietta Manufacturing, the town's largest employer.
In West Berlin, a bomb explodes in a disco packed with American soldiers.

U.S. bombs Tripoli, Libya for its terrorist attack, killing Gaddafi's 15-month-old adopted daughter and two American pilots.
President Reagan and Soviet leader Gorbachev blame each other on their respective national televisions for the failed summit in Reykjavik, Iceland.

1987 Illinois investigator, Steve A. Rhoads, is called in on NEMJC murder
In February, defense attorney for Stephanie Alexander calls for gag order in NEMJC murder case.
A Prentiss County woman, Kathy Odle, is on a 10-member panel that advises the U.S. Department of Education on the implementation of a new law pertaining to the education of the handicapped.
In February, a judge sets tentative date and location for the trial of Stephanie Alexander.
Former Booneville resident, Diane Miller, daughter of Dewey and Sarah Martin of Booneville, an English teacher at Gulfport High School, is appointed to the State College Board by Gov. Bill Alain.
Mrs. Helen Finch White is named Outstanding Citizen.
Elections: Supervisor 1st District, Larry Barron, 2nd District, Jimmy Moore, 3rd District, J.P. Davis, 4th District, H.B. Lindsey, and 5th District, William L. McKinney.
In January, *Chicago Tribune* story claims that Stephanie Alexander confessed to the murder of Stacie Pannell at NEMCC.
Road building, park improvements highlight the Baldwyn progress.
Sadie's Variety Store, owned and operated by Sadie Gault since about 1939, closes.
Wal-Mart celebrates its 12th year in Booneville.
Burton gets a new fire station and truck.
From *Baldwyn History* by Claude Gentry: "Frank James allegedly to have spent a few nights at the Baldwyn Hotel just before the James Gang robbed the bank in Corinth".
Two tornadoes hit Prentiss County with the heaviest damage in Carolina, Gaston and Thrasher communities.

A second change of venue denied in Alexander murder trial.

About 100 Prentiss Countians meet at Thrasher High School gym to oppose Booneville's proposed city expansion of the city limits.

Tommy Davis, of Pisgah, and his dog, Jake, win National Bird Dog Championship in Grand Junction, Tennessee. This is Mr. Davis' 3rd win in the competition.

Trustees at the Northeast Mississippi Junior College vote to change the name to Northeast Mississippi Community College.

Northeast Lady Tigers win Women's National Junior College Tournament. Coach Ricky Ford is named as "Coach of the Year".

It is announced that Booneville will get new National Guard Armory.

Mayor Nelwyn Murphy named Mississippi's Business Person of the Year by the Future Business Leaders of America.

In August, NEMCC President Harold T. White dies in Jackson of an apparent heart attack; Joe M. Childers, dean for 15 years, is named as the new President.

Offices of the chancery clerk and board of supervisors move into the old post office which the county renovated for a Chancery Building.

Eugene Doran is appointed Dean at NEMCC and J. Connie Drown is named assistant to the Dean.

Retired Booneville businessman, Stewart Vail, dies; he opened a Vail and Baddour Store in Booneville, which eventually expanded to five stores known today as Fred's.

NEMCC Tigers and Lady Tigers are ranked in the Top 10 in national basketball; men 8th and ladies 6th.

In December, the only downtown grocery, McGee's, operated by Gordon and Lexie McGee, closes after 46 years in business.

War Memorial and Eternal Flame in front of the Prentiss County Courthouse.

Sadie's Variety Store, a Booneville "institution" for almost 50 years, where of it was said, "If you couldn't find it there, you didn't need it anyway."

The new National Guard Armory in Booneville.

"Old" Post Office "new" Pretniss County Chancery Building in Booneville.

LtCol Oliver North and Rear Admiral John Poindexter testify to Congress on the "Irangate" scandal; Iran-Contra reportedly blames President Reagan.
More than 70 nations pledge to save the Earth's ozone layer.
In Washington, history is made in December as Soviet leader Mikhail Gorbachev and President Reagan sign the first nuclear treaty.
The bottom falls out of stock market as worst crash since 1929.

1988 NEMCC murder trial begins in Aberdeen.
Bank of Mississippi President, C.J. "Junior" Roper, is named Business Person of the Year.
Tim Ford, of Tupelo, son of Dr. and Mrs. John M. Ford Sr. of Baldwyn, is elected Speaker of the Mississippi House of Representatives.
Stephanie Lynn Alexander is found guilty for the murder of Stacie Pannell in Aberdeen.
Booneville city expansion is approved.
Former home economist Claire T. Ross is named Prentiss County's Outstanding Citizen at the Junior Auxiliary's Charity Banquet.
Wheeler Eagles win the state boys 1A title, making them the most winning team in Mississippi State Basketball Tournament history; it's Wheeler's 8th state championship.
Booneville High School Principal Clyde Lindley is named Overall Educator of the Year in Administration by the Northeast Mississippi Chapter of Phi Delta Kappa.
Police Chief John O. "Bobby" Lambert resigns citing health reasons. Captain Bob Jones is appointed acting chief.
Booneville police form a union, voted it out, then voted it back in after learning Tupelo police had formed a union.
Prentiss County Schools are awarded minimum accreditation.
Postal rates increase from 22 cents to 25 cents.
Ground is broken for a four-lane Highway 45 between Guntown and Baldwyn.
Classes begin at the new Booneville High School.
Booneville businessman Jimmy Fisher announces he will build a Western Sizzlin' Steak House and a Days Inn Motel on the land adjacent to Bumper's Drive-In.
Jumpertown science teacher Patsy Johnson receives the 1988 Presidential Award for Excellence in Science Teaching.
Simmons Company of Atlanta, Georgia announces its purchase of Wall-Snugglers and Sleep Craft, Booneville furniture manufacturers, from the Darlene and Maness Bartlett family.
ACT scores were released and Booneville High School students who had taken college prep courses had the second highest scores in the state.
Two tornadoes hit southern and eastern Prentiss County destroying nine homes in the Marietta and Siloam Road areas and damaging the New Site High School Gym.
The first baby in seven years, Alisha Gail Weyhrauch, is born at Baptist Memorial Hospital in Booneville when her parents, Thomas and Brenda Weyhrauch of Booneville did not have time to get to the hospital in Tupelo and went to the Booneville emergency room instead.
Wolverine Tube Inc., manufacturer of copper tubing, announces it will build a $12 million plant in the Booneville-Prentiss County Industrial Park.
Reagan visits Russia which he dubbs "evil".
Ayatollah Khomeini of Iran ends an eight-year war.
In the Persian Gulf, a U.S. warship shoots down an Iranian airliner killing 286.
Hurricane Gilbert, the worst storm in the Western world this century, strikes Mexico twice in three days.
George Herbert Walker Bush, a decorated hero of WW II, sweeps to a 40-state victory defeating Michael Dukakis of Massachusetts for President of the U.S.

1989 Toni Chittom, a local girl and daughter of Mr. & Mrs. Gary Chittom, dances for Ole Miss Rebelette Squad.
A pecan tree called "Big Ike" makes headlines when it is cut down on January 12. It was necessary to cut the tree due to the construction of Highway 45 in Alcorn County. Wheeler residents, James and Betty Zackarevicz are given the job of making furniture from the 150 year old pecan tree, believed to be the fifth largest pecan tree in the world. The tree was cut by Tulon and Andy Jackson of Booneville.
Booneville High School receives national recognition for its College Preparatory Advanced Math Program. The school is cited in an educational research manual published by the Southeastern Educational Improvement Laboratory at North Carolina State University for achieving excellence in mathematical teaching programs.
Dr. Charles B. Romaine, 51, of Cleveland, Tennessee, a board certified general surgeon, announces the open-

New Booneville High School, home of the "Blue Devils."

ing of his office at Baptist Memorial Hospital in Booneville.

It is announced that the first step for the local 911 emergency phone system in Prentiss County is to come up with a workable plan for numbering county roads. South Central Bell gives the group a target date of November 1990 to get the project ready.

Mrs. Virginia Franks Oakley becomes the 13th recipient of the Outstanding Citizen Award presented by the Junior Auxiliary.

Bro. Jimmy Wallis, of Dry Creek, celebrates the first anniversary of his heart transplant on February 17.

Fire caused by lightning destroyes the agriculture building at New Site High School, which will be rebuilt.

Northeast's Tigers finish their season by winning second place in the nation at the National Junior and Community College Tournament in Hutchinson, Kansas.

The county's oldest resident, Susie Baker Green, dies at age 106 on April 9.

Mayor Nelwyn Murphy wins her second term as Booneville Mayor by a margin of 31 votes over her opponent F. Wade Lambert, a former Alderman. Elected Aldermen are Ralph Stutts, David Horn, Larry Downs, Billy Brasel and incumbent Robert Swinney.

Rienzi eighth grader Mitch Isbell is the "official greeter" of President George Bush when the President spoke at the commencement address at MSU's graduation ceremonies on May 13. Isbell, who has spina bifida, said it was a dream come true.

Hardee's, a new fast-food restaurant, opens in Booneville on June 5.

Jumpertown's Mayor, Joe Morgan, is re-elected. Elected as Aldermen were Gary Bridges, Tommy Prentiss, Rex Thorne, Chuck Geno and Debra Moore, the town's first woman alderman.

Rienzi Mayor David Potts is also re-elected. Aldermen elected were Jimmy Bishop, David Lee, Henry Palmer, Willie Lee Huggins and Johnny Stewart.

In Marietta, former Alderman Ronald Burns is elected Mayor. Elected aldermen were Charles R. (Ray) Taylor, Hollis Pharr, C.T. Moore, Kenneth Moreland and former Mayor James C. (Jimmy) Pharr.

Elected to serve as members of the Prentiss County School Board are incumbent Mackie Holder, Harrell Padgett, Larry Jones, Ronnie Hatfield and Betty Glover. Mrs. Glover is believed to be only the second woman to serve on the board. The first was Nelwyn Murphy, Booneville's present Mayor. This is the first election since the Justice Department approved the county's new school district lines.

Marathon Cheese in Booneville announces it will close on August 25, just 3 months short of the company's 27th anniversary.

A research report published by the Mississippi Agricultural & Forestry Experiment Station, a division of MSU, predicts that of the seven counties in the northeastern corner of Mississippi, Prentiss County will prove to have the highest percentage of growth in the five years between 1987-92.

Diana Heylin is named the new librarian at the George E. Allen Library in Booneville.

Northeast Community College receives $2.5 million in Major Economic Impact Authority funds. The money will be used to build a math and science complex.

A massive earthquake rocks San Francisco Bay area with 270 deaths.

The U.S. sends troops into Panama.

A vast oil spill poisons the Alaskan shores.

Tiananmen massacre as Chinese soldiers slaughter students.

Iran mourns the death of Ayatollah Khomeini. Americans best remember Khomeini as the fanatic whose followers held 52 of their fellow Americans hostage in Tehran for 444 days.

1990 The Berlin Wall falls.

Iraq invades Kuwait.

Mrs. Thatcher, Britain's Iron Lady, quits.

The Prentiss County Courthouse is designated a Mississippi Landmark by the State Department of Archives and History.

A lawsuit is filed in federal court in Aberdeen on behalf of the Prentiss County Annexation Committee in an effort to have the present annexation plan set aside.

A new computer lab opens at Rienzi Elementary School, complete with 24 new computers.

A fire destroys the Jacinto Hunting Club building located across from the Jacinto Courthouse.

Reba Bland begins her duties as home economist on February 19. She replaces Betsy McGlohn, who resigned to resume teaching.

New Site's post office becomes a "community post office", meaning the post office "closed" as a postal service operated facility using postal personnel and becomes a community post office contracted to a private individual. A.C. Eaton, who served as New Site's postmaster for 25 years before his retirement in May 1981, is awarded the contract with the U.S. Postal Service to operate the community post office.

Townhouse-Penthouse Inc., a local furniture manufacturer, announcs plans to build a 50,000 square foot addition to its facility.

Thrasher community is to receive a park being funded by a grant from the Land and Water Conservation division of the National Park Service. The Prentiss County Board of Supervisors is to match the funding.

Robert Eastman, an employee of Hercules Tank Company, is electrocuted while preparing to dismantle the water tank on the court square.

Justice Court Judge, Gene Gray, dies at his home at Zion's Rest community February 23 after an extended illness. His wife, Clynese, is appointed by the Board to serve until an election is held.

The Northeast Lady Tigers win their sixth straight state basketball championship.

The Wheeler Eagles win a record ninth state basketball championship.

Jane Turner is named Prentiss County's Outstanding Citizen.

Captain Jerry Barnes is named Assistant Police Chief. He replaces Captain Bobby Jones who retired.

An escapee from a Missouri prison, after first being captured in Marietta, then escaped from the Prentiss County jail. The escapee, David Corey Gist, has still not been captured.

The Board of Aldermen voted 3-2 to make Booneville's Police Chief an elective position again rather than appointed.

Edward McCoy is named principal at Jumpertown School.

Basketball coaching legend Gerald Caveness dies at age 57.

Mayor Nelwyn Murphy vetoed the ordinance changing police chief from an appointive position to an elective position. It is the first time in her five-year tenure as Mayor that she exercised her right to veto an action of the city's Board of Aldermen.

The Justice Department grants pre-clearance on the city's Annexation of 18 square miles, as well as three previous annexations.

Booneville native Phillip Sanders is named Booneville's new post-master.

Governor Ray Mabus and a number of state, county and local Dignitaries are on hand for groundbreaking ceremonies November 9 for the new $4,350,000 Math and Science Complex at Northeast Community College.

In a special election to fill the posts of tax assessor-collector and Justice court judge, southern district, Steve Eaton defeats Anthony Aycock for the tax assessor's post, while Ralph Caver defeats Jeff Floyd to become the new justice court judge.

The Booneville Blue Devils win their first ever State Division 2A title.

A special recognition service is held for Booneville's National Guard. The local Guard was activated due to the crisis in the Middle East and was sent to Camp Shelby for training. From there the unit was scheduled to go to Ft. Hood, Texas.

Booneville High School Band Director Vance Wigginton is named the recipient of the 1990 A.E. McClain Award as Mississippi's Outstanding Young Band Director.

Local ASCS Executive Director, Charles Calvert, retires after 33 Years.

R.J. "Piggy" Bonds, President of WBIP, is chosen for inclusion in the *Who's Who Registry, Platinum Edition, 1992.*

1991 David Corey Gist, escapee from a Missouri prison and from the Prentiss County jail, is arrested in West Memphis, Arkansas on January 2, thanks to a viewer who saw the prisoner profiled on *America's Most Wanted* television program.

Booneville's first policewoman, Tammy Johnson, 24, is sworn in on January 2.

The county's oldest resident, Betty Eulala Glover, dies on January 15 at the age of 101.

Local National Guardsmen, the Tupelo based 155th Armored Brigade, is activated December 6-7 for duty at Camp Shelby and then to Fort Hood, Texas due to the Persian Gulf crisis, were reported to be "surviving"- but missing their families.

Some 100-150 residents of Lebanon Mountain community meet on January 17, at the Baldwyn High School auditorium to oppose a regional landfill being built on Lebanon Mountain.

Local pharmacist, L.C. Wright, is named Prentiss County Tree Farmer of the Year and the Northeast District Tree Farmer of the Year.

Troy Moore, who operated landmark "Troy Moore's Store" for 41 years, dies August 14 at age 72.

Cecil Smith, a member of the Prentiss County Electric Power Association Board of Directors, dies as result of an auto accident on August 29 at age 72. His wife, Betty, was later appointed to fill his unexpired term.

Booneville's Board of Aldermen again pass an ordinance making the office of Police Chief elective and Mayor Murphy again vetoed the ordinance.

Booneville High School is one of 10 Northeast Mississippi schools recognized by the Three Rivers Regional Education Service Agency for achieving Performance Level Four or Five. BHS met level four standards.

Prentiss Countians elect a new chancery clerk, Travis Childers in the September 17 primary.

In the October 8 runoff, Farrell Brumley is elected sheriff and Mattie Perry is elected to serve as circuit clerk. Also elected are 5th District supervisor William L. McKinney, county superintendent of Education Edward McCoy, Justice Court Judge south Ralph Caver, and Justice Court Judge north Floyd Dodds.

Bonnie Breedlove Kemp, an elementary counselor for the Booneville Municipal School System, is selected as Mississippi School Counselor of the Year by the Mississippi Counselor's Association.

Jean Spencer is named the new home economist for Prentiss and Alcorn Counties.

Outgoing Chancery Clerk Phillip Cole is named First District Chancery Court Adminstrator, placing him over the chancery courts of eight counties.

Kenneth Chism is hired as the new principal at Jumpertown School to replace Edward McCoy, county superintendent-elect.

Union of Soviet Socialist Republic is dissolved; President Gorbachev Resigns; Commonwealth of Independent States formed.

1992 The City of Booneville and Prentiss County join the new Northeast Mississippi Solid Waste Management Authority, a consortium made up of six counties and six cities in the area.

State Senator John White is appointed chairman of the Senate's Local and Private Committee. He is also appointed to Appropriations, Environmental Protection, Fees and Salaries, Highways and Transportation, Public Health and Welfare and Wildlife and Fisheries.

State Representative Billy McCoy is awarded the chairmanship of The House Education Committee. He is also appointed to the Appropriations, Transportation, State Library, Congressional Redistricting and Legislative Reapportionment committees.

Mrs. Martha Ruth Martin is named Prentiss County's Outstanding Citizen for 1992 at the Junior Auxiliary's Charity Dinner.

The Wheeler Eagles win their third straight state basketball championship, giving them their 11th state championship, which is tops among all schools in the state.

Lenena Holder, from Prentiss County, wins the title of Miss University at the University of Mississippi.

Booneville Board of Aldermen cited Alan Tollison of Booneville for his bravery in rescuing Teresa A. Marshall from her burning car.

Prentiss County voters favored George Bush and Dan Quayle over Bill Clinton and Al Gore. But nationwide, Clinton is the clear winner, becoming the 42nd President of the United States.

Baldwyn historian and author, Claude Gentry, dies on December 9 after suffering a stroke at the age of 90.

Serbian death camps shock the world.

Bill Clinton beats George Bush to White House.

Rioting takes over Los Angeles after the Rodney King verdict.

1993 The Booneville Post Office sells out of 8,000 Elvis Presley stamps around 3:30 p.m. Friday, January 8, Elvis' birthday, and the first official day the stamps are sold.

The Cairo and the Altitude-Hills Chapel Fire Protection Districts expand, which means the entire fifth district is now in a class 9 fire rating.

It is announced a Captain D's restaurant will soon open in Booneville on Highway 45 beside the new Wal-Mart.

A 16-year-old Jumpertown High School sophomore, Jennie Estes, joins the Dubuque, Iowa Colts, a drum and bugle corps. She is first Prentiss County band member to participate in a Drum Corps International group, the first Jumpertown student to do so, and the first Prentiss County student in over 15 years to join any drum and bugle corps.

A Northeast Community College student, Kristie Ray, is abducted from her home in Tippah County and murdered. Her neighbor, Charles Ray Crawford, 27, is charged with capital murder, rape, sexual battery, kidnapping, burglary and grand larceny in connection with her death.

Booneville businessman Keith Shackelford is the recipient of Prentiss County's 17th Outstanding Citizen Award during the Booneville Junior Auxiliary's annual charity dinner.

A retirement reception is held in honor of R.J. "Piggy" Bonds, who served 41 years as the Prentiss County Republican Party chairman. Special guests at the reception included Mrs. Pat Fordice, wife of Gov. Kirk Fordice, and Senator Trent Lott.

The Northeast Mississippi Regional Solid Waste Management Authority chooses a site in Tippah County for its regional public landfill.

Wheeler Eagles win the North Half Championship honors by defeating West Union 73-68, putting the Eagles in the running for their 4th straight Class 1A title.

The Booneville branch of Deposit Guaranty National Bank on Highway 45 is robbed for $4,000. Riley Lee Ellisor Jr., 38, of Columbia, SC is arrested in Fayette County, Alabama. He is suspected in being involved in a total of seven bank robberies throughout Georgia, Mississippi, Florida and South Carolina. Police Chief Hubert Kitchens says it is the first bank robbery in Booneville to his knowledge.

A meeting is held to discuss the future of the Cunningham house, which according to an oral history handed down through the Cunningham family, says General Nathan Bedford Forrest once spent the night at the house on the eve of the Battle of Brice's Crossroads in 1864. Local attorney Donald Franks offers to fund the restoration of the portion of the house if the house is left on its present site on the corner of State and First Streets, property now owned by the First Baptist Church.

Stanley Groves is honored by his peers as Volunteer of the Year at Baptist Memorial Hospital in Booneville. His wife, Jewel, is the first recipient of the award two years ago.

For the fourth time, the Booneville Board of Aldermen pass an Ordinance making the office of the police chief an elective one and for the fourth time Mayor Murphy vetoed it.

After the qualifying deadline passed for Booneville's city election, 29 qualified for Aldermen and four for Mayor. Nelwyn Murphy chose not seek re-election to a third term.

Former Justice Court Judge Deryl Saylors begins work as the state parole/probation officer in Prentiss County.

Capt. Sam McGee, of the Booneville Police Department, is recognized as Law Enforcement Officer of the Year by the Booneville Rotary Club.

Marietta resident, Clinton Burns, successfully undergoes a heart transplant on April 7 at the University of Alabama Hospital in Birmingham.

A retired Booneville nurse, Christine Whitehead, is credited with saving the life of customer Buddy Clark at a local grocery store after Clark apparently suffered a seizure and was unable to breathe.

New Site High School teacher, LaDoska Bennett, is inducted into the STAR Teacher Hall of Fame, one of only two teachers inducted this year.

Carolina United Methodist Church observes its 135th anniversary on Sunday, June 6.

A dedication ceremony is held June 7 to rename the

R.H. Long Booneville Middle School.

Marietta Springs Park the "Ross B. Pharr Park" in honor of the late fourth district supervisor.

Jennifer Rowland, daughter of Ronny and Diane Rowland, is selected as Booneville's 1993 Miss Hospitality. First alternate was Molly Crow, daughter of Danny and Wanda Crow.

Booneville police officer, Tim Henderson, is hurt while making an arrest at the Aloha Skate Center. The officer's nose was broken and the suspect escaped after someone let him out of the patrol car while officers were making another arrest, said Police Chief Hubert Kitchens.

Miss Mississippi, Prentiss County's Lenena Holder, is honored with a reception by Northeast Community College's Student Government Association on October 26. Holder, a Northeast alumna, was Miss NEMCC in 1989 and represented the school in the Miss Mississippi Pageant. In the Miss America pageant in September, she placed in the Top 15 and was a preliminary talent winner.

White rule ends in South Africa.

In the Middle East, Shalom, salaam, peace agreed upon at last.

A bomb rocks the World Trade Center in New York.

1994 Police Chief Hubert Kitchens resigns. Jerry Barnes is named acting police chief.

Magnolia Regional Health Center in Corinth opens a nurse Practitioner clinic in Rienzi.

Jerry Barnes is officially appointed full time police chief by the Booneville Board of Aldermen.

The new Jumpertown Ambulatory Care Clinic opens in House 42 at The Tennessee Valley Regional Housing Authority.

The Spooktacular Festival is held in downtown Booneville.

Retired Booneville Middle School principal Howard Long is Honored when the school was named the R. H. Long Booneville Middle School

A ribbon cutting ceremony is held for the opening of new 12 mile four-lane segment of Highway 45 from Frankstown to 1 1/2 miles south of the Prentiss-Alcorn line. The ribbon was cut by Mr. & Mrs. Elmer and Susie McCoy, parents of Representative Billy McCoy who

Osborne Creek intersection with new four lane highway 45 at Booneville looking North toward Corinth.

New Caterpillar plant in Booneville.

was instrumental in obtaining legislative approval of the 1987 Highway Program under which the new U.S. 45 Highway was built.

Millions watch on television as former football star O.J. Simpson drives across Los Angeles, facing arraignment on charges of murdering his ex-wife and her friend.

U.S. seizes Haiti without firing single shot.

1995 The Baldwyn Bearcats and the Lady Bearcats successfully defend their Prentiss County basketball tournament titles.

Donte Jones, a Mississippi State signee, is named to the All- American team. He is the first Northeast Tiger

Prentiss County Agri-Center.

to do so since Vince del Negro (1958-60).

The Booneville Blue Devils baseball team advance to the North semifinals before losing two out of three games to eventual state champion West Lowndes.

Northeast Mississippi Community College head football coach Hubert Tucker, 52, is killed in a two-car accident February 20 in Philadelphia, Mississippi. He was returning from Decatur, Mississippi where he had attended NEMCC's basketball games in the state tournament.

Outspoken, crusading Booneville attorney Donald Franks dies at his home on March 26 at the age of 86 of an apparent massive heart attack. He was thought to be the oldest practicing attorney in the state, as well as being a businessman, civic leader, writer, historian, horse breeder, and philanthropist.

Gunter Brewer is named new head football coach at Northeast Mississippi Community College.

A one-car accident on April 30 near Marietta claims the lives of two New Site High School students, Camille Sellars of Booneville and Allen Taylor of Marietta. Leigh Ann Harris of New Site was injured and later died.

Ground-breaking ceremonies are held on July 10 for Caterpillar's new $4.9 million plant in Booneville.

In mid-July, the Paxton Media Group and New York Times Company announce they had signed a letter of intent for PMG to purchase the *Banner-Independent*.

Bud Michael is elected as Prentiss County Sheriff.

"Happy Harold" Campbell signs off the air at WBIP after 26 years at the Booneville radio station. He went to work for Gardner Merchant Foods at NEMCC in the cafeteria.

WBIP Radio Station is sold by longtime owner R.J. "Piggy" Bonds

The body of 17-year-old Bryan Collins of Thrasher is found September 13 in a soybean field near Rienzi, the apparent victim of a motorcycle accident. He had been missing since August 18.

On October 26, the Mississippi legislature authorized $10 million in grants for livestock facilities to be built across the state. Prentiss County receives $400,000 toward its proposed Agriculture Center on Highway 45 North.

On November 9, the Mississippi Department of Economic and Community Development Community Services Division awards Booneville Middle School a $3 million Capital Improvements Grant for an Earth Studies Complex.

On Friday, December 22, the body of 21-year-old Brad Cummings is found off Highway 356 near Pisgah. The investigation of his murder is ongoing.

Alfred P. Murrah Federal Building in Oklahoma City is bombed by terrorist; Timothy McVeigh arrested.

1996 A swearing in ceremony is held January 2 at the courthouse for Prentiss County's newly elected officials, Sheriff Bud Michael, circuit clerk Bud Green, 4th district supervisor Roy Green, justice court judges Buster Spencer and Debra Moore, and north half constable Robert Moore.

Red Kap Industries announces the Booneville plant will lay off 125 workers between January and March.

Kurt Kutrip, former history and government instructor at Booneville High School, becomes principal of Wheeler School. He replaces Jack Robinson who retired for health reasons.

Former fourth district supervisor for two terms, Jim Ramey, dies on January 20 at his home.

Kim Stevens, an eighth grader at Wheeler, wins the Prentiss County spelling bee.

In February, students from kindergarten through college have an unexpected holiday because of several inches of ice and snow that covered Booneville and Prentiss County. However, it was nothing to compare to the ice storm of February 1994.

D. Patrick Eaton is named as the first executive director of the Booneville Area Chamber of Commerce.

Booneville School Superintendent Robert Griffin announces he will delay his retirement until July 1, 1997.

Larry Morgan, principal of Booneville High School, is named assistant superintendent for the 1996-97 school year.

A goundbreaking is held for a new physicians office building at Baptist Memorial Hospital in Booneville. It is also announced that Dr. J. Patrick Benge and Dr. Laura J. Crecillus will open a practice of obstetrics and gynecology. Two Booneville natives, Dr. Robert McKinney

Earth Studies Complex at Booneville Middle School.

and Dr. Nathan Baldwin had previously announced they would open a practice in Booneville.
The skeletal remains of Danny Ray Thompson (42), who had been missing since May 1993, are found by timber cutters in a wooded area near Piney Grove community in Prentiss County. No foul play was suspected. It is speculated that Thompson had a heart attack or seizure while out walking.
Kenny H. Goode, 39, of Hickory Flat, is named managing editor of the *Banner-Independent.*
Mitch Johnson is appointed assistant administrator at Baptist Memorial Hospital in Booneville.
In May, the Prentiss County Board of Supervisors approves paying $24,131 as the county's share of matching funds to be utilized toward the purchase of several hundred acres of land near the Brice's Crossroads Battlefield to improve the historic location. The purchase is a joint effort among several counties.
In June, the 132nd anniversary of the Battle of Brice's Crossroads is observed with what some call the second most historic event in the history of the battlefield, namely the purchase of 838 acres from private owners. The land is to be developed by the Brice's Crossroads National Battlefield Commission. The first phase, which is to include the addition of 3,000 feet of trails, five interpretive exhibits and parking, is scheduled to be complete by October 1997.
Longtime Northeast coach and athletic director, Bill Ward, retires after a 42-year career in athletics on the high school and community college level, with 28 of those years at Northeast Community College.
Booneville is named a certified retirement community. The designation gives the city a share of the state's advertising budget promoting the state and retirement cities in national publications.
Rickey Neaves, a Saltillo native, is named principal of Booneville High School for the 1996-97 school year.
Two representatives from the Center for Small Town Research and Design visit Booneville to "scout" out the downtown area to see how it can be improved.
Mississippi Attorney General Mike Moore visits Booneville and attends a Youth Rally at the West Side Park. Moore presented Booneville High School student Tom Russell with the YES (Youth Empowered by Service) Award. At the time, Russell was only the 20th person to receive the award, which is given by the Attorney General's office recognizing outstanding achievements by young people in the state. Russell organized the Prentiss County Youth Board.
Cedar Drive, in what was formerly known as the Marathon Cheese Road project, is completed, opening up the southeast side of Booneville to Highway 145 without motorists having to drive through the downtown section of Booneville.
It is announced that Red Kap will close, leaving 116 jobless. The Booneville facility, which manufactured dress shirts, had been in operation since the 1950s.
An estimated 1,000 people attend the open house at the new Prentiss County Criminal Justice Center. The facility houses both the police and sheriff's departments, jail, courtroom for city and justice court, and 911 office.
Mrs. Donnie Goddard is named the "biggest rat in town" after raising $2,400 for the American Cancer Society. Nearly $5,000 was raised by seven "rat" contestants.
A $100,000 building, which housed the former Jumpertown branch of the Peoples Bank, is deeded to Jumpertown. Officials utilized the gift as a new city hall, which is located across the street from the old city hall.
The opening of the Booneville Family Clinic is announced by North Mississippi Health Services. Melanie Wallace, M.D., a Booneville native, staffs the clinic.
R.T. Rinehart of Rienzi wins the 1996 True Value/Jimmy Dean Country Showdown in Orlando, Florida and walked away with $50,000, a recording contract and the coveted national title.
Some 600 students from grades one through five of Prentiss County schools meet at Anderson Elementary to share ideas on what will be included in the Kid's Town Playground which is to be built at the West Side City Park during the late spring by volunteers at a cost of approximately $100,000.
The Booneville City School Board awards a contract to Worsham Construction of Corinth to build the Booneville Environmental Education Center behind the

New Brice's Crossroads Museum and Visitor's Center, just over Prentiss County line.

Flag display at Brice's Crossroads Museum and Visitor's Center.

R.H. Long Middle School, expected to be completed in March 1998.

The town of Marietta holds its first Christmas parade on December 7, with Jimmy Pharr as the grand marshal. His granddaugher, Torie Pounds, is the 1996 Christmas Queen.

Some $10,035 is raised at the annual Goodfellows Program. The money will be used to help provide Christmas food boxes to the less fortunate in the county. Over 1,000 Prentiss County families were recipients of the food boxes.

Robert D. Griffin announces he will retire as superintendent of the Booneville School District on December 31. Larry Morgan, present assistant superintendent, will become superintendent January 1, 1997.

A pipe bomb threatens to wreck the Olympics in Atlanta.

O.J. Simpson is acquitted of murder.

Clinton wins his second term as President.

1997 In January Prentiss Countians are to contend with a dusting of snow, ice and sub-zero temperatures.

The old Booneville High School is renovated into "The Landmark Community", offering housing units for senior citizens.

Longtime Booneville Fire Chief, Frank Fleming, dies. William Boyd Cook is named as his successor.

Marietta student Matthew Arnold is the winner of the Prentiss County Spelling Bee. He correctly spelled "formidable" and "marsupial".

Lt. Governor Ronnie Musgrove attends the groundbreaking for the Booneville Environmental Education Center on the campus of Booneville Middle School.

Eudora Kemp is honored as Prentiss County's 1997 Outstanding Citizen by the Booneville Junior Auxiliary.

Dr. Paul Ellzey retires after 44 years as a Booneville physician. He estimates he delivered over 2,000 babies.

Dr. Sam Galloway dies after a brief illness, having practiced medicine in Booneville for over 40 years.

Mitch Savery, Jr. is named the first director of the new Prentiss County Agri-Center.

Sheriff Bud Michael is named Law Enforcement Officer of the Year by the Booneville Rotary Club.

The new Prentiss County Criminal Justice Center

The old Booneville High School, now "The Landmark Community."

Bonnie Kemp, a Prentiss County native and daughter of Wyatt and Evelyn Sparks Breedlove, is hired as principal of Hills Chapel School, replacing Billy Stroupe, who resigned earlier in the year.

Dr. Walter Downs is named Baldwyn Schools Superintendent, Replacing retiring C.L. Shelton.

L.L. Bethay, founder of Prentiss Manufacturing Company, dies at the age of 94.

The building of Kid's Town, a massive playground at the Westside City Park, is built with the public donating 3,000 volunteer man hours, making it the largest volunteer built playground in the state.

Jennifer Spain is selected as Booneville's 1997 Miss Hospitality.

Craig Bishop is selected as Trooper of the Year by his fellow Mississippi Highway Patrol troopers in the nine-county New Albany District of the Mississippi Safety Patrol.

Judy Ramey is elected as Marietta's first female Mayor. Aldermen elected were Ronald Burns, Charles Taylor, Janet Loden, Stanley Ramey and Dale Kennedy.

Elected as aldermen in Booneville are incumbents Joe Eaton, Mitch Barrett and David Bolen. New aldermen elected are Bobby Goddard and Wayne Michael. Mayor Wade Lambert was unapposed for re-election to a second term.

In Jumpertown, Mayor Joe Morgan wins a fourth term. Aldermen elected are Elbert Moore, Jay C. Morgan, Tommy Prentiss, Jimmy W. Ross, and Rex Thorne.

Renzy Lee Cartwright, a World War I veteran, is honored on his 102nd birthday by Superior Home Health in Booneville.

Goode Furniture Co. announces it will close, leaving 149 jobless.

The Cunningham House, reputedly where General Nathan Bedford Forrest spent the night before the Battle of Brice's Crossroads in June 1864, is moved to the Booneville Depot.

An acre of land located on Little Brown Rd 1/2 mile off Highway 30, iss donated by Raymond Wallace of Memphis to Prentiss County to be the future home of the New Hope-Bunkom Hill Fire Station.

A break-in occurrs at the George E. Allen Library and a knife collection was stolen. A Booneville resident is arrested and the 74 knives were recovered.

Patilda Maness resigns as justice court clerk and Paul Wright is appointed to the position.

Louise Womack Peeler, a retired teacher, recipient of the Outstanding Citizen Award, and one of Booneville's most civic minded residents, dies.

Mindy Cadle is selected as the first Miss Fall Festival. It is estimated that around 13,000 people attended

Kids Town at Westside Park in Boonville.

Louise Womack Peeler Memorial Park in downtown Booneville.

Booneville and Prentiss County's sixth annual fall festival.

The Booneville Blue Devil Band recevies "All-Superior" ratings for the 23rd consecutive year.

It is announced Bassett Furniture will close leaving some 300 jobless.

Chassie Mauney joins the Booneville Area Chamber of Commerce as assistant to the director, Patrick Eaton.

A Prentiss County man, Roy Keith Morgan, dies in a deer hunting accident in Blackland on the second day of deer season.

It is announced the Prentiss Manufacturing plant at Jumpertown will close in January meaning the loss of 93 jobs.

O.J. Simpson is found liable for deaths in civil suit.

Diana, Britain's Princess of Wales, is killed in car accident in Paris.

1998 January weather includes two to five inches of snow. Myron Wilson is named new postmaster at Booneville. Booneville Civil War historian, Virgil Robinson, is instrumental in Booneville's obtaining historical markers commemorating the Capture of Booneville on May 30 1862 and the Battle of Booneville on July 1 1862.

William (Bill) Smith is appointed interim judge for the South half of Prentiss County after Buster Spencer's suspension.

The Rev. Bobby Hankins, pastor of First United Methodist Church in Booneville, is named as Outstanding Citizen in 1998 by the Booneville Junior Auxiliary.

Booneville School District maintains a level 5 accreditation rating. The Prentiss County School District improves its rating from 3.5 last year to an accreditation level of 4 this year.

Highway Patrol Trooper Craig Bishop is named 1998 Law Enforcement Officer of the Year by the Booneville Rotary Club.

Kay Stacy of Marietta School and Tammy Mauney of Booneville Middle School are honored by the Booneville Rotary Club as Teachers of the Year.

It is announced that Prentiss Manufacturing Company will close its Adams St. plant in Booneville, meaning the loss of 122 jobs.

Joyce Keeton is named Volunteer of the Year at Baptist Memorial Hospital.

Shelley Cartwright is named Booneville's Miss Hospitality.

The Banner-Independent holds a 100th anniversary celebration.

Booneville resident Barbara Shackelford is named the 1998 Woman Of Achievement for the State of Mississippi. She was sponsored by the Booneville Business and Professional Women's Club of which she is a member.

Linda Clifton resigns as principal of Booneville Middle School to accept a job as principal of Tupelo Middle School.

Beverly Hill is hired as the new principal of Booneville Middle School.

The Brice's Crossroads Visitors and Interpretive Center opens.

The first Tri-State Fair is held at the Prentiss County Agri-Center and is described as a success, with an estimated 20,000-25,000 attendance.

Concord Baptist Church in the Dry Creek Community celebrates its 150th anniversary.

A thousand gallon capacity moonshine still is destroyed in a remote area of the New Hope community and a Prentiss County man is arrested.

Baldwyn native, Shelaine Palmer, is named the new 4-H Youth Agent/Home Economist.

Two teenage Civil War reenactors from Florence, Alabama are injured during a reenactment at Booneville's Fall Festival. As one of the young men opened an ammunition box to get a new round, wind caused a smoldering piece of wadding to fall in causing a large flash fire.

Booneville, in competition with 27 other Main Street cities, receives 'The Best Organization' award, signifying that Booneville is now recognized statewide for its organization skills within the Main Street Association.

Booneville achieves another honor - a listing in the National Register of Historic Places.

It is announced that Lucky Star Industries in Baldwyn will close its Plant, meaning the loss of 325 jobs.

Two new county school board members, Wayne Hall and Benny Eaton, are elected.

The Booneville High School Marching Band wins the Governor's Cup and the Class 2A State Marching Band title in state competition, in Hattiesburg, for the second consecutive year.

Former Georgia newspaper publisher Leonard Woolsey is named the new publisher for *The Banner-Independent* and *The Daily Corinthian*.

Former Northeast Community College instructor, Peggy Wroten, is awarded a large judgement in a federal lawsuit held in Alcorn County. Wroten sued three Northeast officials, President Joe Childers and Deans Connie Drown and Johnny Allen, who were accused of unjustly firing her from her teaching position because she refused to change an "F" to a "W" for withdrawn for basketball standout Dontae Jones during the spring of 1995. The case is being appealed by the Northeast officials.

Democrat President Clinton is faced with impeachment by the Republican controlled House of Representatives on charges of perjury and obstruction of justice.

1999 The City of Booneville is listed in the January issue of 'Site Selection' magazine as one of the nation's top 50 small towns for corporate facilities.

Battle of Booneville marker.

In January, sleet causes roads to glaze over, causing area schools to be canceled for one day.

Prentiss County Superintendent of Education, Edward McCoy, announces he woill not seek re-election.

The George E. Allen Library becomes "automated", making all 13 libraries in the Northeast Regional Library System in Prentiss, Alcorn, Tippah, and Tishomingo Counties connected through central headquarters in Corinth.

Former Booneville Mayor Nelwyn Murphy, the first woman elected to a political office in Prentiss County, dies on January 21 of liver cancer at age 78. Mrs. Murphy served three terms as county superintendent

The Banner-Independent weekly newspaper celebrates its 100th year in 1998.

of education and two terms as Mayor of Booneville.

In January, four funnel clouds are verified in the county but none apparently touched down.

Anna Sparks, a seventh grader at Hills Chapel School, is the winner of the 1999 Prentiss County Spelling Bee.

The Thrasher Rebels finally get to play basketball in their new gymnasium. The Rebels opened with a pair of wins over Houlka. Their old gym was closed in 1995 due to unsafe conditions.

Prentiss County Deputy Michael Hisaw, 27, is killed in the line of duty on March 11 while responding to a disturbance call near Jumpertown.

Booneville's 26th annual Fourth of July Parade is held, starting on Seventh Street and ending in Foster Park.

Attendance is estimated to be around 15,000 for the Celebrate America held on July 3 at Old Bridge Beach at Bay Springs.

"Welcome to Booneville" signs are unveiled at Gaston Road and the Blackland-Osborne Creek Intersections on Highway 45. The signs were made possible thanks to a gift from Caterpillar Inc.

In July, temperatures hovered around 100 and the heat index soared to 110 degrees. The crop outlook was bleak because of the draught.

The old Prentiss County Health Department on north First Street is torn down to make way for a Christian Life Center for the First United Methodist Church.

Burger King opens a restaurant in Booneville.

The National Guard Armory in Baldwyn closes.

In the first primary election, incumbent Sheriff Bud Michael is defeated as was first district supervisor Gayle Floyd. In the race for 2nd district supervisor, incumbent Jimmy Moore and his opponent Glen Green, each received 1,090 votes. In the run-off Green defeated Moore. In the run-off election, three incumbents were defeated— Jimmy Moore, Roy Green and William L. McKinney.

Following the November 2 general election, Randy Tolar, 39, is elected Sheriff. The staff is reduced at the

The Prentiss County Agri-Center, Home of the Tri-State Fair.

A downtown mural done by Diane Guin's art class at Booneville High School.

sheriff's department in order to keep spending in line. Six deputies and four jailers are laid off. Sheriff Bud Michael agrees to employ only four deputies for the remainder of his term, with no overtime allowed.

A box containing 22.5 pounds of processed marijuana comes open at the Booneville UPS office and led to the arrest of four people in Alcorn County.

Two historical markers and the Cunningham House are dedicated during 'Historic Day' held at the historic depot area. The markers signify the Battle of Booneville and the Capture of Booneville during the Civil War.

A recently purchased and renovated GM&O caboose is toured by guests, including U. S. Representative Roger Wicker.

The Booneville Blue Devils win the Class 2A football championship.

Former Booneville Mayor Charles Steen dies on December 11 at age 74. He served the City of Booneville for 24 years, first as Alderman and then as Mayor from 1973 to 1977.

Students in Diane Guin's art class at Booneville High School paint a mural on the north side of the old Masonic building on Main Street across for the courthouse.

Following a shooting massacre in Littleton, Colorado, security measures are stepped up in the Booneville Schools.

It is announced that England/Corsair will open a facility in the former TPI building in the Booneville-Prentiss County Industrial Park, creating 200 jobs.

Hill Robinson, a brick mason from Jumpertown, dies after bricks fell on him at a home under construction in a new subdivision on CR 7126, just off Highway 45 below the Ninth Street bridge. Robinson, 56, had been a brick mason around 40 years.

Dr. Charles Chance of Parsons, Kansas, is named the eighth President of Northeast Community College.

Al Sypniewski becomes the new administrator at Baptist Memorial Hospital in Booneville. He is married to the former Peggy Sherrill of Booneville.

A living history encampment to commemorate the 135th anniversary of the Battle of Brice's Crossroads is held.

The Booneville Historical Commission is awarded with a 1999 Mississippi Municipal Association Summer 'Making Mississippi Move Award' for their dedication to historic preservation with the Cunningham House, reputedly the site where Confederate General Nathan Bedford Forrest spent the night just prior to the Battle of Brice's Crossroads.

Bertrand Piccard and Brian Jones complete the first non-stop balloon flight around the world.

John F. Kennedy Jr., 38-year-old son of President Kennedy, dies with his wife and her sister when the private aircraft he was piloting crashes into the Atlantic ocean.

Clinton survives the impeachment.

All around the world people celebrated in great style to welcome the new millennium.

2000 The Jerry Lee Lewis family buys the old Tays home, making Booneville their primary place of residence. They also own a home in Nesbit, Mississippi.

A Booneville woman, Amy Clement, wins the Miss Alcorn County title.

Blake Jones and Justin Davis of Booneville are winners at the Sqwincher Junior Novice Tennis Tournament at Columbus. Jones is first place winner in singles competition in the 18-year-old division. Davis is the fifth place winner.

Osborne Creek Baptist Church, founded in 1850, holds Sesquicentennial Celebration.

Dennis "Buddy" Whisenant, auto mechanics instructor, retires from Northeast Vo-Tech in Booneville.

The state's farmers may face severe water restrictions due to lack of rainfall.

The old Tays home in Booneville as purchased by the Jerry Lee Lewis family.

Prentiss County Courthouse

The dedication of the Joe M. Childers Hall at Northeast Community College is held.

Booneville attorney, John Ferrell, is elected to the Board of Bar Commissioners of the Mississippi Bar.

Patrick Eaton leaves his post with Booneville Area Chamber of Commerce to direct Northeast Community College fund-raising.

Amy Counce, daughter of Ellis Counce and Lou Ann Counce, is hired as head librarian at George E. Allen Library in Booneville.

Ricky Ford, Northeast Mississippi Community College women's Basketball coach and admissions counselor, is included in the sixth Edition of *Who's Who Among America's Teachers, 2000.*

Jumpertown girl, Noel Anderson, daughter of Mark and Melinda Anderson, is crowned Little Miss Mississippi.

W53AF-TV

Bro. Lealon Owens had been broadcasting his "Glory to God Hour" at the station for 2 years, when God gave him the vision of full-Christian programming on TV-53. Bro. Lealon originated his idea of Christian television in 1987, after the management of the secular station announced that the station would be closing. Just as the Lord and Savior Jesus Christ was born in a cold manger in Bethlehem, so was the birth of Christian television in Booneville, MS. Coming into this world was not an easy task. In December 1987, in a little 10' by 20' tin storage building Christian television programming was given to local viewers. TV-53 was only an UHF station with a 100 watt transmitter.

Bro. Lealon and several dedicated volunteers found a way to make a dream come true. The owners of the station agreed to let him hold a "Praise-a-Thon" for twenty-four hours a day, seven days a week for, not coincidentally, 53 days. "It was 53 days for TV-53". Volunteers manned the phones while many preachers and singing groups took their messages and music to the people and success was achieved. One person called near the end of the Praise a-Thon and pledged $53.00 for TV-53 starting a trend that took TV-53 beyond their goal. At the end of the 53 days, supportive viewers and volunteers had donated monies and auction items to accumulate twenty-six thousand three hundred dollars ($26,300). In January 1988, UBN and a board of directors were formed to oversee the management of the station. Through continued support from viewers and others, TV-53 has prospered by leaps and bounds.

After this time the Lord blessed with a 20X28 addition to the tin building for a temporary studio continue broadcasting until March 1990. UBN purchased 5.4 acres of land, including a house. This Purchase enabled the station to expand to two office and a studio. This was paid off in April 1993, with eleven employees on payroll and six regular volunteers.

When the loan was paid off in 1993, the Lord allowed for several improvements. The station now included four offices, two studios, and a control room with a one thousand watt transmitter and a formal station in Booneville, MS. Since that time Bro. Lealon Owens and the local viewers of W53AF-TV raised monies to build the UBN (LPTV) stations in Russellville, AL, Adarnsville, TN, and Fulton, NIS totaling four successful Christian television stations and one one thousand watt translator station in Tuscumbia, AL now in the company network. On April 26, 1996, UBN was granted income tax exemption under the Internal Revenue Code, 501 (c) (3) and became a business entity known as not-for-profit. This open environment embraces communication where conversations are not guarded and suppressed. It also encourages people to contribute freely, openly, and does not put up barriers or stifle people based on immaterial factors such as age, sex, sexuality, race, etc.

With the passage of time dreams are coming true for UBN. As of today, the dreams of the past have been accomplished. Dreams that without the help of an ever present and merciful God, a dedicated staff, and the continued support of much loved and appreciated viewers, could not have been attained. Recent changes and accomplishments are a result of I-HS love and power. First during the summer of 1996, in Tuscumbia, AL the Lord blessed UBN with a one thousand watt translator station, W46CF-TV. This translator continues the signal from the Russellville, AL station, W59CF-TV into the Shoals area reaching Florence, Muscle Shoals, and Sheffield. Second, WI 8BL-TV completed construction of a six thousand square foot facility in the summer of 1997. TV- 18 is positioned between the two prosperous cities of Savannah and Adamsville, TN

Third, in the fall of 1997 the most glorious example of God's power came into existence: the home office of UBN, North Third Street W53AF-TV. TV-53 has completed a new twenty-three thousand square foot building, which contains seven offices, three studios, a phone room, dressing rooms, a kitchen and break room, a conference room, a bookstore, editing and production rooms, a modem control room, and huge auditorium. This auditorium seats approximately five hundred people.

In the summer of 1998 the Fulton, MS station, W38BX-TV, was upgraded to twenty-two thousand nine hundred watts of effective radiated power. TV-38 has now become W39CD-TV. Completed in the fall of 1998, is a new six thousand five hundred square foot facility at the Russellville, AL station, W59CF-TV. This station is rebroadcast on the translator station W46CF-TV.

The answer to these marvelous works is the Lord and Savior Jesus Christ, the leadership of Bro. Lealon Owens, the management past and present and the local supporting viewers of each station.

Submitted by Jerod Owens

Unity Broadcasting Network

D.T. BEALL CHAPTER #1185, UDC

This chapter was formed January 27, 1909, by Mrs. Mollie Plaxico Allen and its first president was Mrs. Mamie Cross. These early members honored the memory of those who served and those who died and the present members are still endeavoring to instill respect for our founding fathers who fought for our country. They are the reason for the success and happiness that we are enjoying today. The following men are the soldiers who were the ancestors of whom our charter members received their membership *in the UDC organization.

Charter members, admitted February 27, 1909, were ('in order of admittance): Mollie Plaxico Allen, Evelyn Allen, Edna Walthall Alexander, Martha Mitchell Alexander, Stella Miller Bell, Dora Falls Boone, Ella Spain Brown, Claudia Blythe Carter, Mamie Mitchell Cross, Nancy K. Cunningham, Mattie Bums Dalton, Minnie Rinehart Davis, Lillian Elliott, Mminie Anna Taylor, Lummie Bums Threadgill, Fashion Patrick Peeler, Della Rinehart Frazer, Ida Bradsher Gilbert, Maude Walton Hamm, Zue Blythe Hamm, Annie Majors, Margaret Ledbetter, Fannie Gresham Ledbetter, Kate Petty Lacy, Creeina Kimbrell, Elle Walton Kimbrell, Miss Willie Kimbrell, Inez Smith McCarley, Irene Miller McCorkle, Myrtle McMurtry, Mary Tommie Miller, Lou Falls Miller, Clara Augusta Mitchell, Susie Miller, Amanda Carter Huffman, Lula McMillan Patrick, Mattie Walton Peeler, Eva A. Phillips, Lillian Smith Reece, Anna Smith Walker, Grace Walker, Nannie G. Povall Walton, Bettie D. Miller Williams, Daisy Dora Walker, Birdie Hamilton Rinehart, Keturah Fugitt Sanders, Sallie E. Stanley, Annie Stanley Barnett, Siddle Shmiault, Mattle Glen Dalton, Anna Walker, Daisy Peeler Walton, Georgia Moore, Nora Elliott Moore, Ora Elliott Green, Mary Majors Norwood, and Willie Fugitt Cook.

Admitted August 7, 1909, were: Fannie Walthall Howser, Mary Jessie Reynolds, and Mattie Julia Reynolds.

Soldier ancestors were G.W. Plaxico, Co C, 32d Ms.; Rufus P. Walthall, 28th Ms; Phillip P. Mitchell, Co K, I" Tn.; John H. Miller, Co A, 7th Ms Cavalry; George L. Falls, Co 1, 34th NC; H. W. Spain, Co C, 37h Infantry; E. E. Blythe, Co K, 19th Ms; Joshua Y. Cannock, Co A, 2nd Infantry; J. Sutt Bums, Sr., Co C, 32 nd Ms; G. W. Patrick, Sr., Co A 2 nd Ms.; Giles Rinehart, Co B, 26th; James S. Elliott, Co 1, 38th NC; T. J. (or T. G.) **Hamilton, Co** C, I I th Ms Cavalry; A. M. Bradsher, Co C, Elsworth's Ms Reg.; George Walton, Co A, 7th Ms; William Majors, Spy, (twice arrested and ninprisoned); J. M. Ledbetter, 7 ffi Tenn. Sharpshooters; A. L. Petty, Co A Ms Cavalry; G.B. Kimbell, Co B 2 nd Ms.; Henry C. Walton (died at Chattanooga; G. W. Smith, Co K 26h& 32nd Ms; John H. Miller, Co A 7th Ms. Cav.; George R. McMurtrey, Co D I I thSC; Joseph C. Carter, Co B 12d'Ms; Robert C. McMillian, 31st Ms Inf.; A. M. Street, Co C 26 th Ms; John W. Smith, Co K 26th Ms; Phillip Marion Walker, Co C 17'hMs; John H. Milton, Co A Ms. Cav.; J. M. Fugitt, Co C, 26hMs; Dr. W. L. Rogers, 26th Ms Surgeon; T. R. Buffess, Co K 19thMs; J. N. Moore, Co F 23d Ms; and James S. Elliott, Co 1 3 8thNC.

Current members and their ancestors are: Neola Lee Hollingsworth Cleveland, her ancestor, Great Grandfather William Moore Fant, Pvt. Patterson's Reg. Cav.; Sandra Kaye Sartor Ford, Great Great Grandfather John P. Sartor, Capt Bowles I't Ms. Batallion; Rita Kathleen Godwin, Great Grandfather Thomas Randolph Smith, Co B I I th Al. Cav.; Nellie Pauline Nicholson Googe (Real Daughter), Father, Thomas Jefferson Nicholson, C A Ms. Inf. ; Sandra Lewis Gray, Great Great Grandfather, Meridith Reynolds, Pvt. Co E 42dMs.; Phylis Allen Hare, Great Grandfather, Hartwell Bramlett Pitts, Pvt. Co D 6 th MS Cav.; Linda Johnson, Great Great Grandfather, Thrasley Chapman, Pvt. Co H 37th Ms Inf. ; Patsy Lejune Hill Johnson, Great Grandfather, James Thomas Asbury Cartwright, I" Brig. 2d Reg. Ms. Vols.; Marian Eudora Grisham Kemp, Great Grandfather, James Thomas Asbury Cartwright, I't Brig. 2dReg. Ms. Vols.; Mary Nell Walden Whitaker Martin, Great Great Grandfather, John Campbell, Pvt. Co. A 32d Ms. Vols; Gladys Smith Moore, Great Grandfather, William Henry McCoy, Pvt. Co. H 2 d MS Cav.; Helen Edge Perry, Grandfather, Win. Franklin Jobe, Capt. Rice's Co.; Effie Lucille Nicholson Pharr (Real Daughter), Father, Thomas Jefferson Nicholson, Co A Ms. Inf.; Jeri Leigh Overall Potts, Great Great Grandfather, George Washington Finch, Co C OhMs. Cav.; Sara Annece Bonds Pounds, Great Grandfather, James W. Bonds (Killed at Gettysburg), Pvt. Co A 2 nd MS. VOIS; Mary Viola Tunnell Robinson, Great Grandfather, Mark Dempsey Cooper, Co F 41st Ms; Patricia Ann Sparks, Great Great Grandfather, James W. Bonds, Co A 2dMs Inf. Vols.; Mary Charylene Googe Strange, Great Grandfather, Benjammi Julian Kizer, Capt. Co K & G, 26hMs Inf. ; Eleanor P. Pickering Tidwell, Grandfather, Ransone Jay Welch, Sgt. Co G 7th Ms Inf.; Sara Marjorie Oakley Waters, Great Grandfather, John Suttle Bartlett, Pvt. Co H I OhMs Cav.; Helen Rivers Finch White, Grandfather, George Washington Finch, Co. C 6h Ms Cav. Recently deceased members who are greatly missed include: Gladys Marie Miller Sumners, Great Grandfather, William David Floyd, Pvt Co K 32 nd MS Inf, And Great Granduncle, Robert Alexander Floyd, Pvt. Co C 26hMs Inf.

AKERS FAMILY

IN LOVING MEMORY OF

STEPHEN RAY AKERS

October 22, 1970-
October 31, 1987

FUGITT FAMILY

IN LOVING MEMORY OF

PATRICIA ANN HARE FUGITT

"PAT"

January 31, 1948
August 5, 1998
Wife of Carroll Joe (Dickie) Fugitt
Mother of DeAnna Fugitt
Daughter of Ralph and Billie Hare

AKERS, FREDDIE DALE, born Apr. 29, 1938, son of Columbus Eugene and Ena Jewel (Pace) Akers. Freddie is the grandson of William Pinkney and Emma (Smith) Akers and Robert Vernon and Arvie (South) Pace. On May 27, 1961, he and Bettie Raye Smith, daughter of Earl Ray and Delta (White) Smith, were married at Little Brown Free Will Baptist Church in Prentiss County. Bettie Raye is the granddaughter of Andrew and Lennie (Robison) Smith and Webster and Mary (Holley) White.

The Freddie Akers Family (1983). Front row, left: Freddie Akers and wife, Bettie Raye. Back row, left: Sons, Sterling and Stephen

From 1961 to 1974 Freddie and Bettie Raye made their home in Memphis, TN where Freddie was employed as a data technician by the US Postal Service and Bettie Raye was a teacher in the Memphis City Schools. In 1974 health problems mandated an early retirement for Freddie resulting in a move back to Prentiss County where they built a home in the Hill's Chapel Community and at which they continue to reside. Since 1974 Bettie Raye has been employed by Northeast Mississippi Community College as an instructor in the Mathematics Department. Freddie and Bettie Raye received their elementary and high school education in Prentiss County. Freddie attended Burton and New Hope Schools, graduating from the eighth grade at New Hope. Freddie is a 1957 graduate of New Site High School. Bettie Raye completed her elementary education at Hill's Chapel School and graduated from Booneville High School in 1956. She received an associate's degree from Northeast Mississippi Community College in 1958 and a bachelor's degree from Blue Mountain College in 1960. Bettie Raye earned two graduate degrees from Memphis State University, a master's in 1962 and a doctorate in 1975.

To this couple were born two sons: Sterling Dale (b. Feb. 11, 1962) and Stephen Ray (b. Oct. 22, 1970) in Memphis, TN. Sterling Dale attended Sherwood School and Woodland Presbyterian School in Memphis before his parents moved back to Prentiss County. In Prentiss County Sterling attended Hill's Chapel School for two years and graduated from Booneville High School in 1980. He is also a graduate of Northeast Mississippi Community College in 1982, where he was elected to the Hall of Fame and Mississippi State University in 1984 with a degree in civil engineering. After graduation from Mississippi State, Sterling began his career working for the Mississippi State Highway Department but has been employed by Hill Brothers of Falkner, MS since December 1984. He married Jina Maria Vaughn of Iuka, MS Jun. 11, 1988. They have three children: Emily Maria (b. Oct. 20, 1992), Evan Dale (b. Nov. 3, 1994) and Elizabeth Ashley (b. Sep. 8, 1996). Sterling and his family live at 200 Emily Lane in Booneville.

Stephen Ray attended Hill's Chapel School for eight years and was in his senior year at New Site High School when he was killed in an automobile accident Oct. 31, 1987 at the age of 17. He was an honor student throughout his school years and his ambition was to get a degree in mechanical engineering upon completion of high school. Stephen Ray Akers is buried in Little Brown Cemetery in Prentiss County. *Submitted by Bettie Raye Smith Akers.*

AKERS, STEPHEN RAY, born Oct. 22, 1970 at Baptist Hospital in Memphis, TN and lived in Memphis until August 1974, when he moved with his family to Prentiss County. He began his education at Hill's Chapel School in the fall of 1976 and finished the eighth grade in the spring of 1984 at Hill's Chapel. He had attended New Site High School for three years and was in the first semester of his senior year when he was killed in an automobile accident Oct. 31, 1987. He was a member of Little Brown Free Will Baptist Church, where he had perfect attendance in Sunday School for the seven years prior to his death. He enjoyed hunting and took great pride in the care of his guns. He and his older brother engaged in truck farming, especially the growing of sweet potatoes and peanuts.

Stephen Ray Akers' senior photo (1987)

The following poem was written in memory of Stephen on the fifth anniversary of his death and published in the *Booneville Banner Independent* on Oct. 22, 1992.

To Stephen,
You came to us in October,
And for a happy seventeen more,
You were our ray of sunshine
In the smile you always bore.
Dearest Son, you filled our home
With your teasing, taunting love,
But criticism of others, you said, . . .
Should only come from above.
Your independent nature,
Your happy social ways
Belied a deeper inward self
That guided all your days.
Your teachers knew the student.
Oh, how your face is missed!
But we know you're making A's
On Heaven's Honor List.
Your monument we see each day,
And your class, too, gave you fame.
Their book in 1988
In memory bears your name.
Sunday School you never missed,
And you proudly wore your pin.
The room dedicated just to you,
Each Sunday we go in.
The autumn air is crisp and clean;
There are peanuts in the ground,
And sweet potatoes to be dug.
A new place to hunt is found.
Your clean gun's in your closet.
There are shells you'll never load.
But we know that you're now hunting
Better game in God's abode.
Though our emptiness can n'er be filled,
Your memory has the power
To guide us to a fuller life
Until our final hour.
We now can talk without the tears,
And smile and speak your name
God and time can truly heal,
But Octobers are never the same.
Love,
Mama, Daddy and Sterling. *Submitted by Bettie Raye Smith Akers.*

ALLEN, BENJAMIN K., born 1848 in Old Tishomingo County, son of Major Allen and Mary Holmes, who were both born in North Carolina. Benjamin Allen married Mattie Nash in 1881. Mattie Nash (b. 1861) daughter of John Nash (b. 1835, d. 1862) and Mary Elizabeth Kemp. John and Mary married in 1855.

Benjamin K. Allen and Mattie Nash Allen

Benjamin Allen had a cotton gin in Jacinto and was a farmer and a businessman. Benjamin and Mattie Allen had three children: Giffie, Minnie and Major Allen. Benjamin Allen died in 1935. Mattie Allen died Jul. 29, 1950. They are both buried in the Jacinto Cemetery.

Major Washington and Maude Unfress Allen

Major Washington Allen (b. Mar. 23, 1885) son of Benjamin and Mattie Allen married Maude Umfress Jul. 27, 1918. Maude (b. Nov. 23, 1893) daughter of Nathaniel N. Umfress and Matilda Cook. Major and Maude Allen lived in Big Creek, MS. They had three children: Omer, Howard and Marjorie. Major Allen died Oct. 31, 1959 and Maude Allen died Jun. 1, 1986.

Martha Bell Beckett Allen and Omer C. Allen

Omer Allen married Martha Bell Beckett in August 1943. She was the daughter of Lee Roy Beckett and Hilma Smith. Omer and Martha Allen have four children: Mike, David, Camille and Kent. Omer Allen worked for the State Game and Fish Commission and was a farmer and a member of the Methodist Church.

Howard Allen married Betty Sue Johnson in July 1950. She was the daughter of Clarence Johnson and Jimmie Bennett. Howard and Betty Allen have four children: Milton, Linda, Barbara and Steve. Howard Allen is territorial manager of Jostens and Louis Reifer Creations. He is also a farmer, rancher and tree farmer.

Howard and Betty are members of the Methodist Church.

Betty Johnson Allen and Howard Q. Allen

Marjorie Allen married Willard V. Drischel in January 1949. She was a former secretary for Douglas Aircraft and E.J. Dupont. Marjorie and Willard Drischel have three children: Randall, Karla and Cynthia. *Submitted by Howard and Betty Allen, 33 CR 103, Pittsboro, MS 38951.*

Willard V. and Marjorie Allen Drischel

ALLEN, JOHN, born 1742 in Virginia, died 1822 and served in the Revolutionary War. He moved to South Carolina and is buried in Bethel Cemetery in Woodruff, SC. He and his wife (name unknown) had 10 children: William, James, Mary, Caleb, Matthew, Micajah, John, Elizabeth, Lucretia and Susanna.

The John Allen Family. Front row from left: Lena Frances Allen, Lawrence Allen, Boyd Allen and Leona Bryant Allen. Back row from left: Earnest "Buck" Allen, John Allen, Lena Davis Allen and Acker Allen.

James Allen (b. 1776, d. 1825) was a minister for several years. He moved to Woodruff, SC and married Mary Woodruff. They had eight children: Elizabeth, Joseph, John, Anna, James, Moses, Sarah and Mary.

John Allen (b. 1803, d. 1874) was born in South Carolina and moved to Itawamba County, MS. He married Cynthia Frame. They had nine children: Middleton, James, Paulina, Columbus, Otis Bunyan, Lenora, Bodecia, Robert and Joseph.

Otis Bunyan Allen (b. 1847, d. 1931) married Elmyra Hood. They had nine children: Ruth md. Billy Floyd; Solomon md. Sallie Davis; Paulina md. Bill Carlock; Sallie md. Fate Bridges; Mary md. John Davis; Cynthia never married; John md. Lena Davis; Minnie never married and Joe md. Venia Park.

Ruth Allen and Billy Floyd had one child, Ada, who never married.

Solomon Allen and Sallie Davis had 12 children: Columbus, Talmadge and Lawrence never married; Lillian md. Levi Speck Sr.; Bonds md. Lavada Donahue and Clytee Kemp; Oma md. Will Payne; Bonnie md. Eula Morgan; Audrey md. Louise Scott; Nora md. Wade Cowan; Flora, md. Milton Wallis; an infant and R.V. md. Louise Oswalt.

Paulina Allen and Bill Carlock had eight children: an infant, Dewey never married, Elmyra md. Hugh Whitehead, Andrew md. Mallie Pruitt and Louella Windham, Ellis md. Gladys Enis, Willie md. Jim Samples, Alma md. Fred Duncan and Mary md. John Lee Wardlaw.

Sallie Allen and Fate Bridges had no children.

Mary Allen and John Davis had five children: Mamie md. Jack Duggar, Earnest md. Delores Dillard and Charlene Holland Allen. Myrtle md. Vardaman Whitten, Janie md. Leo Wildman and Charles md. Ann Johnson.

John Allen and Lena Davis had five children: Lawrence never married, Boyd md. Daisey Hogue, Earnest md. Leona Bryant, Acker md. Clara Roberts and Lena Frances md. Tony Sappington.

Joe Allen and Venia Park had three children: Winnie md. Cecil Hardy, Loyd md. Charlene Holland and Laynie md. Loyd Melson and Ruble Russell.

Many Allen descendants still live in Prentiss County and throughout the US. *Submitted by Merle Glover.*

ANDERSON FAMILY, The following announcement appeared in the Nov. 22, 1836, *Huntsville* (Madison County, AL) *Democrat*: "Married on 8th instant by John W. Irby, Esq., William Anderson to Miss Cyrena Tipton, daughter of Isaac Tipton, all of this county."

First row, left: Noah Anderson, Arthur Anderson, Matilda Grisham Anderson, Joseph Randolph Anderson and Robert R. Anderson. Second row, left: Lula Park Anderson, John E. Anderson, Joseph D. Anderson and Gillie Anderson.

William (b. 1811 in Alabama) and Cyrena (b. 1822 in Alabama) had children: Isaac (b. 1837), Nancy (b. 1839), Caroline (b. 1841), Sarah (b. 1843), William (b. 1845), Joseph Randolph (b. Aug. 9, 1847), Adeline (b. 1852) and Lewis Mead (b. 1855).

The Andersons moved to Tippah County around 1842 where William farmed and operated a brick kiln near the Pine Grove Community. He and Cyrena are buried in unmarked graves in Clear Creek Cemetery.

Joseph Randolph "Joe" Anderson, farmer and blacksmith (b. Aug. 9, 1847. d. Aug. 5, 1915), married Matilda Jeanette Grisham (b. Feb. 10, 1844, d. Sep. 10, 1914), daughter of Andrew Jackson Grisham and Gillie Olive. Their home was about 200 yards east of County Line Church on the Prentiss/Tippah line. Four of their children died in infancy: Willie J. (b. 1871, d. 1873), James R. (b. 1873, d. 1873), Luther I.M. (b. 1874, d. 1875) and Oscar P. (b. 1880, d. 1881). These infants, their parents and their Grisham grandparents are buried in the Anderson Cemetery in Prentiss County.

Joe and Tildie's other children: Gillie Sarena (b. 1875, d. 1962) md. John Aiken, Noah (b. 1878, d. 1965) md. first Myrtle Lula Park, second Anna Rowland; John Ephraim (b. 1882, d. 1960) md. Lillian Prather, Robert Richard (b. 1884, d. 1959) md. Bess Wallis and Joseph Daniel (b. 1888, d. 1952) did not marry. Some established homes in Tippah County while others lived in Prentiss County.

John E. Anderson lived in the Wheeler and Frankstown communities. He married Lillian Prather, daughter of Tofie Rone and Lizzie Bartlett Prather, Dec. 7, 1903. Their children: Robert Alonzo (b. 1905, d. 1995) md. Elizabeth Black, Clifford Randolph (b. 1906, d. 1907), Rubye June Violet (b. 1908) md. Ezra Davis, Luther Earl (b. 1912, d. 1988) md. Ruby Nix, Joe Forest (b. 1915, d. 1988) md. Blanche Ricks, William Clarence (b. 1918) md. Jennie Stutts and Wesley Milton (b. 1920, d. Jan. 13, 2000) md. Opal Carpenter.

The Anderson children graduated from Wheeler High School where Robert and Earl played on championship basketball teams. During his school days, Clarence and a friend operated a hamburger place called The Dead Rat. Robert and Ruby became teachers and later Robert was a county agent. Earl managed a cheese plant. Joe Forest was a master carpenter. Clarence is the president of his own company. Milton retired from the Air Force.

Robert had two sons, Robert Black md. Nike Poulos and James Franklin md. Meg Murphy.

Ruby's daughters are Vivian Diane who married Coy Lambert and Mary June.

Earl's children: Linda Sue md. Teddy Rex Basil; Freddie Ray md. first Lorene Coleman Scott, second Mary Helen Garza and Ruby Jean md. Lonnie Estes Bell.

Joe Forest's daughter, Jo Carolyn, md. John Scott Beebe.

Clarence's children are William Clarence Jr., who married Karen Sweetser; Jennifer Elise md. Bill Esposito and John Steven md. Trish Kennedy.

Milton's daughter, Kathy Lynne, is married to Russell Lamb. Submitted by Jo Carolyn Anderson Beebe, 645 Hickory Hill, Hiawassee, GA 30546. (706) 896-6290.

ANDERSON, HOPKINS TURNER, son of William Anderson and Amanda Louise Walden Cobb (b. 1868, d. 1940, buried in Marietta) married Ora Brooks Williams (b. 1871, d. 1904, buried in Marietta) daughter of James Lafayette Williams and Elizabeth Hawkins. They had three children: Audie, Lona and Zelma. This is the story of Audie and his descendants, as he is the only one of their children that settled in Prentiss County. Audie (b. 1888, d. 1966) married Lucy Bolton (b. 1889, d. 1959) daughter of Jehu Bolton and Annie Sumners. Aunt Lucy was how she was known in the community. They had eight children:

Bryan (b. 1911, d. 1985) married Era Wren and had three daughters: Sue, Mary Jean and Lucy. They lived in Memphis and have eight grandchildren.

Ora Bell (b. 1913, d. 1992) lived in Jackson most of her adult life and lived in Booneville for several years before her death.

Zera (b. 1914) married Joe Duggar and has one daughter, Jo Carol, who married Jerry Hisaw. They had three children: Anissa (d. 1980), Michael, a deputy sheriff for Prentiss County and killed in the line of duty in 1999 and Wesley, attends NEMCC.

Lorraine (b. 1916) married Victor Berry. They have six children: Thomas, Glen, Audie, Daniel, David and Betty Ray. They have several grandchildren and great-grandchildren and live in Vernon, AL.

Harvey (b. 1919, d. 1989) married Juanita Mathews and lived in Ohio most of his adult years.

A.E. (b. 1923) married Mary Jarman and had three children (Mark, Beth and Ruth) and lives in Huntsville, AL.

Rex (b. 1924, d. 1984) married Rachel Greene. They had one daughter, Patricia, married Hal Hancock from the Pratt Community and they have two sons, Greg married Becky Hawkins and has two sons, Jonathan and Noah, lives in Baldwyn and Jim, who has three daughters (Jessica, Julianne and Jennifer), lives in Massachusetts. Rex then married Margaret Carbone and had three more daughters (Toni, Brenda and Donna, who live in Biloxi) and has one granddaughter.

Dennis (b. 1928) lives in Memphis.

I read recently that what mattered most in your life was how you lived your "dash", that space between the year you were born and the year you die. I believe with all my heart that my Grandma and Grandpa Anderson had a wonderful "dash." They lived through much sickness and four sons serving in the military with three of them serving during WWII. They were good neighbors and absolutely great grandparents. Grandpa taught me about civic duty, good manners and patience. Grandma taught me to love cats, how to warm socks by an open fire and make wonderful teacakes. I know all the other grandchildren have good memories of them, maybe not the same ones, but good ones anyway. They raised a responsible, respectful and concerned family and one in which I am proud to be a part. *Submitted by Patricia Anne Anderson Hancock.*

ANDERSON, WILLIAM HENRY "WICK,"

is listed in *Who's Who In Medicine, 1939-1969* and *Biographical Encyclopedia of America, 1940-1969.*

Family: son of Walter and Mary Elizabeth (Shackelford) Anderson; brothers: Walter, Joe, Albert, Bob, Frank, Tom; sisters: Ethel, Luanna md. Mildred Paulk, Tupelo; two daughters, Jane Elizabeth (Mrs. William Hall Preston Jr.) Nancy Paulk; one grandchild, William A. Preston.

Education: Mississippi College BA; University of Mississippi, BS, MS; Tulane University, MD graduate work, New York Postgraduate Hospital, Mayo Clinic, Rochester, MN.

Career: medical staff, Northeast Mississippi Hospital, Booneville, 1918-1969. Board of Directors, 1918-1949. Surgeon, G.M.&O.RR 1922-1969. President, Mid-South Postgraduate Medical Assembly 1926. Chief of Staff, Anderson Clinic 1928-1969. Health officer, Prentiss County 1929-1940. President, Mississippi State Medical Association 1940.

Editor: *The Mississippi Doctor* (official organ Mississippi State Medical Association) 1926-1960. *The Booneville Independent* (weekly newspaper) 1928-1953. *Progressive Hospitals* (quarterly, Mississippi Hospital Association) 1945-1948. *The Booneville Builder* (tabloid weekly newspaper) 1959-1965. Medical treatises.

Political: Colonel, Gov. Fielding Wright staff, 1948-1952; Advisory Council to Committee on Hospital Care for Mississippi, 1948-1950; Colonel, Gov. Hugh White staff, 1952-1956; Colonel, Gov. J.P. Coleman staff, 1956-1960; Appointed to Commission on Hospital Care for Mississippi, 1950-1960. Honored by Mississippi State Legislature, 1968.

Church: teacher, men's bible class, First Baptist Church, 1939-1969. Deacon, First Baptist Church, 1940-1960.

Other: President Board of Trustees, Booneville schools, 1935-1944. Trustee, Blue Mountain College, Blue Mountain, MS 1934-1956. Vice President, Mississippi Forestry and Chemurgic Association, 1945. President, Booneville Rotary Club, 1945. President, Highway 4 Association, 1948-1950. District Governor, Rotary International, 1954.

Wick Anderson had what he described in others as "a spur in the blood." This certain drive he attributed to genes and inner commitment. The ambitious man is selfish; he desires honor for himself. The man absorbed in life in work in the mind's vision, feels that be has been entrusted with a great mission which he must fulfill. If recognition comes to him, it is of passing moment, for he is under the spell of a righteous cause working its way through him. Such a premise may explain why Wick declined to locate in a large medical center but chose to return to his own hill section to share most deeply in human life. Booneville became his center and for five decades be was a crusader aflame for his "hub of the universe."

Born near Dumas in the struggling wake of reconstruction (his father served four years under Gen. Joe Wheeler), he was the middle one between three older and three younger boys and three girls. He grew up working hard, but with time to roam the Tippah Hills, fish the clear streams and go on an occasional Saturday night fox hunt. At 17, the year his father died, he was the only one in his senior class, no diploma, no commencement. That fall he was allowed to enter the freshman class at Mississippi College after an entrance examination and a month's trial. After collecting payment for a horse, five cows and a yearling from the farm, he managed his tuition, with some added help from an uncle. He cut hair and served tables through four years. His senior year he held the three top campus honors: president of his class, president of the YMCA and editor of the college yearbook.

Wick's old family doctor, who had delivered 10 of the Anderson children, planted in the young boy's mind the desire to study medicine. Nor had he forgotten, at 13, that he and younger brother Bob had successfully stitched a calf ripped open by another farm animal. Also, stories and visits of two uncles, both physicians who died early, had fascinated him.

He went on to earn two degrees from Ole Miss and his MD from Tulane where he was doing special work with neoarsphenamine in the treatment of syphilis, when be decided to locate with Dr. W.H. Sutherland in Booneville. His arrival in town coincided with the peak of the influenza epidemic in 1918. Another plan was borne cold night when he made a house call to a typical poor family in the county. In one room, heated by a meager fire in an old oil drum, the patient lay on a mattress of corn shucks, shivered under thin cotton quilts and subsisted on a diet of fatback and peas. Wick returned to town (he had brought the first closed car to Booneville), made up some money and bought food which he carried back to the family and resolved on a relentless campaign to lift rural income for this section. Over the next three decades, with the help of the banker, the lawyer, the merchant and incessant pounding through the columns of his newspaper, from the stump, through political pressures, trading the support of a gubernatorial candidate for the promise of a helping hand, Prentiss County gradually saw change. First came a county agent to help change farming methods, then a home demonstration agent who, with many new ideas, supervised housewives in making 7,000 mattresses in a communal effort, then the cheese plant brought better herds and better pastures and Booneville's first factory, built entirely by public subscription, provided work for women. In time came other industries, improved schools and finally the junior college and the first Hill-Burton hospital. Mississippi also got its four-year medical school in Jackson.

Wick sat in his legislator's seat to press the button for the appropriation. Mississippi's burgeoning hospital system soon commanded national attention. Fifty-four modern community hospitals placed good medical care within a radius of 30 miles to any resident of the state. These hospitals in turn have given clinical support to the four-year medical school and university teaching hospital in Jackson.

He believed that the greatest sin of the age is greed and next is unenlightenment, ignorance of health, prevention of disease.

Wick Anderson was a man of action. This is a world of work. One can not live in it without working. Above all, one cannot save it without working and he worked, as long as there was life in him, to see that his small part moved toward a better day. *Submitted by Mildred Anderson.*

ARCHER, CLARENCE SINCLAIR,

born 1869, died 1956, eldest son of G.W. Archer and Gennie Archer, married Mary Jane Anderson from Selmer, TN in 1903. One of the first rural mail carriers in the Baldwyn Post Office, he traveled a distance equal to eight times around the world delivering mail in rural southwestern Prentiss County by buggy when possible and by horseback when the mud was too deep. Sometimes he could be heard playing his trumpet as he went through the countryside delivering mail. Many times a patron would meet him at the mailbox to get news of a neighbor or tell him of the birth of a new baby. He was a very kind and gentle person, always helpful and a devoted church worker, serving as Sunday School superintendent, deacon and elder in the Baldwyn Christian Church. He had a deep rich bass voice and enjoyed singing in the church choir. His wife, Mary, joined him in devotion to the church and their home was always open when visiting preachers needed a place to stay.

Clarence S. Archer with rural mail delivery cart

Clarence and Mary Archer had one daughter, Clara Kerr (b. 1904, d. 1992). She married Joel Duke Young (b. 1904, d. 1973) of West Point, MS in 1932. She taught at Wheeler High School for 15 years before finishing her teaching career at Saltillo High School. Duke Young was manager of the Prentiss County Electric Power office in Baldwyn for 23 years, retiring in 1969. They had four children: Mary Joel (b. 1932, d. 1995), Jeannette, Duke Archer and Lunelle.

George W. Arthur Home

Mary Joel Young was a medical technologist, working in the lab of the Baldwyn unit of North Mississippi Medical Center for several years. She married Wayne Pennell (b. 1927, d. 1999) of McComb, IL. They had five children: Robert Joel Pennell, a carpenter in Baldwyn; James Franklin, Steven Wayne, Debora Lee and William Jonathan Pennell, also a carpenter in the Baldwyn area. Wayne had two children, David and Linda Pennell, by a previous marriage.

Jeannette Young married Joseph Crabb Shackelford and they had four children: Joseph Matthew, Linda Carol, Amy Kay and Laura Michelle. All except Linda Carol live in the Baldwyn area. Jeannette Young Shackelford has worked in the insurance business as a secretary and as an insurance agent since 1965. Her husband, Joe, is a native of Prentiss County, is a retired law enforcement officer in Prentiss County and Booneville.

Duke Archer "Arch" Young married Barbara Jean Holloway and they had Greg, Steven and Malcolm. He is an engineer for a heavy equipment company in Birmingham, AL.

Lunelle Young married Randle Miller, a native of Prentiss County and retired manager of the Prentiss County Electric Power office in Baldwyn. She is a retired math teacher, teaching a total of eight years in Booneville, Wheeler, Baldwyn and retired as head of the math and science division at Northeast Mississippi Community College, having taught there 27 years. They have two children: Keith Alan and Martha Elizabeth, who both live in Lee County, MS.

Clarence and Mary Archer had one child, four grandchildren and 16 great-grandchildren.

ARCHER, GEORGE WASHINGTON SMITH,

born 1840 and died 1900, married in 1860 to Jane Elizabeth Pricilla "Gennie" Welch, the pampered daughter of a plantation owner at Yellow Creek in Tishomingo County. They lived in Marietta for the first 10 years of their marriage.

George joined the Confederate Army and was infantryman, gun shop worker and then chaplain in the 32nd Regiment of Mississippi Volunteers. Gennie Archer said when the Civil War began, the Southern boys rode off to join, waving their hats and shouting, "We'll lick the Yankees and be back in three weeks."

George Washington Smith Archer

Gennie told her grandchildren, "When the Yankee armies were ranging about in northern Mississippi, everything was just terrible. There wasn't any law anymore and I never knew what would happen or who would come to the door day or night, a wounded soldier, or a neighbor, or a bushwhacker. Some nights I'd know there was a battle on because I'd hear the big guns booming in the distance and I'd lie awake all night praying and hoping that my husband or my brother or my other kin or friends were not being killed. Many times I've lain across the bed all night with my clothes on to be ready for whatever happened. It was a terrible time!"

Once Union soldiers came to take her father to a northern prison. They decided instead to make sport by giving the old man a chance to run for his life. If he made it safely over the hill, they would let him live. His wife and daughter watched horrified as he ran as hard as he could, bullets whizzing by. As he neared the crest, he fell and his hat flew off. They thought he had been killed, but he got up and ran over the hill, returning unscathed, his hat full of bullet holes.

They settled in Baldwyn about 1870, when it was just a small village. George was minister of the Baldwyn Christian Church, a kind and gentle person, a song writer, poet and portrait photographer. He was a sewing machine repairman, jeweler, repairing watches and making wedding bands from gold coins. His obituary in the Baldwyn newspaper on Nov. 9, 1900 said, "His mechanical skill was of high order and developed into natural genius and many were the inventions of merit constructed at his establishment that would have proved beneficial to both himself and fellow-beings had they been pushed and placed in the market."

George and Gennie had eight children: Jessie, Myrtle, Clarence, Eugene, Hortense, Louis, Nellie and Knowles. Eugene and Louis died as children. The others grew to adulthood in their home next to the Christian Church on North Third Street in Baldwyn. Jessie and Nellie remained there along with Nellie's husband, Oscar Abrams and their two daughters, Blanche and Mary Kate. All the grandchildren remained very close to each other all their lives perhaps because they played together every Sunday afternoon while their parents visited George and Gennie.

Jessie, the only one left in the once bustling home, died in 1949. The house was rented for several years until Blanche Abrams Stults, who had grown up there, her husband, Claude Stults and their four children moved in. In about 1976 she, then widowed and her children grown, sold it to the city of Baldwyn, who tore it down and constructed the Anne Spencer Cox Library on the site.

George and Gennie Archer had eight children, 12 grandchildren and 20 great-grandchildren. Only descendants of Clarence still live in Prentiss County: Jeannette Shackelford and Lunelle Miller and their families and Robert Pennell and his family live in the Baldwyn area.

ARCHER, JESSIE IJENA,

born 1861 and died 1949, the daughter of G.W. and Gennie Archer. A very gifted poet, the 16 year-old Jessie created a legend about the springs at Marietta and wrote the poem, *Nemo-Akim/Purple Shell*.

Jessie Ijena Archer

Nemo-Akim/Purple Shell

When the red man here was monarch, as the old-time legends tell,
Once he owned a priceless treasure, 'twas a shining purple shell,
And it held the power of healing, hid within its mystic hue,
He who touched its polished surface, pain or sickness never knew.

Oft it healed the wounded warrior, with the foe before his face,
Oft refreshed the bleeding hunter, faint, returning from the chase,
Oft when burning, deadly fever smote the red man with its breath,
Purple Shell, the Nemo-Akim, saved him from the sleep of death.

Far across the distant mountain, hunters came o'er rock and dell,
Many weary moons they wandered, just to touch the magic shell,
Long was it the red man's treasure, guarded with a jealous care,
Long it was the red man's blessing, Nemo-Akim bright and fair.

Autumn's painted leaves were burning, dancing, falling soft and still,
When a spring was gurgling, rippling in the sands beneath the hill;
When the mighty Chief Makonah, paused to rest him in the shade,
Gazing on the limpid waters where the gay leaves danced and played.

Then the bright-hued leaves in circles, fluttered round the warrior's head,
"Let the great Makonah listen, he is thirsty now," they said:
"He must drink from Nemo-Akim, then his slumbers will be sweet,
And the leaves shall dance together in the sunlight, at his feet."

Then the Chief, as in a vision, saw them dancing as they fell
And he in the laughing waters, idly dipped the purple shell.
But it slipped between his fingers, bright waves snatched it from his hand,
Then in vain, the mighty sachem, sought it in the shallow sand.

Then he came before his people, on his face in anguish fell,
"Woe my brothers, to Makonah, he has lost the purple shell,
Nemo-Akim! Oh my people, let the careless warrior die.
He has lost the red man's treasure, never shall your tears be dry."

Then from every scattered wigwam, every lodge beside the rill,
Came the warrior and the maiden, to the spring beneath the hill;
Vainly searching, searching, searching, till the red man's heart was sore,
But no hunter, squaw, nor sachem, ever saw the treasure more.

In the sands where Nemo-Akim vanished from Makonah's sight,
Bubbled forth a fresher fountain, it was clear and pure and bright;
And it held the power of healing, still they came and found it true,
He who drank its limpid waters, pain or sickness never knew.

Long, oh! long ago has vanished of the red man's every trace,
From the hillside and the hollows, that were once his dwelling place,
Every token has departed, where his tribe were wont to meet,
And his ashes long have mingled, with the dust beneath our feet.

But that spring is gushing, rippling in the sand beneath the hill,
Where concealed from white man's vision; Nemo-Akim lieth still;
Still its healing balm distilling, through the bubbles as they rise,
From the heart of Nemo-Akim that in viewless splendor lies

Still, when autumn paints the forest, with her tints of red and gold,
Bright leaves dance again in circles, gayly as they did of old;
Holding every breeze enchanted, while they keep their mystic spell,
Thus they hold their yearly revels, o'er the spring of Purple Shell.

And 'tis said the red man's spirit, to this fountain as of yore,
When the midnight moon is beaming, brings his earthen cup once more,
Quaffs again the healing waters, that are gushing, rippling still,
O'er the long lost Nemo-Akim in the sands beneath the hill.

ARMSTRONG, ARCHIE LEANDER,

born Sep. 20, 1902 and died Feb. 8, 1964, the first child born to George Washington Armstrong and Nancy Maudre McCutcheon Armstrong. At age 17, he eloped and married 17 year old Jessie Mae Clark. Shortly after their marriage he was off bearing at a sawmill and his right hand was severed at the wrist. Jessie kept the hand in a box

Archie and Jessie Mae Armstrong

in a chest and when he died she placed his hand in the casket with him. After the accident, he sold Woodmen of the World Insurance. He drove a car and did most of the work other men do with two hands.

Jessie Mae (b. May 9, 1902, d. Jun. 7, 1991) daughter of Steve "Bud" Clark and Izora Umfress Clark. Her siblings are Mary Lou Clark Woodruff and Joseph L. Clark.

They were dedicated members of the Snowdown Church of Christ. Their love for the Lord and their fellowman was evidenced by their commitment to the church and good works. They always opened their home to visiting preachers or anyone in need. They had no children, but their nieces, nephews and other family members enjoyed the hospitality of their home. They left their home to the Snowdown Church of Christ and a fellowship room is dedicated to their memory. They are buried in the Snowdown Cemetery.
Submitted by Lyonel Wade.

ARMSTRONG, CHARLIE GLENN,

born Sep. 1, 1922 and died Jun. 28, 1989, married Mary Ruth Holloway (b. Sep. 4, 1922) May 24, 1941. Glenn was the son of George Washington Armstrong (b. Jan. 18, 1883, d. Oct. 24, 1954) and Doris Clark Wren (b. Jun. 16, 1887, d. 1970) who married in 1920. Glenn, George and Dora are buried in Snowdown Church of Christ Cemetery in Prentiss County. Glenn was the grandson of Charles W. Armstrong (b. Jun. 22, 1864, d. Jun. 16, 1916) and Mary Jane Goodwin (b. May 19, 1864, d. Feb. 9, 1957). They are buried in Armstrong Cemetery in Prentiss County, MS. Also, Glenn was grandson of Stephen Taylor "Bud" Clark (b. Nov. 12, 1857, d. December 1918) and Dicie Ann Williams (b. Sep. 22, 1855, d. Oct. 1899). They are buried at Liberty Hill Cemetery in Alcorn County.

Glenn, Mary Ruth, Cathy, Harold and Gerald Armstrong (standing)

Glenn had six half-sisters, a half-brother, three brothers, a sister (see George W. Armstrong), a half-sister, Nancy Wren Rinehart Rorie and a half-brother, Noel Wren.

Mary Ruth is the daughter of William Dock Holloway (b. Jan. 15, 1893, d. Jun. 13, 1961) and Mary Elizabeth Hardin Holloway (b. Jun. 22, 1892, d. Oct. 1965) married May 3, 1914. They are buried at Old Kemp's Chapel Cemetery in Alcorn County. She is the granddaughter of William Hardin (b. June 1857) and Mary Elizabeth Mollie Vanderford Hardin (b. Jul. 3, 1863, d. Mar. 26, 1944) married Dec. 12, 1886. William is buried at Hardin Family Cemetery, Prentiss County. Mollie is buried at Juliette Cemetery, Alcorn County. She is also granddaughter of Sidney Hafford Holloway (b. June 1869, d. 1903) and Susan E. Blassingame (b. September 1872, d. 1903) married Nov. 23, 1890. They are buried in Chapel Hill Cemetery in the Holloway Community near Burnsville, Tishomingo County, MS.

Mary Ruth's brothers and sisters:

Herman Roy (b. Sep. 6, 1915, d. May 8, 1979) married Eula Fay Boothe Nov. 27, 1937. Eula Fay was born Sep. 10, 1917. Their children are Juanita Holloway Augustine (b. Dec. 24, 1938) and Jimmy Dale (b. Dec. 22, 1943).

Hafford Carrol (b. Oct. 19, 1919, d. Jan. 19, 2000) married Lillian Frances Bullard (twin to Howard). Their children are William Ray, Patricia Carol (b. 1946, d. Sep. 29, 1947), Larry (b. 1948, d. 1964) and Timothy Halford.

Howard Dow, twin to Halford (b. Oct. 19, 1919), married Vera Pauline Dawson (b. Apr. 6, 1920, d. Feb. 2, 1994) Mar. 11, 1938. Their children are Sadie Jo (b. Jul. 14, 1939), Howard Dwight (b. May 17, 1947), Sarah Diane Holloway Rhinehardt (b. Feb. 14, 1949), Donnie Annette Pauline (b. Feb. 18, 1950), Madeline Patricia (b. Jun. 18, 1952), Billy Dawson (b. and d. Jul. 30, 1953).

Mabel Bernice (b. Sep. 26, 1927, d. 1996). Her children are James Daniel Moody (b. Jan. 14, 1949) and Danny Robert Moody (b. Jun. 20, 1951). She married Millard Nash.

Marcus Oather, twin to Marvin Edwin (b. Nov. 26, 1929), his children are Thelma Yvonne (b. Jun. 13, 1952), Brenda Bernice (b. Nov. 16, 1953) and Lois Annette (b. 1966).

Marvin Edwin (b. Nov. 26, 1929) married Jo Ann Ticer (b. Sep. 20, 1934, d. Jan. 1, 1960). Their daughter was Barbara Ann (b. Aug. 14, 1956). Marvin married second Fay Willis.

Curlee Alexander (b. Oct. 2, 1932, d. Jun. 26, 1979) is buried in Old Kemp's Chapel Cemetery.

Mary Ruth and Glenn's children are (1) Gerald Glenn (b. May 8, 1943), children: Ronnie, Keith and Mike; grandchildren, Cody and Cade. (2) Harold (b. Dec. 4, 1945) md. Jo Flanigan. Their children are Gwen, Lynn, Jeremy and Justin. (3) Kathy Ruth (b. Jul. 21, 1952) md. Sherrill Umfress (divorced) then married Perry Walden. Their children are Perry Nicholas and Ross Tyler.

Mary Ruth and Glenn always worked together even transporting cars from Chicago, IL. Lottie gave this courting of Glenn and Mary Ruth a great "boost."
Submitted by Lottie Nash Wade with much love and respect.

ARMSTRONG, GEORGE WASHINGTON,

the first of seven children born to Charles W. and Mary Jane Goodwin Armstrong. George W. (b. Jan. 18, 1883, d. Oct. 24, 1954) married Nancy Maudre McCutcheon (b. Apr. 20, 1885, d. May 13, 1918), daughter of Catherine Loveless McCutcheon (b. Mar. 14, 1853, d. Feb. 19, 1936) and James Robert McCutcheon (b. May 4, 1852, d. May 1, 1923). They are buried in Forked Oak Cemetery in Prentiss County. Nancy Maudre is buried in Armstrong Cemetery in Prentiss County. George W. is buried in Snowdown Cemetery. To George W. and Nancy Maudre were born nine children:

Nancy Maudre McCutcheon Armstrong about 1900.

(1) Archie Lee (b. Sep. 20, 1902, d. Feb. 8, 1964) married Jessie Mae Clark (b. May 9, 1902, d. Jun. 7, 1991). They have no children and are buried in Snowdown Church of Christ Cemetery near Jacinto.

(2) Hester Mae (b. Jul. 27, 1904, d. Jan. 16, 1958) married Oren L. Wade (b. Nov. 19, 1902, d. Mar. 9, 1969) Dec. 21, 1921.

(3) Ila (b. Feb. 17, 1906, d. Dec. 20, 1994) married Robert Sidney Wade (b. Nov. 12, 1900, d. Mar. 9, 1969). They had four children: Eural Wayne, Ava, Annette and Julia.

(4) Artie (b. Jun. 26, 1908) married Noel E. Lambert (b. Dec. 18, 1906, d. May 24, 1992) and had two children, Alvin Gene Lambert and Madrid Lambert Richardson. He is buried in New Lebanon Cemetery in Prentiss County.

(5) Vista (b. Nov. 4, 1910, d. Oct. 18, 1993) married Clifford Rinehart (b. Mar. 7, 1907, d. Aug. 19, 1983) Aug. 7, 1927 and had four children: Loyd, Zelma, Laverne and Joanne.

(6) Infant daughter is buried in Jacinto Cemetery.

(7) Eunice (twin) (b. Mar. 20, 1915) married Freeman Taylor and had two sons: Kenneth Ray (b. Sep. 20, 1940, d. Dec. 7, 1981), buried in Snowdown and Jerry Taylor. Second marriage was to Ted Barnett, a widower with seven children. To this union one son was born, Paul Barnett.

(8) Iness Lavada (twin) (b. Mar. 20, 1915, d. Jun. 16, 1997) married Dalton Kelly Williams (b. Apr. 23, 1910, d. May 6, 1997) Jun. 16, 1934. To this union were born three sons: (1) George (b. Dec. 13, 1936) married Elizabeth Holley in 1957. Two sons were born, Robert and Jeffrey; (2) Randell Kelly (b. Feb. 20, 1941) married Jimmie Pond in 1969 and (3) Dolan Wayne (b. Sep. 27, 1949) married Janis Manigiagli in 1975. Two children were born, Scott and Katie. Dalton and Iness moved to southern California in 1957. They are buried in Green Hills Memorial Park in Rancho Palos Verdes, CA. Their children and grandchildren all live in southern California.

(9) Infant son Carlous is buried in Armstrong Cemetery.

Hester Mae was only 13 years old when her mother, Nancy Maudre, died, leaving her a big responsibility to help raise her five younger siblings. They lived in the Jacinto area and she cared for them with great love and hard work while her father worked to support the family.

On Dec. 21, 1921, she married Oren Leslie Wade and was a kind and loving wife and mother to their eight children: William Dolye, James Edwin, Oren Lyonel (Cotton), Myra, Vonceil, Harold Dean, Hoyt and H.M. (Mackey). Hester died Jan. 16, 1958, of cancer and is buried in Forked Oak Cemetery in Prentiss County. Oren was killed in a car wreck, along with his second wife, Rayde McBride Wade, their young son, brother, sister and family friend Mar. 9, 1969. They too are buried in Forked Oak Cemetery.

In 1920 the widowed George Washington Armstrong with seven children at home married widow Dora Clark Wren with two children, Clyde and Nancy. Dora (b. Jun. 16, 1887, d. Sep. 19, 1970) is buried in Snowdown. To this marriage were born four children: (1) George Warren (b. Apr. 4, 1921) married Lema Woodruff (b. Jul. 27, 1915, d. May 22, 1997) and is buried in Snowdown. They had five children: Bobby, Dillard and Gail and deceased are a baby daughter, Nelda Grace, buried in Armstrong Cemetery and Dorothy Faye (b. Apr. 8, 1955, Sep. 10, 1965), buried in Snowdown. On Dec. 31, 1997, Warren married Betty Highsmith of Corinth. (2) Charlie Glenn (b. Sep. 1, 1922, d. Jun. 28, 1989) married Mary Ruth Holloway (b. Sep. 4, 1922) May 24, 1941. He is buried in Snowdown. They have three children: Harold, Gerald and Cathy. (3) Dora Cleatus (b. Apr. 15, 1924, d. Jun. 30, 1988) married Arlie C. Woodruff (b. Sep. 22, 1919, d. Apr. 2, 1981) and is buried in Snowdown. They had two children, Robbie and Wynell. (4) Arlie

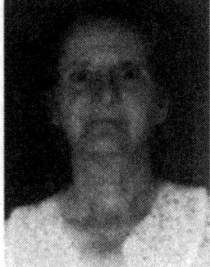

George W. and Dora Clark Armstrong

Allen (b. 1927) married Ann Cappleman from Jasper, AL. They live in Illinois. *Submitted by Lyonel Wade.*

ARMSTRONG, ILA A., born Feb. 17, 1906 and died Dec. 20, 1994, the third of nine children born to George Washington and Nancy Maudre McCutcheon Armstrong. Ila was very close to her siblings and to her daddy and mother who died at the age of 33.

Ila Armstrong Wade and her four grandchildren

On Oct. 30, 1921, Ila became the wife of Robert Sidney Wade. His mother, Martha, became her second mother and taught her and helped care for her during times of sickness and stress as her own mother would have done. She loved her husband's parents and his siblings and their families and got along well with all of them.

Ila loved her husband, Sidney and supported his work with Berea Church of Christ as they reared their four children to love the Lord. She was proud of his work in the community, on the farm in the logwoods and at the sawmill. She could always tell where he was working by the sounds that reverberated around the place. She was the only woman in the community whose husband owned a John Deere tractor that had steel-lug wheels and a magneto. The huge wheel he cranked it with also served as a pulley for the sawmill and his brother's gristmill; he was also a mechanic. In July, Ila always tried to can at least 100 quarts of blackberries and other fruits. At hog-killing time, before they had freezers, she canned the loins and sausages for winter food.

She supported Sidney with the lumber work in his helping their son Eural build a house in Henderson, TN where Eural lived while he attended Freed-Hardeman College. He also cut, sawed, hand planed and hauled the lumber which was used in their daughter Ava's house, which he helped build, at Midway.

Ila was devastated by the wreck on Mar. 9, 1969 which killed Sidney and four other family members, but about a year later in 1970, she moved in with Julia who was teaching in Cherokee, AL. There Ila did babysitting for teachers Ann and Melvin Brown's children, Lisa and Jimmy. Later she cared for Roger and Mary Moore's newborn daughter, Jennifer. These families loved Ila and called her "Granny."

Ila's last home was Oak Grove Court in Iuka, where she worked for her Lord by helping Mrs. Tommie Robinson, Mrs. Josie Clingan and Mrs. Lily Potts. She loved all her neighbors and loved to send get-well cards to the sick.

Ila and Sidney had four children:

1) Eural Wayne (b. Mar. 23, 1923) married Ola Trimble and had Kenneth and Tommy. Ken married Judy Webb and they had Jane and Jill. Tommy married Pat Thomason and they had Melanie, Melinda, Tommy Jr. and Meridith. Eural and Ola have an adopted daughter, Christy, a foster daughter, Debbie and two foster sons, Robert and Alex.

2) Ava (b. Jun. 29, 1932) married Bob Wimbish. They had Ellen, Mary, Robert and Jon. Ellen married Eddie Green and they have Jessie and Allison. Mary married Phillip South and they have Ethan and Audrey. Robert married Tracy Gist and they have Sarah and Molly. Jon married Sharon Curtis and they have Lauryn.

3) Annette (b. Nov. 8, 1943) married Steve Nesbitt and they had Alan and Carla. Alan married Debra Daughety and they have Johnathon.

4) Julia (b. Jul. 29, 1947) married Steve Goodman and they had Amy. *Submitted by Ava, Annette and Julia.*

ARMSTRONG, JOSEPH, born 1797 in Georgia, married Mary Pearson May 15, 1823 in Tuscaloosa, AL. He later married Mary V. Carr (b. 1807 in North Carolina), daughter of Martha Carr. To this union was born 10 children: (1) William A. (b. 1824) married Rachel Bishop, (2) Lucy (b. 1826) married Sion Brown, (3) Sophronia (b. 1830), (4) Baby son, (5) Matilda (b. 1833), (6) Alfred L. (b. 1837), (7) Ephraim W. (b. 1837, d. 1900) married Rebecca C. Burleson and is buried in Armstrong Cemetery northeast of Hamilton, AL; (8) Charles H. (b. 1839, d. 1864), (9) John W. (b. 1843) married Cynthia Safronia Ledbetter and (10) George Miller (b. 1846, d. 1899) married Hannah Isbel Morrow in 1877 in Marian County, AL and later moved to Texas. He is buried in Baker Cemetery in Parker, TX. All the above children were born in Alabama, either Bibb or Marian County.

Charles W. Armstrong and Mary Jane Goodwin Armstrong

Charles H. married Jincy M. Green (b. 1835, d. 1908) Nov. 16, 1859 at the home of her parents, Absalom and Mary Green in Marian County, AL by A.A. Carr, MG. Two sons were born: (1) Joseph A. "Jo Ab" (b. 1860, d. 1926) married Hulie Crane and is buried in Ida, AR and (2) Charles W. (b. 1864, d. 1916). Charles H. was inducted into service Jan. 12, 1864 at Camp Davies, MS in Co. A, 1st Regiment of Alabama Volunteers to serve three years in the US Army. His enlistment papers show him to have black eyes, black hair, dark complexion and five feet, 10 inches tall. He died in Larkins Ford, AL on May 4, 1864 of dropsy, a disease contracted in line of his duty as a soldier of the US Army. He was buried in the area where he died. In 1866 his widow, Jincy M. Armstrong, applied for pension and received $12 monthly until her death Aug. 12, 1908.

Charles W. Armstrong married Mary Jane Goodwin (b. 1864, d. 1957), daughter of Andy and Mary Crane Goodwin. He was a carpenter and bricklayer. In 1898 he was licensed to become Postmaster of Arden Post Office in Prentiss County. They lived most of their life in old Tishomingo County area and are buried in Armstrong Cemetery in Prentiss County. Seven children were born to this union: (1) George Washington (b. 1883, d. 1954) md. Nancy Maudre McCutcheon; (2) Joe Tom (b. 1885) md. Mollie McCutcheon, sister of Nancy Maudre; (3) Mary Eliza (b. 1887, d. 1982) md. Dave Marion Howell; (4) Leander Clinton (b. 1894, d. 1896); (5) J. Guyton (b. 1896, d. 1958) md. Alma Tennison; (6) C. Estella (b. 1898, d. 1989) md. Robert L. Helton; (7) Charlie M. (b. 1900, d. 1966) md. Iva Lucy Carson (b. 1908, d. 1996) and (8) Carle Perry (b. 1905, d. 1974) married Winnie Whitaker (b. 1913, d. 1991) and is buried in Bakersfield, CA. Carle is buried in Summersville, MO. *Submitted by Lyonel Wade.*

ARNETT FAMILY, William Calvin Arnett (b. Apr. 27, 1837, d. Jan. 27, 1902) came to Prentiss County from North Carolina where he married Mary Caroline Rogers (b. Mar. 8, 1839) on Dec. 13, 1860. The two owned property in the eastern part of the county in Big Brown Bottom east of the Blythes Chapel Community. To this union were born three children: Johnny C. (b. Sep. 20, 1862, d. Mar. 20, 1871), D. Williamson (b. Jul. 12, 1865, d. Nov. 10, 1948) and Laura Alice (b. Feb. 15, 1867, d. Feb. 17, 1961). Laura came to the new county of Prentiss at approximately 3 years of age after her parent's prior move to Carbondale, IL where she was born. She married Daniel Clinton Holley Jul. 5, 1891 at the residence of Vina Rogers. The ceremony was performed by J. D. Huddleston and witnessed by J.F. Rogers, A.T. Smith, G. Henry Holley and H.T. Rogers. Daniel Clinton was a farmer and fur dealer and died Oct. 23, 1911. They had 11 children. Plumer Leslie and Calvin Wesley were twins.

Plumer Leslie Holley (b. Mar. 19, 1882, d. Nov. 1, 1976) married Eila Miler Jun. 18, 1916. They had no children.

Calvin Wesley Holley (b. Mar. 19, 1882, d. Nov. 18, 1953) married Belva Brinkley Apr. 21, 1918. They had two children, Wesley Jr. and Lacy B.

Minnie Ethel Holley (b. Jul. 31, 1893, d. Dec. 8, 1976) married James Willis "Jim" Green Aug. 12, 1912. They had four children. Their first son died at birth. Ferrell Holley (b. Apr. 18, 1918, d. Dec. 4, 1965) married Mary Ethel Davis and they had one child, Alys Madgeline. The first daughter was Opal Juanita Green Deaton who married Ruben H. Deaton. Their two children were Shirley Ann Deaton who married Kenneth Moreland and Peggy Sue Deaton who married Edward Simmons. The second daughter was Hazel Mozelle Green who married Ewell O. Brown. The Browns have no children.

Homer Dewey Holley (b. May 1899, d. Jan. 2, 1956) married Oma Eulala Searcy Apr. 2, 1921. They had no children.

Ida Mary Emily Holley (b. Feb. 1, 1902, d. Jan. 28, 1984) married Clovis McKinley Taylor Dec. 23, 1922. They had two children, Mary Alice Taylor Sherman and Clovis McKinley "Mac" Taylor.

Cleetus Reed Holley (b. Feb. 17, 1902, d. Dec. 25, 1959) married Pearl Windham Jan. 7, 1923. They had four children: Emogene Holley Downs, Alma Rose Holley McDonald, Lila Reed Holley Bailey and Laura Lee Holley England.

Guy McKinley Holley (b. Apr. 28, 1897, d. Mar. 7, 1954) married Minnie Mae Maxwell. They had no children.

Waco Selmer Holley (b. Oct. 1, 1906) married Linnie Mae Moreland in 1925. They had five children: Edwin, Charles, Joan, Jimmy and Buddy.

Sidney Kiley Holley (b. Jan. 7, 1905) married Inez Loveless in 1925. They had two children, Sidney Kiley Jr. married Jerry Stark and had one child, Sherry Gay and Evelyn Nell Holley married James Sappington and had one daughter, Sandra Cae; Sidney Kiley Jr. was killed in a plane crash at Baldwyn, MS May 16. 1948. Sidney Kiley Sr. later married Evie Moore and they had one child, Patty Holley who married Jerry Buse.

Cecil Calvert Holley (b. Oct. 31 1911, d. Mar. 6, 1974) married Rosalie Edmondson and had two children, Larry Brent and Lynn Elaine. Lynn died at about 10 years of age.

The sons of Daniel Clinton Holley followed their father's trade. After his death they moved their business to Booneville, MS where they also dealt in seed and fertilizer. The firm was listed as "Holley Brothers." Cecil Calvert later dealt in lumber and building supplies and his business was known as "Holley Builder's Supply." *Submitted by Hazel Green Brown.*

ASHCRAFT, CARL JEFFERSON AND RUTH (BROWN), Carl Jefferson Ashcraft was born Jul. 30, 1902 to Ephraim Green and Martha Jane (Wheeler) Ashcraft. Carl's father, Ephraim, died when

Carl was about 3 years old. Ephraim died of cancer and we are unsure as to exactly when he died or where he is buried.

Carl Jefferson and Ruth (Brown) Ashcraft. Shirley Ashcraft is child.

Ephraim Green Ashcraft was born April 1863 in Tennessee. His mother, Caroline Ashcraft, never married. Caroline was born in November 1835. We find her parents, James and Eleanor Ashcraft, on the 1840 Hardin County, TN census. They lived near Pickwick Dam in an area called Old Hamburg. By 1860 James had died, because he is not listed on the 1860 Old Tishomingo County census with Eleanor and Caroline. We have not been able to find parents for James or Eleanor or from what area they moved.

Martha Jane was born in 1837 in Kentucky. Her parents were George L. Wheeler and Mary Ann (Hendricks). Mary Ann's parents were Auvis (sp?) and John Hendricks (Hindrix?). George died about 1864-65. We do not know his parents, the date of his death or where he is buried. Mary Ann died in 1860 and is buried in an unmarked grave in Old Bucksnort Cemetery in Altitude, MS.

Carl married Ruth Brown Jun. 14, 1928. They eloped. Ruth was born Aug. 16, 1910 in Alcorn County. Her parents were John Oscar and Olive (Vanderford) Brown. Carl and his brother, Bud, married sisters, Ruth and Lerlean Brown.

The Brown Family moved into the Jacinto area about 1810. Jepe and Lizzie Brown, Ruth's grandparents, died the same day during the typhoid fever epidemic and were buried in the same grave. Isaac Mason Brown, Ruth's great-grandfather, was killed in the Civil War and is buried in Liberty, VA in a mass grave. William Vanderford, Ruth's great-grandfather, came to Old Tishomingo County when he was 18 years old. He was a School Master, Methodist preacher, Justice of the Peace and owned his own grist and sorghum mills. Christopher Pleasant Vanderford, Ruth's grandfather, was a physician, who treated his patients with herbs.

Carl and Ruth had eight children: Eloise (b. 1930), Roy Milton (b. 1931), Cleyone Carmon (b. 1932), Zera Grace died as an infant, Geraldine (b. 1938), Bobby Lloyd (b. 1941), Shirley Ann (b. 1943) and Wanda Jean (b. 1951). All seven children still live in Prentiss County.

Carl was a very gifted man. He could play any musical instrument by ear. He loved building things and working with wood. He died Sep. 17, 1963 and is buried in Liberty Cemetery in Booneville, MS.

Ruth was a wonderful mother and a hard worker. She loves to tell stories of being able to pick more cotton in a day than most men and although she was a small woman, she could. She was very talented with flowers and this was always apparent in her house and yard. She is 89 years old and still lives in Prentiss County. *Submitted by Carolyn Whitehead and Eller Drew Cox.*

ASHCRAFT, CLEYONE CARMON "PICK" & ALLIE GASTON (KIZER),

lived in Prentiss County for all, but about 12 years, of their lives.

Allie has deep roots in Prentiss/Old Tishomingo. She is the daughter of Allen Gaines and Ottie Odell (Bolton) Kizer. Her great-grandfather, Benjamin Julian Kizer, was a captain in the Civil War. Her great-uncle, B.J. Kizer, built the first Inn and Tavern in Jacinto, MS. As you read the Old Tishomingo Courthouse records, you will read about the community and political involvement's of Michael Kizer and his father, Francis Kizer (Allie's great-great and great-great-great-grandfathers). Francis Kizer was so politically involved, he was fined $20 for betting on the 1844 Presidential election. Francis is listed as one of the families taking part in the establishment of the county.

Center of photo: Cleyone "Pick" and Allie Ashcraft. Their daughters beginning with the bottom left corner: Carolyn (Ashcraft) Whitehead. Top left corner: Sharon (Ashcraft) Burcham. Top right corner: Marilyn (Ashcraft) Sappington. Bottom left corner: Brenda (Ashcraft) Barnes. Special note: Each person in this picture is 25 years old.

Allie's great-grandmother's, Martha Francis (Gaines) Kizer's, family was one of the first families to settle in the Pharr Flatts/Pleasant Valley area. The Gaines family helped to survey the Natchez Trace and their family lived just off the Trace. They fought in the American Revolution, Civil War and Indian War. The Gaines family has been in Old Tishomingo/Prentiss County for almost 200 years.

Pick's parents are Carl Jefferson and Ruth (Brown) Ashcraft. They named him Cleyone Carmon, but his brother named him "Pick" and "Pick" stuck. Carl's dad, Ephraim Green Ashcraft, born in 1863, died when Carl was about three years old. His mother, Martha Jane, his grandmother, Mary Ann and his seven older brothers and sisters had to raise Carl and his younger brother, Sam. We cannot find Ephraim Green Ashcraft's grave, but Martha is buried near Carl in Liberty Cemetery in Booneville.

Pick's great-great-great-grandfather, James Brown, was listed on the 1840 Old Tishomingo County census. James Brown's oldest son, Isaac Mason Brown of Old Tishomingo County, fought and died in the Civil War. He is buried in a mass grave in Liberty, VA. Isaac's son, Jefferson "Jepe" Davis Brown and his wife, Pamelia "Lizzie" Elizabeth (Abel) Brown, are buried in one grave. They died of typhoid fever on the same day.

Pick's grandmother, Olive (Vanderford) Brown can trace her roots to when the Vanderfords first came to America in 1637 and then to Belgium in 1550. Pick's great-great grandfather, William Vanderford, came to Old Tishomingo County when he was 18. He was a School Master, a Methodist preacher, owned a grist mill and sorghum mill and was Justice of the Peace from 1864-1866. Christopher Pleasant Vanderford, Pick's great-grandfather, was a doctor, who treated his patients with herbs, roots, bark of trees, etc.

Pick is retired from Jesco and Allie is retired from Wal-Mart. They live on Old Marietta Road. They have four daughters: Carolyn (Whitehead); Marilyn (Sappington); Brenda (Barnes) and Sharon (Burcham). They have five grandchildren: Jessica Whitehead (b. 1981), Brandon Barnes (b. 1985), Kyle Barnes (b. 1989), Cliff Sappington (b. 1991) and Keaton Burcham (b. 1994). *Submitted by Carolyn Whitehead and Eller Drew Cox.*

ASHCRAFT, EPHRAIM GREEN AND MARTHA JANE (WHEELER),

Ephraim Green Ashcraft was born April 1863 in Tennessee. His mother was Caroline Ashcraft (b. November 1835). With the information I have, I believe that Caroline never married. Her parents were James and Eleanor Ashcraft of Hardin County, TN. James and Eleanor had five children: William (b. 1828), Ephraim (b. 1830/31), Susan Emeline (b. 1834/40), Caroline (b. 1837) and Angeline.

The Ephraim Green and Martha Jane (Wheeler) Ashcraft Family taken approximately 1906. Back row standing: Buddie Napolium, Henry Sylvester, Granville Lonnie, Minnie Bell and Robert Eaveman. Sitting: Alvie, Carl Jefferson, woman holding child (mother to children) Martha Jane (Wheeler) Ashcraft, child-Sam David, Mary Caroline and older woman (grandmother to children) Mary Ann (Hendricks) (Wheeler) Ashcraft. Man in right corner: Ephraim Green Ashcraft and child-not sure.

Ephraim Ashcraft, Ephraim *Green* Ashcraft's uncle, helped to rear Ephraim Green, but because of the same first name, there is a lot of confusion in reading old documents to tell which Ephraim is being talked about.

Ephraim Green married Martha Jane (Wheeler) Sep. 5, 1883 in Hardin County, TN. Martha's parents were George L. Wheeler and Mary Ann (Hendricks).

Ephraim Green and Martha had nine children: Alvie; Minnie Belle (b. 1887), Granville Lonnie (b. 1889), Henry Sylvester, Robert Eaveman, Buddie Napolium (b. 1898), Mary Caroline (b. 1900), Carl Jefferson (b. 1902) and Sam David (b. 1904).

Ephraim Green Ashcraft made whiskey and farmed for a living. He had cancer on his face. His son, Carl Ashcraft, told his children that part of his nose was gone by the time he died. We cannot find a death date for Ephraim Green or where he is buried. Carl was about two or three years old when his father died and Sam, the youngest child, was a baby.

Martha was about five feet tall, very thin, had blue eyes, brown hair and was considered very pretty. Ruth Ashcraft, Martha's daughter-in-law, said she had pierced ears, but never wore earrings. She put broom straw in her ears when her vision became bad and when her ears became infected, she took the straw out and her vision was better.

Martha did not marry again. Her mother, Mary Ann, moved in with her to help with the home and children. Martha Jane (Wheeler) Ashcraft died in 1937 and is buried near her sons, Carl and Bud in the Liberty Cemetery in Booneville. *Submitted by Carolyn Whitehead.*

ASHCRAFT, JOHN,

the Tuscumbia Community history would not be complete without the John Ashcraft Family record. John Ashcraft (b. Mar. 22, 1851 in Hamburg, Hardin County, TN) served in the Civil War at a very young age. He was one of the last veterans of that war to die in Prentiss County. He died at his home in Tuscumbia on Jun. 17, 1940 and is buried in the Mormon Cemetery, northeast of Booneville. John's parents were William Ashcraft and

Mary Elizabeth "Polly" Fisher. This family moved from Hardin County, TN to old Tishomingo County, MS by 1860.

From left: Emma Leah, Martha Jane Jones Wood Erwin Ashcraft, Minnie Jewel, John Ashcraft and Ruby Ann.

There were four children: John being the oldest, Sarah Elizabeth, Mary J. and Annie. Sarah Elizabeth (b. Jul. 26, 1857, d. Feb. 7, 1930) married Herman Burton Laster Sep. 15, 1879 and they had 10 children. Three died as infants, one died as a youth and the others lived and raised families in the communities of Prentiss County. Mary J. was 1 year old in the 1860 census and would have died young as no further record is known of her. Annie (b. Oct. 22, 1867, d. Feb. 16, 1941) married William Newton Ross and lived in Leedy, Tishomingo County, MS. She, with her husband, Newton and her sister, Sarah Elizabeth, is buried in Liberty Hill Cemetery in Leedy.

John first married Dec. 5, 1868, to Mary Jean Jernigan Warlow Anderson. They divorced after raising some orphan children. She moved to Kelsey, TX where she died in 1925.

On Sep. 11, 1911 John married Martha Jane Jones Wood Erwin. Martha Jane "Mattie" is the daughter of Huey Gilmore Jones and Nancy Emeline Miller. She is a niece to Mary Jean, John's first wife, as "Jennie" is a half-sister to Nancy Emeline Miller. To John and Martha came four children:

Emma Leah (b. Oct. 13, 1912, d. Apr. 3, 1973) married Apr. 18, 1931 Bynum "M." Smith (b. Sep. 5, 1911, d. December 1991). They had nine children: Bynum Jr. (b. and d. Jul. 15, 1931), Mary Dean md. Q.D. Pollard, Bobby Marion md. Susie J. Stinnett, Mildred Ione md. Robert Paige Craven, John David md. Myrtle V. Eaton Margaret Irene md. James Rueben Carson, Glenda Joyce md. Jimmy Gordon Burcham, Judith Ellen md. Therman V. Saylors and Bonnie Lee md. Devin David Ruesch.

Ruby Ann (b. Aug. 18, 1915, d. Jul. 27, 1990) married Oscar Wayland Weatherbee Jun. 9, 1934. Four children came to this union: Doris Ann md. Raymond Lee Oakes, Patsy Darlene md. Dale Edward Clarkson, Larry Wayland md. LaRayne Kimball and Sarah Lucille md. Terrell Kim Johnson.

Minnie Jewel (b. Jun. 3, 1818, d. Jan. 26, 1992) married Lenard Melvin White. Two children, Evelyn Ramona Ashcraft and Truman Raymond Ashcraft, were born to Jewel.

Quoting from the *Volume One of Prentiss County History*, printed in 1981, "The original four acres on which the Tuscumbia School was located were given by John Ashcraft" (in deeds to the School Trust Fund. There was a gentleman's agreement by a handshake that once the property was no longer used as a school, it would revert to the family.)

John and Mary Jean "Jennie" accepted the message of the Mormon missionaries and were baptized members of The Church of Jesus Christ of Latter Day Saints Apr. 16, 1896. The story told was that as John ran his peddling wagon through the communities, he affectingly being called "Uncle John," that if he joined the Mormon Church, he wouldn't have friends enough to bury him when he died, to which he said, "Just take me over the hill and I'll give you a good stink." One of the very earliest and one of the two memories of my grandfather was there was standing room only at his funeral and never had I seen so many cars and wagons of friends and neighbors who attended his funeral. Grandpa John helped build the first chapel for the Mormon Church and was an active member until his death. He loaned his car to the missionaries from time to time, as well as food and shelter. *Submitted by Doris A.W. Oakes, PO Box 791, Eagle, ID 83616-0791, e-mail <dawoakes@worldnet.att.net>*

BARKER, JOHN RAYFORD, born Feb. 19, 1839 in Benton County, AL, died in 1912 and is buried Upper Cane Creek Cemetery, Cleburne County, AL. He married Laura Ann Bailey (b. Nov. 22, 1841, Benton County, AL, d. Feb. 7, 1929, Prentiss County, MS) Feb. 21, 1861 in Calhoun County, AL. Laura Ann is buried Upper Cane Creek Cemetery, Cleburne County, AL.

John Rayford Barker's parents were Charity Betty (Elizabeth) Jackson (b. Apr. 2, 1811) and Ephraim Manley (Manual) Barker (b. Jun. 29, 1811), Laurens, SC. They were married Oct. 2, 1828.

John Rayford Barker and Laura Ann (Bailey) Barker

Laura Ann (Bailey) Barker's parents were Joshua Bailey (b. Sep. 20, 1820, South Carolina, d. Nov. 10, 1905, Haralson County, GA), buried Campground Cemetery, Muscadine, AL and Mary Elizabeth "Betty" Brown (b. 1818, d. ca. 1890). They were married Jan. 14, 1841 in Benton County, AL. Joshua in 1838 served in Captain John Witcher's Georgia Militia Light Horse Cavalry at Cedartown, GA. He is believed to have enlisted at the age of 42 in the 28th Alabama Infantry. He was elected Jun. 6, 1864 to the Office of Constable in Calhoun County, AL and was given exemption from military duty for the remainder of the Civil War by Alabama Governor Watts.

Joshua's parents were Dr. James Bailey (b. Jul. 16, 1785, South Carolina, d. Jul. 17, 1843, Benton County, AL) and Elizabeth Harris (b. 1783). They were married Dec. 23, 1805, Elbert County, GA.

Dr. James Bailey's parents were Allen Bailey (b. ca. 1770, Abbeville County, SC, d. Mar. 1806, McCormick County, SC and Mary "Polly" Bailey.

Allen Bailey's parents were William Bailey (b. 1753, Ireland, d. Abbeville, SC) and Elizabeth Bailey.

William Bailey's parents were Nathaniel Bailey (b. 1718, Ireland, d. 1778, Old 96 District, SC) and Jane Bailey. They immigrated 1768 to Charles Town, SC from Belfast, Northern Ireland.

John and Laura Ann (Bailey) Barker made their home in Cleburne County, AL. Laura Ann moved to Prentiss County, MS after the death of her husband in around 1913. She lived with her daughter, Charity Elizabeth "Lizzie" (Barker) Brown. Laura Ann died in Prentiss County, MS but was carried back to Cleburne County, AL by train to be buried, accompanied by two grandchildren, Molly Azena (Barker) Gardner and Grace Brown. John and Laura Ann had 11 children as follows: Drewery M. (b. Jan. 22, 1862, Calhoun County, AL, d. Sep. 16, 1866); James Robert (b. Dec. 12, 1863, Calhoun County, AL, d. Aug. 9, 1920) became both a lawyer and a Methodist preacher. He is buried Upper Cane Creek Cemetery, Cleburne County, AL. John Thomas (b. Mar. 26, 1866, Haralson County, GA, d. Aug. 23, 1866); Wesley Jackson (b. Jul. 2, 1867, Haralson County, GA, d. Feb. 22, 1949) was a Methodist preacher. He is buried Gadsden, AL. Levi Ornan (b. Sep. 7, 1869, Haralson County, GA, d. Oct. 11, 1948), buried Upper Cane Creek Cemetery, Cleburne County, AL; Ephraim J. (b. Sep. 6, 1871, Haralson County, GA, d. Oct. 20, 1896, buried Upper Cane Creek Cemetery, Cleburne County, AL; Sara Frances (b. Nov. 27, 1873, Cleburne County, AL, d. Feb. 21, 1924), buried Upper Cane Creek Cemetery, Cleburne County, AL; William Eli (b. Apr. 18, 1876, Cleburne County, AL, d. Jan. 28, 1968), buried Booneville Cemetery, Prentiss County, MS. He was a merchant and a farmer in Prentiss County, He married Miley Elizabeth (Tolleson); Charity Elizabeth (b. May 27, 1878, Cleburne County, AL, d. Sep. 7, 1962), buried New Hope Cemetery, Prentiss County, MS. She married Clavin Brown; Desota Alonzo (b. Nov. 18, 1880, Cleburne County, AL, d. Nov. 10, 1961), buried Upper Cane Creek Cemetery, Cleburne County, AL; Rufus (b. Aug. 19, 1883, d. Jun. 17, 1885), buried Upper Cane Creek Cemetery, Cleburne County, AL. *Submitted by Martha Jean (Pike) Lindsey.*

BARKER, WILLIAM ELI AND MILEY ELIZABETH, were married Dec. 25, 1898 in Cleburne County, AL. His parents were John Rayford and Laura Ann (Bailey) Barker. Her parents were Green Berry and Minervia (Edwards) Tolleson.

William Eli was a railroad worker at the time of his marriage to Miley Elizabeth. In 1907, they moved from Cleburne County to Winston County, AL and became a self-employed farmer. In 1915, they moved the family again to Hills Chapel Community, Prentiss County, MS. They bought farm land of 240 acres in which they farmed. William Eli's health failed and they sold the farm and bought a place in the Tuscumbia Community of Prentiss County, MS and opened a business called "Barker's Store" where they sold general merchandise. At Miley Elizabeth's death on Feb. 20, 1955, William Eli closed the business.

William Eli Barker, 1898-1968

William Eli is remembered by his children and grandchildren as a hard-working, honest and faithful Christian man whose values are instilled in his family today. He helped start the Candler's Chapel Baptist Church and later became a deacon in the church. He was a great Bible reader (he read it from back to back). His grandchildren remember him most from his constant Bible questions and his funny tongue twisters that his grandchildren are still passing on to their children today. He died at the age of 92 Jan. 28, 1968, Prentiss County, MS.

Miley Elizabeth is remembered by her family as a loving Christian mother and grandmother who always put her family first. Her sewing talent was well displayed by the beautiful clothes her children wore. She could see an item of clothing in a store and go home and reproduce it. She had a gift for cooking from scratch. She loved animals, especially cats.

William Eli and Miley Elizabeth had nine children:

1) Zuma Gertrude (b. Dec. 11, 1899, Cleburne County, AL, d. Jan. 17, 1965, KS) md. Dec. 9, 1917, Prentiss County, MS to Plummer Holley. Children: William Herschel, Katie Willodeen, Elizabeth Elaine, Bobby Hampton, Jackie Willard, Barbara Louise and Janice Lee.

2) Judson Plasco (b. Sep. 10, 1901, Cleburne County, AL, d. Oct. 6, 1902, Alabama).

3) Vera Pearline (b. Oct. 4, 1903, Cleburne County, AL, d. Jun. 4, 1905, Alabama).

4) Katie Amalie (b. Aug. 25, 1906, Cleburne County, AL, d. Aug. 15, 1978, Prentiss County, MS) md. May 16, 1923, Prentiss County, MS to Elton L. Smith. Children: Richard Lee and Charles Edwin.

5) Rolfe Abner (b. Oct. 16, 1908, Winston County, AL, d. Jun. 27, 1992, Prentiss County, MS) md. Feb. 17, 1933, Prentiss County, MS to Verna Thompson. Children: Jo Ann and Rolfe Aaron.

6) Mollie Azena (b. Mar. 9, 1911, Winston County, AL, d. Jun. 11, 1998) md. Jun. 20, 1942, Prentiss County, MS to Mont Ray Gardner. One daughter, Billie Marie.

7) Herman Franklin (b. Apr. 22, 1913, Winston County, AL, d. Jul. 15, 1993, Prentiss County, MS) md. Apr. 28, 1934, Prentiss County, MS to Martha Bonna Pike. One daughter, Miley Jane.

8) Trana Aliena (b. Mar. 22, 1916, Prentiss County, MS) md. Apr. 28, 1937, Alcorn County, MS to Julian Carey Pike. Children: Julia Elizabeth, Jerry Franklin, Martha Jean and Linda Aliena.

9) Hiram (Harmon) Evan (b. Jun. 27, 1919, Prentiss County, MS) md. Apr. 30, 1938, Prentiss County, MS to Charlene Smart. Children: Harmon Eugene, Larry Evans and Ken David. *Submitted by Maria Malatesta. (See story on Miley Elizabeth (Tolleson) Barker and John Rayford and Laura Ann (Bailey) Barker.*

BARKER-TOLLESON, Miley Elizabeth Tolleson (b. Feb. 10, 1878 in Cleburne County, AL, d. Feb. 20, 1955) md. Dec. 25, 1898 in Cleburne County, AL to William Eli Barker (b. Apr. 18, 1876, Cleburne County, AL, d. Jan. 28, 1968). Miley and William are both buried in the Booneville Cemetery, Prentiss County, MS. Miley Elizabeth and William Eli moved to Prentiss County, where they resided most of their adult life. William was a farmer and a merchant. They had nine children. Her parents were Green Berry Tolleson (b. Aug. 1, 1850, Benton County, AL, d. Dec. 3, 1895), buried at the Lower Cane Creek Cemetery, Cleburne County, AL and Louise Minervia (Edwards) Tolleson (b. May 17, 1854 in Benton County, AL, d. Nov. 19, 1923, buried at the Lower Cane Creek Cemetery, Cleburne County, AL.

Miley Elizabeth Tolleson Barker, 1878-1955

Green Berry Tolleson's parents were William Tolleson (b. May 28, 1812, Denmark) and Mary A. Easterling (b. May 31, 1816.)

Louise Minervia (Edwards) Tolleson's parents were Stephen Edwards (b. Sep. 27, 1818, SC, d. Jul. 11, 1909, buried at the Lower Cane Creek Cemetery, Cleburne County, AL and J.P. Mariah (Chandler) Edwards (b. Feb. 23, 1824, Madison County, GA), d. Apr. 24, 1891, buried at the Lower Cane Creek Cemetery, Cleburne County, AL. They were, married Aug. 25, 1842, Benton County, AL.

Stephen Edwards' parents were William Edwards (b. Jul. 12, 1776 in North Carolina) and Elizabeth (Clayton) Edwards (b. Jun. 1, 1785). Edwardsville, AL was named for him.

J.P. Mariah (Chandler) Edwards' parents were Richardson Chandler (b. Jul. 14, 1796, d. Sep. 30, 1859 in Calhoun County, AL and Frances (Shields) Chandler (b. Nov. 17, 1795, d. ca. 1851 in Benton County, AL.

Richardson Chandler's parents were James Chandler (b. 1781 in Virginia, d. 1809 in Franklin County, GA) and Elizabeth (Stovell) Chandler.

Frances (Shields) Chandler parents were Littleberry and Susannah (Rogers) Shields.

James Chandler, the son of Joseph Chandler (b. ca. 1725 in Virginia, d. 1803 in Caswell County, NC).

Joseph Chandler was the son of John Chandler (b. ca. 1695).

John Chandler was the son of Robert Chandler (b. ca. 1659 in Virginia, d. 1704 in Kent County, VA).

Robert Chandler Jr. was the son of Robert Chandler Sr. (b. ca. 1628).

Robert Chandler Sr. was the son of John Chandler who arrived in Jamestown, VA in 1607 on the ship *Hercules*. He and his son Robert both served as members of the House of Burgesses. *Submitted by Kim Evans. (See story on William Eli Barker.)*

BARNES, OTHA CLAYTON, moved to Prentiss County from a community and church called Red Bud, near the Alabama line in the early 1900s. Later he married Georgia Griggs (These were my great-grandparents.) To them were born William, Adell, J.J. (who was my grandfather) and Annie Lee.

William married Minnie Berry. To them were born Otis, H.C., Avo and Brucie.

Adell married Sam Beasley. They had Luna, Lena and Dena.

J.J. (who was my grandfather) married Minnie Warren. To them were given: Olga, Cecil (who was my father), Ruby and Ray.

Annie Lee married Andrew Nix. They had no children.

Olga married Ruben Ricks. They had three children: Mary Nell, Floyd and Martha.

Cecil (who was my father) married Emma Lou Taylor. Six children were born to them: Ivanell, Nina, Ellis, Jerry, Paul and Mackie.

Ruby passed away at age 12 and Ray at age 3.

Mary married Cleborn Lambert and had three children: Carolyn, Elaine and Jimmy. After they divorced, she married Arnold Murphy. They had one son, Wayne.

Floyd married Shirley Glass and divorced. They had no children.

Martha married Ben Ashmore. They had three children: Betty Jo, Martha Hale and Tim.

Ivanell married Thomas Samples. They had four children: Thomas Jr., Angelia, Charlotte and Fredia.

Nina married L.C. Williams. They had a daughter and a son, Rhonda and Gregory. After they divorced, she married Bob Sparks and had Sue and Emmla.

Ellis Ray married LaRue Talley. They have four children: Mary, Ray, Marie and Elaine.

Paul married Shirley Harp. They had a daughter and a son, Vikki and Rusty.

Jerry married Carolyn Peters. They divorced and he later married Betty Leathers. He has no children by either marriage.

Mackie is not married.

The grandchildren of Ivanell are Bobby Alan McCoy, Sylvia (Austin) Wouldridge, Jessica Newell, Ray Austin Jr., Nikki and Jeremiah. The three stepgrandchildren are Scott Bridges, Michael Hodnett and Alea Hodnett.

I am proud of my two great-grandsons, Brady Alan McCoy and Austin Blake Wouldridge. *Submitted by Ivanell Samples.*

BARNETT, JOSEPH THOMAS, when the call went out through the countryside that the Yankees were near Iuka, Joseph Thomas Barnett and two of his younger brothers, Richard Henry Lee Barnett and Robert James Barnett, got on their horses and rode to Warren's Mill in Itawamba County, not too far from their homes, to enlist in Captain I.W. Warren's company of "Partisan Rangers." That was Sep. 7, 1862. Tommy was 24 years old, Henry was 22 years old and Robert James was 19 years old. The Battle of Iuka was fought Sep. 19 and 20. Tommy's oldest child, Sidney McNalley, was born just a few days later on September 29. Tommy and Robert James survived the next four years of the war, but Henry was not so lucky. He was captured and died Jan. 6, 1863, as a POW in a federal prison, Johnson's Island, Alton, IL. Henry's wife, Emeline Martin and Tommy's wife, Nancy Elizabeth Martin, were sisters and daughters of John Reynolds Martin and Elizabeth Shackelford Martin. Emeline had died in 1862. Sarah Paine Brooks Barnett, their mother, also died in 1862. When their father, Joseph Francis Barnett, died in 1855, the oldest son, John William Brooks Barnett and their Uncle John Barnett were appointed by the court as their legal guardians. Yearly settlements were made with them, paying room, board and schooling to their mother. Tommy's final settlement Oct. 10, 1859, when he became of age, was for $435.53. Joseph Francis and Sarah Paine Barnett and their children came to Tishomingo County, MS from Giles County, TN between 1850 and 1855. The log cabin they built now sits near the entrance to Tishomingo State Park. They are buried in the Barnett-Bullard Cemetery off Highway 30, three miles west of Burton. Most likely, Emaline Martin Barnett and other family members are buried there also. The Barnett's graves are covered with a stone and wood structure. The cemetery is almost inaccessible now and a lot of the headstones are covered by undergrowth and trees.

Tommy and Nancy Martin Barnett's children were: Sidney McNalley (b. 1862, d. 1912), Mary Callena "Callie" (b. 1865, d. 1883), Sarah Elizabeth "Sallie" (b. 1870, d. 1888), Louella (b. 1874, d. 1906) married Cullen Stanley, Horace Edgar (b. 1879, d. ?) married Leland Sykes and Arthur C. (b. 1877, d. ?) married Elizabeth Miller. John Reynolds Martin moved from Bay Springs to Booneville about 1866 and built a plank store where "The Dress Shop" was located in 1961. His son-in-law, Tommy, entered into the mercantile business with him. This was one of the first stores in Booneville, thus earning Tommy the title in his obituary "Pioneer Merchant of Booneville", as John Reynolds died about 1870. Tommy built a house in front of the present day Booneville Church of Christ. The house had a "wide circular porch, French windows inside shutters, ornamental iron on the roof and an iron fence surrounding the lawn on which were Chinese Magnolia trees." This house was torn down in the 1950s.

Several years after Nancy's death (b. 1842, d. 1882), Tommy married Fannie Neil (b. 1869, d. 1922). They had two sons, Eugene (b. 1890, d. 1935) married Lena Rivers Isbell and Roy (b. 1896. d. 1941) married Gretchen Ellis. Tommy died in 1920 of "uremic poisoning" at the age of 82, having outlived a wife, three daughters, a son and several children who had died as infants.

Sidney McNalley Barnett (b. 1862, d. 1912) married Annie Lou Shinault (b. 1865, d. 1936). Their four children were: William Thomas "Will" Barnett (b. 1882, d. 1943) married Annie Stanley and had two sons, Billy and Stanley; Nannie Elizabeth Barnett (b. 1884, d. 1970) married Robert M. Browning and their seven children were Thomas, Barnett, Willie, Mildred, Horace, Carroll and Nannie; Bertha Helen Barnett (b. 1888, d. 1921), first married Allan Robinson and had Elizabeth and Sidney and then married Walter Bolton and their son was Walter Jr. and Mildred Lou Barnett (b. and d. 1900).

Many family members and descendants of Tommy Barnett are buried in the Booneville Cemetery. *Submitted by Betty Browning Ford.*

BEARD, RANZEY EVERETT, born Feb. 3, 1894 and died Aug. 15, 1975, son of Dave Virgil Beard (b. 1852, d. 1931) and Nancy Caroline Wright (b. 1855, d. 1939). On Jun. 10, 1916, he married Docia Mae Rogers (b. May 19, 1893 in Indian Territory, d. Jan. 21, 1951), daughter of Zemeriah Alcie "Alce" Rogers (b. 1866, d. 1930) and Cora Ann Bullard (b. 1867, d. 1948).

Everett and Docia's children are Leonard Lyle (b. Jun. 2, 1918) and Joyce Coraene (b. Sep. 22, 1921).

On Jan. 10, 1945, Leonard Lyle Beard married Wyna Eloise Fortner (b. Apr. 20, 1923). They have one son, Larry Lynn Beard (b. Mar. 13, 1946) who married Shelly Lorene Evans and they have a daughter, Haley Lorene (b. Nov. 23, 1971) who married Tim Hellenbrand.

Docia Rogers Beard, Everett Beard holding Coraene and Leonard is standing (Mrs. Nunley turned a fan on right before the photo was taken!)

Joyce Coraene Beard married John Bolivar Rogers, son of Henry Taylor Rogers (b. 1858, d. 1944) and Harriet Priscilla "Siller" Rhodiann Moreland (b. 1868, d. 1956), Nov. 20, 1938. Coraene and Bolivar's children are: Reeder Joy (b. Feb. 2, 1941) married Wayne Vuncannon (b. Mar. 2, 1941) and Betty Jo (b. Oct. 5, 1944) married William Bernard Scott (b. Jun. 5, 1938). *Submitted by Betty Rogers Scott.*

BELEW FAMILY, there is much we have not been able to prove as yet about the history of the Belews. There are numerous spellings for the surname Belew—such as Ballew, Belue, Bilyeu, etc., but perhaps the original was Beaulieu, which was a French habitation name from any of the extremely numerous places in France. An even older origin and spelling of the name was De Bella Aqua and the connection goes back to King Witta in 300 AD.

At the present time we believe that we trace back to the first known Belew, (Rene') Belew, who appeared in Union County, SC in the early 1700s. He was married to Ann Bullington. Renny was born in 1738 and died in 1797 and his will is in existence in South Carolina. Three of his sons, Renny Reuben and Zachariah, as well as Renny Sr., are on record for service in the American Revolution. The Reuben mentioned here is not the Reuben with whom we are concerned.

According to a book written by Dorothy Howard, a descendant of Renny Belew Sr. and entitled *Dorothy's World, A Childhood in Sabine Bottom,* our Belews entrance to the US was up the coast of FL, possibly from Barbados to Virginia and the Carolinas. This has yet to be proven. Supposedly, they were French Huguenots and first came to the New World in the 1600s. A different theory is that they entered the New World in New England and the Virginia branch worked its way down to the south. We have yet to prove either theory, as it would relate to our particular line of Belews.

For our line we have traced back with proof to Reuben Belew and his wife, Harriet Hale Spain. Harriet's mother was Sarah Spain, who died in South Carolina in 1836, according to probate at the time of her death in Mar. of that year. There was no mention of Sarah's husband at that time and it is presumed that she was a widow. Research by a professional genealogist, Brent Holcomb indicates that her husband and Harriet's father, may have been a John Spain. At the time of Sarah's death, Harriet was married to Reuben and we think she was pregnant with her first child. Reuben Belew (b. Feb. 9, 1810) and Harriet Hale Spain (b. Feb. 23, 1816) were both born in South Carolina. Eliet Jane Belew, their first child, was born in Union County, SC, Aug. 12, 1836 and Harriet would have been 20 years old at the time of her birth. Both Reuben and Harriet are mentioned in the probate papers at the time of Sarah Spain's death.

Sometime between 1836 and 1840, the family removed to Lawrence County, TN according to the 1840 Census in Tennessee. Their second child, John Wesley Belew, was born there Jun. 14, 1838. At some point before 1850, again according to the US Census, the family moved yet again to Tishomingo County, MS which later became Prentiss County, MS. Prior to the move to Mississippi four more children were born in Tennessee: Sarah Ann Belew (b. Feb. 4, 1841), Matilda D. Belew (b. Aug. 26, 1845), Susan Belew (b. Mar. 14, 1847), William Taylor Belew (b. Oct. 27, 1848).

The last four children were born in Mississippi: Frances Belew (b. Oct. 20, 1850), Neal Brown Belew (b. Jul. 1, 1853), Marion Harry Belew (b. Mar. 10, 1857), Missouri Belew (b. Nov. 9, 1859).

Reuben Belew enlisted in a Mississippi regiment Jun. 9, 1861 at the age of 50 for one year's service in the Confederacy. According to his discharge papers, he was six feet tall, blue eyes, gray hair and by occupation when enlisted, a planter. He was discharged Dec. 19, 1861 to return home to care for his children, as Harriet Belew died Oct. 18, 1861. We haven't any record of the cause of Harriet's death, unless it was being constantly pregnant, which was not unusual for those days.

John Wesley Belew enlisted in the Confederacy in September 1861. According to his descendants he never came home again. He was captured at Ft. Donelson after a battle won by the Union on Feb. 10, 1862. He was transported to Camp Morton, Indianapolis, IN and remained a Yankee prisoner there until he died Apr. 4, 1862 of typhoid fever and pneumonia. He is buried in Green Lawn Cemetery in Indianapolis, IN. He was 24 years old at the time of his death. He married Julia Ann Medley of Itawamba County, MS on Sep. 30, 1860 before he left to serve in the Confederacy. He left one son, William D. Belew (b. Aug. 17, 1861). Julia Ann Medley died in 1867 and after the death of her father, William Medley, her son, William D. Belew, became the ward of his paternal grandfather, Reuben Belew and his uncle, William Taylor Belew.

Sarah Ann Belew married James Ratliff Feb. 1, 1866. They had five children: Benjamin Marion Ratliff (b. 1869), Jesse T. Ratliff (b. 1871), Frances Ratliff (b. 1873), William Ratliff (b. 1874) and Harriet Ratliff (b. 1877). We have knowledge of only one of these children, Benjamin Marion Ratliff and he married Alma Ellender Jennings. They had one daughter, Marion Ruth Ratliff, who married Edwin Gordon Kellner Aug. 15, 1941. They had two sons, Stephen Edwin Kellner (b. Dec. 13, 1943 in Fort Worth, TX) married Nancy Gail Royer Jan. 30, 1971. The second son was Stuart Leslie Kellner (b. Jan. 21, 1947 in Missoula, MT) married Mikal Morgan Apr. 29, 1969. Edwin Kellner currently lives in Helena, Montana. Ruth Ratliff Kellner died May 18, 1996.

Matilda D. Belew married William Axley Jones Dec. 21, 1871. There isn't any record, but I believe that the D stands for Delia. Dee was a nickname for Delia and Matilda D. Belew was called Aunt Dee by her nieces and nephews. William Axley Jones served in the Confederacy and had been married previously to Lucy J. Burns. They had one son, James Leroy Jones. Lucy Burns probably died in childbirth. Matilda and William Axley Jones had two daughters, Alice Ada Jones (b. Oct. 10, 1872) and Julia Ann Jones (b. May 11, 1874). William Axley Jones died Mar. 27, 1875 of blood poisoning. Alice Ada Jones married William J. Hampton and Julia Ann Jones married Joseph Absalom Moore Oct. 15, 1891. Around 1880 Matilda D. Jones took the three children, James Leroy Jones, Alice Ada and Julia Ann Jones, to Texas to be near her brothers in Wise County, TX. According to her granddaughter, Nine Jewel Moore, she said she "just closed the door of her house, left everything and took the children in a great hurry to catch a ferry across the Mississippi River." Matilda D. Belew died Aug. 20, 1934, just a few days short of her 90th birthday.

Eliet Jane Belew married Thomas W. Ham Jan. 28, 1855 in Mississippi. They had one daughter they named Harriet. Thomas W. Ham commanded his own regiment in the Confederacy, Ham's Regiment, Mississippi Cavalry, Army of Mississippi, which was mustered into Confederate service May 5, 1864. Colonel Ham was mentioned often in the diaries of the Reverend Samuel Agnew and also mentioned several times in the Official Records of the War of the Rebellion. He was highly respected both as a man and a soldier. Colonel Ham died of wounds near Atlanta, GA, Jul. 30, 1864. Eliet Jane Ham later married A.M. South Jan. 6, 1874, but we know nothing further of them at this time. Eliet Jane died Dec. 3, 1885.

Susan Belew married Judge Middleton Barrett Hunt. The Judge was a name, not a title. Their children were Robert Lee Hunt, Willis Stonewall Hunt, John Embry Hunt, Glenn Marion Hunt, Thomas Jefferson Hunt, Victoria Hunt and Emma Hunt.

We know little of the Hunts with the exception of Robert Lee Hunt. (His parents were great admirers of Robert E. Lee and knew him personally). Robert Lee Hunt married Virginia Maud Plaxco. Robert Lee Hunt (b. May 8, 1882, d. Sep. 19, 1965) had two children, Robert Hunt and Isabelle Hunt. Robert Hunt married and had children and died of a heart attack at an early age and before the death of his mother, who died in her 90's. Isabelle never married, received her doctorate, was a teacher for many years and had an interest in politics.

Marion Harry Belew married Sallie Eskridge Jan. 17, 1889. They had three children: Clara Belew (b. Jun. 7, 1890), Hale Belew (b. Sep. 12, 1892) and Thadius Belew (b. Aug. 6, 1894).

Clara Belew married Harley Burton and some of the Burton family now own the house in Decatur, TX that was built by J.A. Moore for his family. Hale Belew married Esther Gregg Mar. 3, 1925. Esther died Jun. 3, 1945. Thadius Belew married Alice Price and he died in 1973.

Neal Brown Belew married a woman whose first name was Elizabeth, but we do not know her surname. Neal (d. Oct. 11, 1905) and Elizabeth (b. Apr. 27, 1854, d. Jan. 17, 1956) are buried in Pleasant Grove Cemetery in Decatur, TX.

Missouri Belew (b. Nov. 3, 1859) married J.M. Ratliff (b. Dec. 15, 1852). Missouri bore one son, John Reuben Ratliff and died Apr. 5, 1879. John Reuben Ratliff died in Oct. 1879. According to the Mortality Schedule of 1880 in Prentiss County, MS Missouri died of "heart edema" at the age of 20. Her son was listed on the same mortality schedule as having died of "stomach trouble." Reuben Belew died Nov. 7, 1879 and according to the same mortality schedule, the cause of his death was "dropsy." I consulted with Dr. Thomas Recht and his theory is that the deaths of Missouri and Reuben Belew was the result of a strep infection that had damaged their hearts, possibly with Missouri's condition being worsened by the strains of childbirth. There were no antibiotics in those days, so little could be done to combat strep infections. J.M. Ratliff died Feb. 18, 1883, at the age of 30 years, 2 months and 3 days. He is buried in Pleasant Grove Cemetery, Decatur, TX.

William D. Belew, the son of John Wesley Belew, married Mary (Mollie) Merritt in December 1887 in Aurora, TX. They had eight children: May Belew md. Will Willis, Henry Belew md. Elizabeth Alexander, Frank Belew, Lena Belew md. J.Q. Cox Sr., Eula May Belew md. Wright, Reuben Belew md. Clara Patterson, William T. Belew md. Edith Patterson, Vaughn Belew md. Bertha, William D. Belew died Mar. 14, 1953 in Boyd, TX and his wife, Mary died Dec. 4, 1942 in Bowie, TX.

The first Renny Belew held land in South Carolina due to a Royal Land Grant from George III. The Belews were Baptists and lived and attended church near and in the Fairforest area and the Fairforest Baptist Church in South Carolina. It is currently believed that Reuben Belew's father was Jesse Belew, the eighth child of Renny Belew. More research needs to be done for proof. When the families moved to Tennessee and then to Mississippi it was done by wagon train, without roads and with great difficulty and hardship. The foregoing information was collected from verbal family history, National Archives, Chancery Court records, Census records, mortality schedules, correspondence with other descendants and Bible and cemetery records. There seemed to be certain sorrows in their lives and I hope there were joys as well. I have spent so much time with the records that I feel I know them. I think that I probably know more about them than anyone else now living. *Written by Margene Shuler Recht, January 1996, Wailea, Maui, HI*

BENNETT, WILLIAM CHRISTOPHER ANDERSON,

born Jan. 16, 1856 in Belmont, MS died Jun. 17, 1930. He was a farmer by trade and raised his own tobacco, which he smoked in a corncob pipe. Lucinda Jane Hallmark was born Feb. 29, 1856 in Golden, MS died Jul. 30, 1941. They are buried in Friendship Cemetery in Tishomingo County, MS. The date of their wedding is not known. From this union, six children were born:

William Christopher Anderson Bennett and Lucinda Jane Hallmark Bennett

Martha Caroline "Mattie" Bennett (b. Nov. 17, 1874, d. Apr. 4, 1932) married Manley Wilemon and they had three children: Columbus, Dewey and Claudia. Mattie's second husband was William James Denson. Columbus md. to Gertrude Chism and they had seven children: Manley, Myrtle, Luna Mae, Syble, Ellis, Fay and May Belle. Dewey md. to Maggie Brumley and they had 10 children: Cecil, Flavious, Clyde, Aline, Elton, Maxine, Kenneth, Donald, Ronald, Paul and Jean. Claudia (Tincie) md. to Arnie Stanley and they had three children: Estelle, Louise and Edsel.

James Fletcher Bennett (b. Sep. 16, 1877, d. Jan. 24, 1953) md. Mary Frances Gann Jan. 2, 1895 and they had five children: Lucy Belle, Ethel Lee, Carrie Elizabeth, Willie Clifton and Rufus. Lucy md. to Luther Franks and they had five children: Dillard, Vernon, Helen, Syble and Marvin. Ethel md. to Quitman Baxter and they had seven children: Iva Gale, Beatrice, Wyna, Mary Kate, Charles, Jimmy and Maxine. Carrie was first married to John Baxter and they had six children: Clovis, Hershel, Edith, John Jr., Bob and Kathleen. Her second husband was Jesse Carpenter and they had one daughter, Geraldine. Willie Clifton was first married to Myrle Harp and they had five children: Surue, Avanell, Lee, Clyde and Nellie. His second wife was Marie Ryan. Rufus md. to Lloyd Gahagan and they had five children: Mary Effie, Imogene, Juanita, Charlene and Jimmy Earl.

George Washington Bennett md. to Lura Ellen Denson and had 10 children: two sons died in infancy, Clarence, Carlton, Cornelia, Evie, Marie, Allie, Dewdrop and Harold. Clarence first married to Cleo Stepp and had one son, Gerald. Carlton married Mae Crouch and had one daughter, Linda. (Clarence's second wife was Magdalene Bishop.) Cornelia md. Bernard VanDevander and had one daughter, Jewel. Evie md. Noah Bowen and had two children, Marion and Erlene. Marie md. Walter Odom and had one son, Milford. Allie md. Marshall Shields and had one son, Tommy. Dewdrop md. Ozele Shields and had two children, Jesse K. and Peggy. Harold was not married.

Ida Eveline Bennett (b. Jul. 22, 1890, d. Nov. 4, 1962) md. George Washington Denson and had 10 children: two daughters and one son (Jewel, Dimple and George) died in infancy, Zinnie Mae, Violet, R.C., Travis, Audie, Arthur and Fay Virginia. Zinnie Mae first married Clint Horn and they had two sons, Clyde and Harley. Her second husband was Roy Moreland. Violet md. Dorsey Sanders and had four children: Shirley (died in infancy), Ruby Mae, Alta and Buddy. R.C. md. Ruby Estes and had two children, George and Jane. Travis md. Sylvia Gann and had three children: baby that died in infancy, Bobby Travis and Anita. Audie md. Ruby Nichols and had two daughters, Dana and Renee. Arthur md. Jean Wroten and had two children, Mackie and Donna. Fay md. Bobby Owens and had three children: Ray, Ann and Charles.

Annie Lee Bennett (b. May 13, 1896, d. Feb. 24, 1974) md. Albert Erastus Denson and had five children: Ottis, Syble, Maxine, Arlis and Nolan. Ottis md. Reath Moore and had three children: Harold, Sonya and Jerry. Syble md. M.J. "Duke" Lee and had two children, James and Donna. Maxine md. Bill Bradick and had five children: Bill Jr., Dennis, Wanda, Vicki and Brenda. Arlis md. June Wigginton and had one daughter, Diane. Nolan md. Ruby Hall and had four children: Perry Lee (died in infancy), Gerald, Tim and Pam.

Flora Belle Bennett (b. Oct. 8, 1900, d. Jun. 25, 1983) md. John Dewey Denson and had four daughters: Ann Jewel, Ruth, Lorene and Pauline "Polly". Jewel first married Wilbur McFerrin and had three children: Johnny, Linda Ann and Joey. Her second husband was Roy Faulkner. Ruth md. Norris Robertson and had seven children: Norris Jr., Ross, Dan, Ellen, Patricia, Jane and Kathy. Lorene md. John Wax and had three sons: John, Charles and Terry. Polly md. John Norton and had three children: Jim, Fay and Ricky. *Submitted by Lorene Denson Wax.*

BIRMINGHAM, RUBEN,

in 1860 he and his wife Charity lived in Putnam County, TN with their five children: Ephraim R., Sarah J., John J., George W. and William C. Both Ruben and wife Charity, whose maiden name was Roberson, were originally from North Carolina. Ruben was a farmer. There may have been other children from this union.

John and Sarah Birmingham and eight of their 10 children ca. 1905

John J. Birmingham later married Polly Picketts and they had at least six children: sons Sam, John, Robert and Ed, daughters Lenny Lee and Bessy (do not have details about this marriage and the children). John met his second wife in Prentiss County, a young Sarah Elizabeth Borden, whom he married Feb. 25, 1889. There were 10 children from this union: sons George Washington, R. Emily and William Charles; daughters Linnie Ann, Mary Lizzie, May Bell, Elzie, Verna, Johnnie Modeanie and Lois.

One son of John and Sarah Birmingham, George Washington, later married Mollie Bettie Lee and had 10 children. Their sons Garlan and Billy Ray died at a young age, Eulice Warren died in France during WWII, Avis Melvin, J.B. and George Lee. The daughters of George and Bettie were Leinas who died at a very young age, Eula Irene, Carrie Christine and Bettie Ree.

The other children of John and Sarah Birmingham married as follows: R. Emily md. Eva Strickland, William Charles md. Sybil Burcham, Linnie Ann md. Sam Flannagan, Mary Lizzie md. William Monroe Runions, May Bell md. James Runions, Elzie md. Jesse Jones.

George and Bettie Brimingham's children married as follows: Eulice Warren md. Dorothy Cooksey, J.B. md. Zelma Rinehart, Avis Melvin md. Mildred Maness, George Lee md. Clara Sue Floyd, Eula Irene md. Marvin Owens, Carrie Christine md. Harmon Massengill, Bettie Ree md. Lewis Cleveland.

There is much uncertainty about the two last name spellings, of which one is Birmingham and the other is Brimingham. Nonetheless, these two names are the same family line and many descendants still reside in Prentiss County.

BISHOP, LEONARD BENJIMON "BEN,"

born Jan. 1, 1899 in Atwood, AL and died Jan. 8, 1980, son of Margret L. McCarley (b. May 4, 1868, d. 1936) and Dillard G. Bishop (b. Aug. 30, 1864, d. 1936). Ben had four brothers and one sister. He was a farmer and blocksetter at sawmills. He came to Mississippi in 1917 to the Bay Springs area and married Verna May Willis (b. Oct. 11, 1905, d. Jan. 29, 1984) on May 18, 1918. Verna was born in the Piney Grove community of Prentiss County to Luna Howell (b. Jan. 23 1885, d. Jun. 11, 1913) and Dave Willis (b. Feb. 11, 1870, b. Nov. 15, 1921). Verna had two brothers and one sister who died in infancy. Verna was a housewife and operated a country store for over 30 years. In 1944 Ben purchased his own farm and lived there the rest of his life. Ben and Verna were married 62 years and to their union were born three boys and one girl, listed below in order of birth.

From left: Verna May Bishop (age 22), Horace Ernie Bishop (age 5), L.B. Bishop Jr. (age 2) and Cecil Troy Bishop (age 28). Picture was taken just before Christmas 1927.

Cecil Troy Bishop (b. May 7, 1920) married Magdalene Spencer October 1941. On Nov. 4, 1942 he entered the Army and Dec. 10, 1942, his son, Charles Lucian Bishop, was born. Charles Lucian died in 1981. Cecil Troy Bishop served in Europe, Northern Ireland and France from 1943 to 1944. He was wounded Jul. 9, 1944 and was killed in action Sep. 17, 1944; he died for his country.

Horace Ernie Bishop (b. Jul. 11, 1922) entered the Army Nov. 4, 1942 and served in Europe, England, France, Belgium, Holland and Germany. He was discharged January 1946 and on Nov. 23, 1946 he married Mayme Frances Nesler (b. Jan. 29, 1923, d. Jul. 16, 1993). Horace and Mayme had one son, David Ray Bishop (b. Sep. 8, 1947) who resides in Booneville.

Dorothy Maverine Bishop

L. B. Bishop Jr. (b. Sep. 24, 1925, d. Feb. 6, 1982) entered the Navy in September 1943 and served on a destroyer in the South Pacific. He was discharged in June 1946 and married Vernice Tennison Dec. 21, 1946. They had one son, Sammie (b. Jul. 27, 1947, d. Jul. 28, 1947) and two daughters, Kathy (b. Apr. 18, 1952) married Ben Gelton and Judy (b. Apr. 30, 1957). Vernice and Judy reside in Booneville.

Dorothy Maverine Bishop (b. Jul. 30, 1929) married Prentiss Grimes (b. Jul. 16, 1918, d. Jul. 1, 1985) Dec. 8, 1945. She was employed at Blue Bell Manufacturing in Tishomingo from 1954 until they closed. She had two children, a son, Phillip (b. Dec. 11, 1950, d. Mar. 20, 1952) and a daughter, Deborah (b. Aug. 20, 1952). In April 1976, Deborah married Tommy Walker. Dorothy lives in Mt. Nebo Community. *Submitted by Horace E. Bishop, 110 Bishop Street, Booneville, MS 38829. (662) 728-6638.*

BOGGS, ASBERY WASHINGTON, born Apr. 25, 1851 in Tuscumbia, Franklin County, AL and died 1890. He is buried in Strickland Cemetery, northeast of Red Bay, AL. He married Amanda Melvina Weatherbee (b. Oct. 3, 1857 in Alanthus, Franklin County, AL) in 1874 in Alanthus, Franklin County, AL. After Asbery died, Amanda married John Hammond Shell. Amanda and John are buried in Osborne Creek Cemetery on old Highway 45, seven miles south of Booneville, Prentiss County, MS.

Top row: Frank Corbitt, Addison Wesley Boggs, Delbert Corbitt and R.C. Boggs. Front row: Eddie Boggs, Bill Boggs, Earl Boggs (on Bill's knee), Walter Boggs and Frankie Corbitt.

Amanda and Asbery were the parents of six children, all born in Franklin County, AL. The 1900 census shows all the children of Asbery and Amanda living in Prentiss County, MS near Booneville.

Addison Wesley Boggs, the first child, (b. Nov. 3, 1875, d. Oct. 5, 1940) married Louetta Jane Crabb Sep. 2, 1894 in Prentiss County, MS. Louetta died Aug. 17, 1941. Both are buried in O.M. Cemetery, north of Hollis, Harmon County, OK. Louetta was the daughter of Annias Norris Huston Crabb and Sarah Elizabeth Johnson Crabb of Prentiss County, MS.

Addison and Louetta had 13 children. The first, fifth and sixth were still born.

The second child, Benjamin Walter Boggs (b. Dec. 5, 1898, d. Mar. 29, 1971) married Eva Ola Hefner.

The third child, Elizabeth Melvinia Boggs (b. Apr. 19, 1900, d. Aug. 15, 1980) married Richard Fletcher Perry of Corinth, Alcorn County, MS.

The fourth child, Mary Florence Boggs (b. Oct. 4, 1902, d. Nov. 17, 1979) first married Boyce Pringle and second married John Pinky Moldenhauer.

The seventh child, Hubert Lyie Hugh Jefferson Boggs (b.n May 15, 1907, d. Feb. 18, 1958) first married Lorene Hudson and second married Lois Mamie Foster.

The eighth child, William Shelton Boggs (b. Jun. 8, 1909, d. Apr. 14, 1978) md. Melba Lorene Ward.

The ninth child, R.C. Boggs (b. May 2, 1911, d. May 15, 1968) md. Laura Estell Corbitt.

The 10th child, Edna Mae Boggs (b. Jul. 18, 1913, d. Feb. 14, 1970) md. James Floyd Wilhite.

The 11th child, Elsie Vista Boggs (b. Dec. 23, 1915, d. Nov. 26, 1991) md. Delbert Franklin Corbitt.

The 12th child, Annie Lavada Boggs (b. Dec. 11, 1917) first married George Fredrick Burns and then married Jodie Lee Adams.

The 13th child, Claudia Lulu Boggs (b. May 13, 1920, d. May 11, 1972) married Don Leon (Moore) Austin first, married James Erin Miller second and married Raymond Brandenberg third.

Asbery Washington Boggs' father, Kinchen Boggs (b. Nov. 5, 1810) married Mary KcKinnis Feb. 23, 1829 in Morgan County, AL. Kinchen's parents were Samuel Oliver Boggs (b. 1763 near Savannah, GA) and Mary "Pooly" Kent. They married Dec. 12, 1795. It is believed, but not yet proven, that Samuel's father was Joseph Boggs and that he came from Ireland prior to the Revolutionary War. The first available information shows him living near Savannah, GA and a captain in the Continental Army. *Submitted by Earl Boggs.*

BOLEY, GEORGE LEWIS, born Oct. 24, 1792 in South Carolina, was probably the son of John and Mary (Lewis) Boley of Spartanburg, SC. He married Aug. 7, 1816 in Madison County, Mississippi Territory, AL Winnie Robertson (b. Apr. 10, 1801 in North Carolina) (See Robertson). George died Apr. 10, 1845 and Winnie died Jun. 28, 1845, both in Lawrence County, AL. Their oldest son, John Edward (b. 1818, d. 1868), married in 1841 Sarah Manervy Sutton and remained in Lawrence County; some descendants settled in Parker County, TX.

Their remaining children, listed below, born in Alabama, were living in homes of Robertson/Donaldson relatives in Old Tishomingo County, MS later.

On the 1850 Census, James Robertson Boley (b. Sep. 22, 1821, d. after 1900) was listed as a brick mason living in the household of uncle, James H. Robertson in Tishomingo County, MS. He married Dec. 21, 1858 Minervia E. Bell (b. 1838 in Tennessee). Their children were Piney and James Washington (b. 1849, d. 1924). James R. served in Co. B, Commander Thomas Ham, CSA and filed for a pension in 1900. In 1880, he served as delegate for Meadow Creek Baptist Church. Some descendants live in Wise County, TX.

Hiram Carl Boley (b. 1825) farmer, married Mar. 14, 1848 in Tishomingo County, MS Elinder Jane Wilson (b. 1825 in Tennessee, d. after 1855). Their children born in Mississippi: Mary L. (b. 1850), James Washington (b. 1852), Sarah Margaret (b. 1854) (See Payne History) and Francis Adeline (b. 1856). On the 1850 Census, the family was living next door to Hiram's aunt, Berlina Robertson Alexander. Hiram married second on Oct. 21, 1858 in Tishomingo County, MS Catherine H. Hartsfield (b. 1838 in Tennessee), daughter of Jacob and Hannah C. (Spain) Hartsfield. They had a daughter, Harriet (b. 1859 in Mississippi). Apparently before 1869 Hiram and possibly Catherine died, as Uncle L.L. Brown is appointed guardian for three of the children. By 1880, James W., Sarah and Francis are living together near relatives in Wise County, TX.

Martha M. Boley (b. 1828) married Nov. 25, 1847 in Tishomingo County, MS Calvin K. Donaldson (See Donaldson Family).

Sarah Berline Boley (b. Apr. 19, 1830) married Dec. 27, 1949 in Tishomingo County, MS Tully Francis Parker (b. 1824 in South Carolina). Their children: Myra Lenora (b. 1850), Mary Berline (b. 1848) and Louisa Frances (b. Jun. 14, 1854). Sarah Berline died Apr. 17, 1858 in Mississippi. T.F. Parker served the CSA. In 1870 he was the pastor of Meadow Creek Baptist Church. He remarried and the family moved in 1873 to Grayson County, TX later Wise County, TX.

Louise C. Boley (b. Mar. 8, 1832) married Aug. 17, 1850 in Tishomingo County, MS Lawrence Lee Brown (b. Apr. 23, 1825 in Alabama). On the 1850 Census, newlyweds of two months are living with her uncle, James H. Robertson. Lawrence was listed as a merchant and had business dealings with James H. Robertson. Their children: Henry (b. Sep. 4, 1851), Louisa O. (b. 1854), Alice (b. 1858), Lawrence Lee Jr. (b. Jun. 15, 1859), Mary M. (b. 1862), George W. (b. Sep. 13, 1864), William F. (b. Oct. 20, 1868) and Dollie A.V. (b. Sep. 15, 1870). Louise died Mar. 29, 1900; Lawrence died Sep. 25, 1902, both, along with several children, are buried in Booneville Cemetery.

Eliza Jane Boley (b. 1836) married Jun. 3, 1858 in Tishomingo County, MS David L. Pritchard (b. 1831 in Tennessee). Their children: Winnie E. (b. 1859 in Mississippi), David Lafayette (b. 1863) and Mary Clemmie. On the 1850 Census, Eliza Jane, age 14, is living with sister, Martha Donaldson. David, a farmer, served the CSA, became ill and died the way home ca. 1865. He is buried in Atlanta, GA. Eliza Jane died in 1869 in Mississippi.

Susan Boley (b. 1839) married Oct. 10, 1860 in Tishomingo County, MS Uriah Russell Sherrill (b. 1837 in Tennessee). They had a daughter, Mintie. On the 1850 and 1860 Censuses, Susan, age 11 and 21, living with sister, Martha Donaldson; Martha and C.K. Donaldson give "consent" for her marriage to U.R. Sherrill. *Submitted by Paige P. Essary.*

BONDS, JAMES W., son of Wright Walker Bonds Jr. and Sarah Jane Nicholson, married Mary A. Ledbetter, daughter of Banks Ledbetter and Charity Denson on Jan. 5, 1857.

Banks Ledbetter was elected for one term as Tishomingo County Coroner in 1839. He died about 1847 in Tishomingo County. He was the son of James Ledbetter (b. ca. 1775 in Georgia, d. in Putnam County, GA in 1829) and Sarah Camp (b. Dec. 1, 1782, Amhurst County, VA, d. ca. 1840 in Putnam County, GA).

Sarah Camp was the daughter of Samuel Camp (b. 1752 in Durham, CT, d. 1827 in Warren County, GA) and Mary Banks (b. 1753 in Culpepper County, VA, d. 1800 in Warren County, GA). Samuel Camp was the son of Reverend Ichabod Camp (b. 1726 at Durham, CT, d. 1786 in Kaskaskia, IL) and Content Ward (b. 1727, d. 1754 in Middleton, CT). Ichabod Camp was the son of John Camp (b. 1686, d. 1767) and Phoebe Canfield (b. 1687, d. 1774) of Milford, CT. John Camp was the son of Edward Camp II (b. 1650, d. 1721) of New Haven and Milford, CT and Mehitable Smith (b. 1655 in Milford, CT).

Charity Denson was the daughter of Calley Denson (b. ca. 1785 in North Carolina) and Elizabeth Watkins. Elizabeth and Calley were married in Hancock County, GA. Callie died in 1845 in Benton County, AL. Calley probably married a cousin, since his parents were Joseph Denson and Mary Watkins. Joseph and Mary were married in Edgecomb County, NC. Joseph's parents were Benjamin Denson and Mary Whitehead. Putnam County, GA Will Book A, p. 165-166, shows "John Watkins will, wife Charity. Daughters: Polly Strasterland, Elizabeth Denson and Sally Thompson, appointed son-in-law, Calley Denson, executor and wife, Charity W., also. Dated Oct. 6, 1819, proven Mar 26, 1823."

Mary A. Ledbetter Bonds was left a widow when James W. Bonds was killed on Jul. 1, 1863 on the first day of the three day Battle of Gettysburg, after serving the Confederacy for one year, four months and 19 days. They had two sons, James Andrew and Wright Walker. James married Molly Pierce and became the first mayor of Mantachie, MS and later a merchant in Baldwyn, MS. His home in Mantachie, built in 1885, still stands and is now a museum. He and Molly had a daughter, Troy, who married a building contractor, Luther McDonald and a son, Carlton, who was a cotton buyer.

Wright Walker Bonds married Sarah "Josie" Holley and had eight children: Louvenia "Venie" married Charlie McCreary, Tennie married George Washington Scott, Effie married Charles F. Swain,

Mollie married Tom Brown, Luther married (first) Georgia Smith and (second) Etha Parker, Roy Festus married Nellie Smith, Maggie married Jesse Sparks and James Ray married Vera Swinney. *Submitted by Bernice Bonds Janeway.*

BONDS, LUTHER CURTIS, son of Wright Walker Bonds and Sally Josie Holley, was born in Prentiss County and married Georgia Smith, daughter of Jack and Annie Wroten Smith. To them were born, Maedell who married Milford Holder at age 55; Sibyl who married Oneal Brown and had one son, Jackie Neal and Louise who married Floyd Roy and had William Curtis, James Floyd and Johnny. A son was stillborn to Luther and Georgia and Georgia took pneumonia and died. Mother and baby were buried together.

Luther then married Etha Parker, a school teacher who came down from Alcorn County to teach at old Walden School, a two-teacher school. To Luther and Etha was born a daughter, Bernice, who married Raymond Janeway. They had four daughters: Olivia, Gale, Claudia and Pamela.

Etha was born in Tennessee to Octavious and Emma Daniels Parker. She had three brothers: Will, who taught school at Kossuth and Farmington and married Clyde Hubbard, a school teacher from Iuka and had one daughter, Lorraine; Abe married Vallie Wilson from Union City, TN and migrated to Montana and on to California, where at his death he was the top GM dealer in the state. He was very active in civic affairs. He and Vallie had two daughters, Geraldine and Beverly and Clyde who joined the Marines in WWI. Stationed in Great Falls, MT, he met and married Dora Johnson. To them were born Phillip "Bud," Shirley, Tavy and Allan. Clyde and Dora moved to Hamilton, MT and raised their family. They owned a service station business.

In later years, Aunt Dora was live-in companion to Edna Morrison who was sister to the Morrison of Morrison-Knutson Construction Co. that built Hoover Dam with horses and ground slides to move dirt. This company also helped build the Tenn-Tom Waterway. They have a huge office building in San Antonio, TX.

Octavious and Emma had two daughters, Fannie, who married Tom Driskell and had a son, Noel and a daughter, Vera. The already mentioned Etha married Luther Bonds. When Etha was born, Fannie begged her mother to give her that baby, which she did. All her life she loved and cared for Etha like she was her own. I always liked for Aunt Fannie to visit us because then I didn't have to wash dishes or churn. *Submitted by Bernice Bonds Janeway.*

BONDS, WRIGHT W. SR., born about 1776 in South Carolina. It is believed that he was the son of John Bonds Sr. who was a member of the North Carolina House of Commons from 1785 to 1790 and Lucretia Nicholson, whose father, Edward Nicholson was also a member of the North Carolina House of Commons from 1780 to 1782. Wright married Priscilla Eley (believed to have been born about 1803 in South Carolina), the daughter of Josiah Eley and Charity Denby, the daughter of James Denby and Patience Norfleet. When Josiah Eley's will was probated in 1803, the family was residing in Franklin County, NC.

The children of Wright Bonds and Priscilla Eley were: Elizabeth, John Eley (b. 1803), Greenberry (b. 1805), Sarah (b. 1813), William C. (b. 1815), Wright Jr. (b. 1817 in Tennessee), Robert E. (b. 1822) married Julia Canfield, Lemuel P. (b. 1824) married Sarah Scruggs and Michael (b. 1825 in Alabama).

Josiah Eley (b. ca. 1740 in Isle of Wight County, VA) moved before 1772 to Bute County, NC. His will which was dated Sep. 24, 1803 and probated in December 1803, shows that he was an extensive land owner with many slaves.

Priscilla Eley and her father, Josiah were descendants of Robert Eley, who was also the ancestor of President Lyndon Baines Johnson.

The first Eley on record in Isle of Wight county, VA is the Robert Eley who probably came over in the *Primrose* which sailed from Gravesend, England bound for Virginia Jul. 27, 1635. His name is indexed in "Hotten's Emigrants" page 259, as Robert Eelie. Robert Eley on Sep. 17, 1639 patented 600 acres in Isle of Wight County, VA due for his own personal adventure and the transportation of 11 other persons.

Robert Eley, born Feb. 28, 1609 in Covenham, St. Bartholomew, Lincoln County, England. Robert and one of his brothers, Richard came from England to America and settled in Virginia. Succeeding generations used the same given names creating confusion. To correct this, Richard's sons decided to drop the second "e" in their surname and began to spell their name Ely. Robert's four sons retained the "e."

One of the sons of Wright and Priscilla Eley Bonds, Wright Bonds Jr. married Sarah Jane Nicholson who was probably a cousin. Wright Sr. served under Maj. Gen. Andrew Jackson on an expedition against the Creek Indians in 1814. It was probably during this service that he first saw North Alabama and Mississippi Territory. He moved to Tishomingo County, MS sometime prior to 1837 when his name first appears in county records. His name is sprinkled throughout the history of old Tishomingo County. Wright Bonds was one of the committee of four elected to vote on secession, on the condition that all the southern states secede together. When all the other delegates voted to secede, the Tishomingo county delegates also voted to secede. He was listed as one of the last officials to hold office before the Civil War. His signature is also on the list of volunteer soldiers who signed up at Jacinto along with that of his son, James W. Bonds. Wright bonds died Aug. 20, 1862. His son James was killed Jul. 1, 1863 on the first day of the three-day Battle of Gettysburg when Co. A, 2nd Mississippi was entrenched in the railroad cut and sustained heavy fire from the 6th Wisconsin.

Wright Bonds Jr. and Sarah Nicholson had eight children: James W., Mary, Francis, Susan, Elizabeth, Sarah, David and Felix Alfred.

James W. Bonds was 24 years old when he died so far from home, leaving a widow with two young boys, James Andrew and Wright Walker III. James Andrew Bonds later became the first mayor of Mantachie, MS. His home in Mantachie, the "Bonds House," is now a museum.

Wright Walker Bonds III married Sarah Josephine "Josie" Nancy Elizabeth Holley. Their children were Louvenia "Venie" Bonds McCreary, Tennie Bonds Scott, Effie Bonds Swain, Mollie Bonds Brown, Luther Curtis, Roy Festus, Maggie McKinley Bonds Sparks and James Ray. *Submitted by Ann Sparks. Sources: Maureen Holley Crow, Mary Sumners and Loren Bonds, descendant of Greenberry Bonds, brother of Wright W. Bonds Jr.*

BRACKEEN, CARLIE & BESSIE, Carlie Wilburn Brackeen (b. Feb. 9, 1903), son of Josiah

Bonds Reunion, 1930. L-R, front row: Mae Effie Furtick, visitor(?); Linus Scott, Josie Lee McCreary, Tommye Brown, Sara and R.J. "Piggy" Bonds, Eileen McCreary, Benebba Scott, John Sparks, Bernice Bonds. Second row: Roy Bonds, Nellie Smith Bonds, Uncle Ceph Holley, Josie Holley Bonds, Louvenia "Venie" Bonds McCreary, Tennie Bonds Scott, Mollie Bonds Brown, Maggie McKinley Bonds Sparks. Third row: Troy Scott, Luther Bonds, Etha Bonds, Ray Bonds, Vera Bonds, Effie Bonds, James West, Mauveline West, Charles McCreary, George Scott, Myrum McCreary, Lona McCreary, Tom Brown, Jesse Sparks. Fourth row: Lester McCreary, Weiland Brown. Fifth row: Newspaper man (visitor) Tapscott (?), Oma Holley, Dewey Holley, Syble bonds, Maedell Bonds, Esta Lou McCreary Scott, Forrest Sparks, Odell Brown, Ione Brown, Nona Faye Sparks, Lloyd Scott, Troy Scott, Louise Bonds. Photographer was Jetty Nunley, a Booneville "institution" for decades.

Young and Fannie Patrick Smith Brackeen of Booneville. He did not attend school until after age 17. Wanting an education, he went to the high school and asked the principal if he could enroll. It was decided to let him try ninth grade. Carlie asked if he could work as janitor and live at the school. He would arise early to fire the furnace, so the school would be warm when the students arrived. After graduating from Booneville High School in 1926, he worked a year before claiming his bride, Bessie Lou Williams, the daughter of William Austin and Alma Finch Williams. The wedding took place in Booneville Jul. 3, 1927. His ambition for college led him to all kinds of jobs to make the dream a reality. Bessie worked for her Uncle Curtis Williams, the Circuit Clerk. In May 1930, their first son, Billie Edward, was born at the home of his grandparents, William Austin and Alma Williams (where the bank is located on Lake Street at Highway 30). In the fall of 1931, the family left Booneville for Oxford. The next three years, they lived on the Ole Miss Campus in a cottage that the University built for married couples. Carlie again used his determination and energy to make his dream a reality. He painted for the University, kept the golf course, worked on weekends in an Oxford men's store and bought a cow to sell milk to other couples, as well as provide for his own family. Bessie canned vegetables from the garden beside the cottage. In July 1932, their second son, Travis Wilburn, was born. When Carlie was in class, Bessie would keep the golf shop. Once she baby-sat William Faulkner's daughter while William and Carlie golfed.

Carlie and Bessie Brackeen 1930

In 1933, Carlie graduated from Ole Miss with a BA in Education. For the next year, he did work for his MS degree. Then, he and his family returned to Prentiss County where he accepted the job as principle of Burton School. Later he became principle of Gift School in Glen in Alcorn County. In June 1937, their third and last child, a daughter, Wanda Lou, was born in the same home in Booneville where her older brother was born. The state of Mississippi was having a hard time paying its teachers, so Carlie decided to go into business to support his family.

The family moved to Iuka where Carlie opened the Iuka Cash Grocery and Feed Store. In 1948 he built Iuka Cash and Carry on Highway 25 South. He and Bessie raised their three children in their home next to the store (across from present courthouse). In 1963 they founded the Tishomingo County Memorial Garden by donating land for its use. Both are buried there. Carlie died in 1966 and Bessie died in 1998. They had seven grandchildren and when Bessie died, there were five great-grandchildren. *Submitted by Melody Yelverton Hanson.*

BRACKEEN, JOSIAH YOUNG, son of John Pryor and Sarah Priscilla Short Brackeen was born Aug. 22, 1875 in Wheeler, Prentiss County, MS. Josiah was named for his two grandfathers. His two sets of grandparents were Josiah R. Brackeen and Sallie Bullard Brackeen, the daughter of Benjamin Bullard, who was a justice of the peace of old Tishomingo County, MS and Young and Roda Barber (Barker) Short. Josiah married his boss's daughter, Fannie Patrick Smith (b. Sep. 30, 1872) Jan. 2, 1896, the daughter of Vincent Allen Thorp and Elender Susanna Patrick Smith of the New Hope Community. Her grandparents were Moses and Elizabeth Tharp Smith and Lewellyn and Demsey Abney Patrick. All of their grandparents were some of the earliest settlers of the county. Josiah had driven the boss's daughter in a buggy to and from the school where she taught. Before their marriage, Fannie applied for the job as postmaster using her name, Patrick Smith. She got the job and kept it, until it was learned that she was a female. After their marriage, Joe S. (as he was known) became a farmer. The first of the seven children, a son, Claude Pryor, was born in late 1896. Then a second son, Willie Price, was born in 1899. Lula Trice was the first daughter and was born in 1901. Then in 1903 twins, Carlie Wilburn and Carrie Wilord, were born. Three years later, Eula Tommie was born. In 1908 Fannie became pregnant with the last child, a son. In the last trimester of her pregnancy, Fannie was helping a neighbor, who was ill and contracted measles. Both she and the baby died at childbirth. They are buried in New Hope Cemetery.

The Josiah Young Brackeen Family 1908. From left: Lula, Price, Tommie, Josiah, Pryor, Fannie and twins, Carlie and Carrie

Josiah married Victoria Ingram, daughter of John Eliaha and Mary Jane Ingram and their first child was James Roger (b. 1910). William Scott joined the family in 1912. Their only daughter (b. 1916) was named Virginia Priscilla. The youngest son, Luther Woodrow, was born in 1919. In the winter of 1920, Victoria died.

Four years later, Joe S. married Frances Elizabeth Smith Nichols, daughter of William Rush and Mary Jane Smith (not related to the first Fannie Smith). Josiah's second set of twins, Frances Irene and Joseph Eugene, were born in 1924. Smith Junior was born in 1926. The youngest of the living 14 children was Ethel Marie, born in 1927.

During all the years of raising his family, Joe S. not only farmed, but he also carried mail on horseback to Cherokee, AL, ran a hamburger stand on the corner next to the courthouse and also had a little store out front of his home on Highway 30. In 1954 Josiah suffered a heart attack and died in the hospital a short time later. At his death, he had 59 grandchildren. He was buried in New Hope Cemetery next to Fannie Patrick Smith Brackeen and baby son. *Submitted by Wanda Yelverton.*

BRIMINGHAM, TERRIE, daughter of Gene and Sue Green Brimingham, married Yancey Davis of Hamilton, AL. She and Yancey attended Freed-Hardeman University and the University of Alabama. Terrie received a BS degree in computer science and business education from the, University of North Alabama.

Yancey received a BS degree in industrial management from the University of Alabama. He is employed by NTN Bower Co. in Hamilton, AL. Terrie is employed by the Mission Office at the Hamilton Church of Christ. They reside in Hamilton, AL. *Submitted by Zelma Brimingham.*

Yancey and Terrie Brimingham Davis, daughter of Gene and Sue Green Brimingham. Gene is the son of J.B. and Zelma Rinehart Brimingham

BRIMINGHAM, TIMOTHY JASON, a dynamic young man who was a 1995 graduate of Tishomingo County High School. He was a student of Northeast Mississippi Community College with plans to further his education at Freed-Hardeman University in the field of civil engineering.

He was a member of the Mississippi National Guard. While in high school, he was known for his participation on the TCHS football and basketball teams, his friendly personality and leadership abilities. He died at the age of 19 with a brain aneurysm.

Tim Brimingham, son of Gene and Sue Green Brimingham

After his death, a scholarship fund was established in his name. An access street on campus at Tishomingo County High School was named "Brimingham Boulevard" in his honor. Tim's parents are Gene and Sue Green Brimingham of Snowdown Community. *Submitted by Jo Ann Rinehart Sorrell and Sue Green Brimingham.*

BRIMINGHAM, TONY, a graduate of New Site High School in Prentiss County, received a BS degree in physical science from Freed-Hardeman University and a BS degree in civil engineering from Mississippi State University.

In 1994 he married Jana Dillinger Brimingham, who is originally from Indianapolis, IN. She received a BS degree in exercise from Freed-Hardeman University and a master of science degree in exercise science from Mississippi State University. Tony and Jana did live in Hamilton, AL. Tony was employed at NTN Bower Co. in Hamilton and Jana was employed as Director of Winfield Wellness Center in Winfield, AL. Tony served as youth minister of Hamilton Church of Christ.

Recently they moved to Birmingham, AL and are employed there. He is the son of Gene and Sue Green Brimingham of Snowdown Community. *Submitted by Sue Green Brimingham.*

Tony Brimingham, son of Gene and Sue Green Brimingham and his wife, Jana Dillinger

BRIMINGHAM, WARREN "GENE," son of Zelma and J.B. Brimingham, was born Oct. 22, 1948 at Community Hospital, Corinth, MS. He married Nedra Sue Green. They have two living children: Tony, of Birmingham, AL and Terrie Brimingham Davis of Hamilton, AL. Their son Tim died in June 1996 from a brain aneurysm at the age of 19. Gene is employed at Parker Hannifin in Booneville, MS. He was ordained a minister of the Primitive Baptist Church at Sardis, near Rienzi, Feb. 4, 1995. He pastors Mackey's Creek Church in Prentiss County.

Tim Brimingham, Gene Brimingham, Sue Brimingham, Terrie Brimingham Davis, Yancey Davis, Sharon Brimingham Elmore, Tony Brimingham. In front is Tony's wife, Jana Dillinger Brimingham, Jeffery Elmore and April Elmore, children of Ricky and Sharon Elmore and Zelma Brimingham

Sue is a beautician and owns her shop in Snowdown Community. She also worked as a paraprofessional in the exceptional education department at Hills Chapel School in Prentiss County for a number of years. She and Gene live in Snowdown Community and she is a member of the Snowdown Church of Christ. *Submitted by Terrie Brimingham.*

BRIMINGHAM, ZELMA RINEHART, born Aug. 1, 1928, to Clifford Palmer and Vista Armstrong Rinehart. The family lived in Hickory Flat Community in Alcorn County near Clifford's family, T.W. and Nettie Palmer Rinehart. They later moved to Jacinto about 1935.

Zelma attended Juliette, Jacinto and Rienzi schools. She married J.B. Brimingham Dec. 24, 1947 at the home of her cousin, Brother Cleveland Rinehart and his wife, Vickie. Witnesses were his son, Clifford and wife Evelyn. J.B.'s parents were George W. and Bettie Lee Brimingham.

J.B. was a veteran of WWII and the Korean conflict. He served in the US Army from 1944-1946. He later served in the US

J.B. and Zelma Rinehart Brimingham and children, Warren Eugene "Gene" and Sharon Ann.

Air Force (1950-1953) with the 516th Troop Carrier Wing, Memphis, TN. His commanding officer was Theodore Smith of Corinth, MS. J.B. was in the refueling unit of the Motor Pool. He was later employed by the US Army Corps of Engineers, Memphis District, until he sustained a back injury.

Zelma, J.B. and Gene lived in Memphis for a few years, then moved to Snowdown Community in Prentiss County. Sharon was born in Booneville, MS in 1960. Other places in which they lived were Chicago, IL, Prairie, MS and Jacinto, MS. Zelma still lives in Snowdown Community. J.B. died Jul. 12, 1994 from cancer and is buried in Sardis Cemetery in Alcorn County.

Zelma works at the Jacinto Country Store and Souvenir Shop across from historic Jacinto Courthouse during the tourist season.

J.B. was ordained a minister of the Primitive Baptist Church May 29, 1971. He was pastor of Mackeys Creek (Prentiss County), New Providence (near Belmont, MS), Turman's Creek (near Saltillo, TN) and Lone Pilgrim (near St. Louis, MO). He and Elder Cecil Woodruff pastored Sardis Church near Rienzi.

B.J. was a happy, friendly person who made everyone with whom he came in contact feel welcome in his presence. *Submitted by Zelma Rinehart Brimingham.*

BROWN, EWELL ODUS AND HAZEL MOZELLE GREEN, married Jul. 1, 1939, by Reverend G.P. Mayo. No children were born to this union.

Ewell was the third child born to Newton Odus Brown and Pearl Nan Walden Brown. He was born Jun. 14, 1921.

Hazel was the fourth child born to James Willis "Jim" Green and Minnie Ethel Holley Green. She was born Oct. 28, 1922.

Pfc. Ewell Brown and Hazel Green Brown in 1943 just before he left to go overseas. He was in the Battle of the Bulge.

Ewell served in WWII and was in the Battle of the Bulge. He was in the dry cleaning business for 40 years and Hazel was a nurse's assistant for several years and a secretary. Submitted by *Hazel Green Brown.*

BROWN, ISAAC MASON, born in 1828 in Jackson County, AL to James and Agnes Bishop Brown and died Jul. 7, 1862 in the Confederate States Army in Liberty, VA. Martha E. Owen/Owens was born in 1830 in North Carolina. She married her first husband, Thomas Green, Jul. 27, 1846 in Floyd County, GA. They had one daughter, Jane Elizabeth Green (b. Dec. 13, 1847). Jane never married, but had one son, James Richard. When her son was about 9 years old, Jane committed suicide by jumping into a well. Martha E. Owen/Owens married Isaac Mason Brown Mar. 7, 1850. They had seven children.

Isaac M. Brown's and Martha E. Brown's headstones.

William I.M. Brown (b. Dec. 13, 1850 in old Tishomingo County, MS) married Elizabeth Caroline Setters Nov. 7, 1869. Twin, Sarah Frances Brown (b. Dec. 13, 1850) married John L. Chase Aug. 27, 1870. Mary Elizabeth Brown (b. Dec. 7, 1853) married Robert Marcus Maness Oct. 4, 1874. She died Nov. 12, 1933. Ailey C. Brown (b. May 25, 1856, d. August 1858). Addline Isabell Brown (b. Jan. 30, 1859) married Jesse Abels Nov. 16, 1873. She died Dec. 20, 1880. Jefferson Davis "Jeff" Brown (b. 1861) married Pamelia Elizabeth (Lizzie) Abels Dec. 10, 1882. Both died Feb. 12, 1899, because of an ice storm and were buried in the same grave in Juliette Cemetery in Alcorn County, MS. John Thomas Brown (b. Feb. 13, 1871) married Mollie Elizabeth McAdam in 1905. He died Jul. 26, 1956 in Texas.

Grandpa Isaac is buried in Liberty, VA, but the Confederate States Army stone was placed beside Grandma's stone in the Armstrong Cemetery because of the inability to transport it to Liberty, VA. Grandma is buried outside of the cemetery, but the headstones are not on the actual grave site. *Submitted by Eller Drew Cox, 6 CR 316, Corinth, MS 38834-9205.*

BROWN, JAMES FRANKLIN, JR., born Jul. 21, 1877 in Prentiss County, MS, died Sep. 30, 1961, with burial in Mt. Zion Cemetery in McNairy County, TN. "Jim," as he was known, was the son of James Franklin Brown Sr. (b. Feb. 18, 1851 in Marion County, AL, d. Aug. 25, 1923 in Stantonville, McNairy County, TN).

Jim's mother was Martha Jane Tipton Brown (b. Aug. 11, 1849 in Bay Springs, Jasper County, MS, d. Oct. 11, 1918).

Jim was married to Eliza Idella Willis Brown (b. Mar. 15, 1882 in Falcon, McNairy County, TN, d. Oct. 29, 1966), the daughter of Jackson Monroe Willis. This couple lived in the Stantonville, TN area while they reared nine children: William Cecil, James Earl, Mary Jane, Edith Alma, Maggie Lee, Mildred, Willis Alton, Raymond Clay and Wilson Arlon Brown. Most all of the children have stayed and raised their families in this area and around Memphis, TN except Raymond, who resided in Meridian, MS.

Early in their marriage, Jim was a farmer and then he followed the carpenter trade. Later on Jim moved his family to Corinth, MS, except Earl, where he remained until his death. Jim and Della were members of the Church of Christ. He was very much a Bible scholar. You would often find him with his Bible under his arm looking for interested people to discuss the scriptures.

As years passed, the children grew up and had families of their own. Sundays were a day of rest for some, but not for Della as she kept busy cooking Sunday dinner for family members, who came to visit. Very important to Jim and Della were the family reunions, which are still being held in the McNairy County area. *Submitted by Shirley Jean Brown Potter.*

BROWN, JAMES LEAMON, first child of Newton Odus (b. 1893, d. 1985) and Pearl Nan Brown (b. 1892, d. 1988) was born Jan. 19, 1917 in a log house on what was known as the old Thomas Moreland place in the Hills Chapel Community. Leamon attended school at Hills Chapel and Burton. He met his future wife, Eula Mae Moss, at a singing at Blythe Chapel in 1932. After a three-year courtship, Leamon secured Joe Moss's (b. 1897, d. 1977) permission for Eula's hand in marriage. Leamon sold a heifer and purchased the $3 marriage license. On the evening of Mar. 19, 1935, Miss Fanny Searcy carried the couple in her Model A Ford to the Iuka Courthouse where they exchanged wedding vows before Mayor Jernigan. Best man, Alvis Marlar and witness, Nolan Wheeler, paid the mayor's $1 ceremony fee. Eula said, "Leamon had 15 cents left on our wedding night," and Leamon said, "That is about all I've been able to hang on to."

The newly weds started out renting, farming and housekeeping on the John Davis Farm just south of Hills Chapel School. On Dec. 1, 1938, they moved to an 81-1/2 acre farm with a house, barn, spring and a dug well, which they purchased for $150.00. Their move at this time of the year was due to bad roads. The roads were frozen and would support the weight of a 1936 Dodge pickup loaded with their belongings. The next day at sunrise, Leamon, with the help of his brother-in-law, Lester Moss (b. 1922, d. 1997), drove his livestock up beyond Hills Chapel School by the Walden Cemetery, down the Riddle Wind Ridge to their new home. They covered the eight miles and reached the "Sugar Farm", located just north of the old Idumea School in the Burton Community at sunset. I was told the reason it was called the "Sugar Farm" was because the previous owners barely made enough to buy sugar. The Browns purchased 29 more acres of bottom land, which made the "Sugar Farm" 110-1/2 acres total. The "Sugar Farm" sure was sweet to the Leamon Brown Family.

This is a picture of Leamon and Eula Brown's 50th wedding anniversary in 1985 with their sons. From left: Dennis, Tony, Eula, Leamon, James L. and Dwight Brown.

God sure has smiled down upon and blessed the Browns. Through the years, they have been able to scratch out a living, raise their children and send them to college from the resources God provided them off the "Sugar Farm." Leamon and Eula Brown's marriage produced five sons: James L. Brown Jr., Robert Lee Brown (b. 1937, d. 1939), Eldon Dwight Brown, Tony Dale Brown and Dennis Moss Brown. All the sons live in Prentiss County not far from the "Sugar Farm." The Brown's church affiliation was with The New Lebanon Free Will Baptist Church in the Cairo Community of Prentiss County. *Submitted by Tony Brown.*

BROWN, NEWTON ODUS, born Oct. 6, 1893 in Cleburne County, AL to Robertson Wyatt Brown and Mary Emily Hale. Odus moved with his family to Booneville, MS in 1911.

Brown Family. Edwin, Vance, Ewell, Johnny, Leamon, Odus, Pearl, Maylene, Virginia, Beverly. Pearl's father was John Anderson Walden. Pearl's mother was Adella Nancy Elizabeth Penolia Thompson.

He married Pearl Nan Walden Nov. 24, 1915. This union produced eight children as follows: James Leamon Brown, Johnny Wyatt Brown, Ewell Odus Brown, Pearl Maylene Brown, Vance Walden Brown, Edwin Davis Brown, Virginia Dolores Brown Penna and Beverly Jean Brown Taylor. Pearl (b. Dec. 21,

1892 in Booneville, MS, d. Jun. 3, 1988 at almost 96) and Odus (d. Aug. 5, 1985 at almost 92) are buried in Mount Pleasant Cemetery in Prentiss County, MS. Their church affiliation was with the Primitive Baptist Churches at New Hope and Little Flock in Prentiss County, MS.

The children range today in age from 63 to 83. Six children live in Mississippi, one in Tennessee and one in Alabama. From this union, we have approximately 100 offspring. The families have all kinds of vocations, but the original eight children and parents grew up on a farm. We are thankful for our heritage and our parents that carried us to church, taught us to work and manage God's resources. *Submitted by Vance W. Brown.*

BROWN, PEARL MAYLENE BROWN, born Jan. 3, 1925 is the fourth child of Odus and Pearl Walden Brown. After graduating from Booneville High School in 1944, she worked as a nurse's aid in the local hospital until Enis Brown returned from WWII duties. They were married Mar. 18, 1945 and to this union, six children were born, four boys and two girls. Maylene was a homemaker until their divorce in 1964. At this time, she took full responsibility of the children and farm and supported her family by managing the local high school cafeteria for six years. She did bookkeeping and general office work part-time, while attending the local college where she completed work for the AA degree and did studies to attain the status of junior at the University of Mississippi in Oxford. In 1972, she accepted the position of area nutritionist for Head Start centers in six counties. Maylene continued this work for 21 years until retiring in the Spring of 1990.

Pearl Maylene Brown family

The children learned to work, received good education's and became good citizens. All are married with children and good homes. There are 13 grandchildren and three great-grandchildren: nine girls and seven boys. The children are: Enis Trenton Brown Jr. family of Eatonton, GA; Carroll Thomas Brown family of High Point, NC; Elizabeth Nann Brown Bancks family of Jacksonville, FL; Rebecca Dolores Brown Lambert family of New Site, MS; Nathan O'Neal Brown family of Amory, MS and Daniel Wyatt Brown family of Eatonton, GA.

Maylene is content in her retirement years on her farm with the joys of caring for her fruit orchards, garden and lawn and fishing in her lake. She is active in her community and the Baptist Church. She is a member of a Seniors group called "The Joy Makers" and sings in the Senior choir at her church. Also, she does volunteer work at the Baptist Memorial Hospital in Booneville, MS. A supreme joy for her is each homecoming of her children and their families. *Submitted by Maylene Brown, 417 CR 3301, New Site, MS 38859.*

BROWN, ROBERTSON WYATT, born Sep. 3, 1865 in Cleburne County, AL to Peter Ramson Brown and Polly Martha Chandler. The wife of Wyatt, Mary Emily Hale, was born in Cleburne County to John Hale and Darcus Tollison Hale Nov. 25, 1878. Mary Emily died from childbirth Feb. 7, 1904. Robertson Wyatt remarried Martha Ann Edmonson and a son, R.J. Brown, was born Oct. 27, 1910. Martha died from cancer after the family moved from Mississippi back to Alabama. Later Wyatt married Della Morrison.

Papa's brothers and sisters. From left: Selester, Ada, Cindy, Papa Odus, Elzie, Elis and Uncle Joit Johnson walking. Not pictured is Papa's half brother, Uncle R.J. Brown.

The family moved to Booneville, MS in 1911 by covered wagon. Several times my dad told us children about the trip. They brought all their personal items, dogs, cows, seed and plants from Cleburne County. The women and small children came on the train to Paden, MS and they all arrived about the same time after the wagon's 10-day journey. We have today in 1999, some lettuce seed, apple trees and string beans they brought in the covered wagon. My dad was always appreciative of how people on their journey took care of their animals and their personal needs by taking them in for food and shelter.

Most of the family moved back to Calhoun County, AL, after living in Mississippi for seven years. However, my father, Odus Brown, who married Pearl Nan Walden, wished to remain in Mississippi. Also, Lucinda, my father's sister, married R.C. Miller and remained in Mississippi. *Submitted by Johnny Browne.*

BROWNING FAMILIES, the name of Browning is derived from the Saxon baptismal name Brunyn or Bruning, which was popular in England in ancient times. The name in its original form was a combination of Brune, an early form of Brown (which had reference to the color of the complexion or hair of its first bearers) and wyn or win, which was a diminutive or a suffix of endearment. The earliest recorded reference to the name is in England in 1273.

The Brownings in Prentiss and Tishomingo Counties are descended from Francis Browning, who was born in Albemarle County, VA. In 1816 he married Mildred Dollins and they moved to Lincoln County, TN in the 1820s. Their children, all born in Virginia, were John, Ruth, Jane, Soota and William. After Francis died in 1826, Mildred (Milley) remarried and died several years later. The children were raised by the court appointed guardians and relatives.

Ruth K. Browning married John M. Patterson Nov. 13, 1839 in Lincoln County.

Jane Mallory Browning (b. 1820, d. 1862) was married to William M. Moore. They had 11 children. They moved from Lincoln County in the 1840s to Tishomingo County. In 1851 they left with a wagon train for Texas. See William M. Moore Family, *The Leon County Texas History Book.*

Soota D. Browning married Allen Johnston in 1841. They lived in Tennessee and raised a large family. Soota died in the 1850s.

William M. Browning (b. 1824, d. 1892) enlisted in 1847 with Co. E, 3rd Tennessee Volunteers and saw service in Mexico during the Mexican War. His widow, Rachel Simpson Browning, drew a pension until her death in 1904. The family stayed in Tennessee until the 1870s when they moved to Gadsen, AL. They reared four or five daughters.

John Alexander Browning (b. 1817 in Virginia) and Mary Ann Ruth Dollins (b. 1817 in Tennessee) daughter of Taliaferro Dollins and the granddaughter of Presley Dollins (who fought with the first Virginia Militia during the Revolutionary War), were married Dec. 2, 1840, by Rev. John Bell in the Mt. Hebron Cumberland Presbyterian Church where both of their families worshipped. Their family story, as recorded in their Bible, tells us about their six-day journey by wagon in 1844 from Lincoln County to Tishomingo County. They paid $200 for 160 acres about halfway between Jacinto and Cairo. Here they farmed and raised their children, Francis, Joseph, Margaret, Marcus and Martha.

Mary Ann died May 10, 1883 and John died Feb. 27, 1895. Both are buried, along with many other family members in the Old Clausel Hill Cemetery near Cairo. For the family history of Francis Taliaferro Browning (b. 1841, d. 1889), see *Tishomingo County Mississippi History and Families,* 1997.

During the Civil War, Joseph William Browning (b. 1843, d. 1863) joined the "Boone Avengers", Co. H, 26th Regiment, Mississippi Infantry and lost his life at age 18.

Margaret Jane Browning (b. 1843, d. 1904), fondly called "Aunt Sis" by the family and Frances Almeda Browning (b. 1848, d. 1893) never married.

Martha Ellen Browning (b. 1859, d. 1938) married James T. Miller in 1902. Both are buried in The Booneville Cemetery.

Marcus William Browning (b. 1853, d. 1931) married Fannie Elizabeth Lacy (b. 1856, d. 1922). Laura Fuller wrote more of their history in *The Tishomingo County Mississippi History and Families.*

Continuation of this family can be read in the 1981 *History of Prentiss County Mississippi. Submitted by Anne B. Stennett Walker.*

BULLARD, CHARLIE CASTLEBERRY "POO," son of Calvin Curlee and Rhoda Evelyn Elizabeth "Betty" Milligan, was born Dec. 11, 1876 in Tishomingo County, MS. He married Anna Amelia Valentine Brown (b. Valentine's Day 1884) to James Houston and Nancy Curtiss Brown. Charlie was the grandson of William Henry and Rebecca Billings Bullard and the great-grandson of John C. and Rebecca Fortenberry Bullard. Charlie and Anna's children were:

1. Harold Lionel (b. ca. 1905, d. Jul. 14, 1924 accidentally while jumping from a moving train).

2. Herbert Ellis (b. Sep. 20, 1906 in Marietta) married Lela May Richey (b. Jan. 20, 1913 in Bay Springs, MS), daughter of Wesley Robert and Adeline Honeycutt Richey Oct. 18, 1933. The couple had five children: Joyce Ann (b. 1934), Herbert Harold (b. 1935), Billy Hugh (b. 1937), Talmadge Eugene "Bud" (b. 1948) and Brenda Lynette (b. 1951). Ellis and May later moved to Wheeler, MS in 1960. Ellis died Sep. 10, 1974 and May died Apr. 12, 1987 in Booneville, MS.

(Ca. 1910). Charlie Castleberry and Anna Amelia Valentine Bullard. Children from left: Carolyn Avis "Toddie," Harold Lionel and Herbert Ellis.

3. Carolyn Avis "Toddie" (b. Mar. 7, 1909, d. May 8, 1969) married Earnest "Ted" Church Sep. 8, 1934. They had no children.

4. Lois Hester (b. Oct. 16, 1911, d. Aug. 17, 1984) married Charles Lamar Bolton Dec. 24, 1926. He was the son of William Berry Bolton and Launa Nicholson. They had four children: Charles (b. 1932), Margaret Ann (b. 1935), Lucy (b. 1937) and Evelyn Eugenia (b. and d. 1945).

5. Eula Mescal "Chick" (b. 1913) married Leland Davis Apr. 23, 1933. They had eight children: Thomas Leland, Joy, Bill, Ken, Harry, Paula, Susan and Barbara "Katie."

6. Nelson Orville "Bunt" (b. Sep. 29, 1916, d. Sep. 6, 1972) married Ailene Whitfield Dec. 21, 1935. Ailene was the daughter of Tip and Maud Annie Whitfield (b. Mar. 24, 1915 in Franklin County, AL, d. October 1980 in Corinth, MS). Their children were Jerry Dale, Billie Sue and Jackie Louise.

7. Talmadge Albee "Tal" (b. ca. 1922) married Pauline McCutcheon Jul. 25, 1940. He died Feb. 25, 1945 in Germany during WWII. He and Pauline had one child, Peggy Ann.

8. Lola Eugenia "Billie" Bullard (b. ca. 1924, d. Feb. 10, 1944).

Charlie and Anna and their children moved for a short time to Cooper, Delta County, TX in the 1920s. When Anna died there Apr. 9, 1929, of a heart attack at the age of 45, the family brought her body back to Mississippi for burial and remained here. Charlie did not remarry. On Dec. 9, 1958, two days short of his 82nd birthday, he was struck by a train near his home in Rienzi. They are buried together in Zion's Rest Cemetery, Marietta, MS. *Submitted by Lela E. Ungaro.*

BULLARD, JAMES CLEMENT and Cora Evelyn Osborn were married Oct. 1, 1927 in Tishomingo County, MS by Bob Grisham. From this union were born 12 children (eight boys and four girls). Clement was the second child born to William M. "Bill" Bullard and Cordelia Carson Bullard Sep. 15, 1906 in Tishomingo County located in the Hubbard Salem Community. Cora (b. Aug. 8, 1909) was the fourth child of Samuel Taylor and Minnie Tennessee Jane Brown Osborn in Tishomingo County, MS.

James Clement and Cora Evelyn Osborn Bullard

Daddy and momma's first born was Ernest Houston (b. Oct. 7, 1928). Everyone knew him as "Huddy" and he died of cancer Aug. 16, 1986. He lived at home and never married. He and daddy farmed many years. When daddy's health prevented him from farming, Houston worked for his brothers: James Edward "Dick," Clifton and Carl, who are brick layers. He later went to work at NEMCC in the Janitorial Department and worked there until 1986. James Edward "Dick," the second child (b. Aug. 11, 1931), married Ripple Lee Scott Jul. 4, 1953. They have four children: James Michael, Susan Denise Goldman "Dennie," Lesa Dawn Allen and Steven Edward. They live in Prentiss County, MS.

Winston Eugene (b. Aug. 29, 1933, d. Jun. 22, 1935) was the third child.

Harold Eugene "Dorman," the fourth child (b. Sep. 29, 1935), was killed in an automobile accident May 6, 1966. He was married to Jane Gilley. They have a boy. Larry Dean and a girl, Janice Lynn Fox. They live in Prentiss County, MS. Minnie Jane was the fifth child (b. Sep. 18, 1937), finally a girl in the family, married Holland L. Jumper May 25, 1957. They have one son, Holland Dale. Momma named Minnie Jane her mother's name. Her brothers gave her the nickname of "Sissy" and that name stuck. We all call her that today. She really was a big help to momma being the only girl in the family at this time. They live in Dry Creek Community in Prentiss County.

Carl William, the sixth child (b. Jun. 30, 1939) named after Grandpa Bullard, married Mary Lou Lambert Feb. 18, 1961 and they have three boys: William Keith, Robbie Carl and Chad Wayne. They live in Prentiss County, MS.

Shelby Eugene, the seventh child (b. Aug. 28, 1941), married Ann Storey. They have a girl, Regina Ann Greenhill and a boy, Kevin Eugene. Shelby died of cancer Feb. 20, 1976. He served in the Vietnam war 1967 and 1968. They live in Union County, MS.

Clifton Ray, the eighth child (b. Jul. 4, 1943), married Charleen Cartwright Jan. 27, 1964. They have three children: Sonya Renee Stack, who was killed in automobile accident in 1991, Clifton Ray Jr. "Peter" and Paula Darlene Bonds. They live in the Thrasher Community in Prentiss County, MS.

John Wayne was the ninth child (b. Aug. 27, 1945, d. Nov. 10, 1949).

Betty Sue, the 10th child (b. Jul. 16, 1948), married Harold Palmer Jul. 2, 1966. They had two daughters, Jennifer Hope Palmer Potts and Casey Lynn Palmer born Dec. 15, 1977. Casey died Jan. 8, 1978. They live in Rienzi Community in Alcorn County, MS.

Evelyn Darlene, the 12th child (b. Feb. 22, 1955) was named after momma. She married Melvin Wallace "Bud" Davis on Oct. 5, 1979. They have two boys, James Eric and Derrick Wayne. They live in Prentiss County, MS. Daddy and momma moved from Hubbard Salem Community in Tishomingo County, MS to Prentiss County, MS around 1945. They lived on John Weatherbee's place and farmed his land for about 10 years. During this time, Glenda, Evelyn and Betty Sue were born. Daddy moved on Troy Moore's place and they lived there until 1967. Daddy bought some land on Stutts Chapel Road and built a nice home. Daddy died May 29, 1979 at the age of 74 years. Momma died Jul. 11, 1994 at the age of 85 years. Daddy and momma lived a long full life. A life full of hard work raising a big family. All the children grew up having to work hard but we all had a lot of good times and we have a lot of precious memories in our hearts we share when we all get together. Daddy and momma raised 10 children to be grown and now families of their own. As of this date, there are 22 grandchildren, 33 great-grandchildren and two great-great-grandchildren. *Submitted by Betty Sue Bullard Palmer.*

BULLARD, JAMES WINSTON "WINS" OR "WINCE," born sometime around August 1845 in Alabama, the son of Marion Winston Bullard from South Carolina. He married Rebecca Melvina Jackson (b. 1845), daughter of T.J. Jackson.

Jadeene Bullard Wiggins' dad, John Thomas Jr. or Jay, remembered his father John Thomas Sr. referring to his grandfather as "ole T.J." Jackson. Another son, Troy, also remembered talk about "ole T.J." and believes the initials stand for Thomas Jefferson Jackson. Troy Bullard remembers his dad saying the family was related to Stonewall Jackson. None of this has been proven though.

The children of Wins and Rebecca were: Sarah "Sally" E. (b. 1866), Cora Ann (Oct. 26, 1867, d. Dec. 27, 1948), John Thomas (Jun. 27, 1869, d. May 12, 1956), Robert Newton (b. Feb. 26, 1871, d. Feb. 1942 in Bakersfield, CA), Cassie Bianca (b. Jan. 30, 1873, d. Mar. 1, 1953) married a Peoples,

Cora Bullard Rogers and son, Chester Harrison Rogers in 1930.

Marion Columbus "Lum" (b. November 1875) and Viola (b. March 1878).

The son of Sarah Bullard and James Wallace Green was J. Wallace Green (b. Nov. 15, 1889).

The children of Cora Bullard and Zemeriah Alcie Rogers (b. 1866, d. 1930) were: Minnie Vernon (b. Mar. 2, 1891), Docia Mae (b. May 19, 1893 in Indian Territory), Chester Harrison (b. Jan. 27, 1898) and Myrtle Melvina (Mar. 15, 1900, d. 1904).

The children of John Thomas Sr. and Mattie Edna Pannell (b. 1880, d. 1960) were: Lena Bell (b. Apr. 22, 1899), Ruby Viola (b. Nov. 24, 1901), John Thomas "Jay" Jr. (b. Feb. 10, 1906), Edna Pearl (b. Jan. 12, 1908) and Troy Lee (b. Jul. 6, 1918).

The children of Robert Newton and Alice E. Blasingame (b. 1870, d. 1948) were: Noah Newton (b. Jan. 2, 1891), James Thomas (b. Oct. 7, 1895), Eula Lee (b. Feb. 14, 1898), John Robert (b. Mar. 19, 1900), Mattie Dee (b. Mar. 2, 1906) and Lou Allie (b. Aug. 23, 1908, d. December 1979).

The children of Marion Columbus "Lum" Bullard and Ida Mae Wesson (b. 1882) were: Roy (b. 1906), Irene K. (b. 1910) and Joyce (b. 1915).

Apparently, Viola Bullard had no children, but it is family knowledge that she married a man with the surname Nichols.

Several Bullards in this line moved to Texas, mostly in the vicinity of Dallas. Both Cora Bullard Rogers and Cassie Bullard Peoples are buried in Little Brown Cemetery in Prentiss County, MS. *Submitted by William Russell Coatney.*

BULLARD, LLOYD AND DELLIAN, born Nov. 17, 1902, Lloyd was the eighth child of Frank and Jeannie Bullard. They had seven sons and two daughters. Dell (b. Jan. 31, 1903) was the second of eight children; five daughters and three sons born to Sarah Elizabeth and Lowrey Franklin Owens.

Being neighbors, Lloyd and Dell attended the same school, Iduma. They walked a round trip of four miles each day to the two-room, one teacher school, which housed grades one through eight.

What began as a childhood friendship turned into a lifelong commitment. On Jan. 9, 1921, Lloyd and Dell were married unceremoniously as the local preacher stood on the side of his wagon. The following day they left for Florida to take care of Lloyd's brother's children whose mother had recently died. They remained there for about two years.

Lloyd and Dellian Bullard

While still in Florida, their first child, J.L. was born. Their second child, Aaron was born in 1923, after they had returned to Prentiss County. In 1926 a third son was born, Doyle and in 1930 a daughter, Charlene.

Aaron married Eunelle Sparks and made their home in the Burton community of Prentiss County. They had two children, Mackey and Janice and two grandchildren, Jason and Cassie Cutshall. Eunelle died in November 1995.

Charlene married James Edwin Wade and made their home in Memphis. They had three children: Kathy, Randy and Phillip and seven grandchildren: Alex, Anthony and Amanda Short; Brennan, Elleson and Parker Wade and Helen Wade.

J.L. died at the age of 16 and Doyle at the age of 3.

Lloyd worked as a logger, farmer, truck driver, school bus driver and eventually as a painter, the job he retired from at the age of 81. As a school bus driver, he noticed those children on his route who were in need and secretly supplied them with little extras, such as a present so they would have a gift to exchange at the school Christmas party.

Dell is remembered for her wonderful sense of humor, the gleam in her eyes and the delectables she created in her kitchen. Both Lloyd and Dell dearly loved visitors. Even though Dell suffered with heart problems in later years, she was never too sick to enjoy company.

Lloyd and Dell resided in the Burton community and were faithful members of New Hope Primitive Baptist Church. They are buried in New Hope Cemetery, along with their sons, J.L. and Doyle.

Lloyd and Dell enjoyed a long, blissful marriage. They often enjoyed recounting a story from the early days of their marriage. Dell's parents were expected to come for a visit. On the day before their arrival Dell said, "I'll be glad when Papa gets here so I can have him put up my mailbox." Lloyd replied, "And I hope they come soon. I need Mama to patch my overalls." He then proceeded to get his post-hole digger and she got out her needle and thread and they both went to work.

In 1994, after 73 years of marriage, they were parted in death. Dell was buried on Mother's Day, a fitting tribute. Lloyd died six weeks later and was buried one day before Father's Day. *Submitted by Janice Cutshall, granddaughter.*

BULLOCK, LAVERNE RINEHART, daughter of Clifford Palmer and Vista Rinehart of Jacinto, MS attended Jacinto School and Rienzi High School. She married Cecil Bullock, son of Dewey and Annie Bullock of Cairo, on Dec. 25, 1955 at the home of her cousin, Cleveland and Vickie Rinehart. He was a missionary Baptist minister.

Laverne's sister Zelma and her husband, J.B. Brimingham, went with them to get married. They owned a general store near Cairo for many years. He also worked for the Cairo Water Department and the Forestry. Cecil passed away in October 1981. He was a WWII veteran. Laverne still lives near Cairo.

Vaden, Darla, Beverly, Jared and Laverne Bullock

They have two children, Beverly and Vaden. Beverly graduated from Thrasher High School. Vaden is married to Darla Davis Bullock and they have a son Jared, 2 years old. Vaden is employed at Monetech of Iuka; Beverly is employed at Big V Water, Booneville, MS. *Submitted by Beverly Bullock.*

BUNCH, JIMMY DANIEL, born Jun. 14, 1961, married Shelia Densie Davis on Apr. 17, 1980. Shelia Davis Bunch (b. Feb. 27, 1962), daughter of Garvin Earl Davis (b. Dec. 29, 1932, d. Feb. 4, 1994) and Waynona Mayvene Vanderford Davis (b. Nov. 25, 1935) married Jun. 6, 1955.

Jimmy, Catherine, Shelia and Daniel Bunch

She is the granddaughter of Elton Davis (b. Nov. 8, 1904, d. Jan. 2, 1969) and Fannie May Stanley Davis (b. Jul. 26, 1906, d. Apr. 8, 1982). They are buried in the Jacinto Cemetery in Alcorn County. She is also the granddaughter of Winston "Wink" Jasper Vanderford (b. Mar. 9, 1916, d. Apr. 17, 1989) and Ella Missouri Woodruff Vanderford (b. Feb. 21, 1913, d. Sep. 2, 1991) who married Jun. 23, 1933. Garvin, Wink and Ella are buried in the Snowdown Church of Christ in Prentiss County.

Jimmy and Shelia's children are (1) Kathrine Lucille Bunch (b. Nov. 22, 1980) and (2) Daniel Earl Bunch (b. Aug. 17, 1984). Kathrine is a high school graduate of New Site High and is attending Northeast Community College. Daniel goes to school at Thrasher where he plays football. Shelia is a graduate of New Site High. They enjoy camping, fishing and water sports. *Submitted by Kathrine Lucille Bunch.*

BURCHELL, JAMES AND EDNA BEARDEN, James Carroll Burchell (b. Mar. 8, 1929 in Stone County, AR) son of Benjamin J. Burchell (b. Dec. 11, 1888 in Caldwell County, KY, d. Feb. 23, 1937 in Illinois) and Mary Ann Goforth (b. Dec. 19, 1903, d. Dec. 7, 1948). Benjamin was the son of William Abraham Burchell (b. 1836, d. 1892) of Woodford County, KY and Martha Jane Hankins (b. 1851, d. ca. 1918) of Gibson County, TN. William Abraham was the son of William Burchell (b. ca. 1804) and Synthia ? (b. ca. 1807).

On Apr. 16, 1956, James Carroll Burchell married Edna Frances Bearden (b. Mar. 18, 1933, d. Jan. 13, 1989) in Booneville, MS.

From left back row: W.E. Bearden and Koonie Davis. Front row: Henry Clay, Martha Jane, Kattie Lee, Pleas, Emma Lou and Laura Bearden.

Edna Frances Bearden was descended from Pleasant B. Bearden (b. Feb. 23, 1799 in Spartanburg, SC). Pleasant Bearden moved to Lincoln County, TN when he married Margarett Garrett (b. May 2, 1807 in Tennessee). Their children were Mary Ann, Susan, William H., Nancy C., Henry Clay (b. Jun. 20, 1842), who married Martha Jane Blythe (b. Jun. 23, 1845) and Amanda Narcissa.

By the start of the Civil War, Henry Clay Bearden was in Tishomingo County, MS and enlisted in Captain Henry Davenport's company, the Davenport Rifles, 42nd Mississippi Infantry. He was with the 42nd at Gettysburg and was captured on the third day of the battle during Pickett's charge. He was sent to various northern prisons and ended at Johnson's Island in Sandusky, Ohio. At the end of the war, he was released on oath at Fort Delaware.

Henry Clay Bearden married Martha Jane Blythe Jan. 22, 1867. Martha Jane was the daughter of William Carroll "Buck" and Lucinda Blythe. Henry and Martha had two sons, Pleasant Price Bearden (b. May 16, 1868) and William Ellis Bearden.

Pleasant Price Bearden married Laura Frances Drucilla Jane Cox (b. Oct. 30, 1871) on Oct. 30, 1889 in Booneville, MS. Laura was the daughter of Joseph L. Cox and Laura Frances Walden.

Pleasant Price Bearden and Laura Cox had seven children: Kattie Lee, Emma Lou, R.C., William Carlton (b. Sep. 12, 1898 in Prentiss County, MS), Annie May, Mattie Bell and Mabel Annice.

On Jan. 9, 1921, William Carlton Bearden married Nancy Jane (Estes) Griggs (b. Jul. 23, 1902). William Carlton and Nancy Jane Bearden had eight children: Charlene, Henry Clay, Thomas Porter (John), Annie Lee, Edna Frances, Mabel Jane, Ellis Carl and Roy Rogers Bearden.

Edna Frances married Sherman Floyd Harris. They had two sons, Jackie Floyd and Larry Dale. After Sherman was killed in a 1953 tornado, she and her second husband, James Carroll Burchell, moved to Illinois where their son, Mitchell Lynn Burchell, compiler of this history, was born Jan. 31, 1957 (in Chicago). Edna missed her family in Mississippi, so the family moved back. James Myron Burchell was born Apr. 9, 1959. A couple of years later, the family moved to Los Angeles, CA and there, Jerrie and Jeffery were born Jan. 23, 1963.

Edna Frances died of cancer Jan. 13, 1989 and is missed terribly by all who knew her. *Submitted by Mitch Burchell.*

BUTLER, LILBURN CANERDY, born Feb. 4, 1835 in Franklin County, AL, son of George Canerdy and Harriet Elizabeth Duboise Butler. He married Rebecca Elizabeth Winnett Jan. 10, 1854. She was born Jul. 24, 1834 to Jacob and Florence Lynn Winnett. They reared their family in old Warren County, TN.

Their children were as follows:

Katherine Marie Richey, descendant of Lilburn Canerdy and Rebecca Elizabeth Winnett Butler

1-2) George T. Butler (b. Nov. 19, 1854, d. Feb. 11, 1855); infant son (b. and d. Jul. 12, 1856). Both sons are buried at Hopewell Cemetery in the Summitville Community.

3) Tabatha Jane Butler (b. Dec. 23, 1858, d. Apr. 12, 1927) md. Jonathan T. Davis Oct. 13, 1874 in Booneville, MS. She is buried at Booneville Cemetery.

4) Lydia R. Butler (b. May 30, 1861, d. Feb. 6, 1932) md. Jim Fraser.

5) Harriet Elizabeth Butler (b. Sep. 1865, d. Jan. 5, 1940) md. James Robertus Norton. She is buried at Booneville Cemetery.

6-8) W. Robert Butler (b. 1868); Florence B. Butler (b. Dec. 31, 1869, d. Sep. 9, 1925) md. William T. Frasier; John Butler.

Lilburn Canerdy Butler fought for the Confederacy, enlisting in the War Between the States Aug. 5, 1861 at Knoxville, TN. He stood five feet and 10 inches tall, sallow complexion, black hair and dark eyes. Pvt. Butler was soon given the rank of sergeant and served under Capt. Dashill and Lt. McCall in Co. I, 34th Tennessee Infantry, 4th Regiment. He was captured at Coffee County, TN and was imprisoned at Louisville, KY. He was discharged Aug. 22, 1864.

When the Butlers moved to the recently formed Prentiss County, they built in the northern section of the city of Booneville. All the land in this tract, including where the northeast Mississippi Community College now sits, was farmed by the Butler family. The site where they built is located at 1102 North College Street. The white frame Butler home once stood where the Northeast Mississippi Community College president's home now stands. The house was moved and now serves as faculty housing.

Many of Lilburn Canerdy Butler's descendants still reside in this area.

Lilburn Canerdy Butler (d. Feb. 4, 1914) and Rebecca Elizabeth Winnett Butler (d. May 25, 1915) are buried in the family plot at the Booneville Cemetery. *All information on this family was abstracted from "Kinship Treasures from Coffee County, TN" and submitted by Sandra Lewis Gray, great-great-granddaughter.*

CALVERT FAMILY, Charles, Eva, 2-year-old Jean and 2-week old Edwin moved from Quitman County, MS to Prentiss County in October 1957 when Charles became county executive director of the Prentiss County ASCS office. He remained there until retiring in November 1990. Eva began working at Booneville Hospital, later going to Prentiss County FHA where she retired in November 1996. Carlton was born into the family in February 1963.

Jean, Edwin and Carlton are all graduates of Booneville High School and went on to attend NEMCC.

Jean completed her education at Mississippi University for Women with a degree in elementary education. After living and teaching in Columbus, MS and Southaven, MS for several years, she returned to Booneville in 1992 with her three children: Heather Rowland, Calvert and Mollee Malone. In 1995 she married Carroll Martin Jr. of Guys, TN. He brought Lauren and Jonathan to the family. She teaches at Anderson Elementary School in Booneville. Daughter Heather is a second-generation graduate of NEMCC and MUW. She earned a master's degree from Stephen F. Austin University in Nacogdoches, TX. She is presently living in Columbus, MS where she is the executive director of the Columbus Fine Arts Council.

Edwin completed his education at Mississippi State University earning a master's degree in vocational agriculture and extension. He and his family, wife Elizabeth and daughter Samantha, presently live in Mantachie, where he is the district conservationist of Itawamba County.

Carlton has been employed by UPS in Booneville since 1984. He has one daughter, 8-year-old Katelyn. *Submitted by Charles Calvert.*

CALVERY, NANCY ANN DICKEY ROGERS, born in Georgia Dec. 19, 1841. Her family probably lived in Alabama before moving to Mississippi. Nancy's parents are not documented, but her father is believed to be Robert M. Dickey, age 62, born in Georgia, the 1870 Prentiss County census with children: Fannie C. (age 22, born in Georgia); Sarah E. (age 16, born in Georgia); John T. (age 19, born in Georgia) and Louisa (age 7, born in Mississippi). Apparently, the wife is deceased. Robert M. Dickey is mentioned in the Rogers estate court proceedings and Nancy named her last child, Robert.

Nancy Ann Dickey Rogers Calvery, third wife of Zimmery Rogers and second wife of Thomas H. Calvery.

Nancy married Zimmery Rogers, a well-to-do farmer, May 9, 1864. He was 57 and she was his third wife. Three children were born to this union: Tennessee, Henry Clay and Paulina. James Zimmery Rogers died in 1869 and is buried in Blythe's Chapel. Nancy had another son, Sidney Talmage Rogers, born in 1876.

On Jul. 9, 1878, Nancy was married to Thomas H. Calvery (b. 1834) by Rev. J.B. Brite. Thomas was a widower with grown children and lived in Tishomingo County following the timber mills. Three children were born to them: Louvenia, Vineyard Lee (Ben) and Robert Thomas.

After the Civil War, many people fell on hard times and Nancy's family was among them. During her marriage to Calvery, the family became destitute and she allowed Tennessee and Paulina to be taken in by their half-brother, Dr. W.J. Rogers. Henry Clay went to live with his half-brother, G.W. Rogers.

Nancy and Thomas Calvery had moved to Arkansas in 1883 and back in 1884. About this time, Thomas died and Nancy was left with Sidney Talmage Rogers and the three small Calvery children. By 1892, the Rogers estate still was not settled, but sometime after Calvery died, Dr. Rogers moved Nancy back to the Rogers place and she apparently lived there until it was sold.

Henry Clay Rogers, Sidney Rogers and Bob Calvery families were frequent visitors in Ben Calvery's home. A visit might be almost a week, because of difficulty in travel. Ben's son, Monroe Calvery, of Ripley stated that he spent a large part of his young life with his grandmother. Nancy saw after him when he was small. When she visited among her children, she took him with her. Nancy died Easter Sunday, Apr. 12, 1925, while visiting Bob. Monroe was there when she died. She is buried in Antioch No. 2 in Alcorn County.

Her descendants are:
1. Tennessee Queen Victoria Rogers (b. 1865, d. 1951) married in 1883 to John Henry Miller (b. 1854, d. 1920). (See her story.)
2. Henry Clay Rogers (b. 1866, d. 1948) married Roxie Downs, a widow with eight children. They had Lawrence Almous, who married Gertrude ?. Their children were Almous Eugene, James Edward, Carl Willard, Hillard Anna, Doris Ellen and Olen.
3. Paulina Rogers (b. 1868) married ? Cummings.
4. Sidney Talmage (b. 1876, d. 1943) married Eva Floyd (b. 1881, d. 1959). In 1900 he moved to Sheffield, AL and worked for the Southern Railroad. He was killed in a train accident. Children were Gertrude (b. 1904, d. 1985) married Claude Terrell; Sidney Talmage (b. 1908, d. 1967) married Ruby Newsom; Sidney married first ? Acuff and second Leon Webster; David Paul (b. 1919, d. 1988) married Mary Dubois.
5. Louvenia "Dena" (b. 1881, d. 1960) married Joseph Francis Dixon. They had two sons. Dennis married Vera Thornton and had: Mary Jo married Charles Lockhart; Martha Ann married Buford Glissen and Francis married James Butts. Collins married Era Wallace and had Patty and Sherry.
6. Vineyard Lee "Ben" (b. Jan. 12, 1881, d. Nov. 9, 1975) married Jan. 14, 1906 Elizabeth (Lizzy) Cartwright (b. Mar. 6, 1878, d. Oct. 20, 1937). (See his story.)
7. Robert "Bob" Thomas (b. 1886, d. 1958) married Mary Cartwright. They had Clyce, Monroe, Elton, a girl and Vineyard Lee. Mary died in childbirth and Bob married Ruth ? and their children were Pershall, twin girls and perhaps others. *Submitted by Pollye Calvery.*

CALVERY, THOMAS, blacksmith and farmer, settled in Tishomingo County by 1841. The family is listed in the 1845 census of Tishomingo County. Thomas (b. 1796) and his wife, Nancy (b. 1797) were born in Georgia, listed in the 1820 census of Oglethorpe County, GA. The parents of nine children born while the family lived in Georgia: Thomas H. (b. 1824), William (b. 1825), James W. (b. 1828), Nancy H. (b. 1830), Terriesa F. (b. 1832), Drucilla C. (b. 1834) and Martha A. (b. 1836). The family was in Alabama when John C. was born (b. 1838), then Luticia (b. 1841) was born in Tishomingo County. Thomas H. Calvery, the oldest son, a farmer and a mechanic, married Lucinda Word Jun. 17, 1844. He and Lucinda were the parents of Sarah E. Calvery (b. 1847) and George Washington Calvery (b. Nov. 29, 1849). Lucinda died by 1852.

Thomas then married Emily G. They were the parents of Anderson Word Calvery (b. 1854), Thomas Frank Calvery (b. 1856), William L. Calvery (b. 1858), Dock Calvery (b. 1861), James R. Calvery (b. 1866), Mary F. (b. 1869) and Josiah Calvery (b. 1870).

Following the death of Emily, Thomas married Nancy Dickey Rodgers, a widow, on Jul. 9, 1878 in Prentiss County. Thomas and Nancy were parents of three children: Venyard Lee Calvery, Robert Thomas Calvery and Louvenia Calvery. More information about this family can be found in the *History of Tippah County.* George W. Calvery, son of Thomas and Lucinda, married Nancy Jane Payne Dec. 3, 1872 in Prentiss County, making their home in Booneville. Nancy was the daughter of William B. and Nancy Ann (Kizer) Payne. Nancy's grandparents, the Thomas Payne and Francis Kizer families, were among the early settlers of Tishomingo County, MS. In 1836 William B. and the Kizers bought lots in the new city of Jacinto.

While in Booneville, George and Nancy Jane were parents of Isham Calvery (b. 1873), Laura Calvery (b. 1874, d. 1941), Nobie L. Calvery (b. 1877), Bynum (b. 1879, d. 1923), Kirtes Gurley (b. 1880, d. 1961) and Jirdon Pittman (b. 1883, d. 1912). About 1886 the family joined other families for the long trip to Texas. The youngest child, Mettie, was born after they reached Texas. After a time in Booneville, TX the families moved on to Indian Territory (Oklahoma). George and Nancy settled in the little community of Dixie where George leased land from the Indians. He and Nancy were members of the Dripping Springs Baptist Church. The children married and lived in nearby communities.

George and Nancy were buried in the Dixie Cemetery near their children, Mettie and Jirdon.

Thomas Frank Calvery, son of Thomas H. and Emily Calvery, married Clemma Bearden Oct. 22, 1879 in MS. They settled in Grady, Indian Territory (after 1907, Oklahoma). Their children were Walter W. (b. 1880), Maggie B. (b. 1882), Barney Dennis (b. 1884), Roy B. (b. 1889), Nioma (b. 1891) and Wiley B. (b. 1893).

Following the death of Clemma, Thomas Frank married Mrs. Sharp, a widow. They had two children, Al and Vada. *Submitted by Glenda Willmon, a descendant of Kirtes Gurley Calvery.*

CALVERY, VINEYARD LEE "BEN," born in Tishomingo County Jan. 12, 1881, died Nov. 9, 1975, the son of Thomas H. and Nancy Ann Dickey Rogers Calvery. (See her story.) After Thomas died, Ben spent his early life in Prentiss County.

Vineyard Lee (Ben) Calvery, son of Thomas H. and Nancy Ann Dickey Rogers Calvery.

Ben married Elizabeth Cartwright (b. Mar. 6, 1878, d. Oct. 20, 1937), the daughter of James Monroe and Ellen Medford Cox Cartwright. James Monroe was the son of James and Elizabeth Long Cartwright. Elizabeth was the daughter of Samuel Long (d. 1757-1758) and Mary Fryar (d. 1859). They married in 1816 and came to Tippah County from Perry County, TN with John Chishlom in 1836. Ben and Lizzie had five children:

Ed married Clistra Malone and had Belva, Howard and Louvenia. Ed was a mechanic and lived at Kossuth.

Earl married Mavis Carter and had James, Johnnie, Willie and Virginia. He lived up north for many years, but died in Alcorn County.

Orbie Monroe (b. Mar. 15, 1911, d. Jun. 6, 1999) married Edna Earl Rainey (b. Jul. 28, 1915). Edna is the daughter of William Charles and Kitty Urilda Parrish Rainey. William Charles was the son of Hiram Jr. and Delpha Carter Rainey, a grandson of Hiram Sr. and Margaret Blackwood Rainey, great-grandson of Aaron and Nancy Rainey. Margaret was the daughter of Andrew Blackwood and Susanna Robertson, granddaughter of William Robertson (Revolutionary

107

War), great-granddaughter of Col. Charles Robertson (Revolutionary War) of Watauga.

Monroe and Edna had three children: Audrey Durell (b. Jul. 3, 1932) married Oct. 4, 1952 Pollye Gaillard (b. Apr. 19, 1934). Their children: William Durell (b. Jan. 4, 1972) and Alice Elizabeth (b. Jun. 8, 1976), who married Aug. 2, 1994 Randy Edward Cockrell (b. Apr. 5, 1970). They have a daughter Amber Elizabeth (b. Oct. 2, 1996). Billy Dan (b. Apr. 8, 1935) married Betty Wilson and had Michael Dan and then married Francis Mason. Michael married Andrea Soltys and had Benjamin (b. Oct. 24, 1996). Peggy Ann (b. Apr. 8, 1935) married Bruce Wallis. They had Benny Martin, who married Regina Menees and had Emily (b. Dec. 2, 1983), Ben (b. Dec. 14, 1989), Will (b. Jul. 18, 1991) and Jeannie Lynn, who married John Tice and had Parrish Anne (b. Apr. 23, 1997).

Beecher married Lou Burns. Their children were: Bobby, Lloyd and Sandra. He lived at Forrest and is buried there.

Ruby married Cleo Reeves and had Alton Levern, Bonnie and Dale. They lived at Ripley.

Ben was a timber man and a farmer. He was a foreman for Coleman Heading Mill Co. In the winter, he crossed the frozen Hatchie River with wagons. Sometimes his family lived in a tent at the mill site if other housing was not available. They later moved to Kossuth.

About 1933 he moved to Ripley to farm the Joe Dixon place. He also had a blacksmith shop. Lizzie died in 1937 and Ben moved to Kossuth and worked in Ed's shop. He made yard furniture and knives and did blacksmith work until Ed died in 1972. Ben moved to Ripley and lived with Monroe until his death in 1975. *Submitted by Pollye Calvery.*

CARLOCK/GERLACH, HANS CHRISTIAN,

born 1631 in Saxony, Germany. He married Anna Maria Kummer and the Carlock lineage began its trek toward our generation. They had seven children: Edmun, Conrad, Tobecus, Hans, Maria, Johan Christian and Peter.

The Carlock Family Photograph. The family of William "Bill" and Paulina Allen Carlock. Seated from left: William "Bill" Carlock and Paulina Allen Carlock. Standing from left: Alma Carlock, Willie Carlock, Elmira Carlock, Andrew Carlock, Ellis Carlock and Mary Carlock.

Johan Christian Gerlach (b. 1672, d. 1764) married Maria Margaretha. They had five children: Elias, David, unknown, Johan and unknown. They came to America in 1720. Elias Gerlach was naturalized in New York as Elias Gerlof. All the others eventually took the name of Carlock.

David Carlock (b. 1700, d. 1770) married Catherine Volmer. They had six children: Caroline, Conrad, Frederick, Catherine, John Christian and George.

John Christian Carlock (b. 1727, d. 1803) married first Susan Witmer. They had two children, Lemuel and Catherine. Susan and her first child, Lemuel, were killed by Indians. John Christian's second wife was Sarah Whitman. They had eight children: Abraham, Isaac, Emile, Eunice, Moses, Job, Jacob and Mary.

Jacob Carlock (b. 1775, d. 1847) married a Whitney. They had nine children: Duke, John, Mary, James, George, Sarah, Jacob Jr., Joseph and Leutitia. Jacob was a Lutheran preacher, who led immigrants through Kentucky and Ohio.

Jacob Carlock Jr. (b. 1816, d. ?) married a Mary (last name unknown). They had seven children: Jacob, William Violles Culten, Mary, Sarah, Nancy, Frances and Martha.

William Violles Culten Carlock (b. 1834, d. 1915) married first, Elizabeth Tatum. They had four children: John, Mary, Joan and William "Bill." After serving in the Civil War, William V.C. did not return to Mississippi. He went to Obion County, TN where he married Mary Park. They had two children, Isodora and William. The family moved to Mills County, TX in 1879. William V.C. died in Austin, TX, Nov. 14, 1815.

William "Bill" Carlock (b. 1864, d. 1961) married first Mary Crowder. They had one child, Effie Lee, who married John Scott. They had 15 children: Velma married Shorty Kesler; Doc, married Ozella Palmer; R.W. married Bertha Miller; Mary married Fred Cook; infant; J.C. married Isabell Holt; Maude; Brownie married Mary Corbin; Alice married J.C. Harlan first and Louis Standifer second; John married Lottie Wilson first and later married six more times; Jack married Louise Stennett; Roy married Hazel Acres first and Annie Lee Roberts second; Hattie married Norris Burns; Luna married Troy Pace and Jean married Claude McCreary.

William "Bill" Carlock's second wife was Paulina Allen. They had eight children: infant; Dewey; Elmira married Hugh Whitehead; Andrew married Mallie Pruitt first and Louella Windham second; Ellis married Gladys Enis; Willie married Jim Samples; Alma married Fred Duncan and Mary married John Lee Wardlaw.

Mary Carlock (b. 1908, d. 1997) and John Lee Wardlaw had four children: Merle married Billy Glover and had two children, Rick and Jeff; Buddy married Jo Ann Morrow and had two children, Michael and Nancy; Herman married Amanda Ross and had two children, Douglas and Amanda and Charles married Martha Haas first and had two children, Emily and Paula and then married Carolyn Carnathan and they have no children.

Great-grandchildren of Mary Carlock and John Lee Wardlaw are: Corrie and Meredith Glover; Lee and Andrew Wardlaw; Michael, Stephanie and Kyle Morrison; Justin and Kayla Browne and Taylor McKinney.

Many Carlock descendants still live in Prentiss County and throughout the US. *Submitted by Rick Glover.*

CARTWRIGHT, MERRIL AND LAURA,

began their life together Sep. 1, 1950 at the Oak Grove Methodist Church in the Osborne Creek Community, just west of Booneville. Merril Tyson Cartwright was the son of Hettie Mae Carpenter and Claude Wesley Cartwright and was born Dec. 4, 1929. Hettie Mae (b. Feb. 11, 1899, d. Sep. 19, 1977) was the daughter of Fannie Agnes Moore and Lafayette Tyson Carpenter and Claude (b. Sep. 5, 1897, d. Dec. 25, 1983) was the son of Mary Christian and Newton Columbus Cartwright.

Laura Illeen Windham (b. Mar. 25, 1929) was the daughter of Ollie Sallie Ann Carpenter and Andrew Franklin Windham. Ollie (b. Oct. 5, 1895, d. Nov. 1, 1983) was the daughter of Eliza Lenora Jumper and William Lurk Carpenter and Frank (b. Dec. 31, 1882, d. Apr. 16, 1946) was the son of Laura Humphreys and Simeon Windham.

These background families were some of the first families to be in western Prentiss County and they were mostly farming families.

Merril was reared on a farm on the Wyningar Road in the Osborne Creek community. He began school at the Osborne Grammar School, but transferred to Booneville Public School (West Side) in the sixth grade. He graduated from Booneville High School, attended Northeast Mississippi Junior College and received a BS in agricultural education and a master's in agricultural education and school administration from Mississippi State University. His college education was interrupted by a stay in the Army during the Korean Conflict.

Laura was born half way between Jumpertown and Booneville. She and her family moved to Booneville when she was 3 years old. She attended Booneville schools, all 12 years in the West Side Booneville High School building, where she graduated as valedictorian of her class.

Merril became a vocational agriculture teacher. He had known since he was a freshman in high school what he wanted to do and his years as chapter and state president and national vice president in the Future Farmers of America made him even more sure of what he wanted to do. He taught at Merigold, Alcorn Agricultural High School (Kossuth) and Booneville High School. He was the first vocational director of the Prentiss County Vocational Technical School and was the instigator of the vocational complex.

Merril was one of the few from Mississippi to become a national officer. As a vocational agriculture/FFA adviser, he had Mississippi's first American Star Farmer (Ralph G. "Buddy" Smith).

Laura was a secretary at Booneville High School and at Mississippi State University. With her children grown (or almost), she went back to school (she had previously taken courses at Northeast, Blue Mountain and Mississippi State) to Northeast and the University of Mississippi to obtain a BS and master's in business education. She later went back to State and received an educational specialist degree. Afterward, she taught vocational business courses at the Prentiss County Vo-Tech School and chartered the Prentiss County FBLA Chapter.

Between going to school, teaching at schools and being a part of organizations, like the Woman's Club of Booneville and Rotary Club of Booneville, there were children.

Clifton Claude Cartwright was born at Merigold (Cleveland Hospital) Nov. 1, 1953. Christina Carol Cartwright was born at Kossuth (Corinth Hospital) May 13, 1957.

When Cliff and Christi were 4 and 1, the Cartwright clan moved to their farm on Osborne Creek Road (Chris-Cliff Farm) and made their last move. Both children grew up on the farm and they both attended Booneville schools (all three schools), graduating from Booneville High School. The family was a dedicated part of the Booneville First United Methodist Church where Cliff and Christi received "Perfect Attendance" pins for many years.

Both children followed in their dad's footsteps in vocational education youth organizations. Cliff was state president of the FFA and Christi was state president of FHA.

Cliff loved farming and was a part of the operation from the time he was a boy. He attended Northeast and Mississippi State in Pre-Med. He was accepted before age 20 into the four-year program in the University of Mississippi Medical School at Jackson, MS. He did his residency in family medicine at Jackson, TN and began his own solo practice back home in Booneville.

Since Christi loved the work she did in FHA in high school, she majored in home economics. She believed that home and family were important and, after all, she had inherited her "Mammaw" Windham's talent for sewing. She began her undergraduate work at Northeast and graduated from Mississippi University for Women. She received a master of education from the University of Mississippi and an educational specialist from Mississippi State University.

She has taught home economics, which has become family and consumer science in Alcorn County schools, spending most of her years at Biggersville.

Seated: Laura Windham Cartwright and Merril T. Cartwright with Johnny Lee Allen Jr. and Jessica Michelle Allen standing between them. Standing at back: Johnny Lee Allen, Christina Carol (Christi) Cartwright Allen, Clifton Claude Cartwright, Carolyn Stephens Cartwright, Carmen Breaux and Clifton Wesley Cartwright. Easter at Chris-Cliff Farm.

Cliff married Carolyn Jean Stephens Aug. 4, 1973, at the First United Methodist Church in Booneville. Carolyn was born Apr. 5, 1953, to Hazel Marie Roberts (b. Jun. 9, 1926) and Audie Ray Stephens (b. Apr. 13, 1926, d. Jun. 29, 1992). Carolyn had competed her BS at Belhaven College in Jackson, MS and she completed an AD degree in nursing while Cliff did his residency in Jackson, TN. Carolyn would become Cliff's nurse and office manager when they opened their practice in Booneville.

They have one son, Clifton Wesley (b. Dec. 14, 1979 at Jackson, TN).

Christi married Johnny Lee Allen Dec. 21, 1976, at the First United Methodist Church in Booneville. Johnny was born Jan. 5, 1954, to Marie Shipman (b. Jun. 17, 1921, d. Feb. 26, 1990) and Roy Lee Allen (b. Nov. 12, 1912). They, too, were in school, Christi at MUW and Johnny at State. Johnny was also a state FFA president. They competed that work and moved back to Alcorn County where he would teach vocational agriculture until he transferred to Northeast Mississippi Community College. There, he has been an instructor, a department chairman and dean of instruction. They moved to Booneville after Johnny's last advancement to instructional dean.

Christi and Johnny have two children, Jessica Michelle (b. Jul. 9, 1986) and Johnny Lee Allen Jr. (b. Apr. 29, 1991). Both children were born while they lived in Alcorn County on their farm in the Biggersville community.

Merril and Laura Cartwright and their extended family live within a few miles of each other in Booneville, MS. Merril retired from education in 1986 to become a full-time cattle farmer. Laura retired in 1988 to do freelance writing, working as a stringer/correspondent for the Memphis, TN, *Commercial Appeal* and doing features and a weekly column (*Laura Cartwright from Chris-Cliff Farm*) for the *Booneville Banner-Independent*.

CHAMBERS, THOMAS LEE "TOMMIE,"

born Mar. 24, 1905 at Bear Creek, Franklin County, AL, died Nov. 8, 1995 in Prentiss County, MS, lived in the Marietta Community. His parents were Marion Frances and Lola Van Spencer Chambers (b. Aug. 6, 1910 at Wheeler, Prentiss County, MS).

Her parents were Johnny Lee Spencer and Tennie Magnolia Lindsey Spencer. Tommie's brothers: Brad Chambers, Yancey Chambers and Robert Chambers. Sisters: Lula Bell Chambers, Fannie Chambers and Sadie Chambers.

Lola's brothers: John and Jimmie; sisters: Ivene, Magalean, Wilodean, Ruthie and Mildred Spencer.

Tommie spent his childhood years in Prentiss County in the New Site Community where he lived with and between Lula Bell Chambers Taylor and Sadie Chambers Denson and two or three years at Belmont with Dr. Johnson and Bay Springs with his brothers Yancey and Robert Chambers and back to New Site. Lola spent her first two or three childhood years at Wheeler then moved to New Site Community, the Cross Road area on Siloam Road, Watson's place.

Tommie and Lola had a short courtship. They met at an ice cream supper and square dance at her parent's house. They were married Jul. 26, 1926 and raised eight children. Tommie logged in winter and farmed in summer. Lola kept the house clean, cared for the children, helped in the fields and she loved gardening. Lola said times were hard back then and they experienced the hardship of the Depression in the 30s like everyone else. Tommie worked on the WPA for 50 cents a day. The wars in the 40s, we hoped things would get better.

Tommie said after the war, he was tired of share cropping. They managed to buy a farm at Marietta Community in 1948 and things got better. They raised cows, shipped milk, farmed cotton, corn and hay. Tommie drove a school bus for 18 years at Marietta School. Lola still lives at Marietta today. They lived for 69 years together. Their children are Horace Chambers, Louise Chambers Nichols, Helen Chambers Pate, Marjorie Chambers Brosious, Trudy Chambers Voyles, Hoyt Chambers, Ruby Chambers Ross and Wayne Chambers who still lives at Marietta Community.

CHARLWOOD, WARNIE ANNISE POUNDS,

born Oct. 9, 1955 at Booneville, MS and died Feb. 17, 1986 at Tupelo, MS. She died at the age of 30 and is buried in the Jericho Church Cemetery. She was married to David Epting Charlwood of Baldwyn, MS on Apr. 9, 1977. She attended Booneville High School, Northeast Mississippi Community College, Mississippi State University and the University of Mississippi. She worked at the Prentiss County Welfare Office in Booneville and later taught school in Baldwyn.

She left two children: Sara Elizabeth Charlwood (b. Aug. 15, 1979) and John Andrew Charlwood (b. Jan. 8, 1985).

Annise was the only child of Sara Annese Bonds and Oswald Chambers

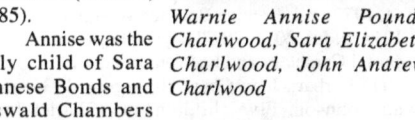
Warnie Annise Pounds Charlwood, Sara Elizabeth Charlwood, John Andrew Charlwood

Pounds, married Dec. 25, 1937. Sara Bonds was born Nov. 1, 1920 at 503 Washington Street, Booneville. Oswald Pounds (b. Aug. 28, 1915, New Site, MS, d. Dec. 19, 1975 at home in Booneville) is buried in Booneville Cemetery.

David Epting Charlwood's father, Knowles Shaw Charlwood (b. Jan. 9, 1929) md. Bettie Ann Davis (b. Apr. 22, 1931 in Union County), the daughter of Sam Davis and Fannie Epting Davis of Union County. David's grandfather was Knowles S. Charlwood Sr. of Buchanan, MI.

Sara Bonds and Oswald Pounds were related and parents and grandparents used the Bible to agree to the wedding.

Nellie Andres Smith (b. Feb. 14, 1894, d. Jun. 10, 1991) md. Jul. 12, 1914 to Roy Festus Bonds (b. Jul. 3, 1894, d. Oct. 13, 1959). They had two children, Sara Annece and Roy Jackson "Piggy" Bonds. Piggy married Shelby Jean Bishop Oct. 17, 1959. They have three daughters and their husbands and five grandchildren.

Nellie Smith's mother was Annie Wroten who married Andrew Jackson "Jack" Smith (b. Sep. 8, 1860), the son of Vincent Allentharp Smith of South Carolina and the grandson of Isaac Smith.

Annie Wroten Smith was the daughter of Christenna Goddard (b. Oct. 15, 1841, d. Apr. 21, 1870) and E. Carrol Wroten (b. Oct. 29 1833, d. May 18, 1901). He was the older son of Elisha and Permelia A. Wroten who came to old Tishomingo County when land became available from the Chickasaw Cession in what is known as sections of land around the Siloam area.

Oswald Pounds' parents were Warnie Elvira Wroten (b. Feb. 15 1891, d. Oct. 23, 1953) and Seth William Alexander Pounds (b. Dec. 10, 1888, d. Sep. 19, 1959).

Warnie Wroten Pounds' parents were Robert W. Wroten (b. 1852 and lived 88 years), the youngest child of Elisha and Permelia A. Wroten and Nancy Ann Randolph (b. Dec. 20, 1852, d. Jun. 18, 1916). They married Aug. 26, 1873 as recorded in the Wroten Bible. Therefore, Annie Wroten Smith and Warnie Wroten Pounds were first cousins.

Annise Pounds Charlwood was acquainted with pain and her two children, Sara and John, knew about someone being ill. Annise was diagnosed with Hodgkins disease when Sara Elizabeth was 2 years old. Annise continued with her job while taking treatment. Her family can never ever forget the prayers, the love, the care offered from acquaintances, friends and loved ones.

John Andrew doesn't remember how his mother fought to live to give birth to him. She was four months pregnant before the realization occurred that it was "not just cancer but a baby." Don't ever say that prayers are not answered in more ways than one can imagine! When time proved that John would live, Annise gave up the battle and said she was ready to go home.

David Charlwood has been blessed with a wonderful wife, Martha. Sara, John and Jacob are my grandchildren. Submitted by *Sara Bonds Pounds*.

CHASE FAMILY,

the following was extracted from The Chases From Old Tishomingo County, MS by Sandra Lewis Gray, Library of Congress Control #00-091074.

Chase Family. Jennie, Columbus Bunyon Chase, Roxie Whitfield Chase, Willie, Charlie, Sylvester, Luther, Tom, Lee, Ollie Lester, Walter and Paul

Columbus Bunyan Chase was born in eastern Prentiss County Nov. 14, 1863, the fifth child of Jonathan Thomas and Mary Ann Chase. He had two brothers, John Marshal and Jefferson Davis and two sisters, Agnes Emaline II and Isabel J. John Marshal and Agnes Emaline were the children of Jonathan Thomas Chase's first marriage to Agnes Emaline Smith who died in childbirth with Agnes Emaline II.

Columbus Bunyan Chase married Roxie Ann Whitfield (b. 1871) and had 11 children:

I) Willie Etta Chase (b. Jan. 22, 1890, d. Oct. 24, 1952) md. Henry Lee Shamblin (b. Oct. 30, 1883, d. Mar. 13, 1963). Both are buried at old Armstrong Cemetery.

II) David Walter Chase (b. Oct. 29, 1891, d. May 3, 1952) md. Essie Marie Thompson (b. 1899). He is buried at old Buck Snort Cemetery.

III) Jennie Pearl Chase (b. Feb. 26, 1894, d. Aug. 21, 1959) is buried at old Armstrong Cemetery.

IV) Luther Clayton Chase (b. Dec. 21, 1895, d. Oct. 11, 1994) md. Noda Lois McCoy (b. Aug. 24,

109

1908, d. Jul. 17, 1974), buried at New Lebanon Freewill Baptist Church Cemetery in Tishomingo County. They had eight children:

1) Gerald Gene Chase (b. 1929) md. Peggy Sue Stacy and second, Jean Turbeville.

2) Ernestine Chase (b. 1931) md. Jessie Baker, has one child Theresa Ann Baker (b. 1955) md. Dean Marcus Simpson, has three children: Dean Ryan Simpson (b. 1978), Mason Albright Simpson (b. 1981), Jessie Lauren Simpson (b. 1983).

3) Veston Eudell Chase (b. 1935) md. Clara Belle Tucker, has four children: (1) Michael Roy Chase (b. 1959) md. Sara Frances Kizer, has two children: Michael Roy Chase Jr. and Heather Leigh Chase. (2) Gregory Lynn Chase (b. 1962) md. Johnya Lamb, one child, Brandon Gregory Chase. (3) Beverly Kay Chase (b. 1968) md. Joseph Eric Medley, two children: Nicholas Aaron Medley and Erica Lynette Medley. (4) Timothy Alan Chase (b. 1973) md. Vickie Stearns.

4) Sadie Lou Chase (b. 1939) md. Roy Buford Gist, three children: (1) Mickey Roy Gist (b. 1959) md. Karen Doris Whitaker and second, Laura Miller, two children: Brian Chase Gist (b. 1984) and Cody Ray Gist (b. 1989). (2) Felicia Joyce Gist (b. 1965) md. Charlie Lee Powers, two children: Emily Nicole Powers (b. 1987) and Jacob Lee Powers (b. 1993). (3) Dana Gail Gist (b. 1967) md. Jeffrey Lee Lyles, two children: Joshua Lewis Lyles (b. 1992) and Sara Danielle Lyles (b. 1996).

5) Linda Quay Chase (b. 1941) md. George Monroe Michael and second, William Joe Hooper, four children: (1) Randy Allen Michael (b. 1962) md. Melody Tudor, one child, Jonathan Erick Chase Michael (b. 1985); (2) Darron Scott Michael (b. 1965) md. Amy Annette Thigpen, one child, Chase Allen Michael (b. 1988); (3) Sally Nicole Hooper (b. 1974); (4) Andy Kevin Hooper (b. 1979).

6) Bobby Wayne Chase (b. 1943) md. Vivian Marie Queen, three children: (1) Peter Anthony Chase (b. 1974); (2) Cynthia Marie Abbott Chase married first, Harold Gene Edmondson and second, Rodney L. Pollard, two children: Matthew Scott Edmondson and Marcus Alan Pollard; (3) Jeffrey Abbot Chase (b. 1963).

7) Sandra Oreda Chase (b. 1949) md. Nathan A. Russell, three children: Matthew Paul Russell (b. 1977); Natheda Kate Russell (b. 1979) and Jonathan Austin Russell (b. 1981).

8) Danny Joe Chase (b. 1952, d. 1983).

V) Thomas Olen Chase (b. Apr. 10, 1898, d. Oct. 4, 1980), buried at Old Buck Snort Cemetery, married Lola Faye Woodruff (b. Oct. 13, 1897), four children:

(1) James Wallace Chase (b. Oct. 6, 1928) md. Jeanette Brackeen, three children: 1) Ronald Quinn Chase Sr. (b. 1955) md. Karen Lowery, three children: Amanda Faye Chase, Ronald Quinn Chase Jr. and Mitchel Craig Chase. 2) Donald Chase (b. 1957). 3) June Carlyon Chase (b. 1961).

(2) Thomas Wilton Chase (b. Oct. 19, 1929) md. Marjorie King, two children: (a) Terry Wayne Chase (b. Sep. 14, 1954) md. Paula Moore, one son, Kelby Shanon Chase (b. May 2, 1990); (b) Sandra Kay Chase (b. Sep. 20, 1960) md. Ronnie Johnson, one daughter, Mallory Leigh Johnson (b. Feb. 5, 1990).

(3) Robert Paul Chase (b. Oct. 27, 1935) md. Sara Langley, two children: Robert Paul Chase Jr. (b. Jun. 25, 1975) and Emily Elizabeth Chase (b. Sep. 13, 1976).

(4) Travis Ray Chase (b. Dec. 19, 1939) md. Linda Sue King, two children: (a) Regina Lynn Chase (b. Sep. 2, 1966) md. Kevin Lane Foster, three children: Audrie Alana Foster (b. Apr. 3, 1990); Hannah Brooke Foster (b. Feb. 5, 1996); Ashlyn Elizabeth Foster (b. Oct. 24, 1997). (b) Cheryl Ray Chase (b. Feb. 11, 1969) md. Scottie Sledge, two children: Carrie Leigh Sledge (b. Jan. 16, 1991), Jimmy Dwayne "J.D." Sledge (b. Feb. 11, 1999).

VI) James Oliver Chase (b. Mar. 17, 1900, d. Nov. 17, 1981), buried at Liberty Memorial Gardens, married Ola Mae Woodruff (b. Apr. 10, 1909), three children:

(1) Opal Euvonne Chase (b. Jan. 4, 1930) md. John Wesley Wilemon, three children: 1) Brenda Wilemon (b. Jul. 25, 1948) md. Richard Cohen, two children: (a) Angela Marlinda Smith (b. Dec. 8, 1966) md. Michel Norigenna, three children: Michel Norigenna Jr. (b. Feb. 10, 1998), Cecilia Christina Norigenna (b. Jul. 7, 1991), David Cunningham (b. Jun. 29, 1994); (b) Ginger Nicole Munsey (b. Aug. 7, 1978). 2) John Jr. Wilemon (b. Jan. 13, 1952). 3) Timothy Jay Wilemon (b. Nov. 9, 1963) md. Lisa Leonna Malone, one child Jessica Lunia Wilemon (b. Sep. 23, 1981) md. Christopher Inman.

(2) David Eudene Chase (b. Nov. 22, 1935) md. Peggy Rhoads, three children: Lura Jo Chase (b. Jul. 21, 1955), one child, David Neil Crook (b. Jul. 18, 1981); Michael Dale Chase (b. Feb. 22, 1957) md. Kathy Whitley, one son, Jeffrey Whitley Chase; Kimberly Ann Chase (b. Jul. 23, 1960) md. Thomas Horgan, one child, Savannah Jo Horgan (b. Jul. 28, 1994).

(3) Billy James Chase (b. Nov. 14, 1937, d. 1970) md. Betty Hallmark, three children: James Murray Chase (b. 1959); Elizabeth June Chase (b. 1963); Kathy Denise Chase (b. 1970).

VII) Lee Roy Chase (b. Mar. 25, 1902, d. Aug. 7, 1977) md. Arbie Arvada Holloway (b. Oct. 2, 1906, d. Aug. 4, 1967). They are buried at Old Bucksnort Cemetery. They had two children: (1) Raymond Troy Chase (b. Aug. 10, 1924, d. Sep. 6, 1992) md. Clara Raye Gray and second, Marie Green, buried at Jumpertown Cemetery, one son, Danny Troy Chase (b. Aug. 14, 1955) md. Kay Kennally, three children: Danielle Tee Chase (b. Sep. 14, 1978), Robert Joey Chase (b. Dec. 19, 1979), Casey James Chase (b. Oct. 14, 1982). (2) Zera Gwendolyn Chase (b. Nov. 11, 1926) md. David Erastus Denson, one son, Randy Dave Denson (b. Jun. 20, 1958) md. Lois Ann Masquelier.

VIII) Charles Homer Chase (b. Mar. 19, 1905, d. _), buried at Armstrong Cemetery, married Callie Johnson (b. Apr. 1, 1900), buried at Old Armstrong Cemetery, two children: Billy Charles Chase (b. Jun. 25, 1936, d. Nov. 8, 1939) and Sylvie Marie Chase (b. 1938) md. Lee Morgan, five children: Roger Lee Morgan, Linda Gayle Morgan, Stanley Dale Morgan, Barry Glenn Morgan and Anita Lynn Morgan.

IX) Kennie Lester Chase (b. Mar. 4, 1907, d. Jun. 4, 1972) md. Bernice Beatrice Westphal (b. Aug. 23, 1914, d. Jul. 20, 1998). They are buried at Liberty Memorial Cemetery and had four children:

(1) Barbara Jean Chase (b. Sep. 4, 1934) md. Dwain Johnson. Five children: (a) (Sharlet Jean Johnson (b. Jul. 20, 1953) md. Ricky Henderson, one son, Ryan Wade Henderson (b. Feb. 18, 1974); (b) Janeth Dean Johnson (b. May 21, 1955) md. Terry Lambert, three children: Bradley Wayne Lambert (b. Sep. 8, 1974, Cary Shane Lambert (b. Dec. 6, 1975) and Derek Tate Lambert (b. Jul. 30, 1984). (c) Melvy Quay Johnson (b. May 28, 1983) md. Jerry Morman, one child: Casandra Nicole Morman (b. Apr. 5, 1983). (d) Gail Angelo Johnson (b. Feb. 18, 1960) md. Fredie Holder. (e) Sharie Annette Johnson (b. Jan. 28, 1963) md. Jerry Jones, two children: Jeremy Dwain Jones (b. Aug. 23, 1984) and Jaran Page Jones (b. Sep. 6, 1989).

(2) Vernon Alvin Chase (b. Mar. 6, 1939) md. Elizabeth Scott, three children: (a) Lisa Michelle Chase (b. Aug. 25, 1962) md. Danny Swinney, two children: Jason Tyler Swinney (b. Oct. 13, 1988) and Jacob Seth Swinney (b. Oct. 1, 1992); (b) Timothy Allen Chase (b. Mar. 3, 1967); (c) Christopher Scott Chase (b. Aug. 5, 1971) md. Tammy Williams, one child, Holly Brooke Chase (b. Dec. 7, 1999).

(3) Sharon Ann Chase (b. Jan. 27, 1944) md. James McLaughlin, two children: (a) Tatia Lynn McLaughlin (b. Aug. 31, 1966) md. Wallace Carpenter III, two children: Haley Anne Carpenter (b. Oct. 8, 1992) and Taylor Lynn Carpenter (b. Sep. 21, 1997).

(b) Lora McClaughlin (b. Aug. 17, 1968) md. Robert Chandler, three children: Caitlin Nicole Chandler (b. Aug. 30, 1991), Macey Marie Chandler (b. Aug. 25, 1994) and Sydney Reed Chandler (b. May 17, 1999).

(4) David Gilbert Chase (b. Sep. 27, 1952) md. Kara McKinney, three children: (a) Tara Linsay Chase (b. Jun. 21, 1977) md. John Eric Herrington; (b) David Chase Jr. (b. Sep. 7, 1984) and (c) Lydia Chase (b. Mar. 18, 1993).

X) Columbus Paul Chase (b. 1909, d. 1962) md. Ruby Lee Richardson (b. 1907, d. 1974) three children: (a) Hilton Ray Chase Jr. (b. 1938) md. Robbie Evelyn Russell (b. 1947), three children: Hilton Ray Chase (b. 1965); Emily Larose Chase (b. 1968) and Jeremy Kenneth Chase (b. 1973). (b) Juanita June Chase (b. 1940) md. Billy Boyd and second, Billy Hill (b. 1935), four children: Michael Wayne Boyd (b. 1958) md. Christy Darlene Jones; Regina Gail Hill (b. 1963) md. Robert Michael McDonald, two children; Billy Miles Hill (b. 1971) and David Alan Hill (b. 1977). (c) Paul Dillard Chase (b. 1943) md. Jayne Evelyn Riley (b. 1947), three children: Christina Michelle Chase (b. 1965), Todd Riley Chase (b. 1967), Jay Paul Chase (b. 1978).

XI) Sylvester Chase (b. Dec. 9, 1911, d. Aug. 21, 1936), buried at Old Forked Oak Cemetery, married Minnie Bell Roy (b. 1917), one child: Bobbie Nell Chase (b. 1936) md. Douglas Fairbanks Alford (b. 1921), five children: (a) Douglas Alford (b. 1952) md. Lamniey Juanita Hall, one child, Christina Yvette Alford (b. 1973); (b) Reva Rebecca Alford (b. 1954) md. Stephen Ray Ferguson; (c) Linda Nell Alford (b. 1959) md. Virgil Walter Duncan, two children: Wesley Mitchell Duncan (b. 1979) and Shannon Laura Duncan (b. 1980); (d) Teresa Ann Alford (b. 1962); (e) Donavan Ray Alford (b. 1971). *Submitted by Sandra Lewis Gray.*

CHASE, JOHN, born 1788 and his wife, Elizabeth born 1792, were both from North Carolina and came to the Altitude Community around 1836. They had five children:

Jonathan Thomas and Mary Chase

1) John Chase Jr. (b. 1819 in North Carolina) md. Nancy Cooper, second, Mary Trotter and third, Elizabeth Jones. He had eight children: Sara Jane (b. 1847), John J. (b. 1851), Mary A.V. (b. 1853), William M. (b. 1856), Eliza (b. 1858), Benjamin (b. 1861), Nancy A. (b. 1866) and Melvina (b. 1868).

2) Nancy Chase (b. 1822 in North Carolina).

3) Lucinda Chase (b. 1826 in Tennessee).

4) Jonathan Thomas Chase (b. Feb. 24, 1828 in Tennessee) md. Feb. 8, 1850 to Agnes Emaline Smith (b. 1828 in Tennessee). They had two children: (1) John Marshal Chase (b. 1851, d. 1918) md. Ann Green McCoy (b. 1851, d. 1949), sister to James Monroe McCoy. They had nine children: Henry, Maudie, Richard, Effie, Samuel, Thomas, Charles, Henrietta and Sadie. John and Ann McCoy Chase are buried at Forked Oak Cemetery. (2) Agnes Emaline Chase II (b. Jul. 20, 1853) md. James Monroe McCoy (b. Nov. 22, 1857), brother to Ann Green McCoy. They lived in the eastern part of Prentiss County and had eight children: William Coley (b. Jan. 2, 1875, d. Jun. 29, 1953); Columbus Curtiss (b. Jan. 4, 1880, d. Jul. 7,

1953); Margaret Emma (b. Sep. 3, 1883, d. Nov. 19, 1965); Henry Marshal (b. Feb. 10, 1885, d. Sep. 29, 1977); Robert Thomas (b. Aug. 9, 1887, d. Aug. 7, 1982); Carrol Blanchard (b. Nov. 29, 1889, d. Sep. 1, 1987); Homer Talmadge (b. Apr. 18, 1898, d. Jun. 26, 1984); James Auther "Cap" McCoy (b. Jul. 4, 1893, d. Sep. 5, 1984).

Agnes Emaline Chase McCoy died Aug. 22, 1944 and James Monroe McCoy died Apr. 21, 1936. They are buried at the New Hope Cemetery. Agnes Emaline Smith Chase died in childbirth with Agnes Emaline II Jul. 20, 1853. It is not known where she is buried. Upon the death of Agnes Emaline Smith Chase, Thomas married a second time to Mary Gambil McClure (b. Apr. 10, 1825) and they had five children.

3) Jefferson Davis Chase (b. 1856) md. Mary E. Rogers and had two children: Clarence H. (b. 1895) and Claudius M. (b. 1897).

4) Isabel J. Chase (b. 1858).

5) Columbus Bunyan Chase (b. Nov. 14, 1863) md. Roxie Ann Whitfield (b. 1871). Children: Willie Etta (b. 1890); David Walter (b. 1891); Jennie Pearl (b. 1894); Luther Clayton (b. 1895); Thomas Olen (b. 1898); James Oliver (b. 1900); Lee Roy (b. 1902); Charles Homer (b. 1905); Kenny Lester (b. 1907); Columbus Paul (b. 1909); Sylvester (b. 1911).

Columbus Bunyan Chase died Sep. 3, 1941 and Roxie Chase died Jan. 18, 1938. They are buried at Armstrong Cemetery.

5) Samuel (b. 1829) was married six times: Elizabeth Smith, Mary Barber, Sara Jane, R.E. Stanton, Lucy Ann Jacobs and M.J. Gambiel.

All information on this family was abstracted from "The Chases of Old Tishomingo County, MS." Submitted by Sandra Lewis Gray, great-great-great-granddaughter. Library of Congress Control Number 00-091074.

CHASE, JOHN MARSHAL, born 1851, was the first born of Jonathan Thomas and Agnes Emaline Smith Chase of the Burton Community. He married Ann Green McCoy (b. Jan. 8, 1871), daughter of William Henry and Sarah McCloud Howell McCoy. She was the sister of James Monroe McCoy that married Agnes Emaline Chase II, sister of John Marshal Chase. They lived in Eastern Prentiss County on a hill above where Mrs. Estel (U.L.) Taylor now lives on County Road 2160. A part of the old potato house remained a few years back. John made brick and some still remain at certain homes around in that community.

They had nine children: Richard M. Chase (b. 1893, d. 1952); Henry Dewey Chase (b. May 13, 1899, d. Nov. 14, 1907); Maudie Bell Chase (b. May 9, 1893, d. Oct. 12, 1894); Effie Chase (b. Dec. 31, 1896, d. Dec. 15, 1980) md. Aubrey M. Harper; Samuel R. Chase (b. May 5, 1901, d. Dec. 1, 1982) md. Ruby Holder; Thomas Chase married Sophia Searcy; Charles Chase (b. Feb. 22, 1905, d. Jan. 26, 1964) md. Irma Tennison; Carlos Alphanso Chase (b. Apr. 22, 1907, d. Feb. 2, 1913); Henrietta "Ettie" Chase (b. Mar. 30, 1910, d. Apr. 14, 1986) md. Johny Pace; Sadie Chase married Joe Rushing.

The fifth child of John Marshal and Ann Green McCoy Chase, Samuel R. Chase, married Ruby Holder. They raised their family at Burton and had three children:

1) Joyce Chase (b. Jun. 12, 1937) md. James D. Phifer, two children: (a) Paula Joyce Phifer (b. Oct. 9, 1961) md. William Steven White, four children: William Steven White Jr. (b. May 25, 1989); Sarah Grace White (b. Jul. 24, 1990); Robert Alexander White (b. Jul. 2, 1991); Mary Madeline White (b. May 12, 1995). (b) James Kevin Phifer (b. Nov. 18, 1969).

2) Raymond Joe Chase (b. Nov. 6, 1939), four children: Jody Chase, Cathy Chase, Charlotte Chase, Annette Chase.

3) James Howard Chase (b. Jan. 11, 1946) md. Virginia Hughes, one child, Melissa Gail Chase (b. Dec. 14, 1973).

John Marshall Chase died in 1918 and Ann Green McCoy Chase in 1949. They are buried in Forked Oak Cemetery in Eastern Prentiss County.

All information on this family was abstracted from "The Chases of Old Tishomingo County, MS." Submitted by Sandra Lewis Gray. Library of Congress Control Number 00-091074.

CHASE, JONATHAN THOMAS and Agnes Emaline Smith Chase were married Feb. 8, 1850. The second child born to this union was Agnes Emaline Chase II (b. Jul. 20, 1853). She was named for her mother who had died during childbirth. She never knew much about her mother to pass on to future generations. She worked hard at a young age, being loaned out to other farm families for labor.

James Monroe and Agnes Emaline Chase McCoy

She married James Monroe McCoy, son of William Henry and Sarah McCloud Howell McCoy. He was born in Monroe County, MS on Nov. 22, 1857 and had eight brothers and sisters: John Laminus (b. Jul. 1, 1855, d. Dec. 4, 1926); Sally (b. Sep. 23, 1860, d. Apr. 12, 1952); William Benjamin (b. Oct. 27, 1862, d. Feb. 21, 1939); George Arthur (b. Jul. 24, 1865, d. Oct. 24, 1942); Daniel Andrews (b. Feb. 21, 1869, d. 1886); Ann Green McCoy (b. Jan. 8, 1871, d. February 1949); Margaret Emily McCoy (b. Oct. 16, 1873, d. Mar. 5, 1939); Otis McCoy (b. May 3, 1875, d. Jan. 12, 1945).

James and Agnes II lived in the Burton Community and had the following eight children:

1) William Coley (b. Jan. 2, 1875, d. Jun. 29, 1953) md. Artie Bell Stokes Shefield and had six children.

2) Columbus Curtiss (b. Jan. 4, 1880, d. Jul. 7, 1953) md. Cora Thompson.

3) Margaret Emma "Maggie" (b. Sep. 3, 1883) md. George Burcham.

4) Henry Marshel (b. Feb. 10, 1885, d. Sep. 29, 1977) md. Della Faye Leeth.

5) Robert Thomas (b. Aug. 9, 1887, d. Aug. 7, 1982) md. Ola Butler.

6) Carrol Blanchard (b. Nov. 29, 1889, d. Sep. 1, 1987) md. Elzie Scroggin.

7) Homer (b. Apr. 18, 1898, d. Jun. 26, 1984) md. Allie Vesta Boyd and second, Louise Boone.

8) James Arthur "Cap" (b. Jul. 4, 1893, d. Sep. 5, 1984).

McCoy Family

James Monroe and Agnes Emaline Chase McCoy are buried at New Hope Cemetery in eastern Prentiss County.

All information on this family was abstracted from "The Chases of Old Tishomingo County, MS." Submitted by Sandra Lewis Gray, great-great-granddaughter. Library of Congress Control #00-091074.

CLARK - WILLIAMS - UMFRESS, my great-grandparents were Stephen Taylor "Bud" Clark and Dicie Ann Williams. Grandpa Bud was the son of William Thomas Clark and Melvina (last name unknown). Grandpa Bud's brothers were John B., Louis C., William, Levi A., James C. and his sisters were Martha J. and Delitha C. They lived in the Tishomingo and later Prentiss County. There is no more information on grandma Dicie's and Melvin's families.

Stephen Taylor and Isora Umfress Clark

Grandpa Bud and Grandma Dicie Ann lived in the Snowdown Community. They owned and lived at what was later known as the Archie and Jessie Armstrong place. At that time it was quite a large farm. Grandpa Bud farmed and had a blacksmith shop. Grandpa Bud and Grandma Dicie's children were William Henry (md. Francis "Fannie" Jane Smith), Alexander "Alex" (md. Josie Wren), Harriet (md. Robert Franklin Smith), Artie (md. Joe Frank Stephenson), Rozela "Rosie" (md. Lee Wren) and my grandmother, Dora Dallas (b. Jun. 16, 1887). She married Oscar Wren who died in the 1918 influenza epidemic. In 1920 she married George Armstrong. The youngest child, Annie, married Athe McGaughey. Aunt Annie was born about a month before Grandma Dicie Ann died in October 1895. Aunt Harriet was the oldest daughter and wasn't married at this time. She took care of the other children and helped Grandpa Bud until he married Isora Umfress in March 1896. They had three children and one son, Joseph "Joe," married Ada Tidwell. They had two daughters, Mary Lou (md. Gordon Woodruff) and Jessie May (md. Archie Armstrong). Grandpa Bud and both wives are buried at Liberty Hill Cemetery. *Submitted by Mauvolene (Rinehart) Dawson.*

CLEVELAND, WEBSTER JR., is a descendant of Basil Harris and Joseph Cleveland, pioneers of Mississippi.

Neola Hollingsworth Cleveland is a descendant of William Hale and James Hollingsworth, who both served in the Revolutionary War.

After graduation from Belmonth High, Webster attended Wood Junior College, University of Mississippi and University of Tennessee in Memphis. He did residencies in Atlanta and Vicksburg and practiced in Tishomingo County for four years. He enlisted in the US Air Force during the Korean Conflict and served as Chief of Surgery at Shaw Air Base in South Carolina for two years. After discharge, he practiced medicine/surgery in Booneville, retiring in 1997.

Neola graduated from Belmont High and then worked in Decatur, AL, almost 12 years. She worked for the Prentiss County Home Bank and Peoples Bank until her children were born. When the children were in kindergarten and school, she entered Northeast Mississippi Junior College; earned a degree in elementary education at Blue Mountain College and attended the University of Mississippi, earning a master's and doctorate in educational education.

Webster and Neola were married Oct. 10, 1956, at Belmont. Craig Webster was born Apr. 10, 1960; Candace Cleveland Forbes Sep. 26, 1961 and Kerry Owen Jun. 28, 1963 in Booneville.

Craig graduated from Booneville High in 1978, attended Northeast, University of Mississippi and

Southern College of Optometry in Memphis and is practicing optometry in Booneville. He married Donna Lee Griffin in 1985. Cameron Webster was born Jan. 11, 1993 and Constance Lee Apr. 30, 1995.

Candy graduated from Booneville High in 1979 and attended Northeast and Mississippi State University, earning degrees in business administration and petroleum engineering. She married James Thomas Forbes of Starkville in 1985 and they moved to Texas. She earned a pharmacy degree at the University of Texas in Austin. Their children are: Anna Lee (b. Dec. 1, 1992), James Callahan (b. Dec. 7, 1994) and Bailey Elizabeth (b. Jan. 28, 1997). They live in Tomball where she is a pharmacist.

Kerry graduated from Booneville High in three years, attended Northeast, Memphis State and the University of Mississippi Medical Center, completing residencies at Methodist, Memphis in Internal Medicine and in Infectious Diseases and is now practicing in Memphis.

All three children were active in scouts and band in high school and at Northeast. Craig played trumpet, Candy played tenor saxophone and oboe and Kerry played French horn and marching French horn. Both boys earned Eagle in scouting and God and Country Awards. Candy was the first girl in Prentiss County to earn a God and Country Award.

Neola is currently a division vice president and local registrar of UDC; past regent and local registrar in DAR; state third vice president and local public relations person in Kappa Kappa Iota; president of Booneville Woman's Club; past president and recording secretary of Booneville Pilot Club with perfect attendance sine 1957; Berea class secretary of First Baptist Church; Empathy of Sunshine Servants and incoming leader with Webster of JoyMakers. Both are members of Chamber of Commerce and Friends of Library.

After solo practice, Webster joined the Medical Clinic. He is a Mason, past president of Jaycees; past state president of SAR; past president and Paul Harris Fellow of Rotary; a member of the American Medical Association, VFW, American Legion and SCV. *Submitted by Webster Cleveland Jr.*

COLE, AUDREY MARIE FLOYD was the eldest daughter of Rocky Lee Floyd (b. Mar. 13, 1896, d. Oct. 27, 1972) and Esther Lee Moorman (b. Dec. 22, 1900, d. Aug. 13, 1946). They were married Jun. 17, 1917. Her grandparents were William Floyd and Sarah Ashcraft and John Moorman and Mary Ellen Cole. Marie was born Dec. 27, 1921 in Prentiss County. Her brothers and sisters are: Willie Ophas Floyd (b. Oct. 1, 1918, d. Dec. 11, 1994); Henry Cecil Floyd (b. May 19, 1920, d. Jul. 7, 1921); Opal Autherene Floyd (b. Mar. 24, 1924, d. Aug. 12, 1951); Troy Ray Floyd (b. Dec. 11, 1926, d. Dec. 11, 1927); Lee Tulen Floyd (b. May 27, 1927); Clettis Earl Floyd (b. Feb. 25, 1932, d. Mar. 24, 1999); Mary Francis Floyd (b. Dec. 17, 1935). Marie's father re-married following Esther Lee's passing to Elviree Whitehead (b. Apr. 1, 1916, d. Mar. 12, 1981). To this union was born Jimmie Lee Floyd (b. Jul. 31, 1949), Jerry Don Floyd (b. Jan. 28, 1951, d. May 30, 1986) and Larry Eugene Floyd (b. May 30, 1952, d. Sep. 8, 1982).

Marie married Walter James Cole (b. Feb. 23, 1913, d. Jul. 18, 1994) Nov. 14, 1936. She was 14 at the time and he was 23. They lived in Prentiss County most of the time, although they did live in Leesburg, LA on two different occasions while Walter was doing farm work and in Florida during part of 1958. The Florida house was a corncrib that had been converted into a house. Walter also had a short stay in Chicago doing factory work.

At the age of 10, Marie was baptized into The Church of Jesus Christ of Latterday Saints. She attended school through the sixth grade at Tuscumbia and Hills Chapel. Two of her children (Kathleen and Don) became Thrasher valedictorians.

Walter and Marie had 12 children: Charles Wayne (b. Sep. 27, 1937, d. May 21, 1939); Aubrey Gene (b. Apr. 13, 1940-Jul. 27, 1988); Audra Dean (b. Jul. 23, 1944-); Billy James (b. Sep. 20, 1946-); Esther Lee (b. Feb. 28, 1949-Mar. 10, 1949); Bobby (b. Jul. 1, 1950-Jul. 1, 1950); Anetta Susan (b. Feb. 6, 1952-); Walter Herman (b. Jul. 24, 1954-); Sarah Kathleen (b. Apr. 15, 1957-); Freddie Don (b. Oct. 16, 1958-); Freda Marie (b. Aug. 13, 1961-) and Johnny Hank (b. Nov. 14, 1966-). All of the children were born in Prentiss County.

From left: Jimmie Lee Floyd, Francis Floyd Stephenson, Tulon Floyd and Marie Floyd Cole (1999).

When Walter and Marie met, he was home from a CCC camp. Walter spotted her, casually walked up and put his arm around her. Marie's date took one look at him and walked away. The rest, as they say, is history.

Marie is a good housekeeper and gardener and about the best cook you'd find anywhere. She learned as a child the basic skills of doing things and working hard and is very talented. She played the guitar and dabbled for a time with painting beautiful pictures. When she was able, she made sure all of her children and grandchildren had one of her hand-made quilts. *Submitted by John T. Larsen.*

COLLIER, AMOS, in the 1820 census of Perry County, TN, Amos Collier and his wife were 26 to 45 years old and had four daughters and one son, all under 10 years of age.

Amos was next found on a jury in 1826 and in April 1829. The 1830 census shows Amos and wife still in Perry County, age 30 to 40, with six sons and five daughters. By 1837 Amos and family were in Tishomingo County, MS.

The 1850 census shows Amos Collier (b. North Carolina) and wife, Nancy, (b. South Carolina) in Southern District, Tishomingo County, with daughter, Alsey, age 18, (b. Alabama) and older children (b. Tennessee). Evidently, the Colliers moved to Alabama by 1832 and squatted there for a time waiting for Indian lands to open up in the Mississippi Territory.

In 1850 their daughter, Sarah, was living near them with husband, James Crumby and six children. Son, George, was 20 and son, Henry, was 36. Henry and wife, Sarah, lived near his parents in the New Site area, east of Booneville. Their children were: Amos, Squire Boone, John, Livonia and Mahala (b. Tennessee) and Allan K., George W. and Mary A. (b. Mississippi). Nearby were son, Abraham, his wife, Emeline and their children, Arthur and Nancy C.

The Collier family was well documented in the *History of Old Tishomingo County* by Fan Alexander Cochran in relation to the first hanging in Tishomingo County. A man was shot while hoeing cotton for Amos. The killer was subsequently hanged by the sheriff on Dec. 5, 1845.

At the August 1863 term of Tishomingo Court, the estate of Amos Collier was put under an administrator to pay off his debts. Dates of his and his wife's deaths are unknown.

In the 1860 census, Amos was 69 and Nancy was 67. Apparently, the family suffered greatly during the Civil War. His children split over the issues involved. Some fought for the Confederacy, some moved north and took the other side. Amos lost nearly everything and died in debt. His family scattered from Illinois to Arkansas. Several of his children died before he did.

When the December 1865 Court met, the report of the administrator was that the remainder of the Collier land would have to be sold to pay off some of the indebtedness and that this would not be enough. Amos had invested in Confederate Treasury Bonds and these, of course, were now worthless. Court proceedings name several children and grandchildren of Amos and Nancy Collier, which are listed below. Their daughter, Sarah, was one of my maternal great-grandmothers.

1. Elizabeth (descendant) married John Finch. Their children were: Paul Finch; Fannie, who married Andrew Cunningham; another daughter, who married A.L. Cunningham; Sarah Crabb; G.W. Finch; Martha Finch and Amos Finch.

2. Henry Collier (descendant). His children were Amos Collier, Samuel Collier and Lavonia, who married William Adams.

3. Jack (descendant). His children were Bud and Mahala Collier.

4. Martha of Itawamba County married Michael McDaniel.

5. Abraham Collier of Arkansas.

6. William Collier (descendant) of Illinois.

7. Frances Draper of Alabama.

Some of the family moved to Texas and Oklahoma after the Civil War. *Submitted by Dennis Ward.*

COUNCE, ELLIS ROBERT, is the great-grandson of William "Colonel" Counce of Lawrenceburg, TN. William Counce was born Nov. 23, 1813 and married Martha Shackelford Oct. 13, 1837 in Lawrence County, TN. Martha was born Jul. 4, 1818, to James P. and Mary Ann Roberts Shackelford. William and Martha Counce had five children: Mary Ann (b. 1839); Elizabeth (b. 1840); Peter H. (b. 1841); Samantha Ann (b. 1843) and Martha Amanda (b. 1844).

In December 1861, Peter enlisted as a private in Co. G of the 53rd Tennessee Infantry from Giles County. He was taken prisoner by federal troops at New Hope Church, GA, Jun. 5, 1864 and confined to Rock Island Barracks, Rock Island, IL. On May 3, 1865, Peter was exchanged for a captured northern soldier in New Orleans, LA. While Peter faced the difficulties of being a Confederate soldier during the Civil War, his family faced their own burdens in Tennessee. Union soldiers raided the Counce farm taking livestock and food and they are believed to have burned the family's kitchen, which was attached to the house. The Counce farm was located near the Lawrence-Giles County line where the house still stands.

After the war, Peter married Evaline White and they had 10 children: John, Hugh, Curt, Phelan, Will, Davy, Icy, Samantha, Gentry and Thelma. After William Counce's death Jan. 9, 1890, Peter moved his wife and children to Prentiss County, MS where he bought land and settled his family. John H. Counce (b. 1885) married Agnes Viola Lyons (b. 1900) in 1915 and they had three children: Ellis Robert (b. 1928), Clovis Eugene "Gene" (b. 1918) and Evaline. Evaline died during infancy.

Ellis Robert Counce served in Utility Squadron One of the US Naval Air based in the Hawaiian Islands during WWII. He is a retired businessman, who lived in Little Rock, AR and Memphis, TN before returning to Booneville. Ellis has one daughter, Amelia Lee "Amy" Counce (b. 1975). *Submitted by Amelia L. Counce.*

CRABB, ANNIAS NORRIS HUSTON, born Feb. 28, 1848 in Tennessee. He died Dec. 11, 1910 in Prentiss County, MS. He married Sarah Elizabeth Johnson, who was born in 1845 in Bay Springs, Tishomingo County, MS and died in 1925. Sarah's parents were Jefferson Johnson and Sarah Jane Carroll.

Both are buried in the Siloam Church Cemetery. Annias and Sarah were blessed with eight children and they were all born in Marietta, Prentiss County, MS.

Addison Wesley Boggs and Louetta Jane Crabb Boggs.

The first child, Normanda Paulie Paralia Crabb, born in 1871, married William Henery Adams Nov. 8, 1889.

The second child, Margaret Artellia Crabb, was born Sep. 2, 1873 and died Jun. 5, 1952 in Hollis, Harmon County, OK. She married William Franklin Kizer Dec. 28, 1890. He died Nov. 15, 1935 in Hollis, Harmon County, OK. Both are buried in O.M. Cemetery, north of Hollis.

The third child, John W. Crabb, born in 1876, married Georgia Randolph Nov. 4, 1894.

The fourth child, Louetta Jane Crabb, was born Jul. 25, 1878 and died Aug. 17, 1941 in Hollis, Harmon County, OK. She married Addison Wesley Boggs in Booneville, Prentiss County, MS (see Asbery Washington Boggs previously in book). Louetta and Addison are buried in O.M. Cemetery, north of Hollis, Harmon County, OK.

The fifth child, Frankie Crabb, born in March 1881, married ? Randolph about 1911.

The sixth child, Annie E. Crabb, born in 1882/1884, married Elija Worten about 1902.

The seventh child, Jeff J. Crabb, born in 1886, married Clemmie Boggs May 6, 1906.

The eighth child, Thomas W. Crabb, was born Oct. 8, 1890 and died Dec. 29, 1925. He married Ada Hall.

Annias Norris Huston Crabb is descended from James Hurd Crabb, who was born Nov. 15, 1826 in Loretta, Lawrence County, TN and died Jun. 27, 1914. On Jan. 7, 1847, James married Dicey Elizabeth Brashears, who was born Jul. 23, 1828 and died Sep. 3, 1869.

James Hurd Crabb descended from Joseph Crabb, who was born May 15, 1805 and died about 1880 in Mississippi. He married Catherine Rogers, who was born Mar. 8, 1804 and died Feb. 20, 1873.

I am descended from Addison Wesley Boggs and Louetta Jane Crabb. Addison and Louetta were my grandparents. *Submitted by Christy Boggs.*

CRABB, JAMES HURD, born Nov. 15, 1826 in Tennessee and died Jun. 27, 1914 in Prentiss County, MS. His first wife was Dicey Elizabeth Brashears (b. Jul. 23, 1828, Lawrence County, TN to Sep. 3, 1869, Prentiss County). They were married Jan. 7, 1847 in Lawrence County.

James and Dicey moved their family to the Prentiss County area of Tishomingo County in 1866 after the birth of their last child. All seven of their children were born in Lawrence County, TN. They were:

1. Hughston Anamos "Norris" Crabb (b. Feb. 28, 1848, to Dec. 1, 1910, Prentiss County) married Sarah Elizabeth Johnson (b. 1845 Mississippi to 1925 Prentiss County) Nov. 11, 1869 in Tishomingo County, MS. They are buried in Siloam Church Cemetery. Their children were Normanda, Margaret, John W., Louetta Jane, Frankie, Annie, Jeff J. and Thomas W.

2. Fountain Rogers Crabb (b. Aug. 13, 1851, to Feb. 12, 1919, Prentiss County) first married M.J. Weaver. Their children were F.E. and A.B. Then, he married Amanda Eleanor Anderson (b. Apr. 4, 1865, Alabama to Sep. 18, 1919, Prentiss County). Fountain and Amanda are buried in Siloam Church Cemetery near Booneville. Their children were Amanda, Ananias, Harvey, Eddie M., Lily J., Thomas and Fountain Houston.

3. William Joseph Crabb (b. Jan. 22, 1853, to Sep. 2, 1873, Prentiss County) married Polly Ann Hathcock (b. 1850 Mississippi) Aug. 15, 1872 in Prentiss County. William is buried in Siloam Church Cemetery.

4. James Walter Crabb (b. Sep. 24, 1856, to Oct. 24, 1937, Booneville) married Elizabeth Elander Hathcock (b. Nov. 4, 1856, Mississippi to Oct. 24, 1940, Booneville). Their children were: James Lonza; Martha Lou; William Walter; James Vester; Menta Lee; Houston Asbury; Oscar Lee; Columbus E.; Daniel Chester; R.C. Elton and J. Prentiss. Elizabeth Hathcock's parents were Fern Hathcock and Lucinda McDaniel.

5. Sarah Narcissa Catherine Crabb (b. June 1858) married George M. Murphy (b. Apr. 1854 in Alabama). Their children were Annie, George W., Robert Frances, Emmett O. and Mandy Earl.

6. Thomas Asberry Crabb (b. Sep. 12, 1861, to Dec. 24, 1940, Prentiss County) married Serena Elizabeth Wesson (b. Aug. 4, 1860, Mississippi to Jan. 30, 1907, Prentiss County). They are buried in Hopewell Primitive Baptist Church Cemetery. Their children were: Willie Sarah Lenora, Mattie B., Nolan, James Oliver, Walter, Robert E. Lee, Clinton, George C., Alice, Clarence and Bruce Alexander.

7. Elizabeth "Betty" Jane Crabb (b. Jun. 14, 1865, to Nov. 29, 1935, Prentiss County) married William A. Hathcock (b. Dec. 15, 1868, Mississippi to Jan. 11, 1944, Prentiss County). They are buried in Little Brown Cemetery near Booneville. His parents were Andrew Jackson Hathcock and Serena Posney. Betty and William's children were: Andrew, Jessie, George William and Serena.

On Jul. 26, 1871 in Booneville, James married his son's mother-in-law, Mrs. Lucinda McDaniel Hathcock (b. Nov. 15, 1826, Alabama to Jun. 21, 1894, Prentiss County). James, Dicey and Lucinda are buried in Siloam Church Cemetery at Marietta.

During the Civil War, James served in the 48th Tennessee Infantry, Co. G under Captain Lewis Miller for the Confederate Army. *Submitted by Pamela Cay Crabb Devin, PMB #439, 1911 SW Campus Drive, Federal Way, WA 98023.*

CRABB, JAMES VESTER, born Mar. 9, 1881 to J. Walter Crabb, a merchant and Elizabeth Heathcock Crabb in eastern Prentiss County. He had two sisters, Lou Crabb Jones and Perminto Crabb Stevens and seven brothers: Houston, Chester, Prentiss, R.C., Will, Oscar and Lum.

In 1902 he married Clara Mattie Tynes, the daughter of Tishomingo County physician, Dr. Henry L. Tynes. They had six children: Audrey Crabb Trantham, Earl Crabb Shackelford, Alton, Humbert, Henry and R.L. He became a member of the Bay Springs Masonic Lodge on Nov. 21, 1903 and remained a member the rest of his life, receiving a 50 year Masonic pin in special ceremonies in 1960.

Dr. J.V. Crabb

Vester and Clara already had a family when he entered medical school. He graduated from the University of Tennessee College of Medicine on Jun. 6, 1914. He first practiced as a family physician in eastern Prentiss County and western Tishomingo County, making house calls at first on horseback. Their car, a Chevrolet touring car, bought about 1919, had a top attached at the windshield which was opened back in good weather. Sometimes Dr. Crabb's hat would fly off and they had to stop, get out and run the hat down.

In about 1927, Dr. Crabb opened an office on Church Street in Booneville and his wife was his nurse and assistant. He served as a family physician in Booneville until a short time before his death. He is best known for his eczema medicine which was good for poison ivy, cuts, scratches and other skin disorders as well as about the only known cure for eczema at the time. People came from far and wide to get it.

In 1982, his great-granddaughter, orthopedic surgeon, Dr. Linda Shackelford, then at William Beaumont Army Medical Center in El Paso, TX set a broken arm for retired army nurse and Prentiss County native Dillard Cunningham. The same arm was broken 50 years before and was set by Dr. Crabb!

He had a great sense of humor, always joking and most idle conversations would include at least one big yarn, especially delighting the grandchildren and great-grandchildren

Dr. Crabb died Jul. 2, 1965 and was buried in Little Brown Cemetery east of Booneville. His wife of over 50 years died Sep. 1, 1970 and was buried beside him. His obituary in *The Booneville Banner* stated: "At the time of his death, Dr. Crabb was one of the oldest practicing physicians in Prentiss County, both in seniority and by right of esteem. His entire life was a career of service, dedicated fully and willingly to humanity. His constructive influence which touched the entire county where he lived so long endures as a last memorial to his rare devotion and service.

"With the passing of years, he established his professional reputation and the demands on his service reached large proportions. He was interested in every aspect of medicine and he labored untiringly to elevate the standards of his profession. He left his work to speak for him and his long record as a family physician needs no commentator." *Submitted by Jeanette Shackelford.*

CRABB, JAMES WALTER, at the time of his death Oct. 24, 1937 in Booneville, James Walter Crabb owned over 1,400 acres, making him one of the largest landowners in Prentiss County. His parents, James Hurd Crabb and Dicey Brashears brought him to the county in 1868. They came from Lawrence County, TN where James Walter was born Sep. 24, 1856.

In February 1874 in Booneville, James married Elizabeth Ellender Hathcock (b. Nov. 4, 1856, Mississippi to Oct. 24, 1940, Booneville). She was the daughter of Fern Hathcock and Lucinda McDaniel. James and Elizabeth are buried in Siloam Cemetery.

They had 11 children, who were all born and died in Prentiss County (unless otherwise noted):

1. James Lonza Crabb (b. Jun. 8, 1876, to Aug. 26, 1876).

2. Martha Lou Crabb (b. Aug. 2, 1877, to Apr. 12, 1952) married Daniel Perry Jones (b. Nov. 1, 1877, to Feb. 4, 1899) Jul. 28, 1898 in Booneville. They are buried in Siloam Church Cemetery. Their children were Rausie and Perry Vestus.

3. William Walter Crabb (b. Nov. 14, 1879, to Jul. 12, 1958) married Nima Goodwin (b. Mar. 25, 1875, Prentiss County to May 14, 1927, Belmont) Nov. 11, 1896 in Booneville. Their children were: Walter, Luther, Audie, Autie Mae, Eula, Era, Lois and Claude. After Nima died, William married Nancy Posey, Ethel Eaton and Lynn Tennison.

4. James Vester Crabb (b. Mar. 9, 1881, to Jul. 3, 1965) married Clara Tyner (b. Sep. 2, 1884, to Sep. 2, 1970). They are buried in Little Brown Church Cemetery. Their children were: Audrey, Henry W., Alden, Earl, Humbert and R.L.

5. Menta Lee Crabb (b. Jul. 16, 1884, to Dec.

25, 1962) married Josiah Ebb Stephens (b. Jul. 25, 1877, to Jun. 16, 1968). They are buried in the Belmont Cemetery. Their children were Carey and Arey.

6. Houston Asbury Crabb (b. Aug. 7, 1885, to Jul. 26, 1972) married Bertha Mai Umfree (b. Mar. 1, 1883, to Nov. 30, 1977). They are buried in the Booneville Cemetery. Their children were La Nova Quay and Clytee Mauveline.

7. Oscar Lee Crabb (b. Feb. 9, 1889, to Feb. 19, 1951, Prentiss County) married Cleora Penny (b. Jun. 18, 1888, to Jul. 28, 1965). They are buried in Little Brown Cemetery. Their children were: O.C., Gladys, Estelle, Ruth, Randall and Gerald.

8. Columbus "Lum" E. Crabb (b. May 1, 1890, to Apr. 11, 1965) married Letra Weems (b. Mar. 29, 1895, to Jun. 27, 1973). They are buried in Booneville Cemetery. Their children were Jewell, Maxcine and Lavern.

9. Daniel Chester Crabb (b. Nov. 6, 1893, to Jan. 4, 1972) married Ida Mae Lewis (b. Nov. 17, 1907, Alcorn County to Nov. 24, 1993) Dec. 22, 1937 in Marietta, MS. They are buried in the Mt. Nebo Church Cemetery. They had one son, Daniel Prentiss.

10. R.C. Elton Crabb (b. Jul. 11, 1897, to Mar. 6, 1973) married Mollie Edna Windham (b. Aug. 20, 1905, to Apr. 30, 1991). They are buried in Booneville Cemetery. They had one son, Charles Elton.

11. J. Prentiss Crabb (b. Dec. 12, 1899, to Dec. 13, 1992, Fairfield, Butler County, Ohio) married Katie Fay Smith. They had one son, James Wilton. *Submitted by Steven Devin, 1911 SW Campus Drive PMB #439, Federal Way, Washington 98023.*

CRABB, JOSEPH, born May 19, 1805 in White County, TN and died after 1880, possibly in Prentiss County, MS. He was the son of Joseph Crabb (b. 1772 in Virginia and died after 1850 in Tennessee), son of Joseph Crabb (b. 1740-49 in Virginia and died in 1798 in Grainger County, TN). Joseph, born in 1805, married around 1824, to Catherine Rogers, born Mar. 8, 1804 in Tennessee and died Feb. 20, 1873 in Prentiss County, MS daughter of William Rogers and Rosey Herd. Joseph Crabb was still living Prentiss County, MS in 1880 with unmarried daughter, Malinda Jane Crabb.

Children of Joseph Crabb and Catherine Rogers were:

(1) Fountain Rogers Crabb, born in 1825 in Lawrence County, TN and died in 1844 in Lawrence County, TN married in 1858 in Lawrence County, TN to Elizabeth Brashears, born in 1822 in Lawrence County, TN and died in 1899 in Lawrence County, TN.

(2) James Hurd Crabb, born Nov. 15, 1826 in Tennessee and died Jun. 27, 1914 in Prentiss County, MS married in 1847 in Lawrence County, TN to Dicey Brashears (sister of Elizabeth), born Jul. 12, 1830 in Lawrence County, TN and died Sep. 3, 1869 in Prentiss County, MS. James Hurd Crabb then married Lucinda McDonald, born in 1826 in Alabama and died in 1894 in Prentiss County, MS. He was a Confederate soldier in the Civil War.

(3) William Perry Crabb, born in 1829 in Giles County, TN and died in 1893 in Yell County, AR, married first in 1850 in Lawrence County, TN to M. Elizabeth Horne, born in 1828 in Tennessee and died Aug. 3, 1878, Prentiss County, MS daughter of John Horne and Nancy Poteet. William Perry married a second time in 1879 in Prentiss County, MS to Mattie Lue Livingston, born in 1857 in Tennessee and died before 1893, possibly in Arkansas. He was a Union soldier in the Civil War, enlisting Dec. 1, 1862 in Corinth, MS as a private of Co. C, 1st Regiment, Alabama Cavalry Volunteers.

(4) Malinda Jane Crabb was born in 1831 in Giles County, TN and died after 1900 in Mississippi.

(5) Elizabeth Ann Crabb, born in 1833 in Giles County, TN and died Apr. 10, 1887 in Prentiss County, MS married Dec. 1, 1853 in Lawrence County, TN to Anderson Horne, born in 1833 and died Sep. 4, 1864 in Mississippi, son of John Horne and Nancy Poteet.

(6) Thomas Wesley Crabb, born Nov. 25, 1834 in Giles County, TN and died May 12, 1902 in Pope County, IL, married first in 1853 in Lawrence County, TN to Rachel Elizabeth Nutt/McNutt, born in 1834 in Bedford County, TN and died May 13, 1894 in Pope County, IL. Thomas married a second time in 1895 in Illinois to Henrietta Travelstead, born in 1845 in Illinois and died in 1938 in Illinois. He was a Confederate soldier in the Civil War.

(7) Rebecca Catherine Crabb, born Jan. 6, 1837 in Giles County, TN and died Feb. 15, 1917 in Prentiss County, MS married in 1866 in Tishomingo County, MS to Nelson Osborn Jenkins, who was born Mar. 10, 1848 in Georgia and died Jul. 27, 1925 in Alcorn County, MS son of James M. Jenkins and Narcissa.

(8) Joseph Crabb, born in 1839 in Giles County, TN and died Nov. 7, 1863 in Point Lookout, MD, married Jul. 5, 1860 in Tishomingo County, MS to Elizabeth Sarah Finch, born in 1843 in Prentiss County, MS daughter of John W. Finch and Elizabeth Collier. Joseph died as a POW He was a Confederate soldier in the Civil War.

(9) Rhoda E. Crabb, born in September 1841 in Tennessee, married Feb. 17, 1876 in Prentiss County, MS to William Thomas Ivey, born around 1837 in Tennessee and died after 1900.

(10) C. A. "Kyle," born Feb. 18, 1844 in Lawrence County, TN, died Mar. 20, 1859 in Prentiss County, MS and is buried in Siloam Cemetery in Prentiss County, MS.

(11) Rosa Narcissa Crabb, born Oct. 16, 1846 in Lawrence County, TN and died Aug. 13, 1887 in Prentiss County, MS married Mar. 29, 1876 in Prentiss County, MS to Elisha Carroll Wroten, born Oct. 29, 1833 and died May 18, 1807 in Prentiss County, MS son of Elisha Wroten and Permelia. *Submitted by Mary Ellen Crabb Ledford, 702 Fouts Drive, Irving, TX 7506-4126 email: ellen@airmail.net.*

CRABB, WILLIAM PERRY, born 1829 in Giles County, TN and died 1893 in Yell County, AR. He was the son of Joseph Crabb and Catherine Rogers.

On Dec. 12, 1850 in Lawrence County, TN, William married Elizabeth Horne (b. 1828 to Aug. 3, 1878 Prentiss County). They moved to what would become the Prentiss County area of Tishomingo County in 1853, returned to Tennessee around 1865, then moved back to the Booneville area by 1878.

William and Elizabeth had 11 children:

1. James Moore (b. Jul. 16, 1852 in Pulaski, Giles County, TN to December 1929 in Texas) married Mattie Julia Stovall Jan. 23, 1883 in Camp County, TX. Their children were Annie Laurie, Nannie, Paul Jerome, Virgil Raney, Julius Ben, Robert Roy, Lonnie Ray and Nonnie May.

2. Rutha Artelia (b. 1853 in Tennessee) married Joshua Callie Mansell Oct. 26, 1876 in Prentiss County. Their children were Amanda Elizabeth, Joseph William, Nancy Catherine, Anderson C. and Francis M.

3. Rosey N. (b. Jan. 06, 1854 in Tishomingo County to Oct. 11, 1922 in Prentiss County) married Christopher Columbus Lester Aug. 20, 1872 in Prentiss County. Their children were Maggie, Columbus, Bud, Clint, Fred, Ida, Lavada, Mary, Rosa and Willie.

4. Mary C. (b. 1856 in Tishomingo County) married James Marion Lee Oct. 31, 1878 in Prentiss County. Their children were Lou Anna, James Franklin, Sarah Mandy, Myrtie Bell and Mary.

5. Nancy Catherine (b. 1859 in Tishomingo County) married Allen Arthur Gentry Nov. 29, 1877 in Prentiss County.

6. Perry Asberry (October 1858 in Tishomingo County to 1931 in Chewalla, TN) married Mary Rebecca Fendley Dec. 27, 1879 in Prentiss County. Their children were William Asbury, James Richard, John Anderson, Walter Jefferson, Christopher Columbus, Roxie, Jeanetta Fredonie and Martha.

7. William T. (b. 1862 in Tishomingo County) married Martha Ellen Harvey Sep. 14, 1893 in Yell County, AR.

8. John A. (b. 1864 in Tishomingo County to 1893 in Arkansas) was married to Martha Ann Johnson on Dec. 15, 1889 in Yell County, AR. Their children were James P., Ola and Emmeline.

9. Joseph M. was born in 1867 in Tennessee.

10. Sarah Elizabeth (b. 1869 in Hardin County, TN to May 23, 1955 in Jonesboro, AR) first married Enoch Morgan Plaxico Nov. 30, 1885 in Prentiss County. They had one daughter named Martha. With her second husband, G.J.L. Bledsoe, who she married Nov. 11, 1897 in Wise County, TX she had one son named Chester. Sarah and her third husband, Charles Wesley Hancock, married Feb. 24, 1910 in Corinth, MS. Their children were Thomas Clifton, Jesse Oliver and Carl.

11. George was born in 1870 in Hardin County, TN.

After Elizabeth's death, William married Mattie Lue Livingston Dec. 30, 1879 in Prentiss County. They had:

12. Henry Livingston (b. Jan. 23, 1881 in Booneville to Apr. 08, 1963 in Carlsbad, NM) first married Emily Darby Gordon Aug. 18, 1903 in Bell County, TX. Their children were Mabel Bee, Benjamin Perry, Mattie Lou, Algee Buel and Dolly May. Henry later married Anna B. Johnson. *Submitted by Jack Ledford, 702 Fouts Drive, Irving, TX 75061-4126.*

CRABB, WILLIAM WALTER, born Nov. 14, 1879 in Booneville, Prentiss County, MS. He was the son of James Walter Crabb and Elizabeth Ellender Hathcock. On Nov. 11, 1896 in Booneville, he married Nima S. Goodwin, daughter of Leander Franklin "Andy" Goodwin and Mary J. Armstrong of Prentiss County. Nima was born Mar. 25, 1875 in Prentiss County and she died May 14, 1927 in Belmont.

William and Nima had eight children:

1. Walter Lee Crabb was born Oct. 16, 1897 in Prentiss County. He died Sep. 27, 1991 in Iuka. On Nov. 25, 1917, he married Ruth Sheppard at Mt. Nebo Church in Booneville. She was born Nov. 5, 1898 and died Jan. 21, 1979. Walter and Ruth are buried in Forked Oak Cemetery near Booneville, They had five children: Herman, Leslie Eugene, Donald Ray, Dorothy and Doris.

2. Luther Garvin Crabb was born Aug. 11, 1900. He died August 1964 in Tampa, FL. He married Christine Elizabeth Fenter. Luther and Christine had nine children: Ralph Lee, Joyce Faye, Archie, Betty Lou, Myrna Geraldine, William Robert, Claude Carlton, Stella Louisa and John Webster.

3. Audie Odell Crabb was born Feb. 19, 1903 in Booneville. He died Oct. 2, 1958 in Sheffield, Colbert County, AL. He married Effie Mae Anglin Jul. 7, 1925 in Tishomingo County, MS. She was the daughter of Charles Marion Anglin and Sarah Elizabeth Vinson. Effie was born Nov. 30, 1901 in Belmont and she died Aug. 23, 1984 in Sheffield. Audie and Effie are buried in the Sheffield Oakwood Cemetery. They had three children: Charles William, William Odell and James Edward.

4. Autie Mae Crabb was born in Booneville. She married Wilfred Frank Kilburn. They had two children, Wilfred Wayne and Syble Laqueta.

5. Eula Crabb was born in Booneville. She married Leonard Moody, son of John Moody and Caroline Shook. He was born May 2, 1907 in Mississippi and died in April 1982 in Belmont. Leonard and Eula had eight children: Leonard Winyard, Carol Sue, Bobby Gene, Kathryn Fae, Kenneth Ray, Myra Jane, Jimmy Jerald and W.D.

6. Era Maryeller Crabb was born Sep. 9, 1912 in Booneville. She died Apr. 13, 1993 in Booneville. She married Arline Grimes in November 1936. They had a daughter named Patsy Donnita.

7. Lois Crabb was born in Booneville. She married Dwelt Pippin in 1936. They had one daughter named Peggy.

8. Claude Crabb was born in Booneville. He married Lucille Sereeka.

After Nima died, William married Nancy Posey Oct. 6, 1934. Then, on Mar. 25, 1941, he married Ethel Eaton and again on May 23, 1948, he married Lynn Tennison, all in Booneville. He was buried next to Nima in Mt. Nebo Freewill Baptist Church Cemetery in Booneville. *Submitted by Mrs. Charles William Crabb, 4634 Windemere Street, Longview, WA 98632.*

CRAWFORD, JOSIAH,
born 1817, Clark County, AL? and died 1862, Tippah County, MS married in 1844 to Malinda/Matilda? (b. 1822 in Tennessee or Alabama). The parents of Josiah or the maiden name of his wife are unknown. Their five children were:

1. William Luther married Annie Bullock.
2. Sarah.
3. Joseph married first to Clara Lou Laird. Their seven children were: J. Richard (Mack?) (b. 1899-1987) married in 1908 in Prentiss County to Ila Yates and had Joe Heath; May married Henry Whitaker (b. 1883-1965) and had Lucille (married Clyde Winberry), Floy, Virginia (married Emmett Ransom) and Hazel (married Norvel Nesbitt); Pansy (b. 1882-1949) married Samuel May and had Josephine; Joseph Earlton; Horner Ford; Vera Lucille (b. 1890-1960) married James Algie Gowdy (b. 1887-1950) and had Harold (married Mary Polk Richardson), James Earlton (married Julia Cour) and Juanita (married Charles Willmore) and Clara (b. 1893-1991) married Henry Hewitt.
4. Thomas B/P born in 1847.
5. Mollie Crawford (b. 1850-1910) married Dr. John Randolph Palmer (b. 1849-1922). Both are buried in Blackland Cemetery. Their children were: Oliver Orlando; Nettie (b. 1882-1945) married Augustus Hargett and had Johnnie (b. 1906-1964), who married Charles Young (b. 1906-1949); Jodie; Lula Mae (b. 1873-1932) married George Martin Chambers (b. 1872 in Booneville) and had 10 children. George, son of Joseph Daniel Chambers (b. 1847-1920) married in 1867 in Prentiss County to Josephine Kremer (b. 1851-1930), daughter of Andrew Kremer (b. 1811 in Baden Baden, Germany and died in 1891 in Jumpertown) and Elizabeth Stoker, daughter of Robert Stoker (parentage traced to Robert Stoker, born 1710 in Whickham Durham, England and died in 1770) and Mary Stack (parentage traced to Anthony Stack (b. 1735 in Bern, Switzerland). Andrew Kremer married the second time to Isabella Dees, daughter of Mark.

Joseph Chambers, son of David P. Chambers (b. 1808 and died in 1870 in Jumpertown) and Charlotte Bolling (b. 1819, Georgia to 1853), possibly the daughter of Samuel Bolling Jr. and Elizabeth Townsend. Children: Samuel married Levina Anderson; Elizabeth married Ebenezer Smith (b. 1810-1875) and their children were Calvin, Peter, David, Joseph, Victoria, Elizabeth and E.B.; Sarah Adeline (b. 1841-1914) married Zacharia Taylor Trantham (b. 1841-1890) and had 11 children; John married Samantha Brown; Martha (b. 1842-1910) married Samuel Wrenn (b. 1840-1890) and had 12 children; Mary; Joseph Daniel; James Martin married Missouri Dees and Robert. David P. Chambers married the second time to Elizabeth Wrenn and had Alice (b. 1863-1932), who married Leonidas Smart (b. 1858-1926) and had John: Minnie, Benjamin, Arthur, Joseph and Myrtle. Joseph and Josephine Chambers had: David Andrew married Annie Windham; Luella married Marcus Heath Yates; George Martin; Etta Belle married William Milton Clark; Joseph Frank married Maude McCord; Laura Josephine married Joseph Andrew Surratt; Mary Elizabeth married Collin Frank Carmichael; John Robert; Edna married Lebert Smith; Claude and Earl Brandon.

David P. Chambers, son of Ann, lived in Spartanburg County, SC and Monroe County, TN and had siblings: Robert; John married first to ? and had Nancy (married William Whalen) and Matthew (married Mary Smith) and married second to Nancy Edwards; Mary (b. 1797-1855) married Elias C. Hutcheson; James L. married Sarah ? and had Elizabeth A. (married Henry G. Sims), John T. (married Sarah Ann Sims), Ann, William, Samuel and Mary; Samuel C. (b. 1805-1840) married Elizabeth, who married second to James Wheeler; William and Jane married James Cameron. Nettie Mae Chambers (b. 1902, Booneville and died 1980 in Bon Aqua, TN), daughter of George Chambers and Lula Palmer (parentage traced to Rev. Thomas Palmer (died 1637) and Joane Jordan), the subject's grandmother married first Denman V. Ross (b. 1899-1941) and second to Luther Glenn Bilbrey, 1902-1982. *Submitted by Clark Sinclair, Houston, TX.*

CROCKETT, WILLIAM AND ELIZABETH C.,
William Cowan Crockett was born Apr. 22, 1803 in Jackson County, GA, the oldest child of Mary Cowan Crockett and John Crockett Jr., both from North Carolina. William was named for his maternal grandfather. The family lived and farmed on the Mulberry Fork in Jackson County, GA. William's grandfather, John Crockett Sr., also lived on Mulberry Fork part of this time.

When William was 9, the family relocated to Franklin County, TN. In 1820 the family was in the northern part of the county, which in 1836 was formed into Coffee County.

Elizabeth Cunnyngham was born in Franklin County, TN, Mar. 30, 1812, the daughter of James Cunnyngham who had been an early pioneer of the county.

In 1824 William Crockett filed a claim for 50 acres of land adjoining his father's and on Sep. 28, 1828, married Elizabeth Cunnyngham. William was 25 and Elizabeth, 16. All eight of the couple's children were born in Franklin/Coffee County over the next 16 years: John C., Mary K. (Polly), Elizabeth Caroline, Sina Angeline, James M., Davy S., William J. and Samuel T. Crockett.

In 1846 William and Elizabeth moved to the southern part of Tishomingo County, MS (later Prentiss County) and purchased 320 acres on Osborne Creek (several miles west of present day Booneville). In 1850 Siney and David attended school. To work the farm, William kept black slaves. Records from 1860 show two slave houses and 13 slaves ranging in age from 2 to 40 years of age. Those who remained on the Crockett farm after the Civil War were Elick (55 in 1870), Ann (40), George (19), Addine (13), Martha (10), Julia (8) and Elick Jr. (6.)

In 1850, the Crocketts' son, John, married Louise Wileman and Elizabeth Caroline married Thomas Humphrey. Sina married Benjamin Wileman in 1853.

Tragedy came early and repeatedly to the Crockett home. Their son, William J., died in 1848, only 5 years old. Polly, who had married neighbor, Robert Hester in 1849, died 13 months later at the age of 19 leaving an infant son, Thomas and James and Davy both died in 1856, 14 and 19 years of age, respectively. John's wife, Louise, apparently died before 1860.

Son, John and sons-in-law, Humphrey and Wileman, all served in the Confederate forces. John was a sergeant in the 22nd Mississippi Infantry. Humphrey was in Ham's Cavalry, ending the war as a corporal. Wileman died in Tennessee in April 1863 leaving Siney a widow with four small children.

In August of that year, the Crocketts' youngest son, Samuel, died at the age of 19. A month later, Elizabeth died, having at 51 years of age outlived five of her eight children.

After the war, Sergeant John Crockett returned home and married Callie Fulgham Dec. 9, 1865. In 1872, Siney married Henry Ross Moores. In succeeding years, William made his home with daughter, Siney.

In 1879 William made out his will. After remembering grandson, Thomas Hester, William's estate was evenly divided between his three surviving children, John, Elizabeth and Siney. After Siney's death in 1881, William lived with daughter, Elizabeth Humphrey in Alcorn County. In 1885 William deeded his farm and home land to his two sons-in law.

Despite his great losses, William Crockett spent his last years surrounded by many grandchildren and great-grandchildren through his daughters, Elizabeth and Siney. He smoked his pipe and rocked the young ones in his lap as he told them stories.

William died Sep. 24, 1890, at the age of 87. His body was buried next to his wife and children on a hilltop near his home and farm on Osborne Creek. *Submitted by Douglas R. Scally.*

CROW, ROBERT LEROY "UNCLE BOB,"
born Feb. 14, 1866, died Oct. 31, 1962. Margaret Emma (Aunt Mag) Crow was born Aug. 27, 1861 and died May 27, 1955. Robert Leroy (Uncle Bob) and Margaret Emma (Aunt Mag) were married Oct. 23, 1892. Mag was born and raised in Alcorn County on Hatchie River, Union Church Community. She was the daughter of James T. and Tempy Miller Crow. Her sisters and brothers were Mary, Francis, Eliza, Martha, Mandy, Bill, John, Frank, Angie and Robert. Bob was the son of John Thomas and Sally Henderson Crow. He had two sisters, Ann Crow Bedford and Mary Crow Daniel. John Thomas and Sally are buried at Gaston Cemetery. James T. and Tempy are buried at Union Cemetery.

Robert Leroy Crow and Margaret Emma Crow

Bob and Mag's children were:

Edgar Phillip (b. Nov. 22, 1893, d. Jan. 14, 1919) md. Mae Huddleston. They had no children.

Robert Clyde (b. Dec. 17, 1897, d. Jun. 1, 1974) md. Dessie Floyd. Their children were Junior, married Vandy Hendrix, had no children; Bruce married Geneva Brackeen, their children Vern, Ellis, Helen, Barbara and Janet; Billy married Kathryn Parker, their children: Larry, Joyce and Tim; Jack married Gerldine Phillips, children Donna, Tommy and Bob; Howard married Jettie Rinehart, children Pam and Patty. Eugene married Maurine Cagle, children Debbie, Myra Lynn and Tiffany; Myrle married Maydene Stennett, child Tammy.

Mary Lillian (b. Aug. 17, 1899, d. Mar. 16, 1990) md. William Franklin "Bill" Johnsey. Their children: Eunice married Billy Moore, had no children; Una Mae married Price "Pud" Turner, their children: Ricky, Sherri and Debbie; Peggy married Max Wade Lancaster, their children Jan and Fred; Bobby married Fay Simmons, had no children; Billy married Nona Fay Lauderdale, their children: Regina, Gary, Tracy and Chad.

The Crow family migrated from South Carolina to Sand Mountain, AL, residing there for a few years. They then moved on to old Tishomingo County, MS near Marietta for about five years. They left there in the early 1840s on their way to Texas. When they reached the eastern edge of Tippah County, which is now Alcorn County, a member of the family became ill. They camped at a spring at the east edge of Hatchie bottom until the family member was well. They liked that part of the country so well they decided to live there instead of continuing on to Texas. They lived in that location, named Crow Mountain, for a number of years. They bought a farm and moved three miles east, which is 1/2 mile west of Union Baptist Church. This land is still in the Crow family. When they moved from Alabama to Mississippi, they brought the first tomato seed to this part of the country, which they shared with their neighbors.

Bob and Mag were cousins. Their grandfathers were brothers. Jim was Mag's grandfather and J. Hugh was Bob's grandfather. Jim was born in South Carolina in 1798, wife Elizabeth Breedlove was born in Georgia in 1797. They are buried at Marietta, MS. J. Hugh was born in Alabama and married a Hamilton. Although Bob and Mag were cousins, they did not meet until they were grown.

When Bob was 19 years old he decided he was going to ride his horse to Hatchie and find his kin. After a few trips, Bob and Mag slipped off and got married. They lived and raised their family in Prentiss County in Gaston and Thrasher Community.

Bob, Mag, Edd and Clyde are buried in Gaston Cemetery. Lillian is buried at Rienzi Cemetery. *Submitted by Peggy Lancaster.*

CUNNINGHAM, JAMES ANDREW, born Feb. 9, 1874 at New Site to Andrew Cunningham (b. 1838, d. 1920) and Frances Green Finch (b. 1838, d. 1908). His grandparents were Hugh Cunningham (b. 1795, d. 1877) and Margaret Upton (b. 1796, d. 1866) and John Finch (b. 1808, d. 1872) and Elizabeth Collier (b. 1817, d. 1863).

"Mister Jim," "Uncle Jim," "Cousin Jim" or "Pappy Jim" as he was known received no formal education until he was in his late teens because he had to work to help support the family. He was one of 15 children.

He attended several different schools in the area pursuing a higher education. He taught school in Prentiss County for a while, then was elected to the State Legislature. He attended Millsaps Law School and began the practice of law in 1906. He was later elected to the State Senate.

Jim was the founder of the law firm of Cunningham & Cunningham. He was a member of the Prentiss County Bar Association, the Mississippi Bar Foundation, The American Bar Association and the American Trial Lawyers Association. He was a member of the Methodist Church where he taught a class for many years. He was also a member of the Sons of Confederate Veterans.

On Apr. 10, 1904 Jim married Nancy Caroline Floyd (b. Jul. 24, 1881, d. Sep. 8, 1964) in Booneville. They had four children: Floyd Wade (b. 1905, d. 1976), Edith (b. 1907, d. 1979), James Andrew Jr. (b. 1914, d. 1956) and William Riley (b. 1918, d. 1950).

At the time of his death, James Cunningham (age 96) was the oldest practicing lawyer in Mississippi. He died Nov. 1, 1970.

DAVENPORT, ROBERT, born Oct. 3, 1811 in Green County, GA. He died Aug. 7, 1896 in Booneville, MS. He is buried in Booneville Cemetery. He was married to Martha Hester (daughter of Stephen Hester and Elizabeth Smith) Jun. 13, 1833 in Clark County, GA. Martha Hester was born Feb. 14, 1819 in Clarke County, GA. She died Mar. 8, 1894 in Prentiss County, MS. She is buried in Booneville Cemetery. Robert Davenport and Martha Hester had the following children:

1. Stephen Davenport, captain in CSA.

2. Henry Davenport was born Jan. 6, 1836 in Clarke County, GA. He was mortally wounded Jul. 3, 1863, at Gettysburg, Pennsylvania.

3. Martha Elizabeth Davenport was born Oct. 23, 1841 in Tishomingo County, MS. She died Jun. 2, 1844.

4. Joseph Hester Davenport was born Jan. 9, 1845 in Tishomingo, County, MS. He died Nov. 21, 1856.

5. Amanda Elizabeth Davenport was born Mar. 6, 1848 in Tishomingo County, MS. She died Aug. 21, 1862 in Tishomingo County, MS.

6. Georgia Ann Davenport was born Feb. 15, 1850 in Tishomingo County, MS. She died in 1852 in Tishomingo County, MS.

7. Francis Anabella Davenport was born Aug. 7, 1852 in Tishomingo County, MS. She died Aug. 19, 1852 in Tishomingo County, MS.

8. Sallie Ann Eliza Davenport.

9. Fanny Easley Davenport.

10. Robert Burton Davenport was born Mar. 9, 1858 in Tishomingo County, MS. He died Mar. 19, 1893 in Texas.

Captain Stephen Davenport was born Oct. 30, 1834 in Clarke County, GA. He died Nov. 8, 1863 in Fulton, MS and is buried in Fulton Cemetery. He was married to Mary E.J. Rives (daughter of Berry C. Rives and Martha Rives) Oct. 21, 1857 in Tishomingo County, MS. Mary E.J. Rives was born Apr. 20, 1841 in Mississippi. She died Jan. 20, 1904 in Prentiss County, MS. She was buried in Booneville Cemetery. Captain Stephen Davenport and Mary E.J. Rives had the following children:

1. William H. Davenport.

2. Mattie Bell Davenport was born in 1863 and she died in 1863, 27 days after birth.

3. Sallie Ann Eliza Davenport was born Feb. 23, 1854 in Tishomingo County, MS. She died Feb. 12, 1934 in Prentiss County, MS. She is buried in Booneville Cemetery in Booneville, MS. She was married to Louis Jones Greene Jr. (son of Lewis Jones Greene Sr. and Lucinda Wincy McDonald) Nov. 13, 1872 in Prentiss County, MS. Louis Jones Greene Jr. was born Oct. 13, 1843 in Tishomingo County, MS. He died Jun. 1, 1932 in Prentiss County, MS. He was buried in Booneville Cemetery in Prentiss County, MS. Sallie Ann Eliza Davenport and Louis Jones Greene Jr. had the following children: Robert Edward Greene; William Henry Greene (b. Mar. 4, 1875 in Prentiss County, MS and died Jul. 15, 1894 in Prentiss County, MS) is buried in Booneville Cemetery in Booneville, MS; Martha Lucinda "Mattie Lou" Greene; Lewis Jones "Jim" Greene; Stephen Davenport "Tobe" Greene; Clifford Porter Greene; Gordon Hamilton Greene; Fannie Nash Greene (b. Mar. 13, 1887 in Prentiss County, MS and died Dec. 23, 1890 in Prentiss County Mississippi) is buried in Booneville Cemetery in Booneville, MS; Sarah Elizabeth "Lizzie" Greene; Mary Easley Greene and Charles Stanley Greene (b. Jan. 5, 1895 in Prentiss County, MS and died Feb. 13, 1896 in Prentiss County, MS) is buried in Booneville Cemetery in Booneville, MS.

4. Fanny Easley Davenport was born Jul. 13, 1856 in Tishomingo County, MS. She died Jan. 28, 1941 in Texas. She was married to William Robert Davenport (son of Smith Davenport and Martha A.B. Hillsman) Aug. 23, 1877 in the home of Robert Davenport in Prentiss County, MS. William Robert Davenport was born Mar. 10, 1850 in Sumter County, GA. He died Aug. 2, 1884 in Prentiss County, MS. He was buried in Booneville Cemetery. Fanny Easley Davenport and William Robert Davenport had the following children: Robert Smith Davenport (b. Apr. 11, 1879 in Mississippi and died Oct. 24, 1952 in Gonzales County, TX); William Edward Davenport (b. June 1880 in Mississippi and died Nov. 27, 1965 in Gonzales County, TX); Peter Nash Davenport (b. Mar. 1885 in Mississippi and died Sep. 12, 1903); Henry Steve Davenport and Martha Davenport. *Submitted by Robert Turner.*

DAVENPORT, WILLIAM ROBERT, born Mar. 10, 1850 in Americus, Sumter County, GA. He died Aug. 2, 1884 in Prentiss County, MS. He was buried in Booneville Cemetery. He was married to Frances "Fannie" Easley Davenport (daughter of Robert Davenport and Martha Hester) Aug. 23, 1877 in the home of Robert Davenport in Prentiss County, MS. Frances "Fannie" Easley Davenport was born Jul. 13, 1856 in Tishomingo County, MS. She died Jan. 28, 1941 in Dewville, TX. She was living from 1887 to 1941 in Dewville, Gonzales County, TX. William Robert Davenport and Frances "Fannie" Easley Davenport had the following children:

1. Robert Smith Davenport was born Apr. 11, 1879 in Booneville, Prentiss County, MS. He died Oct. 24, 1952 in Texas. He was a farmer in Dewville, TX; William Edward Davenport; Henry Steve Davenport and Martha Davenport.

2. Peter Nash Davenport was born Mar. 8, 1885 in Prentiss County, MS. He died Sep. 12, 1903 in Dewville, TX. He was buried in Sandies Chapel Cemetery in Gonzales, TX.

William Robert Davenport

3. William Edward Davenport was born Jun. 14, 1880 in Prentiss County, MS. He died Nov. 27, 1965 in Gonzales County, TX. He was married to Virginia Houston Hurt Dec. 24, 1908 in Dewville, TX. She was born Jan. 19, 1881 in Dewville, TX. She died Sep. 16, 1970 in Dewville, Gonzales County, TX. William Edward Davenport and Virginia Houston Hurt had the following children: William Edward Davenport Jr. (b. Jun. 13, 1910 in Dewville, Gonzales County, TX and died Jan. 2, 1979 in Texas) was living in 1965 in Dewville, TX; Virginia Elizabeth Davenport; John Henry "Sam" Davenport; Clara Angeline Davenport; Fannie Elizabeth Davenport; Tapply Hurt Davenport; Martha Louise Davenport (b. Aug. 11, 1919 in Dewville, Gonzales County, TX) was living in 1965 in Dewville, TX; Robert Huston Davenport and Mary Emaline "Emma" Davenport.

4. Henry Steve Davenport was born Jul. 1, 1882 in Prentiss County, MS. He died May 22, 1954 in Spearfish, SD. He was buried in Spearfish, SD. He married Aleatha Belle Bishop. Aleatha Belle Bishop was born Sep. 2, 1894. She died Jan. 12, 1962. She was buried in Rosehill Cemetery in Spearfish, SD. Henry Steve Davenport and Aleatha Belle Bishop had one child, infant Davenport, born and died in 1925.

5. Martha Davenport was born Dec. 21, 1883 in Aurora, Wise County, TX. She died Jan. 22, 1969 in San Marcos, Hayes County, TX. She was buried in Dewville Cemetery in Nixon, TX. She was married to Thomas Elliott Falls Sep. 14, 1904 in Booneville, MS and after his death, returned to Texas. Thomas Elliott Falls was born Aug. 21, 1876 in Booneville, MS. He died Nov. 21, 1930 in Booneville, MS. He was buried in Booneville Mississippi Cemetery. Martha Davenport and Thomas Elliott Falls had the following children: Francis Hillsman Falls; Sarah Elizabeth Falls; Katherine Anne Falls; Helen Elliott Falls; Thomas Elliott Falls Jr. (b. Jul. 19, 1920 in Booneville, MS) died May 8, 1944, over Berlin, Germany, while piloting a B-17 bomber and he was buried in National Cemetery, Fort Sam Houston in San Antonio, TX and William Robert Falls. *Submitted by Robert W. Turner.*

DAVIS, DARVIS NATHAN and Patricia Ann Foster were married Mar. 9, 1978. Nathan (b. Dec. 26, 1959) is the son of Garvin Earl Davis (b. Dec. 29, 1932, d. Feb. 4, 1994) and Waynona Mayvene Ford Davis (b. Nov. 25, 1935) who married Jun. 6, 1955. He is the grandson of Elton (b. Nov. 8, 1904, d. Jan. 2, 1969) and Fannie May Stanley Davis (b. Jul. 26, 1906, d. Apr. 8, 1982). They are buried in the Jacinto Cemetery in Alcorn County.

Nathan's grandparents are Winston Jasper "Wink" Vanderford (b. Mar. 9, 1916, d. Apr. 17, 1989) and Ella Missouri Woodruff Vanderford (b. Feb. 21, 1913, d. Sep. 2, 1991) who married Jun. 23, 1933. Garvin, Ella and Wink are buried in the Snowdown Church of Christ Cemetery in Prentiss County.

Patricia Ann (b. Apr. 8, 1959) is the daughter of

Rev. Robert Anthy Foster (b. Jan. 15, 1926, d. Apr. 12, 1986) and Annis Dewdrop Dunn Foster (b. May 18, 1931, d. Apr. 9, 1997) who married Dec. 24, 1946. They are buried in New Site Cemetery. She is the granddaughter of William Denver Foster (b. Jul. 10, 1904, d. Jan. 9, 1969) md. Rosie Josephine Vance Foster (b. Nov. 9, 1902, d. January 1958) Sep. 7, 1924.

April, Pat, Nathan Davis

They are buried in Houston, MS. Her grandparents are John Kelly Dunn (b. May 26, 1896, d. Jan. 5, 1968) and Virdie Alice McKinney (b. Jan. 10, 1893, d. Sept. 15, 1968).

Nathan and Pat have one daughter, April LeAnn Davis (b. Aug. 19, 1995). She was born 17 years after her parents married. Grandmother Waynona Davis cared for her while her mother and father worked. *Submitted by Patricia Ann Foster Davis.*

DAVIS, DREXEL EARL and Donna Sue Hayden were married Jun. 6, 1980. Drexel was born Jul. 31, 1956 and is the son of Garvin Earl Davis (b. Dec. 29, 1932, d. Feb. 4, 1994) and Waynona Mayvene Vanderford Davis (b. Nov. 24, 1935) who married Jun. 6, 1955.

Donna, Miranda and Drexel Davis

Drexel is the grandson of Winston Jasper "Wink" Vanderford (b. Mar. 9, 1916, d. Apr. 17, 1989) and Ella Missouri Woodruff Vanderford (b. Feb. 21, 1913, d. Sep. 2, 1991) who married Jun. 23, 1933. Garvin Davis, Winston and Ella Vanderford are buried in the Snowdown Church of Christ Cemetery in Prentiss County.

Drexel is the grandson of Elton Davis (b. Nov. 8, 1904, d. Jan. 2, 1969) and Fannie May Stanley Davis (b. Jul. 26, 1906, d. Apr. 6, 1982). They are buried in Jacinto Cemetery in Alcorn County.

Donna Sue Hayden Davis (b. Aug. 17, 1959) is the daughter of Harold Hayden (b. Jul. 16, 1936, d. Jul. 24, 1993) and Mary Ann Knight. Harold is buried at Little Brown Cemetery in Prentiss County. Drexel enjoys making sorghum molasses.

Drexel and Donna have one daughter, Miranda Nicole Davis (b. May 19, 1982), who goes to school at New Site. Drexel finished high school at New Site and is employed for Horace Huddleston Construction. Donna finished high school at Jumpertown and is employed at Wal-Mart in Booneville. Submitted by *Miranda Nicole Davis.*

DAVIS, GARVIN EARL, born Dec. 29, 1932, died Feb. 4, 1994, married Waynona Mayvene Vanderford (b. Nov. 25, 1935) Jun. 6, 1955. Garvin was the son of Elton (b. Nov. 8, 1904, d. Jan. 2, 1969) and Fannie Mae Stanley (b. Jul. 26, 1906, d. Apr. 6, 1982). They are buried in the Jacinto Cemetery. Garvin was the grandson of Luther T. Davis (b. 1877, d. 1958) and Miranda Davis (b. 1878, d. May 19, 1952) and Fred Stanley (b. Jun. 1, 1888, d. Mar. 21, 1913) and Daisy Stanley (b. Jun. 19, 1887, d. Nov. 23, 1928). They are buried in the Jacinto Cemetery.

Waynona is the daughter of Winston Jasper "Wink" Vanderford (b. Mar. 9, 1916, d. Apr. 17, 1989) and Ella Missouri Woodruff Vanderford (b. Feb. 21, 1913, d. Sep. 2, 1991), who married Jun. 23, 1933. Waynona is the granddaughter of Charlie Edward Woodruff (b. Feb. 25, 1891, d. Dec. 20, 1966) and Minnie Odell Stone Woodruff (b. Apr. 6, 1893, d. May 6, 1961) who married Aug. 2, 1910. They are buried in Snowdown Church of Christ Cemetery. Garvin Earl Davis is also buried in Snowdown Church of Christ Cemetery in Prentiss County.

Garvin and Waynona Davis

Waynona is also the granddaughter of Mark Vanderford (b. Sep. 15, 1879, d. Oct. 3, 1938) and Neal Samantha Maness (b. Jul. 3, 1881, d. Mar. 9, 1958) who married Aug. 20, 1900. They are buried in Juliette Cemetery in Alcorn County.

Garvin and Waynona's children:
1) Drexel Earl Davis (b. Jul. 31, 1956) (see his bio for more information); 2) Anita Gail Davis Wigginton (b. May 15, 1958) (see Sammy Kay Wigginton bio); 3) Darvis Nathan Davis (b. Dec. 26, 1959) (see his bio for more info.); 4) Shelia Denise Davis Bunch (b. Feb. 27, 1962) (see Jimmy Daniel Bunch); 5) Teresa Lynn Davis Murphy (b. Aug. 22, 1963) (see Richard Duane Murphy bio).

Waynona is the sister of James Hulon Vanderford, Hazel Jean Vanderford and Nelda Dean Woodard.

Garvin is the brother of Luther Davis, R.C. Davis, Ray Davis, Leutty Davis, Dewayne Davis and Junior Davis. Garvin had one sister, May Davis born dead.

Garvin and Waynona were members of Snowdown Church of Christ in Prentiss County where he was a deacon. Garvin went to school at Holcut. He was a farmer. He grew pimento peppers and cucumbers. He later became a carpenter. He built houses for lawyers, doctors, school principals and for the plain country folks. He renovated many churches such as First Baptist in Booneville. At Thanksgiving and Christmas he made yard decorations. He cut them out and Waynona helped paint them. *Submitted by Waynona Mayvene Vanderford Davis.*

DAVIS, J.R., born Feb. 15, 1823 and lived with his parents on Beech Creek, on the farm where C.I. Holt now lives, until he was 20 years of age. Then, his father gave him land to cultivate for himself. He planted corn and cotton and thought it would be too much for one, so on Aug. 1, 1844, he married Jemima Ann Hill to help him pick the cotton. From this union there were five sons and five daughters born. Two boys and one girl died in infancy and the others lived to be grown and had families of their own.

Jemima Ann Hill was born Dec. 11, 1825. They were both living in May 1905 and had 35 living and 11 deceased grandchildren and 28 living and six deceased great-grandchildren.

Catherine Arabell Davis Phillips, Daughter Of John Riley Davis

J.R. and Jemima lived on Beech Creek, Wayne County until the fall of 1853, then went to Jasper County, MO, lived there 18 months. They moved back to the Iron Mountain for two and a half years then in the fall of 1857 they moved to Illinois and in the spring of 1858 back to Wayne County. They belonged to the Christian Church a good many years. He was a Confederate soldier for two and a half years and heard Gen. Forrest say "Charge, boys."

John Riley Davis, father of Ara Davis Phillips (md. William Phillips), great-grandfather of Inez Cole and hundreds of grandchildren and great-great-grandchildren.

DAVIS, JAMES BARNEY, moved to Prentiss County about 1918 from Franklin, TN with his siblings and parents, George Washington Carol Davis and Mary Phillips Davis. Barney attended Burcham School and Burton School. Carol Davis served one term as Justice of Peace for the fifth district.

In 1928, Barney met Nona Gladys Elliott, one of the 10 children of Thomas Jordan Elliott and Edna Cobb Elliott from Tishomingo County, at an ice cream supper. During their year of courtship, they attended dances, singings, parties and ice cream suppers. They were married Sep. 8, 1929.

Barney and Gladys Davis, last picture made together in 1972.

Barney and Gladys' first home was a two-room apartment rented from Granny Riley at Holts Spur. Their furnishings consisted of four chairs and a side table (given by Gladys' parents), a stove and a dish safe (given by Gladys's Aunt Inez and Uncle Earnest Rast), a small dresser with a scorched spot purchased by Barney at a Burnsville store, two iron beds and the bare necessities of dishes, flatware, cooking utensils and linens. One iron bed, the small dresser and a gravy bowl still remain in the family.

The newlyweds tried to follow in their parents' footsteps and become farmers but were not very successful. Next, Barney tried the timber business without success. His third career choice was the trucking business, which proved to be successful. He continued in this occupation until his death Aug. 21, 1972. He is buried in the Booneville Cemetery.

Barney and Gladys purchased their first home and 25 acres of land in the Altitude Community. Their second and final home was located at 407 Jacinto Road in Booneville.

Their four children, Eloise, Moise, Shirley Ann and J.B. Davis Jr., attended Hills Chapel Elementary School, graduated from Booneville High School and attended Northeast Mississippi Jr. College. Barney, Gladys and their four children were members of the East Booneville Baptist Church.

Eloise received her BS degree from Florence State University, Master's and AA degrees from the University of Alabama. She began her career as an educator in Alabama where she met her husband, Terrell Livingston. Eloise received state and local honors during her career such as induction into the Library Hall of Fame, several distinguished service and achievement awards and having a library named in her honor. After her husband's death in 1992, Eloise continues to make her home in Alabama.

Moise married a Prentiss County boy, Jasper Jones and they had one daughter, Cynthia. Moise and Jasper completed their education receiving a BS, Master's and AA degrees from Mississippi State, Arkansas State and University of Alabama in Birmingham. They taught school in Arkansas, Mississippi and Alabama. Jasper died in 1992. He is buried in the

Booneville Cemetery. Cynthia married Phillip Rollins. They have two sons, Phillip II and Jason. Their home is in Scottsdale, AZ.

Shirley married her childhood sweetheart, Chick Runions, a Prentiss County boy. They lived in Booneville all their lives. Shirley and Chick were blessed with a talent in singing and playing the guitar. Family and friends enjoyed their entertainment at parties and family gatherings. Chick's claim to fame was that he played in a band in the same theater in Booneville where Elvis Presley performed. Shirley was a secretary/bookkeeper for Western Auto and Etheridge Auto. Chick worked for International Shoe Machine Co. Chick died in 1981. Shirley died in 1997. They are buried in the Booneville Cemetery.

J.B. started working when he was very young delivering papers on a bicycle, a horse, or a scooter. As a teenager he worked at Big Star Grocery. After serving in the Air Force Reserve, J.B. returned to Booneville for a short period of time. He accepted a job in Los Angeles, CA, with the telephone company. Eventually, he moved to Memphis where he met his wife, Ola. J.B. is the owner of Cougar Chemical Co. and AAA Mobile Washing Service. His family (Jeff, Lisa and her husband, John) helps operate the family businesses.

Gladys Davis is an active resident of The Landmark Community. She will celebrate her 89th birthday on Jul. 22, 2000. *Submitted by Moise Jones.*

DAVIS, JONATHAN T. "JAY," came to northeast Mississippi in the early 1870s. He married on Oct. 13, 1874 to Tabatha Jane Butler, daughter of Lilburn Canerdy and Rebecca Elizabeth Winnett Butler. They had 12 children:

Jonathan T. and Tabatha Jane Butler Davis

1) Robert Monroe (b. Jun. 24, 1875) md. Julie Everett. They had one son, George Elkin Davis, who married Virginia Turner and they lived in Corinth. Elkin worked for the post office.

2) Lilburn George Washington (b. Jun. 13, 1878) md. Pearl Livingston. He is buried in Hinkle Cemetery in Alcorn County, MS. They had two children according to the will of Jonathan T. Davis.

3) Ira Dee (b. Apr. 10, 1880) md. Qumy Priddy and they lived in Corinth where he had a construction business. They later moved to Memphis where he died Jul. 23, 1935. He is buried in the Henry Cemetery in Corinth, Alcorn County, MS. They had four children: Ira, J.T. Evelyn and Erna.

4) John A. (b. Mar. 31, 1882) was married and had one son named Owen, according to grandfather's will. John was a brakeman for the railroad and was accidentally killed.

5) Trudie Mae (b. Dec. 5, 1884) md. Aug. 19, 1906 to Marcus Malcom Lewis. They lived around Ramer, TN and Alcorn County before moving back to Booneville. Trudie died Oct. 5, 1971 and Malcom died May 15, 1948. They are buried at Liberty Cemetery. They had four children: Ida Mae, Minnie Lee, Marcus Eugene and James Hardin.

6) Lizzy Lee (b. Mar. 16, 1887, d. May 31, 1891).

7) Hortence Florence (b. Mar. 11, 1889, d. Nov. 4, 1959) md. Clarence Lee Felker. Son, Quitman (md. Elisabeth Eugenia Box Davis) and daughter, Tabatha Jane Felker. They lived in Booneville.

8) Carl A. (b. May 23, 1891) md. Mamie Houston, three children: Paul Lilburn (b. Apr. 10, 1915); Lucille Virginia (b. Oct. 4, 1917) and Laverne (b. Apr. 17, 1927). They lived in Baldwyn, Lee County, MS.

9) unnamed infant child (sex unknown) was born and died Feb. 1, 1893.

10) Harriet Elizabeth Davis (b. Nov. 4, 1894, d. in infancy Apr. 28, 1895).

11) L. Jeannette (b. Jan. 29, 1897, d. Mar. 25, 1980) md. James Robert Felker, five children: Juanita (b. Nov. 18, 1916); William Ralph (b. Dec. 17, 1917); J.R. (b. Jan. 30, 1931); Fred Raymond (b. Sep. 7, 1924) and Neva Hale (b. Oct. 7, 1926). They lived in Booneville.

12) Winnie (b. May 25, 1899) md. Eugene Wheeler. One daughter, two children: John Howard Wheeler born and died in 1923. Daughter, Joyce Wheeler. They lived in Jackson, MS.

The home that Jonathan Davis built in the late 1800s for his family in northwest Booneville no longer stands. It was later referred to as the Schultz Home with its grand stairway and towering magnolia trees on acres of manicured lawn. This picture of tranquility gave way to Wal-Mart in 1990. This was a sad day for our family.

Jonathan T. and Tabatha Jane Butler Davis are buried in the Booneville Cemetery.

All information on this family was abstracted from "Kinship Treasures From Coffee County, Tennessee" and submitted by Sandra Lewis Gray. Library of Congress Card Number 97-77004.

DAVIS, WILLIS MONROE, born Oct. 28, 1821, died Jan. 18, 1912, from Alabama, moved to Mississippi in early 1800s where he met and married Harriet Persons (b. Dec. 2, 1839, d. Dec. 25, 1912). Willis was an early settler in Tishomingo County. He owned several hundred acres and had many children; one of which was David M. (b. Jan. 18, 1875, d. May 18, 1949) md. Ella Cleo Hopkins (b. Aug. 9, 1880, d. Jul. 7, 1957). Another son was James Monroe Davis (b. Oct. 6, 1862, d. May 11, 1940). James Monroe married Sophronia Isabel Hopkins (b. Oct. 18, 1866, d. Nov. 14, 1944). Ella Cleo and Sophronia were sisters. James Monroe was also a land owner in Mississippi and finally settled in Prentiss County. James and Sophronia had three sons and four daughters: James Olon "Popos," Ward Monroe, Leonard Bell, Myrtie Viola, Zena Avis, Essie Ariva and Easther Glenn. Ward Monroe and Leonard Bell both served in WWI.

James Olon (b. Sep. 17, 1892, d. Apr. 20, 1968) md. Rubye Ida Frasier in 1915 and they had two children, Sydney (b. 1919) and Glen (b. 1925). They later divorced and he moved to California and remarried.

Ward Monroe (b. Jul. 20, 1894, d. Feb. 8, 1973) md. Jan. 11, 1921 to Pinkie Ethel Furtick (b. Dec. 20, 1897). They had four children: Roy W. (b. Jul. 13, 1922) died of leukemia in 1952. He married Sophia Johnson (b. Nov. 11, 1919) and they had one child, Janis Lynn (b. Nov. 15, 1951) md. David Allen Pedersen (b. Dec. 21, 1950). Their children are Kristin Lynn (b. Jul. 22, 1979) and Kenneth Roy (b. Mar. 16, 1983). Ward and Pinkie's second child Helen Bernice (b. Apr. 29, 1926) md. Herschel Huddleston

Front from left: Ward Davis, Margaret Davis Hamilton, Pinkie Davis. Back from left: Bernice Davis Huddleston, Maggie David Hudson and Roy W. Davis.

(b. Dec. 12, 1921). They had three boys: Ray (b. May 6, 1947) md. Mary Ruth Jones, two children, Vicki and Christy. The second son, Kenneth (b. Apr. 7, 1952, d. Oct. 24, 1997) md. Linda Kay Senter, two children, Renai (md. David Elliot) and Jason. Ricky, the last of Herschel's sons, was born Aug. 28, 1962 and married Debbie Gann. They have one child, Kevin Wayne.

Maggie Arlene (b. Oct. 31, 1930), the third child of Ward, married Mar. 7, 1953 to Fred Daniel Hudson (b. Sep. 5, 1927). Their boys were Gary Daniel and Larry Wayne. Gary Daniel (b. Nov. 14, 1956) md. Jeanie Sanders (b. Dec. 7, 1956), children: Michael Lee Sanders (b. May 8, 1976), Holly Brooke (b. Feb. 7, 1979) md. Charles Keith Martin (b. Jan. 10, 1974), child, Katelynn Danielle (b. Jul. 16, 1998). Later, Gary married Donna Marie Masek (b. Aug. 1, 1964). Their children were Justin Eugene Terry (b. Jun. 10, 1983), Codie Allen Fulks (b. Jul. 14, 1986) and Kimberly Marie (b. Apr. 1, 1989). Larry Wayne, Arlene's other son, was born Feb. 2, 1958 and is single and works at Quebecore World.

Margaret Ann (b. Feb. 20, 1938) was the last of Ward's children. She married Mar. 12, 1973 to Raymond Tyler Hamilton. Margaret died May 1, 1979 of Khrons disease. They had one child, Erik Tyler (b. Aug. 27, 1973) md. May 23, 1998) to Tracy Chantel DeVaughn (b. Dec. 27, 1973).

Leonard Bell Davis (b. Apr. 17, 1896, d. Sep. 22, 1978) was the third born son of James and Sophronia. He married Aug. 24, 1919 to Beatrice McCombs. Their children are Mary Ethel (b. Jun. 1, 1921) md. Holley Green, child Allys Green Richardson. Second daughter, Mildred (b. Dec. 28, 1922), married Charles Isom. Next was Irene (b. Feb. 18, 1924, d. April 1993) md. Leon Coleman. James Harold (b. Jan. 8, 1926) was the only son of Leonard. He married Thelma Rhoades (b. 1913, d. 1967), one child, Danny Lee (b. 1947, d. 1969). The last girl was Dollie (b. Aug. 28, 1930, d. November 1998) never married.

Fourth child of James was a daughter, Myrtie Viola (b. Feb. 17, 1898, d. Sep. 20, 1984) md. Dec. 22, 1936 to William Evert Caver (b. Feb. 19, 1891, d. Nov. 6, 1972).

The other three daughters never married and lived together in Booneville. Zena Avis (b. Feb. 22, 1899, d. Jun. 13, 1989); Essie Ariva (b. Apr. 7, 1905, d. May 19, 1987) and Easther Glenn (b. Feb. 19, 1910) is still living in Booneville. *Submitted by Larry Wayne Hudson.*

DAWSON, ROBERT "BOB" WINFRED, born to Winfred Bennett Dawson and Mary Kathryn Lee Dawson Aug. 12, 1956 in Booneville, MS. He was considered a miracle baby to Kathryn and Winfred because she had miscarried a few times and was not expected to carry Bob full term. He, as well as his sister, Lana, who was eight years older, were "the apple of their parents eyes."

Bob's father, Winfred, was born Jun. 4, 1922 in Alcorn County. He died Jun. 17, 1987 and is buried at Sardis Cemetery in Rienzi. He had been a resident of Booneville for over 50 years at the time of his death.

Bob's mother, Kathryn, was born Oct. 14, 1925, at Altitude in Prentiss County. She also has been a resident of Booneville for over 50 years.

Winfred's parents were Robert Dawson (b. Feb. 18, 1895, d. Feb. 2, 1942) and Dora Dean Kemp Dawson (b. May 3, 1893, d. Dec. 18, 1957). Robert was a barber by trade. Dora

Major Robert Winfred Dawson

stayed home and took care of their only child, Winfred.

They both were from Alcorn County and are buried at Sardis Cemetery in Rienzi, MS.

Kathryn's parents were Willie P. Lee (b. Jan. 21, 1889, d. Dec. 18, 1968) and Vivian Phillips Lee (b. Sep. 4, 1890, d. Oct. 19, 1981). Willie owned a farm in Rienzi. Vivian stayed home and cared for Kathryn and her eight brothers and sisters. Both Willie and Vivian were longtime residents of Prentiss County. They are buried at Carters Chapel Cemetery in Altitude.

Bob, Ann, Robert and Brad Dawson

Bob's sister is Lana Dawson Harrelson (b. Jan. 3, 1948 in Booneville). She is married to Jerry Wayne Harrelson of Wheeler, MS. They have one son, Richard "Richie" Wayne Harrelson, born May 3, 1973. Lana and Jerry have lived in Iuka, MS for many years. They are both school teachers.

Bob Dawson lived on Miller Circle in Booneville all his childhood years. He graduated from Booneville High School and was a member of First Baptist Church. He attended Northeast Community College with a two year football scholarship as a manager. He then attended Mississippi State University again as a manager with a football scholarship majoring in physical education. He was a member of Pi Kappa Alpha fraternity. Bob graduated from Mississippi State University on Aug. 12, 1978.

Graduation day from Mississippi State University was a very special day for Bob. It was not only his graduation but also his birthday as well as the day he was commissioned into the Marine Corps.

Becoming an officer for Bob was the fulfillment of a youthful dream. The Marine Corps was his life. He served well as an officer for 13 years active duty and then four years in the Reserves. He served in Twentynine Palms, CA; Okinawa, Japan; Camp Lejeune, NC and Denver, CO. At the time of his death Jul. 1, 1997, he had achieved the rank of major.

Bob received many awards while in the Marine Corps including the Navy Commendation Medal and the Navy Achievement Medal. Bob was also a member of First Baptist Church, American Legion, Booneville Blue Masonic Lodge and the Scottish Rites Bodies of Corinth (lifetime member).

Bob worked at Circuit City in Birmingham, AL, as their operations manager from 1993- 1994.

Bob met Ann Pillsbury of Pascagoula, MS in April 1978, during their senior year at Mississippi State University. It must have been fate that brought them together. If it had not taken both of them that summer to graduate, they probably would not have kindled their loving relationship resulting in 18 wonderful years of marriage.

After their graduation from Mississippi State University, Bob went to Quantico, VA, for his officer's training. Ann was 45 minutes away in Washington, DC working for the Republican National Committee. After Bob finished his officer's training, he and Ann were married Jul. 21, 1979, at Pascagoula, MS Their honeymoon was spent traveling to their first duty station at Twentynine Palms, CA.

They have two children: Robert Eugene Dawson (b. Jan. 28, 1982, Twentynine Palms, CA) and Brad Pillsbury Dawson (b. Apr. 12, 1984 at Camp Lejeune, NC).

Tragedy struck Bob in May 1995, when he contracted Encephalitis which caused him to have seizures. He was disabled until his tragic and untimely death Jul. 1, 1997, at Pickwick Lake from a drowning accident. He is greatly missed by his family.

Ann and the boys have decided to live in Booneville to be close to Bob's mom. After all the other places they had lived, they decided there was no finer place to live than Booneville, MS.

DEGRAW, TOMMY CHARLES, born Apr. 19, 1959, married Cathy Marie Hendrix (b. May 28, 1958) Sep. 4, 1980.

Cathy Marie is the daughter of Thurman Leo Hendrix (b. Nov. 14, 1920, d. Mar. 26, 1982) and Alma Fay Vanderford Hendrix (b. May 10, 1925 who married Feb. 22, 1945.

Standing: Cathy Marie Hendrix DeGraw, Tommy Charles DeGraw. Sitting L-R: Amanda Lynn DeGraw and Samantha Nicole DeGraw

She is the granddaughter of Charley Cado Hendrix (b. May 8, 1898, d. Sep. 23, 1966) and Martha Elizabeth McCoy Hendrix Warren (b. Oct. 22, 1901). She is also the granddaughter of Clovis Aaron Vanderford (b. Jun. 1, 1901, d. Jan. 16, 1985) and Ida Sula Richardson Vanderford (b. Jun. 11, 1904, d. Sep. 8, 1989) who married Feb. 20, 1920. They are buried in Kemp's Chapel Cemetery in Alcorn County. Thurman and Cado are buried in Jacinto Cemetery in Alcorn County.

Tommy Charles is son of Charles Franklin DeGraw (b. Sep. 8, 1938 and Lois Lambert DeGraw (b. Dec. 28, 1941). Tommy's grandfather is Leonard Rubeun Lambert (b. Jun. 14, 1912, d. Feb. 28, 1973). His grandmother is Mary Aday Lambert (b. Feb. 5, 1921). He is the grandson of Eva Warhurst DeGraw (b. May 13, 1913, d. May 1, 1983) and John Allen DeGraw who died in 1937. Tommy's great-grandparents are Fred Lambert (d. 1953), Sally Aday (d. 1959) and Robert Aday. Tommy's great-grandparents are Della Warhurst (d. 1959) and Jim Warhurst; also Sam DeGraw and Elizabeth DeGraw.

Tommy and Cathy's children are:

1) Amanda Lynn (b. Nov. 17, 1981) graduated from Thrasher High School in May 2000. She graduated third in her class and received two scholarships to Northeast Community College where she will be attending in the fall of 2000. She was a member of the Prentiss County Band where she played the trumpet. She works at J.C. Penney in Corinth. She enjoys going to the movies and playing miniature golf.

2) Samantha Nicole (b. Jun. 8, 1983, attends Thrasher High School where she was a member of the Prentiss County Band, involved in English and BETA Club. She enjoys swimming and being around friends and family.

Tommy attended Iuka High School and he works at Heartland Building Products in Booneville, MS. He enjoys working on computers, hunting and playing video games.

Cathy graduated Thrasher High School and now works at Quartet Manufacturing in Booneville, MS. She enjoys fishing and reading books.

DENSON, GEORGE MATHES and Effie Luke Denson and their family of seven children were a second-generation pioneer family in the New Site Community of eastern Prentiss County. His parents, William Cicero and Sarah Ford Denson, came from Alabama by covered wagon a few years after the end of the Civil War seeking new land and settled in the New Site Community. After William Cicero Denson's death, the farm was sold to George M. Denson.

Ravanel "Denson" Green, Orville Green, Jim Spencer, Jane Redden, Remel Spencer, Jimmy Spencer, Jim Denson and Salie Denson.

Mr. Denson was a farmer and educator. He earned the name of "Tater" Denson by raising and shipping sweet potato slips all over the nation. He taught school for 38 years at Little Brown, New Site, Crossroads and Prospects. Many times he walked eight miles to school and for most of those years received $40 a month salary. He also served two terms in the state legislature as representative from Prentiss County. Mr. Denson died as result of an automobile accident in 1946. Mrs. Denson had preceded him in death by many years. *Submitted by Remel Spencer, 306 McClamroch Drive, Booneville, MS 38829. (662) 728-5308.*

DENSON, JAMES CLABORNE, son of George Mathes and Effie Rowena Luke Denson of the New Site Community. He was the grandson of William Cicero and Sarah Ann Ford Denson also of the New Site Community. He was the great-grandson of John Perley and Susannah Catherine Gallman Ford of Eva, AL. Lunzada "Sadie" Chambers Denson was the daughter of Marion Franklin Chambers and Martha Davis Chambers. James C. was born Sep. 2, 1897. Sadie was born Apr. 1, 1899.

James C. and Sadie were married Feb. 3, 1918 and spent most of their married life in Prentiss County excepting for about a 10 year period in South Mississippi at Wiggins. From this union six children were born three sons and three daughters. Herschel Winfield (b. Nov. 4, 1919) md. Irene Wilson, had one son, David; James Adron (b. Oct. 6, 1921) md. Annie Bell Odom, had two sons and four daughters: Betty Ann, Peggy Louise, James Donald, Philipp, Sandra Dale and Adrian Lynn; Maxie Remell (b. Jul. 31, 1925) md. James H. Spencer and they had two children, James H. Spencer Jr. and Jane Carroll Spencer; Ravanelle (b. Feb. 8, 1928) md. Orville Green and had one son, James Larry. Wiona (b. Aug. 9, 1934) md. John Stanley Senter and had one son, John Alvin; Marion Mathis (b. Mar. 13, 1942) md. Katie Johnson and had one daughter, Stephanie.

James C. died February 1981 and Sadie died August 1995. They are both buried in Little Brown Cemetery in the New Site Community. Three of the children: Herschel, Adrian and Ravenelle and her husband, Orville, are deceased. All are buried in Little Brown Cemetery with the exception of Herschel who is buried in Allen Line Cemetery in Tishomingo County. All the children, with the exception of Wiona and her husband and family, lived most of their lives in the northeast Mississippi area. Wiona's family lives in Winthrop Harbor, IL.

James C. was a farmer by trade. He and Sadie were married 63 years at the time of his death in 1981.

DENSON JOHN DEWEY, son of George Mathes and Effie Rowena Luke Denson of the New Site Community. He was the grandson of William Cicero and Sarah Ann Ford Denson, also of the New Site Community. He was the great-grandson of John Perley and

Susannah Catherine Gallman Ford of Eva, AL. Flora Belle Bennett Denson was the daughter of William Christopher Anderson and Lucinda Jane Hallmark Bennett of Tishomingo County, MS.

John Dewey Denson and Flora Belle Bennett were married Jan. 13, 1918 in the home of her parents and spent all of their married life in Prentiss County, except for a 10-year period between 1937 and 1947,

John Dewey Denson and Flora Belle Bennett Denson.

which they spent in Oktibbeha County. From this union, four daughters were born. Ann Jewel (b. Sep. 27, 1919) married Wilbur McFerrin of Calhoun County on Jul. 27, 1939 and they have two sons and one daughter: Johnny, Joey and Linda Ann. Jewel's second husband was Roy Faulkner of Gainesville, TX. Ruth Ellene (b. Feb. 19, 1922) married Norris Robertson of Lafayette County on Oct. 5, 1942 and they have three sons and four daughters: Norris Jr., Ross, Dan, Ellen, Patricia, Jane and Kathryn. Sarah Lorene (b. Sep. 28, 1924) was married to John Wax of Oktibbeha County on Mar. 19, 1944 and they have three sons: John D., Charles and Terry. Rose Pauline (Polly) (b. Sep. 21, 1928) married John Norton of Tippah County on May 30, 1947 and they have two sons and one daughter: Jim, Ricky and Fay. John D. and Flora B. had 16 grandchildren, 30 great-grandchildren and 15 great-great-grandchildren. John D. died Apr. 20, 1980 and Flora B. died Jun. 25, 1983. Both are buried in Little Brown Cemetery in the New Site Community.

In the early years of their marriage, John D. engaged in farming and timber work. In the mid 20s, he was employed by the State Highway Department and operated a mule-drawn road grader on Highway 4 East. In 1933 he was moved to Baldwyn and the mule-drawn grader was replaced with a tractor-drawn grader for Highway 45. In 1937 he was transferred to Starkville and they spent the next 10 years there. Back in Prentiss County, he did construction work and was employed by Northeast Mississippi Hospital at the time of his retirement. They were married for 62 years at the time of his death in 1980. *Submitted by Polly Denson Norton.*

DENSON, WILLIAM, the Densons of Prentiss County are descendants of the William Denson who came to Isle of Wight, VA from England in 1637. His descendants migrated to North Carolina, then South Carolina and finally Georgia. In Georgia, another William married Catherine Phillips and they had a son they named William Cicero on Nov. 20, 1826. William Cicero married Sarah Ann Ford on Mar. 31, 1848. William and Sarah had the following children: William Archelaus Perley (b. 1849, d. 1849); John Hillyer (b. 1850, d. 1875); James Washington (b. 1853, d. 1923); Frances Ann (b. 1855, d. 1855); Thomas Cicero (b. 1857, d. 1935); Clayburne Stanley (b. 1859, d. 1950); Ezra Dailey (b. 1861, d. 1944); George Mathes (b. 1867, d. 1946); Martha Emma (b. 1869, d. 1869); Rebecca Dora (b. 1870, d. 1962); Sarah Genettie Catherine (b. 1873, d. 1966) and an unnamed infant (b. 1875).

William and his family lived in Alabama at the time of the Civil War and he served the Confederacy from there. After the war, William sold his land in Alabama and moved to Mississippi about 1872. His last two children were born in Prentiss County.

Family legend says William moved his entire family, including a married son and his family, because one of his sons was getting serious about an Indian maiden that lived nearby. The story goes on to say that the son married in Mississippi, but he named his first child for the Indian maiden.

There are still numerous Denson descendants in Prentiss County, although they do not all carry the name due to the women in the family. William and Sarah also have many descendants from Canada to Mexico and many states in between.

William Denson family descendants 1921. "Bettie" Rorie, Fred Rorie, Walter Rorie, Lionel Rorie, Kye Rorie, Nettie Langford, Grace Langford, Ethel Rorie, Ruby Rorie, Clinton Rorie.

The fifth child of William and Sarah was Thomas Cicero, born Mar. 11, 1857 in Morgan County, AL. He married Martha Ann Gresham on Sep. 18, 1874. Eventually, they went to Indian Territory, now Oklahoma, where Martha died soon after having their 10th child. Tom returned to Mississippi with the children. He then married Adaline Akers and had four more children. After her death, he married Amanda Taylor Barrett and had three more children. Tom had two more wives, Alice Kennedy and then Annie Bridges King. Tom died Feb. 29, 1935 in Belmont, MS and is buried in Little Brown Cemetery near three of his wives and his parents.

The fourth child of Tom and Martha was Sarah Elizabeth "Bettie", born Apr. 12, 1879, at New Site and died Jul. 2, 1957, at New Site. She married James Frederick Withers Rorie on Feb. 2, 1902. Their children are: Clinton Frederick (b. 1902, d. 1971); Ethel Beatrice (b. 1904, d. 1979); Kye Euklet (b. 1908, d. 1978); Lionel Thomas (b. 1913, d. 1990) and Walter Lee, still living. They also raised Fred's daughter, Ruby Bell (b. 1894, d. 1966) and his nieces, Nettie (b. 1902, d. 1999) and Grace, still living. Bettie and Fred always had an open door for anyone in need and various family members from both sides used it from time to time.

Walter married Flossie Mae Wilson on Apr. 15, 1944 and they have one child, Ruby Lee. *Submitted by Walter Rorie.*

DENSON, WILLIAM CICERO and Sarah Ann Ford were married Mar. 31, 1848 in Randolph County, GA. He was born in Georgia Nov. 20, 1826 and died Jan. 10, 1906, with burial in Little Brown Cemetery. She was born in Georgia May 10, 1831 and died Nov. 28, 1920, with burial in Little Brown Cemetery. His parents were born in South Carolina. Her father was born in Virginia, her mother in South Carolina.

William Cicero Denson and Sarah Ann Ford Denson

William C. Denson served four years with the 12th Alabama Cavalry. Farming was his profession. He also served as postmaster at New Site for many years. William and Sarah Denson came from Arbacoochee, AL, by covered wagon in the early 1870s, seeking new land. They were thought to be the first settlers at New Site. The original farmland, plus additional acreage, remain in the family, with their grandson's, George B. Denson's, family still operating the farm.

Twelve children were born to this couple: William A.P., John Hilliard, James Washington, Francis Ann, Thomas Cicero, Clayburne Stanley, Ezra, George Mathes, Martha Emma, Rebecca Dora, Sarah Genetti Catherine and an unnamed infant. Four of the children either died at birth or within the first year.

John Hilliard married Oma Sarah Box and they had two children, Mary Fannie and John Hilliard Jr.

James Washington first married Melta Catherine Millican and they had seven children: Emma Saretha, Lura Ellen, William James, George Washington, James Jr., Rosa Inez and Cornelius Catherine. James W.'s second wife was Eliza Pardue and they had four children: David Cicero, Albert Erastus, Mary Maybell and Felix Artine.

Thomas Cicero first married Martha Ann Grisham and they had 10 children: William Wesley, Tennessee Jane, Mary Emma, Sarah Elizabeth, John T., Elbert C., C. Monroe, Jesse Anderson, Oscar and George Washington. Thomas C.'s second wife was Adaline Akers and they had four children: Samuel Dailey, Sarah Ann, Charley Nathaniel and Houston Hilliard. Thomas C.'s third wife was Amanda Barrett and they had three children: Felix Green, Lee Bryan and Oliver B. Thomas C.'s fourth wife was Alice Kennedy and his fifth wife was Annie B King.

Clayburne Stanley married Margaret Josephine Pierce and they had nine children: Willie Lee, John Sidney, Charlie, Mattie Lee, Thomas C., Mary Frances, James Taylor, Joseph M. and Lucy Josephine.

Ezra first married Ellen Millican and they had nine children: Mary, Katherine, John, William, George, Charlie, Oscar, Jesse and Elmer. Ezra's second wife was Polly Winn and they had four children: Melba, Velica, Polly and Molly.

George Mathes first married Effie Rowena Luke and they had seven children: William Cicero, Minnie Belle, Prince Albert, Lilly Pearl, James C., John Dewey and George Bryan. George M.'s second wife was Ella Elize Lee and they had one son, who died in infancy. George M.'s third wife was Amanda Victoria Lee and they had three daughters: Myrtis Quay, Effie Elizabeth and Lula Fay. George M.'s fourth wife was Pearl Lambert and his fifth wife was Annette Easterland.

Rebecca Dora first married John H. Wood and they had two children, Sarah Annie and William Henry. Rebecca Dora's second husband was James Bashear and her third husband was Jack Jones. They had one son, Robert.

Sarah Genetti Catherine married Levi Jackson Moore and they had nine children: William Jesse Levi, an infant son, George Washington, Minnie Belle, Esther Mae, Olive Glendora, Edgar Linwood, Raymond Leroy and Lexie Virginia.

The farm was sold to the seventh son, George. After William C.'s death in 1906, "Grandmother" continued to live with George's family. George farmed, becoming well known nationwide for his sweet potatoes. He also served in the state legislature and taught school. *Submitted by Ruth Denson Robertson.*

DEVAUGHN FAMILY, the history of the DeVaughns in Prentiss County unfolds backward through Alabama, across Georgia and North Carolina, before finally landing around Fairfax County, VA, the home of ancestor, Thomas DeVaughn I. Little information is known of Thomas' background and whether he was an immigrant to America or native. However, Thomas DeVaughn (b. 1690) is the stopping point for our particular branch of the DeVaughn family. Since genealogy research is an ongoing process, perhaps in the future, our connection will be extended past Thomas.

It is interesting to note that the spelling of the family name has been altered through the years. Up until about the middle of the 1800s, some records show the name to be DeVaughan. Later records indicate that the name was listed as DeVaughn. This is a minor change, but one which often causes difficulty in research.

Thomas' son, Thomas DeVaughn II (about 1708, d. 1793), was a Revolutionary War veteran. He served as a sergeant in the 6th Virginia Regiment and fought at Valley Forge among other sites. He and his wife, Elizabeth, had seven children, each of whom greatly increased the DeVaughn legacy. Thomas is also responsible for the family settling in Nash County, NC.

One of Thomas II's sons, Samuel (b. 1742, d. 1799), was the ancestor of our DeVaughn branch. Samuel and his wife, Elizabeth, had 11 (known) children. Their children began to migrate westward with some settling in Georgia and others moving further on into Alabama. Isham Wilson DeVaughn (b. 1790, d. 1847) was one who moved to Coosa County, AL.

Isham and his wife, Elizabeth, married in Nash County, NC, about 1813, then began migrating west. The couple had eight children, one of whom was William Wilson DeVaughn (b. 1823, d. 1855). William married Rebecca Jarrett and together they had four sons before his death in 1855 in Coosa County, AL.

The eldest son of William, Hamilton McDuffie DeVaughn (b. 1843, d. 1919), married a widow, Sara Gann Stolenaker (b. 1841, d. 1880). The couple moved to Itawamba County, MS sometime after 1871. They had six children. Sara died shortly after the birth of the sixth child and Hamilton remarried. He married Mary Harris (b. 1864, d. 1936) in Itawamba County, MS in 1882. Together they raised his six children and added six more to the family.

William Lungsford (Bill) DeVaughn (b. 1871, d. 1955), second child of Hamilton and Sara, married Josephine (Josie) Watts (b. 1878, d. 1921). Josie was the daughter of Lemuel and Matilda Franks Watts of the Ryans Well Community in Itawamba County. Bill and Josie settled around the Pratt Community and began a family. They had 10 children. Although several children moved away and made their home in other states, the rest remained in the area. Most of the DeVaughn family in Prentiss County today are descendants of Bill and Josie and are continuing to carry on the DeVaughn family line.

The DeVaughn family history does not end at this writing. Indeed, genealogy is a continual update of names, dates and events. Hopefully, this brief overview will encourage family members to delve deeper into their "roots" and discover more of the past of the DeVaughns. *Submitted by Beverly C. DeVaughn.*

DOBBINS FAMILY, among the settlers living in County Waterford, Ireland, was the family of James Dobbins. He died in Carrickfergus, Duneane County in 1665. The earliest record of a Dobbins in America is Samuel, who was born in 1731 in Richmond County, VA and served in the Revolutionary War. His son, Griffin, migrated to Jefferson County, TN. Abner was the next ancestor who appears to have been born in Virginia in 1809 and his son, Creed Fulton, born in Dandridge County, TN in 1845, is our family's Confederate soldier. According to his son, Abner, living at Savannah, heard the fighting across the river at Shiloh. He was 16 and followed the Army, Forrest's Cavalry, into Mississippi. After the war, he came back to this state, settled in Corinth where he met Emma Elizabeth Ferrell and married her there. The Dobbins had a boarding house near the GM&O Railroad. Most of their boarders were railroad workers. Creed augmented their income by painting houses and wallpapering. They reared a large family. James Fulton was the son who settled in Booneville in 1904. His first son, Paul, was born here and Earl arrived in 1907. Van was born four years later. The Dobbins followed the tradition of their father by taking pride in their wallpapering and painting. They hitched the wagon and loaded their ladders and paint equipment to go to houses all over the county. The family lived on five acres located in the curve of McClamroch Drive. The house still stands. Paul married Mary Rugg. They had no children. Earl married Bertie Glen Windham and had one daughter, Jane Cox Davis. Lillian Martin was Van's wife and their children were Vannette, Judith and Jim. *Submitted by Jane Cox Davis.*

DOBBINS, CREED brother of Jim, came to Booneville and married Mary Inez Holmes. Creed was a painter, carpenter and what was more pleasing to him, a fishing guide. He and Inez had five children. Louise married Clarence Doyle and had one son, Clarence Jr. Elton married Eddiewiss Sartin. They had Mary Allice, who became Mrs. George Hartsock Jr. Sue Dobbins married Charles Reid Barnett and the son, Bill, united with Cathy Merchant. Ruth, Creed's and Inez's third child, married Lamar White. They had two children: Alice Ruth, who is married to Lee Burns and her brother, Bobby, who married Ruth Pardue. Phillip Dobbins never married. The youngest son, Charles, married Eva Bolt. They had three children: Charlotte, Patricia and Charles Jr. *Submitted by Jane Cox Davis.*

DOBBS, THOMAS, born in Carroll County, GA, Aug. 9, 1829. His parents were Martin Dobbs (b. 1805 in Gwinnett County, GA) and Elizabeth Garrett (b. 1810 in South Carolina). Thomas married Artela G. Malone about 1848 in Georgia. They moved to Benton County, AL, about 1853. He volunteered in April 1862 to serve in the Confederate Army in the Civil War and served under Captain Wiggington in Co. C, 1st Georgia Infantry. He became a prisoner of war and was imprisoned at Rock Island Prison in Rock Island, IL, until 1865. He returned to Alabama after the war and in 1874 Thomas and his family moved to Marietta in Prentiss County, MS. He purchased land there from Marcus Goodger on Feb. 23, 1874. Thomas' brother, J.R. Dobbs, was part owner of the Saddler House Hotel from 1888 until 1890. School was held there and Thomas' son, Bennett, was one of the teachers. Thomas Dobbs died Feb. 17, 1889, at the age of 59 from pneumonia. He is buried in the Massey Cemetery (a family cemetery) in Marietta, MS. Artela Dobbs died after 1911.

Bennett and Francis Dobbs and their four children: Jeff and Lossie Dobbs (front) and Jim and Roscoe Dobbs (back row). The photo was taken in 1903 in Cooper, TX.

Children of Thomas and Artela Dobbs: Nancy Jane Dobbs (b. 1849, d. 1885) married James Barden Massey about 1870 in Franklin County, AL.

Mary Dobbs (b. 1851, d. before 1900) married T.A. Stennett on Jul. 5, 1881 in Prentiss County, MS.

Martin Dobbs (b. 1852, d. between 1870, d. 1899).

Newman Dobbs (b. 1853, d. ?) married Virginia Ford on Oct. 11, 1877 in Prentiss County, MS.

Jonathan Dobbs (b. 1856, d. between 1870-1899) married Nancy ? about 1878 in Prentiss County, MS.

Bennett Dobbs (b. 1858, d. 1931) married Francis L. Butler on Dec. 4, 1887 in Marietta, MS.

Martha Adeline Dobbs (b. 1861, d. 1930) married Elisha W. Hughes on Mar. 26, 1879 in Prentiss County, MS.

Eliza Dobbs (b. 1862, d. 1918) married William C. Hughes on Dec. 18, 1881 in Prentiss County, MS.

George Dobbs (b. 1866, d. ?) married Lizzie Ballard about 1889.

Elbert Dobbs (b. 1868, d. 1890).

James Monroe Dobbs (b. 1870, d. 1908) married Fredonia Swinney on Oct. 26, 1892 in Prentiss County, MS.

Thomas Dobbs' son, Bennett Dobbs, was born May 18, 1858 in Cleburne County, AL. He taught school in Marietta, MS for a few years at the Saddler House Hotel. He was 30 years old in 1887 when he married Francis L. Butler in Marietta. Bennett became ill with consumption shortly after his marriage and his doctor advised him that he needed to live in a drier climate. He and his wife, Francis, traveled by train to Lamar County, TX in 1888. He taught second grade in a school there. They moved to Acton, TX in 1889 where his uncle, Jonathan (J.R.) Dobbs had moved from Marietta, MS. Two of their children, Thomas Jefferson Dobbs and Roscoe Alexander Dobbs, were born while they lived in Acton, TX. They moved to Lonoke County, AR in 1892, where Bennett taught school. In 1894 they moved to Cooper, TX. Two more children, James and Lossie, were born in Cooper, TX. Bennett and his family moved to Colorado City, TX in February 1907. His brother, Newman Dobbs had also moved there. Bennett built an auto repair shop and two of his sons worked as mechanics in the shop. Bennett also owned a grocery store and was a cotton broker. He died in 1931 in Colorado City, TX at age 72. His widow, Francis, went to live with her daughter, Lossie Dobbs Sanders in Ector County, TX from 1945-1954. Francis Dobbs died in 1954 at her daughter's farm in Ector County, TX. She was 87 years old. *Submitted by Janet Tranum, who is a great-great-granddaughter of Thomas Dobbs.*

DONALDSON, BERKLEY, born about 1784 in Caswell County, NC, the son of Robert and Martha (Walker) Donaldson. He was also known as Buckley/Barkley/Birkley, but it is now believed the correct spelling is Berkley, pronounced in the various dialects of the areas involved. He married Feb. 2, 1811 in Williamson County, TN to Dida Mira Armstrong (b. 1791 in Tennessee and died before 1870 in Mississippi). He served as a private in the Tennessee Militia Infantry until May 11, 1814, during the War of 1812. By 1830 the family was in Wayne County, TN before settling in Hardeman County, TN by 1840. Berkley died there in December 1842.

From left: Katie Donaldson, Calvin K. Donaldson, Dida Mira Armstrong Donaldson, Martha Boley Donaldson and Amanda E. Donaldson.

Shortly after the death of Berkley, it appears that most of his family came to Tishomingo County, MS. Their son, John Berkley Donaldson, was in Tishomingo County as early as 1844 after receiving an original Land Patent in T6, R7. Another son, Robert Grundy Donaldson, came before 1850 receiving a land patent by 1856. The only daughter, Martha

Walker Donaldson Fulghum, moved with her family in 1848. Youngest son, Calvin K. Donaldson, was in Tishomingo County before 1847. Another son, Caswell H. Donaldson (b. 1821, d. 1897), who married first Hannah Bell Maxwell and second Emma, remained in Hardeman County, TN.

John Berkley Donaldson (Feb. 16, 1811, d. Nov. 17, 1881) is buried in Osborne Creek Church Cemetery. He married in Hardeman County, TN on Mar. 21, 1833, to Sarah Fulghum (b. 1812 North Carolina and died after 1850 in Mississippi). Their children were Benjamin Fulghum and Martha A. He married second in 1857 to Amy Ella Hashell (b. 1835, d. after 1881). Their children were Caswell, Tennessee L., Sarah A. and John Berkley Jr.

Martha Walker Donaldson (b. Apr. 19, 1813, d. Feb. 13, 1893) married in Hardeman County, TN on Mar. 16, 1831, to William Fulghum. Both are buried in Osbourne Creek Church Cemetery. (See Fulghum for children and picture).

Robert Grundy Donaldson (b. 1817, d. Dec. 22, 1882) married about 1846 Elizabeth___ (b. 1832 in Alabama and died before 1882). Their children were Berkley William, John Master, Martha Ann, W. Caswell, Ben, Barney, James J., Reubin, Alice E., Thomas R. and Laura. Some children settled in Wise County, TX. The mother, Dida Mira Armstrong Donaldson, lived in this household according to the 1850 and 1860 Census for Tishomingo County. She apparently died after the 1860 Census since she is not listed on the 1870 Census. In 1878, Robert G. gives, in exchange for $5, four acres to be used for a cemetery by the Meadow Creek Baptist Church. The cemetery is still in use today.

Calvin K. Donaldson (b. 1826 and died in 1912 in Texas) married Nov. 25, 1847 in Tishomingo County. Martha M. Boley (b. 1828 in Alabama) died Jun. 5, 1909. Their children, all born in Mississippi, were: Joseph Alexander (b. 1850), Amanda E. (b. 1851), James H. (b. 1856), Kathrine S. (b. 1859), Robert Franklin (b. 1862), Martha A. (b. 1864) and George B. (b. 1865). Calvin K. served in the CSA for two years returning home a cripple. The family moved to Wise County, TX in 1878. Calvin and Martha are buried in Pleasant Grove #2 Cemetery in Wise County, TX. *Submitted by David W. Parker.*

DONALDSON, CALVIN, born in 1925 in Tennessee and came to the Old Tishomingo area with his older siblings about 1840. He married a neighbor, Martha A. Boley in 1847 and they ultimately had seven children: Joseph, Amanda, James, Kate, Robert, Martha and George, who were born and raised in the Booneville area. Martha was the daughter of George L. and Winnie Boley.

Stephen and Amanda Donaldson Wilkinson with children left to right: Henry, William, Dallie, Fred and Amos

When their daughter Amanda was 80 years old (b. in 1931), she wrote a letter for her children and grandchildren, so they would know something about family history and the early life she remembered from her childhood while growing up in Prentiss County during the Civil War. The following descriptions came from that letter. Calvin served with the Mississippi Cavalry for two years and came home a wounded cripple, who could not walk for more than a year. The family lived in a two-room hewed log house on a farm a few miles south of Booneville. Their clothing was rough homespun kind and shoes were made from hides by men, who were too old to go to war. There was only one cow and it produced little milk, so her mother diluted the milk with water in order that each child could have some. One old mule was used for transportation and plowing. The children were all expected to work in the fields as soon as they were old enough, regardless of sex. They raised corn and potatoes to eat, but had no other grain for the four years during the war. It was difficult to raise enough crops for food and when they did, the soldiers, both Union and Confederate, would come by and take everything they wanted. They dug up and boiled dirt from the floor in the smokehouse in order to have salt to eat. It had dripped there previously when they had fresh meat to smoke.

In 1878, Calvin and Martha, along with Amanda's young family and other families, decided to go West on the railroad in hopes of homesteading on new frontier land. The railroad ended at Fort Worth and they finally settled about 30 miles northwest of there on a farm near Aurora, Wise County, TX. Several other related Donaldson families also settled nearby. Martha died in 1909 and Calvin in 1912. They are both buried in Pleasant Grove No. 2 Cemetery, south of Boyd in Wise County, TX.

Additional information about Calvin and Martha's children and grandchildren follows: Joseph Alexander Donaldson, born in 1850, married Mary Anne Burton and had children: Homer, Orrie B., Joe E. and Bertha. Amanda, born in 1851, married Stephen Wilkinson (see Wilkinson Family). Kate S, born in 1861, married Andrew Kyle and later his brother, Martin Kyle. Robert Franklin Donaldson, born in 1862, married Martha E. Smith and they had Russ, Roxanna, Derush, Robert and Moulcy. Martha A. Donaldson, born in 1864, married Benjamin Reed Ray and later Richard A. Stewart. George B. Donaldson, born in 1865, married Martha Henderson and they had Exah Mae, Bertha and Ruth. *Submitted by James L. Slade.*

DOWNS, DAVID ARTHUR, born Nov. 6, 1928, died Jan. 17, 1994 and Betty Jo Morris, born Sep. 4, 1930 were married Apr. 13, 1946 in Frankstown, MS.

Arthur is the son of the late Claude and Mary Alice (Wingo) Downs. Arthur has three brothers: Edward, Earl and Oliver Downs and three sisters: Lillie Mae Downs, Ruby Lancaster and Louise Alexander.

Betty Jo is the daughter of the late Elmer and Hattie Mae (Johnson) Morris. Betty Jo has five brothers: Robert, Edgar, Everett, Roy and Earl Morris and four sisters: Oma Christian, Grace Sheffield, Lona Boren and Billye Joy Caver.

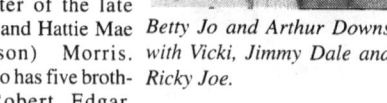

Betty Jo and Arthur Downs with Vicki, Jimmy Dale and Ricky Joe.

Arthur worked at Brown Shoe Co. and Betty Jo began working at Prentiss Manufacturing Co. in 1950 and retired Dec. 31, 1995 after 45 years service. They are members of Gaston Baptist Church.

Children of Arthur and Betty Jo are Jimmy Dale (b. Jan. 12, 1949), Ricky Joe (b. Sep. 1, 1955) and Vicki Lynn (b. Jan. 1, 1959). Jimmy Dale married Sadie Lou Price, daughter of Cecil and Lucille "Lester" Price. They live in Ripley and have two children, Dana Paige and Berkley Dale. Dana is married to Jimmy Horton.

Ricky married Karen Elizabeth Crawford, daughter of Billy and Virlon Bartlett Crawford. They have one son, Levi Brett and live in the Dry Creek Community.

Vicky married Mark Dudley White, son of Jimmy and Martha Dodds White. They have two children, Mark Dudley White Jr. and Brandi Lynn. They live in the Altitude Community.

DUNCAN, CHARLES RILEY, born Mar. 24, 1805 in South Carolina. In 1830 we find Charles in Gwinett County, GA. He married Elizabeth R. Garner on Sep. 12, 1835 in Fulton County, GA. Elizabeth was born Feb. 21, 1817 in South Carolina. They moved to Mississippi in late 1840. On Jan. 15, 1848 we find the family in Tishomingo County. They bought land near Rienzi, Northwest 1/4 Section 1, Tract 6, Range 7, East. They sold this

Charles Riley Duncan

land in 1851 and moved to Altitude Community, Southwest 1/4, Section 3, Tract 5, Range 8, 160 acres on Dec. 24, 1852. They had 10 children:

1-2) Thomas J. (b. 1837) and John F. (b. 1839), both were born in Georgia.

3) Matilda Elizabeth (b. 1841 in Georgia) md. Merideth B. Reynolds on Mar. 28, 1861. They had one child, Martha Elizabeth Reynolds (b. Feb. 21, 1862) md. Walker Smith and second, Jasper Lee Hopkins. She had 10 children. Private Merideth B. Reynolds, Co. E, 42nd Inf. Regt., Mississippi CSA, was hit by grapeshot on Jul. 2, 1863 in Gettysburg and never came home. (See history of Merideth B.

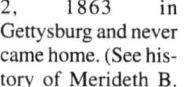

Martha Ann Duncan "Aunt Koon" and James Hill

Reynolds). Second marriage to Thomas Smith, two children: Georgia Thomas Smith (b. Jan. 26, 1880, md. John William Davis); Taylor Smith (b. Jul. 3, 1882, md. Anne Lemore Daniel). Matilda Elizabeth Duncan Reynolds Smith died of a massive heart attack in 1919 and is buried at Smith Chapel Cemetery.

4) James A. Duncan (b. 1844 in Georgia).

5) Charles Perry Duncan (b. Feb. 27, 1844 in Georgia) served as a private in the 2nd Mississippi Cavalry in the War Between the States. He married Rebecca Shotts and they lived in the Prentiss, Alcorn County area where he served as a pastor. Rev. Charles Perry Duncan died May 18, 1920 and is buried near Kossuth in Pleasant Hill Methodist Church Cemetery. They had six children: Thomas Jefferson Duncan, George Duncan, John Franklin Duncan, Charles Duncan, Fannie Duncan and Sally Duncan.

6) Joseph F. Duncan (b. 1849 in Mississippi).

7) Mary Ann Duncan (b. Jan. 24, 1852 in Mississippi) md. Rufus Wiley Langford. They lived in the Blackland Community and had six children: William Bell (b. Dec. 21, 1871); Sally Thomas (b. Mar. 17, 1883); Joseph Oscar (b. Apr. 6, 1875); Martha Genora (b. Apr. 20, 1879); Matilda Elizabeth (b. Jan. 6, 1882) and Evans Mangus (b. Sep. 8, 1885). Mary Ann died in Forth Worth, TX on Dec. 6, 1922 and is buried in Jonesboro, AR, where her son owns a funeral home.

7) Martha M. "Aunt Koon" Duncan (b. Dec. 25, 1857) md. James E. Hill. They lived in the Candler's Chapel Community close to Hills Chapel. They had

no children and later adopted a child. Martha M. Duncan Hill died Dec. 23, 1948 and is buried at Candler's Chapel Cemetery.

9) Nancy Ellen Duncan (b. Mar. 1, 1862) md. Robert C. Anderson. They ran a small store just south of Corinth. They had three children: Emerson (b. 1892), George W. (b. 1895) and Mollie (b. 1898). Nancy Ellen Duncan Anderson is buried at the old Corinth City Cemetery.

10) Sarah Caroline Duncan married Henson.

Elizabeth Garner Duncan died Jan. 12, 1887 and Charles Riley Duncan died Jan. 1, 1895. They are believed to be buried at Mt. Pleasant (old Bucksnort) Cemetery. *Submitted by Sandra Lewis Gray, great-great-great-granddaughter.*

DUNN, JULIUS WASHINGTON, (b. Aug. 12, 1894, d. Jul. 29, 1952) and Florence Virginia "Jennie" Evans (b. Nov. 19, 1896, d. Mar. 27, 1976) were married Jan. 11, 1920 in Prentiss County, MS.

Julius was the son of Sabrey Catherine Barnes and Thomas Henderson Dunn. Jennie was the daughter of Sarah Elizabeth Rogers and Jim Evans.

Julius and Jennie had four daughters: Belva Beatrice Dunn (b. Jul. 21, 1921) md. Grover Estes Jr., son of Grover and Elizabeth Estes of Marietta; Virginia Sue Dunn (b. Nov. 3, 1924) md. Marvin H. Clegg, son of Sam Clegg of Mathiston, MS; Julius Lee Dunn (b. Sep. 17, 1930) md. Roy Lee Morris, son of Elmer and Hattie Morris of Iuka; Patrilla Joan Dunn (b. May 2, 1937) md. Bobby Gerald Maddox, son of Earl and Clara Maddox of New Site.

Julius W. and Jenny Dunn

During WWI Julius served his country in France (Serial #3252349 Co. K, 18th Inf.). He was in the fierce battle of Argonne Forest when the Armistice was signed in 1918.

Julius taught school in Prentiss, Kemper and Quitman County, MS. They lived on a farm northwest of Marietta and moved to Booneville in 1945. He worked as a butcher until his death in 1952.

Julius enjoyed playing the banjo. Julius and Jennie were faithful members of the Church of Christ.

ELDRIDGE, STANLEY, born May 28 to Bethel and Katie Eldridge. He served in the US 8th Air Force. He married Daphene Mathis who was born May 31, 1926 to Dennis and Rachel Smith Mathis on Apr. 19, 1947. They worked at Brown Shoe Co. and live in the Tuscumbia Community where they are members of the Tuscumbia Baptist Church.

Stanley and Daphene Eldridge

Daphene and Stanley had one son, Larry Wayne Eldridge (b. Feb. 13, 1949) who graduated from Northeast Mississippi Community College and worked for TVA as a boilermaker. He died Mar. 22, 1999 and was buried in the Tuscumbia Baptist Cemetery. He is survived by his wife, Kay Grimes Eldridge; one son, Laramie Eldridge; two daughters, Jenny Hatfield and Amy Young; three grandchildren: Bryson and Brooke Hatfield and Terri Leigh Young. *Submitted by Daphene M. Eldridge.*

ELLIS, LEVI A., (b. Dec. 15, 1860 in McNairy County, TN) was the son of William C. and Elizabeth Dodson Ellis. Levi married Dec. 26, 1880 to Nancy Miranda "Sissy" Adams, daughter of Confederate veteran, Marquis D. Lafayette and Elizabeth P. Sides Adams. Levi raised his family around the old Jacinto and Cartersville Community in Alcorn County. He was a veterinarian. Levi died Dec. 22, 1943 and Miranda died Jan. 11, 1948. They are buried at Rowland Mills Baptist Church Cemetery in the Holts Spur Community. They had six children:

Seated: Levi A. Ellis, Elledge Ellis, Miranda Adams Ellis. Back standing: Mary Lou Ellis Pruitt, unidentified, Allice Ellis Whitehurst.

I) Cora E. Ellis (b. February 1883) md. Bob Galyean, one child, Maxine. They lived in TX.

II) Alice Ellis (b. May 7, 1885) md. William R. Whitehurst, lived in Jacinto, one son, William Frank (b. May 1, 1927) md. Eupha Quay Nix. They had five children: (1) Carolyn Denise Whitehurst (b. Oct. 9, 1951); (2) William Ronnie Whitehurst (b. Jan. 21, 1953); (3) Glenda Kim Whitehurst (b. Jan. 29, 1955); (4) Patricia Kay Whitehurst (b. Jan. 4, 1957) and (5) Kathy Jo Whitehurst (b. Aug. 10, 1958). All live in Memphis except William Frank and wife. They moved to Booneville, MS. Alice Ellis Whitehurst died Jan. 17, 1923 and is buried in Hubbard Salem Cemetery in Tishomingo County.

III) Jesse D. Ellis (b. Jul. 8, 1887) md. Leona Taylor, daughter of Thomas L. and Sally Cummings Taylor. They lived in the Roland Mills Community and had five children:

1) Lora Agnes Ellis (b. Jul. 8, 1916, d. May 13, 1996) md. Lewis Roberts. They lived in Florida but retired to Tishomingo County, MS. They have six children: Bobby (b. 1940), Jimmy Wayne (b. 1942), Jesse (died at age 7), Mary Carolyn (b. 1944), Patsy Gail (b. 1946) and Dottie Roberts (b. 1954).

2) Dexter Ellis (b. Feb. 8, 1918) md. Mary Campbell, lived in California and had three children: Rosemary, Wanda and Lana.

3) Evelyn Ellis (b. Apr. 5, 1920) md. Paul Camper.

4) Mary Magdeline Ellis (b. Nov. 2, 1924) md. Garvin R. Gray. They live in Booneville and have two children. (1) Lester Roy Gray (b. Sep. 26, 1943) md. Sandra Kay Lewis, one child, Rhonda Roxanne Gray (b. May 13, 1968) md. Harold W. Lollar Jr., four children: Brandy Elese (b. Mar. 13, 1975); Neil R. (b. Dec. 17, 1976); Timothy R. (b. Sep. 20, 1984); Katherine Marie (b. Jul. 9, 1989). (2) Linda Gray (b. Apr. 3, 1953) md. Paul Bonds, two children: (a) Randy Bonds (b. Aug. 16, 1971, d. Jul. 19, 1982), buried in the Booneville Cemetery. (b) Jessica Bonds (b. Jan. 9, 1980).

5) Augusta Elizabeth Ellis (b. Aug. 25, 1932) md. Frances Lee Jones. They spent many years in TX then retired to Booneville.

Jesse Ellis died Dec. 7, 1975 and is buried across from their old homeplace in Roland Mills Cemetery.

IV) Mary Lou Ellis (b. Aug. 12, 1889) md. Cleve Pruitt, one child, Gladys Pruitt, who married Ledford Qualls, one son, Harold, lives in Burnsville. Mary Lou Ellis Pruitt died Mar. 19, 1969.

V) Fannie E. Ellis (b. 1891) md. John Stockton. They had two children Geneva Stockton (b. Apr. 23, 1919, d. Aug. 13, 1992) and Ruby Stockton. Fannie Ellis Stockton died in 1891 and is buried at New Lebanon Freewill Baptist Church Cemetery.

VI) Martin Elledge Ellis (b. Jul. 31, 1898) never married and died Sep. 2, 1953. He is buried at Rowland Mills Missionary Baptist Church Cemetery. *Submitted by Sandra Lewis Gray.*

ELMORE, SHARON BRIMINGHAM, daughter of Zelma Rinehart and J.B. Brimingham, was born in Prentiss County, MS at Booneville Hospital. She attended Thrasher, Hills Chapel and New Site Schools and later completed a GED. She is married to Richard Elmore. They have two children, Jeffery, age 14 and April, age 7. Jeffery will be in high school next school year and April will be in third grade. She attends Hills Chapel and Jeffery completed the eighth grade at Hills Chapel.

Richard is the son of Joe and Ruby Elmore. He attended school in Copperas Cove, TX. Sharon, Ricky, Jeffery and April live in Snowdown Community in Prentiss County. Sharon is employed by Wal-Mart in Booneville. Ricky has a back injury. *Submitted by Zelma Rinehart Brimingham.*

April, Sharon, Ricky and Jeffery Elmore. Sharon is daughter of J.B. and Zelma Rinehart Brimingham

ENGLAND, JOHN born ca. 1798 in Pennsylvania and died after 1880 in Prentiss County. He married Rebecca (last name unknown), born Mar. 12, 1798 in South Carolina and died Jan. 5, 1880. They had nine children:

(1) Edward J. England was born ca. 1820 in Kentucky. He married Jane (last name unknown). He was enumerated in the Carroll County, GA, 1850 census and the Yalobusha County, MS 1860 census.

(2) Elizabeth England was born ca. 1822 in Illinois. She was single and residing in her father's household for the 1880 Prentiss County census.

(3) Rebecca England was born ca. 1825 in Illinois. She married Thomas J. Gahagan Oct. 5, 1854 in Old Tishomingo County, MS.

(4) Nancy M. England was born ca. 1826 in Georgia. She married Nathan Poole Pettit Apr. 8, 1858 and apparently died shortly thereafter.

(5) William E. England was born ca. 1829. On Sep. 3, 1946, he married Sarah Howard in Carroll County, GA.

(6) John R. England was born Apr. 29, 1931 in Georgia and died Jan. 24, 1903 in Prentiss County. He married Mary R. Pettit Nov. 14, 1858.

(7) Arminda J. England was born Feb. 8, 1839 in Georgia and died Feb. 27, 1908, according to her grave marker; however she was born in 1833 according to census reports. On Feb. 17, 1959, she married William J. Fugitt.

(8) Manda Jane England was born in May 1836 in Georgia and died Jun. 19, 1908 in Prentiss County. She married Richard Fendley Mar. 18, 1860.

(9) Mary Ann Levicey England was born Sep. 7, 1838 in Georgia and died Dec. 8, 1900 in Prentiss County. On Dec. 20, 1860, she married John W. Fugitt. *Submitted by Marjorie Moore Green.*

FALLS, THOMAS ELLIOTT, born Aug. 21, 1876 in Booneville, MS. He died Nov. 21, 1930, near Thrasher, MS. He was a member of the Thrasher Methodist Church and was an outstanding farmer and dairyman and had been a lifelong citizen of Prentiss County. He was the son of the late George L. and Sallie

Elliott Falls, pioneer settlers of this area. He was married to Martha Davenport (daughter of William Robert Davenport and Frances "Fannie" Easley Davenport) Sep. 14, 1904 in Booneville, MS. Martha Davenport was born Dec. 21, 1883 in Aurora, Wise County, TX. She died Jan. 22, 1969 in San Marcos, Hayes County, TX. She was buried in Dewville Cemetery in Nixon, TX. Martha Davenport Falls was also a member of the Methodist Church. In 1905 Thomas and Martha Davenport Falls bought land in the Thrasher Community. They were pioneers in dairying for that area. After Thomas E. Falls' death, Martha D. Falls moved to San Marcos, TX. There she purchased and maintained an apartment house on L.B.J. Drive. It is now the "Lyndon Bains Johnson Shrine", because President L.B. Johnson lived in this apartment house while he attended Southwest Texas College. When Mrs. Thomas E. Falls died, she was survived by four daughters, one son, 10 grandchildren and six great-grandchildren. One son, Thomas Elliott Falls Jr., was a B-17 pilot and was killed in action over Berlin, Germany, during WWII.

Thomas Falls family

Thomas Elliott Falls and Martha Davenport had the following children: Frances Hillsman Falls, Sarah Elizabeth Falls, Katherine Anne Falls, Helen Elliott Falls, Thomas Elliott Falls Jr. and William Robert Falls.

Francis Hillsman Falls was born Jun. 18, 1905 in Prentiss County, MS. She died Jun. 5, 1996 in Phillips County, AR. She was buried in Cypert Cemetery, Cypert, AR. She attended Thrasher public school. She attended college at MSCW and Mississippi Southern before she obtained her teaching certificate. Her first job as a teacher was the 5th and 6th grades at Pisgah Consolidated High School in Rienzi, MS for the school year 1924-25. She then went to Marvell, AR to teach and there she met and married Wallace Berry Turner Apr. 26, 1931 in Booneville, MS. To this union were born four children: Martha Connelly Turner, Thomas Berry Turner, Robert Wallace Turner and William Lee Turner. The Turner family made their home in Phillips County, AR, where Wallace was engaged in farming and Francis was a public school teacher. Martha was a graduate of MSCW and the three boys graduated from Mississippi State University.

Sarah Elizabeth Falls was born Dec. 1, 1908 in Booneville, MS. She died Feb. 21, 1989 in Luling, TX. She was buried in Luling, TX. She was married to Stan N. Donea on May 27, 1934 in Nixon, TX. Stan N. Donea was born Nov. 11, 1896 in Romania. He died Nov. 3, 1982 in San Antonio, TX. He was buried in Luling, TX. There were no children born of this marriage.

Katherine Anne Falls was born May 30, 1912 in Booneville, MS. She was married to James L. Ford May 19, 1941 in San Marcos, Hayes County, TX. James L. Ford was born Jan. 18, 1917 in Dallas, TX. Katherine Anne Falls and James L. Ford had the following children: Mary Ann Ford and Elizabeth Betty Ford.

Helen Elliott Falls was born May 3, 1918 in Booneville, MS. She died Oct. 8, 1988 in Luling, TX. She was married to Albert Scott Morris Jr. on Apr. 19, 1940 in San Marcos, Hayes County, TX. Albert Scott Morris Jr. was born Nov. 21, 1916 in Royce City, TX. He died Jun. 14, 1960 in Luling, TX. Helen Elliott Falls and Albert Scott Morris Jr. had the following children: A. Scott Morris III, Thomas E. Morris and Stephen F. Morris.

Thomas Elliott Falls Jr. (Buddy) was born Jul. 19, 1920 and died May 8, 1944, while as a pilot of a B-17 on a bombing mission over Berlin, Germany, during WWII. His body was recovered after the war and returned to the National Cemetery, Fort Sam Houston, San Antonio, TX. A memorial stone was also placed in the Booneville Cemetery.

William Robert Falls was born Oct. 8, 1924 in Booneville, MS. He died Mar. 15, 1974 in San Marcos, Hayes County, TX. He was married to Sara Jean Wilson on Aug. 1, 1958 in San Marcos, Hayes County, TX. Sara Jean Wilson was born Jan. 27, 1930. William Robert Falls and Sara Jean Wilson had one child, William Robert Falls Jr. *Submitted by Robert W. Turner, PO Box 789, Marianna, AR 72360.*

FENDLEY, RICHARD, born Apr. 12, 1833 in South Carolina and died Nov. 19, 1914 in Prentiss County, MS. He married Manda Jane England on Mar. 18, 1860 in Tishomingo County. To them seven children were born:

(1) Mary Rebecca Fendley was born in April 1861 and died in August 1940. She married Perry Asberry Crabb on Dec. 27, 1879.

(2) Jenette Minerva Ann Fendley was born Oct. 11, 1862 and died Dec. 10, 1949. On Aug. 31, 1882, she married John Willis "Jack" Green.

(3) John Richard Fendley was born Oct. 15, 1864 and died Nov. 19, 1951. On Apr. 18, 1893, he married Lamina Adeline McGlothin.

(4) Martha Fendley was born Feb. 17, 1867 and died Oct. 28, 1867.

(5) Sarah Elizabeth "Sally" Fendley was born Jan. 19, 1869 and died Oct. 29, 1942. On Sep. 3, 1885, she married Liza Anderson Horn.

(6) Mandie F. "Donie" Fendley was born May 7, 1872 and died Aug. 29, 1948. She married William C. Dixon.

(7) Thomas Jefferson "Bud" Fendley was born Jan. 1, 1875 and died Nov. 11, 1964. He married Ethel S. Dunn. *Submitted by Marjorie Moore Green.*

FLOYD, CLETTIS EARL "RED," born in 1932. His parents, Lee and Esther Floyd, had purchased their own farm in 1936. At the age of 4, Red (as he was known), was helping turn the wooded hill into a farm.

Red and Ramona with their family in 1970 when Red was very ill. From left: Esther, Ramona holding Bob, Tom, Red holding Dan, and Ned.

Tuscumbia and Thrasher were schools that Red attended, but after the death of his mother in 1946, he quit school to help the family. Red's brother was living in Florida and Red would travel by bus to Florida and help there. He would then come back to Booneville and help with his father's fields. Red had friends in Utah and started including them in his traveling cycle. He did this until Uncle Sam invited him to join the US Army.

When he was released from the Army, Red went to Utah again. His friends were preparing for college and wanted him to go. He explained that he didn't have a high school degree, but finally took the GED and passed with high scores, except for English. He said that he would read the question, say it how he would say it and then mark the other one! He passed English by one point. Brigham Young University was where he called home for the next three years. He got his bachelor's degree and also found his eternal companion.

Red and Ramona Hill went on a blind date and Ramona knew that night that they would be married. She said that he was always a little slow; it took him three weeks to propose. They were married in March 1958 in the Salt Lake Temple of the Church of Jesus Christ of Latter Day Saints. Ramona is the daughter of Ray and Modean Hill of Montrose, CO. The newlyweds lived out west for a few years, but eventually made their home in the Jacinto Community. Ramona was a homemaker and worked with Red in all that he did. His employment included the Iuka Welfare Office and being an investigator for the state welfare department.

A life threatening illness hit Red in 1968. The family consisted of Tom, Ned, Esther and Dan. Bob was born the next January. Red and Ramona lived day-to-day on faith alone. Eventually, Red's disease was cured. This was accomplished through the faith and prayers of many people. The doctors didn't have an explanation for it.

After this illness, Red decided to do the work he truly loved. He became a saw miller and carpenter with Ramona working by his side. Farming was also a love that he pursued. The family grew many acres of pimento peppers and cucumbers. This was in addition to the huge garden and the other crops grown.

After the children grew up (eventually adding a total of 18 grandchildren to the family), Ramona decided that it was time for her to finish what she had started many years before – her education. She graduated from Northeast Junior College in 1990.

On Mar. 24, 1999, Red died in the home that he had built with his loving wife. *Submitted by Esther Floyd Wheat.*

FLOYD, ROCKY LEE and Esther Lee Moorman represent the laborers of the county. As sharecroppers, they traveled from farm to farm as work permitted. Tishomingo, Baldwyn and Burnsville were just a few places they lived. The family settled in Prentiss County around 1900.

The sharecropping families would live in a house belonging to the landowner. Each year they would give part of what was grown to the owner. If they had their own mules, they would give one third of the corn and one fourth of the cotton. If they didn't own mules, which cost about $200 each, they would give one half of everything. Growing cotton, soybeans and corn provided for the family, if they supplemented it with large gardens and hard work.

Lee and his adult children in 1946 after Esther died. Back row: Marie Floyd Cole, Clettis "Red" Floyd, Opal Floyd Stephenson and Frances Floyd. Front row: Ophas Floyd, Lee Floyd and Tulon Floyd.

Lee was the fourth of 11 children of William Thomas Floyd and Sarah Frances Ashcraft. They were also sharecroppers. As Lee grew older, he worked at a sawmill, a mule powered cotton gin and as a carpenter. Esther Lee Moorman was the daughter of Mary Ellen Cole, who married John Terrell Moorman.

Lee and Esther married on Jun. 17, 1917 in Booneville. They sharecropped in the area and finally purchased their own land in 1936. They built their home and remained there the rest of their lives.

Lee and Esther had eight children: Willie Ophas, 1918; Henry Cecil, 1920, Audrey Marie, 1921; Opal Autherene, 1924; Troy Ray, 1926; Lee Tulon, 1929; Clettis Earl, 1932 and Mary Frances, 1935. Henry and Troy did not live beyond their first years. Opal died in an accident in August 1951. The rest of Lee and Esther's children married and had children, with the number of descendants now greater than 160.

Lee's family was among the earliest members of The Church of Jesus Christ of Latter Day Saints in Prentiss County. They were instrumental in organizing Sunday School and helped the missionaries that traveled throughout the area. Lee served as a local missionary and helped build the chapel that housed the little church.

Music was an important aspect of family life. Lee played the banjo and sang folk songs. These have been passed down each generation and are still enjoyed at family gatherings.

Esther died at the age of 46. She had worked hard every day of her life and taught her children to do the same. Her life was one of service and love. People, who knew her, remember her with love and respect.

Lee married Elvriee Whitehead on Aug. 29, 1948. They had three sons: Jimmy Lee, 1949; Jerry Don, 1951 and Larry Eugene, 1952. Jimmy has four children. Jerry (34) and Larry (29) both died from diabetes.

Lee was 76 when he died in Booneville. He lived a good, long life. Elvriee survived him until 1981. She died in the Memphis Hospital. The legacy of strong families, hard work, music and love for God and nature has been passed to each of Lee's descendants. These have value far beyond this world. We look forward to the day when, again, the circle will be unbroken and we will be together forever. *Submitted by Esther Floyd Wheat.*

FORD, THOMAS, born about 1820 in Alabama. He married Sarah Powers on Dec. 23, 1841 in Madison County, AL. Sarah was born about 1822 in Alabama. Thomas and Sarah died sometime after 1880 in Prentiss County. They had five children: James, Mary, Hickman, Virginia and William.

The Moses Hickman Ford Family. Front row from left: Minnie Williams, Sallie Crumby, Mary Johnson Ford and Moses Hickman Ford. Back row from left: Jodella Clark, Thomas Jefferson Ford and James Oscar Ford.

William Z. Ford (b. 1856, d. 1880) married Mary Moore on Sep. 13, 1877. They had a son named Thomas born in 1880.

Moses Hickman Ford (b. 1850, d. 1928) married Mary Catherine Johnson (b. 1847, d. 1920) on Aug. 24, 1870. She was the daughter of Samuel Jefferson Johnson (b. 1819, d. 1861) and Margaret Jane Carroll (b. 1824, d. 1901) of Prentiss County. Hickman bought a farm near the Siloam Community where he and Mary raised a family. They had nine children, but only five lived to adulthood. They were Minnie, Sallie, Jodella, Thomas and James. Edna, Opal, Launer and Alice died shortly after birth. Hickman and Mary are buried in the Siloam Cemetery, as are most of their children.

Minnie Ford was the oldest, born in May 1872. She married Porter Walker Williams on Jan. 20, 1898. Walker was born in August 1855. Walker owned a farm near the New Site Community. They had a daughter named Anna, who married Evans Gaines. Walker also had two sons from his previous marriage, Austin and Curtis.

Sallie Ford was born in February 1874. She married Robert Crumby on Apr. 27, 1890. Robert was born in October 1871 in Tennessee. Sallie and Robert moved to Memphis, TN where he worked as a policeman. Sallie and Robert are buried in the Poplar Street Cemetery in Memphis. They had seven children: Warnie, Mary, Minnie, Eckford, Lunsford, Ruby and Oran.

Jodella Ford was born in May 1883. She was married to James Austin Clark in 1905. James was born in May 1883. He owned and operated a grocery store in Marietta, MS. He was the son of James and Elizabeth Clark. Della and James had four children: Leonard, Olan, Rubel and Leeland.

Thomas Jefferson Ford (b. 1885, d. 1948) married Mary Louetta Finch (b. 1887, d. 1973) on Mar. 22, 1905. Mary was the daughter of George Washington Finch and Mary Elizabeth Vandevander. Jeff and Mary had three children: Jewell, Herchel and Randle. Jeff later married Minnie Green Fugitt. They had a son named Tommy.

James Oscar Ford (b. 1886, d. 1957) married Charlotte Caroline McCreary (b. 1889, d. 1930) on Oct. 7, 1906. Charlotte was the daughter of Jefferson McCreary (b. 1859, d. 1928) and Margaret Jackson (b. 1866, d. 1949). James and Charlotte had two children, Thomas Oscar and Henry Alvin.

Thomas Oscar Ford (b. 1907, d. 1985) married Clellia Pearl Bolton (b. 1908, d. 1970) in August 1926. Clellia was the daughter of William Calvin Bolton (b. 1885, d. 1970) and Modena Massey (b. 1886, d. 1963). Oscar and Clellia had five children: Ruby, Rachel, Henry, Buddy and John.

Ruby was born Aug. 20, 1927 and married Willie Floyd Robertson on Nov. 10, 1945 in Booneville. They had eight children: Bob, Joe, Don, Doug, Sharon, Sandra, Debra and Sheila.

Henry Alvin Ford was born Dec. 30, 1915. He married Reba Duggar on Jul. 18, 1942. They had two children, Charlotte and Roy. Alvin later married Genola Sterling. They have a son named Jeffery. *Submitted by Joe Robertson Jr.*

FULGHUM, BENJAMIN FRANKLIN "DOCK," born in Tishomingo (now Prentiss) County on Mar. 1, 1850, the youngest of seven children of William and Martha Fulghum. William was born Jan. 29, 1806 in Wayne County, NC, the son of Benjamin and Anna Fulghum. Benjamin was the son of Raiford Fulghum, born 1743 in Wayne County, NC. Raiford was the son of Anthony Fulghum, born in Isle of Wight County, VA and died in North Carolina in 1768. Anthony was the son of Michael Fulgham. Michael was the son of Captain Anthony Fulgham, born in England and died in Isle of Wight County Oct. 19, 1669. Captain Anthony came to Virginia around 1640 and was a large landowner, having secured a number of land grants by virtue of bringing over a number of families from England to the colonies.

Benjamin Franklin "Dock" Fulghum

Back to Prentiss County Fulghums: William and Martha were married Mar. 16, 1831 in Hardeman County, TN and moved to Mississippi in 1848. William farmed 500 acres of land in western Prentiss County, according to the 1850 census. He lived to be "90 years, 2 months and 24 days" according to their gravestones at Osborn Creek Church in western Prentiss County.

Benjamin Franklin Fulghum (Grandpa Dock to all of us great-grandchildren) married Emily Nancy "Nannie" Howard on Jan. 10, 1869. Nannie was the daughter of David and Annie (Belew) Howard of Union County, SC. Nannie died Mar. 8, 1918, at age 78. Their children were William Franklin "Bud" Fulghum, Bettie Mae and Callie. Bettie Mae never married and lived with her father until his death Jul. 9, 1936. Callie married Ovelton Robertson, a farmer and businessman in Prentiss County.

Grandpa Dock enjoyed all of us great-grandchildren and always had apples and pecans when we visited. He would pare the apples and crack the pecans and enjoy watching us eat. He was much respected in Booneville and was elected constable in 1889 and 1911.

William Franklin "Bud" Fulghum was born Jul. 16, 1874. He was married Dec. 24, 1899, to Alice Hester, daughter of Joseph and Martha (Kenningham) Hester of Prentiss County. Grandpa Bud was a farmer most of his life; however, his last 16 years were spent serving as city marshal and justice of the peace. Bud and Alice had four sons: Arthur, Clarence, Clyde and Leslie.

Clyde, born Nov. 30, 1901, met his future bride, Lila Lena Beasley, while working with a highway construction crew in her hometown of Calhoun City, MS. They lived out their lives in Booneville. Clyde (my father) was an auto mechanic for many years and served as marshal and chief of police in Booneville. He later became field representative for a major health insurance company. Lila became a beautician and owned two beauty shops in Prentiss County.

Their children were Charles Henry, David Clyde and Freddie Eugene. Freddie, the youngest, was active in high school and junior college sports and played on two Booneville High School state champion basketball teams. He was a tank commander in the National Guard. He was killed in an explosion and fire at the Armory in Booneville in 1950.

David graduated from Millsaps College in Jackson after serving in the Army of Occupation in Japan following WWII. He resides with his wife, Jean in Memphis, where he is a CPA with an industrial equipment company. Their children are Glenn and Dianne.

Charles Henry served in the Army Air Corps in WWII and graduated from Ole Miss in 1950. He married Margaret Lee Inman of Flora, MS on Aug. 8, 1952. They currently reside in Pascagoula, MS where he retired as city manager in 1986. Margaret retired in 1992 after 33 years teaching elementary school.

Our (Margaret's and mine) three children are Charles H. Jr., Joseph Benjamin (Ben) and Margaret Patricia (Pat).

Charles Jr. attended Ole Miss and got his electrical engineering degree from the University of South Alabama. He is employed by a paper manufacturing company in Jackson, AL. He has two children, Phoebe and Charles Anthony.

Ben received his degree in electrical engineering at Mississippi State University and is now employed with a communication systems developer and manufacturer in the Dallas, TX area. He resides with his wife, Kelly (Reed) Fulghum in Colleyville, TX with their two daughters, Kate and Anne.

Pat graduated from Asbury College in Kentucky and is now Pat Speegle. She now lives in Freeport, FL, with her husband, Troy Speegle, a general contractor. They have three children: Troy David, James Henry and daughter, Jolee.

We have covered a lot of territory since Captain Anthony arrived in the "Colonies" in 1640. Now we are scattered all over the country, but I still feel a strong attachment to Prentiss County. I get back "home" from time to time to look up the few folks I grew up with, who are still around. *Submitted by Charles Henry Fulghum.*

FULGHUM, WILLIAM,

born Jan. 30, 1806 in Wayne County, NC was the son of Benjamin Raiford Fulghum and wife, Anna__ and grandson of Raiford and Winnefred Pierce Fulghum. He married on Mar. 16, 1831 in Hardeman County, TN to Martha Walker Donaldson (See Donaldson). The Fulghums came to Tishomingo County in 1848 to be near her brother's families and her mother, already settled in this area. According to the 1850 Census, William was a farmer with 500 acres. Martha died Feb. 13, 1893 and William died Apr. 14, 1896. Both are buried in the Osborne Creek Church Cemetery.

Picture made before February 1893 at the home of William Fulghum, later owned by Jesse Free. Seated: William and Martha Fulghum. Standing in back: Dock Fulghum, Nannie Fulghum, Bettie Fulghum, Callie Fulghum (Robertson) and Bud (W.F.) Fulghum.

Their children:
(1) Susan A. (b. 1833) married James Franklin Wilemon.
(2) John Mathis (b. Feb. 1, 1834, d. Nov. 19, 1925) married first Mary A. Gentry and second Martha Ann Moore. He served in Co. C, 26th Mississippi Infantry, CSA.
(3) Louisa Jane (b. 1837).
(4) Sarah Elisabeth (b. 1839).
(5) William F. (b. 1842, d. Aug. 22, 1897) married Mary.
(6) Martha Jane (b. 1844, d. Dec. 8, 1915) married in 1868 to Rufus Peyton Walthall.
(7) Zilpha Caroline (b. 1847).
(8) Benjamin Franklin (see below).
(9) James W.B. (b. 1853) went to Texas.
(10) Mary/Mollie E.A. (b. December 1857, d. February 1938) married L.C. Rone.

Benjamin Franklin (aka D.F. or Dock) (b. Mar. 1, 1850, d. Jul. 9, 1936) married Jan. 10, 1870 in Prentiss County, MS to Emely Nancy Ann (Nannie) Howard (See Howard), who was born Feb. 12, 1845 in Union County, SC and died Mar. 8, 1918. Both are buried in Old Booneville Cemetery. D.F. served as a Justice of the Peace and was elected Constable in 1899 and 1911. Their children were:
(1) Martha Ann Caroline "Callie" (b. Apr. 29, 1872, d. Dec. 23, 1934) married Feb. 1, 1900, to Ovelton Bonds Robertson. (See William Bonds Robertson History)
(2) William Franklin "Bud" (b. Jul. 16, 1874, d. Sep. 12, 1949) married Dec. 24, 1899, to Alice Hester. Bud served as City Marshall and Justice of the Peace. Their sons were Clyde Hester, Leslie, Clarence and Arthur.
(3) Bettie May (b. May 27, 1876, d. 1960) never married.

D.F. and Nannie and their children and spouses are buried in the Booneville Cemetery. *Submitted by Virginia H. Lemmon.*

FULGHUM, WILLIAM "WILL" RAPHORD SR.,

born Aug. 20, 1874 and died Feb. 5, 1949 and Lucy Ann (Floyd) (b. Aug. 2, 1890, d. Dec. 9, 1970) were the parents of four children: Elizabeth Moore (b. May 26, 1913, d. Nov. 15, 1919); Lucia Frances (b. Oct. 29, 1914, d. Dec. 16, 1989); William Raphord Jr. (b. Aug. 18, 1919, d. Jan. 6, 1988) and Robert Neal (b. Apr. 26, 1926-).

Front row from left: John M. Fulghum and Martha Moore Fulghum. Back row from left: Noah Jasper Sartin, Maude Fulghum Sartin and William R. Fulghum Sr.

William R. Sr. was a farmer, merchant and cotton buyer. William R. Sr. and brother-in-law, Boone Floyd, had a general mercantile store, Fulghum and Floyd, but went out of business during the depression. William R. Sr. continued to buy cotton, sell fertilizer and insurance. He served on the Board of Aldermen and the Hospital Board. William R. Sr. and Lucy are buried in the Booneville Cemetery with their daughter, Elizabeth, who died at the age of 6.

Frances was married to Wilfred "Chigger" Johnson (b. Mar. 24, 1906, d. Jul. 1, 1950). Wilfred was a mortician for McMillan Funeral Home. They had no children. Wilfred is buried in Booneville Cemetery and Frances is buried in Chicago with her second husband, Louis Garro.

William R. Jr. and Muriel (b. Hall) Fulghum were the parents of three sons: William Larry (b. Mar. 19, 1944), who lives in Montana; Kenneth Blake (b. Feb. 5, 1947), who lives in Mississippi and Russell Clarke (b. Oct. 9, 1950), who lives in Montana. William R. Jr. has three daughters by his second wife, Louise: Lucricia (b. Jan. 9, 1965); Candice (b. Jul. 5, 1967) and Laura (b. Nov. 29, 1973). They live in Mississippi. William R. Jr. is buried in Jackson, MS.

Robert Neal served in the Navy during WWII and on active duty with the National Guard during the Korean Conflict. He is a graduate of Northeast Junior College and Mississippi State University with a degree in accounting and is a retired hospital administrator. Robert Neal and Wilma (Rencher) Fulghum are the parents of one daughter, Cynthia Elizabeth (b. Jul. 6, 1955). Cynthia is a graduate of University of Mississippi with a degree in accounting. Cynthia is married to Larry D. McRight. They have two children: Hunter Dawson (b. Sep. 21, 1981) and Elizabeth Austin (b. Sep. 9, 1986). Larry and Cynthia live in Greenville, MS and after retirement Robert and Wilma moved to Greenville.

William Fulghum was the son of Benjamin and Anna Fulghum of Wayne County, NC, who settled in Booneville in 1848. William (b. Jan. 1, 1806, d. Apr. 14, 1896) and Martha (Donaldson) (b. Mar. 19, 1818, d. Feb. 3, 1893) were my great-grandparents. They lived about three miles south of Booneville, off Highway 45. William was a farmer. They are both buried in Osborne Creek Cemetery.

John M. Fulghum (b. Feb. 1, 1834, d. Nov. 19, 1925) and Martha (Moore) (b. Sep. 8, 1836, d. Feb. 5, 1908) were my grandparents. John's first wife Mary A. (Gentry) died shortly after giving birth to their only child, Oscar. Oscar went to Texas after he was a grown man and is buried in San Francisco. He had a son, Bobby and daughter, Charlene. John and Martha (Moore) had one son, William (Will) Raphord Sr. and one daughter, Maude (Mrs. Jasper Sartin). They lived about eight miles from Booneville in the Meadow Creek Community. John was a farmer. He served in the Confederate Army and was wounded and captured. After the war ended, he walked all the way home from Virginia. John and Martha are buried in the Booneville Cemetery. *Submitted by Robert Neal Fulghum.*

GAINES, HENRY PENDLETON AND JOHN STROTHER,

the Gaines family, brothers, cousins, fathers and sons carried out instructions from Washington to survey a wagon road connecting Colbert's Ferry on the Tennessee with the Tombigbee River. The Spanish in West Florida were interfering with American goods coming to their port at Mobile and this Tennessee-Tombigbee connection would allow a route for goods to come into Alabama via Tennessee and northern Mississippi instead. Meanwhile, another route, known as the Gaines Trace, was being surveyed by the Gaines men as a way for immigrants to settle in northern Alabama.

Gaines Sisters. Standing from left: Martha Francis (Gaines) Kizer married Captain Benjamin Kizer; Rebecca (Gaines) married Dee Matthews; Belva (Gaines) married Cilt Allen and William Ferguson. Sitting from left: Nancy S. (Gaines) married Captain William Moore and Mary A. Gaines married Wister Allen.

Henry Pendleton Gaines and his wife, Nancy (Shipp), moved into a home near where the Gaines men were surveying these new roads. Their home was located just off the Natchez Trace in Old Tishomingo County, the Pharr Flatt area. After the completion of the Trace, Henry and his family moved on to help survey other roads. We are not really sure where he went, but his cousins and uncles were surveying the Gaines Trace in Alabama. We do not believe he moved too far away from northeast Mississippi.

John Strother Gaines was born Aug. 20, 1814, his parents were Henry and Nancy Gaines. John married Eliza "Liza" A. Patten, daughter of Dorn Patten. John must have loved the Pharr Flatts area, because in 1836, he moved his new family back into this area. Possibly, John was still helping with work near and around the Natchez Trace. John Strother Gaines is listed as the first settler in the Pharr Flatts.

Six Gaines infants are buried in the Pleasant Valley Cemetery, where Liza is buried in a marked grave and where we think John Strother Gaines is buried in an unmarked grave. One of their sons, P.H. Gaines, was killed at Kingston, GA, on Oct. 10, 1863, during the Civil War. He is buried in Pleasant Valley Cemetery. Eliza's father, Dorn Patten, is also buried in Pleasant Valley Cemetery.

John and Eliza Gaines had several daughters: Nancy S. married Captain William Moore; Mary A. married Wister Allen; Rebecca Gaines married Dee Matthews; Belva married Cilt Allen and William Ferguson and Martha Francis.

Martha Francis Gaines was born Aug. 29, 1842 in Pharr Flatts. She married Captain Benjamin Julian Kizer on Sep. 10, 1863, as soon as he returned from the Civil War. They had 10 children, who grew up in the Pharr Flatts/Pleasant Valley area.

The Gaines family has a lineage that would make any family proud. Gaines men have fought in the American Revolutionary War, the Civil War, the Spanish American War and the Indian War. The Gaines women raised children, took care of homes and business while their men were away. The Gaines family helped politically and monetarily in the development of the US and for almost 200 years, the extended Gaines family has helped in the growth of northeast Mississippi. *Submitted by Carolyn Whitehead and Gene Kizer.*

GALLOWAY, DR. SAMUEL CALVIN JR.,
began his general practice of medicine in Booneville on Aug. 1, 1951. He was born in Plant City, FL Dec. 13, 1915. His parents were Samuel C. Galloway Sr., who was born in Lincoln County, TN to Alexander Calvin Galloway and Elizabeth Snipes Galloway and Lula Steen Johnston Galloway, who was born in Algoma, MS to Dr. Alonzo Johnston and Alberta Steen Whisenant Johnston. He attended elementary school in Lake Wales and Tampa, FL and middle school in Pontotoc, MS. He graduated from Tippah-Union High School in Cotton Plant, MS in 1933. He attended Chickasaw College in Pontotoc, MS and Erskine College in Due West, SC. He taught math and science and coached at Mississippi Heights Academy and Professor J.B. Brown's Boarding School for Boys at Blue Mountain, MS and worked as a chemist at Electrometalurgical Co. in Sheffield, AL, before serving in WWII. He served in the 42nd Infantry Division and in the European Theater Army of Occupation after the war. Following discharge from the military, he received a BS degree in science from the University of Mississippi and graduated from the University of Mississippi Medical School in Oxford in 1948. He received his MD degree from the University of Illinois School of Medicine in Chicago in June 1950. He served his internship at the Illinois Central Hospital in Chicago.

On Sep. 4, 1949, he married Ruth Barkley of Ripley, daughter of Robert Anderson Barkley, who was born in Union County, MS and Verna McBryde Barkley, who was born at Cotton Plant, MS. Ruth's grandparents were Elijah Wellington Barkley and Effie Craig Barkley of Union County, MS and Patton Anderson McBryde and Jessie McBryde McBryde (cousins) of Ripley, formerly of Cotton Plant. She was a graduate of Ripley High School and Delta State University (then DSTC).

The Galloway children (all born in Booneville) are: Samuel Calvin III (b. Nov. 2, 1951); Robert Barkley (b. Jun. 20, 1954) and Ruth Gail (Cissy) (b. Jun. 29, 1956).

Sam is a graduate of the University of Mississippi and later received his associate degree in nursing from Northeast Mississippi Community College. He is a registered nurse and has been working with Methodist Alliance Home Care in Memphis for the past 15 years.

Bob is a graduate of the University of Mississippi School of Pharmacy and was a practicing pharmacist in Booneville and Corinth for several years and has been with Eli Lilly Pharmaceutical Co. as a sales representative for 15 years. He married Camille Cunningham, daughter of James A. and Avenell Waddle Cunningham of Booneville on Jan. 2, 1977. Camille is a graduate of Mississippi University for Women and received her MS degree in speech pathology from the University of Mississippi. Presently, she is speech pathologist at Thomas Street School in Tupelo. Their children are: Robert Barkley Jr. (b. Aug. 7, 1980) and twins, James Andrew and William Brett (b. May 16, 1983). Presently, Robert Jr. is a sophomore at Northeast Mississippi Community College. Drew and Brett are juniors at Booneville High School.

Cissy received BS and MS degrees in home economics education from the Mississippi University for Women and has been teaching at Booneville High School 21 years. She married Phillip Charles Worley, son of Nelvin Worley and Avenell Trantham Worley of Booneville on Jun. 7, 1981. Phil received BS and MS degrees and specialist in education from Mississippi State University and teaches science at Thrasher High School. Their son, Phillip Cal Worley, was born Mar. 20, 1985. He is a freshman at Thrasher High School at this time.

Dr. Sam Galloway practiced until Apr. 1, 1992, when he retired for reasons of health. He died Mar. 6, 1997. *Submitted by Ruth Galloway.*

GARDNER, GRANNY,
no history on Wheeler would be complete without a Granny Gardner story. The new teacher of Wheeler School back in 1932 was standing in her room when she heard an awful noise coming from somewhere outside. She had been in Wheeler long enough to know everybody so she was more than a little surprised when she saw what was causing the commotion. She had run to the window, looked down the road and, for heavens sake, there was Granny Gardner coming up the road on a wagon that looked like it was doing 50 miles and hour - bump, bump, bump. Her companion was a 10-12-year old boy who was standing in the middle of the wagon, perfectly in control, running the horses as fast as they could go. Granny was holding to the wagon seat with one hand while the other hand was waving her bonnet up and down as she was whooping and yelling as loud as she could. It was like a circus that got loose.

Gladys Milton, the teacher who saw it, hasn't gotten over it yet. It was the best show she ever saw. Granny wasn't any more than 70 years old then and she wasn't going anywhere in particular. Granny was just having fun. Everybody that saw it got a good idea that automobiles just couldn't come close to a wagon and two horses for that kind of enjoyment. Granny, herself, wouldn't think of it as a great accomplishment. At age 90, she could still buck dance. Granny lived to be at least 106 years old, depending on who you talked to.

Sometime later when she started hitting the 90s, one of her fourth generation children, Eloise Garner (Webb), who was still in high school, decided to take a friend along to see Granny. Eloise lived with Rev. Otha Miller and her great-grandmother and she didn't know everything there was to know about Granny. After she and her friend, Sarah, had visited a little while, Eloise started out by saying, "Granny now tell Sarah how far you had to go every Sunday to get to church in the old days."

Granny said, "What? Us? Honey, we went to dances. We'd get up early on Saturday, ride all day, dance all night and go back on Sunday."

That ended the illusion of the hardships and sacrifices of the early Americans, but there was much more to Granny Gardner. God had given her another talent as well, that of comforting and healing. She was the mid-wife, she came when people got sick. She flirted with life and death for all her years. Granny's great-granddaughter, Billie Marie Gardner Hare, says that at age 97 Granny had emergency appendicitis surgery. She had so much poison in her system that they were going to lose her. She told them a certain type of whiskey to bring to her; they brought her whiskey but not the kind requested. She told them that this kind of whiskey would not work. She had to have that specific kind. They found it and she started to turn for the better. Granny had doctored enough in her lifetime to know what kind of poison would kill another kind of poison.

Granny had a little history of her own that she never said much about, at least not in her older days, even though she never forgot it. She was somewhere around 15 years old when the Civil War came. One day in the winter she found a boy out in the cornfield. He had been trying to feed himself by eating dry corn. He wore the Union blue, a Yankee and the enemy, but not to her and her parents. She brought him into the house, fed him, gave him a bed and tried to keep him alive, but he died.

Some years later, people who passed a certain road that went out of Wheeler toward Baldwyn noticed a cut stone on the side of the road. It read "Unknown Soldier." In at least 50 years or more after it was placed there, the stone always had fresh flowers on it. It was just a nice little mystery thing for people like me to wonder about.

Granny's life spanned the three greatest wars of the US, the Civil War of the 1860s and the WWI and WWII of the 1940s, the coming of the railroad in Wheeler in 1861 - which brought soldiers in from the north, the coming of cars in 1910 and a lot of other things that she may have called foolish. Who could have wanted more than two good horses, one good wagon, a pair of shoes and a night of dancing?

That was about half of what Granny was all about, but the other part was the healing which made her a person you'd never want to forget. Several of Granny Gardner's kin and her children's children's children live in Wheeler and surrounding area and still have a memory of her that has been passed down. We have visions that all of her children will come together one day in Wheeler and have an evening of buck dancing.

We know them as good friends, but in this case I will speak for myself and thank Eloise Garner Webb for introducing me to Alice Rogers "Granny" Gardner and in memory to her mother, Essie Miller Garner, who told me who kept the fresh flowers around the stone of the unknown soldier. Granny did it all. *Submitted by Sarah Louise Milton.*

GARDNER, MONT RAY
and Mollie Azena Barker were married Jun. 20, 1942 by Brother G.P. Mayo at his home. Mont Ray Gardner (b. Oct. 30, 1914), son of Ceborn and Lois Gaddis Gardner in Baldwyn, MS.

Mollie Azena (b. Mar. 9, 1911), daughter of William Eli and Miley Elizabeth Tollison Barker in Winston County, AL. Mont was in the Army and stationed at Courtland, AL. After his tour of duty they bought a 80 acre farm in the Tuscumbia Community in 1946. They had one daughter, Billie Marie Gardner, who was born Jul. 11, 1943 in Booneville, MS.

Mont and Azena were remembered by the community as good neighbors and always active in their church, Tuscumbia Baptist, until their health failed. Mont was also a painter part-time and he always did a good job. Azena worked at Prentiss Manufacturing and was remembered by her co-workers as a dear friend and helper. Her niece, Elizabeth Mathis, always remembered what a good cook she was and how she always made you feel welcome.

Mollie Azena Barker Gardner and Mont Ray Gardner

Billie Marie Gardner and Linus Eugene Hare were married in Prentiss County at the home of Brother J.L. Gore on Jun. 30, 1962. They have lived all their married life in the Tuscumbia Community and been active in the Tuscumbia Baptist Church. Linus Eugene Hare was born Dec. 12, 1943. He works at Kimberly Clark in Corinth, MS and Billie works at Dowdle Gas Co. They have two children:

1) Daughter, Monte Jean Hare (b. May 11, 1963) md. Jasper Donald Lambert (b. Jul. 19, 1959), son of Jasper and Rosie Williams Lambert of the Altitude Community. Monte works as business manager for the Booneville City schools and Donald is recruiting and retention NCO for the National Guard in Booneville. They have two children, Molly Nicole Lambert (b. May 21, 1991) and Andrew Donald Lambert (b. Sep. 16, 1995).

2) Son, Kevin Lyn Hare (b. Apr. 17, 1968, a math instructor at Thrasher High School. He is married to Marla Ray Rowland (b. Dec. 30, 1975), daughter of Danny and Marilyn Dees Rowland. Marla is a special

education teacher with the Booneville Separate School District. They have one daughter, Katy Lyn Hare (b. May 21, 1999).

Mont Ray Gardner died Oct. 13, 1995 and Mollie Azena Barker Gardner died Jun. 11, 1998. They are buried at the Tuscumbia Cemetery. *Submitted by Billie Gardner Hare.*

GARNER, WALTER CLEOFUS, son of John H. Garner, who was born in Alabama in 1856. He later moved to Mississippi where he met and married Harriet Elizabeth Lominick (b. 1862, d. 1942). Rita Lou Garner was the daughter of James Asbury Cartwright and Angela Cole Cartwright, who died when Rita was 6 years old.

Mr. and Mrs. W.C. Garner in 1960.

In 1912 the Blackland Community was a thriving west Prentiss County village with a good school, a Methodist church and a Baptist church nearby. W.C. Garner (b. 1889, d. 1970), who had taught in several county schools, bought the local general mercantile store in partnership with his uncle, Walter Prather. In 1914 he married his sweetheart since third grade, Rita Lou Cartwright (b. 1892, d. 1980), who began to work in the store. Later, Mr. Prather sold his share of the Blackland store and built a store at Oak Hill.

The Garners worked hard and the store became the center of the community. It sold everything from nails, groceries and shoes to satin and lace. On cold winter days, members of the community sat around the pot-bellied stove eating sardines, cheese and crackers and playing checkers and dominoes. On the weekend, there was even a barber. During election years, the store was a polling place.

Cleofus and Rita were involved in all aspects of the community, teaching Sunday School and working in PTA In 1929-30, the school had trouble with accreditation and the Garners helped to consolidate the school with Wheeler High School.

Then came the depression and the customers of the store could not pay the bills they had charged. The roads were beginning to be improved and people were going to Booneville to shop, instead of the community store.

In 1930 Mr. Garner drove his Model A Ford to Booneville each day to work, first at the Farm Bureau, then at the Prentiss County Co-op, which he managed for several years. Mrs. Garner continued to operate the store in Blackland for awhile, but because of the depression, they decided to close the store and move to Booneville. Later, they sold the store and the three houses they owned in Blackland.

W.C., as many people called him, decided to become a full-time cotton buyer and opened an office on Market Street. Rita and daughter, Elizabeth, became the office force.

The Garners were active in the life of the town. Cleofus was a faithful member of the Rotary Club and Rita a charter member of the Booneville Pilot Club. Mr. Garner was on the board of trustees of the school when they applied for a Junior College. This was something he worked very hard for and was very proud when the college opened in 1948. The first year of operation, the senior class of Booneville High School became part of the Junior College and the Garner's daughter, Sue, was one of the members of the only graduating class of Northeast Mississippi Agricultural High School.

The Garners had three daughters: Ernestine (Mrs. Stratton Daniel Jr.) of Memphis, TN; Elizabeth of Booneville and Sue (Mrs. Ben Phillips) of Columbus, GA. They have two grandsons, Michel Phillips and Garner Phillips and two great-grandchildren, Benjy and Ivy Phillips, all of Georgia. *Submitted by Sue G. Phillips.*

GENO, TOUSSAINT, a Frenchman living in South Carolina at the turn of the 19th century. Where he came from, nobody knows, that I can find. He owned land and resided in Kershaw County, SC. He drew at least eight pay stubs for his involvement in the Revolutionary War. He left a will that he wrote in 1791. In it two young men were mentioned. The will was probated in 1803. One of the young men was Francis and the other was John Buty.

Francis and John both served their country, as listed in the *Tennesseans in the War of 1812*, Transcribed and Indexed by Byron and Samuel Sistler. I have no more information on John. I have not found a wife for Francis and only one son for him. He was Francis Geno Jr., born about 1807 in North Carolina. After a long, productive life, he died in Tippah County Oct. 10, 1896. He was the father of a large family and group of descendants who have made their homes in many areas of north Mississippi and scattered throughout the nation.

According to Kent Geno's *Out of the Wilderness into Tomorrow*, his grist mill was burned by Union troops during the Civil War. He farmed and was an ordained deacon in the Mt. Olive Baptist Church. According to his obituary in the Southern Sentinel of Ripley, he was a God fearing, God loving man.

He was the father of 12 children: Ann, Martha and Savannah Mahalla were all born in South Carolina. Edney (Edna) M., John, Eliza, Elizabeth M., William Thomas, Francis (Franklin) and Andrew Jackson were born in Tippah County. Rachel D. and Lafayette D. were born in Prentiss County.

Ann and Martha married Strother and Stephen Crawford. Both their husbands died in the early 1860s. Each of the Geno girls produced large families from which sprang a host of Crawfords and descendants, many of whom became teachers, preachers and leaders in their respective communities. After their Crawford husbands died, Ann married A. Brumley and Martha married Mike Cox. Mike lived to 114 years of age and they had seven children.

Savannah Mahalla married James Carter. She died after having only three children, but these children produced leaders for the future of Prentiss County and surrounding counties, plus many who migrated as far away as Oklahoma, Indiana and Oregon.

Edney M. married David Feagan; after he died, she married Emanuel Alexander Mullikin and moved to Arkansas. She had a son by both husbands. These children grew up in Arkansas and their descendants remain there today.

John Geno did not live a full life. He was captured at Fort Donelson during the Civil War. He died Mar. 12, 1862, as a POW in a hospital in St. Louis, MO. Eliza married Matthew Brumley, Apr. 13, 1865 and Elizabeth M. married J.W. Ford, Dec. 22, 1868.

William married Margaret E. Surratt. Though he did not stay around, their large family, reared by a strong mother, stayed to see Prentiss and area counties into the 20th century. Many of their descendants established businesses and contributed much to the development of the forward thinking areas of north Mississippi. In this family, much tragedy came, but with the spirit of hope they overcame and the children became stalwart church, civic and family leaders.

Rachael D. married Nathan Brooks. Nathan lived to the ripe old age of 101 years old. Rachael was the mother of 14 children. She is buried in Jumpertown Cemetery, along with many of the children she gave birth to. They were the fathers and mothers of a host of Prentiss County leaders of yesterday, today and tomorrow.

Francis (Franklin), Andrew Jackson and Lafayette D. all became family men and worked hard. Some of them stayed in the area and some of them departed for the promise of the future that Texas and the West had to offer.

This is only a small part of the history that one man from South Carolina began for the future of Prentiss County, MS. The descendants in Prentiss County alone from Francis Geno Jr. include such familiar sounding names as Geno, Carter, Cox, Michael, English, Johnsey, Eaton, Phillips, Crawford, Brumley, Brooks, Yates, Downs, Dunnam, Perrigo, Padgett, Wirth, Nichols, Shepherd, Hall, Rogers, Kinningham, Ford, Harris, Pounders, Keenum and who knows how many others.

GENTRY, CLAUDE, born Jul. 25, 1902 in Baldwyn. His birthplace was less than 300 yards north of the Brice's Crossroads Visitor's and Interpretive Center which is located at 607 Grisham Street. The center bears a legacy to his love for Brice's Crossroads Battlefield.

"Mr. Claude," as he was known to many, dedicated much of his adult life to the historical preservation of the Battle of Brice's Crossroads.

His log cabin museum, which stood next to his home in Baldwyn from 1961-1998, served as visible proof of his commitment to Brice's Crossroads and to the city of Baldwyn. He was instrumental in organizing anniversary celebrations for the battle in 1954 and 1964. He was responsible for the granite markers on Highway 370 erected by an act of the Mississippi Legislature in 1957 during the term of Governor J.P. Coleman.

Claude Gentry

He moved away for a while to work in Tupelo, but returned to Baldwyn in 1927. He played independent baseball, painted and sold insurance.

Among his many accomplishments were president of the Mississippi Historical Society (1963-1964) and editor of the Northeast Mississippi Historical Journal (1968). He received the "Distinguished Service Award" from the Chicago Civil War Roundtable. He also received an award from the London, England Civil War Roundtable. He was once named Outdoor Writer of the Year by the Mississippi Wildlife Federation. He authored 20 books ranging from the Civil War to religion to fiction and was technical advisor for the filming of the movie, *Shiloh* in 1955. The movie is still shown today at the Shiloh Visitor's Center.

In 1929, he bought motion picture equipment and opened the first conventional theater in Baldwyn. It played silent movies and was located across from Hassell's Appliance Store on Main Street. His wife, Gladys, played the piano to accompany the silent movies. He later opened the old Lyric theater which faced the railroad. He owned and operated two theaters in the 1930s, 40s, 50s and 60s in Baldwyn: The Ritz and the Lyric. Mr. Claude began the city's current newspaper in 1939. He was the first editor of the *Baldwyn Weekly News* or *The Baldwyn News* beginning in 1940.

He published a flyer to advertise his movies and it grew into the present weekly newspaper. He was also a painter, pilot, Sunday School teacher, song leader and businessman.

Mr. Claude died Dec. 9, 1992, at the age of 90. *Submitted by Edwina Carpenter, administrator, Brice's Crossroads Visitor and Interpretive Center.*

GLOVER, ISAAC MARION, born in Old Tishomingo County in July 1846, the seventh of Allen Glover's 20 children. His mother was Sarah Elizabeth Robinson Lindsey, Allen's second wife. Allen and Elizabeth had one other child, Elizabeth Ann *1900,*

"Betsy," born in 1848 about the time of the mother's death.

Isaac Marion Glover and Sarah Elizabeth Glover

When Marion was barely 15, the Civil War began. He enlisted in Iuka on Sep. 1, 1861 in Co. K, 26th Regiment, Mississippi Volunteers. He was captured in Jonesboro, GA in 1864. On his pension application, he listed a disability due to a wound received following the surrender: "I was wounded by a Tory (bushwhacker)."

Marion's story immediately following the war is unaccounted for, but we pick it up on Jul. 18, 1867. On that day in Itawamba County, he married Sarah Elizabeth "Sally" Mullins Johnson Bardin. Sally was born Feb. 3, 1847 in Texas where her parents, John Thomas Mullins and Anna H. Nanney, had moved from Itawamba County. They returned to Mississippi after one year. At the age of 13, Sally married Sylvanus S. Johnson, son of Stephen and Elizabeth Johnson and had a son, Sylvanus. Sylvanus Sr. was killed in the war. Sally's second husband, Henry Horn Bardin, was a widower with several children. That marriage was unsuccessful.

Marion and Sally lived for a time in Union County, MS but eventually settled in the Hopewell Community of Prentiss County. Their children were: John (b. 1871); Henry Franklin (b. 1873) married Lucy Free; Mary Louise "Mollie" married John W. "Bill" Ryan; Joseph Masie (b. Aug. 18, 1878, d. Mar. 28, 1969) married Lydia Ann Boren; Minnie Clara (b. December 1880) married Newton Isaac Keys; Allie Tibytha (b. Sep. 3, 1883, d. Dec. 31, 1976) married Julius Berry Ricks and Marion Lee (b. Feb. 15, 1886, d. Jul. 23, 1973) married Mattie B. Crabb.

In the years following the Civil War, Marion and Sally spent their lives, as did so many southerners, eking out a living in the hot, cotton fields. Their children grew up and had families and perhaps they looked forward to the days when they could sit on the porch and watch their grandchildren at play. However, in 1904, the team of mules that Marion was driving ran away and he was thrown from the wagon and killed. He was 58 years old. He is buried in the Hopewell Primitive Baptist Church Cemetery. Sally died in Paris, TX while visiting her son, Joe and her daughter, Minnie and is buried there.

John apparently died as a child, for no one has memory of him. Henry moved to California; Joe and Minnie moved to Texas, leaving Allie, Mollie and Lee in Prentiss County. *Jo Carolyn Anderson Beebe, 645 Hickory Hill, Hiawassee, GA 30546. (706)896-6290.*

GLOVER, RICHARD I., born 1556 and died 1615 near London, England. His last son from his second wife was Richard Glover II (b. 1611, d. 1696). He came to Rappahannock County, VA on the ship *Assurance de lo* in July 1635. He married Mary Booker in Virginia. They had six children: Richard, Thomas, Robert, William Sr., Benjamin and Samuel.

William Glover Sr. (b. 1653, d. 1713) married Mary Burton Davis. They had four children: Thomas, Charles Worth, Joseph and William Jr. William Glover Sr. served as governor of North Carolina in 1706-1708.

William Glover Jr. (b. 1695, d. 1754) married Mary Norwood. They had seven children: John, Lydia, Sarah, George, William, Benjamin and Joseph.

Billy Glover family photograph 1998 Fourth of July Celebration. Front row children from left: Coral Stephens and Corrie Glover. Front row adults from left: Billy Glover and Merle Wardlaw Glover. Back row from left: Rick Glover, Jessica Stephens, Kathy Glover, Jeff Glover, Meredith Glover and Teresa Glover.

Joseph Glover (b. 1734, d. 1784) moved to Granville County, NC, around 1740. He married Phoebe Mitchell. They had 10 children: John, Elizabeth, Priscilla, William, Daniel, David, Jacob, Mary Ann, Robert and Phoebe Norwood.

John Glover (b. 1752, d. 1821) served in the Revolutionary War under his brother, William, from 1775-1777. He took the Oath of Loyalty with his father, Joseph in 1778. He married Elizabeth Hicks. They had four children: George Washington, Frederick, Larkin and Isham. He migrated to Edgefield, SC, about 1785-1790.

Jones Curtis Glover family photograph 1932 Family Reunion. Seated front row from left: Ebe Glover and Brownlee Glover. Seated second row from left: Mary Brownlee Glover, Billy Glover and Jones Curtis Glover. Standing front row from left: Lavada Glover, Virginia Glover, Sadie Glover, Dennis Glover and Vernon Swindle. Standing back row from left: Bill Cochran, Katie Glover Cochran, Mary Lesley Glover and Ellis Glover.

George Washington Glover (b. 1776, d. 1843) moved to Warren County, GA. He married Elizabeth Jones. They had 11 children: Gracey, Olive, Martha, Seaborn, Stephen, Allen, George, William, Terry, Elizabeth and Simon. George Washington Glover moved to Hernando, DeSoto County, MS in 1840. He died there in 1843.

Allen Glover (b. 1810, d. 1891) was born in Warren County, GA. He married first Harriett Castleberry. They had six children: Mary, Nathan, William, Charles, John and Harriett.

Allen Glover moved to Prentiss County, near what is now Wheeler in the mid-1840s. His second wife was Elizabeth Lindsey. They had two children, Isaac Marion and Elizabeth. Allen Glover bought his home place, two miles south of Wheeler, from the American Land Co. in 1846. The American Land Co. bought the land from the Chickasaw Indian Tribe. The deed was signed by Chief No Ah Chu Nah on May 25, 1836.

Allen Glover and his third wife, Sarah Mills, sold this place to their son, Jones Curtis Glover, on Nov. 12, 1887. They are buried in a family cemetery on the home place. They had 11 children: Drucilla, Melinda, Elias, Emaline, Allen, Caroline, Jones Curtis, Juda, Joseph, Madison and Mary.

Jones Curtis Glover (b. 1859, d. 1945) was born and died the home place south of Wheeler. He was postmaster at Wheeler in 1897-1900. His first wife was Lucinda Mathis. They had seven children: Allen, Elizabeth, Buddy, Tim, Jack, Loula Pearl and Ulysess.

Jones Curtis Glover's second wife was Mary Alice Brownlee Holmes. They had 11 children: Ellis married Mary Lesley; Sadie married Vernon Swindle; an infant girl; Katie married Leon Stephenson; Lavada married Boyce Enis; Virginia married Vardie Wren; Dennis married Edna Samples; Ebe married Ruth Perry; an infant girl; Brownlee married Reba Perry; Billy James married Annie Merle Wardlaw.

Merle and I have two children. James Richard married Katherine Houk. They live in Centreville, VA. Jeffrey Allan married Teresa Haynes. They live in Torreon, Coahuila, Mexico. They have two children, Corrie Louise and Meredith Anne. This completes 12 generations of Glovers.

There are hundreds of Glover descendants throughout the US. *Submitted by Billy J. Glover.*

GOOCH, WESLEY, born 1822 in Tennessee. He came to Tishomingo County, MS and married Jemima Bennett on Feb. 10, 1840 in Jacinto. Jemima was born in 1823 and died in 1897. She is buried in Hopewell Cemetery in Prentiss County. Wesley and Jemima had Sarah (b. 1842), who married B.P. Kennedy in 1858; William M. (b. 1843, d. 1930), who married Emily; Missouri A. (b. 1844), who married G.W. Barrett; Thomas B. (b. 1846, d. 1918), who married Margaret; Jessie A. (b. 1859); Jefferson Davis (b. 1861, d. 1944), who married Mary Melissa Wilburn and Mary J.P. (b. 1864). There is a period of time before the last three children, but they still bare the name Gooch.

Jefferson Davis Gooch (b. Aug. 14, 1861, d. Jan. 1, 1944) married Mary Melissa Wilburn (b. May 6, 1864, d. Apr. 30, 1908) on Jul. 7, 1880. Mary was the daughter of Claibourne B. Wilburn and Sarah Ann Enis. Jefferson Davis and Mary built a house between Hopewell and Marietta in Prentiss County and had 14 children:

Jefferson Davis Gooch

(1) Walter Lee (b. Aug. 16, 1882, d. Nov. 20, 1904) married Annie Lou Crouch.

(2) W.W. "Hub" (b. Sep. 16, 1884, d. Apr. 3, 1958) married Myrtle Barrett.

(3) Wiley Claibourne (b. Nov. 24, 1886, d. Feb. 12, 1970) married Ora Lee Crouch.

(4) M.A. "Maude" (b. Nov. 11, 1888, d. Mar. 6, 1956) married Ward Philpot.

(5) J.A. "Authur" (b. Jan. 11, 1891, d. Sep. 15, 1935) married Edna Gist.

(6) C.V. "Carrie" (b. Apr. 1, 1893, d. Jul. 16, 1977) married Jim Little.

(7) R.D. "Vernon" (b. Feb. 24, 1895, d. Oct. 29, 1966) married Edna Files.

(8) F.M. "Mildred" (b. Feb. 23, 1899, d. ?) married John T. McNeese.

(9) J.C. (b. May 7, 1897, d. Aug. 13, 1929).

(10) R.C. (b. Feb. 22, 1901, d. ?) married Sula Mae Wren.

(11) V.B. "Beaut" (b. Aug. 9, 1903, d. ?) married Clyde Swinney.

(12) J.O. "Odis" (b. Nov. 2, 1905, d. ?) married Jimmie.

(13) & (14) Twins, Leon and Glen (b. Apr. 30, 1908, d. Apr. 30, 1908).

Mary Melissa died the day the twins were born and died. They are buried beside her in Hopewell Cemetery along with Jefferson Davis.

Wiley Claibourne Gooch and Ora Lee Crouch

(b. Dec. 7, 1889, d. Dec. 23, 1965) were married Feb. 4, 1906 in Prentiss County. Their children were Lawrence Lucion, Sibyl, Rodney, Gladys, Pauline, Vandiver, Stanley and Olan. Wiley and Ora Lee crossed the Mississippi River on a ferry and moved to Portageville, MO, where they bought a cotton farm. They are both buried in Portageville.

Lucion (b. Mar. 24, 1907, d. Mar. 18, 1967) stayed in Prentiss County and married Ora D. Ryan (b. Jun. 13, 1907, d. Feb. 13, 1986) on Sep. 21, 1925. Ora D. was the daughter of John William Ryan and Mary Louise Glover. They had one daughter, Sadie Christine Gooch (b. Jul. 23, 1925), who married Rupert Edwin Pike (b. May 18, 1920, d. Sep. 7, 1986) on Oct. 14, 1944. Lucion, Ora D. and Rupert are buried together in the Booneville Cemetery. S*ubmitted by Christine Gooch Pike.*

GOODWIN, LEANDER FRANKLIN "ANDY,"

moved his family to a farm in Prentiss County, MS in the 1890s. They came from Mud Creek, Jefferson County, AL where Leander was born Oct. 6, 1842 to Joshua Richard Goodwin (b. 1801, d. 1895) and Sarah Farrar. He married Mary Jane Crane on Aug. 1, 1865 in Jefferson County. Mary was born Jan. 26, 1845 in Jefferson County and died. Aug. 16, 1927 in Booneville, Prentiss County, MS. Leander died in Golden, Tishomingo County, MS on May 24, 1933. Leander and Mary are buried at Mt. Nemo Church Cemetery in Booneville.

They had the following children:

1) Mary Jane Goodwin (b. about 1865 in Jefferson County, AL).

2) Susan R. Goodwin (b. about 1868 in Jefferson County, AL). It is believed that on Dec. 13, 1889 in Prentiss County, MS she married Joseph Rogers.

3) Samuel Joshua Goodwin (b. Aug. 27, 1870 in Jefferson County, d. Jun. 11, 1949 in Dennis, MS). He married Mary L. Gray (b. 1874, d. 1957), daughter of A.T. and Mattie Gray, on Dec. 8, 1891 in Prentiss County. Samuel was a farmer. He and Mary are buried at Ridge Cemetery in Itawamba County, MS.

4) Thomas Leander Goodwin (b. Oct. 6, 1872 in Jefferson County, d. Oct. 31, 1907 in Booneville) md. Sarah Eleanor Howell, daughter of Elisha Howell and Mary Goodard, on Dec. 4, 1896 in Prentiss County. Sarah was born May 15, 1876 in Mississippi and died Dec. 29, 1966 in Booneville. Thomas was a farmer. He and Sarah are buried in Mt. Nemo Church Cemetery in Booneville. They had one child, Prentiss William Goodwin.

5) Nima S. Goodwin was born Mar. 25, 1875 in Jefferson County and died May 14, 1927 in Belmont, MS. On Nov. 11, 1896 in Booneville, Nima married William Walter Crabb, son of James Walter Crabb and Elizabeth Ellender Hathcock. William was born Nov. 14, 1879 in Booneville and died there on Jul. 12, 1958. Nima and William are buried at Mt. Nebo Church Cemetery in Booneville. They had the following children: Walter, Luther, Audie, Autie Mae, Eula, Era, Lois and Claude.

6) Dennis Perry Goodwin (b. Jan. 26, 1880 in Marion County, AL, d. Jul. 3, 1964 in Booneville), he married on Jan. 1, 1901 to Christine Elizabeth Smith, daughter of Andrew Jackson Smith and Anne Wroten in Prentiss County. Christine was born Feb. 20, 1884 in Mississippi and died in Booneville on Jan. 2, 1967. Dennis was a farmer. He and Christine are buried at Mt. Nebo Church Cemetery in Booneville. They had three children: Harold, Olin and Anne.

During the war, Leander served as a private in the Confederate Army for the 28th Alabama Infantry Volunteers, Co. H. On Mar. 1, 1862, he enlisted in Jonesboro, AL. He served until his company surrendered in North Carolina in 1865. *Submitted by C. Devin.*

GOOGE FAMILY,

the history of the Googe family like the history of other American families, stretches back into the distant past and to a foreign land. Betty Googe Buckley of Starkville provides us with the earliest account of the Googe family dating back into the 1600s when there was a great deal of political and religious conflict occurring in European countries.

Within Germany at this time lived a family of six: father, mother and four sons. The father and mother were being persecuted although it is not known whether for religious beliefs or political beliefs. Subsequently, the mother and father were executed in the presence of the four sons.

Following the execution a nun took charge of the sons and with them worked their way from Germany to London where she booked passage to America for herself and the four boys. Although she was a person possessing strong religious beliefs, the nun did not force her religious beliefs on the four boys in her charge. She did firmly instruct the boys in the merit of hard work and in the development of their learning abilities. About this time the name was changed from Googer to its present form, Googe. The two older boys worked in the new world and repaid the nun for her kindness. It is believed that these earliest known members of the Googe family settled in Virginia and thence in Georgia.

Joseph M. Googe, great-grandfather of Betty Googe Buckley, came to Mississippi from Rome, GA. His son Elias Rogers Googe became a veterinarian practicing on farm animals and chosen hunting dogs in rural north Mississippi and west Alabama. During a flu epidemic the community doctor and his wife fell victim to the flu and died leaving four children. Elias Rogers Googe and his wife took the DeBou children and called them their adopted children. Later one of the DeBou sons married Fannie Elizabeth Googe and lived in Red Bay, AL. At a very young age Elias Rogers Googe enlisted in the Confederate Army serving from 1863 to his discharge at Iuka, MS at the close of the war in 1865. He was later elected sheriff of Itawamba County (1900-1904). Elias Rogers Googe was esteemed by his family and friends as a Christian gentleman and a community leader and joined by his sister Sallie, organized the Sandy Springs Baptist Church and was later buried in the cemetery near this rural church.

Joseph Googe's great-great-great-great grandsons: Joshua Thomas Googe and Benjamin James Googe

Joseph M. Googe, born Mar. 12, 1812, died Nov. 13, 1882; he was married to Elizabeth Rogers Googe (b. Nov. 26, 1820, died Dec. 1, 1884). Their children: Elias Rogers Googe born in Floyd County, GA, Jan. 23, 1845, died Feb. 16, 1926; William J. Googe born Nov. 15, 1859, died Mar. 28, 1879; Sallie A. Googe Pierce born Aug. 23, 1853, died May 15, 1926; Martha J. Googe Moore born Jun. 2, 1856, died Nov. 10, 1883; J. H. Googe born Aug. 3, 1865, died Jan. 3, 1866.

Elias Rogers Googe was married to Sitty Anne Morgan Feb. 22, 1865. Both are buried at Sandy Springs, MS which is south of Marietta. Born to this marriage were 11 children: Alice Lurana Googe Cromeans born Jul. 29, 1866, died Sep. 14, 1916; James Henry Googe born Feb. 19, 1868, died May 11, 1924; Fannie Elizabeth Googe Debou born May 11, 1869, died Dec. 31, 1938; Ann Eliza Googe Warren born Dec. 4, 1871, died May 4, 1943; Martha Fatina Googe born Aug. 11, 1873, died Oct. 17, 1874; George William Googe born Dec. 15, 1876, died May 24, 1956; Mittie Lee Googe born Dec. 28. 1878, died Apr. 2, 1879; Minnie Mae Googe born Dec. 28, 1878, died Jan. 2, 1898; Maranda Googe Dozier born Feb. 6, 1881, died Jun. 11, 1963; Charles Rogers Googe born Aug. 12, 1883, died Jan. 23, 1950 and Virgil E. Googe born Oct. 19, 1885, died Dec. 18, 1957. *Submitted by Kathryn Googe Floyd.*

GOOGE, JAMES HENRY,

a likable person, made many friends. He loved the outdoors and was happy as a timber man. Between 1920 and his death, he cut logs in Tombigbee River bottom and floated rafts of logs down the river to a large mill which was located on the west bank of Tombigbee River just above where the bridge on Highway 78 crossed the river. He would ride a raft of logs down the river and then go to Fulton to visit with his father, Elias Rogers Googe who was living in the home of Samuel Lee and Maranda Googe Dozier. James Henry had asthma and probably had it most of his life. He ran from the measles because he felt that should he catch them he would smother to death. He did, unfortunately, catch the measles (while staying with the Rance Johnson family) and was carried to the Dozier home. Dr. Nanney went to minister his needs, but the measles would not break out and James Henry died May 11, 1924.

James Henry Googe was married to Minnesota Kizer born May 31, 1868, died Aug. 7, 1953. They lived at Pleasant Valley, Pharrtown Community in Prentiss County. Seven children were born to this marriage:

Lillian Googe Files, daughter of James Henry Googe

I. Mary Leon died in infancy.

II. Lillian Googe Files, born Aug. 14, 1903, died Jul. 12, 1933.

III. Rodney Howard Googe, born Oct. 28, 1892, died Feb. 14, 1968, married Visa Allen Pharr, three children: a) Kenneth Howard, Sep. 12, 1917, deceased, married Erma Sparks, three children: 1. Kenneth Darrell Googe, Dec. 7, 1944, married Evonne Shipp, two children, Kenneth Howard II, Mar. 15, 1968, deceased and Melanie Dawn Googe Feb. 27, 1973. 2. James Derwerd Googe May 14, 1951 married Susan Reynolds, three children: Jennifer Nicole, Jan. 27, 1983; Jeffrey Ryan, Aug. 13, 1986 and Jessica Leigh, Jan. 23, 1990. 3. Douglas Clair Googe, Oct. 29, 1962. b) Mary Charylene Googe Apr. 17, 1923 married Dr. W. W. Strange, one son, William H. "Bill," Jul. 20, 1943. c) Gladys Anne, Nov. 17, 1926 married Clinton W. "Frankie" Windham, deceased, three children: 1. Shelia Allen Shepherd, Apr. 30, 1947 married Stan Shepherd (divorced), three children, Roger Allen, Sep. 3, 1973; Jacqueline Dawn Nov. 14, 1974 and Shannon Dawn Feb. 15, 1995. 2. Martha Dawn Googe Windham, May 30, 1949 married Jamie R. Owens II, two children, Jamie Rice Owens III, Feb. 18, 1971 married Sandra Smith, one child Tyler Watson Owens Nov. 8, 1996; Michael Watson Googe Windham Owens Jul. 30, 1974. 3. Clinton W. "Buddy" Windham II, Oct. 8, 1951, deceased married Cathy Clarene Goddard, two children, Jennifer Allen, Mar. 30, 1969 and Jessica Suzanne, Feb. 10, 1976 married to Scott Ritter, one child Bailey Jan. 7, 1997.

IV. Horace Alvin Googe Mar. 6, 1899, died Aug. 9, 1950 married Helen Womack, one child, Dorothy Helen, Sep. 10, 1927, married Charles Robbins, two children, Deborah Helen, May 27, 1955 and Donna Louise, Jul. 7, 1960 married first to Stephen Reed, one child, Ashley Helen Oct. 27, 1980. Second marriage to David Glen Bohannon, one child, Wesley Allen, Nov. 28, 1984.

V. Shelby Greene Googe, Dec. 15, 1905, died Mar. 13, 1960 married Nellie P. Nicholson, three children: a. James Harold, Jan. 19, 1928 married Annie Margaret Rinehart, three children: James Harold Googe Jr., Sep 28, 1959 married Tina Lisa McClinton, three children, Elizabeth Margaret May 7, 1989, Benjamin James, Apr. 5, 1990 and Joshua Thomas Oct. 1, 1992. 2. Sandra Lee Gordon, Aug. 16, 1961, (divorced) one son Drew Gordon, Jul. 13, 1984. 3. April Conious Googe, Apr. 4, 1966 married Sean Weaver Gough, two children, Sarah Ann Gough, Aug. 24, 1997 and Rachel Leigh Gough, Aug. 31, 1999. B. Charles Edwin Googe, May 14, 1930 married Betty Jo Martin, two children, Charles Edwin Jr., Aug. 21, 1956 and Susan Maria, Sep. 26, 1963 married William Jones, two children, Shelby Shea Jones, Jan. 18, 1993 and William Preston Jones, Apr. 29, 1997. C. Kathryn Nell Googe Floyd, Oct. 7, 1938 married Kenneth Eugene Floyd, four children: Melanie Rose, Dec. 4, 1966 married Henein Iskander, two children, Lauren Nicole, Sep 13, 1994 and Natalie Paige, Dec. 28, 1995. Kenneth II "Kenny", Jul. 10, 1968, Mark Jefferson Jan. 4, 1976 (deceased) and Molly Kathryn, Jan. 4, 1976 married Stewart Graham Hodge.

VI. Eugene Virgil Googe, Sep 11, 1894, died Sep. 26, 1978, buried at Memphis, TN.

VII. Clovis Rogers Googe, Mar 3, 14, 1896, died Jun. 12, 1942, married Rosa Mae Baker, one child, Gloria Evelyn, July 23, 1927 married William Winfred Strickland (deceased), three children: Linda Mae, Nov. 23, 1947 married David Walls, two children, David Lynn, Nov. 27, 1967 married Sara Frances Stegall, one son Matthew Ryan, May 17, 1997; Jason Allen Walls, Nov. 4, 1970, one son Johnny Dewayne, Mar. 1, 1991.

Mary Jo, Oct. 11, 1950 married Kenny Street, two children, Amy Leigh, Jan. 13, 1974 and John Kenneth "Kenny," Jan. 27, 1978.

William Winfred II Jul. 2, 1952 (deceased).

The grandchildren and great-grandchildren of James Henry have gone in many directions. A number have gone into the medical profession, several the teaching field and others have chosen public relations, newspaper, accounting, military, computer technology and postal service careers. Totally different fields from James Henrys'. To our knowledge only one, Mark Jefferson Floyd, chose the path of timber cutting.

All of James Henry's children have passed on from this life. However, the Googe name continues, there are two living grandsons, five great-grandsons and three great-great-grandsons bearing the Googe name.

GRAY, LESTER ROY, born Sep. 26, 1943 in Tishomingo County, MS son of Garvin Roy and Mary Magdeline Ellis Gray. He attended the Tishomingo County School District until second grade. when his family moved to Booneville to be closer to their employment. He pursued his education in the Booneville School System and Northeast Mississippi Junior College.

Roy married Sandra Kay Lewis Sep. 4, 1964. Sandra was born Nov. 12, 1946 to James Hardin and Artie Marie Hopkins Lewis of the Tuscumbia Community. Sandra obtained her education from the Prentiss County School system. After owning their own business for many years, Roy was approached with an offer of assuming the position of general manager with Mid-South Express Inc., with offices in Memphis, TN; Newark, NJ; Little Rock, AR; Jackson and Tupelo,

Roy Gray

MS. While there he was responsible for researching transportation rates in the Library of Congress in Washington, DC and the procurement of over six million dollars in transportation bids with the Department of Defense. After years of travel, Roy decided he wanted to spend less time on the road and in 1986 accepted the position of sales manager with Mid-South Frame, later incorporated as Free Spirit Auto Glass, Inc. Since his association the company has grown from a local operation to a multi-state wholesale supplier of OEM automotive glass serving Georgia, Tennessee, Alabama and Mississippi.

Roy is a member of the Civitan Club, the National Rifle Association and Prentiss County Republican Party, where he serves as chairman. Roy has represented Prentiss County as a delegate to the State Republican Convention and has served as county co-chairman for presidential candidate George W. Bush's 2000 campaign. He is a charter member of the Prentiss County Christian Coalition.

Sandra is a member of Friends of the Library, United Daughters of the Confederacy, where she serves as second vice president and a member of the Prentiss County Republican Party where she serves on the Executive Committee. She has represented Prentiss County as a delegate to the State Convention. She served as Prentiss County 1994 Campaign Chairman for US Congressman Roger Wicker and as Prentiss County co-chairman for Candidate George W. Bush in his 2000 presidential campaign. She is a charter member of the Burton Community Historical Society, Inc., charter member of Prentiss County Genealogical and Historical Society and charter member of the Prentiss County Christian Coalition. She is also a past member of the Booneville Business and Professional Women's Club where she held the position of Scholarship Chairman.

Both are members of First Baptist Church of Booneville. They have one child, Rhonda Roxanne Gray (b. May 13, 1968, Tupelo, Lee County, MS). Roxanne married Harold Windal Lollar Jr. and has four children: Katherine Marie Richey (b. Jul. 9, 1989); Timothy Reid Lollar (b. Sep. 20, 1984); Neil Randal Lollar (b. Dec. 17, 1976) and Brandy Elese Lollar (b. Mar. 13, 1975). *Submitted by Sandra Lewis Gray.*

GREEN, J.W., my memories of my birthplace of Prentiss County and New Site, MS the greatest times of all my childhood and home, I would like to begin! I am the granddaughter of J.W. (Jack) Green, one of New Site's residents in Prentiss County.

I am the daughter of their only surviving daughter, Ollie Mae Green, who married Thomas Homer Owens from Itawamba County, MS.

I was born in the home of Jack Green, my grandparents, on May 29, 1930, the third child from the oldest of four children, who was born in Prentiss County. We then moved to Fulton, MS where my parents had five more children, seven girls and two boys. Their names are: Dorothy Oleta, Reba Willodean, Ruby Juanita (which is my name), Mary Joyce, Fairy Nell, Thomas Edward, Hilma Sue, Jack Douglas and Judith Carol. We all married and had children. I, Ruby, married Cecil Beasley of Fulton, MS and bore two children of my own, Steven Keith and Vickie Lynn. She died in October 1997 due to an auto accident. She had no children. Steven had two daughters, Cristy and Michelle, of Dallas, TX.

At Gospel Television Station 53, Booneville, MS May 1997, Mother's Day. Sis, Reba Hankins Program (New Life Ministries).

All my childhood dreams were to move back to Prentiss County. Oh, we loved our grandparents at New Site and to me as a child, it was heaven to get to visit them. Especially at Christmas time, we would all rejoice at the thought of going and I always desired to be like my grandmother, Nettie. They once ran the post office and had the only mercantile store.

Now, getting back to me, I divorced Cecil Beasley and remarried Carl Sturdivant and then Samuel Lawrence, who are now deceased and I remain a widow and am in the gospel work of Jesus Christ as a missionary and teacher. My older sister, Reba Willodean, is a minister of the gospel and for the past 10 years has been ministering at the Booneville, MS television station 53.

We were raised in a Christian home, as my parents were God fearing people. My father was a farmer and we knew what it was to work with our hands. I wish to add, most all of our Green family is noted for their wonderful gospel singing and organ and piano playing. My mother, Ollie, wrote poetry and songs, which we, her children, learned to sing.

My father, Homer, passed away in 1971 at the age of 76 and my mother died at almost 95 years of age in 1997. She had remarried after my father's death to Fred Huling, who was a Godly man.

I appreciate this great book that is being published and all who have participated in making it possible. I am glad to be part of my great heritage of New Site, MS. *Submitted by Ruby J. Owens Lawrence.*

GREENE, THOMAS TAYLOR, born Sep. 23, 1808 in Kentucky, the son of John and Martha Green. Thomas Green acquired land there on Apr. 9, 1855. Thomas Taylor Green married Louisa Hastings on Sep. 22, 1829. She was the daughter of Daniel and Chloe Hastings. Thomas and Louisa had seven children, one of which was Ambrose H. Green (AM) (b. Oct. 15, 1844, d. Jan. 18, 1910). Ambrose H. was born in Alabama. He enlisted in the Civil War in July of 1862 and served in Co. C, 5th Alabama Cavalry under Commander R.O. Pickett and Captain J.D. McClusky. He was discharged at the end of the Civil War in Danville, AL. In 1867 A.H. married Nancy Emiline Gwynne. Nancy was born in February 1847, the daughter of Isom and Mary "Polly" Gwynne. A.H and Nancy Green moved to Prentiss County about 1886. They had nine children: Annie Lee Green; Jesse Green; Viola Green, who married J.D. Wallis; Joe Humphrey Green, who married Della Moore; Daniel Green, who married Oma A. Williams; Albert Green; Andrew Green, who married Willie Thompson and Eliza Green, who married Rufus Ellis.

Greene Family. Back row, from left: Vivian, Nancy, Herman, J.W., Evonell, Nelly, Lamar, Lynn, Lou Della, Joyce, Hughy, Patsy and Rachel. Front row, from left: Patrisha, Louise and William.

Joe Humphrey Green and his wife, Della Moore, daughter of Stephen Lee Moore and Mary Jane Stovall, married on Dec. 21, 1900 and made their home in Marietta, MS. They purchased 80 acres of land on Jan. 11, 1912 and raised their seven children: Horace "Bill" Green, who married Vera Harris; Haszel Green, who married Edmon A. McClusky; Dimple Green, who married Horace Massey; Howard Green (died at birth); Eula Mae Green, who married Clarence

Crowell; Nellie Hester Green, who married Willie G. Schoggen and Herman Green, who married Vivian Williams.

Herman married Vivian Williams, daughter of Thomas Seth Williams and Luella Hallmark. Herman and Vivian purchased the home and farm from his father, Joe, on Nov. 6, 1935. Joe and Della live beside their son, Herman, while Herman and Vivian's family grew to 13 wonderful children, as follows.

Nellie Faye Greene (deceased) married Irv Simmonds and had two sons, Rod Simmonds and Bart Simmonds.

Rachel Greene married Rex Anderson (deceased) and had one child, Patricia Anderson. Patricia married Hal Hancock and has two sons: Greg Hancock, who married Becky and has two sons, Jonathan and Noah and Jim Hancock, who married Jill and has three daughters: Jessica, Jullianne and Jennifer. Rachel's second marriage was to Frank Rossi and they have four children. Frank Rossi Jr. married Robbie and has four children: Rena, Tony, Sarah and Frankie. Laura Leigh Rossi married Jerry Richmond and has two children, Rachel and Jerry Jr. Fred Rossi married Joan and has one child, Margaret. Robert Rossi married Ingrid and has three girls: Valerie, Julie and Emily. Cynthia Jo Rossi is Rachel Rossi's youngest child.

Lou Della Greene married Clearance Thomas and had two children: Mark Thomas, who married Becky Bellamy and has two sons, Seth and Aaron and Carol Thomas, who married Randy Allen and has one daughter, Baylae.

James Williams Greene married Evonell Sparks, daughter of Oliver and Verna Sparks. They have five children. Ricky Greene married Barbara Scott and has three children: Aaron Greene, Jonathon Greene and Brittney Greene. Aaron married Bronzie Swinney and has one daughter, Layken Greene. Terri Greene married Gary Dorrsett and has two sons, Jason and Braden. Terri's second marriage was to Leon Gilson. James Williams Greene Jr. "Jake" married Lynn Timmons. Sharla Greene married Lee Burns Jr. and has two children, Cory and Kara. Malcolm Greene married Norma Jean Pendarvis "Jeannie" and has one child, James Dakota "J.D."

Patsy Greene married Roy Lee Berryhill (deceased) and had one son, Doug Berryhill (deceased). Patsey's second marriage was to Leon Chapple.

Huey Greene had no children.

Lynn Greene married Sarah Moore and has two daughters. Sara Lynn Greene married Barry Childers and has two daughters, Kacie and Carly. Loretta Greene married Dennis Smith (deceased). Loretta's second marriage was to Mike Beasley and they have one son, Austin.

William Greene married Doretha Gentry and has one son, Hugh, who married Venisa.

Joyce Greene married Calvin Barber and has three children. Jim Barber married Brenda Shumpert and has two girls, Kadee and Cacie. Nora Barber married Tony Brown and has two children, Dena and Andrew. Eunice Barber married Barry Fredrick and has four children: Barry Jr. "B.J.," Codey "C.J.," Dalton "D.J." and Ashlyn Joyce "A.J."

Louise Greene married Larry Michael and has three children. Bobby Michael married Amy Smithy and has two children, Ashlynne and Bobby Joe "Bo." Jeff Michael married Melissa and has one son, Chase. April Michael is Louise Michael Panes's youngest child. Louise's second marriage was to Ed Panes.

Nancy Greene married Leroy Livingston and has one daughter, Kimberly Livingston. Kim married Dewayne Lewis and has two children, Aric and Adrienne. Nancy's second marriage was to Ray Smith.

Lamar Greene (deceased-car accident at 21 years old) had no children and Jimmy Lane Greene (died at birth).

James Williams Greene served in the Korean War. He operated with the 7th Fleet under Captain Alford on the USS DDE-499 ship *Reneshaw* based in Honolulu, HI, 1951-1955. J.W. served six months in the Marshall Islands during the hydrogen bomb testings in 1954. He was given an honorable discharge in 1955 and returned home to Marietta, MS where he purchased the farm from his mother, Vivian Greene on Nov. 4, 1960. To this day the original farm is still in the Greene name and every year on the 4th of July the Greenes have their family reunion and reminisce the stories of years past. *Submitted by Sharla Greene Burns.*

GRESHAM, CARROLL,

his story is short for two reasons. First, he lived such a short time. Second, he left very few clues about his life. Carroll is a mystery. The census shows he was born in Tennessee. Old Tishomingo County marriage records show his marriage. The police records of Old Tishomingo County show his was a pauper death. His youngest daughter left a family Bible with both her parents dates recorded. Though his life was short and he left few children, those children left many descendants.

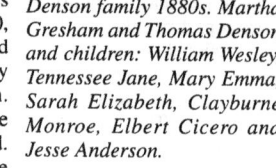
Denson family 1880s. Martha Gresham and Thomas Denson and children: William Wesley, Tennessee Jane, Mary Emma, Sarah Elizabeth, Clayburne Monroe, Elbert Cicero and Jesse Anderson.

Carroll Gresham was born Dec. 19, 1825. He married Lavinia Collier Aug. 22, 1844. Lavinia was born Aug. 25, 1820, to Amos Collier and Nancy Wyatt. They had three children. The boy died before he was 10 years old. The daughters were Nancy Elizabeth (b. 1850, d. 1941) and Martha Ann (b. 1852, d. 1891).

Carroll died Dec. 11, 1858. His grave site is unknown. Lavinia died Aug. 19, 1886. Her grave site is also unknown. There was a Collier Family Cemetery near New Site, but no one can locate the graves now. Only the general location of the cemetery is known. This could be where Lavinia was buried.

Nancy Elizabeth Gresham married Monroe Holloway Dec. 14, 1868. Their children were J.C., Fannie Ann, Dora Bell, Amanda, C.C., Ellie and Bargania. These children married and raised families.

Fannie Ann married John Fugitt Oct. 4, 1887. Dora Bell married W.S. Ellis Oct. 20, 1889. Amanda married E.J. England Dec. 19, 1891. C.C. married Hattie Shamlin Dec. 24, 1898. Ellie married J.A. DeFer Jul. 17, 1895. Bargania married John Walker Lovell Jul. 6, 1896. The children of these couples in turn raised families, many of them in Prentiss County.

Martha Ann Gresham married Thomas Cicero Denson, son of William Cicero Denson and Sarah Ann Ford, Sep. 18, 1873. Their children were: William Wesley, Tennessee Jane, Mary Emma, Sarah Elizabeth, John, Clayburne Monroe, Elbert Cicero, Jesse Anderson, Oscar and George Washington. John, Oscar and George died young. Will raised his family in Tennessee. Emma and Elbert raised their families in Florida. Jesse raised his family in Kansas. Tennie and "Bettie" raised their families in Prentiss County.

Will married Julia Gann Oct. 30, 1895. Tennie married William Lonzo Nicholson Dec. 5, 1897. Emma married Leslie Young Feb. 2, 1902. "Bettie" married James Frederick Withers Rorie Feb. 2, 1902. Monroe first married Sula Hughes Jan. 1, 1905, but they divorced. He later married Nancy Mae Walker. Elbert married Martha Milam Aug. 9, 1912. Jesse married Georgia Parsons Apr. 8, 1906.

Martha Ann died and was buried in Indian Territory, Oklahoma, near present day Ardmore. She and Thomas had moved there shortly before the birth of their last child. Thomas returned to Mississippi after the death of his wife and raised his family in Prentiss County near his parents in New Site. Thomas is buried in Little Brown Cemetery near New Site.

Carroll Gresham left many descendants, including this writer, who is his great-great-granddaughter. *Submitted by Ruby Rorie.*

GRISHAM, ANDREW JACKSON "JACK" SR.,

born about 1815 in Virginia probably, son of George Gresham (died Mar. 16, 1852 in Lawrence County, TN) and his first wife, Miss Waugh. Jack married Gillie (Olive) Mason (daughter of James Olive and Sarah Hartsfield), born about 1824 in Wake County, NC. They moved from Tennessee to old Tishomingo County, near the Tippah County line, before December 1849. Civil War deserters followed Andrew home, executing him in the presence of his family. Distraught, Gillie found life to be unbearable and died soon afterwards. Both were buried in the Anderson Family Cemetery.

Their oldest child enumerated in 1850, Elizabeth (b. 1888) was probably Gillie's stepdaughter, Elizabeth Mason.

Children of Andrew and Gillie were: Ephriam (b. Dec. 19, 1842); Matilda Jeanette (b. Feb. 10, 1844); Martha A. (b. Jul. 22, 1848); James Lemuel (b. Dec. 29, 1849); Rachel Ellen (b. 1851); Andrew Jackson Jr. (b. Dec. 1, 1854); George Washington (b. 1856) and Richard Robert (b. Mar. 16, 1861).

Elizabeth Mason married Isaac G. "Black Ike" Grisham on Jan. 27, 1859. Elizabeth died before 1863. Isaac was called "Black Ike" to distinguish him from his first cousin, Isaac C. "Red Ike" Grisham. Children of Elizabeth and Ike were Nancy Mahala and Mary M. Grisham.

Ephriam "Eaf" Grisham married Elizabeth J. "Bettie" Patterson on Jun. 18, 1867. In 1870, Eaf's orphaned brothers, Jackson, George and Richard lived in his household. Ephraim died Dec. 12, 1925. Their children were William Jack, Manerva R., Charles, Anna Florence, James B., Wesley, Virgie, Phillip V. and Grover Grisham.

Matilda Jeanette "Tilda" married Joseph Randolph Anderson. Matilda died Sep. 10, 1914. Their children were Willie J., James R., Luther I.M., Sarena Gillie, Noah Arthur, Oscar P., John Ephraim, Robert Richard and Joseph Daniel Anderson.

Martha A. "Mattie" married Robert Henry Mitchell (a Baptist preacher) on Feb. 1, 1872. Martha died Nov. 29, 1908, near Rosston, Nevada County, AR. Their children were: Ella, Thomas Edmond, Ada, Laura, Lawrence, Pickens, Cornilia, Austin Quitman, Luther Henry, Ethel, Grover, Willie and Richard Mitchell.

James Lemuel "Jim" married Margaret Amanda Jones on Nov. 7, 1872. Jim died Jun. 12, 1926 in Hamilton County, TX. Their children were: William Richard, James Lemuel Jr., Ida Rose Anna, Charles Ephraim, Jesse Andrew, an infant, Harriet Lou Emma, Addie May and Claude Virgil Grisham.

Rachel Ellen married Hamilton S. Savage. Hamilton and Rachel went to Fannin County, TX about 1873. Their children included: O.W., J.R. and A.L. Savage.

Andrew Jackson "Jack" Jr. married Cordelia "Cora" Ann English on Nov. 3, 1876. Jack died Jun. 22, 1897 in Wolfe City, TX. Their children were: Ellis/Ellison, Willie, Henry Walton, Walker C., Ethel, Hattie, Jessie L., Tinie Beatrice and Robert L. Grisham.

George Washington married Amanda Patterson on Nov. 11, 1883. George died in 1936. Their children were: James Arthur, Pearlie, Boyd, Marshall Mark, Ada Bessie, Richard Roy, John F. and Gillie Grisham.

Richard Robert "Dick" married Phoebe Leander "Lee" "Leah" Welch on Dec. 3, 1885. Richard died in August 1925 in Wolfe City, TX. Their children were:

Opal, Lillian, James Albert, Marvin Henry, Richard Raymond, Ruth, Roy, Clyde Harold, Gladys, Oleta and Frankie Lucille Grisham. *Submitted by Ray R. Weathers, 806 Barkley Drive, Hamilton, TX 76231.*
SOURCES: Barnes, Mrs. Irene, "Marriages of Old Tishomingo County, MS Volume I, 1837-1859." Compiled and printed by Mrs. Irene Barnes, Iuka, MS 1978.
__ebe, Jo Carolyn Anderson.

Gresham, Any Way You Spell It, Volume V, No. 1, Page 3; Volume III, No. 3, Page 11.

Grisham, Hattie in a letter dated Sep. 24, 1964, to Clara Elsie Fergusson Crain.

Barney, Bill, Cemeteries of Prentiss County, MS.
Perry, Rebecca Jane
Taylor, Jack L., DDS
The Prentiss County Historical Association, "Anderson, F7" by Jo Carolyn Anderson Beebe, from "History of Prentiss County, MS."
Tombstones for Gillie Olive Grisham and Andrew Jackson Grisham in (Old Baptist Cemetery) Anderson Family Cemetery on county line of Tippah and Prentiss Counties, MS.
Williamson, Dr. Lee - telephone conversation on Nov. 8, 1987. Dr. Williamson has a family Bible, which records births and deaths.
1850 and 1860 US Census, Tishomingo County, MS and 1870 US Census, Prentiss County, MS.

GRISHAM, JAMES LEMUEL "JIM" SR., born Dec. 29, 1849 in old Tishomingo County near the Tippah County line, was the first Mississippi-born child of Andrew Jackson Grisham Sr. and his wife, Gillie Olive (Mason). Following the untimely and tragic deaths of his parents during the Civil War, Jim and his siblings were scattered. By 1870, Jim was a farm laborer living in the home of Harriett A. (Garner) Jones near Booneville.

On Nov. 7, 1872 in Prentiss County, Jim married Margaret Amanda Jones. Margaret, born Jun. 25, 1855 in Alabama, was the second child of Harriett Garner and William Toliver Jones, a presumed Civil War casualty. Two children, William Richard "Will" (b. Aug. 29, 1873) and James Lemuel "Lem" Jr. (b. Mar. 25, 1876), joined the family before Jim and Margaret decided to go to Texas with an entourage of family and friends.

Will was terrified that he would never see his "Paw" again when Jim swam his horse across the Mississippi River herding his livestock. The Grishams arrived in Fannin County about Sep. 1, 1878, two weeks prior to the premature birth of my great-grandmother, Ida Rose Anna, born Sep. 15, 1878 in Fannin County.

Charles Ephraim "Charlie" (b. Jan. 4, 1881); Jesse Andrew "Jessie" (b. Feb. 20, 1883); an infant son; Harriet Lou Emma (b. Jul. 1, 1886); Addie May (b. Mar. 11, 1889) and Claude Virgil "Verge" (b. Apr. 12, 1891) were the younger children of Jim and Margaret Grisham.

William Richard "Will" married Iona Mae "Mamie" Sewell on Dec. 21, 1898. Will died Mar. 13, 1937.

James Lemuel "Lem" married May Iantha Chumney on Oct. 6, 1901. Lem died Jul. 25, 1951.

Ida Rose Anna married Robert Jeff Fergusson on Nov. 9, 1898. Ida died Jul. 14, 1948.

Charles Ephraim "Charlie" married Myrtie Onie "Myrtle" Deathrage on Aug. 2, 1908. Charlie died May 21, 1951.

Jesse Andrew "Jessie" married Sarah Bertie Sparks on Jul. 22, 1906. Jessie died Mar. 17, 1940.

Harriet Lou Emma married Samuel Floyd "Sam" Williams on Sep. 16, 1906. Emma died Dec. 14, 1965.

Addie May married Benjamin Hill Lassater on Dec. 20, 1908. Addie died in Nov. 1948.

Claude Virgil "Verge" first married Nancy Lee "Nannie" Blackshear on Dec. 20, 1914 and later married Alta P. (Bennett) Young on Jul. 27, 1950. Verge died Apr. 14, 1955.

A Prentiss County neighbor and widower, William Clift Winters, found Margaret's mother, Harriett Jones in Fannin County, TX and married her. William Clift brought Harriett, with her two youngest children, to Langford Cove, Coryell County, TX. To be near her mother, Jim and Margaret moved their family to Hamilton County, TX. Jim and Margaret arrived in the Blue Ridge Community of Hamilton County in time to become charter members of the Blue Ridge Missionary Baptist Church, which was formed on Jul. 10, 1880.

James Lemuel Grisham Sr. died Jun. 12, 1926, at Blue Ridge, Hamilton County and was interred in the Murphree Cemetery in Evant. Margaret Amanda (Jones) Grisham died Nov. 18, 1936, at Blue Ridge, Hamilton County and was buried beside her husband in the Murphree Cemetery in Evant, Hamilton County, TX. *Submitted by D'Ann E. Herrod, 5612 James Avenue, Apartment 119-A, Fort Worth, TX 76134.*

SOURCES: 1850 and 1860 US Census, Tishomingo County, MS; 1870 US Census, Prentiss County, MS; 1880 US Census, Fannin County, TX; 1900, 1910 and 1920 US Census, Hamilton County, TX.

Grisham, James L. and Margaret Amanda Jones - Marriage Record, Prentiss County, MS.

Grisham, Mrs. J.L. – Newspaper obituary, Nov. 20, 1936, "Hamilton Herald Record."

Hamilton County Historical Commission, "James L. Grisham Sr. Family" by Elreeta Crain Weathers, from "A History of Hamilton County, TX," by Taylor Publishing Co., Dallas, TX, 1979, Page 173.

Grisham Sr., James "Jim" Lemuel – Death Record, Hamilton County, TX, Volume 5, Page 23, #592.

Grisham, Hattie in a letter dated Sep. 24, 1964, to Clara Elsie Fergusson Crain.

HALL BROTHERS AND CUNNINGHAM SISTERS, two of Bud and Laura (Moore) Hall's sons married sisters. Leroy (b. 1894, d. 1954) and Amos J. (b. 1897, d. 1977) married Sally Viola (b. 1894, d. 1978) and Ora A. (b. 1901, d. 1972) Cunningham. The girls were the eldest and the youngest daughters of L.N. (Ran) Cunningham (b. 1869, d. 1901) and Elizabeth (Lizzie) Boggs (b. 1874, d. 1947). Their father had been killed shortly after Ora's birth in an argument over a cow. Lizzie never remarried. Viola and Ora had one sister, Tiny (b. 1898, d. 1960), who married Beldon Gann (b. 1898, d. 1960) and a brother, who died as an infant.

Leroy Hall family. Leroy Hall, Arzo Hall, R.B. Hall and Viola (Cunningham) Hall

Sadly enough, Viola was the only one of the three sisters to have any children to live to adulthood. Viola and Leroy had three children: Arzo Lee (b. 1917, d. 1987); Mary Geraldine (b. 1920, d. 1994) and Robert Bly (R.B.). Arzo married Bernice Thelmalou Tyra (b. 1921, d. 1988) from Itawamba County and Hackleburg, AL, on Jun. 12, 1943 and had four sons:

1. Arlis Wayne, who married Betty Dill and had two children, Angela Sue and Arlis Wayne Junior.

2. Marlis Wade, who married Judy Catherine McCreary and had two daughters, Laura Katherine and Shelia Maxine.

3. Randal Lee, who married Ronda Sherron Crowe and had two children, Kevin Lee and Regina Sherron and adopted five children in 1998: Crystal, Jimmy, Harley, Cleo and Summer.

4. Nolan Arzo, who married Donna Annette Lambert and had two children, Ashley Nicole and Dustin Michael. Mary Geraldine was married about three times, but only had children with Charles Leborn Isbell. These children, Mike and Allen and Leborn were all killed in a house fire in 1952. R.B. was also married more than once and had three children: Lance, Melissa Ann and Stacy. Melissa Ann (Missy) married Kenneth Lambert and has a son, Journey Kree. R.B. still lives somewhere in the Goat Island area of Tishomingo County.

Of the grandchildren of Arzo and Bernice, several are married and have families of their own. Shelia married James Frost of the Cairo Community and has a daughter, Hannah. Kevin married Lisa Meeks and has a daughter, Tuesday. Regina married Terry Hester and had two sons, Travis and Ethan. Most of the members of this family still live in the Prentiss County area. *Submitted by Laura Hall.*

HALL, ARLANDER, born 1882 and died 1950, was the first child of Bud and Laura (Moore) Hall. He was known as Lander to the family. He married Virdie Harris (b. 1888, d. 1968) on Dec. 19, 1911. Lander and Verdie had six children: Horace A., Luna Verdie, Manny Boyd, Arlander Junior (Pet), Laura May and Faye. Horace (b. 1912, d. 1985) married Dimple Dewdrop Finch (b. 1913, d. 1976), the daughter of W.W. Finch and Lula Gann on Feb. 26, 1937. They had two children: Mary Jeanette, who married Oneal Smith and has a son, Stuart and a daughter, Sonja and Betty Carolyn, who married Donnie McCombs and has two daughters, Mitzi and Julie. Luna Verdie married Wille Gann and had two daughters: Marjorie Lilly, who married Bluford Miller and has a son, Brad and Janice Marie, who married George Crowe and has two sons, Paul and George. Manny Boyd (b. 1914, d. 1995) married Roberta White on Dec. 22, 1945. Boyd and Roberta had four children:

Boyd Hall family in the early 1980s. Back row standing from left: James Downs, Buddy Hall and Galen Nichols. Middle row: Magelene (Hall) Downs Spradlin, Vaughnda (McCoy) Hall, Boyd Hall, Maeline Hall, Majel (Hall) Nichols and Mark Nichols. Front row: Craig Hall, Stacey Hall, Roberta (White) Hall, Chris Downs, Brad Downs and Benny Nichols.

1) William Boyd (Buddy) married Vaughnda McCoy and has two children, William Craig and Stacey Lee.

2) Majel Delores married Galen Haston Nichols on Mar. 3, 1967 and has two sons, Galen Mark and Benjamin Trevor.

3. Magelene married James Preston Downs and has two sons, James Bradley and Christopher Allen.

4. Maeline is not married and stays with her mother.

Arlander Jr. (Pet) died at the early age of 15 of an unknown illness. Laura May married Hoyt Breedlove and had three children: Janet, who married Doug Bratcher; Pam and Steve, who married Marilyn Spradlin and has two children. Faye married J.T. Smith and moved to Memphis. They have three children: Gary, Marlin and Paul.

Descendants of this family are a little scattered, but most remain in the Tishomingo, Prentiss or Lee County areas. *Submitted by Roberta (White) Hall*

HALL, JAMES LAFAYETTE "BUD," born 1856 and died 1933, may have come to Mississippi with two brothers, John W. and Charlie. A sister, Alma, may have remained in Tennessee. According to Bud's death record found at McMillan's Funeral Home in Booneville, his father's name was Alec, but it is not known if he was ever in Mississippi. An old family story says that Alec, or one of his brothers, shot and killed a Union officer in Tennessee to avoid fighting in the Civil War. After shooting the officer, the family moved to Texas. Thus, the how and when of Bud's arrival in Mississippi are unknown. The 1900 census records state that his parents were from Alabama. Whatever the case, Bud married Laura Moore (b. 1862, d. 1924), daughter of Stephen Moore and Mary Jane Stovall of Tishomingo County (see Moore Family in Tishomingo County History) in January 1880. Bud and Laura had 11 children that lived to adulthood in Prentiss County and two that did not. These children were: Arlander (b. 1882, d. 1950); Charles Henry (b. 1885, d. 1965); Virgil (b. 1886, d. 1957); James Alexander (b. 1888, d. 1924); Ada (b. 1891, d. 1971); Leroy (b. 1894, d. 1954); Jason Guy (b. 1895, d. 1970); Amos J. (b. 1897, d. 1977); Noonan H. (b. 1898, d. 1979); Floyd M. (b. 1900, d. 1981) and Troy (b. 1904, d. 1952).

Members of Bud Hall family. Back row standing: Eulaia (Thornton) Hall, Henry Hall, Omie (Johnson) Hall, Haze Hall, Guy Hall, Amos Hall, ?, Patsy Green, Troy Hall, Basel Hall, (baby) William Green and Herman Green. Middle row kneeling: Floyd Hall, Virgil (Pat) Hall, Corneliar (Stacy) Hall, Ora (Cunningham) Hall, Alvia (Thornton) Hall, J.W. Green and Myrtie Hall. Front row seated: Nellie Green, Allene Hall, Ruby Ann Hall, LouDella Green, Joyce Green and Rachel Green.

Charles Henry Hall married Omie Johnson (b. 1894, d. 1974) on Jan. 3, 1915. They had two sons: Burly Basel (b. 1919, d. 1978), who married Lois Lyle Seago (b. 1921, d. 1985) and Henry Haze. Basel and Lois had a son, Tillman, who married Joyce Ann Bailey. They have two children, Chris and Vickie. Haze was married twice, to Allene Graham and Beatrice Lee, respectively.

Virgil was known by all as Pat. He was born with clubbed hands and feet and blindness. Although physically handicapped, he was known to be quite intelligent and knew all his family members, even distant cousins. He also had a good memory for events and stories.

James Alexander, known as Eleck or Alex to the family, married Nancy Elizabeth (Lizzie) Burns. When he died of tuberculosis, he left Lizzie with three small children to raise: Bernice, Earl Q. and Mary Edna. Bernice (b. 1916, d. 1997) married Marvin T. McKinney and had five children: Sandra, Marvin, James, Marion and Bobby. Earl (b. 1920, d. 1983) married Myrtie Stephens. After her death, he married Connie Trollinger. Mary Edna moved to Memphis, TN and married Ira Cummings. They have two daughters: Cheryl, who married Bill Stegbauer with two children, David and Scott and Patti, who married a Blassingame and has a daughter, Jennifer.

Ada was the only daughter. She married Thomas W. Crabb (b. 1890, d. 1955) and had seven children, but only two daughters lived to adulthood, Eulaia and Floyel. Eulaia married J.D. Tyra. Eulaia and J.D. had three children: Dale, Don and Shelia. Floyel married her distant cousin, Bruce Crabb. Floyel and Bruce had five children: Audrey, Ray, Yvonne, Joyce and Boyce.

Jason Guy was known as Jake by many. Guy married Corneliar Stacy (b. 1897, d. 1961) on Mar. 21, 1920. They had one child, Vernard. Vernard married Elsie Jane Wells and had four children: Becky, Martha, Debra and Buddy.

Noonan H. was known as Trustie by many and viewed by some as strange. He was not the cleanest person and lived in a house with a dirt floor with many dogs inside the house with him. Some treated him as if he were mentally impaired, but that may not have been the case. A family story tells that at one time Trustie was the crispest and cleanest of all his brothers. He started dating a young girl. He might have married her, but she did not feel the same. When she refused him, he began taking care of some of the dogs belonging to his brothers and decided he liked the company of the dogs better. Anyone who knew him would say he was a little odd, but perfectly harmless. Maybe the jilting affected him that way.

Floyd M. was nicknamed Babe. He married Eulalia Thornton (b. 1906, d. 1993). They had one child, Myrtie. Myrtie married Ernie Crowe, but died in her late 40s of cancer.

Troy, nicknamed Bunt, married Alvina (Alvie) Thornton (b. 1908, d. 1998) on Jan. 4, 1925. Troy and Alvie had two daughters, Allene and Ruby Ann. Allene married Buddy Baker and had two children: Kaye, who married Larry Jones and Mike, who married Teresa Cleveland. Ruby Ann married Nolan Denson and had three children: Gerald, Tim and Pam, who married Bill Harris. Kaye and Larry have three children: Tonya, Kayla and Josh. Gerald and Tim each have a daughter, Melissa and Rachel. Pam and Bill have two children, Matthew and Bree Ann.

Many of the members of this family are still living in or near the Prentiss County area. Some reside in Tishomingo County or Itawamba County. Many of the older members are buried in the Pleasant Valley Cemetery, Siloam Cemetery, Saucer Creek Cemetery or Marietta Cemetery.

By some standards, Bud Hall would have been judged a unique individual. It is said that he delivered all of his children and had enough money and land to leave each of them their own home place. He owned land in Mississippi and Tennessee. No one knows how he acquired the money or land, but he knew how to provide for his family in the broadest sense of the phrase. *Submitted by Vickie Hall. For information on Arlander, Leroy and Amos, see related articles.*

HANNON, JAMES EARL, son of Leonard Alney Hannon (b. 1903, d. 1974) and Gertie Faye Martin Hannon (b. 1908, d. 1954). Dyann Hannon is the daughter of Roland Carl McCoy (b. 1913, d. 1979) and Irene Belue McCoy (b. 1919).

James Earl served in the US Armed Services as a paratrooper in the 82nd Airborne Division from 1950 to 1953. Dyann graduated from Booneville High School in 1954 and continued her education at Northeast Mississippi Community College.

James and Dyann were married on Jul. 24, 1955. After about three locations, they made their permanent home in Booneville, MS. They have two sons. James Rickey Hannon (b. 1958) is married to Janet English Hannon. Rickey is lead technician at Galaxy Cablevision in Booneville. Janet teaches 6th grade at Thrasher School. They have a daughter, Amy Hannon, a freshman at Booneville High School and a son, Evan Rickey Hannon, who is in the 4th grade.

James and Dyann's other son, Carlton Mickey Hannon (b. 1961) is married to Cheryl Thorne Hannon. Mickey is an accountant for Crain CPA Firm in Jackson, TN. Cheryl teaches in a private school in Jackson. Mickey has one son by a former marriage, Carlton Broc Hannon, a sophomore at New Site School.

Back row from left: James Rickey Hannon, Janet Hannon, James Earl Hannon, Dyann Hannon, Cheryl Hannon and Mickey Hannon. Seated from left: Evan Rickey Hannon, Carlton Broc Hannon and Amy Dyann Hannon.

James Earl is now retired as maintenance director from Baptist Memorial Hospital. Dyann is an employee of Peoples Bank & Trust Co. and part time secretary of East Booneville Baptist Church. She is also the organist at East Booneville Baptist Church and their son, Rickey, is the pianist. *Submitted by James Earl Hannon.*

HARE, CHARLIE DANIEL, born Oct. 17, 1904, to the late William Isaac (Buck) Hare (b. Sep. 3, 1868, d. Aug. 5, 1954) and Hattie Helen Daniels Hare (b. Nov. 16, 1875, d. Mar. 31, 1946) in Altitude, Prentiss County, MS. William and Hattie had five children: Elton, Esther, Elmer, Blufford and Charlie. Elmer died at 6 months of age. Elton married Kate Pike. Esther married Olen Pike. Blufford married Lena Holly. Charlie married Mable Blanch Smith. Mable's parents were Elliott Louallen and Maude Bell Sims Smith.

William and Hattie Hare family. Taken in 1905. From left: Blufford Hare, William Isaac Hare, Esther Hare, Hattie Hare, Elton Hare and Charlie Hare

Charlie's family operated a country store and corn gristmill in Altitude. His family also did some farming.

On Dec. 21, 1924, Charlie married Mable Blanch Smith. Mable was born in the New Hope Community on Jan. 22, 1906. After their marriage in January 1925, Charlie went to work for the American Snuff Co. driving a pair of horses to a top buggy with rubber tires giving out samples. After awhile, he went to work for Jule Smith Grocery in Booneville for two years. Mable taught school in Altitude for one year. The first of their children, Helen Virginia, was born in Altitude in 1927.

In 1929 Charlie and Mable moved to Houston, TX. Elton, Blufford and their families had already moved to Houston. Elton worked in a sawmill and later became an ironworker. Blufford worked in a lumberyard. At one time, Elton and Blufford worked for their Uncle Charlie Daniels in his lumber business.

Charlie and Mable Hare family. Taken in 1999. Back row from left: Mary Ann Berry, Joy Blomberg, Bill Hare and Charles Hare. Front row: Mable and Charlie Hare. Oct. 6, 1999.

When Charlie and Mable moved to Houston, he went to work for Fairmaid Bread Co. Then in 1932, he started working for the American Snuff Co.

There were four other children born while living in Houston. They are Charles Elliott in 1932, William Richard (Bill) in 1934, Mary Ann in 1935 and Joy Marie in 1938.

In 1941 the American Snuff Co. transferred Charlie to Austin, TX. He continued working for them until he retired on Nov. 1, 1969.

Charlie and Mable are members of the Church of Christ, Charlie serving as an elder for many years. They have attended the same congregation for 55 years.

Charlie loved to garden and fish with his sons and friends. Mable is known as a great cook to all the family. They have a large family. Along with their five children and their spouses, there are 14 grandchildren and spouses, 28 great-grandchildren (two are married) and five great-great grandchildren. All of the family, except one grandson, lives in Texas.

Charlie and Mable's home was always very special for all the family. After living in the same home for 50 years, in 1998, it was time to move into an assisted living home. On Dec. 21, 1999, they celebrated 75 years of marriage. *Submitted by Cecille Hare.*

HARPER, JOHN MAURICE, fifth child born to James A. Harper and Mattie Melton Harper. His brothers and sister include the following: James Hubert, Odus Everett, Aubrey Melton, Joseph Buford, J.Q., Tom Henry, Lottie Harper Holley and George Wilson Harper. John was born Oct. 28, 1906 in Prentiss County, MS. On Nov. 10, 1929, he married Bertha Mae Hisaw, the fourth child of Joseph Bert Hisaw and Myrtle Walker Hisaw. Bertha was born Mar. 12, 1913 in Prentiss County. Her sisters included the following: Zannie Hisaw Crabb, Annie Hisaw Walker, Lena Hisaw Welty, Vera Hisaw Harbor and Vivian Hisaw Crowe. Bert Hisaw had one son, Boone, by a previous marriage.

50th Wedding Anniversary of John M. and Bertha Harper, Nov. 10, 1979.

John and Bertha lived and raised their nine children in Prentiss County. Their youngest son has never lived outside the state of Mississippi. Their children are: Clara Fay, Charlotte Gwen Rachel, Lena Mae, Ouida Joan, Barbara Sue, Noonan Maurice, Linda Jane and Harold Dwain (twins) and Stanley Bert.

John and Bertha lived in the Robinson and Shady Grove Community in the early years of their marriage. They also lived in the Thrasher and Kirkville communities. They moved to the Burton Community in 1937 and lived there until 1952 moving to the Wheeler Community where they resided until their deaths.

John was a farmer and Bertha was a housewife, working on and off at Prentiss Manufacturing, as well as helping John farm. He said, "She was the best helpmate a man could have." Bertha was a good seamstress, sewing clothes for her family and the public. She also had her own fabric store in Wheeler at one time. She enjoyed quilting many beautiful quilts. They both enjoyed having their families visit them.

Fay married Jessie Burns; they had one daughter, Linda, four grandchildren and five great-grandchildren. Rachel married Nonan Harris; they have one daughter, Shirley, two grandsons and one great-granddaughter. Lena married Homer Cole; they had two sons and one daughter: Rusty, Johnny and Velda and seven grandchildren. Joan married Kenneth Scott (divorced); they had one son and one daughter, Kenny and Vanessa. Sue married Tommy Carpenter (divorced); they had two sons, Tim and Bart. Sue married Carl Honeycutt and they had two daughters, Sue Lynn and Richelle. Sue has seven grandchildren. Maurice married Carol Bonner and they have two sons, John and Junior and two grandsons. Jane married Sammy Ryan (divorced) and they had one daughter, Rhonda and one grandson. Dwain married Marla Morgan; they have one son, Devon and two daughters, Brianna and Morgan. Bert married Jan McBrayer; they have three sons, Nathan, Matthew and Micah.

John and Bertha celebrated their 60th Wedding Anniversary on Nov. 11, 1989, at the home of their son, Dwain and Marla Harper in Gardendale, AL. All nine of their children were present, 15 of their grandchildren were present, 11 of their great-grandchildren were present and 2 of their great-great grandchildren were present. John and Bertha were married for 64 years before Bertha's death.

Bertha died Jul. 19, 1994 and John died Jun. 16, 1997. They are both buried in Prentiss County Memorial Gardens near Frankstown, MS. Two granddaughters preceded them in death. Their first grandchild Linda Fay Burns Wilson died May 21, 1994 and Sue Lynn Honeycutt died Mar. 2, 1971. *Submitted by Shirley Eaton.*

HEMBREE, ANDREW P.C. "DOC," migrated with his parents, A.T. and Mary E. Hembree and one brother, Terrell A. Walker Hembree from South Carolina. They were living in Walker County, GA in 1850 and had arrived in old Tishomingo County by 1860. A.T. was not listed with the family on the 1860 census, so it is assumed that he died between 1850 and 1860.

Andrew P.C. Hembree married Dolly Hare Mar. 2, 1871 in Prentiss County, MS. Walker Hembree married Dolly's sister Loduska Hare, Dec. 27, 1869 in old Tishomingo County, MS before the county was divided into Alcorn, Prentiss and Tishomingo. Dolly and Loduska were daughters of William and Nancy Hare.

Andrew P.C. Hembree had several occupations; on the 1870 census he is listed as a house carpenter. He was owner of the Prentiss Hotel in Booneville, MS in the early part of 1900. The family was living in Corinth in 1910; A.P.C. was proprietor of a meat market. He and his mother died after 1910; it is not known where they are buried. Dolly died May 27, 1927 and is buried near Jackson, TN.

Andrew and Dolly had five children: (1) Cator V. Hembree, born Jan. 23, 1875, married first to Earlie and second to Ollie. Cator had three known children: Vasco, Martha Loduska and Martin Cator. Cator V. met his death by gunshot wound in Pontotoc County, MS Apr. 5, 1914 and is buried in the Ecru Cemetery in Pontotoc County, MS. Vasco Hembree was in the Army in 1929. It is not known where he went after that. Martha Loduska married Howard McCoy, died Aug. 11, 1979 and is buried at the Ecru Cemetery. Martin Cator was sheriff of Pontotoc County at one time; he died Nov. 10, 1971 and is buried in the Ecru Cemetery.

(2) Oscar H. Hembree, born 1878, married Alice C. They had an adopted daughter Willie. Oscar died 1947 and is buried in Tippah County, MS.

(3) Andrew Walker Hembree, born 1881 and died after 1910. He never married.

Prentiss Hotel in Booneville, pictured are Dolly Hare Hembree, unknown, Amorilla Hembree Vanstory, unknown and Andrew P.C. "Doc" Hembree and on the balcony is Mary E. Hembree, mother of Andrew P. Hembree, ca. 1900

(4) Amorilla Loduska Hembree, born Nov. 15, 1882 married William Jackson Vanstory Oct. 10, 1906. *Submitted by Margaret Vanstory.*

HENDRIX, DONNIE RAY, born Oct. 7, 1948 married Barbara Ann Davis (b. Mar. 21, 1950) on Aug. 28, 1969. Donnie Ray is the son of Thurman Leo Hendrix (b. Nov. 14, 1920, d. Mar. 26, 1982) and Alma Fay Vanderford Hendrix (b. May 10, 1925) who married Feb. 22, 1945.

L-R: Bonnie Lynn Hendrix, Barbara Ann Davis Hendrix, Donnie Ray Hendrix, Kerry Ray Hendrix

He is the grandson of Charley Cado Hendrix (b. May 8, 1898, d. Sep. 23, 1966) and Martha Elizabeth McCoy Hendrix Warren (b. Oct. 22, 1901). He is also the grandson of Clovis Aaron Vanderford (b. Jun. 1, 1901, d. Jan. 16, 1985) and Ida Sula Richardson Vanderford (b. Jun. 11, 1904, d. Sep. 8, 1989) who married on Feb. 20, 1920. They are buried in Kemp's Chapel Cemetery in Alcorn County. Thurman and Cado are buried in Jacinto Cemetery in Alcorn County.

Barbara Ann Davis Hendrix (b. Mar. 21, 1950) is the daughter of Clarence Junior Davis (b. Dec. 5, 1929, d. Dec. 16, 1995) and Bonnie Ross Davis (b. Aug. 25, 1933). They married Nov. 15, 1947. Bonnie lives in Florida. Junior is buried Chapel Hill Cemetery in Burnsville, MS. Barbara Ann is granddaughter of Clarence Davis buried in Arkansas and Flora Lambert Davis (b. Apr. 19, 1911, d. Jul. 6, 1991) who married in February 1929. She is buried in Antioch Church Cemetery, Burnsville, MS. She is also granddaughter of Charley Clint Ross (b. Jan. 19, 1902, d. Mar. 14, 1966) and Elsie Riley Ross (b. Aug. 31, 1900, d. Jan. 11, 1981) who married Oct. 7, 1922. They are buried in Rowland Mills Missionary Baptist Church Cemetery.

Their children:

1) Kerry Ray (b. Jul. 29, 1970) graduated from Thrasher High School. He served in the US Air Force for four years: Japan, Biloxi, MS and others. He is now self-employed in Los Angeles, CA.

2) Bonnie Lynn (b. Aug. 4, 1974) has a son Nicholas Adam (b. Feb. 18, 1993). Bonnie graduated from Thrasher High School and now works at Quartet in Booneville, MS.

Donnie Ray went to Thrasher High School. He worked 23 years at Tyrone later named Dana. He works at Metal Products. His fun is hunting and fishing.

Barbara graduated from Burnsville High School and attended Northeast Junior College. She works in the school cafeteria at Booneville High School. She enjoys reading and growing flowers. *Submitted by Barbara Ann Davis Hendrix.*

HENDRIX, THURMAN LEO, born Nov. 14, 1920 and died Mar. 26, 1982, married Alma Fay Vanderford (b. May 10, 1925) on Feb. 22, 1945. Thurman was the son of Charley Cade Hendrix (b. May 8, 1898, d. Sep. 23, 1966) and Martha Elisabeth McCoy Hendrix Warren (b. Oct. 22, 1901). Thurman was the grandson of John Alex (b. Jan. 8, 1872, d. Mar. 23, 1947) and Julia E. Bohannon McCoy (b. May 2, 1873, d. Aug. 6, 1960). They are buried in Juliette Cemetery in Alcorn County. Thurman was also the grandson of J. Sim Hendrix (b. Oct. 30, 1856, d. Aug. 2, 1922) and Margaret Patrick Hendrix (b. Jul. 10, 1866, d. Jan. 24, 1943). They are buried in Jacinto Cemetery. Thurman and Cato are buried there also.

Thurman had one sister, Jeffie Margaret Hendrix (b. Nov. 21, 1927, d. Apr. 14, 1998) who married Vester Vanderford (b. Apr. 22, 1923, d. Dec. 16, 1992). He was the son of David and Maude Maness Vanderford. Jeffie, Vester, David and Maude are buried in Williams Cemetery in Alcorn County.

Alma Fay is the daughter of Clovis Aaron Vanderford (b. Jun. 1, 1901, d. Jan. 16, 1985) and Ida Sula Richardson Vanderford (b. Jun. 11, 1904, d. Sep. 8, 1989) who married on Feb. 20, 1920. They are buried in Kemp's Chapel Cemetery in Alcorn County. Fay is the granddaughter of Mark Vanderford (b. Sep. 15, 1879, d. Oct. 3, 1938) and Neal Samantha Maness Vanderford (b. Jul. 3, 1881, d. Mar. 9, 1958) who married Aug. 20, 1900. They are buried in Juliette Cemetery in Alcorn County. Fay is also granddaughter of Green Berry "Bee" Richardson (b. 1869, d. 1945) and Nannie Bell Cox Richardson (b. 1872, d. 1966). They are buried in Sardis Cemetery in Alcorn County. (See Clovis Aaron Vanderford)

Clovis Leo and his mother Alma Fay Vanderford Hendrix

Their children are: 1) Clovis Leo (b. Oct. 12, 1946) did not marry. He lives with Fay. 2) Donnie Ray (b. Oct. 7, 1948) md. Barbara Ann Davis (b. Mar. 21, 1950) (see Donnie Ray Hendrix). 3) Doris Fay (b. Jan. 24, 1951) md. Bradley Rorie (b. Mar. 25, 1948). (See Bradley Rorie). 4) Cathy Marie (b. May 28, 1958) md. Tommy Charles DeGraw (b. Apr. 19, 1959) (see Tommy DeGraw).

Thurman and Fay farmed. He served four years in the US Navy and was stationed in Corpus Christi, TX. Thurman went to Kenosha, WI and worked in construction. Fay stayed in Prentiss County and raised the children. Thurman returned and worked in timber and was hurt and retired. Fay worked at the garment factory at Holcut in Burnsville. The family all enjoy going to Maw Maw Fay's house for good food, card games and lots of love. *Submitted by Samantha DeGraw.*

HILL, DOC JORDAN, born 1870 and died 1948, son of Phelix Johnsey Hill, married Willie Columbia Ann Gooch (b. Oct. 12, 1893, d. Jan. 15, 1955). Their children were as follows:

1) Viola (b. 1895, d. 1973) md. first, Claud Keeton and second, Thurman Isbell.

2) Clara (b. 1897) md. Howard Stubblefield and had two sons, Harold and Malcolm.

3) Ollie (b. 1898) md. Auddie Coggins and had two sons and two daughters. Bernard married Evelyn Holley and they had two daughters. Karen married Steve Brigman and had one son, Jayson. Holley married with no children. Second son married Lenora _ and had four children: Tony, Vickie, Phil and Sherry. Daughter Doris married John Davis and had five children: John Jr., Steve, Mike, Gary, Randy and Charlotte. Daughter Gloria married Duval Hefflin and had two children, Jeph (md. twice with two children, Shannon and Shelly) and Melanie (md. with two children.

4) Essie Hill married Herman Coggins and had two children, one of whom died at birth. The other, Conwell Coggins, married Marilyn Miller and had two children: Joe married Dorothy Morgan and had Jessica and Morgan and Terry who married Mitchell Garner and had Nathan Vance and Ashley Lauren.

5) Dora Hill married Dewey Miller and had Thomas, Carolyn, Bobby and Bill.

6) Leonard Hinds Hill died in 1904.

7) Roy Clyde Hill married Ruby Robertson and had Jerry, Richard, Ted, Larry, Janice and Ronnie. Jerry married Yvonne Thornhill and adopted two sons. Randall Hill (b. Jan. 10, 1968) md. Stacy Ainsworth and had one child, Joshua Caleb (b. Jul. 17, 1998). Michael Hill (b. Sep. 18, 1970) md. Debbie Jones and had one child, Brianna Hill (b. Jan. 15, 1994).

Richard Clyde Hill married Helen Elizabeth Smith and had three sons: Richard Daniel (b. Dec. 17, 1966); Joel Scott (b. Apr. 29, 1969) md. Amy Melisa Polk; Robert Christopher Hill (b. Sep. 18, 1974). Teddy Ray Hill Sr. married Mary Ann Franks in 1960 and had three children: Teddy Ray Jr. md. Ellen Petrie and had five children: David Wesley (b.

Holder Family Reunion. This picture submitted in memory of Lena Bertie (Holder) Thompson and her husband, Lawrence, at whose home this was taken at a family reunion with preaching in the afternoon by Lena's brother, Elmer. Some on this picture are not natural family but church family. Five of Bud Holder's children, his youngest sister and a sister-in-law are present and three of Sid Holder's children are present. All will be numbered by row. Those not known will be listed as unknown. Starting from left with the bottom row. Row #1: (1-2) unknown, (3) Mackie, (4) Kelly Hugh, (5) Clarice, (6) Kenneth, (7) Foy Holland, (8) Mary Frances Holland, (9-10-11) Duard and Audrey Holder's children, (12-13) children of Laura Holder Miller, (14-16) unknown. Row #2: (1) Almour (Holder) Johnson, (2) son Donald, (3) Nolen Johnson, (4) Arminnta (Johnston) Smith, Bud's sister-in-law, (5-6) Oscar and Ora Holder, (7-9) unknown, (10-11) Elmer Lee and Nena Faye Holder, (12-13) Elizabeth and Kellie Holder, (14-15) Bessie and Fate Holland, (16-17) Duard and Audrey Holder, (18-19) Laura (Holder) Miller and child, (20-21) unknown, (22-23) Lula and Elmo Holder, (24-25) Dell and Charlene Bullard. Row #3: (1) unknown, (2) Beulah (McGaughy) Holder, (3) Elder Elmer Holder, (4-8) unknown, (9-10) Annie Mae and Milford Holder, (11) Dora Ella (Holder) Whitfield, Bud's youngest sister, (12) Lee Whitfield, (13) Toy Whitfield's son, (14) Lela Whitfield, (15) Vivian (Thompson) Holder, (16) Evans Holder (17) Lena Bertie (Thompson) Holder, (18-19) unknown, (20) Mrs. Clint Bullard, (21) Clint Bullard, (22) Loyd Bullard. Row #4: (1) unknown, (2) Almie Holder, (3) Dee Bullard, (4) Elder Marlin Bullard, (5) Sallie Owens, (6) Toy Whitfield, (7) unknown, (8-9) Ed and Vearl Hardwick, (10) Frances (Holder) Eaton, (11-12) Edith (Holder) Smith and Clatus Smith, (13-15) unknown, (16) Elmer Holder Jr., (17-18) unknown. This picture donated for use by Nena Faye Holder, 348 Highway 364, Booneville, MS 38829. (662) 728-4755.

Dec. 9, 1992), Rachel Franks (b. Dec. 16, 1995), Anna Petrie, Sara Oakley and Megan Irene (b. May 30, 1997). In 1974 Ted Sr. married Sharon Graham and they have two children: Kari Alice (b. Oct. 29, 1976) md. Ted Slusser of Memphis and Graham Hill.

Larry Wayne Hill married Julie Ann Lane and had two sons, Craig Allen (b. Sep. 10, 1978) and Ryan Wayne (b. Apr. 30, 1980). Janice Carol Hill married Charles Phillip Browning and had two sons, Corey Michael (b. May 19, 1984) and Lee Gullam (b. Feb. 15, 1988).

HOLDER, BUD AND SID, similarities, duplications, circumstances and events that happened in Bud and Sid Holders' lives.

Paternal grandparents were Hawkins Holder and Malissa Ann (Carr) Holder.

Maternal grandparents of Bud were William Honey and Ann Honey. Her maiden name is not known.

Parents were Benjamin Austin Holder and Martha Frances E. Honey.

William Hawkins (Bud) Holder (1859, d. 1932). His children by his first wife, Frances Tennessee Johnston:

(1) Oscar Ervin Holder (b. 1884), (2) Lena Bertie Holder (b. 1888), (3) Elmer Cleveland Holder (b. 1890), (4) Hoyle Kellie Holder (b. 1894),

Children by his second wife, Eliza Harris:

(5) Ursala Holder (b. 1899), (6) Nellie Holder (b. 1900), (7) Austin Holder (b. 1902), (8) Bessie (twin, born in 1904, d. 1905), (9) Essie (twin, born in 1904, d. 1905), (10) Noel Holder (b. 1909), (11) Homer Lee Holder (b. 1911), (12) Ruby Holder (b. 1914).

Maternal grandparents of Sid were Nelson M. Gary and Mary Amanda (Honey) Gary.

Parents were John Oliver Holder and Martha Frances E. Gary.

Joseph Columbus (Sid) Holder (b. 1873, d. 1931). His children by his wife, Minnie Bell (Seago) Holder:

(1) Dora B. Holder (b. 1895), (2) George Arthur Holder (b. 1896), (3) John David Holder (b. 1898), (4) Bessie Ree Holder (b. 1900), (5) Milford Paulie Holder (b. 1902), (6) Fred Owen Holder (b. 1904), (7) Almour Holder (twin, b. 1906), (8) Almie Holder (twin, b. 1906), (9) Lester Columbus Holder (b. 1909), (10) Noel Price Holder (b. 1912), (11) Arlie Garfield Holder (b. 1914), (12) Baby girl (b. and d. in 1920).

Bud and Sid Holder are kin on both sides of the house. It is not known the exact connection of William Honey and Mary Amanda Honey. Nelson Gary and Mary Amanda Honey married in 1847, three years before indexing on the 1850 census.

The Holders, Carrs, Honeys and Garys are found in the Piedmont Counties of South Carolina and only Malissa Ann, who is not found on the 1850 census, is not listed as born in South Carolina.

Bud and Sid's mothers had identical names. Since Sid's mother was the youngest, she was named after Bud's mother. Of 17 children by two marriages, only Bud and Sid's fathers' families and two cousins, the sons of the oldest son of Hawkins, stayed in Mississippi.

Two sons of Bud and Sid were called and ordained to preach, Elmer Cleveland and John David. Elmer's wife died after their fourth child was born, leaving them with out a mother. Arthur died after his fourth child was born, leaving them without a father.

Bud and Sid each had a daughter named Bessie.

Each had twin daughters, Bessie and Essie and Almour and Almie.

Each had a son with part of a president's name, Elmer Cleveland and Arlie Garfield.

They each had a son named Noel. Homer and Arlie were in the service in WWII.

Bud and Sid each had a brother named Thomas Marion. The way some tried to tell which one they were talking about was Bud's brother was called Tom and Sid's T.M.

Bud and Sid each had 12 children. Each moved from Tishomingo County to Prentiss soon after 1900, Bud to Altitude and Sid to Cairo.

With names like William Hawkins and Joseph Columbus, Bud and Sid came natural.

They had two uncles that died in the Civil War, the sixth son, Thomas E., five months after entering and the oldest two months before the war was over, leaving six children without a father. *Submitted by Hassell Holder.*

HOLDER, FRED, born May 13 1904. His parents were Sid and Minnie Holder. His brothers were Arthur, David, Milford, Lester, Price and Arlie. His sisters were Dora, Bessie, twins Almour and Almie and a baby girl that died at birth.

Fred married first Ola Jourdan in 1924. She was the daughter of Claud and Mittie Jourdan. Ola was born Oct. 3, 1908. Their children were Hassell, Marshall, Buddy and Dwaine. Fred married second to Earlene Hopper. They did not have any children. Hassell (b. Nov. 20, 1925) married Maxine Engle on Jan. 31, 1943. Maxine was the daughter of Dank and Essie Engle. Maxine was born Feb. 25, 1926. Their children were:

This picture was taken in the summer of 1944 prior to Hassell leaving for the Army on August 11. Bottom Row: Lional Dwaine, born in 1939. Middle Row: Fred, born in 1904, Ola, born in 1908 and Horace Edwin (Buddy), born in 1934. Top Row: Marshall, born in 1930, Maxine, Hassell's wife, born in 1926 and Hassell, born in 1925.

(1) Ronnie (b. Dec. 15, 1946) married Tanya Ann Twitty on Nov. 21, 1973. Tanya Ann was born Jan. 1, 1957. She was the daughter of Loumis and Audie Twitty. Ronnie and Ann's children were: Jessica (b. May 20, 1977) married Jason Thorton and they do not have any children, Felisha (b. Apr. 10, 1983), Allison (b. May 7, 1986) and Daniel (b. Dec. 14 1988).

(2) Marsha (b. Apr. 17, 1948) married Michael Skelton in 1970 and divorced in 1977. They did not have any children.

(3) Eddie (b. Jun. 13, 1950) married Annette Maness on Mar. 20, 1970. She was born Jul. 7, 1952. She was the daughter of Hugh and Willie Etta Maness. Their children were: Beth (b. Sep. 25, 1972) married Stanley Fleming, Stephanie (b. May 23, 1979) and Natalie (b. May 29, 1984).

(4) Gary (b. Sep. 20, 1951) married first Martha Whitfield in 1973. They did not have any children. They were divorced. He then married Dorothy Taylor (b. Nov. 1, 1960). She was the daughter of Elton and Essie Mae Taylor. They have one daughter, Tee Sha Mae Maxine (b. Feb. 27, 1982).

(5) Ola Mae (b. Mar. 20, 1953, d. Feb. 5, 1965).

(6) Rita Sue (b. Jul. 18, 1958) married Randy Twitty, the brother of Tanya Ann, Ronnie's wife. They were married on Nov. 6, 1973. Randy was born Jun. 12, 1952. Their children are Sarah (b. 1975) married Kelvin Hammett, they have one daughter, Hailey; Scott (b. 1979) married Candace Hubbard on Dec. 4, 1999.

Marshall Holder (b. Aug. 30, 1930) married first to Delephane Lowery, second to Ruth Lindley and third to Carrie Sue Dixon.

Marshall and Delephane's children were: Freddie Ray (b. 1950) married first to Karen Childers and had Bradley and Carla and then married Gail Johnson and had no children; Brenda Gay (b. 1956) married Jimmy Don Bonds and had Monica and Dana and Horace Edwin "Buddy" (b. Sep. 13, 1934) married Doris Nell Carter on Dec. 15, 1954. Buddy died Jun. 4, 1978. Their children were David Owen (b. Apr. 5, 1958) married first Patrica Hart and did not have any children. David married second to Waneth "Kathy" Burcham (b. Feb. 21, 1959) in 1995. They have one son, David Austin (b. 1996).

Janet Elaine (b. Jul. 27, 1960) married Ronald Bowen, who was born in December 1956. They have sons, Matthew Wayne (b. 1987), Riley Holder (b. 1989) and David Austin (b. 1993).

Lisa Renea (b. Mar. 26, 1965) married Adam Jeffery Brazenas. They have a son, Adam Jeffery and a daughter, Samantha Lorain.

Lional Dwaine (b. Apr. 12, 1939) married first Mary Storey. They had two sons, Mike and Keith. After Dwaine and Mary divorced, Mary married a Turner. He adopted Mike and Keith. Dwaine married second Wanda Pritchard. They have one daughter, Karen Sue (b. 1960) married Gary Aschauer. Their children are Jessica Ann (b. 1978), Catherine Annette (b. 1980) and Jacob Dwaine (b. 1983). *Submitted by Marshall Holder, 402 East 5th Street, Corinth, MS 38834. (662) 287-2717.*

HOLDER, JOSEPH COLUMBUS "SID," born in 1873 near the Holder Cemetery, which is on County Road 961, southeast of Burnsville, MS. His parents were John Oliver and Martha Frances E. (Gary) Holder. His brothers were T.M., Willie, Louis and Riley. His sisters were Arry, Lindy, Lular, Mattie, Lonie and twins who died at birth.

Sid married Minnie Bell Seago in 1893. Minnie was the daughter of William Tillman and Martha Frances (Hughey) Seago, who lived in Ingram Mills in Desoto County, MS by 1872 where Minnie was born. She had full sisters, Martha E. and Sarah Ann. In 1878 Martha Frances died and William Tillman moved back to Tishomingo County where he had family. He later married Mrs. Nancy Cobb Montgomery and they had a daughter, Fannie and sons: Chester, Percy and Early.

Picture was made in front of Sid and Minnie Holder's garden at their home place in Cairo, possibly made in the 1920s before Sid's declining health and death in 1931.

Sid and Minnie started married life on a farm in the Berea Community, which is on Highway 365 south of Burnsville. They lived there until sometime after 1900 when they moved to the Cairo Community in northeast Prentiss County. Sid died while they lived there in 1931. Minnie died in 1947 while living with her daughter, Almour in Wheeler. Their children were:

(1) Dora (b. 1895) married Willie Miller. Their children were: Rexford, who married Ruth Castelberry; Hershel, who married Reener Williams; Lopez, who married first Dick Ellis and later a Bryant and Dorothy, who married Dick McCombs.

(2) Arthur (b. 1896) married Ada Hendrix. Their children were: Jewell, who married Terry Whitfield; Inez, who married Vernard Beene; Leister, who married Dan Weed and Beulah, who married Dan Posey.

(3) David (b. 1898) married first Dona Brown. They had one daughter, Moese, who married William Beene. When Moese was 6 years old, her mother died. David later married Lydia Wren.

(4) Bessie Ree (b. 1900) married Cap Scott.

(5) Milford (b. 1902) married first Annie Mae Inman. Their children were Norvell, who died shortly after birth; Clarice, who married Jerry Guess; Kenneth, who married Betty Taylor and Joe, who married Sandra (last name unknown). After Annie Mae's death, Milford married Madell Bonds.

(6) Fred (b. 1904) married first Ola Jourdan. Their children are Hassell, who married Maxine Engle; Marshall, who married 1) Delaphene Lowery, 2) Ruth Lindley and 3) Carrie Dixon; Horace (Buddy), who married Doris Carter Eaton and Dwaine, who married 1) Mary Storey and 2) Wanda Pritchard. Fred married second to Earlene Hopper.

(7) Almour (twin, b. 1907) married Nolen Johnson. They had one son, Donald, who married 1) Dale Arnold and 2) Maxine Godwin.

(8) Almie (twin, b. 1907) married Lee Davis.

(9) Lester (b. 1909) married Bertie Burcham. Their children were Clyne and Clyve (twins), who died shortly after birth and Charles Ray.

(10) Price (b. 1912) married first Carrie Young. They had one son, James Norman. Price married second to Lois Martendale.

(11) Arlie (b. 1914) married Carol Ness. Their children are Chris, Karen, John and Robbie.

(12) An infant was born in 1920 that did not live. *Submitted by Ronnie Holder, 78 CR 2280, Booneville, MS 38829.*

HOLDER, WILLIAM HAWKINS "BUD,"
born in Tishomingo County on Jan. 15, 1859 and died in Prentiss County on Jan. 15, 1932. His parents were Benjamin Austin Holder and Martha Frances E. Honey. She was the daughter of William and Anna Honey, all of them born in South Carolina.

Bud married first Frances Tennessee Johnston. She was related to the General Johnston who was the commanding officer at Shiloh and was killed there. The place and date of Bud's and Frances' marriage is not known. They settled in the Leeddy Community in Tishomingo County. Frances was born in 1865 and died Jan. 18, 1897. Their children were:

This picture of W.H. (Bud) Holder and the unknown lad was possibly taken in the late 1920s before Bud's death in January 1932.

(1) Oscar Ervin (b. 1884) married Ora Hamilton in 1908. Their children were Duard, who married Audrey Huddleston; Vearl, who married Ed Hardwick; Laura, who married Odell Miller and Frances, who married Lee Eaton. A daughter, Vera Maye, was born in 1912 and died in 1914 and an infant son was born and died later.

(2) Lena Bertie "Auntie" (b. 1888) married Lawrence Thompson in 1912 in Prentiss County. They did not have any children of their own, but after Auntie's brother, Elmer's wife died leaving four small children, she and Lawrence raised them.

(3) Elmer Cleveland (b. 1890) married Lula Patrick, place not known. She was born in 1890 in Shiloh, TN, died in 1916. Their children were: Eva Gertrude, who married first Sam Burcham and second George Early; Evans, who married Vivian Thompson; Clinton (Jack), who married Florence Burns and Elmer Lee, who married Nena Faye McCutchen. After Lula died in 1916, Elmer later married Bulah McGaughy. They had one son, Elmer Jr.

(4) Hoyle Kellie (b. 1894) married Elizabeth Marcy in 1919 in Prentiss County. Their children were: Edith, who married Clatus Smith and Kellie Hugh, who married Janie Morgan. After Bud's first wife died in 1897, he married Eliza Harris.

(5) Ursala (b. March 1899, d. November 1899).

(6) Nellie (b. 1900, d. 1902).

(7) Austin (b. 1902) married Vera Price. Their children were Alene, who married Paul Jack Smith and Ilene, who married Kenneth Harris.

(8) Bessie (twin, b. 1904-05) married Fate Holland. Their children were Mary Frances, who married Enoch McCoy, Foy, J.W., Carmon, Billy David and Leland.

(9) Essie (twin, b. 1904-05) married James Pace. Their children were: Audrey, who married J.T. Lambert; Ray, who married Bernice Maness; Lyle, who married Eloise Wilson and Troy, who married Glenda Enlow.

(10) Noel (b. 1909) married Eulaler Murphy in 1929. They had one son, Thomas.

(11) Homer Lee (b. 1911) married first Ivey Lowery. They did not have any children. After her death, Homer married Opal Johnson. They had one son, Harold Lee.

(12) Ruby (b. 1914) married Sam Chase in 1936. Their children were Joyce, who married J.D Phifer and James Howard, who married Virginia Hughes. *Submitted by Mackie Holder, 361 Highway 364, Booneville, MS 38829. (662) 728-6070.*

HOLLEY FAMILY,
Absolom Holley (b. ca. 1770 in Anson County, NC, d. November 1850 in Tishomingo County, MS) married Lucinda (unknown) about 1791 in Anson County, NC.

He was the son of William Holley (b. ca. 1740, d. 1783 in Anson County, NC). Absolom had a brother, Edward Holley (b. ca. 1768).

Found in the Anson County, NC will book is the following: "5 Apr. 1783, Estate of William Holley ... includes 300 acres on Richardson Creek, one grindstone in possession of Mr. Nathaniel Holley; one very nice rifle gun in possession of James Maxfield in McLenburg (sic) County which he refuses to deliver ... Note on Reuben Mathus, Charles Evans, Theophilus Hill, one prayer book."

William Holley was the son of Julius Holley (b. ca. 1720, Anson County, NC, died before 1771 in Anson County). Children of Julius Holley were William, Nathaniel, a daughter who married John Jackson, a daughter who married William Nelson, John, Edward and Thomas.

Absolom and Lucinda Holley were the parents of Elizabeth (b. 1792), Nancy (b. ca. 1793), Mary (b. 1793), Edward (b. ca. 1794), Julius A. (b. 1796), John (b. 1797), William (b. 1798), Absolom B. (b. 1808) and Margaret (b. ca. 1812) all born in Anson County. Elizabeth md. John Chase, Nancy md. John J. Walden, Mary md. John Weldon, John md. Nancy Ann Harris and Margaret md. Archibald Harris.

Julius A. Holley married Sarah B. Horton. Their children were Absolom Jackson, Naomi "Oma," Plummer Douglas, William T., Julius Alexander, James D. "Berry," Lucy A., George Washington, Sarah Amanda, Hardy C.M. and Amanda S. Holley all born in Anson County.

Absolom and his large family moved to Tishomingo County, MS ca. 1842.

Wright Bonds/Josie Holley Family. L-R, bottom row: Wright Walker Bonds III, Roy, Maggie, Luther, Josie, Ray (baby). Top row: Tennie, Effie, Venie, Molly

Plummer Douglas Holley (b. Sep. 2, 1825, d. Oct. 4, 1902 in Prentiss County) married Emely N. Crow, daughter of Nathaniel Sanders Crow and Nancy Buford Johnson Dec. 16, 1848 in Booneville, MS. Children of Plummer Douglas and Emely Crow Holley were John Taylor, Louisa Pernecia Ann, Sarah Josephine Nancy Elizabeth, Sophia N., Cephus Nathaniel, Daniel Clinton, Emma V. and Silvanus.

Sara Josephine "Josie" Nancy Elizabeth (b. Jan. 1858, d. 1953) married Wright Walker Bonds III. Their children were Louvenia "Venie" (McCreary), Tennie M. (Scott), Effie E. (Swain), Mollie (Brown), Luther C., Roy Festus, Maggie McKinley (Sparks) and James Ray.

Amanda S. married Richmond Allen Johnston, son of John A. Johnston and Huldy Phillips. She was then disowned by her father, Julius Holley, according to a descendant. Children of Richmond Allen and Amanda Holley Johnston were Mary f. "Mollie", Bellzee (Hartsfield), Julius W., Howell Brant, James William, Robert D., Huldy L., Eliza A. and Anna E.

Mollie never married but had two children, Thomas Jefferson Johnson and Ella Mae who married William Arthur Saylors. It is said on good authority that the father of these two children was Lee Cartwright. Thomas married Delphia Derryberry. This generation of Johnstons started spelling the name without the "t." *Submitted by Ann Sparks. Sources: Maureen Holley Crow, Wayne Anderson Holley, Vida Brooks Hughes, Texas and Wanza Merrifield, Oklahoma.*

HOLLEY, ABSOLOM B.,
came to old Tishomingo County from Anson County, NC in the 1840s. Absolom B. was the brother of Julius Holley, who also came to Mississippi around the same time. Their father, Absolom, lived with Julius. Julius and his father, Absolom, are buried in the Holley Cemetery at Bunkum Hill.

Absolom B. Holley married Elvin M. and had 10 children. Those children were: Nancy, William S., Louis H., Eveline, Calvin, John, Eliza, Mary J., Sarah A. and Amanda, who was born around 1852.

This picture is of Rosencrantz Holley taken at his son Charles' house.

Louis H. Holley (b. 1833) married Aliza Rogers. Their children were: Rosencrantz, Marion Grant, Syrenthia E. and Nancy E. A Louis Holley has been found on a list of southern soldiers for the Confederacy during the Civil War.

Louis's son, Rosencrantz, was the only one who married. He married Sarah Ann Cochran, daughter of John C. Cochran and Martha Ann Taylor. Rosencrantz and Sarah's children were: Charles Marshall, Lucy Elizabeth and Geneva. Rosencrantz and Sarah are buried in Little Brown Cemetery.

Charles Marshall Holley married Mary Lenora Jones. They had three children: Joseph Grady, Charles Clarence and Zannie Grace.

Joseph Grady Holley married Alma Lou Barnes, daughter of James Burlison Barnes and Rilla Gahagan. Grady and Alma's three children are: Joseph Don, Roy Neal and James "Jamie" Marshall. *Submitted by Brad Holley.*

HOLLEY, JULIUS MARVIN SR.,
Wayne Holley is the descendant of Julius Marvin Holley and Mamie Inez Rummage. Julius Marvin was the son of Edward Nelson Holley and Rachel Leeth. Edward Nelson was the son of Julius Alexander and Sarah Elizabeth Harris.

Edward Nelson and Rachel Leeth were married Dec. 17 1885. There were five children born:

Rena Belle, James Clifton (died in his early 20s), Mary Loula (died at age 2), Julius Marvin Sr. and Mamie A. (married a McNeil).

Rachel Holley passed to a better world in 1897. Edward Nelson married Sallie Shackleford in 1916. Edward Nelson passed to a better world in February 1941. They are buried in the Holley Cemetery.

Julius Marvin Holley Sr., Wayne's dad

Rene Belle married Charles W. Davis. They had two children, Faye Davis and Charles Holley Davis. Faye married Travis Lindley and they had one child named Ann. Holley Davis married Mae Furtick and they have two children, John C. Davis and Lynda A. Davis.

Julius Marvin Holley married Rausie Mayo in 1912. Four children were born: Margie married a Horn, then a Martin; Christine married Julius Tom Hodges; Owen married Annabelle Rodgers and Julius Marvin (Red) Jr. married Dorothy. The marriage ended between Julius and Rausie in 1931.

Margie had two children by Horn, Leroy and Bettie and then a third child with Martin named David. Christine had three children: Thomas Eugene, John Leroy and Leonard. Owen Watson had two children, Shirley Jean and Patricia Ann. Julius (Red) Marvin Jr. had two children, Mark and Tammy.

Front: Mamie Rummage Holley. From Left: William (Bill) Edward, Joe Dee and Wayne Anderson, Wayne's mom and brothers.

Julius Sr. and Mamie moved to Florida. Julius' visits back to Mississippi to see his father were few, probably because of finances. Julius's and Mamie's sons never knew much about the Holley side of the family.

Julius Sr. married Mamie Rummage in 1933 in Booneville. They had four children: William (Bill) Edward married Patricia Prince; Wayne Anderson married B.J. Quire; Joe Dee married Nam Hi and Joe had a twin named Mary Lee, who died at birth.

William Edward was named after both grandfathers, William Rummage and Edward Holley. He was born in Booneville. Bill and Pat have three sons: Edward, Allan and Kenneth. Bill retired from the Air Force with the rank of lieutenant colonel and lives in Florida.

Wayne Anderson was born in Booneville. He was named after Dr. Anderson, who was the doctor that delivered him. Wayne and B.J. had three children: Russell Wayne (died at age 3), Teresa Lynn and James Anderson. Teresa married Vincent and had Marissa Nicole. Teresa married a second time and had Dustin Wayne and then had twins, Kayla and Candance. James Anderson is not married.

Wayne served time in the Army. When he got out, he went into police work. He started as a dispatcher at Winter Haven Police Department. Twenty-five years later, he retired with the rank of captain.

Joe Dee Holley was born in Florida. Joe and Nam Hi have no children. Joe retired from the Army with the rank of sergeant and lives in Columbus, GA.

Julius Marvin Sr. died in 1954 and is buried in Florida. Mamie passed away in 1976 and is buried in Florida. *Submitted by B.J. Holley.*

HOLLEY, WILLIAM CALVIN, son of William Shep and Elizabeth Jane Rogers Holley, was born Jan. 12, 1856. On Sep. 9, 1878, he married Amanda Pierce, daughter of Theophilus and Betty Ferguson Pierce. William Calvin and Amanda Holley made their home in eastern Prentiss County near the Bearden School, known in later years as Ole Burnt School House. To this couple were born nine children: (1) Della Lou Elva Elizabeth Jane (b. Sep. 2, 1880); (2) William Theophilus (b. Apr. 30, 1882); (3) John Shep (b. Dec. 23, 1884); (4) Mary Verda Samantha (b. Jun. 9, 1886); (5) James Gurley (b. Dec. 29, 1888); (6) Hattie Emmaline (b. Sep. 21, 1889); (7) Clovis Price (b. May 4, 1891); (8) Mason Archie (b. Jan. 9, 1893) and (9) an infant son (b. 1894).

Amanda Pierce Holley and children (about 1898). Front Row (L-R): Mother, Amanda Pierce Holley; Hattie Holley Inman; Mason(Mace) Holley; Clovis (Clof) Holley and James (Jim) Holley. Back Row (L-R): Mary Holley White; William(Will) Holley; Della Holley Mayo; John Shep Holley.

Wiliam Calvin Holley passed away in 1894 prior to the birth of his ninth child. Amanda Pierce Holley, widowed with eight children ranging from 1 to 14 years of age, managed to rear her children to adulthood. She passed away in 1950 at approximately 97 seven years of age. (Her mother died when she was a baby and she never knew her exact birth date.) Both William Calvin Holley and Amanda Pierce Holley are buried in Little Brown Cemetery. Their children married in Prentiss County where they, with the exception of James Gurley, continued to live and raise their families.

Della Lou Elva Elizabeth Jane Holley married J. Pardon Mayo, a Free Will Baptist Minister, on Feb. 12, 1903. Della and Pardon Mayo had three children: Vaudie S. Mayo (b. 1906, d. 1974), who married Mary Bell Barnes; Ila Mayo, who married Lloyd Saylors and a son named Milan, who died in infancy. Pardon Mayo passed away Oct. 12, 1957 and Della Holley Mayo passed away Mar. 29, 1969. Both Della and Pardon Mayo are buried in Little Brown Cemetery.

William Theophilus Holley married Mary Jane Moreland on Nov. 24, 1901. To this couple were born the following: Kellous Artin; Arlin (b. Aug. 18, 1904, d. 1963); Artie Bell (b. Jun. 23, 1906, d. 1964); Flossie Ray (b. Dec. 1, 1913) and Vernon Quitman (b. Sep. 26, 1916, d. Aug. 4, 1917). Mary Jane Moreland Holley passed away Apr. 19, 1925 and William Theophilus Holley passed away in 1963. Both are buried in Little Brown Cemetery.

John Shep Holley married Effie Josephine Horn on Jun. 15, 1909. To this couple were born two children: Verda Bell Holley (b. Aug. 23, 1910, d. Mar. 9, 1999) and Voyd Dillard Holley (b. Aug. 19, 1913, d. Jan. 7, 1990), who married Annis Beatrice Isbell on Jun. 3, 1934. John Shep Holley passed away Feb. 25, 1976 and Effie Josephine Holley passed away Sep. 25, 1974. Both are buried in Little Brown Cemetery.

Mary Verda Samantha Holley married William Webster White on Feb. 25, 1904. To this couple were born three children: Kylie Ree White (b. Apr. 15, 1905, d. Dec. 8, 1987), who married Benjamin Levi Moreland on Mar. 7, 1920; Delta Dee White (b. Jul. 11, 1911), who married Earl Ray Smith on Feb. 28, 1937 and Roy Clyder White (b. Aug. 8, 1912, d. Feb. 28, 1996), who married Evelyn Ruth Hoard on Sep. 22, 1934. William Webster White passed away Oct. 23, 1954 and Mary Verda Holley White passed away Nov. 24, 1972. Both are buried in Little Brown Cemetery.

James Gurley Holley married Alma Johnson on Dec. 25, 1918. To this couple were born 12 children: Crystal Crittintine; Hazel June; James W ; Kenneth Clayton; Amanda Christell; Brownell Gayrue; Wallace Lee Rome; Mary Rachel; Madge Delana; Shirley Imogene; Cleburn Obern and Marc. Alma Johnson Holley passed away Dec. 30, 1941 and James Gurley Holley passed away Oct. 21, 1969. Both are buried in Stephenson Cemetery, south of Memphis, TN.

Hattie Emmaline Holley married John H. Inman. To this couple were born five children: Glee; Holley; Paul; Stanley and Mary. Hattie Emmaline Holley passed away in 1982 and John H. Inman passed away in 1972. Both are buried in Little Brown Cemetery.

Clovis Price Holley married Martha Jane Miller. They had no children. Martha Jane Miller Holley passed away May 23, 1967 and Clovis Price Holley passed away Feb. 17, 1978. Both are buried in Little Brown Cemetery.

Mason Archie Holley was never married. He passed away Feb. 24, 1960 and is buried in Little Brown Cemetery. *Submitted by Bettie Raye Smith Akers.*

HONEYCUTT, ROBERT L., born Dec. 7, 1942 in Alcorn County, MS is the oldest of four children of Minnie Virginia Walker (b. Jul. 7, 1920 in Alcorn County) and Looney Lawdy Honeycutt (b. Jan. 20, 1920 in Short, MS, Tishomingo County), who married on Feb. 1, 1941 in Corinth, MS. His siblings: Daniel Wiley (b. Jul. 27, 1944); Michael Dewayne (b. Jun. 26, 1950) and Jimmie Lee (b. Oct. 30, 1948). Dan married Mary Comer Hendrix (Iuka) on Apr. 16, 1981. Wayne married Barbara Jean Barrett (Memphis, TN) on Jun. 21, 1974. They have two daughters, Anna Marie (b. May 28, 1978) and Amanda Elaine (b. Aug. 3, 1982). Jimmie Lee married James Middleton (Jimmy) Whitt (Eupora) on Jul. 5, 1970. They have two children, Susan Leigh (b. Jun. 3, 1972) and James Barry (b. Jan. 18, 1975) and one grandson, Cody.

Growing up in Alcorn County, Robert attended school at Kossuth, Northeast Mississippi Junior College and Mississippi State University. He worked as industrial arts teacher at Oxford High School in Oxford, MS and Lee High School in Columbus, MS. He moved to Booneville in the fall of 1969 to take the job of industrial arts instructor at Northeast Mississippi Community College where he remained until his retirement as the director of vocational technical education.

The Robert L. Honeycutt Family, left: Andrea Lynn, Sue and Robert

At NEMCC he met Sue Carolyn Kimbrell (b. Sep. 18, 1939 in Booneville), who was librarian at Eula Dees Memorial Library. They were married on Aug. 15, 1970. Sue is the daughter of Ruben Avery Kimbrell (b. Aug. 21, 1902 in Clay County and died Mar. 16, 1982) and Anna Lou Maxwell (b. Dec. 6, 1906). See Thomas Stephen Miller, Maxwell and Kimbrell histories.

Sue's paternal grandparents were Charlie David Kimbrell (b. Feb. 13, 1860, d. Jan. 6, 1939) and Ida Maud Glasson (b. Jun. 30, 1867, d. Jan. 10, 1965) of

Clay County, MS; great-grandparents were Ruben "Uncle Rube" Kimbrel (Alabama), Mary A. Barfield (North Carolina), William Avery Glasson and Mary Elizabeth Foster.

Sue and Robert have one daughter, Andrea Lynn (b. Aug. 31, 1974 in Booneville). On Mar. 28, 1998, Andrea married John Luke Mathis (b. Aug. 16, 1974), son of Olivia Holley and Johnny Wayne Mathis, (Alcorn County).

Robert's father, Looney Lawdy Honeycutt, is one of six children of Cora Jane Phillips (b. 1880, d. 1955) and Jessie Green Honeycutt (b. 1874, d. 1937); married on Feb. 20, 1898; siblings: Lloyd, Lennie, Lawrence, Ethel and Elma. A WWII veteran, Looney was a member of the 80th Infantry, 319th Regiment, 3rd US Army. Robert's paternal great-grandparents were Jim Honeycutt, Lucretia Barnes, John Thomas Phillips and Emma E. Kay.

Robert's mother, Minnie Virginia, is one of five children of Madgie Odell Dilworth (b. Dec. 29, 1893, d. Dec. 29, 1969) and Kendall Settle Walker (b. Jul. 30, 1887, d. Aug. 23, 1969); married on Feb. 16, 1916; siblings: Ruby Geraldine, Ruth Settle, Laura Lee and Walter Robert (Bob). Robert's maternal great-grandparents were David Settle Walker, Minnie Christian Barry, Alfred Martie Dilworth, Sidney Antella Quennella (Quinnie) Dotson Caldwell. *Submitted by Andrea Honeycutt Mathis.*

HOPKINS FAMILY, fifth child of Benjamin Franklin and Mary Eliza Campbell Hopkins was Jasper Lee Hopkins (b. Jan. 30, 1872 in Tishomingo County). Jasper was musically inclined and loved to sing and play the organ and accordion.

He married Mary Louartie Deaton on Jan. 25, 1893. She was born Jul. 17, 1875, the daughter of Louis Alvin and Sarah Ellen Hough Deaton. She had five siblings: Annie Deaton, James Emsley Deaton, John Wesley Deaton, George Deaton, Richard Calhoun Deaton and Sophie Deaton.

Jasper Lee Hopkins

They had three children:

I) Rufus Lee Hopkins (b. Nov. 14, 1893) md. Minnie Bell Barnes and had four children:

1. Lucile Hopkins (b. Oct. 11, 1911) md. Richard Guy Hare, four children: (1) Rufus Ralph (b. Apr. 21, 1927) md. Billie Francis South (b. Sep. 4, 1930), one daughter Patricia Ann Hare (b. Jan. 31, 1948, d. Aug. 5, 1998) md. Carroll Joe Fugitt, one daughter, Deanna Carroll Fugitt (b. Mar. 16, 1970). (2) Gerald Wayne Hare (b. May 17, 1935, d. Nov. 13, 1940). (3) Dillard Ray Hare (b. Oct. 22, 1938, d. Oct. 30, 1940). (4) Betty Carolyn Hare (b. Dec. 20, 1943,) md. Robert Wayne Rear (b. Dec. 5, 1940, d. Feb. 6, 1967). Second marriage to Harry Curt Pennington.

Martha Elizabeth Reynolds, only daughter of Merideth B. Reynolds pictured with her aunt, Nancy Ellen Duncan Anderson

2. Estelle Hopkins (b. Oct. 16, 1915) md. U.L. Taylor, two children: Anita Sue Taylor (b. Dec. 6, 1938) and James Harold Taylor (b. Dec. 31, 1943).

3. Lenard Rufus Hopkins (b. Apr. 9, 1913, d. Oct. 11, 1927).

4. Ulysess Lee Hopkins (b. Sep. 10, 1919) md. Evelyn Lucker, two children: Zena Antionette Hopkins and Paul Allen Hopkins.

Refus Lee Hopkins married second, Abbie Stites, three children:

5. Ernest Leo Hopkins (b. Aug. 9, 1926, d. Dec. 10, 1998) md. Mary Wynola Woodruff (b. Jul. 26, 1926, d. Jan. 9, 2000) six children: (1) Larry Ernest Hopkins (b. Sep. 15, 1948, d. Jan. 27, 1998); (2) Jerry Lee Hopkins (b. Aug. 2, 1950); (3) Gary Wayne Hopkins (b. Feb. 5, 1952); (4) John Michael Hopkins (b. Apr. 13, 1953); (5) Mary Elaine Hopkins (b. Feb. 5, 1956); (6) Tommy Eugene Hopkins (b. May 5, 1958).

6. Genell Hopkins (b. Oct. 28, 1932, d. Dec. 19, 1935).

7. Wyvone Hopkins (b. Oct. 7, 1935) md. Johnny Caldwell, one child, Barbara Gail Caldwell.

Refus Lee Hopkins married third, Georgia Bond Stacy. He died in 1961 and is buried in the Booneville Cemetery.

II) Benjamin Emsley Hopkins (b. Nov. 9, 1895) md. Minnie Bell Moreland, four children: (1) Howard Benjamin Hopkins (b. Jan. 31, 1919) md. Mildred Marshall, two children: Carolyn Hopkins and Peggy Hopkins. (2) Lavier Zee Hopkins (b. Feb. 7, 1920, d. May 19, 1999) md. W.D. Freshwater, two children: David Freshwater and Glen Freshwater; (3) Billy Hopkins (b. Dec. 3, 1924) md. Betty Isbell, one child, Emily; (4) Willie Ann Hopkins (b. Dec. 3, 1924) md. John Redding, two children: Andra Redding and Susan Redding. Benjamin Emsely Hopkins died Apr. 20, 1978 and is buried at the Booneville Cemetery.

III) Baby boy, no dates.

IV) Baby boy Hopkins (b. Sep. 8, 1898, d. Oct. 2, 1898). Mary Louartie Deaton died Nov. 14, 1875 and is buried in the Joel Cemetery.

Jasper Lee Hopkins married second, Martha Elizabeth Reynolds Smith (b. Feb. 21, 1862), daughter of Merideth B. and Matilda Elizabeth Duncan Reynolds. Martha Elizabeth "Mattie" had been widowed by Walker Smith of the Tuscombia Community in 1894 and was an extensive land holder. She also had six children: Susan Elizabeth Smith (b. Jan. 4, 1883) md. John Ammon Nunley, died Jun. 23, 1963; Thomas Merideth Smith (b. Aug. 4, 1884) md. Ada Lee Daniel, died Jan. 11, 1964; Florence Smith (b. Sep. 16, 1886, d. Oct. 30, 1889); Rosie Leona Smith (b. Jun. 21, 1888) md. Lonnie Edgar Lessenberry, died Jun. 13, 1967; Joe Taylor Smith (b. Aug. 29, 1890) md. Pearl Daniel, died 1947; Baxter Evans Smith (b. Nov. 27, 1892) md. Maudie Lucile Blackburn, died Jul. 24, 1980). Jasper Lee and Martha Elizabeth Reynolds Smith Hopkins were married Dec. 11, 1898. Jasper fathered four more sons.

V) Noonan Orlanda Hopkins (b. Nov. 15, 1899) md. Gussie Ann McCoy and had five children: Artie Marie, Mattie Moeise, Rosie Ilene, Jasper Coley and Noonon Clyde. Noonon Orlanda Hopkins died May 6, 1881 and is buried at Smith Chapel Cemetery.

VI) Jasper Van Hopkins (b. Jul. 28, 1901) md. Sudie Cox, two children: Madgeline and Arron Hopkins. Jasper Van Hopkins (d. Nov. 13, 1961) and is buried at Smith Chapel Cemetery.

VII) Dewey Wister Hopkins (b. May 4, 1903), seventh son, married Sibyl Smith, three children: Jeanette, Daryl and Dwight. Dewey Wister Hopkins died May 6, 1966 and is buried in the Booneville Cemetery.

VII) Arthur Dayton Hopkins (b. Mar. 23, 1905) md. Grace Breedlove, two children: Ovid Hopkins and Harold Hopkins. Arthur Dayton Hopkins died Feb. 24, 1985 and is buried in Tuscumbia Church Cemetery.

Martha Elizabeth Reynolds Smith Hopkins died May 20, 1923 and is buried at Smith Chapel Cemetery beside her first husband, Walker Smith.

Jasper Lee Hopkins married third, Maggie Lee Harris. Living most of his life in and around the Prentiss County area, Jasper Lee died Sep. 8, 1938 and is buried at Joel Cemetery in Tishomingo County by his first wife Mary Louartie Deaton Hopkins. *Submitted by great-granddaughter, Sandra Lewis Gray.*

HOPKINS, ARTHUR DAYTON, born Mar. 28, 1905 in Prentiss County and died Feb. 24, 1985. He married Nov. 17, 1929, to Grace Juanita Breedlove. She was born Nov. 24, 1912 in Prentiss County and died Jan. 14, 1991. They had two children, Ovid Dayton and William Harold Hopkins. Dayton was an honorable man – his word was his bond. His mother, Mattie Reynolds Smith Hopkins, instilled in all of her sons (Noonan, Van, Wister and Dayton) that they should be proud of their name (Hopkins) and do nothing to bring dishonor to it. Dayton was a successful farmer and dairy farmer most of his life. He was a member of the Masonic Lodge, as was his father (Jasper) and his son (Ovid). Grace Juanita lived about 10 miles east of Booneville. During the winter months, her father (Luther Breedlove) would saddle a mule named Nell for her to ride the muddy roads to school.

When she arrived at school, she would hang the stirrups over the saddle horn and send the mule home to show that she arrived without any mishap. Her

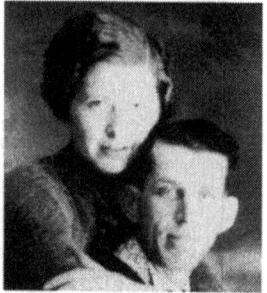
Arthur Dayton Hopkins and Juanita Breedlove Hopkins. Taken probably in 1930-1931.

parents (Luther and Liller Breedlove) would pick her up in the afternoon in a buggy. She and Syble Smith went to school together and were great basketball players for Hills Chapel School. Later in life, they married brothers, Arthur Dayton and Dewey Wister Hopkins, becoming sisters-in-law. After their marriage, Grace played semi-pro basketball for the Tupelo Red Wings of Tupelo, MS. In the early part of WWII, there was a shortage of artillery shells. She was employed at an ammunition factory in Benton Harbor, MI. She worked in a concrete cubicle for safety purposes. She was only supposed to work in this capacity for three months, however, due to manpower shortages, she worked there for nine months. After this time, her fingernails and toenails came off and her hair changed color, because her body had absorbed too much TNT. She and Dayton also worked the rest of the war years as first class machinist in the Mare Island Shipyards at Vallejo, CA. Their oldest son, Ovid Dayton Hopkins (b. May 26, 1932 in Prentiss County) married Betty Jo Holloway of Bragg City, MO, on Jun. 2, 1956 in Kennett, MO. They are retired and live in Memphis, TN. They have two daughters, Melodie Lynn and Candie Dee. Melodie Lynn Hopkins married Jeff Hartline and lives in Nashville, TN. They have three children: Megan Leigh, Wesley Benjamin and Logan. Candie Dee also lives in Nashville. Their second son, William Harold, was born Aug. 23, 1937 in Lepanto, AR. He was married Sep. 19, 1968, to Mary Alice Riddle. He works for the gas and water department and they live in Booneville, MS. They have one daughter, Lisa Dawn Hopkins. She married Walter Allen Davis and lives in Oxford, MS. *Submitted by Ovid Hopkins.*

HOPKINS, BENJAMIN FRANKLIN, born Apr. 4, 1814 in North Carolina, son of Hampton and Susannah Brown Hopkins. He married Sarah Jane Hyatt, a descendent of the Cherokee nation, born Oct. 26, 1812 in Kentucky.

They had 10 children: William A. (b. Aug. 28, 1832); Benjamin Franklin II (b. Apr. 9, 1836); John I.C. (b. Jul. 2, 1837); Mary Jane (b. Feb. 18, 1839); James A. (b. 1841); Margaret M. (b. 1843); Lucinda A. (b. Feb. 22, 1845); Rubin S. (b. 1847); Henery (b. 1849); Larkin C. (b. 1854).

Benjamin Franklin and Mary Eliza Campbell Hopkins

In Jerry Martin's book, *A Place Called Belmont*, we find that "Benjamin Hopkins would surely have to be a significant early settler. Ben Hopkins owned several hundred acres of land in and around present Belmont." It is said that Benjamin Franklin Hopkins donated land for the purpose of building the First Baptist Church of Belmont. Benjamin Franklin Hopkins died May 27, 1862 and Sarah J. "Sally" Hyatt Hopkins died Oct. 24, 1862. They are buried at Joel Cemetery in Dennis, Tishomingo County, MS.

The second son, Benjamin Franklin Hopkins II (b. Apr. 9, 1836) md. Mary Eliza Campbell (b. Dec. 28, 1840), daughter of William M. and Rachel Angeline Shook Campbell. During the War Between the States Benjamin Franklin Hopkins was slightly crippled from a frost bitten leg. He treated illness, fractured bones etc., until the patient could see a doctor. He made shoes for the Confederate soldiers and harnesses for their horses. When the home guard came for him the captain told him to gradually work his way to the back of the line and then he could go home; they needed the shoes and harnesses worse than they needed him.

They had nine children: Julia Adeline (b. May 22, 1861) md. James C. Tittle; William Benjamin (b. Aug. 28, 1864) md. Jerusha Flurry; Sharfonia Isabella Hopkins (b. 1866) md. James M. Davis; Alice B. Hopkins (b. 1869) md. J.L. Lindsey; Jasper Lee Hopkins (b. Jan. 30, 1872) md. first, Louarty Deaton and second, Martha Elizabeth Reynolds; Orlander Rubin Hopkins (b. Jul. 10, 1875) md. Bonnie Alma Harris; Ella Hopkins (b. Aug. 9, 1880) md. David M. Davis; Authur Clinton Hopkins (b. Jan. 11, 1883) md. Mary Lou Flurry; Sarah Angeline Hopkins (b. 1887) md. John W. Deaton.

Benjamin Franklin Hopkins II died Sep. 6, 1918 and Mary Eliza Campbell Hopkins died Dec. 28, 1840. They are buried in the Joel Cemetery in Tishomingo County. For more information on this family see related stories in this book, The Tishomingo County History Book (page 345) and also the Prentiss County History Book, Vol. I, page 302. *Submitted by Sandra Lewis Gray, great-great-great-granddaughter.*

HOPKINS, DEWEY WISTER, born May 4, 1903 to Jasper Lee and Martha Elizabeth Reynolds Hopkins of the Tuscumbia Community. He was the seventh son of Jasper Lee Hopkins and the third oldest of four sons born to Jasper and Mattie. They owned a large farm so the boys learned hard work and discipline at an early age.

During this era, formal education was attained from the Community school, which in this case was the old Providence School with the sessions scheduled to coincide with the farming seasons. At a fairly young age, Wister's family sent him to attend the Memphis Barber School to train for the profession which he pursued throughout his lifetime.

Dewey Wister and Sibyl Smith Hopkins, ca. 1930

He began his barber business in a small shop adjacent to Clint Walden's store, which was located on what is now Highway 30 East or East Church Street. He later built a shop building across from Walden's Sawmill in which he incorporated a bathroom containing a shower installation. Since many homes at that time did not have such, he had many customers that regularly used his facility, thereby creating a most unique source of income for a barber shop, while providing a needed community service. His place of business was known throughout the community as "Hops Barber Shop." He stayed at this location and continued to practice his profession until his death May 6, 1966.

It was through his profession that he first met Sibyl Smith, who came to his barber shop for a haircut. Thus was the beginning of a long and wonderful courtship and marriage.

Sibyl was born in 1912 to Allen and Eliza Pitts Smith, having three brothers: Hartwal, Cecil and Foy. The family farmed in the Hill's Chapel Community.

Sibyl attended Hill's Chapel Elementary, Tishomingo Elementary Boarding School and Thrasher High School. During her school years, she was an outstanding basketball player.

She and Wister were married Dec. 29, 1929. They had three children: Jeanette, Daryl and Dwight. Jeanette married James Wilson of Belmont and they reside in Florence, AL; Daryl, at the time of his death, was married to the former Mary Ann Lemons, of Corinth. Dwight died at the age of 18 months due to heart complications suffered from birth.

Sibyl was an expert seamstress who worked at Blue Bell Industries for many years and also did sewing for a number of people in the community. She possessed the skill of seeing a garment and thereafter making it, creating her own pattern of the required size. She also had a "green thumb" for growing gardens, flowers and shrubs. This was a hobby she actively pursued and at times was the envy of the neighborhood for her achievements. After retirement she moved to Birmingham and later to Anniston, AL, where she died in June 1987. Throughout their lifetime, the church and related activities always had an important role in their work and family activities. They were well-known throughout the entire community for their willingness to help others as needs became known, particularly for young people. Wister and Sibyl are buried at the Booneville Cemetery. *Submitted by Jeanette Hopkins Wilson.*

HORTON, SARAH B., born ca. 1800, probably in Chesterfield County, SC. She was the daughter of Hardaway "Hardy" Horton (b. ca. 1775, d. 1838) and Amy Darden (b. ca. 1775, d. 185_), who is said to have been a "blue blood." Amy Darden, born in Bute County, NC was the daughter of James Darden (b. ca. 1742 in Brunswick County, VA) and Sarah "Sallie" Bobbitt (b. ca. 1747 in Granville County, NC). Earlier Dardens spelled the name Derden, Durden and Dearden. Sallie Bobbitt was the daughter of John Bobbitt (b. ca. 1725 in Bertie County, NC) and Amy Alston (b. 1730 in Bertie County). Amy Alston was the daughter of Richard John Alston. The Alstons of North Carolina owned plantations and slaves and are descended from English royalty. Theirs is an accepted, though not proven royal line.

Hardy Horton was the son of Thomas Horton and Mary Bell. Mary Bell was the daughter of Thomas Bell, a justice of Bute County Court of Pleas and Quarter Sessions in 1765, 1766, 1767, 1770, 1771 and 1773.

Hardy Horton was a large land and slave owner. His will dated Sep. 19, 1838, was proven in court, April session 1839 in Anson County, NC. His will names his daughter, Sally Holley.

Sarah B. Horton married Julius A. Holley in 1817 in Anson County, NC.

Found in Anson County, NC deeds is the following: Feb. 9, 1808, pp. 100, 101 two deeds from Isaac Sheppard to Hardy Horton for 100 acres of land, both sides Lane's Creek, Wit: Luke Derden, William Sheppard. Jul. 9, 1814, Bk Q, pp. 73, 74. From Mark Derden by William Hammond, Sheriff, 200 acres on Carolina Branch of Lane's Creek, Hardy Horton, highest bidder. (A relatively small amount of money was owed Hardy Horton and Mark Derden was 23 years old and single so wonder if this has to do with estate settlement of James Derden. There is no deed to show how and when this land was acquired before 1814. The land description fits that in deed. registered Jan. 2, 1839, Deed. Bk 10, p. 23, by Julius Holley from Hardy Harton (Horton).

Julius and Sarah Horton Holley died in Prentiss County, MS and are buried in Holley Cemetery. *Submitted by Ann Sparks. Source: Maureen Holley Crow Papers.*

HOUSTON, GEORGE BRINKLEY, born Jan. 28, 1942, while his father, Capt. Fred. L. Houston, was helping construct Fort Crowder during WWII in Neosho, Jefferson County, MO. He obtained his name from two great-grandfathers, William Joseph "Joe" Brinkley and George "Bud" Houston.

His parents, Kathryn Rogers Houston and Fred. L. Houston were married on Oct. 6, 1940 by the Rev. Bynum Basden, pastor of the Osborne Creek Baptist Church, where they both were members. His dad was called to active service as a captain in the Corps of Engineers and was stationed at Fort Warren, Cheyenne, WY before and during the early WWII years.

George B. Houston Family. Front Row L-R: George Brinkley Houston, Kathryn Rogers Houston, Jeanne Bailey Houston. Back Row: Jeff Cole and wife Shelaine Houston Cole, Inman Jharel Houston, Deborah Houston Peterson and Paul Peterson

George attended Booneville Elementary, August 1948-June 1956; Booneville High School, August 1956-June 1960; Mississippi College, Clinton, MS, August 1964-May 1964, BA with Honors; University of Arkansas, 1964-65, Fayetteville, AR, graduate study in English Department and New York University, 1969, Continuing Education. Honors included Omicron Delta Kappa, Who's Who in American Colleges/Universities, Assistantship to University of Arkansas to teach English, Class President Sophomore, junior and senior years of college and one of the Outstanding Seniors at Mississippi College.

He was married to Iris Jeanne Bailey on Aug. 22, 1964, at Second Ponce de Leon Baptist Church, Atlanta, GA, by Dr. Dick Houston Hall, pastor, First Baptist Church, Decatur, GA. Jeanne was born Jul. 7, 1943 at Emory Hospital in Atlanta, Fulton County, GA.

Jeanne is the daughter of I.J. Bailey (b. Mar. 30, 1917 in Loganville, GA) and Esther Leonora Gaines (b. Sep. 3, 1921 in Decatur, DeKalb County, GA).

Esther is the daughter of Milton Alexander Gaines (b. May 24, 1883 in Forsyth County, GA) and Bessie Leonora Crow (b. Feb. 10, 1887 in Forsyth County, GA).

IJ's parents are Cicero Hamilton Bailey Sr. (b. Feb. 9, 1874 in Henry County, GA) and Melissa Hattie

Lou McDaniel (b. Aug. 10, 1880 in Rockdale County, GA).

George's employment has included Mississippi College, Dormitory Manager, August 1963-June 1964; University of Arkansas, Teaching Assistant, August 1964-June 1965; J.C. Penney Co., Management, June 1965-June 1988; George B. Houston Associates, Inc., June 1988-June 1992; Haverty's Fine Furniture, Sales Management, June 1992-June 1996; Castleberry Office Furnishings, Sales/Design, June 1996-June 1998 and November 1999 to present; Kemper USA, Inc., Marketing Manager-USA, June 1998-November 1999.

As a member of Briarlake Baptist Church, Decatur, GA, he has served as secretary of deacons, chairman of deacons, Sunday School teacher and chair of the Minister of Music Search Committee.

Their children are Sherry Shelaine Houston Cole, married to Jeffrey Scott Cole and parents of Kelly and Andrew; Deborah Lynn Houston Peterson, married to Paul David Peterson and parents of Matthew and child due in September 2000 and Inman Jharel Houston, engaged to be married to April Ellis on Aug. 5, 2000. Shelaine was born Sep. 18, 1966 in Tulsa, OK; Deborah was born Jun. 27,, 1968 in Shreveport, LA and Inman was born Sep. 1, 1974 in Atlanta, GA.

Jeanne and George have lived in Fayetteville and Little Rock, AR; Tulsa, OK; Shreveport, LA; Teaneck, NJ and Atlanta, GA.

HOWARD, ANNA BELEW, born Oct. 4, 1811 in Union County, SC thought to be the daughter of Jesse Belew, was married on Mar. 20, 1833, to David Howard, son of Thomas and Ursula "Nutty" (Bullington) Howard of Union County, SC. Anna was a member of the Bethlehem Baptist Church near Spartanburg, SC.

Pictured are sisters and brother, ca. 1910: Emely Nancy Ann (Nannie) (Howard) Fulghum, James Christopher (Kit) Howard and Ellender Elisbeth (Howard) Jennings

David died Oct. 24, 1854 in South Carolina, so in 1858, Anna along with her younger children, married daughter and son-in-law, moved to Old Tishomingo County, MS to live next door to brother, Reuben Belew (b. Feb. 9, 1810 in South Carolina, d. Nov. 7, 1879) and wife, Harriet Hale Spain, already living in the Blackland area. He served in Co. F, 23rd Mississippi Infantry, CSA. He was discharged after the death of his wife. He is described as six feet tall with fair complexion, blue eyes and gray hair.

Reuben and Harriet's children:

(1) Eliet Jane (b. 1836 South Carolina, d. 1885) married in 1855 in Mississippi to Thomas W. Ham.

(2) John Wesley (b. 1838 Tennessee, d. 1863) married Julia An Meddy.

(3) Sarah Ann (b. 1841 Tennessee) married in 1866 to James T. Ratliff.

(4) Catherine (b. 1843 South Carolina, d. 1884 Texas) married in 1866 in Mississippi to Reverend James Amasa Smith.

(5) Matilda D. (b. 1845 Tennessee, d. 1934 Texas) married William Axley Jones.

(6) Susan (b. 1847 Tennessee, d. before 1910) married Jud M.B. Hunt.

(7) William Taylor (b. 1848 Tennessee, d. 1912 Texas) married in 1874 to Elizabeth. He married second to Mary Stewart.

(8) Frances (b. 1850 Mississippi, d. 1877).

(9) Neil Brown (b. 1853 Mississippi, d. 1905 Texas).

(10) Marion Harry (b. 1857 Mississippi, d. 1929 Texas) married in 1889 to Sallie Eskridge.

(11) Missouri (b. 1859 Mississippi, d. 1879) married James M. Ratliff.

Many of these children settled in Wise County, TX and are buried in the Pleasant Grove #2 Cemetery in Decatur, TX.

The children of Anna Belew and David Howard, all born in Union County, South Carolina, were:

(1) Ellender Elisabeth (b. Feb. 9, 1834, d. Dec. 5, 1916) married on Nov. 24, 1857 in South Carolina to John Calvin Jennings. Both are buried in Gaston Cemetery.

(2) Joseph (b. Nov. 27, 1835, d. Oct. 21, 1856, South Carolina).

(3) Elliott Jane (b. Sep. 26, 1837, d. Apr. 3, 1876) married on Feb. 6, 1860 in Mississippi to Isca C. Grisham. Both are buried in Osborne Creek Church Cemetery.

(4) Jesse Thomas (b. Feb. 28, 1840, d. Jan. 28, 1862, Mississippi) died of measles while serving as Private in Co. K, 2nd Mississippi Infantry, CSA.

(5) Jason (b. Jan. 22, 1843, d. Jan. 21, 1862 Mississippi) died of pneumonia while serving as Private in Co. K, Mississippi Infantry, CSA.

(6) Emely Nancy Ann (b. Feb. 12, 1845, see Fulghum).

(7) James Christopher "Kit" (b. May 9, 1847, d. Jul. 6, 1921) married Nov. 12, 1891, to Dora Goodger. Both are buried in Deep Creek Cemetery in Wise County, TX.

(8) John Stephen (b. Oct. 13, 1850) lived in Louisiana and married Sep. 7, 1872 Hannah F. Wilkerson.

Another sister of Anna and Reuben that remained in Spartanburg, SC, was Eleanor (b. 1800, d. 1884), who married in 1837 to William Bullington. Their children were:

(1) Jesse Harrison (b. Apr. 27, 1838, d. 1915 South Carolina).

(2) Robert J. (b. ca. 1843, d. 1862) died while serving CSA.

Anna Belew Howard died Aug. 23, 1887 in Prentiss County, MS and is buried in an unmarked grave. *Submitted by Larry G. Gustafson Jr.*

HOWELL, CHARLES LEE "CHARLEY," born in Marion County, AL to Beverly Chester and Harriett Emaline Burlison Howell. The family moved to Tishomingo County, MS about 1890. They lived near Paden, it was there that Charley met and married his first wife, Lee Anna Owens, Dec. 22, 1892. Lee Anna was born Nov. 24, 1871. Charley and Lee Anna had the following children: Loura Effie Howell, born Jan. 30, 1894; John William Howell, born Feb. 4, 1895; Laura Harriett Howell, born Oct. 6, 1896; Oliver Boone Howell, born Mar. 27, 1898; Zelma Cordelia Howell, born Jan. 21, 1900; Lillian Ethel Howell, born Oct. 13, 1901 and Boliver Smith "Doc" Howell, born Aug. 2, 1903, (Doc was named after Dr. Boliver Smith who delivered him). Lee Anna died when Doc was only 2 months

Back row, L-R: Mittie Howell Ryan, Clarence Ryan, Edith Nix?, Charley Howell, Georgia Ann Belue Howell, unknown and unknown. Front row, L-R: Charles Nix

old. She is buried at Forked Oak Cemetery in Prentiss County, MS.

Charley married the second time to Georgia Ann Belue Mar. 24, 1904. Georgia Ann was born Feb. 14, 1875, daughter of Robert N. and Mary A. Dean Belue. Charley and Georgia Ann had the following children: an infant daughter who was born and died November 1904, Mittie Loudemie Howell, born Dec. 30, 1905; Alice Melverdie Howell, born Oct. 8, 1907; Kittie Mae Howell, born Jan. 4, 1910; Thomas Houston Howell, born Dec. 3, 1911; Aaron Clay "Pete" Howell, born May 28, 1914 and Marion Ray Howell, born May 28, 1914.

Charley Lee was a farmer. He farmed in Tishomingo County, but was living in Prentiss County by 1936 as indicated by his voter certificate dated June 1936. He died in Prentiss County, MS May 9, 1944 and is buried at Gaston Cemetery in Prentiss County, MS. Georgia Ann died Oct. 18, 1959 and is buried at Gaston also.

Loura Effie Howell died Jul. 1, 1908 and is buried at Forked Oak Cemetery. John William Howell married Annie Jackson Smith Aug. 26, 1914. He died Feb. 23, 1971 and is buried at Oak Grove Cemetery at Iuka, MS.

Laura Harriett Howell married James Abraham Miller Dec. 3, 1922, she died Feb. 11, 1976 and is buried at Oak Hill Cemetery in Quitman, GA.

Oliver Boone Howell married Nora Tilly; he died Dec. 1, 1973 and is buried at Oak Grove Cemetery in Iuka, MS.

Zelma Cordelia Howell married Herbert A. Nix; she died Jun. 3, 1992 and is buried at Gaston Cemetery.

Lillian Ethel Howell married James Russell Nichols Dec. 21, 1919; she died Dec. 5, 1969 and is buried at East Prentiss Cemetery in Prentiss County, MS.

Boliver Smith Howell married Ovia Olivia Darwin Nov. 5, 1935; he died Apr. 1, 1986 and is buried at Gaston Cemetery in Prentiss County, MS.

Mittie Loudenue Howell married Clarence Ryan; she died Dec. 4, 1994 and is buried at Oaklawn Memorial Park, Booneville, MS.

Alice Melverdie Howell married Leonard Harris Jun. 29, 1929; she died Feb. 8, 1996 and is buried in the Booneville Cemetery, Booneville, MS.

Kithe Mae Howell married William Elmer "Happy" Vanstory, Dec. 22, 1934; she died Dec. 10, 1987 and is buried in the Gaston Cemetery.

Aaron Clay Howell married Lois Lovelace; he died in 1990 and he is buried at Oaklawn Memorial Park in Booneville, MS.

Marion Ray Howell married Ruby Pearl Vanstory Oct. 23, 1933; he died Apr. 10, 1978 and is buried at Oak Lawn Memorial Park in Booneville, MS.

HUDDLESTON, ROBERT GRANVILLE, descendant of Robert Huddleston of Amelia County, VA. The Huddlestons moved to North Mississippi around 1800. Robert's grandson, John B. Huddleston, was a preacher in Tippah County. According to historical records, John B. preached at a church outside of Ripley and held the first service there following the Civil War. John B.'s son, John David Huddleston (b. 1844, d. 1926), was a Civil War veteran and a Primitive Baptist preacher. He helped organize Little Flock Church in Prentiss County over one hundred years ago. John David was married twice and had a total of 12 children. His first wife, Nancy Norton, died in childbirth. Together they had four children: Henderson, Lafayette, Mary and Wiley. John David and his second wife, Josephine Elizabeth Grammar, had eight children: Lee, Cornelius, Ora, Sally, Abner Dalton, Walter, David Arthur and Minnie.

One of John David's sons, Abner Dalton Huddleston (b. 1885, d. 1937), was a Prentiss County farmer, who married Maggie Catherine Jordan (b. 1886, d. 1952). They had three children: Robert

Granville (b. 1913, d. 1998), Luther Grafton (b. 1916, d. 1999) and Ona Mae (b. 1918).

Granville and Edith Huddleston (seated) and their children. Standing from left: Larry Huddleston, Charlotte Deaton, Debbie Huddleston, Norma Church and Gary Huddleston.

Granville married Edith Melton on Jun. 1, 1935, at the Prentiss County Courthouse. Abner gave Granville 25 cents so he and his bride could see a movie and have a bag of popcorn after the wedding ceremony. Edith and Granville lived in Prentiss County for the first few years of their marriage. Granville farmed and cut wood. Near the beginning of WWII, Edith and Granville moved to Memphis, TN where Granville worked for Fisher Aircraft, building gunner turrets on bombers. In 1946, they returned to Prentiss County where Granville built his first house. Granville was a carpenter. For several years, he worked for S&J Construction and for Armstrong Construction, but he was best known for the many fine houses he built in North Mississippi. Even after his "retirement" Granville continued to do what he loved best—carpenter work. He built cabinets, beautiful pieces of furniture, additions to houses and did some remodeling of houses. He worked into his 80s until cancer finally slowed him down. Before his death in May 1998, Granville described himself, "I'm a rich man. True riches have nothing to do with material wealth and everything to do with family and friends." Edith still lives in that first house Granville built.

Terry Huddleston (Mar. 2, 1952-Feb. 29, 1984), son of Granville and Edith Huddleston.

Granville and Edith had six children. Their oldest child, Norma, married F.C. Church. They have three daughters: Wanda, Teresa and Denise. They live in Southaven, MS. F.C. is presently retired. Norma works for Howe K. Sipes Co. in Memphis, TN and is a part-time interior decorator.

Charlotte Huddleston married Thomas Deaton. They live in the Thrasher Community where Thomas is a farmer and Charlotte is an elementary schoolteacher. They have two children, Sherry and Bobby.

Larry Huddleston is married to Diane Sappington. Larry works for S&J Construction and Diane works for Booneville City Schools. They had four sons: Glen, Michael, Scot and Kelly (b. 1972, d. 1989).

Gary Huddleston is married to Donna Crow. Gary owns Huddleston Cabinets and is a lay minister. He is an Army veteran (1966-1968). Gary's wife Donna works for Farmers and Merchants Bank. They have two daughters: Lori and Laci.

Terry Huddleston (b. 1952, d. 1984) was married to Debra Henderson. Terry attended Blue Mountain College. He was a lay preacher and was an assistant manager at J.C. Penney in Tupelo. Terry and Debra had three children: Brian, Kevin and Sharon.

Debbie Huddleston attended Blue Mountain College, Cameron University in Oklahoma and the University of Denver. She is a mental health therapist and works with children in Bainbridge, GA. She is an Army veteran (1986-1992) and served in the Gulf War. *Submitted by Edith Huddleston.*

HUGHES, SAMUEL WATSON, descendent of Orlando Hughes was born 1703 in Glamorgan Wales Great Britain and came to America around 1700, settling in Powhatan County, VA. They established a settlement known as Hughes Creek Plantation. Orlando's descendants spread throughout the US. The branch from his son Josiah had settled in Bedford County, TN by 1820 and Samuel would have been 3 years old at this time.

The Alf Hughes Family. Standing back row, L-R: Laura, Maud. Front row, L-R: Claude, Alf, Jane (with Elbert in lap) and Jessie

Samuel (b. 1817, d. 1900) md. Rebecca Cheeves (b. 1822, d. 1900) and moved to Tishomingo County, MS in what is now the Pisgah Community of Prentiss County. Land records show that Samuel purchased a tract of land from agents representing ShiRaNah of the Chickasaw tribe of Indians in 1852.

Samuel and Rebecca were the parents of Mary Elizabeth, Nancy A., William R., Lucinda C., Samuel W. Jr., John T., Josiah, George W., James E., Charlie, Alfred L. and Rebecca Jane. Samuel and Rebecca spent the rest of their lives in Prentiss County and they and some of their children are buried in the Pisgah Methodist Church Cemetery.

Their son, Alfred Lambert Hughes (b. 1859, d. 1936) md. Fannie Jane Blagg (b. 1861, d. 1934) and they moved to Alcorn County in the Kossuth area. They were the parents of Clayton (d. age 4), Annie (Walker), Florence (Melvin), Laura (Mills), Maud (Lambert), Claude, Jessie (Morris) and George Elbert. All of the daughters married and lived most of their lives in the Corinth area.

Both Claude and George attended Mississippi Agricultural College (Mississippi State University). Claude served in WWI and then settled in Russellville, AR where he was mayor at the time of his death in 1968. He had one son, Claude Allen Hughes Jr.

Alfred and Fannie Jane Hughes are buried in the Hinkle Creek Cemetery in Kossuth, MS.

George Elbert (b. 1902, d. 1975) md. Minnie Mae Smith (b. 1906, d. 1994) from West Point, MS. They lived in Monroe, LA for two years before returning to Kossuth where they lived until Alfred's death. They settled in Columbus, MS where George started a paint contracting business and remained there until his death. Their children are as follows:

Jane Hughes Pittman (b. 1931), a retired school teacher who lives in Columbus, MS; Garry Van Hughes (b. 1935), owner of Hughes Management Companies in Louisville, MS; George Hal Hughes (b. 1938), Dean of Students at Northeast Mississippi Community College in Booneville, MS and Frances Hughes Thompson (b. 1941), manager of the Educational Federal Credit Union, Columbus, MS. *Submitted by Jane Pittman and Hal Hughes.*

HUMPHREY, THOMAS S. AND ELIZABETH CROCKETT, Thomas Stewart Humphrey was born in 1829 in Georgia, the oldest son of William Humphrey from North Carolina. Thomas' mother had died before 1850 and William Humphrey had remarried. The family relocated to Mississippi about 1845 and settled in the southern part of Old Tishomingo. Thomas grew up farming with his father and brothers on their home farm near Blackland, MS.

Elizabeth Caroline Crockett, called Caroline, had been born Apr. 30, 1833 in Franklin (later Coffee) County, TN the daughter of William and Elizabeth Cunnyngham Crockett and had moved to southern Tishomingo County, MS when 13 years old. The family home and large farm were west of Booneville.

The couple married on May 30, 1850 in the Crockett home. Thomas was 21 years old and stood five foot seven inches tall with light colored hair and blue eyes. Caroline was 17, petite with dark hair and eyes. They lived their first year of marriage in Thomas' father's home.

The couple's children were Mary Elizabeth, born in 1851; Louisa Ona Angeline "Onie," born in 1852; John Thompson Humphrey, born in 1854; Modena Emily Adeline "Addie," born in 1856; Virginia Caroline "Callie," born in 1859 and William "Bud" Johnson Humphrey, born in 1861.

By 1860 the family had relocated several miles west into Tippah County and it was here that the opening months of the Civil War found them. On Jan. 26, 1863, Thomas enlisted in Booneville as a private in Captain Ham's Cavalry unit, later known as Companies B and C of the Eleventh Mississippi Cavalry. Thomas re-enlisted in Richmond, VA, for a second year. The spring of 1864 found Thomas back in north Mississippi. On May 5 he re-enlisted at Tupelo for the duration of the war and was promoted to 3rd corporal.

At the war's conclusion, Thomas' unit was surrendered in Citronella, AL. Thomas was paroled 12 days later in Columbus, MS and made the journey of 110 miles back to his family.

James Franklin Humphrey was born Dec. 29, 1864. Sons, Tobe Tandy and Claude Thomas Humphrey, followed in 1868 and 1871, respectively.

The family's oldest daughter, Mary Elizabeth, married in 1866 to Henry Scally, a Mississippi native and young veteran of the war. Mary was 15-1/2 years of age with curly blonde hair. In 1868, Onie married William Pollard. Onie, with dark eyes and long dark hair, was just shy of her 16th birthday. Addie married Martin Kitchens in 1875 and John married Lula Ross in 1880. In 1884, Callie, a schoolteacher, married Dr. George Scally. Callie was 25 and Dr. Scally was 29.

In 1885 Caroline Humphrey's father, William Crockett, deeded his eastern 160 acres and the Crockett home to Thomas Humphrey. Crockett lived with the Humphreys until his death in 1890. Caroline and Thomas' home was a few miles east of Jumpertown on the Ripley-Booneville Road. By this time, grandchildren were being added to the family. Thomas continued to farm and was appointed justice of the peace. He came to be referred to as "Judge Humphrey."

The next few years were harsh with a daughter-in-law and three of the Humphreys' daughters dying in less than five years: John's wife Lula in 1887; Callie in 1888 of consumption; Onie of tuberculosis in 1890 and Addie in 1891. The Humphreys took Callie's children into their home for several years until Dr. Scally remarried in 1895. Gertrude and Alma Scally formed close, lifelong friendships with Uncles Tobe and Claude Humphrey.

The Humphreys' son, James, married Nettie Huggins in 1891; Tobe married Katie Williams in 1899 and Claude married Ruth Rowland in 1917.

About 1887 Judge and Caroline Humphrey moved their home to Wenasoga in northern Alcorn County near Martin Kitchens and Mary and Henry Scally. Mary cared for her parents and was particu-

143

larly devoted to her father. The Humphreys also had a farm hand and a hired girl to help out.

On Oct. 11, 1900, Judge Humphrey died of cancer at the age of 71. His body was buried in the Wenasoga Cemetery beside the Holly Baptist Church and only a short distance from the Humphreys' home. A tall monument was erected to his honor and was inscribed: "A devoted husband and indulgent father."

Caroline survived Thomas by five years, dying on Jul. 1, 1905, at 72 years of age. Her body was buried beside Thomas'. This corner of the cemetery came to be a family plot with a number of the Humphrey children and grandchildren eventually buried there. *Submitted by Douglas R. Scally.*

HURST, DR. JOSEPH LEWIS "JOE" and his wife, Sarah Wallace Hurst were married on Dec. 10, 1949, at the Oxford University Methodist Church in Oxford, MS. Both were students at the University of Mississippi. Dr. Hurst graduated from the University of Mississippi Medical School and completed his studies at the University of Tennessee Medical School in Memphis in December 1952. His internship was completed at Baptist Hospital in Memphis in December 1953. Dr. Hurst received his BS degree in biology and chemistry from the University of Southern Mississippi, where he was a member of the honorary biology fraternity, Alpha Epsilon Delta. At the University of Tennessee, he was a member of the honorary medical fraternity, Phi Chi. Sarah graduated from the University of Mississippi School of Pharmacy and while in Memphis worked at Walgreen's Pharmacy. Sarah and Joe moved to Booneville, MS in January 1954 where Dr. Hurst established his medical practice, becoming a partner with Dr. Paul Ellzey. Later, Dr. Webster Cleveland joined the Medical Clinic, as well as Dr. Samuel Galloway. Sarah worked at Duckworth Drug Co. as a pharmacist.

Sarah and Joe had four children, three of whom survived. Thomas Terry Hurst II was born in 1954, Louann Olivia in 1957 and James Joseph in 1959. The Hursts have been faithful members of the First United Methodist Church since moving to Booneville, Sarah and Joe serving on the administrative board, as teachers and in various other positions. They were also active in civic and community projects, Sarah being a member of the Pilot Club, the Garden Club, the Woman's Club and the Natchez Trace Chapter of the DAR. Joe was active in the Boy Scouts and the Jaycees.

Sarah Wallace and Joseph Lewis Hurst on their wedding day, Dec. 10, 1949.

Sarah worked until Louann was born, then devoted herself to her children and her church. All three children earned degrees from the University of Mississippi. Dr. Hurst retired after 39 years of medical practice in 1993. During that time, he had treated thousands of patients and was a credit to his community. The Medical Clinic was operated with the philosophy of serving patients and the Medical Clinic physicians never refused to see a sick patient based on his ability to pay. His retirement was short lived, however, as he started part-time work with the Mississippi State Department of Health within a month of his retirement. His most rewarding hobbies have been growing and arranging beautiful roses, which he shares with his family and friends and fishing. In 1972 he caught a 26.5-pound striped bass, for which he was awarded the 1972 Tennessee Record.

Joseph was born to Thomas Jesse Hurst (b. 1883, d. 1963) and Belle Terry Hurst (b. 1893, d. 1977) on Apr. 14, 1925 in Hattiesburg, MS. Thomas Jesse's father, John Bonaparte Hurst, hailed from Ireland and settled in Florida, where he married Priscilla Ray Hurst. Belle's father, Lewis Saxon Terry, was a Baptist minister from a long-standing Mississippi family. Thomas Jesse worked 50 years for the Illinois Central Railroad.

Sarah was born to Thomas Randolph Wallace and Lizzie Olive Wallace in Savannah, TN on Sep. 27, 1928. The Olives and Wallaces were long-standing Tennessee and Alabama settlers. Their ancestor, James Olive, hailed from England, settled in North Carolina and fought in the Revolutionary War. Thomas Randolph worked for the US Postal Service for 50 years.

Sarah and Joe have been blessed with loving children, daughters and son-in-law and beautiful grandchildren. Terry married Tierney Horner Collier in 1986 and blessed the family with the birth of Julie Kate in 1987 and Thomas Andrew in 1989. Terry is also the stepfather of Don Collier, born in 1982. James married Marianne Andrews Austin in 1996 and blessed the family with the birth of Joseph Andrews in 1998. James is also the stepfather of JoAnna Austin, born in 1990. Louann married Thomas Joseph McDonald II in 1998.

Dr. Hurst served his country during WWII with the 107th Cavalry, Troop C of the US Armed Forces. He saw active duty in the European Theater for two years, for which he has always felt an enduring sense of pride. *Submitted by Dr. and Mrs. Joseph L. Hurst.*

ISBELL-MOORE, Walter Clarence Isbell, born at New Site, MS Dec. 16, 1889, was a descendant of Elijah Wroten (b. Jan. 1, 1807, d. Oct. 8, 1887), who was born in South Carolina and his second wife, Sarah Ammons (b. Feb. 14, 1814, d. Mar. 15, 1892), born in Tennessee. According to the story handed down, Elijah Wroten's forefather's name was Rowden (or similar spelling) and was a relative of the Queen of England. The Queen sent him to the Colonies during the Revolutionary War to determine the war situation. Arriving in America, he learned why the Colonies were fighting, turned traitor and helped the Colonies fight the British army. The Queen heard of his involvement and put out a decree for his beheading. At this time he changed his name to Wroten. Elijah had a twin brother, Elisha. Mary Jane Wroten (b. 1846, d. 1940), daughter of Elijah and Sarah Wroten, married Thomas Jefferson Johnson, born 1844 in Tishomingo County, MS, the son of Samuel Jefferson Johnson (b. 1817, d. 1861), born in Tennessee and Nancy Carroll (maybe Jane Carroll) (b. 1823, d. 1901), born in North Carolina. Thomas and Mary Jane Johnson's children were: Luther D., Elijah D., William L., Frank, George, Cleveland, Lula, Mattie Bell, Josie Bell, Johnella and Sarah Jane (Jenny or Sally). Sarah Jane "Jenny" married George Isbell.

Clarence and Ester Isbell

At age 17, Thomas Jefferson Johnson joined Hardee's Regiment, Army of Tennessee and served under General Bragg in the battles of Stone River, Chickamauga, Missionary Ridge and Lookout Mountain. Thomas J. Johnson and Mary Jane are buried in the Siloam Cemetery near New Site.

Sarah Jane "Jenny" Johnson (b. 1868, d. 1942), daughter of Thomas Jefferson Johnson and Mary Jane, was born in Tishomingo County and married George Walter Isbell (b. Feb. 18, 1857, d. Oct. 5, 1937), who was born in Alabama. It is believed that he had a sister named Betty and maybe two brothers, but he was orphaned at a young age. George Isbell said that five Isbell brothers left Ireland and emigrated to America, one settling in Alabama, one in Tennessee, one in Texas; it is not known where the other two settled.

The children of George and Jenny Isbell were Walter Clarence (b. 1889, d. 1956) (wife Esther May), Charles Edgar (b. 1891, d. 1935) (wife Jean), Lena Bell (b. 1893, d. 1973) (husband Sam Stockton), Leonard Forrest (b. 1895, d. 1962) (wife Lena Mae), Lula Estell (b. 1898) (married Eddie Beard) and Eva May (b. 1901) (married Frank Woodruff). George Isbell was married prior to his marriage to Jenny Johnson and had a son named Bob who lived in the Vina, AL area. George and Jenny Isbell, Clarence, Lula and Eddie Beard, Forrest and Lena Mae Isbell are buried in the Siloam Cemetery near Esther May Moore (b. Nov. 10, 1901) is a direct descendant of Joseph Gallmann, born ca. 1570-1580 in Abermettminstetten, Switzerland.

Joseph married Kungolt Gallmann before 1602. Their child, Keeinhein Gallman (b. 1602/3, d. 1676), married Anna Ringger (b. 1634, d. 1684). Their child, Hans (Jacob) (b. 1672, d. 1725) married Elizabeth Dubs (b. 1671, d. 1769). Their child, Jacob Gallmann, born ca. 1672 in Switzerland and died October 1738 in Saxe-Gotha, SC, married Jerena StaheIt (b. Oct. 10, 1696) in Switzerland. She died before 1734. Jacob and six of his children arrived in South Carolina Feb. 7, 1734. Jacob and Jerena's children: Henry Gallmann (b. 1705, d. before Feb. 19, 1768) married first wife (unknown), second wife Elizabeth Geiger (b. 1740, d. 1803). Their child, John Conrad, born ca. 1747 and died 1829 in Henry County, GA, married Susannah (?) and she died Jun. 10, 1832 in Henry County, GA. John Gallman served in the Revolutionary. He was a sergeant in the state militia before and after the fall of Charleston, SC (see *South Carolina Patriots in the Revolution* by Moss, page 340: Galdman, Curry....He served as a sergeant in the militia and supplied provision before and after the fall of Charleston A. A. 262: 4620.) Their child: John Conrad Jr. (b. ca. 1773 in South Carolina, d. 1833 in Henry County, GA) married a lady named Elizabeth who died Dec. 27, 1833 in Henry County. Their child Susannah Catherine Gallman, (b. Jul. 10, 1803 in South Carolina, buried in Quercus Grove Cemetery in Switzerland County, IN) married Perley Ford Sep. 17, 1925 in Lawrence County, MS. Perley (b. Feb. 23, 1793, Culpepper, VA, d. September 1769, buried in Lawrence Grove Cemetery, near Eva, AL) won land in the Georgia 1832 Gold Land Lottery which gave special consideration to veterans. Perley and Susannah's children were Joseph (b. 1826), Jessie S. (b. 1827), John G. (b. 1829), Sarah Ann (b. 1831, Henry County, GA), George W. (b. 1833), Susan K. (b. 1835), Thomas C. (b. 1838), David D. (b. 1841) and William F. (b. 1843). Perley and Susannah Ford's daughter, Sarah Ann, was educated to be an English teacher at a university he planned to open at Stilesborough, GA, but she eloped with Cicero "Bill" Denson. They were married Mar. 31, 1848 in a cotton field in Randolph County, GA and her father, Perley Ford, disinherited her. After leaving Georgia, they bought land and settled in northern Alabama where a gold mine was found on their property (documented). William Cicero Denson was a 2nd lieutenant in the 12th Alabama Cavalry, CSA. Their journey which started in Georgia, ended at New Site, MS on Christmas eve 1872. William Denson was the postmaster at New Site from 1879 to 1890. Sarah Ann was a school teacher. Their children were A.P. William (b. 1849, d. ?), John H. (b. 1950, d. 1873), James W. (b. 1853, d. 1923), Frances (b. October 1855, d. November 1855), Thomas C. (b. 1857, d. 1935), Clayburne S. (b. 1859, d. 1950), Ezra (b. 1861, d. ?), George M. (b. 1866, d. 1946), Martha E. (b. May 18, 1869, d. Nov. 29, 1869), Rebecca D. (b. 1870, d. 1962), Sarah Genetta Catherine "Nettie" (b. Jun. 5, 1873, d. Oct. 19, 1966) and infant (b. Sep. 27, 1875).

William C. and Sarah Ann Ford Denson are buried in Little Brown Cemetery near New Site, MS.

Esther May Moore Isbell is also a descendant

of Richard Moore, who settled in Prince George County, VA in 1704. He married Catherine Norwood, had seven children and died in 1726. John Moore, son of Richard, was born in Prince George County, VA but moved to Sumter County, SC. He was married to Tabitha Pace and died in Northhampton County, NC in 1753. Isharn Moore, son of John Moore, was born in Northhampton County and died in Sumter County, SC in 1803. He was married to Ann Singleton. Richard Moore, son of Isham Moore, married Mary Wheeler. He was born in Northhampton County and died in Sumter County in 1792. James Moore, son of Richard Moore, was born in North Carolina in 1785 and moved to Sumter, SC. He married a Miss Thornton and they had one child. Later he married Matilda Thornton and he died in Lawrence County, TN in 1855. William Moore, son of James Moore, born in South Carolina, moved to Tishomingo County and died in 1870. He was married to Sarah Thornton. Hiram Moore, son of William Moore, was born in 1825 in Lawrence County, TN and moved to Tishomingo County, MS. He married Lucinda J. Martin and they had two children, Marion (b. 1856, d. 1909) and Levi Jackson "Jack" Moore (b. 1861, d. 1938). Hiram James fought in the Civil War and died in 1869. Hiram and his wife Lucinda are buried in the Siloam Cemetery near New Site, MS.

Levi Jackson "Jack" Moore, son of Hiram James Moore and Sarah Genetta "Nettie" Catherine Denson were married Dec. 17, 1891. Jack inherited a farm at New Site where they lived their entire lives. On their wedding night, their friends went to their home for a shivaree. Before their friends arrived, Jack had strung wire around the house near the ground. When the party goers arrived and started tripping over the wire, they thought that they had been shot as Jack was inside the house shooting his gun over their heads. After the chaos, they took down the beds and danced. Jack and Nettie owned a store at New Site; she was the postmistress and they farmed. Their children were Levi (b. 1892, d. 1977) married Emma, George W. (b. 1896, d. 1969) married Ruby, Minnie Bell (b. 1899, d. 1968) married Walter Green, Esther May (b. 1901) married Clarence Isbell, Olive (b. 1904, d. 1919), Linwood (b. 1906, d. 1985) married Grace, Raymond (b. 1908, d. 1984) married Opal, Lexie (b. 1911, d. 1999) married Leonard Kennedy and an infant that died.

Esther Mae, daughter of Jack and Nettie, was living with her sister Minnie Bell in Booneville during WWI while attending Booneville High School, when influenza struck her family at New Site. She returned home and took care of her entire family for 29 days without any help.

Clarence Isbell hauled crossties with mules and wagon, that helped build the Illinois Central Railroad through northeast Mississippi.

Walter Clarence Isbell, a WWI veteran having served in Europe and Esther Mae Moore, married Aug. 8, 1920 at the home of the bride's parents with Rev. Lovell performing the ceremony. They were farmers and lived at New Site attending Siloam Methodist Church. Clarence Isbell was a Mason.

The children of Walter Clarence and Esther Mae Moore Isbell were (1) Betra Mae Helen (b. May 21, 1921) married Leonard Nichols (deceased). Their children were (a) Geneva Ann (b. Jun. 12, 1939) married Kenneth Warren who served overseas in the Armed Forces. Ann was reared by her loving maternal grandparents, Clarence and Esther Isbell.

Their children: Elizabeth Ann (b. Mar. 31, 1963) and Barbara Lane (b. Feb. 5, 1966). (b) Denella Fay (b. and d. Jun. 8, 1941, buried at Lilbourn, MO). Helen and Leonard are buried in Siloam Cemetery near New Site, MS.

(2) Sarah Faydell (b. Feb. 20, 1923) married Robert W. "Bob" Wagganer during WWII while both were in the Armed Forces. Robert served overseas in the Armed Forces. Robert was on orders to go to the South Pacific when the war ended. Their children are (A.) Betty Faye (b. Mar. 30, 1946) married Roy Robbins. Their children

(a.) Robert P. Robbins (b. Jun. 11, 1971) married Chrissie Schneiders; their child is Breanna Marie (b. Nov. 15, 1998). (b.) Michelle Ann Robbins (b. Jun. 27, 1973).

(B.) Ronald William (b. Nov. 23, 1951) first married Anna Hauer Fowler deceased. Their child: Grant William (b. Oct. 31, 1978) married Tammi Goodman. No children. Ronald second married Redonna Reynolds. No children. (C.) Stanley Robert (b. Nov. 10, 1956) is a Shriner.

(3) Clarence Kathleen (b. Feb. 12, 1926, d. Apr. 23, 1999) married Jack McDonald (deceased) who served overseas during WWII. Their children:

(A.) Gregory (b. Dec. 21, 1946) first married Dorothy Crawford; their child, Bry-Ann (b. Nov. 7, 1969); second marriage to Patsy Jones, no children. (B.) Clifford (b. Feb. 23, 1948) married June Carsberg, no children. (C.) Darah Fay (b. Apr. 21, 1956) married Bruce Jernigan; their children: Jennifer (b. Nov. 14, 1984) and Jeffrey (b. Dec. 29, 1990). (D.) Gene (b. May 10, 1960) married Theresa Mastri, no children. Jack grew up in Michigan but lived nearly all his life in Miami, FL. Jack and Kathleen are buried in Siloam Cemetery.

4. Dorothy Maxie (b. Dec. 22, 1928) married Robert "Rob" Martin (deceased) who served overseas in the Armed Forces during WWII. Their children: (A.) Jimmie (b. Jan. 26, 1948) a Marine who served in the jungles of Vietnam during the Vietnam War, first married Eva Lewis; their child, Rodney (born Apr. 29, 1971) married Marilyn Young; no children. (2) second married Jenny Henson; their child, David (b. Dec. 28, 1978). (B.) Nancy (b. May 19, 1950) married Jerry Slack; their children: (a.) Laura (b. Mar. 22, 1969) married Greg Burns; no children. (b.) Rusty (b. Dec. 29, 1971) married Jennifer Echols; their children: William (b. Dec. 14, 1995) and Benjamin (b. Jun. 23, 1998). (C.) Kenneth (b. Jan. 23, 1953) married Lucy Holley; their children: Tracey (b. Sep. 12, 1973), Robert (b. Apr. 14, 1978) and Rebecca (b. Jan. 30, 1983). (D) Bruce (b. Sep. 11, 1959) married Anntionette Hopkins; their children, Joshua (b. Jun. 16, 1988) and Danielle (b. Feb. 6, 1998). (E.) Jeffery (b. Jul. 31, 1964) married Rebecca Manness; their children, Samuel (b. Jun. 26, 1994) and Callie (b. Jan. 5, 1997). (F.) Wade (b. Sep. 24, 1966) married Rhonda Landston; their child, Cole (b. Oct. 17, 1996). Rob was buried in Siloam Cemetery at New Site.

(5.) Webber Clemmet (b. Mar. 14, 1932) married Melba Kennedy; no children. Webber served overseas in the Armed Forces during the Korean War.

(6.) Nellie Sue (b. Sep. 1, 1935) married Dr. Fred Rhoads; their children:

(A.) Deborah (b. Jan. 17, 1955) married Colonel Stanley Yarbrough, USAF; their children: a. Shannon Michelle (b. Mar. 21, 1978) and Thomas Frederick (b. Jan. 2, 1988).

(B.) Timothy (b. May 30, 1960) married Robbie Ann Yeomans; their children: a. Joshua Timothy (b. Sep. 25, 1991), Caleb Frederick (b. Apr. 15, 1994) and Anna Caitlin (b. Aug. 6, 1996).

(7.) Nettie Jane (b. May 8, 1939) married Edgar Weaver Martin, who served overseas in the Armed Forces. Their children: a. Thomas Edgar (b. May 18, 1965) married Elizabeth Napier; no children. b. Paul Weaver (b. Mar. 29, 1967). c. Stephan David (b. Jul. 17, 1974).

Clarence and Esther Isbell's descendants are engaged in the following occupations: university professor, minister, barber, teachers, registered nurses, radio engineer, musician, chemist, administrators, office managers, custom farmers, welders, social worker, and many more too numerous to mention. *By Faydell Isbell Wagganer, with contributions by my brother, sisters and their families and Robert W. Ford, author of Dr. John Perley Ford*

JANEWAY, RAYMOND ALEXANDER AND RAYE BERNICE BONDS,

Raymond was born in 1921, seventh of 10 children in Strawberry Plains, TN to Dudley Alexander Janeway and Lockie Denton Janeway. Dudley worked for the railroad and died when Raymond was 8 years old. Lockie's great grandmother was a full blood Cherokee married to an Army officer of the Confederacy. She was formerly married to a James Keeler and they had a daughter, Pearl, who married Lawrence Shetterly. Pearl still lives in Kingsport, TN. Lawrence worked for Owens-Corning. They had a son, Lynn and a daughter, Betty in Kingsport. They had a son, James Jr. whose wife was Christine. They had a son and they still live in the Strawberry Plains area. Dudley had been previously married and had four daughters. Ruth married Dixon Watson. They had two sons who were majors in the First Army in WWII. Vergie married Clergy Harmon, who was a building contractor. They had two sons, Harold and Richard and two daughters, Dorothy and Aldean. Carrie married Johnny Pilger and they lived in the Chicago area, children unknown. Lucy married a Shetterly, brother to Lawrence and they lived in Virginia in the DC area. He worked for the government. To the Dudley/Lockie union was born Raymond, then Edith who married Ray Sharp. Ray died but Edith still lives in Kingsport. Ray worked for Mead Paper Co. They had two daughters, Patsy and Carolyn. Lockie and Dudley's third son was Y. J., known as "Cotton," who died recently near Strawberry Plains. His wife's name is unknown to the writer, but they are believed to have had two sons.

Dudley and Lockie's youngest son, Dixon married and had two daughters.

They live in the Strawberry Plains area and are retired.

Raymond Janeway and Bernice Bonds (b. Oct. 29, 1924) were married Nov. 3, 1943 in Bound Brook, NJ. During WWII, Raymond was working for Bakelite at Oak Ridge, TN where "The Bomb" was being processed. The company sent him to Bound Brook to another plant for training. Bernice was working at Ford Motor Co. in Memphis making piston pins for Liberator Bombers. To them was born Trechia Olivia in Jefferson City, TN in 1945. Olivia married Jimmy Miller, son of Raymond and Sara Copeland Miller and to them was born Trechia Janeway Miller. With a degree in English from Ole Miss, Trechia opted for the profession of a dental hygienist. She was a cheerleader and dancer in high school and college. Their son, Michael Ray, a mechanical engineer, married Ellen Westmoreland, a paralegal. To them was born Anna Morgan and Abby Kate, who have seven living grandmothers. Ellen's parents are Johnny and Laverne Westmoreland of Potts Camp, MS.

Gale (b. Feb. 10, 1947) retired after 30 years from Northeast Mississippi Community College as secretary to the Vocational Department. Until her retirement she was the only secretary that department had had. She also served a term as president of Junior Auxiliary. She married Julian Johnson, son of Troy and Frances Lillian Coffey Johnson. They lived in Carthage, MS in Leake County, where Troy was born and had an automobile dealership until his death. Troy had a twin brother, Roy, in Senatobia, MS who was an attorney and an elected district attorney at one time. Troy and Lillian also had a daughter, Sara Ann, who died at age 13 from complications from high blood pressure and kidney failure. Lillian was a school teacher and took Julian to Senatobia to be near Roy's family and to a teaching position in that area. Julian was working for the highway department when Northeast Junior College needed a teacher for civil technology. He is still there but could retire. Gale and Julian had two daughters. Jennifer Nicole was salutatorian of her graduating class at Booneville High School. She was band drum major her senior year in high school. This carried over into her two years of junior college. She was first chair flutist. She graduated cum laude from Ole Miss with a BS degree in biology. She took necessary courses at the Tupelo satellite of the University of Mississippi for her teaching certificate. After working a year in a doctors clinic, she went to the University of North Alabama for two years and earned a BS degree in nursing science, graduating at the top of her class. During the second year at UNA, she married Michael Privett, son of Rowan and Evelyn Privett of Oxford, MS. Michael is a Marine. After a four year stint in service, he returned to Ole Miss, majoring in geology. After going through ROTC training and earning a BS degree he was commissioned 2nd Lieutenant in the Marine Corps. Michael is a third generation Marine. His dad retired as staff sergeant. He has an uncle on his mother's side who is a retired one star general. They retired in Tupelo. Michael and Jennifer are at present in Quantico, VA where he is in officer's training and she is a nurse in critical care at the Fredericksburg hospital. Cori Leigh graduated from Booneville High School and Northeast Community College, where she played clarinet in the band. She graduated from Mississippi State University with a degree in elementary education. She teaches sixth grade. She married Chris Sebren of Starkville, MS son of Evelyn Sebren of Starkville and Don Sebren of Jackson, MS. He graduated from Mississippi State with a sports management degree. He was one of the original staff of the T-Rex hockey team in Tupelo. They have a son, Tyler Cole.

Marsha Claudia (b. Jan. 27, 1949 in Memphis, TN) graduated from Booneville High School and Northeast Junior College. She went to work with the unemployment office in Tupelo. There she met David Hill. When they married, one had to go. Since David had seniority, Claudia was it. She went to work as secretary for the engineer at Tombigbee River Valley Water Management District, where she is approaching retirement. David was born in Amory to Madge and Thomas Wilson. David is a sales representative. He has a business degree from Mississippi State. They have a daughter, Leslie Anne. She graduated from Tupelo High School, attended Northeast Community College and will transfer her two years of credit to Mississippi State University. She plans to be a counselor.

Pamela Renee (b. Mar. 10, 1951, the morning her dad died that evening from injuries received in an automobile accident the night before) graduated from Booneville High School and attended Northeast Junior College. She works in the chancery clerk's office in Prentiss County for the board of supervisors. She married Roger Henderson, son of Ray W. and Martha Jane Henderson. He is in maintenance for Johnson at Caterpillar. They have a son, John Ashby. John graduated from Booneville High School, Northeast Junior College and the University of Mississippi with a degree in psychology, earned a master's degree in psychology at the University of Tennessee at Chattanooga and a PhD in industrial psychology at the University of Tennessee, Knoxville. He is a consultant. He married Greta Dunnam of Pascagoula, MS. She is the daughter of Gary and Gloria "Gigi" Dunnam of Pascagoula. She graduated with a PhD in pharmacy from the University of Mississippi. *Submitted by Bernice Bonds Janeway.*

JOHNSEY, WILLIAM FRANKLIN

"BILL," born Nov. 19, 1904, died Dec. 7, 1962, son of Bert and Addie Stoop Johnsey. Bert and Addie are buried in Rienzi Cemetery. Bill's brothers were Harry, Ned, Melvin and Wallace. His sisters were Mary Johnsey Ray, Kathlene Johnsey Cummings and Lucy Johnsey Latch.

Bill married Mary Lillian Crow (b. Aug. 17, 1899, d. Mar. 16, 1990) on Dec. 27, 1925, daughter of Robert "Bob" and Margaret "Mag" Crow. Bob and Mag are buried in Gaston Cemetery in Prentiss County. Bill and Lillian are buried in Rienzi Cemetery.

Lillian had two brothers, Edd and Clyde.

Bill and Lillian had four daughters and two sons.

Willie Eunice (b. Jan. 5, 1927) first married J.R. Felker, they divorced. She then married Billy Moore. She has no children.

Bottom Row, from left: Bill Johnsey, Bob Johnsey, Billy Johnsey and Lillian Johnsey. Top Row, from left: Una Mae Johnsey (Turner), Eunice Johnsey (Moore) and Peggy Johnsey (Lancaster).

Una Mae (b. Nov. 9, 1930, d. Jun. 29, 1999) is buried in Lebanon Cemetery in Corinth, MS. She first married Ival Ashby. They have one son, Richard Howard "Rick" (b. Apr. 1, 1951). They divorced. She then married Price "Pud" Turner. They have two daughters, Sherri Lynn (b. Jun. 14, 1956) and Debra Price "Deb" (b. Sep. 2, 1958). Pud adopted Richard Howard "Ricky," now Turner. Richard married Linda Dunn. They have three children: Richard Clint (b. Jun. 10, 1976), Whitney Leeann (b. Nov. 15, 1979) and Benjamin Price (b. May 25, 1982). Sherri married Ricky Stewart; they have one daughter, Amber Nicole (b. Apr. 30, 1980). They divorced. Sherri then married H.C. Bates.

Bottom Row, from left: Peggy Johnsey (Lancaster), Billy Joe Johnsey and Una Mae Johnsey (Turner). Top Row, from left: Bob Johnsey and Eunice Johnsey (Moore).

Peggy Joyce (b. May 27, 1932) married Max Wade Lancaster on May 17, 1952. They had three children. Their first child was Janet Rhena "Jan" (b. Aug. 25, 1961). She first married Keith Richardson, they divorced having no children. She then married Jeff Haley. They have two children, Jill Elaina (b. Oct. 22, 1989) and Jake Andrew (b. Apr. 18, 1994). Max and Peggy's second child was a son, stillborn Jan. 21, 1965. Their third child, Fred Clayton (b. Jul. 9, 1966). He first married Molly Walters, they divorced having no children. He then married Tammy Andrews.

The fourth child born to Bill and Lillian Johnsey was Quida Alline (b. Dec. 25, 1934, d. Mar. 14, 1935).

The fifth child was Bobby Bert (b. Aug. 21, 1936, d. Dec. 26, 1992). He is buried in Liberty Cemetery, Highway 30 East, Booneville, MS in Prentiss County. He married Faye Simmons. They had no children.

The sixth child of Bill and Lillian was Billy Joe (b. Apr. 23, 1939). He married Nona Faye Lauderdale. They have four children. Regina (b. Feb. 4, 1964) married Chris Ramey. Gary (b. born Sep. 27, 1965), Tracy (b. Feb. 26, 1972) and Chad (b. Nov. 23, 1975) married Julie Raper, they have two children, Justin and Josh. *Submitted by Mrs. M.W. Lancaster.*

JOHNSON FAMILY,

Bell Johnson and John Alexander Hartsfield lived and raised their family in the New Chandler Community. They had a beautiful place with large magnolia trees in their yard. The blooms were abundant on the trees and people admired them because they were new to that area. Johnny, as he was called, operated a county store on his property.

Bell Johnson (b. Nov. 1, 1863, d. Dec. 19, 1943) and Johnny Alexander Hartsfield (b. Aug. 15, 1855, d. Jan. 29, 1934) were married in November. To them were born James Allen "Jim Allen" (b. Aug. 19, 1883, d. Jul. 13, 1964) and Minnie (b. Oct. 1, 1885, d. Dec. 11, 1969).

Jim Allen married Marcella Vest (d. Jul. 18, 1972) on May 14, 1913. They had no children but were good to the children who frequented the store, which they inherited with the home from Jim Allen's dad.

Johnny "Papa" Hartsfield

Minnie married O'Dell Mathis (d. Jan. 5, 1957) on Jul. 24, 1904. They had three children: 1) Dennis (b. Dec. 16, 1905, d. Dec. 16, 1968) married Rachel Smith (d. Mar. 7, 1997) on May 14, 1912, they had five children: Prentiss Warren (b. Mar. 22, 1924, d. Mar. 11, 1995), Syble Daphene (b. May 31, 1926), Melvin Grady (Apr. 15, 1929, d. Sep. 3, 1950 in Korean War), Willadean (b. Jan. 25, 1931, Feb. 10, 1931), L.Q. (b. Feb. 15, 1933). 2) Alfred (b. Jan. 7, 1904) married Ilene George (d. Mar. 5, 1951 of liver cancer) on Jan. 19, 1928. they had five children: Mildred (b. Apr. 15, 1929, Jo Ann (died as a toddler), Gerald (b. Dec. 12, 1931, d. Mar. 20, 1995), Jimmy Dale (b. Apr. 16, 1936), Barry Donald (b. Jul. 21, 1940). 3) Brant (b. Oct. 1, 1924, d. Apr. 16, 1937) a good boy and well liked, died of spinal meningitis. One photo remains of him in which there is a resemblance to L.Q.

Larry Wayne Eldridge, son of Daphene and Stanley, died Mar. 22, 1999 on his Uncle Warren's birthday; Chris Mathis, grandson of Warren Mathis was killed in an auto accident.

JOHNSON, EUGENE AND BERTHA WINSETT,

in 1940 when I was 4 years old, our family moved a mile and a half up the road from where I was born to the Dewey Floyd farm where we milked 20 or so cows and farmed 60 some odd acres of bottom land and all the new ground we could clear. I say we because even at 4 I was expected to do as much work as a 4 year old could do. The depression was a fresh memory in my parent's minds and every one of us helped feed ourselves. We had it better than most folks because we always had butter and milk.

Bertha Ediston Winsett, ca. 1926 and Eugene V. Johnson, ca. 1925

Interestingly enough, the building we used as a milk barn was also "the old" Robertson school house where my daddy had gotten all eight years of the only formal schooling he ever had.

The actual part where classes were held was now

a hay barn. I remember that the stage was still there and the little niches which held the coal oil lamps were there and even two of the lamps had survived. I can remember yet the stories my dad told about how strict the teachers were.

About the pranks some of the bigger boys tried to get away with. Those were certainly the days when the "spare the rod and spoil the child" rule was about the only rule there was. The thing about it was you were bound to get another good whipping at home as soon as some tattle tale told on you. And as far as the education my dad received there, well I'll just tell you I'd put him up against college educated fellow any day. Common sense is what you had to have to feed a family of five back there in the 30s and 40s.

Because, boy could that Mose Eugene Johnson eat. He could eat a whole chicken any day. He was 13 in 1940. He went to war in 1945 just as that awful war was over and served two years in the US Army and 23 in the US Air Force.

We all missed him when he went to the service but none more than my oldest sister, Ethel Marie. That meant that she took on his share of the work being the next oldest and all. She was 11 in 1940. A 9 year old Georgia Lee was the daredevil of the bunch. She could sing like an angel at church Sunday morning and dance a hole in her shoes that night.

Here it is the middle of 2000 and we are all still surviving.

Our parents are both gone and buried at Liberty Cemetery. They were Eugene Vardaman and Bertha Ediston Johnson. Vardaman Lee Johnson was born Jun. 8, 1942. We are all proud of him. He served in the US Air Force for 26 years and is at present still aiding the cause of peace in another country. *Submitted by Zu Ann Johnson King.*

JOHNSON, FRANK AND LUCY, Frank was a farmer. They lived in Prentiss County almost all of their lives. Their land and home was near Siloam Church. They had seven daughters and two sons.

Frank and Lucy Johnson Family. This picture was made at Bay Springs in 1951 or 1952 at a family reunion with a potluck lunch. Some went swimming in the creek.

At this time all the family, children, grandchildren and the first three great-grandchildren are in the picture.

One of the grandsons now owns the land and has built his house where the old home was.

Only two of the children are still living, Trudy Stacy and Bobbie Corbin. *Submitted by Wanda Malone Sanders, 109 Melody Lane, Senatobia, MS 38668.*

JOHNSON, THOMAS J./DELPHIA DERRYBERRY, Thomas Jefferson Johnson was born January 2, 1880, in Prentiss County, the son of Mary F. "Mollie" Johnston, who never married. Family legend is that the father of Thomas and his younger sister, Ella Mae (Saylors), was Lee Cartwright. Mollies's parents were Amanda Holley, daughter of JUlius and Sarah Horton Holley, and Richmond Allen Johnston, son of John A. Johnston and Huldy Phillips. Mollie was shunned by some of her sibilings and her mother's family. But her aunt, Amanda Harriet Johnston Smith, was her mainstay. Mollie apparently did not always lead a strictly conventional life in the eyes of polite society, but she was a woman much loved and respected by her children and their families. And her epitaph reads "she lived and died a Christian."

On July 30, 1899, in Prentiss County, Thomas Jefferson Johnson married Delphia Derryberry, born April 6, 1881, to Thomas Jefferson Johnson married in McNairy County, Tennessee in July 1878. Julia Brigman is believed to be the daughter of Moses Brigman who during the course of the Civil War, served in Co G, 1st Alabama Confederate Cavary and was mustered out of Co F, 11th Illinois Union Cavalry on June 9, 1865.

Thomas C. Derryberry was the son of an intriguing character, Pitzer Miller "Pitts" Derryberry. Pitzer was born February 15, 1835, probably in Tippah County, Mississippi, possibly in McNairy County, Tennessee. In 1857 in Hardeman COunty, Tennessee, Pitzer married Susan Carper, who had a child, Ida, from a previous marriage. Susan was the daughter of Sampson Carper and Savinia (or Lavinia) Austin. Sampson Carper is reputed to have been an outlaw who ran the old Mattamora Hill stagecoach stop near Pocahontas, Tennessee during the pre-Civil War era. A minor Civil War battle, the Battle of Davis Bridge, was fought partially in Sam Carper's yard and is so mentioned on historical markers at the site. Sam Carper and members of his family were killed in an area feud about 1860.

When the Civil Warstarted, Pitzer was living near Pochohntas and joined Forrest's Third Cavlry, along with his first cousin, PJM (Pleasant Jasper Marion) Derryberry. In 1870, Pitzer was named admistrator and a non-resident heir to the estate of his father, JOhn T. Derryberry, of Tippah County, Mississippi. Pitzer's mother was Kizziah Woodward, who is said to have died in Texas while on a visit with a brother.

Old family letters, land records and jury lists show Pitzer residing at Cuba, Mississippi (west of Corinth in Alcorn COunty) after the turn of the century. Records indicate Pitzer was a large landowner, but records also indicate he had several wives who are reported to have ended up with most of his property.

In his final years Pitzer was in Prentiss COunty with his son, Thomas. HIs will shows he was estranged from his current wife as he stated " I make no arrangements for my wife because of her treatment of me". He died on February 9, 1916, during WWI and was buried at Liberty Cemetery east of Booneville,, where a Confederate marker has been placed at the approximate site of his grave which has been lost with time. Pitzer was a brother to Alex Derryberry who was Sheriff of Alcorn County and the grandfather of Roscoe Turner, the aviator.

Thomas J. Jonson and Delphia Derryberry had the following children: 1. Eugen JOhnson, who married Bertha Winsett; children Marie. MOse, Georgia, ZuAnn, and Vardaan. 2. Emma Lee, who married Howard Lawrence; children William H. (killed in WWII), Gerald and Jimmy Glen. 3. Charles Johnson, who married Vera Wren; children Billy Edward and Betty Jane. 4. Gladys who married Roy Lawrence; children Wayne, Martha, Mary Ethel, and Jacky. 5. Harlan Johnson who married Charlene Armstrong; children Carl, Bobby, andf Pat. 6. Draynon JOhnson who married Juanita Duren; children Raymond and Ricky. 7. Mary Evelyn who married Ernest Ashmore; children William Gail and Douglas. 8. Bonnie Lou who married first Aubrey Melton Harper, and second, Aaron Teulon Whisenant. Bonnie nd Aubreyhad one daughter, Mattie Maxine Harper, who married John Lyle Sparks and had Ann, Jerry, Edwin, and Ricky. Bonnie and Teulon had William Wyatt "Gus" Whisenant who married Thelma Ruth Caldwell and had Stephanie Renee and William Brian.

JOHNSTON, JOHN A./HULDY PHILLIPS, born 1800 in North Carolina. At this time, little is known of him, other than the fact that his name appears in county records as an early settler of old Tishomingo County. One researcher lists his parents as Tom Johnston Sr. and Anne Allen of Johnston County, NC. He married Huldy Phillips who was born in 1806.

According to a story on page 206 of the *Families of Alcorn County, MS*, Vol. II, Huldy Phillips was the daughter of Lazarus Phillips and Rachel Sanders. Lazarus Phillips is said to be the descendent of William Phillips (b. ca. 1720) who was a sergeant in the Revolutionary War. Rachel Sanders was the daughter of Quakers, Benjamin Sanders and Leah Smith. Rachel Sanders was dismissed from the Quakers for marrying out of the order.

Grave of Mollie Johnston, daughter of Richmond Allen Johnston and Amanda Holley, beloved mother of Thomas J. and Ella Johnson

Also according to that story, "the Sanders family can be traced to Robert Saunders who died in 1439 in Northamptonshire, England. A later descendant, Laurence Saunders, was burned at the stake in 1555 for preaching against pestilent popery, idolatry and superstition and for not renouncing his Protestant faith for Catholicism."

One of the sons of John A. Johnston and Huldy Phillips was Richmond Allen Johnston (b. ca. 1834 in Tennessee) who married Amanda Holley (b. between 1841-44 in North Carolina), daughter of Julius Holley and Sarah Bobbitt Horton (see her story in this volume). According to a Holley descendant, Amanda was disowned by her father when she married Richmond Allen Johnston.

Richmond Allen and Amanda Holley Johnston were married Dec. 24, 1858 and their children were Mary F. "Mollie" Johnston (b. Feb. 14, 1860, d. Mar. 14, 1929); Bellzee Johnson (md. John Hartsfield), Julius W. Johnson (md. Sarah Francis Rogers), Howell Brant Johnson (b. 1869, d. 1959) md. Aurilla McAlpin), James William Johnson (md. Pearl Williams), Robert D. Johnson, Huldy L. Johnson, Eliza A. Johnson and Anna E. Johnson.

Mollie Johnston never married, but had two children, Thomas J. Johnson and Ella Johnson. About this time the name began to be spelled minus the "t." Some say it was because of hard feelings over Mollie's status as an unwed mother.

The story is that both Mollie's children had the same father, Lee Cartwright, even though the children were born nine years apart. Lee Cartwright was unmarried at the time these children were born, but he later married. The whys and wherefores of this situation will never be known, but Mollie was probably shunned and ill-treated. Many of the Johnson/Johnston descendants grew up never knowing they were related to the Cartwrights and Holleys. This writer's grandmother wouldn't talk about it at all and was embarrassed by the facts. But an inquiring mind wants to know. This writer has visited Mollie's grave at Smith's Chapel Cemetery in the Tuscumbia Community and was glad to see the original spelling of the name on her stone and the inscription "she lived and died a Christian."

Why should there be a stigma attached to her name? I dare say there wasn't any for the gentleman in question. Mollie's son, Thomas J. Johnson, married Delphia Derryberry. Mollies's daughter, Ella, married William Arthur Saylors. Mollie has many descendants who should surely praise her name. *Sources:*

Maureen Holley Crowe, William Rorie, Margaret Carson and LDS Church on-line. *Submitted by Mollie's great-great-granddaughter, Ann Sparks.*

JUMPER, SAMUEL FRANKLIN, born Jan. 29, 1909, to James Douglas Jumper and Hattie Murphy Jumper. Sam grew up and married Ruthie Irene Koon. They raised three children: Douglas Jumper, Leista Belue and Dennis Jumper.

Sam, for most of his life, was a political leader in Prentiss County. He was chosen to serve as trustee of the Jumpertown School District, which became an accredited high school during his term.

Sam F. Jumper with his great-granddaughter, Misty D. Mitchell in 1983.

He was elected constable of the second district, to complete the term of the late Claud Crofford. He was elected to the following four-year term.

Sam then was selected as deputy sheriff for three terms to Sale Martin, Ben Holley and George Rutherford.

In 1964 he was elected supervisor of the second district. He served continuously for three more four-year terms until 1976 when he retired.

One of his ambitions was completed before his retirement by paving the New Bryant and Jumpertown-Blackland roads, which afforded a north-south and east-west paved road through his district.

He was a third degree Mason of the Booneville Masonic Lodge and a 32nd degree member of the Corinth Scottish Rite Lodge.

Sam never sought recognition that he might easily have won. He felt it was the small things that count in life. He loved Christ and his family. He made friends with all who came in contact with him.

Sam Jumper was a lifelong resident of Jumpertown until his death on Feb. 9, 1984. *In loving memory, Martha Jumper Mitchell.*

KENNEDY, DAVID, nor Elizabeth Kennedy ever lived in Prentiss County, MS but many of their descendants certainly did. Two of their youngest sons, Dock Riley and wife, Sarah Jane Tyra, Robert Russell "Dick," and wife, Margaret Malissa Frederick, along with their children, all moved to Tishomingo County before 1883. Both families lived along side of each other and farmed the area around McDougal Creek near Mt. Pleasant Church. Much of the farm is now a part of the Bay Springs Lake, but the old homesteads still remain located behind the Mt. Pleasant Church and Cemetery. The land for the church and cemetery was donated by Dock Riley and Sarah Jane Kennedy. Both couples and several of their children are buried there. As their families expanded the sons and daughters married, had their own families and migrated throughout the country, many of which settled in Prentiss County.

Children of Dock Riley and Sarah Jane Kennedy were: Nancy Adeline married Lemial Houston Kennedy; Malissa married Lewis Harp; Mandy; Cansady married L.H. Horton; Margaret married T. Tipton; James Garner married Modennie "Dennie" Wright; Emma married George Tipton; Mary married Laster Smith; Bytha; Thomas Woodruff "Tom" married Annie Paden; Kizzie married ? Ward and Jessie married Minnie Ward.

Robert Russell "Dick" and Margaret Malissa "Liz" Kennedy's children: Joseph David "Joe" who married (1) Alice Price, (2) Nancy Elizabeth Armanda Lambert Grammer and (3) Lillie Johnson; Mary Ann married Colonel Wilson; Sarah Jane married ? Mills;

Robert Russell and Margaret Malissa Kennedy Family. Front Row from left: James Hamilton, Geneva, Margaret Malissa, Robert Russell and Martha Malinda. Back Row from left: Dovie Lorraine, Lydia Angeline, Sarah Jane, Mary Ann, Joseph David and Kemp Bashaw (K.B.). Not Pictured: William Russell (Bill).

William Riley "Bill" married (1) Matilda Adams and (2) Geneva Horton; Dovie Lorraine married Leroy Ramsey Paden; Lydia Angeline married James D. Dean; Kemp Bashaw married Dena Horton; James Hamilton "Jim" married Sarah Francis Crumby; Martha Malinda married Walter Hunt; Geneva married Oscar Searcy and Myrtie Elvira.

The earlier Kennedy ancestors tended to hold on to Irish Lore and traditions. Although very clannish, they tended to be very superstitious, although deeply religious. The following story has been passed down through generations about Robert Russell Kennedy:

One winter night before retiring to bed, Dick Kennedy walked across his front porch before walking inside. He looked up to see the reflection of a human face in a cedar tree in the yard. The "face" he identified as that of their youngest daughter, Myrtie Elvira. Quite shaken, he hurried inside to relay the news to his wife. He announced, "Myrtie Elvira is going to die." He proclaimed this event as a "sign" from God. Less than one week later, the 2-1/2 year old Myrtie died as a result of typhoid fever. Records he kept were included in his personal effects following his own death many years later. Handwritten notes appeared from time to time in his handwriting proclaiming, "It has been 16 days since Myrtie died" or "Myrtie died 113 days ago," etc. His personal grief is evident as this man struggled to cope with yet another loss in his already tragic life. As a young man, his own aging father had been taken from his family to die for a cause that he so deeply believed in to be right. These families believed that all of their family's painful secrets had been left behind in the Freedom Hills of north Alabama. *Submitted by Paula Kennedy Clack.*

KENNEDY, JOSEPH DAVID, the Kennedy family came to Prentiss County, MS via Tishomingo County from Marion County, AL. Some of the first Kennedys in Prentiss County were the Joseph David Kennedy family. This set of Kennedys lived in or around the New Site area. Joseph David Kennedy was the son of Robert Russell and Margaret Malissa (Frederick) Kennedy from Marion County, AL. Robert Russell was the son of David Stephenson Kennedy, born ca. 1797 in Tennessee. David bought land in Marion County, AL in the early 1800s where he raised his family until his death in October 1862. David Kennedy and family were farmers in the north Alabama area who owned no slaves. He depended on his family's help and support to work the farms. They were a religious but clannish bunch and believed in strong family values. Their family values would be tested during the American Civil War.

As the war began, all young men in the area were given the choice of fighting for the South, being jailed and charged for treason against the South, or death. Most of the men in Alabama were forced to fight for the South, but some left the area and fought for the North, as was the case of the Kennedy boys: James J., William S. and George W. Kennedy. In late September 1862, George W. Kennedy was granted a furlough to go home on a few days pass. Obviously, seeing the condition of his son, saddened David. He left his home in Alabama and crossed the enemy lines to visit William S. and James J. in Glen, MS probably for no other reason than to take them warm clothing and food as the weather was beginning to turn cold. Some Southern Guerrillas, who rebelled against Northern Sympathizers, hearing of this went to the home of David, charging him with having visited his sons. They hanged him to death and gave a black man a plug of tobacco to bury the corpse. Family lore passed down says that the family later found the body by his feet sticking out of the ground in a shallow grave in a clay root of a tree. They took the body back to the family plot for a Christian burial. Recently, I visited Marion County, AL, where I was taken to the area of the hanging. The stories are still passed down of David Kennedy's ghost that still haunts the area today.

Joe D. Kennedy Family. First row seated from left: Houston, Joe D., James G. (in lap of Joe D.), Leonard, Nancy Elizabeth, Martha (in lap of Nancy Elizabeth). Back row standing from left: Margaret, Alice, Viola and Johnnie.

Robert Russell and Dock Riley Kennedy left north Alabama thinking that they were leaving the past behind them. However, they still stayed as close to the family heritage as possible. They often returned to Alabama to the old home place that cost their families so much grief, but also stood for so much richness in family value. Robert Russell Kennedy's family migrated to Prentiss County where many of the Kennedys still remain today. The family values are still there as are the close family ties in all of the Kennedys. *Submitted by Barbara Kennedy Moore.*

KIMBRELL, RUBEN AVERY "SHORTY," born Aug. 21, 1902 in Clay County, MS as the only son of Ida Maud Glasson (b. Jun. 30, 1867, d. Jan. 20, 1965) and Charlie David Kimbrell (b. Feb. 13, 1860, d. Jan. 6, 1939), who married on Feb. 19, 1885. He had four sisters: Oma Pearl (b. May 13, 1886, d. Oct. 13, 1890), Myrtle (b. Jan. 12, 1886, d. ?), who married W. Columbus Gibson on Feb. 21, 1909; Mary E. (b. Jul. 30, 1892, d. Nov. 18, 1967), who married H.P. Williams on Jan. 11, 1911 and Norine F. (b. May 3, 1905, d. Aug. 12, 1941), who married Aubrey M. Briscoe on Jun. 6, 1929.

"Shorty" began working with Southern Bell Telephone and Telegraph Co. in 1923. He met Anna Lou (Ann) Maxwell, daughter of Mary Frances Miller and Robert Belton Maxwell Jr. They were married on Aug. 12, 1934. Ann worked for Southern Bell as a switchboard operator in Booneville. When their daughter, Sue Carolyn, was born Sep. 18, 1939, Ann resigned with 15 years of service. On Aug. 1, 1947, Shorty was promoted to line foreman, headquarters in Tupelo, MS and remained in that position until he retired on Sep. 1, 1967. An outdoorsman, he enjoyed deer hunting with his nephews, Ross, Ruben and J. C. Williams.

Shorty's paternal grandparents were Mary A Barfield, born in North Carolina ca. 1838 and Ruben

"Uncle Rube" Kimbrel, born in Alabama ca. 1836. Both died in 1904. Ruben's father, David Kimbrel was born ca. 1810, North Carolina. His mother's first name was Rebecca. She was born ca. 1810 in Georgia; died in the 1860s and buried in Oktibbeha County, MS.

Maternal grandparents were William Avery Glasson, born in Mississippi on Sep. 9, 1844 and Mary Elizabeth Foster. They were married on Sep. 7, 1866 in Chickasaw County, MS. His father was Awbrey B. Glasson, a Georgia farmer, born in 1804 and died in the 1870s. His mother was Elvira C., born ca. 1817 in South Carolina and died in April 1880. Awbrey and Elvira were married ca. 1833. Mary Elizabeth Foster's father was Washington "Wash" Foster and her mother was Amanda Spruell, buried in Heidlenheimer, Bell County, TX.

The R.A. Kimbrell Family in the 1940s. From left: Anna Lou Maxwell Kimbrell, Ruben Avery "Shorty" Kimbrell and daughter, Sue Carolyn.

Shorty and Ann's only child, Sue Carolyn, attended Booneville High School, Northeast Mississippi Junior College and Mississippi College in Clinton. After graduation she taught for five years at New Site Attendance Center in Prentiss County. In September 1966 upon completion of her master's degree, she became assistant librarian at Northeast Mississippi Junior College. In 1976 she became library director and remained in that position until her retirement on May 31, 1991. While working at NEMJC she met and married Robert L. Honeycutt from Kossuth, MS. Employed at NEMJC, Robert served in several areas: industrial arts instructor, vocational guidance counselor and vocational-technical director.

Ruben Avery "Shorty" Kimbrell died Mar. 16, 1982 and is buried in the Booneville Cemetery on the Maxwell Family plot. See articles on Maxwell, Thomas Steven Miller and Robert L. Honeycutt. *Submitted by Sue K. Honeycutt.*

KITCHENS, FRANCIS/SAMUEL SPARKS

Frances Kitchens was born in 1824 in Alabama, the daughter of James Matlock Kitchens, a Primitive Baptist preacher, and Sarah "Sally" Brown. James Matlock Kitchens was born on August 7, 1796, on French Broad River in Tennessee. Sally Brown was born on Sep 16, 1796, in Georgia, according to the 1850 census of Walker County, Alabama.

James Matlock Kitchens and Sally Brown were married in 1813 in Lawrence County, Alabama. ALso listed on the 1850 census in the household of James M. Kitchens, was Christopher Kitchens, male aged 80, born in Virginia. This was probably the father of James Matlock Kitchens. All that is known of Sally's family is that she had a brother, Thomas Brown and a sister, Frances Brown who married John D. Randolph.

According to Walker County, Alabama history, James Matlock Kitchens moved to Alabama in 1812 at age 16 along with a brother and an uncle, James Acuff (So, possibly, James Matlock Kitchens' mother was an Acuff). Early marriage records show numerous marriages between Acuffs and Kitchens in Grainger County, Tennessee.

James M. Kitchens and the Brown siblings moved to Walker County in 1836 and helped constitute the Sulphur Springs Primitive Baptist Church. James Matlock Kitchens was ordained a minister in May of 1845 and served the church until December 1867 when ill health caused his resignation. He is said to have descended from a Henry Kitchens who sat in the Virginia House of Burgesses.

James Matlock Kitchens and Syntha "Sally" Brown had the following children: John, Nancy (married James F. Robinson), Mary Polly (married Harvey Hamilton), Christopher C. (married Sarah Ann Taylor), William, Samuel, James Matlock, Jr. (married Mary D. Files), Jesse (married Eleanor Brown), Matilda (married John "Jack" Brown), Elizabeth, Susan, and Frances who married Samuel E. Sparks, the son of Thomas and Rutha White Sparks, and the father of James M. Sparks who moved his family to Prentiss County, Mississippi around 1880.

KIZER, ALLEN GAINES,
born Aug. 31, 1902 in Prentiss County, MS. His parents were Sidney Michael Kizer (b. 1872) and Nancy Jane (Miller) (b. 1869), both born in Prentiss County, MS.

Allen has family roots steeped in the development of the US and Prentiss County. His middle name "Gaines" is from his grandmother's family, who can trace their lineage from their arrival in Virginia about 1640, all the way to Sir John Gams, 1559 in Newton Brecon County, Wales. The Gaines family has many books written about their accomplishments since arriving in America in 1640.

Allen Gaines Kizer and Ottie Odell (Bolton) Kizer.

Allen's great-great-great grandfather, Francis Kizer, is listed as one of the families taking part in the establishment of the county – that's old Tishomingo County. The Kizer name is repeatedly written in the old courthouse records and history records of old Tishomingo and Prentiss County.

Allen was a farmer and he loved to hunt. He was a quiet man, who minded his own business, but always wanted to know what was going on politically in his community and in his country. He married Ottie Odell Bolton on Dec. 9, 1928.

Ottie was born Jul. 29, 1913. Her parents were William Calvin Bolton, born in 1885 and Modenia R. (Massey), born in 1886, from Alabama. Ottie was 15 years old when she married Allen, who was 26 years old. She was a beautiful, fun-loving, easygoing young woman. She loved parties, gospel singings, picnics and going barefooted. Allen was mature, serious and interested in politics – something Ottie never gave a thought. But, these differences must have bound them together, because they had been married 50 years when Allen died.

Ottie's family, the Boltons, the Masseys and the Jarnigans can trace their roots into the early 1800s in Alabama. There were many preachers in their family. I guess that is why Ottie grew up loving revivals, singings and picnics.

Allen and Ottie had eight children: Annie Lou (b. 1930); Lena Pearl (b. 1932); Allie Gaston (b. 1934), named "Allie" after her dad and "Gaston" because of the Gaines family; Earl Ray (b. 1936); Donnie Gene (b. 1943); Nancy Jane (b. 1946); Lana Kay (b. 1951) and Steve (b. 1954). Donnie died in 1974 in an accident. Steve lives in Pigeon Forge, TN but the rest of the children live in Prentiss County.

Allen Gaines Kizer died Jul. 7, 1978 and is buried in Pleasant Valley Cemetery. His son, mother, father, sisters, grandparents, great-grandparents, cousins, aunts and uncles are buried in Pleasant Valley Cemetery.

Ottie loved her home, her garden and raising chickens, but the thing that has always brought her the most happiness is having her family (children, grandchildren and great-grandchildren) near her. When she has those she loves around her, we can see that mischievous sparkle in her eyes that made Allen fall head-over-heels in love with her. Ottie is 86 years old, still lives in Prentiss County and is still very beautiful. *Submitted by Carolyn Whitehead.*

KIZER, CAPTAIN BENJAMIN JULIAN,
born Mar. 24, 1837 in old Tishomingo County, MS to Michael and Sallie (Cook) Kizer. Benjamin had one older brother, Michael, born in 1836, but we have lost track of Michael. Benjamin goes on to play an important role in helping develop Prentiss County. Benjamin's mother, Sallie, died when he was 3 days old. His father, Michael, then marries Mary Margaret (Box) and they have 10 children.

Captain Benjamin Julian Kizer – Civil War Veteran

Benjamin Julian Kizer enlisted in the Confederacy on Aug. 16, 1861. His occupation was listed as schoolteacher. He was captain of Co. K in the 26th Mississippi Infantry. He served until the fall of Ft. Donelson, when his regiment was captured. He entered the 32nd Mississippi until his regiment was paroled, then he rejoined them. In April 1865, he is listed as "prisoner of war", captured at Hatcher's Run, VA. He served in the war until his surrender at Appomattox Courthouse Virginia in 1865.

Captain Benjamin Julian Kizer married Martha Francis Gaines on Sep. 10, 1863. Martha's parents were John Strother Gaines, born in 1814 and Eliza (Patton) Gaines, who was born in 1817. The Gaines family helped to survey the Natchez Trace. John Strother's family was one of the first families to settle near the Trace in an area today called Pharr Flatts in old Tishomingo County.

John Strother died Nov. 10, 1879 and is buried in Pleasant Valley. Eliza (Patton) died Jan. 17, 1904 and is buried next to her husband and near her father, Dorn Patton in Pleasant Valley.

After the war, Benjamin returned to teaching, but later served as postmaster of Hazel Dell, which was located in the eastern part of Prentiss County. Benjamin's signature is on many documents of old Tishomingo records showing he helped make decisions to develop old Tishomingo County and then Prentiss County. Benjamin served as justice of the peace and on the board of supervisors. Benjamin's reputation was as an honest, well-educated man, who loved politics, had a "little temper", but helpful to his fellowman.

Benjamin and Martha Kizer had 10 children: John Strawther, Minnesota, William Hayman, Michael Sidney, Noonan Clayton, Mittie Rebecca, Clifford Gaines, James Rodney, Earnest Earl and Ollie Pearl. Each of these children went on to play active roles in the development of Prentiss County, MS.

Captain Benjamin Julian Kizer died Mar. 24, 1908 and Martha Francis (Gaines) Kizer died Feb. 16, 1913. They lived and served in Prentiss County all of their lives. They are both buried in the Pleasant Valley Cemetery in Booneville in Prentiss County, MS. Captain Kizer served his *country* and then served in his *county*. He carried on a "Kizer" tradition. *Submitted by Carolyn Whitehead and Gene Kizer.*

KIZER, JOHN STROTHER,
eldest child of Captain Benjamin and Martha Gaines Kizer.

He was born in Tishomingo County in 1865 and lived in Prentiss County until his death in 1938.

He was a farmer and owned part of the land that was once owned by his father, Captain Benjamin Kizer and his grandfather, John Strother Gaines, one of the early settlers to the area. A portion of the land is still owned by the Kizer family.

Strother was married three times. His first marriage was to Tina "Tiny" Perry. They had two children, Dora and Beldon.

Dora married Monroe Moreland and was a housewife. They had one son, Dallas. The Morelands lived their entire life in Prentiss County. Dallas' descendants continue to live in Prentiss County.

John S. Kizer, Minnesota Kizer Googe, Willie Kizer and Sydney Kizer. Picture taken in 1938.

Beldon enlisted in the Army during WWI. While he was stationed in New Bedford, Massachusetts, he married Annie Wood. They had five children: Eileen, Beldon Jr., Raymond, Shirley and Gayle.

Shortly after Beldon's birth, Tina passed away.

Strother then married Nannie Baxter. They had three children: Baxter, Estella and Olen. Baxter and Estella never married. Olen married Eva Ward. They had two children, Sue and Tommy.

Olen was a businessman and spent most of his life in Prentiss County, but his later years were spent in Osyka, MS where his descendants still live.

Baxter lived in Prentiss County most of his life and Estella passed away at the age of 16.

Nannie passed away at an early age.

Strother's third marriage was to Willie Cobb. They had five children: Gara, Wauchita, Helen, Eugenia and James.

Strother also had a stepson, Floyd Ferguson, who married Willowdean Strickland. They had five children: Floyd Jr., who died soon after birth; Billy; Barbara; Marilyn and Cynthia.

Floyd was a farmer and lived most of his life in Prentiss County. Most of his descendants live in Itawamba County.

Gara married J.G. Cleveland and they had six children: Charles, James (deceased), Clara, Gerald, Dorothy and Tommy (deceased).

Gara was a housewife and lived most of her life in Prentiss County. She now resides at Lee Manor in Lee County. Most of her family lives in Prentiss County.

Wauchita married William Robertson. She worked in the Tigrett Drugstore for many years. Most of her life was spent in Prentiss County.

Helen married Alfred Frebel. They had four children: Alfred Jr., Sylvia, James and Helen Ann. Helen was secretary at the Hialeah Church of Christ for over 30 years. Shortly after Helen's marriage, she moved to New York, then to South Florida where she still lives with her husband.

Eugenia taught school in Mississippi and Virginia. After her retirement, she lives part-time in Booneville. She never married.

James married Reba Blunt. They had four children: Shelia, Sonja, James Jr. and Mona.

James retired from the Air Force, afterwards working for the FAA and the city of Owensboro, KY. He lived the last several years of his life in Kentucky where most of his family continue to live.

Strother's descendants live in many parts of the US: Mississippi, Tennessee, Kentucky, Florida, New York, Massachusetts, North Carolina and Texas. *Submitted by Eugenia Kizer.*

KIZER, SIDNEY MICHAEL, born Jan. 14, 1872 in Prentiss County, MS to Captain Benjamin Julian Kizer and Martha Francis (Gaines) Kizer. He was the fourth son and one of 10 children.

Sidney Michael married Nancy Jane (Miller) on Oct. 31, 1895. Nancy Jane was born Dec. 24, 1869 and her parents were William T. Miller (b. Jul. 18, 1829 in Alabama) and Jane Miller (b. Nov. 22, 1835). We do not know anything about the Millers or what area they moved from to Prentiss County. William died Mar. 22, 1897 and Jane died Mar. 28, 1896. They are buried in the Pleasant Valley Cemetery.

Sidney Michael and Nancy Jane had three children: two daughters, Willie Lou, born 1900 and Nellie, who died as a teenager and one son, Allen Gaines Kizer, born Aug. 31, 1902.

Sidney Michael and Nancy Jane (Miller) Kizer – parents; son – Allen Gaines Kizer (see how his hand is like his dad's); daughters – Nellie Rue and Willie Lou. Made about 1907.

Sidney Michael lived in Prentiss County all of his life. He was a farmer. Nancy Jane (Miller) Kizer died Jan. 24, 1932 and is buried in Pleasant Valley Cemetery near her parents. Sidney Michael died Nov. 25, 1950 and is buried next to Nancy in the Pleasant Valley Cemetery. *Submitted by Carolyn Whitehead and Allie (Kizer) Ashcraft.*

KIZERS, FRANCIS, B.J. AND MICHAEL, the Kizers were among the first settlers in old Tishomingo/Prentiss County. Francis Kizer is listed as one of the families taking part in the establishment of the county. Francis was born in 1785 in Alabama. As we look through the old records, we see the "Kizer" name very often. In October 1836, B.J. Kizer bought four lots and Francis Kizer bought two lots in downtown Jacinto. On Nov. 7, 1836, Benjamin J. Kizer was granted a license to open an Inn and Tavern in the town of Jacinto. This was at the same time the Jacinto Courthouse was being built.

From the many times we see the "Kizer" name, we know they were a motivated, community active and very political family. We see Francis Kizer listed in the old courthouse records paying a $20 fine for violating the gambling laws by betting on the 1844 Presidential election. In 1836 Francis was appointed overseer to open and cut a road from Rodens Creek as far as where a road leading from James Mackey's to Pontotoc crosses. In 1837 Michael, David and Benjamin J. Kizer were listed as "hands" to help build part of the Ripley Road. In Deed Book E, page 29, Francis Kizer sold a slave to Charles Williams. This was dated Dec. 9, 1839. Francis Kizer died Mar. 18, 1848 in Tishomingo, MS. We are unsure as to where he is buried. He had three wives, but we only have the name of his third wife, Susan Moore, from Morgan County, AL. These are his children: Michael, Nancy Ann (who married William Payne), Benjamin, Francis Jr., George W., Mary C., Andrew, David A., Margaret and Thomas.

Michael, the first-born to Francis, was born in 1815 in Tennessee. According to the circuit county minutes 1836-1844, Michael Kizer and William Rowsey had an affray (fighting). He must have turned out just fine, because we see that he signed many sureties and his name is signed on many major issues in helping to establish the county and then in 1851, he was selected to serve on the jury. Michael married Sallie Cook and they had two sons, Michael (b. 1836) and Benjamin Julian (b. 1837) in Mississippi. Sallie died three days after giving birth to Benjamin. Michael's second marriage was to Mary Margaret Box on Jul. 20, 1837 in old Tishomingo County and they had 10 children.

We lost touch with the first-born, Michael, but Benjamin Julian Kizer becomes well-known in old Tishomingo/Prentiss County. For 160 years of Prentiss County history, we see the *Kizers*. *Submitted by Gene Kizer, Glenda Willmon and Carolyn Whitehead.*

KNIGHT, JOHN RILEY, one of three children born to William Calvin Knight and Elvine Frances (Moore) Knight. He was born in 1874. His siblings were Berry Knight, who left home at age 17 and was never heard from again and Annabelle Knight. He was born in Tennessee. He met his wife, Mary Elizabeth (Robinson) Knight in Alcorn County. They married on Aug. 29, 1897 in Ripley, MS. They set up house in Dry Creek where John Riley sharecropped until he could buy his homestead there. At some point he sold that homestead and bought one in Jumpertown. His youngest son, Bonnie Benjamin, still lives there.

John Riley Knight and MaryElizabeth Knight

John and Mary had seven boys and two girls. Their names are as follows: Claude Oscar, Laudie Bell, Berry Franklin, Johnny Weston, Vonnie Calvin, Bonnie Benjamin, William Washington (died at 6 months), Mary Maudie, who married a Cartwright and Frances Lucielle, who married a Williams. Frances Lucielle is my mother.

I was born after my grandparents died. But I always felt I knew them. I was raised with the wonderful stories of them. I know my grandpa played the fiddle while his children danced. I know it was my grandpa's crystal blue eyes that won my grandma's heart, that when they were old my grandpa use to slip some hard candy or an apple or orange under my grandma's pillow so the kids wouldn't see it and she could have it. But most of all I knew they loved each other with a rare love for each other and their children.

The last thing my grandpa did was to spin a top for my brother. He had a massive heart attack and died in my mother's arms. Both are buried in Jumpertown. He died Dec. 4, 1949 and she died shortly afterwards in 1950. John Riley Knight loved a good joke, where my grandma was a serious, petite woman. She loved her flowers and working outside.

Her parents were Mary Elizabeth (Swendle) Robinson and Benjamin Franklin Robinson. Her grandparents were Henry Robinson and Shirley Robinson on her daddy's side and Seith Swendle (mother unknown) on her mother's side. John Riley Knights grandparents were William Thomas Knight and Eliza (Emmons) Knight on his daddy's side. At this time we have no knowledge of his mothers side.

Frances Lucielle and Bonnie Benjamin are the only Knight children still living. *Submitted by Patricia Elliott, PO Box 1075, St. Croix Falls, WI 54024.*

LAMBERT, CHARLIE, born 1865 and died 1939, was the son of Josiah Lambert and Avis Willis Lambert. Charlie was the grandson of John Lambert (b. 1770, d. 1851), our earliest ancestor found in America. Charlie married Vina Jane Carpenter (b. 1865, d. 1948) on May 16, 1891. They had nine children: Mark, Ethel, Bill, Cora, Omar, Audie, Dell, Columbus and Maggie.

Mark Lambert (b. 1892, d. 1981) was married to Nellie Lauderdale on Apr. 13, 1922. They had four children: Molene, John Watson, Earline and Peggy. Mark and his family lived on a farm near the old Tuscumbia School.

Ethel Lambert (b. 1894, d. 1921) married Will Dodds on Nov. 10, 1912. Their first child, Alice, died when she was only 6 years old in 1920. Homa was born Dec. 11, 1916. He married Dell Lambert on Apr. 10, 1938. They have one son, Jerry and two grandchildren. Homa died in September 1999 and was buried in the Liberty Cemetery in Prentiss County, MS.

Cora Lambert (b. 1890, d. 1981) was married to Ferdie Johnson (b. 1896, d. 1972) on Jan. 9, 1916. They had four sons: Fred, Carmon, Eber and Cefus. Eber and Carmon are deceased.

Bill Lambert (b. 1898, d. 1970) married Mary Kate Ford on Mar. 12, 1923 in Prentiss County, MS. They have a daughter, Rachel Lambert.

Omar Lambert (b. 1900, d. 1991) was married to Fannie Nunley (b. 1905, d. 1977). They had nine children: J.C., R.D., Cleborn (Bug), Earnest (Bay), Flora Marie, Harmon, Billy Joe, Omar Lee and Bernice. R.D. was killed in WWII at Luzon, PI

Audie Lambert (b. 1902, d. 1987) married Vernon Hare on Apr. 28, 1927. He later married Annie May Lambert.

Dell Lambert (b. 1904, d. 1987) married Walter C. Carpenter on Oct. 26, 1933. They had nine children: L.C. (deceased), Raymond, Rual, Jewell (deceased), Hubert, Jannie Ree, Ruben (deceased), Peggy and Violene.

Columbus "Dob" Lambert (b. 1906, d. 1964) married Iduma Lawson on Mar. 24, 1932. They had six children: Hershel, Martha Jane, Ethel, Bobby, Mary Lou and Charlie.

Maggie married Earnest Smith on Oct. 1, 1928. They had three children: Charles, Ileene and Etheleene. *Submitted by Maggie Smith.*

LAMBERT, JACKSON ANDREW "JACK,"

the 10th child born to James Clyde and Lucretia Willis Lambert, was born Jun. 6, 1861. He married Francis Louise Claunch. She was born in 1864 and died in 1886 in a tragic accident. Her clothes caught fire while burning corn stalks in the field and she burned to death. She is buried in Forked Oaks Church Cemetery in the old section. Her grave is marked with a white stone post.

After Louise's death, Jackson married her sister, Martha Howard. Their parents were Love Claunch and Nancy Lucinda Owens. Jack and Martha Howard lived at Burnsville, MS for awhile, then moved to Cairo, MS. They built a home and lived there until both died.

The children of Jack and Millie Francis Louise Claunch were Hattie (b. Jun. 28, 1883) and James Thomas "Tom" (b. Jan. 31, 1886). Thomas was 6 weeks old when his mother died.

The 14 children of Jack and Martha Howard Claunch were: Ludie Mae (Born Oct. 5, 1889); George (b. Jan. 9, 1892); Minnie Lee Lambert (b. Feb. 4, 1893); Willie Aaron "Will" Lambert (b. Feb. 19, 1895); Deaniour Clay (b. Mar. 8, 1897); Kellous Ocia (b. Sep. 6, 1898); Grady Alvin (b. Jan. 29, 1900); Clarence E. (b. Dec. 4, 1902); Charles Homer (b. Aug. 31, 1903); Maudie Louise (b. Mar. 19, 1905); Noel E. Lambert (b. Dec. 18, 1906); Tressie Geneva Lambert (b. Apr. 29, 1908); Esther Lambert (b. Jan. 14, 1911) and Jewel Lambert (b. Jul. 3, 1912).

Jackson A. Lambert had 16 children. They lived on a farm near the New Lebanon Church, which Jack helped to build. Jack was a big impressive figure of a man. He had a mustache and his grandchildren can remember him sitting on the bench of a horse-drawn wagon. Jack had large crops of corn, cotton and cane and a sorghum mill and made molasses to supplement their income. They all worked hard, but it was a loving, caring family. There was a big barn in which to keep the hay for their animals, an apple orchard and everything they needed to put away food for the winter. Their water came from a deep well in the front yard where a shelter was built around it. The water was pulled up with a windlass, rope and bucket and carried into the house. It was such good water! The yards at that time did not have a lawn as we know it today. There was no grass growing to cut. The soil was sandy and packed hard and kept clean by cutting the weeds and sweeping it. Jack died suddenly with a heart attack at his home, just down the road from New Lebanon Church. At his death, Jackson was 76. Francis Eliza Claunch Lambert was 21 at her death. Jack's place was sold to his sons, Deaniour Clay Lambert and Noel E. Lambert and his daughter, Jewel Lambert Nixon. *Submitted by Melvin V. Lambert and Edna Earl Fuller.*

LAMBERT, JAMES THOMAS "TOM,"

born Jan. 31, 1886 in Prentiss County, MS was 6 weeks old when his mother burned to death. After that, Tom lived with his grandparents, Love and Nancy Claunch, whom he always called Paw and Maw. Love and Nancy lived on what is presently known as the Charles Homer Lambert field. Tom lived with them until he married Arra Louette Tennison, daughter of Hiram Tennison and Nancy Elledge. They filed for their marriage affidavit on Aug. 15, 1903 and were married Aug. 16, 1903, by Rev. L.M. White. M.G. Arra was born Aug. 11, 1884 in Tishomingo County, MS and died October 12.

James Thomas "Tom" Lambert and Arra Louette Tennison Lambert

Tom sawmilled and farmed most of his life. He lived at East Prentiss where he cut out a tract of land. He sold his mill to Jim Phillip Rollen, then moved to Bay Springs where he bought two steam sawmills. He owned eight pair of mules and two pair of oxen. He built 8-10 houses for his workers, which were made from 20-inch wide boards of yellow rich pine. Some of Tom's workers were Martin Tennison, Bent Cook, Joe Swim, Olen Belue and Sid Wright. Arra did a lot of cooking for these hands.

Tom later owned the Bonds place, where he had another mill (located on Highway 365, three miles from Cairo, MS) and surrounding land. He bought his half-brother, Will Lambert's place. He owned land from Cairo to Burton, MS. Some of the old place names are The Tin Top, Joe Moss Place and the Belue Place. He had a mill at the Tin Top and it was there that a mud valve blew out, burning Tom from the knee down when he was 60 years old. He built a church at his place and called it, The First Church of God, which Edwin Parker later bought and turned it into a home.

The old store that Tom owned in 1945 was later moved to his son Gravin's place by Leonard Clark and Gravin, to a place across the road from Gravin's house that was a half mile from Tom's place.

Children of James Lambert and Arra Tennison are:

1. Audrie Fae Lambert (b. Jun. 25, 1904 in Prentiss County, MS, d. Mar. 9, 1907 in Prentiss County of meningitis) is buried in Fairview Church of God Cemetery.
2. Goven Hewell Lambert (b. Dec. 14, 1907 in Prentiss County, d. May 29, 1974 in Lee County, MS).
3. Gravin Clemon Lambert (b. Jun. 5, 1911 in Tishomingo County).
4. Hessel Irene Lambert (b. Aug. 6, 1914 in Prentiss County, d. Aug. 14, 1968 at her home in Cairo Community, Prentiss County).
5. Marvin Duell Lambert (b. May 5, 1918 in Prentiss County).
6. Willie Clesta Lambert (b. May 28, 1921 in Prentiss County).
7. Melvin Millard Lambert (b. born Aug. 17, 1922 in Prentiss County).
8. J.T. Lambert (b. Sep. 27, 1927 in Prentiss County). *Submitted by Melvin V. Lambert*

LAMBERT, JOHN,

born 1770 and died 1851, is our earliest ancestor that we have been able to find in America. We have been unable to locate his parents. Our branch of the Lambert family could have arrived in America anytime after 1623 when the earliest known Lambert arrived in Jamestown, VA. It is not known how long John Lambert lived in South Carolina after his birth. It appears that John may have lived his entire life near Indian Territory (McNairy County, TN). By 1812, it appears that he was living in what is now McNairy County, TN. McNairy County is just north of old Tishomingo County, MS.

McNairy County lies just over the Mississippi-Tennessee border and although in another state, the distance between the two places where they lived could have been as little as 15-20 miles. They reportedly lived in the Hamburg Community, which was very close to where the Battle of Shiloh was fought in the Civil War. The Hamburg Road in existence during the war is still in existence today. John moved to Tishomingo County, MS after 1837. John would later own a farm in the Burnsville area in Tishomingo County, MS. John's sons and daughters would move into present day Alcorn, Prentiss and Tishomingo County, MS and they would go in to present day McNairy County, TN to raise their families.

When the 1850 census was taken in September 1850 in Tishomingo County, John was 80 years old and living in the Yellow Creek area, three miles northeast of Burnsville, MS with his daughter, Nancy, who was 30 years of age, Berry (Tuckberry), who was 8 and Mary, who was 6. John told the enumerator that he was 80 years old and that he owned property and that he was born in South Carolina.

This would make his birth year approximately 1770. When John died in February/March of the following year (1851) at Burnsville, MS he was 81 years of age and he had lived under the reign of King George III and 13 American presidents – from George Washington to the first year of the presidency of Millard Fillmore.

Although he did not leave a will, we have records of the appraisal and inventory of his estate. He left 247 acres, a house, household items, cows, hogs and farm related items and equipment.

John asked that his property be divided among his children. They were listed as William (b. 1812); James Clyde (b. 1819); Hickman (b. 1823); Josiah (b. 1824); Rebecca (1817, d. 1825); Thomas (b. 1826?) and Nancy (b. 1830). No mention of a wife was made, meaning his wife had predeceased him.

He was buried with many of his descendants and their wives in the Possum Trot Cemetery, which is on his farm and is a Lambert family cemetery. His marker has long since disappeared, but in 1997, some of his descendants made up and got him a new marker. *Submitted by Melvin V. Lambert with help from Ralph Lambert.*

LAMBERT, JOHN WATSON,

born Jan. 20, 1927 to Mark and Nellie Lauderdale Lambert in the Tuscumbia Community. He attended school at Tuscumbia, Booneville High School and Northeast Mississippi Junior College before entering the Army during WWII. He served in France and Germany and later in the Korean Conflict.

Watson Lambert Family

He married Geraldine Bullard in 1950 and they lived in the Tuscumbia Community before moving to Houston, TX where they lived for five years. While in Texas two daughters were born to them: Deborah Kay (b. Sep. 15, 1956) and Donna Marie (b. Dec. 18,

1957). Their son, John Rodney, was born in Jackson, MS on Feb. 18, 1952. They returned to the Tuscumbia Community in 1960 and made it their home.

Their children attended Thrasher High School and Northeast Mississippi Junior College. John Rodney lives in the Tuscumbia Community; Deborah Kay lives in Oxford, MS and Donna Marie lives in Booneville. Donna Marie married David Inman in 1976. They have three children: Heather Daonna who married Luke Ledbetter in 1998, Tiffany Nicole and William David Dustin. They attend Jumpertown High School.

LAMBERT, MELVIN MILLARD and Letty Marie Worley were married on Feb. 15, 1941 in the home of Harley Owen "H.O." Moss, J.P. at Cairo, Prentiss County, MS. They lived at different places in Prentiss County, MS. They first lived close to the New Lebanon Church at Cairo, MS and then they lived in June Skinner renter house (This is where Marie's parents, Arthur and Lona Dickson Worley, would live later). They lived in the Snowdown Community where Judith was born in 1941. They lived in a house close to Melvin's brother, Garvin Clemon Lambert (a lot of the Lambert's would live in this house as time went by). From there, Melvin and Marie moved to Oregon to build ships for WWII. Melvin was a ship fitter and Marie worked in an apartment complex.

Mr. and Mrs. Melvin Lambert with Judith Ann and Roy Gene

While there, Melvin got his call to go to war. So, he moved back to Mississippi. When Melvin went for his medical exam, the service doctors found him to be a diabetic.

In 1943, Melvin and Marie bought 20 acres of land from his father, James Thomas Lambert, for $500. There was a two-room house on the land located in Cairo Community in the northeast corner of Prentiss County. They lived there for a while, then moved to a renter house owned by Homer Lambert, Melvin's uncle. Roy, the first son, was born Sep. 15, 1944. This is while they were still at the renter house.

The old two-room house that was on their land when they bought it from James Thomas was torn down. They started building a new house in 1944 when Roy was less than a year old. They moved in the new house in 1945 and Joyce was born there in 1946.

Melvin and Marie moved to Georgia to sawmill. Johnny Wayne was born in Hahira, GA. After that, they moved back to Mississippi. Melvin bought a truck and started trucking. He trucked up to 1959. Then he turned it over to his son, Roy. Roy and Johnny both trucked for many years.

Their next two children, Patricia Paulette (b. 1954) and Melvin Vicky Lambert (b. 1959), were born in Booneville Hospital, Prentiss County, MS. When Vicky was about a year old, Melvin Millard went to work for Bowyer Johnson Construction Co. as a grader driver and then to Worsham Construction Co. as a Road Foreman. He worked there for more than 30 years. He was the foreman on the ITT plant in Corinth and part of the Natchez Trace in Tishomingo County. He supervised the building of the bridges on Hwy. 365 and Hwy. 72 at Burnsville. He had to take early retirement in 1973 because of a heart problem and emphysema.

In 1997 he had surgery to relieve fluid pressure on his brain, which left him totally incapacitated. His family cared for him at home until he passed away Apr. 20, 2000 at 2:30 p.m. in Magnolia Hospital in Corinth, MS.

LANGSTON FAMILY, originally from Jones County, Joe Ray Langston and Dot Langston moved to Booneville in Prentiss County in 1964. Joe Ray had graduated that same year from the Jackson School of Law. When Joe Ray opened his office, Dot served as his secretary. Moving to Booneville with Joe Ray and Dot were their three children. Ten-year-old Cindy, 7 year-old Joey and 6 year-old Shane became students in the Booneville/Prentiss County School System. Cindy graduated from Booneville High School in 1972. Joey and Shane finished high school at the prestigious Baylor School in Chattanooga, TN. Cindy later attended Northeast Community College and graduated from Mississippi State University and University of Mississippi Law School. Joey and Shane both graduated from Millsaps College and the University of Mississippi Law School.

Joe Ray Langston with Keaton Langston in 1986.

The Langston Family in 1997

Cindy Langston married Tyson Bridge of Oxford in 1998. She is the proud mother of two children, Casey Lott and Bryce Lott. Their father, Duncan Lott, is also a successful Booneville attorney. Cindy formed the law firm of Langston and Associates in Jackson, MS in 1995.

Joey married Tracie Arnold in 1983. Tracie provided the Langstons with the "roots" they lacked. She is the daughter of Prentiss countians, Bob and Kathleen Arnold. Tracie's grandparents were Bonner and Lucille Arnold of Wheeler. Joey and Tracie have three sons: Keaton Cashe Langston (b. 1985), Joe-Colby Ray Langston (b. 1987) and Kane Arnold Langston (b. 1992). Tracie was the teacher for the Prentiss County School system's first kindergarten class in 1985. She later became the office manger for Langston, Langston, Michael, Bowen & Tucker before devoting herself to the full-time job of raising the Langston boys and managing the Langston home. The Joey Langston family lives in one of Mississippi's most beautiful homes, a fully colonnaded home just south of downtown Booneville. The Langstons travel internationally but most enjoy spending time with their sons at sporting events or at their lakehouse near Pickwick, TN.

Shane is married to the former Michelle Stamps of Lookout Mountain, TN. They have two beautiful daughters, Cody Raye (b. 1986) and Jacqueline King (b. 1989). Shane's family currently lives in Madison County, MS. In 1995, Shane was given an award for his accomplishments, "Mississippi's Most Outstanding Trial Lawyer". Shane is a senior partner in the Jackson, MS, firm of Langston, Frazer, Sweet and Freese.

Joey Langston practices in Booneville and is the senior partner of one of Mississippi's most successful law firms, Langston, Langston, Michael, Bowen & Tucker, P.A. The firm is presently located in one of Mississippi's finest office buildings at 100 South Main Street in downtown Booneville. Langston, Langston, Michael, Bowen & Tucker, P.A. is the same firm that started as "The Law Office of Joe Ray Langston" in 1964. Joey Langston began serving as the attorney for the Prentiss County Board of Supervisors in 1988, a job previously held by his father.

Not having roots in Prentiss County, the Langstons needed a "boost" to establish their law practice. That boost came in 1967 when Joe Ray and family launched a campaign for the office of County Attorney. They won! Those opposing Joe Ray's candidacy complained that he was not raised in Prentiss County. His campaign slogan became "while not a Prentiss Countian by birth, I am a Prentiss Countian by choice!"

The Langstons have shown a commitment to education and hard work. The present day results are three Mississippi law firms that enjoy a nationwide law practice with emphasis on personal injury, mass tort litigation and criminal defense work.

Dot still lives in the family home on Downing Drive in Booneville. The Langstons have been in Prentiss County for 35 years. With their roots firmly set, Booneville and Prentiss County will have Langstons for many decades to come.

The Joey Langston Family in 1999

LARSEN, JOHN T., born Oct. 20, 1950 in Rankin County, MS moved to Prentiss County in 1973 immediately following a two-year stint as a missionary for The Church of Jesus Christ of Latter-day Saints in California. He met and married Kathleen Cole, the 1976 valedictorian of Thrasher High School.

John and Kathleen were married on Jul. 6, 1976 in the Salt Lake City Temple. On Feb. 4, 1981, daughter, Kari Suzanne, was born. She in 1999, was also the Thrasher Valedictorian. On Apr. 28, 1984, Daniel Joseph Larsen would join the family, followed 10 years later, on Jun. 4, 1994, by Katie Marie Larsen.

John was born the son of Sallie Comfort Herrod and John Willie Herrod as the sixth of 13 children but was adopted in 1960 by Leonard Alfred and Nellie Orrilla Arter Larsen of Colorado.

(Sarah) Kathleen, born Apr. 15, 1957, came from a family of 12, the daughter of Walter and Audrey Marie Floyd Cole. Her grandparents were Lee and Ester Floyd and James Huston and Lee Retter Vetito Cole. Kathleen's family has been in the area dating back to the mid to early 1800s.

Children of John and Kathleen Larsen. From left: Daniel, Kari and Katie

Over the years, Kathleen and John have been active in the church and Scouting program. Both are recipients of Scouting's District Award of Merit and John received the Silver Beaver Award, a national honor presented by the local Scout Council. Kathleen has served in numerous positions in the LDS Cub Pack and John was Scoutmaster of Troop 96 for 13 years.

John has served as counselor to three Booneville Bishops, J.C. Morris, Wayne Whipple and Bobby Smith, as well as a member for 8 years, of the Tupelo Stake Presidency in the LDS Church. On Nov. 14, 1999, he was called and ordained the Bishop of the Booneville Ward. Kathleen is a graduate of Northeast Mississippi Community College and was a long-time employee of Prentiss Manufacturing. John has been in the printing trade since 1973, first with Reinbold Printing and then with Mid-South Graphics of Ripley. *Submitted by John Larsen.*

LECROY, JESSE, the LeCroy family has lived in Mississippi for about 150 years. Of French Huguenot extraction, their forebears first settled in North Carolina, then migrated through Georgia to Alabama prior to the Civil War. The great-grandfather of the Mississippi branch of this family was Mordecai LeCroy, the youngest of 12 children born in Alabama. He followed his sweetheart, Martha Stokes, to Union County, MS around 1850 and married her, first settling on Rock Pile Hill. Later the family moved to the Oak Hill Community in western Prentiss County. Their children were Will, Jesse, Sally, Alexander, Robert and Emma.

Jesse and Dezzie LeCroy and their son, Mordecai in front of the old family home around 1915

The second son of this family was Jesse. He was a teacher and farmer. He married Dezzie Morgan and moved to the Blackland community around 1906. Their only child was James Mordecai LeCroy. Dezzie Morgan was afflicted with a debilitating nerve disease, which caused her death at the age of 45. The son, Mordecai, graduated from Mississippi State in electrical engineering in 1932 and did graduate work at Harvard University. In 1934 he married Catherine Brinkley, who as a child had once been a close neighbor. They established their home with Mordecai's father, then a widower. Mordecai served in WWII with the final rank of lieutenant colonel and later was a member to the Mississippi Legislature from Prentiss County. He was a farmer and cotton ginner.

Four daughters: Louise, Olivia, Jessica and Evelyn were all reared in the family home in Blackland. Louise taught at NEMCC for many years and later became a stockbroker and a real estate broker. She married an attorney, Jack Dubard and had two children, John and Amy. Later she married Claude Sanders, a retired brigadier general in the Marine Corp. Olivia was a model and died after a long illness. Jessica is an attorney and a foreign service officer in Washington, DC. She has served in several embassies throughout the world. Evelyn was a human resources consultant in Dallas for many years. She is married to Dr. Robert Hootkins, a nephrologist and they live in Austin, TX with their three children: Robert Jr., Mary Catherine and Helen.

Five generations of LeCroys have lived in the old family farmhouse where Louise now resides. In 2006, LeCroys will have lived in this house for 100 years. *Submitted by Louise Sanders.*

LEDBETTER, WILLIAM RILEY, born Mar. 5, 1837 in Tennessee, son of James P. Ledbetter and Susan A. Smith. His siblings were David Pinkney Ledbetter, Ellen Ledbetter Tanner and James Monroe (Rowe) Ledbetter.

Riley was first married to Parilee Farris, daughter of Commodore Farris and Jane Wardlow, around 1856/1857 in McNairy County, TN. Parilee and Riley had two daughters, Margaret Ann and Mary Josephine (Mollie). After Parilee's death (after 1860/before 1864), Riley married Martha Ann Farris. Since their marriage license bond (Oct. 4, 1864, McNairy County, TN) gives her name as Martha Ann Bishop, she is believed to be the daughter of Elisha and Hellena Farris of Tishomingo County, MS who first married J.M. Bishop in Tishomingo County (1860). Riley and Martha had eight children: James David, John Riley, Rosetta, William F. (died ca. 1874 at age 18), Samuel Taylor, George H., Dock Smith and Dora.

According to his military records, William Riley Ledbetter served as 2nd Lieutenant, Co. F, 18th Regiment (Newsom's), Tennessee Cavalry (Confederate). The regiment was engaged in action at Tuscumbia Creek and Brice's Crossroads.

The Ledbetter family left McNairy County in the 1870s and settled in Lee County, MS. By 1880, Riley's siblings, David and Ellen and families had also settled nearby. His brother and sister-in-law, James Monroe (Rowe) and Densy, followed and were living in Lee County by 1900.

Riley's sister, Ellen, married Richard Tanner in McNairy County, TN (1865) and James Monroe, his brother, married Densy C. Barnes in McNairy County (1874). Riley's brother, David Pinkney, first married Josephine Blalock. His second wife was Fannie Belle Horton. David Ledbetter and family left Mississippi and settled in Arkansas around 1920 before moving to southeastern Missouri.

William Riley Ledbetter died Nov. 15, 1892. According to his Confederate Grave Registration, he is buried in Old Pleasant Valley Cemetery, west of Guntown. His wife, Martha, is most likely buried there, as well. Sadly, the cemetery has been vandalized and headstones have been removed or destroyed. William Riley Ledbetter's headstone was replaced by the US Department of Veteran's Affairs (National Cemetery System/Memorial Program Service). It was set in Old Pleasant Valley Cemetery on Dec. 27, 1999 in the location where his grave is believed to be next to the headstone of his mother (Susan A. Ledbetter).

Riley's children married and settled in north Mississippi. Margaret married Taylor Moore and lived in the Tupelo area. Mollie married John McCarthy and lived in Lee County. James married Frances Carpenter and lived in Prentiss County. John Riley married Callie Kitchens (daughter of Lewis D. Kitchens and Cynthia C. Stewart) and lived in the Glenfield Community in Union County. Etta married Emps Keeton and lived in Prentiss County. Samuel Taylor, a Methodist minister, married Mary Surratt and served churches in Tippah, Alcorn, Benton and Prentiss counties. George married Amie Carpenter and moved from Union County to Texas. Dora married John Young and lived in Corinth. Dock married Susie Young and lived in the Glenfield Community in Union County. *Submitted by Brenda Ledbetter Rayman.*

LEWIS, MARCUS MALCOLM, Trudie Mae Davis (b. Dec. 5, 1884), daughter of Johnathan T. and Tabatha Jane Butler Davis, married Marcus Malcolm Lewis on Aug. 19, 1906. He was born Apr. 4, 1874 to Amos Hardin and Mary Jane Hughes Lewis of McNairy County, TN. Malcom farmed and worked as a barber. They had four children.

1) Ida Mae Lewis (b. Nov. 17, 1907 in Alcorn County, MS) md. Daniel Chester Crabb. They farmed in East Prentiss County and had one child, Daniel Prentiss Crabb (b. Jun. 30, 1941), married Brenda Frances Lacy. They have one daughter, Nelda Darlene Crabb (b. Sep. 30, 1968) md. John Richard Shook, one child, Elijah Chet Shook. A member of Martin Hill Freewill Baptist Church, Ida Mae Lewis Crabb died Nov. 24, 1993 and is buried at Mt. Nebo.

James Hardin and Marie Hopkins Lewis

2) Minnie Lee Lewis (b. Dec. 18, 1908 in Okolona, Lee County, MS) md. Dayton Elkin Mink. They worked with the garment industries in North Mississippi. They had no children. They liked to go up on the river for the weekend and fish. They were members of Carolina Methodist Church. Minnie Lee Lewis Mink died May 17, 1996 at the home of her caregivers, her brother, James and his wife, Marie Hopkins Lewis. She is buried in the Booneville Cemetery.

3) Marcus Eugene Lewis (b. Jun. 8, 1911 in Ramer, McNairy County, TN served in the US Air Force as a master sergeant during WWII. He married Georgia Lou Christian. They moved to Lockport, IL where he was an electrician for Reynolds Aluminum. They have two children: Marsha Gail Lewis (b. Mar. 16, 1955) md. Harry Bennett Craig, resides in Madison, AL and Barbara Jean Lewis (b. May 3, 1957) md. Jeff Gates, one son, Trevor Gates, resides in Memphis, TN. Marcus Eugene Lewis, a member of the Baptist Church, died Mar. 2, 1965 and is buried in the Booneville Cemetery.

4) James Hardin Lewis (b. Jul. 8, 1920 in Ramer, McNairy County, TN) md. Artie Marie Hopkins Lewis on Jul. 19, 1941. James Hardin Lewis was a private first class in the 45th Inf. Div., 179th Regt. during WWII and served in five major campaigns including Sicily, Salerno, Anzio and Southern France, then crossed the Rhine River into Munich, Germany. During WWII he was in the European-African-Middle-Eastern Theater of Operation. He received the Infantryman's Badge and Bronze Star Medals for meritorious achievement in combat against the armed enemy. He was in the Military Police. After returning home, he farmed and later worked as a master carpenter.

Marie Hopkins Lewis worked in the garment industry. She was a great homemaker and known throughout the community for her delicious caramel cakes, candy and chocolate oatmeal cookies. Many times I can remember my mother working all day at the factory and cooking a big dinner for a visiting preacher and his family who was holding our revival.

Lewis Family. Malcom, Marcus, Trudie Mae; standing: Ida Mae and Minnie Lee

They provided the kind of loving home with Christian values, tender guidance and discipline that most children dream of. They had two children, Sandra Kay Lewis (b. Nov. 12, 1946) md. Lester Roy Gray with one child, Rhonda Roxanne Gray (b. May 13, 1968). James Gaylon Lewis (b. Feb. 21, 1951) md. Mary Lou Bearden, two sons: Franklin Gale Lewis (b. Aug. 3, 1969) and Michael Paul Lewis (b. Mar. 20, 1976). They lived in the Tuscumbia Community and were members of East Booneville Baptist Church. As a deacon and teacher, they attended every service faithfully. James Hardin Lewis died Jul. 10, 1998 and is buried in the family plot at Booneville Cemetery. *Submitted by Sandra Lewis Gray, granddaughter.*

LINDSEY, ERBEL GOODWIN "E.G.," born May 31, 1946, Itawamba County, MS to Herbel Buford Sr. and Martha Annie Lou (Goodwin) Lindsey. His grandparents were George Martin Lindsey and Annie Mazie (Rouse) and James A. Goodwin and Bessie M. (Carter). He married Martha Jean Pike, daughter of Julian Carey and Trana Aliena (Barker) Pike. Her grandparents were James Edgar "Ed" Pike and Julia (Lyle) and William Eli Barker and Miley Elizabeth (Tolleson).

The E.G. Lindsey Family. Back Row L-R: Kim, Scotty, Meloney, Martha Jean, Eric. Front Row L-R: Jeffrey, Madison, E.G., Madelyn, Ethan and Kristie

Erbel Goodwin is an auto body instructor at Northeast Mississippi Community College. Martha Jean owns and operates an antique shop in Saltillo. In 1955, Martha Jean became a member of the Natchez Trace Chapter Daughters of the American Revolution. Her Revolutionary War ancestor was Allegany McGuire, who resided during the American Revolution in Virginia. He assisted in establishing American independence while acting in the capacity of orderly sergeant. He served under Captain Charles Scott at Williamsburg, Yorktown and Hampton, other times under General Lincoln and General Gates.

Erbel Goodwin "E.G." and Martha Jean have three children: Jeffrey Martin (b. Apr. 26, 1968, Prentiss County, MS), married Dec. 28, 1991, Prentiss County, MS to Mary Meloney (Green), the daughter of Roy and Brenda (Moreland) Green. Jeff and Meloney had one child, Madelyn Kate (b. May 5, 1997, Lee County, MS); Eric Glen (b. Jan. 26, 1971, Lee County, MS) married on Aug. 14, 1993 in Prentiss County, MS to Kristie Elizabeth (George), the daughter of Will and Judy (Holland) George. Eric and Kristie have one child, Ethan George (b. Feb. 5, 1997, Lee County, MS); Scotty Goodwin (b. May 26, 1972, Lee County, MS) married on Jul. 29, 1995 in Prentiss County, MS to Kimberly Sue (Cole), daughter of Aaron and Ann (Gray) Cole. Scotty and Kim have one child, Madison Paige (b. Jul. 12, 1997, Lee County, MS). *Submitted by Eric Glen Lindsey.*

LINDSEY, GEORGE MARTIN, born Feb. 28, 1889, son of Walter and Drusilla "Drillie" (Cromeans) Lindsey and the grandson of Evens Martin and Georgia Ann (Lipsey) Lindsey, who he was named from and Jim and Sally (Tittle) Cromeans from Itawamba County, MS. George Martin married Annie Mazie Rouse (b. Jun. 17, 1891, Itawamba County MS). Annie Mazie was the daughter of John and Bell (Houston) Rouse and granddaughter of John W. and Martha Rouse and Sarah Rebecca (Wren) (b. Feb. 27, 1838, Alabama) and Robert Kern Houston (b. Aug. 20, 1829, South Carolina). Robert Kern served as sergeant in Co. K, 42nd Mississippi Infantry of the Confederate States of America.

George Martin worked as a mail carrier, farmer, sawmill operator and merchant. Annie Mazie worked as a housewife and merchant.

George Martin and Annie had four children: Audrey Hortense (b. Aug. 13, 1912, Itawamba County, MS); Herbel Buford (b. Mar. 21, 1914, Itawamba County, MS) and lived in Prentiss County, MS; Arcula B.D. (b. Aug. 1, 1916); Fonza Angie (b. May 7, 1919, Itawamba County, MS); Curthel Cutha (b. Jan. 7, 1922, Itawamba County, MS, d. Mar. 3, 1938, Itawamba County, MS); Zelbert I (b. Nov. 25, 1924, Itawamba County, MS, d. Jul. 17, 1972); Eunice Vivian (b. Apr. 4, 1927).

Annie Mazie (Rouse) (b. 1891, d. 1930) and George Martin Lindsey (b. 1889, d. 1975)

Annie Mazie died Nov. 18, 1930, leaving George Martin with small children as young as 18 months old to raise. He then married Bessie M. (Carter) Goodwin Aug. 1, 1939. They lived their last years in Red Bay, Franklin County, AL. Martin died Jun. 14, 1975 and Bessie died Nov. 12, 1978.

George Martin Lindsey is remembered by his children and grandchildren as a hard working, honest and faithful Christian man whose values are instilled in his family today. *Submitted by Fonza Brewer.*

LINDSEY, HERBEL BUFORD SR., son of George Martin and Annie Mazie (Rouse) Lindsey was born in Itawamba County, MS Mar. 21, 1914. He was married to Martha Annie Lou Goodwin (b. Jun. 21, 1926), daughter of James A. and Bessie Molendia (Carter) Goodwin and the granddaughter of Benjamin and Rhoda (Massey) Goodwin and Levi Russell and Martha (Johnson) Carter.

He joined the Army Sep. 23, 1942 as a private. Herbel farmed and was an automotive mechanic.

Martha Annie Lou is remembered by her family as a loving Christian mother and a grandmother who always put family first.

Herbel and Martha Annie Lou had nine children as follows:

1) Herbel Buford Jr. "H.B." (b. Sep. 26, 1942, Itawamba County, MS) married on Nov. 23, 1966 in Prentiss County, MS to Annette (Thorne), children: Herbel Buford III (Traye) (b. Aug. 30, 1969, Prentiss County, MS), married Mar. 12, 1995 to Stephanie (Sellers), child Blake Martin (b. Aug. 26, 1998 Lee County, MS); Trayce Annette (b. Jul. 31, 1971, Prentiss County, MS).

2) Betty Lou (b. Apr. 9, 1944, Itawamba County, MS), children: John Richard Shook (b. May 8, 1966, Prentiss County, MS), married Jun. 24, 1989 in Prentiss County, MS to Darlene (Crabb), child Elijah Chet (b. Nov. 28, 1996, Alcorn County, MS); Tammy Lynn (Shook) Ross (b. Jun. 29, 1970, Lee County, MS) married Michael Todd Ross Apr. 18, 1998, Lee County, MS.

Herbel Buford Lindsey Sr. Family

3) Erbel Goodwin (b. May 31, 1946, Itawamba County, MS) married Martha Jean (Pike) on Sep. 6, 1967, Prentiss County, MS, children: Jeffrey Martin (b. Apr. 26, 1968, Prentiss County, MS), married Dec. 28, 1991, Prentiss County, MS to Mary Meloney (Green), child, Madelyn Kate (b. May 5, 1997, Lee County, MS); Eric Glen (b. Jan. 26, 1971, Lee County, MS) married Aug. 14, 1993, Prentiss County, MS to Kristie Elizabeth (George), child, Ethan George (b. Feb. 5, 1997, Lee County, MS); Scotty Goodwin (b. May 26, 1972, Lee County, MS) married Jul. 29, 1995, Prentiss County, MS to Kimberly Sue (Cole), child Madison Paige (b. Jul. 12, 1997, Lee County, MS).

4) Margaret B. (b. May 18, 1948, Itawamba County, MS) married Jun. 21, 1968, Prentiss County, MS to Charles Cleveland Cheatham, children: Dana Charline (b. Dec. 1, 1970, Prentiss County, MS); Janie Dawn (b. Jul. 22, 1974, Prentiss County, MS).

5) Jackie Eugene (b. Aug. 4, 1950, Itawamba County, MS) married Jul. 14, 1979 to Rebecca "Becky" Burchfield, children: Jonathan Eugene (b. Jun. 2, 1981, Lee County, MS); Callie Emaranda (b. Nov. 11, 1987, Lee County, MS).

6) Hobert Larry (b. Mar. 6, 1953, Itawamba County, MS), married Mar. 1, 1975 in Prentiss County, MS to Linda Sue Lovell, children: Hobert Larry II "Hobie" (b. Apr. 17, 1976, Lee County, MS); three stepdaughters: Angela Rene (Wildman) (b. May 5, 1967) married Jun. 21, 1985, Prentiss County, MS to Charles Michael Tennison, child, Charles Michael Tennison II (b. Nov. 21, 1990); Jennifer Lynn (Nix) (b. Nov. 26, 1968) married Sep. 2, 1988 to Robert Elton Davis, children: Robert Elton Davis II (b. Aug. 11, 1991); Shailyn Dinae (b. Sep. 13, 1994); Cindy Diane (Nix) (b. Apr. 28, 1971) married Feb. 25, 1989 to Michael Allen Barnes, children: Lynzee Ann (b. Jan. 26, 1991); Nicholas Skylar (b. Aug. 30, 1995); Stephen Michael (b. Jul. 23, 1996).

7) James Matthew "Mac" (b. Sep. 9, 1956, Prentiss County, MS) married Jan. 23, 1976, Prentiss County, MS to Lafonda (McCreary), child, James Matthew II "Matt" (b. Apr. 10, 1985, Lee County, MS).

8) Mary Ann (b. Aug. 14, 1959, Prentiss County, MS) married May 9, 1980 to Roy Neal Holley, children: Carter Neal (b. Mar. 3, 1987, Lee County, MS); Collin Lindsey (b. Aug. 30, 1990, Lee County, MS).

9) George Edward (Jobe) (b. Mar. 22, 1961, Prentiss County, MS), married Mar. 29, 1986 to Lisa Carrol (Holliday), children: Edward Jobe (b. and died. Oct. 19, 1992); Anna Carrol (b. May 3, 1994, d. May 5, 1994).

Herbert Buford Sr. died Jan. 27, 1988. Martha Annie Lou died Nov. 6, 1989. Both are buried at Liberty Cemetery, Prentiss County, MS. *Submitted by Margaret Cheatham.*

LINDSEY-MARTIN, my family of Lindseys are the descendants of James (b. 1799, Tennessee) and Nancy (b. 1800, Tennessee), according to the 1850 census of Coosa County, AL.

Walter Lindsey Family. Front Row L-R: Lucus, Walter, Baby Will, Druesilla, Lona, Vel, Hightower and wife Jesse (Houston). Back Row L-R: Thomas L., George Martin and Zechariah Benjamin

Evens Martin Lindsey (b. Jul. 1, 1837, Alabama) son of James and Nancy, married Georgia Ann Lipsey on Jun. 17, 1855, Coosa County, AL. W. Suttle, Probate Judge of Coosa County, AL issued the license and R.R. Dickinson, M.G, married them. Georgia Ann Lipsey was the daughter of Hiram and Caroline Lipsey, Coosa County, AL. Hiram Lipsey died Dec. 21, 1859 and was buried in Old Bethany Methodist Church Cemetery at Stewartville, Coosa County, AL.

Evens Martin and Georgia Ann raised 10 children: James Hiram "Jim," Nancy Callie, Rocksann, Walter (b. May 15, 1862, Alabama, d. Dec. 27, 1930, Itawamba County MS), Josephine, John L., Emmer, Alonzo (b. October 1870, Mississippi) and lived his adult life in Wheeler, MS, Scotter (b. September 1871, Mississippi), Willie Wernie (b. Apr. 5, 1880, Mississippi, d. May 4, 1955, Alcorn County, MS).

Evens Martin fought in the Civil War. He enlisted in Lawrence County, AL in July 1862, Co. A Stewarts Battalion under Gen. Joe Patterson. He was on detached duty with Capt. Dupree Scotts, captured Apr. 7, 1865 and paroled at Vicksburg, MS in June 1865.

Evens Martin and Georgia Ann Lipsey came to Fulton, MS, Itawamba County from Alabama around 1870, then back to Alabama to Cherokee, AL, Colbert County. This is when Georgia Ann died around 1895 and was buried in the Moonhtown Cemetery in Cherokee, AL. He then married Sarah Ann Garrett on Aug. 11, 1898 in Franklin County, AL. At her death, he moved to Prentiss County, MS, Blackland Community and married Emilene "Jumper" Kelly on Apr. 12, 1905, Prentiss County, MS. Evens Martin died Jan. 18, 1909 and was buried in the Hodges Chapel Cemetery, Prentiss County, MS.

Walter Lindsey, fourth child of Evens Martin and Georgia Ann (Lipsey) Lindsey, was born May 15, 1862 in Alabama. He married Druesilla "Drillie" Cromeans (b. May 2, 1862, Itawamba County, MS), daughter of Jim and Sally Tittle Cromeans. Walter and Drusilla's children were Joseph Hightower (b. Feb. 22, 1883, d. Jul. 18, 1958, Prentiss County, MS); James Warren (b. Jan. 28, 1885, d. Aug. 15, 1922); Leonard (b. 1887, d. 1908); George Martin (b. Feb. 28, 1889, d. Jun. 14, 1975, Franklin County, AL); Zechariah Benjamin "Dutch" (b. Apr. 6, 1892, d. Jul. 22, 1963); Thomas L. (b. Jan. 28, 1895, d. Nov. 2, 1965), Lucus Quitman (b. Mar. 28, 1897, d. May 3, 1980); Lona, Lavelyier Alma "Vel" (b. Jul. 8, 1898, d. October 1983, Prentiss County, MS) and William Lester (b. Mar. 24, 1904, d. Dec. 10, 1975, Prentiss County, MS).

Walter died Dec. 27, 1930 and Druesilla died Mar. 28, 1918. Both are buried in Sandy Springs Cemetery, Itawamba County, MS. *Submitted by Jeffrey Martin Lindsey.*

LIVINGSTON, LEMMIE MAE, born Jul. 20, 1916 in Prentiss County, MS was the youngest child of William Gordon and Samantha Louise Waddle Livingston. As a child she was known as Lemmie, but in later life preferred to be called Mae.

Mae grew up in the Hills Chapel vicinity of Prentiss County where her father was a farmer as was his father before him.

Mae met Roy Claiborne Manuel at the peanut shed located behind the Livingston Grocery owned by her cousin. They married Apr. 17, 1937 in Prentiss County. Roy was the son of Tom Manuel who lived at that time in Memphis, Shelby County, TN and Arrie "Missy" Wilburn of Prentiss County. She was the daughter of Claiborne B. and Sarah Enis Wilburn of Prentiss County. After their marriage the couple moved to Arkansas, then to Memphis where two sons were born: Claiborne Haskell Manuel (b. Feb. 19, 1938 in Memphis) married Bobbye Arnold of Iuka, MS has five children. Gordon Wayne (b. Jan. 31, 1943 in Memphis) married Helga Anna Fruhwein of Germany and has three children.

A short time after Wayne was born, Roy entered the US Navy. Mae and the two boys moved back to Prentiss County and lived near Massey's store east of Booneville. Claiborne attended D.A. Hill School until his second year. In the winter, when Roy returned home, the family moved to Lupanta, Mississippi County, AR where they lived when a third son, George Dale was born Nov. 4, 1946. George has no children.

The couple farmed and moved around a lot. They were living in Luxora, Mississippi County, AR on May 3, 1949 when son number four, Billy Ray, was born. Billy married Wanda Louise Staley and they had two children and one grandchild. He next married Heather Griffen. They had no children. Son number five, Johnny Mack (b. Aug. 25, 1951 in Tampa, Hillsborough County, FL) married Brenda Kelly of Idabel, OK. He next married Charlotte Cain of Idabel, OK and they have three children and two grandchildren.

Then it was back to Arkansas where Jerry Lee was born in the backseat of a car on the way to the hospital on Aug. 2, 1954 near Luxora. Jerry married Betty Williston of Idabel, OK and had one daughter. He next married Betty Casey of New Town, ND and they had three children.

The seventh and youngest son, Danny Gerald, was born Oct. 19, 1958 also in Luxora, AR. Danny married Karen Dickenson of Idabel, OK and they had three children.

Mae and Roy moved to Iron Stob, a community southwest of Idabel, OK on Dec. 11, 1961. It was to be the last farm job they took. Mae was really upset about the move because she knew that her oldest son was coming in for Christmas from the military and if she moved far away from Memphis she would not get to see him. She was right. Johnny remembers the move as cold and miserable in the back of a cotton trailer all the way from Luxora, AR.

The boys attended school in nearby Idabel. They survived the move and are scattered abroad now themselves.

Clay lives in Memphis; Wayne lives in Augusta, GA; George, Billy and Johnny live in Idabel; Jerry lives in New Town, ND and Danny lives near Ft. Smith, AR.

After retiring from farming, the family moved to Idabel and Roy took a job near Leary, TX at the Lone Star Ammunition Plant where he worked on a line making munitions. Later he worked in Idabel at the Kellwood sewing factory as a night watchman. Mae went to work in Tootie's Restaurant and later worked at McCurtain Memorial Hospital in housekeeping.

Mae and Roy divorced in 1976. Mae chose to stay in Idabel after the divorce. She next married Dewey Day and they later divorced.

Roy died Sep. 5, 1983 as an indirect result of an attack by intruders in August 1981. He is buried at Denison Cemetery in Idabel, McCurtain County, OK. Mae will celebrate her 84th birthday this July. *Submitted by Charlotte Manuel.*

LIVINGSTON, WILLIAM GORDON, born Feb. 28, 1869 in Mississippi. His obit says Tennessee, but that is incorrect. He may have lived in Tennessee for a time, but that has not yet been confirmed.

William married Samantha Louise Waddle on Dec. 5, 1900 in Itawamba County, MS where Samantha lived with her parents, William O. and Mary Ann Beam Waddle.

William was a farmer and Samantha helped in the fields in addition to taking care of the home and children. Cora Alice was born Mar. 28, 1902 in Prentiss County where the couple made their home. Cora married William Audie Whitley. William was born Oct. 14, 1894. Cora died May 17, 1986 and William died Apr. 5, 1932. They are both buried at Liberty Hill Cemetery in Alcorn County.

Ida Bell was born Jun. 22, 1904 in Prentiss County She married R.C. Shamlin on Dec. 11, 1919. Ida died Jul. 3, 1991 in West Memphis, Crittendon County, AR and R.C. died May 21, 1985. They are both buried at Mt. Pisgah Cemetery in Prentiss County.

Young Leander (b. Mar. 7, 1906 in Prentiss County) was named for his grandfather. He married Emma Jean Byford (b. Jul. 23, 1915) on Jul. 4, 1935. Young Leander died Jun. 11, 1983 and Emma died Nov. 13, 1997. They are both buried at Mt. Pisgah Cemetery in Prentiss County.

Hester Claudie (b. Sep. 7, 1907) married Carl Huddleston (b. 1903). Hester died Jul. 27, 1982 and Carl died in 1969. They are also buried at Mt. Pisgah Cemetery in Prentiss County

Lemmie Mae (b. Jul. 20, 1916 in Prentiss County) married Roy Claiborne Manuel, son of Tom Manuel and Arrie "Missy" Wilburn who was from Prentiss County also. Roy was born Oct. 26, 1914 and died Sep. 5, 1983 in Idabel, OK where he is buried at the Denison Cemetery.

Lemmie remembers Christmas most of her childhood. The other girls were older and they always got bigger dolls!

William Gordon Livingston died May 13, 1952 and Samantha Louise died Oct. 23, 1959. They are both buried at Mt. Pisgah Cemetery, though their graves are not together as they were separated for years. They never divorced.

Many of their grandchildren and great-grandchildren still live in Prentiss County as several generations of their ancestors did. *Submitted by Charlotte Manuel.*

LOLLAR, HAROLD WINDAL "BUBBA" JR., born May 20, 1953, son of Julia Young and Harold W. Lollar Sr. of Clarksdale, Coahoma County, MS. He grew up in Meridian and was educated in the Meridian Public School System. He holds the bachelor of theology degree from Andersonville Baptist Seminary and the associate of divinity degree in pastoral ministry from New Orleans Baptist Theological Seminary. An ordained southern Baptist minister, Bubba has pastored churches in Clarke and Sunflower counties before moving to Prentiss County to become associate pastor of First Baptist Church, Booneville in 1988. After five years at FBC, Bubba resigned to begin a student ministry at the Baptist Student Union, Northeast Mississippi Community College. He also sponsored the fellowship of Christian athletes during his two years at Northeast.

Lollar Family. Front: Katherine Marie and Tim. Back: Roxanne, Bubba and Neil Lollar

In the early stages of then State Senator Roger F. Wicker's congressional campaign, Bubba was asked to become his church coordinator. After 10 months of a very aggressive campaign and a tremendous victory, newly elected Congressman Wicker then asked Bubba to become the district director of Mississippi's First Congressional District. Bubba has been responsible for the Tupelo and Southaven District offices as well as representing Congressman Wicker in his absence at events throughout the 24 county First District.

Bubba is a member of First United Methodist Church, Booneville, where he serves as minister of music and worship. He is a past president of the Booneville Kiwanis Club, a member of the Tupelo Luncheon Civitan Club and a graduate of Leadership Prentiss County.

Bubba is married to the former Roxanne Gray (b. May 13, 1968 in Tupelo, Lee County, MS). She is the daughter of Roy and Sandra Lewis Gray of the Tuscumbia Community. Roxanne holds the master of arts degree in communication with an emphasis in theater from the University of Memphis and the bachelor of arts degree in theater from the University of Mississippi. She is a graduate of Booneville High School.

Roxanne has served as an instructor at northeast Mississippi Community College since 1992, where she teaches such classes as oral communications, acting, movement for the actor, voice and diction and fundamentals of theater. While at Northeast she has directed such productions as *The Pirates Of Penzance, Lend Me A Tenor, Crazy For You, Brigadoon, You Can't Take It With You* and *Painting Churches*.

In addition to her directing credits, Roxanne has served as choreographer for such NEMCC musical productions as *Guys and Dolls* (1986 and 1886), *The Flower Drum Song, Bye Bye Birdie, Fiddler On The Roof, The Sound Of Music, The Music Man, The Trials Of The Big Bad Wolf* and *Meet Me In St. Louis*. In 1999 Roxanne co-authored *The Oral Communications Workbook* which is now in its second edition. She was honored to be selected for inclusion in the 2000 edition of *Who's Who Among America's Teachers*.

In addition to fulfilling her duties at NEMCC, Roxanne serves as pianist and children's choir coordinator at First United Methodist Church in Booneville. They have four children: Brandy Elease Lollar (b. Mar. 13, 1975), Neil Randal Lollar (b. Dec. 17, 1976), Timothy Reid Lollar (b. Sep. 20, 1984) and Katherine Marie Richey (b. Jul. 9, 1989). *Submitted by Sandra Lewis Gray.*

LONG, ROBERT HOWARD, one of five children of Prentiss County natives R.L. and Hattie Mae Youngblood Long, I graduated from Booneville High School and attended two years of junior college. I went to Mississippi State University where I completed my education receiving a bachelor of science degree and a master's degree. I married JoAnn Bruce of Wheeler on Dec. 31, 1950.

Mr. and Mrs. Howard Long

A member of the Mississippi National Guard, I was serving when the Guard was mobilized in 1950 during the Korean War. After a short training period in Fort Jackson, South Carolina, I was called for duty in Korea where I spent parts of 1951 and 1952 in the area of fighting. Upon returning home, my teaching career began.

I began my teaching career in Biggersville. Later I taught at Wheeler. A new junior high school had just been completed in Booneville and I was privileged to become the principal there. When schools were integrated, I was asked to head the school in the black community. Being well accepted by all, I had many good years as principal in that system. After those 19 years, I went back to Booneville Junior High School where I retired in 1994. Upon retirement I had a total of 42 years in education with 33 of those being in the Booneville School System. All 42 years were enjoyable as I dealt with so many students and adults.

After retirement I had a very unusual honor bestowed upon me. The school that I first opened in Booneville was named in my honor. To me this is the highest honor an educator can receive.

Growing up I had such a great time with my brothers and sister. I was taught at an early age to work and to be a responsible person. I was very fortunate to be born into a Christian home. Becoming a Christian at an early age, I was taught the importance of Christianity. I attended church regularly. I have had the privilege of serving many years in my church as a Sunday school teacher for young boys. I was ordained as deacon at a young age.

One of the best trips I have ever made was to Wheeler, MS where I met a young lady who later became my wife. She has been my right-hand helper through all these years. She is a retired secretary of First Baptist Church in Booneville, MS where she served many years.

I have received many honors that I will always cherish. One such honor was being selected as Prentiss County's Outstanding Citizen in 1995.

I have had the opportunity to work all these years in my church and the school system. I have served my country in the military and am proud to be a veteran. The Lord has wonderfully blessed me! *Submitted by Howard Long.*

LOVELL, JOHN WALKER, born Jul. 24, 1879 in Prentiss County, MS. His parents were William E. and Martha Farmer. John married Gannie Holloway, daughter of Monroe and Nancy Holloway. John and his Irish bride reared a large family near Altitude and later moved near the Thrasher Community.

John W. and Gannie Lovell

John W. Lovell was a farmer by trade but is best remembered as a singing teacher. He taught at Bucksnort and Burcham schools, as well as many other local schools and churches. A small fold-up organ accompanied him in his buggy when he went to the schools and churches to teach music.

John died Mar. 18, 1934. Gannie passed away on Apr. 27, 1937. Both are buried in Liberty Church Cemetery in Prentiss County. *Submitted by Ray Lovell, grandson of John Lovell.*

LYLE FAMILY, seems to have originally been of Norman extraction, the original ancestor, Robert de Insula, having come to England in the train of William the conqueror in 1066. He was rewarded with large possessions in Wales. The family branched out in different directions.

After some time, members of the family settled in Renfrewshire, Scotland. In 1489 with the return of King James IV (of Scotland) the Lyle estates were declared forfeited and the family was forced to leave Renfrewshire. Some migrated to county Antrim, Ireland about 1606. They were Scotch Presbyterians.

William Lyle Family. Back Row L-R: William, Oral, Ethel, Julia, Tildon Estes, Lula (Lyle) Estes. Front Row: American, Bonnie and Willie

The Browndodd family in Ireland: Daniel Lyle, whose ancestry was Scotch, married in Ireland about 1650 to Amelia Clotworthy, daughter of Sir John Clotworthy who was prominent in county Antrim affairs in 1630-1660. Daniel was drowned in early manhood on a voyage to America.

Samuel Lyle was Daniel's son. He married Janet Knox of Knoxtown in the church at Raloo. Janet was the daughter of David Knox who married Sally Locke. The Houstons that came to the colony of Virginia were their neighbors.

James Lyle was their son. He married about 1700 to Margaret Snuddy, daughter of William Snuddy and Jane Adams Snuddy. James lived and died in the old Lyle home.

Robert Lyle was James' son. He married in Ireland to Ann Jane Locke, a daughter of Thomas Locke who died in 1753.

When in Ireland, the Rev. John Wesley was entertained by Robert Lyle and preached to the people in one of his fields.

David Lyle was the son of Robert Lyle. He married on Dec. 27, 1735 in Ireland to Mary Blair, daughter of Samuel Blair. David never reached America. He died while in passage. His widow and two children arrived in 1746. Mary Lyle went to Virginia and later to South Carolina. It was here that Robert Lyle, son of Daniel and grandson of Robert Lyle, lived in the Abbeville District.

Robert Lyle was a Revolutionary War soldier and was at Yorktown with George Washington when Cornwallis surrendered to the American army. Robert Lyle married about 1765 and had several children.

Charles Lyle (b. Jun. 23, 1784) was the son of Robert Lyle. He married Nancy Kirby in 1810. There were 11 sons. This family went from South Carolina to Georgia (Carrolton County).

James Lyle, son of Charles Lyle, married Jane Davis, daughter of James Davis and Judith Grisham, They moved to Itawamba County and are both buried at Mt. Pleasant Cemetery near Fulton.

William Franklin Lyle, son of James Lyle, moved to Lee County and is buried at Kirkville. He married Mary Bonna Houston, daughter of Samuel McIntosh (Troop) Houston and America Jane Underwood. They are also buried at Kirkville in Lee County.

Julia (Lyle) Pike (b. Jul. 22, 1889) Itawamba County, MS was the daughter of William Franklin Lyle. Julia (Lyle) was married to James Edgar Pike on Dec. 17, 1906 in Prentiss County, MS. Julia was an art teacher at Hills Chapel School in Prentiss County and James Edgar was a farmer. Julia and James Edgar later moved to Lee County, MS where Julia died. James Edgar moved back to Prentiss County. Julia and James Edgar had six children: Randyle Lyle, James Wythel, Absolom Keith, Julian Carey, Martha Bonna and Rupert Edwin (see Lyle/Pike line for Pike lineage).

Julian Carey Pike, son of Julia (Lyle) and James Edgar Pike, was born Dec. 3, 1913, Prentiss County, MS married Trana Aliena (Barker). They had four children: Julia Elizabeth (Mathis), Jerry Franklin, Martha Jean (Lindsey) and Linda Aliena (Martin). (See Pike/Barker line for Pike lineage). *Submitted by Linda (Pike) Martin.*

MADDOX, BOBBY GERALD, born Oct. 3, 1930 and Patrilla Joan Dunn born May 2, 1937 were married Feb. 16, 1957 in Booneville, MS. Bobby is the son of Clara Cook (b. Jan. 16, 1911) and Robert Earl Maddox (b. Feb. 16, 1909, d. Jul. 18, 1948). Bobby has three brothers: Billy Harold (his twin), Robert Eugene and Larry Donald and three sisters: Barbara Maddox Hughes, Wilma Maddox Underwood and Gretta Faye Maddox Hood.

Patrilla is the daughter of Florence Virginia "Jennie" Evans (b. Nov. 29, 1896, d. Mar. 27, 1976) and Julius Washington Dunn (b. Aug. 12, 1894, d. Jul. 29, 1952). Patrilla has three sisters: Belva Beatrice Dunn Estes, Virginia Sue Dunn Clegg and Julius Lee Dunn Morris.

Bobby was in the National Guard when the Booneville Unit was mobilized in 1950 during the Korean Conflict. He was stationed most of the time in Fort Jackson, SC. He retired from the guard at age 60 with 40 years service. He began working at Brown Shoe Co. in 1955, the year it opened and worked there until Booneville plant closed. After that he worked for the Booneville Street Department until he retired.

Center: Bobby and Patrilla Maddox. L to R: Drew, Jane and Phil Allen, Bob, Trina, Jennie, Carol and Trey Maddox, Sarah and Josh Allen.

Patrilla began working in the office at Prentiss Manufacturing Co. in 1955 and continued there until it closed. They are members of the Booneville Church of Christ.

Children of Bobby and Patrilla are Bobby Gerald Maddox Jr. "Bob" (b. Aug. 27, 1963) and Patricia Jane Maddox (b. Mar. 5, 1965).

On Jul. 15, 1989, Bob married Trina Bullock (b. Jan. 19, 1965). Trina is the daughter of Nada Darlyne Mauney and Charles Wayne Bullock of Ripley. Trina and Bob have two children: Bobby Gerald Maddox III "Trey" (b. Jan. 19, 1991) and Jennie Carol Maddox (b. Jun. 26, 1996).

On Sep. 19, 1987 Jane married Philip Scott Allen (b. Jun. 17, 1960). Phil is the son of Vistan Chisholm and Billy Allen from Collinsville, MS. Jane and Phil have three children: Andrew Scott Allen (b. Aug. 25, 1989), Joshua Ryan Allen (b. Nov. 26, 1992) and Sarah Elizabeth Allen (b. May 26, 1994). They live in Crowley, TX.

MADDOX, DELLA ARMINTA GRISSOM,

born Jun. 8, 1888 and died May 2, 1958, the daughter of William "Billy" and Josephine Grissom. She married Thomas Lacurga Maddox on Apr. 14, 1904.

All of Della's seven children were born in Crooked Oak Community of Colbert County, AL. These children were Ruby Pearl, Robert Earl, William Luther, Velma Josephine, Mamie Florene, AnnieMae Katherine and Charles Elbert "Joe."

Della Grissom Maddox (early 1900s).

Della "MaMa" Maddox and some of her grandchildren. Front row: Bob and Billy Maddox. Second row: Robert Maddox, Barbara Maddox, Greta Faye Maddox, Bobby Joe Wells, Jim Wheeler, Wilda Maddox and Pat Wheeler. Third row: Jo Ann Wheeler, "Mama" Maddox, Billy Wells and Marie Cartwright.

In February 1925 Della's husband, Thomas, died of pneumonia. Della and her children moved to Prentiss County to be near her eldest daughter, Ruby Maddox Cartwright. Della's children stayed in Prentiss County and began having children of their own. Della continued to "mother" her children as well as her grandchildren. She became known as "MaMa Maddox" to all who loved her. She instilled in them the virtue of serving others. Her life was a gift of love and she gave it unselfishly. *Submitted by Cindi Smith, Lovell, great-granddaughter.*

MALONE, SANDY AND MOLLIE MOORE,

the Sandy and Mollie Moore Malone family moved from Colbert County, AL, to Prentiss County in about 1910. He bought land west of the Siloam Road. Two of the three rooms in the house were made of logs. They had six children. Only one is still living, Quay Thornton. Her son now lives on the land.

Sandy and Mollie Malone Family. This picture was made while one of the sons, Flay, was home on furlough before going overseas during WWII.

Sandy was a farmer. He had two gray mules and he traveled to different farms cutting hay. Sometimes he would have to spend the night away from home.

Wrather Malone married Pernie Johnson. They had three children: Leamon, Wanda and Betty. They finished high school in Marietta. *Submitted by Wanda Malone Sanders, 109 Melody Lane, Senatobia, MS 38668.*

MARTIN, ROY C.,

born Jun. 6, 1913 in Keokuk Falls, OK to Owen R. Martin and Alice Smith. Roy lived his early life in Savannah, TN. He completed high school in Corinth, MS where his father was a successful merchant.

Mamie Maxine Lacy was the only child of Minnie Bane and William Henry Lacy, born Jul. 24, 1916 in Gainesville, TX. She is a descendant of Thomas Lacy, born in York County, England in 1650. The pedigree of the Lacy family can be traced back to Charles the Great.

Roy and Maxine Lacy Martin on their 50th Wedding Anniversary, Sep. 15, 1985.

Roy and Maxine met through friends in Booneville and were married Sep. 15, 1935. Roy and Maxine lived for a time in Jackson, TN and Birmingham, AL. They owned and operated the Martin's Family Store in Booneville.

Maxine died Feb. 1, 1995 and Roy died Mar. 7, 1997. They are buried in the Booneville Cemetery. They raised five children in Booneville and all graduated from Booneville High School and Northeast.

Larry Calvin Martin (b. Aug. 31, 1937) married Brenda Bethay on Aug. 28, 1961. They have no children. Larry is retired from the Federal Aviation Administration and Brenda is retired from the Social Security Administration. They live in Havana, FL.

Ronny Lacy Martin (b. Mar. 6, 1940) married Elizabeth Strong on Jul. 3, 1966. They had one son, Ron Brent Martin (b. Nov. 2, 1968). They were divorced in 1983. Ronny married Mary Nell Walden Whitaker on Jul. 15, 1994. Brent married Robbin Cantrell of Jackson, MS on Dec. 31, 1990. They have three children: Brittany, Drew and Bethany. They live in Jackson, MS.

Mamie Alice Martin (b. Dec. 8, 1941) graduated from MSCW and taught school. William Edward (Billy) Tays (b. Apr. 23, 1937) and Mamie were married Jun. 26, 1965. They have a daughter, Allison Lacy Tays (b. May 21, 1974) and a son, Matthew William Tays (b. May 25, 1976). Bill died Mar. 1, 1990. Allison graduated Summa Cum Laude from Millsaps College and is a CPA in Nashville. Matt graduated Cum Laude from Freed-Hardeman University and is completing a civil engineering degree at Tennessee Technological University. Mamie is administrative assistant to the academic dean at Magnolia Bible College in Kosciusko, MS.

Gary Wayne Martin and Cary Dwain Martin were the first twins born in the Booneville Hospital on Highway 45 on Dec. 16, 1949.

Gary married Carolyn Green from Jumpertown, born Nov. 10, 1954. They were married on Aug. 17, 1973 and both graduated from the University of Mississippi. Gary has been with BanCorp South in Tupelo since 1974. Carolyn teaches at Thomas Street School. They have two sons, Benjamin Andrew Martin (b. Sep. 19, 1981) and Stephen Alan Martin (b. Aug. 4, 1986).

Cary married Pamela O'Quin from Jackson, MS on Apr. 4, 1980. They had no children. Pamela was killed in a car accident on Feb. 1, 1996. Cary married Portia Kennon on Jan. 4, 1997. Cary works with the Jackson Public Schools. Portia is office administrator for Edward Earl Jones, Inc. and they make their home in Brandon, MS. *Submitted by Mamie M. Tays.*

MARTIN, SETH

and Frances Halbert brought their young family to Tishomingo County from Hardin County, TN about 1839. They had lived near their fathers, Jonathan Martin and William Halbert, on Turkey Creek in Hardin County. In Tishomingo County, they settled in an area that is now in Prentiss County, near east Prentiss and Friendship. The land for Friendship Church and Cemetery was theirs at one time and was donated to the church by their daughter and son-in law, Elizabeth and Charles Ryan.

Elizabeth Martin Ryan (1829-1900).

Frances and Seth's children included:

William H. (b. 1825), who married Frances Pratt. (See William H. Martin Story).

Elizabeth (Dec. 4, 1829, d. Jun. 15, 1900), the wife of Charles Ryan. They raised a large family in Prentiss County where many descendants still live. Some of their children moved to Texas and Oklahoma. (See Letter from Dr. Ryan).

Moses W. (b. 1835), who married Lydia Moore. (See Moses Martin Story).

John R. (b. 1838 in Tennessee). His wife was Sarah C. and they had two daughters, Maggie age 3 and Dollie Lee age 2, with them on the 1880 Prentiss County Census.

Frances (b. 1839 in Mississippi), who married George W. Howell in 1861 and moved to Missouri where George died during the Civil War. He had enlisted in the Union Army. There was one son, Dock, who married Belle Greene. The 1880 census shows Doctor B. as a 17 year-old in the household of his grandfather, Gilbert Howell.

There were other children, but these are the only ones we have information on.

In June of 1854, Seth gave to his daughter, Elizabeth Ryan, an assortment of livestock.

Recorded in Itawamba County, the deed describes in detail the color and markings of 13 head of cattle, 19 pigs, 6 sheep and a bay mare. Elizabeth signed the deed, accepting the gift under "the several statutes made and provided for the benefit of married women."

Seth died before 1860 and Frances' father, William Halbert, was listed in the census with her. Frances and her son, John R. and granddaughter, Mattie Belle, daughter of Moses W., sold land to Elizabeth and Charles Ryan in 1879. Frances was in the 1880 census, living next door to her son John and his family.

Seth and Frances were cousins. Their mothers, Frances (Frankie) Taylor Martin and Susannah Taylor Halbert, were the daughters of Richard Taylor and Hannah Vernon. Both Richard and Hannah were born in Virginia and died in Knox County, TN.

Hannah Vernon's parents, Jonathan Vernon and Rebecca Worth, were Quakers, born in Chester County, Pennsylvania. Sometime before 1750, the Vernons, along with some others of their religion, came to Charlotte County, VA, which is where Hannah married Richard Taylor in 1773. The young couple moved to Stokes and Surry Counties, North Carolina, along with the Vernons. From there they moved on to Knox County, TN.

William Halbert, born in Wales in 1682, died in Essex County, VA in 1718 and married Mary Cook of Essex County. The line proceeds through (1) their son Joel and his wife Frances Jones, to (2) Joel II and his wife Martha Williams (?), to (3) William, born about 1776 in Surry County, NC, married about 1797 in Stokes County, NC, to Susannah Taylor. Susannah was born about 1780 in Surry County, NC and died before 1860 in Tennessee.

Other lines in the Martin-Halbert ancestry include the Fearnes of Derby, England, the Fawcetts of Yorkshire, England and the Worths of Nottinghamshire, England. All these families came to Chester County, Pennsylvania, before the Revolution.

Today, there are many descendants of the Seth Martins in north Mississippi with names such as: Goddard, Weems, Williams and Deaton. Many others moved on West. The world is much smaller now, thanks to communication and we are able to know and enjoy our distant relatives. *Submitted by Ruby Williams Magers, 2103 Reagan Cove, Tupelo, MS 38801. (662) 840-3737.*

MARTIN, WILLIAM H., son of Seth Martin and Frances Halbert and grandson of Jonathan Martin and Frances Taylor, was born in Hardin County, TN about 1825. William H. married Frances Euphrisia Pratt in Monroe County, MS in 1846 and proceeded to buy land in Tishomingo County, MS the same year, the location being S-6, T-6, R-9 in what is now Prentiss County. The land was bought in partnership with Joseph and Nancy J. Martin. William and Frances had their first child at that location, Mary J., born 1847. In 1847 William H. and Joseph Martin sold the land to Chesley Garrison. (Back in Hardin County, TN, Chesley had been the administrator of Jonathan Martin's estate.) William and Frances next bought land in S-30, T-6, R-9, which was very close to the Itawamba County line and very close to the Lemuel Christian family in Itawamba County. At this location were born James Wilson Martin in 1850 and Susanna E. Martin in 1853. In 1853/1854, William and Frances sold the land to Moses L. and Margaret L. Martin.

About 1854, the Martin family moved to Van Buren County, AR, Turkey Creek Township. Here Joseph Holbert Martin was born in 1856 and Seth Martin was born in 1860. Family lore says that one day they came home and soldiers were setting up picket lines across their farm.

So, about 1862, the Martin family moved to Franklin County, IL and settled in the Crittenden Community. Their old friends from Mississippi, the Christian family, settled in adjoining Perry County. By 1870, three members of the family had departed. Seth apparently died young, Mary J. apparently married and Frances Pratt Martin died. William H. Martin then married Samantha Paralee Christian McCullough, a widow who had traveled with the Christian family to Illinois. They had a child, Laura, born in 1870.

In 1877, the Martins and the Christians left Illinois and traveled together to Wise County, TX. William Martin died about 1878 and in 1879, the surviving members of the two families, still traveling together, made their last move by wagon to the Barrel Springs community of Montague County, TX. *Submitted by Frank Martin.*

MASSEY, JAMES BARDEN, born in Alabama on Jan. 7, 1849, to James A. and Sarah Ann Jones Massey. He married in 1870 to Nancy Jane Dobbs, the daughter of Thomas and Artela Malone Dobbs. She was born Aug. 21, 1849 in Georgia. On Dec. 2, 1873, James and Nancy purchased land in Prentiss County, moving from Franklin County, AL. There was excepted from the deed one acre, which was a cemetery, now named Massey Cemetery. Several family members and relatives are buried there. Records reveal that J.B. was a delegate to the annual meetings of the Regular Primitive Baptist Church Association from 1889-1920.

James Barden Massey

J.B. and Nancy only had three children, the first two being born in Franklin County, AL:

1. James Thomas (b. 1871, d. ?) married Mary Elizabeth Stennett and had Allen and Rausi.

2. George Sylvester (b. Dec. 11, 1872, d. May 28, 1955) married Jun. 29, 1898 to Mary Della Stennett, daughter of George Leesaw and Elizabeth Martin Stennett. Della was born Jun. 26, 1876 and died May 1, 1955. To this union were born 10 children, not unusual for that time. What is unusual is there were four sets of twins in the family. Their first two children were born in Prentiss County. Sometime between 1901-1904, George and Della moved to Hood County, TX where two of his uncles had settled. The first two sets of twins were born in Granbury, TX. I suppose Della needed help, so they moved back to the family farm in Mississippi close to both grandparents. Little did they know that there would be two more sets of twins. Their children are:

a. Edgar Watson (b. 1899, d. 1979) married Bessie Holley and had Dale, Larry, Bonita and Helen Delores.

b. Bonnie (b. 1901, d. 1918) died from complications with mumps.

c. James Herman (b. 1904, d. 1991), Hermitage, TN married Christine Gist and had Kenneth and Martha Ann.

d. George Thurman (b. 1904, d. 1986), Prentiss County, married Martha LaRue Gann and had Ruby Earlene, Nellie Louise, George Thurman Jr. and Harold Ray.

e. Marvin (b. 1907, d. 1999), Wesson, MS married Nell Swilley and had Gene.

f. Melvin (b. 1907, d. 1993), Prentiss County, married Mary Earl Thomas (b. 1910, d. 1988).

g. Horace (b. 1910, d. 1996), Prentiss County, married Demple Green (b. 1915, d. 1993) and had Jerry, Robert and Billy.

h. Gladys (b. 1910, d. 1963) married Herman Wilson (b. 1912, d. 1980).

i. Wade (b. 1912, d. 1997), Laurel, MS married Erma Sullivan and had Barbara.

j. Wayne (b. 1912), Memphis, TN married Marie Bennett and had Joe Wayne and Jack.

3. Sarah Ann Rosetta (b. 1876, d. 1962) married William Dewitt Tyra and had Jessie Ona and Nancy Alma. Rosetta married second to Joseph Porter Hester and had Lizzie Lois, James Barry and Lassi Irene. Rosetta married third to James Elliott Shackelford.

Nancy Jane died Mar. 19, 1885. James Barden married in 1892 to Rebecca Yow (b. 1851, d. 1931). He died Feb. 15, 1931 and is buried, as are both wives in the Massey Cemetery in the Zions Rest Community of Prentiss County. *Submitted by Melinda Massey Dickerson, 404 Peg Lane, Amory, MS.*

MASSEY, JERRY HOYLE, born Jun. 20, 1935, at home on the Massey farm in Prentiss County, MS. His parents were Horace and Demple Green Massey. Horace was the son of George Sylvester and Mary Della Stennett Massey. Demple was the daughter of Joe Green (b. Mar. 8, 1877, d. Oct. 21, 1936) and Della Moore Green (b. Feb. 4, 1879, d. Jan. 14, 1934). Joe's parents were Ambrose H. Green (b. Oct. 15, 1844, d. Jan. 18, 1910) and Nancy Emiline Gwynne Green (b. February 1847, d. Nov. 5, 1931). Della's parents were Stephen Lee Moore (b. Apr. 18, 1834, d. Sep. 28, 1910) and Mary Jane Stovall Moore (b. Dec. 25, 1842, d. Jul. 28, 1896). Since Jerry's father was a schoolteacher, he started to school when he was five years old. He finished high school young and went to Northeast Mississippi Junior College, graduating in 1954. He attended Mississippi State University one semester and then volunteered into the US Army in January 1955 for three years of duty.

On Jul. 29, 1956, Jerry and Jo Ann Smith were united in marriage at the home of the Rev. Eugene Digby in Fulton, MS. Jo Ann was working in Memphis, TN at that time. In December of that year, Jerry was sent to Korea to serve his last year in the peacetime efforts there. He was discharged as staff sergeant in December 1957. Jerry began working in January for the Velsicol Chemical Corporation in Memphis and applied for enrollment at the Christian Brothers College School of Engineering. Sputnik had been sent up in 1957 and the engineering field was wide open. It took four years to earn his degree, graduating in June 1962 with a degree in mechanical engineering. He went to work immediately for E.I. duPont, de Nemours Co., Inc. in Chattanooga, TN where he held different positions. Jerry was a junior achievement leader for duPont for some time. He was ordained as Deacon at Bartlebaugh Baptist Church in Harrison, TN on May 6, 1968. Very active in the Royal Ambassador Organization of our church, Jerry served as association director in Hamilton County, TN and Catoosa County, GA, after we moved there. He enjoyed working with young people.

We were transferred by duPont to South Boston, VA in 1983. Jerry's melanoma reappeared that year and he died there on Jan. 31, 1985. He is buried in the Massey Cemetery by the path he helped make going down to the creek to fish as a boy.

Our oldest son, Michael Lee, was born in Memphis, TN on Oct. 20, 1958. He has a degree in agriculture economics and a master's of business administration from the University of Georgia. He is co-owner of a feed and seed distribution center in Louisiana. Michael married Lillian Clair Giardina in 1989 and they have two children, John Lucas (b. Sep. 15, 1993) and Sarah Kate (b. May 1, 1997).

Our second son, Mark Edwin, was born in Memphis, TN on Aug. 26, 1960. He has a degree in mechanical engineering from the University of Tennessee at Chattanooga and works in the steel building industry near Knoxville, TN. Mark first married Allison Aslinger in Chattanooga and they divorced. He then married Cheryl Coleman in 1995. They have one son, Gabriel Spencer (b. Dec. 12, 1997). Cheryl has two sons by a previous marriage, Justin (b. Nov. 6, 1982) and Mark (b. Jul. 24, 1984).

Our daughter, Melinda Kay, was born in Chattanooga, TN on Christmas Day 1967. She has a degree in physical therapy from the Medical College of Georgia and now lives in Amory, MS. Melinda married Thomas McLain Dickerson in 1995 and they have two sons, Clayton Eli (b. Nov. 25, 1997) and Aidan Noah (b. Aug. 22, 1999). *Submitted by Jo Ann Smith Massey, 100 South Franks Road, Booneville, MS.*

MATHIS, DENNIS, born Dec. 16, 1905 in Prentiss County, MS to Minnie Hartsfield and Odell Mathis, who were married Jul. 24, 1904. Dennis married Rachel Smith May 14, 1913 in Prentiss County. Rachel was born Dec. 4, 1904 in Prentiss County to Verge and Savannah Swinney Smith. Dennis retired from Brown Shoe Co. and Rachel was a housewife.

When Dennis was in high school he was picked by the Memphis Chicks to play pro baseball. His parents were afraid for him to travel so far from home.

Dennis Mathis, Rachel Mathis and grandchildren, Larry Eldridge and Lana Mathis and great-grandchild Jenny Eldridge

Rachel and Dennis were members of Sardis Primitive Baptist church where Dennis was a deacon. They were true to their church especially helping others and had a feeling for members that didn't have a way to church. They were always there to carry them.

Dennis died Dec. 16, 1968 and Rachel died Mar. 7, 1997. Born to them were Prentiss Warren (b. Mar. 22, 1924, d. Mar. 11, 1995 of cancer of the esophagus), Willadean (b. Jan. 25, 1931, d. Feb. 10, 1931), Melvin Grady (b. Apr. 15, 1929, killed in Korean War Sept. 3, 1950), Syble Daphene (b. May 31, 1926) and L.Q. (born Feb. 15, 1933).

Prentiss Warren Mathis married Maxine Gilley when he was young. They were blessed with a son, Prentiss Gayle (b. Dec. 22, 1946). Prentiss Gayle married Shirley Kelly first, they had one daughter, Karen and she has two daughters. His second wife was Rona Montgomery and they had one son, Chris who was killed in an auto accident.

L.Q. married Elizabeth Pike Mar. 9, 1956, they have one daughter Lana Quinn. She married Mark Duncan Tapp May 22, 1976 and they have two children, Shannon Elizabeth and Justin Mark.

Daphene Mathis married Stanley Eldridge Apr. 19, 1947 and has one son, Larry Wayne. He had two daughters, Jenny Eldridge Hayfield and Amy Eldridge Young and one son, Laramie. Larry Wayne died Mar. 22, 1999 with cancer and was survived by his wife, Kay Grimes, daughters and son.

MATHIS, L.Q. AND JULIA ELIZABETH PIKE, L.Q. was the descendant of Dennis Clifford Mathis and Rachel Smith Mathis. Elizabeth was the descendant of J. Carey Pike and Trana Barker Pike.

L.Q. and Elizabeth Mathis, Mark and Lana Tapp, Justin Tapp and Shannon Tapp.

L.Q. was born Feb. 15, 1933 in Prentiss County. After graduation from Thrasher High School, he served two years with the US Army stationed in Germany. After completing his service in the Army, he attended Northeast Mississippi Community College. He is retired from the Mississippi Department of Transportation.

Elizabeth was born Jul. 30, 1938 in Prentiss County. She graduated from Thrasher High School in 1956 and Northeast Mississippi Community College in 1995. She is a teacher at Booneville Headstart Center.

L.Q. and Elizabeth have one daughter, Lana, who is married to Mark Tapp. Lana is office manager for Dr. Ken Goodwin and Dr. Mindelyn Austin and Mark is vice president of the Booneville Farmers and Merchants Bank. Lana and Mark have two children, Shannon Elizabeth and Justin Mark. Shannon is presently a senior at Mississippi State University pursuing a bachelor of science degree in educational psychology. Justin is a freshman at NEMCC pursuing a bachelor of science degree in Forestry.

L.Q. and Elizabeth make their home in the Tuscumbia Community and are active members of the Tuscumbia Baptist Church.

L.Q. had two brothers, Prentiss Warren Mathis and Melvin Mathis, and one sister, Daphine. Melvin was killed during the Korean War. Warren died in March 1996 after a battle with esophageal cancer. Daphine and her husband, Stanley Eldridge, who are both retired, reside in the Tuscumbia Community.

Elizabeth has two sisters, Martha Jean Lindsey and Linda Alena Martin and one brother, Jerry Franklin Pike. Martha is married to E.G. Lindsey and she is an antique dealer and resides in the Big V Community. Linda is a secretary for the vocational education department at Northeast Mississippi Community College. She resides in Booneville. Jerry is a painting contractor and resides in the Smith Chapel Community. *Submitted by Elizabeth Pike Mathis.*

MAXWELL, SCOTSMAN JAMES, father of Robert Belton Maxwell Sr., came to America from Europe. Born to Robert Belton Maxwell Sr. and wife, Mary Caroline Smith, were Robert Belton Jr., Cordelia, Fannie, Ella, Flemmon Hodges, Charlie Smith, Benjamin and John Courson.

Robert Belton Maxwell Jr. (b. Mar. 4, 1862, d. Apr. 17, 1944) was married on Feb. 10, 1885, to Mary Frances Miller (b. May 12, 1867, d. Nov. 29, 1941), daughter of Thomas Steven Miller. Their children were Myrtle Ollie (b. Dec. 3, 1885, d. Jul. 17, 1964); Jessie Pernecy (b. Oct. 11, 1890, d. Apr. 28, 1992); Sarah Elizabeth (b. Jul. 25, 1894, d. Nov. 20, 1979); Thomas Samuel (b. Dec. 21, 1896, d. Apr. 9, 1971); Minnie Mae (b. Jul. 26, 1900, d. Apr. 8, 1973); Otha Lee and Luther Hick (twins, b. Feb. 7, 1904), Luther died Jul. 21, 1905 and Otha died Jul. 4, 1976 and Anna Lou (b. Dec. 6, 1906).

Robert Belton Maxwell Jr. and wife, Mary Frances (Mollie) Miller, 1936.

Robert Belton Jr. (Uncle Bob) was a blacksmith. Even though it was developed to heal lame animals, his patented "Maxwell Liniment" was used for treatment of sore muscles, stiff joints, chest congestion and sore throats.

The Maxwell children made Booneville their home. Myrtle ran The Booneville Floral Co.

Jessie married John Guy Adair on Dec. 24, 1911. They operated a bedding plant farm. Their only child, Mary Avis, married George Settle (Biggersville). Their children are Raymond Adair, Evelyn Ann and Edward Maxwell. By his first marriage to Mary Love McGinty (Yazoo City), Raymond has two sons, Raymond Adair Jr. and Jason Thomas. He later married Sue Walden. Evelyn married William Sloan Farrior (North Carolina). Edward married Rebecca Bassett (Alabama). They have two children: Christopher Maxwell and Jennifer Gale.

Sara married Horace Greely Rogers. They ran a grocery store on Smith Street.

Thomas, an employee of the US Postal Service, married Elizabeth Gish. They had three children: Elizabeth Ann, Mildred Tate and Daisy Roberta (Bobbie).

Minnie Mae, employee of Southern Bell Telephone and Telegraph Co., married Guy M. Holley on Jul. 29, 1937. Guy was co-owner of Holley Brothers, seed and fur business.

Otha, an employee of the US Postal Service, married Grace Gault. They had one child, Mary Gault, who married Houston Nabers. Their children are Mary Grace and Stephen Maxwell. By her first marriage to Mike Gibson (Tennessee), Mary Grace has one son, Michael Bryan, who married Lisa Horn. By her second marriage to Joseph Randall Troupe (West Point), she has one daughter, Martha Gault (Marty). Marty married Reginald Baine Smith (Humphreys County). They have one child. Steve married Mickie Caver. They have one daughter, Jessie Elizabeth. Analyn Kirksey (Tupelo) was Steve's first wife.

Anna Lou married Ruben Avery "Shorty" Kimbrell (Pheba) on Aug. 12, 1934. They were employees of Southern Bell Telephone and Telegraph Co. Sue Carolyn, their only child, married Robert L. Honeycutt (Kossuth) on Aug. 15, 1970. Their only child, Andrea Lynn, married John Luke Mathis (Alcorn County) on Mar. 28, 1998. (For additional information see T.S. Miller, R.A. Kimbrell and R.L. Honeycutt articles.) *Submitted by Mary Gault Nabers.*

MAYO, JOSHUA VAUDRY "BILL," born Feb. 26, 1899 in Marietta, MS and died Nov. 25, 1952 in Chicago, IL, is buried in Kirkville Cemetery. Bill's parents are Robert Henry (Bud) Mayo (b. Jan. 1, 1865, d. Oct. 24, 1949) and Amanda "Jane" Allred (b. Aug. 22, 1868, d. Apr. 15, 1932). Bill married on Aug. 16, 1918 in Prentiss County to Edna Gertrude Williams (b. Apr. 17, 1899 in Marietta, MS, d. Jul. 10, 1991 in Blackland, MS).

Joshua Vaudry (Bill) Mayo and his sister, Ethel (Mayo) Files, while he was at Parchman about 1934.

She is buried with most of her children in the Blackland Cemetery. Edna's parents are William Lafayette Williams (b. Feb. 19, 1862, d. Jan. 26, 1933) and Mary Ellen (Mollie) Cheeves (b. Apr. 2, 1866, d. Nov. 22, 1940).

Bill and Edna had 11 children:

1. Vaudry "Dayton" (b. May 8, 1919, d. Apr. 25, 1993). Dayton married Nettie Louise (Gus) Gram on Oct. 22, 1942 in Prentiss County and had three children: Donna Kay, Enza "Jan" and Delana Elizabeth.

2. Mary "Louise" (b. Oct. 29, 1920, d. Oct. 11, 1997). Louise married William Thomas (Jake) Stone on Oct. 17, 1936 in Prentiss County and had two children, Shirley Ann and Thomas "Leroy."

3. Lois Lavene (b. May 18, 1923, d. Mar. 24, 1986). Lois married Waymon Johnson Graves on Aug. 16, 1940 in Prentiss County and had four children: Betty Lynn, Terry Wayne, James David (Ricky) and Charles Michael. Then she married James George on Jul. 25, 1958 in Prentiss County and had two children, Sandra Ann and Sherry Ann.

4. Edna Venelle (Nellie) (b. Feb. 12, 1928, d. Jul. 2, 1951 in Powers, Oregon). Nellie married Jimmy King on Apr. 23, 1945 in Oregon Coos County and had one daughter, Gloria Jean.

5. Clinton "Virdo" (b. Apr. 26, 1930, d. Apr. 9, 1978). Virdo married Arglis (Nina) Quentero in July 1950 in Germany and had one son, Clinton Christopher. Then he married Christa Ulrich in 1959 in Germany and had two children, Marie Elizabeth (Lucy) and Jimmy Wayne.

Edna Gertrude (Williams) Mayo in her home in Blackland. She was about 80 years old.

6. James "Howard" (b. Jun. 11, 1932, d. Jan. 16, 1998). Howard married Mary Lee (Poodle) Bridges on Nov. 25, 1950 in Prentiss County and had one son, James "Gary." Then he married Henrietta Benbow on Nov. 29, 1955 in Prentiss County and had five children: Mary Louise, Kimberly Ann, James Howard Jr., Joan Ann and Theresa Marie.

7. Everett "Clayton" (b. Mar. 1, 1935). Clayton married Mary Alice Blankenship on May 14, 1955 in Tippah County and had one daughter, Nina Gale. Then he married Dorothy Parker on Dec. 24, 1980 in Jackson County.

8. Ludie "Irene" (b. May 14, 1937, d. Apr. 3, 1995). Irene married William Edward (WE) Eaton on May 22, 1953 in Tippah County and had four children: Roy Baxor, Phyllis Ann, Cathy Gertrude and Richard Dwayne.

9. Virginia Dale (Ginnie) (b. Feb. 16, 1941). Ginnie married Danny Cagle on Apr. 12, 1958 in Prentiss County and had two children: Steven Keith and Mickey Dale.

10. Barbara Jane (Boonie) (b. Sep. 29, 1942). Boonie married Paul Franklin Moore on May 29, 1961 in Prentiss County and had four children: Tommy Franklin, Renita Kay, Lawanda Ann and Tanya Gay.

11. Stanley Dwight (b. Aug. 6, 1944, d. Jul. 31, 1965). Stanley never married.

Bill walked with a limp, but it was said he ran to work every day. To outsiders Bill was a good man and would do anything for you, but to his kids he was very mean and hard on them. In the early 1930s, he was arrested for taking part in making corn whisky and went to Parchman for a couple of years. Edna, on the other hand, was the kindest and sweetest woman you would ever meet. She loved everybody and did not seem to have a care in the world. Bill and Edna have 32 grandchildren, 47 great-grandchildren, 23 great-great-grandchildren and one great-great-great-granddaughter to date. *Submitted by Theresa Buckley, 210 Hillside Ct., Janesville, WI 35345, (608) 754-6607.*

MAYO, ROBERT HENRY "BUD," was born in Mississippi on Jan. 1, 1865 and died Oct. 24, 1949. He married on Jul. 6, 1885 in Itawamba County to Amanda "Jane" Allred (b. Aug. 22, 1868 in Fayette, AL, d. Apr. 15, 1932). Her Parents were Joshua Henry Allred and Mary Amanda (Mandy) McCarver. All are buried in the Kirkville Cemetery. Bud and Jane raised four children in Marietta, MS.

1. Fleeta (b. Dec. 19, 1888, d. Nov. 3, 1964) married Tran Harp in Prentiss County on Sep. 15, 1907. They had eight children: Kermit (b. 1909), Kelcy (b. 1911), Gladys (b. 1913), Sybal (b. 1916), Vester (b. 1918), Ray (b. 1921), Hubert (b. 1928) and Winnie (b. unknown). Most of the Harps are buried in Mark Tree, AR.

2. Ethel (b. Feb. 26, 1896, d. Jul. 1, 1938) married Thomas G. Files in Prentiss County on Sep. 3, 1918. She never had any children and died from cancer. She and Tom are buried in Kirkville Cemetery.

3. Joshua Vaudry (Bill) (b. Feb. 26, 1899, d. Nov. 25, 1952 in Chicago, IL) married Enda G. Williams in Prentiss County on Aug. 16, 1918. They had 11 children: Vaudry "Dayton" (b. 1919), Mary "Louise" (b. 1920), Lois Lavene (b. 1923), Edna Venelle (Nellie) (b. 1923), Clinton "Virdo" (b. 1930), James "Howard" (b. 1932), Everett "Clayton" (b. 1935), Ludie "Irene" (b. 1937), Virginia Dale (Ginnie) (b. 1941), Barbara Jane (Boonie) (b. 1942) and Stanley Dwight (b. 1944). Bill is buried in Kirkville Cemetery. Edna and most of her children are buried in Blackland Cemetery.

Grandpa Bud Mayo

4. Monroe Kirk (MK) (b. 1908, d. Nov. 19, 1953) never married. He died in Meridian Mental Hospital where he is buried in Sedar Haven Cemetery.

Bud was a farmer by trade and described as an honest, quiet, kind man with a reserved temper. He was short and heavy built with a big nose. When his grandchildren would make fun of his big nose, he would give all the other kids candy but them. Jane was tall and heavy and had a limp to her walk. She was a hard worker despite the way she felt. A tornado came though in the middle of the night and destroyed the homestead. The mattress was in the tree. Jane hit her face on the tree and it left a scar. Jane died at age 63 of an illness. Bud died at age 84 of a heart attack. Names in parenthesis are nicknames. Names in quotations are real names used instead of their first name.

MCCARTHY, JOHN, in the 1840s a blight hit the potato crop in Ireland. Because they had become so dependent on potatoes for food, over a million people died of starvation. More than a million others immigrated. Two young Irish Catholics named Daniel (b. 1834, d. 1909) and Elizabeth (b. 1836, d. 1908) McCarthy were among them.

Records show that they settled in Lexington, KY, when they arrived in America. In 1860 John, their first child, was born. Their other children, all born in Kentucky, were Mary, Daniel, Nannie, Elizabeth, Nellie, James and Julia.

John and Mollie McCarthy in 1910.

In the late 1870s, they began their journey south down the Cumberland and Tennessee Rivers in search of the fertile land and good climate they had heard about. Their first stop was in McNairy County, TN where John (b. 1860, d. 1927) met Mary "Mollie" Josephine Ledbetter (b. 1860, d. 1935). They were married on Feb. 7, 1880 in New Hope, TN.

By June 1880 John and Mollie, along with Daniel and his family, had arrived in the Baldwyn area.

John and Mollie began farming and by 1900 they owned their farm in the Jericho Community. Their children were William "Will" Daniel (b. 1881, d. 1936); Bonnie (b. 1885, d. 1967); Birtie (b. 1885, d. 1958); John "Jack" Riley (b. 1888, d. 1952); James "Jim" Patrick (b. 1889, d. 1962); Edward "Edd" Payne (b. 1891, d. 1972); Nannie (b. 1894, d. 1960); Marion "Bud" Taylor (b. 1897, d. 1964) and Fred (b. 1901, d. 1949).

After years of successful farming, John and Mollie moved to Baldwyn and built and operated the McCarthy Gin. Grandchildren still remember visiting Grandpa John at the gin on Saturday afternoon. He would pull out his money box and give them a quarter, which would buy them a milkshake and a sack of candy and have money left. John and Mollie lived in the big white house on Main Street near the gin.

Sons, Bud and Edd, joined their dad in business and later built an ice plant. They delivered ice around the Baldwyn area by wagon. Edd married Florrie Snell and their children were Quana, Carrol, Gene and Babe. Bud married Zellie O'Dell Young and their children were Mary Elizabeth, O'Dell and JoAnn.

Will married Wilma Hickey and owned a store on Main Street in Baldwyn. Their children were Esque, Zeallia and Zana Lee.

Maggie married Jake Epting and their children were John, Paul and Jaka Lee. After Jake died Maggie married John Lesley.

Bonnie married George White and farmed. Their children were Rufus, Mary, Albert, Boyd, Birtie, Clifton and Sara.

Birtie, Bonnie's twin sister, married Claude White and owned a store at Jericho. They had one son, Leslie.

Jack married Julia Haygood and farmed in the Bethany Community. Their children were Francis, Taylor, Hazel, John and Annie Laurie.

Jim married Jaka Holland and farmed in Baldwyn. Their children were John Holland, C.W., Dan and Maury.

Nannie married Gene Ford and farmed. Their children were Mac and Evaline.

Fred married Lillian Waldrop and moved to Red Bay, AL, where he operated a store and had one son, Fred Jr.

Daniel and Elizabeth McCarthy are buried in St. Thomas Catholic Church Cemetery in Saltillo. John and Mollie are buried in Baldwyn City Cemetery. *Submitted by David Frazier, 488 CR 833, Guntown, MS 38849. (662) 365-8538.*

MCCOY, DUVAL CLARINE WHITE, born Mar. 3, 1923, was the second daughter of William Ernest White, who was born Jul. 28, 1895 and died Sep. 30, 1970. He married Martha Estelle Taylor on May 4, 1919, after he returned from WWI. She was born Apr. 11, 1896 and died Apr. 4, 1992. They are buried in Mackey's Creek Cemetery east of Booneville.

Granville and Clarine McCoy

Clarine met James Granville McCoy while she was still in high school. He was born Jan. 1, 1917, to Robert Levi "Bob" McCoy and Tersie Phifer McCoy. They dated about two and a half years. She graduated from Burton High School in May 1941. He was drafted into the army in August 1941. They were married his first furlough home on Nov. 28, 1941. He came home one more time before going to the South Pacific and was gone three years and seven months. He came home in August 1945. The war was over August 14, 1945.

During the war he was in Australia, New Caledonia, Guadalcanal, Fiji, Bougainvillea of Solomon Islands and Leyte and Cebu of the Philippines. He saw action on Guadalcanal, Bougainvillea, Leyte and Cebu.

Clarine worked at Blue Bell Manufacturing Co. during the war. After Granville came home she worked a while, then helped him when he went into business for himself. Later she worked with the child development Program, then as remedial reading aide in the school system.

After Granville returned from the army, he was an auto mechanic, a car dealer for American Motors, then after terminating his business, took a job as maintenance foreman for South Central Plastics.

Granville and Clarine had two children, Melba Jo (b. Feb. 20, 1957) and Terry Lee (b. Dec. 18, 1958). Both graduated with honors from NEMCC in Booneville and Mississippi State University in Starkville. Melba is math and science department head at NEMCC and is married to Randy Gene Morgan. He is first vice president and EDP auditor for BanCorp South in Tupelo. He was born Apr. 12, 1956.

Terry is senior vice president of F.T. Mortgage Co. of Dallas, TX. He married Deborah Lee Jordan of Ripley, MS on May 17, 1980. She was born Sep. 6, 1959.

Terry and Debbie have three daughters: Emily Jordan (b. Nov. 30, 1982), Jessica Lee (b. Apr. 30, 1986) and Valerie Taylor (b. Jul. 13, 1991). *Submitted by J.G. and Clarine McCoy.*

MCCOY, GUSSIE ANN, born Dec. 7, 1900 in the Altitude Community of Prentiss County was the first child of William Coley and Artie Bell Stokes McCoy. On Jul. 20, 1918 she married Noonon Orlanda Hopkins (b. Nov. 15, 1899), son of Jasper Lee and Martha Elizabeth Reynolds Hopkins of the Tuscumbia Community. The Hopkins farmed and at times were the custodians of the old county home. Although working in the fields and house work kept the family busy in the daylight hours,

J.C. Hopkins, Clyde Hopkins, Noonon and Gussie McCoy Hopkins, Moeise Hopkins Crabb, Ilene Hopkins and Marie Hopkins Lewis (ca. 1943).

Noonon found time at night to read to his children: sometimes the local and world events from the newspaper and other times scripture from the Bible. Gussie sewed and hand made most of the clothes for the girls. While the family worked the farm she stayed home to cook their meals on a wood cook stove, churn and make butter, wash dishes and (before the black wash pot) take the family wash down to the spring, January through December. She was known throughout the community for her delicious cornbread and biscuits. They could always squeeze another friend or field hand in at their dinner table. In autumn after all the cotton had been picked for the last time, you could go by in the afternoons and see Gussie out in the field with her pick sack, picking scrap cotton, to make extra money for the grandchildren's Christmas gifts.

It was such a joy to spend the day with them. They expected you to work and do your part. On peddler days we were given a coin to spend. Gussie always had a dozen or so of freshly laid eggs to sell. Uncle Marsh McCoy drove one of the peddler trucks and she was always happy to catch up on the latest McCoy happenings from Wheeler.

They lived in the Tuscumbia Community and were members of the Tuscumbia Baptist Church. Noonon Orlanda Hopkins died May 6, 1981 and Gussie Ann McCoy Hopkins died Dec. 23, 1981. They are buried in Smith Chapel Cemetery. They had five children:

I) Artie Marie Hopkins (b. Mar. 8, 1920) worked as secretary for the superintendent of education and later for the garment industry. She married James Hardin Lewis and they lived in the Tuscumbia Community and were members of the East Booneville Baptist Church. They have two children:

(1) Sandra Kay Lewis (b. Nov. 12, 1946) md. Lester Roy Gray. They have one child, Rhonda Roxanne Gray (b. May 13, 1968) md. Harold Windal Lollar Jr., four children: Kate, Tim, Neil and Brandy.

(2) James Gaylon Lewis (b. Feb. 21, 1951) md. Mary Lou Bearden, two children: Franklin Gale Lewis (b. Aug. 3, 1969) md. Sandi McVey, one child, Stephanie Nicole Lewis and Michael Paul Lewis (b. Mar. 20, 1976).

II) Mattie Moeise Hopkins (b. Jul. 18, 1921) worked as a cosmetologist and later a secretary for a construction company. She married Clyne Houston Crabb and they lived in Pensacola, FL. Mattie Moeise Hopkins Crabb, a Baptist, died Feb. 4, 1998 and is buried at Lindsey Cemetery in Tishomingo County, MS. They had two children:

(1) Martha Carolyn Crabb (b. Oct. 1, 1943) md. Frank Raughton, one son, David Frank Raughton (b. Feb. 10, 1959). Martha Carolyn Crabb Raughton died Feb. 6, 1996 and is buried at Beulah Cemetery in Pensacola, FL.

(2) Michael Houston Crabb (b. Mar. 23, 1955) md. Sonja Michelle Bell, two children: Michelle Crabb (b. Aug. 1, 1976) and Michael Kevin Crabb (b. Jan. 26, 1980).

III) Rosie Ilene Hopkins (b. May 7, 1923) md. Morris Patterson Campbell. They live in Belmont and she is a housewife and a member of First Baptist Church of Belmont. One son, Mickey Dale Campbell (b. Dec. 7, 1951) md. Shelia Simpson.

IV) Jasper Coley Hopkins (b. Nov. 4, 1926) retired from Brown Shoe Co. and State Highway Dept. He married Anisa Gerelene Morgan and they live in the Tuscumbia Community and are members of the Tuscumbia Baptist Church.

V) Noonon Clyde Hopkins (b. Jul. 3, 1931) retired from Rogers LP Gas Co. He married Martha Rose Sanders, they live in the Tuscumbia Community, are members of Smith Chapel Freewill Baptist Church and they have four children:

(1) Jerry Clyde Hopkins (b. Jan. 17, 1958) md. Catherine Ann Cook, one child: William Coley Hopkins (b. Oct. 21, 1991). Second marriage to Annett White.

(2) Patricia Diann Hopkins (b. Apr. 24, 1959) md. Timothy Ray Ashmore, three children: Kenneth Jason Bearden (b. Aug. 26, 1980); Tiffany Diann Bearden (b. Aug. 27, 1984) and Kimberly Dianna Anisa Ashmore (b. Aug. 29, 1988).

(3) Belinda Carol Hopkins (b. Dec. 25, 1961) md. Danny Ray Bishop, three children: Stephanie Suzanne Bishop (b. May 23, 1981), Brittany Roseanne Bishop (b. Nov. 3, 1985) and Daniel Shane Bishop (b. Oct. 28, 1986).

(4) Robin Renee Hopkins (b. Sep. 19, 1963) md. Ricky Dale Johnson, two children: Anna Nicole Johnson (b. Mar. 14, 1988) and Joshua Brett Johnson (b. Jan. 25, 1993). Note: All of Gussie Ann McCoy Hopkins' great-granddaughters carry the name Ann. *Submitted by Sandra Lewis Gray, granddaughter.*

MCCOY, JAMES THOMAS, born Feb. 6, 1894 in Prentiss County, MS. His parents were George Arthur McCoy (b. Jul. 24, 1865) and Kate Edna Hunt McCoy (b. Mar. 2, 1870). Both parents were born in Monroe County, MS. His brothers and sisters were: Charlcy, Houston, Austin, Otis, Lillian, Joe, Kellous, Lois, Lou and Rowland.

Thomas married Leona Phifer on Jul. 28, 1915. Leona was born Aug. 19, 1895 in Tishomingo County, MS. Her parents were Jacob Wilson Phifer (b. Feb. 22, 1851) and Mary Elizabeth Johnson Phifer (b. Jul. 19, 1858). Both were born in Tishomingo County, MS. Thomas and Leona's children were: Shields (b. Jan. 9, 1917); Clin Earl (b. Jan. 4, 1919) and Mary Kate (b. May 27, 1927). The family lived on a farm in the Blythes' Chapel Community in the 1930s. In the 1940s, Thomas gave up farming and began carpenter work. He worked on the nuclear plant at Oak Ridge, TN. When that work ended, he returned to Booneville in Prentiss County and secured employment with the Northeast Mississippi Junior College as a janitor. He was employed there until his retirement.

Taken in 1962. From left, seated front row: Kate (McCoy) Smith and daughter, Nancy Smith; Clin Earl McCoy; J.T. and Leona McCoy and Shields McCoy. Standing back row: Peggy Ann McCoy and mother, Bertha (Clin's wife); Jack Smith (Kate's husband); Bernice McCoy (Shields' wife) and John McCoy (Shields' and Bernice's son).

In 1962 the children returned to Booneville to celebrate the 47th wedding anniversary of their parents. The children had increased in number. On Jul. 29, 1944, Shields married Bernice Deaton, who was born Mar. 5, 1912. Bernice was the daughter of John Wesley Deaton (b. Mar. 1, 1871) and Sarah Angeline Hopkins Deaton (b. Mar. 18, 1878). The parents resided in the Thrasher Community. A son was born to Shields and Bernice on Jul. 25, 1946. He was named John Shields. John became ill in 1950. His physician, Dr. L.L. McDougal Jr. advised Shields and Bernice to move to Phoenix, AZ, so that John could have the benefit of a mild climate. They moved Oct. 19, 1950 and after three years, John had regained his health.

Clin had spent 37 months overseas in WWII, going from North Africa to Sicily, then on to England and across the channel to France and Germany, serving in the 65th Field Artillery. Before he left to go overseas, he had married Bertha Nichols, who was born Mar. 3, 1924 in Birmingham, AL. After Clin was discharged from the Army, he returned home and began working for the Mississippi Forestry Service, but soon resigned to take a job with Seal Test as a salesman in Alabama. He and Bertha had a daughter and they named her Peggy Ann. She was born Aug. 3, 1946.

Jack A. Smith spent many months overseas in WWII, also. He was in the US Air Force stationed in England and flew many missions over Germany as a gunner on a B-17 bomber. Jack and Mary Kate married on Mar. 7, 1948. Jack's father was Austin Smith and his mother was Ola Holley Smith. Jack secured employment with Kimberly Clark in Memphis, TN. He was later transferred to a new plant in New Milford, CT. When a plant was built in Augusta, GA, Jack was transferred to that location. They bought a home just across the state line from Augusta in Aiken, SC. A daughter was born Jan. 27, 1956 and was named Nancy Carol.

The picture shows the entire family at that 47th anniversary. We have some wonderful memories of that day. Some of the group shown in the picture have died since that time: Thomas died Nov. 18, 1969, age 75; Leona died Jan. 4, 1993, age 97; Clin died Mar. 9, 1982, age 63; Bertha died Jan. 15, 1990, age 65 and Bernice died Jun. 14, 1997, age 85. *Submitted by Shields McCoy.*

MCCOY, LILLIAN MARIE, born Nov. 22, 1910 in the Altitude Community of Prentiss County, MS was the fifth child of William Coley and Artie Bell Stokes McCoy, raised in the Altitude and Tuscumbia Community. She graduated from Thrasher High School and attended Blue Mountain College for women. In May 1936 she married Eugene Allen (b. Apr. 27, 1909 in Ellis County, TX), son of Junie Etta Smith and Martin Luther Allen. Although born in

Texas, his family was originally from Prentiss County and moved back shortly before the untimely death of his father in October 1913. The Allens farmed and raised cattle in the Tuscumbia Community and were loved by all who knew them. They were members of the Booneville Church of Christ. Lillian Marie McCoy Allen died Aug. 7, 1998 and Eugene Allen died Mar. 15, 1983. They are buried at the Smith Chapel Cemetery. They had three children:

I) Anita June Allen (b. May 28, 1937) md. Charles Johnson. They are retired and reside at Jacinto, where they are members of the Jacinto Church of Christ. Five children: (1) Charles Keith Johnson (b. Sep. 22, 1959) md. Kim Lindsey, one child, Jarett Johnson (b. Apr. 1, 1980); (2) Philip Gene Johnson (b. Apr. 19, 1961) md. Denice Wren, three children: Monica Jean Johnson (b. Mar. 29, 1983), Courtney Gail Johnson (b. Aug. 15, 1985) and Philip Andrew Johnson (b. Jan. 26, 1988); (3) Kathy Renee Johnson (b. Sep. 5, 1964) md. John Warnick, two children: Joshua Deven Warnick (b. Nov. 14, 1984) and Jonathan Robert Warnick (b. Aug. 19, 1994); (4) Sharon Marie Johnson (b. May 31, 1966) two children: Britny Danielle Johnson (b. Apr. 4, 1990) and Lindsey Marie Johnson (b. Jul. 1, 1999); (5) Michelle June Johnson (b. Mar. 7, 1972) md. Kenny Saylors, one child, April Michelle Saylors (b. Sep. 29, 1991).

II) Peggy Jean Allen (b. Oct. 9, 1938) md. Carl Franklin Bates. Peggy works with the Thrasher School system. They live in Tuscumbia where they are members of the Tuscumbia Baptist Church. They have two children: (1) Pamela Jean Bates (b. Nov. 16, 1958) md. Gerald Johnson, two children, Jeffery Johnson (b. Feb. 22, 1982) and Jessica Lynn Johnson (b. Jun. 22, 1988). (2) Carl Franklin Bates Jr. (b. Jan. 26, 1969, d. Jan. 29, 1969).

III) Joe L. Allen (b. Jul. 9, 1940, d. Nov. 23, 1999) md. Sarah Jane Reed. Joe had his own company, Allen Contracting, Inc. They live at Thrasher and are members of the Booneville Church of Christ.

(1) Eddie Joe Allen (b. Oct. 13, 1958) md. Lisa Bullard, three children: Misty Dawn Allen (b. Oct. 8, 1980); Amanda Jo Allen (b. Jul. 31, 1984) and Jennifer Erin Allen (b. Dec. 17, 1985).

(2) Rhonda Kim Allen (b. Jan. 26, 1960) md. Ralph David Williams, two children: Kathryn Allen Williams (b. Oct. 30, 1993) and John David Williams (b. Jan. 17, 1998).

(3) Trenton Clay Allen (b. Oct. 9, 1967). *Written by Sandra Lewis Gray and submitted by Peggy Allen Bates.*

MCCOY, MARGARET EMMA "MAGGIE," born Sep. 2, 1882 daughter of James Monroe and Agnes Emaline Chase McCoy of the Burton Community, married George A. Burcham (b. Feb. 11, 1877). They lived in the Jacinto Community and had nine children:

James md. Vera Yearber; Clint md. Verona Rinehart; Berdie md. Lester Holder; Vester md. Elva Mae McAnally; Bertha Lee md. Tom Searcy; Garvin md. Earline Brown; Hardings md. Jettie Smith; Marvin md. Kellie "K.T." Harris; Mauvelene md. Junior "J.L." Hendrix.

George A. Burcham died Oct. 4, 1938 and Margaret Emma McCoy died Nov. 19, 1965. They are buried at Jacinto Cemetery in Alcorn County, MS. *Submitted by Sandra Lewis Gray. (See family reunion photo on previous page)*

MCCOY, WILLIAM COLEY, born Jan. 2, 1875 in Prentiss County, MS son of James Monroe and Agnes Emaline Chase McCoy. He was the grandson of William Henry and Sarah McCloud Howell McCoy and Jonathan Thomas and Agnes Emaline Smith Chase. (See related stories on Chasand McCoy).

He had seven siblings: Columbus Curtiss md. Cora Thompson; Margaret Emma md. George Burcham; Henry md. Della Fay Leeth; Robert Thomas md. Ola Butler; Carrol Blanchard md. Elzie Scroggin; Homer Talmadge md. Louise Boone and second, Allie Vesta Boyd; James Arthur "Cap" md. Vivian Pope.

On Feb. 22, 1900 William Coley married Artie Bell Stokes Sheffield. She was born Oct. 16, 1865 to Wiley Henry and Barbary Ann Pollard Stokes. She had three siblings: Rosa Ann Stokes md. J.H. Slaughten; Wiley Henry "Bud" Stokes md. Pantha Ella Hare and Dora Alice Stokes md. Bogle Mullinix.

William Coley and Artie Bell Stokes McCoy

Artie Bell, a widow, had been married previously to William Henry Sheffield and had three sons: Henry C. "Mac" Sheffield md. Pearl L. Lambert; William Elton Sheffield md. Loney Bell King and Frank P. Sheffield.

In 1918 they moved into their new home in the Tuscumbia Community. The house was made with hand hewed timber from their farm at Altitude. They tore down the old house, took the timber and built a barn for the farm animals at their new home. Coley, a successful farmer, was an excellent violinist, also. They had six children, all born at Altitude.

I) Gussie Ann McCoy (b. Dec. 7, 1900) md. Noonon Orlando Hopkins, five children: Artie Marie, Mattie Moeise, Rosie Ilene, Jasper Coley and Noonon Clyde.

II) Dessie Lee McCoy (b. Jun. 8, 1902, d. May 13, 1976) is buried at Forest Lawn Memorial Gardens in Corinth. She married Archie Curtiss and had two children: Billy Foye Curtiss and Archie Lee Curtiss.

III) Ernest Belmer "Pete" McCoy (b. Dec. 2, 1903, d. Sep. 18, 1999) is buried at Smith Chapel Cemetery. He married Sula Curtiss and had two children, Billy C. McCoy and Selby McCoy.

IV) Artie Mae "Jackie" McCoy (b. Nov. 2, 1905, d. Jul. 26, 1917) is buried at Old Buck Snort, Mt. Pleasant.

V) Lillian Marie McCoy (b. Nov. 22, 1910, d. Aug. 7, 1998) is buried at Smith Chapel Cemetery. She married Eugene Allen and had three children: Anita June Allen, Peggy Jean Allen and Joe L. Allen.

VI) Sophia Agnes McCoy (b. Mar. 4, 1912, d. Jun. 6, 2000) md. Ellis Elsmar Thompson and had four children: Bobby Gerald, Barbara Nell, Joyce and Ruby Dean.

Artie Bell Stokes McCoy developed tuberculosis and died Oct. 15, 1928. She is buried at Old Buck Snort Cemetery in the Altitude Community.

William Coley McCoy died Jun. 29, 1953 of heart failure and is buried beside his wife and daughter at Old Buck Snort Cemetery. *All information on this family was abstracted from The Chases of Old Tishomingo County Mississippi by Sandra Lewis Gray, great-granddaughter. Library of Congress Control Number 00-091974.*

MCCREARY, ANDREW, born around 1806 and moved to Prentiss County from Alabama and South Carolina. He married Frances Taylor in South Carolina. Together they had six children before her death around 1839 near Bull Mountain, AL. Their children were: Francis Marion, Sarah Ann, Alex, Nancy, Margaret and Andrew. After Frances' death, Andrew married Francis McClendon in Itawamba County, MS. They had seven children: Archibald, Gorden, Clarissa, William, Elizabeth,

Francis Marion McCreary

Unidentified, Raymond Burcham, Arnold Burcham, Ruth Helen Burcham, Jane Harris Hubbard, Joyce Burcham McKibbens, Jimmy McCoy, Charles Ray Burcham, Paul Jack Burcham and Morris Burcham. 2nd Row: Vivian McCoy, Kellie T. Harris Burcham, Earline Brown Burcham son william in lap, Charles Ray Holder, George Burcham, Barbara Lee Searcy in lap, Maggie McCoy Burcham, Bertha Lee Burcham Searcy, Verona Rinehart Burcham, Homer McCoy and Tom McCoy. 3rd Row: J. A. Cap McCoy, Marvin Burcham, Garvin Burcham, Smith Burcham in arms of Hardings Burcham, Jettie Smith Burcham with James Earl (John) Burcham, James Burcham, Vera Yearler Burcham, Margaret Burchan, Doris McCoy Nichols, Dolly Rogers, Rick Rogers Tom Searcy, Clint Burcham, Lum McCoy and Lee Shamlin. Back Row: Vester Burcham, Talmage McCoy, Junior (J. L.) Hendrix, Mauvelene Burcham Hendrix, unidentified, Sally Price Burcham, Vivian McCoy, Jennie Chase, Regina Rogers, Willer Chase Shamblin and Allie McCoy.

Amanda and Maria Ann. After the death of Andrew's second wife, he married twice more, Lucinda Roberts and Sally Locumberry Milam.

Andrew's eldest son, Francis Marion (b. 1826, d. 1906) married Sarah Ann Pounds on Nov. 30, 1843 in old Tishomingo County. They had six children: John, James, Martha Ann, Jefferson, Benjamin and Nancy Jane. John married Sallie Pardue. James married Mathilda ?. Martha Ann married Benjamin F. Wright. Benjamin married Mary Louise Smithers. Nancy Jane married George W. Hallmark.

Jefferson McCreary family. Back row standing from left: Luther McCreary, Lottie McCreary and Laura McCreary. Front row: Jefferson McCreary, Colus McCreary, Arthur McCreary and Margaret Catherine (Jackson) McCreary.

Jefferson (b. 1859, d. 1928) married Margaret Catherine Jackson (b. 1866, d. 1949) on Dec. 31, 1884. They had nine children: Laura (b. 1885, d. 1913); Arie (b. 1888, d. 1888); Charlotta Caroline (Lottie) (b. 1889, d. 1930); Luther Jefferson (b. 1891, d. 1968); Arthur Marion (b. 1896, d. 1980); Andrew Colus (b. 1898, d. 1984) and two daughters and a son, who died as infants without names. Laura married William Clark and raised a family in Prentiss County. Lottie married James Oscar Ford and also raised a family in Prentiss County. Arthur moved to Texas to raise a family and Colus moved to Tennessee to raise his family.

Luther Jefferson married Annie Belle Robinson (b. 1892, d. 1968) on Dec. 21, 1913. They had two children, Opal Irene and Thurman Colus (b. 1917, d. 1981). Opal married Russell Fugitt, but had no children. Thurman married Maxine Cross from Saint Joseph, MO in 1945. They had three daughters: Connie, Judy and Jane. Connie married Jim McCoy and had four daughters. Judy married Marlis Hall and has two daughters, Laura and Shelia. Jane married Eddie Tennison and has a daughter, Christy. Shelia married James Frost and has a daughter, Hannah. Christy married Keith Ryan and has a son, Cody.

Many of the early members of the McCreary family are buried in Pleasant Valley, Cotton Springs, Friendship and East Prentiss Cemeteries of Prentiss County. The descendants of this family are still mostly in the Prentiss County area. *Submitted by Judy (McCreary) Hall.*

MCHUGH, PETER, born in County Leitrim, Ireland in 1848 and with his brother, John, immigrated to America in 1867 where they joined their brother, Thomas, who had come in 1857.

Peter left New York where he had been a blacksmith and made his way to Prentiss County, MS. While there, he married Margaret Katherine Haley, daughter of another Irishman, Michael Haley. Peter and Kate had five children while in Booneville: William Thomas, John, Peter, Ella and Molly.

During his years in Booneville, Peter was involved in the fur and hide trade, the scrap iron business and continued to practice his blacksmithing skills. In 1891 he was working on a patent for a locking washer, but unfortunately, never applied for the patent.

In 1898 Peter, Kate and the three surviving children moved to Dyer in Gibson County, TN where Katherine, Margaret, Alice, William Wallace, Edward Bruce and Charles Omega were born.

Peter McHugh died in 1920 and his wife, Kate, died in 1927. *Submitted by Pat Jones.*

MCKAY, WILLIAM AND JANE, came to Itawamba County, MS before 1850 from South Carolina. William was born about 1788 in Ireland and Jane was born about 1794 in South Carolina. Their children were: William F., who married Julia Patterson; Hugh Jackson (Jack), who married Matilda J. Reece; Michael, who married Mahala Ables; Samuel, who married Permelia Caroline Ables; Mary, who married J.E. Farrer; John, who married Margaret (Belinda) Montgomery and Nancy, who married John Haney.

Hugh Jackson McKay married Matilda Josephine Reece on Oct. 17, 1848 in Itawamba County, MS. Their children were: John; Nancy, who married Jack Bolin; William; Matilda, who married J.S. McNair in Prentiss County, MS; Andrew Jackson, who married Victoria Ashley; Cordona (Callie), who married John Rainey; twins, Mary F., who married L.H. Marrow in Prentiss County, MS and settled in Tennessee and Robert Franklin, who married Fronie Bell Oswalt in Prentiss County and after her death married Mrs. Bessie Ledbetter and settled in Corinth, MS and Thomas M. They also may have had Harvey, Matterson and Benjamin.

Thomas M. McKay was born Nov. 1, 1862 and married Georgianna (Susie) Pruitt in Itawamba County, MS on May 9, 1880. Her parents were Marion Pruitt and Sarah Ingles. To this union was born Mary Alice, James William, Lebra Dovie, Charlie and Jesse, who married Lois Josephine Nicholson, daughter of William Alonzo Nicholson and Tennessee Jane Denson. Jesse and Lois had James Earl, William Marshall, Lorraine and Bobby Lee.

Front from left: Donald, Randy and Tommy. Back from left: James, Marshall, Jesse and Bobby.

James married first Helen Sevelle Weems, daughter of Leslie Exel Weems and Ella Mae (Mamie) Brown and had three children: Jimmy Darrell (stillborn), Mamie Eloise (stillborn) and Patsy Joy. His second wife was Joe Hyde, by whom he had Tommy, Sharon, Donald, Becky and David.

Marshall married Josephine Imperapore, who he met in Italy during WWII. They had one child, Randy and live in Memphis.

Lorraine was married first to Hollis Hatcher and had one son, Hollis Jr. Both died young in accidents. Her second husband is Milton Downs and they live in Booneville.

Bobby married Helen Thorton, who had three children. Bobby and Helen had one son, Ronnie Lee. Bobby is a retired fireman in Booneville.

Robert Franklin was born in 1868 and died in 1951. Robert and Fronie Bell Oswalt had: Carrie Lee, who married William Denson Spencer; Effie Myrtle, who married Riley Grammer; Almus Allen, who married Nomie Wren; Julius Harmon, who never married; George Elzie, who married Mary Newton; Sara Linnie Lou and Velena (Lena) May, born in 1908, who married Ellis Carpenter. Velena and Ellis had Maxine, who married James Columbus Farr. Maxine and James had James, Lois, Martha, Joseph, Jackie and Nancy Jean, who married Clifford Bible. Velena, Maxine and Nancy live in Moss Point, MS. *Submitted by Lorraine Downs.*

MCKINNEY, JAMES THOMAS, born Jul. 7, 1867 in Franklin County, AL, the son of Sampson (b. 1836, d. 1900) and Nancy Ann Crowell (b. 1844, d. 1927) McKinney. He married on Jul. 18, 1890, to Lydia Belzoria Crow, the daughter of Zachariah (b. 1845, d. 1906) and Mary Hunt (b. 1853, d. 1933) Crow. *James Thomas McKinney Family. Bottom row, from*

left: Troy, Belzoria, James Thomas and Roy. Second row, from left: Ray, Elva, Vera, Rather, Romey, Nina, Clayton and Robert.

Belzoria was born Feb. 16, 1873 in Franklin County, AL. Their first six children were born in Franklin County. They purchased a farm in the East Prentiss Community about 1905. They operated a general store on their property in addition to farming. Jim was also known as a good blacksmith. Belzoria wove her own fabric from the wool of her sheep. They attended the East Prentiss Baptist Church where some of their children are still members. Jim attended the Bay Springs Masonic Lodge. Their children are:

1. William Edgar (b. 1892, d. 1894) buried in Franklin County, AL.

2. Romey Austin (b. 1894, d. 1956), Montgomery, AL, married Mary Lois Holley (b. 1900, d. ?) and had Randall, Holley, Mary Ruth and Betty Jean.

3. Nina Lodemia (b. 1896, d. 1991), Prentiss County, married Eldon Reese Pounds (b. 1893, d. 1953) and had Lola Faye, James Thurman (deceased), Lorene Avenell, Erlene Remell, Mary Helen and Virginia Ann.

4. Clayton Samuel (b. 1898, d. 1976), Prentiss County, married Luna E. Gilley (b. 1902, d. 1974) and had Herman Clayton (b. 1922, d. 1923), Chester Lee, Lester Kenneth and Clayton Samuel Jr.

5. Robert Andrew Dowe (b. 1900, d. 1989), Prentiss County, married Minnie Mae Gilley (b. 1903, d. 1985) and had Edith Marie, Lydia Evelyne and William Dowe.

6. Rather Lee (b. 1903, d. 1949), Prentiss County, married Erma Cleo McCreary. They had five children: Pauline, Margie Maurine, William Lee, James Thomas and Mary Elizabeth.

7. Eva Dell (b. 1906, d. 1907) is buried in Old Friendship Cemetery.

8. Vera Alene (b. 1908), Prentiss County, married Joe Dave Smith (b. 1903, d. 1996). See their story.

9. Elva Ione (b. 1911, d. 1951), Prentiss County, married Talmadge Moore (b. 1912, d. 1975) and had Nellie Ruth, Peggy Carolyn and Sharon Janet (b. 1950, d. 1995).

10. Arthur Troy (b. 1913, d. 1995), Birmingham, AL, married Ellawill Cowan (?, d. 1998) and had Melinda.

11. James Roy (b. b. 1913 – twin), Tuscaloosa, AL, married Jimmie Sue Clayton Johnston.

12. Ray (b. b. 1919), Prentiss County, married Helen Faye Brown. They have James Ray, Shirley Faye, Kara Sue and Sara Lou (twins) and Johnny Arthur.

The three youngest sons, Roy, Troy and Ray, were in WWII at the same time. James Thomas died Dec. 19, 1951 and Lydia Belzoria died Jul. 14, 1956. They and several of their children are buried in the East Prentiss Church Cemetery. *Submitted by Vera McKinney Smith, 100 South Franks Road, Booneville, MS.*

MCKINNEY, PAUL RAY, married Lisa Dawn Woodard on Feb. 14, 1987. Paul Ray was born Dec. 17, 1964 and is the son of Mr. and Mrs. L.B. McKinney.

Lisa Dawn Woodard (b. Jan. 3, 1969) is the daughter of Nelda Dean (b. Dec. 16, 1943) and John Ellis Woodard (b. Sep. 7, 1938) who married Dec. 23,

1961. She is the granddaughter of Winston Jasper "Wink" Vanderford (b. Mar. 9, 1916, d. Apr. 17, 1989) and Ella Missouri Woodruff Vanderford (b. Feb. 21, 1913, d. Sep. 2, 1991) who married on Jun. 23, 1933. They are buried in the Snowdown Church of Christ Cemetery in Prentiss County. Lisa has one brother who is buried in the Snowdown Church of Christ Cemetery. She has no sisters.

John, Lisa and Nelda Woodard

Paul Ray and Lisa have two children: Justin Cody McKinney (b. Dec. 25, 1988) and Courtney Danielle McKinney (b. Apr. 26, 1994). Justin stayed with his great-grandmother, Ella Missouri Woodruff Vanderford while his mother worked. He gave her much joy until her death Sep. 2, 1991. He enjoys fishing and hunting. Justin Cody and Courtney Danielle are going to school at Hills Chapel. *Submitted by Lisa Dawn Woodard McKinney.*

MELTON, CORNELIAS, born Sep. 15, 1768 in Albemarle, VA, died April 1821 in Rutherford County, NC and married Dicey Green about 1768 in Albemarle, VA. He is found on the 1820 census of Rutherford County, NC.

His will was probated in Rutherford County and names sons: Abner, Marvel, Lindsey, Frederick Green and Hiram. It also mentions wife and daughters but their names are not given. One daughter's name is mentioned but is not legible.

According to one researcher, Cornelias was the son of Silas Melton (b. 1725, d. 1783) of Albemarle, VA and Catrina _, of Louisa, VA. Silas Melton was the son of William Melton (b. Dec. 11, 1707, d. 1751/55) and Elizabeth Farr/Pharr (b. ca 1698, d. ca. 1751). William Melton was born in Kingston upon Thames, Surrey, England. He died in Hanover, VA.

Hiram Melton was born in 1809 in Rutherford County, NC. We are uncertain as to his wife. It has been said he was married to a Summer or Sumner girl of Dutch descent who was the sister of Zilpha Summer, the wife of James Young. But one researcher says that Hiram's wife was a Gowing.

Nothing is known of Hiram Melton from his birth in North Carolina until he turned up near Enville in McNairy County, TN about 1836, where he was a wealthy land owner. We are told Hiram in later years was obese, weighing about 400 pounds at his death. He was murdered, shot in the back from ambush while eating his breakfast beneath a large shade tree in September 1866. He is buried in O'Neal Cemetery near Enville, TN near Melton and Young relatives.

Hiram Melton was the father of William Walter, Nancy Eleanor, Mary Jane, John Quincy, James, Louisa, Henry, Caroline, Elizabeth and Isaac.

Four of Hiram's sons were never heard of after the Battle of Shiloh. They were most likely killed in the battle and thrown into one of the mass graves. In the book, *Confederates In The Attic,* the author mentions a northerner whose ancestor fought at Shiloh and picked up a rifle dropped by a fallen soldier. Scratched into the stock of the rifle was the name "Melton." The descendant still owns the rifle dropped by a Melton at Shiloh.

John Quincy Melton (b. Jun. 15, 1838, d. Mar. 10, 1898) md. Ellen Catherine Young (b. Oct. 15, 1842, d. Feb. 13, 1908), daughter of James Young and Zilpha Sumner. John Quincy Melton served in Co. B, 21st (Wilson's) Tennessee Cavalry. His muster sheet shows he attained the rank of 4th sergeant and that he owned his bay horse valued at $450-$500. His muster sheets also show that he was enlisted at Jack's Creek in Hardin County by Capt. Wharton for a period of three years and was never paid. This company saw action at Brice's Crossroads.

John Quincy Melton, a small man and unable to read or write, was a messenger for General Nathan Bedford Forrest. His wife, Ellen Catherine, taught him to read after the war. She is said to have heard the roar of cannon during the Battle of Shiloh.

The children of John Quincy Melton and Ellen Catherine Young were James Wesley, Flora Eunice, George, Isaac B., Mattie, Hiram B., Narcis and John Noah.

John Quincy and Ellen Catherine Young Melton are buried at Piney Grove in Prentiss County.

Mattie Melton (b. Jul. 19, 1877, d. Feb. 6, 1949) md. James A. Harper (b. Nov. 2, 1872, d. Jul. 17, 1956), son of Henry J. Harper and Mary Holloway, who are buried in Hinkle Creek Cemetery in Alcorn County.

Jim Harper was a male nurse. His father, Henry J. Harper, was in the Medical Corps in the Confederate Army, probably as an orderly. He enlisted in Co. A, 43rd Mississippi Infantry in Aberdeen, MS. He was taken prisoner at Corinth and is on a list of paroled Confederate prisoners, wounded and nurses, delivered at Iuka, MS. He was captured again at Vicksburg and appears on a roll of prisoners of war captured by Major General U.S. Grant.

Mattie Melton Harper was said by her daughter-in-law, Bonnie Johnson Harper Whisenant, to be the best woman she ever knew. Bonnie named her only daughter Mattie Maxine (Harper Sparks) after Mattie Melton. Aubrey Melton Harper said that his father was a hard man but that his mother was wonderful to him. Jim and Mattie are buried at Forked Oak in Prentiss County where Mattie was a faithful member.

Children of James and Mattie Melton Harper were James Hubert, Odus Everett, Aubrey Melton, Joseph Buford, John Maurice (see his story), J.I., Tom Henry, Lottie Lucille and George Wilson.

MELTON, HIRAM, according to historical records, Hiram Melton (b. 1808, d. 1886) moved to Enville, TN from North Carolina with his wife and three small children in 1836. They had seven more children after moving to Tennessee. Hiram reportedly acquired large tracts of land in the area where he settled. He was shot from ambush as he sat having breakfast under the shade of a tree in his yard. He is buried at O'Neals Cemetery near Finger, TN.

John Noah Melton (1883-1964)

Hiram's fourth child, John Quincy Melton (b. 1838, d. 1898), married Ellen Catherine Young (b. 1842, d. 1908) in Tennessee in 1860. The first of their nine children was born near Corinth, MS in 1865. John Q. and his family settled around Jacinto. He donated land for the Baptist church and the cemetery at Piney Grove. John Q., his wife Ellen and numerous descendants are buried in the Piney Grove Cemetery.

John Noah Melton (b. 1883, d. 1964) was the youngest child of John Q. and Ellen Melton. He was a schoolteacher and a farmer. He married Sally Augusta Pardue (b. 1889, d. 1923). She was the oldest daughter of Rufus and Minnie Cunningham Pardue. John and Sally had seven children before her death at age 34 as the result of a fire.

Humbert Melton (b. 1908, d. 1975) married Zera Grace Gentry. They were both schoolteachers in Prentiss County. Humbert was an Army veteran. They had three children: James, an infant daughter Sarah Jane (died Feb. 6, 1949) and Janis.

Amos Melton (b. 1909, d. 1974) married Forrest Sparks. He owned Booneville Meat Packing Co. They had four children: an infant son who died in 1934, Sue (b. 1936, d. 1962), Brenda and Wayne.

John and Sally had an infant son who died in 1911.

Lucille Melton (b. 1914) married Johnny Knight. They had 13 children: John Hollis, Billy Wayne, Evelyn, Bobby Gene, Lloyd, Shirley, Charles (b. 1946, d. 1964), Sarah, Martha, Melton, Harold, Keith and Cathy. Many years after Johnny's death in 1965, Lucille married Travis Johnson. He and Lucille lived happily until his death in 1998.

Ernestine Melton (b. 1916) married Marion B. Miller. He was a WWII veteran and a preacher. They had seven children: Humbert Wayne, Jerry, Jimmy, Sarah, Karen, Glenn and Betty. Their family settled in Alabama.

Edith Melton (b. 1919) married Robert Granville Huddleston. He was a carpenter. She was a homemaker and worked at Prentiss Manufacturing for 20 years. They had six children: Norma, Charlotte, Larry, Gary, Terry (b. 1952, d. 1984) and Debbie.

Stella Melton (b. 1921) married Marlin Short. He was a WWII veteran. They had five children: Ronnie, Kay, Gail, Gordon and Donna.

Several years after Sally's death, John Noah married his second wife, Gertrude Timbes (b. 1901, d. 1979). They had no children. Gertrude had one child by a previous marriage, Geraldine Yow Tate (b. 1920, d. 1952). John was a great fan of baseball, especially the St. Louis Cardinals. He remained active and enjoyed gardening and playing with his grandchildren until his death at age 81. *Submitted by Charlotte Deaton.*

MELTON, JOHN NOAH born Oct. 17, 1883 and died Dec. 24, 1964 married Sallie Pardue (b. Mar. 9, 1889, d. Jun. 23, 1923). Their children:

1-2) Humbert married Zera Grace Gentry and Amos married Forrest Sparks, daughter of Jesse and Maggie Bonds Sparks. Their children were an infant son who didn't survive, Kathryn Sue, Wayne and Brenda Faye.

While a young child, Sue was diagnosed with a heart defect and was advised by doctors that she should live a very sheltered, careful life and shouldn't marry or attempt to have children. But Sue was determined "to have a life." She went to Memphis where she attended art and modeling classes and met a young sailor from Maryland, Randall Mason and was married. They lived for a time in California and then returned to Memphis. Randy, apparently unable to cope with the serious condition of his young wife, abandoned her. Sue found employment and lived for a while with her Uncle John Sparks and family in north Memphis, sharing her younger cousin Ann's room. Ann and Sue became good friends as well as cousins. With her health deteriorating, Sue soon returned to her parents' home in Booneville. She was a brave young woman who knew she was on borrowed time. She begged one eminent heart surgeon with Bethesda Hospital in Maryland to perform life saving surgery, but she was regrettably too ill by this time to be a viable candidate for the surgery. She never lost her wonderful sense of humor and died at the age of 25. She is buried in the Booneville Cemetery.

Wayne was married to Beth Richardson and they had Susan Annette (md. Randy King and had Holly) and Sonya Elizabeth (md. Mike Jones and had Michael and Jon William). Susan and Sonya are both teachers in Prentiss County schools. Brenda first married Charles Smith and they had Karen Sue, Greg, Brian and Matthew. Brenda then married Larry Laurence and they had Lara Ellen. Brenda is a nursing instructor and lives in San Antonio with Larry and Lara. Wayne's two grandsons are the fifth generation to live on his grandfather Jesse Sparks' old homeplace in the 5th District.

Karen Smith Bouldin is now married to Taylor Rushing. Her children are Brandy, Bobbie and B.J. Bouldin. They live in Jackson, TN. Greg Smith married Lisa Pendergrast and they have Cade and Caleb.

3-6) Lucille (md. Johnny Knight); Ernestine (md. Marion Miller); Edith (md. Granville Huddleston) and Stella (md. Marlin Short).

John Noah's second wife was Gertrude Timbes.

MICHAEL, HESTER UTASKA (CAVER),

born Sep. 6, 1887 in Prentiss County, MS to William Shelton Caver and Cora Farris (Blagg) Caver. Hester married Reuben Hill Michael on Dec. 14, 1902. Reuben Hill Michael was born Feb. 16, 1884, to James Daniel and Mary Ellen Michael. Their family consisted of the following children:

Hester Utaska (Caver) Michael

(1) Verda Lee (b. Dec. 1, 1903, d. Feb. 8, 1904).

(2) Mabel C. (b. Feb. 2, 1906, d. in Blytheville, AR) married Fant Windham on Sep. 12, 1928.

(3) Jodie B. (b. Apr. 6, 1908, d. Apr. 1, 1998 in Prentiss County, MS) married Frank "Vardaman" Chambers (b. Dec. 26, 1903, d. Feb. 7, 1975) on May 20, 1925..

(4) Benjamin Franklin (d. at birth 1909).

(5) George Franklin (b. Jul. 27, 1910, d. Nov. 30, 1933) married Olive Storey on Oct. 9, 1932.

(6) William Daniel (b. Feb. 12, 1913) married Ruby Guy Michael on Aug. 31, 1935.

(7) Mary Farris (b. Apr. 18, 1915) married Wesley Davidson on Dec. 15, 1936.

(8) Ima Lou (d. at birth 1917).

(9) Ura Gladys (d. at birth 1917). Ima and Ura were twins.

(10) Ruby Ester (b. Mar. 16, 1919) married Andrew Leroy Storey on Apr. 8, 1936.

(11) Dorothy Nell (b. Jul. 14, 1921) married Tom Stanford on Oct. 11, 1940.

(12) Caver (d. at birth 1924).

Daughter, Dorothy Nell, was born in Crosett, AR. All other children were born in Prentiss County, MS.

Hester and Reuben Hill were divorced and Hester went on to live out her life staying most of her time with daughter, Jodie B. She would stay periodically with her other children. She was dearly loved for her quiet, loving manner. Hester died Jan. 21, 1957 in Memphis, TN while staying with Jodie B. She is buried in the Carolina Methodist Church Cemetery in Prentiss County. Reuben Hill Michael died Jun. 20, 1969 and is buried in Crossroads Cemetery.

William Shelton Caver was born Feb. 6, 1865 in Old Tishomingo County, MS. His mother is Margaret Caver, born Aug. 5, 1829 in South Carolina. William died Feb. 4, 1949 in Prentiss County and is buried in the Crossroads Cemetery at Jumpertown. Cora Farris Blagg was born May 29, 1869 in Mississippi. Her father was a Blagg and her mother was a Rowsey. Cora Farris Caver died May 29, 1869 and is buried in the Old Windham Cemetery in Prentiss County.

James Daniel Michael was born Jan. 25, 1861 in Prentiss County and died May 18, 1937. He married Mary Ellen Carmichael (formerly Michael) on Oct. 13, 1881. Mary Ellen died Oct. 24, 1947. James Daniel and Mary Ellen are both buried in the Carolina Methodist Church Cemetery. *Submitted by Mrs. Ruby Storey.*

MICHAEL, JAMES DANIEL,

born Jan. 25, 1861 in Prentiss County, MS to George W. Michael and Elizabeth Jane Bridges. He married Mary Ellen (Michael) Carmichael on Oct. 13, 1881 in Prentiss County. Mary Ellen was born Jan. 28, 1865, to Martin Luther Michael and Mary (Funderburg) Michael. James Daniel and Mary Ellen's children were as follows:

The James Daniel Michael Family. Front Row: Mary Etta, James Daniel, James Clifford, Mary Ellen, Ruth Inez. Back Row: Eugenia Notree, Annie Lou, Reuben Hill and Georgia Martin.

(1) Georgia Martin (b. Jun. 18, 1882 in Prentiss County, d. Nov. 25, 1933) married John Windham on Jun. 27, 1897.

(2) Reuben Hill (b. Feb. 16, 1884 in Prentiss County, d. Jun. 20, 1969) married Hester Utaska Caver on Dec. 14, 1902.

(3) James Clifford (b. Aug. 14, 1888 in Prentiss County, d. Mar. 19, 1971) married Quay Mathews on May 19, 1918.

(4) Eugenia Notree (b. Jan. 24, 1890 in Prentiss County, d. 1966) married first Frank Eaton on May 11, 1905 and second Arthur Daniel Hurst.

(5) Mary Etta (b. Dec. 9, 1895 in Prentiss County, d. Jul. 8, 1973) married Joseph Walker Green on Jan. 21, 1912.

(6) Annie Lou (b. Mar. 1, 1898 in Prentiss County, d. Mar. 9, 1996) married William Henry Smart on Dec. 20, 1913.

(7) Ruth Inez (b. Dec. 3, 1903 in Prentiss County) married first Dixie Carter and second Charles Brooks.

James Daniel Michael's father, George W. Michael, was born Oct. 27, 1833 in Rutherford County, NC. His mother, Elizabeth Jane (Bridges) Michael, was born Sep. 17, 1837 in North Carolina. Their children were: Sarah E. (b. Nov. 27, 1857, d. Jul. 1, 1911), James Daniel, Georgiana F. (b. Aug. 13, 1862, d. Jan. 5, 1911), Mary Etta (b. May 22, 1865, d. Apr. 28, 1889) and John William (b. 1869, d. ?). George died Jul. 9, 1906 and Mary Ellen died Aug. 26, 1911. Both are buried in the Carolina Methodist Church Cemetery.

Mary Ellen's father, Martin Luther Michael, was born in 1837 in North Carolina. Her mother, Martha Lou (Kistler) Michael, was born May 28, 1839 in North Carolina. Their children were: Benjamin Franklin (b. Sep. 19, 1859, d. Aug. 19, 1922), Mary Ellen, Hope Alice (b. 1869, d. ?), Columbus T. (b. 1879, d. ?) and Price A. (b. 1882, d. Aug. 26, 1968). Martin Luther died in 1929 and Martha Lou died Jan. 15, 1916. Martha Lou is buried in the Carolina Methodist Church Cemetery. *Submitted by Ruby Carolyn Williams.*

MILLER, JOHN HENRY AND TENNESSEE "TENNIE" ROGERS,

William Carol Miller (b. 1826, d. 1905) and Sarah Ann Green (b. 1825, d. 1904), buried in Miller Cemetery near Hackleburg, AL, were the parents of John Henry Miller (b. Feb. 14, 1854, d. Dec. 5, 1920), who married Tennessee "Tennie" Rogers on Sep. 27, 1883. Tennie (b. Mar. 1, 1865, d. Jun. 26, 1951), daughter of Zimri Rogers (b. Mar. 15, 1807 in Kentucky and died Jun. 5, 1869 and buried in Blythe's Chapel on a plot donated by Zimri and his second wife, Elizabeth) and Nancy Ann Dickey (b. Georgia on Dec. 19, 1841), the third wife of Zimri. Nancy Ann died Apr. 12, 1925. In the late 1870s and early 1880s, Tennie received her education while living with her half-brother, Dr. W.J. Rogers in Marietta, MS.

John Henry Miller Family in 1906. Front row, from left: Ollie, John Henry, Tennie and Eila. Back row, from left: R.C., Luna, Baxter and Alton.

John Henry had moved from Marion County, AL, to Little Brown Church Community on Brown's Creek in southeast Prentiss County where in 1882, he purchased 120 acres of farmland and another 80 acres in 1886. He was five feet, five inches tall and chubby built. He wore pants, rather than overalls and a derby hat. While living and farming at Brown's Creek, John Henry and Tennie had the following children:

1. Luna Ethel Miller (b. 1884, d. 1970) married Joe Vandevander on Jul. 4, 1909 and lived in the Zion's Rest Community. Both are buried in the Massey Cemetery. They had two daughters: (a) Daisy Mae married Sidney Johnson (b. 1933) and had Darrell, Jerry, Dudley, Ramelle and Jack. Sidney and Daisy live in an assisted living facility in Germantown, TN. (b) Frances Louise (b. 1918) married Paul Leathers (b. 1936) and had a daughter, Bettie Wade, who married Milton "Bud" Nichols. Their daughters are Wanda, Linda Kay and Jimmie Ann. Louise was the manager of Kuhn's in Booneville.

2. Thomas Baxter Miller (b. 1886, d. 1964) married Loner Maye Newborn Dec. 25, 1910. After living in New Mexico a number of years, where Florrie Faustine was born in 1913, they later moved to Thrasher, MS. (a) Florrie first married Earl Moreland and had a daughter, June Forrest (deceased in 1953). Florrie's second husband was Oscar Jones of Clover, SC. Their children are Ernest James, Dorothy and Edmond. Florrie died Apr. 1, 1998 and is buried in Clover. (b) Nelle Mae Joyce Miller (b. 1922) married James Franklin Baxter of Louisville, AL (b. 1945) and they had a son, Joe Frank. Joyce is living in Crowne Health Care in Eufaula, AL, since her husband's death. (c) Dorothy Elizabeth Miller (b. 1925), retired elementary teacher, resides in Florence, AL, with her husband, Dellmer Heffington. (d) James Hale Miller (b. 1929, d. 1981), claim agent for Illinois Central Railroad, married Shirley Asher (b. 1959), lived in Paducah, KY and had two children, David and Kristin.

3. Courtney Alton Miller (b. 1889, d. 1964) married Ona Floyd (b. 1910) and had two daughters: (a) Jewel (b. 1912, d. 1996) married Chester "Bud" Morgan and had a son, James Chester Morgan. (b) Gladys was born Nov. 26, 1916. Her mother died when Gladys was only 1 month old. Gladys married Guy Morgan (b. 1934) and after his death, married Herbert Sumners (b. 1966). Alton married his second wife, Radie Davis (b. 1917). To them were born Katie Lee, Cleo, Fannie Mae, Robert, Frieda, Geraldine and Clovis Glen. Alton lived at Baldwyn, MS.

4. R.C. "Doc" Miller (b. 1892, d. 1968) married Sinda Brown and to this union were born: Anuel Faye, Harold, Mary Wyatt, Johnnie Marie, Marion Brown "Dick", Frances, Kathryn, Martha Sue and Bobby Junior. R.C. is buried in Morris Hill Cemetery in Hoover, AL.

5. Eila Lee Miller (b. 1896, d. 1962) married P. Leslie Holley, who worked for Holley's Seed and Feed Store in Booneville.

6. Ollie Mae Miller (b. 1899, d. 1989) served as postmistress at Thrasher (1924-1926) and married Paul Tubbs. They lived in Sheffield, AL and had a son, John Ladell.

John Henry Miller purchased a 30-acre farm at Thrasher and he, Tennie and Ollie moved there in 1918. Tennie was a great lover of flowers, spending many happy hours in her garden and sharing flowers with friends and neighbors. In later years, she became an artist with her embroidering and quilting. John Henry and Tennie are laid to rest in the Booneville Cemetery in Booneville, MS. Baxter and Maye Miller and Leslie and Eila Holley are also buried in the Booneville Cemetery. *Submitted by Dorothy M. Heffington.*

MILLER, THOMAS STEVEN, of the Hopewell Community (Prentiss County) was the son of Joel Miller (b. Jul. 7, 1805, d. Jul. 1852) and Mary Miller (b. Apr. 10, 1809, d. ?).

Thomas Steven (b. Feb. 11, 1828, d. 1908) married Ellen Monica (Menacky) Wyatt Long (b. Jan. 20, 1828, d. ?). Their children were Joel Darling, William Milton, John Thomas, J.H. (Jerry), Pernecie Vashtie, Sara Jane (Sallie) and Mary Frances.

Joel Darling was born Mar. 24, 1849 and died while still a child. William Milton (b. Apr. 19, 1851, d. ?) was married twice and had two children: Lula, who married Dave North and Luther. John Thomas (b. Jan. 29, 1857, d. ?) married Sannie Bettys. Their children were Wyatt, Otha and Jason. J.H. (Jerry) (b. Mar. 12, 1862, d. May 28, 1931) married Margaret (Mag) Pettit. They had three children: Thomas, Clifford and Myrtle. Pernecie Vashtie (Necie) (b. Sep. 12, 1874, d. Jun. 29, 1936) married Samuel (Mack) Swinney. She was "Uncle Mack's" second wife. They had no children. Sara Jane (Sallie) (b. Apr. 9, 1860, d. ?) married Richard (Dick) Keisler. Their children were John (married Alice Crabb), Sam (married Ora Hardin), Minnie (married Walter Crabb) and Ellen (married George Crabb). Mary Frances (b. May 12, 1867, d. Nov. 29, 1941) married Robert Belton Maxwell Jr. (b. Mar. 4, 1862, d. Apr. 17, 1944), son of Robert Belton Maxwell Sr., on Feb. 10, 1885, at her Hopewell home with Reverend John Lytal of Baldwyn performing the ceremony. She and her husband lived in the Hopewell Community, until late December 1906 when they moved to Booneville. Mary Frances was a housewife and mother. Her husband was a blacksmith.

Their first child, Myrtle Ollie, was born Dec. 3, 1895 and died Jul. 7, 1964. Jessie Pernecy (b. Oct. 11, 1880, d. Apr. 28, 1992) married John Guy Adair. Their only child, Mary Avis, married George S. Settle. They have three children: Raymond Adair, Evelyn Ann and Edward Maxwell and four grandchildren. Sarah Elizabeth (b. Jul. 25, 1894, d. Nov. 20, 1979) married Horace Greely Rogers. Thomas Samuel (Tom) (b. Dec. 21, 1896, d. Apr. 9, 1971) married Elizabeth Gish. They had three children: Elizabeth Ann, Mildred Tate and Daisy Roberta (Bobbie). Minnie Mae (b. Jul. 27, 1900, d. Apr. 9, 1973) married Guy M. Holley. Otha Lee and Luther Hick, twins, were born Feb. 6, 1904. Luther died Jul. 21, 1905. Otha married Grace Gault. They had one daughter, Mary Gault, who married Houston Nabers. Their two children are Mary Grace and Steven Maxwell. Otha died Jul. 4, 1976. Anna Lou, born Dec. 6, 1906, married Ruben Avery "Shorty" Kimbrell. They had one daughter, Sue Carolyn, who married Robert L. Honeycutt. The Honeycutt's have one daughter, Andrea Lynn. (See Maxwell, Kimbrell and Honeycutt histories in this book.) *Submitted by Ann Kimbrell.*

MOFFITT, KENNETH RANDAL, descendant of Andrew Jackson Murren, the first white settler of Henderson County, TN. In 1799, Mr. Murren moved from North Carolina to Henderson County with his 12-year-old son. After building a one-bedroom cabin and leaving his son in the care of the local Cherokee Indian tribe, he went back to North Carolina for the rest of his family.

Dana Giddens Moffitt is the descendant of Francis Giddens of Franklin County, TN a gunsmith during the Revolutionary War. His home in Franklin,

Kenneth Randal Moffitt family. From left: Jennifer, Randy, Dana and Kenneth in 1998.

TN is currently on the National Registry of Historic Homes.

After graduation from Lexington High School in Lexington, TN Randy received his bachelor of science in business management from the University of Tennessee at Martin. Dana graduated from Huntingdon High School in Huntingdon, TN and received her bachelor of science in liberal arts from University of Tennessee at Martin in 1969.

Randy and Dana were married on Mar. 26, 1967. Randy served in the US Marine Corps Reserve Unit 1965-1971, earning sergeant E5 rank.

In 1969, Randy began his professional career as an industrial engineer with the HIS Corporation, Sportswear Division in South Fulton, TN. Dana began her career as a regional day care licensing supervisor with the Tennessee Department of Public Welfare.

Several re-locations later, they made their home in Bruceton, TN and began their family. Kenneth Gray Moffitt was born Feb. 20, 1972 and Jennifer Rebecca Moffitt was born Apr. 11, 1977.

The Moffitts moved to Prentiss County in November 1978. Randy joined Prentiss Manufacturing Co. as their chief engineer and advanced to vice president of manufacturing. While raising their family, they have been active in the community with Boy Scouts and Girl Scouts, City Park baseball, softball, football and cheerleading. Kenneth achieved the coveted Eagle Scout award at age 14. Ken and Jennifer were active in their high school, both playing French horn in the Booneville Blue Devil Band. The family belongs to First United Methodist Church.

Dana was a homemaker for 12 years enjoying her volunteer work with Booneville Junior Auxiliary until 1982, when Jennifer began school. Dana started her library career as a library assistant in the Booneville City School System. In 1991 she accepted the position of librarian for the George E. Allen Library. Her love for people, books and order made her realize this was her dream position. In 1994 she joined the Natchez Trace Chapter DAR. She is a member of the Booneville and Prentiss County Historical Commission.

Kenneth graduated from Booneville High School in 1990 and attended Mississippi State and Otis Parsons School of Art and Design in Los Angeles, CA. His artistic talents enabled him to start his own business in decorative art called Paint The Town.

Jennifer graduated from Booneville High School and in 1997 from Northeast Mississippi Community College with full honors. She graduated from Mississippi State in 1999 Magna Cum Laude with a degree in business management.

Randy and Dana make their home in Booneville, MS. *Submitted by Dana Moffitt.*

MOORE - GREEN FAMILY, the fourth child of Walter Lee Green and Minnie Bell Green was Wilfred Lee. He was born Jun. 23, 1929 in Jackson, TN. He attended public schools in Jackson, graduating from Jackson High School in 1947.

Wilfred was given the nickname Bo or Bodie at a very young age and is still known by that today. He worked for Western Auto for 10 years. He then went to work at the Jackson Post Office for 27 years, from which he retired.

Wilfred married Helen Lorraine Sanderson on Mar. 16, 1952. Their first child, Wilfred Lee Jr., was born Jul. 14, 1953. He has always been known as Fred or Freddie. He graduated from North Side High School in 1971 and then attended college at Tennessee Tech in Cookeville, TN. On Apr. 10, 1976, he married Rheanne Daster. Their children are: Elaine

Wilfred Lee and Lorraine Green.

Michelle, born Mar. 10, 1980; Lee Russel, born Sep. 14, 1982 and Kathryn Helen, born Dec. 27, 1991. Elaine is in her second year at Union University. Lee and Kathryn are students at Trinity Christian Academy in Jackson, TN. Fred and Rheanne are divorced. He later married Margaret Christensen.

Wilfred and Lorraine's second child, Jeannie Lorraine, was born Aug. 27, 1958. She graduated from North Side High School in 1976, obtained a bachelor of music degree from Lambuth College and later earned a degree in nursing from Union University. She is a registered nurse and works at Methodist Hospital of Jackson.

Jeannie married Dwayne Alan Tignor on Jun. 4, 1977. They have two children. Amanda Lorraine, born Sep. 27, 1979, graduated from Trinity Christian Academy, attended Lambuth University for two years and is now in nursing school at Jackson State Community College. Michael Alan was born Jan. 10, 1982 and is a senior at Trinity Christian

Celebrating Nettie Moore's birthday in 1949.

Academy, where he is very active in numerous activities.

Laura Beth, Wilfred and Lorraine's third child, was born Mar. 20, 1963. She married William Henry Bozza Jr. on Aug. 7, 1980. She obtained a degree in radiologic technology from Jackson State Community College and works as a registered radiologic technologist at Jackson-Madison County General Hospital in Jackson. Their children are Elizabeth Ann, born Jan. 30, 1981 and Meghan Alyss, born Oct. 7, 1989. "Beth" Ann graduated from Trinity Christian Academy and is attending Jackson State Community College. "Ali" attends Trinity Christian Academy.

Bodie and Lorraine have owned and operated a furniture store, Lobo Sales, since 1987. They make their home in Jackson, TN, as do all of their children. *Submitted by Daisye Stephenson.*

MOORE, BUCK, born 1901 near Bay Springs in Tishomingo County, MS and died 1988. He was the son of William Casper Moore (b. 1861, d. 1936) and Ella Montgomery Moore (b. 1868, d. 1953).

Buck had seven brothers and four sisters: Jim married Maude Tipton; Elvie married Jourd Harris; Tinie married Clofus Magers; Hardie married Arie Pounds; Bardie married Emma Pounds; Bob married Grace Wardlow; Belvie married Monroe Pounds; Buck married Helen Bostick; Henry married Erin Brown; Brewer married Byrd Moore; Pozy married Icy Griffin and Pernie never married.

Buck, at one time or another, was a service station owner, Chevrolet dealer, timber broker and motel and restaurant owner/operator. He was a man of sterling character, who was known for his integrity and business acumen. He was a devout Christian and an active member of the Baptist Church wherever he lived, serving in various positions of leadership. He is buried in Memorial Gardens in Belmont, MS.

Buck and Helen Moore, 1939

Helen Bostick was born Sep. 2, 1913, near Golden, MS, Tishomingo County, the daughter of George Austin Bostick (b. 1876, d. 1944) and Ellen Estelle Hale Bostick (b. 1887, d. 1923).

Helen had four sisters and two brothers: Clayton married Pearl Miller and later married Leighvelia Cooke; Blanche married Lenzie Morse and after his death, she married his brother, Johnny Morse; Beatrice married Beryl Williams; Helen married Buck Moore; Ora Lee married John Flora; Sylvia married Albert Glover and Charles married Opal Hicks.

Helen attended Blue Mountain College and Mississippi State College for Women and taught school a few years in early life before becoming associated with her husband in business. She, too, has been an active member of the Baptist Church, serving in all phases of the work. She taught Sunday school classes for 60 years. She is an avid reader, a lover of history and an expert seamstress. She enjoys quilting and doing genealogical research. She makes her home in Booneville in the house they built in 1964.

Buck and Helen married on Sep. 22, 1935. They are parents of one son, Jerry Buck, born May 26, 1937 in the old hospital in Booneville. Incidentally, rooms were $3 per day! Jerry attended grammar school in Booneville but graduated from high school in Douglas, GA and went on to graduate from the University of Georgia in Athens. He married Evalyn Dale Jenkins in 1957. They make their home in Athens where he is engaged in business.

They are parents of two children. Jody Evalyn was born Aug. 15, 1961 in Jesup, Georgia and is married to Andy Waddell. They live in Milledgeville, GA. Jerry Buck Jr. (Jay) was born Jun. 1, 1968 in Orangeburg, SC. He married Victoria Lorraine (Lori) Watson on May 7, 1988 in Crawfordville, GA. They have two children: Jayson Elliott (b. Mar. 9, 1994) and Cameron Elias (b. Apr. 28, 1997). They reside in Eatonton, GA. *Submitted by Helen Bostick Moore, 1999.*

MOORE, EBENEZER SCOTT, born in South Carolina and was 48 in 1850, married Martha Alexander who was born in Tennessee and was 49 in 1850. They lived in Alabama until moving to Mississippi where they purchased land in 1841 from Joseph Alexander, who was probably related to Martha. Her mother, Ann Alexander, born in Tennessee, was 68 in 1850 when she was living with Ebenezer and Martha in the Carrollville District of Old Tishomingo County. Sarah Alexander, sister to Martha, was living with them in 1850 and 1860 and was 45 in 1850. Ebenezer's brother, William K. Moore, whose wife, Abigail, was born in Tennessee, also moved from Alabama to Mississippi prior to the 1870 census. Ebenezer and Martha had eight children.

Margaret Ann (b. 1828, d. 1895) md. Bartholomew Stovall on Aug. 17, 1852 and had two children, Sarah M. (d. 1854) and Martha Ann (b. 1854, d. 1856). She was back living with her parents in 1860. On Dec. 26, 1866, she married Henry C. Parker who was the widower of her sister, Jane. In 1870 Margaret, Henry and his four children were living near her parents. Henry owned land and was farming. They later moved to Thrasher where he was a county supervisor.

William Jarvis "Bill" (b. 1830 in Alabama) is probably the William J. Moore who married Virginia A.P. Moore on Jan. 12, 1860. They were living with her parents, E.J. Moore in 1860 and he was teaching school. There are a few records of a William J. Moore from the Civil War. A marriage license was issued on Nov. 14, 1868, to W.J. Moore and Mattie A. Gary and witnessed by W.W. Thomas, but was later voided. Bill died in Arkansas.

Sarah Molissia (b. 1831 in Alabama) md. W.J. Stovall on Oct. 21, 1852.

Jane Caroline (b. 1833 in Alabama, d. 1866 in Alabama) md. H.C. Parker (b. 1830, d. 1909) on Nov. 23, 1857. They had four children: William M., Henry Allen, Nancy A. "Nannie" and Leonidus. Jane is buried in the Moore Cemetery. Her epitaph says, "As a wife devoted, as a mother affectionate, as a friend ever kind and true." H.C. Parker was buried in the Gaston Cemetery as was his daughter Nannie. Margaret and the other three children were buried in the Old Camp Ground Cemetery.

Martha Amna (b. and died. 1836, lived only 4 months).

Rufus Allen (b. 1837, d. 1856).

Armanellia Abigail (b. 1838, d. 1871) md. Columbus Marion Young on Jul. 28, 1858. Both were born in Alabama. Their children were John Franklin (b. 1859, d. 1868) and Columbus Jefferson (b. 1861). They were living on her parent's farm in 1860. Columbus joined the 2nd Regiment, Co. K, 60 day volunteers (Davidson's Infantry) Dec. 5, 1861 in Corinth. His equipment was a double barrel shotgun. He was paid for 39 days to Jan. 13, 1862. The family Bible shows his death date as Jan. 20, 1862, but the Army record was incomplete. Armanella, a widow and Columbus, age 8, were living with her parents in 1870. At some point she married a Mr. Faris.

James Franklin "Jim" (b. 1841 in Mississippi, d. 1862) was living with his parents and attending school in 1860. He enlisted Aug. 24, 1861 in Iuka in Co. C, 26th Regiment, Mississippi Volunteers for a term of three years. He was taken prisoner at the surrender at Fort Donelson, TN on Feb. 16, 1862 and died of typhoid fever Mar. 25, 1862 in the prison hospital at Camp Morton, Indianapolis, IN. He was buried in Green Lawn Cemetery.

Ruth Tersia (b. 1846, d. 1921) md. William Washington Thomas. (See William Washington Thomas Family).

A church, also used as a school, was built on Ebenezer's property and was known as Moore's Church, a congregation of the Cumberland Presbyterian Church. There was also a cemetery known as Moore's Cemetery. On Aug. 28, 1872, two years before his death, Ebenezer donated this property by deed to the Trustees of the church and their successors in office. On Nov. 14, 1873, the church and cemetery were deeded to Trustees of a Methodist Church. After a few years this church disbanded. Later this land reverted to Ebenezer's descendants. The church building is no longer there and the cemetery is overgrown and most of the markers gone.

Ebenezer died Mar. 2, 1874 and Martha died Jun. 12, 1874. They were probably buried at Moore's Cemetery. After their deaths there was a lawsuit regarding their farm property by R.T. Thomas vs. W.M. Parker. It was settled by a decree of the Chancery Court of Prentiss County, ordering the property to be sold to the highest bidder at the courthouse door. The land was purchased by William Washington Thomas and H.C. Parker who were married to Ruth Thomas and Margaret Ann Parker, daughters of Ebenezer and Martha. Most of this land remained in the Thomas family until the 1940s. *Submitted by Nall Thomas Wiygul*

MOORE, JAMES RAY, born 1917 and died 1982, the youngest son born to Jim Moore (b. 1890, d. 1976) and Sarah Maude Tipton Moore (b. 1893, d. 1973). In 1937 he married Ruby Christine Taylor, the only daughter of Burlin Taylor (b. 1904, d. 1980) and Lora Floyd Taylor (b. 1904, d. 1985).

Ruby Yvonne Moore was born in 1938 to Ray and Ruby Moore. She married Paul Ray Mayo, son of Lester and Ruth Mayo. They were blessed with four children: Danny, Ricky, Dennis and Amy Mayo. Danny and his first wife had two children, Leslie Mayo and Scotty Mayo. He is presently married to Cammie Crabb Mayo and they have one child, Camrie and are expecting in early 2000. Ricky Mayo, their second child, lost his life in 1978 in an automobile accident. Their third child was named Dennis Mayo and he married Lori Stevenson Mayo. They were blessed with three children: Whitney, Hunter and Preston Mayo. Their youngest child was named Amy Mayo. She married Harvey Shook and they were blessed with two sons, Tyler and Dylan Shook.

The second child of Ray and Ruby Moore was named Martha Raye Moore. She was born in 1940. She married Johnny Lee Barnes, the son of Flora Mae and Delmus Barnes. They were blessed with two sons, Terry and Garry Barnes. Terry married Phyllis Smith and they were blessed with two daughters, Alanah and Alexandria Barnes. Garry married Cindy Taylor and they were blessed with two children, Jeremy and Taylor Barnes.

Sandra Jane Moore was born in 1949 to Ray and Ruby Moore. She married Larry H. Harris, son of Reable and Herschel Harris. They were blessed with three daughters: Angela (Angie) married Brad Wilemon; Lori married Michael Rogers and Leigh Anne lost her life in a car accident in 1995. The entire family still all live in Prentiss County with the exception of Terry Barnes and his family. They live in Tupelo, MS. *Submitted by Amy Shook.*

MOORE, JAMES TYSON SR., son of Berry Tyson Moore and Ida Elizabeth Knight, both born in the 1870s. He was the youngest child of eight children born to Tyson and Ida Moore. His sisters were Ruby Glenn Michael, Junie Lynn Wallis, Gladys Dean Saylors and Doris Pauline Geno. His brothers, William Van Dorn and Cullen Morton, both died before they were 2 years old and Charles Malcolm Moore died in a car accident in 1960. James T. was always a special brother to his sisters and they often called him "Jamie." After the sisters got older and they lost their beloved parents, James took it upon himself to visit them weekly and sometimes daily, until their deaths. All of them lived into their 80s with the exception of Pauline, who died at age 76.

James Tyson Moore Sr. Family. From left: Betty Moore Childers, Jimmy Moore, James Tyson Moore Sr., Annie Frances Green Moore, Berry Green Moore and Peggy Moore Carter.

James T. Moore married Annie Frances Green in April 1939. They were married in a double wedding ceremony with Marvin (Spud) Tollison and Ruth Murphy Tollison and these two couples have celebrated their anniversaries together almost every year since. Annie Frances Green is the third child of Joseph Clayton Green and Delia Lou Ledbetter Green. She had nine brothers and sisters, six of whom are still living. Harvey Green, Wallace Green, Bobby Green and Gladys Green Brown are deceased. Those still living are Ruby Smart, J.M. (Whim) Green, Myrtle Blassingame, James Fred (Bud) Green and Mae Dean Lambert.

Shortly after James and Frances married, they moved from the Blackland Community to a 100-acre farm in Jumpertown and there they built a small house with timber cut from the farm. They started growing cotton, soybeans and corn and milking a few cows, by hand of course. Then in 1953, James T., along with his father B.T. Moore and his brother, Charles M. Moore, built one of the first mechanical Grade A Dairy barns in the county. James eventually bought the entire operation and his family milked up to 150 cows a day for the next 40 years.

In 1951, James and Frances bought an additional farm at the edge of Dry Creek called "Sugar Orchard" to supplement the row crops on the home place. The Sugar Orchard was mostly a cotton farm and we four children spent our days working in those fields, either chopping or picking, whatever was needed. The fieldwork came after we helped with the morning milking and we always knew that the late afternoon would bring another milking session before our days work was done. Our daddy was a firm believer in work and we were taught early in life that hard work never hurt anyone. I can honestly say that it never hurt any of us! Our mother, Frances, was really the leader in the dairy barn operation and could tell you how many gallons of milk were produced and which cow produced the most on any given day. She was also on a first name basis with the milk truck drivers that came to our barn every day.

After a week of farm work, we always looked forward to church on Sundays at Jumpertown Methodist Church, where we were all active members. We had many aunts, uncles and cousins to spend Sunday afternoons with, either at the Moore grandparents or the Green grandparents. We have a rich heritage of family and love and we cherish that more each year.

James and Frances had four children, all still living. Betty Lou was born in 1940 and married Danny B. Childers. They have three daughters: Cherry Eaton, Robin Fancher and Dana Bullard. A son, Christopher Bruce, died at birth. Betty and Danny reside in the Blackland Community. James Tyson Jr. (Jimmy) was born in 1943 and married Ernestine Eaton. They have two daughters, Marti Downs and Delia Essary. Jimmy was elected supervisor of the second district in 1976 and served 24 years. His grandfather B.T. (Tice) Moore served in the same capacity for 20 years. Jimmy and Tina live in Jumpertown. Peggy Jo was born in 1948 and married Raiford Carter. They have two children: a daughter, Fran Massingill and a son, Will. Peggy and Raiford Live in Tupelo. Berry Green Moore was born in 1952 and married Charlotte Burchum. They have two sons, Josh and Grant. Berry and Charlotte bought the dairy operation at James' and Frances' retirement and have since acquired some of the original farmland.

All four Moore children were educated and graduated from Jumpertown High School, with Peggy and Berry both going on to Mississippi State University to earn degrees in education. They have both taught in Prentiss County and Tupelo School Systems. James T. and Frances have 11 great-grandchildren in addition to their nine grandchildren. James died Dec. 16, 1996, at the age of 79 and is buried in the Jumpertown Cemetery next to his parents. Annie Frances is still living and continues to live in the same house they built 61 years ago. She is 79 years old. *Submitted by Betty Lou Moore Childers.*

MOORE, LEVI JACKSON, married Sarah C. Genetti Denson in 1891. They had nine children. The oldest, Levi, married Emma Chaffin, had four sons and lived near Birmingham, AL. George married Ruby Rorie. They had one son, George Jr., who was killed in the Korean War in 1951. All three are buried in New Site Cemetery.

Summer reunion 1994. Back row from left: Christine Green, Wilfred Green, Marydell Kanavel. Front row from left: Daisye Stephenson, Randall Green and Lorraine Green.

Minnie Bell married Walter Lee Green in 1918 and they had five children. Minnie Bell and Walter were born and raised within a quarter mile of each other. Their first three children were born in Prentiss County. At one time they had a restaurant in Booneville. In 1927 they moved to Jackson, TN because Walter had gotten a job as a railway mail clerk and his headquarters was in Jackson.

Their first child, Daisye Dewdrop, was the first grandchild in the Jack Moore family. Daisye came back to Prentiss County her senior year in high school, after her parents had divorced. She graduated from New Site High School in 1936. Then she went back to Jackson and got a job as a clerk in the S.H. Kress and Co. Store. Daisye met Harold Stephenson while working at Kress and left them in 1940 to marry Harold. At that time, the Kress Stores would not allow married women to work there.

Harold was a water well driller and had started his own business before he and Daisye met. He drilled wells in many counties in West Tennessee.

Daisye and Harold had two children, Daisye Jeanette and Everett Harold Jr. Jeanette was born in 1942 and Everett in 1947. They both graduated from Jackson High School.

Jeanette graduated in 1960 and went to Georgia Tech in Atlanta, GA. She was one of the first females to go there. She met Joseph Bass on a work assignment in California and they married in 1968. They had three children: Joshua Aaron, born Dec. 18, 1971; Sarah Josephine, born Sep. 6, 1974 and Jeremiah Stephen, born Sep. 30, 1976.

Everett started his college career at Auburn University in Alabama. After two years there he transferred to the University of Tennessee at Knoxville. He earned a bachelor of science degree there. He then attended Virginia Tech in Blacksburg, VA and obtained a master of science degree. At this point, he went to work for Union Camp Corporation for three years. He went back to Virginia Tech, started work on his PhD and decided he did not especially like that. He went back to work at Union Camp and worked there for about 16 years, at which time it was bought out by International Paper Co. Everett remains employed with International Paper.

Jeanette has worked for the Florida Public Service for a number of years, even though she lives in the state of Georgia. She lived in Thomasville for years, but has now moved to Whigham. *Submitted by Daisye Stephenson.*

MOORE, MINNIE BELL, born Jun. 6, 1899 and died Feb. 20, 1968, daughter of Jack and Nettie Moore, married Walter Lee Green (b. 1897, d. 1959), son of Jack and Nettie Green. Walter and Minnie Bell had five children: Daisye Dewdrop (b. Jan. 3, 1919), Walter Randall (b. Jan. 7, 1921), Thelma Marydell, (Dell) (b. Jul. 17, 1925), Wilfred Lee, (Bodie) (b. Jun. 23, 1929) and Minnie Bell, (Nickey) (b. Apr. 11, 1932).

Summer Treat. Front from left: Bodie and Randall Green and Bob Kanavel. Second row: Nickey and Daisye Green and Uncle Raymond Moore. Behind fence: Neighbor and Glen Kanavel.

Daisye, Randall and Dell were born in Prentiss County. The Green family moved to Jackson, TN when Dell was 3 years old. Walter was a mail clerk on the Gulf, Mobile and Ohio railroad. The couple separated when Nickey was quite young. Daisye married Harold Stephenson and had two children. Randall married Christine Greg and had five children. Wilfred married Lorraine Sanderson and had three children.

When Dell was 11, the Kanavel family moved close by. At 12, Bob Kanavel invited Dell to a hayride for which his mother was a chaperone. A few months later, the Kanavels moved across town and they lost touch.

After a ruptured appendix forced Dell to miss school for a year, she decided to finish school at New Site. She lived with her mother's brother, George Moore, his wife, Ruby and son, Junior, for two years. They became her second family. Upon graduation, Dell returned to Tennessee and worked for Southern Bell.

Bob Kanavel had joined the Navy and was home on leave when Pearl Harbor was attacked. He visited Dell and asked that they correspond. Bob then headed for the South Pacific and spent two years on Guadalcanal and other Pacific islands. After several severe attacks of malaria, Bob returned in December 1943. Robert Franklin Kanavel (b. Jun. 24, 1924) married Dell on Jan. 1, 1944. The couple was stationed in Oregon until the war ended.

Bob was sent to Korea in 1950. In 1951, he returned to Millington, TN where Anna Marie was born Jan. 6, 1953. Bob Jr. arrived on Dec. 14, 1956 in Norfolk, VA, followed by Charles Kenneth on Apr. 16, 1958 in Jacksonville, FL and Sandra Dell, Dec. 31, 1962 in Sanford, FL. Bob retired after 20 years of service, then worked for the US Department of Agriculture for 22 years, retiring in Florida where they now live.

Nickey married James Tully Gill (b. January 1933). Jim was Navy, also and was stationed in England and in Guantanamo, Cuba. His family was able to live with him. Vickey Lynn was born Sep. 14, 1954 and James Tully Jr. in October 1958. The couple later moved to Texas.

Rheumatic fever suffered in childhood damaged Nickey's heart. She had open-heart surgery several times and died of heart problems on Aug. 23, 1972. Vickey was killed in 1976 and was buried in Texas. Jim later remarried. *Submitted by Dell Green Kanavel.*

MOORE, MINNIE BELL, born Jun. 6, 1899 and died Feb. 20, 1968, daughter of Jack and Nettie Moore, married Walter Lee Green (b. 1897, d. 1959), son of Jack and Nettie Green.

Walter and Minnie Bell had five children: Daisye Dewdrop (b. Jan. 3, 1919), Walter Randall (b. Jan. 7, 1921), Thelma Marydell (b. Jul. 17, 1925), Wilfred Lee (b. Jun. 23, 1929) and Minnie Bell, nicknamed Nickey, (b. Apr. 11, 1932).

The couple separated when Nickey was very young. Daisye married Harold Stephenson and they had two children. Dell married Robert Kanavel and they had four children. Wilfred married Lorraine Sanderson and they had three children. Nickey married James

Tully Gill and they had two children. Randall married Charlie Christine Greg (b. Aug. 24, 1924) on her 18th birthday. The couple had five children: William Randall (b. Dec. 19, 1944), Charles Lee (b. Oct. 8, 1948), Thomas Milton (b. Jul. 19, 1950), Carmen Christine (b. Mar. 26, 1952) and Robert Sidney (b. Apr. 19, 1954).

As a teen, Randall joined the National Guard and participated in helping with flood control when the Mississippi River overflowed and many areas were underwater. The men in the National Guard were called to active duty before Pearl Harbor was bombed and we actively entered WWII. Randall was fortunate to be able to enter flight training and became a pilot. He flew P-40s for six months in the Caribbean and B-17s for six months as a member of the Eighth Air Force, completing many bombing raids over Germany. His first child was 5 months old when he returned from Europe. When the war ended, Randall remained in the National Guard and retired as a major. Randall retains his love of planes and flying and has instilled that love in his children, especially in his youngest son, who at present is a pilot with Fed Ex.

Walter and Minnie's children in 1940

Randall worked for several large companies in the southeast, including Quaker Oats and Walt Disney World, but always kept his home in Jackson, TN where he resides today. *Submitted by Dell Green Kanavel for Walter R. Green.*

MORGAN, JAMES SAMUEL "SAM," born Nov. 25, 1878 in Hackelburg, AL, to Harrison Morgan and Martha Savannah Walker Morgan. Harrison was the son of Jimmy Morgan, born about 1816 in South Carolina, died in 1886 and buried in the Old Bethel Cemetery in Colbert County, AL. Harrison Morgan (b. Jul. 28, 1847) married Martha Savannah Walker (b. Sep. 15, 1852). To this union were born Obie J. (b. 1872), William A. (b. 1874), Harriet Lou (b. 1876), James Samuel (b. 1878), Lang A. (b. 1880), Henry (b. 1882), Dellar (b. 1884), Robert (b. 1886), Drewey (b. 1888), Annie L. (b. 1890), Ollie B. (b. 1892) and Alma (b. 1894). Eight of their children were born in Hackelburg, AL. The youngest four were born in Mississippi. They lived near New Site, MS. Harrison worked and delivered mail at Ida Post Office from Jul. 30, 1906, to Apr. 15, 1916. This office was closed in 1916 and the mail was sent to the New Site Post Office. Harrison died Feb. 8, 1918 and Martha Savannah. Walker Morgan died Nov. 16, 1920. They are both buried in Pleasant Valley Cemetery in Prentiss County.

This is a wedding picture of Sam and Elizabeth Morgan made in Denton, TX Nov. 30, 1904.

In 1902 James Samuel (Sam) Morgan went to Denton, TX where most of the older brothers lived. On Nov. 30, 1904, James Samuel married L. Elizabeth Wroten (b. Aug. 29, 1885) in Denton County, TX. To this union were born Shelby (b. Sep. 6, 1906), Florence (b. Oct. 25, 1908), Elmer (b. May 10, 1910), Chessie (b. Jul. 24, 1911), Raymond (b. May 10, 1913) and Bessie (b. Nov. 20, 1914). James Samuel and Elizabeth brought their family to Prentiss County, MS and stayed a while. Elizabeth got sick and they went back to Denton, TX. Elizabeth died Feb. 16, 1916 and was buried in Shiloh Cemetery in Denton County, TX which is west of Lewisville, TX.

Shelby, the oldest child, married Amanda Phifer McCoy, a widow with two children, Clay McCoy and Elaine McCoy. Shelby and Amanda Morgan had children Tharon, Earlene, Vernon, Shirley, Margie and Larry Morgan.

Florence Morgan married Buster Hisaw and their children were Eugene, William, Tommy, Gwendlyn and Raymond Earl.

Elmer died at a young age.

Chessie Morgan married Joe Tolar and their children were Helen and Bobby Tolar.

Raymond Morgan married Laverne James and their children, Janice, James David, Randy, Karon, Cynthia and Donnie Morgan.

Bessie Morgan married Lee Huddleston.

These are the children and grandchildren of James Samuel and Elizabeth Wroten Morgan. After the death of Elizabeth, James Samuel came back to Mississippi with the children. He later married Minnie Ray (b. Apr. 1, 1901) and their children are Nona (b. Jan. 7, 1920), Woodrow (b. Feb. 7, 1922), Gordon (b. Apr. 14, 1925), James (b. May 22, 1926), Clara (b. Mar. 14, 1931) and Billy (b. Jan. 10, 1935). They lived in Prentiss County. This is just a brief listing of James Samuel (Sam) Morgan and Elizabeth Wroten Morgan and descendants. Several live in Prentiss County and in different parts of the US. James Samuel Morgan died Oct. 10, 1956 and was buried in Pleasant Valley Cemetery where his parents were buried. *Submitted by Myra Moore.*

MORGAN, SHELBY, born Sep. 6, 1906, to James Samuel Morgan and Elizabeth Wroten in Denton, TX. Shelby came as a small boy to Booneville, MS where he went to school and began surveying. On Sep. 23, 1926, he married a widow, Amanda Phifer McCoy, who had two children: Clay (b. May 2, 1919) and Elaine (b. Mar. 19, 1924). Amanda was born Nov. 27, 1899 in Tishomingo County to Jacob Wilson Phifer and Elizabeth Phifer. To this union was born Tharon (b. Sep. 7, 1927), Earlene (b. Jun. 15, 1930), Euel Vernon (b. Jun. 4, 1932, d. Jul. 30, 1933), Shirley (b. Mar. 20, 1937), Margie (b. Aug. 15, 1940) and Larry (b. Nov. 1, 1946). Shelby and Amanda lived in Prentiss County at this time, where Shelby was the county land surveyor from 1935 to 1943. In 1945 they moved to Tishomingo County. Larry was the only child born in Tishomingo County. Shelby was a land surveyor in Tishomingo County and also worked with the Corps of Engineers in different states. Around the year 1960, they moved back to Prentiss County out east of Booneville on Highway 30. Shelby was a land surveyor for over 40 years.

Tharon married Betty McBride (b. Aug. 20, 1932). They have one child, Machiel (b. Oct. 5, 1966). Tharon and Betty make their home in Iuka, MS. Tharon is a retired school principal.

Earlene married Clete Rowsey (b. Dec. 8, 1924). To this union was born Danny (b. Oct. 7, 1953) and Jackie (b. Jun. 7, 1957). Danny married Linda Suitor (b. Jun. 8, 1953) and from this marriage was born: Andrew (b. May 20, 1974), Danica (b. May 2, 1976) and Daniel (b. Oct. 5, 1977). Andrew married Mary Ellen Mitchell. Danica married Michael Moore. Danny later divorced and married Diane Wegman (b. Jun. 17, 1952). Clete passed away on Jul. 7, 1988. Later Earlene married Marion Lentz (b. Feb. 18, 1928) and they make their home in Booneville, MS.

This is the last picture we had made together. Back row from left: Larry Morgan, Margie Walden, Elaine Claunch and Tharon Morgan. Front row from left: Shirley Walden, Shelby Morgan, Amanda Morgan, Earlene Rowsey Lentz and Clay McCoy.

Shirley married Gerald Walden (b. Jan. 11, 1934). To this union was born Sheila (b. May 27, 1956) and Gary (b. Sep. 26, 1957). Sheila married Terry Hunkapiller (b. Mar. 9, 1956) on Apr. 11, 1975. To this marriage was born Myra (b. Mar. 9, 1976). Sheila later divorced and married Eddie Holley (b. Jun. 10, 1958). They have two children: Mona Lea (b. Jun. 29, 1984) and Mykel (b. Oct. 13, 1988). Myra married J.J. Moore (b. Nov. 29, 1975) on Apr. 18, 1997 and to this union was born Trevin Hall (b. Jul. 27, 1999). Gary married Kathy Hardin (b. Apr. 2, 1957). They have two children: Julie (b. Jun. 20, 1984) and Joshua (b. Jul. 8, 1987). Gerald and Shirley make their home in Booneville, MS.

Margie married Roy Walden (b. Nov. 24, 1936). To this union were born Rhonda (b. Jan. 31, 1961) and Randy (b. Aug. 21, 1970). Rhonda married Jim Burcham (b. Jun. 19, 1959). They had one child, Brandon (b. Nov. 4, 1980). Rhonda later divorced. Randy married Natache Cagle (b. May 12, 1971) and to this union was born Molly Ann (b. May 5, 1997). Roy and Margie make their home in Cairo, MS.

Larry married Joyce Caldwell (b. Mar. 6, 1946). To this union were born Jennifer (b. Aug. 28, 1971) and Michelle (b. May 29, 1976). Jennifer married Mark Cowan (b. Mar. 6, 1969). Michelle married Todd English (b. Aug. 28, 1974). Larry and Joyce make their home in Booneville, MS where Larry is superintendent of Booneville Schools.

Shelby passed away on Apr. 14, 1971 and Amanda lived to be 93 years old (died Mar. 10, 1993). They are buried in Forked Oak Cemetery in Prentiss County. *Submitted by Sheila Walden Holley.*

MORRIS, J.C. JR. AND MILDRED RUTH HAMBLIN, first met when as an 11 year-old, J.C. picked up milk with his dad from the Hamblin farm. Mildred, a spirited 5 year-old, informed her friends that she was going to marry J.C. and 13 years later, she did!

J.C. Morris was born in the Geeville Community in Prentiss County on Nov. 11, 1917, the oldest child of Jesse Clinton "Clint" (b.

J.C. and Mildred Ruth Hamblin Morris of Baldwyn, MS.

1889, d. 1966) and Viola "Crick" Roberts Morris (b. 1892, d. 1977). Their other children were: Katherine "Mavauline" (b. 1922), James "Thomas" (nicknamed "Bucket" in school) (b. 1928, d. 1972) and Martha "Nell" (b. 1930).

Mildred Ruth Hamblin was born in the Blair Community in Lee County on Jul. 18, 1923, the oldest child of Robert Loyd "Rob" (b. 1900, d. 1981) and Pansy Lee Hickey Hamblin (b. 1902, d. 1993). Their other children were Sarah "Agnes" (b. 1930), James Robert (b. 1934, d. 1937) and Bobby Wayne (b. 1938).

J.C. and Mildred had their first date on Friday, Oct. 13, 1939 and married on Oct. 10, 1941 in Tupelo, MS. J.C. had joined the Army in September 1939 and the first 13 years of their marriage were spent moving, courtesy of Uncle Sam. They also endured two long separations, when J.C. was sent to Germany during WWII and to Korea for 19 months during that conflict.

J.C. left the Army in 1954 and the family settled in Booneville, then moved to Baldwyn in 1957. He attended Northeast Mississippi Junior College and Mississippi State University where he earned a bachelor's degree in history and a masters degree in guidance counseling. When he left active duty in 1954, he enlisted in the National Guard in Baldwyn. Later on, he enlisted in the Air Force National Guard in Costa Mesa, CA and when he retired from military service in November 1977, J.C. had served 36 years.

In 1962 the family moved to Fullerton, CA, where J.C. worked as an educator and guidance counselor until his retirement in 1979. Mildred worked for Catalina Swimwear in Fullerton until her retirement in 1979. They returned to Baldwyn, MS in July 1980, where they continue to live.

J.C. and Mildred have five children: Deborah Jeanne Moseley (b. Sep. 14, 1942), Thomas Wayne (b. and d. Aug. 28, 1946), Ricki Lee Ericksen (b. Feb. 24, 1948), David Alan (b. Apr. 25, 1950) and James "Kevin" (b. Dec. 27, 1951). All of their children have returned with their families to live in Prentiss County, except Kevin, who lives with his family in Orem, UT.

During their army travels, they lived in Kentucky, Wisconsin, Minnesota, Colorado and Louisiana. While living in Brainerd, MN, they came in contact with the Church of Jesus Christ of Latter-Day Saints and joined the church in 1948. They have been active in church activities for over 50 years, both serving in many positions of leadership. They are members of the Booneville Ward.

They both enjoy good health and lead active, productive lives. They have been blessed (so far) with 11 grandchildren, eight step-grandchildren, five great-grandchildren and four step-great-grandchildren. Their home is the center of family activity. In 1999, they celebrated their 58th wedding anniversary.

Though they have traveled and lived in many places, Prentiss County has always been home to them. *Submitted by Deborah Moseley.*

MOSELEY, WAYNE WOODS, born Nov. 18, 1942 in Milford, CT the oldest child of Arthur Easton Moseley and Mildred Marion Woods. They moved to West Hoosick, a small hamlet in upstate New York, when Wayne was a baby. Wayne's only sibling, Carol Marion Moseley, was born May 10, 1947.

Wayne was raised on a 32-acre farm in Buskirk, NY attending school in nearby Cambridge. He went to school with two great-grandsons of Grandma Moses, the celebrated painter who lived in nearby Eagle Bridge.

Wayne graduated from Cambridge Central School, receiving a New York State Regents Scholarship and attended the State University of New York Agricultural and Technical Institute at Canton. Later, he moved to Scottsdale, AZ and within a year, joined the Church of Jesus Christ of Latter-Day Saints. One year later, he left to serve a two-year mission for the church in Argentina, South America.

After returning to the US, he moved to California, married and raised a family of five children, three boys and two girls. That marriage, unfortunately, ended in divorce after 19 years. He had a career for over 25 years in computer programming and data base management.

Deborah Jeanne Morris was born Sep. 14, 1942 in Baldwyn, MS, the oldest child of J.C. Morris and Mildred Ruth Hamblin. Her paternal grandparents are Jesse Clinton "Clint" Morris and Viola "Crick" Roberts, both of Baldwyn, MS. Her maternal grandparents are Robert Loyd "Rob" Hamblin and Pansy Lee Hickey, both of Baldwyn.

During the 1950s and 1960s, Rob and Pansy Hamblin lived in Booneville, where they owned the Bridge Cafe on Market Street. Deborah's first job was working in the cafe as a teenager, helping out during busy lunch hours when they fed the Blue Bell employees.

Deborah's other siblings are Ricki Lee Ericksen (b. Feb. 24, 1948), David Alan Morris (b. Apr. 25, 1950) and James "Kevin" Morris (b. Dec. 27, 1951).

Wayne and Deborah Moseley on their wedding day.

Deborah's early years were spent traveling with her family, courtesy of the US Army. Her dad left active military duty in 1954 and moved the family to Booneville, where she attended seventh through ninth grades. In 1957, the family moved to Baldwyn, where she completed high school and graduated in 1960. She graduated from Northeast Mississippi Junior College in 1962.

In late 1962, the family moved to Fullerton, CA. Deborah graduated from California State University, Fullerton in 1965, with a bachelor's degree in theater arts and speech. She accepted a summer job working for Pacific Bell in the "America the Beautiful" Exhibit at Disneyland and liked working for the phone company, staying on with them for 22 years.

Wayne and Deborah met in church and on Aug. 10, 1990, they were married in the LDS Temple in Los Angeles. They lived in Riverside, CA for two years before moving to Mississippi. They built a home in Baldwyn and have settled into country living.

They love to travel and do genealogy research, tracing their lines back many generations. Wayne has discovered 13 Mayflower ancestors and over 25 Revolutionary War ancestors. Deborah has Revolutionary War and Civil War patriots in her lines.

Wayne's family has lived in New England for many generations, while Deborah's ancestors lived in Virginia and the Carolinas before migrating into Tennessee, Alabama and Mississippi. *Submitted by Deborah Moseley.*

MOSS, JOSEPH "J.B." OR "BENTON," fifth child born to Joseph Leviticus (Levi) Moss (b. 1845, d. 1923) and Vina Robbins Moss (b. 1845), was born Feb. 18, 1875 in Blount County, AL. His grandparents were James H. and Elizabeth Green Moss. Joseph Benton's brothers and sisters were Mahalia Cordelia, John Henson, Rhoda Elizabeth, Joseph Andrew, Henry V, Lueler and Bessie Pearl Moss.

Joseph Benton, Charley and Martha Jane Defoor Moss. Back Row standing: Joseph Monroe Moss and Harley Moss.

In the early years of Benton's life, Levi Moss moved his family from Blount County, AL, to a farm in Franklin County, AL, located between Vina and Atwood just below Holly Springs Church.

On Sep. 9, 1894, Joseph Benton Moss married Martha Jane Defoor in Hackleburg, AL. Their seven children, all born in Franklin County, AL, were Joseph Monroe, Harley, Charley, Chester, Ruth Beatrice, Eunice Emeline and James (Jim) Benton Moss.

Joseph Benton and Martha Jane Defoor Moss moved their young family to Prentiss County, MS on Nov. 19, 1919, to a homestead located on the present County Route 2241 in the Burton Community. Their home was on a ridge along the road that goes to Leamon and Eula (Moss) Brown's farm.

Iduma School, which was located on property adjacent to the Moss' property, consolidated with Piney Grove School in 1923 and Burton School was built.

Joseph Benton Moss, a Free Will Baptist minister, was responsible for four or five congregations including New Lebanon and Little Brown. He was a Mason, a Justice of the Peace and a circuit preacher, who traveled from church to church in northeast Mississippi, southwest Tennessee and northwest Alabama teaching music and "Singing Schools." As a member of the Moss Quartet, along with his children Joe, Harley and Ruth, he enjoyed attending and singing gospel hymns at "all day singings with dinner on the ground."

Benton Moss also farmed the land with mule and plow, was a bee keeper, made molasses, hand-wove baskets, built furniture and split ties for railroad tracks, fences and roof shingles.

The children of Joseph Benton and Martha Jane Moss marriage is as follows: Joseph Monroe Moss married Minnie Pearl Pharr; Harley Moss married Lottie Crabtree, then Bertha Dial; Charley N. Moss married Maymie E. Samples; Chester N. Moss married Luna Rogers; Ruth Beatrice Moss married Thomas Luther South; Eunice Emeline Moss married Erwin Jackson Searcy and James (Jim) Benton Moss married Dora McAnally, then Willie Mae Floyd. Many descendants of Joseph Benton and Martha Jane Defoor Moss still live in the Burton Community and Prentiss County.

On Dec. 13, 1951, Joseph Benton Moss went to meet his Lord. He and Martha Jane Defoor Moss are buried in Forked Oak Cemetery in Prentiss County, MS. He was the first person laid to rest in the third cemetery east of the church. *Submitted by Peggy Mann.*

MURPHY, RICHARD DUANE, born Jun. 17, 1959, is the son of Aubrey Vasco Murphy Jr. (b. Jun. 28, 1930, d. Jan. 10, 1978) and Nellie Ruth Bishop Murphy (b. Mar. 27, 1933). Aubrey and Nellie married Sep. 6, 1953. Aubrey is buried in Booneville Cemetery.

Richard's grandparents are Aubrey Vasco Murphy Sr. (b. Oct. 30, 1907, d. Apr. 15, 1994) and Lillie Gambill (b. Sep. 21, 1908, d. _) who married on Apr. 18, 1925. They are buried in Booneville Cemetery. Aubrey married Vera Faye Pierce Murphy (b. Jan. 1, 1921) on Jun. 16, 1949. Also, Andrew Jackson "Jack" Bishop (b. Jan. 10, 1903, d. Mar. 26, 1985) married Rachel Matilda Downs Bishop (b. Dec. 9, 1903, d. Mar. 22, 1992) on Aug. 22, 1923. They are buried in Booneville Cemetery.

Teresa Lynn, Vanessa Lynn, Rodney Duane, Andrew Vinson and Richard Duane Murphy

Teresa Lynn Murphy (b. Aug. 22, 1963) is the daughter of Garvin Earl Davis (b. Dec. 29, 1932, d. Feb. 4, 1994) and Waynona Mayvene Vanderford Davis (b. Nov. 25, 1935) who married Jun. 6, 1955. She is the grand daughter of Elton Davis (b. Nov. 8, 1904, d. Jan. 2, 1969) and Fannie May Stanley Davis (b. Jul. 26, 1906, d. Apr. 8, 1982). They are buried in the Jacinto Cemetery in Alcorn County. She is also the granddaughter of Winston Jasper "Wink" Vanderford (b. Mar. 9, 1916, d. Apr. 17, 1989) and Ella Missouri Woodruff Vanderford (b. Feb. 21, 1913, d. Sep. 2, 1991) who married Jun. 23, 1933. Garvin, Wink and Ella are buried at the Snowdown Church of Christ in Prentiss County.

Richard and Teresa's children are Rodney Duane Murphy (b. Oct. 23, 1980); Vanessa Lynn Murphy (b. Oct. 31, 1984) and Andrew Vinson Murphy (b. Jan. 23, 1989). *Submitted by Richard Duane Murphy.*

NASH, ELGIN ALVIN "DICK," born Jun. 9, 1900 and died Nov. 23, 1965, the son of Robert Edward "Bob" and Nancy Elizabeth (Rorie) Nash. Dick married Beulah Mae Vanderford (b. Oct. 28, 1903) on Sep. 11, 1921. Beulah is the daughter of Mark and Neal Samantha (Maness) Vanderford. Dick and Beulah have a daughter, Lottie V. Nash Wade (b. Sep. 24, 1924).

Elgin and Beulah Vanderford Nash with Lottie Nash Wade, 1942.

Dick and Beulah lived in the Hickory Flatt Community all their lives. They farmed and grew almost all their food for themselves and others. Dick and his father had a sawmill on the home place, which provided work for the community men. Dick was bailiff of 3rd District, Alcorn County, for two terms or eight years. He was deputy sheriff under sheriffs Bert Coleman, Hillie Coleman and "Little Bert" Coleman,

Dick and Beulah always had a garden in the summer and canned and froze food for the winter. In the winter, Beulah made quilts for the family and always had a quilt for those who had a fire or some other tragedy. She sewed all Lottie's clothes. Lottie was 16 years old when she got her first "store bought "dress. She went to Miss Nunley's studio in Booneville to get her a picture made.

Marylane Wade Koch, Robert Koch, Laura Ellen Beeler Wade, William Nash Wade, Lottie Nash Wade, Dylan Armstrong Wade, William Doyle Wade, Jean Eagle Wade, Leslie Alvin Wade, Chelsea Elizabeth Wade, Circa 1990.

Lottie married William Doyle Wade on Apr. 20, 1946. Rev. C.C. Rinehart performed the ceremony. Lottie and William Doyle have three children: William Nash "Bill," Marylane Louise Wade Koch and Leslie Alvin. Leslie has both his papas' names, Oren Leslie Wade and Elgin Alvin "Dick" Nash.

There are three great-grandchildren: Dylan Armstrong Wade, Chelsea Elizabeth Wade and Meredith Grace Wade Koch.

Lottie went to Hickory Flat school, where her father, Dick, also went to school. Her namesake was Lottie Bass Rinehart, a teacher at Hickory Flatt School. Miss Monota Carpenter, who boarded with the Nashes, mentored Lottie to become a teacher in her later life. Lottie worked in Smith's Drug Store in Rienzi on Saturdays until 1942 when she moved to Memphis.

Dylan Armstrong Wade, Chelsea Elizabeth Wade and Meredith Grace Wade Koch.

Summers spent with her Granny and Papa Nash were special and memorable times for the grandchildren. They would watch the clock to be ready for 11:00 a.m. when Papa Nash would take them to swim in Hurricane Canal and play on the sandbar. They loved to go on a pick-up ride to visit preacher Cleveland C. Rinehart. For Bill this was a special treat to visit with C.B. Curlee at the store to talk about the Civil War, visiting "Soggy Sweat" at the county courthouse and experiencing other activities at the courthouse.

Marylane remembers trading eggs to the peddler for candy and going to the storm house for safety. She values summer experiences such as milking cows, gathering eggs, playing in the corn shed, eating tommy-toe tomatoes and picking blackberries and muscadines. She too had her share of homemade dresses; Granny Nash made her a quilt from material from her dresses. Granny also made shirts for Bill and Leslie. A special treat for all was Granny's homemade teacakes.

Dick was killed almost in front of his home in an accident involving a drunk driver. His was the first burial in Kemp's Chapel Cemetery, beside the Kemp's Chapel Baptist Church built on land donated by Dick and brother Arch Nash. Beulah and Lottie gave the land for the cemetery.

The home place land owned by Bob and Nannie Nash is still the home of Beulah, where another house was built at the original homeplace. Lottie still owns the Boshears place given to her by her dad in 1943.

Dick and Beulah always taught by example to be mindful of other people's needs. They were very caring and giving of themselves. *Respectfully submitted with love by Bill, Marylane and Leslie.*

NEWBORN, JAMES HASWELL, born Oct. 14, 1845 in Lawrence County, TN, son of Asa D. Newborn and Lucinda Mewborn or Newborn. Asa married Lucinda, his cousin, on Oct. 27, 1844, when she was not quite 15 years old. Asa's first wife is unknown, but she and Asa had four children. One of the sons, Francis J. "Frank," has descendants who live in Prentiss County. Maye Newborn Miller stated that her half-uncle, Frank, was part Indian. Asa died in April 1854 and Lucinda married James Campbell Queen about 1859.

James Haswell Newborn (1845-1901)

James Haswell taught school for a period of time after the Civil War. He and Nancy Elizabeth Davis were married on Nov. 25, 1869 and lived on upper Beech Creek in Wayne County, TN. Elizabeth's parents were John Riley Davis, a veteran of the battle of Shiloh and Jemima Ann Hill Davis. One of Elizabeth's brothers, Eliphus Davis, moved to the Prentiss County area in 1898 and a sister, Arra Bell Katherine Davis, who married William Jackson Phillips, moved from Wayne County, TN to Prentiss County, MS in 1900. Arra Bell and Eliphus have many descendants in this area.

All the children of James Haswell and Elizabeth were born in their log home on Beech Creek. He raised stock, sheep, clover and corn and they also raised a patch of cotton with the family picking out the seeds by hand. The Newborn family had an orchard and bees were kept providing two of their staple foods.

A life-changing decision was made on Mar. 1, 1898, when the Newborns, their children, John C., Arrie, Ethel and Maye, left Beech Creek and crossed the Tennessee River at Pittsburg Landing and moved to Prentiss County, Mississippi near Candler's Chapel. Included in the party were their daughter, Alice Newborn Hill, her husband, Mose Hill and their four children: Allen Newborn, a son, (spelled his name Newburn) and Amanda, his wife of one day. Maye related a horrifying experience in crossing the river at Pittsburg Landing. The boat was heavily loaded and several in the party had to wait. An accident occurred when a member of their group waiting lost his horse when a steamboat passing by frightened it causing it to run away forcing the remaining party to cross the high river in a canoe. Maye was only 9 and afterwards she was always afraid of water.

James Haswell homesteaded a farm near Candler's Chapel. He got wet in the cold, winter weather and developed pneumonia. He died Jan. 26, 1901, less than three years after moving to Mississippi. He is buried in Candler's Chapel Cemetery. There is a bought marker at his and Elizabeth's burial site.

Elizabeth bought a farm at Hill's Chapel after James Haswell's death. John C. with help cleared the land and built the house. Arrie married James Allen "A1" Wheeler in 1904 and Ethel married Joe Wheeler in 1905. On Nov. 20, 1908, land was deeded by Elizabeth and her children for a church and school at Hill's Chapel. The deed specified that no organ or musical instrument be used in the church house thereon.

In 1911 most of the Newborn family moved to New Mexico with the exception of Arrie, who purchased her mother's farm in 1920. A1 and Arrie's son, Blake, bought the farm in 1948 and lived there until his death in 1990. His widow, Bertie Mae Wheeler, still resided there in 2000, when she died.

Mose Hill, for whom Hill's Chapel was named and his wife, Alice, lived in Portales, NM. Elizabeth and John C., as well as Ethel and her family and Allen and his family, lived in Texico, NM. Maye and her husband, Baxter Miller, lived near Hagerman, NM. Ethel and her family later moved to California. Allen moved his family to Grove, OK. Baxter and Maye came back to Prentiss County and resided in Thrasher. After John C.'s death in 1922, Elizabeth lived with Alice and later with Allen before returning to Prentiss County to live with Arrie and Maye. She died Mar. 21, 1929, at Arrie's at her old home place.

There are only three surviving grandchildren of James Haswell and Elizabeth Newborn: Earl Hill of Nogales, AZ, son of Mose and Alice Hill, born Aug. 15, 1906; Joyce Miller Baxter of Eufaula, AL, daughter of Baxter and Maye Miller, born Aug. 12, 1922 and Dorothy Miller Heffington of Florence, AL, sister of Joyce, born Nov. 28, 1925. *Submitted by Dorothy M. Heffington.*

NICHOLSON, OLLIE RINEHART, daughter of Thomas Wister and Nettie Palmer Rinehart, born March 1915 and died Apr. 1984 at Tupelo Hospital. She married Richard Nicholson. Their children were Nettie Lou and twin boys, Dwight and Dewey

Nicholson. Nettie Lou married Vernon Hughley. Their children are Venita (who married Steve Wheeler and lives in Memphis), Richard (who also lives in Memphis) and Leigh (who married Curtis Winslow of Booneville). Dwight and Dewey live in Booneville. Nettie Lou's second marriage was to Thomas Harris and they lived in Booneville. She died in 1993 of a heart attack.

Children of Thomas Wister and Nettie Palmer Rinehart. Sitting, l-r: Dora Rinehart Walden, Flora Rinehart Carpenter, Verona Rinehart Burcham, Audrey Rinehart Searcy and Ollie Rinehart Nicholson. Standing, Clifford Palmer Rinehart, Ralph Lomax Rinehart, Roy Sylvester Rinehart, James K. Vardaman Rinehart and Alice Rinehart Enis (Missing is Evelyn Rinehart, who died at 17 with a growth behind her eye).

Ollie was a beautician and owned a shop in Booneville for many years. Her sisters, Alice Enis and Audrey Searcy, were also beauticians, working at Ollie's shop for a while.

Ollie was a member of Sardis Primitive Baptist Church. Her brother Clifford Palmer Rinehart, was pastor for many years. Her parents and grandparents were members of this church. She is buried in Booneville Cemetery by the side of her husband. *Submitted by her niece, Zelma Brimingham*

NICHOLSON FAMILY, not much is known of the Nicholsons before 1860. There were two brothers, John N. and William Alonzo and a sister, Jinks, that we know of, but we do not know their parents.

John N. was born May 18, 1861 and died Aug. 16, 1933 and is buried in Little Brown Cemetery. He first married Theressa Hampton, by whom he had John Buyan, Jim, Vonie, Annie and a child that drowned. By his second wife, Arrie Lilly Cates, he had a son, Roy.

From left: Colious, Lon, Lois, Tennie and Lee Nicholson.

John Buyan, born in 1888 and died in 1975, was a builder in the community. In the early 1900s, he built approximately 40 houses and a church in the Booneville Fish Lake area. He was married to Lorena Evelyn Lowery. Their children are: John; R.B.; Vera Lee, who married Brown Kennedy; Sadie Antaleen, who married William Tuggle Jones; Ruth, who married H.L. Boone; J.C. (Red) and Connie Pearl.

Jim's children were: Lucian, Opal, Newt, Sidney, James, Edna Hicks and Clemmie, who Brown Kennedy married first. He was married to Roxi L. Lowery.

Annie married John Westly Skelton. They had Ruth Lawson, Lorrena Randle, Vivian Ashcraft, Forrest, John Millard, Isiah, Herbert, Joy (male), Billy and Glenn Skelton. Glenn lives in Baldwyn and is married to Estelle Inman and has two daughters: Judy Schueren, who lives in Ohio and Sue Munn, who lives in Diamond Head, Mississippi.

William Alonzo (Lon) (b. Jul. 16, 1874 and died Oct. 9, 1951) was married to Tennessee (Tennie) Jane Denson (b. 1877 and died in 1965), daughter of Thomas Cicero Denson and Martha Jane Grisham. Martha's parents were Carroll Grisham and Levina Collier. Lon and Tennie had nine children. They were:

1. William Colious, who died at the age of 11 when he accidentally shot himself while turkey hunting with his sister, Lois.

2. Lois (b. Sep. 6, 1900 and died Jul. 10, 1985) married Jesse McKay.

3. Lee S. died young.

4. Clara Flora Allen first married a Mr. Davis and had Geraldine and Noel and then was married next to Otis Allen and had a daughter, Barbara, who lives in Illinois.

5. James Thomas (b. 1909, d. 1955).

6. Charles Clifford (b. 1910, d. 1969) married Flora Bell Allred and has a daughter, Onedia Bracken, who lives in Guntown.

7 and 8. Twins, Jessie and Essie, died in infancy.

9. Lilly Pearl lives in Jackson, TN and has a daughter, Corinna Fortuna, who lives in Illinois.

The twins, Jessie and Essie and Colious are buried in Little Brown Cemetery with their Uncle John N. Nicholson. *Submitted by Patsy Nicholas.*

NICHOLSON, THOMAS JEFFERSON, "another of the gallant boys who followed General Robert E. Lee has answered the last call. One by one the dear old boys who wore the gray are passing away and on last Friday, Thomas J. Nicholson passed over the river and was gently laid to rest in the Marietta Cemetery. He was born Mar. 3, 1843 in Franklin County, AL and served for four years in the Civil War and after that took up the task of bringing peace and progress back to his country. He served faithfully in the war and was just as true and faithful a citizen. He lived in the Zion Rest Community in Prentiss County for over 70 years. He was a faithful and devoted member of the Church of Christ." (from obituary).

Thomas J. Nicholson with two grandsons, Charles and James Googe

Thomas J. Nicholson was twice married, first to Sallie Armstrong who passed away in 1904. To this union 11 children were born, five boys and six girls: Robert Andrews, William Lucien, David W., Thomas J., Martin Luther, Laura Ophelia, Louise Alice, Mary Florence, Mattie Pearl, Jessie Alma and Ann Elizabeth.

His second marriage was to Lavada Finch Howell. He and Lavada had six children, one dying in infancy. Two daughters are still living and are members of the United Daughters of Confederacy. They are now receiving a pension since they are daughters of a Confederate soldier.

I. Nellie Pauline (b. Dec. 30, 1909) married Shelby Greene Googe (deceased). Their children are (A) James Harold Googe (b. Jan. 19, 1928) married Annie Margaret Rinehart; three children: (1) James Harold Jr. (b. Sep. 28, 1959) married Tina Lisa McClinton, three children: Elizabeth Margaret (b. May 7, 1989), Benjamin James Googe (b. Apr. 5, 1990) and Joshua Thomas Googe (b. Oct. 1, 1992). (2) Sandra Lee Gordon (b. Aug. 16, 1961) divorced; one son, Drew Gordon (b. Jul. 13, 1984). (3) April Conious Googe (b. Apr. 4, 1966) married Sean Weaver Gough; two children, Sarah Ann (b. Aug. 14, 1997) and Rachel Leigh (b. Aug. 31, 1999). (B) Charles Edwin Googe (b. May 15, 1930) married Betty Jo Martin; two children, Charles Edwin Jr. (b. Aug. 21, 1956), Susan Maria (b. Sep. 26, 1963) married William Jones; two children, Shelby Shea (b. Jan. 18, 1993) and William Preston (b. Apr. 29, 1997). (C) Kathryn Nell Googe (b. Oct. 7, 1938) married Kenneth Eugene Floyd; four children: (1) Melanie Rose Floyd (b. Dec. 4, 1966) married Henein Iskander; two children, Lauren Nichole (b. Sep. 13, 1994) and Natalie Paige (b. Dec. 28, 1995). (2) Kenneth Eugene II "Kenny" (b. Jul. 10, 1968) (3) Mark Jefferson (b. Jan. 4, 1976) deceased, (4) Molly Kathryn (b. Jan. 4, 1976) married Stewart Graham Hodge.

Joseph Nicholson, youngest child of Thomas J. Nicholson

II. Effie Lucille Nicholson (b. Aug. 30, 1914) married Fred Pharr; four children: (A) Floyd Jack (b. Apr. 7, 1934); four children: Wilda Ann, David Ross, Michael Keith and Anthony Duane, 11 grandchildren and two great-grandchildren. (B) Martha Sue Flanders (b. Jul. 18, 1936), two children, Martha Raye Nugent (b. Dec. 15, 1953) and Jennifer Kay Davis (b. Dec. 12, 1959), four grandchildren: Tracy Alaine and Christy Lynn Nugent and Kelly Rebecca and Michael Clay Davis, one great-grandchild, Abby Alaine Criger. (C) Mary Faye Rhodes (b. Aug. 12, 1946), two children, Ginger Alaine Carson (b. Jun. 8, 1967) and Michael Earnest Guy Jr. (b. Mar. 1, 1972), three grandchildren: Taylor, Bailee and Bronson. (D) Tommie Jean Griffin (b. Sep. 1, 1942), two children, Felicia Dawn Shephard (b. Jul. 17, 1965) and Jason Marty Griffin (b. Nov. 12, 1962), four grandchildren: Thomas, Jared, Greta and Jason.

III. Arlis Nicholson married Eula Wren, both deceased, one son, Winfred.

IV. Sallie Medlin, deceased, two daughters, Betty Jean and Nell.

V. Joseph Nicholson married Doris McCoy, both deceased, no children.

NUNLEY FAMILY, came from Great Britain through the Carolinas and Virginia into Georgia. They were farmers. Some owned large plantations before the Civil War. There are, various spellings of the name.

Israel Nunnally fought in the Revolutionary War and lived until 1826. His wife, Margaret Gibson Nunnally, drew a pension. His son, Horatio, was a lieutenant in the Georgia Militia in 1810 when his son, James Archer, was born in Green County. By 1924, Horatio was a captain. On Oct. 2, 1832, Horatio was the presiding J.P. when his son, James, married Margaret Pinson in Walton County, GA. To them were born Nathan Pinson (b. 1835) and Thomas Jefferson (b. May 5, 1837). On

Thomas Jefferson Nunally and Arminda Jane Anderson

L to R: James William Washington (Billy), Nathan Sidney (Nate), Thomas Jefferson (T. J.) Jr., Margaret Jane (Sis), Joseph Wyatt, Francis Marion, Jasper Lafayette, Mary Elizabeth (Lizzie) and Emma Estelle (Isacc Newman is not show)n Nunally.

Oct. 2, 1858, Thomas married Arminda Jane Anderson (b. Oct. 27, 1839). They moved to Kemps Creek, AL.

During the Civil War James A. served with a Georgia Regiment. His sons, Nathan and Thomas served in the 48th Alabama Regiment, CSA. Nathan was killed at Chickamauga. Thomas, a sergeant, lost a finger during the Second Battle of Manassas.

Slaves were treated kindly and wanted to remain at the Nunnally Plantation after the war.

Seated from left: Bernard Ray, Finis Nathan Nunley (father) and Truman Sidney. Standing from left: Dolly Maness Nunley (mother) and Vera.

Nobody had to work until the Yulelog was burned at Christmas. Slaves cut the largest backlog and soaked it in the creek until the celebration began.

Thomas and Arminda moved to Cullman, AL, where they are buried near Holly Springs in the Primitive Baptist Nunnelley Cemetery. His children were James William Washington "Bill," Nathan Sidney, Thomas Jefferson Jr., Margaret Jane, Joseph Wyatt, Francis Marion, Jasper Layfayette, Mary Elizabeth, Isaac Newman and Emma Estelle.

Nathan Sidney was born Jan. 26, 1861. He came to Tishomingo County, part of which later became Prentiss County. Dec. 17, 1882, he married Sally Elizabeth Gilley (b. Oct. 30, 1868), daughter of Thomas Gilley and Martha Ann Williams. When Tom refused to give 14 year-old Sally's hand, she and Nath eloped. Around 1894 they moved to Texas for two years. The first year Nath made l500 bushels of corn. The second, he made a tow sack full. They moved back to Prentiss County and lived near Altitude, where they had a large farm and a blacksmith shop. Their house had two open hallways. The closed-in back porch held a weaving loom and spinning wheel. The Nunnelley School burned then consolidated with Hills Chapel.

Front row from left: Mary Lynn, Benny Carol, Bernard Larry. Middle: Arlene and Bernard Ray Nunley. Back row from left: Reba Ilene and Ouida Jeanette. (Not pictured, Nathan Joel)

Nath and Sally are remembered as good, honest, hard-working neighbors, always ready to help. They were Primitive Baptist and are buried at Mt. Pleasant (Buck Snort) Cemetery with their children: Thomas Lee, Clovis and Emma "Emer." Their other children were Arminda Jane "Arrie" married Almos Vinson; Mattie L. married Sam Free; Annie married Will Ross, then Jim Lambert; Fannie married Omer Lambert; Randolph married Virgie Smith; Lear married Milburn Davis; Maggie died in Texas; Finis Nathan was born in Texas on May 20, 1895.

In 1914 Finis Nathan married Dolly Maness (b. Aug. 11, 1899), daughter of Irene Carpenter and Tom Maness. Finis changed the spelling to Nunley. His first son, Marlon, died in infancy; Bernard Ray (b. Jun. 6, 1917); Vera (b. May 4, 1922) md. Cecil Case and moved to Corinth; Truman Sidney (b. Mar. 17, 1928) was a Korean War veteran, married Connie Harp and moved to Corinth. Finis and Dolly are buried at Mt. Olive Church of God.

On Dec. 18, 1937, Bernard Ray Nunley married Tisha Arlene Lambert (b. Feb. 21, 1920), daughter of Myrtle Rose McAnally and Marcus Dewitt "MM" Lambert. Bernard began preaching at the age of 16. He helped establish Mt. Olive Church of God in 1941. Besides his physical labor, he donated all the lumber used to box the first church building. Myrtle Lambert and her children gave the land. Bernard pastored the church for several years. His ministry spanned 66 years at the time of his death. He is buried beside his father and mother.

Nathan Joel Nunley

Bernard and Arlene Nunley had seven children: Ouida Jeanette, Leamon Joe (died in infancy and is buried at McAnally Cemetery), Reba Ilene, Benny Carol, Bernard Larry, Mary Lynn and Nathan Joel. Bernard Larry served in the Marines in Vietnam. A retired Air Force sergeant, he lives with his wife, Martha Grooms in Prattville, AL. Their sons are Brandon Kirk and Nathan Eric. Benny and Joel are in construction business. Their sons are James Derek, who is presently in Bosnia with the National Guard and Nathan Ray. Derek is married to Angela Mullins. Ouida married James Woods. Her children are Debra, Darlene and Michael Ray, who married Ginger Pace. Debra married Bobby Davis. Their sons are Joshua and Caleb. Darlene married Bobby Williams. Their sons are Jonathan and Justin. Reba married Bill McGaughy. Her children are Tim and Angela Michelle. Tim married Kim Cook. Their son is Timmy Jared "T.J." Michelle married Sam Stacy. Their daughter is Kelsey. Mary married James Gargus. Their children are Amy Lynn and Bryant Floyd. Bryant served aboard the USS *LaSalle*, Flagship of Commander, US Navy, during the Persian Gulf War. He is married to Jamie Lynn Ludlam. Amy is married to Shawn Michael Coleman. Their daughter is Rachel Katelyn. Mary teaches school. *Submitted by Bernard Larry Nunley and Mary Lynn Gargus.*

OAKLEY, CLAUDE AUBURN, lifelong residents of Prentiss County, Claude Auburn Oakley (b. May 5, 1888, d. Feb. 25, 1955) and Ruth Smith (b. Jul. 7, 1891, d. Dec. 15, 1972) were married on Aug. 26, 1909. Claude was the fifth of 12 children born to George Washington Oakley (b. 1855, d. 1935) and Amanda Frances Young Oakley (b. 1853, d. 1913) (see George Washington Oakley History). Ruth was the oldest of three daughters born to Stephen Taylor Smith (b. Nov. 9, 1848, d. Feb. 4, 1927) and Sallie Grisham Smith (b. Mar. 22, 1872, d. May 16, 1959) (see Smith-Grisham Family History). The Oakley and Grisham families had lived less than one mile apart in the Osborne Creek Community and Claude and Ruth raised their children "across the road" from Ruth's parents. Ruth had attended Mississippi State College for Women, but traded a college education to marry the "love of her life." Around 1947, they built a "new" house on Hwy. 45 (now Hwy. 145) about five miles south of Booneville. Part of that property and the house is now the site of Morgan Moving and Storage.

Oakley children and spouses in 1948. Seated: Effie (Mrs. Murray Spain), Virgie (Mrs. Jude Garner), Jude Garner, Claude, Plato. Standing: Bun Grisham, Maye (Mrs. Otis Spain), Ruth Smith (Mrs. Claude Oakley), Louise (Mrs. Pink Oakley), Mary Carpenter (Mrs. Jesse Oakley), Ruth Wilkerson (Mrs. Plato Oakley), Otis Spain, Lillian Daniels (Mrs. Bob. Oakley) and Plato.

Claude was a cotton buyer and farmer. He had a cotton-buying office in Baldwyn originally, then moved to Booneville and began a partnership with Mr. John Curlee. Their office was located in the old Will Barnett building where the parking lot now is on West College Street by Dickerson's Furniture. This area was the location of several cotton offices including Mr. Will Fulgum's, Milton Grisham's, W.C. Garner's and Carlton Bonds. Around the early 1950s he moved into the office on East Church Street adjoining the back of the Hatcher Law Offices. Claude's greatest love, however, was training bird dogs. Quail season meant that hunters from as far away as St. Louis would converge on the Oakley house to board "weeks at a time."

Ruth was known for her generous hospitality and fine Southern cooking and a visit to her house always meant something good to eat. Each holiday was a special occasion at the Oakley house, for everyone came home to fellowship with family and feast on Mama Oakley's fabulous meals. The yard was always full of grandchildren and cousins playing some form of ball, while the Oakley sons and sons-in-law sat on the breezeway replaying the week's ballgames or boasting about the "big one" that got away.

Summers and July 4th in particular, meant a fishfry at the artesian well, which was located in a pasture behind the house. A truck or wagon would make several trips from the house to the picnic site loaded with lawn chairs, food and, of course, dozens of Oakley children and grandchildren. The day would be filled with plenty of food, games and the "forbidden" swim in the George Oakley pond.

Claude served as a substitute mail-carrier and was also a trustee at Osborne Creek School, where the children attended until they could start to Wheeler High School. At Wheeler the boys played basketball.

Claude and Ruth Oakley were members of Osborne Creek Baptist Church and are buried in Osborne Creek Cemetery.

Children of Claude Auburn Oakley and Ruth Smith Oakley:

1) George Smith Oakley (b. Nov. 1, 1911, d. Jul. 21, 1986) md. Oct. 14, 1962 to Dorothy Lee Woodruff White (b. Jan. 20, 1929). Stepdaughter, Carolyn White Jones (b. l947).

2) Virgil Neil Oakley (b. Feb. 20, 1914, d. Dec.

1, 1991) md. Apr. 8, 1933 to Mary Christine Smith (b. Oct. 10, 1915). Children: Betty Ruth Oakley Wallace (b. 1934) and Gladys Lee Oakley Slappy (b. 1941).

3) Luei Hebron "Tate" Oakley (b. Oct. 9, 1917, d. Apr. 16, 1979) md. Feb. 8, 1947 to Frances Henrietta Yates (b. Feb. 27, 1923). Children: Charlotte Ann Oakley Whitehead (b. 1947), Shirley Ruth Oakley Cole (b. 1947), Frances Yates Oakley Green (b. 1953).

4) Sara Majorie Oakley Franks (b. Jul. 8, 1921) md. Jul. 16, 1937 to Jesse Dee Franks (b. Jan. 31, 1919, d. Feb. 5, 1987). Children: Mary Ann Franks West (b. 1941), Gloria Dee Franks Smith (b. 1943), Stephen Guest Franks (b. 1946) and Majorie Kaye Franks Cozort (b. 1947).

5) William Claude "Billy" Oakley (b. Apr. 23, 1925, d. Oct. 5, 1990) md. Nov. 5, 1946 to Sarah Elizabeth "Sue" Stuart (b. Jan. 23, 1926). Children: William Kenneth Oakley (b. 1947, d. 1989), Richard Stuart "Dick" Oakley (b. 1948). Phillip Claude Oakley (b. l951), Gary Smith Oakley (b. l952), Susan Gail Oakley Heath (b. l957).

6) Martha Ruth Oakley Brooks (b. May 30, 1928) md. Jun. 4, 1950 to Truman Darnell Brooks (b. Sep. 27, 1921). Children: Martha Wanda Brooks Mosley (b. 1951) and Larry Oakley Brooks (b. 1955). Submitted by *Shirley Oakley Cole*.

OAKLEY, GEORGE WASHINGTON,

born Mar. 3, 1855 in Lauderdale County, AL and died Apr. 30, 1935 in Prentiss County, MS and Amanda Frances Young (b. Mar. 17, 1856 in Lauderdale County, AL, d. Aug. 1, 1913 in Prentiss County, MS) were married on Apr. 6, 1880 in Prentiss County. G.W.'s widowed mother, Mary Elizabeth Blassingame Dalton Oakley (b. Feb. 4, 1822 in Tennessee; d. Aug. 19, 1894 in Prentiss County, MS) moved to Prentiss County from Lauderdale County, AL, after the Civil War (ca. 1866). George's father was Jesse Alexander Oakley (b. 1816 in Williamson County or Maury Co, TN; d. Jul. 10, 1862). He was taken prisoner of war and died in a Union Prison in St. Louis.

George Washington Oakley Family, 1893. Front: Tom, Maye, Clad, (middle) G.W., Amanda, Pink, (back) Virgie, Grandmother Mary Blassingame, Jesse and Bob.

In an Oct. 5, 1939, article in the *Baldwyn Home Journal*, D.J. Hill remembered the Oakley family: "The founder of this family was Jesse Alexander, a native of Tennessee, leaving his childhood home he came to Lauderdale County, AL, was twice married. Mr. Oakley showed his patriotism by joining the Texans and fighting with them to gain their independence from Mexico (b. 1835, d. 1836)." Family accounts indicate that Jesse had lived and owned property in Texas and that his first wife was possibly buried there. Jesse and his two young sons, James (b. 1842, Alabama) and William (b. 1844, Alabama), returned to Lauderdale County, AL. Jesse married Mary Dalton, a widow, on Dec. 21, 1848 in Lawrence County, TN. Mr. Hill continued, "At the breaking out of the hostilities between the States, Jesse did not enlist, but his sons, William and James, did and did active and valuable service. William captured a Yankee commander and his company. I have seen the sword surrendered at Plato Oakley's in good state of preservation, hilt and blade measuring 42 inches. The other son, James, was shot and killed near Savannah on the day before the great Battle of Shiloh on Apr. 6-7, 1862. The father was captured by the Yanks and thrown into prison at St. Louis where he died." Jesse had gone to claim the body of James when he was captured. He is buried at Jefferson Barracks National Cemetery in St. Louis (grave JBNC 5266). William served with Co. H, Maury Grays, Maury County, TN and later reorganized with the 4th Alabama Infantry Regiment. He was killed at Gaines' Mill.

Oakley House at Osborne ca. 1910. Back L-R: Plato, George Washington, Amanda Young Oakley, Claude, Ruth Smith Oakley. Front L-R: Johnnie, Maggie, Effie, Maye, Tom, Sid and John.

Jesse and Mary had six children: Thomas Campbell Oakley (b. 1849, d. 1925), Elizabeth Oakley (Mrs. Lemuel O. Jones (b. 1851, d. 1933), John Oakley (b. 1853), George Washington, Jessie Alexander Oakley Jr. (b. 1856, d. 1938) and Ann Oakley (b. 1859). Mr. Hill noted that Mary moved to Prentiss County with her four sons, located in the Oak Hill Community "where they have lived and died, except one year, all of them moved to Missouri but soon came back home."

G.W.'s children at Virgie and Jude Garner's 50th wedding anniversary in 1948. Seated: Jude Garner, Virgie O. Garner, Claude, Tom, Maggie (Mrs. Bun Grisham). Standing: Maye (Mrs. Otis Spain), Sidney, Effie (Mrs. Murry Spain), Plato. Jesse, Bob and Pink were deceased.

Jesse's parents were born in Virginia: William Oakley (b. ca. 1784/5 in Virginia, md. 1806, d. Mar. 15, 1822 in Maury County, TN) and Elizabeth Gray (b. ca. 1786 in Virginia, died in Maury County after 1850). William moved to the Tennessee community of Fly (S SW of Nashville) around 1800. DAR records list the parents of William as being James Oakley Sr. (b. 1755 in Amelia County, VA, d. Apr. 13, 1848 Maury County, TN) and Janet MacKinney (b. Aug. 1, 1759, Virginia; d. July 1839). James moved from Amelia County, VA to Maury County, TN by way of Henry County, VA where he married in 1783. James received a pension as a veteran of the Revolutionary War.

George and Amanda raised 12 children, seven boys and five girls. George built a home in the west Prentiss Community of Oakhill and later in the Osborne Creek Community (present site of the Thomas Garner house). George was a landowner and farmer. His Oakley boys were notorious for playing pranks on each other as well as on unsuspecting neighbors. One farmer awakened to find his wagon on the roof of his barn! Amanda, however, was equal to the task of raising her prankster sons. An Oakhill neighbor, Guy Garner, remembered her "jumping into the creek and taking on the whole bunch" when she found the boys in their favorite swimming hole against her orders. This spunk served her well as a midwife and nurse; she was known to ride "far and wide" on horseback late into the night to deliver a baby or care for the sick. Amanda died at age 58. George never remarried and he died at age 80 in the Osborne Creek home of his youngest son, Plato.

Children of George Washington Oakley and Amanda Frances Young Oakley: 1) Elizabeth Virginia "Virgie" Oakley (b. 1881, d. 1961) md. Julius David "Jude" Garner (b. 1878, d. 1960); 2) Jesse William Oakley (b. 1882, d. 1920) md. Mary Parthenia Carpenter (b. 1883, d. 1979); 3) Robert Samuel "Bob" Oakley (b. 1884, d. 1940) md. Mary Lillian Daniels (b. 1886, d. 1992); 4) George Pinkney "Pink" Oakley (b. 1886, d. 1912) md. Mattie Louise Hamm; 5) Claude Auburn Oakley (b. 1888, d. 1955) md. Ruth Smith (b. 1891, d. 1972); 6) Thomas Dewitt Oakley (b. 1890, d. 1964) md. (first) Mamie Pearl Tays (b. 1887, d. 1933) and (second) Jetty Pauline Rogers Warren (b. 1901, d. 1967); 7) Lena Maye Oakley (b. 1892, d. 1960) md. Otis S. Spain (b. 1895, d. 1964); 8) Sidney R. Oakley (b. 1894, d. 1966) md. Mary Katherine Spain (b. 1896, d. 1988); 9) Julius Plato Oakley (b. 1896, d. 1984) md. Mary Ruth Wilkinson (b. 1900, d. 1982); 10) Mary Effie Oakley (b. 1898, d. 1988) md. Murry Jefferson Spain (b. 1894, d. 1982); 11) Margaret Irene Oakley "Maggie" (b. 1901, d. 1982) md. George Bunyan "Bun" Grisham (b. 1900, d. 1989); 12) Johnnie Frances Oakley (b. 1902, d. 1917).

OWENS SIBLINGS,

Annie Ophelia Owens (b. Dec. 9, 1924) married Paul Stearling Simmons (b. Jan. 26, 1924), the son of Sudie Jim Simmons. They farmed and sharecropped before leaving Prentiss County in the early 1950s to live near Ophelia's mother in Biloxi. Three sons were born to them, Jerry Lee (b. Nov. 25, 1945), Terry Wayne (b. Feb. 27, 1948) and Larry Gene (b. Sep. 20, 1955).

Jerry married Judy Ella Webb. They had three girls. Lisa Ann married Nikolas Ioannis Petrou from Greece. They had John Nick (b. Jun. 17, 1986), Stravoula Nick (Voula) (b. Dec. 12, 1988) and Stephanie Lynn (stillborn Nov. 25, 1993). Lisa is now married to Joseph Kiehm II.

Paula Gean (b. Jun. 28, 1969) died of cancer on Apr. 25, 1990. She had one son, George.

Sharron Maurice (b. Apr. 13, 1972) married Daniel Uriebe Sr. They had Jessica (b. Mar. 13, 1989) and Daniel Uriebe Jr. Sharron is now married to Hugo Navarrate.

Jerry and his wife Mary (?) live in Ocean Springs. His children and grandchildren live in New Orleans, LA.

Terry married Julie Ann Coley. They have two children, Brandon Dwayne (b. Jan. 29, 1981) and Megan Renae (b. Aug. 18, 1987). They live on the Mississippi Gulf Coast.

Larry married Nelda Faye Raphel. They have two children, Tera Lee (b. Dec. 28, 1976) and Paul Jason (b. Oct. 4, 1980).

Tera married Odis Lindsey. They have one child, Sadie Faye. They all live in Moyock, NC.

Paul Stearling Simmons died Oct. 5, 1978, at the Mobile Infirmary in Mobile, AL, while undergoing heart surgery. Ophelia resides in Ocean Springs.

Melton Leon Owens (b. Jul. 30, 1930) married Vina Mae Buckeridge. They left Prentiss County in the late 1950s. They had two children: Retha Jewel (b. Oct. 25, 1948). She married Richard King. They had one son, Richard W. King.

Danny Leon Owens (b. Apr. 14, 1951) married Edith Eaton. They had three daughters. Anita Owens married Dean Skelton. She has three children: Daniel, Darren and Mason. They live in Fort Riley, Kansas. Also, twins, Sharon Kay and Rita, were born. Rita married Kevin Nuget. Sharon has three children by William Warden: Shannon, Shana and Tiffany. Danny is now married to Jane Bates and makes his home in

Biloxi, MS. Melton Leon died of cancer on Aug. 20, 1969. He is buried near Gulfport.

Lealon Lamar Owens (b. Jul. 30, 1932) married Jewel Dee Case Lambert. He has four children. Brenda and Rickey are by a marriage to Mary Rosa Michaels (b. Jan. 18, 1936, d. Mar. 25, 1975). He and Jewel have Jerold and Tabatha. Jewel also has a son, Billy Wayne Lambert.

Brenda Gay Owens is married to Gary Jolly. She had three sons by marriage to David Baker: Steven Douglas, Mark Anthony and Kelly Lamar.

Rickey Lamar Owens is married to Barbara Jean Kennedy (B.J.). He has three sons. Rickey Lamar Jr. and Britt Leonard by former wife, Carolyn Bromley. He and B.J. have a son, Hunter Cade Owens.

Jerold Lealon Owens (b. Jun. 25, 1971) is married to Cathy McKinney.

Tabatha Jewel Owens (b. Jun. 16, 1975) is married to Steve Wilbanks. Their children are Noah Lamar and Siera Mckagin.

Lealon is founder and president of Unity Broadcasting Network in Booneville, MS.

John Travis Owens (b. Mar. 21, 1942) attended Wheeler School and left Prentiss County in 1959 to live with Grandma Sudie and work with his Uncle Paul in the carpenter trade. He married Mary Ruth (Judy) Hickman. Three children were born to them.

Regenia Deniece Owens (b. Jul. 29, 1964) married Charles Maxwell Powell. They have a daughter, Charlene Ruth (b. Sep. 13, 1984).

John Steven Owens (b. Sep. 13, 1984) married Judy Darlene Fryery. They have four children: Cindi Lynn (b. May 17, 1985); John Steven Jr. (b. Sep. 7, 1987); James Travis (b. Feb. 22, 1990) and Danielle Naomai (b. Aug. 19, 1991). Tina Louise Owens married Thomas Gregory Schauger. They have three children: Thomas Gregory Jr. (b. Dec. 20, 1987), Chanda Arial (b. Mar. 17, 1991) and Megan Victoria (b. Mar. 4, 1994). They all make their home on the Mississippi Gulf Coast.

Velma Erline Owens (b. Sep. 9, 1945) married Curtis Lyle Smith on Mar. 14, 1970. She had two children, Harold Wayne Smith (b. Mar. 6, 1967) and Lori Lynn Smith (b. Oct. 30, 1969) by a former marriage to Bobby H. Smith.

Harold married Sonja Lee Shirley. They have a son, James Kyle Wayne Smith (b. Apr. 17, 1994). Their home is in Marietta, MS.

Lori married Brian Guy Stennett. They have twin daughters, Courtney Noel and Candace Lea (b. Nov. 23, 1988). Their home is in Booneville, MS.

Curtis had two sons, Tony and Gary. (see Smith-Jarnagan story)

Mary Evelyn Owens (b. Oct. 25, 1947) married Luther Wayne Smith on Mar. 25, 1966. They have no children. Evelyn is owner and operator of Evelyn's Beauty Shop in Burton Community beside their home.

Edith Grace Owens (b. Feb. 25, 1950) married Murl Pannell. He died in an auto accident in Tennessee on Jul. 28, 1990. They had three children: Gregory Murl Pannell (b. Nov. 6, 1967) is married to Anna White. He has twin daughters, Molly Virginia Ann and Megan Desiree (b.Aug. 8, 1988). Anna has a son, Paul. Greg and Anna are expecting their first child in January 2000; Keri Mae Pannell (b. May 23, 1968) and Tresi Lara Pannell (b. Sep. 30, 1970). They all reside in Tupelo, MS.

Jimmy Earl Owens (b. Jul. 8, 1954) graduated from Wheeler High School in 1972. He left Prentiss County to work with his brother, Travis. He married Shirley Brown in 1976. They have one daughter, Katlyn Mechelle (b. Nov. 6, 1989). They make their home near Ocean Springs, MS.

Timmy Earnest Owens (b. Jan. 13, 1959) is married to Delsie Powers. He has one child, Brandi Necole (b. Oct. 20, 1984), by his first wife, Brenda Fair. Delsie has two children, Cristal and Josh Powers. Timmy lives in the house his dad left him south of Booneville on Meadow Creek Road. *Submitted by Erline Smith and Evelyn Smith.*

OWENS, AUDIE LEE BALDWYN, Prentiss County, MS was the birthplace of Audie Lee Owens (b. 1906, d. 1985). He was the son of Andrew Jackson Owens and Belle Victoria Grissom Owens.

Andrew Jackson Owens, born Nov. 8, 1877, was the son of William Elias Owens (b. 1820 in South Carolina and died in 1890 in Prentiss County) and Emmiline Parks Owens (b. 1844 in Mississippi and died in 1915 in Baldwyn, Prentiss County, MS). They are buried in the Hopewell Cemetery in Baldwyn. A detailed account of this family can be found in the *History of Prentiss County Mississippi*, published by the Prentiss County Historical Association in 1984.

Della Pauline Owens and Audie Lee Owens

Andrew Jackson Owens married Belle Victoria Grissom on Mar. 22, 1900 in Prentiss County, MS. She was the daughter of William Thompson Grissom (b. Mar. 20, 1854 in Mississippi and died Oct. 13, 1933), who married Millie Ann Epps (b. Aug. 2, 1855 in Alabama and died Feb. 20, 1937). They are buried in Pratt's Cemetery in Baldwyn, MS. Their children are:

1. Belle Victoria Grissom (b. Feb. 22, 1881).
2. Autry L. Grissom (b. 1889).
3. Henry A. Grissom (b. 1894).
4. Ollie Grissom (b. 1896).
5. Marion Elmer Grissom (b. 1898).
6. Martin L. Grissom (b. 1891).

Belle Victoria Owens and Andrew Jackson Owens

Family records state that William Thompson Grissom was the son of Abraham Newton Grissom (b. 1823, d. 1905) and Amanda Mathilde Williams (b. 1833, d. 1898). Abraham Grissom was the son of Martin Grissom (b. 1784, d. 1864) and Elizabeth Gregory (b. 1793, d. 1871). Martin Grissom was the son of Drury Grissom (b. 1760, d. 1829).

Milly Ann Epps Grissom was the daughter of Eli Epps (b. 1815 in North Carolina, d. ?) and Sarah Elizabeth Wiley (b. 1818 in Alabama, d. ?). They were married Aug. 10, 1842 in Itawamba County, MS. Their known children are: June (b. 1844); James (b. 1849) and Millie Ann (b. 1855 in Alabama). Records indicate that Eli Epps was the son of Pleasant Marvel Epps (b. 1789 in North Carolina and died 1860, d. 1870) and his first wife (name unknown), but definite proof is lacking.

The union of Andrew Jackson Owens and Belle Victoria Grissom was blessed with four children:

1. R.C. Owens (b. Jan. 9, 1901 in Mississippi, d. Mar. 22, 1969 in Texas) married Jan. 9, 1921 to Gladys Jean Drigger (b. Jun. 22, 1904, d. Jan. 28, 1987 in Texas).
2. William E. Owens (b. 1904 in Mississippi, d. 1967 in Tennessee) married Lucy T. (unknown) (b. 1913).
3. Romie (b. after 1910 in Mississippi) married Dolly (unknown). Both died in 1975 in Texas.
4. Audie Lee Owens (b. Oct. 22, 1906 in Baldwyn, Prentiss County, MS, d. Mar. 20, 1985 in Memphis, TX) second marriage was to Della Pauline Richards (b. Oct. 12, 1914 in Mt. Pleasant, TX, d. Sep. 18, 1994 in Longview, TX).

After the birth of their last child, Andrew Jackson Owens and Belle Victoria Owens moved to Mt. Pleasant, TX around 1915. She died there Jul. 16, 1939 and he died at Tyler, TX, Jul. 2, 1955. Both are buried in Snow Hill Cemetery in Mt. Pleasant, TX.

Audie Lee Owens first married Dovie Leigh Smith in Mt. Pleasant, TX. They were later divorced. They were the parents of two boys:

1. L.W. (Dub) Owens (b. Dec. 11, 1928 in Mt. Pleasant, TX) first married Mary Herley, who died in 1976 in Lufkin, TX. Their children are: Mark Owens, Beth Owens and Matthew Owens.
2. Harold Weldon Owens (b. May 18, 1930 in Mt. Pleasant, TX) married two times. The only known child is Tommy Lee Owens, born in 1968 in Gregg County, TX.

Audie Lee Owens next married Della Pauline Richards on Sep. 19, 1936. Pauline "Polly" was the daughter of Lonnie Richards and Ophelia Melissa Hudgins Richards of TX. Audie and Pauline made their home in Tyler, TX where he retired from Southwestern Transportation Co. After they retired, they moved to Memphis, TX where Audie died Mar. 20, 1985. Pauline Owens moved to Longview, TX where she died Sep. 18, 1994. Both are buried in Snow Hill Cemetery in Mt. Pleasant, TX.

Audie and Pauline Owens were the parents of two children:

1. Charolotte Ann Owens (b. Nov. 14, 1944 in Tyler, TX) married Jerry Don Hester in Tyler, TX on Jun. 15, 1963. They have one daughter, Nikki Lynn Hester, born Sep. 27, 1976 in Texas. Jerry and Ann Hester live in Longview, TX.
2. Russell Arlen Owens (b. Nov. 23, 1940 in Pittsburg, Camp County, TX) married Betty Jean Terrell (b. Oct. 26, 1941 in Tyler, TX) on Sep. 9, 1960 in Tyler, TX. Betty is the daughter of Douglas Charles Terrell and Doris Cotten Terrell of Tyler, TX. Russell and Betty Owens live in Beaumont, TX. They are the parents of: (1) David Arlen Owens (b. Sep. 2, 1961 in Tyler, TX) married Connie Leigh Zimmerman Aug. 17, 1985 in Jefferson County, TX. David and Connie are the parents of Seth Arlen Owens (b. Mar. 8, 1990); Randi Leigh Owens (b. Feb. 8, 1993) and Beau Brenden Owens (b. Jun. 24, 1994). David and Connie Owens live in Lumberton, TX. (2) Aimee Belle Owens (b. Nov. 3, 1966 in Tyler, TX) married Glenn Keith Smith on Feb. 7, 1987 in Beaumont, TX. They are the parents of Brittnie Belle Smith (b. Apr. 25, 1990) and Lauren Jean Smith (b. Sep. 5, 1995). Aimee and Glenn Smith live in Beaumont, TX. (3) Jennifer Marie Owens (b. Aug. 14, 1969 in Beaumont, TX) married Travis Scott Burke on Jul. 27, 1996 in Beaumont, TX. They have one daughter, April Marie Burke (b. Oct. 10, 1995) and live in Franklin, TN. *Submitted by Russell A. Owens.*

OWENS, JOHN HOWARD, second son of William Joseph Owens (b. 1865, d. 1918) and Mary Emma Calton (b. 1870, d. 1968), grandson of Bill and Alice Owens and Luke and Janie Calton, was born Dec. 23, 1901. Howard lived in and around Prentiss County all of his life. He attended school in the eastern part of the county, possibly Paden or Blythes Chapel. He told stories of walking two miles to school and carrying his lunch of molasses and cornbread in a tin bucket.

Howard had three brothers and four sisters: Bradford, Hansel, Frank, Rachel, Madie, Lydia and Hattie.

In February 1923 Howard married Lillian Childers. Six children were born to them. Three died in infancy and are buried in unmarked graves in Liberty Cemetery. The three living were Annie Ophelia,

Melton Leon and Lealon Lamar. Their marriage ended when Lealon was just an infant. Howard raised the children. Lillian later married Calvin Hessler making their home in Biloxi, MS.

Bertha Mae Simmons was born Oct. 16, 1922 in Gloster, MS. Her mother was Sudie Jim, the daughter of Jim Simmons and Mary Fraser, the great-granddaughter of William Thomas and Susan Kistler Fraser.

John Howard and Bertha Owens on their wedding day

Bertha Mae was raised by her Grandpa Jim, never knowing who her father was. Sudie Jim never revealed her secret. Bertha never had a birth certificate or ever attended school a day in her life.

Around 1940, Sudie came back to Prentiss County with her two sons, Paul Stearling and James David and other daughter, Mary Ethel. They lived south of Booneville on the Counce farm and in the Jess Free house before moving from place to place around the county. Mary Ethel and James David Simmons graduated from Wheeler High School. Their home is on the Mississippi Gulf Coast. Sudie Jim (b. 1903, d. 1981) is buried in Biloxi, MS.

Bertha Mae married Lum Gentry on Jul. 17, 1943. He died about a month later. She had one son, John Travis. John Howard and Bertha Mae married on Nov. 11, 1944. He adopted Travis and raised him as his very own.

Howard and Bertha lived on both Walter McCord's and John Curlee's place north of Rienzi, farming a few acres of corn and cotton with a pair of old mules named Neg and Ned. Sharecropping was how they made their living. Two of their best friends were Guy and Lois Joyner with whom they farmed many years.

While on these farms, Velma Erline, Mary Evelyn and Edith Grace Owens were born. A son was stillborn. Howard made a little wooden box and buried him in the corner of the garden near the house. When they were ready to move he, along with Guy Joyner, moved baby Owens to Liberty Cemetery.

Around 1953, the Owens family moved to the Bert Gifford farm at Thrasher, sharecropping with him for two years. Jimmy Earl Owens was born.

From there the Owens moved to Bill Jackson's place at Blackland, later moving to Osborne Creek to help Guy Joyner on a farm he had rented.

Tired of being obligated to one man, Howard moved his family near Wheeler. He rented a house from the Gooches. There, Timmy Earnest Owens, the last of six children was born.

Howard and Bertha bought an acre of land on the Booneville and Wheeler Road. They proceeded to buy an old two-story house for $250, tear it down and with that lumber, built their first home. That was in 1962. A fire destroyed their home in 1967. Their insurance built another house, but family records and pictures were forever gone.

After years of struggling with a heart condition and high blood pressure, Bertha died May 23, 1969. Although having no formal education, she could read and write very well. She made all her daughters' clothes, making her own patterns. She taught us many trades.

With health gone, her only regret was having to leave her two young sons behind. We gave her a promise to take care of them. Bertha Mae is buried beside Baby Owens in Liberty Cemetery.

Howard later sold the house and bought one on Meadow Creek Road. He died Nov. 7, 1982. He is buried beside Bertha.

No diplomas, no degrees to brag of, but indeed, teachers of good, of Godly morals, of righteous living, of honest, working hard and loving. These were parents to brag about. *Submitted by Erline and Evelyn Smith.*

PAYNE, THOMAS FRANKLIN MARION,

born Jun. 1, 1840 in Old Tishomingo County, MS, son of William B. Payne (b. Jul. 12, 1812 in Georgia and died Oct. 12, 1886, of tuberculosis in Wise County, TX) and Nancy Ann (Kizer) Payne (b. Sep. 11, 1828 in Tennessee and died Jan. 27, 1897 in Mississippi). Thomas's siblings, all born in Mississippi, were Sarah E. Roberta (b. 1843) married John Roach; William R. (b. 1846) married Amanda Bane; Nancy J. (b. 1848) married George Calvery; Martha Ann (b. 1851) married Felix Alford Bonds, L.B.C. (b. 1855) and John R. (b. 1859).

At age 23, he married on Dec. 25, 1863, to Mary T. Robertson (age 16), born Feb. 3, 1847 in Old Tishomingo County, the second daughter of James Harlow Robertson and wife, Manerva (Swinney) Robertson (See Robertson Family). She was baptized at age 15 in 1862 at Meadow Creek Baptist Church, providing evidence that the James H. Robertson family attended this church located in Old Tishomingo County. The church burned ca. 1920 and today is a United Methodist Church with the old cemetery still in existence.

Thomas Franklin Marion Payne and wife, Mary T. (Robertson) Payne, ca. 1864.

Thomas Franklin Marion Payne volunteered to serve for the Tishomingo Rifles, Co. A, 2nd Regiment and served as Captain in Co. B., 7th Regiment of the Mississippi Cavalry, CSA. He and his father ran a gin in Booneville. Their children were: Euastus W. (b. 1865), Manerva Ann (b. 1866), James William (b. 1868), Mary Alice (b. 1869), Thomas Thadeous (b. 1871), Fanny Belle (b. 1872), Sallie Ruberta (b. 1875), Michael Whitfield (b. 1877), John Edgar (b. 1880) and Sidney Overton (b. 1881).

The Payne family moved to Wise County, TX ca. 1778-1779, along with his father, (mother did not go) two sisters, their husbands and family. They operated a grocery-dry goods store in Keeterville, TX and later farmed and raised cattle in Indian Territory.

Mary T. Payne died Sep. 25, 1882, at age 35 of bilious fever and congestion. Thomas F.M. married second on Oct. 11, 1883 in Keeterville, TX to Sarah Margaret Boley, daughter of Hiram Carl and Elinder Jane (Wilson) Boley (See Boley History). Their children were Walter Calhoon (b. Nov. 2, 1884), W.B. Jr. (b. Dec. 9, 1886, d. Jan. 24, 1887), Sintor (b. Nov. 29, 1887), Odie, twins-Leslie and Bessie and Victoria and Homer. Some family members are buried in Keeterville Cemetery in Wise County, TX. *Submitted by Michael O. Parker.*

PERRIGO, WILLIAM HERSCHEL, on Feb.

9, 1949, William Herschel Perrigo, son of Elgie and Mary Tine Lancaster Perrigo, married Virginia Christine Hughes, daughter of John and Lydia Lauderdale Hughes. They made their home in the Pisgah Community and farmed, raising cotton and soybeans. Christine worked for MAP, Inc. and at Pisgah Headstart since it began in 1965. Herschel later owned and operated H & H Fertilizer, then worked for Terra, Inc. until his retirement. Herschel passed from this life on Dec. 1, 1995, leaving Christine, six children, 10 grandchildren and two great-grandchildren. Born to this marriage were: William Hughes (b. Nov. 9, 1949), Deborah Paulette (b. Feb. 20, 1952), Jacky Wayne (b. Jan. 23, 1957), Don Wade (b. Aug. 30, 1962), Anita Daphne (b. Jul. 1, 1965) and Rocky Edward (b. Nov. 2, 1969).

Christmas 1985 - The Perrigo Family. From left, Front Row: Christine, Mary Tine and Herschel. Back row: Hugh, Anita, Jacky, Paulette, Don and Rocky.

William Hughes (Hugh) married Linda Gable, daughter of Roy and Gladys Gable. They had two daughters, Ginger Dawn (b. Jan. 17, 1973) and Kristi Marie (b. Sep. 14, 1974). Ginger married Chuck Farris, son of Frank and Sharon Trollinger. They had three children: Joshua Dakota (b. Oct. 11, 1990), Casey Lane (b. Jul. 8, 1993) and Karlin Paige (b. Apr. 13, 1998). Kristi married Scott Slack, son of Jerry and Nancy Slack, on Dec. 27, 1995. Hugh served in the Vietnam War from 1968 to 1971. After his return, he was partners with Herschel in H & H Fertilizer business in Pisgah. Hugh died at the Veteran's Hospital in Memphis, TN on Jan. 22, 1997.

Paulette married Bud Sims, son of J.E. and Wade Sims, on May 15, 1969. They had Mikel Ray (b. Apr. 9, 1970), Tawanna Gail (b. Oct. 11, 1973) and Gordon Kyle (b. Dec. 11, 1982). Mikel married Lori Stroupe and had one daughter, Kaylee Elizabeth (b. Jan. 18, 1997). Tawanna married Brad Nash, son of Randal Nash and Carolyn Hearn on Aug. 6, 1994. They have one daughter, Olivia Jade born Aug. 24, 1999.

Jacky Wayne married Mary Sue Smart, daughter of H.C. and Ruby Smart on Jun. 4, 1976. They had two sons, Justin Paul (b. Mar. 4, 1980) and Coy Evan (b. Jan. 28, 1985).

Don married Judith Jumper, daughter of Dennis and Judy Jumper, on Oct. 20, 1984. They have two children, Dennis Shawn (b. Feb. 23, 1976) and Mary Samantha (b. Aug. 16, 1991).

Anita married Michael Bruce Gardner, son of Danny and Martha Gardner, on Nov. 1, 1991. They had two children: Donovan Brock (b. May 30, 1986) and Abbie-Michaela Christine (b. Jun. 26, 1996).

Rocky married Felesha Bullock, daughter of Richard Bullock and Arbadella Whitman, on Oct. 17, 1992. On their seventh wedding anniversary in 1999, Kristen Grace Perrigo was born.

Herschel had one brother, Bobby, who was killed in an accident 1963, leaving behind his wife, Melba Caldwell Perrigo and one daughter, Amy. He had one sister, Joy, who married Robert (Bob) Osborne. They had three children: Diane Green, Renee Henley and Darrell Osborne. His father, Elgie, died Sep. 16, 1980. Mary Tine carried on the family tradition of Sunday dinner (after attending worship at Pisgah United Methodist Church) for many years.

Christine was the baby of eight children. She had one sister and six brothers, better known as "The Hughes Boys": Paul (Goob), Charlie, Robert, Gordon (Homer), Raymond (Scrap) and Herschel. Goob and Charlie never married. Robert married Mauveline English. Homer married MoAnn Childers. Raymond married Frances Foy and had one son, Greg. Herschel married Annie Rhea Henderson and had one son, Samuel. All of the Hughes brothers are deceased. Christine's surviving sister, Sulu Devader, married Leland Garner and had one son, Thomas Dewey. Many Sunday afternoons and holidays were spent at the

"Hughes" house on the hill, laughing and reminiscing of the pranks and tales told by the brothers.

The Perrigo descendants all graduated from Jumpertown High School and remain residents of Prentiss County. *Submitted by Mary Sue Perrigo.*

PHILLIPS FAMILY, how do I began to tell such a remarkable story of such a sweet and caring lady? Perhaps, I should start by introducing her: Nellie Tolbert Hill was born Sep. 2, 1903, somewhere between Waynesberg and Clifton, TN. Let us began with some of her earliest memories as told in her own words.

"I have wonderful memories of my childhood, my brothers and sisters playing a game called Annie Over. First, they would throw the ball over the house, then holler Annie Over. We played games like that to keep busy because there were no stores around. When we were not at play we worked. We drew water from the well for the stove, picked corn and hoed cotton. We never were made to do our work, you just did it because we liked to eat and take our baths. We did not have luxuries like today's children. We were hard workers. That was the way our parents taught us to be and their parents taught them.

I can remember my grandmother very well. She lived with us until I was 10 years old. My grandfather I just can't recall, but I heard mommy tell that he had died in a Civil War prison camp. It was in 1913 when we moved to Mississippi, grandmother said she was not crossing any river so she stayed in Tennessee. On the trip there were 11 wagons driven by mules. It was a long and bumpy ride. The women and children would have to get out of the wagon when we came to banks and hills so it would not be hard on the mules.

It took three days. It was on the last night when we camped beneath a bank, a car's headlight boogered the mules. Cars were very few back then, so daddy and all the men folks had to calm them down. The next day the mules were ready to go again. Daddy was taking us to our new home, because our old home in Tennessee had burned. The wagon was packed with things folks had given us and I wondered where that dusty road would lead. We finally made it to our new home, a small saw mill house with enough room for sleeping, eating and love, so it was just right.

Daddy took a job in the woods and mommy was a mid-wife. Folks would come from miles around to see her, because of sickness and such. Back then, doctors were as few as cars, you just didn't see many. I remember mommy going to the home of Mrs. Whitfield when she was having a baby. We had to hold her head up for two days and nights, if she laid back she would quit breathing. Finally, she had the baby and everything was all right. However, I knew three other times when the mothers died from what they called the German Flu. I used to watch mommy and I always wanted to be a nurse. I am blessed that she was there seeing after all of us children.

I had six brothers and six sisters. We all share lots of birthday parties together, but as the years went by the small house seemed to get a little lonelier, because my brothers and sisters would either get married or move away. It was the year 1920 when a young man named Cliff Phillips and I began to date. He asked for my hand but I felt that I was too young. Soon after he was drafted into the service. I made a promise to wait for him and that we would marry when he returned. While he was over, we wrote letters to each other. We talked about our plans to marry and I often wondered if that would happen.

Three long years past when he returned home and on Mar. 2, 1924 we married. It was a beautiful day, the preacher married us on the outside in a buggy. Cliff had told some of the boys overseas that he was going home to get married and raise a large family, so that is just what he did. We had seven wonderful children: Inez, Marorie Queen, Cathleen, Gerald Dean, Emogene, Max and Diana. I had made four quilts and Cliff had two Army blankets and that was all we started out with. I am blessed to have lived in Prentiss County where I am surrounded by family and friends." *Submitted by Jennifer Dill.*

PHILLIPS, BASCOM LEE, in March 1930, Bascom Lee and Willie Summers Phillips purchased the Will Free homestead near Altitude in Prentiss County and moved their family to the four-room house. Mr. Phillips, using the old mare, Fanny and a team of mules raised cotton and row crops. He and Willie married Sep. 13, 1903, after the death of his first wife, Ellen Irene (b. Aug. 19, 1876, d. Jul. 18, 1901), the older sister of Willie.

Few facts are known about the Phillips family. Bascom and two brothers, Marvin and John Allen, were children of Franklin and Evaline Fisher Phillips.

Willie Summers Phillips was the daughter of William Dallas and Mary Margaret McCarley Summers. Family history of siblings, Isaac and Samuel (Bud) Summers, have been researched and recorded by other family members.

With her marriage to Bascom, Willie became stepmother to Cleo (b. Aug. 24, 1898, d. Jul. 19, 1995). Bascom and Willie Summers Phillips were parents to Bessie (b. Dec. 28, 1904, d. Oct. 30, 1997); Gladys (b. Dec. 15, 1908); Herman (b. Nov. 24, 1906 and died in 1930); Roy Lee (Nov. 28, 1912, d. Nov. 3, 1995); Zola (b. Aug. 21, 1917); Alva (b. Oct. 9, 1919); Mary Glenn (b. Sep. 7, 1921) and Rubel (b. Aug. 24, 1923 and died in 1925).

The oldest son, Herman Wheeler, died in 1930 while a student at the University of Southern Mississippi, Hattiesburg. He was a promising student, popular and active on campus. Condolences poured into the Phillips home after his death occurred while playing basketball at school. Proceeds from life insurance were instrumental in purchasing the family farm.

Mary Glenn (b. Sep. 7, 1921) married Ides Burton (Jack) Rutherford (b. Sep. 28, 1916, d. Feb. 24, 1996) on Nov. 5, 1941, shortly before he reported to the Army. Most of his military service was spent at Camp Shelby, Hattiesburg, MS. He served in the Quartermaster Corps as a cook. As a civilian, he farmed, worked at service stations and later returned to grocery work, which he enjoyed. Mary Glenn was a homemaker for many years, caring for her parents when they aged. She began work at Northeast Mississippi Hospital in Jan. 1963 and retired as ward secretary in June 1984 after 21-1/2 years. They had two daughters, Shirley Ann (b. Mar. 16, 1944) and Glenda Katherine (b. May 3, 1951). Shirley married Jerry Milton Few in 1964 in Columbus, MS and divorced in Birmingham, AL in 1968. They had two children, Jerry Richard (Rick) (b. Mar. 12, 1965) and Sherry Ann (b. Aug. 9, 1968). Jerry married Connie Faye Parrish and they were parents of Jerry Richard Few Jr. (b. Apr. 5, 1985). Sherry married Jerald Wayne Key Jr. on Sep. 26, 1992 and they are parents of Jerald Wayne (Jaye) III (b. Oct. 1, 1993) and JennyAnn Few Key (b. Feb. 19, 1996). Glenda married William Dale Newborn (b. Feb. 15, 1950) on Jun. 12, 1971 and they are parents of Michael Dale (b. Dec. 22, 1977) and Scottie Glenn (b. Jul. 14, 1982).

Shirley graduated from Mississippi State College for Women in 1964 and worked briefly with the Extension Service before beginning work with the Social Security Administration in 1965. She returned to Birmingham Southern College and received a master of arts in public and private management in 1987 and is now working as the Alabama area administrative assistant for the Social Security Administration.

Glenda attended Northeast Mississippi and Jefferson State Junior Colleges before beginning work in childcare. She attended Birmingham Southern College and received a bachelor's degree in 1990. She is a resource and referral counselor with Childcare Resources.

Descendants of Bascom and Willie Phillips have been respected, productive and contributing members of communities in Prentiss and Alcorn Counties. Second and third generation members of this family carry on these values and the work ethic instilled by their ancestors. *Submitted by Ms. Mary G. Rutherford.*

PIERCE, SIRRAH JAMES, was not born in Prentiss County MS but he married twice in the county. Sirrah was born about 1851 in possibly Lawrence County, TN son of James Parrilla and Sarah Greenhaw Pierce. He married first Pemelia A. Rickman, daughter of George W. and Sarah E. Irvine Rickman, on Mar. 3, 1873 in Prentiss County, MS. Pemelia was born about 1847 in Lawrence County, AL. To this union four children were born: John Thomas (b. 1882, d. 1967); Prentice R. (b. 1883, d. _); Ada A. (b. 1885, d. _); Maggie D. (b. 1888, d. _). Sirrah married second, Katie Thompson on Feb. 4, 1897 in Prentiss County, MS.

John Thomas Pierce was born in McNairy County, TN which might indicate that the family moved across the road. John married Willie Verlon Laster (b. 1889, d. 1945), daughter of Harmon Burton and Sarah Elizabeth Ashcraft Laster, on Oct. 8, 1905 in Prentiss County, MS. To this union three children were born: Erskine Chalmers (b. 1906, d. 1988); Stella Mae (b. 1912, d. 1985) and James Herman (b. 1917, d. 1979). They had eight grandchildren. Two of the grandchildren named a son after John Thomas Pierce as he was a powerful man to only stand about 5 foot tall. He was one of the best carpenters in Marshall County. His granddaughter cherishes her childhood memories of summer days spent swinging on his porch. *Submitted by Lynn Pierce Appling McCandless, granddaughter.*

PIKE, JAMES TILFORD AND MARY JANE VAWTER, married Nov. 12, 1841 in Tishomingo County, MS. James Tilford, born Sep. 12, 1819, Robertson County, TN, died Oct. 9, 1887, Prentiss County, MS buried on the Old Gilbert Howell Place, tombstone removed and put in Holley Cemetery, all located in Prentiss County, MS. His parents were Mary (b. ca. 1803) and John Pike Jr. (b. ca. 1796, d. Jun. 18, 1873). His grandparents were believed to be John Sr. and Sarah (Byrd) Pike, Robertson County, TN. James Tilford was a gifted fiddle player.

Mary Jane Vawter, born May 6, 1823 Maury County, TN, died Mar. 30, 1870 buried in Pleasant Site Cemetery, Franklin County, AL. Her parents were Rhoda (McQuire) (b. Nov. 16, 1785, d. Aug. 28, 1824, Maury County, TN) and John Vawter (b. Jan. 16, 1778, North Carolina). Mary Jane Vawter's grandparents were Sarah Holliday b. Feb. 12, 1757, Virginia, d. Mar. 22, 1836, Maury County, TN) and Allegany McGuire (b. Aug. 6, 1757, Cumberland County, VA, d. Jun. 18, 1843, McNairy County, TN). They were married Jun. 27, 1782.

James Tilford Pike, 1819-1887

Allegany McGuire who resided in Virginia during the American Revolution, assisted in establishing American independence, while acting in the capacity of orderly sergeant. He served under Capt. Charles Scott at Williamsburg, Yorktown and Hampton. Other times, he served under Gen. Lincoln and Gen. Gates.

Mary Jane and James Tilford's children were: John Hawkin "Hawk" (b. Aug. 15, 1842, Tishomingo County, MS, d. Jul. 5, 1909, Navarro County, TX) married Mary Frances "Molly" Greenhill Nov. 13, 1872. The 1880 census of Itawamba County, MS lists John Hawkin as a physician. He served as a private, CSA, Co. H., 26th Mississippi Regiment (Col. A.E. Reynolds and also Davenport's Battalion Calvary (State Troops) Butler's Co. Calvary Reserves, State of Mississippi. He was wounded at Richmond, VA; Alfred B. (b. May 6, 1844, Tishomingo County, MS) served as private in the CSA Davenport's Battalion Cavalry Reserves, state of Mississippi; Juliann Frances (b. Feb. 7, 1846, Tishomingo County, MS, d. Aug. 23, 1868) married David Hunt Jan. 13, 1868, Tishomingo County, MS; Rufus Pinkney (b. Feb. 29, 1848, Tishomingo County, MS, d. Oct. 12, 1916, Galveston, TX) married Ello Octavia (Mallow), died Mar. 2, 1927, Galveston, TX; David Niven "Dink" (b. May 7, 1850, Tishomingo County, MS). David lived in Texas and moved to Prentiss County, MS the last years of his life. He is buried in Holley Cemetery, Prentiss County, MS; Cephas Jasper (b. Sep. 7, 1852, Tishomingo County, MS, d. Dec. 2, 1944, Prentiss County, MS, buried in Holley Cemetery, Prentiss County, MS) married Martha Jane (Holley) and at her death, married Matilda Ann (Sims); Mary Jane (b. Jan. 31, 1856, Tishomingo County, MS) married W.S. George, they lived in Texas; James Tilford (b. Nov. 14, 1859, Tishomingo County, MS). *Submitted by Julian Carey Pike.*

PIKE, JAMES EDGAR, born Mar. 29, 1882, died Apr. 12, 1941, buried at Holley Cemetery, Prentiss County, MS and Julia (Lyle) (b. Jul. 22, 1889, Itawamba County, MS, d. Apr. 21, 1931, Lee County, MS) married Dec. 17, 1906, Prentiss County, MS.

James Edgar Pike's parents were Cephas Jasper Pike (b. Sep. 7, 1852, Tishomingo County, MS, d. Dec. 2, 1944, buried in Holley Cemetery, Prentiss County, MS) and Mary Jane (Holley) (b. Dec. 5, 1857, d. May 19, 1885, buried at Holley Cemetery, Prentiss County, MS) married Nov. 2, 1876, Prentiss County, MS.

Julia Lyle Pike's parents were William Franklin Lyle (b. Nov. 5, 1856, d. August 1931, buried in Kirkville Cemetery) and Mary Bonna (Houston) (b. Nov. 20, 1865, d. Jun. 28, 1899, buried at Kirkville Cemetery). William Franklin was a schoolteacher and Justice of the Peace in Lee County, MS.

William Franklin Lyle's parents were James Lyle (b. Dec. 14, 1811) and Jane (Davis) (b. Apr. 29, 1818) daughter of James Davis and Judith (Grisham). They moved to Itawamba County and are both buried at Mt. Pleasant Cemetery near Fulton.

Mary Bonna (Houston) Lyle's parents were Samuel McIntosh "Troop" Houston (b. Aug. 6, 1830, buried at Kirkville Cemetery, Lee County) married America Jane (Underwood), buried at Kirkville Cemetery, Lee County. Samuel McIntosh "Troop" Houston served in Civil War, Co. F, 32nd MS Infantry CSA.

James Edgar "Ed" Pike, 1882-1941 and Julia (Lyle) Pike, 1889-1931

James Edgar and Julia Lyle Pike had six children: Randyle Lyle (b. Dec. 30, 1907, Prentiss County, MS) married Virginia (Haskin), two children Donald and Virginia (Ginger). They divorced and he later married Neva (Dalton) Hamilton, one stepson, Billy Hamilton. Randyle and Neva reside in Kennwick, WA; James Wythel (b. Oct. 1, 1909, Prentiss County, MS, d. May 1970, buried in Castaic, CA) married Louise LaForge, one son, Douglas. They divorced and he later married Mary Fay Gahagan, five sons: Nicky, Billy, Tom, Eddie and David; Absolom Keith (b. Sep. 29, 1911, Prentiss County, MS, d. Apr. 15, 1983, Castaic, CA buried in Holley Cemetery, Prentiss County, MS). Keith, as everyone called him, never married. He was a retired California State Agricultural Inspector and a veteran of WWII, serving in the US Navy; Julian Carey (b. Dec. 3, 1913, Prentiss County, MS) married Apr. 28, 1937 to Trana Aliena (Barker), daughter of William Eli and Miley Elizabeth (Tolleson) Barker. They have four children: Julia Elizabeth, Jerry Franklin, Martha Jean and Linda Aliena. Carey and Trana reside in the Tuscumbia Community, Prentiss County, MS; Martha Bonna (b. Apr. 13, 1916, Prentiss County, MS) married Apr. 28, 1934, Prentiss County, MS to Herman Franklin (Frank) Barker, son of William Eli and Miley Elizabeth (Tolleson) Barker. They have one daughter, Miley Jane. Martha and Frank lived in North Miami, FL until they retired. They then moved to Prentiss County to live close to their daughter. Frank died Jul. 15, 1993, Prentiss County, MS and was buried in the Booneville Cemetery, Prentiss County, MS and Rupert Edwin (b. May 18, 1920, Prentiss County, MS, d. Sep. 7, 1986, buried in the Booneville Cemetery, Prentiss County, MS) married Oct. 14, 1944 to Christine (Gooch), two children Brenda Sue and Jimmy Doyle.

Julia and James Edgar made their home in East Prentiss County. James Edgar was a farmer. Julia was a homemaker and art teacher. James Edgar and Julia moved to Lee County, MS, where James Edgar farmed and Julia taught art. The home they lived in while in Lee County is now listed on the National Registry of Homes as the oldest home in Lee County. Julia died while they were living in Lee County. James Edgar moved back to Prentiss County after her death. *Submitted by Martha Bonna (Pike) Barker.*

PIKE, CEPHAS JASPER AND MARTHA JANE HOLLEY, were married Nov. 2, 1876, Prentiss County, MS. Cephas Jasper (b. Sep. 7, 1852, Tishomingo County, MS, d. Dec. 2, 1943, Prentiss County, MS) parents were James Tilford and Mary Jane (Vawter) Pike.

Mary Jane (b. Dec. 5, 1857, Tishomingo County, MS, d. May 19, 1885, Prentiss County, MS) parents were Absolom Jackson "Jape" Holley (b. Mar. 13, 1822 in North Carolina, d. Feb. 1, 1913) and Mary Jane (Rogers) Holley (b. Jan. 28, 1836, Tennessee, d. Mar. 21, 1904). Absolom and Mary Jane were married Jan. 6, 1850. They are buried in the Holley Cemetery, Prentiss County, MS.

Cephus J. Pike Family, Front Row: L-R Matilia (Sims), Gladys, Cephus. 2nd Row: L-R Clovis, Olen, Kate, Clyde. 3rd Row: L-R Henry, June, Nick, James "Ed", Julia (Lyle) Pike, Tilford, Edna.

Absolom Jackson "Jape" Holley's parents were Julius Holley (b. 1796, d. 1857) and Sarah B. (Horten) Holley (b. 1796, d. 1877).

Mary Jane (Rogers) Holley's parents were James Zimri Rogers (b. Mar. 15, 1807, Kentucky, d. Jun. 5, 1869, Tishomingo County, MS) and Amy (Davis) (b. Dec. 23, 1811, Tennessee, d. Mar. 1844, Tishomingo County, MS) were married May 24, 1827, Tennessee. James Zimri was a Mason and member of the Marietta, Prentiss County, MS Lodge.

Cephas Jasper and Martha Jane lived in east Prentiss County. He was a farmer and Martha Jane was a housewife. Their children were: Ena B. (b. Sep. 23, 1877, d. Feb. 20, 1943, buried at New Hope Cemetery, Prentiss County, MS) married Mar. 7, 1909 to Jo Mitch Riddle; Tilford J. "Tif," (b. Jul. 31, 1880, d. Feb. 20, 1956, buried at Holley Cemetery, Prentiss County, MS) married Nov. 8, 1906 to Annie (Pounds); James Edgar "Ed," (b. Mar. 29, 1882, d. Apr. 12, 1941, buried at Holley Cemetery, Prentiss County, MS) married Dec. 24, 1906 to Julia (Lyle); Nick Franklin (b. Aug. 11, 1884, d. Mar. 27, 1922, buried at Evergreen Cemetery, Harris County, TX).

After Mary Jane's death, Cephas Jasper married Mathilda Ann (Sims) Jan. 5, 1886. She was the daughter of Henry J. and Nancy L. (Johnson) Sims. Cephas and Mathilda had eight children all born in Prentiss County, MS: Cephas Pinckney (b. Nov. 22, 1886, d. Feb. 2, 1888, buried at Holley Cemetery, Prentiss County, MS); Henry Harrison (b. Nov. 7, 1888, d. Jul. 11, 1974, buried at Rosewood Cemetery, Harris County, Houston, TX) married Jan. 12, 1910 to Peachie Arlevia (Finch); Julia Murl (June) (b. Apr. 14, 1891, d. Nov. 27, 1963, buried in Vicksburg, MS) married to Jack Taylor; Clovis Cleveland (b. Mar. 5, 1895, d. Nov. 20, 1946, buried at Holley Cemetery, Prentiss County, MS); Olen Blanchard (b. Mar. 19, 1895, d. Aug. 16, 1973, buried in McComb, MS) married to Ester (Hare). Ester died and Olen remarried Ruby (Grisham); Katie Lou (b. Feb. 23, 1897) married to Elton Hare; Clyde William (b. Sep. 1, 1899, d. Dec. 10, 1972, buried at Jackson, MS) married to Helen; Gladys Goldia (b. Jul. 20, 1902) married to Paul Ballard of Tupelo, MS. *Submitted by Jerry Pike.*

PIKE, JULIAN CAREY AND TRANA ALIENA BARKER, Julian Carey Pike, son of James Edgar "Ed" and Julia (Lyle) was born Dec. 3, 1913, Prentiss County, MS, married Apr. 28, 1937, Alcorn County, MS to Trana Aliena (Barker), daughter of William Eli and Miley Elizabeth (Tolleson) Barker.

Julian Carey and Trana Aliena (Barker) Pike

Trana and Carey resided in Corinth, MS where they owned and operated a small cafe for one year. They later moved to Prentiss County where they purchased a farm. They were active members of the community. The community where they live is called the Smith Chapel Community, named after the Smith Chapel Church, in which the land to build the church was donated by Carey and Trana.

Trana finished school as the Salutatorian, Class of 1935 of Burton High School, Prentiss County, MS. She worked for 30 years at Prentiss Manufacturing Co.

Carey and Trana have four children: Julia Elizabeth (b. Jul. 30, 1938) married Mar. 9, 1956 to L.Q.

Mathis; Elizabeth and L.Q. have one daughter, Lana Quinn (b. Jul. 29, 1959) married May 22, 1976 to Mark Duncan Tapp. Lana and Mark have two children, Shannon Elizabeth (b. Sep. 9, 1977) and Justin Mark (b. Jan. 10, 1981). Jerry Franklin (b. Apr. 4, 1944) married Barbara Gail (Thorne). Jerry and Barbara have two daughters, Maria Lynn (b. Feb. 6, 1968) married Jun. 4, 1995 to Peter Malatesta. Maria and Pete have two sons William Peter (b. Aug. 9, 1996) and Benjamin Julian (b. Mar. 18, 1998); Jeania Gail (b. Jun. 27, 1971) married Jan. 12, 1997 to Bryan Alan McCutchen.

Martha Jean (b. Jan. 11, 1949) married Sep. 6, 1967 to E.G. Lindsey. They have three sons: Jeffrey Martin (b. Apr. 26, 1968) married Dec. 28, 1991 to Mary Meloney (Green). Jeff and Meloney have one daughter, Madelyn Kate (b. May 5, 1997); Eric Glen (b. Jan. 26, 1971) married to Kristie Elizabeth (George). Eric and Kristie have one son, Ethan George (b. Feb. 5, 1997); Scotty Goodwin (b. May 26, 1972) married Jul. 29, 1995 to Kimberly Sue (Cole). Scotty and Kim have one daughter, Madison Paige (b. Jul. 12, 1997).

Linda Aliena (b. Jul. 30, 1952) married Apr. 16, 1971 to Charles Bruce Martin. Children, Kimberly Aliena (b. Oct. 8, 1973) married Mar. 6, 1999 to Christopher Gerald Evans; Carey Bruce (b. Jan. 28, 1979). *Submitted by Scotty Lindsey, 501 East Skyline Drive, Booneville, MS 38829.*

PIERCE, ALBERT LEVI, on Jun. 23, 1907 Albert Levi Pierce (b. Dec. 7, 1888, d. Jun. 15, 1974) and Martha America Mayo Pierce (b. Jun. 2 1889, d. Dec. 15, 1972) were wed. On Sep. 29, 1924 they gave birth to Quindel Pierce.

On Sep. 23, 1916 William Marcus Lambert (b. Mar. 8, 1855, d. May 2, 1932) and Pearl Jeanette Kitty (b. Jul. 18, 1882, d. Jun. 2, 1944) were wed. On Dec. 12, 1927 they gave birth to Dillard Fay Lambert.

Quindel and Dillard Fay were wed Jun. 5, 1943 in New Site, MS on the front porch of Rev. George Pardon (Uncle Pardon) Mayo.

Almost immediately Quindel was drafted to serve in the US Army during WWII and left for boot camp in September 1943. He saw action in Germany and Austria and was discharged in 1945. On Mar. 13, 1950 Janice Marie Pierce was born and on Sep. 25, 1959 Timothy Guy Pierce joined the family. Both children were born at the Northeast Mississippi Hospital in Booneville, MS.

Quindel worked at Firestone in Booneville from 1951-1963 at which time he became a Whirlpool appliance dealer until he retired in 1990. Fay has worked in the home as homemaker, wife and mother since the birth of Janice Marie.

On Mar. 25, 1977 Julie Deanna Nicholson was born to Janice Pierce Nicholson and Sidney Newman Nicholson.

In 1982 Jenna Lee Tigrett was born to Janice Pierce Tigrett and Kenneth Darrell Tigrett (b. Mar. 17, 1946) on September 11. Four years later Joey Pierce Tigrett came into the world on Aug. 1, 1986.

Shortly before Easter 1996 the family welcomed the first grandchild, Katlyn Elizabeth Nicholson on Apr. 2.

On May 16, 1999 Quindel passed away leaving behind a loving family and many dear friends.

At present all members of this Pierce family reside in Booneville, MS.

PIKE, JAMES TILFRED, born Sep. 12, 1819 in Tennessee to John Pike (b. 1796, d. 1873) and Mary Choat (b. 1803). His mother was the daughter of Volentine and Dosha Choat. James lived for a while in Alabama before moving to Tishomingo County, MS, where he got a job with John Vauter. He married John's daughter, Mary Jane (b. May 6, 1823) on Nov. 12, 1841, Old Tishomingo County, (present day Prentiss County). They had John H. (b. Aug. 15, 1842), who married Mollie Greenhill, Alfred B. (b. May 6, 1842), Julianne Francis (b. Feb. 29, 1848), David N. (b. Mar. 7, 1850), Cephas Jasper (b. Sep. 7, 1852), Mary Jane (b. Jan. 31, 1856), who married W.S. George and James Tilfred (b. Nov. 14, 1858). Mary died Mar. 30, 1870 and James Tilfred moved to Texas for a brief time before returning to Mississippi. He died Oct. 9, 1887.

Ceafus Pike became a farmer and lived near Holley Cemetery in Prentiss County. He married Mary Jane Holley (b. Dec. 5, 1857, d. Feb. 19, 1885), the daughter of Absalom J. Holley (b. 1822, d. 1913) and Mary Jane Rogers (b. 1836, d. 1904). They had four children: Roena Belle (b. Aug. 23, 1877, d. 1943), who married Joe Mitch Riddle, Tilford J. "Tiff" Pike (b. Jul. 31, 1879, d. Feb. 26, 1956), who married Annie Pounds, James Edgar "Edd" Pike (b. Mar. 27, 1882, d. Apr. 12, 1941), who married Julia Lyle and Nixon F. Pike (b. Aug. 11, 1884). Mary Jane died when Nick was 9-months-old and Ceafus married Matilda Sims. They had eight children.

James Tilfred Pike

Edd Pike married Julia Lyle (b. Jul. 22, 1889, d. Apr. 21, 1931) in Prentiss County on Dec. 24, 1906. Julia was the daughter of William Franklin Lyle (b. Nov. 5, 1856, d. Feb. 8, 1931) and Bonna Houston (b. Nov. 20, 1865, d. Jun. 28, 1899). Edd and Julia had Randyl Lyle (b. Dec. 31, 1907), who married Virginia Hasken and Neva Dalton; James Wythel (b. Oct. 2, 1909, d. Apr. 15, 1985), who married Mary Faye Gahagan; Absalom Keith (b. Sep. 29, 1911, d. 1971), who never married; Julian Carey (b. Dec. 3, 1913), who married Trana Barker; Martha Bonna (b. April 1916), who married Frank Barker and Rupert Edwin.

Rupert was born May 18, 1920 and married Christine Gooch (b. Jul. 23, 1926) on Oct. 14, 1944. Christine was the daughter of Lucian and Ora D. Gooch. Rupert was a painter by trade, which included both houses and cars. He played the harmonica for entertainment. He died Sep. 7, 1986. To Rupert and Christine were born Brenda Sue (b. Jul. 18, 1945) and Jimmy Doyle (b. Jan. 18, 1955), who married Carolyn Harper and had Justin and Alexandra. Brenda married Derryl Anthony Scott (b. Mar. 12, 1941) on Oct. 29, 1965. Derryl is the son of Leroy and Erin Scott. Brenda and Derryl "Pete" had Kelley Michelle (b. May 26, 1966) and Sabrina Svetlana (b. Dec. 4, 1970). Brenda is a teacher with the Booneville School District and still lives in Booneville. Kelley married Nathan Baldwin (b. Jun. 9, 1964). Alexandria Michelle Baldwin was born Feb. 10, 1999. *Submitted by Brenda Pike Scott.*

PINSON, WALLACE WEAVER, born Mar. 19, 1889 and died Mar. 31, 1968, lived in the Cairo Community of Prentiss County. He was the youngest of four children born to John David Pinson (b. January 1852, d. Mar. 20, 1931) and Laura Hagan Pinson (b. January 1855, d. Feb. 01, 1901). His siblings were Alice Pinson (b. 1877), Martha J. Pinson (b. March 1881) and James Alvin Pinson (b. Oct. 29, 1882).

Wallace and Bertie Wright Pinson

John and Laura Pinson were married in 1873. They were buried in New Hope Cemetery.

As a young man, Wallace helped John in the logging business. On Dec. 12, 1912, he married Bertie Wright (b. Jan. 23, 1895, d. Jun. 6, 1960) of the Forked Oak Community. Bertie was the daughter of Bill Wright (b. Jan. 2, 1862, d. Sep. 5, 1905) and Sallie Claunch Wright (b. Feb. 14, 1866, d. Feb. 27, 1932). They were buried in Forked Oak Cemetery.

Wallace and Bertie were the parents of Irene Pinson Umfress (b. Jan. 28, 1917, d. Jun. 30, 1991), who lived in Pontotoc, MS; Edith Pinson Jourdon (b. Jan. 16, 1919) of Iuka, MS; Oliver Wendell Pinson (b. Aug. 15, 1921, d. May 4, 1945) who died aboard the USS *Little* during WWII; James Waymon Pinson (b. Dec. 7, 1930, d. Feb. 2, 1956), who lived in Valdosta, GA and died in a truck accident and Syble Pinson Mitchell (b. May 20, 1932), who lives in Kenosha, WI.

Wallace and Bertie spent their lives on the farm at Cairo. He grew vegetables, fruit, corn, poultry and cattle. Wallace enjoyed squirrel hunting and attending all day singings. Bertie busied herself keeping the family fed and clothed. She was a seamstress and sewed many quilts.

Wallace and Bertie joined New Lebanon Freewill Baptist Church in 1928. They are buried in the cemetery there near Wendell, Waymon, Irene, Syble's husband, Robert Mitchell and Edith's husband, Almous Jourdon. *Submitted by Harrol W. Umfress.*

POLLARD, JOHN W., born Jan. 7, 1801, Greenville County, SC married Barbara Stone on Mar. 25, 1822. She was born Dec. 1, 1802 in Pickens County, AL.

They had 13 children:
1) Luallin G. (b. Mar. 17, 1823);
2) Mary Jane Pollard (b. Jul. 25, 1824);
3) Casper Parham (b. Mar. 27, 1826);
4) A. Datia Nash (b. Oct. 23, 1832);
5) Nancy (b. Mar. 15, 1829);
6) Lattamore (b. May 21, 1831);
7) John R. (b. Oct. 23, 1832) md. Malinda Hamby. He joined the Confederacy and was killed at the Battle of Chickamauga;
8) Margaret C. (b. May 22, 1834;
9) Barbara (b. Dec. 27, 1836 in South Carolina) md. Henry Stokes and lived in Pickens County, AL before moving to Prentiss County. They had four children: Rosa Ann, Wiley Henry "Bud," Artie Bell and Dora Alice. Barbara Ann Pollard Stokes died Oct. 29, 1914 and is buried at Mt. Pleasant Cemetery.
10) Mariah Harrison Pollard (b. May 23, _, d. May 19, 1841);
11) Emily Pollard (b. Dec. 2, 1841);
12) Wiley Pollard (b. Jul. 18, 1845) md. Nancy Ellen Burcham Jan. 11, 1903 in Prentiss County, MS. They had five children: Marcus Browning (b. Nov. 2, 1903); Charley Lattimore (b. Nov. 14, 1905); Barbara Luvada (b. Dec. 31, 1907); Odell Auren (b. Sep. 12, 1910); Julius Andrew (b. Oct. 5, 1913). Wiley Baxter Pollard died Sep. 22, 1922 and is buried at Mt. Pleasant Cemetery.
13) Mariah Harrison.

Army of Confederate States Certificate of Disability for Discharge: Pvt. John W. Pollard, Co. F, 2nd Bn., AL of Capt. Lumsden's Artillery of the Jones Legion Regt. of Confederate States was enlisted by Lt. Vaughn of the regiment at Columbus, MS on Dec. 16, 1861 to serve three years. He was born in Greenville District in the state of South Carolina, is 62 years of age, 5'10" high, dark complexion, gray eyes, gray hair and by occupation when enlisted a carpenter. During the last two months said soldier has been unfit for duty 60 days. Station: Knoxville. Date: Nov. 21, 1862. I certify that I have carefully examined the said John W. Pollard of Capt. Lumsden's Co. and find him incapable of performing the duties of a soldier because of general ability and old age. Frank Ramsey, post surgeon, M.C. Young, act surgeon,

Medical Board Examination. Discharged Nov. 21, 1862 at Knoxville, TN. John E. Toole, commanding the post.

John W. Pollard died Jun. 23, 1865. Barbara Pollard died Sep. 4, 1860.

Most of the information above was given to me by Steve Taylor who was so kind to share this wealth of his many years of research. *Submitted by Sandra Lewis Gray.*

POUNDS, JAMES ELBERT JR., born Oct. 23, 1886 and died Dec. 29, 1969, son of James Elbert Pounds Sr. (b. Oct. 25, 1857, d. Feb. 6, 1924) and Martha Thornton Pounds (b. Jun. 17, 1864, d. Jul. 15, 1937), was the third of 12 children. He was reared in Prentiss County, MS, west of New Hope Primitive Baptist Church and New Hope School. On Mar. 20, 1913, he married Arrie Smith (b. Aug. 9, 1891, d. Apr. 19, 1979). She was also from the New Hope Community, the daughter of Walter Pierce Smith (b. Sep. 12, 1855, d. Apr. 4, 1922) and Willie Ann Bullard Smith (b. Oct. 24, 1862, d. Jan. 27, 1948). He taught school for two years. Preferring the life of a farmer in 1920 he and Arrie bought a home and farm just south of New Hope School.

Elbert and Arrie were interested in the welfare of the school children and the people of the community. Both believed every child should have a chance for an education. Elbert was trustee of New Hope School a number of years. Arrie was the person to whom children were sent in case of minor accidents or illness. For example, a child fell into a ditch and she wrapped him in blankets and dried his clothes before a wood burning fireplace. He then returned to school.

Elbert worked with others from the school districts of Burton, New Hope and Hills Chapel in establishing Burton High School for the students of those districts. Later, after all his children had gone to college, he was instrumental in the establishment of Northeast Mississippi Junior College at Booneville, MS. He was a member of the first board of trustees of the college.

Elbert and Arrie had five children:

1. Elbert Smith Pounds (b. Nov. 11, 1914) earned a degree from Mississippi State University and taught mathematics near Jackson, MS. There he met and married Marguerite Alford of Jackson, also a teacher. Smith served in WWII in the finance department of the Army. After the war, he returned to Jackson and worked for the Veterans Administration. After retirement, they continue to live in Jackson.

2. Dorris Dean Pounds (b. Jun. 3, 1916, d. Jul. 16, 1996) graduated from Blue Mountain College in Blue Mountain, MS. She taught English, shorthand and typing in Mississippi and worked in Memphis, TN as a secretary. Wishing to learn of other sections of the US, she taught in Nevada, Oregon and Taos, NM. There she met and married Jack Boyer of Taos. She lived there until her death. She and Jack had two children, Jeffery Lynn Boyer (b. October 1955) and Sheryl Yvonne Boyer. Jeff has a MA degree in archaeology and is an archaeologist for the state of New Mexico. He married Ginger Nolan. They live in Taos, NM and have two children, Meghann Boyer and Miles Boyer. Sheryl, loved by all the Pounds family, died at age 29.

3. Norma Rhea Pounds (b. Aug. 29, 1920) graduated from Blue Mountain College in Blue Mountain, MS. She taught mathematics in Mississippi and Germantown, TN. On Jun. 12, 1948, she married Milford Umfress, also from Prentiss County, MS, but working in Memphis, TN. They continue to live in Memphis and have two daughters, Marilyn Rhea Umfress (b. Aug. 30, 1953) and Sandra Jean Umfress (b. May 28, 1956). Marilyn graduated from Memphis State University and earned a MA degree in library science from George Peabody College in Nashville, TN. She is a librarian in the Memphis/Shelby County Public Library System. Sandra earned a BA from Memphis State University. After graduation she worked as a computer software consultant. On May 14, 1983, she married Stephen Atkerson of Smyrna, GA and now lives in Atlanta, GA. They have three children: Eden Michelle Atkerson (b. Sep. 19, 1988), Nathaniel Everette Atkerson (b. Dec. 2, 1991) and Matthew Stephen Atkerson (b. May 25, 1993).

4. Willie Pierce Pounds (b. Jul. 9, 1923, d. Aug. 17, 1983) served in the artillery branch of the Army in WWII. He fought under General Patton in the Battle of the Bulge and was in Czechoslovakia when the war ended. Willie returned home and graduated from Mississippi State University. After graduation he was employed by Delta Air Lines and lived in Jackson, MS at the time of his death.

5. M. Yvonne Pounds (b. Dec. 13, 1925) graduated a registered nurse from Kings Daughters Hospital. She worked in Jackson, MS as a nurse and joined the Air Force Nurse Corps in 1955. In 1971 she married William Dougherty. Lt. Col. Yvonne Dougherty retired from the Air Force in 1975. At the time of her retirement, she and her husband lived in Biloxi, MS. After retiring she obtained a BS degree from William Carey College in Biloxi, MS. She continues to live in Biloxi.

Elbert and Arrie loved their home and community and continued to live there until their deaths. They are buried in New Hope Cemetery. *Submitted by Norma Pounds Umfress.*

REYNOLDS, MERIDETH B., born in 1835 in North Carolina according to the 1860 Tishomingo County census. He married Matilda Elizabeth Duncan on Mar. 28, 1861. He enlisted in the War Between the States in May 1861, served in Co. E, 42nd Inf. Regt. under the command of Col. Davenport. This regiment would be one of the many combined to number 15,000 men under the command of Confederate Gen. George E. Pickett. Forming a line one and a half mile long and engaging in the bloodiest battle of the war known as "Pickett's Charge" on Jul. 3, 1863 in Gettysburg. On Jul. 2, 1863 Pvt. Merideth B. Reynolds was wounded by grape shot and taken to a doctor. His left arm was amputated and he was dismissed and never heard from again. It is believed that while trying to make the trip back home to Mississippi in the July heat, infection set up in the wound and proved to be too much for Pvt. Merideth Reynolds to bear.

Pvt. Merideth B. Reynolds, Co. E, 42nd Inf. Regt., Mississippi CSA

Martha Elizabeth Reynolds (b. Feb. 21, 1862) was his only child. At the young age of 23, Matilda Elizabeth Duncan Reynolds found herself a widow with a child to support.

Matilda's parents, Charles Riley Duncan (b. Mar. 24, 1805 in South Carolina) and Elizabeth R. Garner Duncan (b. Feb. 21, 1817 in South Carolina) welcomed Matilda and Martha Elizabeth "Mattie" into their home. They had nine children other than Matilda.

Matilda Elizabeth Duncan Reynolds at 39 years of age married Thomas Smith (b. Mar. 28, 1813). He was 27 years her senior and had 13 children. He had two more children with Matilda. A second daughter, Georgia Thomas Smith (b. Jan. 26, 1880) md. John William Davis and a third child, a son, Taylor "Bulb" Smith (b. Jul. 3, 1882) md. Anne Lenore "Nora" Daniel.

Martha Elizabeth Reynolds and Walker Smith (b. Oct. 27, 1856) md. Feb. 5, 1882. Walker was a farmer and road foreman. Walker Smith died Sep. 23, 1894. Martha Elizabeth was left with extensive land holdings. Her second marriage was to Jasper Lee Hopkins on Dec. 11, 1898.

Martha Elizabeth Reynolds had 10 children (six by Walker and four by Jasper). They were: Susan Elizabeth Smith, Thomas Merideth Smith, Florence Smith, Rosie Leona Smith, Joe Taylor Smith, Baxter Evan Smith, Noonon Orlando Hopkins, Jasper Van Hopkins, Dewey Wister Hopkins and Arthur Dayton Hopkins.

Martha Elizabeth "Mattie" Reynolds Smith Hopkins died with tuberculosis on May 20, 1923. She is buried at Smith Chapel Cemetery by her first husband, Walker Smith. Matilda Elizabeth Duncan Reynolds Smith died of a massive heart attack in 1919 and is buried at Smith Chapel Cemetery beside her second husband, Thomas Smith.

After much research by great-grandson Ovid Hopkins, a Civil War monument was placed at Smith Chapel in memory of Pvt. Merideth Reynolds by great-great-granddaughter Sandra Lewis Gray, who also submitted this history.

RHOADS, HUMBERT CLYDE, born Nov. 27, 1912 to William Joshua Rhoads (b. Nov. 24, 1879, d. Jul. 30, 1954) and Launa Maggie Crouch (b. Oct. 15, 1883, d. Jul. 27, 1940), the daughter of William M. Crouch (b. Apr. 1, 1836, d. 1914) and Sarah "Sallie" Powers (b. Dec. 1, 1844, d. 1918).

William M. Crouch was the son of John Crouch (b. Jan 1, 1814) and Polly (unknown) Crouch (b. Jan. 1, 1814). William enlisted in the 1st Alabama Infantry, CSA and was wounded at Greensboro, NC.

William Joshua Rhoads, son of William A. Rhoads (b. 1852) and Sarah J. Gahagan (b. 1862), served two terms as justice of the peace in Prentiss County, MS. He also served as a county supervisor and had a record number of roads graveled and improved during his term in office. William A. Rhoads was the son of Pleasant Rhoads (b. 1826) and Amy G. (unknown) Rhoads (b. 1833). Sarah J. Gahagan was the daughter of Francis M. Gahagan (b. Jan. 1, 1838) and Amanda Pettit (b. Feb. 22, 1846, d. Feb. 13, 1936), the daughter of Joshua Pettit III (b. 1802) and Mary (unknown) Pettit (b. 1805). Francis M. Gahagan enlisted in the 26th Mississippi Infantry, CSA and was captured at Fort Donelson along with two brothers-in-law, Benjamin and Nathan Pettit on Feb. 16, 1862. He died a prisoner of war at Camp Morton, Indianapolis, IN.

On Nov. 28, 1929, Humbert Clyde Rhoads married Eula Mae Stockton (b. May 29, 1912, d. Oct. 27, 1995), daughter of Samuel C. Stockton (b. Jul. 31, 1888, d. Sep 15, 1971) and Lena Bell Isbell (b. Sep 29, 1893, d. May 13, 1973), daughter of George W. Isbell (b. Feb. 18, 1857, d. Dec. 2, 1937) and Sally (Sarah) Jennifer Johnson (b. Oct. 10, 1867, d. Oct. 7, 1942). Sally Johnson was the daughter of Thomas Jefferson Johnson (b. Oct. 11, 1844, d. Mar 17, 1907) and Mary Jane Wroten (b. Oct. 8, 1847, d. Apr. 23, 1940). Thomas J. Johnson was the son of Samuel J. Johnson (b. 1817, d. 1861) and Margaret Jane Carroll (b. 1823, d. 1901). Thomas Jefferson Johnson served in the 32nd Mississippi Regiment, CSA. Eula Mae Stockton was a first cousin five times removed to Richard Stockton, who was a signer of the Declaration of Independence. His grandfather, also Richard Stockton, purchased 6,000 acres from William Penn which is now Princeton, NJ. Samuel C. Stockton was the son of Josephus Stockton (b. Jun. 25, 1845, d. Feb. 19, 1910) and his second wife, Tennessee "Tennie" Vance (b. Sep 25, 1860). Josephus Stockton was a Civil War veteran. He enlisted in the 2nd Mississippi Infantry at Jacinto, MS. After the war Josephus was a Missionary Baptist minister. When Josephus died in 1910 he still carried a minie ball in his leg, a souvenir of his service for the Confederacy.

Humbert Clyde Rhoads and Eula Mae Stockton Rhoads had four daughters, Sammie Clydean Rhoads (Garvin), born Sep 12, 1930 in Chicago, IL; Peggy Joann Rhoads (Chase) born Oct. 27, 1934 in Prentiss County, MS; Rita Kay Rhoads (Doktor) born Jul. 22,

1943 in Prentiss County; Patricia Diane Rhoads (Shannon) born Feb. 23, 1952 in Prentiss County and one son, Charles "Charlie" Humbert Rhoads born Oct. 3, 1939 in Prentiss County.

RICKS FAMILY, the Ricks families of Prentiss County can trace their ancestry to Jonas (b. 1734, d. 1821) and Gwyn Ricks, Quakers of Rowan County, NC. Jonas was a blacksmith, cooper and farmer. It is believed that they had eight children, one of whom was Edward, born Aug. 4, 1769.

John Benton Ricks

Edward married Jane Mendenhall in Guilford County, NC in 1792. They had six children, including John, born Jul. 4, 1798.

John married Massey Robbins in 1819. They moved to Alabama about 1825. Six of their eight children moved into Mississippi to Pontotoc and Itawamba Counties. Ransom and wife, Nancy Gilliland Ricks, were the first to arrive, followed by Edward with his mother and sisters, Leah and Pheba. Ruben and Nathan also came. Eventually, they all resided in present day Prentiss County. Ransom and Nancy's children were Andrew, Mary, Lucinda, Martha, Sarah, John, James, Margaret and Harvey.

On Jan. 13, 1853, Edward (the younger) married Rebecca Anne Pratt, daughter of Jonathan and Susannah Pratt, who lived east of Baldwyn. They had nine years of marriage and five children: John Benton (b. 1854, d. 1947), Carroll Clayton (b. 1856, d. 1941), Aaron Dean (b. 1857, d. 1946), Parthena Frances "Fannie" (b. 1858, d. 1934) and Ed B. (b. 1861, d. unknown).

Edward enlisted in the 19th Mississippi Infantry, Co. K, nicknamed the Baldwyn Rifles, on Feb. 17, 1862. He was killed at the Battle of Antietam at Sharpsburg, MD, on Sep. 17, 1862, the single bloodiest day in American military history. His brother, Ransom, was captured on Aug. 17, 1863, only a few miles from his home. He was sent to a prison in Alton, IL and from there to Fort Delaware, Delaware. He was released on Jun. 7, 1865 and is believed to have made it back to Mississippi where he soon died and was buried in a cemetery, now abandoned, at Carrollville.

About five years after Edward was killed, Rebecca married Abner Ausborn Jones. In the late 1800s, they joined the migration of Mississippians to Texas. Also moving were Carrol, Ed and Fannie Ricks Boren and the Jones children, Ab and Kindness. John and Aaron Ricks and Abner's son, Will Jones, remained in Prentiss County.

Aaron married Sina Downing. Their children were Westley, Walter, Dennah, Emma and Grady.

John married Sarah Anne "Sallie" Vinson on Dec. 30, 1877. Her parents were John H. Vinson and Naomi H.S. Long. John and Sallie had five sons named after Primitive Baptist preachers: Julius Berry, Oscar Orlando, Abner Morris, Talbert Dalton and Roscoe Phillip. Jessie Parthenia was their only daughter.

Julius (b. 1878, d. 1972) married Allie Glover. Children: Roxie Avo, Ruby Benton Floyd, Eddie Clarence, Clara Vinson, Luther Lloyd, Mary Blanche, Bertie Dean, stillborn boy and Ora Mae.

Oscar (b. 1880, d. 1976) married Matilda Modena Miller. Children: Sadie, Leonard, Bessie Mae, Helen and Gladys Hale.

Jessie (b. 1882, d. 1904) married Dan Ryan. Their child: Guy Ryan.

Abner (Ab) (b. 1884, d. 1946) married Ivy Hardy. Children: Gordon, Annabell Lee, Aileen, infant son and Alton.

Talbert (Tab) (b. 1887, d. 1978) married Della Hooper. Children: Bolivar, Alan, Holbert, Virginia and Vergie Mae.

Roscoe (Rock) (b. 1890, d. 1984) married Lois Ray. Children: Lillian, John Ray and Arlis. *Submitted by Jo Carolyn Anderson Beebe, 645 Hickory Hill, Hiawassee, GA 30546. (706) 896-6290*

RINEHART, CLIFFORD PALMER, born Mar. 7, 1907, died Aug. 19, 1983, son of Thomas Wister and Nettie Belle (Palmer) Rinehart. Married on Aug. 7, 1927 to Vista Lee Armstrong (b. Nov. 4, 1910, d. Oct. 18, 1993), daughter of George W. and Nancy Maudre (McCutcheon) Armstrong. They lived in the Jacinto Community in Alcorn County, MS where they reared four children: Zelma, Loyd, Laverne and Jo Ann.

Clifford was ordained as a minister of the Primitive Baptist religion at Sardis Primitive Baptist Church (east of Rienzi) in 1941. He was pastor of several churches during his ministry: Sardis, New Providence, Hopewell, Little Flock, Mt. Herman and Little Hatchie.

Elder Clifford Palmer and Vista Armstrong Rinehart on their 50th Anniversary

In addition to the ministry, Clifford also taught school at Snowdown, Juliette, Hickory Flat and Jacinto schools. Clifford and Vista owned a general store in Jacinto during the 1940s and 1950s. During the late 1950s and 1960s, Clifford sold Watkins products in Alcorn County. He served as a member of the Alcorn County Draft Board for a number of years. In his latter years, he was site director for the Jacinto Senior Citizens Center. Vista helped him by serving meals, quilting with the ladies quilting group and joining in the group's activities. They loved being a part of the community and being able to see their friends on a daily basis.

Vista was an excellent cook who was noted for her special chocolate cakes. She was the manager of the Jacinto School cafeteria for several years. Her children and grandchildren have many cherished memories of the fabulous meals she prepared.

Clifford's heritage in Alcorn County began with Elias Rinehart, who was one of the first settlers of Jacinto. He and his brothers moved to Mississippi from South Carolina, they purchased 4,000 acres of land in the Tishomingo County area, which now consists of Alcorn, Prentiss and Tishomingo countries. Elias was one of the founders of Jacinto. He also donated the land for Sardis Primitive Baptist Church and the adjoining cemetery. He helped organize Sardis Church and was a deacon there. He had a son, Lorenza Dowd Rinehart who married Caroline Branstrutter in 1841. Clifford's paternal grandparents were Sanford Sylvester and Mary Jane Parker Rinehart. His maternal grandparents were Elijah and Haley (Farris) Palmer. Clifford had the following brothers and sisters: Roy, Ralph, KV, Dora, Flora, Verona, Ollie, Audrey Mae, Alice and Evelyn who died at the age of 17.

Vista's parents, George Washington and Nancy Maudre Armstrong had seven other children: Archie, Carlos, Artie, Ila, Hester, Eunice and Iness (twins). After Maudre's death, George married Dora Clark. They had four children: Warren, Glen, Allen and Cleatus. Vista had a step-sister, Nancy Wren and step-brother Noel Wren. Her paternal grandparents were Mary Jane (Goodwin) Armstrong an Charlie Armstrong. Her maternal grandparents were Robert and Catherine McCutcheon. *Submitted by Zelma Rinehart Brimingham.*

RINEHART, EVELYN, daughter of Thomas Wister and Nettie Palmer Rinehart, died at the age of 17 with a growth behind her eye. She attended Rienzi High School and had a great personality.

Our grandmother Rinehart said many times she would go to the foot of the stairs to tell her to come down and remember her death. *Submitted by Zelma Brimingham*

RINEHART, LEONARD PALMER, born Jan. 31, 1912 the son of Frank Sylvester Rinehart, born Aug. 12, 1872 and Margaret Francis (Fanny) Green, born Jun. 20, 1883. Frank and Fanny were married on Jul. 28, 1901 in Tippah County. Frank was a farmer. He and Fanny lived in the Dry Creek Community near the Prentiss and Tippah County line when Leonard was born. Leonard's siblings were Jessie (half-brother), Ellie, George, Harrison, Tom, Pearl and Charles (Jack). Frank died Apr. 10, 1948 and Fanny died Feb. 14, 1966. They are buried in the Sardis Cemetery east of Rienzi.

Leonard Palmer and Pauline McCoy Rinehart

Earnest Pauline McCoy born Sep. 21, 1915 daughter of Joel William McCoy, born Jan. 4, 1889 and Keziah Clementine Goddard, born Sep. 1, 1887. They were married in Prentiss County on Dec. 13, 1911. They lived in Prentiss County where Joel was a farmer. Pauline's siblings are John Thomas, Lavona Warerien, Mary Ophelia, Flora Rena and William Clyde (Billy). Joel died Jun. 21, 1963 and Keziah died May 22, 1948. They are buried in the Oak Hill Cemetery.

Leonard Rinehart and Pauline McCoy were married in Prentiss County on Dec. 30, 1936. Leonard like his father was a farmer. He planted mainly cotton, soybeans and corn. He would also have dairy cows and raise hogs to sell and for home use. In the winter of 1951, they lived on the Bill Cox Dairy Farm. During an ice storm that winter, they had to milk the cows by hand for about two weeks instead of using electric milkers. Leonard started out farming with only a mule or a horse, like so many other farmers did in the 1920s and 1930s. But as the years passed, he was able to buy large tractors and equipment to do his farming and soybean combines to harvest.

Leonard retired from farming around 1977. He then started raising and selling bantam chickens. He and Pauline enjoyed trips each month to First Monday Trade Day at Ripley, MS. While Leonard sold and traded his chickens, Pauline would enjoy looking for old glassware. Leonard had a disabling stroke in

March 1991. Leonard died Jul. 3, 1994 and was buried in the Booneville Cemetery on July the 4th.

Leonard and Pauline's children are: (1) Joel Sylvester (b. Feb. 11, 1949) married Wilda Jean Butler. Their children are Joel Wesley (b. Oct. 2, 1976) and Jessica Lauren (b. Nov. 13, 1983). (2) Henry Erastus (b. Oct. 26, 1953) married Sarah Joyce Culwell. Their children are Hank Shannon (b. Aug. 13, 1977) and Leigh Ellen (b. Oct. 2, 1982). (3) Janet Rena (b. Jul. 27, 1955) married Johnny Bonds Roy. Their children are Christina Rena (b. Nov. 22, 1986) and Sarah Marie (b. Jan. 7, 1990). *Submitted by Janet Roy.*

RINEHART, LOYD, son of Clifford Palmer and Vista Armstrong Rinehart, was born May 10, 1930 and died from cancer April 1999. He attended Jacinto School and Rienzi High School. He married Earline Lambert Rinehart on Jun. 19, 1950. Other than a few years of living near military bases while Loyd served in the Mississippi National Guard during the Korean Conflict, they have lived in Booneville, MS. He owned and operated Rinehart's Tire Store from 1970-1995. Loyd loved music and played the guitar. He made copies of tapes and gave many to his friends and relatives

Earline and Loyd have one son, Michael Loyd Rinehart and two grandchildren, Clifford Palmer and Anne Elise Rinehart. They live in Natchez, MS. Earline is the daughter of Mark and Nellie Kate Lauderdale Lambert.

The family lived in Tuscumbia Community of Prentiss County. Earline attended Tuscumbia School Booneville High School and Northeast Mississippi Community College. She was employed at Garment factories until a back injury prevented her from working. She still lives in Booneville. *Submitted by Earline Lambert Rinehart.*

RINEHART-NICHOLSON, Ollie Rinehart Nicholson, daughter of Thomas Wister and Nettie Palmer Rinehart, was born in March 1915 and died in April 1984 at Tupelo Hospital. She was married to Richard Nicholson. Their children were Nettie Lou and twin boys, Dwight and Dewey Nicholson.

Nettie Lou married Vernon Hughley. Their children are Venita who married Steve Wheeler and lives in Memphis; Richard, who also lives in Memphis and Leigh who married Curtis Winslow of Booneville. Dwight and Dewey live in Booneville. Nettie Lou's second marriage was to Thomas Harris and they lived in Booneville. She died in 1993 of a heart attack.

Children of Thomas Wister and Nettie Palmer Rinehart. Sitting L-R: Dora Rinehart Walden, Flora Rinehart Carpenter, Verona Rinehart Burcham, Audrey Rinehart Searcy and Ollie Rinehart Nicholson. Standing: Clifford Palmer Rinehart, Ralph Lomax Rinehart, Roy Sylvester Rinehart, James K. Vardaman Rinehart and Alice Rinehart Enis. Missing is Evelyn Rinehart, who died at 17 with a growth behind her eye.

Ollie was a beautician and owned a shop in Booneville for many years. Her sisters, Alice Enis and Audrey Searcy, were also beauticians and worked at Ollie's shop for a while.

Ollie was a member of Sardis Primitive Baptist Church. Her brother, Clifford Palmer Rinehart, was pastor for many years. Her parents and grandparents were members of this church. She is buried in Booneville Cemetery by the side of her husband. *Submitted by her niece, Zelma Brimingham.*

RINEHART, THOMAS WISTER, the first Rineharts to enter the US were from Germany. They settled in South Carolina. Elias Rinehart and family moved to the south for a warmer climate. Elias Rinehart (b. 1802 in Germany, d. 1876 in US) had 12 children. When he moved south, he bought 4,000 acres of land in Tishomingo County, MS, of which Jacinto was the county seat. He helped organize a bank in Jacinto. A builder, Elias built a levee across the Tuscumbia River and charged a toll until he was repaid. He furnished land for Sardis Primitive Baptist Church and cemetery. Elias and five generations of Rineharts are buried there. He was a deacon of the church. He wanted to give each child 320 acres of land and it was handed down through six generations.

Thomas Wister and Nettie Palmer Rinehart

Thomas Wister Rinehart was the fourth generation. His father, Sanders Sylvester Rinehart was the first of three generations of elders of Sardis Church. Second generation was Eugene Sylvester Rinehart, brother of Thomas Wister Rinehart. The third generation elder was Clifford Palmer Rinehart, son of Wister Rinehart. Clifford Rinehart's grandson, Gene Brimingham, is also an elder.

Elder Sanders Sylvester Rinehart died and left his land to his three sons: Eugene Sylvester, Thomas Wister and Lee Rinehart. Thomas Wister was a deacon of Sardis Church most of his life. He married Nettie Bell Palmer the first Sunday in November 1900 at the home of Elijah Palmer, Nettie Bell's father. They were married 54 years.

Thomas Wister (b. Jun. 9, 1881, d. Feb. 21, 1959) and Nettie (b. Jan. 22, 1881, d. Sep. 4, 1954) had 12 children: Dora Lee (b. 1902), Flora Jane (b. 1903), Roy Sylvester (b. 1905), Clifford Palmer (b. 1907), Verona (b. 1909), Ralph Lomax (b. 1913), Ollie Eunice (b. 1915), a stillborn in 1917, Alice Marie (b. 1918), Audrey Mae (b. 1921) Evelyn (b. 1923) and James K. Vardaman (b. 1926).

Wister and Nettie believed in better schools, churches and government. They fed and clothed poor people and gave away more than most people had. They taught their children by the Holy Bible.

Their home was always open to relatives and church family alike. Wister had a new home built just before the depression, large enough to accommodate many people. I remember one night we had 68 people for a church association. Wister had a porch halfway around the house and many sermons were preached there. Nettie was an excellent cook and people came to eat her cooking. The minister usually finished his sermon saying, "Come on, all you people to Brother Rinehart's for food." My memories of this home are good.

Wister Rinehart was hired by the US government to help set up the AAA program. He was a promoter of the John Rankin Tombigbee Waterway, but didn't live to see it finished.

The three children living today in the year 2000 are Alice Rinehart Enis, Audrey Rinehart Searcy and James K. Vardaman Rinehart. *Submitted by Audrey Rinehart Search*

ROACH, JOHN HARRISON, born in 1841 in Tennessee. A few years later, his family moved to Tishomingo County, MS where his father was a farmer.

In August 1861, John enlisted from that county to serve in Co. C of the 26th Mississippi Infantry under the command of Col. A.E. Reynolds. This regiment saw action at Fort Donelson, Vicksburg, the Wilderness, Spotsylvania, Cold Harbor and surrendered at Petersburg in 1865. He received a pension for this service.

After the war, he married Sarah E. Payne, daughter of William B. and Nancy Kizer Payne. John and Sally moved to Booneville where they had five children: Katie, William Lon, Mittie Estella, Nanny and Mary Elizabeth. John Harrison was a shoemaker and he opened his store beside the Post Office. The ads he placed in *The Pleader* stated that his shoes were made of the finest French calf and guaranteed to fit.

He later expanded his business to Corinth and Iuka where he kept on hand saddles, buggy whips and wagon harnesses, which he could also repair.

When his wife, Sarah died in 1878, he married Sally Patrick, daughter of G.W. and Martha E. Butler Patrick. John Harrison Roach died in 1922 and is buried in the Booneville Cemetery. *Submitted by Alyce Lawson Teaney.*

ROBERTSON, CHRISTOPHER HENRY, born Dec. 7, 1857 in Old Tishomingo County, MS near Booneville, was the son of James Harlow and Manerva (Swinney) Robertson (See Robertson History). He married Theodosia Annie Young in Booneville on Dec. 9 1883.

Christopher Henry Robertson and Annie Young Robertson at their home in Decatur, Wise County, TX ca. 1920

Annie was born Dec. 30, 1860, daughter of Washington Pinkney and Elizabeth (Stephens) Young (married Sep. 9, 1854; children: William M., James W. and Josiah) of Blythe's Chapel Community. The Stephens came from Jackson County, AL, by covered wagon pulled by oxen to the Free State of Tishomingo in early 1839. The Young families came before 1840, as they are listed on the 1840 Census for Tishomingo County. The daughter of John William and Nancy Stephens, Elizabeth Young, born Nov. 13, 1836 in Jackson County, AL, married second Benjamin Franklin Robinson. She died Jan. 31, 1915 and is buried at New Lebanon Freewill Baptist Church. John William, born in 1800 in Greenville District, South Carolina, died in 1857 and is buried at Blythe's Chapel. Nancy was born in 1800 in South Carolina. The Stephens children: Randolph, Jane, Lucinda, Josiah, Barbary, Daniel P, Liny, William Alexander and John Wesley.

Washington Pinkney Young, born ca. 1835 in Madison County, AL, died before Feb. 12, 1861 in Old Tishomingo County, the son of Mason and Eleanor (Miller) Young (married Jul. 28, 1831 in Madison County, AL). Their children were Columbus M., Elender A., Unity C. and John W. Eleanor Miller, born ca. 1809 in South Carolina, died before Apr. 19, 1855 and is thought to be buried in an unmarked grave in Blythe's Chapel Church Cemetery. She was daughter of Fredrick Miller, born Dec. 26, 1770, died Jul. 25, 1852 and wife, Polly, born Jan. 8, 1773. Their children were Josiah, Unity, Joel, Annie and Eliza.

Mason Young born, Jul. 25, 1811 in Tennessee, died Jul. 12, 1887. He married second, Sarah E. Davis. Both are buried in Blythe's Chapel Church Cemetery. Mason was son of Edmond and Ruth (Mason) Young (married in 1807 in Burke County, NC; children: Joseph and John). Ruth Young, born Oct. 6, 1786 in North Carolina and died Nov. 1, 1873, was the daughter of Michael Mason. He died in Alabama. Edmond Young received pension for service during the War of 1812. He served in Captain John B. Dempsey's company, Tennessee Militia, entering at Shelbyville, TN, Sep. 24, 1813, until Dec. 23, 1813. He was discharged at Huntsville, AL. He was born Jan. 3, 1785 in North Carolina and died Aug. 6, 1877. Both Ruth and Edmond are buried in Blythe's Chapel Church Cemetery. All of these families lived in Blythe's Chapel area. Shortly after marrying, Christopher Henry and Annie Robertson moved to Searcy, AR. He was in the grocery business. Their first three children were born there:

(1) Lillian Jenara married Robert Daniel Donaldson, grandson of Robert Grundy and Elizabeth Donaldson of Prentiss County. (See Donaldson family)

(2) James Pinkney married Effie Spain, daughter of Marion Francis and Ida Cora (Lowery) Spain of Prentiss County.

(3) Marion Boyd married Ruth Alvada Johnson. Their only daughter is Anna Louise Robertson Estes of Rancho Palos Verdes, CA.

About 1891, the family moved to Decatur, Wise County, TX where he owned a farm in the Pleasant Grove Community and was also in the grocery business. Four additional children were born here: Roy Nathaniel, Una Elizabeth, Buna and Hortense. They were long time members of the Baptist Church, including the Decatur First Baptist Church. Theodosia Annie Robertson died Jul. 4, 1921; Christopher Henry Robertson died Jun. 29, 1941. Both died in Decatur, TX and are buried there in the Oaklawn Cemetery. *Submitted by Anna Louise Robertson Estes.*

ROBERTSON, JAMES HARLOW,

an early settler of Old Tishomingo County, MS received two original land patents in 1837 in the Meadow Creek area of present day Prentiss County, MS. He came from Lawrence County, AL with his mother, Temperance and sisters. Temperance died in early 1845; James H. was administrator for her estate. In the third and fourth Tishomingo County, MS Administrations (1839-1840), James was elected to the Board of Police; listed as a drygoods store merchant in Carrollville in the southwest part of the county; worked on railroad construction through Booneville and in 1872 helped in building the county home.

Sons of James Harlow Robertson. From left: Christopher Henry Robertson, William Bonds Robertson, Burket Swinney Robertson, James Wiley Robertson and Nathaniel Whitfield Robertson. Picture was made when William visited his brothers in Oklahoma and attended a double wedding for son of Burket on Jul. 7, 1918. Picture was probably made by their nephew, James W. Payne, son of sister, Mary T. Payne, who had a Picture Gallery in Wellington, TX.

The 1850 Census for Old Tishomingo County shows James as a merchant with Real Estate valued at $600. The 1860 Census Post Office Blackland indicates he is a farmer with Real Estate valued at $5,000, Personal Estate $15,000, with nine slaves. Following the Civil War, the 1870 Census shows that he is living in T5, R7 still as a farmer with Real Estate valued at only $500 and Personal Estate at $800.

His father was James Robertson Sr. of Wake County, NC; moved in 1813 to Lawrence County, AL, near Moulton, before Alabama became a state. It is believed that James Sr. was the son of John Robertson Sr. (b. ca. 1729 Virginia, d. before 1803 in Wake County, NC), wife, Amy Temple (b. 1731 Virginia, d. after 1803); John, son of Christopher Robertson (b. ca. 1710 Virginia-before 1791 in North Carolina), his first wife, _____ Isham.

James Robertson Sr. and Temperance ___ were married in Raleigh, NC. Their children were: Lott (b. 1783) unmarried; Willis (b. 1787) remained in North Carolina; Pollie (b. 1788) no information; Higdon (b. 1785) married in 1825 to Mary Ponder and remained in Lawrence County, AL; Candace (b. 1800) no information; Winnie (b. 1801, d. 1845) married George Lewis Boley (See Boley); Amy (b. 1804) no information; Sarah (b. 1806, d. after 1880) married Oct. 7, 1847 in Tishomingo County to Elisha Folsom; James Harlow (b. 1805) (See below); Nancy (b. 1807) no information; Berlina (b. 1813, d. after 1880) married Joseph Alexander Jul. 11, 1833 in Lawrence County, AL. They moved with James H. and family to Tishomingo County ca. 1837. Joseph was Justice of the Peace and died in 1845. Their children were: James (b. 1834 Alabama), others born in Mississippi: Sarah M. (b. 1837), Temperance (b. 1840), William (b. 1842), Julianna F. (b. 1844) married Sep. 12, 1859, to Elisha T. Smith.

In 1832 while still in Lawrence County, AL, James Harlow Robertson purchased a land patent of 80 acres for $100.25 near the community of Landersville, next to his brother, Higdon Robertson and brother-in-law, George Boley. His father, James Sr., died ca. 1830. By 1836 James H. moved to the newly opened Indian Lands of Tishomingo County. He married Mar. 19, 1844, to Manerva Swinney (b. September 1827, Georgia), daughter of Wiley Swinney and first wife, Harriet Smith (See Swinney). Their children were:

(1) Temperance Sophira A. (b. Feb. 24, 1845, d. Sep. 10, 1916) married Jul. 19, 1862, John C. Hodges. He was in the lumber business and was elected Sheriff in 1877. He died in 1878 leaving Tempie with seven small children: James D. (b. 1863), John Lewis (b. 1865), Sidney E. (b. 1866), Emma E. (b. 1868), Cora A. (b. 1871), Prentiss (b. 1874) and Reuben R. (b. 1876). Tempie and John are buried in Old Booneville Cemetery.

(2) Mary T. (See Payne Family History).

(3) James Wiley (See Family History).

(4) William Bonds (See Family History).

(5) Burkett Swinney (b. Mar. 31, 1853, d. Sep. 16, 1928) is buried in Reed, Oklahoma Cemetery. He married Feb. 19, 1880, Alice E. Justice. Their children were: Ora Victoria (b. 1880), Emma (b. 1885), James David (b. 1888), Claude Everett (b. 1892), Tempie (b. 1896), Luther Henry (b. 1899) and Orna Alice (b. 1906). The family moved to Wise County, TX ca. 1896 to Greer County, OK in 1901.

(6) Nathaniel Whitfield (b. Oct. 7, 1855, d. Jan. 15, 1938) is buried in Reed, Oklahoma Cemetery. He married Aug. 20, 1885, to Sarah Olive Jones. Their children were Ora Belle (b. 1889), James Henry (b. 1890), Pearl (b. 1893), Bettie Lee (b. 1895), Ella Bar (b. 1899), Houston (b. 1902) and Roy (b. 1905). Nathaniel went to Briar, TX before 1880 and settled in Reed, Greer County, OK in 1900.

(7) Christopher Henry (See Family History).

(8) Fannie (b. 1859, d. ca. 1878/80) was living with sister, Tempie Hodges, on the 1870 Census. First wife of James Harlow Robertson, Manerva Swinney, died between 1860 Census and before he remarried Nov. 3, 1867, Mrs. Martha Ann Jones Wadsworth. Their only child was Luther Higdon (See Family History).

James Harlow Robertson died Apr. 12, 1885 and is buried with Masonic honors by Booneville Lodge #305 (established Jan. 24, 1868) where he was a charter member. Burial location has not been found, but it is assumed that he was buried in a now unmarked grave in the Meadow Creek area. The descendants of James Harlow Robertson placed a marker to his and his family's memory in the Old Booneville Cemetery on Oct. 17, 1998. *Submitted by Bettie Parker Gustafson*

ROBERTSON, JAMES WILEY,

born Mar. 14, 1849 in old Tishomingo County, MS. He was the third child of James Harlow Robertson (b. 1805, d. 1885) and Manerva Swinney (b. 1827, d. after 1860), who had a total of three daughters and five sons. He married Millie Ann Jones Nov. 8, 1868 in Lamar County, GA.

Millie Ann Jones Robertson and James Wiley Robertson

She was born Nov. 28, 1850, to Aaron F.F. Jones (b. 1792, d. about 1879) and Mary Ann Wadsworth (b. 1825, d. 1870) and grew to womanhood in Pike County, GA. She was the fifth child of seven daughters and three sons in the Jones family.

By 1880, James Wiley and Millie Ann had moved to near Boonesville, Wise County, TX where they resided until moving to Southwest Indian Territory (Oklahoma) in 1901. With their children, the Robertsons settled just East of Vinson, Harmon County, OK. It is here, the Cave Creek Cemetery, that they are buried. In 1913 the Robertsons moved to Stillwater, Payne County, OK, so Reuben, the youngest of the family, could attend college.

The children of James Wiley and Millie Ann are:

Eudora Eleanor, born Dec. 18, 1869 in old Tishomingo County, MS, died Aug. 8, 1947 in Harmon County, OK and is buried at Cave Creek Cemetery in Harmon County, OK. She married William Alonza Head Dec. 25, 1887 in Wise County, TX.

Wiley Edward was born Jan. 29, 1872 in Prentiss County, MS and died Feb. 28, 1872 in Prentiss County, MS.

Minerva Velula was born May 5, 1873 in Prentiss County, MS and died Apr. 20, 1906. She married Joe W. Williams on Sep. 16, 1894 and divorced later.

Etna Pearl was born Aug. 21, 1875 in Prentiss County, MS and died Jul. 1, 1880 in Prentiss County, MS.

Colin Hodges was born Mar. 29, 1878 in Prentiss County, MS and died Nov. 22, 1968 in Amarillo, Potter County, TX. He is buried in Cave Creek Cemetery in Harmon County, OK. He married Laura Caughey on Feb. 5, 1903 and married Una Mae Tillman on Jan. 31, 1927, at Mangum, Greer County, OK.

Iora Myrtle was born Jun. 3, 1880 in Prentiss County, MS and married W. Robert Park on Nov. 24, 1898.

183

Wiley Wadsworth, born Dec. 29, 1882 in Wise County, TX, died Apr. 13, 1917 and is buried in Cave Creek Cemetery in Harmon County, OK. He married Beatrice Nixon Clayton on Feb. 15, 1906 in Brown County, TX.

Olsie Lolie, born Jun. 3, 1885 in Wise County, TX and died in OK.

Mary Pearl, born Jul. 5, 1887 in Wise County, TX, died Apr. 18, 1978 in El Paso, TX and is buried in Texline, Dallam County, TX. She married John R. Teague on May 5, 1912 in Clayton, Union County, NM.

Reuben Boyd, born Dec. 9, 1889 in Wise County, TX, died May 29, 1969, at Okmulgee, OK and is buried in Hoffman, Okmulgee County, OK. He married Jewel McCarty on Jun. 1, 1920 in Harmon County, OK. Jewel died Jul. 12, 1934 at Little Rock, AR. Reuben's second marriage was to Grace Marie Fuller, Feb. 13, 1937 at Eufaula, OK.

James Wiley died his birthday at the age of 76 years, Mar. 14, 1925 and was buried in Cave Creek Cemetery, near Vinson, Harmon County, OK. Millie Ann died at the age of 84 years, on Jan. 1, 1935, near Vinson, Harmon County, OK and was buried in Cave Creek Cemetery, near Vinson, Harmon County, OK.

James Wiley appears in the following US Censuses: 1850, Tishomingo County, MS with his parents; 1870, Prentiss County, MS, with his wife, Millie A. and child, Eudora E.; 1880, Wise County, TX with his wife, Millie A. and children Eudora E., Manerva V., Etna P. and Colan H.; 1910, Harmon County, OK, with his wife, Millie and children Lola O., Reuben B. and Mary P. and 1920, Harmon County, OK, age 71 years, with wife, Millie, age 69 years, living with daughter, Eleanor E. Head, who was listed as the head of family, along with her family. *Submitted by James McCarty Robertson.*

ROBERTSON, LUTHER HIGDON, the youngest son of James Harlow Robertson (See Robertson History) and the only child by his second wife, Martha Ann Jones. His father married Nov. 3, 1867 in Old Tishomingo County, MS, Mrs. Martha Ann Jones Wadsworth, older sister of Millie Ann Jones, wife of his son, James Wiley Robertson. The Jones sisters were the daughters of Aaron Francis Flourney Jones and Mary Ann (Wadsworth) Jones of Georgia.

Mr. and Mrs. Luther Higdon Robertson, made at their home in Gloster, MS, ca. 1930

Martha Ann was born about 1841 in Georgia and first married William C. Wadsworth. They had a son, William B., born ca. 1860 and a daughter, Sophronia C., born ca. 1862; both born in Georgia and both had died by 1900.

Luther Higdon Robertson was born Jul. 22, 1869 in Old Tishomingo County. He married Nov. 29, 1892, Mary Taylor Jobe, born Nov. 20, 1866, daughter of Wiley Taylor Jobe and Phoebe (Lawson) Jobe of Old Tishomingo/Alcorn County.

Children, all born in Prentiss County were:

George Boyd (b. 1894) married Annie Ruth Hale.

Luther Paul (b. 1897) married Clara Wiley Grady (b. 1898).

Sallie (b. 1899), Emma (b. 1901), both died young.

Ella Agnes (b. 1904) married Nolan Dickerson.

Luther was a farmer. He lived on the old Robertson homeplace in the Meadow Creek area and then moved to the Pisgah area and then moved to Gloster, Amite County, MS, ca. 1913. He died Jul. 6, 1939 and is buried in Gloster, Mississippi Cemetery. Mary died Apr. 1, 1962 and is buried with Luther in Gloster Cemetery.

Luther's mother, Martha Ann, was a Baptist. She lived with his family in later years and died at his home on Aug. 22, 1909 and was buried in Prentiss County.

On Jul. 30, 1900, Luther H. Robertson deeded two acres of land for the sum of $1 to the Trustees of Robertson School to be used for school purposes. This one-room schoolhouse was located in later years, on the property of James Benjamin Floyd, then Dewey Floyd, the grandfather and father of J. Robert Floyd of Booneville. One of the teachers was Bonnie Robertson (later Mrs. Homer Parker) and great-niece of Luther H. Robertson. She taught the years of 1920-21 and 1921-22 as an Assistant receiving $60 the first year; $62.50 the second year; subject to change, according to average attendance. Superintendent of Public Education for Prentiss County at that time was J.W. Taylor. *Submitted by Gene Gustafson Sr.*

ROBERTSON, WILLIAM BONDS, second son of James Harlow Robertson (See Family History) and wife, Manerva Swinney. He was born Apr. 13, 1851 and died Dec. 11, 1930. He is buried in Old Booneville Cemetery. He married Dec. 22, 1874, Nancy Mahalia Hawkins (b. Mar. 20, 1848, d. Feb. 16, 1918), daughter of William Graves Hawkins and wife, Sarah Jane Adkins, the granddaughter of Joseph G. and Elizabeth G. Montague Hawkins, lines going back to Captain Thomas Graves of Jamestown, VA and Peter Montague of Virginia.

Mr. and Mrs. William Bonds Robertson, ca. 1900.

William Bonds Robertson was a farmer and long time Baptist; children:

(1) Orie Brooks (b. Oct. 8, 1875, d. Aug. 17, 1878) is buried in Meadow Creek Cemetery.

(2) Ovelton Bonds (b. Mar. 20, 1877, d. Aug. 27, 1941) married Martha Ann Caroline (Callie) Fulghum (b. Apr. 29, 1872, d. Dec. 23, 1943). They are both buried in Old Booneville Cemetery. They had Callie Bonds (Bonnie) (b. Aug. 9, 1901, d. Jul. 27, 1946), who married May 29, 1925, Homer William Parker (b. Jul. 31, 1895, d. May 3, 1968). Both are buried in Booneville Cemetery. Their children were:

1) William Raymond Parker (b. Jul. 22, 1926, d. Mar. 6, 1992) married Mar. 2, 1946, Shirley May Holland (b. Aug. 2, 1928, d. Feb. 11, 1990). Both are buried in Booneville Cemetery. Children: Donald Raymond, living in Clarksville, TN; Robert Dale was born and died in 1951 and is buried in Booneville Cemetery and Bonnie Louise married Roger Lee Unsell and is living in Clarksville, TN. Their children are Kevin Lee and Crystal Lynn. Raymond married second Beulah Martha Wallace McDaniel of Iuka.

2) Homer O'Neil Parker (b. Aug. 13, 1930) is retired and living in Memphis, TN. He married first Era Charline Geno. They have a son, Michael O'Neil, who is working for Northwest Airlines and living in Cordova, TN. He married Rebecca Sue Bivens and they have a son, Daniel O'Neil. O'Neil married second to Sarah Anne Floyd and their children are: David Walter, who is working for International Paper and living in Germantown, TN. He married Jeanne Maureen Roberts. Their children are Fletcher O'Neil and Chad Ryne. O'Neil and Sarah's other child is Paige Susette, who is a kindergarten teacher for Harding Academy and living in Bartlett, TN. She married Michael Christopher Essary and they have Chelsea Ann and Michael Christopher II.

Robertson family, Summer of 1929: 1st row, from left: Alice Floyd Robertson, James Odus Robertson, William Bonds Robertson, Callie Fulghum Robertson, Ovelton Bonds Robertson, William Henry Robertson, Mollie Floyd Robertson, unknown, unknown. 2nd row: Ruby Robertson (Hill), Homer W. Parker, Bonnie Robertson Parker, Mable Robertson (Howell), Raymond Parker, Mary Elizabeth Robertson, unknown, unknown. 3rd row: Pauline Robertson (Young), Ethel Robertson (Hanley), Henry Robertson, Guy Robertson, Harold Robertson.

3) Bettie Virginia Parker (b. Apr. 11, 1938), living in Rosemark, TN married first Dorman Lee Holland and had two daughters: Bonnie Ruth Crawford, working for Ezon Co. and living in Memphis, TN and has a son, Christopher Wayne and Virginia Lynne (Ginger) Lemmon, working for Hilton Hotel Corporation and living in Atoka, TN and has two daughters: Amber Michelle and Audrey Nichole.

Bettie married second Larry Gene Gustafson and had two sons: Larry Gene Jr., working for Smith & Nephew and living in Atoka, TN and has sons, Cody Gene and Holden Wakefield Thomas. He is now married to Jessica Dawn Lawrence and has a son, Parker Hayes Lawrence Gustafson and stepdaughters: Brittany Nicole and Alexandra Leigh Howard. Bettie and Larry's other son is William Clifton, who is working for Christie Cut Stone and living in Atoka, TN.

(3) Norie Jane (b. Oct. 12, 1878, d. Oct. 1, 1879) is buried in Meadow Creek Cemetery.

(4) Baby Boy (b. and d. May 16, 1881) is buried in Meadow Creek Cemetery.

(5) James Odus (b. Jan. 4, 1883, d. Apr. 5, 1936) married Nov. 22, 1906, Sarah Alice Floyd. Both are buried in Old Booneville Cemetery.

(6) William Henry (b. Jan. 9, 1891, d. Jul. 26, 1977) married Jun. 25, 1911, Mary Etta (Mollie) Floyd. They are both buried in Old Booneville Cemetery.

Additional information on the William Bonds Robertson family is found in the First Edition of the Prentiss County History. *Submitted by Bonnie R. Crawford.*

ROBERTSON, WILLIAM GUY, (Continued from Prentiss County History Vol. I, page 374). William Guy Robertson died Jun. 13, 1997 and Doris Tays Robertson died Feb. 3, 1989.

Marie's son, David Andrew Spain, died Sep. 1, 1996. His stepdaughter, Ami Patrice Lambert, died in Nov. 1992. David had a son, Andrew Blake Spain (b. Nov. 22, 1987).

Laura and Jerry's daughter, Melissa, has one son, Michael Taylor (b. Dec. 18, 1998).

Guy Wayne's daughter, Ashley, married Michael Douglas Minton of Somerset, PA on Jul. 30, 1994.

Peggy and Bobby's daughter, Dena, married George William Cutshall III of Iuka on Aug. 12, 1995.

Two other daughters, Kelly Ann and Amy Carol, were born Jun. 1, 1986. William Leonard Spain divorced Alice Jeanice Johnson Spain in December 1985 and he married Terecia Annette Kendrick on Sep. 23, 1989.

Cindy Palmer married, but later divorced David Myrick. She had daughters, Jennifer Leigh (b. Mar. 17, 1980) and Staci Nichole (b. Apr. 14, 1990).

Dawn Lise Palmer married Randall Lynn DeArmond and had twin sons, Palmer Randall and Andrew Lynn (b. Mar. 31, 1992).

Christopher Eugene Palmer married Bridgette Michelle Parmer.

Ovid James Robertson (no other information on him).

James Sidney Robertson died Sep. 6, 1984.

Harold Ray Robertson married Debbie McDonald on Apr. 6, 1993. They have one daughter, Lauren Elizabeth, born Feb. 24, 1996.

Billy (William Ovid) was born Jul. 7, 1940.

Ruby Robertson married Clyde Hill. James Jerry Hill married Yvonne Thornhill and adopted two sons: James Randal Hill (b. Jan. 10, 1968) md. Stacy Ainsworth (b. Dec. 12, 1970) and had one child, Joshua Caleb Hill (b. Jul. 17, 1998). Michael Jerry Hill (b. Sep. 18, 1970) md. Debbie Jones (b. Oct. 5, 1970) and had one child, Brianna Hill (b. Jan. 15, 1994).

Richard Clyde Hill married Helen Elizabeth Smith and had three sons: Richard Daniel (b. Dec. 17, 1966); Joel Scott (b. Apr. 29, 1969) md. on Dec. 27, 1997 to Amy Melisa Polk; Robert Christopher Hill (b. Sep. 18, 1974).

Teddy Ray Hill Sr. married Mary Ann Franks in 1962 and had three children: (1) Teddy Ray Jr. married Ellen Petrie and had son David Wesley (b. Dec. 9, 1992); daughter Rachel Franks (b. Dec. 16, 1995) and triplets, Anna Petrie, Sara Oakley and Megan Irene (b. May 30, 1997). (2) Jessica Marie (b. Nov. 6, 1963). (3) John Gregory (b. Aug. 21, 1967) md. Amy Justice on Jan. 10, 1998. Ted and Mary Ann divorced in 1970. Ted married Sharon Graham Hill on Mar. 23, 1974 and had two children, Kari Alice (b. Oct. 29, 1976) md. Ted Slusser of Memphis, TN on Jun. 6, 1999 and Graham Hill (b. Mar. 1, 1981).

Larry Wayne Hill married Julie Ann Lane and had two sons, Craig Allen (b. Sep. 10, 1978) and Ryan Wayne (b. Apr. 30, 1980).

Janice Carol Hill married Charles Phillip Browning and had two sons, Corey Michael (b. May 19, 1984) and Lee Gullam (b. Feb. 15, 1988).

Pauline Robertson Young (d. Feb. 28, 2000). Her son, Bobby, has two children, Shayne and Slade. Her son, Eddie and his wife, Tammy, have two children, Kim and Olivia. Her daughter, Paulette, married Sonny Watkins and they have Megan Lee (b. Sep. 25, 1987).

ROBINSON, WILLIAM RENARD "ROOF," born Apr. 17, 1886 and died Mar. 19, 1956, son of John and Liza Robinson, married Jettie Bell Curtis (b. Mar. 30, 1886, d. Jun. 18, 1971), daughter of Elijah W. and Lou Cindy Russell Curtis. They lived in the Prentiss, Lee and Itawamba counties and reared seven of eight children. James Mozie (b. Jun. 29, 1911, d. Feb. 15, 1975); Beatrice (b. Oct. 18, 1913, d. Feb. 5, 1976); Lonzo Evin "Red" (b. Aug. 21, 1915, d. May 29, 1985); William Renard Jr. (b. Jan. 14, 1919); Leonard Franklin "Little Red" (b. Apr. 4, 1921, d. 1956); Coyce Lee (d. as infant of two weeks); Luecoy (b. May 23, 1925); Ernie Bell (b. Jun. 6, 1928).

Hubert Algie Shouse (b. Oct. 19, 1908, d. Nov. 22, 1947), son of Ernest Lafayette Shouse and Lucy Manley Shouse, married Hessie Lou Magers (b. Jul. 30, 1910, d. Mar. 19, 1998), daughter of Auskie and Neomia Maxwell Magers. They lived in Prentiss, Lee and Itawamba counties and reared seven of eight children. Hershel Lee (b. Aug. 18, 1930) md. Nicole Craviosier; Opal Ernestine (b. Dec. 17, 1932, d. Mar. 24, 1994) md. George Frazer Davis; Wilbur Algin (b. Apr. 28, 1934) md. Cleo Cowart; William Clofus "Billy" (b. Feb. 12, 1941) md. Mary Ann Edge; Luther James (James Luther) (b. Mar. 23, 1944) md. Brenda Hooper; Betty Lou (b. Mar. 20, 1946, d. Mar. 23, 1946), Carolyn Joyce (b. Apr. 11, 1947) md. Boyce Monroe Hutcheson. Howard Elvin, the eldest, (b. Sep. 29, 1928) md. Ernie Bell Robinson on Jul. 24, 1948.

Howard and Ernie Bell have made their home in and around Prentiss County. Their occupations have included farming, gas station owner/operators, factory work and other ways of earning a living for their four children.

Front L-R: Catherine, Ernie Bell, Howard. Back: Barbara, Junior and Judy

Catherine (b. Jun. 23, 1949) md. Robert Quitman Ashcraft on Aug. 12, 1967. They have three children, two of which died as infants: Curt (b. Apr. 11, 1975) and Robert Howard (b. Sep. 29, 1976). Melissa (b. Nov. 2, 1970) was married to Brit Ross Mansir on Sep. 16, 1995. They have one daughter, Lena Catherine (b. Dec. 24, 1996). Catherine and her family all live in Booneville. She works for The Department of Human Services and Quitman is disabled.

Barbara (b. Apr. 17, 1957) married Tommy Guzman on Oct. 26, 1989. They live in Black Fish, AK. Barbara has two daughters by a previous marriage to Larry Junior Wilbanks. April Michell (b. Jul. 1, 1975) married Thomas Franklin Greenwood on Nov. 28, 1998. They are proud parents of one son, Thomas Franklin Greenwood Jr. "T.J." (b. Sep. 30, 1999). Kimberly Dawn (b. May 22, 1980) md. James Magee on Apr. 4, 1997. They are proud parents of two sons, Clayton James (b. Mar. 11, 1998) and Kyle Elisha (b. Nov. 23, 1999). Tommy has two sons, Richard Thomas Guzman and Chadwick Dewayne Lucas. Barabara and Tommy have lived in the Black Fish area and greatly appreciate their friends and neighbors.

Judy (b. May 23, 1963) md. John Steven Bryan on Oct. 24, 1992. They live and work in Booneville. They are not parents but they spend a lot of time spoiling nieces and nephews. They spend their free time enjoying their time together.

Howard Elvin Jr. "Junior" (b. Mar. 29, 1968) md. Carla Moore on Feb. 10, 1989. They live and work in the Marietta area. They have one son, Tyson Blake (b. Jul. 9, 1991). They are very involved in school and community activities. Junior and Tyson have both been involved in the sport of racing with Carla being their supporter.

ROGERS-ARNETT AND ROGERS-BULLARD, Rogers-Arnett: William G. Rogers, born May 29, 1833 in Tennessee, son of Williamson Rogers (b. 1805, d. 1875) and Melviannie Cook (b. 1812, d. 1898). Their oldest child, William, was 6 years old when his family packed up their wagon and moved from Lawrence County, TN to Old Tishomingo County, MS in 1839. There, on Apr. 26, 1860, he married Sarah Ann Arnett, born in July 1840 in North Carolina.

Their children: Marian W. (b. 1864); Zemeriah Alcie (b. Apr. 24, 1866); Vianna A. (b. 1868); Sarah A. (b. 1870); William F. (b. May 1872) married Elvie (b. November 1877) and had a son, Roosevelt (b. 1901) and a daughter, Mabel (b. 1907); Dora Ella (b. 1874); Hugh L. (b. 1876); Mary J. (b. December 1879) and Roena "Rose" M. (b. March 1881).

Through the years William farmed the land and reportedly died Nov. 14, 1918 in Paragould, AR. It is not known when or where Sarah Ann passed away, though she's shown still living with William on the 1910 soundex.

Rogers-Bullard: Known for his red hair and his ability to shape metal, Zemeriah Alcie "Alce" Rogers, son of William G. Rogers (b. 1833, d. 1918) and Sarah Ann Arnett (b. 1840, d. ?) was born Apr. 24, 1866, near New Site. On Apr. 26, 1890, he married Cora Ann Bullard, born Oct. 26, 1867 in Guntown, MS and the daughter of James Winston "Wins" Bullard (b. 1846, d. ?) from Alabama and Rebecca Melvina Jackson (b. 1845, d. ?) from Georgia.

Alce owned 80 acres, but only farmed 15, growing corn, oats and watermelons. The family used to sell eggs from brown Leghorn chickens for 10 cents a dozen. Noted for his blacksmithing skills, Alce could make a part for a broken gun or wagon with ease even if he had no pattern to follow.

"Alce", Cora Bullard Rogers and son, Chester

Alce and Cora's children were: Minnie Vernon (b. Mar. 2, 1891); Docia Mae (b. May 19, 1893 in Indian Territory); Chester Harrison (b. Jan. 27, 1898) and Myrtle Melvina (b. Mar. 15, 1900. d. in 1904).

Minnie Vernon Rogers married Tom Rayburn and had children, Troyce, Pauline and DeLora, later divorcing in 1937. Vernon or "Vernie" passed away in Memphis, TN in October 1978.

Alce's son, Chester, remembers New Site as a settlement when he was growing up. There was a gristmill, a general store and a horse smithy. Jack Green owned the general store and when it came time for food, he would insist everyone in the store come eat at the long table he had that would seat 15 to 20 people. Chester further recalls that on election nights, paper was used to cast your vote.

As a youth, Chester remembers setting traps and shipping furs to a company in St. Louis, MO. Mink would fetch $10-$12 a pelt, an all black polecat $7, while possum or muskrat were 50 cents each.

Zemeriah Alcie Rogers died Mar. 27, 1930 and Cora Ann passed away on Dec. 27, 1948. Both are buried in Little Brown Cemetery.

Submitted by Lee Coatney.

ROGERS, CHARLES FLOYD TALMAGE, was instrumental in a renewed search into the life of his great-grandmother, Nancy Dickey Rogers Calvery. He was the grandson of Sidney Talmage Rogers Sr. (b. Sep. 15, 1876 in Prentiss County, died Mar. 28, 1943 in Sheffield, AL) and Eva Lilly Floyd (b. Oct. 12, 1881, died Sep. 17, 1959 in Sheffield, AL) and the son of Sidney Talmage Rogers (b. Jan. 14, 1908 in Sheffield, AL, died August 1967 in Pompano Beach, FL) and Ruby Newsom (married Dec. 20, 1930).

In searching for his family, he wrote, called and met many of his family connections, uncovering interesting facts about Nancy. Although he never got to the end of his search, he spurred renewed interest in other family members to dig some more.

Charles died Jan. 8, 1998 at Tuscumbia, AL. He was a native of Colbert County, AL. Charles held a doctor of divinity degree from South Western Baptist Seminary of Fort Worth, TX and was pastor of churches in Alabama, Tennessee, Texas and Mississippi.

He was the father of five children: Stephen, Deborah, Peggy, Kathy and Connie. *Submitted by Pollye Calvery.*

ROGERS, CHESTER HARRISON,

son of Zemeriah Alcie "Alce" Rogers (b. 1866, d. 1930) and Cora Ann Bullard (b. 1867, d. 1948), born Jan. 27, 1898. Chester left Mississippi in his late teens and hitched a ride on a train with his cousin, Wallace Green, as far as Lewisville, AR. From there, Chester ended up in a small town called Ferris about 10 miles south of Dallas, TX. It was in Ferris that he eventually met and married Girtie Lee Wiser, born Feb. 5, 1907 and the daughter of William Harry Wiser (b. 1874, d. 1962), born in Coffee County, TN and Alva Rilla Moore (b. 1883, d. 1969), born in Itawamba County, MS.

From left: Girtie Lee Wiser Rogers holding Martha and Chester Rogers holding Lynn.

Chester inherited his father Alce's creative talents, but rather than metal, his element was wood. Chester had the ability to draw up plans for anything from a piece of furniture or a new garage to renovating a house. With skilled hands, he crafted things that were both useful and beautiful, even down to the delicate and intricate finishing touches.

Chester and Girtie Lee's children: Chester Lynn (b. Dec. 2, 1926 in Ellis County, TX, d. Jan. 24, 1994 in Dallas County, TX) and Martha Ann (b. Sep. 30, 1928 in Ellis County, TX).

On Mar. 28, 1953 in Idabel, OK, Lynn Rogers married Jilcye "Jill" Marie West Childers. Their children: Griffin Michael Childers Rogers (b. Jun. 3, 1948); Jilcye Lynn (b. Apr. 2, 1954); Kent West (b. Sep. 16, 1957) and Beverly Claire (b. Jan. 20, 1961).

Martha Ann Rogers married Doyle Francis Coatney, born May 23, 1922 in Appanoose County, Iowa, on Oct. 15, 1948. Doyle passed away on Nov. 14, 1972. Their children are: Bonnie Lee (b. Oct. 28, 1953) and William Russell (b. Dec. 18, 1956) both born in Dallas County, TX.

Chester Harrison Rogers died in Lancaster, Dallas County, TX on May 24, 1990. Girtie Lee Wiser Rogers preceded him in death on May 17, 1986, also in Lancaster. They are buried in Laurel Land Memorial Park in Dallas, TX. *Submitted by Martha Rogers Coatney Brashear.*

ROGERS, HENRY TAYLOR,

born Mar. 2, 1858, died Jan. 29, 1944, was the youngest son of Williamson Rogers (b. 1805, d. 1875) and Melviannie Cook (b. 1812, d. 1898). On Sep. 7, 1893, he married Harriet Priscilla "Siller" Rhodiann Moreland, born Jan. 26, 1868, died Oct. 22, 1956, daughter of Thomas Moreland (b. 1830, d. 1889) and Harriet Stacy (b. 1837, d. 1918).

Their children: Luda Bell (b. Aug. 4, 1897, d. Dec. 30, 1994), who married Ollie Edgar Goff (b. Mar. 13, 1877, d. Mar. 25, 1963); Henry Dalton (b. Jul. 2, 1900), who married Cora Graham (b. Mar. 25, 1896, d. May 25, 1963); Luna Mae (b. Sep. 4, 1907), who is still living and married Chester Moss (b. Sep. 18, 1906, d. Nov. 19, 1984); John Bolivar (b. Jan. 4, 1909, d. Nov. 15, 1977), who married Joyce Coraene Beard (b. Sep. 22, 1921) on Nov. 20, 1938.

The children of Luda Bell Rogers and Ollie Edgar Goff: Clyde Orbra, born Jan. 1, 1913; Bessie Blanch (b. Jan. 28, 1916, d. Sep. 12, 1963); Alma

Henry holding Luna and "Siller" Moreland Rogers holding Bolivar. Luda and Dalton standing

Lucille (b. Jun. 18, 1919, d. May 27, 1987) and Lottie Mae (b. Dec. 12, 1923).

The children of Henry Dalton Rogers and Cora Graham: Henry Frank (b. Oct. 9, 1936) and Velma Lee (b. Apr. 24, 1934) married a Knight.

The children of Luna Mae Rogers and Chester Moss: Annie Mae (b. Aug. 16, 1925) married a Tidwell; Max Ray (b. Jan. 11, 1927, d. May 27, 1998); Eloise (b. Oct. 17, 1932) married a Wilson and Harriet Jane (b. May 1, 1939) married a Davis. *Submitted by Coraene Beard Rogers.*

ROGERS, JOHN BOLIVAR,

born Jan. 4, 1909, the youngest son of the youngest son of one of the original settlers of Old Tishomingo County, MS. His parents were Henry Taylor Rogers (b. 1858, d. 1944) and Harriet Priscilla "Siller" Rhodiann Moreland (b. 1868, d. 1956). On Nov. 20, 1938, Bolivar married Joyce Coraene Beard, the daughter of Ranzey Everett Beard (b. 1894, d. 1975) and Docia Mae Rogers (b. 1893, d. 1951). Bolivar passed away on Nov. 15, 1977 and is buried in Little Brown Cemetery.

Back: Coraene Beard Rogers and Bolivar Rogers. Front: Reeder Joy and Betty Jo.

Coraene Beard Rogers still lives on an original 27 acres from the section of land that her great-great-grandfather, Williamson Rogers, settled around 1839 in Old Tishomingo County. For 160 years this parcel of land has been the only portion of the old homestead that has continuously remained in the Rogers name and has never been sold.

Coraene and Bolivar's children are Reeder Joy (b. Feb. 2, 1941) married Wayne Vuncannon (b. Mar. 2, 1941). Betty Jo (b. Oct. 5, 1944) married William Bernard Scott (b. Jun. 5, 1938).

The children of Reeder Joy Rogers and Wayne Vuncannon: Jeffery Wayne (b. Oct. 11, 1964) married Dale Renee Cox (b. Jul. 17, 1963) and Sherry Dawn (b. Feb. 19, 1969) married Mark Jeffery Mize (b. Aug. 18, 1969).

The children of Betty Jo Rogers and William Bernard Scott: William Bruce (b. Jan. 25, 1966) married Lori Jean Nicholson (b. Nov. 6, 1973) and Cristy Deonne (b. Aug. 15, 1970) married Brad Morgan (b. Feb. 26, 1972).

The children of Jeffery Wayne Vuncannon and Dale Renee Cox: Jamie Lynn Duncan (b. Oct. 17, 1982); Casey Nicole (b. Dec. 10, 1985) and Lindsey Michele (b. Jul. 19, 1988).

The children of Bruce Scott and Lori Nicholson: William Blake (b. Oct. 17, 1994) and John Bryson (b. Mar. 26, 1997).

The children of Cristy Deonne Scott and Brad Morgan: Eric Brandon (b. May 6, 1986), James Brett (b. Mar. 21, 1997) and Brinten Scott (b. Jul. 29, 1999). *Submitted by Reeder Rogers Vuncannon.*

ROGERS, WILLIAMSON,

born Jan. 14, 1805 in Kentucky. It is possible that he spent some time in Maury County, TN before settling in Lawrence County, TN where on Aug. 11, 1832, he married Melviannie "Vianna" Cook (b. Sep. 16, 1812, from Tennessee).

Around 1839, Williamson packed his possessions, his wife and first five children and headed

Williamson Rogers' justice of the peace desk.

for Mississippi to settle a section of land in Old Tishomingo County near New Site. The parents of Williamson are unknown, but it is probable that James Zemeriah "Zimry" Rogers, born Mar. 15, 1807 in Kentucky, who settled nearby, is Williamson's brother. Family knowledge believes this Rogers line originated in Cook County, IL.

Williamson and Vianna's children were: William G. (b. May 29, 1833) married Sarah Ann Arnett (b. July 1840) on Apr. 26, 1860; Elizabeth Jane (b. Aug. 23, 1835) married a Nichols and had a daughter, Vianna Ellen (b. 1872); Eliza Ann (b. Apr. 3, 1837) married William L. Holly on Aug. 28, 1851; Ellison, Eliza's twin (b. and d. Apr. 3, 1837); Mary Caroline (b. Mar. 8, 1839) married William C. Arnett on Dec. 13, 1860 and died Sep. 20, 1890; Sarah Catherine (b. Feb. 23, 1841); James McDaniel (b. Dec. 10, 1843, d. Nov. 29, 1885); Thomas Jefferson (b. Jul. 12, 1844) married Mary Jane (b. July 1844) and had a son named Williamson (b. 1869) and daughters, Willie (b. August 1881), Mary (b. August 1883) and Nancy (b. July 1885); Charlotte Susanna (b. Nov. 26, 1848) never married; Martha Minerva (b. Dec. 21, 1850); John F. (b. Feb. 17, 1855) served as justice of the peace in Jacinto in 1866, constable in 1867-1868 and never married and Henry Taylor (b. Mar. 2, 1858) married Harriet Priscilla "Siller" Rhodiann Moreland on Sep. 7, 1893.

From 1852 to 1855, Williamson Rogers served as justice of the peace in Jacinto. On the 1860 census, the value of his real estate was placed at $2,000 and his personal worth at $800. Primarily a farmer, Williamson owned some livestock: a steer, several cows, "one grey mair," numerous hogs and some sheep.

Twenty-seven acres of Williamson's original homestead has never been sold and has remained in the Rogers name for the past 160 years. It is currently owned by his great-great-granddaughter, Coraene Beard Rogers.

Williamson Rogers passed away from consumption on Apr. 3, 1875. He is buried in Little Brown Cemetery and his headstone inscription reads: "Not lost, blest thought, but gone before where we shall meet to part no more."

Melviannie died Jul. 31, 1898. Buried in Little Brown Cemetery, her gravestone is etched: "As a wife devoted. As a mother affectionate. As a friend ever kind and true." *Submitted by Bonnie Coatney.*

RORIE-HENDRIX,

James Bradley Rorie (b. Mar. 25, 1948) married Doris Fay Hendrix (b. Jan. 24, 1951) on Nov. 27, 1970.

Doris Fay is the daughter of Thurman Leo (b. Nov. 14, 1920, d. Mar. 26, 1982) and Alma Fay Vanderford Hendrix (b. May 10, 1925) married Feb. 22, 1945. She is the granddaugther of Charley Cado Hendrix (b. May 8, 1898, d. Sep. 23, 1966) and Martha Elizabeth McCoy Hendrix Warren (b. Oct. 22, 1901); Clovis Aaron (b. Jun. 1, 1901, d. Jan. 16, 1985) and Ida Sula Richardson Vanderford (b. Jun. 11, 1904, d. Sep. 8, 1989) married on Feb. 20, 1920, buried in

Kemp's Chapel Cemetery in Alcorn County. Thurman and Cado are buried in Jacinto Cemetery in Alcorn County.

James Bradley Rorie, son of James Elwyn Rorie (b. Dec. 14, 1919) and Elizabeth Mary Lou Holloway (b. Nov. 9, 1922) who married Jan. 6, 1946. Bradley is grandson of Clifton Loranzie "Tip" Holloway (b. Mar. 1, 1901, d. Jan. 20, 1973) and Mary Lee Watson (b. Apr. 3, 104, d. May 3, 1971) who married Aug. 14, 1920, are buried in Hopewell Cemetery in Alcorn County; also grandson of Sanford Stanley (b. Dec. 22, 1881, d. Sep. 29, 1960) and Clara Sue Smith Rorie (b. Aug. 10, 1887, d. May 6, 1971) and are buried in Sardis Cemetery in Alcorn County.

James Bradley had four brothers: Clifton Stanley (b. Sept. 30, 1946, d. Jul. 13, 1987, Old Kemps Chapel Cemetery), Marcus Lee (b. Jun. 22, 1949, d. 1983, Snowdown Chrch of Christ Cemetery), Lonnie Wade (b. Oct. 27, 1955) and twin Donnie Wane (b. Oct. 27, 1955).

William Randy Rorie, James Bradley Rorie, Mary Fay Rorie Phillips, Doris Fay Hendrix Rorie

Bradley and Doris Fay have two children, William Randy (b. Dec. 12, 1971) graduated Thrasher High School in 1991 and works for Gibhart Electrical in Tunica, MS; Mary Fay (b. Mar. 27, 1975) married Toy Calvin "Tripp" Phillips (b. October 1976) and have a son Toy Calvin "T.C." Phillips IV (b. Aug. 16, 1999). Mary graduated Thrasher High School in 1994 and also attended Northeast Junior College at Booneville, MS. She and Tripp are managers and part-owners of Sonic in Booneville.

Bradley attended Reinzi High School and Biggersville High School. He served two years in the US Army and worked at Tyrone, later named Dana for 23 years. He now works Wolverine Tube in Booneville. His interests are hunting and fishing.

Doris attended Jacinto Elementary School, then graduated from Thrasher High School May 10, 1970. She was a homeworker while raising the children. Her interest is sewing, crafts, flowers, fishing and babysitting her grandson. She is Hardee's "Special Biscuit Maker" in Booneville, MS.

ROY, ARTHUR, born Oct. 22, 1847 in Danaleith County, Moray Shile, Scotland, son of Alexander and Margaret George Roy, came to America as a young man in 1870. His trunk had a false bottom in which his money was hidden. He completed his American Naturalization in Corinth, Alcorn County, MS on Jul. 22, 1884.

Arthur married on Apr. 5, 1877, to Francis Dowd (b. Feb. 9, 1855), daughter of Alfred and Amanda Smith Dowd. They raised

The Arthur Roy Family. Back: John, Sandy, Annie, Mandy and Francis. Front: Willie K., Arthur, Jennie, Francis and Rosa

their family of three sons and five daughters in Alcorn County. Two girls died in infancy. Annie married Marcus Wiginton; Alexander "Sandy" married Ida Brown; Mandy Eviline married Emit Nagle; John Arthur married Verdie McEwen; Francis "Frank" Jessie; Jennie; William Kendrick married Mattie Bell Johnson and Rosa Mitchell married Marshall Brown. Arthur died Feb. 12, 1920 and Francis died Nov. 25, 1912.

William Kendrick (b. Feb. 3, 1894, d. Jun. 8, 1954) married on Feb. 13, 1915 in Tishomingo County, to Mattie (b. Nov. 27, 1896 in Alabama, d. Sep. 27, 1972). Willie, or W.K. as he was known, was a farmer but most of his life a saw-miller. When he would get timber to cut, he would load up the mill and his family and move to the new location. The first thing he did was cut enough lumber to build them a house. He would then go on with his saw-milling. He used oxen or mules to log out the trees to be loaded on wagons and later trucks.

Willie and Mattie's children were born in Alcorn, Tishomingo and Prentiss Counties, where today in Prentiss County a son, grandchildren and great-grandchildren live, while others are in other counties in Mississippi, Louisiana and Tennessee. Their five children are:

(1) Conna Bynum (b. Dec. 29, 1915, d. Apr. 15, 1965) married Frankie Miller. Their children are Sue Jean, Doris Dean, Jimmy Wayne and Kenny Lane.

(2) Minnie Bell (b. Oct. 9, 1917) married first Sylvester Chase and had a child, Bobbie Nell. She later married Thomas Crumby and had children, Myra Ann, Tommy Ray, Linda Sue, James Owen, Dwain and Donald George.

(3) Floyd Arthur "Bollie" (b. Oct. 6, 1919 in Prentiss County) married Nov. 12, 1938, to Annie Louise Josephine Bonds (b. Feb. 28, 1915, d. Jun. 7, 1995). Bollie and Louise have lived in Prentiss County as have their three sons and their families since they were married. Bollie spent most of his life as a farmer. Their sons are: 1) William Curtis (b. Oct. 28, 1939) married first Nancy Wheat and had one daughter, Molly Elizabeth. He married second Mary Rosamond. 2) James Floyd (b. Oct. 3, 1941), 3) Johnny Bonds (b. Mar. 2, 1947) married Janet Rinehart and had two daughters, Christina Rena and Sarah Marie. Bollie and Louise had one daughter, Francis Louise (b. and died Jun. 24, 1951).

(4) Cleo Mary (b. Jan. 31, 1922, d. Jun. 12, 1994) married Guy Elton Cole. In Prentiss County, they raised their family of 11 children: Billy Joe, Betty Jane, Eddie Wayne, Terry Gene, Mary Christine, Patsy Ann, Jackie Faye, Debra Lynn, Brenda Gail, Lisa Gay and Shelia Rena.

(5) William Nathan "Hoover" (b. Jan. 26, 1924, d. Jul. 26, 1987) married Jane Martin. Their family was raised in south Mississippi and Louisiana. Their children are Dwight Kendrick, Patty Karen, Ronnie Lee, Paul Edward and Mary Jane.

All three sons and one son-in-law of W.K. and Mattie served in WWII; Conna in the Navy and Bollie, Hoover and Thomas in the Army.

From the many descendants of Arthur and Francis, there are very few male Roys in the last generation to carry the Roy name forward. *Submitted by Bobbie Alford, 1200 Clear Creek Road, Lumberton, MS 39455. (601) 796-4369*

RUSHING-HOUSTON, Mittie Etta Rushing (b. Feb. 1902, d. 1986) daughter of James Edward Rushing and Nancy C. Hellums married Thomas Graham Houston (b. 1889, d. 1938) son of John Lucky Houston and Martha Jane Crowder in 1918. They were blessed with five children: James Thomas "J.T." (b. Mar. 26, 1921), Rayburn B. (b. Apr. 29, 1926, d. Sep. 18, 1926), Martha Geraldine (b. Sep. 1927), Nelwyn B. (b. May 29, 1935) and Charles Rushing (b. Apr. 2, 1939).

Tom enlisted in 1918 and honorably discharged in 1919. Mittie and Tom lived in Mississippi and Alabama. They followed the sawmills. Then they bought J.E. Rushing's place as he was retiring from farming. Mr. Rushing continued to live on the place for the rest of his life.

Thomas Graham Houston and Mittie Etta Rushing on their Wedding Day

Mittie and Tom began rebuilding the old house, keeping only one room of the original structure. While the rebuilding was being done, Tom became ill and was taken to Memphis to the old Marine Hospital where he died of a perforated ulcer. Mittie came back on the train with his body, not knowing how she was even going to get from Booneville to the house. To her surprise, when the train arrived, it was met by the neighbors. It was November 1938 and she was 36 years old and expecting her fifth child.

Friends came and finished the house so that Mittie and the children had a place to live. the following April Charles was born.

Mittie saw loss and tragedy over the years. She had already lost a baby, Rayburn Bostick, who only lived about five months. She lot Tom and had four children to raise.

In 1946 tragedy struck again when a motorist struck J.T. killing him just down the road from the house. He was 25 years old. The entire community suffered along with Mittie because of the loss.

In the years that followed , with a strong will and abiding faith, she was able to raise the three remaining children: Geraldine, Nelwyn and Charles. It was her pleasure to see all of them married and to be able to know all of her grandchildren before her death in 1986.

Geraldine married A.C. Roberts Dec. 23, 1946 and had two children, Shirley June and Dennis Houston.

Nelwyn married first Mary Sue Turner Nov. 3, 1957 and had three children: Miram Sunell, Cecelia Joy and Norris Turner; married second Margaret Belinda Norwood Jun. 29, 1996.

Charles married Dorothy Jeanne Russell and had one child, Charles Russell.

Mittie was a member of the Paden Eastern Star and Forked Oak Baptist Church. She worked at the Burton School Lunch Program and also qualified to work WPA.

Tom and Mittie are buried at Forked Oak Cemetery. *Submitted by Geraldine Roberts.*

RUSHING, JAMES EDWARD, born Jul. 20, 1865 in Mississippi, died December 1947 in MS, son of Abel Rushing and Mary F. Tennison. He married first Nancy Caldonia Hellums (b. Mar. 21, 1869 in Mississippi, d. Apr. 16, 1920, heart attack) on Sep. 17, 1891 in bride's home near Burnsville, MS by Rev. Carroll Patterson; married second C.V. "Miss Lummie" Dunn Dubois (b. 1877) ca. 1925.

James Edward Rushing, Nancy Caldonia Hellums Rushing and all their children

As a young man, James Edward worked on the railroad. Later he farmed until retirement. He was a member of Forked Oak Baptist Church and a Mason.

James and Nancy had nine children: Elton (b. Oct. 10, 1892), Mary Elizabeth (b. Dec. 9, 1894), Willie Blanche (b. Dec. 8, 1896), Minnie (b. Feb. 2, 1899), Mittie Etta (b. Feb. 1, 1902), Bluford (b. Feb. 10, 1904), Leonard H. (b. Jan. 17, 1906), Thomas Byram (b. Jun. 17, 1908) and Hester (b. Apr. 15, 1912).

Elton married Artie Byram and had two children, Madine married Bryson Barber and Cutheran married Mayo ___.

Mary Elizabeth "Bessie" married Harry A. Houston; children: Helen married first Willie Scruggs and second Gavin Cushman, Herman married Sarah Lafayette, Marie married Allen Prestige, James, Quay married Ellis Prestige, Kenneth Wayne married Alice Nelson and Billy Dwayne.

Willie Blanche married John Houston and had one child, Cortez Eugene who married first Leotice Street, second Earline Woodruff and third Peggy ___.

Minnie married Nelson Tillman and had two children, Vhonda married Harvey Davis and Virgil married first Eddie Hercheck and second Ronald Smith.

Mittie Etta married Thomas Graham Houston; children: James Thomas "J.T.", Rayburn Bostick, Martha Geraldine married A.C. Robert, Nelwyn B. married first Mary Sue Turner and second Margaret Belinda Norwood and Charles married Dorothy Russell.

Bluford married Lillian Woodruff; children Dyonne married Claude Potts and Euvonne married L.G. Asbil.

Leonard H. married Liza Wileman; children Juanita married Dee Massey and Laverne married Claude Kennedy.

Thomas Byram married Sadie Ruth Chase; children Laquita married James Pate and Sarah Joe married Joe Maxey.

Hester married Harold D. Austin; children Martha married L.C. Crotts and Monnette married Ray C. Smith.

The Rushing home was open for boarders. Some of the Houston young men from Parsons, TN boarded there while working at the sawmills. In fact, Mr. Rushing is said to have said that the boll weevils got his cotton and the Houstons got his girls.

After Mr. Rushing retired, he, Miss Lummie, his sister Melinda and brother Hiram lived together. After Mr. Rushing's death Miss Lummie went to Alabama to live with her son, Bill Bubuois where she died and is buried near Russellville. *Submitted by Belinda Houston.*

RUSHING, REBECCA SUE ANN, born August 1852 daughter of Abel Rushing and Mary Tennison. On Jul. 22, 1870 in Lee County, MS, she married George T. Johnson, born in Mississippi in September 1852. George and Sue Ann divorced in 1900.

Their first child, John Henry (b. Jul. 19, 1871) married Mattie Launa Harrison in 1907. Their children are William Eugene (b. July 1909) and Frances Launa (b. December 1911). Mattie died in 1914. John married Maude Fink in 1917. Their daughter, Josephine, was born July 1919.

Mary Josephine "Josie" (b. Apr. 2, 1873) married John Dutch Rider in January 1893. Their children are Eulie (b. November 1893), Eva (b. 1899), Owen Looney (b. November 1901), Tandy (b. 1905), Poley (b. 1908) and Vester (b. 1910).

Jesse Clayton (b. Jan. 27, 1877) married Ida Bell Coggins February 1900. Their children are Dessie Mae (b. April 1901), Essie Lee (b. April 1902), Annie Pearl (b. August 1905), Georgia Bell (b. April 1909), Eddie Carlton (b. June 1911) and Leonard (b. September 1921).

The fourth child by census records was Andrew, born December 1879. Family members remember him as "Lude."

Willie Edward (b. Dec. 10, 1880) married Martha Miranda Robinson February 1908. Their children: Maudie Launa (b. April 1910); Lula Mae (b. March 1914); Arthur William (b. September 1917); Robert Leo (b. February 1919); Jesse Leon (born in 1920); Blanche (b. October 1922); Eva Cordella and James Willie, birth dates unknown; William Edward Jr. (b. March 1932) and James Dolan (b. 1933).

Amanda L. "Mandy" (b. Sep. 16, 1883) married William Lee Rider October 1897. Their children are Lee Etta (b. 1898); Lillie Mae (b. 1900); Lou Alma (b. 1903); Ruel Vernon (b. 1906); Sudie (b. February 1908; Glen Franklin (b. October 1910); Reuben Leon (b. August 1913) and Kathleen and Marie, birth dates unknown.

Ovie C. (b. Jun. 13, 1884) married Caleb Gibson Kennedy July 1900. Their children are Minnie Rozena (b. April 1902); Willie Jesse (b. September 1904); Mattie Lou (b. March 1907) and Edna (b. 1918).

Robert Porter (b. Jun. 8, 1886) married Louisa E. "Lou" McCoy July 1907. Their children are Lola Pearl (b. August 1908); Dora L. (b. 1909); Ora M. (b. 1911); Ruth Eveline (b. September 1912) and Robert Arlie "Jack" (b. February 1914).

Luther Coleman (b. Feb. 18, 1889) married Virdie Evelyn McCoy Feb. 24, 1907. Their children are my father, Hermon William (b. April 1909, d. November 1994); James Wilburn (b. March 1914); Beatrice (b. July 1917); Alton Otto (b. May 1921); Mildred Irene (b. February 1924); Helen Virginia (b. June 1926) and Luther Coleman Jr. (b. January 1929, d. June 1987).

James Lester (b. Aug. 1, 1893) married Annis Reynolds May 1921. Their sons are James Eldred (b. 1922); Lester Leon (b. January 1924) and John Clayton (b. April 1927).

Rebecca Sue Ann Rushing Johnson died Christmas Day 1905 and is buried near her parents and daughter, Josie Rider in Forked Oak Cemetery in Prentiss County. George died in Alcorn County February 1917 and is buried in an unmarked grave near daughter, Mandy Rider in Liberty Hill Church Cemetery. *Submitted by Bobby Glen Johnson.*

RYAN, DR. CHARLES, this letter was written almost 100 years ago by Dr. Charles Ryan from Burtons, MS, Jun. 13, 1902 to his granddaughter, Minnie Ryan in Hillsboro, TX.

My Dear little Minnie,

I wrote a letter to your Pa and Ma last Monday, the 9th of this month and I wanted to write one to you, so bad that I was nearly sick, but I felt so weak, tired and lazy that I did not get started off on it, so I decided to put it off a few days longer. Now, I am up at your Aunt Mollie Shack's and although I feel pretty stupid, I concluded that I would write you a little short letter today. All are well up here except Lexie. She is fretting with toothache.

I staid Wednesday night at your Aunt Fan's.

Dr. Charles Ryan (1820-1902).

She has something like a 10-acre field full of young chickens, goslings, ducks and turkeys and it keeps her busy to see to them. She also has plenty of English peas, beans, Irish potatoes and other garden stuff. Other crops look fine although they need rain. Well, I did not get to finish this letter the day I commenced it and it is now Thursday the 18th and I have just come back to your Aunt Molly Shacks from a little trip through the country selling some medicine, but money is terrible scarce. I did not sell much. Well, I must tell you about going to Forked Oak last Saturday to a Lodge of the "Eastern Star." That is a Lodge of Masons for Women. Your Aunt Fannie went with me.

Now you may bet we had a high old time. Plenty of good things to eat and all the lemonade we could drink and seemed like all the little girls and boys in the county must have been there. Most of them were good-looking and well behaved. Some of them looked very much like you. Some like Annie Laurie and Lelia May. Some like Laurence. All dressed fine and seemed so lively and happy that I almost forgot that I was old.

Well, the next day, Sunday, I went to an old fashioned singing at Oak Ridge where they had agreed to sing in the old-fashioned songbooks for the satisfaction of the old folk. Well we had a grand old time there. But it seemed like somebody was missing. When I get into a crowd of people here I can generally see some of my children and a host of grandchildren and great-grandchildren, but some are missing. I can't see your Pa nor your Ma nor you nor Laurence nor Annie Laura nor Lelia May nor Willie Earl. Neither can I see your poor old long lost Aunt Kizzie, Aunt Bettie, Aunt Verdie and the worst missed of all, your poor old Mama. So you see there are a great many missing links in the family chain. And while I occasionally meet with very pleasant things, I also meet some very sad things and the sad things strike so hard that they cut me down faster than the pleasant things can build me up.

Well, I guess I will go down to the old home today and go to the Lodge tomorrow at Bay Springs. And if I can keep stout enough I want to go down below Kirkville next week to see old Uncle Billie, who is in very bad health. Well, Minnie, it will soon be time, I guess, for you and all the school children to go to school and you know I want you all to be good children and to beat all others in everything you undertake to learn. Now, Minnie, I don't want you to be long in answering this letter. You have no idea how much good it does me to get letters from you. Sidney seems to be healthy and stout and plump as a guinea hog, able to do good work. Lexie is rather on the puny list, weak and not able to stand much. It will soon be time for us to go back home or go to Texas, but we are not able to get to Texas, so I guess we will go back to the old home. Give love to Pa and Ma and all the little ones, accept a double share for yourself and be sure to write a great long letter to your . . . very soon.

Good Bye. CRyan.

P.S. This is 20th day of June/02 and all our kin are well so far as I know at present.

Minnie was the daughter of Charles Alonzo Ryan and Cora Apperson. Alonzo died in Dallas, TX about 1950-1955. Their other children were Annie Laurie, Lelia May, Willie Earl and Earnest. (Charles Alonzo was the son of Dr. C. and Eliz.) "Aunt Fan" is Fannie Ryan Goddard, wife of George T. Goddard. "Aunt Mollie Shack" is Mary J. (Molly) Ryan, who married James E. Shackleford. "Kizzie" was Kiziah A. Ryan, who married A.J. Wilson and lived in Indian Territory in Oklahoma in 1880. "Mama" referred to Elizabeth Martin, wife of Dr. C. Ryan. "Aunt Verdie" was Melverdie Ryan, wife of Stephen Millican. She died young and her children, "Lexie" and "Sidney," lived with other family members. "Aunt Bettie" was "Aunt Bet Stephens," another daughter of Charles and Eliz. Ryan.

"Old Uncle Billie" most likely referred to William Richard Ryan, an older brother of Charles. Dr. Ryan died Oct. 7, 1902, a little over three months after he wrote this letter. He is buried with other family members in Friendship. The "old home" he referred to was across the road from Friendship Church and Cemetery. I believe he gave the land for the cemetery. *Submitted by Ruby Williams Magers, 2103 Reagan Cove, Tupelo, MS 38801. (662) 840-3737.*

SCOTT, SAMUEL C., born 1794 in Tennessee. He moved to Alabama where he married Elizabeth Pritchard (b. 1806) in Lauderdale County on Nov. 21, 1830. Their children were James (b. 1832); Margaret (b. 1834) married Cicero Farrar on Oct. 10, 1850;

Tempe (b. 1836) married George W. Henley on Jan. 4, 1858; William (b. 1837); Samuel Berry (b. May 1838) married Mary E. Hodges and Caroline (b. 1843) married Thomas Pate on Dec. 28, 1857.

Charley Scott and Berry Scott

Samuel Berry Scott enlisted in the Army of the Confederacy at Guntown, MS, on Apr. 30, 1861 under Captain John F. Booth. He was mustered into service at Lynchburg in Co. E, 2nd Regiment, Mississippi Infantry. He served throughout the war and on Apr. 2, 1865 he was captured near Petersburg, VA. He was a prisoner of war at Point Lookout Maryland until he was released Jun. 19, 1865.

After returning from the war to Lee County, MS, Berry married Mary E. Hodges on Mar. 28, 1867. They had four children: Charley Marcella (b. Mar. 7, 1875), Nettie, (b. April 1882), Sammie (b. October 1890) and Dora. Mary died sometime between 1912 and 1915.

Charley Marcella Scott married Georgia Ann Charles on Feb. 8, 1894 in Prentiss County, MS. Georgia was born Apr. 11, 1875 to John Charles and Mary Jane Merchant. They had 10 children, four of whom died early: Claudie (b. Jul. 12, 1895, d. May 28, 1905), Leslie (b. Sep. 1, 1900), Myrtle (b. Aug. 28, 1903, d. Feb. 18, 1904), an infant, Effie Hazel (b. Jan. 31, 1905, d. Nov. 10, 1990) married Clifton Beggs, Lula Geneva (b. Aug. 7, 1907) married Odis Hatfield, Leroy Percy (b Jan. 16, 1910, d. Nov. 13, 1987) married Erin Anderson, Mildred Lena (b. Jul. 7, 1912) married Elmer Castleberry, Gara Elois (b. Sep. 11, 1915, d. Oct. 14, 1989) married Homer Parham and Clyde (b. May 1, 1918, d. January 2000) married Pat Shappley.

Leroy Percy Scott married Erin Allene Anderson on Apr. 19, 1933, after her graduation at Pine Grove School in Dumas, MS. She was the daughter of Luther Madison Anderson and Maud Ellen Gross. To them were born Ripple Lee (b. Aug. 24, 1934) who married James Edward Bullard, Clara Jean (b. May 20, 1936) married Harold Thompson, Gerald Denson (b. Jun. 22, 1939) married Linda Floyd, Derryl Anthony "Pete" (b. Mar. 12, 1941) married Brenda Pike, Donna Kay (b. Jul. 17, 1943) married Jimmy Deaton. Leroy was a farmer who later became an engineer and foreman on the construction of many buildings in Prentiss County.

Derryl and Brenda were married Oct. 29, 1965 in Booneville in Prentiss County, MS. They had two children Kelley Michelle (b. May 26, 1966) and Sabrina Svetlana (b. Dec. 4, 1970). Kelley married Nathan Baldwin Jul. 25, 1986 and they have Alexandria Michelle Baldwin (b. Feb. 10, 1999). *Submitted by Derryl "Pete" Scott.*

SHINAULT, WILLIAM M., one of the earliest settlers on Twenty-mile Creek in Old Tishomingo County and present day Prentiss County. He and his wife, Sarah Elizabeth Mann, were living in what is now Prentiss County, near the present Booneville-Baldwyn airport before 1850. He had extensive land holdings, which were divided among his wife, six living children and the children of a daughter, who preceded him in death, prior to and at his death in 1898. William M., Sarah and other family members are buried in Osborne Creek Church Cemetery in Prentiss County and many of their descendants still live in Prentiss County.

William M. Shinault (b. Oct. 2, 1819 in Limestone County, AL, d. died Oct. 30, 1898 in Prentiss County) married Sarah Elizabeth Mann (b. Feb. 29, 1829 in Tennessee, d. Jan. 31, 1902 in Prentiss County). This marriage produced seven children who lived to maturity: Lee O., Emma, Etna, Tennie, William Walter, Annie Lou and Charlie R.

Lee O. Shinault (b. in 1847 in Mississippi, d. 1918-1922 in San Antonio, TX).

Emma T. Shinault (b. 1849, d. Oct. 29, 1923 in Jackson, TN) married Felix W. (Luke) Wadley (b. Sep. 15, 1831, d. Mar. 23, 1923 in Jackson, TN), a merchant.

Etna A. Shinault (b. in 1853 in Mississippi, d. Nov. 2, 1936) married William Crawford (b. 1848, d. 1909) on Feb. 29, 1876. The family lived 40 years in Wheeler, MS. They had nine children who lived to maturity: William D., Annie Ernest, Bessie, Sadie, Cora, J.C., Berdie and Luther. Tennie Shinault (b. Oct. 12, 1856, d. Feb. 5, 1893) married Dr. George Ellis. It is believed she had three children: Gertrude, Baxter and another son(?). The family moved from Prentiss County to Memphis, TN. Dr. George Ellis is believed to be the son of Dr. James B. Ellis of Ripley, MS and whose family came to Ripley from Marshall County, MS.

William Walter Shinault (b. Mar. 12, 1862, d. Jan. 8, 1929) married Siddie A. Burress on Feb. 5, 1889. They had six children: Annie, Sarah, Ottis, Charlie, Willie and Frank. After Siddie's death, he married Kate Grisham in 1914.

Annie Lou Shinault (b. Feb. 3, 1865, d. Dec. 5, 1936) married Sidney M. Barnett (b. 1862, d. 1912). Their three children were William Thomas, Nannie and Bertha. They lived in Booneville, MS. Annie Lou attended Bethlehem Academy in Kentucky from 1877 to 1880.

Charlie R. Shinault (b. Nov. 14, 1867, d. Jan. 12, 1926) married Josephine Pillow. They had one daughter named Josephine. Charlie was a practicing physician in Helena and Little Rock, AR. He was president of the Arkansas Medical Society in 1903 and instrumental in getting the first Arkansas State medical examining law passed.

The following paragraphs contain information about William M. and Sarah E. Shinault's grandchildren and great-grandchildren.

William and Etna Crawford's family: William E. Crawford (b. Nov. 8, 1877, d. Dec. 28, 1951) married ___ and had one son. Annie Maude Crawford married George Taylor. They had one daughter, Louise Taylor. Ernest T. Crawford (b. Apr. 8, 1881, d. Mar. 4, 1957) married Lucy J. Daniel (b. Jul. 4, 1883, d. Dec. 14, 1924) on Oct. 8, 1905. They had four daughters: Mary, Bessie, Ruby and Virginia. Bessie Crawford married ___McCrary and had four daughters. They lived in Memphis, TN. Sadie Eudora Crawford (b. 1882, d. 1911) married ___Seay and had one son, who was raised by her sister, Berdie. Cora Bell Crawford married Boyce Burgess and had three children: Jessie, Annie and Luther. They lived in Tupelo, MS. Julius Charles "Jack" Crawford (b. 1886, d. 1912). Berdie Lee Crawford married Dr. McDougal. They had no children and lived in Wewoka, OK. Luther Harbert Crawford (b. Oct. 25, 1895, d. Jun. 28, 1955) was a WWII veteran. His wife was Alice Garner (b. 1900, d. 1977). Their daughter is Marjorie. Etna's line can be traced to the present time.

Dr. George and Tennie Ellis family: Gertrude Ellis (b. 1876), it is possible that she married a man named Rabb. She lived in Memphis. Baxter Ellis (b. 1878) was a doctor in Memphis or the surrounding area. It is known he had one son, Baxter Ellis Jr and another son, born 1879/1880. The name is illegible on the census. Tennie could have had other children prior to her death in 1893.

William Walter and Siddie Shinault family: Annie T. Shinault (b. Jan. 7, 1890, d. Jan. 5, 1937) married Julius Berry and had one daughter, Margaret Sale Berry (b. 1915, d. 1979); Sarah Charlene Shinault (b. Jan. 24, 1894, d. Dec. 11, 1982) married Arthur B. Shultz, they had no children. Ottis Mann Shinault (b. Aug. 1, 1898, d. Nov. 30, 1979) never married. Charlie R. Shinault (b. Mar. 24, 1899, d. Jan. 10, 1976) married Gwendolyn Sutherland (b. 1902, d. 1996). Their three sons are twins, Charles L. and Ottie and Jerry. Charlie L. Shinault married Bettie Sue Morris. Their daughters are Elizabeth, Charlene and Diane. Gulf Shores, AL, is their home. Ottie Mann Shinault died about 1972. His wife was Mary Lou Dandy. They had two daughters and a son, Richard. Charlie L. and Ottie were WWII pilots. Charlie had a career as air traffic controller in Houston and New Orleans. Ottie trained helicopter pilots at Fort Rucker, AL. Jerome "Jerry" Shinault married Betty___. They have three daughters, Sarah, Jill and Pat. Jerry is an attorney in Mobile, AL. Willie Rice Shinault (b. 1892, d. 1904) drowned. Frank Hamer Shinault (b. ca. 1900, d. ca. 1958) married Gladys___. Their four sons are Edward, William, Gerald and Robert. They live in California.

Sidney M. and Annie Lou Barnett family: William Thomas Barnett (b. 1882, d. 1943) married Annie Stanley. Their two sons are William Thomas "Billy" and Stanley. Nannie Elizabeth Barnett (b. Sep. 12, 1884, d. Jan. 11, 1970) married Robert M. Browning (b. 1884, d. 1952). Their seven children are Thomas, Willie, Mildred, Barnett, Horace, Carroll and Nannie. Allan and Bertha H. Robinson had two children, Sidney M. Robinson and Elizabeth Robinson. Bertha's second husband was Walter Bolton. They had one son, Walter Bolton Jr., who was a pharmacist in Memphis. Annie Lou's line can be traced to the present time.

Charlie R. and Josephine Shinault family: Their daughter Josephine married first ___ Demann and second ___ Thompson and had one son. *Submitted by Betty Browning Ford, 135 Pine Ridge Road, Tuscumbia, AL 35674 and Josie Browning Keeton, 754 CR 5031, Booneville, MS 38829, October 1999.*

SHOUSE FAMILY, the Shouse family in Prentiss County is descended from Johann Adam Schauss (b. 1704, d. 1770) who immigrated to Pennsylvania from Albisheim (Rheinland-Pfalz), Germany in 1736. Johann was granted free passage to America on the Dutch ship *Harle*, so that he might ply his trade as miller for the German-Moravians in the newly founded settlement of Bethlehem, PA. Johann and his children became active in the Moravian-German Unity movement at that time and the Schauss family members provided trade skills such as milling, blacksmithing and ship building. In 1753 Phillip Schauss (b. 1728, d. 1810), son of Johann, joined Count Zinzendorf and two other Moravians and moved south to settle North Carolina and the settlement that is now Winston-Salem, NC. Around 1800 the spelling of the Schauss name became "Shouse."

The whole Ernest and Lucy Shouse family

S.E. "Ed" Shouse was renowned in North Carolina as a cabinetmaker "extraodinaire" at a relatively young age. He made his living by traveling to areas where trade was good and crafting the finest of furniture. This led him to the booming Muscle Shoals/Florence, AL area where he wed America Josephine Dotson in 1888. Ed and Josephine would have only one child, Ernest Lafayette Shouse, as Ed would die of pneumonia at the age of 30, one year later.

Ernest Shouse would live a difficult childhood as a fatherless child. At the age of 12, Ernest was adopted by his Uncle Will and Aunt Jo Dotson. Will and Jo, by all accounts, gave Ernest the loving family he had never known. He was given a good religious education and taught to live by a strong work ethic, traits for which he would be known for the rest of his life. As a teenager, Ernest learned to sawmill and soon operated his own mills. Ernest met and fell in love with his Aunt Jo's younger sister, Lucy Manley of Lawrenceburg, TN. Since Lucy's father didn't approve of the courtship, Ernest and Lucy eloped and married in 1907.

When Ernest and Lucy Shouse moved into Mississippi they would become the first Shouse's living in the state. Residing near Frankstown, Ernest continued to be successful as a sawmiller and was active as an elder in the Church of Christ. Ernest was killed in a sawmill accident at one of his mills in Nashville, GA in 1954. Lucy lived in Booneville until her death in 1982. They had 11 children: Hubert, Grace, Vivian (died as an infant), Homer, Dexter, Edna, Theo, Sam, Zelma, Juanita and. J.V.

Hubert Shouse married Hessie Magers and they lived in Prentiss County most of their lives. Their children were Howard, Herschel, Opal, Wilbur, Billy, James, Carolyn and Betty. Howard and Ernie Bell Shouse live in Booneville, as does Carolyn (Mrs. Boyce) Hutcheson. Billy and Ann Shouse reside in the Wheeler Community.

Homer Shouse married Ruby Senter and raised their family in Marietta. Their children were Helen, Vernon, Louise, J.W. and Lynnette. Ruby continues to make her home in Marietta, since Homer's death in 1978. Helen was married to the late Raymond Glover and had two children, Lannie and Lynn, six grandchildren and one great-grandchild. Helen is married to Curtis Greenhill and lives in Wheeler. Vernon was married to the late Patsy (Wallace) Shouse and had three children: Sam (Birmingham, AL), Tana (Mobile, AL) and Teresa (Corinth) and four grandchildren. Vernon lives in Booneville. Louise is married to Bennie Vickers and presently lives in Jacksonville, FL. They have one child, Karen living in Arlington, VA. J.W. and Jo Shouse presently live in Camden, TN. They have two children, Kevin (Omaha, NE) and Phil (Auburn, AL) and one grandchild. Lynnette is married to Gary Thornton and lives in New Site with their son, David.

Edna married Youal Thornton and lives in New Site. They have two sons, Norris and James, who also lives in the area. Norris and Joann Thornton have three sons: Michael, Marlon and Raben (Lake Worth, FL) and four grandchildren. James and Patricia Thornton have two daughters, Tammy Bullard and Tina Hutchens.

Theo married Nettie Corbin and lives in Booneville. They had two children, Charles and Peggy. Charles and his wife, Kathy, have three children: Brandi, Penni (Mrs. Glenn) Cooper and Mickey and one grandchild. The late Peggy (Mrs. Jerry) Glover has one son, Brian, who is living in Wheeler.

Zelma (Shouse) Darwin and her family live in Sparks, GA and J.V. Shouse and his family live in Morganfield, KY.

SMART, HENRY CLIFFORD, born Jul. 31, 1918, son of William Henry Smart and Annie Lou Michael Smart and Ruby Lucille Green (b. Jan. 25, 1919) the daughter of Joseph Clayton Green and Delia Lou Ledbetter Green were married Jul. 18, 1936.

Clifford spent over 40 years as a Baptist minister in small churches in Prentiss and Tippah Counties. Ruby spent the majority of her life working in the home. For many years they operated Smart's Grocery in Jumpertown and worked a dairy farm.

H.C. and Ruby Smart and Children, Christmas 1977. Anita Turner, Lynn Corbin, Mary Sue Perrigo, Jerry Smart, Bobby Smart, Billy Smart, Martha Prather and Gilford Smart.

Clifford and Ruby had eight children, four girls and four boys, Billy Joe and Bobby Henry (b. Oct. 30, 1940); Charles Gilford (b. Dec. 7, 1943); Martha Louise (b. Jan. 3, 1946); Jerry Leon (b. Apr. 19, 1952); Mary Sue (b. Mar. 30, 1958); Ruby Lynn (b. Sep. 8, 1960) and Anita Joy (b. Dec. 7, 1962).

The Smart children all graduated from Jumpertown High School and seven attended college and five graduated from college and they all lived in Prentiss County the majority of their lives. They all married and had children of their own.

Billy married Janice Morris, daughter of Burnis and Susie Morris on Dec. 22, 1962. They had one daughter, Lori Jo Smart (b. Aug. 15, 1968). Janice died Dec. 7, 1994.

Bobby married Sharon Michael, daughter of Virginia and Bonard Michael, on Aug. 21, 1964. They never had children.

Gilford married Jane Nicholson, daughter of Ray and Janice Nicholson, on Aug. 20, 1965. They had two sons, Charles Kevin, (b. Sep. 14, 1972) and Lonnie Ray (b. Nov. 20, 1977).

Martha married J.C. Prather, son of R.C. and Erma Prather, on Sep. 4, 1964. They had two sons, Cary Bret (b. Apr. 1, 1969) and Kelly Bart (b. Sep. 10, 1971).

Jerry married Cindy Newcomb, daughter of J.E. and Beatrice Newcomb, on Jan. 4, 1975. They had one daughter, Brandi Nicole (b. Oct. 4, 1977).

Mary Sue married Jacky Perrigo, son of Herschel and Christine Perrigo, on Jun. 4, 1976. They had two sons, Justin Paul (b. Mar. 4, 1980) and Coy Evan (b. Jan. 28, 1985).

Lynn married Freddie Corbin, son of Eugene and Kathleen Corbin, on Nov. 14, 1980. They had two daughters, Holly Smart (b. Dec. 15, 1986) and Annie Ruby (b. Jun. 30, 1992).

Anita married Tommy Turner, son of Tom and Bobbie Turner, on Jul. 26, 1985. They had two children, Bric Thomas (b. Sep. 17, 1986) and Mariah Lucille (b. Aug. 20, 1996).

Lori Jo Smart, daughter of Billy and Janice, married Mark Taylor, on Aug. 20, 1994 and they had one daughter, Jana Marie (b. Apr. 13, 1997). They have one son, Adam Taylor (b. Jan. 25, 1985).

Charles Kevin Smart, son of Gilford and Jane, married Rhonda Robinson on Aug. 21, 1999. *Submitted by Ruby Smart.*

SMITH, ARTHUR ELIGAH, born May 18, 1873 in Booneville, Prentiss County, MS, died Sep. 4, 1942. He married Noonie Hopper Sep. 23, 1889.

Arthur Eligah and Noonie had five children: Tyne Walker (b. Jan. 13, 1901, d. Jun. 26, 1971) married Valcour Clayton Aug. 13, 1923; Daylon Clayton (b. Nov. 4, 1903, d. May 16, 1964); Youlas Warren (b. Apr. 18, 1907, d. Sep. 16, 1959; Eligah Daniel (b. Aug. 18, 1909, d. Sep. 14, 1969) married Taffa Lee Bonds Jun. 21, 1929; Bynum M. (b. Sep. 5, 1911). *Submitted by Margaret Smith Carson.*

SMITH, BYNUM M., born Sep. 5, 1911 in Booneville, Prentiss County, MS, d. Dec. 27, 1991 in Iuka, Tishomingo County, MS. He married twice, first Vada Faye Smith Whitaker Mink in Booneville, MS; second Emma Leah Ashcraft Apr. 18, 1931 in Corinth, MS.

Bynum and Emma had nine children: Bynum M. Jr. (b. Jul. 15, 1931, d. less than one year of age); Mary Dean (b. Dec. 1, 1932) married Q.D. Pollard Aug. 23, 1953 in Booneville; Bobby Marion (b. Feb. 9, 1935) married Susie Jane Stinnett Mar. 5, 1955 in Washington, DC; Mildred Ione (b. May 12, 1938) married Robert Paige Craven Jun. 27, 1957 in Quitman, MS; John David (b. Feb. 6, 1941) married Myrtle Viola Eaton Feb. 9, 1962 in Booneville; Margaret Irene (b. Jan. 3, 1943) married an unknown person Jun. 1, 1963 in Booneville, her children: Elizabeth Leigh Carson (b. Dec. 1, 1966), Rebecca Carol Carson (b. Aug. 16, 1968), Joseph Reuben Carson (b. May 21, 1970) all born in Iuka, MS; Glenda Joyce (b. Jan. 17, 1946) married Jimmy Gorden Burcham Sep. 21, 1964 in Booneville; Judith Ellen (b. Jan. 25, 1950) married Thermon "V" Saylors Aug. 2, 1968 in Booneville and Bonnie Lee (b. Nov. 2, 1954) married Devin David Ruesch Jul. 26, 1974 in Provo, UT. *Submitted by Margaret Smith Carson.*

SMITH, ELIJAH, born Feb. 12, 1834 in Anson County, NC, died 1903 in Booneville, Prentiss County, MS. He married twice, first Nancy Nicholdson, Dec. 20, 1855 in Tishomingo County, MS; second Amanda Harriett Johnston, Dec. 22, 1859 in Tishomingo County, MS.

Elijah and Amanda had 10 children: James M. "Dock" (b. 1862, d. in Texas); Mary Callie (b. 1864, d. in Mart, TX) married J.R. "Jim" Calvery, Apr. 17, 1887; Thomas Frank (b. 1866, d. in Texas) married Rachel Carpenter; Virgal Henry (b. Jun. 18, 1868, d. Jul. 13, 1946) married Savannah Swinny Jan. 17, 1893; Winnie Francis (b. Apr. 18, 1869, d. Dec. 8, 1914) married Price Henderson; Della F. (b. Oct. 19, 1871, d. Apr. 2, 1914) married Will G. Winfield Dec. 18, 1900; Arthur Eligah (b. May 18, 1873); Tandy Hill (b. Sep. 24, 1874, d. Apr. 16, 1956) married R. Mintie Johnston Dec. 1, 1893; Tintas Walker "Tyne" (b. 1878, d. in Texas) married Bertha; Edward D. (b. August 1883, d. 1929) never married. *Submitted by Margaret Smith Carson.*

SMITH, HENRY BUFORD, born Nov. 22, 1903, ancestors settled in what is now the eastern part of Prentiss County. On Jan. 5, 1843, Vincent Allen Tharp Smith (b. May 20, 1812, d. Jun. 19, 1897), son of Mose and Lousette (Tharp) Smith from Pike County, GA, married Elender Ann Susanne Pactrick (b. Jan. 5, 1828, d. Feb. 11, 1911), daughter of Lewellen and Nellie Dempsey Pactrick from Alabama. Vincent Allen was a farmer and

Henry Buford and Myrtie Jarnagin Smith with children, Louise and Curtis Lyle

postmaster at Brown's Creek Post Office in 1895-1896. One of their 10 children was Joseph Andrew Jackson Smith (b. Dec. 7, 1851). He married Harriet Melbra Shackelford. Grandpa Joe, as he was called, had a truly remarkable means of showing hospitality. "When eating at his table, the bowls were never passed around, you passed your plate to him, he filled it as he pleased. You never went away hungry, maybe too full."

Joseph Andrew and Melbra had 11 children. There was Oscar Harmon, Willis Allen, Dan, Menirva, Marcus, Elliot, Laster, Blanche, William Tankley, Electa "Leckie" and Riley Bell.

Oscar Harmon Smith (b. Jan. 25, 1883) married Hattie Bell Beard (b. Jul. 6, 1884), daughter of David and Nancy Beard, farmers in Tishomingo County. Hattie was the sister of Porter, Gennie, Molly, Dora, Lillie, Everet, Eddie and Etner.

Six children were born to Oscar and Hattie Bell: William Arnold, Henry Buford, Luther Earl, Kelly Adel, Chester Randel and Eula Pearl.

Myrtie Wilson Jarnagin's (b. Dec. 26, 1905) family was among the first settlers in eastern Prentiss County. Her father, James Oscar Jarnagin (b. Oct. 15, 1873, d. Nov. 24, 1957) married Dora Evelena Wright (b. May 20, 1883, d. May 10, 1949). She was the daughter of Reverend James Monroe Wright (b. Jan. 3, 1857) and Mary Jane White (b. Apr. 4, 1859).

Dora was the granddaughter of John Francis Wright and Mary Anne Elizabeth Windham.

The Jarnagins came from Cherokee, AL. Myrtie had a sister, Mamie (b. Nov. 26, 1908, d. May 31, 1927). She is buried in Friendship Cemetery. Her brother, Earnest Clayton (b. Aug. 25, 1903, d. Aug. 1, 1969), is buried in East Prentiss. They were never married.

Henry Buford Smith attended school at Oak Ridge. Myrtie attended school at East Prentiss.

On Apr. 22, 1927, the Reverend C.J. Orlander joined their hands in marriage. Three children were born to this union: Mamie Louise (b. Feb. 11, 1929), Curtis Lyle (b. Jul. 10, 1933) and Billy Harold (b. Oct. 13, 1941).

Louise married Melvin Lee White on Oct. 1, 1947. To them was borne son, Dale Lee White (b. Aug. 1, 1948). He married Angela Barrett. They had two children, Christopher Lee (b. Mar. 3, 1970) and Brandi Nicole (b. Oct. 13, 1971). Chris married Leslie Bolton. They had one son, McKinzie Elton Lee White (b. Jun. 23, 1993). Chris is now married to Cindi Horn.

Brandi has two children by marriage to Mark Moreland: Jessica Helena Nicole (b. Apr. 26, 1989) and Justin Barrett (b. May 23, 1991) Brandi is now married to Jeff Davis.

Melvin died Jul. 27, 1994. He is buried in Liberty Memorial Cemetery. Louise lives at Hills Chapel. Dale is married to Rhonda Borden Ackers. They make their home in Iuka, MS.

Curtis served in the US Army (1954-1956) in the 41st Signal Corps, Co. C, Fort Chaffee, AR and Fort Ord, CA. He was discharged from USAR in April of 1962. He earned the rank of SP4. He married Barbara Windham. To them were born two sons, Tony Curtis (b. Jul. 8, 1954) and Gary Wayne (b. Mar. 6, 1959). Tony married Sabre Howell and they had one child, Kayla Suzette (b. Oct. 19, 1982). He later married Kayann Mayo. A daughter was born to them, Lesa Kayann (b. Nov. 9, 1991). Tony died May 19, 1996, as a result of a gunshot wound. He is buried in the Booneville Cemetery.

Gary had one daughter, Summer Noel Smith (b. Sep. 13, 1992). She lives in Searcy, AR, near her grandmother, Barbara. Gary married Donna A. Silky of Strafford, MO. A month after their marriage on Jun. 5, 1995, Gary died in an automobile accident in Springfield, MO. He is buried in the Mt. Pisgah Cemetery near Springfield, MO.

On Mar. 14, 1970, Curtis married Erline Owens Smith. She had two children, Harold Wayne and Lori Lynn Smith (see Owens-Simmons). They reside in Booneville.

Billy Harold Smith served six years (1962-1968) in the Army National Guard, Co. R, 398th Regiment, Fort Chaffee, AR. His rank was sergeant, E-5. On Dec. 24, 1962, he married Saundra Dawnell Bullard (b. Nov. 23, 1944). Two children were born to this union, Tori Dawn (b. May 20, 1966) and George Bradford (b. Sep. 11, 1971). SSgt. Brad is now serving in the US Air Force. He resides in Seattle, WA. Billy, Saundra and Tori make their home in Booneville.

Henry Buford worked as a farmer, sawmill worker and later as a carpenter with his brother, Arnold until he died Dec. 2, 1968.

Myrtie worked many years in the garment industry until she retired. She married Woodrow Wilson Schoggins. He died Sep. 22, 1977. Myrtie died Oct. 20, 1983. She and Buford are buried in East Prentiss Cemetery. *Submitted by Erline Smith.*

SMITH, HUBERT RAY, born Jan. 11, 1906, died Apr. 29, 1970, son of Lonnie Douglas Smith (b. 1875, d. 1970) and Dorcas Howell Smith (b. 1878, d. 1940), was reared in the New Hope Community of Prentiss County, MS. Hubert had one brother, Argyle F. Smith (b. 1901, d. 1983), of Fulton, MS and two sisters, Annie Lou Wigley (b. 1907, d. 1970) of Huntsville, AL and Mauveline Smith Wilemon of the Burton Community in Prentiss County, Mississippi. Hubert's grandparents were Columbus Washington Smith and Matilda Carter Smith and Elisha Andrews Howell (b. 1842, d. 1923) and Mary Ann (Molly) Goddard Howell (b. 1848, d. 1919). His great-grandparents were Vincent Allen Thorpe Smith and Ellen Patrick Smith and Gilbert Howell (b. 1816, d. 1894) and Sarah Nabors Howell (b. 1814, d. 1861).

Hubert received a bachelor of science degree from Mississippi Agricultural and Mechanical College (now Mississippi State University) in 1931 and a master of education degree in 1954. He taught agriculture and science for 35-1/2 years in schools in Tishomingo, Prentiss and Alcorn counties. One of his students was Thelma Christine Umfress (b. Dec. 21, 1915, d. Jul. 22, 1995), whom he married on Aug. 18, 1934.

Hubert Ray Smith and Thelma Christine Umfress Smith

Christine was the daughter of Alvie Dean Umfress (b. Oct. 19, 1881, d. Jan. 15, 1971) and Nellie Jane Stricklin Umfress (b. Apr. 28, 1885, d. Apr. 24, 1965). Christine had three brothers: Wayne Armon Umfress (b. Feb. 1, 1914) of Pontotoc, MS; Milford Henry Umfress (b. Mar. 3, 1918) of Memphis, TN and Clastie Umfress (b. Jan. 29, 1920) of Senatobia, MS. Christine was reared in the Cairo Community of Prentiss County and graduated from Holcut High School in 1935.

Hubert and Christine were Baptists and lived most of their married life in the Smith home place a mile and a half north of New Hope. In addition to teaching, Hubert farmed and raised livestock. Christine worked for many years at Brown Shoe Co. in Booneville. She was an avid gardener and loved flowers. They are both buried in the New Hope Cemetery.

The marriage of Hubert and Christine produced three sons: Hubert Ray Smith, Jr. (b. Dec. 1, 1937), Gene David Smith (b. Mar. 15, 1941, d. Jan. 16, 1943) and Don Edwin Smith (b. Sep. 26, 1944).

Ray resides in Alexandria, VA, where he is a dentist. Ray married on Mar. 16, 1965, to the former Marjorie Cameron Pulman of Alexandria. Ray and Margie have two children: Anne Carter Smith Papp (b. Jul. 31, 1968) married on May 24, 1997 Richard Douglas Papp of Atlanta, GA and Douglas Dean Smith (b. Mar. 2, 1971).

Don is a dentist in Kosciusko, MS. Don married on Nov. 2, 1968, to the former Brenda Margaret Frazier of Jackson, MS. Don and Brenda have one son, Don Edwin (Win) Smith Jr. (b. Feb. 24, 1970). Win is a dentist with his father in Kosciusko and married on Jun. 26, 1993, to the former Pamela Mechelle Moore of Kosciusko. Win and Mechelle have one son, Don Edwin Smith III (b. Jun. 29, 1999), whom they call Edwin. *Submitted by Dr. Don E. Smith.*

SMITH, JOE DAVE, born to Willis Allen and Etna Rozella Beard Smith Feb. 3, 1903 in the Mackey's Creek Community of Prentiss County. Willis Allen was the son of Joseph Andrew Jackson and Harrietta Milberry Shackelford Smith. Etna Rozella was the daughter of Dave Virgil and Nancy Caroline Wright Beard. On Sep. 19, 1926, Joe Dave married Vera Alene McKinney. They were married by Will Rhoads, Justice of the Peace, at his home in Prentiss County. Vera is the daughter of James Thomas and Lydia Belzora Crow McKinney. She was born Oct. 18, 1908 in Prentiss County.

Joe Dave, Vera and Hoyt Smith in 1928

Dave and Vera started their married life in a house on her parents' farm. It was probably built when Uncle Clayton married, since Mama refers to it as "Clat's house." It seemed to be the beginning home for the McKinney kids as they married. They made one crop there, then they became sharecroppers, meaning they lived on someone else's farm and worked their land for a share of the profit and a house to live in. The farms they shared can be remembered according to which child was born there, Hoyt was born at the McKinney house; Boyd on Will Caver's farm in the Candlers Chapel Community; Nelene on the Frank Whitlow farm in the same community; JoAnn on the Luther Taylor farm in the Hills Chapel Community and Mac on the Harold Smith farm in the New Hope community. From there, they moved to the Tuscumbia Community and worked the farm owned by Milton Pardue. They made one crop there, then became landowners.

Their first farm was north of the South Prentiss School. They later sold that land and purchased the farm just east of the school. Junior was born after we moved there. Joe Dave never owned a tractor and farmed all his life with a team of mules. We also milked several cows and sold milk. Children of Joe Dave and Vera are:

1. Willis Hoyt (b. 1927, d. 1989) married Betty Jean Rushing and had Shelly. Later, he married Mable Gattis, but was divorced from both wives.

2. Boyd Wythel (b. 1929) married Betty Whybrew and had Cathy and Marty. They divorced and he married Juanita Baer later.

3. Nelene (b. 1934) married James Mitchell Pannell (b. 1930, d. 1989) and had Shelia and Janet.

4. JoAnn (b. 1937) married Jerry Massey (b. 1935, d. 1985) and had Michael, Mark and Melinda.

5. Luther McKinney "Mac" (b. 1942, d. 1964) never married.

6. J.D. Junior (b. 1947) married Josie Bohannon and had Kelly, Nicholas and LeAnn.

All of their sons and sons-in-law served their country in the military. Hoyt was in the US Navy from 1945 until retirement in 1974. Boyd was in the US Army in the Korean War. Junior was in the US Army in the Vietnam War. Mitchell was in the US Army in the Korean War. Jerry was in the US Army at the end of the Korean War. Mac was waiting to be drafted to Vietnam when he drowned.

Dave lived 93 years in Prentiss County. He died Sep. 15, 1996 and was buried in the East Prentiss Church Cemetery. He and Vera have long been members of East Prentiss Baptist Church. *Submitted by Nelene Pannell, PO Box 82, Booneville, MS.*

SMITH, STEPHEN TAYLOR AND SALLIE GRISHAM SMITH FAMILY, Stephen Taylor Smith (b. Nov. 9, 1848, d. Feb. 4, 1927) was elected as a supervisor of Prentiss County, MS, Second District in 1899. He served for eight years and "in this capacity served his people very faithfully," according to his obituary. He was born in Georgia and moved to the Prentiss County area shortly after the Civil War. He married Sallie Grisham (b. 1872, d. 1959) Sep. 20, 1890.

Stephen's parents were Capt. John Smith and Mary Neil Gardner (no dates available), who lived near Barnsville, GA before moving to this area. Stephen's siblings were Frederick Page Smith, married Mollie?; Dr. Robert G. Smith (b. 1851, d. 1887), married Amanda Shepherd; Dr. Boliver Rogers Smith (b. 1853, d. 1930), never married and a sister Burke, died at approximately 13 years of age before the family moved to Mississippi. Dr. Robert G. practiced medicine in the Burton Community from 1875 until his death in 1887. At that time, his brother Dr. Boliver, who had practiced medicine for two years in Marietta with Dr. Warren and at his home in the Osborne Creek Community, moved to Burton and took up that practice for approximately 45 years. Robert and Boliver are buried in the Forked Oak Church Cemetery. Stephen Taylor and Sallie are buried in the Osborne Creek Cemetery. John Smith and his wife Mary Neil's burial site have not been determined at this time.

Stephen Taylor Smith and granddaughter Marjorie Oakley Franks, age 3 or 4 years

At the beginning of the Civil War, Stephen, approximately 13 years old was too young to fight, but this did not deter him from helping the cause. He volunteered to guard Yankee prisoners. When he turned 15, Stephen ran away and joined his father and his father's brothers in the Confederate Army. Their mustering out pay was $50 in silver and some horses.

Sallie Grisham Smith's parents were Hardin William Grisham (b. 1832, Tennessee, married Oct. 29, 1853, Tishomingo County, MS, d. 1884, Prentiss County, MS) and Sarah Ann Felitha Quemina Massey (b. 1834, Anderson District, SC, d. 1922, Prentiss County, MS). Their homeplace, where Sallie grew up was on the Osborne Creek-Wheeler Road around the present site of the Wilmer Keeton house. Hardin William joined the Confederate Army about May 1861 and served for a time in the company of Col. Mark Lowery and Capt. Swinney. He was discharged "for sore feet," according to the application for pension filed by his widow Sarah. Other children of Hardin William and Sarah were Harriet Elizabeth "Betty" (md. Daniel L. Prichard); Eugenia Meridian (md. Frank Elder); Martha Lou (md. Jeff Mitchell); William Hardin "Will" (md. Susan Elizabeth Muse); George Alexander (md. Mary Susan Davis), Robert (md. Edna Augusta Blanchard), James Washington "Jim" (md. Ollie Frances Campbell), Charlie Norton (?) and Daniel Lee (?). Hardin William's father was George William Grisham (b. ca. 1795, Virginia, d. ca. 1850, Old Tishomingo County, MS). His mother's name is unknown and she apparently died shortly after his birth. George William's second wife was Elizabeth Gordon (b. Jan. 15, 1818, Georgia, d. Jan. 12, 1900, Prentiss County). Hardin William and Sarah are buried in Osborne Creek Cemetery.

Stephen Taylor Smith and Sallie Grisham Smith holding infant daughter Ruth

Stephen and Sallie Smith were a prosperous, well-respected family of Prentiss County, owning many acres of farmland. They lived in a large home on Osborne Creek Road. Stephen was 24 years older than his wife. He had been "smitten" early on with the young Sallie. Family members often repeated that Stephen told friends and family that he was waiting for Sallie to grow up and become his wife and he dated all of her sisters while he waited. As a bachelor of 42, Stephen married the 18 year-old Sallie. They became the parents of three daughters: Ruth (b. Jul. 7, 1891, d. Dec. 15, 1972, md. Claude A. Oakley); Lura Mae (b. May 29, 1894, d. Oct. 9, 1980, md. Harvey P. Franks) and Marjorie Marie Taylor (b. Dec. 10, 1897, d. June 1994). The only descendants from the Stephen Taylor and Sallie Grisham Smith family came from the Claude and Ruth Oakley marriage (see Claude Oakley Family History).

Marjorie Marie Smith Taylor, "Miss Marie" to most was a graduate of Mississippi Normal Institute (now University of Southern Mississippi). She taught in Prentiss County schools for many years. She married Blanchard Taylor in 1926, but divorced some years later. Lura and Harvey lived all of their married lives in Memphis, TN.

Sallie Grisham Smith with her three daughters, L-R: Lura, Ruth and Marie

After Stephen died in 1927, Sallie operated a small store from the back of her home for a few years. In the late 1920s or very early 1930s, that house burned and Sallie built a new house in the same spot. She continued to live in the same house and managed her farmland for 32 years until her death in 1959. For much of that time her daughter Marie lived with her. Daughter Ruth, husband Claude and their large Oakley family lived across the road. The Smith and Oakley properties and homesites are located at the intersection of Highway 45 and south end of Osborne Creek Road. *Submitted by Gloria Franks Smith, great-granddaughter.*

SMITH, THOMAS, born Mar. 26, 1813 in Anson County, NC, died May 22, 1889 in Booneville, Prentiss County, MS. Body interred in Booneville, Prentiss County, MS, Smith Chapel.

He married twice, first Winferde Ratliff, Jan. 6, 1833; second Matilda Duncan Reynolds in Booneville, Prentiss County, MS Oct. 31, 1878.

Thomas and Winferde had 13 children: Elijah (b. Feb. 12, 1834); Joseph (b. Jun. 17, 1835, d. before 1889) married Elizabeth Caudle; Macy (b. Dec. 26, 1837, d. Jul. 1, 1917 in Ennis, TX) married twice, first Robert "Bob" Alexander Floyd Oct. 9, 1853 and then Vol Ennis, Sep. 16, 1865; Culpepper (b. Apr. 27, 1839, d. Jun. 10, 1862) married Francis Vanderford Mar. 21, 1860; Martha Ann (b. Dec. 14, 1840); Susan (b. May 15, 1844); Elizabeth (b. Mar. 8, 1846) married Robert James Whitesides Jan. 15, 1871; Jefferson (b. Mar. 16, 1848, d. 1909) married Louisa W. Bonds Jan. 9, 1871; Henry (b. Jun. 17, 1850); Ratliff A. (b. Oct. 27, 1853, d. Sep. 21, 1914) married Martha Jane Kelton Jan. 5, 1875; Manizer (b. May 20, 1855, d. before 1860); Walker (b. Oct. 27, 1856, d. Sep. 23, 1894) married Mattie Reynolds Feb. 5, 1882; Christopher Evans (b. Sep. 5, 1859) married Sarah Victoria McHaffy Nov. 9, 1899. *Submitted by Margaret Smith Carson*

SMITH, THOMAS "TOM," born 1878 and died 1955, the son of Jefferson Smith and grandson of Thomas Smith Jr., who settled in the Tuscumbia Community in Prentiss County in 1854. Tom married Anna Johnson in 1905. They had three sons: Earnest (b. Oct. 6, 1906); Lonnie (b. Oct. 26, 1907) and Charlie (b. 1913). Anna and Charlie were killed when a tornado struck their home near Rienzi, MS, on Mar. 20, 1913.

My grandfather, Thomas, went through much agony and turmoil during the next year or so. He married Cordelia Lambert, the daughter of Bill Lambert, on Christmas Day in 1914. They had six children: Dorothy, Juanita, Sylvester, Hestle, Jettie and Lester. Cordelia died Feb. 20, 1969. Thomas and Cordelia are buried in the Smith Chapel Cemetery.

Earnest Smith married Maggie "Tea" Lambert on Oct. 1, 1928. Tea (b. Jun. 11, 1911) was the youngest child of Charlie Lambert and Vina Jane Carpenter Lambert, both of Prentiss County. Earnest and Tea had three children: Charles Edward (b. Mar. 20, 1930); Ileene (b. Oct. 30, 1931) and Etheleene (b. Jun. 2, 1941). Earnest died Mar. 10, 1992 and Etheleene died Mar. 22, 1999.

Charles Smith enlisted in the Army in 1948. During his military career, he served in various countries, including Japan, Korea, Panama Canal Zone and Vietnam. During his tour in Japan, he married Kuniko Kumazawa on Oct. 31, 1951. They have three children: Kinu Diane (b. Mar. 2, 1953); Kenneth Wayne (b. Aug. 12, 1954) and Sheila Ann (b. Sep. 13, 1962). Charles retired from the Army in 1972 and entered into real estate sales in Augusta, GA. He opened his own company in March 1983 and retired from real estate in 1994.

Diane Smith married Ralph Carney on Jun. 2, 1973. They have four children: Jerry Edward (b. Jun. 15, 1974); Bradford Lee (b. Apr. 23, 1976); Allison Diana (b. Mar. 28, 1985) and Valerie Elise (b. Dec. 2, 1987). Ralph is an office service technician with Earthgrains Bakery and Diane is a real estate broker in Augusta, GA. Jerry is employed by The Carpet Mart in Augusta, GA. Brad and his wife, Kimberly Napier, live outside Asheville, NC, where Brad works as a mechanical engineer for Meritor Corporation and Kim is a pharmacist for CVS.

Kenneth Smith married Mary Peacher on Jul. 14, 1971. They have one son, Erik Wayne Smith, born Sep. 24, 1971. Kenneth and Mary own a new home construction business in Augusta, GA. Erik married Chasity Rene Bolyard on May 18, 1996. They have one son, Caleb Wayne, born Sep. 14, 1998. Erik is the owner of S & S Hydro, Inc. Landscaping Co. Chasity is a nurse with the Augusta Health Department.

Sheila married Mark Atkins on Nov. 28, 1978. They have two daughters, Dana Kay (b. Dec. 15, 1978) and Crystal Lynn (b. Jan. 27, 1982). Sheila is a real estate broker in Augusta, GA. Mark is a trim contractor of new homes. Dana is a junior at Augusta State University. *Submitted by Charles Smith.*

SMITH, ILEENE, is the second child of Earnest and Maggie "Tea" Lambert Smith (b. Oct. 30, 1931). She married Tulon Floyd on Jul. 18, 1949. They have two daughters, Retha Gail (b. Dec. 13, 1950) and Nioka Kay (b. Mar. 7, 1953). Ileene married David Riddle on Jan. 22, 1966.

Retha Gail Floyd was married to Johnny Cummings on Jan. 10, 1969. They have one son, Greg (b. Oct. 25, 1969). Gail married Jimmy Sisenea on Feb. 17, 1994.

Greg Cummings married Leeja Lauderdale on Oct. 3, 1986. They have three children: Cody Lee (b. Jan. 22, 1987), Wesley Tyler (b. Jan. 8, 1989) and Whitney LeeAnn (b. May 8, 1990). Greg is a lieutenant with the Booneville Fire Department. Leeja works for the Prentiss County government.

Nioka Kay Floyd married Tommy Thorne on Nov. 3, 1971. They have one daughter, Wendy Kay (b. May 31, 1975). Kay married Juan Gonzalez. Kay is a nurse in Tampa, FL.

Wendy Kay Thorne has a son, Corey (b. Apr. 21, 1992). Wendy married Perry McVey on Nov. 16, 1995. They have one daughter Brookelyn McKayle (b. Jul. 11, 1996). Perry died May 12 1999.

Etheleene Smith Kelley

Etheleene Smith (b. Jun. 2, 1941) the youngest child of Earnest and Maggie "Tea" Lambert Smith married John Kelley on Nov. 11, 1959. They have six children: John J. (b. Jun. 27, 1961); Susan (b. Aug. 18, 1963); Richard F. (b. Aug. 10, 1964); Thomas P. (b. Feb. 8, 1968); Cassandra (b. May 8, 1969) and Patricia (b. Nov. 5, 1973). Etheleene died Mar. 22, 1999.

John Kelley is married to Lynn Novack. They have two children: John (b. Sep. 29, 1983) and Tom (b. May 14, 1988).

Susan Kelley is single and lives near her father in Booneville, MS.

Richard Kelley is married to Colleen Hamilton. They have three children: Richard (b. Jun. 10, 1982); Nicole (b. Jan. 17, 1984) and Joseph (b. Mar. 1, 1985).

Thomas P. Kelley has one son, Michael (b. Aug. 28, 1985). Cassandra Kelley is married to Dennis Prisant. They have four children: Robert (b. Jun. 8, 1990); Matthew (b. Jul. 4, 1991); Jordan (b. Sep. 24, 1994) and Ryan (b. Mar. 16, 1998).

Patricia Kelley is married to Jason Kimbrell. They have two children: Paige (b. May 7, 1993) and Jason (b. Oct. 4, 1994). *Submitted by Ileene Riddle.*

SMITH, WILLIAM ARNOLD, William Arnold Smith was born to Oscar & Hatties Belle Smith in 1903. They lived in the Mackey Creek-Burton community east of Booneville. W.A. married Ethel Pardue in November 1922. They had two children, Maxine and Glen. W.A. always loved working with wood, so he began the trade of carpentry. He and his only son, Glen SMith, worked together in the 1950's building many Prentiss County homes. During that time, Glen Smith COnstruction was incorporated. On August 22, 1961 W.A. Smith was killed in an automobile accident. Glen continued to uphold the reputation of "Building Good Homes" in Prentiss County. During the sixties Glen became co-owner of Builders Supply Inc., then Smith Lumber Company was opened in the seventies. Smith Lumber was located on the site of the old Booneville Cotton GIn on 145N between the Ford and Chevrolet dealerships. By the nineties Glen had sold his business and was semi-retired. He developed Smith Subdivision from 40 acres of farmland and named the streets afterr his first three grandchildren: Glenwood Street (David Glen Stutts), Carleigh Lane (Carleigh Vick), and Hollie Haven (Hollie Stutts). All in all , Smith Construction has built over 300 quality homes in Prentiss County, leaving a legacy of family homes for years to come. *Submitted by Vicki Stutts.*

W.A. and Glen Smith

SOUTH, WILLIAM MARION, born 1871 and died 1943. A farmer by trade, son of Joseph and Mary Elizabeth Wright South, grandson of Samuel Bryan and Elizabeth Williams South and great-grandson of Ricky and Becky James South.

Will South's first wife, Dillor Johnson South (b. Dec. 18, 1875, d. Oct. 8, 1889, buried in Palestine Cemetery), daughter of Andrew and E.J. Johnson, died during childbirth shortly before her 15th birthday. Their child died around the age of 2.

Will South's second wife was Flora Jones South (b. 1863, d. 1900, Palestine) whose family lived in Tishomingo County. Three children were born of this union while they were residing in Hill County, TX: Rosie (b. 1893, Forked Oak) married Rufus Tennison, Thomas Luther (b. 1895, Forked Oak) married Ruth Beatrice Moss and Mary Jane (b. 1898, Forked Oak) married Austin Lowery.

Will South's brother, J.T. "Tom" South, who married Nancy Jane Mayo, died at 23 on Nancy Jane's birthday Sep. 15, 1897 leaving his wife and infant daughter, Alta Bell South Hill (b. 1896).

Will South married his third wife in 1902, his dead brother Tom South's widow Nancy Jane Mayo South. Will and Nancy lived on the present CR 131 at Paden in Tishomingo County. Their children were: Ruth August South Defoor (b. 1904), Alfred Clayton (b. 1906, twin) married Ravelle Mock, Alpha Lois (b. 1906, twin) married Monroe Whitehead, then Tracy Mauldin; William Albert (b. 1909) married Lola Robinson, Annie Laurie "Laura" married Tom Felker (b. 1912), Samantha Cordelia (b. 1916) married Earl Wilson, Martha Rachel (b. 1921) married Homer Dee Carter.

William Marion South, his three wives: Dillor Johnson, Flora Jones and Nancy Jane Mayo, plus many of their parents, children, grandchildren, brothers and sisters are buried at Palestine Church, Paden, MS and Forked Oak Church in Prentiss County.

Many descendants of William Marion, Tom, Flora and Nancy Jane South still live in Prentiss and Tishomingo Counties. *Submitted by Peggy Mann*

SORRELL, JO ANN (RINEHART) SORRELL, daughter of Clifford Palmer and Vista Rinehart attended Jacinto School and graduated from Rienzi High School in 1960. Jo Ann taught in Hills Chapel School in Prentiss County from 1972 through 1977. She married Mark Stephen Sorrell on Jul. 10, 1991. They lived in Dalton, GA for 18 years where both were teachers in the Whitfield County School System. Jo Ann taught visually impaired; Mark taught eighth grade algebra and Georgia history. In July 1999, Mark and Jo Ann moved to Madison, AL to be near children and grandchildren. Both are continuing their teaching and coaching careers in Madison. Jo Ann received her BS degree in education from Jacksonville State University and her MEd degree from the University of Mississippi and has completed further studies at Mercer University, North Georgia College and West Georgia College. Mark received his BS degree from the University of Tennessee at Chattanooga and his MEd degree from West Georgia College. He is originally from Kingsport, TN; his parents are the late Wesley Ray Sorrell and Doris (Hunnicut) Sorrell.

Jo Ann has two children from a prior marriage to Guy Sanford Johnson from Rienzi, MS: Nathan Guy Johnson and Anita Carol (Johnson) Denson. (Their paternal grandparents are Guy Johnson and the late Velma Green Johnson of Rienzi, MS.) Nathan is a 1980 graduate of Bradshaw High School in Florence, AL. He attended Auburn University and Mississippi State University; he received a BS degree in civil engineering from Mississippi State University. He owns Johnson and Associates Engineering, Inc. in Huntsville, AL. Nathan is married to Susan (Boerner) Johnson. Susan is the daughter of Robert H. and Dorothy (Dot) Bolling Boemer of Huntsville, AL. Nathan and Susan have four children: Lauren Elizabeth age 12, Caleb Guy age 9, Caroline Grace and Carmen Leigh (identical twins) age 7. Susan and Nathan met when they were students at Auburn University. Susan has a BS degree in early childhood education from Auburn University and an MEd degree in early childhood education from Alabama Agricultural and Mechanical University in Huntsville. Nathan, Susan and children live in Huntsville, AL.

Anita Johnson Denson is a 1981 graduate of Bradshaw High School in Florence, AL. She received a BS ARC degree in architecture from Mississippi State. She is married to Michael "Mike" Denson. Mike is the son of Edward and Pat Denson of Decatur, AL. Anita and Mike have one daughter, Emma Caroline, age 2-1/2 years, who is named for two great-great-grandmothers and Eli Nathaniel, born Jan. 4, 2000. Mike attended Auburn University and Mississippi State University. He has a BS degree in industrial engineering from Mississippi State University. He has a software development company in Decatur, AL where they reside; Anita is the owner of The Design (architecture) Firm in Decatur.

SOUTH, THOMAS LUTHER "T.L.," son of William Marion (b. 1871, d. 1943) and Flora Jones South (b. 1863, d. 1900), born May 26, 1895 in Hill County, TX. His grandparents were Joseph and Mary Elizabeth Wright South. His great-grandparents were Samuel Bryan and Elizabeth Williams South and his great-great-grandparents were Ricky and Becky James South.

Thomas Luther South served in the US Army during WWI, Service Number 2124480, Oct. 6, 1917 to May 19, 1919; unassigned, Co. G, 128th Infantry, A.E.F. He fought in the battle at Montfaucon Sector, Oct. 1-20 and Nov. 5-8, 1918. He was captured by the Germans on Nov. 8, 1918, just three days before the Armistice was signed on Nov.

Thomas Luther South, WWI, 1917-1919.

11, 1918, ending WWI. At some point during his tour of duty, his family was notified that he had been killed in action. The Paden, MS family met the train every day for three days expecting Luther's body to arrive. After three days, the family was advised that the army's notification of Thomas Luther South's death was in error. It seems that another soldier named Luther South had been killed in action.

Thomas Luther South also served in the Civilian Conservation Corps, Co. 2424, CCC, Mississippi SCS-23, assigned at Ripley, MS, Jul. 12, 1940 to Mar. 3, 1941, under Superintendent Howard T. Jones, Camp Miss SCS-23.

Thomas Luther South married Ruth Beatrice Moss on Jul. 24, 1926. Children born to this union were Thomas Justus (b. 1927, d. 1929, Palestine Cemetery), William Manuel (b. 1928), James Bendell (b. 1930, d. 1983, Forked Oak), Luther Armon (b. 1932), Orville Truman (b. 1939) and Peggy Ann South (b. 1946). Surviving children of T.L. and Ruth South still live in and around the Burton/Hills Chapel areas of Prentiss County.

In 1934, T.L. and Ruth South used $250 of his $1,500 war bonus to purchase the 57-acre Robert McCutchen farm, located one fourth mile below Forked Oak Church in Prentiss County. T.L., a farmer and sawmill worker, was a member of the Forked Oak Missionary Baptist Church.

T.L. South had two full sisters: Rosie South, who married Rufus Tennison and Mary Jane South, who married Austin Lowery; one stepsister, Alta Bell South Hill (the daughter of Will South's brother, Tom and Nancy Jane Mayo South) and several half-brothers and sisters (children of Will South and Nancy Jane

Mayo South): Alpha Lois South (b. 1906, twin), who married James Monroe Whitehead, then Tracy Mauldin; Ruth August South Defoor (b. 1904); Anna Laurie South Felker (b. 1912); Cordelia South Wilson (b. 1916); Martha Rachel South (b. 1921), who married Homer D. Carter; William Albert South (b. 1909) and Alfred Clayton South (b. 1906, twin).

Thomas Luther (b. 1895, d. 1975) and Ruth Beatrice Moss South (b. 1909, d. 1991) are buried in the Forked Oak Church Cemetery in Prentiss County. *Submitted by Peggy Mann.*

Standing from left: Luther Armon, James Bendell and William Manuel. Seated: Thomas Luther, Ruth Beatrice, baby, Peggy Ann and Orville Truman South. Summer of 1947.

SOUTH, WILLIAM MARION,
born 1871 and died 1943, a farmer by trade, the son of Joseph and Mary Elizabeth Wright South, grandson of Samuel Bryan and Elizabeth Williams South and great-grandson of Ricky and Becky James South.

Will South's first wife, Della Johnson South, along with their child, died during childbirth shortly before her 15th birthday.

Will South's second wife was Flora Jones South (b. 1863, d. 1900, Palestine), whose family lived in Tishomingo County. Three children

Children of William Marion and Flora Jones South. Rosie South (Tennison) (1893), Mary Jane South (Lowery) (1898) and Thomas Luther South (1895). Picture taken around 1914-1915.

Children of William Marion and Flora Jones South, Tom and Nancy Jane Mayo South and William Marion and Nancy Jane Mayo South. (Will South married Flora Jones; Tom South married Nancy Jane Mayo. Flora Jones South (1863-1900) and Tom South died. Will South married his brother Tom's widow, Nancy Jane Mayo South. Picture made on Jul. 4, 1950, at Monroe and Alpha Whitehead's home in the Burton/Forked Oak Community. Standing from left: Alpha Lois South Whitehead Mauldin (1906, twin of Alfred), Rutha August South Defoor (1904), Annie Laurie South Felker (1912), Thomas Luther South (1895), Cordelia South Wilson (1916), Alta Bell South Hill (1896, daughter of Nancy Jane Mayo and Tom South), Mary Jane South Lowrey and Martha Rachel South Carter (1921). Seated from left: William Albert South (1909), Nancy Jane Mayo South (mother of all except Thomas Luther South and Mary Jane South Lowrey) and Alfred Clayton South (1906, twin of Alpha Lois).

were born of this union while they were residing in Hill County, TX: Rosie South (b. 1893), who married Rufus Tennison; Thomas Luther South (b. 1895), who married Ruth Beatrice Moss and Mary Jane South (b. 1898), who married Austin Lowery.

Will South's brother, Tom, was married to Nancy Jane Mayo South and they had one child, Alta Bell South (Hill) (b. 1896). Tom South died.

Will South's third wife was his dead brother's widow, Nancy Jane Mayo South. Will and Nancy Jane Mayo South lived on the present County Route 131 in Paden in Tishomingo County. Their children were Ruth August South Defoor (b. 1904); Alfred Clayton South (b. 1906, twin; Alpha Lois South (b. 1906, twin), who married Monroe Whitehead, then Tracy Mauldin; William Albert South (b. 1909); Annie Laurie South Felker (b. 1912); Cordelia South Wilson (b. 1916) and Martha Rachel South (b. 1921), who married Homer D. Carter.

William Marion South, his three wives (Della, Flora and Nancy Jane), plus many of their children and grandchildren are buried at Palestine Church in Paden, MS. Many descendants of Will, Flora and Nancy Jane South still live in Prentiss and Tishomingo Counties. *Submitted by Peggy Mann.*

SPARKS, JESSE LEE,
born Oct. 22, 1891 and died Mar. 7, 1964, the youngest son of James M. and Martha Jane Roberts Webb Sparks. Jesse and older brother, Charles, were the youngest of nine children and the first to be born in Prentiss County, MS, the others having been born in Walker County, AL. James and Martha Jane joined by letter the Old Mackey's Creek Church.

Jesse attended Burnt School House and Jacinto Male Academy.

While in Booneville for the Sparks brothers livestock show, Jesse noticed a beautiful young lady and crossed the street to make her acquaintance. She was Maggie McKinley Bonds (b. Jan. 27, 1897, d. Apr. 4, 1970), the daughter of Wright Walker Bonds III and Sarah Josephine Holley and said by some to be the prettiest girl in Prentiss County in her day.

Jesse Lee Sparks and Maggie McKinley Bonds

Jesse was hot-tempered but always had a twinkle in his eye and was something of a prankster. Maggie was quiet and modest and as beautiful inside as out. He and Maggie were married on Sep. 7, 1914, when she was 17 and he was 23.

Times were hard for rural southerners in those days. Jesse worked briefly for the US Postal System and the Mississippi Highway Department and did some timber cutting for a sawmill, but he was always a farmer at heart, making his a hard but rewarding life. Due to his dawn to dusk days in his fields and Maggie's frugal management, they were able to build a comfortable and attractive home on present day South Lake Street in Booneville in the early 1950s.

Jesse never learned to drive. He once ordered an automobile, but when it arrived, a man offered him more than he had paid for it, so he sold it. He apparently didn't want an automobile very badly, but his young daughters, Forrest and Nona Faye, were so disappointed, they squalled.

Jesse and Maggie lived much as the Amish people do, very self-sufficiently. Jesse did purchase a Sears Roebuck victrola (an early wind-up record player) and after they moved to town, a radio and later a telephone and television!

Jesse never owned a tractor, but walked behind his horse and plow and carried his produce to market in a wagon pulled by old Maud, even as late as 1963, which was very much the age of the automobile. His love of tilling the soil, which he no doubt inherited from his father and grandfather, along with Maggie's talents as a cook, provided a bountiful table. They and their little farm and home made wonderful memories for their city-raised grandchildren and they are still sorely missed after all these many years.

Jesse Sparks raised a fine crop the last summer of his life, even though he had a heart condition and emphysema (the Sparks curse). He never smoked, drank nor gambled and was never heard to complain of his lot in life. He was not perfect, had a reputation of being quick tempered, but never ever having heard him curse, this writer, his granddaughter, has never met a man she respected as much as her beloved granddaddy Sparks.

Jesse and Maggie came from long lines of Primitive Baptists, but sometime in their married life, they joined what some would no doubt refer to as a cult. They met with people of their belief in their various homes. This writer does not know what prompted this change of direction in their religious lives but, knowing what Christian people they were and that they certainly lived their religion daily, has full confidence that our God does not hold their denomination against them as mortals do. They loved the same Lord and Savior as do the Baptists, Methodists, etc.

Jesse and Maggie remained deeply devoted to one another all their married lives until parted by his death in 1964 at the age of 73. (For more on James M. Sparks, see *Prentiss County History* Volume 1 and the children of Maggie and Jesse, see other stories in this issue.) *Submitted by Ann Sparks.*

SPARKS, JOHN LYLE,
when John Sparks (son of Jesse Lee and Maggie Bonds Sparks) and Maxine Harper (daughter of Aubrey Melton Harper and Bonnie Lou Johnson) married, they did not know they were third cousins once removed! What a shock it was to Maxine when her daughter, Ann, amateur genealogist, uncovered this deep dark secret decades later.

John Lyle Sparks and Mattie Maxine Harper

Plummer Doug Holley (b. 1825, d. 1902) was the great-grandfather of John Sparks (b. 1925, d. 1982). Amanda Holley, Plummer's sister, was the great-great-grandmother of Maxine Harper. (See Holley family stories *in Prentiss County History* Volume I.)

John and Maxine were high school sweethearts who quit school and got married on Sep. 25, 1943. John soon realized he had better finish his education and tried to join the Army, but was too nearsighted to be accepted. He was drafted into the Navy and was in the states when their war baby, Ann, was born Sep. 2, 1944. Maxine visited him in Norfolk, Virginia in 1945 and remembers being awakened by the corner newsboy shouting, "Extra! Extra! President Roosevelt dead!" John was later stationed on a supply ship in the Philippine Islands. While John was in the Navy, Maxine divided her time equally between her parents and his, leaving Ann in the care of her Grandmother Sparks while she spent her days in the local garment factory.

John joined up for a second hitch in the Navy, but when promised schooling did not materialize, he wanted out. His dad, Jesse, wrote a letter pleading hardship and got him out early.

Two sons were born, Jerry Lyle (b. Apr. 3, 1947) and John Edwin (b. Dec. 11, 1950).

In 1952, John moved the family to Bowling Green, KY, where he attended Bowling Green Business University for six months and finished accounting courses he had started at the hometown junior college.

In late summer of 1952, the Sparks family moved to Shelby County, TN where John went to work for the duPont Co. in the accounting department.

John became an avid fisherman, spending most weekends and vacations at Grenada Lake, fishing for crappie and leaving Maxine a "week-end widow" at home with the kids.

In 1962 Maxine's oldest child graduated high school and her fourth child and third son, Eric "Ricky" Wayne, was born July 27.

Ann, Jerry and Edwin graduated from Frayser High School and Ricky from Frayser Christian Academy. Ann and Jerry joined the workforce after high school and Jerry married Linda Jo Sheppard. They had two daughters, Lori Lynn and Leigh Ann. Jerry and Linda divorced. Lori married first Bruce Lambert and second Gerald Young. She has a daughter, Meghan Elise Lambert and two sons, Conner Lee and Zachary Joseph Young. Jerry and Lori and family still live in Memphis.

Leigh Ann married John Kolbe and they have two daughters, Madison Paige and Samantha. They live in Fairfax, SC.

Edwin and Ricky both graduated from Christian Brothers College in Memphis with degrees in chemical engineering. Edwin married Connie Beth Caldwell and they have a daughter, Kristin Michelle, a sophomore in high school and a son, Michael Alan, a freshman at Mississippi State. Edwin and family live in Pascagoula, where Edwin is a plant manager and Connie a school librarian.

Ricky married Regina Lynn Hollandsworth, a classmate at Frayser Christian Academy. They have two sons, Eric Wayne, 11 and John Christopher, 9. They live in Louisville, KY, where they are all very active in soccer, softball, basketball and in their church where Ricky is a deacon.

John Sparks died of a heart attack on Easter Sunday, Apr. 11, 1982, at the age of 56 after having been retired (early) from duPont for one month.

Maxine is living at Grenada Lake where she and John had planned to retire together. But she is planning to move soon back to her hometown, Booneville and daughter, Ann, is looking forward to having her mother near. *Submitted by Ann Sparks.*

SPARKS, MARTHA JANE ROBERTS, born about 1849, daughter of John Green Roberts (b. Nov. 20, 1815, d. September 1862) and Elizabeth Martha "Mariah" Ferguson (b. Sep. 19, 1824, d. 1889). John and Elizabeth are buried at old Flatwoods Cemetery in Nauvoo, AL near Jasper. It has been said that John Green Roberts was killed in a feud or a duel over a horse. John Green Roberts was born in Georgia and Elizabeth Ferguson in Alabama according to census records. On the 1860 Walker County, AL census, John Green Roberts is listed as an illiterate farmer (with 400 acres) but his wife Elizabeth is not listed as illiterate, although the majority of adult women on that census were. But on the bill of sale of a parcel of land sold in 1859, they both "made their mark."

John Green Roberts, son of Isaac Newton Roberts (b. ca. 1795, d. after 1840) and Nancy Myers (b. ca. 1797, d. after 1850). Isaac Newton Roberts married Nancy Myers Oct. 1, 1812 in Jackson County, GA. He is on the 1805 Greene County, GA tax list. Isaac had 420 acres in Greene County, GA in 1836. Samuel Yancey Ferguson had adjoining land. Several of Isaac N. Roberts' children moved to Texas where one, Chandler Roberts was a Texas Ranger.

Nancy Myers, daughter of Abraham Myers (b. 1760 in Philadelphia, PA) and Sarah Roberson.

Elizabeth Ferguson, daughter of Samuel Yancey Ferguson (b. Mar. 19, 1800 in Chester District, SC) and his first wife, Malinda Wood (died Jan. 5, 1831). Samuel Yancey Ferguson was a justice of the peace in Morgan County, AL in 1825, 1833 and 1834 according to the Morgan County marriage book.

Samuel Yancey Ferguson, son of Adams Ferguson (b. ca. 1755, probably in Chester District) and Elizabeth "Betty" Barber (died ca. 1825, buried in Old Hopewell Baptist Cemetery near Richburg, SC). Adams Ferguson, son of James S. Ferguson and Agnes Adams of Chester District, SC.

"Pa" Ferguson, an impeached governor of Texas, was also a descendant of Adams Ferguson. Both "Pa" and "Ma" Ferguson were governor of Texas. "Ma" was elected some years after her husband was impeached for "irregularities in his administration."

Martha Jane Roberts, first married a Webb, by whom she had two sons; widowed and married James M. Sparks, son of Samuel Sparks and Frances Kitchens (see Kitchens story and Sparks stories). Martha Jane Roberts Webb and James M. Sparks joined old Mackey's Creek Church when they moved to Prentiss County and are buried in Old Friendship Cemetery at Bay Springs. *Submitted by Ann Sparks. Source: Mrs. Herb Roberts, Abilene, TX.*

SPARKS, THOMAS/RUTHA WHITE, The earliest documentation of Thomas Sparks and his wife Rutha White finds them in Lawrence County, Alabama circa 1818. Thomas Sparks is listed on the 1820 and 1830 Lawrence County censuses as head of his household. Because the 1840 census lists Rutha as head of her household, researchers have assumed that Thomas died prior to that census, but no documentation of his death has been found. And there being a Thomas Sparks on the 1840 Lawrence County census with a much younger wife, this writer believes that Thomas Sparks and Rutha seperated and Thomas then started a second family with a new wife. There is circumstantial evidence to support this theory.

In 1824, 1826, 1829, and 1839 Thomas Sparks was a constable or Justice of the Peace. In 1841 Thomas Sparks was a constable in the beat of Capt. D.K. McVay, in 1844 a JP in the beat of Capt. Joseph Wood, in 1847 a JP in the beat of Capt. John J. McCluskey, and in 1855 a tax collector, according to Lawrence County, Alabama bond records.

In early 1835 Thomas and Rutha had their last child together and Rutha subsequently moved to Walker County, ALabama. About 1835/36 one Thomas Sparks married Julina McWhorter in Lawrence County, where she died in 1857. According to a descendant, Thomas Sparks, aged 59, who appears on the 1860 McLennan County, Texas census in the James D. Wallace household, was from Lawrence County, Alabama and the widower of Mrs. Julina Sparks.

This writer is convinced that Thomas Sparks, husband of Rutha wWhite , and Thomas Sparks, husband of Julina McWhorter, were one and the same man. It seems odd that Thomas, husband of Rutha, "disappeared" from Lawrence County just as Thomas, husband of Julina "appears". At no timedo the Lawrence County censuses show two Thomas Sparkses. It seems coincidental that both men with the same name would be elected to the same county offices.

Thomas, husband of Rutha, is sadi to have come from Tennessee just prior to moving to ALabama, and so this writer has searched in vain for years in Tennessee records for some trace of Thomas and Rutha.

Thomas, husband of Julina, is known to be the son of John Sparks and Sarah Tickle (or Tickell) who lived in Morgan County, Georgia from about 1800 to about 1824.

GEORGIA INTESTATE RECORDS lists one Samuel White, deceased 1810, wife Ann, children WIlliam, Jiney and Ruthey in Jasper County, Georgia, which borders Morgan County. Furthermore,

EARLY LAWRENCE COUNTY, ALABAM MARRIAGES lists one Ann White who married a JM Speck in 1820. This Samuel and Ann White are most probably the parents of Rutha White Sparks. After the death of her husband, Ann White followed her daughter and son in law to Lawrence County, Alabama, where ahe married JM Speck. Placing the Whites in Morgan County, Georgia, one can logically place Thomas Sparks, husband of Rutha, there also.

James Sparks, the firstborn of Thomas and Rutha, named a daughter born in 1864 Alice McWhorter Sparks.

Descendants of Thomas and Rutha and descendants of Thomas and Julina speak of a son, John C. Sparks, who went to Texas and was a Texas Ranger.

Children of Thomas and Rutha White Sparks were James Sparks (born April 11, 1816 in Alabama Territory), Samuel Sparks (born about 1818 in ALabama Territory, 2nd gr grandfather of writer), William Sparks, (born 1821 in Alabama), Nancy (McVay) (born 1823 in ALabama), Elijah Sparks (born about 1828 in ALabama), John C. Sparks (born about 1829 in Alabama), Stephen Green Sparks (born about 1832 in Alabama) and Eli Allen Sparks (born January 22, 1835, near Moulton, Lawrence County, Alabama). Son James and grandson James M. moved from Walker County, Alabama to Prentiss County, Mississippi with their families.

SPENCER, JAMES HARME AND MAXIE REMEL DENSON, from the pages of life ... James Harme Spencer and Maxie Remel Denson began dating in 1946 and were married on Dec. 17, 1949. He owned a grocery store at Zion Rest. We lived there about a year, sold the store and moved to a house on Highway 4 from Booneville to Bay Springs.

James H. Spencer was the son of John L. Spencer and Tennie Lindsey Spencer. He was born May 19, 1922 and died Feb. 2, 1993.

From left: James H. Spencer Jr., Remel Denson Spencer and Jane Carol Spencer Redden.

Remel Denson Spencer was born Jul. 31, 1925. She was the daughter of Jim Denson and Sadie Chambers Denson. I started to work at Blue Bell Shirt Factory in Booneville. Jimmie went to work at Barber's Milk Co. Then we moved to Battle Creek, MI. Jimmie went to work at Post Cereals and I went to work at a Cookie Factory and then transferred to Post Cereals. We both worked on the late shift.

I got pregnant with Jim, that is James H. Spencer Jr. and Jim was born Jan. 31, 1952. We came home when Jim was 3 months old; we were sure proud of that day.

Jimmie went back to work for Barber's Milk Co. and when Jim was about a year old, I started work at Prentiss Manufacturing Co. We had moved to a house on Northeast Brewer Street. We sold the house and rented until we got the house we live in built, then we moved into our new house. We only had Jim for about seven years; he started to school and was in the first grade when Jane Carol came along on Apr. 7,

From left: Jane Carol Spencer Redden, James H. Spencer Sr. (Jimmy) and James H Spencer Jr. (Jim).

1959. So, our family was complete. We obeyed the Gospel before we went up north, at the Booneville Church of Christ, where we were in regular attendance along with our children. We were blessed with grandchildren. Jim had three children: James H. Spencer III, Rachel Spencer and Andrew Spencer. Jane Carol Spencer had one child, Cory Marrell. *Submitted by Remel Spencer.*

SPENCER, JOHN L., born Nov. 18, 1888 in Fulton in Itawamba County and died May 30, 1963, to Jim Spencer and Callie Lindsey Spencer. He married Aug. 15, 1909, to Tennie Magnaria Lindsey (b. Feb. 23, 1892, d. Dec. 2, 1984), who was born in Alabama to Jim Lindsey and Amy Bruner Lindsey. To their union were born these children:

Family of John L. Spencer and Tennie Magnaria Lindsey Spencer. Made in 1958. From left: Lillard Ivean Spencer Ivey; James H. Spencer (Jimmie); Mary Magdalene Spencer Bishop; Willo Dean Spencer Estes; Tennie Spencer; Edna Pauline Spencer Lytal; John L. Spencer; Lola Van Spencer Chambers and Ruth Lee Spencer Heartwell.

1. Lola Van Spencer (b. Aug. 6, 1910) married Tommie Chambers and had eight children.

2. Lillard Ivean Spencer (b. Oct. 9, 1912, d. Mar. 14, 1996) married Arlin Ivey and had eight children.

3. Edna Pauline Spencer (b. Oct. 12, 1914, d. Dec. 27, 1986) married Arlis Lytal and had eight children.

4. Ruth Lee Spencer (b. Aug. 1, 1917, d. Oct. 21, 1998) married Tommie Heartwell and had two children.

5. James H. Spencer (Jimmie) (b. May 19, 1922, d. Feb. 5, 1992) married Remel Denson and had three children.

6. Mary Magdalene Spencer (b. Nov. 5, 1924) married Cecil Bishop and had one child.

7. Willo Dean Spencer (b. Apr. 15, 1927) married John Estes and had three children.

They also have 33 grandchildren, plus great-great grandchildren. *Submitted by Magdalene Bishop.*

STENNETT, HERSCHEL G., born Nov. 4, 1927 in Prentiss County, MS, to Gordon Merritt Stennett and Ruby Swaim Stennett. He had one older brother, William Eugene Stennett, who preceded him in death.

Herschel grew up in the Zion's Rest Community and graduated from Marietta High School. While in high school, he worked in the afternoons at the Booneville Independent learning to operate a linotype machine.

He was a veteran of the Korean Conflict.

On Sep. 10, 1955, he married Anne Catherine Browning, the daughter of William Marcus (Willie) and Lula Parker Browning of Prentiss County. Herschel and Anne had one daughter, Christy Anne Stennett, born Mar. 31, 1961. On May 18, 1984, Christy married Scott Bradley Watts, son of Bob and Evelyn Cloninger Watts of Hollywood, FL. They have one son, Christopher Scott Stennett Watts, born Oct. 14, 1987. Scott, Christy and Christopher live in Valdese, NC.

Herschel and Anne moved to Ripley, MS, where they owned and published the weekly newspaper, *The Southern Sentinel,* from Jan. 1, 1972 until Jul. 31, 1985. Herschel died of colon cancer Jun. 5, 1986, at the Baptist East Hospital in Memphis. He is buried in the Booneville Cemetery.

On Jan. 16, 1993, Anne married Luther Lamar Walker of Elberton, GA. Lamar is a native of Prentiss County. His parents were Audie and Alva Etta Sumners of the Marietta Community. Lamar's first wife, Jane Edwards, died in October 1989. He and Jane had three children: Kay, Marty and Phil. Lamar has eight grandchildren. *Submitted by Christy Stennett Watts*

STOKES, YOUNG THOMAS, born, married and raised his family in Prentiss County. Born Mar. 19, 1895 to Alfred Stokes and Amanda "Mandy" Skelton Stokes, he married Bessie Lou Jones (b. Jul. 17, 1918) daughter of George Riley Jones and L. Leona Nicholson Jones.

That marriage resulted in five children, all of which were born and raised in Prentiss County: Virginia V. Stokes married Edmon W. Provins and had three children. Riley Alfred Stokes married Onesta Stacey and had four children. I. Rummell Stokes married Arlo Milam and had five children. Golden Stokes married Howard Bray and had five children. Glenda R. Stokes married Edward Taylor and had two children. So there are a lot of grandchildren that resulted in the union of Young Thomas and Bessie.

All of his children and grandchildren remember "Tom" as a gentle giant. He was a big, strong man but very quiet and gentle.

Young Thomas Stokes died in 1963 and is missed very much by those that were lucky enough to have had him in their life. He and Bessie are buried in Lindsey Cemetery in Tishomingo County.

This is not so much a history of a family as it is a tribute to a man that left many fond memories. A tribute to the best grandfather anyone could ever have. This is for you "Pa" Stokes from all your children and grandchildren. *Submitted by his grandson, Waylon Stokes Provins*

STOREY, ANDREW LEROY, born Oct. 31, 1914 in Prentiss County, MS. His parents were William Henry and Nellie Kate (Suitor) Storey. On Apr. 8, 1936 he married Ruby Ester Michael, daughter of Reuben Hill and Hester (Caver) Michael. Ruby was born Mar. 16, 1919. Leroy and Ruby made their home in the Pisgah Community and have been an integral part of that community for many years. Until retiring, Leroy farmed the Storey home place that joins the Pisgah Methodist Church grounds. Ruby worked many years at the Blue Bell plant in Booneville as well as sharing in the family duties on the farm. Their marriage produced these children, all born in Prentiss County:

The Leroy Storey Family, September 1954. From left: Andrew Leroy Storey, Ruby, Carolyn, Ralph, Gene and Crandall.

(1) Roy "Gene" (b. Jan. 24, 1938) married first Lynda Sue Deaton and second Lou (Kendall) McPhail. His children are Randle Gene (b. Mar. 22, 1962) and Daryl Wayne (b. Mar. 6, 1971).

(2) Martha Sue died at birth, Apr. 21, 1941 and is buried in the Pisgah Methodist Church Cemetery.

(3) Ruby "Carolyn" (b. Jun. 10, 1942) married first Jimmy Inman and second Dwayne Williams. Her children are Patricia Ann (b. Jul. 16, 1968) and Dwayne Alan (b. Aug. 16, 1979).

(4) Crandall Lee (b. Jun. 19, 1944) never married.

(5) Ralph Andrew (b. Aug. 28, 1945). died in a motorcycle accident on Sep. 2, 1979 and is buried in the Pisgah Methodist Church Cemetery.

The Storey family traces it's roots back several generations. Leroy's family tree goes as follows: 1) William Henry Storey (b. Dec. 17, 1880, d. Jun. 22, 1956). 2) Leander Lafayette Storey (b. Jan. 26, 1852, d. Jan. 11, 1930. 3) William George Storey (b. Jun. 16, 1821, d. Jun. 28, 1856). 4) Andrew M. Storey (b. Feb. 26, 1800, d. after 1852). 5) George Storey (b. May 1, 1770, d. May 19, 1857). 6) Anthony Storey (b. 1746, d. Sep. 12, 1783). 7) George Storey (b. about 1725, d. January 1805).

The Michael family can also be traced back several generations starting with Ruby's father, Reuben Hill Michael. 1) Reuben Hill Michael (b. Feb. 16, 1884, d. Jun. 20, 1969. 2) James Daniel Michael (b. January 25, 1861, d. May 18, 1937). 3) George Washington Michael (b. Oct. 27, 1833, d. Jun. 9, 1906). 4) Daniel Michael, (b. 1794, d. Mar. 22, 1846). 5) Conrad (Johann) Michael (b. Jan. 1, 1763, d. Mar. 27, 1839). 6) Jacob Michael, dates unknown. *Submitted by Gene Storey.*

STOREY, NELLIE KATE SUITOR, born Feb. 21, 1887 and died Nov. 22, 1969, one of 11 children born to William Newton Suitor (b. Jan. 15, 1845, d. Jan. 17, 1922) and Mary Alice Lusk (b. Feb. 28, 1845, d. Jun. 1, 1891) of the Hinkle Community in Alcorn County, MS. Nellie Kate married on Jun. 12, 1904, to William Henry Storey (b. Dec. 17, 1880, d. Jun. 22, 1956). There were 11 children born to Nellie Kate and William Henry Storey, all born in Prentiss County. They are:

Nellie Kate Suitor Storey, March 1968.

1. William Clarence (b. Sep. 16, 1905 in Prentiss County, d. Jan. 18, 1977 in Texarkana, AR) married Jan. 18, 1931, to Edna Bayne Easley (b. Jan. 19, 1911 in Texarkana, AR). They had one daughter, Doris Okay (b. Dec. 12, 1931).

2. Walter Franklin (b. Nov. 4, 1907, d. Mar. 30, 1998) married Dec. 8, 1935, to Prudence Irene Strange (b. May 12, 1918). Their children are: Joseph Franklin (b. May 28, 1937); Mary Elizabeth (b. Nov. 20, 1938); Barbara Nell (b. Sep. 12, 1941) and Irma Charlene (b. Feb. 20, 1944).

3. Albert Newton (b. Aug. 17, 1910, d. Oct. 11, 1958) was crippled at the age of 17. He remained single and lived with Nellie Kate until his death.

4. Henry Leander (b. Nov. 9, 1912) married Helen Johnson. They had one daughter, Louise. Henry died May 29, 1954 in Mt. Clemens, MI.

5. Andrew Leroy (b. Oct. 31, 1914) married Apr. 8, 1936, to Ruby Ester Michael (b. Mar. 16, 1919). Their children are: Roy Gene (b. Jan. 24, 1939); Martha Sue died at birth on Apr. 20, 1941; Ruby Carolyn (b. Jun. 10, 1942); Crandall Lee (b. Jun. 19, 1944) and Ralph Andrew (b. Aug. 28, 1945, d. Sep. 2, 1979).

6. Nellie Viola (b. Aug. 3, 1916) married Jul. 28, 1933, to Carl Tice (b. Aug. 2, 1911). Their children are: Betty Jane (b. Mar. 7, 1934); Carl O'Neil (b. Oct. 5, 1935); Bobby Harold (b. Feb. 14, 1945) and Marjorie Carole (b. May 26, 1947).

7. Robert Harold (b. Sep. 5, 1918, d. Sep. 1, 1991) married Nov. 22, 1945, to Mary Virginia

Blassingame. Their children are: Mary Ann (b. Dec. 3, 1947); Robert Harold Jr. (b. Oct. 8, 1949); Nita Jo (b. Jan. 28, 1951); James Franklin (b. Aug. 9, 1953); Christopher Scott (b. Jul. 4, 1961 and Susan Glenn (b. Jul. 17, 1964).

8. Mary Alice (b. Mar. 2, 1920, d. Feb. 23, 1990 in Texarkana, TX).

9. Eunice (b. Aug. 10, 1924) married May 31, 1946, to Harold Thomas Stott (b. Sep. 30, 1924). Their children are: Judith Anne (b. Mar. 1, 1947); Harold Thomas Jr. (b. Feb. 3, 1953) and Jeffrey Norris (b. Jan. 17, 1962).

10. Joseph Duane (b. Jun. 12, 1929, d. May 21, 1930).

11. Betty Lou (b. Sep. 3, 1932) married Hugh McCord.

The Storey family of Prentiss County has it's roots centered in the Pisgah Community. Nellie Kate Suitor Storey is buried in the Pisgah Methodist Church Cemetery. William Henry, also buried in Pisgah, is one of five generations of Storeys buried in this cemetery. *Submitted by Crandall Storey.*

SUTHERLAND, WADE HAMPTON, born Feb. 18, 1875 near New Site. He married Daisy Dickinson (b. 1877, d. 1957) and they had two sons and five daughters.

Dr. Sutherland practiced medicine at Kirkville for 16 months and at Wheeler for five years. He then went to Booneville and in 1916 he built a small clinic near present day City Hall and renovated an old jail into a 15-bed hospital. This was the first hospital in Northeast Mississippi. In the 1920s he built the four-story building on what is now College Street to house his clinic. The Sutherland building is believed to have contained the first elevator in Prentiss County. Dr. Sutherland's clinic was on the top floor of the building and served as offices for Dr. W.H. Sutherland, Dr. R.B. Cunningham and Dr. H.B. Sutherland.

Dr. W.H. Sutherland studied medicine at Tulene University, Chicago; University of Tennessee Medical Department, Memphis; New York, Boston, Mayo Clinic and Edinburgh, Scotland.

He was a member of the Missionary Baptist Church, a Mason, Eastern Star and Shriner.

After practicing as a physician in Booneville for more than 50 years Dr. W. H. Sutherland died Dec. 16, 1959.

SWINNEY, WILEY, an early settler to Old Tishomingo County, present day Prentiss County, MS, is first found with Georgia Volunteers Militia for the War of 1812. A private and 3rd sergeant from Aug. 23, 1813-Mar. 8, 1814 in Capt. William Butler's company, drafted infantry, 2nd Regiment earning $72.52 for service. In 1824, Walton County, GA he has a water mill on the Apalachee River. In the fall of 1830, he meets with others to plan repair or replacement of the bridge over the river at Richardson's Store; 1830 Household Heads #214. He is listed in 1831 as owner of 17 slaves in Green's Militia District. On 1832 Cherokee Land and Gold Lottery, he wins prize in drawing of land lots.

Wiley (b. Apr. 3, 1791 in North Carolina) son of William Swinney of Chatham County, NC and wife, Elizabeth Lassiter, daughter of Jotham Lassiter of Chowan and Wake County, NC and wife, thought to be, Prudence ___. Wiley married ca. 1818 in Georgia to Harriet Smith. Their children, born in Georgia:

James W. (b. 1821, d. before 1877) married in 1857 Mary E. Rogers. He served in Co. K, 2nd Division, Mississippi Infantry, CSA.

Burket D. (b. 1825, d. 1847).

Manerva (b. 1827, d. after 1860) married Mar. 19, 1844, James Harlow Robertson (See Robertson).

Sophia Ann Gennett (b. ca. 1829) married Moses T. Wright.

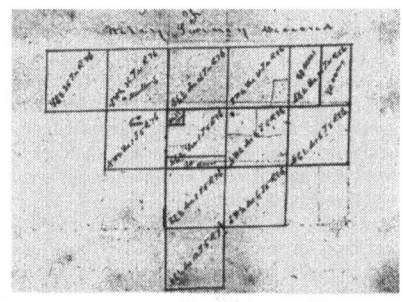

Plan for Division of Land of Estate of Wiley Swinney to wife, Mrs. Mahala Swinney, daughter, Sabra J. Elder, son, William Swinney and son, Wiley Swinney. Includes parts of Townships 4 and 5, Range 7E and 8E and Sections 1, 6, 12, 31, 35 and 36; showing dwelling, gin and mill. Dated April 1860.

The Swinneys leave Walton County, GA. Wiley purchases 80 acres in April 1837 in Chambers County, AL. Marriage records found for Wiley Swiney and Mahala Calvig (b. Nov. 29, 1837) and William Clifton and Harriet Swinney (b. Dec. 30, 1838). Apparently records are our Wiley and Harriet. Family tradition states; Wiley "wealthy in land and slaves, he began seeing the younger woman, Malaha; Harriet divorced him after Mahala had several children. He continued to provide well for Harriet." It appears that "divorce" was unavailable, not valid or whatever the circumstances of the time.

Descendants of Wiley Swinney, Veteran of War of 1812, unveil marker in Old Swinney Family Cemetery. From left: Shirley Garrett Lassiter of Clovis, NM, Bettie Parker Gustafson of Rosemark, TN, Charlotte Garrett Tignor of Erick, OK, LaDeane Robertson Dowdle of Caledonia, MS, Reuben Boyd Robertson of Lago Vista, TX, Ann Robertson Estes of Rancho Palos Verdes, CA, Madge Swinney Palumbo of Booneville, O'Neil Parker of Memphis, Jenta Boone of Clinton, MS and James McCarty Robertson of Cordell, OK.

The group including Wiley's brother, Timothy, wife, Elizabeth Alred and family; Mahala's brother, Thomas Calvery and family, came to Old Tishomingo County ca. 1838/9. Wiley purchased seven Land Patents totaling 1,128 acres in the Tuscumbia area beginning October 1840 through 1856.

Records indicate that Harriet did receive a divorce ca. 1835/6 on file in Alcorn County MS. Wiley and Mary Mahala Calvery (b. Jun. 9, 1821, Georgia, d. Oct. 20, 1861) again married May 29, 1844 in Tishomingo County. Their children were:

Thomas (b. 1838, d. 1871) married first Matilda Molton, second Elizabeth Rogers. He served in Co. A, 2nd Mississippi Infantry, CSA.

Rebecca (b. 1840, d. 1865) married James Simmons.

Nancy Ann (b. 1841, d. 1854).

Sabra Jane (b. 1842, d. 1861) married Thomas N. Elder.

Wiley Jo (b. 1843, d. 1864) served in the Tishomingo Rifles, Co. A, 2nd Mississippi Regiment, CSA.

Henry (b. 1844, d. 1845).

Edmond (b. 1846, d. 1858).

William T. (b. 1848, d. 1879) married in 1869 Mary Lillian Mayes. He served in Co. D, 6th Mississippi Cavalry, CSA.

Mary Francis (b. 1851, d. 1853).

John was born and died in 1854.

Other marriages for Harriet appear in Old Tishomingo County; Wiley's Will lists both "Harriet Hudson or Harriet Graham." Tishomingo County 1850 Census, Northern Division shows Harriet in household of W. Hudson; then about the time of the writing of Wiley's Will, Harritt Hudson marries William A. Graham Aug. 11, 1856. Finally, on 1860 Tishomingo County Census, Post Office Jacinto, Harriet Graham, age 69, is living next door to son, James W. Swinney. She is not found on 1870 Census. Deeds made to Harriet by Wiley support family tradition that he "provided well for her."

Wiley served in 1841 as Officer for Election at Keyes polling place and was a member of the Jacinto Masonic Lodge #142, chartered in 1851. He was listed as a farmer on the 1850 Census with real estate valued at $3,500. His Will written in 1856 contained 23 pages, two codicils, speaking first to children of second marriage; then children of first marriage.

Wiley died Mar. 23, 1858. It took 20 years to settle his estate; first executor, H.W. Elder died; son, T.N. Elder was appointed. Fourth Accounting of estate in 1865, executor reports no activity; nothing in hands of executor; slaves in his control in 1862 had escaped; nothing realized from their services. In the end there seemed to be nothing left to pass on but a disagreement about amount owed executors. Most of children having died, it was left to the next generation of grandchildren to make amends.

Property is no longer in the Swinney family today. Present owners relate stories of old homeplace, location of blacksmith shop, old mill, orchard, bits of dishes, old bricks, handmade on place and old cemetery located in back on Graveyard Hill. Only childhood tales, rocks and indented spots give witness of many members of Swinney family buried there, sure to include Wiley, Malaha, James William, Burket, Rebecca, Nancy Ann, Sabra Jane, Wiley Jo, Henry, Edmond, Mary Francis, John B. and probably Harriet.

On Oct. 17, 1998, 50 descendants walked the 300 yards to the old graveyard and held a service placing a marker in memory of a War of 1812 soldier on the grave site of Wiley Swinney. "A man's influence can long outlive the life that sheds it." *Submitted by H. O'Neil Parker.*

TAPP, MARK DUNCAN, born Jun. 25, 1957 in Baldwyn, MS to Richard Clyde Tapp and Virginia Dare Rice Tapp. He was one of four children: Betsy Rose, Richard Stevenson and Arty Rice. Upon graduation from Baldwyn High School in 1975, Mark attended Northeast Mississippi Community College. On May 22, 1976, he married Lana Quinn Mathis.

Shannon, Mark, Lana and Justin

Lana (b. Jul. 29, 1958 in Booneville, MS) to L.Q. Mathis and Julia Elizabeth Pike Mathis. Mark managed a Texaco station in Baldwyn while Lana attended NEMCC. Mark and Lana W. have one daughter, Shannon Elizabeth (b. Sep. 9, 1977) and one son, Justin Mark (b. Dec. 10, 1980).

After selling auto parts for Davidson Chevrolet and automobiles for Larry McKay Chevrolet for several years, Mark was employed with the Sunburst Banking System in Baldwyn from Jul. 1984 until September 1992. In September 1992, he was employed by Farmers and Merchants Bank and opened a branch office in Booneville where he continues to serve as vice president and manager. Lana was employed with Northeast Mississippi Community Services where she enjoyed serving the elderly and the handicapped for 13 years. She served the public for 1-1/2 years working for Travis Childers in the Prentiss County Chancery Clerks Office as a deputy court clerk. She continues meeting the public as receptionist/dental assistant with Dr. Ken Goodwin, a friend and local dentist.

Mark and Lana, in support of and love for their children and community, have both been active in many school, church and civic activities. Mark coached little league baseball for eight years. Mark and Lana were active members of the Booneville High School Athletic Booster Club from 1992-1999 with Mark serving as president in 1995. With Mark being a Baldwyn Bearcat for so many years and Booneville and Baldwyn being big rivals in every sport, it was a challenge for Lana and the children to convert him to being a Booneville Blue Devil.

Shannon was a varsity cheerleader for three years and Justin lettered in football four years with two undefeated seasons and Booneville competing in the state football championship both his junior and senior years. Shannon excelled both academically, graduating in the BHS Hall of Fame sixth in her class. Their parents and grandparents were very proud of both their athletic and academic accomplishments. Shannon attended Northeast Mississippi Community College and graduated in the Hall of Fame from Mississippi State University as an honor graduate and will continue her education at the University of Mississippi Medical Center School of Health Related Sciences seeking a degree in occupational therapy. She is engaged to be married in the spring of 2002 to James Thomas "Tommy" Fraiser.

Justin, following in his Uncle Arty's footsteps, has attended Northeast Mississippi Community College and will continue his education at Mississippi State University pursuing a bachelor of science degree in forestry resources.

TENNISON, EUGENE, arrived on the scene in the home of Vester T. and Birdie McCutchen Tennison on Feb. 8, 1926 in the Burton Community near Booneville, MS.

Gene was a man of action and many talents. He participated in school and 4-H Club activities. He represented Mississippi at the 4-H Club Congress at the national convention in Chicago in 1941.

Eugene Tennison

Gene served in the Army during WWII. After serving his country, he continued his education, graduating from Mississippi State University and for life he remained an avid Bulldog booster. He also graduated from George Peabody College for Teachers, now Vanderbilt University and the Southern Baptist Theological Seminary at Louisville, KY.

He was called into the ministry while teaching at Amory and was ordained and licensed for the ministry there in 1954. He taught at Okolona, Amory, was principal at Iuka High School, Iuka Elementary and Tishomingo Elementary. He will always be remembered by the many students he touched as a dedicated teacher, principal and friend.

Brother Gene, as he was lovingly called, served as pastor of Tishomingo Baptist Church for 19 years, as well as music director for several years. He pastored at Fayette, AL and served First Baptist Church in Booneville as music director. He was a talented pianist and his beautiful voice brought joy and comfort to many throughout his life.

Brother Gene endeared himself to all who were privileged to know him. He was a beloved pastor, teacher, counselor, mentor and friend. "He could speak with kings and never lose the common touch." He was a giver. He was a compassionate person who could relate to youth or adults. In his eloquent manner, he always said the right thing at the right time and shared his talents, means and love with everyone.

He was a life member of the Mississippi Retired Teachers Association and served on the scholarship committee. He was also active on the local level.

Brother Gene served as a counselor at Timber Hills Mental Health Center from 1979 until 1986.

Brother Eugene Tennison passed from this life on Sep. 23, 1999, after a long illness. He was laid to rest in Forked Oak Cemetery. He is survived by one sister, Margie Harper; a brother, Curtis Tennison; a niece, Carolyn Ashmore; a great-niece, Vickie Lambert and a great nephew, Larry Ashmore, all of Burton. *Submitted by Ruth Dawson of Tishomingo.*

THOMAS, CLAUDE BAXTER, born 1877 and died 1937, son of William Washington and Ruth Tersia Moore Thomas (See William Washington Thomas Family) married Eleanor Victoria Smith (b. 1887, d. 1969) on Jun. 4, 1919. After their marriage they resided in Booneville.

Baxter received his education in the Booneville schools. He later attended a boarding school in Huntingdon, TN and took the Civil Service exam. He secured an appointment to the Railway Mail Service on the Southern Railroad out of Memphis where he served 14 years. He transferred to the Mobile and Ohio Railroad in 1919 where he served 18 years until his death. During the time he lived in Booneville he also operated a farm which he inherited from his parents. He was known as an outstanding baseball player and was catcher and manager for the YMCA team in the Commercial League in Memphis where they were the league's pennant winner in 1911. He was a Mason, on the board of directors of the Farm Bureau and was chairman of the board of stewards of the First Methodist Church in Booneville at the time of his death. He, with the help of Robert McMillan, dug trees from his farm and planted them in front of the church, where they still stand. He was well known for his diligence, honor and honesty, traits which he learned from his father.

Claude Baxter Thomas and Eleanor Victoria Smith on their wedding day

Eleanor was the daughter of Robert Burton Smith and Evelina (Julena) Williams Smith, pioneer residents of Prentiss County. She was a 1910 graduate of I.I.&C. (now MUW) and attended the Chautauqua Institute, Chautauqua, NY the summer of 1911. She taught elementary school at Collins and Como, MS for seven years before returning to Booneville to serve as Prentiss County Home Demonstration Agent in 1917-18. After her marriage she continued to be active in the Sunday School Department of the First Methodist Church, teaching a boy's Sunday School class and later heading the Primary Department. She was active in staging Christmas pageants for a number of years, an activity she enjoyed both in the church and during her teaching career. She was an organizing member of the Natchez Trace Chapter MSDAR and a charter member of the Booneville Woman's Club and had a lifelong interest in genealogy and preservation of family records and mementos. After her husband's death she operated the Thomas Kindergarten for 18 years. Both are buried in the Booneville Cemetery. Their daughters, Julia Ruth (b. 1922) and Nell Smith (b. 1924) were born in Booneville. Julia Ruth is a graduate of MSCW and taught elementary school in Marks and Tupelo before her marriage to John Malvin McElroy (b. 1920) of Baldwyn in 1948. He is a graduate of Mississippi State University and was a partner and later owner of Buster McElroy and Co. in Baldwyn. After her marriage she was a manager with World Book Encyclopedia until her retirement in 1990. Their children are Thomas Melvin (b. 1950) and Richard Hartness (b. 1951).

Tommy is a graduate of Mississippi State University, where he was a member of the football team and the University of Mississippi School of Law and is in the private practice of law in Tupelo. He married Charlotte Jean Gower (b. 1951) of Baldwyn in 1972. She is a graduate of Mississippi College and is a freelance writer of children's music curriculum. Their children are Thomas Melvin Jr. "Mel" (b. 1978), a student at Birmingham Southern College and Charles Gower "Chuck" (b. 1981), a senior at Tupelo High School. Both are outstanding at sports.

Richard is a graduate of Mississippi State University with a master's degree in business administration and was a member of the football team. His marriages to Martha Jane Watkins of Aberdeen in 1973 and Diane Elizabeth Lewis in 1984 ended in divorce. He married Janice Elene Smithey Howard (b. 1954) in 1988. They are living in San Diego, CA where he is a partner in Indigo Investments. Janice is a partner in Howard-Steen Interior Architecture. Their children are Kristina Nicole (b. 1990) and Michelle Julia (b. 1993), both in elementary school.

Nell is a graduate of Bowling Green College of Commerce. She worked in the accounting field in Tupelo until her marriage in 1956 to Frank Mitchell "Mike" Wiygul, MD of Shannon. He is a graduate of the University of Mississippi and Harvard Medical School and was employed in several medical capacities in Jackson, MS until his retirement in 1990. Their children are Frank Mitchell III "Mitch" (b. 1957), Robert Baxter (b. 1959) and Thomas Jacob "Tom" (b. 1960).

Mitch is a graduate of the University of Mississippi and received a PhD in chemistry from Johns Hopkins University. He is employed in the computer modeling and simulation field in Baltimore, MD.

Robert is a graduate of Millsaps College and the University of Mississippi School of Law. He is employed in the area of environmental law in Denver, CO. He married Julia Hamilton Weaver (b. 1963) in 1995. She is a graduate of Rhodes college in Memphis and has a master's degree in divinity from Harvard University. She is employed in the field of community development. They have one child, Amelia Hayes (b. 1997).

Tom is a graduate of Mississippi State University with a master's degree in business administration. He is a certified public accountant in Jackson, MS. He married Catherine Mary Lewis (b. 1964) in 1993. She is a graduate of Millsaps College and was employed in the field of accounting prior to the birth of their children, Thomas Jacob Jr. (b. 1996) and Emma Catherine (b. 1997). *Submitted by Nell Thomas Wiygul.*

THOMAS, DAN, born 1879 and died 1952, son of William Washington Thomas and Ruth Tersia Moore, married Myrtle Irene Compton (b. 1892, d. 1970), daughter of Richard Washington Compton and Pierce King Lewis. Dan was born and reared in Prentiss ings.

County and attended school in the public schools. He later attended Mississippi A&M College and received a bachelor's degree in textile engineering in 1909. He later returned and received a bachelor's degree in agriculture in 1918. He remained at the college as herdsman of the dairy herd for a year, then he went to Greensboro, AL and taught in the high school. Irene was born in Wayne, AL and received her advanced education at Alabama Teachers College. She taught school at Greensboro, AL and there met her future husband. They were married on May 28, 1924. They bought a farm and moved to Tupelo, MS and there reared a family of five children and raised registered Jersey cattle.

The oldest child, William Pierce (b. Jun. 8, 1925, d. Feb. 14, 1990), after high school, attended Mississippi State University and DePaul University in Chicago, where he was selected to go to Los Alamos, NM to do secret work, which we later found out was the development of the atomic bomb. Bill transferred to Kirtland AFB in Albuquerque, NM where he married Betty Lou McFadden (b. Apr. 3, 1923) on Jun. 7, 1947. They made their home in Albuquerque. They have two daughters, Susan Irene Thomas (b. Aug. 20, 1949) married Robert William Weidenmeyer, II (b. Jul. 19, 1946) on Nov. 1, 1969. They live in Houston, TX. They are the parents of Heather Marie (b. Jan. 14, 1975) and Robert William Weidenmeyer III (b. 1978, d. 1999). Heather married Michael Gabor Nagy (b. May 15, 1969) on Jul. 19, 1997. They make their home in Houston, TX where she is a science teacher and he is a pharmaceutical salesman. Their second daughter, Debra Ann Thomas (b. Oct. 6, 1952) married William Gary Gillespie (b. Jan. 18, 1947) in 1975 and they had one son, Geremy Smith Gillespie (b. Jul. 13, 1977). This marriage ended in divorce and Debbie later married Howard Lee Smith in 1988. Howard (b. Oct. 16, 1949), reared in California, pursued advanced degrees and is now Dean of the Business School at the University of New Mexico in Albuquerque.

The second child of Dan and Irene was Martha Irene Thomas, born Oct. 10, 1927. She married Keitte Sanders "Sandy" Yon Jr. (b. 1926, d. 1973) on Jun. 8, 1947. Sandy served four years in the US Marines and after his education, became financial advisor for the University of Georgia, College of Education. Martha and Sandy had four daughters. Martha married Harold Lyle Nix (b. Sep. 10, 1920) on Jan. 25, 1975 and they make their home in Athens, GA. Harold was a professor at the university until his retirement. Children of Martha and Sandy Yon are Kit Sandra Yon (b. Sep. 3, 1948), who married Jim McCord on Aug. 30, 1969 and this marriage ended in divorce. She married Jay Britten Miller Jr. (b. Jun. 15, 1946) on Aug. 10, 1974 and they have three children: Martha Elisabeth Miller (b. May 11, 1976), Lillian Munson Miller (b. May 27, 1979) and Jay Britten Miller III (b. Jul. 11, 1990). The second child of Martha and Sandy was Dana Lanette Yon (b. Dec. 12, 1949), who married Terence Britton (Terry) Phillips (b. Aug. 21, 1939) on Sep. 2, 1978. There are no children to this marriage. The third child was Cynthia Jean (Cindy) Yon (b. Feb. 7, 1958), who married Theodore Lloyd Piper (b. Jun. 19, 1957) on Apr. 30, 1983. They have two daughters, Sara Brooke Piper (b. Aug. 11, 1985) and Kelly Lynn Piper (b. Sep. 19, 1987). This marriage ended in divorce. Cindy later married Glenn Edward Niske (b. Apr. 7, 1952) on Nov. 7, 1993 and they live in Columbia, SC. The fourth daughter was Patricia Jane Yon (b. Jun. 24, 1962), who married Jeffrey Joseph Ridgway (b. Dec. 10, 1959) on Jul. 20, 1984. They have two children, Matthew Joseph Ridgway (b. Sep. 28, 1988) and Mindy Nicole Ridgway (b. Mar. 4, 1991).

Dan and Irene's third child, Barbara Eula (b. May 5, 1929) was stillborn. The fourth child, Daniel McMillan Thomas (b. Aug. 20, 1931), married Marilakin Key Howard (b. Mar. 18, 1932) on Dec. 28, 1955. Dan practiced veterinary medicine for 19 years in Forest, MS and then joined USDA as a meat and poultry inspector. Marilakin was a practicing dietitian. They have four children: Martha Key Thomas (b. Jul. 19, 1957) married Charles Leonard Smith (b. Nov. 7, 1957) on Feb. 20, 1982 and they have two daughters, Josie Carol Smith (b. Dec. 16, 1985) and Martha Irene (Missie) Smith (b. Jul. 26, 1988). Martha, a RN and Leonard, a salesman, make their home in Clifton, VA. The Thomas's second child, Linda Carol Thomas (b. Apr. 5, 1960) married William Bryan (Bill) Tucker (b. Feb. 17, 1960) of McComb, MS, on Aug. 11, 1984 and they have two children, Amanda Joyce Tucker (b. Apr. 7, 1988) and William Bryan Tucker Jr. (b. Oct. 29, 1990). Bill is a professor in dairy science at Mississippi State University in Starkville, MS and Linda is a registered dietitian. The third child, Daniel McMillan (Danny) Thomas Jr. (b. Jul. 18, 1962), married Leigh Kirby Graves (b. Oct. 6, 1965) on May 30, 1987 and they have three children: Kirby Elizabeth Thomas (b. Jul. 4, 1990), Daniel Lakin Thomas (b. Apr. 16, 1993) and William Taylor (b. Feb. 22, 1995). Danny, a CPA and Leigh live in Jackson, MS, where he is controller for KLLM Trucking Co. Dan and Marilakin's fourth child is William Lakin Thomas (b. May 10, 1966), a chemical engineer with Shell Chemical Co. He is not married and lives in Atlanta, GA. The fifth child of Dan and Irene is Sarah Ruth Thomas (b. Jul. 1, 1933), who married James Franklin Deckard (b. Jan. 18, 1928) on Jun. 26, 1954. Ruth is a registered nurse and Jim retired from Levi Strauss Co. as an industrial engineer. They live in Knoxville, TN and have three children: Michael Thomas Deckard (b. Aug. 7, 1956), who married Jo Ann Gentry (b. Feb. 11, 1955) on Feb. 8, 1985. They have no children and live in Cookville, TN where Mike is a Forester with the State of Tennessee. Shirley Jo Deckard (b. Sep. 27, 1957) married Larry Jaffe Moore (b. Nov. 7, 1950) on Sep. 26, 1987 and they have one daughter, Sarah Louise Moore (b. Aug. 3, 1988). Shirley is a registered nurse and Larry is a self-employed carpenter. They live in Knoxville, TN. The third child is Pamela Lynn Deckard (b. Sep. 28, 1961), who married Kenny Ray Gorman (b. Jul. 16, 1954) on May 6, 1980 and they have two daughters, Nikki Marie Gorman (b. Mar. 25, 1981) and Elizabeth Danyell Gorman (b. Sep. 1, 1989). This marriage ended in divorce. Pam is a chemical engineer with the US Energy Department in Oak Ridge, TN and she lives in Powell, TN. The last child of Dan and Irene is Minnie Effie Thomas (b. Jan. 6, 1936), who married James Horton Curlin (b. 1936, d. 1995) on Mar. 27, 1965. Minnie and Jim had two children. Thomas Horton Curlin (b. Feb. 16,1971) married Dana Justine Hixon (b. Dec. 9, 1973), on Aug. 9, 1992 and they live in Cordova, TN and have no children. Tom is a financial analyst with Morgan Keegan and Dana is a registered pharmacist. Donna Kaye Curlin is not married and is an accountant and office manager for an accounting firm in Memphis, TN. *Submitted by Daniel M. Thomas.*

THOMAS, EFFIE GERTRUDE, married Clayborn Wilburn and they had one child, Tyndall Baxter. This marriage ended in divorce and the names of Gertrude and Tyndall were changed back to Thomas. Tyndall Baxter Thomas (b. 1904, d. 1961) married Frances Inez French Moore (b. 1914) on Sep. 25, 1943. Frances was born and reared in Water Valley, MS and is the daughter of John Edward and Amber Romuy.

Tyndall was an employee of the Redstone Arsenal Space Center in Huntsville, AL. Frances is a licensed practical nurse and served on the licensing board for the state of Mississippi. They made their home on property that has been in the Thomas family for four generations, dating back for well over 150 years. Frances had one son by a previous marriage, William Allen "Sonny" Moore (b. Jul. 12, 1936). Sonny lives with his mother.

There were four children born to Tyndall and Frances. Their first child was a son, David Lammone (b. Aug. 2, 1944). He married Lynn Anderson (b. 1945, of Albuquerque, NM) on Jun. 7, 1967 and they have three children: William David Thomas (b. Jan. 8, 1981), Christopher Michael Thomas (b. Mar. 15, 1983) and Jennifer Louise Thomas (b. December 1985). Lammone had a successful career in the US Air Force and after retirement, he and Lynn make their home in Bossier City, LA where he is an area supervisor for the Pizza Inn franchise.

Tyndall and Frances' second child, Gloria Estelle Thomas (b. Mar. 18, 1947) married Tom Stephens (b. Jul. 13, 1945). Gloria and Tom live on the Thomas Estate, east of Booneville. Gloria is employed by Quartitt and Tom is a self-employed carpenter. They have two children, Rhonda Gale Stephens (b. Feb. 21, 1965) married Lynn Lambert (b. May 14, 1968). They are the parents of two children, Kyle Lambert (b. May 12, 1990) and Stephanie Brooke Lambert (b. Sep. 10, 1998). Rebecca Ann Stephens (b. Feb. 17, 1969) the second child of Gloria and Tom, married Samuel Howell on Jun. 26, 1987 and they had one son, Samuel Lee Howell Jr. (b. Oct. 31, 1987). Rebecca's second husband is Carleton Rick Skelton (b. Jun. 2, 1961). They were married Apr. 20, 1991 and have one daughter, Tiffany Estelle Skelton (b. Aug. 31, 1993).

Tyndall and Frances' third child was a daughter, Oretia Gertrude "Rita" Thomas (b. Aug. 14, 1949). She married Jerry Miller in 1969 and they had one son, Johnny Miller (b. Dec. 8, 1970). This marriage ended in divorce. Rita's second husband is Glen Daugherty (b. October 1933). They have one daughter, Frances Rose Daugherty (b. May 17, 1978). Rita and Glen live in Water Valley, MS.

The fourth child of Tyndall and Frances is Cynthia Runez "Dingle" Thomas (b. Nov. 21, 1954) lives on the Thomas Estate. Dingle is a registered pharmacist and works for the Veterans Administration Hospital in Memphis, TN. She has one daughter, Amber Melissa "Amy" Thomas (b. Feb. 4, 1971). Amy married Jody Pitts (b. Jul. 4, 1969) on Jun. 24, 1995 and live in Booneville, where she is a science teacher in the Baldwyn public schools. Jody is employed by Eaton Paper Co. They have one daughter, Aby Kensington (b. Jul. 18, 1999). *Submitted by Daniel M. Thomas.*

THOMAS, JOHN, married Temperance "Tempie" C. Rogers. John was born in South Carolina and died prior to Nov. 26, 1878, when his property was deeded by his heirs to William Washington Thomas "for the consideration that W.W. Thomas, son and heir of said John Thomas deceased has paid off and discharged two notes executed by said deceased". This property had been purchased by John in 1872. It is unclear where his previously owned property was located but they lived in the 4th District, Northern Division, Old Tishomingo County when their children were born. After Tempie's death they lived in the Carrollville District near Meadow Creek.

John and his brother Miles were charter members of Shady Grove Methodist Church near Meadow Creek which was an active church until disbanded in the late 1950s. Many of the family members are buried there although the older graves are not marked. In 1998 the Mississippi Annual Conference of the Methodist Church transferred the cemetery to the Board of Trustees of Shady Grove Cemetery of Prentiss County.

Tempie was born in Tennessee and died prior to the 1860 census. Gertrude Thomas, Tempie's granddaughter, said John and Tempie were going on a trip in their wagon. Tempie got sick in Memphis, died there and was buried in Temple Cemetery, which has been done away with. Another granddaughter, Tempie Bell Hicks Hobson, said she died in Prentiss County in 1851 at the birth of her daughter Rean. One family member says she was part Indian but no proof has been found. Tempie could not read or write.

John had 12 children, but it is unclear whether all of these were also Tempie's children.

199

Nancy Caroline was 16 in 1850. She never married and was living with her father in Prentiss County at the time of his death.

Barnaby was 14 in 1850. He married Mary E. Honnell Apr. 26, 1860 and in July 1860 they were living with her parents near Rienzi. They had two children, Rosana and Frances. He enlisted Mar. 7, 1862, in Capt. Lowrey's Regiment, Mississippi Volunteers, which later became Co. A, 32nd Regiment, Mississippi Infantry and records show he served until furloughed for 30 days from Apr. 13, 1864. He was paid through June 1864. His army records are incomplete. He died before his father.

Eliza Jane was 13 in 1850. She married William W. Taylor Jul. 21, 1859 near Booneville. They were living near her father in 1870 but by 1881 they were living in Tippah County and later moved to Wise County, TX. They had four children: Nancy Ann (b. 1861), Mary Isabelle "Molly" (b. 1863), John Taylor (b. 1867) and Modena (b. 1874). Eliza died in 1926 in Decatur, TX and is buried in Bethel Cemetery near Decatur. William died in 1892.

Elbert was 12 in 1850 but was not listed on the 1860 census.

William Washington was born in 1839, (See William Washington Thomas Family).

Miles J. (b. 1841, d. 1926) was a Confederate war veteran. He cut off his fingers with a pocket knife after being shot swimming the Tennessee River during the battle at Shiloh. He married Tennessee "Tennie" Lue Taylor Dec. 5, 1867 and they lived close to John Thomas in 1870 but moved to Tippah County before 1880. Many of their descendants live in Ripley. Tennie was the sister of William Taylor who married Eliza Thomas.

John Carson was 6 in 1850. He and his brother George and sister Martha were in Johnson County, TX in August 1879, but he apparently returned to Mississippi and married S. Emma Wright in Prentiss County, Dec. 22, 1879. They later returned to Johnson County.

Martha Ann was 5 in 1850. She married Henry Paschal Hicks in Johnson County, TX and had two children, Tempie Bell Hicks Hobson and John Carson. She also had an adopted son, Charles Thomas Hicks, who was Henry's nephew.

George W. was 3 in 1850. He was living in Johnson County in 1879, but it is said he moved on to Oklahoma or California.

Calvin Taylor "Doc" was 2 in 1850. He married Sallie Davenport Dec. 11, 1876 in Prentiss County and moved to Texas. He was living in Texhoma, OK in 1926.

Mahala Angeline was born in 1850. She married George W. Ray Aug. 17, 1873 in Booneville and by 1879 they had moved to Johnson County, TX.

Arena Isabell (Rean) (b. 1851) lived with her father until his death and then went to Texas with her brother John Carson and his wife Emma in 1880. She stayed for some time with her sister, Martha Ann Hicks in Decatur, TX before marrying Dan Harmon in Wise County.

THOMAS, WILLIAM WASHINGTON "BILLY," son of John Thomas and Temperance C. "Tempie" Rogers Thomas (See John Thomas Family) and Ruth Tersia Moore, daughter of Ebenezer Scott Moore and Martha Alexander Moore (See Ebenezer Scott Moore Family), were married in Prentiss County Feb. 4, 1869 by Reverend J.W. Honnell, M.G., the first minister at the First Methodist Church of Booneville.

Billy, born Jul. 11, 1839, five miles east of Kossuth, MS in Old Tishomingo County, was a Confederate war veteran having served four years. He enlisted Jun. 8, 1861 in the 2nd Regiment, 1st Brigade, Army of Mississippi to serve for one year when it was first organized at Blackland. This regiment was transferred to the Confederate service Sep. 19, 1861 and the designation was changed to Co. F, 23rd Regiment, Mississippi Volunteers, Blackland Gideonites. He was captured at Fort Donelson, TN Feb. 16, 1862 and was imprisoned at Camp Morton, IN until exchanged about Sep. 20, 1862. He was again captured near Nashville, TN Dec. 15, 1864 and was received at the Military Prison, Louisville, KY Dec. 20, 1864. He was discharged there Dec. 24, 1864 and sent to Camp Douglas, IL where he remained until Jun. 30, 1965 where he was discharged on General Orders from #109 AGO Washington, DC dated Jun. 6, 1865.

Ruth was born Oct. 31, 1846 in the Carrollville District of Old Tishomingo County. After their marriage they lived on her father's farm until they bought farmland east of Booneville in 1872, some of which is still owned by the descendants of their daughter Gertrude. Billy was known for his industry, economy and integrity. According to a memorial written by a close friend and printed in a local newspaper at the time time of his death, he gave financial aid to many who needed it to a far greater extent than most people knew and according to his friend, often said that his worst fault was "pinching for dollars". He wore a beard according to the fashion of the time and was meticulous about keeping it clean and neatly trimmed. Billy and Ruth were active members of Shady Grove Methodist Church where he was a steward for many years. His father, John Thomas and uncle Miles Thomas were charter members of the church. Ruth died Mar. 11, 1921 and Billy died Apr. 1, 1926. Both are buried in Shady Grove Cemetery.

There were nine children born to the family. Walter Hafford (b. 1869, d. 1871) and William Fletcher (b. 1871, d. 1872), the two oldest and Elvia Pearl (b. 1886, d. 1886) the youngest, lived less than a year.

Effie Gertrude (b. 1873, d. 1958) was the first child to reach adulthood. She married Clayborn B. Wilburn in Corinth Aug. 16, 1903 (see Effie Gertrude Thomas family).

Martha Ozella (b. 1875, d. 1954) graduated from the Vicksburg Sanitarium in 1909 with a nursing degree and was one of the group of 29 nurses who were first registered in 1914. She helped organize the Mississippi Association of Graduate Nurses in 1911 and was an officer in the association for five years. She was the first trained nurse to work at the 15-bed hospital opened in Booneville in 1917 by Dr. W.H. Sutherland. During WWI she served as a Red Cross nurse in Hot Springs, AR among other places. In 1927 she went to Vicksburg as a Red Cross nurse to help the flood victims. She later worked as county health nurse from 1930 to 1937. The first telephone in Prentiss County was listed in Ozella's name. She never married but was close to her nieces and nephews. She is buried in Shady Grove Cemetery.

Claude Baxter Thomas (b. 1877, d. 1937) was the fifth child (See Claude Baxter Thomas family).

Dan Thomas (b. 1879, d. 1952) was the sixth child (See Dan Thomas family).

Eula Hortense (b. 1881, d. 1967) married James C. McCarthy (b. 1875, d. 1958) and lived in Tupelo. They had two sons. Charlie Scott moved to California as a young man and married there. He had a son and a daughter. Curtis Wright (b. 1909, d. 1980) married Martha Jo Seal (b. 1911, d. 1984) and lived in Tupelo. They had no children.

Anna Lillian (b. 1884, d. 1940) never married, taught school in Laredo, TX and later was a beauty parlor operator at Bry's Department Store in Memphis before returning to Booneville to live at their parent's homeplace with Ozella and Gertrude, where all three lived until their death. Lillian is buried in the Shady Grove Cemetery.

TIMBES, BUFORD CULLEN, sixth child born to Samuel Levi Timbes and Missouri Etta (Sudie) Robinson Timbes. He was born Jun. 2, 1908 and died Feb. 14, 1961. On Nov. 2, 1924, he married Ruby Pearl Holder, born May 24, 1908, to Denier Holder and Annie Holder. They made their home in the Cairo Community of Prentiss County. Two children were born to this union:

Bobby Neal (b. Mar. 5, 1931, d. Jul. 25, 1987) married Quay Pruitt (b. Dec. 1930, d. Jun. 26, 1983) on Oct. 27, 1949. They have four children: (1) Barbara Kay (b. Aug. 26, 1950) married Dwayne McLemore. They have two children, Lee Pruitt (b. Jun. 21, 1984) and Benjamin Neal (b. Dec. 26, 1987). (2) Ricky Neal (b. Jul. 9, 1955) married Teressa Byrd. They have two children Natalie Nichole (b. Aug. 19, 1975) and Deanna Ashlea (b. Jul. 2, 1982). (3) Margaret Lynn (b. Jan. 3, 1962) married Larry Stanford. They have two children, Matthew Jamison (b. Jan. 23, 1988) and Morgan Allison (b. Jul. 2, 1994, d. Oct. 22, 1994). (4) James Cullen Timbes (b. Sep. 27, 1964) presently is unmarried and has no children.

Buford Cullen and Ruby Pearl have a second child, Johnnie Ruth Marlar (b. Sep. 16, 1939) married to Harold Marlar. She has two children, by a previous marriage to Lucien Puckett. (1) Kathy Sue Hubbard (b. Oct. 8, 1956) married to Mike Hubbard. Kathy has two children by a previous marriage to Edward Murphy. They are Edward Scott (b. Aug. 17, 1974) and Kimberly Leanne (b. Jul. 16, 1991). (2) Stanley Lawayne Puckett (b. Sep. 1, 1966). Lawayne has one child from a previous marriage to Cindy Pate. Brittany Pearl (b. Nov. 1, 1989). Scott Murphy has two daughters, Shae'a Lyn (b. May 6, 1995) and Chastity Leanne (b. Jul. 30, 1996).

Ruby Timbes resides in Iuka, MS, as well as her daughter, Johnnie and all of her children and grandchildren. Bobby and Quay's children reside in Iuka with the exception of Barbara who makes her home in Corinth, MS. Buford Cullen, is buried in New Lebanon Cemetery located in the Cairo Community, along with Bobby, Quay and their granddaughter, Morgan Stanford. *Submitted by Margaret Stanford.*

TIMBES, JAMES GARLON, second child of Samuel Levi and Missouri Etta (Sudie) Robinson Timbes. James Garlon Timbes (b. Aug. 31, 1900, d. Feb. 2, 1958) married Sep. 2, 1921 to Onnie Mae Trimble (b. Feb. 23, 1905, d. Oct. 27, 1999). They made their home in the Cairo Community of Prentiss County with their three sons: James Cecil "J.C.", James Wallace "J.W." and Charles Edward.

James Cecil (b. Jul. 30, 1922) was first married to Imogene Spradling of Mantachie and to this union five children were born: (1) Martha Joan (b. Jan. 8, 1943) married Bobby Joe Lambert. They have two sons, Michael Joe and David Scott. Joan and Bobby divorced. Joan married Reece Lee Wilson. They have one daughter, Cindy Lee Wilson. (2) James David Timbes (b. Jun. 23, 1947, d. Jun. 23, 1954). (3) Donald Jurone Timbes (b. Feb. 13, 1949) married Kathy Lee Chanez. They have two sons. (4) Sandra Jane (b. Feb. 25, 1955) married Michael Graham. They have two daughters. (5) Susan Marie (b. May 30, 1957) married Glenn Eurin. They have one son. She divorced and married Preston Reeves. They have two sons and one daughter. She again divorced and is married to Jim Collins.

James Wallace "J.W." (b. Sep. 8, 1925, d. Oct. 1, 1980) married Louise Bishop (b. Jun. 23, 1926). They made their home in Booneville where he was co-owner of Cox-Blythe Drug Store. Their children are: (1) Janice Carolyn (b. Feb. 24, 1945) married to James J. Downs. They have three children: Steven James (b. Apr. 11, 1965); Angelia Michelle (b. Oct. 3, 1968) and David Timbes (b. Dec. 27, 1970). Steven James married Vicki George on Aug. 10, 1985. They have two children: Steven Case (b. Jun. 7, 1989) and Holland Alixis "Allie" (b. Apr. 13, 1994). Angelia Michelle married James Christopher "Chris" Jones. They have two children, Carolyn Krischelle (b. Aug. 7, 1994) and Hunter Jakob (b. May 6, 1999). (3) David Timbes married Lisa Marie Ozbirn on Jun. 1, 1991. They have one child, Jake Evan (b. Jun. 26, 1999). (2) Sherion Janell (b. Nov. 19, 1947) married James W. Jones. They have two children, Bryan Todd (b. Dec. 23, 1971) and Michael Scott (b. Oct. 3, 1975).

Bryan Todd married Lucesita Wing Sie Tam on Jun. 7, 1997. Michael Scott married Audra Cech on May 16, 1995.

Charles Edward married Margret Ann Logsdon on Oct. 19, 1960. They had two children: Ronald Edward (b. Jan. 1, 1962) and Dianna Lynn (b. Apr. 21, 1963). Ronald Edward married Rebecca Marie Smith of Denver, CO, on Oct. 4, 1969. They have two children: Tyler James (b. Feb. 2, 1993) and Darbie Marie (b. Jan. 8, 1995). They make their home in Pensacola, FL. Dianna Lynn married Jimmy Lee Melton Jr. They have two children: Joshua Lee (b. Oct. 8, 1989) and Carolann Lynn (b. Aug. 26, 1990). Charles and Margret Ann divorced and he later married Sue Jenkins. They have one daughter, Ellen Kay (b. Jun. 7, 1968). Ellen married William Glenn Montgomery. They have one son and two daughters: John William (b. Jun. 10, 1990; Serra Elizabeth (b. Jan. 19, 1996) and Jessica Rena (b. Sep. 9, 1999). *Submitted by Louise (Mrs. J.W.) Timbes.*

TIMBES, SAMUEL LEVI AND SUDIE, the Timbes family came to America from either Scotland or Ireland in the 1700s. Samuel Levi Timbes (b. Jul. 8, 1804, South Carolina) married Mary "Polly Ann" Polk (b. Sep. 4, 1811, Georgia) and lived in Tennessee for a while where her brothers also lived. They came in the 1830s to old Tishomingo County and settled in the southern part, which later became Prentiss County, along with her cousin, Pinkney Polk. The Timbes and the Polks settled adjoining land. Samuel was a farmer and raised stock and Pinkney farmed and owned a store, a water grist mill and a cotton gin. The community was known as Polk's Mill Pond and was located southwest of Burton. The farms consisted of a total of 400 acres.

Samuel Levi Timbes and "Sudie" Robinson Timbes, 1937.

Samuel Levi and Mary had two sons: James Leander Polk Timbes (b. Oct. 3, 1840, d. Oct. 12, 1891) and William Curtis Rodney Timbes (b. Oct. 2, 1847, d. Nov. 6, 1884). Samuel Levi and Mary lived all their adult lives in Prentiss County and Mary was the first person to be buried in Forked Oak Cemetery. The exact dates of their death is unknown at present.

The sons of Samuel Levi and Mary continued to live in the Polk Mill Community for many years. James Leander Polk Timbes remained on the farm all his life except during the Civil War when he served in the 10th Mississippi Cavalry, Co. B, Capt. I.J. Warren's Co. of Partisan Rangers (1862-1864).

James Leander Polk Timbes married Cassie Caroline Owens (b. Dec. 26, 1837, d. Oct. 12, 1909) on May 25, 1858. They were married near Whiteoak in Franklin County, AL, by Gilbert Howell, Justice of the Peace. She was the daughter of Franklin Mabry Lowrey Owens (b. 1807, Alabama, d. 1893, Prentiss County). We are unsure of her mother's name.

James Leander Polk Timbes and Cassie Caroline Owens Timbes had 11 children. They were as follows: (1) William Crawford (b. Sep. 25, 1859, d. Jul. 22, 1927); (2) Calvin Franklin (b. Mar. 8, 1861, d. Nov. 17, 1939); (3) Mary Jane (b. Aug. 19, 1862, d. Sep. 15, 1888); (4) James Edward (b. Jun. 12, 1866, d. Dec. 3, 1914); (5) Manervia Caroline (b. Jan. 12, 1866, d. Sep. 9, 1897); (6) Anna Eliza (b. Feb. 24, 1868, d. Aug. 23, 1938); (7) Samuel Levi (b. Dec. 26, 1869, d. Aug. 23, 1938); (8) Columbus Allen (b. Apr. 21, 1872, d. Mar. 14, 1957); (9) Sarah Ethel (b. Jan. 12, 1874, d. Aug. 12, 1891); (10) Martha Marilda (b. May 17, 1875, d. Aug. 24, 1939); (11) John Pinkney (b. Mar. 4, 1878, d. Jun. 3, 1957).

The seventh child, Samuel Levi, was named for his grandfather, Samuel Levi Timbes, born in South Carolina in 1804. On Dec. 22, 1891, he married Missouri Etta (Sudie) Robinson (b. Mar. 26, 1876, d. Jul. 26, 1941), the daughter of B.F. and Elizabeth Robinson. They lived most of their adult life in Prentiss County in what is now the Cairo Community. Eight children were born to this union as follows: (1) Virlon Cleo (b. Nov. 1, 1898, d. Oct. 5, 1979); (2) James Garlon (b. Aug. 31, 1900, d. Feb. 2, 1958); (3) Marion Timbes (b. Jan. 24, 1903, d. Dec. 18, 1903); (4) Nola Mae (b. Nov. 18, 1903, d. May 19, 1974); (5) James Edward (Eddie) (b. May 21, 1906, d. Sep. 14, 1922); (6) Buford Cullen (b. Jun. 2, 1908, d. Feb. 14, 1961); (7) Willie Archer (b. Jan. 28, 1910, d. Apr. 24, 1987) and (8) Audrey Quay (b. Aug. 4, 1913, d. Sep. 28, 1999). Samuel Levi and Sudie's home was destroyed by a tornado on Sunday night, Apr. 5, 1936. Two of their sons' homes were also destroyed, that of Buford Cullen and Willie Archer. No one was injured, as all of the family got in the storm house just as the tornado struck. All the deceased named in the Levi and Sudie Timbes family are buried in New Lebanon in Prentiss County with the exception of Marion, who is buried in Forked Oak in Prentiss County. *Submitted by Maxine U. Wade.*

TIMBES, WILLIE ARCHIE, sixth child born to Samuel Levi Timbes and Missouri Etta "Sadie" Robinson Timbes. Willie Timbes was born Jan. 28, 1910 and he died Apr. 28, 1987. He married on Feb. 6, 1932, to Mamie Elliott, who was born Jun. 1, 1916. They made their home at the old Timbes home place in the Cairo Community. They farmed most of their lives and Willie drove a school bus. In his later years, he worked for the Tishomingo County Hospital, where he managed the laundry department. Mamie Timbes has since moved to Corinth. They had three sons:

Willie Archie and Mamie Timbes taken May 6, 1982, on their 50th Wedding Anniversary.

Morris Waymon Timbes (b. Nov. 18, 1935) married Shirley Johnson (b. Nov. 18, 1936). Morris worked for the United Food and Commercial Workers International Union and retired as an international representative. Morris and Shirley live on part of the old Timbes home place. They have three children. Michael Waymon Timbes married Jamie Dixon and has one child, Patrick Timbes. Mike also adopted Jamie's daughter, Christy, who is a teacher in the Lee County School System. Mike and Jamie live in Corinth.

Kathryn Annette Timbes was married to Kent Clark and they had three children. April Star, the oldest, is a student at Northeast Mississippi Community College. Brandy Annette, the middle, is also a student at Northeast. William Bradley is a student at Tishomingo County High School. They live in Burnsville, where Kathryn has raised them by herself. Pamela Annell Timbes married Steve Butler. She has one stepson, Shade Butler and he is a student at Alcorn Central. They live in Corinth.

Dean Timbes (b. Apr. 10, 1943) second son of Willie and Mamie Timbes married Dot McKee Timbes (b. born Nov. 7, 1942). Dean is a Baptist preacher and has pastored churches in both Mississippi and Alabama. They currently live in Albertville, AL, where Dean is pastor of Mount Calvary Baptist Church. Dean and Dot have two daughters, Kerry Deane and Marcia Jill. Kerry married Mark McMillen and they have one child, Hannah Claire McMillen. They live in Canterment, FL, where Kerry teaches school. Jill married David Williams and they live in Camp Lejeune, NC. Jill works for the state of North Carolina.

Ronnie Dale Timbes (b. Jul. 28, 1954) third son of Willie and Mamie married Debbie Ivy and had three children: Derrick, Erica and Rayce. Ronnie owns Ronnie Timbes Body Shop and Used Cars. Derrick works for his dad, Erica attends New Site High School and Rayce also attends New Site High School. Ronnie lives at the old home place with his current wife, Mary Fair Timbes. *Submitted by Morris W. Timbes.*

TOLLISON, DANIEL, born 1745 in South Carolina, seems to be our earliest known relative. His wife's name was Sarah (b. 1759). Her last name was possibly Wilson and this could be where the Wilson name begins to be passed down. Daniel died in 1821 in Union County, SC. His estate was auctioned and Sarah bought most of it, with a few close friends and relatives buying most of the other. Sarah and Daniel had several

John Wilson Tollison and Nancy Elizabeth Franks Tollison, ca. 1920

children. The only proven one was Wilson, born 1784 and died 1870 in Greenville County, SC. Wilson's wife was Sarah Hannah Thomason, born 1784 and died 1865 in Greenville, SC. Wilson and Sarah's children were: Isaac (b. 1803), James (b. 1805) married Phoebe Young, Steven (b. February 1809), Louise or Lavice (b. 1811) married Hugh Bullard in 1843, Sally Matilda (b. 1813), Susan (b. 1815), Nances (b. 1817) and Rebecca (b. 1819). Wilson and Daniel were extensive land owners as there are many land deeds in the early 1800s. Wilson was in the South Carolina State Militia during the Revolutionary War, a private under Daniel Fielder (b. Oct. 10, 1814, d. Mar. 7, 1815).

There is some speculation as to Daniel's siblings and Wilson's siblings. My research group in South Carolina has suggested these: Daniel Sr., born 1740 or 1745, died before August 1821 in Union County, SC; wife, Sarah Wilson; children: Daniel Jr. (b. 1760-70), Erasmus (b. 1760-70), John (b. 1760-70) (not John of Spartanburg), James (b. 1760-70, Methodist preacher, died 1800), David (b. 1765-70) married Hannah Harris, Vina (b. 1760-70) married Thomas Benson), Abraham (b. 1780-90) married Elizabeth and Wilson (b. 1784).

I think Daniel Sr. and David Sr. are brothers and John of Spartanburg, SC could be a cousin. Their father was the famous Erasmus Sr., who eludes us all. They all appear to be about the same age, live in close proximity to each other most of their lives and all their children have similar repeating names. (See James Tollison, father of William M. Tollison for conclusion). *Submitted by Diane Tollison.*

TOLLISON, JOHN WILSON, born April 1845 in South Carolina, county unknown, died Apr. 5, 1928, son of William Madison Tollison. He came with his brothers, Bill and Bob and two sisters, Lou E. and Sarah. Settled in Ellistown, Union County, MS near New Albany. John, Bill, and Bob moved to Tippah County, MS and lived in the Dry Creek Community the rest of their lives. John Wilson married Nancy Elizabeth Franks (b. May 16, 1841, d. Dec. 23, 1942), daughter of Lemuel Franks of Holland. They are buried in the Jumpertown Cemetery near Booneville, MS at the far back end of the cemetery near the road.

John was a very kind and well liked man and Nancy was known by most grandchildren as "Granny Franks." She was blind in her old age and used to swat at the children with her cane when they played tricks on her. John died in 1928 when daddy was 12 years old, of prostate cancer.

Back: Dawn Gott (Tollison), Bill Roys, Hayden Roys, Denise Tollison Roys, Garry Tollison. Front: Diane Tollison, Willie Lee "Bill" Tollison, Beverly Tollison and April Lewis Tollison.

The children of John Wilson and Nancy Elizabeth Franks Tollison: (I) William Nickolas "Nick" (b. Nov. 16, 1873 in Union County, MS, d. Apr. 8, 1939) married Vallie Walls (b. Apr. 22, 1881, d. Dec. 2, 1956). Children: Ellen Lou Ella, Nancy Annie Mae, John Dee Andrew, William Samuel "Sam", James Edward, Julie Melverta, Clarence Lesley, Roy Curtis, Henry Nolan, Dorothy Ione (Raper) and Troy Walter.

(II) Henry Hezekiah (b. Jan. 21, 1875 in Union County, MS, d. Nov. 11, 1953) married Mariah Coley (b. Jul. 27, 1877, d. Mar. 24, 1949); children: Newton, Edgar, Mary Odell, Nannie, Lucille and Lillie Belle.

(III) Lemuel B. (b. Sep. 3, 1879 in Union County, MS, d. May 2, 1953) married Mallie Ingram (b. Feb. 19, 1889, d. ?); children: Garfield, William, Lawrence, and Maggie.

(IV) George Washington (b. Jun. 18, 1882 in Union County, MS, d. Sep. 19, 1952) married Susan Isabelle Wages (b. 1886, d. 1959); children: (1) Flora Estella, (b. Feb. 20, 1907) married William Duffie Hatchel (b. 1895), children: Myrtle Lois, Mary Francis and Elmon Clyde. (2) Louis Allen, (b. Jul. 22, 1909) married Irene Clowes, children: Emma Sue, Richard and Shirley Belle. (3) Nancy Elizabeth "Lizzie" (b. Feb. 6, 1911) married Albert "Red" Brazil, children: Charles and Vivian "Vicki". (4) Willie Lee "Bill" (b. May 28, 1916) married Beverly Miron (b. Aug. 19, 1935) on Nov. 30, 1959, children: (a) Dawn Michelle (Gott) (b. Jul. 3, 1960), (b) Diane Kim (b. Dec. 9, 1961), (c) Denise Irene (b. Sep. 23, 1964) married William George "Bill" Roys, children: Hayden Hilton Roys (b. May 19, 1994) and Logan Mitchell Roys (b. Apr. 11, 1997) and (d) Garry Lee (b. Apr. 15, 1966) married April Lewis, one child William Joseph Tollison (b. Mar. 31, 1998). (5) Lula Mae (b. Jul. 1, 1914) married J.D. Walk (b. 1912), children: Judy and Steven. (6) James Wilson "JW" or "Jack" (b. Aug. 2, 1920) married Louise Hopkins. (7) Tabitha Myrtle "Bitha" or "Monk"(b. Aug. 3, 1918) married Bruce Ware Walk (cousin to J.D. Walk). (8) John Wesley "Wes" or "Johnny" (b. Jan. 14, 1923) married Gladys Davis, children: David and Becky and (9) Edna Florence "Flo" (b. Apr. 22, 1926) married John Pacillas, children: John "Bob" and Michael "Mike".

(V) Mary Elizabeth "Lizzie" (b. Oct. 1, 1885 in Union County, MS, d. Sep. 5, 1973) married Tom Walls, children: Clara Belle Willard, Buela Peddie, Annie Lou Flannagin, Gladys Willard, Jewel Page, Alice Gaskin, Ruebel Walls, Millard Walls, Vivian Partain and Ellen Willard.

(VI) Marion "Dee" (b. Mar. 28, 1888 in Union County, MS, d. Nov. 16, 1962) married Mary F. Jumper (b. Sep. 23, 1895, d. Jun. 24, 1975), children: Jettie Mae, Ruey Mancel, Winnie Fay and Leola.

(VII) Sarah Lou (b. Mar. 16, 1890 in Union County, MS, d. Mar. 8, 1972), married Will D. Pannell (b. Jul. 15, 1885), children: Clara, Claudie, Inez, Olene and Louise.

(VIII) Joshua "Josh" (b. Mar. 27, 1892 in Union County, MS, d. Sep. 14, 1927) married Georgeann Davis (b. Nov. 7, 1895, d. Jan. 23, 1964), sons: Grady Franklin, James Ray, Ernest and Joe Marvin. Two other children died when they were young; Isaac died of a snake bite at age 12 (per Aunt Lula)and Bilbo died as a baby. No other information is available on them.

TOLLISON, WILLIAM MADISON,

born January 1824 in South Carolina. The place has not been pinpointed, but it is assumed to be Chester or Fairfield County because of other family origins. He was married to Mary (Chilcoat) first in Lawrence County, AL, then to Martha (Rogers) and then to Mary Jane Pannell, daughter of Richard Walter "Dicky" Pannell. Mary Jane's sister, Elizabeth was married to William James Wages, my other great-great-grandfather around 1846. Mary Jane was an older bride and said to be slightly mentally impaired. William was a faithful soldier in the Civil War. He enlisted in Ellistown, MS Feb. 8, 1863 and was released from service Jun. 7, 1865. He was said to have been captured twice by the Yankees. The first time, he broke loose and returned to his regiment. The second time he was captured, he was being transported on a ship and a box from overhead fell loose and hit him in the back. This injury was said to have crippled him. He supposedly spent a long time in a hospital mending, but from the records of the Civil War, I've found him to have spent most of his time in three different prison camps (Memphis, Alton, IL and Fort Delaware, DE). He had been gone so long and walked stooped over when he returned home that his children were frightened of him. Fort Delaware was known to be the "dread of the South" for its awful conditions. He must have suffered greatly. He died between 1916 and 1920. He does not appear in the 1920 census, but does in the 1900 for Chickasaw County, MS. Aunt Lula (b. July 1914) says she, as a very small child, remembers him slightly as walking stooped over. It is still a mystery as to where he is buried. I feel it is somewhere near or in Ellistown Cemetery. There are many unmarked graves listed in the Union County Cemetery book, or he could have been buried at an old homestead. He also could have been living with one of his children at the time of death. He was around 90 years old. His third wife is buried in Troy, MS in Schooner Valley Cemetery.

Back: Lewis Tollison, Nancy Elizabeth "Liz" Tollison, John Wesley Tollison, Susan Isabelle Wages Tollison, Flora Tollison. Front: Lula Tollison Walk, Bitha Tollison Walk, James Wilson "Jack" Tollison, Willie "Bill" Tollison

William M. Tollison's parents were Phoebe Young (b. 1800?, d. 1840) and James (b. 1805), son of Wilson. There are no records of James after the 1840 Chester County, SC census, where he is listed as head of household, no wife and young children residing with him. There are not many other clues about him other than his name and that he fits in with Wilson's children. Uncle "Jack's" name is James Wilson and also there is John Wilson Tollison who is William M. Tollison's son.

William M. Tollison's children were: John Wilson (b. 1845, MS, d. Apr. 5, 1928) married Nancy Elizabeth Franks, Sarah Elizabeth (b. 1847) never married, Jane "Mary Jane" (b. 1849), Lou E. (b. Jun. 2, 1852, d. 27 May 1962) married G.M. Rakestraw, Henry Bell, Robert "Bob" (R.L.) married Barbara Pannell, daughter of R. Walter Dicky Pannell and William (b. April 1865) never married.

William Madison Tollison's siblings were: Levy (b. 1852) married Elizabeth Wright, John Thomas (b. 1826, d. 1863) married Mary Ann Roberts, Sarah (Stone) (b. 1820?) and Feriba (b. 1828?).

Phoebe Young's (William's mother) sisters were Nancy Young Roberts, Evey Free and Barbara Free. Her brothers were John and William.

Phoebe's parents were William and Dolly (Polly or Mary) Young of Chester County, SC. I don't have much confirmed beyond this for her, but have some families I could probably connect. James' family will be listed with Wilson Tollison family. (See Wilson Tollison family.) William Young's siblings were John and Phillip (b. 1875). Researchers assume that his father's name was William, also.

TUCKER, FLEMMA DUPREE CARPENTER,

daughter of James Frederick Hambright Carpenter and Sarah Narcissus Bartlett Carpenter. For many generations her family has been prominent in the history of the development of Prentiss County.

Mrs. Tucker was a member of the Booneville Woman's Club and the Society of Mayflower Descendants.

Hers was a devoted Christian home in which she spent her formative years and its guiding influence and high ideals did much to shape the course of her life.

Flemma DuPree Carpenter Tucker, husband Albert Jackson Tucker.

She was a member of the Booneville First United Methodist Church following her membership at the Blackland Methodist Church. At both churches, she was a leading spirit. Her whole being was permeated and motivated by faith, hope and a religious zeal.

From early life, she had faith in the church that was a most natural, congenial and effective channel through which she gave expression to the dominant qualities of her life.

She taught in the Junior Department in both the Blackland and Booneville churches for a total of 59 years.

Mrs. Tucker taught in the Prentiss County Schools for 45 years. She received her education in the Iuka Normal Institute and Union University with special work in other colleges. She was a student of academic excellence. The scholarship preparations she made for her teaching career were varied and comprehensive.

Mrs. Tucker was a distinguished figure in the educational field of Prentiss County because of her important work in teaching the youth of this section through which she established the quality of her talents.

She had great initiative and the many developments in education were called into existence and they owed their subsequent growth to her wise leadership.

It was a wise combination found in Mrs. Tucker as an educator and as a religious leader. It has been said that the end of all education is the building of character.

A woman of mental and physical strength, she had the understanding, as well as sympathetic and inspirational leadership that marked her as an educator of genius. She has been characterized as a teacher of judgment, diplomacy and leadership. She was a builder of character both in the schoolroom and the Sunday school room.

She was not simply a teacher and a friend and instead of a taskmaster, she was a very human person who won trust and affection. These are some of the qualities that made her career so distinguished as a teacher.

She was most generous, not only in giving material gifts but in her understanding of the frailties of others. Many have been turned to a better life by a quiet word or a counsel from her. She positively swayed the lives and aspirations of her students, a host of youth with whom she came in contact.

A force was ever present and exerted toward thorough scholarship, clean living, laudable ambition and a confident optimism which will be treasured and continued as a source of power in the lives of the students she leaves behind.

It was the earnest and sustained interest, which she had in her students for which she will be remembered.

She has stepped with triumph across the threshold and reflected the beauty and radiance of Him in which she gave her best, her choicest and most generous gift.

Flemma Dupree Carpenter Tucker was born Jul. 22, 1881 and died Feb. 20, 1971.

The other children of this family were: Mary Parthenia Carpenter Oakley (b. Dec. 10, 1883, d. Jan. 2, 1979); Miles Edgar Carpenter (b. Mar. 4, 1886, d. Sep. 5, 1958); James Madison Carpenter (b. Oct. 17, 1888, d. Jul. 4, 1983); Frederick Boone Carpenter (b. Feb. 22, 1891, d. Feb. 25, 1968); Gracie Mae Carpenter (b. May 4, 1893, d. Sep. 13, 1897); Annie Lois Carpenter Lanning (b. Jul. 10, 1896, d. Jul. 17, 1978) and Flecia Clyde Carpenter (b. Jul. 13, 1899, d. Jan. 21, 1900). *Submitted by Marjorie Oakley Waters.*

UMFRESS, ALVIA DEAN, born Oct. 19, 1881 and died Jan. 20, 1971, grew up in the Cairo Community of Prentiss County. He was the eldest child of Nathaniel Napoleon Umfress (b. Jan. 18, 1849, d. Jan. 3, 1898) and Matilda Cook Umfress (b. Jan. 3, 1853, d. Dec. 17, 1939), who are buried in Little Flock Cemetery. His paternal grandparents were James H. Umfress (b. 1809, d. Feb. 28, 1884) and Elizabeth Weaver Umfress (b. Mar. 6, 1808, d. Jun. 5, 1873), who are buried in Little Flock Cemetery.

Alvia's siblings were Bertha Mai Umfress Crabb (b. Mar. 1, 1883), James Cleveland Umfress (b. Nov. 8, 1884), Martin Luther Umfress (b. Nov. 11, 1886), William Baxter Umfress (b. Mar. 12, 1888), George Elmer Umfress (b. Oct. 27, 1891) and Maude Ethyl Umfress Allen (b. Nov. 23, 1893).

On Nov. 2, 1911, Alvia married Nellie Jane Stricklin (b. Apr. 28, 1885, d. Jan. 24, 1965) of Holcut, MS. Her parents were Henry Lee Stricklin (b. Dec. 13, 1855, d. Jun. 30, 1945) and Emma Louise Odom Stricklin (b. Mar. 8, 1855, d. Jun. 5, 1906). They are buried in Mt. Gilead Cemetery.

Nellie's siblings were: Hattie Laura Stricklin Holt (b. Jan. 12, 1879), Nanie Ella Stricklin Glen (b. Jun. 9, 1880), Minnie Lee Stricklin Elledge (b. Jan. 1, 1882), George Wesley Stricklin (b. Dec. 28, 1883), Columbus Jessie Stricklin (b. Dec. 18, 1886), Dora Angeline Stricklin White (b. Aug. 18, 1888), Mattie Elizabeth Stricklin Strickland (b. Mar. 22, 1890) and Pearl Sanford Stricklin Pope (b. Jul. 9, 1892).

Alvia and Nellie were the parents of Wayne Armon Umfress (b. Feb. 1, 1914), Thelma Christine Umfress Smith (b. Dec. 21, 1915, d. Jul. 25, 1995), Milford Henry Umfress (b. Mar. 3, 1918) and Clastie Umfress (b. Jan. 29, 1920).

The Umfress children were taught the value of hard work on the farm where poultry, cattle, corn, soybeans, sorghum, fruits and vegetables were grown. Alvie also raised timber. He was known for the excellent sorghum molasses he milled and the prize watermelons he grew. It was not unusual for him to cut a watermelon at Thanksgiving or Christmas, that he had saved from the fall crop. Nellie made excellent strawberry cobbler pies with fresh berries from Alvia's strawberry patch. She enjoyed gathering the family together for big country breakfasts.

In early April 1936, a tornado badly damaged their home and destroyed the barn, but they were repaired and rebuilt. Children and grandchildren enjoyed visits to their home throughout the years.

Alvia and Nellie were members of New Lebanon Freewill Baptist Church and are buried in the cemetery beside the church, not far from their home. *Submitted by Harrol W. Umfress.*

UMFRESS, CLASTIE, youngest child (b. Jan. 29, 1920) of four born to Alvia Dean Umfress (b. Oct. 19, 1881, d. Jan. 20, 1971) and Nellie Jane Stricklin Umfress (b. Apr. 28, 1885, d. Apr. 21, 1965) in the Cairo Community located in Prentiss County, MS. Clastie was reared in the Cairo Community and graduated from Burton High School in 1941. After graduation from high school he worked in Bristol, Connecticut, until he was drafted into the US Army Infantry. Clastie served in Algiers, North Africa, where he did guard duty at General Dwight D. Eisenhower's headquarters for six months. He continued with the 34th Infantry Division, 133rd Regiment to Naples, Italy. After a short time he traveled to the Anzio Beachhead on the West Coast of Italy and then marched north through Rome in sight of the Pole Valley, where he was wounded in action on Oct. 22, 1944, by German artillery. He was evacuated to Naples Hospital, where he underwent several surgeries and was flown back by plane as a litter patient to Longview, TX. He was discharged in July 1945. Clastie received four Battle Stars, Good Conduct Medals and a Purple Heart during his service in the European African Middle Eastern Theater.

From left: Vivian Jane Umfress, Clastie Dean Umfress, Clastie Umfress and Mary Vivian Umfress.

Clastie was married on Jun. 7, 1953, at the Friendship Methodist Church in Enterprise in Union County, MS to Mary Vivian Spencer, born Jan. 16, 1935 in Union County in Enterprise, MS as the youngest child of John Collins Spencer (b. Oct. 17, 1890, d. Jun. 2, 1938) and Odell Vivian Baker (b. Oct. 1, 1896, d. Feb. 21, 1969). Mary Vivian has one living brother, Eucie Dwayne Spencer (b. Nov. 11, 1932) and three brothers are deceased. Mary Vivian graduated from the Macedonia High School (now West Union) as valedictorian of her 1952 class. She was the high scorer for the Macedonia basketball team and received a scholarship to Northwest Junior College. She attended Northwest from Fall 1952 through Spring 1954, graduated with special distinction and was Salutatorian. She met Clastie while working at Northwest Junior College. Vivian is Past Worthy Matron of the Senatobia chapter of the Eastern Star.

Judy Carol Umfress and Clastie Dean Umfress. Alan Anderson Umfress and Allison Carol Umfress.

Clastie and his wife owned and operated a jewelry store in Senatobia, MS. Clastie is a graduate of the Southern College of Watchmaking and Jewelry Repair in Memphis, TN. He is a life member of the DAV, VFW, American Legion and the Military Order of the Purple Heart. Both are members of the First Baptist Church in Senatobia, Mississippi. They are parents of two children, Clastie Dean Umfress (b. Nov. 2, 1954) and a daughter, Vivian Jane Umfress (b. Nov. 26, 1957). Clastie Dean Umfress married Judy Carol Spaur on Oct. 21, 1977 and they have two children, Allison Carol Umfress (b. Jun. 22, 1990) and Alan Anderson Umfress (b. Feb. 2, 1995). Clastie Dean Umfress is a dentist and resides with his family in Olive Branch, MS. Vivian Jane Umfress is a CPA and lives and works in Memphis, TN. Vivian Jane graduated from the University of Mississippi with a bachelor's and master's degrees in Accountancy. *Submitted by Mary Vivian Umfress, 305 North West Street, Senatobia, MS 38668. (601) 562-8314*

UMFRESS, GEORGE ELMER, sixth child born to Nathaniel Napoleon Umfress and Matilda Cook Umfress, born Oct. 27, 1891 in Prentiss County. His father died in 1898, leaving his mother with seven children to rear. His mother was a very strong lady and handled her children well. She continued to live in the old home place west of Cairo with her two sons, Will and Luther, until the house was destroyed by a tornado Sunday night, Apr. 5, 1936.

George Elmer and Virlon Timbes Umfress.

The three of them were in the house and were blown out into the fields, though not seriously injured. One wall of the house was left standing with Luther's bed still intact up against it. George Elmer's heritage is discussed in another article, but little is known of his mother's family, except her parents were Andrew Jackson Cook and Artie Mencie Stone Cook, with a brother named James Cook and a sister, Emily Cook, who married O.L. Howard.

George Elmer served in the US Navy during WWI aboard the USS *Lamberton*. Upon returning home from service, he married his long-time sweetheart, Virlon Cleo Timbes, born Nov. 1, 1898, daughter of Samuel Levi Timbes and Missouri Etta (Sudie) Robinson Timbes, on Dec. 5, 1920.

George Elmer and Virlon Cleo made their home in Prentiss County for several years where their first child, Samuel Lamar, was born Jan. 29, 1922. Following the sawmill trade, they moved to Yalobusha County, MS, where Eula Mae (b. Jun. 2, 1927) and Evelyne Maxine (b. Dec. 8, 1929) were born, before moving on to Arkansas to farm with his brother, James Cleveland Umfress. They soon returned to Prentiss and Tishomingo Counties (Holcut-Cairo Community). In the early 1930s, they bought a farm from Will Lambert on the Prentiss/Tishomingo County line and made it into a loving, happy home for their three children. They continued to live there the remainder of their lives. They were a dedicated, loyal family to their church, friends and community. The three children attended Prentiss County Schools at Clausel Hill, New Hope and Burton. Lamar graduated from Burton in 1941.

Children: Mae, Lamar and Maxine Umfress

George Elmer died Mar. 30, 1952 and Virlon Cleo died Oct. 5, 1979. They are buried in New Lebanon Cemetery in Prentiss County.

Eula Mae graduated from Holcut High School in 1946 and on Jun. 1, 1950, married Andrew Jackson "Jack" Sims. She received a BS degree from the University of North Alabama and is a retired teacher/librarian. Jack graduated from Burton High School and received his BS and MA degrees from Mississippi State University. He served three years in the US Army during WWII with 35 months in the South Pacific. He is a retired school teacher/administrator. They have made their home in Florence and Lauderdale County, AL, many years. They have one daughter, Andrea Dee Sims Black, born Oct. 24, 1960. She is a doctor of optometry in Jasper, AL. She is married to Kenneth Black and they have one daughter, Leah Black. *Submitted by Maxine U. Wade.*

UMFRESS, MILFORD HENRY, born Mar. 3, 1918 third child of Alvia Dean Umfress (b. Oct. 19, 1881, d. Jan. 20, 1971) and Nellie Jane Sricklin Umfress (b. Apr. 28, 1885, d. Apr. 21, 1965). He is the grandson of Nathaniel Napoleon Umfress (b. Jan. 18, 1849, d. Jan. 3, 1898) and Matilda Cook Umfress (b. Jan. 3, 1853, d. Dec. 17, 1939). Milford grew up in the Cairo Community where he worked on the family farm. He finished school at Burton High School. He served three and a half years in WWII, of which two and a half were with the 8th Air Force in England. After the war Milford worked for Firestone Tire and Rubber Co. in Memphis, TN retiring after 33 years.

On Jun. 2, 1948, Milford married Norma Rhea Pounds (b. Aug. 20, 1920) of the New Hope Community. She taught school for a number of years. Their two daughters are Marilyn Rhea Umfress (b. Aug. 30, 1953) and Sandra Jean Umfress Atkerson (b. May 28, 1956). Marilyn is a graduate of the University of Memphis and is a librarian with the Memphis and Shelby County Library System. Sandra graduated from the University of Memphis. On May 14, 1983, she married Steve Atkerson of Atlanta, GA. They reside there with their three children: Eden Machelle Atkerson (b. Sep. 19, 1988), Nathaniel Everette Atkerson (b. Dec. 2, 1991) and Matthew Stephen Atkerson (b. May 25, 1993). *Submitted by Milford Umfress.*

UMFRESS, NATHANIEL NAPOLEON, married Mrs. Margaret C. Brooks (b. 1838 in South Carolina) Feb. 12, 1870 in Tishomingo County, MS. Margaret had two children by a previous marriage, Emma and Jane Brooks. They had one daughter, Julia Ann Umfress (b. Nov. 17, 1871, d. Jul. 19, 1905). Julia Ann married Charles J. Wheeler on Jan. 1, 1897. Margaret Brooks died in 1873.

Nathaniel Napoleon's second marriage was to Mary Jane Lauderdale Jones on Nov. 17, 1874. They had one child, James Franklin Umfress (b. Sep. 16, 1875). They soon divorced and he was raised by Mary Jane and changed his name from Umfress to Jones. On Nov. 23, 1879, Nathaniel Napoleon married Matilda Cook (b. Jan. 3, 1853, d. Dec. 17, 1939), daughter of Andrew Jackson Cook and Artie Mencie Stone Cook. She had a brother, James Cook and a sister, Emily Cook, who married O.L. Howard. Both Nathaniel Napoleon and Matilda are buried at Little Flock Cemetery south of Burnsville in Tishomingo County. To this union seven children were born.

Nathaniel Napoleon and Matilda Cook Umfress

(1) Alvia Dean (b. Nov. 18, 1881, d. 1971) married Nellie Jane Stricklin (b. Apr. 28, 1885, d. Jan. 24, 1965) and is buried in New Lebanon Cemetery.

(2) Bertha Mai (b. Mar. 1, 1883, d. Nov. 30, 1977) married Houston Asberry Crabb (b. Aug. 7, 1885, d. Jul. 23, 1972) and is buried in Booneville Cemetery.

Children of Nathaniel Napoleon and Matilda Cook Umfress.

(3) James Cleveland (b. Nov. 8, 1884) married Louise Hale and is buried in Helena, AR.

(4) Martin Luther (b. Nov. 11, 1886, d. Nov. 25, 1961) is buried in New Lebanon Cemetery. He served in WWI and never married.

(5) William Baxter (b. Dec. 3, 1888, d. Sep. 26, 1970) divorced after six months of marriage. He served in WWI and is buried in New Lebanon.

(6) George Elmer (b. Oct. 27, 1891, d. Mar. 30, 1952) married Virlon Cleo Timbes (b. Nov. 1, 1898, d. Oct. 5, 1979). He served in WWI. They are buried in New Lebanon Cemetery.

(7) Maude Ethel (b. Nov. 23, 1893, d. ?) married Major Washington Allen and is buried in Big Creek, Mississippi Cemetery.

George Elmer and Virlon Cleo Timbes Umfress have three children Samuel Lamar, Eula Mae and Evelyne Maxine.

The generations we have traced in this history for our own family are: (1) Nathaniel Sr. and Mary Umfress (2) Benjamin and N. Penelope Umfress (3) James H. and Elizabeth Weaver Wiggington Umfress (4) Nathaniel Napoleon and Matilda Cook Umfress (5) George Elmer and Virlon Cleo Timbes Umfress.

In this research, the name Umfress is spelled many ways, such as: (Humfress) (Humphras) (Humphries) (Humphress) (Humphreys). *Submitted by Maxine Umfress Wade.*

UMFRESS, NATHANIEL SR., the Umfress family came to America from Ireland. Nathaniel was a member of the Umfress family, which settled in the Cheraw District of the Colony of South Carolina about the mid-1700s. He and his wife Mary were born about 1770. The couple owned property and resided in Marlboro County, SC and was listed there in the Federal Census of 1790, 1800 and 1810.

Children born to this marriage were: Benjamin Sr., Nathaniel Jr., John, William, Lane (b. 1782, d. 1793) and Samuel. Most of this family lived out their life in South Carolina as landowners and farmers. Many of them are buried in the Sandy Grove Cemetery.

Benjamin Sr. (b. 1787, d. Nov. 2, 1863) is buried in Sandy Grove Church Cemetery in Kershaw County, SC, along with his wife, N. Penelope (b. 1785, d. Apr. 26, 1871). Benjamin Sr. and N. Penelope had seven children: James H., Mary "Polly", Melissa Martha "Milley", Nathaniel A. "Nathan", Benjamin J. Jr., Nancy Penelope and William. This family also stayed in South Carolina with the exception of James H.

James H. Umfress (b. Nov. 18, 1809, d. Dec. 28, 1884) married Elizabeth Weaver Wigginton (b. Mar. 6, 1808) in 1828. They were both born and married in South Carolina. They left South Carolina about 1835, moving to Georgia and Alabama and by 1840 we were in Itawamba County, MS. The 1870 Federal Census shows them to be living in Tishomingo County in the Burnsville Community. Elizabeth died Jun. 5, 1873 and was buried in Little Flock Cemetery near Burnsville, Tishomingo County, MS. On Dec. 11, 1876, James H. married Sarah Evaline Haynie in Alcorn County. James H. died Dec. 28, 1884 and was also buried in Little Flock Cemetery.

James H. and Elizabeth had a large family. Listed are children's names, dates of birth and death and where lived.

(1) Middleton C. (b. 1830, d. Dec. 13, 1867) Alabama/Mississippi

(2) Francis Marion "Frank" (b. May 5, 1834, d. Nov. 22, 1905) Mississippi/Alabama

(3) Calvin Commodore (b. Mar. 7, 1835, d. Dec. 21, 1910) Mississippi/Tennessee

(4) William A. "Bill" (b. 1837) Mississippi/Texas

(5) Hugh L.D. (b. 1839, d. Jul. 17, 1862) Mississippi

(6) Malinda (b. 1841, d. Oct. 31, 1867) Mississippi/Alabama

(7) Elizabeth A. (b. May 13, 1840, d. Jan. 21, 1899) Mississippi

(8) Allethia "Letha" (b. May 13, 1842) Mississippi/Texas

(9) Martha Jane (b. 1845, d. 1917) Mississippi/Tennessee

(10) Nathaniel Napoleon (b. Jan. 18, 1849, d. Jan. 8, 1898) Mississippi

James H. and four of his sons served in the Confederate Army. James H. served as a Confederate Captain from Mar. 12, 1862, until Apr. 26, 1865. He served under General J.E. Johnston, Co. F. Son, Hugh L.D., enlisted at Jacinto on Mar. 1, 1862 and was a private in Richard E. Clayton's Co. A, 2nd Regiment, Mississippi Volunteers. He was wounded in the battle of Gaines Mill, Henrico County, VA and died Jul. 19, 1862 from wounds sustained.

Son, Francis Marion "Frank," also enlisted at Jacinto. He served under the command of Col. William Faulkner. He was discharged at Iuka, MS, after the surrender in 1865. On Nov. 22, 1872 in Tishomingo County, he married Mary Elizabeth Robinson, daughter of Alexander Robinson and Sarah Louisa Reynolds Robinson. They had six children: Izora, Noonan, Calvin, Louisa, "Lou," Elizabeth "Betty" and Mary. Frank and Mary separated while she was expecting her last child. Frank stayed in Colbert County, AL, where he is buried and Mary came to Prentiss County where she died and is buried in Jacinto Cemetery. Many people in Prentiss and Alcorn County will remember this youngest child as "Little Mary" Umfress, who would "hop a ride" on the "running board", ride the milk truck, or walk any distance. She even met a "mad dog" in the road one time and lay down and kicked it off until it left. She was one strong-willed lady! She is buried at Jacinto Cemetery in Alcorn

County. Two other sons, Middleton C. and Calvin Commodore, also served in the Confederate Army. *Submitted by Maxine Umfress Wade, great-great-great-granddaughter.*

UMFRESS, WAYNE ARMON,
born Feb. 1, 1914 was reared in the Cairo Community of Prentiss County, MS. He is the eldest child of four born to Alvia Dean Umfress (b. Oct. 19, 1881, d. Jan. 20, 1971) and Nellie Jane Stricklin Umfress (b. Apr. 28, 1885, d. Apr. 21, 1965). His sister was Thelma Christine Umfress Smith (b. Dec. 21, 1915, d. Jul. 25, 1995) of Booneville, MS. His brothers are Milford Henry Umfress (b. Mar. 3, 1918) of Memphis, TN and Clastie Umfress (b. Jan. 29, 1920) of Senatobia, MS.

Wayne Armon and Irene Pinson Umfress.

On Dec. 29, 1939, Wayne married Eunice Irene Pinson (b. Jan. 28, 1917, d. Jun. 30, 1991) of the Cairo Community. She was the eldest of five children born to Wallace W. Pinson (b. Mar. 19, 1887, d. Mar. 31, 1968) and Bertie Wright Pinson (b. Jan. 23, 1895, d. Jun. 25, 1960). Her sisters are Edith Pinson Jourdon (b. Jan. 16, 1919) of Iuka, MS and Syble Pinson Mitchell (b. May 26, 1932) of Kenosha, WI. Their brother, Oliver Wendell Pinson (b. Aug. 15, 1921, d. May 4, 1945), was killed during a kamikaze mission aboard the USS Little in the Pacific during WWII. Their brother, James Waymon Pinson (b. Dec. 7, 1930, d. Feb. 24, 1956), was killed in a truck accident in Florida. Irene, Wendell, Waymon and their parents are buried in New Lebanon Cemetery in the Cairo Community.

The Harrol Umfress Family. From left: Harrol, Alison, Karen, Jennifer U. Scott and Lois Cochran Umfress.

Wayne and Irene grew up on nearby farms. They graduated from Burton High School and attended Wood Junior College before their marriage. During WWII, they lived in Baltimore, MD, where they worked for the Martin Aircraft Co. Their son, Harrol Wayne Umfress, was born in Baltimore on Jan. 23, 1944, his maternal grandmother's birthday.

After the war they returned to Mississippi and earned bachelor's degrees from Mississippi State University. Later Irene earned a master of arts in education degree from the University of Mississippi. Early in their careers, they taught school at Unity in Lee County and at Strayhorn in Tate County. In 1951 they moved to Pontotoc where Wayne worked as a sanitation agent in Pontotoc County for the State Department of Health, where he worked until his retirement. Irene taught school for many years, retiring as an English teacher at Pontotoc Junior High School.

The Umfresses are members of First Baptist Church in Pontotoc, where Irene was a Sunday school teacher and active in Women's Missionary Union. She was an avid reader. Wayne enjoys gardening and raising cattle. Harrol earned a bachelor of science in pharmacy from Ole Miss. He worked for the Walgreen Co. for 25 years and works at Bruno's Food World in Tupelo.

Harrol married Lois Nell Cochran (b. Mar. 14, 1945), daughter of Shelby and Iva Maxcy Cochran of northeastern Pontotoc County on Aug. 8, 1971. Lois is a graduate of Blue Mountain College and earned a masters degree from Ole Miss. She teaches at Itawamba Community College. They reside in the Furrs Community of Pontotoc County and are parents of three daughters. Jennifer Claire Umfress Scott (b. Jan. 18, 1972) is a graduate of Blue Mountain College where she earned a bachelor of arts in education. She married Kevin Lane Scott (b. Apr. 28, 1971) of Lee County on Jul. 31, 1993. They are the parents of Aimee Kiersten Scott (b. Jul. 23, 1996) and Andrew Wayne Scott (b. Jan. 14, 1999) and live in Lexington, TN where Lane is a Baptist minister. Karen Monette Umfress was born Dec. 2, 1974, to Harrol and Lois. She is a graduate of the University of Mississippi, where she earned a bachelor of science in biology and lives in Fairfax, VA. She teaches in the Fairfax County Schools. Alison Faith Umfress (b. May 1, 1977) earned a bachelor of science in physical therapy from the University of Mississippi Medical Center and works at the North Mississippi Medical Center in Tupelo, MS.

Irene Pinson Umfress died the last day of Jun. in 1991 of complications from colon cancer and was buried in New Lebanon Cemetery near her childhood home at Cairo. Through the years, she and Wayne returned to New Lebanon for Decoration Day on the fourth Sunday in May where they enjoyed "Dinner on the Ground" and visiting with friends and relatives. Wayne lives at their home in Pontotoc. *Submitted by Harrol W. Umfress.*

VANDERFORD, CLOVIS AARON,
born Jun. 1, 1901, died Jan. 16, 1985, son of Mark (b. Sep. 15, 1879, d. Oct. 3, 1938) and Neal Samantha Maness Vanderford (b. Jul. 3, 1881, d. Mar. 9, 1958) married Ida Sula Richardson (b. Jun. 11, 1904, d. Sep. 8, 1989) daughter of Green Berry "Bee" (b. 1869, d. 1945) and Nannie Bell Cox Richardson (b. 1872, d. 1966) on Feb. 20, 1920. Aaron and Sula are buried in Kemp's Chapel Cemetery.

Clovis Aaron and Ida Sula Richardson Vanderford, ca. 1980

Mark and Neal in Juliette Cemetery, Bee and Bill in Sardis Cemetery, all in Alcorn County. Born to Aaron and Sula were 11 children:

1) Milton Waldrep (b. Jul. 24, 1921) married Martha Hatcher (b. Dec. 7, 1924) on Jun. 8, 1940. Their children are Johnny (b. Nov. 18, 1943) and Jimmy (b. Jul. 7, 1941).

2) Weada Bell (b. Jul. 2, 1924, d. Jul. 14, 1924), died of crib death.

3) Alma Fay, twin (b. May 10, 1925) married Thurman Hendrix (b. Nov. 14, 1921, d. Mar. 26, 1982) on Feb. 22, 1945.

Clovis Leo (b. Oct. 12, 1946). Donnie Ray (b. Oct. 7, 1948) married Barbara Ann Davis (b. Mar. 21, 1950) on Aug. 28, 1969. Their children are: Kerry Ray (b. Jul. 29, 1970), Bonnie Lynn (b. Aug. 4, 1974). Lynn's son is Nicholas Adam (b. Feb. 18, 1993). Doris Fay (b. Jan. 24, 1951) married Bradley Rorie (b. Mar. 25, 1948) on Nov. 27, 1970. Their children are William Randy (b. Dec. 12, 1971) married Amy Whitehead. Mary Fay (b. Mar. 27, 1976) married Toy Calvin "Tripp" Phillips.

Cathy Marie (b. Apr. 19, 1959) married Tommy Charles DeGraw (b. May 28, 1958) on Sep. 4, 1980. Their children are Amanda Lynn (b. Nov. 17, 1981) and Samantha Nicole DeGraw (b. Jun. 8, 1983).

4) Alta May, twin (b. May 10, 1925, d. Feb. 9, 1986) married Sherman Walker. Their children are Jessie Mae and Janice Fay.

5) Rufus Elton "Top" (b. Jun. 16, 1928) married Daisy Walton Herrington "Pat" (b. Apr. 1, 1944) on Aug. 3, 1964. Shirley Nell Miles (b. Dec. 12, 1951), Sybil Diane (b. Feb. 6, 1955), Deborah Ruth (b. Dec. 31, 1956), Penny Lou (b. May 1, 1965), Sylvia Jean (b. Dec. 12, 1967).

6) L.Q. (b. Oct. 18, 1932) married Kathleen Cook (b. Dec. 24, 1939) on Jun. 9, 1958. Their daughter Kathy (b. Apr. 8, 1961) married Donald Stewart (b. Jun. 9, 1952) on Jun. 29, 1979. Their children are Kim (b. Dec. 31, 1986) and Wesley (b. Apr. 21, 1981).

7) Cletes Melvin (b. Feb. 28, 1937) married Charlene Cook (b. Dec. 24, 1939) on Jun. 30, 1958. Their son, Douglas (b. Jan. 9, 1962) married Sandy Lyons on Jun. 6, 1980. Children are: Justin (b. May 23, 1982 and Adam (b. Nov. 20, 1984).

8) Thedus Ray (b. Jun. 3, 1940) married Betty Miles. Their children are Clinton Ray, Charles Dewayne and Linda Diane Bruce.

9) Bobby Hue (b. Feb. 6, 1943) married Imogene Herrington (b. Feb. 8, 1949). Their children are Patsy Jean, Ricky Hue, Gerald Dewayne.

10) Brenda Joyce, twin, (b. Sep. 22, 1945) married Jimmy Sonnenberg. Their children are Mark and Christopher.

11) Linda Loyce, twin, (b. Sep. 22, 1945) married J.W. Hosey. Their children are James William and Glenda. Linda Loyce married Wendall Byrd. Their daughter is Carla Deanne.

Aaron and Sula had a big family, but all knew they had big hearts. Cards and games were played with the whole family, cousins and friends. Square dances, candy breakings, frying chicken and others were fun. Sula never knew who she was cooking for. Aaron was so kind, gentle and lived by the Golden Rule. *Submitted by Fay Hendrix.*

VANDERFORD, HAZEL JEAN,
born Apr. 9, 1939 daughter of Winston Jasper "Wink" Vanderford (b. Mar. 9, 1916, d. Apr. 17, 1989) and Ella Missouri Woodruff Vanderford (b. Feb. 21, 1913, d. Sep. 2, 1991) married Jun. 23, 1933. They are buried in Snowdown Church of Christ Cemetery.

Hazel Vanderford

Hazel is the granddaughter of Charlie Edward Woodruff (b. Sep. 25, 1891, d. Dec. 20, 1966) and Minnie Odell Stone Woodruff (b. Apr. 6, 1893, d. May 6, 1961) married Aug. 2, 1910 in Selmer, TN. They are buried in the Snowdown Church of Christ Cemetery, also other grandparents are Mark Vanderford (b. Sept. 15, 1879, d. Oct. 3, 1938) and Neal Samantha Maness Vanderford (b. Jul. 3, 1881, d. Mar. 9, 1958) married on Aug. 20, 1900. They are buried in the Juliette Cemetery in Alcorn County.

Hazel still lives at the homeplace where she and her parents lived. She took care of her parents until their death. She did not marry but she is very close to her nieces and nephews. She has worked at many factories, Paden, also worked a big garden at the same time.

She and her sister Waynona Davis (b. Nov. 25, 1935) spend much of their time together. Waynona's husband died Feb. 4, 1994. She has a brother James Hulon Vanderford and another sister Nelda Dean Woodard (b. Dec. 7, 1938). They enjoy going to flea markets collecting "Aunt Jemimia's items, etc." Garvin, Waynona and Hazel enjoyed gardening, making quilts and crafts as Christmas scenes.

She is a member of the Snowdown Church of Christ in Prentiss County. *Submitted by Hazel Jean Vanderford*

VANDERFORD, JAMES HULON, born Mar. 25, 1934 married Lula Fay Floyd (b. Nov. 14, 1936) on Dec. 12, 1953. James Hulon is the son of Winston Jasper "Wink" Vanderford (b. Mar. 9, 1916, d. Apr. 17, 1989) and Ella Missouri Woodruff Vanderford (b. Feb. 21, 1913, d. Sep. 2, 1991) who married on Jun. 23, 1933. They are buried in Snowdown Church of Christ Cemetery in Prentiss County.

James Hulon is the grandson of Mark Vanderford (b. Sep. 15, 1879, d. Oct. 3, 1938) and Neal Samantha Maness Vanderford (b. Jul. 3, 1881, d. Mar. 9, 1958) who married on Aug. 20, 1900. They are buried in Juliette Cemetery in Alcorn County. James Hulon is also grandson of Charlie Edward Woodruff (b. Feb. 25, 1891, d. Dec. 20, 1966) and Minnie Odell Stone Woodruff (b. Apr. 6, 1893, d. May 6, 1961) who married on Aug. 2, 1910. They are buried at the Snowdown Church of Christ Cemetery in Prentiss County. James Hulon has three sisters: Hazel Jean Vanderford (b. Apr. 9, 1939), Waynona Mayvene Vanderford Davis (b. Nov. 25, 1935) and Nelda Dean Vanderford Woodard (b. Dec. 7, 1938).

Wayne, Lula Faye and James Vanderford

Lula Fay Floyd is daughter of Richard Floyd (b. Apr. 7, 1902, d. Apr. 19, 1966) and Leona Ellen Newborn (b. Aug. 28, 1900, d. Jul. 17, 1975) married August 1928. They are buried in the Snowdown Church of Christ in Prentiss County. Lula Fay Floyd Vanderford is the granddaughter of Ishmael Wheeler Newborn (b. Jun. 12, 1877, d. Jul. 23, 1940) and Jimmie Estelle Lee Boyd (b. May 7, 1882, d. May 30, 1976) md. Oct. 4, 1899 in Wayne County, TN. They are buried in East Prentiss Cemetery.

James Hulon and Lula Fay have one son, James Wayne Vanderford (b. Jul. 20, 1965). He went to school at Jumpertown and is now a CPA in Memphis, TN. James Hulon worked for the Forestry Commission and Lula Fay worked in the cafeteria at Jumpertown School before retiring. James now upkeeps the Snowdown Church of Christ grounds and building. Lula Fay baby-sits. James enjoys fishing. *Submitted by Lula Fay Floyd Vanderford.*

VANDERFORD, WINSTON JASPER "WINK," born Mar. 9, 1916 and died Apr. 17, 1989 married Ella Missouri Woodruff (b. Feb. 21, 1913, d. Sep. 2, 1991) on Jun. 23, 1933. Wink was the son of Mark (b. Sep. 15, 1879, d. Oct. 3, 1938) and Neal Samantha Maness Vanderford (b. Jul. 3, 1881, d. Mar. 9, 1958). Ella was the daughter of Charlie Edward (b. Feb. 25, 1891, d. Dec. 20, 1966) and Minnie Odell Stone Woodruff (b. Apr. 6, 1893, d. May 6, 1961). Wink and Ella Vanderford and Charlie and Minnie Woodruff are buried in Snowdown Church of Christ Cemetery in Prentiss County. Mark and Neal Vanderford are buried in Juliette Cemetery in Alcorn County.

Ella and Winston Vanderford on their 50th anniversary

Their children are:
1) James Hulon (b. Mar. 25, 1934) md. Eula Fay Floyd (b. Nov. 14, 1936) on Dec. 12, 1953. Child: James Wayne (b. Jul. 20, 1965).
2) Waynona Mayvene Vanderford Davis (b. Nov. 25, 1935) md. Garvin Earl Davis (b. Dec. 29, 1932, d. Feb. 4, 1994) on Jun. 6, 1955. Children:
   a) Drexel Earl Davis (b. Jul. 31, 1956) md. Donna Sue Hayden (b. Aug. 17, 1959) on Jun. 6, 1980, child, Miranda Nicole Davis (b. May 19, 1982).
   b) Anita Gail (b. May 15, 1958) md. Sammy Kay Wigginton (b. May 28, 1958) on Jul. 15, 1977, children: Samuel Curtis (b. Jul. 8, 1978) and Samantha Gail (b. Jan. 19, 1982).
   c) Darvis Nathan (b. Dec. 26, 1959) md. Patricia Ann Foster (b. Apr. 8, 1959) on Mar. 9, 1978, one child, April Leann (b. Aug. 9, 1995).
   d) Sheila Denise (b. Feb. 27, 1962) md. Jimmy Daniel Bunch (b. Jun. 14, 1961) on Apr. 17, 1980, children: Kathrine Lucille Bunch (b. Nov. 22, 1980) and Daniel Earl Bunch (b. Aug. 17, 1984).
   e) Teresa Lynn (b. Aug. 22, 1963) md. Richard Duane Murphy (b. Jun. 17, 1959) on Jun. 14, 1980, three children: Rodney Duane (b. Oct. 23, 1980); Vanessa Lynn (b. Oct. 31, 1984) and Andrew Vinson (b. Jan. 23, 1989).
3) Hazel Jean Vanderford (b. Apr. 9, 1939).
4) Nelda Dean Woodard (b. Dec. 16, 1943) md. John Ellis Woodard (b. Sep. 7, 1938) on Dec. 23, 1961, one child, Lisa Dawn (b. Jan. 3, 1969) md. Paul Ray McKinney (b. Dec. 17, 1964) on Feb. 14, 1987, children: Justin Cody (b. Dec. 25, 1988) and Courtney Danielle (b. Apr. 26, 1994).

Winston and Ella lived on his father's farm and later bought their farm from Jay White. Wink enjoyed fishing and hunting. Ella, Hazel, Waynona and Garvin did many crafts, made quilts and sewed clothes. Ella enjoyed painting pictures, her garden, flowers and yard. Wink was working in the garden where he died with a heart attack. The family worked together and played together. *Submitted by Hazel Vanderford and Waynona Vanderford Davis.*

VANSTORY, WILLIAM ELMER "HAPPY," born near Jackson, TN Mar. 30, 1912. His parents were William Jackson "Jack" and Amorilla Hembree Vanstory. The family moved to Prentiss County in the early 1920s. Happy, as he came to be known, grew up in the Carolina Community. He married Kittie Mae Howell Dec. 22, 1934.

Happy was a carpenter and brick mason. His skill as a craftsman is still evident in many homes in Prentiss County and surrounding areas. He enjoyed whittling and wood working. His whittling advice was "when whittling a dog, take a block of wood and cut off all that doesn't look like a dog." After he retired from brickwork he worked several years in the maintenance department of Northeast Mississippi Hospital. Happy died Nov. 18, 1985 and is buried in the Gaston Cemetery.

Kittie Mae Vanstory was a housewife, wonderful cook, seamstress and gardener. She was an active member of Thrasher Baptist Church and enjoyed visiting with family and friends.

Happy and Kittie Mae had three children: a daughter (b. and d. Jul. 4, 1943), son William Tommy (b. Feb. 15, 1946) and daughter Mary Ann (b. Jan. 6, 1950).

Tommy graduated from Thrasher High School in 1963. He attended Northeast Community College and worked for American Seating Co., then transferred to Mississippi State University. He received his BS degree in accounting from MSU in 1968.

Tommy married Margaret Harwood Dec. 17, 1966 and moved to Memphis after graduation from MSU where he was employed by Ernst and Ernst accounting firm. Margaret completed her nursing studies at St. Joseph Hospital in Memphis and received a diploma in nursing in 1969.

L-R: Tommy Vanstory, Mary Vanstory, Kittie Mae Howell Vanstory, William E. "Happy" Vanstory, Ann Vanstory Goff, Amy Goff.

Tommy joined the US Navy in December 1968 and went through basic training at Great Lakes Navy Base. After his basic training he was stationed on Guam in the Mariana Islands. He served as a disbursing clerk. Margaret joined him there in June 1969 and their daughter, Mary Margaret was born on Guam Dec. 10, 1969.

After four years in the Navy, Tommy, Margaret and little Mary returned to Mississippi. Watkin, Ward and Stafford CPA's in West West Point, MS employed Tommy. Margaret worked as a registered nurse in Columbus. The family moved to Corinth in 1981.

Mary graduated from Corinth High School in 1987, attended Northeast Community College for two years, then received her BS degree from Memphis State University in 1992. She now lives in Atlanta GA.

Tommy is a partner in Hardwick, Vanstory and Co., CPA, with offices in Corinth and Booneville. Tommy and Margaret converted the old Booneville Hardware warehouse into office space in 1995. Tommy is active in preservation efforts to save historic buildings in Booneville and northeast Mississippi.

Tommy and Margaret moved back to his home place on Thrasher road in 1998 Tommy has been an active member of the Baptist church, the Rotary Club and The Chamber of Commerce. He enjoys woodworking, duck hunting and antique hunting.

Ann Vanstory graduated from Thrasher High School in 1968, Valedictorian of her class. She married Martin Franklin "Frank" Goff Jun. 28, 1968. Ann and Frank lived in Columbus, GA when their daughter Amy Maylene was born Oct. 8, 1970.

Ann married a second time to Richard "Dick" McMillan and now resides in Tupelo, MS. She is an assistant vice-president for The Peoples Bank and Trust Co. Active in the Big Brother/Big Sister program, she enjoys shopping, traveling and antiquing.

Amy Goff graduated from University of Mississippi and now resides in Memphis, TN.

VANSTORY, WILLIAM JACKSON "JACK, born Dec. 18, 1882 in Alcorn County, MS. His parents were John H. and Arvazena Goddard Vanstory. When Jack was but a boy his father deserted the family and Jack spent his youth with the George Yarber family. Jack married Amorilla Hembree Oct. 10, 1882 in Alcorn County, MS. He was a blacksmith and inventor. He had at least two inventions patented, one for a mowing machine part and another for a milk cooler.

L-R: William E. "Happy" Vanstory, Lucille Vanstory Sauer, Kittie Mae Howell Vanstory, Bobby Ray Howell on shoulder of George Crawford, Ruby Vanstory Howell, Ray Howell, Jack Vanstory and Rilla Hembree Vanstory.

Jack and Amorilla had eight children with five living to be adults. They lived at Corinth during the early years of marriage, moved to Jackson, TN around 1912, then back to Rienzi around 1919, then to Prentiss County in the 1920s.

Their first daughter, Lena Arvazena Vanstory (b. Nov. 28, 1908) graduated from Booneville High School in 1927 and taught school for a period of time. She married George Crawford Dec. 21, 1930. Lena died Mar. 20, 1992 and is buried at Parkburg Baptist Church near Jackson, TN.

The second daughter, Ruby Pearl Vanstory (b. Feb. 10, 1910) married Marion Ray Howell Oct. 21, 1933. Ruby worked many years for Blue Bell in Booneville and was famous for her speed sewing. She once entered a sewing contest. The first person to finish making a garment was to win a new sewing machine. Ruby was going so fast that all the other contestants just stopped and watched Ruby sew. She won the sewing machine. Ruby and Ray had one son Bobby Ray Howell. Ruby died Nov. 19, 1992 and is buried in Oaklawn Cemetery in Booneville, MS.

Jack and Amorilla's first son, William Elmer Vanstory (b. Mar. 30, 1912) "Happy," as he came to be known, was a carpenter, brick mason and a talented carver. He could make most anything from wood, brick or concrete. Happy married Kittie Mae Dec. 22, 1934. They had three children: a daughter b. and d. 1943), William Tommy (b. Feb. 15, 1946) and Mary Ann (b. Jan. 6, 1950). Happy died Nov. 18, 1985 and is buried at Gaston Cemetery in Prentiss County.

Jack and Amorilla's next child was Minnie Lucille (b. May 25, 1915). Lucille married Albert Sauer. She worked at Hunter Fan Co. in Memphis, TN. She lived near Southaven after retirement and was active in community service, Lucille died Jan. 14, 1987 and is buried in Carolina Cemetery, Prentiss County, MS.

Jack and Amorilla had twins Murry and M.J. (b. Oct. 31, 1919). M.J. died that same year. Murry died in 1920. They are buried in Rienzi Cemetery, Alcorn County, MS.

Next came Walker Russell Vanstory, born Nov. 5, 1921. Walker was nicknamed "Houlagan." He said he and Happy got their nicknames from the cartoon "Happy Houlagan." Walker served in the Army during WWII, was a prisoner of war in the Pacific islands and received several medals. He married Agnes Pauline Mitchell Jan. 19, 1946. He was a cabinet maker and worked for years for the Baptist Hospital in Gadsden, AL. Walker and Polly had one son Russell Ray "Rusty," (b. Nov. 11, 1956). Walker died Feb. 24. 1998 and is buried in Holly Pond Cemetery, Holly Pond, AL.

Jack and Amorilla's last child was Mary Elizabeth (b. May 10, 1926). Mary died Aug. 30, 1932 at 6 years of age and is buried in Carolina Cemetery, Prentiss County, MS.

Amorilla died Mar. 28, 1957 and Jack died Jun. 1, 1970. They are buried in Carolina Cemetery, Prentiss County, MS. *Submitted by Tommy Vanstory.*

WADE, EVELYNE MAXINE UMFRESS, third and youngest child of George Elmer and Virlon Cleo Timbes Umfress.

Maxine Umfress Wade and Lyonel "Cotton" Wade.

She was born Dec. 8, 1929 in Yalobusha County where her parents had moved following the sawmill trade. They also moved to Arkansas for a short time before returning to the Holcut-Cairo Community in Prentiss County when she was about 3 years old.

Mike and Linda Wade and children: Brad, Robyn and Kassie.

She attended Clausel Hill, New Hope and Burton Schools in Prentiss County before starting to Holcut School in Tishomingo County where she graduated in 1947. She received her BS degree in business education in 1954 from Mississippi State University. After 44 years (eight as a schoolteacher and 36 in the administrative office of the Tishomingo County School District) she retired in 1992.

Her first two years of teaching were at New Candler in Prentiss County where she taught with John Simmons, Principal, Miss Ethel Mae Johnson, Mrs. Virlon Garrett Davis, Mrs. Clyde Pippin and Howard Essary. She then taught five years at Paden and one at Burnsville before going to the office of the County Superintendent of Education in Tishomingo County to work for Mr. Cleston Scruggs, superintendent.

On Sep. 21, 1949, she married Oren Lyonel "Cotton" Wade (b. Mar. 30, 1929), son of Oren L. Wade and Hester Armstrong Wade. They recently celebrated their Golden Wedding Anniversary. Lyonel, self-employed, worked in road construction and as a lime/fertilizer vendor. He was elected first district supervisor and served on the Tishomingo County Board of Supervisors for 12 years (1976-1988). He was then employed by Bonds Co. in Burnsville until his retirement in early 1999. They have made their home in Iuka since 1956, where they are members of the Iuka Church of Christ.

Lyonel and Maxine have one son, James Michael "Mike" (b. Jul. 15, 1961). Mike attended Iuka schools, graduating in 1979. He also graduated from Northeast Mississippi Junior College in Booneville. He received his BS degree and MBA from the University of Southern Mississippi. On Aug. 11, 1987, Mike married Linda Colene Montgomery, born Jul. 1, 1963, daughter of Colon and Bessie Montgomery of Brookhaven, MS. Linda also has a BS degree from the University of Southern Mississippi and a MA degree in accounting from the University of Mississippi. They are now living in Collierville, TN. They have three children: Michael Bradford "Brad" (b. Apr. 24, 1989 in Mobile, AL), Robyn Nicole (b. Sep. 4, 1991 in New Orleans, LA) and Kathrine Elizabeth "Kassie" (b. Jan. 20, 1993 in Memphis, TN). *Submitted by Maxine Wade.*

WALDEN, LONON GERALD, born Jan. 11, 1934 and Shirley Jean Morgan (b. Mar. 20, 1937) were married on Apr. 24, 1954 in Prentiss County. To this union were born two children: Sheila Jean (b. May 27, 1956) and Gary Len (b. Sep. 26, 1957). Gerald and Shirley attended school at Holcut High. Gerald graduated in 1954 and Shirley was in the class of 1955. They lived in Tishomingo County from 1944 until 1961. They now make their home east of Booneville, MS. Gerald worked for the Mississippi State Highway Department for 36 years and retired in 1990. Sheila married Terry Hunkapiller on Apr. 11, 1975. From this marriage was born Myra Dawn (b. Mar. 9, 1976). Sheila later divorced and married Charles Edwin (Ed) Holley (b. Jun. 10, 1958) on Oct. 17, 1980. To this union were born Mona Lea (b. Jun. 29, 1984) and Mykel Jerad (b. Oct. 13, 1988). They made their home east of Booneville, MS. Myra married T.J. Moore (b. Nov. 29, 1975) on Apr. 18, 1997 and to this union was born Trevin Hall (b. Jul. 27, 1999). Gary married Kathy Hardin (b. Apr. 2, 1957) on Jun. 2, 1978 and to this union were born Julie Marie (b. Jun. 20, 1984) and Joshua Allen (b. Jul. 8, 1987). They made their home east of Corinth, MS.

This is a picture of their family. Back row from left: Ed Holley, Sheila Holley, T.J. Moore and Gary Walden. Middle row from left: Shirley Walden, Gerald Walden, Myra Moore holding Trevin Moore and Kathy Walden. Front row from left: Mykel Holley, Mona Holley, Joshua Walden and Julie Walden.

Gerald is the third child of Charlie and Mona Wheeler Walden and was born Jan. 11, 1934. Charlie and Mona were married in Prentiss County and lived for several years near Tishomingo County in Cairo, MS. Charlie Walden died May 28, 1984 and Mona died Mar. 11, 1998. They were both buried in Liberty Methodist Cemetery. Shirley is the third child of the late Shelby and Amanda Phifer Morgan. Shelby and Amanda married in Prentiss County and lived in Tishomingo County for several years. Both are buried in Forked Oak Cemetery.

This is the family of Gerald and Shirley Morgan Walden, their births, marriages, children, their parents and where they lived. Gerald and Shirley have been married for 45 years. Since Gerald's retirement in 1990, they have traveled and seen lots of the US. They both like to fish. Their family means a lot to them. Their son, Gary, works with the Mississippi Highway Department. Their daughter, Sheila, works with the Prentiss County Chancery Clerk Office. Myra, the oldest granddaughter, is a nurse. *Submitted by Shirley Morgan Walden.*

WALDEN, CHARLIE FRANK, born Aug. 29, 1905, eighth child of Franklin and Claudia Walden, who were married on Oct. 31, 1889. To this union ware born 14 children. Franklin Walden was the son of Alexander (b. 1823 in North Carolina) and Nancy Harris Walden (b. 1832 in North Carolina), who were married on Dec. 21, 1851 in old Tishomingo County, MS. Charlie F. Walden married Jun. 8, 1929 in Prentiss County, a widow, Mona Wheeler Whitley, who had one child, Tommy Whitley (b. Sep. 3, 1926).

Charlie (b. Aug. 29, 1905) and Mona Walden (b. Aug. 5, 1908) lived near Booneville, MS and at Cairo, MS, near Holcut for several years. Charlie was a farmer and mill worker. Charlie and Mona Walden were the parents of Charlene (b. Jul. 8, 1930), Harold (b. Feb. 12, 1932, d. 1932), Gerald (b. Jan. 11, 1934), Bobby (b. Oct. 3, 1936), Juanette (b. Oct. 30, 1939), Billy (b. Mar. 15, 1946) and Don (b. Mar. 19, 1948, d. 1948).

Charlene married Clevis Crane (b. Oct. 7, 1912, d. 1987) on Jan. 22, 1955. To this union was born Debra (b. Sep. 28, 1955), Ronnie (b. Jun. 12, 1957) and Rebecca (b. Nov. 4, 1958). Debra married Jim Rogers (b. Sep. 12, 1954) and they have two children, James (b. Dec. 13, 1972) and Jennifer (b. Nov. 13, 1978). Ronnie married Delinda Belue (b. Jun. 23, 1959) and they have two children, Stephen (b. Oct. 10, 1976) and David (b. Feb. 29, 1980). Rebecca married Anthony Fowler (b. Oct. 23, 1958) and they have two children, Natalie (b. Oct. 5, 1978) and McKinley (b. Oct. 29, 1988). Rebecca later divorced and married Frank Walker. Charlene makes her home on Highway 30, east of Paden, MS.

This is a picture of them a few years ago. Back row from left: Bob Walden, Tommy Whitley, Billy Walden, Juanette Anglin and Gerald Walden. Front row from left: Charlene Crane, Charlie Walden and Mona Walden.

Gerald married Shirley Morgan (b. Mar. 20, 1937) on Apr. 24, 1954. To this union were born Sheila (b. May 27, 1956) and Gary (b. Sep. 26, 1957). Sheila married Terry Hunkapiller on Apr. 11, 1975. From this marriage was born Myra (b. Mar. 9, 1976). Sheila later divorced and married Ed Holley (b. Jun. 10, 1958) on Oct. 17, 1980. To this union were born Mona Lea (b. Jun. 20, 1984) and Mykel Jerad (b. Oct. 13, 1988). Myra married T.J. Moore (b. Nov. 29, 1975) on Apr. 18, 1997 and to this union was born Trevin Hall (b. Jul. 27, 1999). Gary married Kathy Hardin (b. Apr. 2, 1957) on Jun. 2, 1978. To this marriage were born Julie Marie (b. Jun. 20, 1984) and Joshua Allen (b. Jul. 8, 1987). Gerald and Shirley make their home in Booneville, MS.

Bobby married Joann Nichols (b. May 22, 1938) on Jun. 9, 1956. To this union were born Vicky (b. May 13, 1960) and Kenny (b. May 26, 1963). Kenny married Norma Thorne, but later divorced and married Tracy Carter (b. Nov. 2, 1962) on Sep. 9, 1994. They have one child, Amanda (b. Oct. 9, 1995). Bob and Joann make their home in Paden, MS.

Juanette married Lawayne Anglin (b. Jun. 7, 1939). To this union were born Dennis (b. Mar. 5, 1960), Timothy (b. Mar. 8, 1963) and Tammie (b. Mar. 27, 1969). Dennis married Becky Broyles (b. Oct. 20, 1959). They have three children: Casey (b. Nov. 28, 1981), Matthew (b. May 2, 1983) and Lucinda (b. Oct. 22, 1986). Timothy married Janis Marlor (b. Jun. 18, 1963). They have three children: Stephany (b. Sep. 22, 1984), Kelsey (b. Apr. 7, 1987 and died in 1987) and Andrew (b. Aug. 10, 1988). Tammie married Randy Pittman but later divorced and married Matt Crocker. They have one child, Seth Thomas (b. Aug. 16, 1996). Juanette and Lawayne make their home in Iuka, MS.

Billy married Rita King (b. Oct. 25, 1949). To this union was born Bradley (b. Dec. 7, 1971) and Gregory (b. Oct. 29, 1975). Bradley married Tracy Rowan (b. Oct. 21, 1971) on Jul. 23, 1994 and to this union was born Brittany. Billy and Rita make their home on Highway 30, east of Booneville, MS.

This is a brief list of the Waldens. Charlie passed away on May 28, 1984. Mona passed away Mar. 11, 1998 and both are buried in Liberty Methodist Cemetery. *Submitted by Gary Walden.*

WALDEN, SANDRA KAY HOUSTON, born Jul. 1, 1944 in Booneville, MS to Captain Fred L. and Virginia Kathryn Rogers Houston. Her middle name, Kay, was for her mother. At the time of her birth, her father was serving in the US Army Corps of Engineers stationed in Oak Ridge, TN. She attended. Booneville schools graduating from high school in 1962. During high school, Sandra was a cheerleader for four years and was elected Miss BHS as a senior. She served as Booneville's Jr. Miss and was selected Miss Hospitality in 1962.

The Joseph Neil Walden Jr. Family. L-R: Joseph Neil Walden Jr., Sandra Houston Walden, Leslie Walden, Joseph Neil Walden III

After high school, Sandra attended Northeast Mississippi Junior College for one year before continuing her education at the University of Mississippi. While at Northeast, she was selected Most Beautiful for the 1962-1963 school year and served in the Student Government Association. During Sandra's three years at Ole Miss, she was a member of Delta Delta Delta serving as historian her senior year and received the Crymes Award in Home Economics.

Sandra graduated Jan. 31, 1966, from Ole Miss with a bachelor of science degree. On Jun. 11, 1966, she was married to Joseph Neil Walden Jr. at Booneville's First Baptist Church. Neil graduated from St. Paul's School, Concord, NH 1963. His parents are Joseph Neil Walden Sr. of Brownsville, TN and Ida Jean Beaver Walden of Memphis, TN. In the fall of 1966 Sandra began her career in education while Neil finished his degree from Vanderbilt University. He graduated on Jun. 4, 1967, with a bachelor of arts. Sandra and Neil returned to Booneville in the fall of 1968 while Neil awaited his assignment with the US Navy.

In November 1968, Neil began US Navy Officer Candidate's School in Newport, RI. On Apr. 11, 1969, Neil was commissioned ensign in the US Navy and on Apr. 20, 1969, their first child, Joseph Neil Walden III, was born in Newport at the Naval Hospital. Following their time in the Navy, Neil and Sandra returned to Booneville where Neil went into business with his father at Walden Body Co. On Aug. 3, 1971, their second child, Leslie Ann Walden, was born in Booneville.

In the fall of 1974, Sandra began teaching at Wheeler High School. In 1979, she was selected Star Teacher by Mississippi's Economics Council. On Aug. 16, 1975, Neil received his master of arts degree from Memphis State University and on May 14, 1978, Sandra received her master of arts degree from the University of Mississippi. After Neil and his father sold their business, Neil taught at Northeast Mississippi Junior College.

In July 1979, Neil, Sandra, Joseph and Leslie moved to Bailey, CO. Neil went into business for himself and Sandra began teaching at Platte Canyon High School in the fall of 1980. She also continued post graduate studies at the University of Northern Colorado and Colorado State University. In 1985, she was selected Platte Canyon's Educator of the Year.

Joseph graduated from Platte Canyon High School in 1987 as Valedictorian of his class and Leslie graduated from Platte Canyon in 1989 as Salutatorian of her class. After high school, Joseph went to the University of Colorado, Boulder, where he graduated Phi Beta Kappa in 1991. In 1995, he graduated from Duke School of Law. After high school, Leslie went to Vanderbilt University, Nashville, where she graduated cum laude in 1993. While at Vanderbilt she served as treasurer of Alpha Delta Pi. Both Leslie and Joseph went to Atlanta, GA following their graduations. Joseph first worked with the Solicitor's Office in DeKalb County, then Cobb County's District Attorney's office as an assistant district attorney. Currently, he is an assistant district attorney with DeKalb County. Leslie has been associated with AON and Alexander and Alexander since graduating from Vanderbilt. She was selected in 1996 to participate in Rotary International Group Study Exchange to Sir Lanka.

In 1996, Neil and Sandra moved from Colorado to Birmingham, AL when GeoMet, Inc., a coalbed methane operating company, acquired his company's major natural gas project in China. Currently, Neil serves as president and chief financial officer of GeoMet Operating, Inc. He frequently travels to China as his company continues to develop coalbed methane projects both domestically and internationally.

Sandra continues her career as an educator after 24 years of teaching. She is presently employed by Jefferson County Schools, Birmingham and is also working as a consultant in career education.

In December 1999, Neil and Sandra purchased a vacation home with a view of Pike's Peak near Evergreen, CO. When they retire, they plan to spend their summers and Christmas holidays in Colorado and the remainder of the year in the South.

WALES, CORNELIUS J. "C.J.," born in Georgia and moved to Waterloo, AL in about 1863 where he met and married Rebecca Parker, a widow from just across the state line in Tennessee. While living in Waterloo, C.J. and Rebecca had two children, Winston and George Hardy Wales. Rebecca also had a son, William T. "Billy" Parker by her first husband. In the late 1860s the Wales family moved to Prentiss County, MS and purchased farm land in the Mount Pisgah Community and raised their family adding five more boys: Timethis, Cornelius Madison, Carl S., Bob and Addison.

Bill and Velma Wales and children: Billy, Bobby and Harry in 1947

Cornelius Madison "C.M." became a dentist and set up practice in Booneville during the late 1800s until mid-1900s. The other Wales boys chose different professions ranging from railroad section supervisor, chaplain at Blue Mountain College, school teacher and farmer. Dr. C.M. married Mattie Clemmie Davis, the only child of James M. "Jim" and Janie Hester Davis. Dr. C.M. and Clemmie purchased a small tract of land and built a home in the "Big V" Community (crossroads of Hwy. 4 and 30, two miles east of Booneville) and raised four children: Winona Wales Gentry, James Hester Wales, William Wallace "Bill" Wales and Grace Wales Morgan. Bill Wales worked as a carpenter in Booneville and throughout the US during the Great Depression.

Bill met and married Velma Josephine Maddox, daughter of Thomas and Della Maddox and raised three boys: William Wallace "Billy" Wales Jr., Bobby Joe Wales and Harry Mack Wales. Bill and Velma purchased land about a quarter mile south of the "Big V" and built a home (currently home of Joey Lindsey). Bill Wales had another son by a previous marriage, Jimmy Richard "Jim" Wales, who married Nell Prince and has two boys, Jimmy and Johnny Wales. Jim and Nell still reside in Germantown, TN.

Billy Wales married Martha L. Holley, the youngest daughter of Ben F. and Mildred Holley. After a tour in the Army with the Mississippi National Guard. (1951-1952), Billy attended Mississippi State College obtaining a BS degree in aeronautical/aerospace engineering. After working 30 years for the NASA, Billy retired in 1988. Billy and Martha live in Huntsville, AL and have four children: Steven Wallace Wales, Eleanor Jo Wales Johnson, Martha Elaine Wales and David Holley Wales. Billy and Martha have four grandchildren: Marcy and Ben Wales and Nick and Jack Johnson.

Bobby Joe Wales spent four years in the USAF after graduation from Booneville High School, during which time he met and married Gail Lee Hudson, a Texas girl. Bobby and Gail live in the Houston, TX area where they have four children: Robby Wales, Kenneth Wales, Kimberley Wales Shuttlesworth and Michael Wales. Bobby and Gail have three grandchildren. Bobby works for Continental Air Lines in Houston.

Harry Mack Wales spent four years in the Army at Homestead AFB, FL where he met and married Linda Ann Jewett. Harry and Linda make their home in Denver, CO where Harry works for the Air Force. Harry and Linda have two boys, Billy and Brian and two grandchildren. *Submitted. by William W. Wales Jr.*

WARDLAW, ROBERT, born near Glasgow or Dunfermline, Scotland about 1670. He married a Hutson (first name unknown). They had three children: James, John and William. Records were not found to prove that Robert Wardlaw ever came to America.

William Wardlaw (b. 1715, d. 1761) did come to America, first to Philadelphia and then to Virginia about 1735. He was an elder in the New Providence Presbyterian Church of New Providence, VA. He married Jeannette Harper. They had seven children: James, John B., Hugh, Joseph, William Jr., Margaret and Robert.

Hugh Wardlaw (b. 1740, d. 1802) moved to South Carolina where he was an elder in the Greenville Soluda Church of Due West, SC. He was a captain of a Whig Militia in the Revolutionary War. He married Elizabeth Coalter. They had 12 children: William, an infant, James, John, David, Margaret, Joseph, Robert, Jane, Hugh Hutson, Elizabeth and Agnes.

William Wardlaw (b. 1764, d. 1839) was born in Virginia and died in Harris County, GA. He and his first wife, Margaret Hall, had six children. He and his second wife, Margaret McCulley, had 12 children: Mary, Absolam, Samuel McCulley, David, Jane, Robert, Micajah, Lucinda, William, John, Joseph and Francis Marion.

Samuel McCulley Wardlaw (b. 1805, d. 1877) was born in Gwinnett County, GA. He married Jane Austin before moving to Itawamba County, MS. They had 10 children: William, James, Mary, John, Margaret, George W., Samuel, Martha, Ann and Charles.

George W. Wardlaw (b. 1840, d. 1912) married Sarah Ann Carter in Itawamba County, MS. They had eight children: J.W.,

L-R: Bill Wardlaw, Jo Ann Wardlaw, Mike Wardlaw, Nancy Wardlaw

George, John Samuel, Della Ann, Henry Oscar, Zenoba, Sarah and Mary. George W. was a Primitive Baptist Minister. One church he pastored, was Westemoreland, near Bissell in Lee County, where he and Sarah are buried.

Henry Oscar Wardlaw (b. 1871, d. 1940) first married Inez Price. They had six children: Clarence md. Eddie Williams; Wiley md. Lillie Tapp; Lena Grace md. Bob Moore; John Lee md. Mary Carlock; Jimmie Lou md. George Amon and an infant.

Henry Oscar's second wife was Lee Anna Billingsley. They had no children. His third wife was Rebecca Carolyn Griffin. They had two children: Addie Mae md. Morris Jones and Henry Oscar Jr. md. Jewel Prather.

John Lee Wardlaw (b. 1904, d. 1973) and Mary Carlock had four children: Annie Merle md. Billy Glover; William Oscar "Buddy" md. Jo Ann Morrow; Herman Douglas md. Amanda Ross and Charles Ray md. Martha Haas first and Carolyn Carnathan Gault second.

John Lee Wardlaw and Mary Carlock had eight grandchildren:

1. James Richard Glover md. Katherine Houk.
2. Jeffrey Allan Glover md. Teresa Haynes.
3. Michael Wardlaw md. Nancy Jo Park.
4. Nancy Wardlaw md. Leslie Morrison.
5. Douglas Wardlaw md. Debra Hendry.
6. Amanda Wardlaw md. Alan Browne.
7. Emily Wardlaw md. Dennis Grubbs.
8. Paula Wardlaw md. James McKinney.

John Lee and Mary had 10 great-grandchildren: Corrie and Meredith Glover; Lee and Andrew Wardlaw; Michael, Stephanie and Kyle Morrison; Justin and Kayla Browne and Taylor Ray McKinney.

Wardlaw descendants are scattered over the US. *Submitted by Bill Wardlaw.*

WATERS, MARJORIE OAKLEY, an entrepreneur before there was such a word.

She and her husband, Milton, opened a cloth/fabric store in downtown Booneville that was the beginning of Marjorie's entrepreneurial efforts. At that first "fabric" store, she sold pieces of material at reasonable prices to folks who needed to save money or who had very little to spend.

A young wife on a limited budget could buy a piece of material for a quarter and with a little talent in sewing, her daughter would have a new dress for school! All made possible from the efforts of the Waters duo. That little store was the beginning of the fabric business for them and it would grow into really big business for Marjorie Waters and for Booneville, MS.

She had smaller stores in several locations in downtown Booneville before. As she puts it: "Milton

Marjorie Oakley Waters

built me the building on the corner where Goddard's Jewelry is now located."

She had gotten to know one of the gentlemen who aided and abetted her getting into the fabric business, L.D. Hancock, when he sold her candy and razor blades in the Waters' first business. Marjorie and Milton had run a little country store in the Osborne Creek Community, a store that had been run a way back in the past by her parents, Mary Carpenter and Jesse William Oakley. Mr. Oakley had supported his family as a cattle buyer and a merchant and Miss Mary taught children to play the piano, something she continued to do for most of her life.

Marjorie Oakley had been moved into the Osborne Creek Community when she was only 18 months old. She lived in what was, during her growing up years, a very aristocratic community.

She grew up in the Oak Grove Methodist Church, led the singing and taught Sunday school. Some students still around remember thinking, "She was the best Sunday school teacher we ever had." The church was small (still is) and she taught those classes wherever there was a spot in someone's car in cold weather or on a log outside in warm weather. She has in her home one of the little chairs that she raised money to buy for her "little ones." She sold subscriptions to the *Banner* to buy them!

Attended the Osborne Grammar School through the eighth grade and remembers that Miss Alma Trantham was teacher/principal. She graduated from Wheeler High School in 1937 and was offered a college education by "Auntie Tucker" but, "I was too much of a Mama's girl to stay away and I didn't quite last a semester," Marjorie said.

The kind of education that she would have gotten probably wouldn't have readied her to be the businesswoman she was to become anyway.

Milton took her as a bride on May 22, 1940. He spent time in the Navy, sold insurance and cars and worked for Billingsley Chevrolet. The couple ran the old Rees Court for a couple of years until Marjorie yelled, "No more." Then she worked for Sherman's, managing the ladies department and finding her niche in life as a storeowner. Hence, The Fabric Shops. They started in 1958.

The little stores were their "learning" years. "We just got material from everywhere," she said. "It might be left-overs, junk, from saleouts, but it was good material. Good useable material." They got lots of their material from Hancock's, but they purchased a great deal of their better material on their own.

"We went anywhere that we could find a bargain," she said. "Then we would sell it at a price that local folks could live with."

They went to mills in North Carolina and to New York twice a year. She recalls, "Milton said, 'If I build that big store, you have to promise that all you will take out of it for one year will be money for your lunch.' And that's what I did. It paid for itself. It just took off." Milton went from cars to cloth! They had found a business where there was a big need in the area. There was the first big one on that corner, but she added others, at Baldwyn, Iuka and Corinth.

Marjorie lost her Milton on Jul. 31, 1968, but stayed on in her business until 1971 and didn't really quit then. The Drapery Shop was her next endeavor, but that didn't intrigue her like the fabric business had.

Today in 1999, she would probably call herself retired, but Marjorie Oakley Waters will never retire. She still has rental properties, business buildings and apartments and they require constant work. A practically full time business.

Though she started out as an Oak Grove Sunday school teacher, she transferred with her husband in 1950 to the First United Methodist Church in Booneville. That church has and still does feel her strong presence. She's been a Sunday School teacher there, president of Circle IV of the United Methodist Women and a Trustee.

The Waters Patio between the church and the Education Building was built by her in memory of her husband. There are draperies all over the church and parsonages that she lovingly placed there, because she loves her church.

She has been a member of the Pilot Club of Booneville, but today she is just a member of the Ladies Civitan Club.

She spends a lot of time on her family history. Marjorie's family is old stock, Carpenter-Hambright, she has complete records back to the Revolutionary War and an active member in the Daughters of the American Revolution (DAR). She particularly enjoys being a part of the United Daughters of the Confederacy (UDC) and she's an authenticated member there, too.

If she has a worry in the world, it is "what will happen to all the wonderful and important papers that prove my heritage," she said.

Her home at 600 West College Street is reminiscent of her mother's time in life. It's the old McCorkle home and she restored it, keeping in mind its original lines. Inside the home, her antiques and modern comfortable furniture match perfectly.

Marjorie Oakley Waters lives her life to the fullest. She doesn't let her age bother her: "I'm proud of all my years," she said.

The outside of her home is decorated for every season: Easter, Christmas and Halloween. Halloween seems to be her favorite for public involvement. She had 250 kids at Halloween. "I had lots of candy, 250 bags and the children love to come by." She sits out front and they love to see all the decorations, especially the witch. "That scares them to death," she laughingly said.

Marjorie Oakley Waters was an entrepreneur before the term was even known about. That is true. She proved that women can be entrepreneurs, maybe even paved the way for others.

She has continued to live her life being a strong person, helping others, traveling and living life to its fullest.

Bibliography: Sarah Marjorie Oakley Waters (b. Aug. 29, 1918) married William Milton Waters (b. Apr. 30, 1917, d. Jul. 31, 1968) on May 22, 1940. Her parents were Mary Parthenia Carpenter Oakley (b. Dec. 10, 1883, d. Jan. 2, 1979) and Jesse William Oakley (b. Apr. 10, 1881, d. Feb. 16, 1920). They married on Feb. 21, 1903. *Submitted by Laura W. Cartwright.*

WEATHERBEE BROTHERS, after John Wesley and Mary Frances (White) Weatherbee moved from Wheeler, Prentiss County, MS to the Stutts Community, northwest of Booneville where John Wesley and Mary Frances died, they left these four boys, who then settled on their own farms just north of the canal, which runs through the north side of the Stutts' farm. They lived and raised their families farming until they died, with the exception of Oscar Wayland, who moved in 1958 with his family to Phoenix, AZ, for his health. Another brother, not in the picture, had already moved to Phoenix, William Wesley Weatherbee. William and Oscar are buried in the same cemetery in Phoenix, AZ.

From left: Robert Leandor, Oscar Wayland, Charles Livingston and John Wesley. Taken in 1956.

In the picture, are from left: Robert Leandor "Lee", Oscar Wayland, Charles Livingston "Charlie" and John Wesley Jr. Charlie is the oldest of the children of John and Mary Frances. He served in WWI in the French trenches. He nor Lee never married, but they were grandfather images to many of the nieces and nephews. *Written by Doris A.W. Oaks, PO Box 791, Eagle, ID 83616-0791. Submitted by Larry W. Weatherbee, Hughson, CA.*

WEATHERBEE, JOHN WESLEY, born Jun. 19, 1863 and died d. May 7, 1935, Alanthus, Franklin County, AL, married Nov. 5, 1885 in Franklin County, AL Mary Frances White (b. 1866, d. 1933), Pleasant Site, Franklin County, AL. (See picture of John Wesley Weatherbee family.) John was the third and only son born posthumously as his father, Charles Wesley Weatherbee, died Mar. 29, 1863, at the Alton, Madison County (IL) Military Prison. His mother was Martha "Patsy" (Hall) Weatherbee. Rev. Moses Livingston and Mary Arminda (Patterson) White were the parents of Mary Frances.

Seated from left: Mary Frances (White) with Myrtle Viola on lap, William Wesley and John Wesley with Robert Leander on lap. Back from left: Hannah Elizabeth, ?, Duncan, Mary Jane. Taken about 1905.

John and Mary Frances had 11 children. The first five were born in Fordton, Franklin County, AL and the last six were born in Wheeler, Prentiss County, MS.

1. Charles Livingston Weatherbee (b. Nov. 4, 1886, d. Mar. 25, 1972) never married. He is buried in Hodges Chapel Cemetery, northeast of Wheeler, Prentiss County, MS.
2. Hannah Elizabeth Weatherbee (b. Nov. 3, 1888, d. May 18, 1910) married Apr. 6, 1906 in Booneville, Prentiss County, MS to Henry A. Beck. "Lizzie" is buried in Osborne Creek Cemetery. They had two sons, Charlie Wade Beck (b. May 9, 1907, d. 1985) and Emmitt Wesley Beck (b. Dec. 14, 1909, d. Jan. 24, 1990).
3. Sarah Rebecca Weatherbee (b. Mar. 3, 1890, d. Apr. 15, 1891) is buried in the Weatherbee Cemetery in Franklin County, AL.
4. Mary Jane Weatherbee (b. Feb. 7, 1892, d. Mar. 22, 1956) married Oct. 11, 1911, to Lewis Jackson Davis (b. Feb. 21, 1891, d. Nov. 30, 1967) and is buried in Hodges Chapel Cemetery in Wheeler, Prentiss County, MS. Jane and Jack had issue of six children (all born in Wheeler, MS): Flora (b. Dec. 16, 1912, d. Dec. 20, 1912) is buried in Hodges Chapel Cemetery; Clara Vernell (b. Apr. 2, 1914, d. Nov. 5, 1968) is buried in the Sandhill Cemetery in Philadelphia, Neshoba County, MS; Sula Estelle (b. Feb. 17, 1917, d. Feb. 27, 1994) is buried in Memphis, Shelby County, TN; Forrest Charlene (b. Apr. 17, 1919); Alma Marie (b. Apr. 29, 1921) is unmarried; Clarence Jackson (b. Dec. 4, 1923, d. May 26, 1925) is buried in Hodges Chapel Cemetery.
5. William Wesley Weatherbee (b. Feb. 26, 1894, d. May 11, 1954) married Mar. 24, 1917, to Mary Hespey Ann Dickinson (b. Apr. 18, 1901, d. Oct. 9, 1989). Both are buried in Greenwood Memorial Cemetery in Phoenix, Maricopa County, AZ. Will and Hespey have three children: Charles William (b. May 9, 1918); Catherine Luvenia Estelle (b. Jan. 23, 1922, d. after 1989) and Robert Wesley (b. Oct. 5, 1928).
6. Robert Leander Weatherbee (b. Feb. 8, 1898, d. Mar. 30, 1982) never married and is buried in Booneville Cemetery in Prentiss County, MS.
7. Amanda Modena Weatherbee (b. Oct. 1, 1900, d. Dec. 6, 1901) is buried in Osborne Creek Cemetery in Booneville, Prentiss County, MS.
8. Myrtle Viola Weatherbee (b. Feb. 5, 1903, d. Jul. 17, 1999) married Aug. 21, 1921, to Herman Bradford Miller (b. Jan. 1, 1901, d. May 12, 1967). Both are buried in Prentiss Memorial Gardens. There are three children: Helen Sue (b. Apr. 28, 1932); Marilyn Yvonne (b. May 20, 1935) and Charles Bradford (b. Dec. 3, 1938).
9. Oscar Wayland Weatherbee (b. Mar. 9, 1906, d. May 19, 1959) (See other item.)
10. John Wesley Weatherbee (b. Dec. 29, 1908, d. Apr. 7, 1965) married Dec. 6, 1930, to Dora Alma Palmer (b. Oct. 7, 1907, d. Mar. 26, 1997). Both, as well as all deceased children, are buried at Sardis Cemetery in Rienzi, Alcorn County, MS. John and Alma had issue of eight children: Hugh Thomas (b. Oct. 17, 1932, d. Dec. 23, 1950); Cecil Roy (b. Feb. 23, 1935); John Robert "Bobby" (b. Apr. 18, 1939, d. Jun. 17, 1994); Donnie Ray (b. Jan. 22, 1941); Mollie Joe (b. Nov. 12, 1942); Zandra Nell (b. Oct. 18, 1944); Dora Annette (b. Nov. 2, 1948) and Virginia Lynn (b. Oct. 5, 1950).
11. Mollie Weatherbee (b. Nov. 20, 1911, d. Dec. 4, 1995) married Dec. 24, 1933, to Henry Lee Palmer (b. Mar. 26, 1912, d. Feb. 7, 1999) and had issue of four children: Wilma Lee (b. May 8, 1935); Frances Charlene (b. Feb. 26, 1939); Jerry Wayne (b. Jun. 6, 1945) and Mollie Regina (b. Mar. 30, 1947). *Written by Doris A.W. Oaks, P.O. Box 791, Eagle, ID 83616-0791, email:<dawoakes@worldnet.att.net> Submitted by Charles W. Weatherbee, New Smyrna, FL.*

WEATHERBEE, OSCAR WAYLAND AND RUBY, have four children:

From left: Patsy Darlene, Ruby Ann (Ashcraft), Sarah Lucille standing in front, Doris Ann, Oscar Wayland and Larry Wayland. Taken about 1953.

1. Doris Ann (b. Jul. 11, 1935) married Jan. 2, 1962, to Raymond Lee Oakes (b. Oct. 23, 1937) and has three children, all born in Boise, Ada County, ID: Glenn Eric (b. Dec. 8, 1964); Roger Wayland (b. Jun. 10, 1966) and LeAnn Kay (b. Aug. 14, 1967) married May 18, 1996, to Luis Rafael Martinez (b. Oct. 18, 1962).
2. Patsy Darlene (b. Dec. 2, 1939) married Nov. 18, 1960, to Dale Edward Clarkson (b. Jun. 21, 1931) and has 11 children. The first four were born in Mesa, Maricopa County, AZ. The rest were born in Kanab, Kane County, UT: (1) Loretta (b. Dec. 2, 1961) married Jan. 7, 1983, to Calvin Dirk Clayson. They have five children. (2) JoAnn (b. Mar. 22, 1963) married Oct. 8, 1983, to Jeffrey Charles Michelsen. They have a family of seven. (3) Larry Dale (b. Jul. 27, 1965) married May 25, 1988, to Deborah Suzette Olsen. They have three children. (4) Barry Edward (b. Jun. 15, 1968) married Sep. 26, 1992, to Pamela Leigh Price. They have four boys. (5) Benjamin Kyle (b. Apr. 5, 1971) married Dec. 18, 1992, to Tiffany Lee Bartlett. They have two children. (6) Daniel Wayland (b. Apr. 17, 1973) married Mar. 29, 1996, to Stephanie Tan Burr. They have two children. (7) Carrilyn (b.

May 6, 1975). (8) John Ryan (b. Oct. 28, 1976) married May 7, 1999, to Chelsea Kristine Van Noy. (9) Timothy Scott (b. Sep. 10, 1978). (10) James Patrick (b. Jul. 26, 1980). (11) Natalie (b. Jun. 19, 1982).

3. Larry Wayland (b. Feb. 5, 1942) married Jun. 9, 1965, to LaRayne Kimball (b. Sep. 15, 1943) and has seven children: (1) Elissa Ann (b. Jan. 30, 1968 in San Leandro, Alameda County, CA) married Dec. 19, 1987, to Jeffrey Michael Stone. They have five children. (2) Melinda Marie (b. Jul. 10, 1969 in Nampa, Canyon County, ID) married Jun. 17, 1989, to Nathan Merville Harvey (b. Nov. 21, 1966, d. May 15, 1998). They have four children, one deceased. (3) Carolee (b. Jul. 4, 1971 in Nampa, Canyon County, ID). (4) Brian Wayland (b. Dec. 14, 1972 in Turlock, Stanislaus County, CA) married Aug. 10, 1996, to Louisa Lopez. (5) Jill Janae (b. May 20, 1976 in Turlock, Stanislaus County, CA. (6) Tara Nicole (b. Dec. 10, 1977 in Turlock, Stanislaus County, CA. (7) David Brent (b. Dec. 27, 1976 in Turlock, Stanislaus County, CA.

4. Sarah Lucille (b. Jan. 21, 1950) married May 14, 1976, to Terrell Kim Johnson (b. Dec. 7, 1951) and has two children, Tersa Ann (b. Dec. 9, 1981) and Tyson Oscar (b. Sep. 11, 1984), both born at Steamboat Springs, Toutt County, CO. *Written by Doris A.W. Oaks, PO Box 791, Eagle, ID 83616-0791. Submitted by Sarah L.W. Johnson, Green River, WY.*

WEEMS, BARTHOLOMEW, born in 1735, probably son of Thomas Weems (b. 1704) and Elinor Jacobs (b. 1710), came to Abbeville, SC, from Augusta County, VA, after 1765. He married Margaret Rosemond and, according to wills and records, had children: John, Bartholomew Jr., James, Samuel, Isabelle Keown, Elizabeth Jordon, Mary Ferguson and Sarah. Bartholomew and Bartholomew Jr. were members of Cedar Spring ARP Presbyterian Church. Bartholomew died Dec. 25, 1800 and Margaret died in 1823 in Abbeville, SC. Bart Jr. was in Alabama by 1819 and died in Lawrence County, AL, before 1860. Records indicate (not proven) that he had these children: James (b. 1800 in South Carolina); George McComb; Andrew Mc; Bartholomew (b. 1818 in South Carolina); Rebecca; Sarah and one more daughter.

Top from left: Wedding Day Mamie Brown and Leslie Elijah Weems. Bottom from left: Unidentified, Letra Crabb and Clifton Brown.

My great-grandfather was Bartholomew, born in 1818 in South Carolina. He was married to Malinda Haney in 1843 in Itawamba County, MS. They were living in Lawrence County, AL in 1850 and returned to Itawamba by 1860. Bart and Malinda had nine children: James B., John Andy, Martha, Josephine, Mary F., Madora J., William Calvin, M. Glath and Rebecca.

James B. (b. 1846 in Alabama) first married Aminda J. Howell. They had a daughter, Nancy D. His second marriage was to Martha Taylor. They had five children: George Andy, Malinda, Monroe, Huey and William Perry. George Andy (b. 1884 in Mississippi and died in 1963) was married to Annie Morgan. Their children were Luther, Martha and Lula Mae, who is married to R.C. Byran and lives in Belmont, Mississippi.

John Andy was born in Alabama in 1847. His children were: Anton C.; Savanah, who married Sid Butler and Varnarie, who married John Absolm McRae.

Martha and Josephine never married.

M. Glath (b. Mississippi in 1862) married Elizabeth (Betsie) Stacy. They had Forrest, a girl (b. 1895); Derrell (b. 1897), who married Lillian Franks and Hattie (b. 1898).

William Calvin, my grandfather, was born in Mississippi in 1860. He married Margaret (Maggie) Caroline Ryan, daughter of Dr. Charles Ryan and Elizabeth Martin, daughter of Seth and Francis Martin. In 1902 and 1903, he was postmaster of Millican, after which the mail was moved to New Site. In his duties as an officer of the law in Booneville, he shot and killed someone and we believe this caused him to take his life in 1922. William and Maggie's children were: Lula K., Luther A., Leslie Exel, Letra, William Bryan and Lillian.

Lula married Lidge Johnson. They had two children, Bruce and Sidney.

Luther never married.

Leslie Exel, my father, (b. 1889) married Ella Mae (Mamie) Brown, daughter of Elijah Franklin Brown and Martha (Mattie) Johnson, daughter of Thomas Jefferson Johnson and Mary Jane Wroten. Leslie carried mail horseback from New Site to Booneville. When he died in 1931, he worked for the state grading the roads in New Site. Leslie and Mamie had six children: Curtis Golden Herschel; Nella Newel; twins, Calvin Thurman and Elijah Herman; Helen Sevelle and Leslie Jay Webster. Curtis died young. Nella married Lloyd Scott and had one son, Celestial. She died young. Calvin (b. 1919) first married Ivey Davis and had one son, John Wayne. His second marriage was to Vera Joyner and they have two sons, Calvin Ernest, who lives in New Orleans and Sidney Mitchell. Calvin and his son, Mitch, both live in New Site. Herman (1919, d. 1982) married four times and had two sons by his third wife, Anzie Howell. They are Elijah Curtis and Phillip Earl. Helen (b. 1921) first married James Earl McKay, by whom she had Jimmy Darrell, Mamie Elois and Patsy Joy. By her second marriage to Cecil Groseclose, she had Wanda Lynn and James Calvin. She then married Bill Forney and then Emmett Blumgren. Leslie (b. 1926) married Melba Davis in Mobile, AL. They had Donna, Dwayne, Rebecca, Michael and David.

Letra (b. 1895) married Columbus (Lum) Crabb and had three girls: Jewel, Maxine and Laverne. Lum and Letra lived on the bottom floor of the jail in Booneville, since he was the jail keeper.

William Bryan (b. 1897) married Mytle Miller.

Lillian (b. 1905) married Carrol McGlaun. They had one daughter, Kathleen, who married Clyde Pardue. *Submitted by Helen Weems Blumgren, 501 General Gibson Drive, Spanish Fort, AL.*

WHISENANT, AARON TEULON, born Jan. 6, 1904 and died December 1976, the son of Doyle Bailey Whisenant (b. November 1873 in Mississippi) and Mary Jane Collum (b. April 1880 in Mississippi). Doyle Bailey was the son of Thomas Martin Whisenant (b. 1846 in Georgia) and Lucinda Franks of Cherokee and Colbert Counties in Alabama. Thomas Martin Whisenant was the son of George Robert (b. 1821 in Georgia) and Mary Whisenant. George Robert was the son of John Nicholas Whisonant II, son of John Nicholas Whisonant and Mary Carpenter. John Nicholas II was born in 1775 in South Carolina. During the War of 1812, Nicholas served in Captain Robert Caldwell's company in South Carolina. *(Source: Raymond C. Whisnant, Dallas, TX)*

Teulon's siblings were: Fannie May, William A., Dennis, Elvis "Whis", Rose and Avo.

The Whisenants are of Swiss descent.

Aaron Teulon Whisenant married Willie Pardue and they had one daughter, Jean. After they divorced, Teulon married Bonnie Johnson Harper (see Johnson/Derryberry stories), who was divorced from Aubrey Melton Harper. Bonnie had a daughter, Maxine Harper. Bonnie and Teulon had one son, William Wyatt "Gus" Whisenant (b. Jun. 11, 1946 in Booneville, MS).

Aaron Teulon Whisenant was an excellent automobile mechanic. He was as good hearted a man as ever lived. He was a generous and hospitable host to Bonnie's relatives all through their marriage.

He was also an excellent grandfather to his step-grandchildren, treating them as if they were of his blood. His son and step-grandchildren have wonderful memories of his storytelling and singing abilities, of tree houses built by "Paw" and fishing trips on his Wednesday afternoons off. He was the daily supplier of "funny books" and candy when he arrived home from the shop. He was an avid reader, especially of westerns, Louis L'Amour and Zane Grey.

Front, from left: William Wyatt "Gus" Whisenant and Jerry Lyle Sparks. Middle: Patricia Ann Sparks, Aaron Teulon Whisenant, Bonnie Johnson Harper Whisenant and Gale Gahagan. Back: Maxine Harper Sparks and Jean Whisenant Gahagan. Taken in early 1948.

Bonnie lived to serve her children, grandchildren and relatives by the score. She was a wonderful country cook. She was quick to laughter, had a quiet sense of humor and could be a talented mimic of speech patterns and mannerisms.

Maxine Harper married John Lyle Sparks. (See Sparks story.)

"Gus" Whisenant graduated from Booneville High School where he was in the Blue Devils marching band and on the football squad. He graduated from Delta State College and is a CPA in Corinth and very active in civic affairs.

While at Delta State, Gus met and married Thelma Ruth Caldwell, the daughter of Frank Caldwell and Lola Delia McCain. They have one daughter, Stephanie Renee (b. Feb. 26, 1970 in Booneville), who is a teacher and talented pianist and contemporary gospel singer. She married "Wes" Westmoreland of Saltillo.

Their son, William Brian Whisenant (b. Jun. 15, 1975 in Corinth), graduated from Alcorn Central High School and Mississippi Southern and is currently in New York pursuing a career in show business. He is a talented musician, singer and actor, working this summer (of 2000) in an off-Broadway stock company with leads in "West Side Story", "Forever Plaid", etc.

Aaron Teulon Whisenant died in 1976 and Bonnie in 1995. They are sorely missed by their family. *Submitted by Ann Sparks.*

WHITE, JAY J., born Dec. 20, 1907 and died Jul. 26, 1999 married Edith Woodruff White (b. Jul. 10, 1911) on Jan. 13, 1929. Jay was the son of Amos and Anna White. Edith was the daughter of Charlie Edward (b. Feb. 25, 1891, d. Dec. 20, 1966) and Minnie Odell Stone Woodruff (b. Apr. 6, 1893, d. May 6, 1961). Jay has several brothers and sisters. Edith had only one sister, Ella Missouri Woodruff Vanderford (b. Feb. 21, 1913, d. Sep. 2, 1991) who married Winston Jasper "Wink" Vanderford (b. Mar. 9, 1916, d. Apr. 17, 1989). They had no children, but helped care for her nieces, nephews and great-nieces and great-nephews.

On Jan. 13, 1999 they celebrated their 70th wedding anniversary. They were given a reception with over 100 family members and friends attending by the congregation of Snowdown Church of Christ, where they were members for nearly 64 years. They were married in Belmont by her grandfather, who was a minister. The ceremony took place in front of a roaring January fireplace at her grandparent's home. They had not been married long before the Great Depression set in. They had it rough but got by. They raised their own food along with stock, cows, pigs and chickens.

Edith and Jay White

They met when she was 6 years old, but it wasn't until years later that they got struck on each other. He came to visit his sister who lived close by and they just decided to get married. Her mother did not want her to get married. She was only 17 years old and the family had moved from the Altitude area to Belmont for the specific reason of sending Edith and her sister to high school. She never went a day. She and Jay got married a month after the family moved to Belmont.

In the 1940s, Jay began doing carpentry and also sawmill work. Carpentry was his summer job and saw milling his winter job. Edith quilted in the winter and worked a big yard and garden in the summer. She also took in washing and ironing from family members who did work outside the farm.

Jay went into the Army during WWII but was honorably discharged because of a condition with his eye. Jay was born at Gillis Mill, TN which is not far from Waterloo, AL. Edith was born in Glendale. The couple settled down in the Snowdown Community where they lived and worked for many years. The couple remembered how the Snowdown Community received its name. Edith said, "An old church had burnt and volunteers had built a new one. The last day they worked on it, a man asked, "what are we going to call it?" Since it was snowing, one of them suggested it to be called "Snowdown." The snow didn't stick, but the name did."

Edith is now in the Tishomingo Manor nursing home. *Submitted by Anita Wigginton.*

WHITEHEAD, DON AND CAROLYN (ASHCRAFT), were born in Booneville, Prentiss County, MS in the Northeast Mississippi Hospital, both being delivered by Dr. S.L. Pharr. They are graduates of Booneville High School in 1969 and 1970. They both grew up on Old Marietta Road in Booneville. They have many fond memories of riding the school bus and going to Booneville High School, since this is where they met and fell in love. They were married Jul. 24, 1971 in Booneville. In June 1971, they purchased their first home with approximately five acres on Old Marietta Road.

Don, Carolyn and Jessica Whitehead

Carolyn's parents are Cleyone "Pick" and Allie (Kizer) Ashcraft. Don's parents are J.B. and Christine (Mann) Whitehead. Their parents still live on Old Marietta Road.

Don attended Mississippi State University from August 1975 until January 1980, where he received a master of science in ruminant and monogastric nutrition. In January 1980, Don went to work for Cargill. He and Carolyn moved to Corinth where they bought a home in the Box Chapel Community. Carolyn began selling real estate in Corinth and also began volunteering in the community.

In August 1981, Don was transferred to Mayfield, KY. Don and Carolyn moved there taking with them a baby girl, Jessica Jo (b. Sep. 8, 1981 in Tupelo, MS). Carolyn began a new career as a stay-at-home mom. The family decided that "traveling" would become their new hobby. They also became very active in the First Baptist Church.

In September 1983, Don was transferred to Nashville, TN. This is where they decided to try "condo living," so they purchased a condominium in River Plantation. In Nashville, Carolyn was still a stay-at-home mom, but began volunteering at Vanderbilt Children's Hospital. In Nashville, Jessica completed first grade at David Lipscomb Elementary.

Don began a new career with the Tennessee Farm Bureau Insurance Co. in 1989 and the family moved to Columbia, TN on Apr. 1, 1990. Don has been selling insurance now for over 10 years and knows that he has found his niche in life. Carolyn is still a stay-at-home mom, but she is also a very active volunteer in many organizations. She has been guest speaker at many women's religious retreats and meetings. Jessica is a senior at Columbia Central High School and will graduate May 18, 2000. She is still undecided about where to attend college, but she has visited Northeast Community College, Ole Miss and Mississippi State in Mississippi, as well as universities in Alabama and Tennessee. Don, Carolyn and Jessica are all very active volunteers with the Republican Party, nationally and locally.

The Whiteheads are very happy to call Booneville their hometown. Since Jessica's grandparents still live in Prentiss County, she also has many pleasant memories of Prentiss County, especially on Old Marietta Road, even though she has never lived there. They all continue to stay abreast of the happenings in Prentiss County via the *Banner Independent* delivered weekly to their home. *Submitted by Don and Carolyn Whitehead.*

WHITEHEAD, J.B., first born to James Monroe and Alpha Loice (South) Whitehead in Paden, MS on May 18, 1924. J.B. left Prentiss County for the first time in 1943 when he volunteered to serve in the army. Traveling by troop train, Camp Shelby was his first stop in this four-year adventure. He served as an anti-craft gunner in the South Pacific and as an MP in Juarez, Mexico and El Paso, TX. Being an MP prepared him to work after the army as a deputy sheriff for Sheriff Jimmy Thomas.

Jimmy, Donny, Tommy, Christine and, seated, J.B. This picture was taken May 11, 1987 on 40th anniversary.

Mary "Christine" Mann was born June 22, 1930, to George Washington and Perla Jane (Moon) Mann in Becker, MS. She was the seventh daughter in a family of eight girls and two boys. Christine had to mature early, because by the tender age of 14, she had lost both of her parents. At 14, she boarded a bus with all of her belongings and moved to Booneville, MS. She lived and worked at the old Booneville Hospital, while training to be a nursing assistant. Because of her love for helping others, nursing was natural to Christine. Being a nurse was her occupation, but it was also her vocation.

On a cold winter night in December 1946, Deputy Whitehead had to inform a skinny young woman that she was illegally shooting fireworks in the city limits of Booneville, this skinny young woman was Christine Mann. On May 11, 1947, J.B. and Christine Mann were married on the front porch of Rev. Pardon Mayo.

On Jun. 18, 1948, God blessed J.B. and Christine with their first child, a little girl, Mary Diane. Mary Diane was to be with them only a short time. She died of a heart valve problem in Memphis, TN and is buried in Forked Oak Cemetery in Burton, MS. J.B. and Christine were blessed with three sons: Donny (b. Feb. 10, 1951); Tommy (b. Jul. 28, 1956) and Jimmy (b. Jul. 15, 1964).

Christine became a LPN and surgical nurse, serving over a span of 44 years in many capacities in the medical profession, working at the Medical Clinic and the Northeast Mississippi Hospital. She retired in 1984. J.B. continued in law enforcement in Prentiss County, until he became a heavy equipment operator, he retired from the TVA.

The Whiteheads joined Fairview Baptist Church in 1949, where they are still active members. For these 50 years, Christine has taught children of all ages and positively influenced their lives.

In 1956 the Whiteheads bought a home on Old Marietta Road. This farm is still home today and full of memories of raising three sons. Retirement has not found the Whiteheads sitting around the farmhouse. They have two grandchildren, Jessica Jo Whitehead of Columbia, TN (b. Sep. 8, 1981) and Tyler Ray Whitehead of Booneville (b. Feb. 17, 1995). J.B. still maintains the 165-plus acre farm, while Christine is active with DAR, as well as, volunteer work. *Submitted by J.B. and Christine Whitehead.*

WIGGINTON, SAMMY KAY, born May 28, 1958, married Anita Gail Davis (b. May 15, 1958) on Jul. 15, 1977. Sammy is the son of Leland Selmer Wigginton (b. Mar. 28, 1918) and Gloria Mae Denson Wigginton (b. Dec. 28, 1926). His grandparents are Doc. D. (b. Jan. 4, 1894, d. May 5, 1977) and Alam Crawford Wigginton (b. Sep. 21, 1898, d. Sep. 1, 1924) and George Denson (b. Apr. 9, 1900, d. Apr. 24, 1985) and Lona Mae Denson (b. Feb. 17, 1900, d. Jul. 10, 1988).

Samantha, Anita, Samuel and Curtis Wigginton

Anita is the daughter of Garvin Earl Davis (b. Dec. 29, 1932, d. Feb. 4, 1994) and Waynona Mayvene Vanderford Davis (b. Nov. 25, 1935) who married on Jun. 6, 1955. Anita's grandparents were Jasper "Wink" Vanderford (b. Mar. 9, 1916, d. Apr. 17, 1989) and Ella Missouri Woodruff Vanderford (b. Feb. 21, 1916,

d. Apr. 17, 1991) who married Jun. 23, 1933. Garvin, Wink and Ella are buried in Snowdown Church of Christ Cemetery in Prentiss County.

Anita is the granddaughter of Elton (b. Nov. 8, 1904, d. Jan. 2, 1969) and Fannie May Stanley Davis (b. Jul. 26, 1906, d. Apr. 8, 1982). They are buried in the Jacinto Cemetery in Alcorn County.

Sammy and Anita's children are (1) Samuel Curtis Wigginton (b. Jul. 8, 1978) a high school graduate from New Site High and formerly employed for Horace Huddleston Construction and (2) Samantha Gail Wigginton (b. Jan. 19, 1982) a high school graduate from New Site High attending Booneville Academy of Cosmetology.

Anita and Sammy are both graduates of New Site High. Sammy is employed at Monotech in Iuka and Anita is employed in the Prentiss County School System at Hills Chapel School. *Submitted by Samantha Gail Wigginton.*

WILKINSON, JOHN AND SARAH, settled on a farm a few miles south of Booneville in Old Tishomingo County, MS about 1840.

Their children, born in the Booneville area and their year of birth are: James W. (b. 1842); William (b. 1843); Stephen (b. 1845); John P. (b. 1847); Samuel (b. 1849); Benjamin (b. 1851); Hannah (b. 1854) and Henry (b. 1858).

William married Nancy A. Doggett of Prentiss County about 1867. John Perry Wilkinson married Frances Elizabeth Pickens about 1871. Their children were Sara Frances (b. 1871), Lou V. (b. 1873), Luther David (b. 1875), Henry Robert (b. 1879), John R. (b. 1880) and twins Perry Reece and Stephen Rice (b. 1884). Samuel J. Wilkinson married Paralee Martin in 1867. Their children were: Lindy, William and Henry.

Stephen A. and Amanda Donaldson Wilkinson with children left to right: Henry, William, Dallie, Fred and Amos

Stephen A. Wilkinson married Amanda E. Donaldson in 1871. Their children, born in Prentiss County, were: Henry Dow (b. 1872), who married Viola Narcissus Bradford and died in Cotton County, OK; William J. (b. 1875), who married Estelle DeArmond and died in 1946 in Fort Worth, TX and Dallie Mae (b. 1877), who married Ernest Preston Slade and died in 1965 in Oklahoma City. Stephen, Amanda and their children left Prentiss County in 1878 going by rail to the end at Fort Worth, TX. They acquired farmland about 30 miles northwest of there, near Aurora in Wise County, TX where two more sons were born: Fred L. in 1880 and Amos T. in 1881. Stephen died in 1916 and Amanda in 1935. Both are buried in Pleasant Grove Cemetery #2, south of Boyd, Wise County, TX. Amanda's parents, Calvin K. and Martha Boley Donaldson of Prentiss County, moved with them to Texas. *Submitted by James L. Slade.*

WILLIAMS, JOHN LEE, born Aug. 15, 1920, to John W. and Cassie Lee Smith Williams. He is the oldest of their four children. Upon graduation from Marietta School, he was awarded the Sears & Roebuck Scholarship for $75 and the Daily Journal Scholarship for $100 to attend MSU. Because his daddy was ill at the time, he declined the scholarships to stay home and run the family farm. Farming and machinery have always been his passion. At the age of 12, he made a cultivator from scrap parts that his daddy later sold for a cow. When he was 20, he was baptized in the old Wildman pool in Hurricane Bottom. John Lee was drafted for WWII in 1942 to serve in the Air Force. While in service, he attended Centenary College in Shreveport, LA. Afterwards, he worked for B.F. Avery as a service manager and was an implement dealer for Minneapolis Moline and White Farm Equipment. He served as a trustee for both Marietta and New Site Schools. He also served as Election Commissioner for eight years.

Their Wedding Day, Jan. 22, 1948, John Lee Williams and Eunice Helen Reeves were married by Brother W.L. Whitner in Tishomingo County.

His wife of 52 years, Eunice Helen Reeves Williams, born Jan. 6, 1927 to Noah and Minnie Montgomery Reeves. She grew up in a large family with 14 siblings. Eunice was the next to the youngest of the family. Studying the Bible and singing were a large part of her home life. It was a regular occurrence for the family to gather and sing hymns at night before going to bed.

John Lee and Eunice Williams with their oldest daughter, Judy.

When her daddy lay dying, he called for his children to sing by his bedside. She was 15 at the time. Her family walked to church every Sunday morning and evening for services. Eunice was baptized at the age of 13 in Red Bud Creek, which was just a stone's throw from her front porch. During the war, Eunice, two sisters, one brother and her mother ran the family farm. After marrying in Tishomingo County on Jan. 22, 1948, the couple made their home in Marietta.

They have four children: Judy Marlyn Williams (b. Jul. 28, 1949) a resident at North Mississippi Regional Center in Oxford, MS; William Noah "Bill" (b. Jan. 27, 1952) married Janette Phillips. They have a son, Daniel Lee. Bill farms and restores antique tractors. They live on John and Cassie's old home place. Ralph David (b. Aug. 25, 1956) married Kim Allen. They have Kathryn "Katie" Allen and John David. Ralph's daughter Jessica attends NEMCC. Williams Truck and Trailer Service is their family business. Janie Marie (b. Jul. 17, 1965) married Mark Cole. Mark manages the Piggly Wiggly in Batesville, MS where they live with their children, Ashlee Marie and Clayton Ryan-Allen Cole.

Today, John Lee and Eunice remain in Marietta and attend the Church of Christ. After retiring from 31 years in the garment industry, Eunice enjoys canning, gardening and her grandchildren. John Lee farms, raises cattle and goes fishing as much as possible with his grandchildren. *Submitted by Janie Williams Cole.*

WILLIAMS, WILLIAM AUSTIN, son of Porter Walker and Rachel Caroline Wilson Williams, was born at New Site on Apr. 1, 1883. He was the grandson of James William (Bill) and Sarah Rush Williams, who were born in Georgia. Bill died of pneumonia while serving in the Confederate Army. Austin's maternal grandparents were William David and Nancy E. Carter Wilson. Nancy was born in old Tishomingo County (now Prentiss), the daughter of Joseph Edward and Eliza A. Carruth Carter.

Austin married Alma Canzada Finch on Jan. 7, 1906. She was the daughter of George Washington and Mary Elizabeth Vandevander Finch. Alma was born Mar. 8, 1881, at New Site at the old Finch homeplace. Her grandparents were John W. and Sarah Elizabeth Collier Finch and William Levi and Sarah Evans Stennett Vandevander. Alma,

William Austin Williams and Alma Canzada Finch in 1905.

known as Lamb, attended the Oakland Normal Institute of Itawamba County in 1902-1905. She was excellent in mathematics. She loved music and all the family enjoyed her humming as she worked. Her houseplants always looked as if they had just come from a nursery. She joined New Hope Church and loved attending the services. She always wore a big hat and was a real Southern lady. She seemed to know everyone and could tell how they were related to her family.

Austin and Alma had only one daughter, Bessie Lou, who was born in 1906. The family lived next door to the Williams' grandparents. Austin farmed, but soon he began to use his creative abilities and began to do all kinds of different things to earn a living. He went to St. Louis to a school to learn to teach auto mechanics. When he returned to Booneville, he started a school, but it had to be closed when the war took too many of the students. The family moved to Booneville and lived there, except for the time when they lived near their oil well. He, at one time, had a bentonite plant east of Booneville, drilled an oil well near New Site near the Natchez Trace, worked on Wilson Dam, delivered mail, carved and made gun stocks, made cement culverts, grave markers and street signs. He always was very well read and was constantly thinking on how to do things in a better way. He built their last home on Bryant Street to look like clapboard siding, but it was solid concrete that had been poured in forms that he designed to look like siding. Even the bathtub was concrete!

Austin died in 1959 and Alma died in 1967. They are both buried in the Siloam Cemetery. *Submitted by Keith Yelverton.*

WILSON, ELLIS WAYNE, born Apr. 24, 1916, son of George Oliver and Fannie (Lee) Wilson of New Site and Alma Bell Gardner, born Sep. 25, 1917, daughter of William Flournoy and Leoma (Hodges) Gardner of Wheeler, were married on Jan. 4, 1943. Ellis was serving in the US Army at the time and Alma was teaching school at Valley Elementary near Belmont, MS. They had two sons, Max Ellis (b. Jul. 24, 1944) and George Wayne (b. Mar. 15, 1948).

Ellis and Alma Wilson's home, bought in 1952 and moving back home in 1976.

213

Ellis was granted an honorable discharge from the Army in September 1945, after serving his country 4-1/2 years in the States and Europe. He and Alma then settled in the New Site area to farm with Ellis' father. Later they moved to Wheeler to help Alma's parents.

In 1952, they bought their first home across from Wheeler School and by this time Ellis decided to do mechanic work. This had been his trade since his teenage years working around his father's saw mill and later having formal training in the Army. On May 28, 1956, he took a job with Dealers Transport Co. in Louisville, KY as a mechanic. Alma took a job with the Wheeler Headstart and later in kindergarten work in Kentucky.

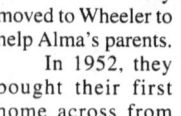

Staff Sergeant Ellis Wilson, World War II (Mar. 29, 1941-Sep. 28, 1945).

In 1976 Ellis took early retirement with Teamsters pension and they moved back to their old home in Wheeler. A new home was planned and built from the "woods up" instead of "grounds up." Timber was cut from his father's farm at New Site and sawed at a nearby mill. The lumber was hauled to Wheeler and stacked to dry. This was probably one of the last houses built in Wheeler from native heart pine. Ellis and Alma moved into their new house May 15, 1978 and are still living there.

Their oldest son, Max, attended schools at Wheeler, Northeast Mississippi Community College and graduated from Mississippi State University. He married Judy Carol Hill from the Blackland Community. They reside in Memphis, TN where he is involved with construction work and she is a real estate agent. They have two sons, Alan Max (b. Feb. 2, 1970) and Brent Edward (b. Feb. 16, 1971). Alan attended Germantown High School, Crichton College and Mid-American Baptist Theological Seminary in Memphis, TN. He is Children's Minister at Longview Heights Baptist Church in Olive Branch, MS. He is married to Lisa Carole King and they have two children, Billy Max (b. Aug. 11, 1995) and Alyssa Carole (b. May 16, 1997). Brent attended Germantown High School and graduated from Millsaps College in Jackson, MS. He received a degree in accountancy and is a certified public accountant in Jackson. He is married to Rebecca Leigh Thames.

Their youngest son, Wayne, graduated from Wheeler High School, Northeast Mississippi Community College, Mississippi State University and Stanford University (in Palo Alto, CA). He is married to Peggy Karen Sellers of Huntingdon, TN. They have four children: Zachary Hugo (b. Jun. 21, 1982), Rachel Lenore (b. Sep. 21, 1983), Tyler Wayne (b. Sep. 22, 1986) and Lee Ellis (b. Jan. 21, 1991) all of whom are honor students at Wheeler School. Wayne is a professional engineer working with NASA and Karen is a teacher with the Booneville School System. They reside in the Wheeler Community on the site where Ellis and Alma bought their first home. *Submitted by Ellis W. Wilson.*

WILSON, JOHN THOMAS, born Feb. 1, 1889 and Feb. 25, 1967, the son of Samuel Thomas and Hannah Jane Kennedy Wilson. Thomas was a Mason in the Burnsville Lodge. He and his twin brother worked for the railroad at Holcut. Thomas married Hattie Marie Goodin, daughter of John Starlin and Mollie Sillester Fennel Goodin of the Red Bay, AL, area. They are buried in the Vaughn Cemetery in Tishomingo County. Thomas and Hattie were the parents of 12 children:

1. Rosie Bell (b. Jul. 10, 1916) married Monroe West and had two sons, James David "Popeye Wilson" and Billy Ray West. Rosie married Hafford Odell McDougal and had three children: Mary Sue, Martha and Shirley.

2. Leona Jane (b. Mar. 7, 1919) married Dee Newcomb and had a daughter, Mable. She is buried at Liberty Hill Baptist in Alcorn County.

Thomas and Hattie Wilson

Leona married D. L. Parsons and had two daughters, Verie and Helen. Children, Thaddous and Martha Sue, are buried at Mt. Gilead Baptist in Iuka, MS.

3. Samuel Thomas "Bud" (b. May 26, 1921, d. November 1997) married Doris Scruggs and had: Linda, Eugene, Brenda, Dale and Gary. Bud married Retha Fortsyte. Bud is buried at New Salem Baptist in Iuka.

4. James Edward (b. Feb. 2, 1923) married Hester Lovelace and had two sons, Edward and David. They live at Cairo in Prentiss County.

5. Buster "Buss" (b. Jun. 15, 1925, d. Feb. 13, 1991) married Nancy Lou Clanton and had: Myron Lynn, Jerry Neal and Remona Jean. Buss is buried in Houlka, MS.

6. Robert Gip "Rab" (b. Dec. 24, 1927, d. Apr. 2, 1989) married Annie Mae Burleson and had: Barbara, Danny and Larry Don. Rab is buried by his parents at Sardis Baptist Church in Iuka, MS.

7. John Henry (b. Oct. 16, d. Sep. 30, 1986) never married. He is buried at Sardis.

8. Rufus Edward "Ed" (b. Mar. 24, 1937, d. Apr. 8, 1997) married Opal Carlise and had: Mary Jo, Dwayne and Shyanna. Ed is buried at Sardis.

9. Betty Ruth (b. Sep. 2, 1940, d. Nov. 16, 1994) married George Washington Smith and Harold Aldridge and had one son, George Junior "Tony" Robinson. She is buried at Sardis Baptist in Iuka, MS.

10. An infant son is buried at Sardis Primitive Baptist in Alcorn County near Jacinto.

11. Annie Mae (b. May 24, 1930, d. Jun. 6, 1936) is buried in Liberty Hill.

12. Mattie Jane is buried at Mt. Gilead in Iuka, MS. *Submitted by Rosie Wilson McDougal, daughter.*

WILSON, MARGARET JANE, born 1888 and died 1973, the daughter of Samuel Thomas and Hannah Jane Kennedy Wilson. Margaret Jane married John Henry Bain (b. 1884, d. 1970). He was the son of Alford Ashworth and Mollie Brown Bain. All of the above are buried at Liberty Hill Baptist Church in Alcorn County, MS.

Henry and Margaret Jane Wilson Bain

You will find Wilson descendants in Alcorn, Prentiss and Tishomingo Counties.

Margaret and Henry had five children:

1. Annie (b. Jun. 9, 1909) married Elmer Harris and had James Arthur and Betty Jean.

2. Benjamin Howard "Buck" (b. Mar. 9, 1921) married Evelyn Jamison Hood and had Howard David, Margaret Ann, John Mitchell and Evelyn Christine.

3. Maggie Evelyn (b. Mar. 13, 1915) never married.

4. Lora Christine (b. Mar. 19, 1924) married Vernon Stout.

5. Lula Maebelle (b. Apr. 25, 1912) married William Roy Harris and had Aaron and Ruth Wayne.

Henry and Margaret farmed and raised their family around Glen. *Submitted by Mary Sue Wright, great-niece.*

WILSON, ROBERT PINKNEY, born Feb. 1, 1889 and died d. Jul. 26, 1964, the son of Samuel Thomas and Hannah Jane Kennedy Wilson. They are buried at Liberty Hill in Alcorn County. Robert married Leola Christine Woodruff, daughter of Joseph and Nancy Woodruff. Robert and Leola raised their family in the Cairo Community. They are buried in the Snowdown Church of Christ Cemetery. Robert had a twin brother, John Thomas. They both worked for the railroad at Holcut.

Robert and Leola Woodruff Wilson

Robert and Leola were the parents of nine children:

1. Cecil (b. May 15, 1917, d. Nov. 12, 1985) married Rachel Reno. They had three children: Paulina, C.J. and Gerald. Cecil and Gerald are buried at Snowdown.

2. Ruby (b. Feb. 20, 1922, d. April 1999) married Mitchell Bain and had two sons, Rickey and James Robert "Jim" and twin daughters, Ruby Joyce and Betty Jane. Ruby is buried at Liberty Hill, Alcorn County.

3. William Edward "Edd" (b. Jan. 2, 1925) married Willard Evelyn Hendrix. Their children are Wanda Lee, Wilma Christine (b. 1949, d. 1949), Donald Edward, Hilda Nadene, William Mitchell and Bobby Wayne.

4. Samuel Clayton (b. Jul. 15, 1920, d. Jun. 14, 1948) was a WWII veteran. He was killed working for the district on a dozer. He is buried at Liberty Hill.

5. Daniel Elvie "Dan" (b. Sep. 22, 1929) married Gwen Jackson. He worked for the police department in Booneville. His children are Danny, Ronnie and Sherry.

6. Lloyd (b. Jan. 19, 1927, d. Sep. 14, 1938) is buried at Liberty Hill.

7. Daisy (b. Feb. 29, 1936) married Charles Odell Thornburg. They have eight children: Robert Charles; Larry Wayne; Johnny Ellison; Randell Odell (b. 1956, d. 1980) was killed in the service and buried at Snowdown Church of Christ; Rita Mae; Retha Kaye; Clayton Junior and Tamela Ann.

8. James Pinkney (b. Jan. 2, 1934) married Rita MacMillian. They both served in the Army. James was principal at Booneville School. They have four children: James David, Diane Lynn, Dinese Faye and Douglas Lee.

9. Nina Ruth (b. Apr. 18, 1940) married Junior Ray Frost. Their children are Albert Ray, Brenda Jean, Russell Lloyd, Roy DeWayne and Wilma Christine. They live in the Cairo Community and are active in the fire department. *Submitted by children and grandchildren of Robert and Leola Wilson.*

WILSON, RUFUS EDWARD, born Dec. 31, 1896 and died Jul. 5, 1921, the son of Samuel Thomas and Hannah Jane Kennedy Wilson. Rufus married Lottie Christine Woodruff, daughter of Joseph and Nancy Woodruff of the Cairo community in Prentiss County, MS. Rufus and two of their children are buried at Sardis Primitive Baptist Church in Alcorn County near Jacinto.

Rufus Edward and Lottie Woodruff Wilson with Hilda and Effie

Rufus and Lottie had four children:

Miles Jasper (b. Feb. 8, 1916, d. Feb. 9, 1916) is buried in Sardis.

Effie Norine (b. Jan. 16, 1917) married Howard Petty. They lived in Homasassa, FL. They had a daughter, Barbara Ann.

Lottie Mae (b. Jul. 21, 1919, d. Feb. 9, 1925) is buried in Sardis.

Hildreth Christine "Hilda" (b. Dec. 10, 1921) married Eugene Petty. They lived in Florisant, MO. They had four children: Bobbie Jean, Dennis Eugene, Sharon Lynn and Ronald. *Submitted by Billy West, great-nephew.*

WILSON, SAMUEL THOMAS, born August 1862 and died in 1938. He was the son of William Thomas and Margaret Rebecca Pickens Wilson. Margaret was born in Irdell County, NC. William was born in Tennessee.

Samuel Thomas and Hannah Kennedy Wilson and children: William "Bill", Margaret, Rufus and twins, Thomas and Robert.

William Thomas served with the Mississippi 15th, Co. F in the Civil War. He died at the Battle of Fishing Creek (or the Battle of Mill Springs as named by the North) in Nancy, KY on Jan. 19, 1862. He joined at Corinth, MS and mustered in at Grenada with the Yalobusha Rifles. Margaret died giving birth to Samuel, a son his dad never knew either. He was raised by his mother's sister, Arabella Brown and her husband, Daniel. Margaret and Arabella were cousins of General Andrew Pickens.

Samuel Thomas married Hannah Jane Kennedy (b. 1862, d. 1941). She was the daughter of John Gibson and Martha Jane South Kennedy. John Gibson served with the 7th Alabama Regiment, Co. D, CSA. After the war, he pastored Mt. Gilead Baptist Church in Iuka, MS. This is where he and Martha are buried. Samuel Thomas and Hannah Jane are buried at Liberty Hill Baptist Church in Alcorn County, MS.

Sam and Hannah were the parents of five children. The children made their homes in the Alcorn, Prentiss and Tishomingo Counties. Their descendants still live in these counties and have made leaders in their communities.

William "Bill" David Gibson Wilson (b. 1885, d. 1956).

Margaret Jane Wilson Bain (b. 1883, d. 1970).
John Thomas Wilson (b. 1889, d. 1967).
Robert Pinkney (b. 1889, d. 1964).

Rufus Edward Wilson (b. 1896, d. 1921).

These five family histories are recorded in this book. *Submitted by grandchildren of Bill and Bess Wilson.*

WILSON, STITH C., born 1853 and died 1942, son of Joseph Nelson Wilson (b. 1826, d. 1911) and Martha Pardue, married Sarah McCoy (b. 1854, d. 1951). They are buried in East Prentiss Cemetery. They had three sons William Joseph, George Oliver and Charles Cleveland.

Joe married Hattie Trimue and they had two daughters, Gertrude and Eleanor.

Charlie married Elmira Hasslet. They had one son and two daughters: Charlie Jr., Louise and Sarah (Sally). Charlie Jr. died in 1958 and was buried in North Port, AL. He had no children.

George Oliver (b. Oct. 6, 1885, d. Jul. 29, 1953) married Fannie Lee in 1908. They had four sons (Horace Windel, Herman Edward, Oliver Thelman and Ellis Wayne) and a daughter (Katie Lee). Horace (b. Sep. 14, 1909, d. Nov. 18, 1997) married Mary Evelyn Gardner (b. Nov. 23, 1912, d. May 18, 1993). They had two daughters, LeDell and Barbara Nell.

Herman (b. Oct. 28, 1911, d. Apr. 12, 1980) married Gladys Massey (b. Jun. 4, 1910, d. Nov. 23, 1963). They had no children.

Thelman (b. Feb. 17, 1914) died as an infant in July 1915.

Ellis (b. Apr. 24, 1916) married Alma Bell Gardner (b. Sep. 25, 1917) on Jan. 4, 1943. They had two sons, Max Ellis (b. Jul. 24, 1944) and George Wayne (b. Mar. 15, 1948). Max married Judy Carol Hill and they had two sons, Alan Max (b. Feb. 2, 1971) and Brent Edward (b. Feb. 16, 1972). Alan married Lisa Carole King and they had one son (Billy Max) and one daughter (Alyssa Carol). Brent married Rebecca Leigh Thames. Wayne married Peggy Karen Sellers and they had three sons: Zachary Hugo (b. Jun. 21, 1982), Tyler Wayne (b. Sep. 22, 1987) and Lee Ellis (b. Jan. 21, 1991) and a daughter, Rachel Lenore (b. Sep. 21, 1983). *Submitted by Wayne Wilson.*

WILSON, WILLIAM "BILL" DAVID GIBSON, born 1885 and died 1956, the son of Samuel Thomas and Hannah Kennedy Wilson. He married Nancy Elizabeth "Bess" Bain, daughter of Alford Ashworth and Mollie Brown Bain.

Bill and Bess Wilson lived in Booneville, MS. He worked for the railroad. She was a housewife. They are buried, along with her parents, at Liberty Hill Baptist in Alcorn County. The parents of Bill are buried at Mt. Gilead Baptist in Iuka, MS.

Nancy Elizabeth "Bess" and William "Bill" Wilson

Bill had one sister, Margaret Jane and brothers, Thomas and Robert (twins) and Rufus.

Bill and Bess were the parents of 10 children:
1. Mary md. Henry Crowder.
2. John md. ?
3. Minnie md. Oscar Rodgers.
4. Ethel md. Covel Graham.
5. Ward md. Hazel Cooper.
6. Edna md. Clifford Smith.
7. Ola md. Bob Neeley.
8. Eula md. J.V. Downs, Harvey Horton.
9. Earline md. Junior Copeland.
10. Douglas md. Eloise Moss.

Bill and Bess still have grandchildren and their offspring still living in the Prentiss County area. *Submitted by Ward Wilson family.*

WINTERS, HARRIETT A. (GARNER) (JONES) AND WILLIAM TOLIVER JONES, were married about 1850 in Alabama. Their four older children: Lemuel O. Jones (b. Jun. 20, 1852); Margaret Amanda Jones (b. Jun. 25, 1855); William Richard "Bill" Jones (b. Nov. 16, 1857) and James H. "Jim" Jones (b. Oct. 13, 1859) apparently were born in Alabama, while their youngest, Martha Ann Jones, was born Jan. 9, 1862, near Baldwyn, now Prentiss County, MS. It is presumed that William Toliver died during the Civil War. The widowed Harriett Jones was enumerated at Booneville, Prentiss County in 1870 with her five fatherless children and a laborer James Lemuel Grisham, who would marry Margaret Amanda Jones on Nov. 7, 1872 in Prentiss County.

In 1878 Harriett Jones, with her two youngest children, accompanied James Lemuel and Margaret Amanda Grisham to Fannin County, TX.

Also about 1878, the first wife of William Clift Winters died in Coryell County, TX. William Clift (b. Nov. 4, 1836), son of Henry Figin Winters and Sarah F. "Sally" Renfro, was a very lonely man. He decided to ride his mule back to Prentiss County to marry his former neighbor, the Widow Jones. Upon arrival in Booneville, William Clift learned that his intended bride had gone to Texas. This news did not deter him. He was a determined man! William Clift, astride his mule, followed Harriet Jones to Texas.

William Clift took his new wife with her two younger children, James H. and Martha Ann, to Langford Cove (now Evant) in Coryell County before 1880. William Clift Winters (d. Jun. 27, 1914), his mother, Sarah F. "Sally" Renfro Winters (b. Sep. 13, 1798, d. Feb. 10, 1880) and Harriett Garner (Jones) Winters (b. Jul. 15, 1833, d. Sep. 24, 1906) were interred in Murphree Cemetery in Evant, Hamilton County, TX.

Lemuel O. Jones married Betty Oakley. Their children were: Emma, Sidney R., Roxie J. and Tom Jones.

Children of Margaret Amanda and James Lemuel Grisham Sr. were: William Richard; James Lemuel Jr.; Ida Rose Anna; Charles Ephraim; Jesse Andrew; an infant son; Harriet Lou Emma; Addie May and Claude Virgil Grisham. Margaret Amanda and James Lemuel were buried in Murphree Cemetery in Hamilton County, TX.

William Richard Jones married Julia Tucker. William and Julia were buried in the Blackland Cemetery near Booneville, Prentiss County. Their children were Oscar Newton and William Toliver Jones, II.

James H. Jones married Pernina Jane Coker on Dec. 22, 1880 in Hamilton County, TX. James was ambushed and murdered as he went to tend his horses on May 30, 1882. Jim was buried in Murphree Cemetery in Evant, Hamilton County, TX. They had one son, William Charles Jones, Sr., DDS.

Martha Ann Jones married Joseph Evans Snider. Their children were: Bertha May; Ethel Gertrude; Enoch Marmaduke; Annie Myrtle; William Sidney; Maude Coilla; Maggie Eleanor; Joseph Lemuel; Jess; Addie Laura and James Snider. Martha and Joseph were buried in Murphree Cemetery in Evant, TX. *Submitted by Elreeta Crain Weathers, great-granddaughter of Margaret Amanda Jones Grisham, 806 Barkley Drive, Hamilton, TX 76531, ecw@htcomp.net. SOURCES: Crain, Clara Elsie Fergusson. Grisham, James "Jim" Cornelius. Grisham, Sr. James "Jim" Lemuel – Death Record, Hamilton County, TX, Volume 5, page 23, #592. Grisham, Mrs. J.L. – Newspaper obituary, Nov. 20, 1936, "Hamilton Herald-Record". Grisham, Margaret Amanda Jones – Death Record, Hamilton County, TX, Volume 5, page 49, #1341. Gurney, Bill – "Cemeteries of Prentiss County, MS." Hamilton County Historical Commission, "James L. Grisham, Sr. Family" by Elreeta Crain Weathers, from "A History of Hamilton County, TX", Taylor Publishing Co., Dallas, TX, 1979, Page 173. Jones, Mrs. William C., "In*

Memoriam – In Memory of My Husband" published in the "Hamilton (Tex) Herald-News", Feb. 21, 1958. Mayben, Norma. Marriage Record, Prentiss County, MS for James Lemuel Grisham and Margaret Amanda Jones. Perry, Rebecca Jane. Tombstones, Murphree Cemetery, Evant, TX. 1870 US Census, Prentiss County, MS; 1880 US Census, Fannin County, TX and 1900, 1910 and 1920 US Census, Hamilton County, TX.

WOMACK, LEE MONROE, the Womack family came from England to the state of Virginia and migrated to old Tishomingo County by the way of the Carolinas, Tennessee and Alabama.

L.M. Womack family. "Golden Wedding Anniversary" Dec. 26, 1950, Booneville, MS. Helen, Earl, Bertha, Louise and Mr. and Mrs. Lee Womack.

Lee Monroe Womack (b. Sep. 10, 1874, d. Nov. 28, 1952) was the son of William Pinckney Womack (b. Jan. 14, 1831, d. Jan. 10, 1898) and Lydia Moore Womack (b. Aug. 13, 1837, d. Nov. 24, 1912). Lee married Ada Belle Hughes (b. Dec. 1, 1882, d. Dec. 30, 1969), the daughter of Mr. and Mrs. Elisha Wroten Hughes, on Dec. 25, 1900. Both are buried in the Booneville Cemetery. They were the parents of Carrie Helen, Lydia Bertha, Earl Brewer and Myrtis Louise. The family lived in Marietta before moving to Booneville. Lee Womack was an extensive landowner, merchant and ginner. He was elected to the Prentiss County board of supervisors from the fourth district for two terms (1920-1924 and 1924-1928). He served as the president of the board for both terms. He was elected sheriff of Prentiss County for the 1928-1932 term.

Carrie Helen Womack (b. Sep. 22, 1901, d. Mar. 10, 1989) married Harace A. Googe (b. Mar. 6, 1899, d. Aug. 9, 1950) in June 1920. He was the son of Mr. and Mrs. Henry Googe of the Pleasant Valley Community. Both are buried in the Booneville Cemetery. They had one daughter, Dorothy Helen (b. Sep. 10, 1927). Harace Googe was a lumberman, merchant and co-owner of the Marietta Gin Co., a Booneville Gin and the Ozark Gin Co. Dorothy Helen graduated from Mississippi State University and received a master's degree from Memphis State University. She retired from the Memphis City School System. She married Charles Robbins (b. Aug. 28, 1927) on Sep. 18, 1954. He was office manager of the Illinois Central Railroad of Memphis. They have two daughters, Deborah Helen (b. May 27, 1955) and Donna Louise (b. Jul. 7, 1960). Deborah and Donna are both graduates of Memphis State University with master's degrees. Deborah has 45 hours beyond her master's. Both are employed by the Memphis City School System. Deborah married Teddy Ray Pierce Mar. 11, 1979. Donna married Stephen William Reid Aug. 11, 1979. They have one daughter, Ashley Helen Reid (b. Oct. 27, 1980), who is a student at the University of Mississippi. Stephen and Donna are divorced. Donna married David Bohannan in 1982. They have one son, Wesley Alan (b. Nov. 28, 1984). He is a student of Southaven Middle School. Dorothy's family lives in Southaven and will be buried in the Booneville Cemetery.

Lydia Bertha (b. May 16, 1905, d. Dec. 14, 1995) graduated from Mississippi Southern University and taught school at Pisgah and Belmont. She married Carroll Yarber (b. Apr. 20, 1900, d. Aug. 1, 1984) of Belmont. They built and operated the Town Motel and Restaurant. Carroll has been associated with the banking business in North Mississippi for over 50 years. He served as director emeritus of the Bank of Mississippi.

Earl Brewer Womack (b. Jul. 9, 1907, d. Sep. 14, 1973) married Annie Lou Houston on Mar. 8, 1930, the daughter of Mr. and Mrs. Ortha Houston of Kirkville. Annie Lou resides at the Landmark Retirement Home. Earl is a veteran of WWII; served as deputy sheriff under his father and Jim Thomas and was appointed game warden with the Mississippi Wildlife and Fish Commission. The Earl B. Womack Hunting Association in Prentiss County is named for him.

Myrtis Louise Womack (b. Apr. 9, 1915, d. Sep. 19, 1997) graduated from Delta State Teacher's College and received a master's degree from Georgia Peabody College. She taught in the Prentiss County High Schools, Kossuth High School, West Point High School and the Northeast Mississippi Junior College. She married LaBeaume Woolridge (Het) Peeler (b. Feb. 25, 1906, d. Apr. 24, 1973) on Jun. 14, 1945, the son of Mr. and Mrs. Walton Peeler. He was a veteran of WWII and a salesman.

Bertha, Carroll, Earl, Louise and Het are buried in the Booneville Cemetery. *Submitted by Dorothy Googe Robbins.*

WOODARD-MCKINNEY NELDA DEAN, born Dec. 16, 1943. Nelda is the daughter of Winston Jasper "Wink" Vanderford (b. Mar. 9, 1916, d. Apr. 17, 1989) and Ella Missouri Woodruff Vanderford (b. Feb. 21, 1913, d. Sep. 2, 1991) who married on Jun. 23, 1933. Nelda is the granddaughter of Charlie Edward Woodruff (b. Feb. 25, 1891, d. Dec. 28, 1966) and Minnie Odell Stone Woodruff (b. Apr. 6, 1893, d. May 6, 1961). Winston and Ella Vanderford and Charlie and Minnie Woodruff are buried in the Snowdown Church of Christ Cemetery in Prentiss County.

Justin, Paul Ray, Lisa, Courtney McKinney

Nelda is also the granddaughter of Mark Vanderford (b. Sep. 15, 1879, d. Oct. 3, 1938) and Neal Samantha Maness Vanderford (b. Jul. 3, 1881, d. Mar. 9, 1958) who married on Aug. 20, 1900. They are buried in Juliette Cemetery in Alcorn County.

John and Nelda have one daughter, Lisa Dawn Woodard McKinney (b. Jan. 3, 1969) who married Paul Ray McKinney (b. Dec. 17, 1964) on Feb. 14, 1987. Their children are Justin Cody McKinney (b. Dec. 25, 1988) and Courtney Dawn McKinney (b. Apr. 26, 1994). Nelda has one brother, James Hulon Vanderford (b. Mar. 25, 1934), two sisters: Waynona Mayvene Vanderford Davis (b. Nov. 25, 1935 and Hazel Jean Vanderford (b. Apr. 9, 1939).

Justin's great-grandmother, Ella Missouri Woodruff Vanderford, baby-sat him until her death Sep. 2, 1991. He gave her many hours of joy. *Submitted by Nelda Dean Vanderford Woodard.*

WOODRUFF, CHARLIE EDWARD, born Feb. 25, 1891 and died Dec. 28, 1996) married Minnie Odell Stone (b. Apr. 6, 1893, d. May 6, 1961) on Aug. 2, 1910 in Selmer, TN. Charlie was the son of Joseph Hightower (b. Jul. 16, 1867, d. Apr. 24, 1944) and Nancy Caroline Smith (b. Oct. 11, 1864, d. Oct. 31, 1901), married Jul. 21, 1888.

Charlie's siblings: Clora M. Woodruff Rickman (b. May 2, 1889, d. Apr. 17, 1922); Gordon E. Woodruff (b. Feb. 25, 1893, d. Dec. 19, 1967); Lila N. Woodruff Pounds (b. Mar. 6, 1895, d. Sep. 6, 1948); Blunt M. Woodruff (b. Feb. 19, 1897, d. Dec. 6, 1992); Lottie L. Woodruff Wilson Wroten (b. Apr. 17, 1898); Leola C. Woodruff Wilson (b. Apr. 26, 1900, d. Dec. 27, 1968).

Charlie and Minnie Woodruff

Nancy died and was buried in Tennessee. Joseph married Johnnie Lucinda Smith Woodruff (b. Nov. 20, 1871, d. Mar. 30, 1952) on Aug. 17, 1902. Their children were: William Kelly (b. Jan. 4, 1904, d. Aug. 9, 1970); Joseph M. (b. Aug. 28, 1906, d. Dec. 29, 1986); Daniel B. (b. Feb. 2, 1908, d. Mar. 10, 1972); Leah A. Woodruff Edge (b. Nov. 17, 1909, d. Mar. 17, 1969); Fannie M. Woodruff Strickland (b. Sep. 29, 1911, d. Aug. 2, 1957); Douglas M. Woodruff (b. Aug. 9, 1914, d. Oct. 20, 1992).

Charlie and Minnie are buried in the Snowdown Church of Christ Cemetery in Prentiss County. Charlie's father and stepmother are buried in the Snowdown Church of Christ Cemetery in Prentiss County. Joseph Hightower first taught school, preached and was buried in Snowdown.

Charlie and Minnie Woodruff's children:

1) Edith Woodruff (b. Jul. 10, 1911) md. Jay J. White (b. Dec. 20, 1907, d. Jul. 26, 1999) on Jan. 13, 1929. Jay was the son of Amos and Anna White. They are buried in Tennessee. Jay and Edith had no children. Jay is buried in the Snowdown Church of Christ Cemetery in Prentiss County.

2) Ella Missouri Woodruff (b. Feb. 21, 1913, d. Sep. 2, 1991) md. Winston Jasper "Wink" Vanderford (b. Mar. 9, 1916, d. Apr. 17, 1989) on Jun. 23, 1933. Wink's parents were Mark Vanderford (b. Sep. 15, 1879, d. Oct. 3, 1938) and Neal Samantha Maness (b. Jul. 3, 1881, d. Mar. 9, 1958) who married on Aug. 20, 1900. They were buried in Juliette Cemetery in Alcorn County. Ella and Wink's children are as follows:

a) James Hulon (b. Mar. 25, 1934). (See James Hulon Vanderford.)

b) Waynona Mayvene Vanderford Davis (b. Nov. 25, 1935). (See Garvin Earl Davis.)

c) Hazel Jean (b. Apr. 9, 1939). (See Hazel Jean Vanderford.)

d) Nelda Dean Vanderford Woodard (b. Dec. 16, 1943.) (See Nelda Dean Woodard.)

Charlie and Minnie Woodruff lived in Alcorn and Prentiss County when they died. *Submitted by Waynona Davis.*

WREN, JAMES ALBERT AND MARY JANE DOWNING, were my great-great-grandparents. They were married in Itawamba County, MS on Jun. 11, 1866.

Grandpa James Albert was born in Madison or Marion County, AL in 1846. I don't have any information on Grandma Mary Jane's family. She was born in 1844, died in 1915 and is buried at Jacinto Cemetery.

Grandpa James A. was the son of George W. Wren born in 1804 in Virginia and his mother was Mary Ann Hughes. His parents were married on Sep. 6, 1827. They were believed to be farmers. Their children born in Alabama were Robert H. (b. Jun. 8, 1828), Martha (b. 1829), George (b. 1833), Nancy (b. 1835), Sara R. (b. 1837), William R. (b. 1841), Mary T. (b. 1845), James Albert (b. 1846). The last three children

James Albert and two of his sons

were born in Itawamba County, MS and they were Elizabeth C. (b. 1849), Francis W. (b. 1851) and Andrew J. (b. 1853). They were probably farmers or merchants.

Although, great-great-grandpa James Albert lived in Mississippi, he went to Rock Hill, SC to join the South Carolina Volunteers. He was with Co. H, 12th Regiment of the Confederate Army. He was only 15 years old at that time. He fought with the SC Vol. until the end of the war. He was with his CO at Appomattox on Apr. 9, 1865 at the surrender of the Confederate Army. When the war was over he returned to his parents in Itawamba County, MS. There, he met and married grandma Mary Jane Downing. They had a daughter, Nancy (b. Nov. 18, 1866). Nancy lived until Sep. 28, 1876. She is buried at the Salem Cemetery in Itawamba County, MS. Their other children were George Washington (b. Oct. 9, 1869) md. Mertie Whitlock; Martha (b. Sep. 9, 1870) was the mother of my grandfather, Oscar Wren. She married William L. Gilley. She died in 1956 and was buried in Jonesboro, AR.

James Robert (b. 1872); Bell (b. November 1874); Alonzo C. (b. Sep. 5, 1877); Wister A. (b. Nov. 14, 1879); Walter Lee (b. May 5, 1884) md. Rozela "Rosie" Wren, daughter of Stephen T "Bud" and Dicie Ann (Williams) Clark. They had another son named Charles H. (b. 1881). Oscar, my grandpa, was claimed as their son and went by the Wren name. He was born Apr. 25, 1887 and died Dec. 4, 1918 of influenza.

At some time grandpa and grandma Wren moved to the Snowdown Community. He worked for the postal service as a mail carrier and carried mail back and forth between the post office and the trains somewhere in what was then known as Tishomingo County. Grandma Mary Jane died in 1915. Grandpa James Albert lived until 1934. They are both buried in the Jacinto Cemetery. There is a marker for grandma but I haven't been able to locate one for grandpa. *Submitted by Mauvolene (Rinehart) Dawson.*

WREN, NANCY JANE, daughter of Oscar and Dora Dallas (Clark) Wren. (See Wren-Clark-Armstrong Families). She married John Henry Rinehart, son of John and Elzetta (Rogers) Rinehart. They lived in the Rienzi Community. Grandpa Rinehart farmed and had part interest in a gristmill with his brother, Frank Rinehart. Grandpa also had a Sorghum mill that he pulled by wagon to people's farms where he processed their sugarcane into sorghum molasses. They are both deceased and are buried at Sardis Cemetery.

Nancy Jane, Jimmy and Mauvolene

My parents, John and Nancy, had three children. Their first child was a son who died soon after his birth and was never named. I was their second child and they named me Marion Mauvolene. I was born Aug. 16, 1931 at Rienzi, MS. Their third child was my brother, James Harold "Jimmy" (b. Nov. 5, 1933). My mother and father were divorced when Jimmy and I were small children. My father died in December 1962 and is buried at in the National Cemetery in Corinth, MS.

After my parents divorced, my mother Nancy, Jimmie and I moved to the Snowdown Community where we lived with grandpa George and grandma Dora Armstrong." See Wren-Clark-Armstrong families." Grandpa and Grandma farmed a big farm. They raised cotton, corn and vegetables. They also had a big orchard where they grew all kinds of fruit. They raised and sold sweet potatoes. I remember the good times we had there. Back then your neighbors were there for you when you had trouble or were sick. They made homemade ice-cream on Saturday night and the boys played music or listened to the radio. We went to church at Snowdown Church of Christ on Wednesday night and Sunday.

After Jimmy and I were grown, my mother worked in the shirt factory in Rienzi, MS. She then married Irving Rorie and they had a store at Jacinto, MS. Mister Irvin died and is buried at Sardis. My mother became disabled and came to live with me in Memphis in 1969. She died in 1989 and is buried at Jacinto.

Jimmy married Denise Depardiue who is from France. They live in North Carolina and are divorced. They had four sons. One son, 1) David, died and is buried in North Carolina where they live. Their other sons are 2) John Wayne who has three children: Lisa Marie (married Christan and has a son Brandon); 3) Richard lives in Chicago and has never married and 4) Jean Claud who has a son, Zachary Scott and also lives in North Carolina.

I married James Ferrell Davis and was divorced. I have four daughters: Peggy Jean, Nancy Carol, Patricia Ann and Dixie Renau. Peggy was married to Walter Ray Hodge II. They are divorced and have a daughter, Jeralynne (Hodge) Moser, who has three children: Christopher Lee Bryant whose father, Billy Bryant, is deceased. She was married to Bryan Moser and they are divorced. Their children are Shelby Daniel and Gregory Keith. Peggy has a son, Walter Ray Hodge III. He was married to Kim Johnston and they are divorced. He is now married to Stephanie (Grant) Hodge and his children live with them. His daughter is Chelsea Rae and son is Andrew Dawson (Drew) Hodge. Nancy Carol married Tommy Shears and they are divorced.

They have two daughters, Laura Lynn who married Cliff Magowan and they have a daughter, Brooke Daniel and a son, James Tanner. Carol's other daughter is Amy Jo Shears and she is not married. Patricia Ann married Kenneth Wayne Cozart and has one daughter, Melissa Ann (Cozart) Crawford who married Stephan Crawford. They have a son, Kevin Wayne and a daughter, Jordyn Renee. Dixie Renau was married to Hatem Houtari who we believe was killed during the Gulf War. They had one son Michael Wayne.

After I was divorced from James Ferrell Davis, I married Freeman John Dawson and we have two sons: Dan Freeman married Cindy (Sims), has two daughters, Kathryn Louise "Katie" and Emily Caroline. Youngest son, Gary Brett, married Charlene Timbs and has a daughter, Brettney Jean. Freeman is deceased and was buried near Boliver, TN. I live in Southaven, MS with my daughter, Dixie and a grandson, Michael Wayne. *Submitted by Mauvolene (Rinehart) Dawson.*

WREN-CLARK-ARMSTRONG, my grandparents were Oscar and Dora Dallas (Clark) Wren. Oscar was the son of Martha (Wren) Gilley who was married to William Gilley. His grandparents were James Albert and Mary Jane (Downing) Wren who raised him. He went by the Wren name. His uncles were George Washington who married Mertie Whitlock, James Robert, Alonzo C., Wister A., Walter Lee who married Rozela "Rosie" Clark. (See Clark Williams.) His other uncle was Charles H. He had one aunt named Bell.

Oscar, Dora, Noel and Nancy

Grandma Dora was the daughter of Stephen Taylor "Bud" and Dicie Ann (Williams) Clark. Grandma's brothers were William Henry, Alexander "Alex" and her sisters were Harriet Smith, Artie Stephenson, Rozela "Rosie" Wren, Annie McGaughey. She had one half-brother, Joseph "Joe" Clark and two half-sisters, Mary Lou Woodruff and Jessie May Armstrong.

When my grandparents first married, they lived with his grandparents, James A. and Mary J. Wren. Grandpa Oscar and Grandma Dora later owned a house and farm, which they rented out after they moved to the Jacinto Community. It was just north of the Bluehill Firetower and was sold to Archie Tennison after Grandpa Oscar died.

Grandpa Oscar and Grandma Dora moved to the Jacinto Community where they owned a mercantile and grocery store. They had two children, Melvin Noel (b. 1908) was the oldest. They had a daughter, Nancy Jane (b. Sep. 21, 1909). Noel died from Pneumonia in 1928 and is buried at Jacinto.

Grandma Dora, Noel and Nancy, all had influenza and that left Grandpa Oscar to care for them as so many other people were sick and dying. When they were almost well, he became sick and died Dec. 4, 1908. He is buried at the Jacinto Cemetery.

After Grandpa Oscar died, grandma Dora in 1920 married George Washington Armstrong, son of Charlie and Mary Jane Armstrong. They lived for some years in the Jacinto Community. They moved to the Snowdown Community where Grandpa Armstrong farmed and sold Woodman of the World Insurance.

They later sold their farm to Irving Lambert. The farm was across the road from the Archie and Jessie Armstrong places. They had four children: Warren, Glenn, Allen "Poochy" and Cleatous who married Arlie Woodruff.

Grandpa Armstrong had four children by his first wife. They were Hester Wade, Ila Wade, Artie Lambert, Vista Rinehart and twins, Iness Williams and Eunice (Taylor) Barnett. He also had one son, Archie, who married grandma's half sister, Jessie May Clark.

Grandpa Armstrong and Grandma Dora are both buried at the Snowdown Church of Christ Cemetery. *Submitted by Mauvolene (Rinehart) Dawson.*

YATES, CHARLIE EDGAR, born 1892 and died 1974, son of William David and Julia Green Yates. He married Martha Florence (1892, d. 1972), daughter of Anna Caver and Jacob Berry Moore, on Aug. 13, 1911. Both came from early pioneer families in the Dry Creek and Jumpertown area. They had seven children. Hoyle Heath (b. 1918, d. 1920) and Jacob Lamont (b. 1925, d. 1926) died in infancy.

Charlie Cullen (b. 1912, d. 1992) married Lucille Michael (b. 1912, d. 1971), the daughter of Alice Geno and Joe Michael in 1931. Cullen farmed and ran service stations and worked for MDOT until his retirement. He married Betty Latham in 1971. Cullen and Lucille had six children.

Eugene (b. 1934) married Hazel Simmons and they had Monty Gene and Edwin. Monty married Diane Sullivan and has two daughters and a stepson. Edwin married Wanda Hicks and has Jeremy.

Charlie Edgar and Martha Florence Yates. Taken in 1961 at home of David Yates in Osborne Creek

Elizabeth (b. 1935) married Norman English (b. 1935, d. 1998) and had Norma Jo. She married (1) Marcus Stroupe and had Lori, (2) Davy Whitley and had Marci and (3) Billy Jones. Lori married Mikel Sims and has a daughter, Kaylee.

Keith (b. 1937) married Jettie Maness and had Ronald, Teresa, Benjy, Jennifer and Johnny. Ronald married (1) Charlotte Ford and had Christy and Heather, (2) Lisa Gray and had Lana. Teresa married Charles Cole and has Justin and Jordan. Benjy married (1) Carolyn Davis, (2) Kathy Davis and has Katlin and Jared. Jennifer married Andy Copeland and has Nikki and T.J. Johnny is married to Keri Jackson.

Millard (b. 1939, d. 1999) married Patricia Tedford and had Frankie, who married (1) Jill Brooks, (2) Jacqui Thweatt and has Wesley and Landon. Herbert married Jamie Sallis and has Kelsey and Cullen. Steven married (1) Angela Eaton, (2) Misty Michael. Millard loved to play his guitar and banjo and sing and was pastor at Fairview Baptist Church at the time of his death.

Sandra (b. 1943) married Harvey L. (Buster) Green in 1963 and has three daughters. Sonya married Jarrod Holloway; Melanie married Todd Swinney and has Carter and LaWanna.

Francile (b. 1951) married Rickie Davis and has Cassandra, who married Tim Stewart. She has a son, Rickie Cade and two stepchildren. Madonna married Kevin Michael and has Tristan and Lily. Penny married Shea Padgett and has twin daughters, Emma and Parker. *Submitted by Francile Yates Davis, 130 CR 8401, Rienzi, MS 38865.*

YATES, GALE, born in 1921, was the third son of Martha Florence and Charlie Edgar Yates. He married Ellie Pearl Yates (b. 1926, d. 1993) in 1946. She was the daughter of Ivey Cartwright and Earl Sappington. They had Rosemary, Gale Jr., Mitchell and Ricky. Gale worked at Baptist Hospital and farmed before retiring.

David Moore Yates, William Heath Yates (cousin), Gale L. Yates and Charlie Cullen Yates. David, Gale and Charlie are brothers.

Billy Joe (b. 1927) married Mary Lou (b. 1930), daughter of Mr. and Mrs. Grover Estes in 1950. He worked at Brown Shoe Co. and attended NEMCC and graduated from Mississippi State University. They moved to Missouri where he taught school until he retired. They have five sons: (1) Roger (b. 1954) married Bonnie Williams and has Shannon and Amy; (2) Gregory (b. 1956) first married Debbie Harness, then Marcia Finley and has Brian; (3) Gilbert (b. 1958) married Renea Christenson; (4) Gary (b. 1961) first married Paula Hill, then Nancy Dimond and has Amanda ? and Stewart and (5) Mark (b. 1963) married Denise ? and has Nicole.

Mary Ann (b. 1927, twin) married Dexter Crow (b. 1926, d. 1993). They had a daughter, Linda, who married David Smith. They lived in Battle Creek, MI, for years before retiring to New Site.

David Moore (b. 1931) was the youngest child. He served in the US Air Force for four years. He married Shirley, daughter of Alice Avery and Michael O'Connor, on Aug. 9, 1952 in Sault Ste. Marie, MI. David attended NEMCC and graduated from MSU. Shirley attended MCMT, Soo Branch, MSU and graduated from the University of Michigan. They moved to Missouri in 1962 and taught at R-14 School at Lonedell and R-2 School at New Haven for 19 years. They came back to Mississippi and David worked at Plumrose and Prentiss Manufacturing and Shirley at Brown Shoe, Jitney Jungle and Prentiss Manufacturing before retiring. They have three children: Michael (b. 1953) first married Connie Hoerstkamp and had Joshua and Michele and then married Janie Biggs and had Chelsea and Cameron. They live in Hallsville, MO. He is district manager for B&G Co. Industrial Cleaners. David Jr. (b. 1955) first married Donna Struebberg and had David III. He then married Cindy Gale. He has three stepchildren, a grandson, Drake and two step-grandchildren. He is a graduate of Marymount College and lives in Hermann, MO. Susan (b. 1958) graduated from Burge School of Nursing in Springfield, MO. She is married to Terry Schroeder and has Amanda, a student at the University of Iowa and Paul, a sophomore at Sycamore High School in Sycamore, IL. She works at the University of Illinois at DeKalb. Terry works at a print shop and is an electrician. *Submitted by Shirley O'Connor Yates, 11 CR 7381, Booneville, MS 38829.*

YATES, WILLIAM H. "BILLY," born about 1807 in Madison County, KY, to Joshua Yates and his wife, Martha Stewart. William "Billy" died in 1887 in Prentiss County, MS. His parents had moved to Bedford County, TN by the 1812 tax list and he married there about 1827 to Mary Ann Moore, daughter of James Moore and wife, Mary, maiden name unknown. Mary Ann Moore Yates was born in North Carolina about 1803 and died

William H. "Billy" Yates 1807-1887.

in old Tishomingo County, MS by 1860-1861. She is likely buried in an unmarked grave near her daughter, Sarah. This family first moved to Marshall County, MS in the early to mid 1840s and then on to old Tishomingo County. Most of the children settled in northeast Mississippi. They are listed as follows:

1. Joshua W. Yates was born in 1829 in Tennessee. He married in 1856 a young widow, Lydia Emaline -?- McElory, in Mississippi and evidently died in the Civil War, leaving two children, William Joshua Yates and Texanna Yates (a daughter).

2. James T. Yates (b. 1831 in Tennessee and died in 1868-70 in Mississippi) married Aug. 11, 1861 (Tippah County record) Martha Jane Jumper, daughter of Charles Gunrod Jumper and his first wife, Elmira Catherine Jowers. James T. and Martha Jane Jumper Yates had three children: Margaret Rebecca Yates (wife of Henry L. Davis); John Henry Yates, who married Matilda Jane Wooley (grandparents of William Hershel McDowell) and William Franklin Yates, who married first Alice Taylor, second Sally Taylor Sawyer and third Emma Inlow Burns. These families all lived mainly in Tippah County, MS and are documented in *Tippah County Mississippi Heritage, Volumes I and II.*

3. Mary Ann Yates married James (Monroe) H. Miller.

4. William H. Yates died Jul. 3, 1863 in the Battle of Gettysburg in the Civil War. He married in 1856 in Mississippi to Mary Ann Lester and left two sons, William David and John Yates. Mary Ann then married Blake Mauldin.

5. John Patton Yates was born in 1836 in Bedford County, TN and died in 1883 in Sharp County, AR. He married Jan. 27, 1856, to Julia Ann Spain, a daughter of James and Lydia Gambill Spain, another Bedford County, TN family, who moved to Mississippi. In fact, Lydia Gambill Spain became the second wife of old "Billy" Yates, following the death of his wife, Mary Ann.

6. Elijah Marion Yates was born by 1838 in Tennessee and evidently died before 1870. He married Mary Elizabeth Jane Mullins in Mississippi. He served with the "Blackland Gidoenets" in the Civil War.

7. Hardin Harrison Yates and his family were written up in *Prentiss County History, Volume I.*

8. Martha Jane Yates (b. 1843, d. 1915) married in 1861 to Henry Washington Spain.

9. Margaret Caroline Yates (b. 1847, d. 1880) married in 1864 to Phillip James Jumper, son of James A. and Eliza James Jumper.

10. Sarah F. Yates (b. 1850, d. 1852) was born in Marshall County, MS and was buried in Jumpertown Cemetery.

11. George W. Yates (b. 1854) married in 1871 in Alcorn County, MS to Mary E. Carpenter. *Submitted by Mrs. Bobbie D. McDowell.*

YATES, WILLIAM H. "BILLY" (YEATES), settled in what is now the Jumpertown area of present Prentiss County, MS in 1852. It was still a part of Tishomingo County at that time. He was the son of Joshua Yates (b. 1776, d. 1849) and wife, Martha Stewart (b. 1775/1780, d. 1840/1843). Both Joshua and Martha were born in North Carolina, place unknown. They both died in Bedford County, TN and are believed buried in unmarked graves at the site of the extinct Sugar Creek Baptist Church near Flat Creek. They were married Sep. 17, 1795 in Madison County, KY.

Joshua's parents have not been proved, but he is believed the son of a John Yates of Madison County. At least two likely siblings were Margaret "Peggy" Yates, wife of William Stewart, who is believed a brother of Martha Stewart Yates and John Yates (b. 1770, d. 1850), who reared a large family in Kentucky. The Stewarts moved to Tennessee with the Joshua Yates family by 1810 to 1812. In Kentucky, the Yates families were members of the Viney Fork Baptist Church, located in the eastern part of the county. Viney Fork was constituted in 1797 and first called "The United Baptist Church of Christ on Muddy Creek." Joshua Yates was a farmer and Primitive Baptist preacher. Both the Yates and Stewart families were connected with the Sugar Creek Baptist Church, on the waters of the Duck River in Bedford County, TN. After Martha's death about 1843, he then married Sarah J. Moore Pybass on Jan. 25, 1844 (Lincoln County, TN record). One of her Pybass sons ended up in northeast Mississippi.

The 10 children of Joshua and Martha are proved by Bedford County, TN, court records (copies in my files). They are listed here:

1. Elizabeth Yates (b. 1796, d. 1851) married in 1817 or 1818 to Joseph Patton, who died before Dec. 18, 1851 in Marshall County, MS. This family moved

to Mississippi before 1849. The Pattons were gone from Marshall County records by 1860.

2. Sarah Yates (b. 1798, d. 1872) was born in Kentucky and married in Bedford County, TN to John Patton (b. 1789, d. 1862). They moved to Lawrence County, MO.

3. Hannah Yates (b. 1800, d. 1885) was born in Kentucky and died in present Benton County, MS. She married in 1822 in Bedford County, TN to Samuel Patton Balch, son of Amos Balch and Ann Patton. This family moved to Tippah County, MS after the 1850 census.

4. Anna Yates (b. 1802, d. 1885) was born in Kentucky and died in Bedford County, TN. She married Joseph Morton and reared a large family.

5. William H. "Billy" Yates (b. 1807, d. 1887) was born in Kentucky and died in Prentiss County, MS. He first married, about 1826 or 1827 in Benton County, TN to Mary Ann Moore (see their story).

6. Rebecca Yates (b. 1810, d. 1843/1849) was also born in Kentucky and died in Bedford County, TN. She was the wife of Tyra Harrison and left a large family named in the court proceedings of Joshua's estate settlement.

7. Nancy Yates married Joseph Bartlett and was said to have lived in Cape Girardeau, MO.

8. Isabella "Ibby" Yates was born about 1815 in Bedford County, TN and married about 1835 to Elijah Vickers. They lived in Lincoln County, TN.

9. Martha "Patsy" Yates (b. 1818, d. 1880) lived in Bedford County, TN where she married Jesse Brown.

10. Malinda Yates (b. 1820, d. 1845) married John Umpstead Bledsoe, who died during the Civil War.

The parents of Martha Stewart Yates and William Stewart, who married Margaret Yates, have not been found. William and Margaret Stewart reared a large family in Bedford County, TN. Their children married into the Dixon, Holt, Hix, Gurley and Gambill families there. A daughter, Jemima Stewart (b. 1799, d. 1871), was born in Kentucky, married Jesse Gurley in Bedford County, TN and moved to Marshall County, MS where Jesse died in 1844. Jemima Stewart Gurley died in 1872 in Alcorn County, MS.

Joshua and Martha Stewart Yates were ancestors of my late husband, William Hershel McDowell. These families were documented by personal research here in Mississippi in Bedford County, TN and in Richmond, Madison County, KY. *Submitted by Mrs. Bobbie D. McDowell.*

YATES, WILLIAM HEATH "BUD," born to William David and Julia Green Yates on Feb. 10, 1882. He had an older sister, Mary (Mrs. John W. Jumper) (b. 1880, d. 1943) and he was the oldest son of 12 children.

He married (1) ? McCombs and had a son, Arnold, who lived and died in Missouri. He had two daughters. His second wife was Alisha Tarrant (Toddy) Moore (b. 1896, d. 1971), daughter of Jacob Berry Moore and Anna Caver Moore. They married on Feb. 10, 1915 and lived in Prentiss County for several years before moving to Arkansas in 1922 and later to California.

He and Toddy had seven children:
Julia Edith (b. 1916) married Tom Cole in 1938. He was a widower with two sons. They lived in Salinas for many years and Edith still does. Tom died in 1988.

William Heath Yates

Velma Azilee (b. 1917, d. 1999) married Pete Durham in 1942. They had six children: Charles, Viola, David, Allen, Frances and Carol. Azilee also had a son, Billy Zeb.

They moved to California and stayed for many years and then came back to Mississippi. Viola died in Arkansas, leaving a husband and five children.

Winona (b. 1920, d. 1976) married David Baker (died in 1994) and had two sons, David Allen Jr. and Gary Lynn (b. 1945, d. 1968). She died of a heart attack and her son of cancer in Salinas, CA.

Anna Helen (b. 1922) was born in Prentiss County just before the family moved to Craighead County, AR. She married Ralph Patterson in California and had four children: Phyllis, Jack, Ralph and Timothy (b. 1959, d. 1992). She is divorced and lives in Salinas, CA.

Hazel Maxine (b. 1926) was born in Arkansas. She married (1) ? Pitts and had a son, Jerry (b. 1942); (2) John Lumsden and had Richard (b. 1947). They live in Salinas, CA.

William Heath (b. 1928, d. 1997) was the only son. He married Betty Baze in 1948 in Greenfield, CA. They had seven daughters and one son. He moved his family and his parents to Mississippi twice. He bought a farm and also ran the Sinclair station with his cousin, Cullen Yates. Betsy (Riehle) (b. 1949) has two sons; Martha (Hicks) (b. 1952) has Nathan. Winona (b. 1954) is single. Susan (Bishop) (b. 1956) has three sons. William "Bill" (b. 1959) has two children; Jane O' Toole (b. 1962); Jo Ann Smithers (b. 1964) has two stepchildren and Elizabeth Calderon (b. 1968) has Victor. The family lived in Salinas and then El Centro. Jane is the only child born in Booneville, MS. William died in 1997 while visiting his daughter, Susan, near Cloverdale, CA.

Wanda (b. 1933) married Milton Mocettini in 1953. They have four children: Mark, Kari, Paul and Todd. They and their family live in the Salinas area.

Toddy died in 1971 and Bud in 1977 at age 95. They are buried in the Jumpertown Cemetery where most of their brothers and sisters are buried.

William and Charlie Yates married sisters, Florence and Toddy Moore, so their children were double first cousins. *Submitted by Betty Baze Yates, 1681 Aurora El Centro, CA 92243.*

YOUNG, MYRTLE MAY, born 1879, purchased the Prentiss Hotel in 1921 from an aunt. The Prentiss Hotel was located at 212 Front St. across the street from the courthouse. Myrtle, known to everyone as "Burt," managed that hotel until her death on Dec. 2, 1952. After Burt's daughter, Emma Harris Jeffries' husband died Oct. 15, 1947, she helped her mother at the Prentiss Hotel, where she raised her two children, Linda Young Jeffries (b. 1936, d. 1977) and Earl Dwight Jeffries Jr. (b. 1944). The hotel was also home to Burt's mother, Emma Blythe Young, until her death on Jun. 4, 1948. It was also home to two of her siblings, Guy Young and Zena Young Burns.

Guy Young's many descendants are listed in the first Prentiss County History and Genealogy Book. Zena married William Marshall Burns (b. 1888, d. 1920) who was born in West Texas. They had one child, Robert Lane "Bob" Burns Sr. (b. 1915, d. 1989). He married twice. His first wife was Virginia Green and they had one daughter, Marylenn and a son who died in his first year of life. Marylenn married Bobby Wroten and they lived in Corinth with their sons, Bo and Brent. After her divorce from Bobby, who has since died, she moved to Florida to be with mother.

Robert Burns married Marjorie Harris from Guntown and they had a son, Robert Lane Burns Jr. "Robin" who is now an optometrist in Georgia. He is married and has two children.

Burt was also close to her sister, Lula Frances "Lucy" Young (b. 1875, d. 1953) who married Edgar Price Spain (b. 1882, d. 1949). They had a son, Edwin Price Spain (b. 1919, d. 1982) who married Rebecca Foley and had a daughter, Lula Young Spain. Becky and Lucy live in Walls, MS. They also adopted a daughter, Lula Young Spain (b. 1923, d. 1966) who married William Riley Cunningham (b. 1918, d. 1950).

At one time the Prentiss Hotel was a center of activity in Booneville and the center of the Young Harris family as well. At Thanksgiving and Christmas the hotel rooms were reserved for family. After eating a big meal, sometimes in shifts, the family would go outside and gather pecans from the trees that surrounded the hotel. They would then return to their homes and sell the pecans, sending the money to Burt and Emma to pay the property taxes on the hotel! After Burt's death, the family gradually stopped coming together every Thanksgiving and by the time Zena died in 1956, the hotel was primarily a boarding house. The hotel was sold to the city in 1967 and demolished. Emma moved with Linda to August Circle until Linda's death in 1977.

Dwight attended Northeast MS Junior College and Mississippi State University, where he majored in civil engineering. In 1971 he took a job with the Coahoma County Road Department. In 1983 he moved to Pineville, LA and worked on the Lock and Dam project. On Sep. 27, 1986 he married Joan Elizabeth Utley (b. 1946), a Detroit, MI native.

Emma lived at Traceway Manor in Tupelo from 1989 until her death on Oct. 27, 1991. *Submitted by Dwight Jeffries.*

INDEX

A
ABLES 163
ACKERS 191
ACUFF 149
ADAIR 159, 166
ADAMS 8, 54, 55, 57, 112, 113, 123, 148, 195
ADAY 119
ADKINS 184
AGNEW 66
AIKEN 19
AIKENS 20
AINSWORTH 136, 185
AKERS 12, 87, 120, 139
ALAIN 69
ALDRIDGE 214
ALDRIN 66
ALEXANDER 32, 39, 60, 69, 70, 71, 86, 122, 167, 183, 200
ALFORD 110, 180, 187
ALLEN 4, 5, 13, 14, 16, 18, 27, 34, 42, 66, 67, 81, 86, 109, 126, 130, 132, 147, 157, 161, 162, 172, 203, 204, 213
ALLEY 27, 40
ALLRED 159, 172
ALRED 197
ALSTON 141
AMMONS 144
AMON 209
ANDERSON 20, 22, 28, 29, 59, 63, 84, 113, 115, 123, 129, 132, 139, 181, 189, 199
ANDREWS 144, 146
ANDROS 51
ANGLIN 114, 208
ANNA 86
APPERSON 188
APPLING 177
ARCHER 27, 40, 44, 57
ARMSTRONG 44, 66, 111, 114, 121, 122, 147, 172, 181, 182, 217
ARNETT 185, 186
ARNOLD 17, 25, 27, 54, 66, 67, 78, 138, 152, 155
ARTHUR 57
ASBIL 188
ASCHAUER 137
ASHBY 146
ASHCRAFT 5, 18, 112, 124, 150, 172, 177, 185, 190, 210, 212
ASHER 165
ASHLEY 14, 40, 163
ASHMORE 147, 161, 198
ASLINGER 158
ATKERSON 180, 204
ATKINS 192
AUGUSTA 86
AUSTIN 51, 144, 147, 159, 188, 209
AVERY 213
AYCOCK 73

B
BABB 28
BACON 51
BAER 191
BAGGETT 41
BAILEY 134, 141
BAIN 15, 214, 215
BAIRD 28, 60
BAKER 10, 72, 110, 131, 134, 175, 203, 219
BALCH 219
BALDWIN 77, 179, 189
BALDWYN 11
BALL 40
BALLARD 121, 178
BALTIMORE 50
BANE 38, 157, 176
BANKS 5
BARAGONA 27
BARBER 24, 30, 36, 40, 111, 132, 188, 195
BARCROFT 28
BARDIN 129
BARFIELD 140, 148
BARKER 18, 127, 128, 154, 156, 178, 179
BARKLEY 127
BARNES 5, 32, 34, 73, 75, 123, 133, 138, 139, 140, 153, 154, 167
BARNETT 58, 66, 86, 121, 189, 217
BARNEY 133
BARRETT 79, 120, 129, 139, 191
BARRON 18, 69
BARRY 140
BARTLETT 31, 43, 71, 86, 122, 202, 210, 219
BARTON 7
BARTRAM 53
BASDEN 41, 42, 141
BASHEAR 120
BASS 168
BASSETT 159
BATES 16, 146, 162, 174
BAXTER 150, 165, 171
BAZE 219
BEALL 58
BEAM 155
BEARD 16, 23, 27, 144, 186, 190, 191
BEARDEN 153, 161
BEASLEY 39, 41, 125, 131, 132
BEAVER 208
BEAVERS 30
BECK 210
BECKET 46
BEDFORD 14
BEEBE 5, 129, 181
BEELER 171
BEENE 137
BEGGS 189
BELCHER 14
BELEW 125, 142
BELL 57, 86, 141
BELLAMY 132
BELSHER 8
BELUE 134, 142, 208
BENBOW 160
BENEDICT 22
BENGE 76
BENNETT 28, 33, 74, 120, 129, 133, 158
BENSON 201
BERKELEY 50, 51
BERRY 29, 40, 135, 189
BERRYHILL 132
BETHAY 16, 79, 157
BETTERSWORTH 58
BETTYS 166
BIBLE 163
BIENVILLE 52
BIGGS 218
BILBREY 115
BILLINGSLEY 34, 209
BISHOP 13, 26, 33, 39, 72, 79, 80, 109, 116, 153, 161, 170, 196, 200, 219
BIVENS 184
BLACK 27, 40, 204
BLACKBURN 140
BLACKSHEAR 133
BLAGG 143, 165
BLAIR 8
BLALOCK 153
BLANCHARD 192
BLAND 73
BLANKENSHIP 160
BLANKFIELD 20
BLASSINGAME 31, 32, 134, 168, 174, 197
BLEDSOE 114, 219
BLOMBERG 135
BLUMGREN 211
BLUNT 150
BLYTHE 86
BOBBITT 141
BOEMER 193
BOERNER 193
BOGGS 113, 133
BOHANNAN 216
BOHANNON 130, 136, 191
BOLEN 79
BOLEY 121, 122, 176, 183, 213
BOLIN 163
BOLLING 115, 193
BOLT 18, 121
BOLTON 125, 149, 189, 191
BOLYARD 192
BONDS 8, 9, 73, 74, 76, 86, 109, 123, 137, 138, 145, 146, 173, 176, 187, 190, 192, 194
BONNER 135
BOOKER 129
BOONE 33, 54, 86, 111, 162, 172
BOOTH 40, 189
BOOTHE 56
BORDEN 23
BOREN 122, 129, 181
BOSTICK 166, 167
BOULDIN 164
BOUTWELL 34
BOWEN 137
BOWLES 86
BOX 118, 120, 149, 150
BOYD 34, 110, 111, 162, 206
BOYER 180
BOYLSTON 52
BOZZA 166
BRACKEEN 110, 115
BRACKEN 172
BRADFORD 213
BRADLEY 28, 40
BRADSHER 86
BRADY 67
BRANSTRUTTER 181
BRASEL 72
BRASHEAR 186
BRASHEARS 113, 114
BRATCHER 133
BRAY 196
BRAZENAS 137
BRAZIL 23, 202
BREAUX 109
BREEDLOVE 15, 18, 24, 73, 79, 116, 133, 140
BRENT 40, 50
BREWER 76, 154
BRIDGE 152
BRIDGES 31, 38, 72, 120, 160, 165
BRIGMAN 136, 147
BRIMINGHAM 15, 23, 123, 172, 181, 182
BRINKLEY 11, 43
BRISCOE 148
BRISTOW 34
BROCK 14, 40
BROMLEY 175
BROOKS 128, 138, 165, 174, 204, 218
BROSIOUS 109
BROSNESS 42
BROWN 6, 7, 12, 16, 17, 25, 28, 29, 31, 56, 58, 60, 86, 115, 127, 132, 137, 138, 140, 149, 162, 163, 165, 166, 187, 211, 214, 215, 219
BROWNDODD 156
BROWNE 209
BROWNING 5, 6, 12, 137, 185, 189, 196
BROWNLEE 129
BROWNY 42
BROYLES 208
BRUCE 19, 156
BRUMBLEY 24
BRUMLEY 16, 38, 73, 128
BRYAN 41, 185
BRYANT 60, 137, 217
BUBUOIS 188
BUCHBERGER 44
BUCK 167
BUCKERIDGE 174
BUCKLEY 130, 160
BUFFESS 86
BULLARD 24, 36, 65, 151, 162, 168, 180, 185, 186, 189, 190, 191, 201
BULLEN 7
BULLINGTON 142
BULLOCK 115, 157, 176
BUMPERS 16, 18
BUMS 27, 38, 86
BUNCH 117, 206
BURCHAM 16, 18, 23, 31, 67, 111, 137, 138, 162, 169, 172, 179, 182, 190
BURCHELL 5
BURCHFIELD 154
BURDETTE 9
BURGESS 189
BURKE 175
BURKS 13, 42
BURLESON 31, 43, 214
BURLISON 142
BURNS 40, 43, 45, 72, 74, 79, 121, 132, 134, 135, 138, 145, 218, 219
BURR 55, 210
BURRESS 14, 24, 40, 189
BURTON 12, 13
BUSH 68, 71, 72, 74
BUTLER 23, 29, 111, 118, 121, 153, 162, 182, 201, 211
BYFORD 155
BYRAM 188
BYRD 29, 31, 32, 177, 200, 205

C
CABELL 10
CABOT 47
CADDLE 23
CADILLAC 52
CADLE 79
CAGLE 33, 42, 115, 160, 169
CAIN 33, 155
CALDERON 219
CALDWELL 15, 140, 169, 195, 211
CALHOON 176
CALTON 175
CALVERT 73
CALVERY 176, 185, 186, 190, 197
CAMERON 28, 115
CAMPBELL 76, 86, 123, 140, 141, 161, 192
CAMPER 123
CANDLER 29
CANNOCK 86
CANTRELL 157
CARANFOR 44
CAREY 41
CARLISE 214
CARLOCK 209
140, 149, 162, 163, 165, 166, 187, 211, 214, 215, 219
CARMICHAEL 31, 32, 115, 165
CARNEY 192
CARPENTER 16, 23, 31, 39, 41, 110, 128, 135, 150, 151, 153, 163, 171, 172, 173, 174, 182, 190, 192, 202, 203, 209, 210, 211, 218
CARPER 147
CARR 137
CARROLL 125, 144, 180
CARRUTH 213
CARSBERG 145
CARSON 148, 172, 190, 192
CARTER 13, 42, 61, 67, 86, 128, 137, 154, 165, 167, 168, 191, 193, 194, 208, 209, 213
CARTERET 51
CARTWRIGHT 28, 38, 39, 41, 42, 43, 67, 79, 81, 86, 109, 128, 138, 147, 150, 210, 218
CASE 173
CASEY 155
CASH 63
CASTELBERRY 137
CASTLEBERRY 129, 189
CATES 172
CATHIE 38
CAUDLE 192
CAUGHEY 183
CAVALIER 51
CAVENESS 73
CAVER 15, 19, 20, 73, 118, 122, 159, 165, 191, 196, 217, 219
CECH 201
CHAFFEE 65
CHAFFIN 30
CHAFFIN 63, 64, 168
CHALMERS 8
CHAMBERLAIN 61
CHAMBERS 109, 115, 119, 165, 195, 196
CHAMPION 15
CHANCE 83
CHANDLER 110
CHANEY 42
CHANEZ 200
CHAPEL 54
CHAPMAN 31, 67, 86
CHAPPLE 132
CHARLES 189
CHARLWOOD 109
CHASE 5, 15, 109, 110, 111, 138, 162, 180, 187, 188
CHEATHAM 154
CHEEVES 143, 159
CHILCOAT 202
CHILDERS 5, 70, 73, 81, 84, 132, 137, 167, 168, 175, 176, 186
CHISHOLM 19, 20, 157
CHISM 74
CHITTOM 66, 71
CHOAT 179
CHRISTENSEN 166
CHRISTENSON 218
CHRISTIAN 16, 28, 31, 122, 153, 158
CHUMNEY 133
CHURCH 18, 143
CHURCHILL 61
CLACK 148
CLANTON 214
CLARK 23, 30, 31, 32, 43, 44, 56, 74, 111, 115, 125, 151, 163, 181, 201, 217
CLARKE 32
CLARKSON 210
CLAUNCH 151, 179
CLAY 56, 65
CLAYSON 210
CLAYTON 163, 184
CLEGG 123, 156
CLEMENT 83
CLEVELAND 86, 111, 112, 134, 144, 150
CLIFFORD 28
CLINTON 74, 78, 81
CLOAR 40
CLOTWORTHY 156
CLOWES 202
COALTER 209
COATNEY 5, 185, 186
COBB 117, 137, 150
COCHRAN 129, 138, 205
COFFEY 145
COGGINS 136, 188
COHEN 110
COKER 31, 215
COLBERT 6
COLE 18, 24, 44, 67, 73, 112, 117, 124, 125, 128, 135, 141, 142, 152, 154, 174, 179, 187, 213, 218
COLEMAN 34, 118, 128, 158, 173
COLEY 111, 174, 202
COLIOUS 172
COLLICOATTE 10
COLLIER 112, 114, 116, 132, 144, 172, 213
COLLINS 29, 31, 58, 76
COLLUM 211
COLSON 17
COLTER 31
COLTHARP 38
COMB 34
COMER 63
COMFORT 152
COMPTON 198
CONWILL 41
COOK 11, 59, 63, 78, 86, 149, 150, 156, 158, 173, 185, 186, 203, 204, 205
COOKE 167
COOLIDGE 60
COOPER 23, 86, 110, 190, 215
COPELAND 145, 215, 218
CORBIN 32, 38, 190
CORNELIUS 38, 39
CORNWALLIS 54, 55
COSBY 36
COULTER 42
COUNCE 43, 84, 112
COUR 115
COWAN 7, 115, 163, 169
COWART 185
COX 13, 31, 121, 128, 136, 140, 181, 186, 205
COZART 217
COZORT 174
CRABB 5, 18, 63, 64, 65, 66, 67, 112, 113, 114, 115, 124, 129, 130, 134, 135, 153, 154, 161, 166, 167, 203, 204, 211
CRABTREE 170
CRAIG 153
CRAIN 133, 215
CRANE 130, 208
CRANMER 47
CRAVEN 190
CRAVIOSIER 185
CRAWFORD 19, 21, 29, 31, 32, 42, 63, 74, 115, 122, 128, 145, 184, 189, 207, 212, 217
CRECILLUS 76
CRIGER 172
CROCKER 208
CROCKETT 115, 143

CROFFORD 148
CROMEANS 130, 154, 155
CROOK 110
CROSS 86, 163
CROTTS 188
CROUCH 129, 180
CROW 75, 115, 138, 141, 143, 146, 163, 191, 218
CROWDER 187, 215
CROWE 4, 133, 134, 135, 148
CROWELL 17, 132, 163
CROWSON 27, 40
CRUM 15
CRUMBY 112, 125, 148, 187
CULWELL 182
CUMMINGS 76, 123, 134, 146, 192
CUNNINGHAM 18, 23, 29, 59, 60, 62, 63, 64, 65, 66, 67, 86, 112, 113, 116, 127, 133, 134, 164, 197, 219
CUNNYNGHAM 115, 143
CURBOW 41
CURLEE 173, 176
CURLIN 199
CURTIS 185
CURTISS 18, 162
CUSHMAN 188
CUSTER 57
CUTSHALL 184

D

DALTON 30, 86, 174, 178, 179
DANDY 189
DANIEL 30, 122, 128, 140, 180, 189
DANIELS 25, 134, 173, 174
DARDEN 141
DARE 47
DARWIN 57, 142, 190
DASTER 166
DAUGHERTY 199
DAVENPORT 116, 124, 200
DAVIDSON 8, 16, 165
DAVIS 7, 8, 14, 17, 23, 25, 31, 32, 33, 40, 43, 67, 69, 70, 83, 86, 109, 116, 117, 118, 119, 121, 122, 129, 135, 136, 138, 139, 140, 141, 153, 154, 156, 165, 171, 172, 173, 178, 180, 183, 185, 186, 188, 191, 192, 202, 205, 206, 207, 209, 210, 211, 212, 213, 216, 217, 218
DAWS 5
DAWSON 111, 118, 119, 198, 217
DAY 40, 155
DE SOTO 6
DEAN 63, 142, 148
DEARDEN 141
DEARMOND 185, 213
DEATHRAGE 133
DEATON 18, 27, 45, 140, 141, 143, 158, 161, 164, 189, 196
DEBOU 130
DECATUR 56
DECKARD 199
DEDE 44
DEES 15, 31, 43, 115, 127
DEFER 132
DEFOOR 170, 193, 194
DEGRAW 119, 136, 205
DEMANN 189
DENSON 109, 110, 119, 120, 132, 134, 144, 145, 163, 168, 172, 193, 195, 196, 212
DENTON 145
DEPARDIUE 217
DEPOYSTER 15
DERDEN 141
DERRYBERRY 138, 147, 211
DEVAUGHAN 121
DEVAUGHN 118, 120, 121
DEVIN 5, 113, 114, 130
DIAL 170
DICKENS 57
DICKENSON 155
DICKERSON 158, 184
DICKEY 165
DICKINSON 197, 210
DIGBY 158
DILL 24, 133, 177
DILWORTH 140
DIMOND 218
DIXON 53, 124, 137, 138, 201, 219
DOBBINS 121
DOBBS 67, 121, 158
DODD 42
DODDS 18, 73, 122, 150
DODSON 123
DOGGETT 213
DOKTOR 180
DONALDSON 121, 122, 126, 183, 213
DONEA 124
DORAN 70
DORRSETT 132
DOTSON 190
DOUGHERTY 180
DOWD 187
DOWDY 31, 45
DOWE 163
DOWNING 181, 217
DOWNS 72, 79, 122, 128, 133, 163, 168, 170, 200, 215
DOYLE 43, 121
DOZIER 130
DRIGGER 175
DROWN 70, 81
DUBARD 153
DUBOIS 187
DUBS 144
DUCKWORTH 59, 60, 61
DUDLEY 145
DUGARD 42
DUGGAR 125
DUKE 34, 39, 66
DUNCAN 8, 29, 38, 110, 122, 123, 140, 180
DUNN 123
DUNN 40, 117, 123, 124, 146, 156
DUNNAM 128, 146
DURDEN 141
DUREN 147
DURHAM 219
DUTTON 9, 10
DUVAL 66
DYER 51
DYKES 29

E

EARLY 138
EARNEST 5
EASLEY 116, 124, 196
EASTERLAND 120
EASTMAN 58, 73
EASTRIDGE 5
EATON 16, 17, 60, 67, 73, 76, 79, 80, 81, 84, 113, 115, 128, 135, 138, 160, 165, 168, 174, 190, 218
ECHOLS 145
EDEN 61
EDGE 27, 33, 37, 39, 185
EDISON 57, 60
EDISTON 147
EDMONDSON 110
EDWARDS 115
EDWIN 179
EINSTEIN 63
EISENHOWER 62, 63, 203
ELDER 19, 20, 192, 197
ELDRIDGE 15, 16, 123, 146, 159
ELEY 9
ELLEDGE 36, 151, 203
ELLIOT 118
ELLIOTT 86, 117, 124, 150, 201
ELLIS 16, 123, 131, 132, 137, 142, 189
ELLISOR 74
ELLZEY 78, 144
ELMER 75
ELMORE 123
EMMONS 150
ENGLAND 34, 123, 124, 132
ENGLE 137, 138
ENGLISH 16, 17, 38, 128, 132, 134, 169, 176, 218
ENIS 129, 182
ENLOW 138
ENNIS 192
EPPS 175
EPTING 109, 160
ERICKSEN 31, 170
ESCHWEILER 44
ESKRIDGE 142
ESSARY 168, 184, 207
ESTES 36, 38, 74, 123, 156, 183, 196, 218
EURIN 200
EVANS 27, 123, 156, 179
EVERETT 118

F

FAIR 175, 201
FALLS 86, 116, 123, 124
FANCHER 168
FANT 86
FARIS 167
FARMER 42, 156
FARR 163, 164
FARRAR 130, 188
FARRER 163
FARRIOR 159
FARRIS 153, 176, 181
FAULKNER 120, 204
FAWCETT 158
FEAGAN 128
FEARNES 158
FELKER 118, 146, 193, 194
FENDLEY 114, 123, 124
FENNEL 214
FENTER 114
FERDINANO 48
FERGUSON 110, 126, 139, 150, 195
FERGUSSON 133, 215
FERRELL 28, 84, 121
FEW 177
FILES 129, 149, 160
FINCH 61, 69, 86, 112, 114, 116, 125, 133, 178, 213
FINK 188
FINLEY 218
FISHER 51, 71, 177
FLAKE 40
FLANAGAN 23
FLANDERS 172
FLEMING 29, 78
FLOOD 44
FLORA 167
FLOWERS 40
FLOYD 18, 19, 27, 31, 42, 44, 61, 62, 66, 68, 73, 82, 86, 112, 115, 116, 124, 125, 130, 131, 152, 165, 167, 170, 172, 173, 184, 189, 192, 206
FLURRY 141
FOLEY 219
FOLSOM 183
FORBES 112
FORBUSH 34
FORD 5, 32, 58, 66, 71, 84, 86, 116, 119, 120, 121, 124, 125, 128, 132, 144, 145, 151, 160, 163, 184, 189, 218
FORDICE 74
FORNEY 211
FORREST 14, 56, 74, 79, 83, 164
FORTSYTE 214
FORTUNA 172
FOSTER 110, 116, 117, 140, 149, 206
FOWLER 17, 145, 208
FOY 176
FRAISER 18, 198
FRANK 178
FRANKLIN 52, 53, 54, 55
FRANKS 14, 19, 20, 21, 61, 68, 72, 74, 76, 121, 136, 174, 185, 192, 202, 211
FRASER 176
FRASIER 118
FRAZER 86
FRAZIER 160, 191
FREBEL 150
FREDERICK 148
FREDRICK 132
FREE 23, 126, 129, 173, 202
FREED 40
FREEMAN 38
FRENCH 199
FRESHWATER 140
FREUD 61
FRIDAY 60
FROST 24, 133, 214
FRUHWEIN 155
FRYERY 175
FUGHUM 43
FUGITT 31, 60, 86, 88, 123, 125, 132, 140, 163
FULGHAM 115, 125
FULGHUM 43, 60, 122, 125, 126, 142, 184
FULGUM 173
FULLER 151
FULPER 44
FUNDERBURG 165
FURR 28
FURTICK 118, 139

G

GABLE 176
GADDIS 127
GAGE 54
GAHAGAN 34, 123, 178, 179, 180
GAINES 125, 126, 141, 149, 150
GALE 218
GALLMAN 119, 120, 144
GALLMANN 144
GALLOWAY 78, 127, 144
GALYEAN 123
GAMBIEL 111
GAMBIL 111
GAMBILL 43, 170, 218, 219
GAMER 14
GAMS 149
GANG 69
GANN 118, 121, 132, 133, 158
GARDNER 14, 19, 21, 33, 45, 127, 128, 176, 192, 213, 215
GARFIELD 57
GARGUS 173
GARNER 11, 19, 20, 36, 122, 127, 128, 133, 136, 173, 174, 176, 180, 189, 215
GARRETT 23, 121
GARRISON 14, 30, 158
GARRO 126
GARVIN 180
GARY 137, 167
GATES 49, 153, 177
GATTIS 191
GAULT 159, 166, 209
GEIGER 144
GENESSE 30
GENETTI 168
GENNETT 197
GENO 17, 31, 32, 72, 128, 167, 184, 218
GENTRY 14, 34, 41, 74, 114, 126, 128, 132, 164, 176, 199, 209
GEORGE 28, 64, 65, 146, 154, 178, 179, 200
GIARDINA 158
GIBSON 35, 148, 159, 172
GIDDENS 166
GIFFORD 66, 67, 176
GILBERT 33, 86
GILL 168
GILLESPIE 199
GILLEY 16, 159, 163, 173, 217
GILSON 132
GISH 159, 166
GIST 73, 110, 129, 158
GLASSON 139, 140, 148, 149
GLEN 203
GLENN 36, 64
GLOVER 5, 19, 21, 72, 73, 128, 129, 130, 167, 181, 190, 209
GODDARD 77, 79, 109, 130, 158, 181, 188, 191, 206
GODWIN 63, 86, 138
GOFF 186, 206
GONZALEZ 193
GOOCH 19, 40, 45, 129, 130, 136, 178, 179
GOODARD 130
GOODE 77
GOODGER 142
GOODIN 214
GOODMAN 145
GOODWIN 18, 113, 114, 130, 154, 159, 181, 198
GOOGE 27, 86, 130, 131, 172, 216
GOOGER 130
GORDON 19, 114, 131, 172, 192
GORE 74, 127
GORMAN 199
GOSNOLD 48
GOUGH 131, 172
GOWDY 115
GOWER 198
GOWING 164
GRADDICK 68
GRADY 184
GRAHAM 17, 25, 134, 137, 186, 197, 200, 215
GRAM 159
GRAMMAR 142
GRAMMER 148, 163
GRANT 56, 57, 164, 217
GRAVES 159, 184, 199
GRAY 5, 18, 19, 23, 33, 35, 73, 86, 110, 111, 118, 123, 130, 131, 140, 141, 153, 154, 156, 161, 162, 180, 218
GREEN 16, 17, 27, 31, 41, 43, 44, 68, 72, 76, 82, 86, 110, 111, 118, 119, 123, 124, 131, 134, 145, 154, 157, 158, 164, 165, 166, 167, 168, 169, 170, 174, 179, 181, 185, 190, 218, 219
GREENE 116, 131, 132, 157
GREENHAW 68, 177
GREENHILL 179, 190
GREENWAY 27
GREENWOOD 185
GREG 168, 169
GRESHAM 86, 120, 132, 133
GRIFFEN 155
GRIFFIN 13, 27, 45, 67, 76, 78, 112, 166, 172, 209
GRIGORY 36
GRIMES 114, 123, 159
GRISHAM 19, 30, 38, 39, 86, 120, 132, 133, 142, 156, 172, 173, 174, 178, 189, 192, 215
GRISSOM 65, 157, 175
GROOMS 173
GROSECLOSE 211
GROSS 189
GROVES 74
GRUBBS 209
GUIN 83
GULLETT 5, 17, 31, 42
GULLICK 31
GUNTHORPE 45
GUNTHROP 29
GURLEY 34, 219
GURNEY 215
GUSTAFSON 5, 142, 183, 184
GUY 172
GUZMAN 185
GWYNNE 131, 158

H

HAAS 209
HALBERT 157, 158
HALE 21, 111, 167, 184, 204
HALEY 146, 163
HALIFAX 53
HALL 5, 13, 81, 110, 113, 128, 133, 134, 141, 163, 169, 209, 210
HALLMARK 17, 110, 120, 132, 163
HAM 142
HAMBLIN 169
HAMBLIN 170
HAMBY 5, 179
HAMILTON 9, 10, 32, 36, 55, 86, 118, 138, 149, 178, 193
HAMM 60, 86, 174
HAMMETT 137
HAMMOND 141
HAMPTON 5, 42, 172
HANCOCK 114, 132, 209
HANEY 163, 211
HANKEE 8
HANKINS 28, 36, 80
HANNON 134
HARBIN 28
HARBOR 135
HARDEN 31
HARDIN 17, 166, 169, 207, 208
HARDING 60
HARDWICK 29, 138
HARDY 181
HARE 23, 39, 66, 86, 88, 127, 128, 134, 135, 140, 151, 162, 178
HARGETT 115
HARMON 145, 200
HARNESS 218
HARP 148, 160, 173
HARPER 13, 36, 111, 135, 147, 164, 179, 194, 198, 209, 211
HARRELSON 119
HARRIS 24, 28, 38, 41, 76, 111, 121, 128, 131, 133, 134, 135, 137, 138, 140, 141, 142, 162, 166, 167, 172, 201, 208, 214, 219
HARRISON 20, 21, 28, 41, 56, 142, 188, 219
HARTLINE 140
HARTON 141
HARTSFIELD 132, 138, 146, 147, 159
HARTSOCK 121
HARVARD 50
HARVEY 66, 114, 211
HARWOOD 206
HASHEL1 122
HASKEN 179
HASKIN 178
HASSLET 215
HASTING 17
HASTINGS 131
HATCHEL 202
HATCHER 163, 205
HATFIELD 36, 72, 123, 189
HATHCOCK 113, 114, 130
HATHORN 28
HAWK 53
HAWKINS 184
HAYDEN 117, 206
HAYES 31, 57
HAYFIELD 159
HAYGOOD 160
HAYNES 67, 129, 209
HAYNIE 204
HEARD 11
HEARN 33
HEARST 66, 67
HEARTWELL 196
HEATH 174
HEATHCOCK 113
HEFFINGTON 165, 166, 171
HEFFLIN 136
HEFLIN 40
HELLUMS 187
HEMBREE 135, 206
HENDERSON 16, 18, 22, 75, 110, 122, 143, 146, 176, 190
HENDRIX 115, 119, 135, 136, 137, 162, 186, 187, 205, 214

HENDRY 209
HENLEIN 47
HENLEY 189
HENRY 31
HENSON 18, 25, 123, 145
HERCHECK 188
HERD 114
HERLEY 175
HERRINGTON 110, 205
HERROD 133, 152
HESTER 18, 39, 45, 115, 116, 125, 126, 133, 158, 175
HEYLIN 72
HICKEY 17, 160, 170
HICKMAN 175
HICKS 20, 34, 129, 167, 172, 199, 200, 218, 219
HIGHTOWER 21
HILL 17, 19, 21, 22, 23, 24, 31, 34, 62, 81, 86, 110, 117, 122, 124, 136, 146, 165, 171, 174, 177, 185, 193, 194, 214, 215, 218
HILLSBOROUGH 54
HILLSMAN 116
HINCKLEY 67
HISAW 82, 135, 169
HIX 219
HIXON 199
HOARD 139
HOBSON 199, 200
HODGE 131, 172, 217
HODGES 13, 59, 139, 183, 189, 213
HOERSTKAMP 218
HOLDER 23, 28, 72, 74, 75, 110, 111, 137, 138, 162, 200
HOLIDAY 34
HOLIFIELD 36
HOLLAND 24, 138, 154, 160, 184
HOLLANDSWORTH 195
HOLLEY 4, 5, 12, 36, 136, 138, 139, 140, 141, 145, 147, 148, 154, 158, 159, 161, 163, 165, 166, 169, 178, 179, 194, 207, 208, 209
HOLLIDAY 63, 154, 177
HOLLINGSWORTH 86, 111
HOLLOWAY 16, 110, 132, 140, 156, 164, 187, 218
HOLLY 134, 186
HOLMES 33, 121, 129
HOLT 117, 203, 219
HONEY 137, 138
HONEYCUTT 135, 139, 140, 149, 159, 166
HONNELL 57, 200
HONNOLL 27, 28
HOOD 156, 214
HOOKER 50
HOOPER 110, 181, 185
HOOVER 60
HOPKINS 16, 17, 18, 25, 118, 122, 131, 140, 141, 145, 153, 161, 162, 180, 202
HOPPER 137, 138, 190
HORGAN 110
HORN 15, 67, 68, 72, 124, 139, 159, 191
HORNE 33, 114
HORNER 144
HORTEN 178
HORTON 31, 32, 42, 138, 141, 147, 148, 153, 215
HOSEY 205
HOUCH 29
HOUCK 45
HOUGH 140
HOUK 129, 209
HOUSTON 5, 11, 29, 36, 67, 118, 141, 142, 154, 156, 178, 179, 187, 188, 208, 216
HOUTARI 217
HOWARD 123, 125, 126, 142, 151, 184, 198, 199, 203
HOWE 56
HOWELL 40, 111, 130, 142, 157, 162, 172, 191, 199, 201, 206, 207, 211
HOWSER 86
HOYLE 28
HUBBARD 137, 200
HUDDLESTON 16, 18, 24, 115, 118, 138, 142, 143, 155, 164, 165, 169, 173
HUDGINS 175
HUDSON 48, 118, 197, 209
HUFFMAN 59, 86
HUGGINS 27, 72, 143
HUGHES 10, 111, 121, 132, 138, 143, 153, 156, 176, 216
HUGHEY 137
HUGHLEY 172, 182
HULING 131
HUMFRESS 204
HUMPHRAS 204
HUMPHRESS 204
HUMPHREY 115, 143
HUMPHREYS 204
HUMPHRIES 204
HUNKAPILLER 169, 207, 208
HUNNICUT 193
HUNT 17, 142, 148, 161, 163, 178
HUNTER 63
HURST 144
HURST 144, 165
HURT 32, 36, 116
HUSTON 152
HUTCHENS 24, 190
HUTCHESON 66, 67, 115, 185, 190
HUTCHINS 23
HUTCHINSON 50
HUTSON 29
HYATT 140, 141
HYDE 163

I

IMPERAPORE 163
INGE 8, 28
INGLES 163
INGRAM 202
INMAN 110, 125, 137, 139, 152, 172, 196
IRWIN 66
ISBELL 5, 65, 72, 133, 136, 139, 140, 144, 145, 180
ISHAM 183
ISKANDER 131, 172
ISOM 118
IVEY 31, 38, 114, 196
IVY 32, 201

J

JACKSON 7, 34, 41, 56, 71, 125, 138, 163, 176, 185, 214, 218
JACO 28, 30, 42
JACOBS 111, 211
JAMES 16, 17, 69, 145, 169, 218
JANE 111
JANEWAY 5, 9, 145, 146
JARNAGIN 191
JARNIGAN 149
JARRETT 121
JARVIS 22
JEAN 16
JEFFERSON 54, 55, 86
JEFFREYS 51
JEFFRIES 219
JENKINS 114, 167, 201
JENNINGS 142
JERNIGAN 145
JESSUP 63
JEWETT 209
JOBE 86, 154, 184
JOCHUM 45
JOHNSEY 146
JOHNSEY 115, 128, 146
JOHNSON 9, 16, 18, 27, 28, 35, 36, 50, 53, 54, 57, 64, 65, 71, 73, 77, 86, 109, 110, 112, 113, 114, 118, 119, 122, 124, 125, 126, 129, 130, 134, 137, 138, 139, 144, 145, 146, 147, 148, 151, 154, 161, 162, 164, 165, 178, 180, 183, 185, 187, 188, 192, 193, 194, 196, 201, 207, 209, 211
JOHNSTON 127, 137, 138, 147, 163, 190, 217
JOLLY 175
JOLSON 60
JONES 14, 18, 23, 24, 28, 29, 33, 34, 40, 50, 71, 72, 73, 75, 81, 83, 110, 113, 117, 118, 120, 123, 129, 131, 132, 133, 134, 136, 138, 142, 145, 158, 163, 164, 165, 172, 173, 174, 181, 183, 184, 185, 193, 194, 196, 200, 204, 209, 215, 216, 218
JORDAN 115, 142, 161
JOURDAN 137, 138
JOURDON 179, 205
JOWELL 11
JOWERS 218
JUMPER 16, 17, 31, 32, 38, 43, 148, 176, 202, 218, 219
JUSTICE 183, 185

K

KANAVEL 168, 169
KATHLEEN 86
KAY 140
KEELER 145
KEENUM 17, 67, 128
KEETON 19, 20, 21, 25, 80, 136, 153, 189
KEISLER 166
KELIO 24
KELLAM 44
KELLEY 193
KELLY 45, 155, 159
KELTON 18, 192
KEMP 5, 28, 34, 73, 78, 79, 86, 118
KENDALL 196
KENDRICK 24, 27, 185
KENNALLY 110
KENNEDY 29, 32, 34, 45, 64, 66, 79, 83, 120, 129, 145, 148, 172, 175, 188, 214, 215
KENNINGAHAM 125
KENNON 157
KERR 35
KEY 15, 177
KEYS 129
KIEFT 50
KIEHM 174
KILBURN 114
KILPATRICK 31
KIMBALL 211
KIMBELL 58, 86
KIMBREL 140, 149
KIMBRELL 86, 139, 148, 149, 159, 166, 193
KING 5, 18, 24, 65, 66, 74, 110, 120, 147, 160, 162, 164, 174, 208, 215
KINNINGHAM 128
KIRBY 156
KIRKSEY 159
KISTLER 165, 176
KITCHENS 9, 10, 74, 75, 143, 149, 153, 195
KITTY 179
KIZER 86, 110, 113, 126, 127, 130, 149, 150, 176, 182, 212
KLINGHOFFER 69
KNIGHT 17, 117, 150, 164, 165, 167, 186
KNOTT 32, 39
KNOX 55, 156
KOCH 171
KOLBE 195
KOON 148
KREMER 115
KUMAZAWA 192
KURKENDALL 31
KUTRIP 76
KYLE 122

L

LABBEARE 20
LACEY 13
LACY 86, 153, 157
LAFAYETTE 188
LAFORGE 178
LAIRD 115
LAMB 110
LAMBERT 5, 18, 23, 24, 34, 66, 67, 71, 72, 79, 110, 119, 120, 127, 133, 135, 138, 145, 150, 151, 152, 162, 168, 173, 175, 179, 182, 184, 192, 193, 195, 198, 199, 200, 204, 217
LANCASTER 31, 115, 116, 122, 146, 176
LANDERS 42
LANDSTON 145
LANE 137, 185
LANEY 33
LANGFORD 120, 122
LANGLEY 110
LANGSTON 152
LANNING 203
LARSEN 31, 112, 152, 153
LASSATER 133
LASSITER 197
LASTER 23, 177
LATCH 146
LATHAM 218
LAUDERDALE 16, 18, 115, 146, 150, 151, 176, 182, 192, 204
LAURENCE 164
LAWRENCE 5, 131, 147, 184
LAWSON 151, 172, 182, 184
LAWYER 44
LEATHERS 165
LECROY 153
LEDBETTER 9, 24, 31, 32, 33, 39, 86, 152, 153, 160, 163, 168, 190
LEDERER 51
LEDFORD 114
LEE 23, 34, 56, 72, 114, 119, 120, 134, 172, 213, 215
LEETH 111, 162
LEGARDO 49
LEMMON 126, 184
LEMMONS 40
LEMONS 141
LENNON 67
LENTZ 31, 169
LEONARD 24, 44, 175
LESLEY 129, 160
LESSENBERRY 140
LESTER 12, 114, 218
LEVICEY 123
LEWELLEN 14
LEWIS 18, 24, 28, 56, 83, 110, 111, 114, 118, 123, 131, 132, 140, 141, 145, 153, 156, 161, 162, 180, 198, 202
LEWIS 17
LEWSFORD 43
LIEBKNECHT 57
LINCOLN 7, 9, 56, 177
LIND 45
LINDLEY 24, 41, 71, 137, 138, 139
LINDSEY 61, 63, 64, 69, 109, 128, 129, 141, 154, 155, 156, 159, 162, 174, 179, 196
LIPSCOMB 28
LIPSEY 154, 155
LISTON 65
LITTLE 17, 129
LIVINGSTON 40, 114, 117, 118, 132, 155, 210
LIVINGSTONE 57
LOCKE 156
LOCKIE 145
LOCUMBERRY 163
LODEN 79
LOGSDON 201
LOKEY 19
LOLLAR 123, 131, 155, 156, 161
LOMINICK 14, 128
LONG 9, 22, 75, 156, 166, 181
LOPEZ 211
LOTHENORE 30
LOTT 74, 152
LOVEJOY 56
LOVEL 23
LOVELACE 142, 214
LOVELESS 20
LOVELL 5, 18, 24, 64, 145, 154, 156, 157
LOWENSTEIN 23
LOWERY 12, 33, 42, 45, 110, 137, 138, 172, 183, 193, 194
LOWREY 29, 200
LOWRY 40
LUCAS 185
LUCKER 140
LUDLAM 39, 173
LUKE 119, 120
LUMSDEN 179, 219
LUSK 196
LUTER 28
LYLE 154, 156, 178, 179
LYLES 110
LYONS 112, 205
LYTAL 166, 196

M

MABUS 73
MACKEY 150
MACKINNEY 174
MACMILLIAN 214
MADDOX 27, 34, 123, 156, 157, 209
MAGEE 185
MAGERS 158, 166, 185, 188, 190
MAGOWAN 217
MAHAFFY 63, 64, 65
MAJORS 86
MALATESTA 179
MALLOW 178
MALONE 110, 121, 157, 158
MANESS 19, 20, 79, 117, 136, 137, 138, 171, 173, 205, 206, 216, 218
MANLEY 185, 190
MANN 170, 189, 193, 194, 212
MANNESS 145
MANNIN 11
MANSELL 114
MANSFIELD 54
MANSIR 185
MANUEL 155
MARCY 138
MARLAR 200
MARLOR 208
MARQUETTE 51
MARRELL 196
MARROW 163
MARSHALL 24, 33, 34, 74, 140
MARTENDALE 138
MARTIN 19, 20, 21, 27, 69, 74, 86, 118, 121, 134, 139, 141, 145, 148, 154, 155, 156, 157, 158, 159, 172, 179, 187, 211, 213
MASEK 118
MASK 38, 43
MASON 24, 49, 53, 132, 164, 183
MASQUELIER 110
MASSENGILL 42
MASSEY 5, 23, 121, 125, 131, 134, 154, 158, 188, 191, 192, 215
MASSINGILL 168
MASTRI 145
MATHER 52
MATHEWS 165
MATHIS 16, 18, 123, 129, 140, 146, 156, 159
MATTHEWS 126
MAUDRE 181
MAULDIN 193, 194, 218
MAUNEY 17, 27, 32, 80, 157
MAXEY 188
MAXWELL 122, 139, 148, 149, 159, 166, 185

MAY 115
MAYES 8, 197
MAYO 127, 139, 159, 160, 167, 179, 191, 193, 194, 212
MCALPIN 147
MCANALLY 23, 162, 170, 173
MCBRAYER 33, 135
MCBRIDE 169
MCBRYDE 127
MCCAFFERTY 31
MCCAIN 211
MCCANDLESS 177
MCCARLEY 86, 177
MCCARTHY 63, 153, 160, 200
MCCARTNEY 66
MCCARTY 184
MCCARY 17
MCCAY 45
MCCLAIN 23, 73
MCCLENDON 162
MCCLINTON 131, 172
MCCLOUD 111
MCCLURE 111
MCCLUSKEY 195
MCCLUSKY 131
MCCOMBS 35, 36, 118, 133, 137, 219
MCCORD 115, 176, 197, 199
MCCORKLE 86
MCCORMICK 56
MCCOY 5, 13, 18, 23, 32, 35, 36, 73, 74, 75, 81, 86, 109, 110, 111, 119, 133, 134, 135, 136, 138, 140, 160, 161, 162, 163, 169, 172, 181, 186, 188, 215
MCCRARY 189
MCCREARY 31, 125, 133, 138, 154, 162, 163
MCCUISTON 60
MCCULLAR 59, 61, 62
MCCULLEY 209
MCCULLOUGH 158
MCCUTCHEN 138, 179, 193, 198
MCCUTCHENS 29, 36
MCCUTCHEON 181
MCDANIEL 112, 113, 142, 184
MCDONALD 40, 110, 114, 116, 144, 145, 185
MCDOUGAL 12, 60, 161, 189, 214
MCDOWELL 38, 218, 219
MCELORY 218
MCELROY 14, 17, 31, 40, 67, 198
MCEWEN 187
MCFADDEN 199
MCFERRIN 120
MCGAUGHEY 111, 217
MCGAUGHY 138, 173
MCGEE 14, 26, 40, 70, 74
MCGILL 17, 32
MCGINTY 159
MCGLAUN 211
MCGLOHN 73
MCGLOTHIN 124
MCGUIRE 154, 177
MCHAFFY 192
MCHUGH 163
MCINTIRE 41, 42
MCKAY 163, 172, 198, 211
MCKEITHEN 28
MCKINLEY 58, 194
MCKINNEY 69, 73, 76, 82, 110, 117, 134, 163, 164, 175, 191, 206, 209, 216
MCLAUGHLIN 110
MCLEMORE 200
MCMATHEWS 7
MCMILLAN 60, 61, 86, 198, 206
MCMILLEN 201
MCMILLIAN 86
MCMURTREY 86
MCMURTRY 86
MCNAIR 163
MCNEESE 129
MCNEIL 139

MCNUTT 114
MCPHAIL 196
MCQUIRE 177
MCRAE 211
MCRIGHT 126
MCVAY 195
MCVEY 161, 193
MCWHORTER 195
MEDDY 142
MEDLEY 110
MEEKS 133
MELTON 2, 135, 143, 164, 201
MENACKY 166
MENDENHALL 181
MERCHANT 121, 189
MERRIFIELD 138
MEWBORN 171
MICHAEL 19, 38, 63, 76, 78, 79, 82, 83, 110, 128, 132, 165, 167, 190, 196, 217, 218
MICHAELS 31, 33, 175
MICHELS 24
MICHELSEN 210
MIDDLETON 139
MILAM 132, 163, 196
MILES 205
MILLER 19, 30, 69, 86, 110, 115, 127, 133, 136, 137, 138, 139, 142, 145, 148, 149, 150, 159, 164, 165, 166, 167, 171, 181, 182, 187, 199, 210, 211, 218
MILLICAN 120, 188
MILLS 30, 129, 148
MILTON 19, 40, 86, 127
MINCEY 43
MINK 153, 190
MINTON 184
MINUIT 49
MIRON 202
MITCHELL 28, 38, 61, 62, 63, 86, 129, 132, 148, 169, 179, 192, 205, 207
MIZE 18, 186
MOBLEY 42
MOCETTINI 219
MOCK 193
MOFFITT 166
MOHLER 28
MOLTON 197
MONTAGUE 184
MONTGOMERY 137, 159, 166, 201, 207, 213
MOODY 114
MOON 212
MOONEY 18
MOORE 20, 21, 38, 41, 59, 60, 61, 67, 69, 72, 73, 76, 77, 79, 82, 86, 110, 115, 120, 123, 124, 125, 126, 130, 131, 132, 133, 134, 144, 145, 146, 148, 150, 153, 157, 158, 160, 163, 166, 167, 168, 169, 185, 186, 191, 198, 199, 200, 207, 208, 209, 216, 217, 218, 219
MOOREHEAD 39
MOORES 115
MOORMAN 112, 124, 125
MORELAND 72, 139, 140, 150, 154, 165, 186, 191
MORGAN 27, 31, 72, 76, 78, 79, 80, 110, 130, 135, 136, 138, 153, 161, 165, 169, 186, 207, 208, 209, 211
MORMAN 110
MORRIS 14, 17, 31, 40, 122, 123, 124, 153, 156, 169, 170, 189, 190
MORRISON 209
MORROW 43, 209
MORSE 56, 167
MORTIMER 58
MORTON 18, 56, 62, 219
MOSELEY 5, 31, 170
MOSER 217
MOSES 31, 170
MOSLEY 174

MOSS 144, 152, 170, 186, 193, 194, 215
MOUNGER 28
MULLIKIN 42, 128
MULLINIX 63, 162
MULLINS 129, 173, 218
MUNN 172
MUNSEY 110
MURDOCK 14
MURLEY 31
MURPHY 31, 65, 69, 70, 72, 73, 74, 81, 113, 117, 138, 148, 167, 170, 171, 200, 206
MURREN 166
MUSE 192
MUSGROVE 78
MYERS 195
MYRICK 185

N
NABERS 159, 166
NABORS 21, 191
NAGEL 20
NAGLE 187
NAGLES 58
NAGY 199
NANNEY 129
NAPIER 145, 192
NASH 171, 176
NAVARRATE 174
NEAVES 77
NEELEY 215
NEGRO 76
NELSON 14, 19, 40, 138, 188
NESBITT 115
NESS 138
NEWBORN 15, 23, 165, 171, 177, 206
NEWBURN 171
NEWCOMB 5, 40, 44, 190, 214
NEWHOUSE 59, 60
NEWPORT 48
NEWSOM 185
NEWTON 163
NICHOLAS 172
NICHOLDSON 190
NICHOLS 34, 40, 44, 109, 128, 133, 142, 145, 161, 165, 208
NICHOLSON 9, 34, 86, 131, 132, 163, 171, 172, 179, 182, 186, 190, 196
NICOLET 50
NICOLLS 51
NILSON 20
NISKE 199
NIX 123, 142, 154, 199
NIXON 31, 66
NOBLES 10
NOLAN 36, 180
NORIGENNA 110
NORMENT 57
NORTH 71, 166
NORTON 120, 142
NORWOOD 86, 129, 145, 187, 188
NOVACK 193
NUGENT 172
NUGET 174
NUNLEY 17, 18, 140, 151, 172, 173
NUNNALLY 172
NUTT 114

O
OAKES 5, 210
OAKLEY 20, 41, 72, 86, 173, 174, 192, 203, 209, 210, 215
OAKS 210, 211
O'CONNOR 218
ODLE 34, 69
ODOM 15, 119, 203
OLIVE 19, 25
OLSEN 210
O'QUIN 157
ORICK 40
ORLANDER 191
OSBORNE 176
OSWALD 65

OSWALT 163
OTIS 53
O'TOOLE 219
OVERALL 86
OWEN 17, 30
OWENS 12, 13, 20, 40, 61, 85, 130, 131, 142, 151, 174, 175, 176, 191, 201
OZBIRN 200

P
PACE 12, 38, 111, 138, 145, 173
PACILLAS 202
PACTRICK 190
PADEN 148
PADFIELD 34
PADGETT 17, 72, 128, 218
PAINE 55
PALMER 17, 24, 27, 42, 72, 81, 115, 171, 172, 181, 182, 185, 210
PANES 132
PANNELL 17, 21, 33, 69, 71, 175, 191, 202
PAPP 191
PARCROFT 28
PARDUE 120, 121, 164, 191, 193, 211
PARHAM 189
PARK 28, 183, 209
PARKER 5, 41, 43, 115, 122, 160, 167, 176, 183, 184, 196, 197, 208
PARKS 33, 43, 63, 175
PARMER 185
PARRISH 177
PARSON 23
PARSONS 132, 214
PASHUTA 45
PATCH 41
PATE 109, 188, 200
PATRICK 86, 136, 138, 182, 191
PATTEN 40, 126
PATTERSON 35, 36, 86, 132, 163, 210, 219
PATTON 43, 149, 219
PAYNE 42, 150, 176, 182, 183
PEACHER 192
PEDERSEN 118
PEELER 5, 58, 79, 86, 216
PENDARVIS 132
PENDERGRAST 165
PENN 51, 180
PENNINGTON 140
PENNY 114
PEPPER 30
PEREZ 5
PERKINS 30, 58
PERRIGO 128, 176, 177, 190
PERRY 32, 73, 86, 129, 133, 150
PERSONS 118
PETERSON 141, 142
PETRIE 136, 185
PETROU 174
PETTIT 123, 166, 180
PETTY 86, 215
PHARR 67, 72, 75, 78, 86, 130, 164, 170, 172, 212
PHIFER 35, 111, 138, 160, 161, 169, 207
PHILLIPS 28, 86, 115, 117, 119, 128, 138, 140, 147, 171, 177, 187, 199, 205, 213
PHILPOT 129
PICCARD 83
PICKENS 213, 215
PICKERING 86
PICKETT 131, 180
PIERCE 120, 126, 130, 139, 170, 177, 179, 216
PIKE 5, 16, 18, 22, 60, 130, 134, 154, 156, 159, 177, 178, 179, 189
PILCHER 45
PILGER 145
PILLOW 189
PILLSBURY 119

PINGER 44
PINSON 35, 172, 179, 205
PIOMINGO 6
PIPER 199
PIPPIN 24, 114, 207
PITTMAN 143, 208
PITTS 86, 141, 199, 219
PLAXICO 86, 114
POINDEXTER 71
POLK 115, 136, 185, 201
POLLARD 23, 31, 110, 143, 162, 179, 180, 190
PONDER 183
POPE 162, 203
POSEY 113, 115, 137
POSNEY 113
POTEET 114
POTTS 28, 72, 86, 188
POUNDERS 128
POUNDS 109, 180
POUNDS 5, 9, 24, 27, 40, 61, 78, 86, 109, 163, 166, 178, 179, 180, 204, 216
POVALL 86
POWELL 27, 175
POWERS 35, 36, 110, 125, 175, 180
PRATHER 21, 25, 128, 190, 209
PRATT 157, 158, 181
PRENTISS 11, 17, 38, 72, 79
PRESLEY 63
PRESTIGE 188
PREWITT 32
PRICE 10, 11, 57, 58, 61, 62, 122, 138, 148, 209, 210
PRICHARD 20, 61, 192
PRIDDY 118
PRINCE 29, 139, 209
PRISANT 193
PRITCHARD 19, 137, 138, 188
PRIVETT 146
PROVINS 5, 196
PRUITT 17, 33, 123, 163, 200
PUCKETT 200
PUTNAM 68
PYBASS 218

Q
QUALLS 123
QUAYLE 74
QUEEN 110, 171
QUENNELLA 140
QUENTERO 160
QUINN 17
QUIRE 139

R
RABB 189
RADCLIFF 23
RAINEY 57, 163
RAKESTRAW 202
RALEIGH 48
RAMEY 76, 79, 146
RAMPLEY 18
RANDLE 172
RANDOLF 42
RANDOLPH 14, 31, 40, 86, 109, 113, 149
RANKIN 39, 41
RANSOM 115
RAPER 36, 146
RAPHEL 174
RAPHORD 126
RAST 117
RATLIFF 63, 142, 192
RAUGHTON 161
RAY 74, 122, 146, 181, 200
RAYBURN 35, 36, 185
RAYMAN 163
REAGAN 67, 68, 69, 71
REAR 140
REDD 31
REDDEN 119
REDDING 140
REDUS 30
REECE 34, 86, 163
REED 125, 130, 162
REES 58
REEVES 200, 213
REID 33, 216

REINER 44
RENCHER 126
RENFRO 215
RENO 214
REVELS 57
REYNOLDS 8, 31, 86, 122, 130, 140, 141, 145, 161, 180, 188, 192, 204
RHOADES 118
RHOADS 5, 69, 110, 145, 180, 191
RHODES 13, 172
RICE 86, 197
RICHARDS 8, 175
RICHARDSON 41, 43, 110, 115, 118, 119, 135, 136, 146, 164, 186, 205
RICHERSON 28
RICHEY 26, 131, 156
RICHIE 62
RICHMOND 132
RICKARD 4
RICKETTS 34
RICKMAN 177, 216
RICKS 19, 25, 129, 181
RIDDLE 7, 23, 140, 178, 179, 192, 193
RIDE 68
RIDER 188
RIDGWAY 199
RIEHLE 219
RILEY 39, 110, 117, 135, 148, 150
RINEHART 15, 31, 32, 58, 59, 77, 86, 111, 115, 131, 162, 171, 172, 181, 182, 187, 193, 217
RINGGER 144
RITCHIE 19
RITTER 130
RIVES 7, 116
ROACH 31, 176, 182
ROBBINS 130, 145, 170, 181, 216
ROBERSON 195
ROBERT 188
ROBERTS 15, 29, 32, 33, 35, 36, 39, 42, 67, 109, 112, 123, 163, 170, 184, 187, 195, 202
ROBERTSON 5, 63, 64, 65, 66, 120, 125, 126, 136, 150, 176, 182, 183, 184, 185, 197
ROBINSON 8, 28, 31, 39, 51, 76, 80, 83, 86, 128, 149, 150, 163, 182, 185, 188, 189, 190, 193, 200, 201, 203, 204
ROBISON 36
RODGERS 139, 215
ROENTGEN 58
ROGERS 20, 22, 23, 44, 57, 86, 111, 113, 114, 123, 127, 128, 130, 138, 139, 141, 147, 159, 165, 166, 167, 170, 174, 178, 179, 185, 186, 197, 199, 200, 202, 208, 217
ROLFE 49
ROLLEN 151
ROLLINS 118
ROMAINE 71
ROMMEL 62
ROMUY 199
ROOSEVELT 58, 60, 61, 62
ROPER 71
RORIE 5, 41, 120, 132, 136, 148, 168, 171, 186, 187, 205, 217
ROSAMOND 187
ROSEMOND 211
ROSETTA 158
ROSS 42, 71, 79, 109, 115, 135, 143, 154, 173, 209
ROSSI 132
ROUSE 154
ROWAN 67, 208
ROWDEN 144
ROWLAND 75, 127, 143
ROWSEY 165, 169

ROY 110, 182, 187
ROYS 202
RUESCH 190
RUGG 58, 121
RUMMAGE 138, 139
RUNIONS 118
RUSHING 12, 35, 36, 62, 111, 164, 187, 188, 191
RUSSELL 42, 77, 110, 185, 187, 188
RUTHERFORD 20, 148, 177
RUTLEDGE 15
RYAN 13, 129, 130, 135, 142, 157, 158, 163, 181, 188, 211

S
SAGE 28
SALK 63
SALLIS 218
SAMPLES 129, 170
SANDERS 24, 35, 36, 60, 73, 86, 118, 147, 153, 157, 161
SANDERSON 166, 168
SANFORD 34, 41
SAPPINGTON 45, 143, 218
SARTIN 64, 121, 126
SARTOR 86
SAUER 207
SAVAGE 40, 132
SAVERY 78
SAVOY 39
SAWYER 218
SAYLOR 30
SAYLORS 16, 18, 25, 40, 74, 138, 139, 147, 162, 167, 190
SCALLY 31, 32, 115, 143, 144
SCHAUGER 175
SCHAUSS 189
SCHNEIDERS 145
SCHOGGEN 132
SCHOGGINS 23, 191
SCHROEDER 218
SCHUEREN 172
SCHUSTER 44
SCOGGINS 23
SCOPES 60
SCOTT 5, 22, 34, 66, 110, 132, 135, 137, 138, 177, 179, 186, 188, 189, 205
SCROGGIN 5, 111, 162
SCRUGGS 188, 207, 214
SEAGO 134, 137
SEAL 200
SEARCY 24, 35, 111, 148, 162, 170, 172, 182
SEAY 21, 189
SEBREN 146
SEGORIA 44
SELLARS 76
SELLERS 154, 214, 215
SENTER 24, 118, 119, 190
SEREEKA 115
SETTLE 159, 166
SEWALL 52
SEWELL 40, 133
SHACK 188
SHACKELFORD 24, 74, 81, 112, 113, 158, 190, 191
SHACKLEFORD 139, 188
SHAMBLIN 109
SHAMLIN 132, 155
SHANNON 181
SHAPPLEY 189
SHARP 31, 32, 38, 39, 43, 145
SHAW 34
SHEARON 33
SHEARS 107
SHEFFIELD 18, 122, 162
SHEFIELD 111
SHELTON 79
SHEPHARD 172
SHEPHERD 128, 130, 192
SHEPPARD 114, 141, 195
SHERIDAN 8
SHERMAN 67
SHERRILL 83
SHETTERLY 145
SHINAULT 189

SHINNAULT 19
SHIPLETT 44
SHIPMAN 109
SHIPP 126, 130
SHIRLEY 175
SHMIAULT 86
SHOOK 18, 29, 43, 114, 141, 153, 154, 167
SHORT 164, 165
SHOTTS 122
SHOUSE 185, 189, 190
SHULTZ 189
SHUMPERT 132
SHUTTLEWORTH 209
SIDES 123
SILKY 191
SILLESTER 214
SIMMONDS 132
SIMMONS 40, 115, 174, 176, 191, 197, 207, 218
SIMPSON 75, 78, 80, 110
SIMS 16, 31, 115, 134, 176, 178, 179, 204, 217, 218
SINCLAIR 115
SINGLETON 145
SISENEA 192
SKELTON 33, 137, 172, 174, 196, 199
SKINNER 36
SKUTT 33
SLACK 145, 176
SLADE 122, 213
SLAPPY 174
SLATER 55
SLAUGHTEN 162
SLEDGE 110
SLUSSER 137, 185
SMART 31, 32, 33, 38, 115, 165, 176, 190
SMITH 2, 5, 12, 13, 17, 18, 20, 21, 22, 23, 24, 29, 30, 31, 33, 34, 36, 38, 39, 41, 42, 48, 56, 58, 59, 60, 61, 62, 63, 64, 65, 66, 67, 73, 80, 86, 109, 110, 111, 114, 115, 116, 122, 130, 132, 133, 134, 136, 138, 139, 140, 141, 142, 143, 146, 147, 148, 151, 153, 157, 158, 159, 161, 162, 163, 164, 167, 173, 174, 175, 176, 180, 183, 185, 187, 188, 190, 191, 192, 193, 197, 198, 199, 201, 203, 205, 213, 214, 215, 216, 217, 218
SMITHERMAN 41
SMITHERS 163, 219
SMITHEY 198
SMITHY 132
SNELL 160
SNIDER 215
SNIPES 127
SNUDDY 156
SOMESETT 54
SONNENBERG 205
SORRELL 193
SOUTH 31, 140, 170, 193, 194, 212, 215
SOUTHERN 18, 34
SPAIN 5, 30, 41, 42, 43, 61, 79, 86, 142, 173, 174, 183, 184, 185, 218, 219
SPARKS 2, 5, 6, 9, 24, 29, 35, 39, 41, 62, 79, 82, 86, 130, 132, 133, 138, 141, 147, 148, 149, 164, 194, 195, 211
SPAUR 203
SPECK 195
SPEEGLE 125
SPENCER 13, 15, 16, 34, 73, 76, 109, 119, 163, 195, 196, 203
SPIGHT 12, 14, 60, 61
SPRADLIN 133
SPRADLING 200
SPRAGGINS 28
SPRUELL 149
STACEY 196

STACK 115
STACY 24, 32, 64, 65, 66, 67, 69, 80, 110, 134, 140, 173, 211
STAGGS 36
STAHELT 144
STALEY 155
STAMPS 152
STANFORD 165, 200
STANLEY 18, 44, 57, 58, 86, 116, 117, 171, 189, 213
STANTON 111
STEARNS 110
STEELE 17, 25
STEEN 64, 65, 66, 67, 83
STEGALL 131
STEGBAUER 134
STENNETT 115, 121, 158, 175, 196, 213
STEPHENS 41, 109, 114, 129, 134, 182, 188, 199
STEPHENSON 56, 111, 112, 124, 129, 166, 168, 217
STERLING 125
STEVENS 16, 18, 33, 76, 113
STEVENSON 51, 167
STEWART 72, 122, 142, 146, 153, 205, 218, 219
STINNETT 190
STITES 18, 140
STOCKTON 123, 144, 180
STOKER 115
STOKES 18, 28, 111, 153, 161, 162, 179, 196
STOLENAKER 121
STOLL 44
STONE 38, 61, 117, 159, 179, 203, 204, 205, 206, 211, 216
STOOP 146
STOREY 5, 39, 137, 138, 165, 196, 197
STORY 41
STOTT 197
STOUT 214
STOVALL 114, 131, 134, 167
STRANGE 19, 86, 130, 196
STREET 86, 131, 188
STRICKLAND 131, 150, 203, 216
STRICKLIN 191, 203, 204, 205
STRONG 157
STROUPE 79, 176, 218
STRUEBBERG 218
STUART 174
STUBBLEFIELD 136
STURDIVANT 131
STUTTS 72, 193
STUYVESANT 51
SUITOR 169, 196
SULLIVAN 54, 158, 218
SUMMER 164
SUMMERS 42, 177
SUMNER 164
SUMNERS 4, 86, 165, 196
SURRATT 115, 128, 153
SUTHERLAND 19, 20, 59, 189, 197, 200
SWAIM 196
SWAIN 138
SWEENEY 27
SWENDLE 150
SWILLEY 158
SWINDLE 129
SWINEY 197
SWINNEY 18, 33, 69, 72, 110, 121, 129, 132, 159, 166, 176, 182, 183, 184, 197, 218
SWINNY 190
SYPNIEWSKI 83

T

TAM 201
TANNER 153
TAPP 159, 179, 197, 209
TAPSCOTT 60
TATE 164
TATUM 38

TAYLOR 23, 24, 30, 36, 42, 44, 72, 76, 79, 86, 109, 111, 123, 133, 137, 138, 140, 149, 153, 158, 160, 162, 167, 178, 180, 184, 189, 190, 191, 192, 196, 200, 211, 217, 218
TAYS 30, 41, 42, 83, 157, 174
TEACH 52
TEAGUE 184
TEANEY 182
TEDFORD 218
TENNISON 13, 29, 35, 36, 42, 111, 113, 115, 151, 154, 163, 187, 188, 193, 194, 198
TERRELL 175
TERRY 144
THAMES 214, 215
THARP 190
THATCHER 66, 72
THIGPEN 110
THOM 24
THOMAS 59, 132, 158, 167, 189, 198, 199, 200, 212, 216
THOMASON 201
THOMPSON 8, 18, 22, 23, 33, 36, 77, 109, 111, 131, 138, 162, 177, 189
THORNBURG 190
THORNE 72, 79, 134, 154, 179, 193, 208
THORNHILL 136, 185
THORNTON 24, 27, 39, 41, 134, 145, 180, 190
THORTON 137, 163
THRASHER 38
THREADGILL 86
THREET 39
THWEATT 218
TICE 196
TICKELL 195
TICKLE 195
TIDWELL 23, 33, 42, 86, 111, 186
TIERNEY 44
TIGNOR 166
TIGRETT 32, 179
TILDEN 57
TILLMAN 137, 183, 188
TILLY 142
TIMBES 18, 35, 66, 67, 164, 165, 200, 201, 203, 204, 207
TIMBS 217
TIMMONS 43, 132
TINDLEY 36
TINKLE 20
TIPTON 148, 166, 167
TITTLE 18, 141, 154, 155
TOLAR 82, 169
TOLLESON 154, 178
TOLLISON 31, 43, 127, 167, 201, 202
TOMBAUGH 60
TOMMIE 86
TOWNSEND 115
TOWNSHEND 54
TRANTHAM 44, 113, 115, 127, 209
TRANUM 121
TRAVELSTEAD 114
TRIMBEL 24
TRIMBLE 31, 200
TRIMUE 215
TRIPLETT 22
TROLLIGER 27
TROLLINGER 134, 176
TROOP 156
TROTTER 110
TROUPE 159
TRUE 58
TRUMAN 62, 63
TRYON 54
TUBBS 165
TUCKBERRY 151
TUCKER 28, 41, 76, 110, 199, 202, 203, 215
TUDOR 47, 110

TUNNELL 86
TURNER 5, 73, 115, 116, 118, 124, 137, 146, 187, 188, 190
TUTOR 36
TWEED 57
TWITTY 137
TYLER 56
TYNER 113
TYNES 113
TYRA 27, 133, 134, 148, 158
TYSON 29

U

UMFREE 113
UMFRESS 31, 111, 179, 180, 191, 203, 204, 205, 207
UNDERWOOD 40, 156, 178
UNSELL 184
UPCHURCH 34
UPTON 116
URIBARRI 52
URIEBE 174
UTLEY 219

V

VAIL 64, 70
VAN NOY 211
VANCE 117, 180
VANDERFORD 116, 117, 119, 135, 136, 164, 171, 186, 192, 205, 206, 211, 212, 216
VANDEVANDER 125, 165, 213
VANDIVER 10, 20, 31, 32
VANSTORY 5, 135, 142, 206, 207
VAUGHN 63
VAUTER 179
VAWTER 177, 178
VERDELL 22
VERNON 158
VEST 146
VETITO 152
VICK 193
VICKERS 190, 219
VINSON 114, 173, 181
VOYLES 109
VUNCANNON 186

W

WADDELL 167
WADDLE 16, 18, 45, 127, 155
WADE 40, 171, 201, 204, 205, 207, 217
WADLEY 189
WADSWORTH 183, 184
WAGES 202
WAGGANER 145
WALDEN 60, 61, 69, 86, 138, 141, 157, 159, 169, 172, 182, 207, 208
WALDROP 160
WALES 29, 208, 209
WALK 202
WALKER 6, 31, 32, 40, 43, 63, 86, 121, 132, 135, 139, 140, 169, 196, 205, 208
WALLACE 19, 28, 34, 64, 77, 79, 144, 174, 184, 190
WALLIS 5, 11, 14, 17, 29, 31, 33, 40, 41, 45, 72, 131, 167
WALLS 131, 202
WALTERS 146
WALTHALL 57, 86, 126
WALTON 86
WARD 27, 28, 43, 77, 112, 148, 150
WARDEN 174
WARDLAW 129, 209
WARDLOW 153, 166
WARHURST 119
WARNICK 162
WARREN 119, 130, 135, 136, 145, 174, 201
WASHINGTON 6, 53, 54, 55
WASSON 32, 39

WATERS 5, 41, 42, 86, 203, 209, 210
WATKINS 185, 198
WATSON 33, 145, 167
WATTS 121, 196
WAUGH 132
WAX 120
WAYNE 6, 55
WEATHERBEE 5, 210
WEATHERS 133, 215
WEAVER 41, 113, 198, 203, 204
WEBB 127, 174, 194, 195
WEED 137
WEEMS 59, 114, 158, 163, 211
WEGMAN 169
WEIDENMEYER 199
WEIR 28
WEISE 44
WELCH 86
WELDON 138
WELLS 30, 35, 134
WELTY 135
WESLEY 29, 156
WESSON 113
WEST 174, 214, 215
WESTMORELAND 145, 211
WESTPHAL 110
WEYHRAUCH 71
WEYMOUTH 48
WHALEN 115
WHARTON 164
WHEAT 124, 125, 187
WHEELER 19, 63, 64, 115, 118, 145, 171, 172, 204, 207, 208
WHIPPLE 54, 153
WHISENANT 83, 127, 147, 164, 211
WHISNANT 211
WHITAKER 36, 86, 110, 115, 157, 190
WHITE 5, 18, 31, 32, 43, 48, 65, 67, 69, 70, 74, 86, 111, 112, 121, 122, 133, 134, 139, 149, 160, 161, 173, 191, 195, 203, 206, 210, 211, 216
WHITEHEAD 74, 112, 125, 127, 149, 150, 174, 193, 194, 205, 212
WHITEHURST 32, 41, 123
WHITESIDE 39
WHITESIDES 192
WHITFIELD 109, 111, 137
WHITLEY 110, 155, 208, 218
WHITLOCK 217
WHITLOW 29, 191
WHITMAN 176
WHITT 139
WHITTEN 23
WHYBREW 191
WICKER 83, 155
WIGGINGTON 121
WIGGINTON 73, 117, 204, 206, 212, 213
WIGINTON 187
WIGLEY 191
WILBANKS 175, 185
WILBURN 129, 155, 199, 200
WILCUT 40
WILDER 29
WILDMAN 154
WILEMAN 20, 115, 188
WILEMON 13, 110, 126, 167, 191
WILKERSON 142, 173
WILKINSON 213
WILKINSON 122, 174, 213
WILLIAMS 12, 20, 21, 25, 36, 39, 50, 86, 110, 111, 125, 127, 131, 132, 133, 137, 143, 148, 150, 158, 159, 160, 162, 165, 167, 173, 175, 183, 188, 193, 194, 196, 198, 201, 213, 217, 218
WILLIAMSON 133
WILLIS 24, 151

WILLISTON 155
WILLMON 150
WILLMORE 115
WILSON 20, 21, 27, 33, 42, 59, 80, 119, 120, 124, 135, 138, 141, 146, 148, 158, 176, 186, 193, 194, 200, 201, 202, 213, 214, 215, 216
WIMBERLY 29, 30, 32
WINBERRY 115
WINDHAM 16, 17, 28, 32, 38, 67, 109, 114, 115, 121, 130, 165, 191
WINFERDE 192
WINFIELD 18, 190
WINGO 122
WINN 120
WINNETT 118
WINSETT 146, 147
WINSLOW 51, 172
WINTERS 133, 215
WINTHROP 50
WINZELL 32
WIRTH 128
WISER 186
WITHERS 132
WITT 9
WIYGUL 167, 198
WOLFE 53
WOMACK 79, 130, 216
WOOD 29, 32, 39, 120, 150, 195
WOODARD 117, 163, 164, 205, 206, 216
WOODRUFF 12, 15, 23, 35, 36, 44, 110, 111, 116, 117, 140, 144, 164, 171, 173, 188, 205, 206, 211, 212, 214, 216, 217
WOODS 5, 16, 170, 173
WOODWARD 147
WOOLEY 218
WOOLMAN 53
WOOLRIDGE 216
WOOLSEY 81
WOOTEN 45
WORLEY 36, 127, 152
WORTEN 113
WORTH 158
WREN 44, 111, 129, 137, 147, 154, 162, 163, 172, 181, 216, 217
WRENN 115
WRIGHT 27, 35, 36, 40, 61, 73, 148, 163, 179, 191, 193, 197, 200, 202, 205, 214
WROTEN 81, 109, 114, 130, 144, 169, 180, 211, 216, 219
WYATT 28, 132, 166

Y

YAEGER 63
YARBER 216
YARBROUGH 145
YATES 16, 17, 43, 115, 128, 174, 217, 218, 219
YEARBER 162
YEATES 218
YELVERTON 213
YEOMANS 145
YOKUM 17
YON 199
YOUNG 8, 34, 36, 40, 44, 45, 59, 66, 67, 115, 123, 132, 133, 138, 145, 153, 155, 159, 164, 167, 174, 182, 183, 185, 195, 201, 202, 219
YOUNGBLOOD 40, 156
YOW 158

Z

ZACKAREVICZ 71
ZELONES 44
ZIMMERMAN 175
ZINZENDORF 189

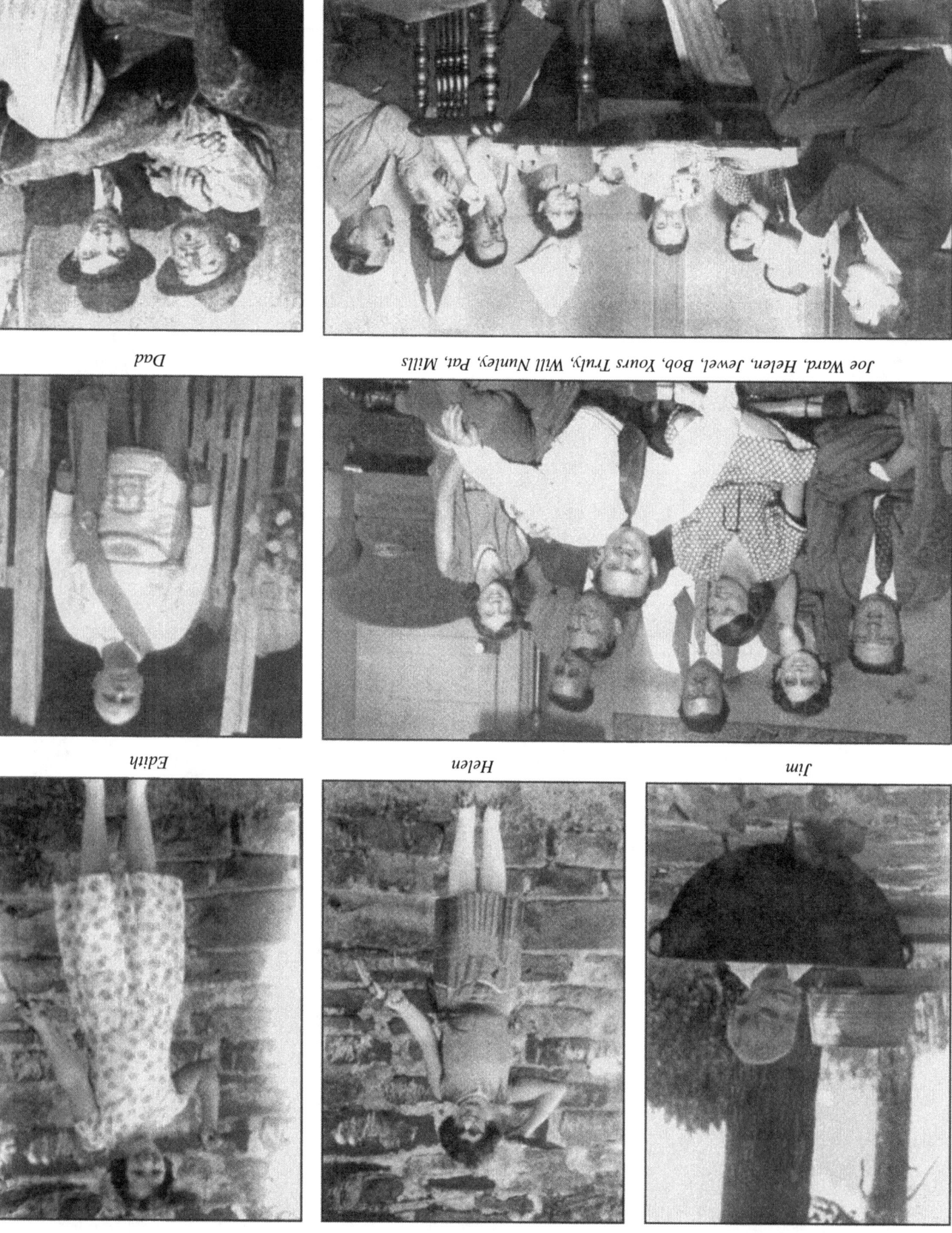

The Line up

Haden Sutherland & True Gullett

Joe Ward, Helen, Jewel, Bob, Yours Truly, Will Nunley, Pat, Mills

Dad

Jim

Helen

Edith

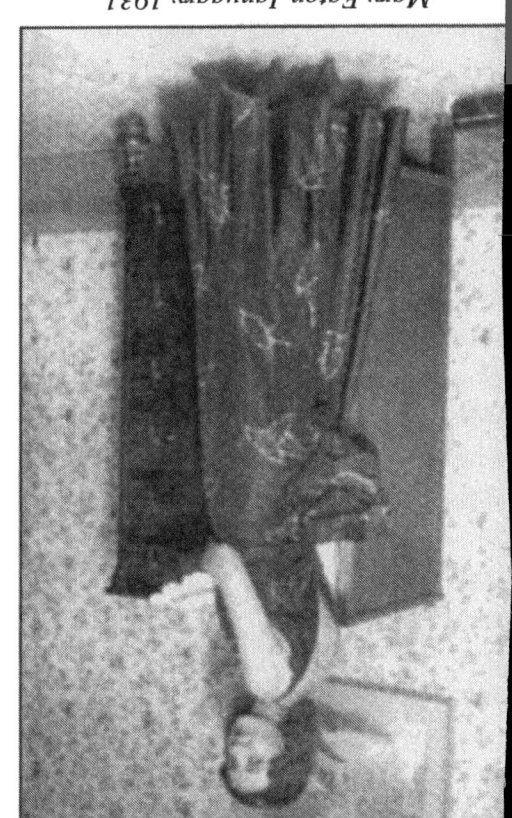
Mary Eaton January 1931

Helen, Milly, Jewel and Jetty

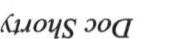
Doc Shorty

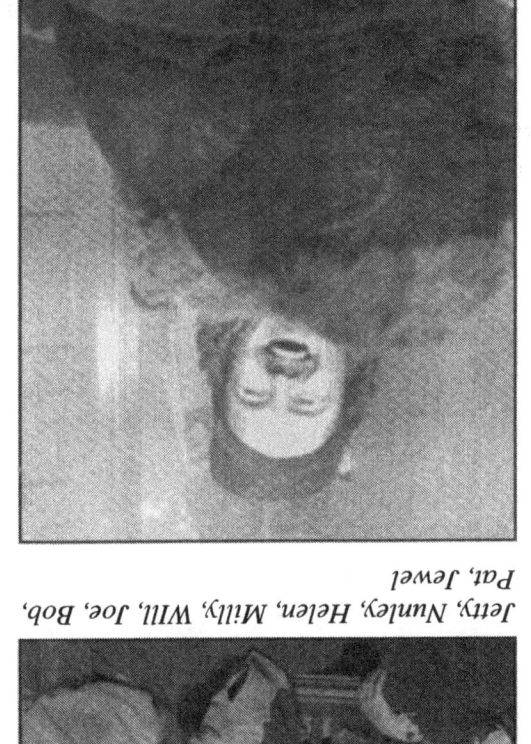
Jetty, Nunley, Helen, Milly, Will, Joe, Bob, Pat, Jewel

Helen and Jetty

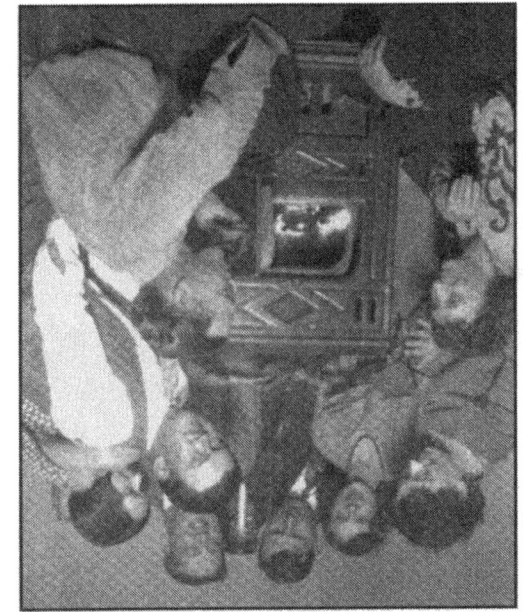
Pat as Santy

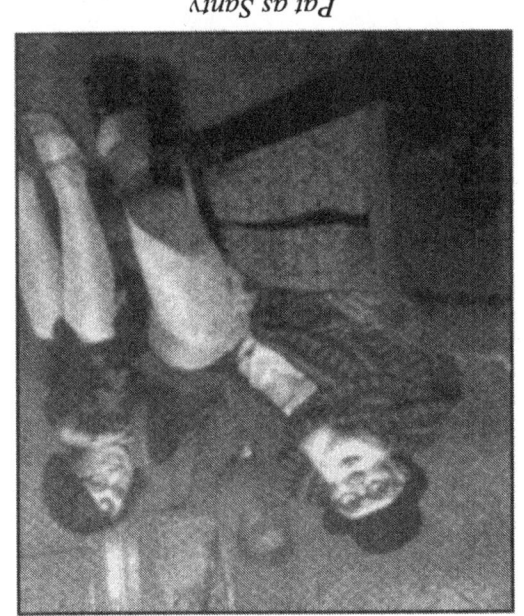
Santy and gang

Pat and Mills